Society THE BASICS

D1033471

Society THE BASICS

FIFTH CANADIAN EDITION

John J. Macionis
KENYON COLLEGE

S. Mikael Jansson
UNIVERSITY OF VICTORIA

Cecilia M. Benoit
UNIVERSITY OF VICTORIA

PEARSON

Toronto

Vice-President, Editorial Director: Gary Bennett
Editor-in-Chief: Michelle Sartor
Senior Acquisitions Editor: Lisa Rahn
Marketing Manager: Lisa Gillis
Senior Developmental Editor: Patti Altridge
Project Manager: Marissa Lok
Manufacturing Manager: Susan Johnson
Production Editor: Nidhi Chopra, Cenveo Publisher Services
Copy Editor: Susan Broadhurst
Proofreader: Trish O'Reilly
Compositor: Cenveo Publisher Services
Photo Researcher: Christina Beamish
Permissions Researcher: Lynn McIntyre
Art Director: Julia Hall
Cover Designer: Julia Hall
Cover Image: Getty Images

Credits and acknowledgments of material borrowed from other sources and reproduced, with permission, in this textbook appear on the appropriate page within the text or page 501.

Original edition published by Pearson Education, Inc., Upper Saddle River, New Jersey, USA. Copyright © 2012 Pearson Education, Inc. This edition is authorized for sale only in Canada.

If you purchased this book outside the United States or Canada, you should be aware that it has been imported without the approval of the publisher or the author.

Copyright © 2013, 2008, 2005 Pearson Canada Inc. All rights reserved. Manufactured in the United States of America. This publication is protected by copyright and permission should be obtained from the publisher prior to any prohibited reproduction, storage in a retrieval system, or transmission in any form or by any means, electronic, mechanical, photocopying, recording, or likewise. To obtain permission(s) to use material from this work, please submit a written request to Pearson Canada Inc., Permissions Department, 26 Prince Andrew Place, Don Mills, Ontario, M3C 2T8, or fax your request to 416-447-3126, or submit a request to Permissions Requests at **www.pearsoncanada.ca**.

10 9 8 7 6 5 4 3 V0TX

Library and Archives Canada Cataloguing in Publication

Macionis, John J.
    Society : the basics / John J. Macionis, S. Mikael Jansson, Cecilia M.
Benoit. — 5th Canadian ed.

Includes bibliographical references and index.
ISBN 978-0-13-209145-9

    1. Sociology—Textbooks. I. Benoit, Cecilia, 1954- II. Jansson, Mikael,
1959- III. Title.

HM586.M32 2012   301   C2011-906792-7

ISBN 978-0-13-209145-9

Brief Contents

Contents

1 Sociology: Perspective, Theory, and Method 1

2 Culture 35

13 Family and Religion 337

14 Education, Health, and Medicine 372

Boxes

Maps

Preface

The world today challenges us like never before. The economy is uncertain, not only here at home, but also around the globe. Technological disasters of our own making threaten the natural environment. There's anger about how our leaders in Ottawa are doing their jobs. No one should be surprised to read polls that tell us many people are anxious about their economic future, unhappy with government, and worried about the state of the planet. Many of us simply feel overwhelmed, as if we were up against forces we can barely grasp.

That's where sociology comes in. For more than 150 years, sociologists have been working to understand better how society operates. We sociologists may not have all the answers, but we have learned quite a lot. A beginning course in sociology is your introduction to the fascinating and very useful study of the world around you. After all, we all have a stake in understanding our world and, as best we can, improving it.

Society: The Basics, Fifth Canadian Edition, provides you with all the basics about how this world works. You will find this book to be informative and even entertaining. Before you have finished the first chapter, you will discover that sociology is more than useful—it is also fun. Sociology is a field of study that can change the way you see the world and open the door to many new opportunities. What could be more exciting than that?

A Word about Language

This text has a commitment to describe the social diversity of Canada and the world. This promise carries with it the responsibility to use language thoughtfully. The book uses the terms "Aboriginal" and "First Nations" rather than the word "Indian." Similarly, we use the term "visible minority" to refer to people of non-white backgrounds. Most tables and figures refer to "visible minorities" as well, because this is the term Statistics Canada uses when collecting statistical data about our population.

Students should realize, however, that many individuals do not describe themselves using these terms. For example, in this text, the term "Aboriginal" refers to people whose ancestors lived here prior to the arrival of Europeans. Here again, however, most people in this broad category identify with their historical society, such as Ojibwe, Blackfoot, Tla-o-qui-aht, Haida, or Kwantlens and Iroquois. "First Nations" refers to Canada's Aboriginal peoples who are neither Inuit nor Metis. Likewise, across Canada, people of Spanish descent identify with a particular ancestral nation, whether it be Argentina, Mexico, some other Latin American country, or Spain or Portugal in Europe. The same holds for Asian Canadians. Although this term is a useful shorthand in sociological analysis, most people of Asian descent think of themselves in terms of a specific country of origin, say, Japan, the Philippines, Taiwan, or Vietnam.

On a global level, this text avoids the word "American"—which literally designates two continents—to refer to just the United States. For example, referring to the term "the U.S. economy" is more precise than "the American economy." This convention may seem a small point, but it implies the significant recognition that we in this country represent only one society (albeit a very important one) in the Americas, which also include our own country, Canada.

New to this Edition

Innovation: New Features in the Fifth Canadian Edition

Each new edition of *Society: The Basics* has broken new ground. The Fifth Canadian Edition has been energized with many fresh ideas, new features, and innovative teaching tools. Sociology never stands still—and neither does this text! Here is a brief overview of what's new in *Society: The Basics*, Fifth Canadian Edition.

Updated statistics   We live and breathe statistical data in our jobs as sociologists. Having current statistical information in the text is paramount. The Fifth Canadian Edition incorporates statistical data from the 2006 Census conducted by Statistics Canada.

A new look   As instructors understand, today's students are visually oriented—in a world of rapid-fire images, they respond to what they see. As a result, this new edition of *Society* offers an exciting new look that is clean, attractive, and sure to boost student interest.

From the first pages of each chapter, *Society: The Basics*, Fifth Canadian Edition, encourages students to use images to learn. Bold, vibrant, and colourful photos pull students into the chapter material and provide not just visual appeal but teaching opportunities as well.

Complete accessibility   The promise of this new edition: Every student in every class will be able to immediately understand the material on every page of the text. This promise does not mean that we have left out any of the content that you expect. We prepared this revision with the greatest care and with an eye toward making language and arguments as clear as they can be.

Student annotations   For the first time, every chapter of *Society* now includes annotations—written by the authors—that help students gain the most from what they read. With these annotations, students have the text author leaning over their shoulders and pointing out many important points and lessons. At the beginning of each chapter, students find a **Chapter Overview**, which states key learning objectives.

Figures and maps that come to life   The text's colourful figures now include annotations that point out key patterns and trends. Coupled with captions found below the figures, students will quickly understand the purpose of each figure and learn how to gain the most from graphic material.

Maps, too, now include annotations that highlight national and global patterns by comparing the everyday lives of individuals living in different places. These annotations make national and global trends clear by presenting them in terms of the everyday lives of people living in different places in Canada and around the world.

Window on the World

GLOBAL MAP 3–1 Child Labour in Global Perspective

Industrialization extends childhood and discourages children from work and other activities considered suitable only for adults. This is why child labour is uncommon in Canada and other high-income countries. In lower-income nations of the world, however, children are a vital economic asset, and they typically begin working as soon as they are able. How would childhood in, say, the African nations of Chad or Somalia differ from that in Canada?

Sources: Global March against Child Labour (2006), World Bank (2006), and UNICEF (2008)

"Critical Review" and "Check Your Learning"

Another new and useful student-centred feature is "Check Your Learning." After theoretical discussions—those parts of the chapters that some students expect to be difficult—there is a "Critical Review" that points out the value and strengths of the theoretical approach and also highlights its limitations. Then students find "Check Your Learning," which poses a question or asks for an explanation. Responding to these items allows students to assess their learning before they move on in the chapter.

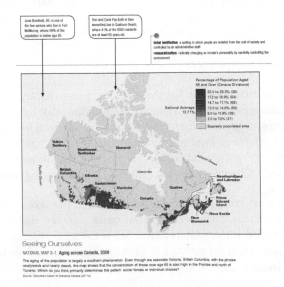

Seeing Ourselves

NATIONAL MAP 3–1 Aging across Canada, 2006

The aging of the population is largely a southern phenomenon. Even though we associate Victoria, British Columbia, with the phrase newlyweds and nearly deads, the map shows that the concentration of those over age 65 is also high in the Prairies and north of Toronto. Which do you think primarily determines this pattern: social forces or individual choices?

Source: Calculated based on Statistics Canada (2011a)

Seeing Sociology in Everyday Life photo essays

Each chapter ends with a one-page photo essay that develops a key theme of the chapter in terms of everyday experiences and popular culture. The hint box helps students to think critically about the photo essay and prepares them to answer the questions which apply sociology to their lives.

New "Making the Grade" end-of-chapter material

Everyone in university or college is familiar with the process of reviewing textbook chapters and creating study notes that highlight the important material that is likely to be found on tests. *Society: The Basics*, Fifth Canadian Edition, now includes a **Visual Summary** that highlights all the key material of the chapter in a clear and colourful way and shows how the ideas flow from section to section. Next to this graphic summary is a listing of the chapter's key concepts along with their definitions.

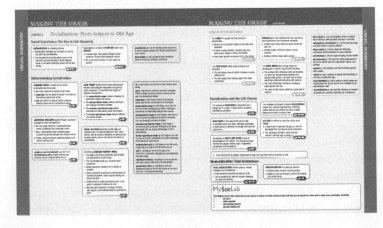

New box feature "Seeing Sociology in the News" Each chapter features a recent news article from the press that illustrates the application of sociology in understanding current events, politics, pop culture, and everyday life.

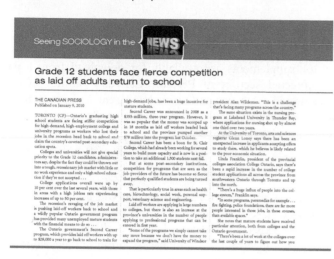

New Canadian Content: Chapter-by-Chapter Highlights

In the Fifth Canadian Edition, all of the Canadian population based statistics have been updated based on the 2006 Census.

Plus

Chapter 1 "Sociology: Perspective, Theory, and Method"

- **Updated**: Thinking about Diversity: Race, Class, & Gender. Research with First Nations, Inuit, and Metis Peoples of Canada, focusing attention on new national guidelines in ethical research.
- **New**: Seeing Sociology in the News. Grade 12 students face fierce competition as laid off adults return to school

Chapter 2 "Culture"

- **New** Figure 2–2 Cultural Values of Selected Countries
- **New**: Thinking about Diversity: Race, Class, & Gender. Early Rock and Roll: Social Divisions and Cultural Change
- **New**: Seeing Sociology in the News. Afghanistan photos on display at Calgary museum tells story of "open-ended" war

Chapter 3 "Socialization: From Infancy to Old Age"

- **Expanded** discussion of Charles Horton Cooley's Theory of the Looking-Glass Self
- **Revision** of Seeing Sociology in Everyday Life. Are We Grown Up Yet? Defining Adulthood
- **New**: Seeing Sociology in the News. Vancouver the Cyberbullying Capital of Canada

Chapter 4 "Social Interaction in Everyday Life"

- **New**: Thinking about Diversity: Race, Class, & Gender. Physical Disability as a Master Status
- **New**: Seeing Sociology in the News. The *Toronto Star*: For Teenagers, Body-to-Body Contact Says It All

Chapter 5 "Groups and Organizations"

- **New**: Seeing Sociology in the News. Professor Suspended after Joke about Killing Students on Facebook
- **Updated** Diversity Snapshot. Figure 5–4 Women as a Percentage of Total Canadians Employed in Management Positions

Chapter 6 "Sexuality and Society"

- **Updated** Table 6–1 on more liberal attitudes among Canadians about social behaviours
- **New**: Thinking about Diversity: Race, Class, & Gender. A Third Gender: The *Muxes* of Mexico
- **New**: Seeing Sociology in the News. Gay Activist Student Marc Hall Drops Court Case, Leaving Catholic School Board . . .

Chapter 7 "Deviance"

- **Updated** national map. The Severity of Crime across Canada
- **Updated** graph (Figure 7–1) showing that crime has been decreasing in Canada since the early 1990s
- **New**: Seeing Sociology in the News. Ex-Employees Turn to Cyber Crime after Layoffs

Chapter 8 "Social Stratification"

- **New**: Seeing Sociology in Everyday Life. When Class Gets Personal: Picking (with) your Friends
- **New**: Seeing Sociology in Everyday Life. Nickel and Dimed: On (Not) Getting By in America
- **New**: Thinking about Diversity: Race, Class, & Gender. The Power of Class: A Low-Income Student Asks, "Am I as Good as You?"
- **New**: Seeing Sociology in Everyday Life. As CEOs Get Richer, the Great Mansions Return
- **Updated** Figure 8–3 Distribution of Income Before and After Transfer Payments and Taxes, Canada, 2009, showing that income inequality has started to increase in our country in recent times.

Chapter 9 "Global Stratification"

- **New**: Seeing Sociology in the News. The Child Catchers
- **New**: Seeing Sociology in Everyday Life. How much social inequality can we find if we look around the world?

Chapter 10 "Gender Stratification"

- **Updated** Figure 10–2 Percentage of Employed Women and Men Aged 15 and Older, 1976 to 2010

- **New**: Seeing Sociology in the News. Women on Board: Breaking the "Bamboo Ceiling"
- **New**: Thinking about Diversity: Race, Class, & Gender. Female Genital Mutilation: Violence in the Name of Morality

Chapter 11 "Race and Ethnicity"
- **Updated** Table 11–1 Visible Minority Categories, Age 15 and Over, Canada, 2006
- **New**: Seeing Sociology in the News. Discrimination to Blame for Prosperity Gap . . .
- **New**: Seeing Sociology in Everyday Life. Is our society becoming more accepting of racially and ethnically mixed couples and friendship groups?

Chapter 12 "Economics and Politics"
- **New**: Thinking Globally. Want Equality and Freedom? Try Denmark
- **New**: Controversy & Debate. The Market: Does the "Invisible Hand" Look Out for Us or Pick Our Pockets?
- **New**: Seeing Sociology in the News. U.S. May Allow Women into Combat—A Move Canada Made Decades Ago

Chapter 13 "Family and Religion"
- **New**: Seeing Sociology in the News. UK court upholds prenuptial deal for heiress
- **Updated** Seeing Ourselves National Map 13–1 Cohabitation across Canada
- **New**: Controversy & Debate. Ectogenesis and the Mother as Machine

Chapter 14 "Education, Health, and Medicine"
- **New**: National Map 14–1 Teachers' Salaries across Canada and other societal shifts
- **New**: Thinking about Diversity: Race, Class, & Gender. Schooling in the United States: Savage Inequality
- **New**: Diversity Snapshot. National Map 14–2 Proportion of Students Following Various Pathways after High School, by Province, 2004
- **New**: Seeing Sociology in the News. The Barriers Come Down: Distance Education Is the Way for Many
- **New**: Seeing Sociology in Everyday Life. The Twenty-First-Century Campus: Where Are the Men?

Chapter 15 "Population, Urbanization, and Environment"
- **New**: Thinking about Diversity: Race, Class, & Gender. What's Happened to the Girls? China's One-Child Policy
- **New**: Seeing Sociology in the News. School Grants Encourage Green Living

Chapter 16 "Social Change: Modern and Postmodern Societies"
- **New**: Seeing Sociology in the News. Social Movements 2.0
- **New**: Thinking Globally. A Never-Ending Atomic Disaster

Supplements for Instructors

Instructor supplements are available for download from a password protected section of Pearson Canada's online catalogue (**vig.pearsoned.ca**). Navigate to your book's catalogue page to view a list of those supplements that are available. See your local sales representative for details and access.

Instructor's Manual

This text offers an instructor's manual that will be of interest even to those who have never chosen to use one before. The manual provides the expected detailed chapter outlines and discussion questions and much more—summaries of important developments, recent articles from *Teaching Sociology* that are relevant to classroom discussions, suggestions for classroom activities, and supplemental lecture material for every chapter of the text.

MyTest

This online, computerized software allows instructors to create their own personalized exams, to edit any or all of the existing test questions, and to add new questions. Other special features of this program include random generation of test questions, creation of alternative versions of the same test, scrambling question sequence, and test preview before printing.

Test Item File

This key author-created supplement reflects the material in the textbook—both in content and in language—far better than the testing file available with any other introductory sociology textbook. The file contains over 2000 items—more than 100 per chapter—in multiple-choice, true-false, and essay formats. All of the questions are identified by level of difficulty.

PowerPoint® Slides

These PowerPoint slides combine graphics and text in a colourful format to help you convey sociological principles in a visual and exciting way. Each chapter of the textbook has approximately 15 to 25 slides that communicate the key concepts in that chapter. For easy access, they are available in the instructor portion of MySocLab for *Society: The Basics*, Fifth Canadian Edition.

peerScholar

Firmly grounded in published research, peerScholar is a powerful online pedagogical tool that helps develop your students' critical and creative thinking skills. peerScholar facilitates this through the process of creation, evaluation and reflection. Working in stages, students begin by submitting a written assignment. peerScholar then circulates their work for others to review, a process that can be anonymous or not depending on your preference. Students receive peer feedback and evaluations immediately, reinforcing their learning and driving the development of higher-order thinking skills. Students can then re-submit revised work, again depending on your preference. Contact your Pearson Representative to learn more about peerScholar and the research behind it.

ClassPrep

ClassPrep is a dynamic database of all the instructor resources that accompany Pearson's leading Canadian introductory sociology textbooks. This powerful tool allows professors to search the database by topic, then view and select material from PowerPoint®, image libraries, lecture outlines, classroom activities and more. Professors can access ClassPrep through MySocLab.

Multimedia Guide

This teaching guide that can accompany any Pearson introductory sociology text helps professors bring sociological concepts to life in the classroom with material to which students relate. Featuring 20 scenes from Hollywood feature films, documentaries, TV episodes, and over 30 songs, this guide provides

- A synopsis of the film or documentary and the relevant scene, the scene location on the DVD, and an explanation of how the selection relates to sociology
- The cultural context of album and song as well as an explanation of how the song relates to sociological issues
- 5–10 discussion questions + 1 assignment follow each scene and song

NOTE: Pearson Canada does not provide the films, documentaries, television episodes or songs.

CourseSmart for Instructors

CourseSmart goes beyond traditional expectations—providing instant, online access to the textbooks and course materials you need at a lower cost for students. And even as students save money, you can save time and hassle with a digital eText that allows you to search for the most relevant content at the very moment you need it. Whether it's evaluating textbooks or creating lecture notes to help students with difficult concepts, CourseSmart can make life a little easier. See how when you visit **www.coursesmart.com/instructors**.

Technology Specialists

Pearson's Technology Specialists work with faculty and campus course designers to ensure that Pearson technology products, assessment tools, and online course materials are tailored to meet your specific needs. This highly qualified team is dedicated to helping schools take full advantage of a wide range of educational resources, by assisting in the integration of a variety of instructional materials and media formats. Your local Pearson Education sales representative can provide you with more details on this service program.

Pearson Custom Library

For enrolments of at least 100 students, you can create your own textbook by choosing the chapters that best suit your own course needs. To begin building your custom text, visit **www.pearsoncustomlibrary.com**. You may also work with a dedicated Pearson Custom editor to create your ideal text—publishing your own original content or mixing and matching Pearson content. Contact your local Pearson Representative to get started.

Student Resources

MySocLab (www.mysoclab.com)

The moment you know   Educators know it. Students know it. It's that inspired moment when something that was difficult to understand suddenly makes perfect sense. Our MyLab products have been designed and refined with a single purpose in mind—to help educators create that moment of understanding with their students.

MySocLab delivers **proven results** in helping individual students succeed. It provides **engaging experiences** that personalize, stimulate, and measure learning for each student. And, it comes from a **trusted partner** with educational expertise and an eye on the future.

MySocLab can be used by itself or linked to any learning management system. To learn more about how MySocLab combines proven learning applications with powerful assessment, visit **www.mysoclab.com**.

MySocLab—the moment you know.

CourseSmart for Students

CourseSmart goes beyond traditional expectations—providing instant, online access to the textbooks and course materials you need at an average savings of 60%. With instant access from any computer and the ability to search your text, you'll find the content you need quickly, no matter where you are. And with online tools like highlighting and note-taking, you can save time and study efficiently. See all the benefits at **www.coursesmart.com/students**.

In Appreciation

John Macionis

I would like to dedicate this book to my wife, Amy. We have travelled a very long way together on our life journey. Amy, you bring me such deep joy simply by being the magnificent woman you are. Keep getting better!

With best wishes to my colleagues and love to all,
John Macionis

Jan J. Macionis

S. Mikael Jansson and Cecilia Benoit

First of all, we want to acknowledge the vast amount of work that went into the U.S. version of this text by John Macionis and by the people at Pearson. We also would like to thank the following friends and colleagues for helping out in the myriad tasks directly involved in the writing of this and earlier editions: Megan Alley (Victoria); Beverley Maclean-Alley (Victoria); Fran Rose (University of Victoria); Alan Hedley (University of Victoria); Lori Sugden (University of Victoria); Bill McCarthy (University of California, Davis); and Zheng Wu (University of Victoria), Helga Hallgrimsdottir (University of Victoria), Josephine MacIntoch (University of Victoria), and Peyman Vahabzadeh (University of Victoria).

We would like to thank the people we worked with at Pearson Education Canada on this fifth edition for their many hours of hard work: including Lisa Rahn, Senior Acquisitions Editor; Patti Altridge, Senior Developmental Editor; Lisa Gillis, Marketing Manager; Marissa Lok, Project Manager; and Nidhi Chopra, Associate Project Manager from Cenveo.

It goes without saying that every colleague knows more about some topics covered in this book than the authors do. For that reason, we are grateful to the hundreds of faculty and students who have written to offer comments and suggestions. More formally, we are grateful to the following people who have reviewed some or all of this manuscript, or the manuscript of the previous Canadian edition:

Mary Frankoff, Heritage College

William Gottschall, St. Francis Xavier University

Kelly Henley, St. Clair College

Mythili Rajiva, Saint Mary's University

Oliver Stoetzer, Fanshawe College

Finally, we remain in debt to David Stover and Dawn du Quesnay, who started us on this project and guided our earliest efforts in ways that remain influential.

Finally, we would like to dedicate this fifth edition of the book to our daughter, Annika, who is now 18 years of age and embarking on the road to higher education. We very much appreciate your understanding of our erratic work schedules and lengthy sociological discussions. We are unable to express in words the love we feel for you, Annika. Thanks most of all for your friendship, which we look forward to in the years ahead.

S. Mikael Jansson
Cecilia Benoit

About the Authors

John Macionis

John J. Macionis (pronounced "ma-SHOW-nis") was born and raised in Philadelphia, Pennsylvania. He earned a bachelor's degree from Cornell University and a doctorate in sociology from the University of Pennsylvania.

His publications are wide-ranging, focusing on community life in the United States, interpersonal intimacy in families, effective teaching, humour, new information technology, and the importance of global education. In addition to authoring this best-seller, Macionis has also written *Sociology*, the best-selling hardback text in the field, now in its fourteenth edition. He collaborates on international editions of the texts: *Sociology: Canadian Edition; Society: The Basics, Canadian Edition;* and *Sociology: A Global Introduction. Sociology* is also available for high school students and in various foreign-language editions.

In addition, Macionis and Nijole V. Benokraitis have edited the best-selling anthology *Seeing Ourselves: Classic, Contemporary, and Cross-Cultural Readings in Sociology,* also available in a Canadian edition. Macionis and Vincent Parrillo have written the leading urban studies text, *Cities and Urban Life*. Macionis's most recent textbook is *Social Problems* (Pearson Prentice Hall), now in its fourth edition and the leading book in this field. The latest on all the Macionis textbooks, as well as information and dozens of internet links of interest to students and faculty in sociology, are found at the author's personal website: **www.macionis.com** or **www.TheSociologyPage.com**. Additional information, instructor resources, and online student study guides for the texts are found at the Pearson site: **www.pearsoncanada.ca**.

John Macionis is Professor and Distinguished Scholar of Sociology at Kenyon College in Gambier, Ohio, where he has taught for more than 30 years. During that time, he has chaired the Sociology Department, directed the college's multidisciplinary program in humane studies, presided over the campus senate and the college's faculty, and taught sociology to thousands of students.

In 2002, the American Sociological Association presented Macionis with the Award for Distinguished Contributions to Teaching, citing his innovative use of global material as well as the introduction of new teaching technology in his textbooks.

Professor Macionis has been active in academic programs in other countries, having travelled to some 50 nations. He writes, "I am an ambitious traveler, eager to learn and, through the texts, to share much of what I discover with students, many of whom know little about the rest of the world. For me, traveling and writing are all dimensions of teaching. First, and foremost, I am a teacher—a passion for teaching animates everything I do."

At Kenyon, Professor Macionis teaches a number of courses, but his favourite class is Introduction to Sociology, which he offers every semester. He enjoys extensive contact with students and invites everyone enrolled in each of his classes to enjoy a home-cooked meal.

The Macionis family—John, Amy, and children McLean and Whitney—live on a farm in rural Ohio. In his free time, Macionis enjoys tennis, swimming, hiking, and playing oldies rock-and-roll (he recently released his third CD). Macionis is an environmental activist, focusing on the Lake George region of New York's Adirondack Mountains, where he works with a number of organizations, including the Lake George Land Conservancy, where he serves as president of the board of trustees.

Professor Macionis welcomes (and responds to) comments and suggestions about this book from faculty and students. Write to him at the Sociology Department, Palme House, Kenyon College, Gambier, OH 43022, or send e-mail to **macionis@kenyon.edu**.

Mikael Jansson

Mikael Jansson is a Scientist at the Centre for Addictions Research of BC, Co-Chair of the Human Research Ethics Board, and Adjunct Assistant Professor in the Department of Sociology at the University of Victoria. Having lived in Sweden, Canada, Mexico, and Finland, he moved 10 times before deciding to study migration at the University of Western Ontario. Now his work includes teaching (Introductory Sociology, Demography, Research Methods and Statistics), research, and parenting. He is an avid (but slow) bicyclist and brings a bicycle with him whenever he travels. Recent trips have taken him through Kenya, Italy, Switzerland, China, Vietnam, and Sweden.

Mikael is a co-investigator on longitudinal research projects on changing lives and health over the life course. His research is focused on youth (including street-involved youth) and personal service workers such as food and beverage servers, hair stylists, and sex workers. He just started a five-year research project about people working in the sex industry. This cross-Canada study has several sub-projects and Mikael is focusing on the families of sex workers with the goal of understanding how partners and children support each other while one family member is working in the sex industry.

You can read more about the research projects he is involved in by searching for his name at the University of Victoria website (**www.uvic.ca**). You can reach Mikael at **mjansson@uvic.ca**. You are invited to work with him in Victoria on his research projects. Most students are funded through their own scholarships or work as research assistants.

Cecilia Benoit

Cecilia Benoit is a Professor in the Department of Sociology at the University of Victoria and Scientist at the Centre for Addictions Research of BC. The courses she teaches include Introductory Sociology, Sociology of Health across the Life Course, and Sociology of Social Inequality.

Her research includes investigation of inequality in access to maternity care for families in Canada and internationally, and health inequities among different vulnerable populations at different stages in the life span. These include Aboriginal girls and women in Vancouver's Downtown Eastside, female adolescents confronting stigmas associated with obesity and asthma, homeless female and male youth and emergent adults, frontline service workers in female-dominated low-prestige and stigmatized occupations, women, men and transgendered people involved in the sex industry, pregnant and early parenting women using addictive substances, and legally-blind adults confronting disability stigmas.

Cecilia is currently leading two CIHR-funded projects that adopt an intersectionality lens: "Team Grant on contexts of vulnerabilities, resiliencies and care among people in the sex industry" and "Interventions to promote health and healthy equity for pregnant and early parenting women facing substance use and other challenges." Both of these studies, similar to the bulk of Cecilia's research, involve extensive community engagement; she has received numerous awards for her scholarship and community outreach activities. Cecilia is the author/coauthor/coeditor of a number of scholarly works, including *Midwives in Passage* (1991), *Women, Work and Social Rights* (2000), *Professional Identities in Transition* (1999), *Birth by Design* (2001), *Reconceiving Midwifery* (2004), *Ethical Issues in Community-based Research with Children and Youth* (2006), and *Valuing Care Work* (2011). You can find out about Cecilia's research by checking out her website at **http://web.uvic.ca/~cbenoit/** or contact her at **cbenoit@uvic.ca**.

The Benoit-Jansson family (or should that be the Jansson-Benoit family?) live in a small house close to the University of Victoria. Together with their daughter, Annika, they enjoy the lakes and forests on Vancouver Island, spending their leisure time fly-fishing in the spring, swimming in the summer, and gathering wild mushrooms in the fall (these being the only three seasons in Victoria). They like to bike all year around.

1 Sociology: Perspective, Theory, and Method

- What makes the sociological perspective a new and exciting way of seeing the world?

- Why is sociology an important tool for your future career?

- How do sociologists conduct research to learn about the social world?

This chapter introduces the discipline of sociology. The most important skill to gain from this course is the ability to use what we call the *sociological perspective*. The chapter then introduces *sociological theory*, which helps us build understanding from what we see using the sociological perspective. The chapter continues by explaining how sociologists "do" sociology, describing three approaches to conducting research and four methods of data collection.

From the moment he first saw Tonya, as they both stepped off the subway train, Duane knew she was "the one." As the two walked up the stairs to the street and entered the building where they were both taking classes, Duane tried to get Tonya to stop and talk. At first, she ignored him. But after class they met again, and she agreed to join him for coffee. That was three months ago. Today, they are engaged to be married.

If you were to ask people in Canada, "Why do couples like Tonya and Duane marry?", it is a safe bet that almost everyone would reply, "People marry because they fall in love." Most of us find it hard to imagine a marriage being happy without love; for the same reason, when people fall in love we expect them to think about getting married.

But is the decision about whom to marry really just a matter of personal feelings? There is plenty of evidence that if love is the key to marriage, Cupid's arrow is carefully aimed by the society around us.

Society has many "rules" about whom we should and should not marry. Until recently, Canadian society ruled out half of the population as possible marriage partners because our laws did not allow people to marry someone of the same sex, even if a couple was deeply in love. But there are other rules as well. Sociologists have found that people, especially when they are young, are very likely to marry someone close to them in age, and people of all ages typically marry someone of the same race, of similar social class background, of much the same level of education, and with the same degree of physical attractiveness (Feng Hou & Myles, 2008; Schwartz & Mare, 2005; Schoen & Cheng, 2006; Chapter 13, "Family and Religion," provides details). People end up making choices about whom to marry, but society narrows the field long before they do.

When it comes to love, our decisions do not result simply from what philosophers call "free will." Sociology teaches us that our social world guides our life choices in much the same way that the seasons influence our choice of clothing.

The Sociological Perspective

Sociology is *the systematic study of human society*. At the heart of this discipline is a distinctive point of view called the *sociological perspective*.

Seeing the General in the Particular

Years ago, Peter Berger (1963) described the **sociological perspective** as *seeing the general in the particular*. By this he meant that sociology helps us see *general* patterns in the behaviour of *particular* people. Although every individual is unique, society shapes the lives of people in various *categories* (such as children and adults, women and men, the rich and the poor) very differently. We begin to see the world sociologically by realizing how the general categories into which we fall shape our particular life experiences.

This text explores the power of society to guide our actions, thoughts, and feelings. We may think that marriage results simply from the personal feeling of love. Yet the sociological perspective shows us that factors such as our sex, gender, age, race, education, and social class guide our selection of a partner. It might be more accurate to think of love as a feeling we have for others who match up with what society teaches us to want in a mate.

Seeing the Strange in the Familiar

At first, using the sociological perspective may seem like *seeing the strange in the familiar*. Consider how you would react if someone were to say to you, "You fit all the right categories, which means you would make a wonderful spouse!" We are used to thinking that people fall in love and decide to marry based on personal feelings. But the sociological perspective reveals to us the initially strange idea that society shapes what we think and do.

Because we live in an individualistic society, learning to see how society affects us may take a bit of practice. Consider the decision by women to bear children. Like the selection of a mate, the choice of having a child—or how many to have—would seem to be very

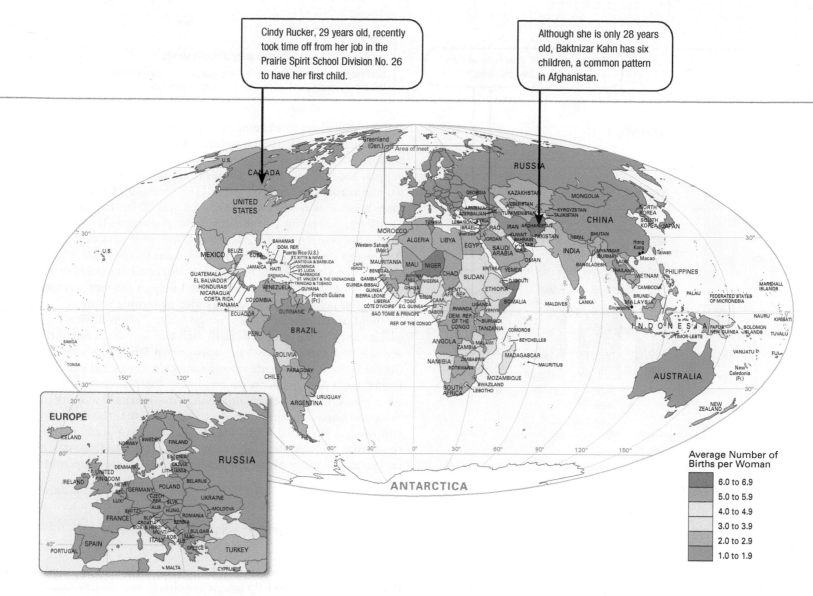

Window on the World

GLOBAL MAP 1–1 Women's Child-bearing in Global Perspective

Is child-bearing simply a matter of personal choice? A look around the world shows that it is not. In general, women living in low-income countries have more children than women in high-income nations. Can you point to some of the reasons for this global disparity? In simple terms, such differences mean that if you had been born into another society (whether you are female or male), your life might be quite different from what it is now.

Sources: Martin et al. (2010), Population Reference Bureau (2010), United Nations Development Programme (2010), and Central Intelligence Agency (2011).

personal. Yet there are social patterns here as well. As shown in Global Map 1–1, the average woman in Canada has slightly fewer than two children during her lifetime. In the Philippines, however, the "choice" is about three; in Guatemala, about four; in Ethiopia, about five; in Afghanistan, about six; and in Niger, about seven.

What accounts for these striking differences? Because low-income countries provide women with less schooling and fewer economic opportunities, women's lives are centred in the home and

they are less likely to use contraception. The strange truth is that society has much to do with the familiar decisions that women and men make about child-bearing.

Seeing Society in Our Everyday Lives

The society in which we live has a lot to do with our choices in food, clothing, music, schooling, jobs, and just about everything else.

sociology (p. 2) the systematic study of human society

sociological perspective (p. 2) the special point of view of sociology that sees general patterns of society in the lives of particular people

Diversity Snapshot

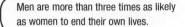

Men are more than three times as likely as women to end their own lives.

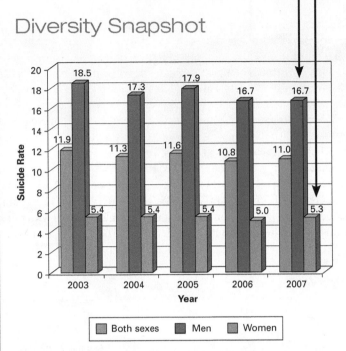

FIGURE 1–1 **Rate of Death by Suicide, by Gender, for Canada**

Rates indicate the number of deaths by suicide for every 100 000 people in each category for 2003 to 2007.

Source: Statistics Canada (2011a).

Even the most "personal" decisions we make turn out to be shaped by society.

What could be more personal than the lonely decision to end your own life? Emile Durkheim (1858–1917), one of sociology's pioneers, showed that social forces are at work even in such an intensely personal action as suicide. Examining official records in and around his native France, Durkheim (1966, orig. 1897) found that some categories of people were more likely than others to take their own lives. He found that men, Protestants, wealthy people, and the unmarried each had much higher suicide rates than women, Catholics and Jews, the poor, and married people. Durkheim explained these differences in terms of *social integration*: Categories of people with strong social ties had low suicide rates and more individualistic people had high suicide rates.

In Durkheim's time, men had much more freedom than women. But despite its advantages, freedom weakens social ties and thus increases the rate of suicide. Likewise, more individualistic Protestants were more likely to commit suicide than more tradition-bound Catholics and Jews, whose rituals encourage stronger social ties. The wealthy have much more freedom than the poor—but, once again, at the cost of a higher suicide rate.

A century later, Durkheim's analysis still holds true. Figure 1–1 shows suicide rates for women and men in Canada between 2003 and 2007. In 2003, there were 11.9 recorded suicides for every 100 000 people. Suicide was more common among men than among women across the life cycle. Men (16.7 per 100 000) are more than three times as likely as women (5.3 per 100 000) to take their own lives. Following Durkheim's logic, the higher suicide rate among men reflects their greater wealth and freedom. Conversely, the lower rate among women follows from their limited social choices. Yet we also know that while males commit suicide more often than females, females are more likely to *attempt* suicide. The reason behind this complex gender patterning requires that we build on Durkheim's ideas but go beyond them if we are to understand the personal actions of men and women in our society. On first glance, it does not appear that Durkheim's theory fits the statistics on suicide among Canada's Aboriginal peoples: Even though Aboriginals are poorer and less independent than non-Aboriginals, the rate of suicide among Aboriginals is more than twice the Canadian rate. Why do you think this is the case? Do you think it is related to the legacy of colonial oppression, the residential school system, and continuing racism and alienation experienced by many Aboriginal peoples in Canada (see Chapter 11, "Race and Ethnicity")?

Seeing Sociologically: Marginality and Crisis

Anyone can learn to see the world using the sociological perspective. But two situations help people see clearly how society shapes individual lives: living on the margins of society and living through a social crisis.

From time to time, everyone feels like an "outsider." For some categories of people, however, being an *outsider*—not part of the dominant category—is an everyday experience. The greater people's social marginality, the better they are able to use the sociological perspective.

For example, no African-American grows up in the United States without understanding the importance of race in shaping people's lives. Songs by the rapper Jay-Z express the anger he feels, not only about the poverty he experienced growing up, but also about the many innocent lives he has seen lost to violence in a society with such wide racial disparities. His lyrics, and those of many similar artists, which are spread throughout the world by the mass media, show that some people of colour in the United States—especially African-Americans living in inner cities—feel as if their hopes and dreams are crushed by society. As noted above, Aboriginal people in Canada often feel the same way. But white North Americans, as the dominant majority, think less often about race and the privileges it provides, believing that race affects only non-white people and

global perspective the study of the larger world and our society's place in it

high-income countries
nations with the highest
overall standards of living

middle-income countries
nations with a standard
of living about average for the
world as a whole

low-income countries
nations with a low standard
of living in which most
people are poor

not themselves as well. People at the margins of social life, including women, Aboriginals, gays and lesbians, people with disabilities, and the very old, are aware of social patterns that others rarely think about. To become better at using the sociological perspective, we must step back from our familiar routines and look at our lives with a new curiosity.

Periods of change or crisis make everyone feel a little off balance, encouraging us to use the sociological perspective. The sociologist C. Wright Mills (1959) illustrated this idea using the Great Depression of the 1930s. As the unemployment rate in North America soared to 25 percent, people without jobs could not help but see general social forces at work in their particular lives. Rather than saying, "Something is wrong with me; I can't find a job," they took a sociological approach and realized, "The economy has collapsed; there are no jobs to be found!" Mills believed that using what he called the "sociological imagination" in this way helps people understand their society and how it affects their own lives. The Seeing Sociology in Everyday Life box on page 6 takes a closer look.

The Importance of a Global Perspective

As new information technology draws even the farthest reaches of the planet closer together, many academic disciplines are taking a **global perspective,** *the study of the larger world and our society's place in it*. What is the importance of a global perspective for sociology?

First, global awareness is a logical extension of the sociological perspective. Sociology shows us that our place in society shapes our life experiences. It stands to reason, then, that the position of our society in the larger world system affects everyone in Canada.

The world's 213 nations can be divided into three broad categories according to their level of economic development (see Global Map 9–1 on page 230). **High-income countries** are the *nations with the highest overall standards of living*. The 69 nations in this category include Canada and the United States, the nations of Western Europe, Israel, Saudi Arabia, Japan, New Zealand, and Australia. Taken together, these nations generate most of the world's goods and services, and the people who live in them own most of the planet's wealth. Economically speaking, people in these countries are very well off, not because they are smarter or work harder than anyone else but because they were lucky enough to be born in a rich region of the world.

A second category is **middle-income countries,** *nations with a standard of living about average for the world as a whole*. People living in any of these 101 nations—many of the countries in Eastern Europe, South Africa and some other African nations, and almost all of Latin America and Asia—are as likely to live in rural villages as in cities and to walk or ride tractors, scooters, bicycles, or animals as to drive automobiles. On average, they receive 8 to 10 years of schooling. Most middle-income countries also have considerable social inequality within their borders, meaning that some people are extremely rich (members of the business elite in nations across North Africa, for example) but many more lack safe housing and adequate nutrition (people living in the shanty settlements that surround Lima, Peru, or Mumbai, India).

The remaining 43 nations of the world are **low-income countries,** *nations with a low standard of living in which most people are poor*. Most of these countries are in Africa and a few are in Asia. Here again, a few people are very rich, but the majority struggle to get by with poor housing, unsafe water, too little food, and—perhaps most serious of all—little chance to improve their lives.

Chapter 9 ("Global Stratification") explains the causes and consequences of global wealth and poverty. But every chapter of this text makes comparisons between Canada and other nations for four reasons:

1. **Where we live shapes the lives we lead.** As you saw in Global Map 1–1 on page 3, women living in high-income compared to low-income nations have very different lives, as suggested by the number of children they have. To understand ourselves and appreciate how others live, we must understand something about how countries differ, which is easy to do by paying attention to the global maps found throughout this text.

2. **Societies throughout the world are increasingly interconnected.** Historically, people in Canada took only passing note of countries beyond our own borders. In recent decades, however, Canada and the rest of the world have become linked as never before. Electronic technology now transmits pictures, sounds, and written documents around the globe in seconds.

   One effect of this new technology is that people all over the world now share many of the same tastes in food, clothing, movies, and music. High-income countries such as Canada influence other nations, whose people are ever more likely to gobble up our hamburgers, dance to the latest hip-hop music, and speak English.

   But the larger world also has an impact on us. We all know about the contributions of famous immigrants such as Adrienne Clarkson, governor general of Canada from 1999 to 2005 (who came to Canada as a refugee from Hong Kong), and Naheed Nenshi, mayor of Calgary since 2010 (who is the son of immigrants from Tanzania). About 250 000 immigrants enter Canada each year, bringing their skills and talents along with their fashions and foods, greatly increasing the racial and cultural diversity of this country.

The Sociological Imagination: Turning Personal Problems into Public Issues

As Mike opened the envelope, he felt the tightness in his chest. The letter he dreaded was in his hands—his job was finished at the end of the day. After 11 years! Years in which he had worked hard, sure that he would move up in the company. All of those hopes and dreams were now suddenly gone. Mike felt like a failure. Anger at himself—for not having worked even harder, for having wasted so many years of his life in what had turned out to be a dead-end job—swelled inside him.

But as he returned to his workstation to pack his things, Mike realized that he was not alone. Almost all of his colleagues in the tech support group had received the same letter. Their jobs were moving to India, where the company was able to provide telephone tech support for less than half the cost of employing workers in Vancouver.

By the end of the weekend, Mike was sitting in his living room with a dozen other ex-employees. After comparing notes and sharing ideas, they realized that they were simply a few of the victims of a massive outsourcing of jobs that is part of what analysts call the "globalization of the economy."

In good times and bad, the power of the sociological perspective lies in making sense of our individual lives. We see that many of our particular problems (and our successes as well) are not unique to us but the result of larger social trends. Half a century ago, sociologist C. Wright Mills pointed to the power of what he called the *sociological imagination* to help us understand everyday events. As he saw it, society—not people's personal failings—is the main cause of poverty and other social problems. By turning personal problems into public issues, the sociological imagination is also the key to bringing people together to create needed change. In this excerpt,* Mills (1959:3–5) explains the need for a sociological imagination:

When society becomes industrialized, a peasant becomes a worker; a feudal lord is liquidated or becomes a businessman. When classes rise or fall, a man is employed or unemployed; when the rate of investment goes up or down, a man takes new heart or goes broke. When wars happen, an insurance salesman becomes a rocket launcher; a store clerk, a radar man; a wife lives alone; a child grows up without a father. Neither the life of an individual nor the history of a society can be understood without understanding both.

Yet men do not usually define the troubles they endure in terms of historical change. . . . The well-being they enjoy, they do not usually impute to the big ups and downs of the society in which they live. Seldom aware of the intricate connection between the patterns of their own lives and the course of world history, ordinary men do not usually know what this connection means for the kind of men they are becoming and for the kinds of history-making in which they might take part. They do not possess the quality of mind essential to grasp the interplay of men and society, of biography and history, of self and world. . . .

What they need . . . is a quality of mind that will help them [see] what is going on in the world and . . . what may be happening within themselves. It is this quality . . . [that] may be called the sociological imagination.

WHAT DO YOU THINK?

1. As Mills sees it, how are personal troubles different from public issues? Explain this difference in terms of what happened to Mike.

2. Living in Canada, why do we often blame ourselves for the personal problems we face?

3. By using the sociological imagination, how do we gain the power to change the world?

*In this excerpt, Mills uses "man" and male pronouns to apply to all people. As far as gender was concerned, even this outspoken critic of society used the conventional writing practices of his time.

Trade across national boundaries has created a global economy. Large corporations make and market goods worldwide. Stock traders in Toronto pay close attention to the financial markets in Tokyo and Hong Kong even as wheat farmers in Saskatchewan watch the price of grain in the former Soviet republic of Georgia. Because most new Canadian jobs involve international trade, greater global understanding has never been more important.

3. **Many social problems that we face in Canada are far more serious elsewhere.** Poverty is a serious problem in this country, but as Chapter 9 ("Global Stratification") explains, poverty in Latin America, Africa, and Asia is both more common and more serious. In the same way, although women have lower social standing than men in Canada, gender inequality is much greater in the world's lowest-income countries.

4. **Thinking globally helps us learn more about ourselves.** We cannot walk the streets of a distant city without thinking about what it means to live in Canada. Comparing life in various settings often leads to unexpected lessons. For instance, in Chapter 9 we visit a squatter settlement in Chennai, India. There, despite a desperate lack of basic material goods, people thrive in the love and support of family members. Why, then,

We can easily see the power of society over the individual by imagining how different our lives would be had we been born in place of any of these children from, respectively, Bolivia, Burma, and South Korea.

are so many poor people in Canada angry and alone? Are material things—so central to our definition of a "rich" life—the best way to measure human well-being?

In sum, in an increasingly interconnected world, we can understand ourselves only to the extent that we understand others. Sociology is an invitation to learn a new way of looking at the world around us. Is this invitation worth accepting? What are the benefits of applying the sociological perspective?

Applying the Sociological Perspective

Applying the sociological perspective is useful in many ways. First, sociology is at work guiding many of the laws and policies that shape our lives. Second, on an individual level, making use of the sociological perspective leads to important personal growth and expanded awareness. Third, studying sociology is excellent preparation for the world of work.

Sociology and Public Policy

Sociologists have helped shape public policy—the laws and regulations that guide how people in communities live and work—in countless ways, including health care, education, juvenile justice, divorce law, and social welfare. Canadian researcher Robin Bagley's (1984) work on sex offences against minors had a major impact on public policy, leading among other things to the 1988 enactment of section 212 of the Criminal Code, which prohibits attempts to purchase sex from persons under 18 years of age (Lowman, 1987).

Sociology and Personal Growth

By applying the sociological perspective, we are likely to become more active and aware and to think more critically in our everyday lives. Using sociology pays off in four ways:

1. **The sociological perspective helps us assess the truth of "common sense."** We all take many things for granted, but that does not make them true. One good example is the idea that we are free individuals who are personally responsible for our lives. If we think that we decide our own fate, we may be quick to praise successful people as superior and consider others with fewer achievements as personally deficient. A sociological approach, by contrast, encourages us to ask whether common beliefs are really true and, to the extent that they are not, why they are so widely held.

2. **The sociological perspective helps us see the opportunities and constraints in our lives.** Sociological thinking leads us to see that, in the game of life, we have a say in how to play our cards, but it is society that deals us the hand. The more we understand the game, the better players we will be. Sociology helps us learn more about the world around us so that we can pursue our goals more effectively.

3. **The sociological perspective empowers us to be active participants in our society.** The better we understand how society operates, the more effective citizens we become. As C. Wright Mills explained in the box on page 6, it is the sociological perspective that turns a private problem (such as being out of work) into a public issue (a lack of good jobs). As we come to see how society affects us, we may decide to support society as it is or we may set out with others to change it.

4. **The sociological perspective helps us live in a diverse world.** North Americans represent just 5 percent of the world's population and, as the remaining chapters of this book explain, much of the other 95 percent lives very differently than we do. Still, like people everywhere, we tend to view our own way of life as "right," "natural," and "better." The sociological perspective prompts us to think critically about the strengths and weaknesses of all ways of life, including our own.

Just about every job in today's economy involves working with people. For this reason, studying sociology is good preparation for your future career. In what ways does having "people skills" help police officers perform their job?

Careers: The "Sociology Advantage"

Most students at colleges and universities today are very interested in getting a good job. A background in sociology is excellent preparation for the working world. Of course, completing a bachelor's degree in sociology is the right choice for people who decide they would like to go on to graduate work and eventually become a professor or researcher in this field. Throughout Canada and the United States, tens of thousands of men and women teach sociology in universities and colleges. But just as many professional sociologists work as researchers for government agencies or private foundations and businesses, gathering important information on how people live, what they think, and how they spend their money. In today's cost-conscious world, agencies and companies want to be sure that the products, programs, and policies they create get the job done at the lowest cost. Sociologists, especially those with advanced research skills, are in high demand for this type of evaluation research (Deutscher, 1999).

In addition, a smaller but increasing number of people work as clinical sociologists. These women and men work, much as clinical psychologists do, with the goal of improving the lives of troubled clients. A basic difference is that sociologists focus on difficulties not in the personality but in the individual's web of social relationships.

But sociology is not just for people who want to be sociologists. People who work in criminal justice—including jobs in police departments, probation offices, and correction facilities—also gain the "sociology advantage" by learning what categories of people are most at risk of becoming criminals or victims, how effective various policing policies and programs are at preventing crime, and why people turn to crime in the first place. Similarly, people who work in the health care field—including physicians, nurses, and technicians—also gain a sociology advantage by learning about patterns of health and illness within the population, as well as how factors such as race, ethnicity, gender, and social class affect human health.

According to the Canadian Association of University Teachers, sociologists are hired for hundreds of jobs in fields such as advertising, banking, criminal justice, education, government, health care, public relations, and research. In almost any type of work, success depends on understanding how various categories of people differ in beliefs, family patterns, and other ways of life. Unless you have a job that never involves dealing with people, you should consider the workplace benefits of taking courses in sociology.

The Origins of Sociology

Like the "choices" people make, major historical events rarely just "happen." Even sociology itself is the result of powerful social forces.

Social Change and Sociology

Striking changes in Europe during the eighteenth and nineteenth centuries made people think more about society and their place in it, spurring the development of sociology. Three kinds of changes were especially important in the development of sociology: the rise of a factory-based economy, the explosive growth of cities, and new ideas about democracy and political rights.

A New Industrial Economy

During the Middle Ages, most people in Europe plowed fields near their homes or engaged in small-scale *manufacturing* (a term derived from Latin words meaning "to make by hand"). By the end of the eighteenth century, inventors were using new sources of energy—the power of moving water and then steam—to operate large machines in mills and factories. As a result, instead of labouring at home or in tightly knit groups, workers became part of a large and anonymous labour force under the control of strangers who owned the factories. This change in the system of production took people away from their homes, weakening the traditions that had guided community life for centuries.

The Growth of Cities

Across Europe, landowners took part in what historians call the *enclosure movement*—they fenced off more and more farmland to create grazing areas for sheep, the source of wool for the thriving textile mills. Without land, countless tenant farmers had little choice but to head to the cities in search of work in the new factories.

positivism a scientific approach to knowledge based on "positive" facts as opposed to mere speculation

As cities grew larger, these urban migrants faced many social problems, including pollution, crime, and homelessness. Moving through streets crowded with strangers, they faced a new, impersonal social world.

Political Change

Economic development and the growth of cities also brought new ways of thinking. In the writings of Thomas Hobbes (1588–1679), John Locke (1632–1704), and Adam Smith (1723–1790), we see a shift in focus from people's moral duties to God and king to the pursuit of self-interest. Philosophers now spoke of *personal liberty* and *individual rights*. Echoing these sentiments, our own Charter of Rights and Freedoms clearly states that "every individual is equal before and under the law and has the right to the equal protection and equal benefit of the law without discrimination and, in particular, without discrimination based on race, national or ethnic origin, colour, religion, sex, age or mental or physical disability" (Department of Justice, 1982).

The French Revolution, which began in 1789, was an even greater break with political and social tradition. As the French social analyst Alexis de Tocqueville (1805–1859) declared, the change in society in the wake of the French Revolution amounted to "nothing short of the regeneration of the whole human race" (1955:13, orig. 1856). As the new industrial economy, enormous cities, and fresh political ideas combined to draw attention to society, the new discipline known as sociology developed in France, Germany, and England, the countries where these changes were greatest.

Science and Sociology

Throughout history, the nature of society has fascinated people, including the brilliant philosophers K'ung Fu-tzu, or Confucius (551–479 BCE), in China and Plato (427–347 BCE) and Aristotle (384–322 BCE) in Greece.[1] Later, the Roman emperor Marcus Aurelius (121–180), the medieval thinkers Saint Thomas Aquinas (c. 1225–1274) and Christine de Pizan (c. 1363–1431), and the great English playwright William Shakespeare (1564–1616) wrote about the workings of society.

It was the French social thinker Auguste Comte (1798–1857) who coined the term *sociology* in 1838 to describe this new way of thinking. This makes sociology among the youngest of the academic disciplines—far newer than history, physics, or economics, for example.

Comte (1975, orig. 1851–54) saw sociology as the product of three stages of historical development. During the earliest *theological stage*, from the beginning of human history to the end of the European Middle Ages about 1350 CE, people took the religious view that society expressed God's will.

What we see depends on our point of view. When gazing at the stars, lovers see romance but scientists see thermal reactions. How does using the sociological perspective change what we see in the world around us?

With the dawn of the Renaissance in the fifteenth century, Comte explained, the theological stage gave way to a *metaphysical stage* in which people came to see society as a natural rather than supernatural phenomenon. The English philosopher Thomas Hobbes (1588–1679), for example, suggested that society reflected not the perfection of God so much as the failings of selfish human nature.

What Comte called the *scientific stage* began with the work of early scientists such as the Polish astronomer Copernicus (1473–1543), the Italian astronomer and physicist Galileo (1564–1642), and the English physicist and mathematician Isaac Newton (1642–1727). Comte's contribution came in applying the scientific approach, originally used to analyze the physical world, to the study of society.[2]

Comte's approach is called **positivism,** *a scientific approach to knowledge based on "positive" facts as opposed to mere speculation.* Comte thought that knowledge based on tradition or metaphysics was really only speculation. A positivist approach to knowledge, however, is based on *science.* As a positivist, Comte believed that society operates according to certain laws, just as the physical world operates according to gravity and other laws of nature. Comte believed that by using science, people could come to understand the laws not only of the physical world but also of society.

By the beginning of the twentieth century, sociology had taken hold in the United States (two decades earlier than in Canada) and showed the influence of Comte's ideas. Today, most sociologists

---

[1] The abbreviation BCE means "before the common era." We use this throughout the text instead of the traditional BC ("before Christ") to reflect the religious diversity of our society. Similarly, in place of the traditional AD (*anno Domini*, "in the year of our Lord") we use the abbreviation CE ("common era").

[2] Illustrating Comte's stages, the ancient Greeks and Romans viewed the planets as gods; Renaissance metaphysical thinkers saw them as astral influences (giving rise to astrology); by the time of Galileo, scientists understood planets as natural objects moving according to natural laws.

Grade 12 students face fierce competition as laid off adults return to school

THE CANADIAN PRESS
Published on January 9, 2010

TORONTO (CP)—Ontario's graduating high school students are facing stiffer competition for high-demand, high-employment college and university programs as workers who lost their jobs in the recession head back to school and claim the country's coveted post-secondary education spots.

Colleges and universities will not give special priority to the Grade 12 candidates, administrators say, despite the fact they could be thrown out into a tough, recessionary job market with little or no work experience and only a high school education if they're not accepted . . .

College applications overall were up by 10 per cent over the last several years, with those in areas with a high jobless rate experiencing increases of up to 50 per cent.

The recession's ravaging of the job market is pushing laid-off workers back to school and a wildly popular Ontario government program has provided many unemployed mature students with the financial means to do so . . .

The Ontario government's Second Career program, which provides laid off workers with up to $28,000 a year to go back to school to train for high-demand jobs, has been a huge incentive for mature students.

Second Career was announced in 2008 as a $355-million, three-year program. However, it was so popular that the money was scooped up in 18 months as laid off workers headed back to school and the province pumped another $78 million into the program last October.

Second Career has been a boon for St. Clair College, which had already been working for several years to build more capacity and is now in a position to take an additional 1,500 students next fall.

But at some post-secondary institutions, competition for programs that are seen as the job-providers of the future has become so fierce that perfectly qualified students are being turned away.

That is particularly true in areas such as health care, biotechnology, social work, personal support, veterinary science and engineering.

Laid off workers are applying in large numbers to colleges, but there is also an increase at the province's universities in the number of people applying to professional programs that can be entered in first year.

"Some of the programs we simply cannot take any more because we don't have the money to expand the program," said University of Windsor president Alan Wildeman. "This is a challenge that's facing many programs across the country."

The same situation exists in the nursing program at Lakehead University in Thunder Bay, where applications for nursing shot up by almost one third over two years.

At the University of Toronto, arts and sciences registrar Glenn Loney says there has been an unexpected increase in applicants accepting offers to study there, which he believes is likely related to the poor economic situation.

Linda Franklin, president of the provincial colleges association College Ontario, says there's been a rapid increase in the number of college student applications all across the province from southwestern Ontario through Toronto and up into the north.

"There's a huge influx of people into the college system," Franklin says.

"In some programs, paramedics for example . . . fire fighting, police foundations, there are far more people interested in those jobs, in those courses, than available spaces."

She notes that mature students have received particular attention, both from colleges and the Ontario government.

"There's been a lot of work at the colleges over the last couple of years to figure out how you

continue to consider science a crucial part of sociology, but we now realize that human behaviour is far more complex than the movement of planets. We are creatures of imagination and spontaneity, so human behaviour can never be explained by any rigid "laws of society." In addition, early sociologists such as Karl Marx (1818–1883) were troubled by the striking inequalities of the new industrial society. They hoped that the new discipline of sociology would not only help us understand society but also lead to change toward greater social justice.

Sociological Theory

The desire to translate observations into understanding brings us to the important part of sociology known as *theory*. A **theory** is *a statement of how and why specific facts are related.* The job of sociological theory is to explain social behaviour in the real world. For example, recall Durkheim's theory that categories of people with low social integration (men, Protestants, the wealthy, and the

unmarried) are at higher risk of suicide. Seeing Sociology in the News explains one consequence for young people of the recent economic recession.

Sociologists conduct research to test and refine their theories. See Figure 1–2 (on page 12), which shows the suicide rates for women and men across different countries.

In building theory, sociologists face two basic questions: What issues should we study? And how should we connect the facts? In answering these questions, sociologists look to one or more theoretical approaches as "road maps." Think of a **theoretical approach** as *a basic image of society that guides thinking and research.* Sociologists make use of three theoretical approaches: the *structural-functional approach*, the *social-conflict approach*, and the *symbolic-interaction approach*.

The Structural-Functional Approach

The **structural-functional approach** is *a framework for building theory that sees society as a complex system whose parts work*

would accommodate this growing demand by mature students," Franklin says.

Mature students apply at various times of the year because they cannot predict when they will get laid off, she said, which can mean missing the cutoff date for applications.

In Windsor, the institution opened an additional number of paramedic courses for retraining adults because there wasn't a way to accommodate this segment in the regular cycle, Franklin said.

"A lot of work has been done there to figure out how we can pre-orient the way we're delivering education to meet quite different needs of the adult learners."

But Grade 12 graduates won't be getting the same kind of attention from the Ontario government.

Like mature students, Grade 12s are eligible to apply for financial help through the Ontario Student Assistance Program. But only unemployed workers can apply for support through Second Career.

Nor will they be given priority for scarce spaces in either colleges or universities despite being up against an influx of mature students.

That's got some Grade 12 students and their parents worried.

Laura Schoof, 17, will be graduating from Vincent Massey Secondary School in Windsor this spring and has applied to three Ontario colleges' medical radiation programs.

"There are more people in their late 40s going in, that's more people applying," said Schoof. "I've been really stressing about getting my grades up and pretty much worrying about getting in."

She believes Grade 12 students should be given priority over mature students because laid off workers could more easily find a job if they were turned away from college.

That doesn't appear to be in the pipeline, however, at either the college or university level.

"No, not right now," said University of Windsor's Wildeman. "We want to be as accessible as we can to as many people as possible who want to get a university education. It's not a question of choosing between the two."

It's the same story at the University of Toronto, where Loney says there will be no special consideration given to high school students.

"You'd have to think through whether someone who is 18 and coming out of high school has a greater claim on the space than somebody who's older and has done some things already," Loney said.

"It's not obvious that one has a greater claim on a space than someone else."

The ultimate answer, say the administrators, is for the Ontario government to fund more spaces,

then there would be no need to pick and choose between high school graduates and mature students.

John Milloy, the minister of training, colleges and universities, could not be reached for comment.

WHAT DO YOU THINK?

1. This article describes the recent surge in community college and university enrolments in Ontario, and a similar trend is occurring across the country. How does this rise in community college and university enrolments reflect not just personal choices by individuals but also larger changes in society?

2. Can you point to other personal choices people have been making that may be linked to the weaker economy? What are they?

3. Did the weakening economy affect your life in terms of work? What about your decision to attend college or university? Did you do so because of lack of job opportunities after finishing high school or because of recent unemployment as a mature student? Do you feel there is competition between these two groups for spots in your college or university?

Source: "Grade 12 students face fierce competition as laid off adults return to school," 9 January 2010. © The Canadian Press.

together to promote solidarity and stability. As its name suggests, this approach points to **social structure,** *any relatively stable pattern of social behaviour.* Social structure gives our lives shape in families, the workplace, or the college classroom. This approach also looks for each structure's **social functions,** *the consequences of a social pattern for the operation of society as a whole.* All social patterns, from a simple handshake to complex religious rituals, function to tie people together and to keep society going, at least in its present form.

The structural-functional approach owes much to Auguste Comte, who pointed out the need to keep society unified when many traditions were breaking down. Emile Durkheim, who helped establish sociology in French universities, also based his work on this approach. A third structural-functional pioneer was the English sociologist Herbert Spencer (1820–1903). Spencer compared society to the human body: Just as the structural parts of the human body—the skeleton, muscles, and internal organs—function together to help the entire organism survive, social structures work together to preserve society. The structural-functional approach, then, leads

sociologists to identify various structures of society and to investigate their functions.

Sociologist Robert K. Merton (1910–2003) expanded our understanding of social function by pointing out that any social structure probably has many functions, some more obvious than others. He distinguished between **manifest functions,** *the recognized and intended consequences of any social pattern,* and **latent functions,** *the unrecognized and unintended consequences of any social pattern.* For example, the obvious function of this country's system of higher education is to give young people the information and skills they will need to hold jobs after graduation. Perhaps just as important, although less often acknowledged, is higher education's function as a "marriage broker," bringing together young people of similar social backgrounds. Another latent function of higher education is to limit unemployment by keeping millions of people out of the labour market, where many of them might not easily find jobs.

But Merton also recognized that not all effects of social structure are good. Thus a **social dysfunction** is *any social pattern that may*

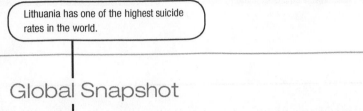

Lithuania has one of the highest suicide rates in the world.

theory (p. 10) a statement of how and why specific facts are related

theoretical approach (p. 10) a basic image of society that guides thinking and research

structural-functional approach (p. 10) a framework for building theory that sees society as a complex system whose parts work together to promote solidarity and stability

social structure (p. 11) any relatively stable pattern of social behaviour

social dysfunction (p. 11) any social pattern that may disrupt the operation of society

Global Snapshot

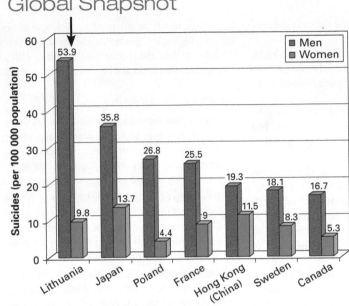

FIGURE 1–2 Suicide Rates of Men and Women in Canada and Selected Countries, 2009

Canada's suicide rate is high compared with that of some nations and low compared with that of still other nations. How do these data support or contradict Durkheim's theory of suicide? Why?

Sources: Statistics Canada (2011a); World Health Organization (2009a).

and conflict. In general, its focus on stability at the expense of conflict makes this approach somewhat conservative. As a critical response, sociologists developed the social-conflict approach.

> **CHECK YOUR LEARNING**   How do manifest functions differ from latent functions? Give an example of a manifest function and a latent function of automobiles in Canada.

The Social-Conflict Approach

The **social-conflict approach** is *a framework for building theory that sees society as an arena of inequality that generates conflict and change.* Unlike the structural-functional emphasis on solidarity and stability, this approach highlights how factors such as class, race, ethnicity, gender, and age are linked to inequality in terms of money, power, education, and social prestige. A conflict analysis rejects the idea that social structure promotes the operation of society as a whole, focusing instead on how any social pattern benefits some people while hurting others.

Sociologists using the social-conflict approach look at ongoing conflict between dominant and disadvantaged categories of people—the rich in relation to the poor, white people in relation to visible minorities, and men in relation to women. Typically, people on top try to protect their privileges while the disadvantaged try to gain more for themselves.

A conflict analysis of our educational system shows how schooling reproduces class inequality from one generation to the next. From a structural-functional point of view, "tracking"—the channelling of young people into particular types of training—benefits everyone by providing schooling that fits students' abilities. But conflict analysis argues that tracking often has less to do with talent than with social background, meaning that well-to-do students are placed in higher tracks while poor children end up in lower tracks.

In this way, young people from privileged families get the best schooling, which leads them to college and university and later to high-income careers. The children of poor families, by contrast, are not prepared for high education and, like their parents before them, typically get stuck in low-paying jobs. In both cases, the social standing of one generation is passed on to the next, with schools justifying the practice in terms of individual merit (Bowles & Gintis, 1976; Davies & Hammack, 2005; Davis & Guppy, 1997; Oakes, 1982, 1985).

Many sociologists use social-conflict analysis not only to understand society but also to reduce inequality. Karl Marx championed the cause of workers in what he saw as their battle against factory owners. In a well-known statement (inscribed on his monument in London's Highgate Cemetery), Marx declared, "The philosophers have only interpreted the world, in various ways; the point, however, is to change it."

disrupt the operation of society. Globalization of the economy, a rising flow of immigrants, and increasing inequality of income are all factors that—in the eyes of some people—disrupt existing social patterns. As these examples suggest, what is helpful and what is harmful for society is a matter about which people often disagree. In addition, what is functional for one category of people (say, a banking system that provides high profits for Bay Street executives) may well be dysfunctional for other categories of people (workers who lose pension funds invested in banks that fail or people who cannot pay their mortgages and end up losing their homes).

> **CRITICAL REVIEW**   The main idea of the structural-functional approach is its vision of society as stable and orderly. The main goal of sociologists who use this approach, then, is to figure out "what makes society tick."
>
> In the mid-1900s, most sociologists favoured the structural-functional approach. In recent decades, however, its influence has declined. By focusing attention on social stability and unity, critics point out, structural-functionalism ignores inequalities of social class, race, ethnicity, and gender, which cause tension

social functions (p. 11) the consequences of a social pattern for the operation of society as a whole

manifest functions (p. 11) the recognized and intended consequences of any social pattern

latent functions (p. 11) the unrecognized and unintended consequences of any social pattern

social-conflict approach (p. 12) a framework for building theory that sees society as an arena of inequality that generates conflict and change

gender-conflict approach a point of view that focuses on inequality and conflict between women and men

race-conflict approach (p.14) a point of view that focuses on inequality and conflict between people of different racial and ethnic categories

feminism support of social equality for women and men

THINKING ABOUT DIVERSITY: RACE, CLASS, & GENDER

W.E.B. Du Bois: A Pioneer in Sociology

One of sociology's pioneers, William Edward Burghardt Du Bois saw sociology as a key to solving society's problems, especially racial inequality. Du Bois earned a Ph.D. in sociology from Harvard University and established the Atlanta Sociological Laboratory, one of the first centres of sociological research in North America. He helped his colleagues in sociology—and people everywhere—see the deep racial divisions in his country. White people can simply be "Americans," Du Bois explained, but African-Americans have a "double consciousness," reflecting their status as citizens who are never able to escape identification based on the colour of their skin.

In his sociological classic *The Philadelphia Negro: A Social Study* (1899), Du Bois explored Philadelphia's African-American community, identifying both the strengths and the weaknesses of people wrestling with overwhelming social problems on a day-to-day basis. He challenged the belief—widespread at that time—that Blacks were inferior to whites, and he blamed white prejudice for the problems African-Americans faced. He also criticized successful people of colour for being so eager to win white acceptance that they gave up all ties with the Black community, which needed their help.

Despite notable achievements, Du Bois gradually grew impatient with academic study, which he felt was too detached from the everyday struggles of people of colour. Du Bois wanted change. It was the hope of sparking public action against racial separation that led Du Bois, in 1909, to participate in founding the National Association for the Advancement of Colored People (NAACP), an organization that has been active in supporting racial equality for more than a century. As the editor of the organization's magazine, *Crisis*, Du Bois worked tirelessly to challenge laws and social customs that deprived African-Americans of the rights and opportunities enjoyed by the white majority.

Du Bois described race as the major problem facing his country in the twentieth century. Early in his career, as a sociological researcher, he made enormous contributions to the study of racial inequality. Later, as an activist, he believed that political reform might overcome deep racial divisions. But by the end of his life, he had grown bitter, believing that little had changed. At the age of 93, Du Bois emigrated to the African nation of Ghana, where he died two years later.

WHAT DO YOU THINK?

1. If he were alive today, do you think that Du Bois would still consider race a major problem in the twenty-first century? Why or why not?

2. How much do you think African-Americans today experience "double consciousness"?

3. In what ways can sociology help us understand and reduce racial conflict?

Sources: Based on Baltzell (1967), Du Bois (1967, orig. 1899), Wright (2002a, 2002b), and personal communication with Earl Wright II.

Feminism and the Gender-Conflict Approach

One important type of conflict analysis is the **gender-conflict approach,** *a point of view that focuses on inequality and conflict between women and men.* The gender-conflict approach is closely linked to **feminism,** *support of social equality for women and men.*

The importance of the gender-conflict approach lies in making us aware of the many ways in which our society places men in positions of power over women, in the home (where men are usually considered the "head of the household"), in the workplace (where men earn more income and hold most positions of power), and in the mass media (how many hip-hop stars are women?).

Another contribution of the gender-conflict approach is making us aware of the importance of women to the development of sociology. Harriet Martineau (1802–1876) is regarded as the first woman sociologist. Born to a wealthy English family, Martineau made her mark in 1853 by translating the writings of Auguste Comte from French into English. She later documented the evils of slavery and argued for laws to protect factory workers, defending workers' right to unionize. She was particularly concerned about the position of women in society and fought for changes in education policy so that women could look forward to more in life than marriage and raising children.

In Canada, Nellie McClung (1873–1951) was a pioneer of women's rights who started school at age 10 and received a teaching

Daniel Grafton Hill (1923–2003) is a well-known authority on Black history and a Canadian sociologist, civil servant, and human rights specialist. Helen Caroline Abell (1917–) is a well-known and respected Canadian sociologist involved with international studies in the field of rural sociology.

certificate six years later. McClung was a supporter of suffrage for women and a well-known advocate for Prohibition, factory laws for women, formal compulsory education, reform in Canadian prisons, and equal representation for women in the political realm. While an elected Liberal MLA in Alberta, she became a member of the "Famous Five," who in 1927 petitioned the Government of Canada to include women in the definition of "person" in the *British North America Act*. The Famous Five's success in 1929 meant that women could be appointed to the Senate.

All chapters of this book consider the importance of gender and gender inequality. For an in-depth look at feminism and the social standing of women and men, see Chapter 10 ("Gender Stratification").

The Race-Conflict Approach

Another important type of social-conflict analysis is the **race-conflict approach,** *a point of view that focuses on inequality and conflict between people of different racial and ethnic categories.* Just as men have power over women, white people have numerous social advantages over Aboriginal peoples, including, on average, higher incomes, more schooling, better health, and longer life expectancy.

An important contribution to understanding race was made by William Edward Burghardt Du Bois (1868–1963). Born to a poor Massachusetts family, Du Bois enrolled at Fisk University in Nashville, Tennessee, and then at Harvard University, where he earned the first doctorate awarded by that university to a person

of colour. Du Bois then founded the Atlanta Sociological Laboratory, which was an important centre of sociological research in the early decades of the twentieth century. Like most people who follow the social-conflict approach (whether focusing on class, gender, or race), Du Bois believed that scholars should not simply learn about society's problems but also try to solve them. He therefore studied the Black communities across the United States, pointing to numerous social problems ranging from educational inequality and a political system that denied people their right to vote, to the terrorist practice of lynching. Du Bois spoke out against racial inequality and participated in the founding of the National Association for the Advancement of Colored People (NAACP) (E. Wright, 2002a, 2002b). An important contribution to understanding race in Canada was made by Daniel Grafton Hill (1923–2003), who is especially remembered for his sociological writings on Black history and human rights. See the Thinking about Diversity box on page 13 for more on Du Bois.

The fact that women and Black North Americans were second-class citizens reduced the attention paid to the work of the scholars and activists mentioned above. By the mid-twentieth century, however, Canadian sociologists were bringing their accomplishments to new generations of students.

CRITICAL REVIEW The various social-conflict approaches have gained a large following in recent decades but, like other approaches, they have met with criticism. Because any conflict analysis focuses on inequality, it largely ignores how shared values and interdependence can unify members of a society. In addition, say critics, to the extent that it pursues political goals, a social-conflict approach cannot claim scientific objectivity. Supporters of social-conflict analysis respond that all theoretical approaches have political consequences.

A final criticism of both the structural-functional and the social-conflict approaches is that they paint society in broad strokes—in terms of "family," "social class," "race," and so on. A third theoretical approach views society less in general terms and more as the specific, everyday experiences of individual people.

CHECK YOUR LEARNING Why do you think sociologists characterize the social-conflict approach as "activist"? What is it actively trying to achieve?

The Symbolic-Interaction Approach

The structural-functional and social-conflict approaches share a **macro-level orientation,** meaning *a broad focus on social structures that shape society as a whole.* Macro-level sociology takes in the big picture, rather like observing a city from a helicopter and seeing how highways help people move from place to place or how housing differs

micro-level orientation a close-up focus on social interaction in specific situations

symbolic-interaction approach a framework for building theory that sees society as the product of the everyday interactions of individuals

● APPLYING THEORY ●

Major theoretical approaches

	Structural-Functional Approach	Social-Conflict Approach	Symbolic-Interaction Approach
What is the level of analysis?	Macro level	Macro level	Micro level
What image of society does the approach have?	Society is a system of interrelated parts that is relatively stable. Each part works to keep society operating in an orderly way. Members generally agree about what is morally right and morally wrong.	Society is a system of social inequalities based on class (Marx), gender (feminism and gender-conflict approach), and race (race-conflict approach). Society operates to benefit some categories of people and harm others. Social inequality causes conflict that leads to social change.	Society is an ongoing process. People interact in countless settings using symbolic communications. The reality people experience is variable and changing.
What core questions does the approach ask?	How is society held together? What are the major parts of society? How are these parts linked? What does each part do to help society work?	How does society divide a population? How do advantaged people protect their privileges? How do disadvantaged people challenge the system seeking change?	How do people experience society? How do people shape the reality they experience? How do behaviour and meaning change from person to person and from one situation to another?

from rich to poor neighbourhoods. Sociology also uses a **micro-level orientation,** *a close-up focus on social interaction in specific situations.* Exploring city life in this way occurs at street level, where you might watch how children invent games on a school playground or observe how pedestrians respond to homeless people they pass on the street. The **symbolic-interaction approach,** then, is *a framework for building theory that sees society as the product of the everyday interactions of individuals.*

How does "society" result from the ongoing experiences of tens of millions of people? One answer, detailed in Chapter 4 ("Social Interaction in Everyday Life"), is that society is nothing more than the reality that people construct for themselves as they interact with one another. That is, we human beings live in a world of symbols, and we attach meaning to virtually everything, from the words on this page to the wink of an eye. We create "reality," therefore, as we define our surroundings, decide what we think of others, and shape our own identities.

The symbolic-interaction approach has roots in the thinking of Max Weber (1864–1920), a German sociologist who emphasized understanding a particular setting from the point of view of the people in it. Since Weber's time, sociologists have taken micro-level sociology in a number of directions. Chapter 3 ("Socialization: From Infancy to Old Age") discusses the ideas of George Herbert Mead (1863–1931), who explored how our personalities develop as a result of social experience. Chapter 4 ("Social Interaction in Everyday Life") presents the work of Canadian-born sociologist Erving Goffman (1922–1982), whose *dramaturgical analysis* describes how we resemble actors on a stage as we play out our various roles. Other contemporary sociologists, including George Homans and Peter Blau, have developed *social-exchange analysis*, the idea that interaction is guided by what each person stands to gain and lose from others. In the ritual of courtship, for example, people seek mates who can offer them at least as much—in terms of physical attractiveness, intelligence, and social background—as they offer in return. Social constructionist theory of knowledge, which maintains that humans generate knowledge and meaning from their experiences and not from an objective reality, is a late modern outgrowth of the symbolic-interaction tradition. Social constructionism calls into question the empiricism, including medical empiricism, that underlies other sociological models (Nettle, 2006).

Sports: Playing the Theory Game

Who doesn't enjoy sports? Children and teens may play as many as two or three organized sports. For adults who don't participate themselves, weekend television is filled with sporting events and whole sections of our newspapers are devoted to teams, players, and scores. What can we learn by applying sociology's three theoretical approaches to this familiar element of Canadian life?

Structural-Functional Approach According to the structural-functional approach, the manifest functions of sports include recreation, getting in shape, and letting off steam in a relatively harmless way. Sports have important latent functions as well, from building social relationships to creating jobs. Perhaps the most important latent function of sports is to encourage competition, which is central to our society's way of life.

Of course, sports also have dysfunctional consequences. For example, colleges and universities that try to field winning teams sometimes recruit students for their athletic skill rather than their academic ability. This practice not only lowers a school's academic standards but also short-changes athletes, who spend little time doing the academic work that will prepare them for future careers (Upthegrove, Roscigno, & Charles, 1999).

Social-Conflict Approach A social-conflict analysis points out how sports are linked to social inequality. Some sports—tennis, swimming, golf, and skiing—are expensive, so participation is largely limited to the well-to-do. Football, baseball, and basketball, however, are accessible to people at almost all income levels. Thus the games people

All Olympic Games involve outstanding athletes. However, the sports that are central to the Summer Games, including track and field events, have a higher share of athletes who are visible minorities. By contrast, the Winter Olympics have fewer minorities and more well-to-do athletes. Can you explain why?

play are not simply a matter of choice but also a reflection of their social standing.

Throughout history, men have dominated the world of sports. The first modern Olympic Games, held in 1896, excluded women from competition. Through most of the twentieth century in Canada, even hockey teams barred girls based on the traditional ideas that they lack the strength and the stamina to play sports and that they risk losing their femininity if they do. Women competed in hockey for the first time at the 1998 Winter Olympics, but are still banned from competing in some sports, including ski jumping, as was the case at the 2010 Winter Olympics. Although our society long excluded Black people from professional sports, opportunities have expanded in recent decades. In 1947, Jackie Robinson broke through the "colour line" to become the first African-American player in Major League Baseball, playing for the Brooklyn Dodgers. More than 50 years later, professional baseball retired Robinson's number 42 on all teams. In 1958, Canadian-born William O'Ree made headlines as the first Black player to be recruited into the National Hockey League. In 2008, African-Americans (12.8 percent of the U.S. population) accounted for 10.2 percent of Major League Baseball (MLB) players, 67 percent of National Football League (NFL) players, and 77 percent of National Basketball Association (NBA) players (Lapchick, 2009). But racial discrimination still exists in professional sports. For one thing, race is linked to the positions athletes play on the field, a pattern called "stacking." The

○ **CRITICAL REVIEW** Without denying the existence of macro-level social structures such as the family and social class, the symbolic-interaction approach reminds us that society basically amounts to people *interacting*. That is, micro-level sociology shows us how individuals construct and experience society. However, by emphasizing what is unique in each social scene, this approach risks overlooking the widespread influence of culture, as well as structural factors such as class, gender, and race. Some scholars also challenge the notion of the continuous social construction of

reality and argue for a "realist" perspective that calls attention to the limits of constructionism, maintaining instead that there is one objective physical reality (Sayer, 1992; Taylor & Ashworth, 1987).

○ **CHECK YOUR LEARNING** How does a micro-level analysis differ from a macro-level analysis? Provide an explanation of a social pattern at both levels.

The Applying Theory table, on page 15, summarizes the structural-functional, social-conflict, and symbolic-interaction approaches.

positivist sociology the study of society based on scientific observation of social behaviour

empirical evidence (p. 18) information we can verify with our senses

science a logical system that develops knowledge from direct, systematic observation

figure shows the results of a 2009 study of race in Major League Baseball. Notice that white players are most concentrated in the central "thinking" positions of pitcher (66 percent white) and catcher (62 percent white). By contrast, Black players represented only 5 percent of pitchers, and there were no Black catchers. At the same time, 9 percent of infielders are Black players, as are 32 percent of outfielders (positions characterized as requiring "speed and reactive ability") (Lapchick, 2009).

More broadly, Blacks represent a large share of players in only five major sports: basketball, football, baseball, boxing, and track. And across all professional sports, the vast majority of managers, head coaches, and team owners are still white (Lapchick, 2009).

Who benefits most from professional sports? Although some players get sky-high salaries and millions of fans follow their teams, the vast profits that sports generate are controlled by a small number of people—predominantly white men. In sum, sports in our society are bound up with inequalities based on gender, race, and wealth.

At the micro level, a sporting event is a complex, face-to-face interaction. In part, play is guided by the players' assigned positions and the rules of the game. But players are also spontaneous and unpredictable. Following the symbolic-interaction approach, we see sports less as a system and more as an ongoing process.

From this point of view, too, we would expect each player to understand the game a little differently. Some players enjoy stiff competition; for others, love of the game may be greater than

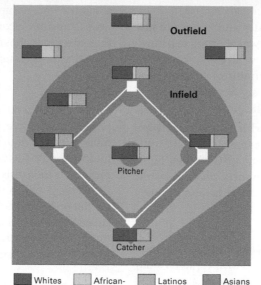

Whites African-Americans Latinos Asians

Diversity Snapshot

"Stacking" in Professional Baseball

Does race play a part in professional sports? Looking at the various positions in professional baseball, we see that white players are more likely to play the central positions in the infield, while people of colour are more likely to play in the outfield. What do you make of this pattern?

Source: Lapchick (2009).

the need to win. In addition, the behaviour of any single player is likely to change over time. A rookie in professional baseball, for example, may feel self-conscious during the first few games in the big leagues but go on to develop a comfortable sense of fitting in with the team. Jackie Robinson played minor-league basketball in 1946 in Montreal and was revered in that cosmopolitan city. Coming to feel at home on the field in New York the next year was a different story. At first, he was painfully aware that many white players and millions of white fans resented his presence. In time, however, his outstanding ability and his confident, co-operative manner won him the respect of the entire nation.

The three theoretical approaches provide different insights into sports, and none is entirely correct. Applied to any issue, each approach provides part of a complex picture. To fully appreciate the power of the sociological perspective, you should become familiar with all three.

WHAT DO YOU THINK?

1. Describe how a macro-level approach to sports differs from a micro-level approach. Which theoretical approaches are macro-level, and which one is micro-level?

2. Make up three questions about sports that reflect the focus of each of the three theoretical approaches.

3. How might you apply the three approaches to other social patterns, such as the workplace or family life?

Three Ways to Do Sociology

Keep in mind that each approach is helpful in answering particular types of questions. As the Seeing Sociology in Everyday Life box on pages 16–17 shows, the fullest understanding of society comes from using all three approaches.

All sociologists want to learn about the social world. But just as some may prefer one theoretical approach to another, many sociologists favour one research orientation. The following sections describe three ways to do sociological research: positivist, interpretive, and critical sociology.

Positivist Sociology

One popular way to do sociological research is **positivist sociology,** which is *the study of society based on scientific observation of social behaviour.* As explained earlier, positivist research discovers facts through the use of **science,** *a logical system that develops knowledge from direct, systematic observation.* Positivist sociology is sometimes called

concept a mental construct that represents some aspect of the world in a simplified form

variable a concept whose value changes from case to case

measurement a procedure for determining the value of a variable in a specific case

reliability consistency in measurement

validity actually measuring exactly what you intend to measure

empirical sociology because it is based on **empirical evidence,** which is *information we can verify with our senses.*

Scientific research often challenges what we accept as "common sense." Here are three examples of widely held beliefs that are not supported by scientific evidence:

1. **"Differences in the behaviour of females and males are just 'human nature.'"** Wrong. Much of what we call "human nature" is constructed by the society in which we live. We know this because researchers have found that definitions of "feminine" and "masculine" change over time and vary from one society to another (see Chapter 10, "Gender Stratification").

2. **"Canada is a middle-class society in which most people are more or less equal."** Not true. As Chapter 8 ("Social Stratification") explains, the richest 5 percent of Canadian families control about 40 percent of the country's wealth, while the poorest 5 percent of Canadian families have a negative wealth—they live in debt.

3. **"People marry because they are in love."** Not exactly. In Canadian society, as already discussed, many social rules guide the selection of mates. Around the world, as Chapter 13 ("Family and Religion") explains, research indicates that marriages in most societies are arranged by parents and have little to do with love.

These examples confirm the old saying that "it's not what we *don't* know that gets us into trouble as much as the things we *do* know that *just aren't so.*" The Seeing Sociology in Everyday Life box on page 19 explains why we also need to think critically about the "facts" we find in the popular media and on the internet.

We have all been brought up hearing many widely accepted "truths," being bombarded by "expert" advice in the popular media, and feeling pressure to accept the opinions of those around us. As adults, we need to evaluate more critically what we see, read, and hear. Sociology can help us do that. Sociologists (and everyone else) can use science to assess many kinds of information.

Concepts, Variables, and Measurement

Let's take a closer look at how science works. A basic element of science is the **concept,** *a mental construct that represents some aspect of the world in a simplified form.* Sociologists use concepts to label aspects of social life, including "the family" and "the economy," and to categorize people in terms of their "gender" or "social class."

A **variable** is *a concept whose value changes from case to case.* The familiar variable "height," for example, has a value that varies from person to person. The concept "social class" can describe people's social standing using the values "upper-class," "middle-class," "working-class," and "lower-class."

The use of variables depends on **measurement,** *a procedure for determining the value of a variable in a specific case.* Some variables are easy to measure, as when a nurse checks our blood pressure. But measuring sociological variables can be far more difficult. For example, how would you measure a person's social class? You might start by looking at the clothing people wear, listening to how they speak, or noting where they live. Or trying to be more precise, you might ask about income, occupation, and education. Because there are many ways to measure a complex variable like social class, researchers must make decisions about how to *operationalize* a variable, stating exactly what they are measuring.

Statistics

Sociologists also face the problem of dealing with large numbers of people. For example, how do you report income for thousands or even millions of individuals? Listing streams of numbers would carry little meaning and tell us nothing about the people as a whole. To solve this problem, sociologists use *descriptive statistics* to state what is "average" for a large population. The most commonly used descriptive statistics are the *mean* (the arithmetic average of all measures, which you calculate by adding all the values and dividing by the number of cases), the *median* (the score at the halfway point in a listing of numbers from lowest to highest), and the *mode* (the score that occurs most often).

Reliability and Validity

For a measurement to be useful, it must be reliable and valid. **Reliability** refers to *consistency in measurement.* A measurement is reliable if repeated measurements give the same result time after time. But consistency does not guarantee **validity,** which is *actually measuring exactly what you intend to measure.* Valid measurement means more than hitting the same spot somewhere on a target again and again; it means hitting the exact target, the bull's eye.

Say you want to know just how religious the students at your university or college are. You might ask students how often they attend religious services. But is going to a house of worship really the same thing as being religious? Maybe not, because people take part in religious rituals for many reasons, some of them having little to do with religion; in addition, some strong believers avoid organized religion altogether. Thus even when a measure yields consistent results (meaning that it is reliable), it can still miss the intended target (and therefore lack validity). Good sociological research depends on careful measurement, which is always a challenge to researchers.

Correlation and Cause

The real payoff in scientific research is determining how variables are related. **Correlation** means *a relationship in which two (or more) variables change together.* But sociologists want to know not just how variables change but which variable changes the other. The scientific ideal is to determine **cause and effect,** *a relationship in which change in one variable causes change in another.* As noted earlier, Emile Durkheim found that the degree of social integration (the cause)

correlation (p. 18) a relationship in which two (or more) variables change together

cause and effect (p. 18) a relationship in which change in one variable (the independent variable) causes change in another (the dependent variable)

SEEING SOCIOLOGY IN EVERYDAY LIFE

Is What We Read in the Popular Press True? The Case of Extramarital Sex

Every day, we see stories in newspapers and magazines that tell us what people think and how they behave. But a lot of what you read turns out to be misleading or worse.

Take the issue of extramarital sex, meaning married or common-law people having sex with someone other than their spouse or partner. A look at the covers of the many "women's magazines" at the supermarket checkout or a quick reading of the advice column in your local newspaper might lead you to think that extramarital sex is a major issue facing today's couples.

The popular media seem full of stories about how to keep your spouse or partner from "cheating" or pointing out the clues that tip you off when he or she is having an affair. Most of the studies reported in the popular press and on websites suggest that more than half of people in intimate relationships—women as well as men—cheat.

But is extramarital sex really that widespread? No. Researchers who conduct sound sociological investigation have found that, in any given year, only 3 to 4 percent of married or common-law people have an extramarital relationship, and no more than 15 to 20 percent have ever done so. Why, then, do surveys in the popular media report rates of extramarital sex that are so much higher? We can answer this question by taking a look at who fills out pop surveys.

First, people with a personal interest in a topic are most likely to respond to an offer in the popular media or online to complete a survey. For this reason, people who have some personal experience with extramarital sex (either their own behaviour or their partner's) are more likely to

show up in these studies. In contrast, studies correctly conducted by skilled researchers carefully select subjects so that the results are representative of the entire population.

Second, because the readership of the magazines and online sources that conduct these surveys is, on average, young, their surveys end up attracting a high proportion of young respondents. And one thing we know about young people who are in an intimate relationship is that they are more likely to have sex. For example, the typical married or common-law person who is age 30 is more than twice as likely to have had an

extramarital relationship than the typical married or common-law person over age 60.

Third, women are much more likely than men to read the popular magazines that feature sex surveys. Therefore, women are more likely to fill out these surveys. In recent decades, the share of women, especially younger women, who have had extramarital sex has gone up. Why are today's younger women more likely than women a generation or two earlier to have had extramarital sex? Probably because women today are working out of the home and many are travelling as part of their job. In general, today's women have a wider social network that brings them into contact with more men.

Chapter 6 ("Sexuality and Society") takes a close look at sexual patterns, including extramarital relationships. For now, just remember that a lot of what you read in the popular media and online may not be as true as some people think.

WHAT DO YOU THINK?

1. Can you think of other issues on which popular media surveys may give misleading information? What are they?

2. Explain why we should have more trust in the results of sound research carried out by skilled sociologists than in the surveys conducted by the popular media.

3. Do you think companies are likely to sell more magazines or newspapers if they publish "research" results that distort the truth? Explain.

Sources: Black (2007); Parker-Pope (2008); and T.W. Smith (2006).

---

affected the suicide rate (the effect) among categories of people. Scientists refer to the cause as the *independent variable* and the effect as the *dependent variable*. Understanding cause and effect is valuable because it allows researchers to *predict* how one pattern of behaviour will produce another.

Just because two variables change together does not necessarily mean that they have a cause-and-effect relationship. For instance, the marriage rate in Canada falls to its lowest point in January, which also happens to be the month when the national death rate is

highest. Does this mean that people drop dead because they don't marry or that they don't marry because they die? Of course not. More likely, it is the cold and often stormy weather across much of the country in January (perhaps combined with the post-holiday blues) that is responsible for both the low marriage rate and the high death rate.

When two variables change together but neither one causes the other, sociologists describe the relationship as a *spurious*, or false, correlation. A spurious correlation between two variables usually results

interpretive sociology the study of society that focuses on discovering the meanings people attach to their social world

critical sociology the study of society that focuses on the need for social change

from some third factor. For example, delinquency rates are high where young people live in crowded housing, but this is not because crowded housing causes youngsters to "turn bad." Both crowded housing and delinquency result from a third factor: poverty. To be sure of a real cause-and-effect relationship, we must show that (1) variables are correlated, (2) the independent (causal) variable occurs before the dependent variable, and (3) there is no evidence that a third variable has been overlooked, causing a spurious correlation.

The Ideal of Objectivity

A guiding principle of science is *objectivity*, or personal neutrality, in conducting research. Ideally, objective research allows the facts to speak for themselves and not be influenced by the personal values and biases of the researcher. In reality, of course, achieving total neutrality is impossible for anyone. But carefully observing the rules of scientific research will maximize objectivity.

The German sociologist Max Weber noted that people usually choose *value-relevant* research topics—in other words, topics they care about. But once their work is under way, he cautioned, researchers should try to be *value-free*. That is, we must be dedicated to finding truth as it *is* rather than as we think it *should be*. For Weber, this difference sets science apart from politics. Researchers (unlike politicians) must stay open-minded and be willing to accept whatever results come from their work, whether they personally agree with them or not.

Weber's argument still carries much weight in sociology, although most researchers realize that we can never be completely value-free or even aware of all our biases (Demerath, 1996). In addition, keep in mind that sociologists are not "average" people: Most are highly educated white men and women who are more politically liberal than the population as a whole. Sociologists need to remember that they, too, are influenced by their social backgrounds.

Interpretive Sociology

As noted above, not all sociologists agree that science is the only way—or even the best way—to study human society. This is because, unlike planets or other elements of the natural world, humans do not simply move around as objects that can be measured. On the contrary, people are active creatures who attach *meaning* to their actions, and meaning is not easy to observe directly. Therefore, sociologists have developed a second research orientation, known as **interpretive sociology**, *the study of society that focuses on discovering the meanings people attach to their social world*. Max Weber, the pioneer of this framework, argued that the proper focus of sociology is *interpretation*, or understanding the meanings people create in their everyday lives.

The Importance of Meaning

Interpretive sociology differs from positivist sociology in three ways. First, positivist sociology focuses on action—on what people do—because this is what we can observe directly; interpretive sociology focuses on people's understanding of their actions and their surroundings. Second, positivist sociology claims that objective reality exists "out there"; interpretive sociology counters that reality is subjective, constructed by people in the course of their everyday lives. Third, positivist sociology tends to favour *quantitative* data, numerical measurements of outward behaviour; interpretive sociology favours *qualitative* data, researchers' perceptions of how people understand their world. In sum, the positivist orientation, close to science, is well suited for research in a laboratory, where investigators stand back and take careful measurements of what people do. The interpretive orientation, while not rejecting science outright, claims that we learn more by interacting with people, focusing on subjective meaning, and learning how people make sense of their everyday lives. This type of research is best carried out in a natural setting.

Weber's Concept of Verstehen

Max Weber claimed that the key to interpretive sociology lies in *Verstehen* (pronounced "fair-SHTAY-en"), the German word for "understanding." It is the interpretive sociologist's job not just to observe *what* people do but also to share in their world of meaning, coming to appreciate *why* they act as they do. Subjective thoughts and feelings, which scientists tend to dismiss because they are difficult to measure, are the focus of the interpretive sociologist's attention.

Critical Sociology

Like the interpretive orientation, critical sociology developed in reaction to what many sociologists saw as the limitations of positivist sociology. In this case, however, the problem involves the central principle of scientific research: objectivity. Positivist sociology holds that reality is "out there" and that the researcher's job is to study and document how society works. But Karl Marx, who founded the critical orientation, rejected the idea that society exists as a "natural" system. To assume that society is somehow "fixed," he claimed, is the same as saying that society cannot be changed. Positivist sociology, in his view, ends up supporting the status quo. **Critical sociology,** by contrast, is *the study of society that focuses on the need for social change*.

The Importance of Change

Rather than asking the positivist question "How does society work?" critical sociologists ask moral and political questions, especially "Should society exist in its present form?" Their answer to this question, typically, is that it should not. Critical sociology does not reject science completely; Marx (like critical sociologists today) used scientific methods to learn about inequality. But critical sociology does reject the scientific neutrality that requires researchers to try to be "objective" and limit their work to studying the status quo.

SUMMING UP

Three Research Orientations in Sociology

	Positivist Sociology	Interpretive Sociology	Critical Sociology
What is reality?	Society is an orderly system. There is an objective reality "out there."	Society is ongoing interaction. People construct reality as they attach meanings to their behaviour.	Society is patterns of inequality. Reality is that some categories of people dominate others.
How do we conduct research?	Using a scientific orientation, the researcher carefully observes behaviour, gathering empirical, ideally quantitative, data. Researcher tries to be a neutral observer.	Seeking to look "deeper" than outward behaviour, the researcher focuses on subjective meaning. The researcher gathers qualitative data, discovering the subjective sense people make of their world. Researcher is a participant.	Seeking to go beyond positivism's focus on studying the world as it is, the researcher is guided by politics and uses research as a strategy to bring about desired social change. Researcher is an activist.
Corresponding theoretical approach	Structural-functional approach	Symbolic-interaction approach	Social-conflict approach

One recent account of the critical orientation, echoing Marx, claims that the point of this type of sociology is "not just to research the social world but to change it in the direction of democracy and social justice" (Feagin & Hernán, 2001:1). In making value judgments about how society should be changed, critical sociology rejects Weber's goal that sociology be a value-free science and emphasizes instead that sociologists should be activists in pursuit of greater social equality. For example, Whitehead, Dahlgren, and McIntyre (2007) argue that sociological research should specifically aim to reduce "social inequities"—differences in social position that are unfair and unjust.

Sociologists using the critical orientation seek to change not only society but also the character of research itself. They often identify personally with their research subjects and encourage them to help decide what to study and how to do the work. Often researchers and subjects use their findings to provide a voice for less powerful people and advance the political goal of a more equal society (Feagin & Hernán, 2001; Hess, 1999; Perrucci, 2001).

Sociology as Politics

Positivist sociologists object to taking sides in this way, claiming that critical sociology (whether feminist, Marxist, or of some other critical orientation) becomes political, lacks scientific objectivity, and cannot correct for its own biases. Critical sociologists respond that *all* research is political in that it either calls for change or does not; sociologists thus have no choice about their work being political, but they can choose *which* positions to support.

Critical sociology is an activist approach that ties knowledge to action and seeks not just to understand the world as it exists but also to improve it. In general, positivist sociology tends to appeal to researchers who try to be apolitical or who have more conservative political views; critical sociology appeals to those whose politics ranges from liberal to radical left.

Research Orientations and Theory

Is there a link between research orientations and sociological theory? There is no precise connection, but each of the three ways to do sociology—positivist, interpretive, and critical—does stand closer to one of the theoretical approaches presented earlier in this chapter. The positivist orientation is linked to the structural-functional approach (because both are concerned with the scientific goal of understanding society as it is), the interpretive orientation is linked to the symbolic-interaction approach (because both focus on the meanings people attach to their social world), and the critical orientation is linked to the social-conflict approach (because both seek to reduce social inequality). The Summing Up table provides a quick review of the differences among the three ways to do sociology. Many sociologists favour one orientation over another; however, because each provides useful insights, it is a good idea to become familiar with all three. In fact, when sociologists conduct research, they often draw upon ideas from all three orientations.

If you ask only male subjects about their attitudes or actions, you may be able to support conclusions about "men" but not more generally about "people." What would a researcher have to do to ensure that research data support conclusions about all of society?

Gender and Research

In recent years, sociologists have become aware that research is affected by **gender,** *the personal traits and social positions that members of a society attach to being female or male.* Gender can affect sociological research in five ways (Eichler, 1988; Giovannini, 1992):

1. **Androcentricity.** *Androcentricity* (literally, "focus on the male") means approaching an issue from a male perspective. Sometimes researchers act as if only men's activities are important, ignoring what women do. For years, sociologists studying occupations focused on the paid labour of men and overlooked the housework and child care traditionally performed by women. Research that tries to explain human behaviour cannot ignore half of humanity.

    Gynocentricity—seeing the world from a female perspective—can also limit good sociological investigation. However, in our male-dominated society, this problem arises less often.

2. **Overgeneralizing.** This problem occurs when sociologists gather data only from men but then use that information to draw conclusions about all people. For example, a researcher might speak to a handful of male public officials and then form conclusions about an entire community.

3. **Gender blindness.** Failing to consider gender at all is called *gender blindness.* The lives of men and women differ in many ways. A study of growing old in Canada might suffer from gender blindness if it overlooked the fact that most elderly men live with spouses but elderly women generally live alone.

4. **Double standards.** Researchers must be careful not to judge men and women by different standards. For example, a family researcher who labels a couple "man and wife" may define the man as the "head of the household" and treat him as important while assuming that the woman simply engages in family "support work."

5. **Interference.** Another way gender can distort a study is if a subject reacts to the sex of the researcher, interfering with the research operation. While studying a small community in Sicily, for instance, Maureen Giovannini (1992) found that many men treated her as a *woman* rather than as a *researcher*. Some thought it inappropriate for an unmarried woman to speak privately with a man. Others denied Giovannini access to places they considered off limits to women.

There is nothing wrong with focusing research on people of one sex or the other. But all sociologists, as well as people who read their work, should be mindful of how gender can affect an investigation.

Research Ethics

Like all other scientific investigators, sociologists must be aware that their work can harm as well as help subjects and communities. For this reason, the Canadian Sociology and Anthropology Association (CSAA) (1994)—the major professional association for sociologists in Canada—provides formal guidelines for conducting research.

Sociologists must try to be skilful and fair-minded in their work. They must disclose all research findings without omitting significant data. They should make their results available to other sociologists who may want to conduct a similar study.

Sociologists must also make sure that subjects taking part in a research project are not harmed, and they must stop work right away if they suspect that any subject is at risk of harm. Researchers are also required to protect the privacy of individuals involved in a research project, even if they come under pressure from authorities, such as the police or the courts, to release confidential information.

research method a systematic plan for doing research

experiment (p. 24) a research method for investigating cause and effect under highly controlled conditions

survey (p. 24) a research method in which subjects respond to a series of statements or questions on a questionnaire or in an interview

participant observation (p. 26) a research method in which investigators systematically observe people while joining them in their routine activities

THINKING ABOUT DIVERSITY: RACE, CLASS, & GENDER

Research with First Nations, Inuit, and Metis Peoples of Canada

In a society as racially, ethnically, and religiously diverse as Canada, sociological investigators will inevitably confront people who differ from themselves. Learning—in advance—how to conduct ethical research with people of diverse cultural backgrounds and histories can not only facilitate the research and ensure that no hard feelings remain when the work is completed, but also keep avenues open for future collaborations.

Canada's national research funding agencies—the Canadian Institutes of Health Research (CIHR), the Natural Sciences and Engineering Research Council of Canada (NSERC), and the Social Sciences and Humanities Research Council of Canada (SSHRC)—and the First Nations, Inuit, and Metis peoples of Canada have worked together to produce consensus guidelines for conducting research that aims to meet the goals of all parties involved. In December 2010, CIHR, NSERC, and SSHRC jointly released the second edition of the *Tri-Council Policy Statement: Ethical Conduct for Research Involving Humans*. Chapter 9 in this second edition of the policy statement discusses the latest thinking about ethical

research involving Canada's Aboriginal peoples. This chapter, developed with Aboriginal partners, emphasizes the need for equitable partnerships and provides safeguards specific to First Nations, Inuit, and Metis people.

Chapter 9 cautions researchers to be aware of the "apprehension or mistrust" of traditional research conducted *on* (*not with*) Canada's Aboriginal peoples. Such research was predominantly driven by the needs and concerns of researchers and often had little or no benefit to Aboriginal communities—and sometimes even resulted in harm. Some of the guidelines that researchers hoping to conduct research with First Nations, Inuit, and Metis peoples should follow include:

1. Researchers must meaningfully liaise with the Aboriginal community that their research is likely to affect, including with community leaders.
2. First Nations, Inuit, and Metis representatives should be invited to join ethical review boards, where appropriate.
3. Researchers and ethical review boards should also include the voices of commu-

nity members who do not have a voice in formal leadership.
4. Researchers must ensure that the research has real benefits for—and that the results are widely distributed to—the participating community.

WHAT DO YOU THINK?

1. What are some likely consequences of researchers' not being sensitive to the different histories and cultures of Canada's First Nations, Inuit, and Metis peoples?
2. What do researchers need to do to avoid these problems?
3. Discuss the research process with classmates from various cultural backgrounds. What similar or different concerns would be raised by these people when taking part in research?

Sources: CIHR (2007); CIHR, NSERC, and SSHRC (2010).

Researchers must also get the *informed consent* of participants, which means that the subjects must fully understand their responsibilities and the risks that the research involves and agree to take part before the work begins.

Another guideline concerns funding. Sociologists must include in their published reports all sources of financial support. They must avoid accepting money from a source if there is any question about a conflict of interest. Researchers must never accept funding from any organization that seeks to influence the research results for its own purposes.

The federal government also plays a part in research ethics. Every Canadian college and university that seeks federal funding for research involving human subjects must have a Human Research Ethics Committee (HREC) to ensure that the proposed research adheres to the guidelines stated in the second edition of *Tri-Council Policy Statement: Ethical Conduct for Research Involving Humans* (Canadian Institutes of Health Research, Natural Sciences

and Engineering Research Council of Canada, and Social Sciences and Humanities Research Council of Canada, 2010).

Finally, there are global dimensions to research ethics. Before beginning work in another country, an investigator must become familiar enough with that society to understand what people *there* are likely to regard as a violation of privacy or a source of personal danger. In a diverse society such as our own, the same rule applies to studying people whose cultural background differs from that of the researcher. The Thinking about Diversity box offers tips on the sensitivity that outsiders should apply when studying Aboriginal communities in Canada.

Research Methods

A **research method** is *a systematic plan for doing research*. Four widely used methods of sociological investigation are experiments, surveys, participant observation, and the use of existing sources.

None is better or worse than any other. Rather, just as a carpenter chooses a particular tool for a particular job, researchers select a method according to whom they want to study and what they want to learn.

Testing a Hypothesis: The Experiment

The **experiment** is *a research method for investigating cause and effect under highly controlled conditions*. Experiments closely follow the logic of science, testing a specific *hypothesis*, a statement of how two (or more) variables are related. A hypothesis is really an educated guess about how variables are linked, usually expressed as an *if–then* statement: *If* this particular thing were to happen, *then* that particular thing will result.

An experimenter gathers the evidence needed to reject or not to reject the hypothesis in four steps: (1) State which variable is the *independent variable* (the "cause" of the change) and which is the *dependent variable* (the "effect," the thing that is changed). (2) Measure the initial value of the dependent variable. (3) Expose the dependent variable to the independent variable (the "cause" or "treatment"). (4) Measure the dependent variable again to see what change, if any, took place. If the expected change took place, the experiment supports the hypothesis; if not, the hypothesis must be modified.

Successful experiments depend on careful control of all factors that could affect what the experiment is trying to measure. Control is easiest in a research laboratory. But experiments in everyday locations—"in the field," as sociologists say—have the advantage of letting researchers observe subjects in their natural settings.

Illustration of an Experiment: The "Stanford County Prison"

Prisons can be violent settings, but is this due simply to the "bad" people who end up there? Or, as Philip Zimbardo suspected, does prison itself somehow cause violent behaviour? To answer this question, Zimbardo devised a fascinating experiment that he called the "Stanford County Prison" (Haney, Banks, & Zimbardo, 1973; Zimbardo, 1972).

Zimbardo thought that once inside a prison, even emotionally healthy people are likely to engage in violence. So Zimbardo treated the *prison setting* as the independent variable capable of causing *violence*, the dependent variable.

To test this hypothesis, Zimbardo and his research team first constructed a realistic-looking "prison" in the basement of the psychology building on the campus of Stanford University in California. Then they placed an ad in a local newspaper, offering to pay young men for their help with a two-week research project. They administered a series of physical and psychological tests on each of the 70 men who responded and then selected the healthiest 24.

The next step was to assign randomly half of the men to be "prisoners" and half to be "guards." The plan called for the guards and prisoners to spend the next two weeks in the mock prison. The prisoners began their part of the experiment when real police officers "arrested" them at their homes. After searching and handcuffing the men, the police drove them to the local police station, where they were fingerprinted. Then police transported their captives to the Stanford prison, where the guards locked them up. Zimbardo started his video camera rolling and watched to see what would happen next.

The experiment turned into more than anyone had bargained for. Both guards and prisoners soon became embittered and hostile toward one another. Guards humiliated the prisoners by assigning them jobs such as cleaning toilets with their bare hands. The prisoners resisted and insulted the guards. Within four days, the researchers had removed five prisoners who displayed signs of "extreme emotional depression, crying, rage and acute anxiety" (Haney, Banks, & Zimbardo, 1973:81). Before the end of the first week, the situation had become so bad that the researchers were forced to end the experiment.

The events that unfolded at the "Stanford County Prison" supported Zimbardo's hypothesis that prison violence is rooted in the social character of jails themselves, not in the personalities of individual guards and prisoners. This finding raised questions about our society's prisons and led to some basic reforms. Zimbardo's experiment also shows the potential of research to threaten the physical and mental well-being of subjects. Such dangers are not always as obvious as they were in this case. Therefore, researchers must carefully consider the potential harm to subjects at all stages of their work and halt any study, as Zimbardo did, if subjects suffer harm of any kind.

CRITICAL REVIEW In carrying out the "Stanford County Prison" study, the researchers chose to do an experiment because they were interested in testing a hypothesis. In this case, Zimbardo and his colleagues wanted to find out if the prison setting itself (rather than the personalities of individual guards and prisoners) is the cause of prison violence. The fact that the "prison" erupted in violence—even when using guards and prisoners with "healthy" profiles—supports their hypothesis.

CHECK YOUR LEARNING How might Zimbardo's findings help explain the abuse of a 16-year-old Somali boy in 1993 by two Canadian soldiers participating in the United Nations peacekeeping efforts in Somalia or the abuse of Iraqi prisoners by American soldiers after the 2003 invasion of Iraq?

Asking Questions: Survey Research

A **survey** is *a research method in which subjects respond to a series of statements or questions on a questionnaire or in an interview*.

The most widely used of all research methods, the survey is well suited to studying what cannot be observed directly, such as political attitudes or religious beliefs or sexual practices.

A survey targets some *population*, for example, unmarried mothers or adults living in rural Alberta. Sometimes every adult in the country makes up the survey population, as in polls taken during national political campaigns. Of course, contacting a vast number of people is all but impossible, so researchers usually study a *sample*, a much smaller number of subjects selected to represent the entire population. Surveys using samples of as few as 1500 people commonly give accurate estimates of public opinion for the entire country.

Beyond selecting subjects, the survey must have a specific plan for asking questions and recording answers. The most common way to do this is to give subjects a *questionnaire* containing a series of written statements or questions. Often the researcher allows subjects to choose possible responses to each item, as on a multiple-choice test. Sometimes, though, a researcher may want subjects to respond freely, to permit all opinions to be expressed. Of course, this free-form approach means that the researcher later has to make sense of what can be a bewildering array of answers.

Focus groups are a type of survey in which a small number of people representing a target population are asked for their opinions about some issue or product. Here a sociology professor asks students to evaluate textbooks for use in his introductory class.

In an *interview*, a researcher personally asks subjects a series of questions, thereby solving one problem common to the questionnaire method: the failure of some subjects to return the questionnaire to the researcher. A further difference is that interviews give participants freedom to respond as they wish. Researchers often ask follow-up questions to clarify an answer or to probe a bit more deeply. In doing this, however, a researcher must avoid influencing the subject even in subtle ways, such as by raising an eyebrow as the subject offers an answer.

Illustration of Survey Research: Longitudinal Studies of Hidden Populations

How do you contact and stay in touch with research participants who are not members of mainstream society? Some individuals cannot be reached through a straightforward survey because they belong to what academics call hard-to-reach or hidden populations (Spreen & Zwaagstra, 1994). Such populations share three main characteristics: (1) there is no known list of the members of the population; (2) acknowledgment of belonging to the group is threatening because membership involves fear of prosecution or of being the object of hate or scorn; and (3) members are distrustful of non-members, do whatever they can to avoid revealing their identities, and are likely to refuse to co-operate with outsiders or to give unreliable answers to questions about themselves and their networks. Intravenous drug users and those who trade sex for money are examples of two hidden populations. Yet the need for reliable research on the individuals who are members of these populations has become urgent, given public concern over high rates of sexually transmitted infections (STIs), hepatitis, HIV infections, HIV transmission, and generally poor health status among these groups (Heckathorn, 1997).

One of the more powerful ways to understand health changes over time is to use a longitudinal research design and collect data from individuals repeatedly for as long as possible. But this again is problematic for studies of hidden populations, because members are unlikely to freely give their real names and reliable contact information.

Cecilia Benoit and Mikael Jansson, two of the authors of this text, are leading a research project in British Columbia that adopts a longitudinal design to better understand the causal links between youth marginalization, street involvement, and health. Youth qualify for the project based on their weak attachment to parents or guardians and the school system and their strong association with the street economy. They are interviewed twice in the first month of contact and then every few months for as long as they

Participant observation is a method of sociological research that allows a researcher to investigate people as they go about their everyday lives in some "natural" setting. At its best, participant observation makes you a star in your own reality show, but living in what may be a strange setting far from home for months at a time is always challenging.

are willing to participate in the study (to a maximum of four years). Because of particular characteristics of this hidden population, combined with distrust of academics and others in positions of authority, several sampling techniques are being used to increase the probability of obtaining a reliable sample. Four non-profit community organizations are helping to establish respondent contact strategies to advertise the study and access the various subgroups of marginalized youth. The study is also widely advertised in shelters, drop-in centres, and other places that marginalized youth concentrate.

A final method of recruiting research participants is a technique known as respondent-driven sampling (Heckathorn, 1997). The technique begins with a small number of research participants who serve as "seeds." The seeds are given three recruitment coupons to hand to peers they believe may want come forward for an interview (based on the rationale that reclusive participants are more likely to respond to the appeals of their peers). The seeds are paid a nominal fee for each peer who comes forward for an interview (paid at the seed's third interview).

In the Field: Participant Observation

Participant observation is *a research method in which investigators systematically observe people while joining them in their routine activities.* This method allows researchers to study everyday social life in any natural setting, from a nightclub to a religious seminary. Cultural anthropologists use participant observation to study other societies, calling this method *fieldwork.*

At the beginning of a field study, most researchers do not have a specific hypothesis in mind. In fact, they may not yet realize what the important questions will turn out to be. This makes most participant observation *exploratory* and *descriptive*, falling within interpretive sociology and producing mostly qualitative, rather than quantitative, data. Compared with experiments and surveys, participant observation has few hard-and-fast rules. But this flexibility allows investigators to explore the unfamiliar and adapt to the unexpected.

Participant observers try to gain entry into a setting without disturbing the routine behaviour of others. Their role is twofold: To gain an insider's viewpoint, they must become participants in the setting, "hanging out" for months or even years, trying to act, think, and even feel the same way as the people they are observing; at the same time, they must remain observers, standing back from the action and applying the sociological perspective to social patterns that others take for granted.

Because the personal impressions of a single researcher play such a central role, critics claim that participant observation falls short of scientific standards. Yet its personal approach is also a strength: Where a high-profile team of sociologists administering a formal survey might disrupt a setting, a sensitive participant observer often can gain important insight into people's behaviour.

Illustration of Participant Observation: Street Corner Society

Did you ever wonder what everyday life was like in an unfamiliar neighbourhood? In the late 1930s, a young graduate student at Harvard University named William Foote Whyte (1914–2000) set out to study social life in a rather rundown section of Boston. His curiosity led him to carry out four years of participant observation in this neighbourhood, which he called "Cornerville."

At the time, Cornerville was home to first- and second-generation Italian immigrants. Most were poor, and many Bostonians considered Cornerville a place to avoid, a slum inhabited by criminals. Wanting to learn the truth, Whyte set out to discover for himself exactly what life was like inside this community. His celebrated book, *Street Corner Society* (1981, orig. 1943), describes Cornerville as a community with

Youth Marginalization, Street Involvement and Health: Using Tables in Research

A table provides a lot of information in a small amount of space, so learning to read tables can increase your reading efficiency. When you spot a table, look first at the title to see what information it contains. The title of the table below tells you that the table presents characteristics of a representative sample of all youth in Victoria, British Columbia, and also a group of street-involved youth in Victoria.

Across the top of the table, you will see that the first column lists the characteristics described in the middle column for the representative sample of all youth and in the third column for the street-involved youth. Reading down each column, note the categories within each variable; even though the percentages in each column add up to a number very close to 100, they do not total exactly 100 percent because of rounding errors.

Starting at the top left, we see that the youth in both samples are aged 14 though 18 and that the street-involved youth are a little older than

the random sample since there are almost three times as many 18-year-olds (27%) as there are 14-year-olds (10%) in the street-involved youth sample. Moving down the table, we see that there are slightly more females than males in both samples.

The two groups of youth differ quite markedly in the remaining three characteristics displayed. First, there are many more youth in the street-involved youth sample who claim an Aboriginal background (31%) than do so in the random sample (2%). Second, the youth in the two groups have very different sexual orientation, since 59% of street-involved youth labelled themselves heterosexual compared to 88% of youth in the random sample.

But the biggest differences between these two groups of youth is found in the third remaining group of percentages that shows who the youth lived with while they were 12 years old. While 62% of youth in the random sample lived

with both biological parents throughout that year, only 15% of street-involved youth did so. Remarkable also is the high number of street-involved youth who lived the whole year before they became teenagers with foster parents (7%).

WHAT DO YOU THINK?

1. Statistical data, such as those in the table in this box, are an efficient way to convey a lot of information. Can you explain why?

2. Looking at the table, how do you think the future life course of these two groups of youth will differ? Explain.

3. Do you see any ways in which this group of street-involved youth in Victoria may differ from marginalized youth in other areas of Canada? If so, what are they?

Randomly Selected Youth Compared to Street-Involved Youth in Victoria, British Columbia, Selected Characteristics

Age	Random Sample	Street Youth	Sexual Orientation	Random Sample	Street Youth
14	21%	10%	Heterosexual	88%	59%
15	20%	17%	Homosexual	2%	4%
16	21%	17%	Bisexual	5%	32%
17	23%	28%	Other	1%	3%
18	14%	27%	Missing	4%	2%
Total	99%	99%	Total	100%	100%
Gender					
Male	49%	43%	**Living Situation while 12 Years Old**		
Female	51%	57%	Both biological parents	62%	15%
Total	100%	100%	Mother only	11%	21%
			Mother and partner	9%	7%
Aboriginal Background			Father only	1%	6%
Yes	2%	31%	Foster parents	0%	7%
No	98%	68%	Other	17%	43%
Total	100%	99%	Total	100%	99%

Note: These percentages are calculated based on original data collected by Cecilia Benoit and Mikael Jansson in Victoria, British Columbia, from two groups of youth. The first is a group of 484 youth who were randomly selected and the second consists of 164 street-involved youth.

its own code of values, complex social patterns, and particular social conflicts.

To start, Whyte considered a range of research methods. He could have taken questionnaires to one of Cornerville's community centres and asked local people to fill them out. Or he could have invited members of the community to come to his Harvard office for interviews. But it is easy to see that such formal strategies would have gained little co-operation from the local people and produced few insights. Whyte decided, therefore, to ease into Cornerville life and slowly build a personal understanding of this rather mysterious place.

Soon enough, Whyte discovered the challenges of even getting started in field research. As an upper-middle-class WASP graduate student from Harvard, he stood out on the streets of Cornerville. Even a friendly overture from such an outsider could seem pushy and rude. Early on, Whyte dropped in at a local bar, hoping to buy a woman a drink and encourage her to talk about Cornerville. Looking around the room, he could find no woman alone. He thought he might have an opportunity when he saw a man sit down with two women. He walked over and asked, "Pardon me. Would you mind if I joined you?" Instantly, he realized his mistake:

> There was a moment of silence while the man stared at me. Then he offered to throw me down the stairs. I assured him that this would not be necessary, and demonstrated as much by walking right out of there without any assistance. (1981:289)

As this incident suggests, gaining entry to a community is the vital—and sometimes hazardous—first step in field research. "Breaking in" requires patience, ingenuity, and a little luck. Whyte's big break came in the form of a young man named "Doc," whom he met in a local social service agency. Whyte complained to Doc about how hard it was to make friends in Cornerville. Doc responded by taking Whyte under his wing and introducing him to others in the community. With Doc's help, Whyte soon became a neighbourhood regular.

Whyte's friendship with Doc illustrates the importance of a *key informant* in field research. Such people not only introduce a researcher to a community but often remain a source of information and help. But using a key informant also has its risks. Because any person has a particular circle of friends, a key informant's guidance is certain to "spin" the study in one way or another. Moreover, in the eyes of others, the reputation of the key informant, for better or worse, usually rubs off on the investigator. So although a key informant is helpful early on, a participant observer must seek a broader range of contacts.

Having entered the Cornerville world, Whyte quickly learned another lesson: A field researcher needs to know when to speak and when to shut up. One evening, Whyte joined a group discussing neighbourhood gambling. Wanting to get the facts straight, he asked innocently, "I suppose the cops were all paid off?"

> The gambler's jaw dropped. He glared at me. Then he denied vehemently that any policeman had been paid off and immediately switched the conversation to another subject. For the rest of that evening I felt very uncomfortable. The next day, Doc offered some sound advice:

> "Go easy on that 'who,' 'what,' 'why,' 'when,' 'where' stuff, Bill. You ask those questions and people will clam up on you. If people accept you, you can just hang around, and you'll learn the answers in the long run without even having to ask the questions." (1981:303)

In the months and years that followed, Whyte became familiar with everyday life in Cornerville and even married a local woman with whom he would spend the rest of his life. In the process, he learned that the common stereotypes were wrong. In Cornerville, most people worked hard, many were quite successful, and some even boasted of sending children to college. Even today, Whyte's book makes for fascinating reading about the deeds, dreams, and disappointments of immigrants and their children living in one ethnic community, and it contains the rich detail that can only come from years of participant observation.

CRITICAL REVIEW To study the community he called Cornerville, Whyte chose participant observation—a good choice because he did not have a specific hypothesis to test, nor did he know at the outset exactly what the questions were. By moving into this community for several years, Whyte was able to come to know the place and to paint a complex picture of social life there.

CHECK YOUR LEARNING Give an example of a topic for sociological research that would be best studied using (1) an experiment, (2) a survey, and (3) participant observation.

Using Available Data: Existing Sources

Not all research requires that investigators collect new data. Sometimes sociologists make use of existing sources: data collected by others.

The data most widely used by researchers are gathered by government agencies such as Statistics Canada. Data about other nations in the world are found in various publications of the United Nations and the World Bank.

SUMMING UP

Four Research Methods

	Experiment	Survey	Participant Observation	Existing Sources
Application	For explanatory research that specifies relationships between variables Generates quantitative data	For gathering information about issues that cannot be directly observed, such as attitudes and values Useful for descriptive and explanatory research Generates quantitative or qualitative data	For exploratory and descriptive study of people in a "natural" setting Generates qualitative data	For exploratory, descriptive, or explanatory research whenever suitable data are available
Advantages	Provides the greatest opportunity to specify cause-and-effect relationships Replication of research is relatively easy	Sampling, using questionnaires, allows surveys of large populations Interviews provide in-depth responses	Allows study of "natural" behaviour Usually inexpensive	Saves time and expense of data collection Makes historical research possible
Limitations	Laboratory settings have an artificial quality Unless the research environment is carefully controlled, results may be biased	Questionnaires must be carefully prepared and may yield a low return rate Interviews are expensive and time-consuming	Time-consuming Replication of research is difficult Researcher must balance roles of participant and observer	Researcher has no control over possible biases in data Data may only partially fit current research needs

Using available information saves time and money. This method has special appeal to sociologists with low budgets. And, in fact, government data are usually more extensive and more accurate than what researchers could obtain on their own.

But using available data has problems of its own. Data may not be available in the exact form that is needed. For example, you may be able to find the average salaries paid to professors at your school but not separate figures for the amounts paid to women and men. Further, there are always questions about how accurate the existing data are. In his nineteenth-century study of suicide, described earlier, Emile Durkheim used official records, but he had no way to know whether a death classified as a suicide was really an accident or vice versa.

Illustration of the Use of Existing Sources: Studying Media Narratives

Media representations of human activity constitute an important source of data collected by others. Academic analysis of media's place in the production and reproduction of dominant knowledges has been greatly influenced by the work of sociologist Stuart Hall (1978) and other contributors to the field of cultural studies (Kitzinger, 2000; Pateman, 1988; Sacks, 1996; Watkins & Emerson, 2000). These approaches to media illustrate how the transmission of social knowledge, values, and meanings changes over time.

Because media representations of key social categories such as gender, class, race, and sexuality are important loci of self and personal identity construction (Seale, 2003), subjugating media stories can negatively affect a person's sense of self and emotional well-being, whether or not these stories are actually true. In addition, contemporary media create social understanding between spatially distanced or socially segregated groups. The standard images found in the media become taken as truth unless the audience has the empirical knowledge to reject them. Thus, in the absence of personal experience with, for example, members of ethnic and visible minorities (Ungerleider, 1991), media stories can serve as key cultural sites where negative labels are created and taken up by the majority of citizens.

Hallgrimsdottir, Phillips, and Benoit (2006) compared media stories of people who work in the sex industry with these individuals' self-reports of their personal backgrounds and experiences of what they do for a living. The authors aimed to describe the level of similarity between media depictions of sex workers and their own description of their lives. The authors relied on two different kinds of data. First, they analyzed the print media discussion of the sex industry in one metropolitan region of Canada, the capital metropolitan region of Victoria, British Columbia. In doing so, they focused on the years 1980 to 2004 in a single regional daily newspaper, the Victoria *Times Colonist*. Articles were located using both a computerized and a paper subject index and represent the sum of newspaper coverage of sex industry–related work. Each article was analyzed in terms of both explicit and embedded content to generate a long list of themes. A subsequent pass through the data was used to collapse these themes into a series of narrative categories and, in a final reading of the data, each article was assigned once to a single category. Second, the authors compared these media narratives with the self-reported experiences of sex workers—their background and personal lives, work experiences, and health and well-being—in the same city and over a comparable time period (Benoit & Millar, 2001).

Not surprisingly, the researchers found that most media narratives of the sex industry were not reflected in the personal stories of sex workers themselves. The interview data showed instead that media narratives follow relatively rigid and standardized cultural scripts in which individuals in the sex industry are presented as having poor moral character and breaking the law, as well as causing social disruption and spreading contagious diseases. These cultural scripts organized the media narratives by directing what was included as newsworthy and what was left out of news accounts. The researchers also found that the contents of these cultural scripts can be used to understand how stigma is reproduced in our society.

CRITICAL REVIEW The main reason why Hallgrimsdottir and colleagues chose to use existing media sources is that they provided a context for understanding the interview data. Using existing sources alone can sometimes be problematic because they were not created with the purpose of answering sociologists' questions. For this reason, using such documents requires a critical eye and a good deal of creative thinking.

CHECK YOUR LEARNING What other questions about the media and human activity might you wish to answer using existing sources?

Putting It All Together: Ten Steps in Sociological Research

The following 10 questions will guide you through a research project in sociology:

1. **What is your topic?** Being curious and using the sociological perspective can generate ideas for social research at any time and in any place. Pick a topic you find interesting and that you think is important to study.

2. **What have others already learned?** You are probably not the first person with an interest in some issue. Visit the library and search the internet to see what theories and methods other researchers have applied to your topic. In reviewing the existing research, note problems that have come up to avoid repeating past mistakes.

3. **What, exactly, are your questions?** Are you seeking to explore an unfamiliar setting? To describe some category of people? To investigate cause and effect between variables? Clearly state the goals of your research and operationalize all variables.

4. **What will you need to carry out research?** How much time and money are available to you? What special equipment or skills does the research require? Can you do all of the work yourself?

5. **Are there ethical concerns?** Might the research harm anyone? How can you minimize the chances for injury? Will you promise your subjects anonymity? If so, how will you ensure that anonymity will be maintained?

6. **What method will you use?** Consider all major research strategies and combinations of methods. The most suitable method will depend on the kinds of questions you are asking and the resources available to you.

7. **How will you record the data?** The research method you use guides your data collection. Be sure to record information accurately and in a way that will make sense to you later on (it may be months before you write up the results of your work). Watch out for any personal bias that may creep into your work.

8. **What do the data tell you?** Determine what the data say about your initial questions. If your study involves a specific hypothesis, you should be able to confirm, reject, or modify it on the basis of your findings. Keep in mind that there will be several ways to interpret your results, depending on the

stereotype a simplified description applied to every person in some category

CONTROVERSY & DEBATE

Is Sociology Nothing More Than Stereotypes?

"Children in public daycare suffer from maternal deprivation!"

"People in Canada? They're rich, they love to marry, and they love to divorce!"

"Everybody knows that a man cannot be a feminist!"

All people—including sociologists—make generalizations. But many beginning students of sociology may wonder how sociological generalizations differ from simple stereotypes.

All three statements at the top of this box are examples of **stereotypes**, *exaggerated descriptions applied to every person in some category.* First, rather than describing averages, each statement paints every individual in some category with the same brush; second, each ignores facts and distorts reality (even though many stereotypes do contain an element of truth); third, each sounds more like a "put-down" than a fair-minded assertion.

Good sociology, by contrast, involves generalizations but with three conditions. First, sociologists do not indiscriminately apply any generalization to individuals. Second, sociologists are careful that their generalizations square with available facts. Third, sociologists

offer generalizations fair-mindedly, with an interest in getting at the truth.

Recall, first, that the sociological perspective reveals "the general in the particular"; therefore, a sociological insight is a generalization about some category of people. Consider, for example, the first statement above, that children in public daycare suffer from maternal deprivation. This statement is inaccurate, since evidence shows that children in well-organized and adequately funded daycare are as socially adapted as children who spend their early years at home with their mothers. The key to successful child development, then, is quality of care—not maternal attachment.

Second, sociologists shape their generalizations to available facts. A more factual version of the second statement above is that, by world standards, the Canadian population—on average—has a very high standard of living. It is also true that our marriage rate is one of the highest in the world. And although few people take pleasure in divorcing, our divorce rate is high as well.

Third, sociologists strive to be fair-minded and have a passion for truth. The statement that a man cannot be a feminist is not good sociology

for two reasons. First, the statement is simply not true because, as you know, many men identify themselves as feminists and strive to enhance women's equality. Second, it seems motivated by gender bias—in this instance, in the reverse of the usual direction.

Good sociology, then, stands apart from harmful stereotyping. But a sociology course is an excellent setting for talking over common stereotypes. The classroom encourages discussion and offers the factual information you need to decide whether a particular belief is valid or just a stereotype.

CONTINUE THE DEBATE . . .

1. Do people in Canada have stereotypes of sociologists? What are they? Are they valid?

2. Do you think taking a sociology course dispels people's stereotypes? Does it generate new ones?

3. Can you identify a stereotype of your own that sociology challenges?

theoretical approach you apply, and you should consider them all.

9. **What are your conclusions?** Prepare a final report explaining what you have learned. Also, evaluate your own work. What problems arose during the research process? What questions were left unanswered?

10. **How can you share what you have learned?** Consider making a presentation to a class or maybe even to a meeting of

professional sociologists. The important point is to share what you have learned with others and to let them respond to your work.

The Controversy & Debate box discusses the use of the sociological perspective and reviews many of the ideas presented in this chapter. This box will help you apply what you have learned to the important question of how the generalizations made by sociologists differ from the common stereotypes we hear every day.

CHAPTER 1 SOCIOLOGY: PERSPECTIVE, THEORY, AND METHOD

"WHY DO COUPLES MARRY?" We asked this question at the beginning of this chapter. The commonsensical answer is that people marry because they are in love. But as this chapter has explained, society guides our everyday lives, affecting what we do, think, and feel. Look at the two photographs, each showing a couple who, we can assume, is "in love." In each case, can you provide some of the rest of the story? By looking at the categories that the people involved represent, explain how society is at work in bringing the two people together.

Jada Pinkett met Will Smith in 1995 when she auditioned for a part on his hit show, *The Fresh Prince of Bel Air*. Two years later, they married. What social patterns do you see?

In 1997, during the fourth season of her hit TV show *Ellen*, Ellen DeGeneres "came out" as a lesbian, which put her on the cover of *Time* magazine. Since then, she has been an activist on behalf of gay and lesbian issues. Following California's brief legalization of same-sex marriage in 2008, she married her long-time girlfriend, Australian actress Portia de Rossi.

HINT: Society is at work on many levels. Consider (1) rules about same-sex and other-sex marriage, (2) laws defining the number of people who may marry, (3) the importance of race and ethnicity, (4) the importance of social class, (5) the importance of age, and (6) the importance of social exchange (what each partner offers the other). All societies enforce various rules that state who should or should not marry whom.

Applying Sociology in Everyday Life

1. Analyze the marriages of your parents, other family members, and friends in terms of class, race, age, and other factors. What evidence can you find that society guides the feeling we call "love"?

2. Figure 13–3 on page 349 shows the Canadian divorce rate over the past few decades. Using the sociological perspective, try to identify societal factors that caused the divorce rate to rise or fall.

3. Explore your local area and draw a sociological map of the community. Include the types of buildings (e.g., "big, single-family homes," "rundown business district," "new office buildings," "student apartments") found in various places and guess at the categories of people who live or work there. What patterns do you see?

MAKING THE GRADE

CHAPTER 1   Sociology: Perspective, Theory, and Method

The Sociological Perspective

The **SOCIOLOGICAL PERSPECTIVE** reveals the power of society to shape individual lives.
- C. Wright Mills called this point of view the "sociological imagination," which transforms personal troubles into public issues.
- Being an outsider or experiencing social crisis can encourage the sociological perspective.

pp. 2–5

The Importance of a Global Perspective

Global awareness is an important part of the sociological perspective because our society's place in the world affects us all.

pp. 5–7

Applying the Sociological Perspective

Applying the **SOCIOLOGICAL PERSPECTIVE** has many benefits:
- helping us understand the barriers and opportunities in our lives
- giving us an advantage in our careers
- guiding public policy

pp. 7–8

The Origins of Sociology

Rapid social change helped trigger the development of sociology:
- rise of an industrial economy
- explosive growth of cities
- new political ideas

pp. 8–9

AUGUSTE COMTE named sociology in 1838.
- Early philosophers tried to describe the ideal society, but Comte wanted to understand society as it really is.
- Karl Marx and many later sociologists used sociology to try to make society better.

pp. 9–10

✓ *The countries that experienced the most rapid social change were those in which sociology developed first (p. 9).*

Sociological Theory

 macro-level

The **STRUCTURAL-FUNCTIONAL APPROACH** explores how social structures work together to help society operate.
- Auguste Comte, Emile Durkheim, and Herbert Spencer helped develop the structural-functional approach.

pp. 10–12

The **SOCIAL-CONFLICT APPROACH** shows how inequality creates conflict and causes change.
- Two important types of conflict analysis are the **gender-conflict approach**, linked to **feminism**, and the **race-conflict approach**.
- Karl Marx helped develop the social-conflict approach.

pp. 12–14

 micro-level

The **SYMBOLIC-INTERACTION APPROACH** studies how people, in everyday interaction, construct reality.
- Max Weber and George Herbert Mead helped develop the symbolic-interaction approach.

pp. 14–16

---

sociology (p. 2) the systematic study of human society

sociological perspective (p. 2) the special point of view of sociology that sees general patterns of society in the lives of particular people

global perspective (p. 5) the study of the larger world and our society's place in it

high-income countries (p. 5) nations with the highest overall standards of living

middle-income countries (p. 5) nations with a standard of living about average for the world as a whole

low-income countries (p. 5) nations with a low standard of living in which most people are poor

positivism (p. 9) a scientific approach to knowledge based on "positive" facts as opposed to mere speculation

theory (p. 10) a statement of how and why specific facts are related

theoretical approach (p. 10) a basic image of society that guides thinking and research

structural-functional approach (p. 10) a framework for building theory that sees society as a complex system whose parts work together to promote solidarity and stability

social structure (p. 11) any relatively stable pattern of social behaviour

social functions (p. 11) the consequences of a social pattern for the operation of society as a whole

manifest functions (p. 11) the recognized and intended consequences of any social pattern

latent functions (p. 11) the unrecognized and unintended consequences of any social pattern

social dysfunction (p. 11) any social pattern that may disrupt the operation of society

social-conflict approach (p. 12) a framework for building theory that sees society as an arena of inequality that generates conflict and change

gender-conflict approach (p. 13) a point of view that focuses on inequality and conflict between women and men

feminism (p. 13) support of social equality for women and men

race-conflict approach (p. 14) a point of view that focuses on inequality and conflict between people of different racial and ethnic categories

macro-level orientation (p. 14) a broad focus on social structures that shape society as a whole

micro-level orientation (p. 15) a close-up focus on social interaction in specific situations

symbolic-interaction approach (p. 15) a framework for building theory that sees society as the product of the everyday interactions of individuals

VISUAL SUMMARY

See the Applying Theory table on page 15.

✓ To get the full benefit of the sociological perspective, apply all three approaches.

Three Ways to Do Sociology

POSITIVIST SOCIOLOGY
uses the logic of science to understand how variables are related.
- tries to establish cause and effect
- demands that researchers try to be objective

pp. 17–20

INTERPRETIVE SOCIOLOGY
focuses on the meanings that people attach to behaviour.
- People construct reality in their everyday lives.
- Weber's *Verstehen* is learning how people understand their world.

p. 20

CRITICAL SOCIOLOGY uses research to bring about social change.
- focuses on inequality
- rejects the principle of objectivity, claiming that all research is political

pp. 20–21

See the Summing Up table on page 21.

✓ **GENDER**, involving both researcher and subjects, can affect all research (p. 22).

✓ All researchers must follow professional ethical guidelines for conducting research (pp. 22–23).

Research Methods

The **EXPERIMENT** allows researchers to study cause and effect between two or more variables in a controlled setting.
- example of an experiment: Zimbardo's "Stanford County Prison"

p. 24

SURVEY research uses questionnaires or interviews to gather subjects' responses to a series of questions.
- example of a longitudinal survey: street-involved youth

pp. 24–26

Through **PARTICIPANT OBSERVATION**, researchers join with people in a social setting for an extended period of time.
- example of participant observation: Whyte's Street Corner Society

pp. 26–28

Researchers use data collected by others from **EXISTING SOURCES** to save time and money.
- example of using existing sources: Hallgrimsdottir and colleagues' media research

pp. 28–30

See the Summing Up table on page 29.

✓ Which method the researcher uses depends on the question being asked.

✓ Researchers combine these methods, depending on the specific goals of their study.

---

positivist sociology (p. 17) the study of society based on systematic observation of social behaviour

science (p. 17) a logical system that develops knowledge from direct, systematic observation

empirical evidence (p. 18) information we can verify with our senses

concept (p. 18) a mental construct that represents some aspect of the world in a simplified form

variable (p. 18) a concept whose value changes from case to case

measurement (p. 18) a procedure for determining the value of a variable in a specific case

reliability (p. 18) consistency in measurement

validity (p. 18) actually measuring exactly what you intend to measure

correlation (p. 18) a relationship in which two (or more) variables change together

cause and effect (p. 19) a relationship in which change in one variable (the independent variable) causes change in another (the dependent variable)

interpretive sociology (p. 20) the study of society that focuses on discovering the meanings people attach to their social world

critical sociology (p. 20) the study of society that focuses on the need for social change

gender (p. 22) the personal traits and social positions that members of a society attach to being female or male

---

research method (p. 23) a systematic plan for doing research

experiment (p. 24) a research method for investigating cause and effect under highly controlled conditions

survey (p. 24) a research method in which subjects respond to a series of statements or questions on a questionnaire or in an interview

participant observation (p. 26) a research method in which investigators systematically observe people while joining them in their routine activities

stereotype (p. 31) a simplified description applied to every person in some category

---

MySocLab

Visit MySocLab at www.mysoclab.com to access a variety of online resources that will help you to prepare for tests and to apply your knowledge, including
- an eText
- videos
- self-grading quizzes
- glossary flashcards

2 Culture

- What is culture?

- Why is it so important to understand people's cultural differences?

- How does culture support social inequality?

This chapter focuses on the concept of "culture," which refers to a society's entire way of life. Notice that the root of the word *culture* is the same as that of the word *cultivate*, suggesting that people living together actually "grow" their way of life over time.

Check out this Ernst & Young report, which gives practical tips to business leaders around the globe on how to diversify their workforces and increase their competitive edge: http://www.ey.com/GL/en/Issues/Business-environment/Leading-across-borders—inclusive-thinking-in-an-interconnected-world

Ernst & Young (E&Y), one of Canada's largest corporate finance firms, pays a lot of attention to cultural diversity these days. The company employs more than 3000 full-time people at 14 offices across Canada, with just less than half of its employees located at its headquarters in the hub of Toronto's financial district. With a population of almost 5 million, Toronto is the fifth largest and most ethnically diverse city in North America. Vancouver is equally diverse. Nearly 40 percent of Vancouver's current population is of visible minority background, with immigrants of Chinese, Indian, and Filipino origin making up the three most numerous groups. Given these population statistics, it is no wonder that E&Y offices in these two cities are strong supporters of the firm's diversity initiatives. Driven by a corporate value statement calling for an "inclusive and flexible environment," over the past few years E&Y has hosted a series of ethnic diversity networking events in Toronto, Vancouver, and other Canadian cities where it has branch offices. The company has a full-time director of leadership and manager of diversity with responsibilities ranging from benchmarking the company's progress in diversifying its workforce and clientele to changing corporate culture to creating a truly inclusive environment (Workplace Diversity Update, 2004). In 2011, E&Y was selected as one of Canada's "Best Diversity Employers," with 30.6 percent of its employees and 28 percent of its managers of visible minority background (http://www.canadastop100.com/diversity/).

What has been the result of this diversity initiative? A substantial increase in its share of business is with local ethnic groups. Italian, Chinese, South Asian, and Portuguese native-language speakers spend more than $25.1 million annually in the Greater Toronto Area alone. Any company would do well to follow Ernst & Young's lead.

Canada is one of the most *multicultural* of all the world's nations. This cultural diversity reflects our long history of receiving immigrants from all over the world. The ways of life found around the world differ not only in terms of languages and forms of dress but also in terms of preferred foods, musical tastes, family patterns, and beliefs about right and wrong. Some of the world's people have many children, while others have few; some honour the elderly, while others seem to glorify youth. Some societies are peaceful and others are warlike, and they embrace thousands of different religious beliefs and ideas about what is polite and rude, beautiful and ugly, pleasant and repulsive. This amazing human capacity for so many different ways of life is a matter of human culture.

What Is Culture?

Culture is *the ways of thinking, the ways of acting, and the material objects that together form a people's way of life.* When studying culture, sociologists consider both thoughts and things. *Nonmaterial culture* consists of the ideas created by members of a society, ranging from art to Zen; *material culture* refers to physical things, everything from armchairs to zippers.

The terms *culture* and *society* obviously go hand in hand, but their precise meanings differ. Culture is a shared way of life or social heritage; **society** refers to *people who interact in a defined territory and share a culture.* Neither society nor culture could exist without the other.

Culture shapes not only what we do but also what we think and how we feel—elements of what we commonly but wrongly describe as "human nature." The warlike Yanomamö of the Brazilian rain forest think that aggression is natural, but halfway around the world the Semai of Malaysia live quite peacefully. The cultures of Canada and Japan both stress achievement and hard work, but members of our society value individualism more than the Japanese, who value collective harmony.

Given the extent of cultural differences in the world and people's tendency to view their own way of life as "natural," it is no wonder that we often feel **culture shock**, *personal disorientation when experiencing an unfamiliar way of life.* People can experience culture

culture (p. 36) the ways of thinking, the ways of acting, and the material objects that together form a people's way of life

society (p. 36) people who interact in a defined territory and share a culture

culture shock (p. 36) personal disorientation when experiencing an unfamiliar way of life

Human beings around the globe create diverse ways of life. Such differences begin with outward appearance: Contrast the women shown here from Ethiopia, India, and Canada and the men from Republic of China, Ecuador, and Papua New Guinea. Less obvious but of even greater importance are internal differences, since culture also shapes our goals in life, our sense of justice, and even our innermost personal feelings.

shock right here in Canada when, say, Jamaican Canadians shop in an Iranian neighbourhood in Montreal, university students from Kingston visit the Mennonite countryside in Southern Ontario, or Vancouverites travel through a small native community in Northern British Columbia. But culture shock can be intense when we travel abroad. The Thinking Globally box on page 38 tells the story of a researcher making his first visit to the home of the Yąnomamö people living in the Amazon region of South America.

January 2, high in the Andes Mountains of Peru. In the rural highlands, people are poor and depend on one another. The culture is built on co-operation among families and neighbours who have lived nearby for many generations. Today, we spend an hour watching a new house being built. A young couple invited their families and friends, who arrived around 6:30 in the morning, and right away everyone began building. By mid-afternoon, most of the work had been done, and the couple then provided a large meal, drinks, and music that continued for the rest of the day.

All societies contain cultural differences that can provoke a mild case of culture shock. This woman travelling on a British subway is not sure what to make of the woman sitting next to her, who is wearing the Muslim full-face veil known as the *niqab*.

No particular way of life is "natural" to humans, even though most people around the world view their own behaviour that way.

Confronting the Yąnomamö: The Experience of Culture Shock

A small aluminum motorboat chugged steadily along the muddy Orinoco River, deep within South America's vast tropical rainforest. The anthropologist Napoleon Chagnon was nearing the end of a three-day journey to the home territory of the Yąnomamö, one of the most technologically simple societies on Earth.

Some 12 000 Yąnomamö live in villages scattered along the border of Venezuela and Brazil. Their way of life could hardly be more different from our own. The Yąnomamö wear little clothing and live without electricity, cars, or other conveniences that most people in Canada take for granted. They use bows and arrows for hunting and warfare, as they have for centuries. Many of the Yąnomamö have had little contact with the outside world, so Chagnon will be as strange to them as they are to him.

By 2:00 in the afternoon, Chagnon had almost reached his destination. The hot sun and humid air were becoming unbearable. Chagnon's clothes were soaked with sweat and his face and hands were swollen from the bites of gnats swarming around him. But he scarcely noticed, so focused was he on the fact that, in just a few moments, he would be face to face with people unlike any he had ever known.

Chagnon's heart pounded as the boat slid onto the riverbank. He and his guide climbed from the boat and walked toward the Yąnomamö village, stooping as they pushed their way through the dense undergrowth. Chagnon describes what happened next:

I looked up and gasped when I saw a dozen burly, naked, sweaty, hideous men staring at us down the shafts of their drawn arrows! Immense wads of green tobacco were stuck between their lower teeth and lips, making them look even more hideous, and strands of dark green slime dripped or hung from their nostrils—strands so long that they clung to their [chests] or drizzled down their chins. My next discovery was that there were a dozen or so vicious, underfed dogs snapping at my legs, circling me as if I were to be their next meal. I just stood there holding

my notebook, helpless and pathetic. Then the stench of the decaying vegetation and filth hit me and I almost got sick. I was horrified. What kind of welcome was this for the person who came here to live with you and learn your way of life, to become friends with you? (1992:11–12)

Fortunately for Chagnon, the Yąnomamö villagers recognized his guide and lowered their weapons. Reassured that he would survive the afternoon, Chagnon still was shaken by his inability to make any sense of these people. And this was to be his home for a year and a half! He wondered why he had given up physics to study human culture in the first place.

WHAT DO YOU THINK?

1. As they came to know Chagnon, might the Yąnomamö, too, have experienced culture shock? Why?

2. Can you think of an experience you had that is similar to the one described here?

3. How can studying sociology help reduce the experience of culture shock?

The co-operation that comes naturally in small communities high in the Andes Mountains of Peru is very different from the competitive lifestyle that is natural to so many people living in Manitoba or Halifax. Such variations come from the fact that we are creatures of culture who join together to create our own way of life. Every other animal, from ants to zebras, behaves very much the same all around the world because their behaviour is determined by instincts, biological programming over which the species has no control. A few animals—notably chimpanzees and related primates—have some capacity for culture, as researchers have learned by observing them using tools and teaching simple skills to their offspring. But the creative power of humans is far greater than that of any other form of life. In short, *only humans rely on culture rather than instinct to ensure their survival* (Harris, 1987; Morell, 2008). To understand how human culture came to be, we need to look back at the history of our species.

Culture and Human Intelligence

Scientists tell us that our planet is 4.5 billion years old. Life appeared about 1 billion years later. Fast-forward another 2 to 3 billion years and we find dinosaurs ruling Earth. It was only after these giant creatures disappeared—some 65 million years ago—that our history took a crucial turn with the appearance of the animals we call primates.

symbol anything that carries a particular meaning recognized by people who share a culture

People throughout the world communicate not just with spoken words but also with bodily gestures. Because gestures vary from culture to culture, they can occasionally be the cause of misunderstandings. For instance, the commonplace "thumbs up" gesture we use to express "Good job!" can get a person from Canada into trouble in Greece, Iran, and a number of other countries, where people take it to mean "Up yours!"

The importance of primates is that they have the largest brains relative to body size of all living creatures. About 12 million years ago, primates began to evolve along two different lines, leading humans away from the great apes, our closest relatives. Some 3 million years ago, our distant human ancestors climbed down from the trees of Central Africa to move around in the tall grasses. There, walking upright, they learned the advantages of hunting in groups and made use of fire, tools, and weapons; built simple shelters; and fashioned basic clothing. These Stone Age achievements mark the point at which our ancestors embarked on a distinct evolutionary course, making culture their primary strategy for survival. By about 250 000 years ago, our species, *Homo sapiens* —Latin for "intelligent person"—had emerged. Humans continued to evolve so that by about 40 000 years ago, people who looked more or less like us roamed the planet. With larger brains, these "modern" *Homo sapiens* developed culture rapidly, as the wide range of tools and cave art that have survived from this period suggests. By 12 000 years ago, the founding of permanent settlements and the creation of specialized occupations in the Middle East (in portions of modern-day Iraq and Egypt) marked a turning point. About this time, the biological forces we call instincts had almost disappeared, replaced by a more efficient survival scheme: *fashioning the natural environment to our purposes.* Ever since, humans have made and remade their world in countless ways, resulting in today's fascinating cultural diversity.

How Many Cultures?

How many cultures are there in Canada? One indicator of culture is language; the Canada 2006 Census lists more than 200 nonofficial mother tongues spoken in this country, most of which were brought by immigrants from nations around the world (Statistics Canada, 2007a).

Globally, experts document almost 7000 languages, suggesting the existence of as many distinct cultures. Yet the number of languages spoken around the world is declining, and more than half are now spoken by fewer than 10 000 people (Lewis, 2009). Experts expect that the coming decades may see the disappearance of hundreds of these languages, including Han (northwestern Canada), Gullah, Pennsylvania German, and Pawnee (all three spoken in the United States), Oro in the Amazon region (Brazil), Sardinian (Sardinia, Italy), Aramaic (the language of Jesus of Nazareth in the Middle East), Nu Shu (a language of southern China that is the only one known to be spoken exclusively by women), and Wakka Wakka and several other Aboriginal tongues spoken in Australia. What accounts for the decline? Likely reasons include high-technology communication, increasing international migration, and an expanding global economy, all of which are reducing global cultural diversity (Barovick, 2002; Hayden, 2003; UNESCO, 2001).

The Elements of Culture

Although cultures vary greatly, they all have common elements, including symbols, language, values, and norms. We begin our discussion with the one that is the basis for all of the others: symbols.

Symbols

Like all creatures, human beings sense the surrounding world, but unlike others, we also give the world *meaning*. Humans transform the elements of the world into *symbols*. A **symbol** is *anything that carries a particular meaning recognized by people who share a culture*. A word, a whistle, a wall of graffiti, a flashing red light, a raised fist— all serve as symbols. The human capacity to create and manipulate symbols is almost limitless; think of the variety of meanings associated with the simple act of winking an eye, which can convey such messages as interest, understanding, or insult.

Societies create new symbols all the time. The Seeing Sociology in Everyday Life box on page 40 describes some of the "cyber-symbols" that have developed along with our increasing use of computers for communication.

We are so dependent on our culture's symbols that we often take them for granted. We become keenly aware of the importance of a symbol, however, when it is used in an unconventional way, as when a young man wears an upside-down Christian cross as a

New Symbols in the World of Instant Messaging

MOLLY: gr8 2 c u!

GREG: u 2

MOLLY: jw about next time

GREG: idk, lotta work

MOLLY: no prb, xoxoxo

GREG: thanx, bcnu

The world of symbols changes all the time. One reason that people create new symbols is that we develop new ways to communicate. Today, more than 135 million people in North America (most of them young and many of them students) use mobile text messaging on a regular basis (Nielsen Media Research, 2008).

Here are some of the most common text messaging symbols:

b   be

bc   because

b4	before
b4n	'bye for now
bbl	be back later
bcnu	be seeing you
brb	be right back
cu	see you
def	definitely
g2g	got to go
gal	get a life
gmta	great minds think alike
gr8	great
hagn	have a good night
h&k	hugs and kisses
idc	I don't care
idt	I don't think
idk	I don't know
imbl	it must be love
jk	just kidding
jw	just wondering

j4f	just for fun
kc	keep cool
l8r	later
lmao	laugh my ass off
ltnc	long time no see
myob	mind your own business
no prb	no problem
omg	oh my gosh
pcm	please call me
plz	please
prbly	probably
rt	right
thanx	thanks
u	you
ur	you are
w/	with
w/e	whatever
w/o	without
wan2	want to
wtf	what the freak
y	why
2l8	too late
?	question
2	to, too, two
4	for, four

WHAT DO YOU THINK?

1. What does the creation of symbols such as these suggest about culture?

2. Do you think that using such symbols is a good way to communicate? Does it lead to confusion or misunderstanding? Why or why not?

3. What other kinds of symbols can you think of that are new to your generation?

Sources: Lenhart (2010), Berteau (2005), and J. Rubin (2003).

symbol of Satanism. Entering an unfamiliar culture also reminds us of the power of symbols; culture shock is really the inability to "read" meaning in unfamiliar surroundings. Not understanding the symbols of a culture leaves a person feeling lost and isolated, unsure of how to act, and sometimes frightened.

Culture shock is a two-way process. On one hand, the traveller *experiences* culture shock when meeting people whose way of life is dramatically different. For example, North Americans who consider

dogs beloved household pets might be put off by the Masai of eastern Africa, who ignore dogs and never feed them. The same travellers might be horrified to find that, in parts of Indonesia and in the northern regions of the People's Republic of China, people roast dogs for dinner.

On the other hand, a traveller can *inflict* culture shock on others by acting in ways that offend them. A Canadian who asks for a cheeseburger in an Indian restaurant is likely to offend

language a system of symbols that allows people to communicate with one another

cultural transmission the process by which one generation passes culture to the next

Sapir-Whorf thesis the idea that people see and understand the world through the cultural lens of language

Hindus working there because they consider cows sacred and never to be eaten. Global travel provides endless opportunities for misunderstanding.

Symbolic meanings also vary within a single society. By ordering all Canadian flags to be removed from provincial government buildings in Newfoundland and Labrador in 2004, the then premier, Danny Williams, gained support from some people who saw the flag as a symbol of federal oppression rather than national pride.

Language

> December 10, southern China. I approach Dashi late in the afternoon a little worried about finding a room in such a small rural village. After I gesture to a boy about 12 years old that I am looking for a place to rest my head, he hops onto the back of my loaded bicycle and points down the road. Several turns later he leaves me after pushing me toward a row house with the typical open-air living room on the main floor where six or seven people sit and watch TV. Somewhat reluctantly, a friendly older woman rents me a room upstairs and shows me the corner of the kitchen at the back of the main floor where I can wash up using water heated on the wood stove. Returning from my dinner, I am greeted by a woman outside and subsequently by a lot of good-natured laughter inside. It suddenly dawns on me that, except for the older woman, there are only women in their early twenties inside watching TV. The interaction with the woman outside just now takes on a different meaning; I interpreted her gestures to mean that she wanted one of my cigarettes. My head is full of questions the next day as I ride south toward Vietnam. I cannot stop thinking about my interaction with the young boy who guided me to the brothel.

The heart of a symbolic system is **language**, *a system of symbols that allows people to communicate with one another.* Humans have created many alphabets to express the hundreds of languages we speak; several examples are shown in Figure 2–1. Even rules for writing differ: Most people in Western societies write from left to right, people in northern Africa and western Asia write from right to left, and people in eastern Asia write from top to bottom.

Language allows much more than communication; it is the key to **cultural transmission**, *the process by which one generation passes culture to the next.* Just as our bodies contain the genes of our ancestors, our cultural heritage contains countless symbols created by those who came before us. Language is the key that unlocks centuries of accumulated wisdom.

FIGURE 2–1 Human Languages: A Variety of Symbols

Here the English word *read* is written in 12 of the hundreds of languages humans use to communicate with one another.

Language skills may link us to the past, but they also spark the human imagination to connect symbols in new ways, creating an almost limitless range of future possibilities. Language sets humans apart as the only creatures who are self-conscious, aware of our limitations and our ultimate mortality yet able to dream and hope for a future better than the present.

Does Language Shape Reality?

Does someone who speaks Cree, the language spoken by Aboriginal people who originated from the James Bay area of Canada, experience the world differently than other Canadians who think in English or French? Edward Sapir and Benjamin Whorf claimed that the answer is yes, because each language has its own distinct symbols that serve as the building blocks of reality (Sapir, 1929, 1949; Whorf, 1956, orig. 1941). Further, they noted that each symbolic system has words or expressions not found in any other symbolic system. Finally, all languages connect symbols with distinctive emotions, so as multilingual people know, a single idea may "feel" different when it is expressed in Hindi rather than in Persian or Dutch.

Formally, the **Sapir-Whorf thesis** holds that *people see and understand the world through the cultural lens of language.* In the decades since Sapir and Whorf published their work, however, scholars have taken issue with this proposition. Current thinking is that although we do fashion reality out of our symbols, evidence does not support the notion that language *determines* reality in the way Sapir and Whorf claimed. For example, we know that children understand the idea of "family" long before they learn that word; similarly, adults can imagine new ideas or things before devising a name for them (Kay & Kempton, 1984; Pinker, 1994).

values culturally defined standards that people use to decide what is desirable, good, and beautiful and that serve as broad guidelines for social living

beliefs specific ideas that people hold to be true

Values and Beliefs

We teach our children middle-class values such as hard work, competition, and respect for authority, which are all important for individual achievement in Canadian society. In applauding such characteristics, we are supporting certain **values**, *culturally defined standards that people use to decide what is desirable, good, and beautiful and that serve as broad guidelines for social living.* Values are what people who share a culture use to make choices about how to live.

Values are broad principles that underlie **beliefs**, *specific ideas that people hold to be true.* In other words, values are abstract standards of goodness and beliefs are particular matters that people accept as true or false. For example, surveys show that most Canadian adults agree that their country should provide equal opportunities to all groups, including women and men (Adams, 1997). Yet, in reality, the proportion of women in the House of Commons was only 22.1 percent in 2011, though this number has been increasing ever so slowly in the last decade (Inter-Parliamentary Union, 2011).

Key Values of Canadian Culture

Because Canada is a country of native peoples and immigrants from many different countries, few values command the support of everyone. Even so, a number of dominant values have emerged. A national report commissioned by the federal government (Citizens' Forum on Canada's Future, 1991:35–45) identified seven important cultural values.

1. **Equality and fairness in a democratic society.** Canadians across the country express a belief in fairness for all citizens, including Aboriginal peoples, citizens of Quebec, and visible minorities.

2. **Consultation and dialogue.** As citizens, we should aim to settle our differences peacefully, by talking over our problems, learning about one another, and arriving at agreed upon solutions to our problems.

3. **Importance of accommodation and tolerance.** Accommodating the traditions and customs of Canada's Aboriginal peoples and ethnic groups, including those of francophone Quebecers, were central to this cultural value.

4. **Support for diversity.** Support for the country's many diversities—regional, ethnic, linguistic, cultural—is another central value that we share as a nation.

5. **Compassion and generosity.** People in Canada value the safety net provided by the welfare state, particularly its universal health care system and attractive social services, pension plans, openness toward refugees, and commitment to reduce regional disparities.

6. **Attachment to Canada's natural beauty.** Canada's wilderness is legendary, and Canadians believe that their governments should do more to protect the natural environment from pollution and other hazards of industrialization.

7. **Our world image: commitment to freedom, peace, and non-violent change.** Canadians want to be seen from abroad as a free, peaceful, and non-violent society that, as a nation, plays an active role in international peacekeeping.

Values: Sometimes in Conflict

Looking over the list above, we see that these dominant cultural values are often difficult to realize. For example, recent federal governments have tended to present an image of Canada as "one" nation bound together by shared values, traditions, and beliefs, yet simultaneously promote fiscal responsibility over public funding of social programs. Results of the 2005 *Canadian Values Study* (National Post, The Dominion Institute, and Innovative Research Group, 2005), indicate that many Canadians do not necessarily agree with this government sentiment. While about two-thirds (64%) of Canadians polled agree that "Canada's strong fiscal responsibility over the past decade is a key foundation of our recent economic growth," the vast majority (79%) agree with the statement: "We have a pressing social deficit in Canada that is measured by problems such as homelessness, waiting lists for health care and lack of access to post secondary education." Those who supported the idea that Canada is confronting a "social deficit" (44%) also tended to agree that the government should increase its social spending budget.

Such conflicts in values inevitably cause strain, leading to awkward balancing acts in our beliefs and actions. Sometimes we decide that one value is more important than another; in other cases, we may simply learn to live with inconsistencies. While Canadians appear to be more liberal overall in their attitudes about moral issues, there remain notable differences, including along regional lines (Angus Reid Public Opinion, 2007). This was confirmed in a 2011 survey showing that British Columbia has the lowest percentage of people in Canada—just 17 percent compared to 36 percent in the rest of western Canada—who believe that all the poor have to do to improve their lives is "pull themselves up by their own bootstraps" (Todd, 2011).

In *A Fragile Social Fabric? Fairness, Trust, and Commitment in Canada*, sociologist Raymond Breton and colleagues (2004) attempt to assess the strength of the national social fabric as well as the extent to which it is fragmented along the main lines of social differentiation in Canadian society. The authors recommend ways in which support for diversity according to ethnicity, social class, gender, and region can strengthen the value of "one" nation of diverse cultures.

Emerging Values

Like all elements of culture, values change over time. People in Canada have always valued hard work. In recent decades, however, we have placed increasing importance on leisure—having time off from work to do things such as reading, travel, or community service that provide enjoyment and satisfaction. Similarly, although the importance of material comfort remains strong, more people are seeking personal growth through meditation and other spiritual activity.

Values: A Global Perspective

Values vary from culture to culture around the world. In general, the values that are important in higher-income countries differ somewhat from those in lower-income countries.

People in lower-income nations develop cultures that value survival. This means that people place a great deal of importance on physical safety and economic security. They worry about having enough to eat and a safe place to sleep at night. In addition, lower-income nations tend to be traditional, with values that celebrate the past and emphasize the importance of family and religious beliefs. These nations, in which men have most of the power, typically discourage or forbid practices such as divorce and abortion.

People in higher-income countries develop cultures that value individualism and self-expression. These countries are wealthy enough that most of the people take survival for granted, focusing their attention instead on which "lifestyle" they prefer and how to achieve the greatest personal happiness. In addition, these cultures tend to be secular and rational, placing less emphasis on family ties and religious beliefs and more emphasis on people thinking for themselves and being tolerant of others who differ from them. In higher-income nations, women have social standing more equal to men, and there is widespread support for practices such as divorce and abortion (World Values Survey, 2008). Figure 2–2 shows how selected countries of the world compare in terms of cultural values.

Norms

Middle-class Canadians are reluctant to reveal to others the size of their paycheque, while people in China tend to share such "personal"

Global Snapshot

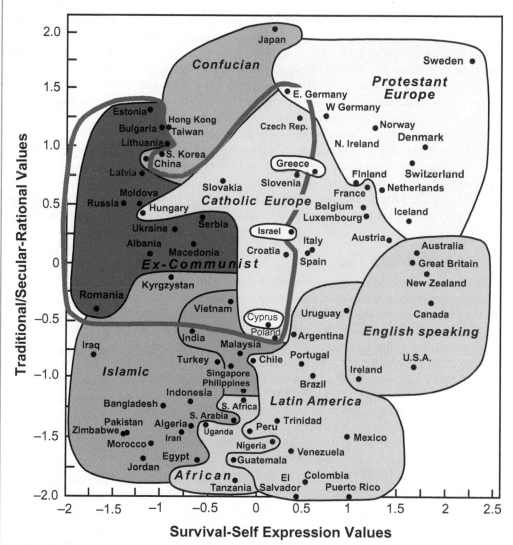

FIGURE 2–2 Cultural Values of Selected Countries

A general global pattern is that higher-income countries tend to be secular and rational and favour self-expression. By contrast, the cultures of lower-income countries tend to be more traditional and concerned with economic survival. Each region of the world, however, has distinctive cultural patterns, including religious traditions, that affect values. Looking at the figure, what patterns can you see?

Source: Inglehart and Welzel (2010).

information eagerly. Both patterns illustrate the operation of **norms**, *rules and expectations by which a society guides the behaviour of its members.*

Sociologist William Graham Sumner (1959, orig. 1906) coined the term **mores** (pronounced "MORE-ayz") to refer to *norms that are widely observed and have great moral significance.* Certain mores

norms (p 43) rules and expectations by which a society guides the behaviour of its members

mores norms that are widely observed and have great moral significance

folkways norms for routine or casual interaction

include *taboos*, such as our society's insistence that adults not engage in sexual relations with children.

People pay less attention to **folkways**, *norms for routine or casual interaction*. Examples include ideas about appropriate greetings and proper dress. A man who does not wear a tie to a formal dinner party may raise an eyebrow for violating folkways or "etiquette." If he were to arrive at the dinner party wearing *only* a tie, however, he would violate cultural mores and invite a more serious response.

As we learn cultural norms, we gain the capacity to evaluate our own behaviour. Doing wrong (say, downloading a term paper from the internet) can cause both *shame*—the painful sense that others disapprove of our actions—and *guilt*—a negative judgment we make of ourselves. Only cultural creatures can experience shame and guilt. This is what the writer Mark Twain had in mind when he remarked that people "are the only animals that blush—or need to."

Ideal and Real Culture

Values and norms suggest how we should behave more than they describe actual behaviour. We must remember that ideal culture always differs from the real culture that actually occurs in everyday life. To illustrate, only about 15 percent of Canadians in a recent poll think that it is morally acceptable for married men and women to have an affair (Angus Reid Public Opinion, 2009). However, more than 10 years ago, almost 22 of Canadian males and 14 percent of Canadian females reported having had an affair while married (Angus Reid, 1997b). A number of prominent politicians from Canada and elsewhere have publicly endorsed sexual fidelity in marriage but practise the opposite—not to mention some members of the Canadian clergy who took vows of celibacy during their ordination yet later broke them. But a culture's moral standards are important all the same, calling to mind the old saying, "Do as I say, not as I do."

Technology and Culture

In addition to symbolic elements such as values and norms, every culture includes a wide range of physical human creations called *artifacts*. The Chinese eat with chopsticks rather than knives and forks, the Japanese place mats rather than rugs on the floor, and many men and women in India prefer flowing robes to the close-fitting clothing common in Canada. The material culture of a people can seem as strange to outsiders as their language, values, and norms.

A society's artifacts partly reflect underlying cultural values. The warlike Yąnomamö carefully craft their weapons and prize the poison tips on their arrows. By contrast, our society's embrace of individuality and independence goes a long way toward explaining our high regard for the automobile: In 2009, Canadians owned about 560 cars per 1000 residents—near the top per capita of any

country. Even in an age of high gasoline prices, many of these automobiles are the large sport utility vehicles that we might expect rugged, individualistic people to choose.

In addition to expressing values, material culture reflects a society's level of **technology**, *knowledge that people use to make a way of life in their surroundings.* The more complex a society's technology, the easier it is for members of that society to shape the world for themselves.

Gerhard Lenski argued that a society's level of technology is crucial in determining what cultural ideas and artifacts emerge or are even possible (Nolan & Lenski, 2007). He pointed to the importance of *sociocultural evolution*—the historical changes in culture brought about by new technology—which unfolds in terms of four major levels of development: hunting and gathering, horticulture and pastoralism, agriculture, and industry.

Hunting and Gathering

The oldest and most basic way of living is **hunting and gathering**, *the use of simple tools to hunt animals and gather vegetation for food.* From the time of our earliest human ancestors 3 million years ago until about 1800, most people in the world lived as hunters and gatherers. Today, however, this technology supports only a few societies, including the Dene Aboriginals of northwestern Canada, the Pygmies of Central Africa, the Khoisan of southwestern Africa, the Aborigines of Australia, and the Semai of Malaysia. Typically, hunters and gatherers spend most of their time searching for game and edible plants. Their societies are small, generally with several dozen people living in a nomadic, family-like group, moving on as they deplete an area's vegetation or follow migratory animals.

Everyone helps search for food, with the very young and the very old doing what they can. Women usually gather vegetation—the primary food source for these peoples—while men do most of the hunting. Because the tasks they perform are of equal value, the two genders have rough parity (Leacock, 1978).

Hunters and gatherers do not have formal leaders. They may look to one person as a *shaman*, or priest, but holding such a position does not excuse that person from the daily work of finding food. Overall, hunting and gathering is a simple and egalitarian way of life. Limited technology leaves hunters and gatherers vulnerable to the forces of nature, however. Storms and droughts can easily destroy their food supply and they have few effective ways to respond to accidents or disease. Looking back at these societies, we see that many children died in childhood and only half lived to the age of 20.

As people with powerful technology steadily close in on them, hunting and gathering societies are vanishing. Fortunately, studying their way of life has provided us with valuable information about our socio-cultural history and our fundamental ties to the natural environment.

hunting and gathering the use of simple tools to hunt animals and gather vegetation for food → **horticulture** the use of hand tools to raise crops

pastoralism the domestication of animals → **agriculture** large-scale cultivation using plows harnessed to animals or more powerful energy sources → **industry** the production of goods using advanced sources of energy to drive large machinery → **post-industrialism** (p. 46) the production of information using computer technology

Horticulture and Pastoralism

Horticulture, *the use of hand tools to raise crops*, appeared around 10 000 years ago. The hoe and the digging stick (used to punch holes in the ground for planting seeds) first turned up in fertile regions of the Middle East and Southeast Asia, and by 6000 years ago these tools were in use from Western Europe to China. Central and South Americans also learned to cultivate plants, but rocky soil and mountainous land forced members of many societies to continue to hunt and gather even as they adopted this new technology (Chagnon, 1992; Fisher, 1979).

In especially dry regions, societies turned not to raising crops but to **pastoralism**, *the domestication of animals*. Throughout the Americas, Africa, the Middle East, and Asia, many societies combine horticulture and pastoralism.

Growing plants and raising animals allows societies to feed hundreds of members. Pastoral peoples remain nomadic, but horticulturalists make permanent settlements. In a horticultural society, a material surplus means that not everyone has to produce food; some people are free to make crafts, become traders, or serve as full-time priests. Compared with hunters and gatherers, pastoral and horticultural societies are more unequal, with some families operating as a ruling elite and men increasing their power at the expense of women.

Because hunters and gatherers have little control over nature, they generally believe that the world is inhabited by spirits. As they gain the power to raise plants and animals, however, people come to believe in one God as the creator of the world. The pastoral roots of Judaism and Christianity are evident in the term *pastor* and in the common view of God as a "shepherd" who stands watch over all.

What would it be like to live in a society with simple technology? That's the premise of the television show *Survivor*. What advantages do societies with simple technology afford their members? What disadvantages do you see?

Agriculture

Around 5000 years ago, technological advances led to **agriculture**, *large-scale cultivation using plows harnessed to animals or more powerful energy sources*. Agrarian technology first appeared in the Middle East and gradually spread throughout the world. The invention of the animal-drawn plow, the wheel, writing, numbers, and new metals changed societies so much that historians call this era the "dawn of civilization."

By turning the soil, plows allow land to be farmed for centuries, so agrarian people can live in permanent settlements. With large food surpluses that can be transported by animal-powered wagons, populations grow into the millions. As members of agrarian societies become more and more specialized in their work, money is used as a form of common exchange, replacing the earlier system of barter. Although the development of agrarian technology expands human choices and fuels urban growth, it also makes social life more individualistic and impersonal.

Agriculture also brings about a dramatic increase in social inequality. Most people live as serfs or slaves, but a few elites are freed from labour to cultivate a "refined" way of life based on the study of philosophy, art, and literature. At all levels, men gain pronounced power over women.

People with only simple technology live much the same the world over, with minor differences caused by regional variations in climate. But agrarian technology gives people enough control over the world that cultural diversity dramatically increases (Nolan & Lenski, 2007).

Industry

Industrialization occurred as societies replaced the muscles of animals and humans with new forms of power. Formally, **industry** is *the production of goods using advanced sources of energy to drive large machinery*. The introduction of steam power, starting in England about 1775, greatly boosted productivity and transformed culture in the process.

Agrarian people work in or near their homes, but most people in industrial societies work in large factories under the supervision of strangers. In this way, industrialization pushes aside the traditional cultural values that guided family-centred agrarian life for centuries.

Industry also made the world seem smaller. In the nineteenth century, railroads and steamships carried people across land and sea faster and farther than ever before. In the twentieth century, this process continued with the invention of the automobile, the airplane, radio, television, and computers.

high culture cultural patterns that distinguish a society's elite

popular culture cultural patterns that are widespread among a society's population

subculture cultural patterns that set apart some segment of a society's population

Industrial technology also raises living standards and extends the human lifespan. Schooling becomes the rule because industrial jobs demand more and more skills. In addition, industrial societies reduce economic inequality and steadily extend political rights.

It is easy to see industrial societies as "more advanced" than those relying on simpler technology. After all, industry raises living standards and stretches life expectancy to the seventies and beyond—about twice that of the Yąnomamö. But as industry intensifies individualism and expands personal freedom, it weakens human community. Also, industry has led people to abuse the natural environment, which threatens us all. And although advanced technology gives us labour-saving machines and miraculous forms of medical treatment, it also contributes to unhealthy levels of stress and has created weapons capable of destroying in a flash everything that our species has achieved.

Post-Industrial Information Technology

Going beyond the four categories discussed by Lenski, we see that many high-income societies, including Canada, have now entered a post-industrial era in which more and more economic production makes use of *new information technology*. **Post-industrialism** refers to *the production of information using computer technology*. Production in industrial societies centres on factories that make *things*, but post-industrial production centres on computers and other electronic devices that create, process, store, and apply *ideas and information*.

The emergence of an information economy changes the skills that define a way of life. Mechanical abilities are no longer the only key to success. People find that they must learn to work with symbols by speaking, writing, computing, and creating images and sounds. One result of this change is that our society now has the capacity to create symbolic culture on an unprecedented scale as people work with computers to generate new words, music, and images.

Cultural Diversity

Take a stroll down Queen Street in Toronto or through Vancouver's Gastown and it will soon become obvious to you that Canada is a culturally diverse society. As noted at the beginning of the chapter, heavy immigration over the past century and a half has turned Canada into one of the most multicultural of all high-income countries. In 1901, 12.8 percent of the population were born outside of Canada. More than 75 percent of these people were born in Europe and almost 60 percent came from the United Kingdom. By 2001, the percentage of the population born outside of Canada had increased to 18.4 percent and more than half of these people were born outside of Europe. By 2006, there was a further

increase to just under 20 percent. This diverging immigration is also reflected in the much greater diversity in the background of Canadians today (see Table 11–1 on page 282 for details of the ethnic diversity in Canada in 2006). Statistics Canada predicts that if this trend continues, between 25 and 28 percent of the Canadian population could be foreign-born by 2031 (Statistics Canada, 2011b). To understand the reality of life in Canada, we must move beyond shared cultural patterns to consider the importance of cultural diversity.

High Culture and Popular Culture

Cultural diversity can involve social class. In fact, in everyday talk, we usually use the term *culture* to mean art forms such as classical literature, music, dance, and painting. We describe people who attend the opera or the theatre as "cultured," thinking that they appreciate the "finer things in life."

We speak less kindly of ordinary people, assuming that everyday culture is somehow less worthy. We are tempted to judge the music of Beethoven as "more cultured" than the blues, couscous as better than cornbread, golfing as more polished than bowling, fly fishing as more refined than bait fishing, ballet as better than ultimate fighting, and the music of Ben Heppner as superior to that of Céline Dion. These differences arise because many cultural patterns are readily available to only some members of a society. Sociologists use the term **high culture** to refer to *cultural patterns that distinguish a society's elite* and **popular culture** to describe *cultural patterns that are widespread among a society's population*.

Common sense may suggest that high culture is superior to popular culture, but sociologists are uneasy with such judgments for two reasons. First, neither elites nor ordinary people share all of the same tastes and interests; people in both categories differ in numerous ways. Second, do we praise high culture because it is really better than popular culture or simply because its supporters have more money, power, and prestige? For example, there is no difference between a violin and a fiddle; however, we name the instrument one way when it is used to produce a type of music typically enjoyed by a person of higher position and the other way when it produces music appreciated by people with lower social standing.

Subculture

The term **subculture** refers to *cultural patterns that set apart some segment of a society's population*. People who ride "chopper" motorcycles, people who enjoy hip-hop music and fashion, Vancouver Eastside drug users, jazz musicians, Calgary cowboys, campus computer "nerds," and West Coast wilderness campers—all display subcultural patterns. See the Thinking about Diversity box on pages 54–55 about subcultures and rock and roll.

It is easy but often inaccurate to put people in subcultural categories because almost everyone participates in many subcultures without having much commitment to any one of them. In some cases, ethnicity and religion can be strong enough to set people apart from one another, with tragic results. Consider the former nation of Yugoslavia in southeastern Europe. The civil war there in the 1990s was fuelled by extreme cultural diversity. This *one* small country made use of *two* alphabets, embraced *three* major religions, spoke *four* major languages, was home to *five* major nationalities, was divided into *six* separate republics, and absorbed the cultural influences of *seven* surrounding countries. The cultural conflict that plunged this nation into civil war shows that subcultures are a source not only of pleasing variety but also of tension and even violence.

Many people view Canada as a "mosaic" in which many nationalities make up the Canadian cultural identity. But given our cultural diversity, how accurate is the "mosaic" image? Some authors writing on the country's two dominant groups, English-speaking and French-speaking, maintain that Canadians make up "two solitudes" (Rocher, 1990), as is evident in the lack of formal and informal interaction among the French-speaking and English-speaking intellectual elites within the Royal Society of Canada (Ogmundson & McLaughlin, 1994).

Others argue that subcultures involve not just *difference* but also *hierarchy*. Too often what we view as "dominant" or "mainstream" culture are patterns favoured by powerful segments of the population, while what we view as "subculture" are, in fact, the patterns of less-advantaged people, such as high school dropouts (Tanner, Krahn, & Hartnagel, 1995) or youth who belong to the electronic dance music culture, which includes raving, clubbing, and partying (Riley, Griffin, & Morey, 2010). Hence, sociologist John Porter (1965) characterized Canada as a "vertical mosaic," in which a privileged male elite consists overwhelmingly of people of British origin (Bell & Tepperman, 1979; Reitz, 1980). While researchers disagree on the extent to which Canada is a closed society that has marginalized some groups at the expense of others (Beaman & Beyer, 2008; Curtis, Grab, & Guppy, 1999), why is it that the cultural patterns of rich skiers in Whistler, for example, tend to seem like less of a "subculture" than the cultural patterns of street youth in the urban core of our cities (Baron, 2004; Benoit, Jansson, Hallgrimsdottir, & Roth, 2008)? Why do those who alter their bodies through cosmetic surgery seem like less of a subculture than those who tattoo themselves (Atkinson, 2003; Yamada, 2008)? Some sociologists prefer to level society's playing field by emphasizing multiculturalism and shedding light on the variety of experiences of the different cultural groups that find their home in Canada (Breton, 2005) and other high-income countries (Kymlicka, 2010).

A generation ago, most people regarded tattoos as a mark of low social status. Today, this cultural pattern is gaining popularity among people at all social class levels. Kat Von D is a tattoo artist on the television show *L.A. Ink*.

Multiculturalism

In recent years, Canada has been facing the challenge of **multiculturalism**, *a perspective recognizing the cultural diversity of Canada and promoting equal standing for all cultural traditions*. This movement represents a sharp turning away from the past, when our society did not recognize the cultural mosaic. Today, we spiritedly debate how to balance a celebration of cultural differences with our shared value of equality.

Multiculturalists point out that, from the outset, the European immigrants to the so-called New World (of course, "new" only to those who came from abroad) exploited the various Aboriginal cultures; some First Nations peoples were decimated, while others were severely reduced in numbers and marginalized on reserves (Dickason, 1992). After Confederation in 1867, people of British origin gained the top political positions in the country, viewing those of other backgrounds (Aboriginal peoples, the French, Southern Europeans, the Chinese, and so on) as being of "lower stock." As Porter (1965:62) states,

> After all, Canada was a British creation, though indifferently conceived by British statesmen of the day. In the first decades of Canada's existence, who would have doubted that the British were destined to an uninterrupted epoch of imperial splendour? Although the French participated in Confederation, Canada's political and economic leaders were British and were prepared to create a British North America. Born British subjects, they intended to die as such.

multiculturalism (p. 47) a perspective recognizing the cultural diversity of Canada and promoting equal standing for all cultural traditions

Eurocentrism the dominance of European (especially English) cultural patterns

As a result of this hierarchy, Canadian historians have tended to focus on the descendants of the English and other Northern Europeans, describing historical events from their point of view. And historians have tended to push to the margins the perspectives and accomplishments of Aboriginals and Canadians of African, Asian, and Latin American descent. Multiculturalists condemn this singular pattern as **Eurocentrism**, *the dominance of European (especially English) cultural patterns*. Molefi Kete Asante, a leading advocate of multiculturalism, argues that like "the 15th-century Europeans who could not cease believing that the Earth was the centre of the universe, many today find it difficult to cease viewing European culture as the centre of the social universe" (1988:7).

Few Canadians would deny that our way of life has wide-ranging roots. But multiculturalism is controversial because it asks us to rethink norms and values that form the core of our culture. One currently contested issue surrounds language. In 1969, the Official Languages Act made both French and English the official languages of Canada—and so the country became officially bilingual. However, as noted in the excerpt from the Citizens' Forum on Canada's Future mentioned above, many tensions remain over the actual implementation of Canada's language policy.

Another controversy centres on how our nation's schools should teach culture. Proponents defend multiculturalism, first, as a strategy to present a more accurate picture of Canada's past. Proposed educational reforms seek, for example, to tone down the simplistic praise commonly directed at Christopher Columbus and other European explorers by acknowledging the tragic impact of the European conquest on the Aboriginal peoples of this hemisphere. Moreover, a multicultural approach recognizes the achievements of many women and men whose cultural backgrounds have, up till now, confined them to the sidelines of history.

Second, proponents claim, multiculturalism enables students to grasp our country's even more diverse present. The 2006 census showed that Toronto has a greater proportion of immigrants (45.7 percent) than other major cosmopolitan cities such as Sydney (31.7 percent), Los Angeles (34.7 percent), and New York City (27.9 percent) (Statistics Canada, 2006a).

Third, proponents assert, multiculturalism can strengthen the academic achievement of Canada's Aboriginal and visible minority children, who may find little personal relevance in Eurocentric education (Adams, 2007; Banting, Courchene, & Seidle, 2007; Ghosh, 1996). National Map 2–1 takes a closer look at language diversity in different parts of Canada.

Fourth and finally, proponents of multiculturalism consider it needed preparation for living in a world in which nations are increasingly interdependent. Multiculturalism, in short, teaches global connectedness.

Although multiculturalism has found favour in recent years, it has drawn criticism too. Most troubling to opponents of multiculturalism is its tendency to encourage divisiveness rather than unity, by encouraging people to identify with only their own category rather than the nation as a whole. As critics see it, a multicultural approach moves Canada along the road that has led to social collapse in the former Yugoslavia and elsewhere.

Moreover, critics contend that multiculturalism erodes any claim of universal truth by evaluating ideas according to the race (and gender) of those who present them. Our common humanity, in other words, dissolves into an "Aboriginal experience," "Chinese experience," "European experience," and so on.

Finally, critics doubt that multiculturalism actually benefits minorities. Multiculturalism seems to demand precisely the kind of ethnic and racial separations that our nation has struggled for decades to end. As well, an Aboriginal-centred or Afrocentric curriculum may well deny children important knowledge and skills by forcing them to study only certain topics from a single point of view. Is there any common ground in this debate? Virtually everyone agrees that we all need to gain greater appreciation of our nation's cultural diversity. But precisely where the balance should be struck is likely to remain a divisive issue for some time to come (Banting et al., 2007; Breton, 2005; Breton et al., 2004; Davies & Guppy, 1998).

Counterculture

Cultural diversity also includes outright rejection of conventional ideas or behaviour. **Counterculture** refers to *cultural patterns that strongly oppose those widely accepted within a society*.

During the 1960s, for example, a youth-oriented counterculture rejected mainstream culture as too competitive, self-centred, and materialistic. Instead, hippies and other counterculturalists favoured a collective and co-operative lifestyle in which "being" was more important than "doing" and the capacity for personal growth—or "expanded consciousness"—was prized more highly than material possessions such as fancy homes and cars. Such differences led some people to "drop out" of the larger society and join countercultural communities.

Countercultures are still flourishing. At the extreme, small militaristic communities (made up of people born and bred in North America) or bands of religious militants (from other countries) exist in Canada and the United States, some of them engaging in violence intended to threaten our way of life.

Cultural Change

Perhaps the most basic human truth is that "all things shall pass." Even the dinosaurs, which thrived on this planet for 160 million years, exist today only as fossils. Will humanity survive for millions of years to come? All we can say with certainty is that, given our reliance on culture, the human record will show continuous change.

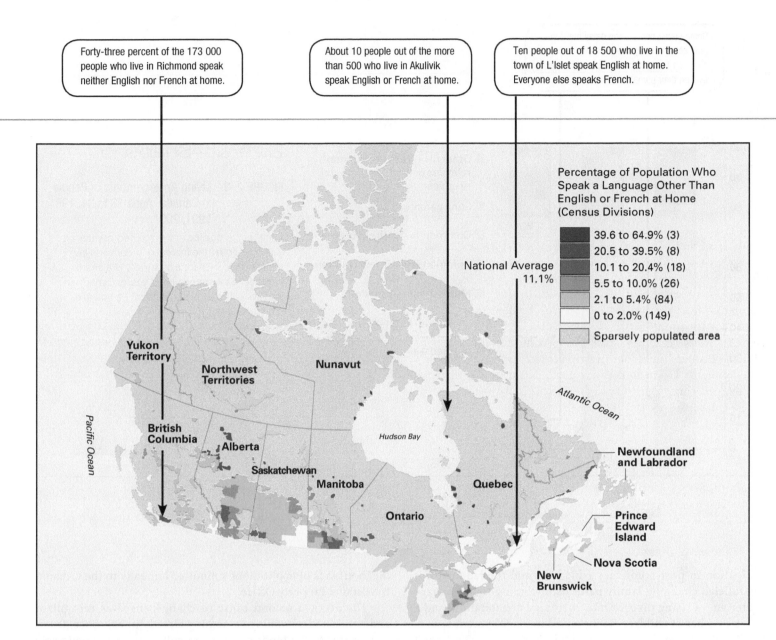

Forty-three percent of the 173 000 people who live in Richmond speak neither English nor French at home.

About 10 people out of the more than 500 who live in Akulivik speak English or French at home.

Ten people out of 18 500 who live in the town of L'Islet speak English at home. Everyone else speaks French.

Percentage of Population Who Speak a Language Other Than English or French at Home (Census Divisions)

	39.6 to 64.9% (3)
	20.5 to 39.5% (8)
	10.1 to 20.4% (18)
	5.5 to 10.0% (26)
	2.1 to 5.4% (84)
	0 to 2.0% (149)
	Sparsely populated area

National Average 11.1%

Yukon Territory

Northwest Territories

Nunavut

Pacific Ocean

British Columbia

Alberta

Saskatchewan

Manitoba

Hudson Bay

Ontario

Quebec

Atlantic Ocean

Newfoundland and Labrador

Prince Edward Island

Nova Scotia

New Brunswick

Seeing Ourselves

NATIONAL MAP 2–1 Nonofficial Home Languages across Canada, 2006

The map shows that the percentage of households that speak nonofficial languages at home varies greatly across Canada. The largest number of Canadians who speak a language other than French or English live in Toronto, Montreal, and Vancouver, with Toronto the leader. Somewhat surprising is the level of relative language homogeneity in large parts of southern Quebec. What is the cause of this? What other trends do you see?

Source: Calculated based on Statistics Canada (2007a).

Figure 2–3 on page 50 shows that the living arrangements of young Canadian adults aged 18 to 34 have changed in the few years between 1981 and 2001 (Clark, 2007). These changes are remarkable: Only half as many people in this age group were married and had children in 2001 as compared to 1981. Conversely, there was a 30 percent increase in the proportion who were living with their parents. Some things have changed only slightly: Today, as a generation ago, most women and men look forward to raising a family. Yet raising a family today is an experience quite different from raising one in earlier times. The important point is that change in one dimension of a cultural system usually sparks changes in other dimensions. For example, women's rising

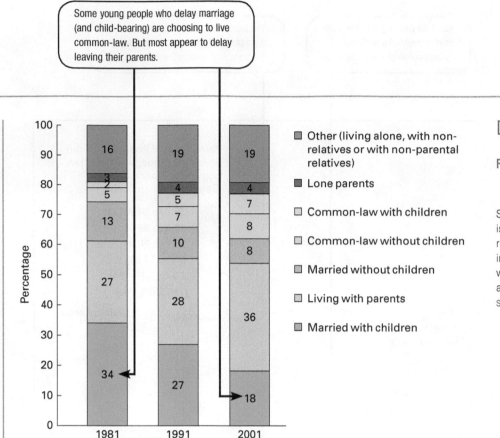

Some young people who delay marriage (and child-bearing) are choosing to live common-law. But most appear to delay leaving their parents.

Legend:
- Other (living alone, with non-relatives or with non-parental relatives)
- Lone parents
- Common-law with children
- Common-law without children
- Married without children
- Living with parents
- Married with children

Diversity Snapshot

FIGURE 2–3 **Living Arrangements of People in Canada, Ages 18 to 34, 1981, 1991, 2001**

Some of the decline in the married population is explained by the increase in common-law relationships. Nevertheless, there is a sharp increase in the proportion of young Canadians who live with their parents. What do you think are the causes for these changes?

Source: Clark (2007).

participation in post-secondary education and the labour force has paralleled changing family patterns, including first marriage at a later age, a rising divorce rate, increased cohabitation, and a growing number of children being raised in single-parent households (Balakrishnan, Lapierre-Adamcyk, & Krotki, 1993; Benoit & Hallgrimsdottir, 2011; Wu, 1999). Such connections illustrate the principle of **cultural integration**, *the close relationships among various elements of a cultural system.*

Some parts of a cultural system change more quickly than others. William Ogburn (1964) observed that technology moves quickly, generating new elements of material culture (such as test-tube babies) faster than nonmaterial culture (such as ideas about parenthood) can keep up with them. Ogburn called this inconsistency **cultural lag**, *the fact that some cultural elements change more quickly than others, disrupting a cultural system.* How are we to apply traditional ideas about motherhood and fatherhood in a culture where a woman can now give birth to a child by using another woman's egg, which has been fertilized in a laboratory with the sperm of a total stranger?

Cultural changes are set in motion in three ways. The first is *invention,* the process of creating new cultural elements, such as the telephone (1876), the airplane (1903), and the computer (late 1940s). The process of invention goes on constantly, as indicated by

the thousands of applications submitted annually to the Canadian Intellectual Property Office.

Discovery, a second cause of change, involves recognizing and better understanding something already in existence, from a distant star to the foods of a foreign culture to the athletic abilities of women. Many discoveries result from painstaking scientific research, and others happen by a stroke of luck, as when Marie Curie unintentionally left a rock on a piece of photographic paper in 1898 and discovered radium.

The third cause of cultural change is *diffusion,* the spread of objects or ideas from one society to another. The ability of new information technology to send information around the world in seconds means that the extent of cultural diffusion has never been greater than it is today.

Certainly, Canadian society has provided many significant cultural contributions to the world, including the renowned classical music of pianist Glenn Gould and the popular novels of Margaret Atwood, who was awarded the 2000 Booker Prize for her acclaimed novel *The Blind Assassin.* Sometimes, though, we forget that diffusion works the other way, so that much of what we assume is "Canadian" actually comes from elsewhere. Most clothing, furniture, clocks, newspapers, money, and even the English language are derived from other cultures around the world (Linton, 1937a).

Ethnocentrism and Cultural Relativism

December 10, a small village in Morocco. Watching many of our fellow travellers browsing through a tiny ceramics factory, we have little doubt that North Americans are among the world's greatest shoppers. We delight in surveying hand-woven carpets in China or India, inspecting finely crafted metals in Turkey, or collecting the beautifully coloured porcelain tiles we find here in Morocco. Of course, all these items are wonderful bargains. But one major reason for the low prices is unsettling to people living in rich countries: Many products from the world's low- and middle-income countries are made by children—some as young as five or six—who work long days for pennies per hour.

We think of childhood as a time of innocence and freedom from adult burdens such as work. In low-income countries throughout the world, however, families depend on income earned by their children. So what people in one society think of as right and natural, people elsewhere find puzzling or even immoral. Perhaps the Chinese philosopher Confucius had it right when he noted that "all people are the same; it's only their habits that are different."

Just about every imaginable idea or behaviour is commonplace somewhere in the world, and this cultural variation causes travellers both excitement and distress. Australians flip light switches down to turn them on, but North Americans flip them up. The Japanese name city blocks; North Americans name city streets. Egyptians stand very close to others in conversation; North Americans are used to maintaining several feet of "personal space." Bathrooms lack toilet paper in much of rural Morocco, causing considerable discomfort for North Americans, who recoil at the thought of using the left hand for bathroom hygiene, as the locals do.

Given that a particular culture is the basis for everyday experiences, it is no wonder that people everywhere exhibit **ethnocentrism**, *the practice of judging another culture by the standards of one's own culture.* Some small degree of ethnocentrism is necessary for people to be emotionally attached to their way of life. But ethnocentrism can also generate misunderstanding and sometimes even leads to conflict.

Even language is culturally biased. Years ago, people in North America or Europe referred to China as the "Far East." But this term, unknown to the Chinese, is an ethnocentric term for a region that is far east *of us.* The Chinese name for their country translates as "Central Kingdom," suggesting that they, like us, see their society as the centre of the world. The map shown on the right challenges our ethnocentrism by presenting a "down under" view of the Western Hemisphere.

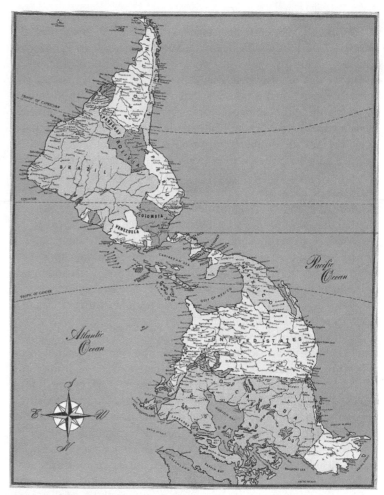

The view from "Down Under"—North America should be "up" and South America "down," or so we think. But because we live on a globe, "up" and "down" have no meaning at all. The reason this map of the Western Hemisphere looks wrong to us is not because it is geographically inaccurate; it simply violates our ethnocentric assumption that Canada should be "above" the rest of the Americas.

The alternative to ethnocentrism is **cultural relativism**, *the practice of judging a culture by its own standards.* Cultural relativism can be difficult for travellers to adopt: It requires not only openness to unfamiliar values and norms but also the ability to put aside cultural standards we have known all our lives. Even so, as people of the world increasingly come into contact with one another, the importance of understanding other cultures will become ever greater.

As noted in the opening to this chapter, businesses in Canada are realizing that success in the global economy depends on cultural sophistication. IBM, for example, now provides technical support

ethnocentrism (p. 51) the practice of judging another culture by the standards of one's own culture

cultural relativism (p. 51) the practice of judging a culture by its own standards

for its products using websites in more than 30 languages (IBM, 2010). In the past, companies paid little attention to cultural differences, sometime with negative consequences. General Motors learned the hard way that its Nova wasn't selling well in Spanish-speaking nations because the name in Spanish means "no go." Coors' phrase "Turn It Loose" startled Spanish-speaking customers by proclaiming that the beer would cause diarrhea. Braniff Airlines translated its slogan "Fly in Leather" into Spanish so clumsily that it read "Fly Naked"; similarly, Eastern Airlines' slogan "We Earn Our Wings Daily" became "We Fly Every Day to Heaven," discouraging timid air travellers. Even poultry giant Frank Perdue fell victim to poor marketing when his pitch "It Takes a Tough Man to Make a Tender Chicken" was transformed into the Spanish phrase "A Sexually Excited Man Makes a Chicken Affectionate" (Helin, 1992).

Widespread ethnocentrism in the world certainly contributes to armed conflict between nations. At the same time, today's military is often called on not only to fight but also to win the hearts and minds of the local people in an unfamiliar setting. The Seeing Sociology in the News box on page 56 gives a cultural understanding of Canada's military role in the Afghan war.

But cultural relativism creates problems of its own. If almost any behaviour is the norm *somewhere* in the world, does that mean everything is equally right? Does the fact that some Indian and Moroccan families benefit from having their children work long hours justify child labour? Because we are all members of a single human species, surely there must be some universal standards of proper conduct. But what are they? And in trying to develop them, how can we avoid imposing our own standards on others? There are no simple answers to these questions. But when confronting an unfamiliar cultural practice, it is best to resist making judgments before grasping what members of that culture think of the issue. Remember also to think about your own way of life as others might see it. After all, what we gain most from studying others is better insight into ourselves.

In the world's low-income countries, most children must work to provide their families with needed income. These young girls work long hours in a brick factory in the Kathmandu Valley, Nepal. Is it ethnocentric for people living in high-income nations to condemn the practice of child labour because we think youngsters belong in school? Why or why not?

A Global Culture?

Today more than ever, we can observe many of the same cultural patterns the world over. Walking the streets of Seoul, South Korea; Kuala Lumpur, Malaysia; Chennai, India; Cairo, Egypt; or Casablanca, Morocco, we see people wearing jeans, hear familiar music, and read ads for many of the same products we use at home.

Societies around the world now have more contact with one another than ever before, thanks to the flow of goods, information, and people:

1. **Global economy: The flow of goods.** International commerce is at an all-time high. The global economy has spread many consumer goods—from cars and TV shows to music and fashion—throughout the world.

2. **Global communications: The flow of information.** The internet and satellite-assisted communications enable people to experience events taking place thousands of miles away, often as they happen. In addition, English has long been the dominant language of the internet, helping spread the English language around the world. It was not until late 2009 that a person could register a web address in Korean, Chinese, Arabic, or another language that uses a non-Latin script.

3. **Global migration: The flow of people.** Knowledge about the rest of the world motivates people to move where they imagine life will be better, and modern transportation technology, especially air travel, makes relocating easier than ever

before. As a result, in most countries, significant numbers of people were born elsewhere (including some 6.19 million people living in Canada, about 20 percent of our country's population).

These global links help make the cultures of the world more similar. But there are three important limitations to the global culture thesis. First, the flow of information, goods, and people is uneven in different parts of the world. Generally speaking, urban areas (centres of commerce, communication, and people) have stronger ties to one another and rural villages remain isolated. In addition, the greater economic and military power of North America and Western Europe means that nations in these regions influence the rest of the world more than the rest of the world influences them.

Second, the global culture thesis assumes that people everywhere are able to *afford* the new goods and services. As Chapter 9 ("Global Stratification") explains, desperate poverty in much of the world deprives people of even the basic necessities of a safe and secure life.

Third, although many cultural elements have spread throughout the world, people everywhere do not attach the same meanings to them. Do children in Tokyo understand hip hop the way young people in Vancouver or Winnipeg do? Similarly, we enjoy foods from around the world but know little about the lives of the people who created them. In short, people everywhere look at the world through their own cultural lenses.

Theoretical Analysis of Culture

Sociologists investigate how culture helps us make sense of ourselves and the surrounding world. Here we will examine several macro-level theoretical approaches to understanding culture. A micro-level approach to the personal experience of culture, which emphasizes how individuals not only conform to cultural patterns but also create new patterns in their everyday lives, is the focus of Chapter 4 ("Social Interaction in Everyday Life").

The Functions of Culture: Structural-Functional Analysis

The structural-functional approach explains culture as a complex strategy for meeting human needs. Drawing from the philosophical doctrine of *idealism*, this approach considers values to be the core of a culture (Parsons, 1966; R.M. Williams, 1970). In other words, cultural values direct our lives, give meaning to what we do, and bind people together. Countless other cultural traits have various functions that support the operation of society.

Thinking functionally helps us understand unfamiliar ways of life. Consider the Old Order Mennonite farmer in Southern Ontario plowing hundreds of acres with a team of horses. His methods may violate the Canadian cultural value of efficiency, but from the Amish point of view, hard work functions to develop the discipline necessary for a highly religious way of life. Long days spent working together not only make the Amish self-sufficient but also strengthen family ties, unify local communities, and result in lower rates of overweight and obesity compared to other Canadians.

Of course, Amish practices have dysfunctions as well. The hard work and strict religious discipline are too demanding for some, who end up leaving the community. Also, strong religious beliefs sometimes prevent compromise and, as a result, slight differences in religious practices have caused the Amish to divide into different communities (Kraybill, 1989, 1994). This is not unlike the situation found in tightly controlled Mennonite communities in Manitoba, as Miriam Toews chronicled in her award-winning novel *A Complicated Kindness* (Toews, 2005).

If cultures are strategies for meeting human needs, we would expect to find many common patterns around the world. **Cultural universals** are *traits that are part of every known culture*. Comparing hundreds of cultures, George Murdock (1945) identified dozens of cultural universals. One common element is the family, which functions everywhere to control sexual reproduction and to oversee the care of children. Funeral rites, too, are found everywhere because all human communities cope with the reality of death. Jokes are another cultural universal, serving as a safe means of releasing social tensions.

○ **CRITICAL REVIEW** The strength of structural-functional analysis lies in showing how culture operates to meet human needs. Yet by emphasizing a society's dominant cultural patterns, this approach largely ignores cultural diversity. Also, because this approach emphasizes cultural stability, it downplays the importance of change. In short, cultural systems are neither as stable nor as universal as structural-functional analysis leads us to believe. The Applying Theory table on page 57 summarizes this theoretical approach's main lessons about culture and places it alongside two other approaches that we consider next.

○ **CHECK YOUR LEARNING** In Canada, what are some of the functions of sports, Canada Day celebrations, and Thanksgiving?

Inequality and Culture: Social-Conflict Analysis

The social-conflict approach draws attention to the link between culture and inequality. From this point of view, any cultural trait benefits some members of society at the expense of others.

THINKING ABOUT DIVERSITY: RACE, CLASS, AND GENDER

Early Rock and Roll: Social Divisions and Cultural Change

In the 1950s, rock and roll emerged as part of North American popular culture. Rock soon grew to become a cultural tide that swept away musical tastes and traditions and changed both Canada and the United States in ways we still experience today.

Early in the 1950s, mainstream "pop" music was largely aimed at white adults. Songs were written by professional composers, recorded by long-established record labels, and performed by well-known artists such as bandleader Guy Lombardo and His Royal Canadians, Dick Toddy, Percy Faith, and Dorothy Collins. The United States featured Perry Como, Eddie Fisher, Doris Day, and Patti Page. Just about every big-name performer was white and the vast majority were male.

The 1950s was also a time of rigid racial segregation. This racial separation meant that the cultures of white people and Black people were different. In the subcultural world of Black musicians, music had different sounds and rhythms, reflecting jazz, gospel singing, and rhythm and blues. All of these musical styles were the creations of composers and performers working with Black-owned record companies and broadcast on radio stations to an almost entirely Black audience.

Class, too, divided the musical world of the 1950s, even among whites. A second musical subculture was country and western, a musical style popular among poorer whites, especially people living in the U.S. South and in eastern parts

of Canada. This subculture included Nova Scotian country music stars Wilf Carter (also known as Montana Slim), Hank Snow, and Don Messer. Like rhythm and blues, country and western music had its own composers and performers, its own record labels, and its own radio stations.

In the early 1950s, there were a variety of musical worlds in North American society, separated by the walls of race and class. There was little "crossover" music, meaning that very rarely, if ever, did performers or songs from one world gain popularity in another.

This musical segregation began to break down around 1955 with the birth of rock and roll. Rock was a new mix of many existing musical patterns, drawing on mainstream pop but including country and western and, especially, rhythm and blues.

The new rock and roll music drew together musical traditions, but it soon divided society in a new way—by age. Rock and roll was the first music clearly linked to the emergence of a youth culture; rock was all the rage among teenagers but was little appreciated or even understood by their parents. One reason for this age split was that, in the prosperous 1950s, young people had more money to spend and record companies realized that they could make a fortune selling music to the new "youth market."

Within a few years, the emerging youth culture presented young people with many new

musical stars, many of whom definitely were not people who looked or acted like their parents. The rock and roll performers were men (and a few women) who looked young and took a rebellious stand against "adult" culture. The typical rocker was a young man who looked like what parents might have called a "juvenile delinquent" and who claimed to be "cool," an idea that most parents did not even understand.

The first band to make it big in rock and roll was Bill Haley and the Comets. These men (Haley lowered his stated age to gain greater acceptance) came out of the country and western tradition (Haley's earlier bands included the Down Homers and the Saddlemen). Haley's first big hits in 1954—"Shake, Rattle, and Roll" and "Rock around the Clock"—were recordings of earlier rhythm and blues songs.

Very quickly, however, young people began to lose interest in older performers such as Bill Haley and turned their attention to younger performers who had a stronger juvenile delinquent image—musicians sporting sideburns, turned-up collars, and black leather jackets. By the end of 1955, the unquestioned star of rock and roll was a poor white boy from Tupelo, Mississippi, named Elvis Aron Presley. Elvis knew country and western music from his rural roots, and after he moved to his adopted hometown of Memphis, Tennessee, he learned all about Black gospel and rhythm and blues.

Why do certain values dominate a society in the first place? Many conflict theorists, especially Marxists, argue that culture is shaped by a society's system of economic production. Social-conflict theory, then, is rooted in the philosophical doctrine of *materialism*, which holds that a society's system of material production (such as our own capitalist economy) has a powerful effect on the rest of the culture. This materialist approach contrasts with the idealistic leanings of structural-functionalism.

Social-conflict analysis ties our society's cultural values of competitiveness and material success to our country's capitalist economy, which serves the interests of the nation's wealthy elite. The culture of capitalism

teaches us to think that rich and powerful people work harder or longer than others and that they therefore deserve their wealth and privileges. It also encourages us to view capitalism as somehow "natural," discouraging us from trying to reduce economic inequality.

Eventually, however, the strains of inequality erupt into movements for social change. Two examples are the civil rights movement and the women's movement. Both sought greater equality, and both encountered opposition from defenders of the status quo.

CRITICAL REVIEW The social-conflict approach suggests that cultural systems do not address human needs equally,

Before the 1950s ended, Presley had become the first superstar of rock and roll, not only because he had talent but also because he had great crossover power. With early hits including "Hound Dog" (a rhythm and blues song originally recorded by Big Mama Thornton) and "Blue Suede Shoes" (written by country and western star Carl Perkins), Presley broke down many of the walls of race and class (but not gender) in the North American music scene.

Presley went on to a 20-year career as "the King." But during that time, illustrating the expanding and changing character of culture, popular music developed in many new and different directions. By the end of the 1950s, popular musical styles included soft rock (Ricky Nelson, Pat Boone), rockabilly (Johnny Cash), and dozens of doo-wop groups, both Black and white (often named for birds—the Falcons, the Penguins, and the Flamingos—or cars—the Imperials, the Impalas, the Fleetwoods). Rock and roll became an international phenomenon, including a substantial following in Canada, but until the 1960s and the development of rock music nearly all of its stars were from the United States. Certain Canadian pop performers of the 1950s and early 1960s—among them the Crew-Cuts and Paul Anka—were seen as "rock and roll" stars in some circles.

During the 1960s, rock music grew even more popular and increasingly diverse, including folk music (the Kingston Trio; Peter, Paul, and Mary; Bob Dylan), surf music (the Beach Boys, Jan and Dean), and the "British invasion" led by the Beatles.

At first, the Beatles were very close to the clean-cut, pop side of rock, but they soon shared the spotlight with another British band that was proud of its "delinquent" clothing and street fighter looks—the Rolling Stones. During the 1960s, the hard rock of the Beatles and the Stones was joined by softer "folk rock" performed in Canada by Neil Young, who was joined by American artists in bands such as Buffalo Springfield and Crosby, Stills, Nash & Young.

Mainstream rock continued with bands like the Who, and rhythm and blues gave birth to "Motown" (named after the "motor city," Detroit) as well as "soul" music, creating dozens of stars who were increasingly more likely to be female, including Aretha Franklin, the Four Tops, the Temptations, and Diana Ross and the Supremes. Many Canadian bands appeared during this time, including Ritchie Knight and the Mid-Knights and Jon & Lee & the Checkmates.

During this period, the American west coast developed a different, more political rock music performed by Jefferson Airplane, the Grateful Dead, and Janis Joplin. West coast spinoff musical styles included "acid rock," which was influenced by drug use and performed by the Doors and Jimi Hendrix. The jazz influence also returned to the world of rock, creating such "jazz rock" groups as Chicago and Blood, Sweat, and Tears.

This brief look at the early decades of rock and roll shows the power of race, class, and gender to divide and separate people, shaping different subcultural patterns. It also shows the power of music to bring people together. We also see that the production of culture—in terms of music as well as movies and music videos—has become a megabusiness. But most of all, it shows us that culture is not a rigid system that stands still but is better described as a living process, changing, adapting, and reinventing itself over time.

WHAT DO YOU THINK?

1. Many dimensions of our way of life shaped rock and roll. In what ways do you think the emergence of rock and roll changed North American culture?

2. Throughout this period of musical change, most musical performers were men. What does this tell us about our way of life? Is popular music still dominated by men today?

3. Can you carry on the story of musical change in Canada to the present? (Think of disco, heavy metal, punk rock, rap, and hip hop.)

Source: Based on Stuessy and Lipscomb (2009) and Encyclopedia of Music in Canada (2011).

---

allowing some people to dominate others. This inequality in turn generates pressure toward change.

Yet by stressing the divisiveness of culture, this approach understates ways in which cultural patterns integrate members of a society. Thus we should consider both social-conflict and structural-functional insights for a fuller understanding of culture.

CHECK YOUR LEARNING How might a social-conflict analysis of university and college fraternities and sororities differ from a structural-functional analysis?

Evolution and Culture: Sociobiology

We know that culture is a human creation, but does human biology influence how this process unfolds? A third way of thinking, standing with one leg in biology and the other in sociology, is **sociobiology**, *a theoretical approach that explores ways in which human biology affects how we create culture.*

Sociobiology rests on the theory of evolution proposed by Charles Darwin in his book *On the Origin of Species* (1859). Darwin asserted that living organisms change over long periods of time as a result of *natural selection*, a matter of four simple principles. First, all living

The Canadian Press

Afghanistan photos on display at Calgary museum tells story of "open-ended" war

BY BILL GRAVELAND
March 8, 2011

CALGARY—A dramatic photo of a young Afghan boy sitting by a wall with his two prosthetic legs in plain sight offers a rare glimpse at the human side of the conflict that has racked Afghanistan over the last decade.

"It's my favourite," says Stephen Thorne, a reporter for The Canadian Press, who took the photo.

"I think at the time I was there it was about 100 Afghans a month who were killed or disabled by landmines. We were in a traffic jam in Kabul and I looked out the window of the truck and there was this kid.

"He's got two prosthetic legs and the look on his face just tells his story."

It's just one of the arresting photos and gripping videos now on display at the Military Museums in Calgary as part of the exhibit "Afghanistan: A Glimpse of War." It will be in Calgary until July.

It was originally unveiled at the Canadian War Museum in Ottawa and is mostly comprised of photos from Thorne and video from documentary filmmaker Garth Pritchard from Priddis, Alta. Both men have made several trips to Afghanistan.

Dean Oliver, director of research and exhibitions at the Canadian War Museum, said the exhibit is unique and continues to be updated.

"It is unusual in that Afghanistan is an ongoing conflict," Oliver said. "It has had a beginning in which we are gathered, but it hasn't had an end. So there were some challenges for us as a museum in presenting historical material that was open-ended.

"It isn't a narrative or a chronology. We made no effort really to try and tell the history of Canada's involvement in the Afghan war, in large part, because the records aren't yet available."

Thorne came back from Afghanistan with a load of memories and a deep appreciation for what people there have been going through.

"Two things impressed me about the time I spent in Afghanistan: one is the commitment and bravery of our troops—I saw them do things I couldn't believe—and the other was the strength and fortitude of the Afghan people who at that time had been through 25 years of war.

"This was kind of the pinnacle of my career."

Lt.-Col Dan Drew, who served three tours in Afghanistan, said the exhibit will help Canadians understand what soldiers are doing over there.

"One thing I'm really proud of is the Canadian people are really behind the military," said Drew, who is stationed at CFB Suffield in Alberta.

"It's up to us to help them understand what we're doing over there. It's a fairly abstract sort of idea to most people because it's the other side of the world, a different culture. So yeah, I think it's a great thing we're doing."

WHAT DO YOU THINK?

1. Do you think that the exhibit will increase Canadians' cultural understanding of our military role in Afghanistan? Of the Afghan people?

2. Do you think it makes a difference who takes the photos that are displayed in an exhibit such as this one? What kinds of photos might an Afghan villager whose home is in ruins take, or a mother who has just buried her son?

3. If the people of the world were able to greatly increase cultural understanding, do you think we might expect to put an end to war? Why or why not?

Source: Afghanistan photos on display at Calgary museum tells story of 'open-ended' war, by Bill Graveland, 8 March 2011. © The Canadian Press.

---

things live to reproduce themselves. Second, the blueprint for reproduction is in the genes, the basic units of life that carry traits of one generation into the next. Third, some random variation in genes allows each species to "try out" new life patterns in a particular environment. This variation enables some organisms to survive better than others and to pass on their advantageous genes to their offspring. Fourth and finally, over thousands of generations, the genes that promote reproduction survive and become dominant. In this way, as biologists say, a species *adapts* to its environment, and dominant traits emerge as the "nature" of the organism.

Sociobiologists claim that the large number of cultural universals reflects the fact that all humans are members of a single biological species. It is our common biology that underlies, for example, the apparently universal "double standard" of sexual behaviour. As the sex researcher Alfred Kinsey put it, "Among all people everywhere in the world, the male is more likely than the female to desire sex with a variety of partners" (quoted in Barash, 1981:49). But why?

We all know that children result from joining a woman's egg with a man's sperm. But the biological significance of a single sperm is very different from that of a single egg. For healthy men, sperm is a "renewable resource" produced by the testes throughout most of the life course. A man releases hundreds of millions of sperm in a single ejaculation (Barash, 1981:47). A newborn girl's ovaries, however, contain her lifetime supply of follicles, or immature eggs. A woman releases a single egg cell from the ovaries each month. So although men are biologically capable of fathering thousands of offspring, a woman is able to bear only a relatively small number of children.

Given this biological difference, men reproduce their genes most efficiently by being promiscuous—by readily engaging in sex. But women look at reproduction differently. Each of a woman's

APPLYING THEORY

Culture

	Structural-Functional Approach	Social-Conflict Approach	Sociobiology Approach
What is the level of analysis?	Macro level	Macro level	Macro level
What is culture?	Culture is a system of behaviour by which members of societies co-operate to meet their needs.	Culture is a system that benefits some people and disadvantages others.	Culture is a system of behaviour that is partly shaped by human biology.
What is the foundation of culture?	Cultural patterns are rooted in a society's core values and beliefs.	Cultural patterns are rooted in a society's system of economic production.	Cultural patterns are rooted in humanity's biological evolution.
What core questions does the approach ask?	How does a cultural pattern help society operate? What cultural patterns are found in all societies?	How does a cultural pattern benefit some people and harm others? How does a cultural pattern support social inequality?	How does a cultural pattern help a species adapt to its environment?

pregnancies demands that she carry the child, give birth, and provide care for some time afterwards. Efficient reproduction on the part of the woman therefore depends on selecting a man whose qualities (beginning with the likelihood that he will simply stay around) will contribute to her child's survival and, later, successful reproduction.

The double standard certainly involves more than biology and is tangled up with the historical domination of women by men. But sociobiology suggests that this cultural pattern, like many others, has an underlying "bio-logic." Simply put, the double standard exists around the world because women and men everywhere tend toward distinctive reproductive strategies.

CRITICAL REVIEW Sociobiology has generated intriguing insights into the biological roots of some cultural patterns. But this approach remains controversial for two reasons.

First, some critics fear that sociobiology may revive the biological arguments of a century ago that claimed the superiority of one race or sex. But defenders counter that sociobiology rejects the past pseudo-science of racial and gender superiority. In fact, they say, sociobiology unites all humanity because all people share a single evolutionary history. Sociobiology does assert that men and women differ biologically in some ways that culture cannot easily overcome. But far from claiming that males are somehow more important than females, sociobiology emphasizes that both sexes are vital to human reproduction and survival.

Second, say the critics, sociobiologists have little evidence to support their theories. Research to date suggests that biological forces do not *determine* human behaviour in any rigid sense. Rather, humans *learn* behaviour within a culture. The contribution of sociobiology, then, includes explaining why some cultural patterns are more common and seem easier to learn than others (Barash, 1981).

CHECK YOUR LEARNING Using the sociobiology approach, explain why some cultural patterns, such as sibling rivalry (the fact that children in the same family often compete and even fight with each other), are widespread.

Because any analysis of culture requires a broad focus on the workings of society, the three approaches discussed in this chapter are macro-level in scope. The symbolic-interaction approach, with its micro-level focus on people's behaviour in specific situations, will be explored in Chapter 4 ("Social Interaction in Everyday Life").

Using an evolutionary perspective, sociobiologists explain that different reproductive strategies give rise to a double standard: Men treat women as sexual objects more than women treat men that way. While this may be so, many sociologists counter that behaviour—such as that shown here—is more correctly understood as resulting from a culture of male domination.

Culture and Human Freedom

This entire chapter leads us to ask an important question: To what extent are human beings, as cultural creatures, free? Does culture bind us to each other and to the past? Or does it enhance our capacity for individual thought and independent choice?

As symbolic creatures, humans cannot live without culture. But the capacity for culture does have some drawbacks. We may be the only animals who name ourselves, but living in a symbolic world means that we are also the only creatures who experience alienation. In addition, culture is largely a matter of habit, which limits our choices and drives us to repeat troubling patterns, such as racial prejudice and gender discrimination, in each new generation.

Our society's emphasis on personal achievement urges us toward excellence, yet this same competitive behaviour also isolates us from one another. Material things comfort us in some ways but divert us from the security and satisfaction that come from close relationships and spiritual strength.

For better and worse, human beings are cultural creatures, just as ants and bees are prisoners of their biology. But there is a crucial difference. Biological instincts create a ready-made world; culture forces us to choose as we make and remake a world for ourselves. No better evidence of this freedom exists than the cultural diversity of our own society and the even greater human diversity around the world.

Learning about this cultural diversity is one goal shared by sociologists. The Thinking Globally box offers some contrasts between the cultures of Canada and the United States. Wherever we may live, the better we understand the workings of the surrounding culture, the better prepared we will be to use the freedom it offers us.

Canada and the United States: Two National Cultures or One?

Canada and the United States are two of the largest high-income nations in the world, and they share a common border of about 6400 kilometres. But do they share the same culture?

One important point to make right away is that both nations are *multicultural*. Not only do both countries have hundreds of Aboriginal societies, but immigration has also brought people from all over the world to both Canada and the United States. In both countries, most early immigrants came from Europe, but in recent years most immigrants have come from nations in Asia and Latin America. Vancouver, for example, has a Chinese community about the same size as the Latino community in Los Angeles.

Canada differs from the United States in one important respect—historically, Canada has had *two* dominant cultures: French (about 16 percent of the population) and British (roughly 36 percent). Almost one-third of people in Quebec (where French is the official language) and New Brunswick (which is officially bilingual) claim some French ancestry.

Are the dominant values of Canada much the same as those of the United States? Seymour Martin Lipset (1985) finds that they differ to some degree. The United States declared its independence from Great Britain in 1776; Canada did not formally separate from Great Britain until 1982, and the British monarch is still Canada's official head of state. Thus, Lipset continues, the dominant culture of Canada lies between the culture of the United States and that of Great Britain.

The culture of the United States is more individualistic, and Canada's is more collective. In the United States, individualism is seen in the historical importance of the cowboy, a self-sufficient loner, and even outlaws such as Jesse James and Billy the Kid are regarded as heroes because they challenged authority. In Canada, it is the Mountie—Canada's well-known police officer on horseback—who is looked on with great respect. Canada's greater emphasis on collective life is also evident in stronger labour unions: Canadian workers are almost three times as likely to be members of a union as workers in the United States (Steyn, 2008).

Politically, people in the United States tend to think that individuals should do things for themselves. In Canada, much as in Great Britain, there is a strong sense that government should look after the interests of everyone. The U.S. Constitution emphasizes the importance of "life, liberty, and the pursuit of happiness" (words that place importance on the individual), while Canadian society is based on "peace, order, and good government" (words that place importance on the government; Steyn, 2008). One clear result of this difference today is that Canada has a much broader social welfare system (including universal health care) than the United States (which has only recently introduced a limited system of public health care). It also helps explain the fact that about one-third of all households in the United States own one or more guns, and the idea that individuals are entitled to own a gun, although controversial, is widespread. In Canada, by contrast, few households have a gun and the government restricts gun ownership, as in Great Britain.

WHAT DO YOU THINK?

1. Why do you think some Canadians feel that their way of life is overshadowed by that of the United States?

2. Ask your American friends to name Canada's capital city. Are you surprised by how few know the answer? Why or why not?

3. Why do many people in the United States not know very much about either Canada or Mexico, countries with which they share long borders?

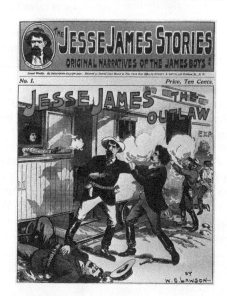

The individuals that a society celebrates as heroic are a good indication of that society's cultural values. In the United States, outlaws such as Jesse James (and later, Bonnie and Clyde) were regarded as heroes because they represented the individual standing strong against authority. In Canada, by contrast, people have always looked up to the Mountie, who symbolizes society's authority over the individual.

CHAPTER 2 CULTURE

WHAT CLUES DO WE HAVE TO A SOCIETY'S CULTURAL VALUES? The values of any society—that is, what that society thinks is important—are reflected in various aspects of everyday life, including the things people have and the ways they behave. An interesting way to "read" a culture's values is to look at the "superheroes" who are celebrated. Take a look at the characters in the two photos below; in each case, describe what makes the character special and what each character represents in cultural terms.

A long-time superhero important to North American culture is Spider-Man. In all three *Spider-Man* movies, Peter Parker (who transforms into Spider-Man when he confronts evil) is secretly in love with Mary Jane Watson, but—in true superhero style—he does not allow himself to follow his heart.

Captain Canuck is a Canadian comic book superhero who first appeared in the mid-1970s. The original story featured Canadian secret agent Tim Evans, who had special powers because of his contact with extraterrestrials and controlled the world from his location in Canada. Later appearances by Captain Canuck saw him fighting a global conspiracy and taking on the biker gang Unholy Avengers.

HINT: Superman (as well as Spider-Man and Captain Canuck) define North American society as good; after all, Superman and Captain Canuck fight for "truth, justice, and the North American way." Many superheroes have stories that draw on great people in our cultural history, including religious figures such as Moses and Jesus: They have mysterious origins (we never really know their true families), they are "tested" through great moral challenges, and they finally succeed in overcoming all obstacles. (Today's superheroes, however, are likely to win the day using force and often violence.) Having a "secret identity" means that superheroes can lead ordinary lives (and means that we ordinary people can imagine being superheroes). But to keep their focus on fighting evil, superheroes must place their work ahead of any romantic interests ("Work comes first!"). Buffy also illustrates the special challenge to "do it all" faced by women in our society: Constantly called on to fight evil, she still must make time for her studies as well as her friends.

Applying Sociology in Everyday Life

1. What traits define popular culture "heroes" such as Clint Eastwood's film character Dirty Harry, Sylvester Stallone's film characters Rocky and Rambo, and Arnold Schwarzenegger's character The Terminator?

2. How do the culture of Canada and the everyday life of its citizens differ from the way of life portrayed in the worlds of popular culture heroes?

3. Watch a Disney film such as *Finding Nemo, The Lion King, The Little Mermaid, Aladdin,* or *Pocahontas*. One reason for the popularity of these films is that they share dominant popular culture themes. Explain the main cultural messages in one of these films.

MAKING THE GRADE

CHAPTER 2   Culture

What Is Culture?

CULTURE is a way of life.
- Culture is shared by members of a society.
- Culture shapes how we act, think, and feel.

pp. 36–39

CULTURE is a human trait.
- Although several species display a limited capacity for culture, only human beings rely on culture for survival.

pp. 36–39

CULTURE is a product of evolution.
- As the human brain evolved, culture replaced biological instincts as our species' primary strategy for survival.

pp. 36–39

We experience **CULTURE SHOCK** when we enter an unfamiliar culture and are not able to "read" meaning in our new surroundings.
- We create culture shock for others when we act in ways they do not understand.

pp. 36–39

culture (p. 36) the ways of thinking, the ways of acting, and the material objects that together form a people's way of life

society (p. 36) people who interact in a defined territory and share a culture

culture shock (p. 36) personal disorientation when experiencing an unfamiliar way of life

✓ Approximately 200 nonofficial mother tongues are spoken in Canada. Worldwide, there are roughly 7000 different languages (p. 39).

The Elements of Culture

CULTURE relies on symbols in the form of words, gestures, and actions to express meaning.

pp. 39–40

LANGUAGE is the symbolic system by which one generation transmits culture to the next.

p. 41

VALUES are abstract standards of what ought to be (for example, equality of opportunity).
BELIEFS are specific statements that people who share a culture hold to be true (for example, "A qualified woman could be elected prime minister").

pp. 41–44

NORMS, which guide human behaviour, are of two types:
- **MORES** (for example, sexual taboos), which have great moral significance
- **FOLKWAYS** (for example, greetings or dining etiquette), which are matters of everyday politeness

p. 44

symbol (p. 39) anything that carries a particular meaning recognized by people who share a culture

language (p. 41) a system of symbols that allows people to communicate with one another

cultural transmission (p. 41) the process by which one generation passes culture to the next

Sapir-Whorf thesis (p. 41) the idea that people see and understand the world through the cultural lens of language

values (p. 41) culturally defined standards that people use to decide what is desirable, good, and beautiful and that serve as broad guidelines for social living

beliefs (p. 41) specific ideas that people hold to be true

norms (p. 44) rules and expectations by which a society guides the behaviour of its members

mores (p. 44) norms that are widely observed and have great moral significance

folkways (p. 44) norms for routine or casual interaction

Values and norms (standards for how we should behave) reflect **IDEAL CULTURE**, which differs from **REAL CULTURE** (what actually occurs in everyday life).

p. 44

Technology and Culture

Culture is shaped by **TECHNOLOGY**. We understand technological development in terms of stages of socio-cultural evolution:
- hunting and gathering
- horticulture and pastoralism
- agriculture
- industry
- post-industrial information technology

pp. 44–46

technology (p. 45) knowledge that people use to make a way of life in their surroundings

hunting and gathering (p. 45) the use of simple tools to hunt animals and gather vegetation for food

horticulture (p. 45) the use of hand tools to raise crops

pastoralism (p. 45) the domestication of animals

agriculture (p. 45) large-scale cultivation using plows harnessed to animals or more powerful energy sources

industry (p. 46) the production of goods using advanced sources of energy to drive large machinery

post-industrialism (p. 46) the production of information using computer technology

✓ Members of societies that possess sophisticated technology should be careful not to judge cultures with simpler technology as inferior (p. 46).

61

Cultural Diversity

We live in a culturally diverse society.
- This diversity is due to our history of immigration.
- Diversity reflects regional differences.
- Diversity reflects differences in social class that set off **HIGH CULTURE** (available only to elites) from **POPULAR CULTURE** (available to average people).

p. 47

A number of values are central to our way of life. But cultural patterns are not the same throughout our society.
- **SUBCULTURE** is based on differences in interests as well as in life experiences.
- **MULTICULTURALISM** is an effort to enhance appreciation of cultural diversity.

pp. 47–50

- **COUNTERCULTURE** is strongly at odds with conventional ways of life. Cultural change results from
- invention (for example, the telephone and the computer)
- discovery (for example, the recognition that women are capable of political leadership)
- diffusion (for example, the growing popularity of various ethnic foods and musical styles)

p. 50

high culture (p. 47) cultural patterns that distinguish a society's elite

popular culture (p. 47) cultural patterns that are widespread among a society's population

subculture (p. 47) cultural patterns that set apart some segment of a society's population

multiculturalism (p. 48) a perspective recognizing the cultural diversity of Canada and promoting equal standing for all cultural traditions

Eurocentrism (p. 48) the dominance of European (especially English) cultural patterns

counterculture (p. 50) cultural patterns that strongly oppose those widely accepted within a society

cultural integration (p. 51) the close relationships among various elements of a cultural system

cultural lag (p. 51) the fact that some cultural elements change more quickly than others, disrupting a cultural system

ethnocentrism (p. 52) the practice of judging another culture by the standards of one's own culture

cultural relativism (p. 52) the practice of judging a culture by its own standards

- **CULTURAL LAG** results when some parts of a cultural system change faster than others.
- We create culture shock for others when we act in ways they do not understand. How do we understand cultural differences?

p. 51

- **ETHNOCENTRISM** links people to their society but can cause misunderstanding and conflict between societies.
- **CULTURAL RELATIVISM** is increasingly important as people of the world come into more and more contact with each other.

pp. 51–52

✓ Global cultural patterns result from the worldwide flow of goods, information, and people (pp. 52–53).

Theoretical Analysis of Culture

The **STRUCTURAL-FUNCTIONAL APPROACH** views culture as a relatively stable system built on core values. All cultural patterns play some part in the ongoing operation of society.

pp. 55–57

The **SOCIAL-CONFLICT APPROACH** sees culture as a dynamic arena of inequality and conflict. Cultural patterns benefit some categories of people more than others.

pp. 55–56

SOCIOBIOLOGY explores how the long history of evolution has shaped patterns of culture in today's world.

pp. 56–58

cultural universals (p. 54) traits that are part of every known culture

sociobiology (p. 56) a theoretical approach that explores ways in which human biology affects how we create culture

See the Applying Theory table on page 57.

Culture and Human Freedom

- Culture can limit the choices we make.
- As cultural creatures, we have the capacity to shape and reshape our world to meet our needs and pursue our dreams.

pp. 58–59

MySocLab

Visit MySocLab at www.mysoclab.com to access a variety of online resources that will help you to prepare for tests and to apply your knowledge, including
- an eText
- videos
- self-grading quizzes
- glossary flashcards

3 Socialization: From Infancy to Old Age

- Why is social experience the key to human personality?

- What familiar social settings have special importance to how we live and grow?

- How do our experiences change over the life course?

Having completed macro-level Chapter 2 ("Culture"), we turn now to a micro-level look at how individuals become members of society through the process of socialization.

On a cold winter day in 1938, a social worker walked quickly to the door of a rural Pennsylvania farmhouse. Sent to investigate a case of possible child abuse, the social worker entered the house and soon discovered a five-year-old girl hidden in a second-floor storage room. The child, whose name was Anna, was wedged into an old chair with her arms tied securely above her head so that she couldn't move. She was wearing filthy clothes, and her arms and legs were as thin as matchsticks (K. Davis, 1940).

Anna's situation can only be described as tragic. She was born in 1932 to a single mother of 26 with mental health problems who lived with her strict father. Angry about his daughter's "illegitimate" motherhood, the grandfather did not even want the child in his house, so for the first six months of her life, Anna was passed among various welfare agencies. But her mother could not afford to pay for her care, and Anna returned to the hostile home of her grandfather.

To lessen the grandfather's anger, Anna's mother kept the child in the storage room and gave her just enough milk to keep her alive. There she stayed—day after day, month after month, with almost no human contact—for five long years.

Learning about Anna's rescue, the sociologist Kingsley Davis immediately went to see the child. He found her with local officials at a county home. Davis was stunned by the emaciated girl, who could not laugh, speak, or even smile. Anna was completely unresponsive, as if alone in an empty world.

Social Experience: The Key to Our Humanity

Socialization is so basic to human development that we sometimes overlook its importance. But in this terrible case of an isolated child, we can see what humans would be like without social contact. Although physically alive, Anna hardly seems human. We can see that without social experience, a child is not able to act or communicate in a meaningful way and seems to be as much an object as a person.

Sociologists use the term **socialization** to refer to *the lifelong social experience by which people develop their human potential and learn culture.* Unlike other species, whose behaviour is biologically set, humans need social experience to learn their culture and to survive. Social experience is also the basis of **personality**, *a person's fairly consistent patterns of acting, thinking, and feeling.* We build a personality by internalizing—taking in—our surroundings. But without social experience, as Anna's case shows, personality hardly develops at all.

Human Development: Nature and Nurture

Anna's case makes clear the fact that humans depend on others to provide the care needed not only for physical growth but also for personality to develop. A century ago, however, people mistakenly believed that humans were born with instincts that determined their personality and behaviour.

The Biological Sciences: The Role of Nature

Charles Darwin's groundbreaking study of evolution, described in Chapter 2 ("Culture"), led people to think incorrectly that human behaviour was instinctive, simply our "nature." Such ideas led to claims that our economic system reflects "instinctive human competitiveness," that some people are "born criminals," or that women are "naturally" emotional and men are "naturally" rational.

People trying to understand cultural diversity also misunderstood Darwin's thinking. Centuries of world exploration had taught Western Europeans that people around the world behaved quite differently from society to society. But Europeans linked these differences to biology rather than culture. It was an easy, although incorrect and very damaging, step to claim that members of technologically simple societies were biologically less evolved and therefore "less human." This ethnocentric view helped justify colonialism: If Native peoples were not human in the same sense that the colonialists were, Native peoples could be exploited, even enslaved, without a second thought. This was the experience for Canada's Aboriginal peoples, who were viewed by Canada's former colonial powers as "savages" and "barbarians" (Dickason, 1992; Francis, 1998).

socialization (p. 64) the lifelong social experience by which people develop their human potential and learn culture

personality (p. 64) a person's fairly consistent patterns of acting, thinking, and feeling

The personalities we develop depend largely on the environment in which we live. As William Kurelek shows in this painting, *Prairie Childhood*, based on his childhood in the Alberta prairies, a young person's life on a farm is often characterized by periods of social isolation and backbreaking work. How would such a boy's personality be likely to differ from that of his wealthy cousin raised in a large city, such as Montreal?

William Kurelek, *Prairie Childhood*. The Estate of William Kurelek and the Isaacs Gallery, Toronto.

The Social Sciences: The Role of Nurture

In the twentieth century, biological explanations of human behaviour came under fire. The psychologist John B. Watson (1878–1958) developed a theory called *behaviourism*, which held that behaviour is not instinctive but learned. Thus people everywhere are equally human, differing only in their cultural patterns. In short, Watson rooted human behaviour not in nature but in *nurture*.

Today, social scientists are cautious about describing *any* human behaviour as instinctive. This does not mean that biology plays no part in human behaviour. Human life, after all, depends on the functioning of the body. We also know that children often share biological traits (such as height and hair colour) with their parents and that heredity plays a part in intelligence, musical and artistic talent, and personality (such as how you deal with frustration). However, whether you develop your inherited potential depends on how you are raised. For example, if children do not use their brain early in life, it fails to develop fully (Begley, 1995; Goldsmith, 1983).

Without denying the importance of nature, then, nurture matters more in shaping human behaviour. More precisely, *nurture is our nature*.

Social Isolation

As the story of Anna shows, cutting people off from the social world is very harmful. For ethical reasons, researchers can never place human beings in total isolation to study what happens. But in the past, they have studied the effects of social isolation on non-human primates.

Research with Monkeys

In a classic study, the psychologists Harry and Margaret Harlow (1962) placed rhesus monkeys—whose behaviour is in some ways surprisingly similar to human behaviour—in various conditions of social isolation. They found that complete isolation (with adequate nutrition) for even six months seriously disturbed the monkeys' development. When returned to their group, these monkeys were passive, anxious, and fearful.

The Harlows then placed infant rhesus monkeys in cages with an artificial "mother" made of wire mesh with a wooden head and the nipple of a feeding tube where the breast would be. These monkeys also survived but were unable to interact with others when placed in a group.

But monkeys in a third category, isolated with an artificial "mother" covered with soft terry cloth, did better. Each of these monkeys would cling to the "mother" closely. Because these monkeys showed less developmental damage than the earlier groups, the Harlows concluded that the monkeys benefited from this closeness. The experiment confirmed how important it is that adults cradle infants affectionately.

Finally, the Harlows discovered that infant monkeys could recover from as much as three months of isolation. But after about six months, isolation caused irreversible emotional and behavioural damage.

Studies of Isolated Children

The rest of Anna's story squares with the Harlows' findings. After her discovery, Anna received extensive social contact and soon showed improvement. When Kingsley Davis (1940) revisited her after 10 days, he found her more alert and even smiling (perhaps for the first time in her life!). Over the next year, Anna made slow but steady progress, showing more interest in other people and gradually learning to walk. After a year and a half, she could feed herself and play with toys.

But as the Harlows might have predicted, Anna's five years of social isolation had caused permanent damage. At age eight, her mental development was still less than that of a two-year-old. Not until she was almost 10 did she begin to use words. Because Anna's mother had a mental disability, perhaps Anna was also affected. The riddle was never solved, however, because Anna died at age 10 of a blood disorder, possibly related to the years of abuse she suffered (K. Davis, 1940, 1947).

A more recent case of childhood isolation involves a California girl abused by her parents (Curtiss, 1977; Rymer, 1994). From the time she was two, Genie was tied to a potty chair in a dark garage. In 1970, when she was rescued at age 13, Genie weighed only 27 kilograms (59 pounds) and had the mental development of a one-year-old. With intensive treatment, she became physically healthy, but her language ability remains that of a young child. Today, Genie lives in a home for adults with developmental problems.

id Freud's term for the human being's basic drives ← **ego** Freud's term for a person's conscious efforts to balance innate pleasure-seeking drives with the demands of society → **superego** Freud's term for the cultural values and norms internalized by an individual

○ **CRITICAL REVIEW** All evidence points to the crucial role of social experience in forming personality. Human beings can sometimes recover from abuse and short-term isolation. But there is a point—exactly when is unclear from the small number of cases studied—at which isolation in infancy causes permanent developmental damage.

○ **CHECK YOUR LEARNING** What do studies of isolated children teach us about the importance of social experience?

Understanding Socialization

Socialization is a complex, lifelong process. The following sections highlight the work of six social scientists spanning the disciplines of psychology and sociology—Sigmund Freud, Jean Piaget, Lawrence Kohlberg, Carol Gilligan, Charles Horton Cooley, and George Herbert Mead—who made lasting contributions to our understanding of human development.

Sigmund Freud's Elements of Personality

Sigmund Freud (1856–1939) lived in Vienna at a time when most Europeans considered human behaviour biologically fixed. Trained as a physician, Freud turned to the study of personality and eventually developed the celebrated theory of psychoanalysis.

Basic Human Needs

Freud claimed that biology plays a major part in human development, although not in terms of specific instincts, as is the case in other species. Rather, he theorized that humans have two basic needs or drives that are present at birth. First is a need for bonding, which he called the "life instinct," or *eros* (named after the Greek god of love). Second, we share an aggressive drive he called the "death instinct," or *thanatos* (the Greek word for "death"). These opposing forces, operating at an unconscious level, create deep inner tension.

Freud's Model of Personality

Freud combined basic human drives and the influence of society into a model of personality with three parts: id, ego, and superego. The **id** (Latin for "it") represents *the human being's basic drives*, which are unconscious and demand immediate satisfaction. Rooted in biology, the id is present at birth, making a newborn a bundle of demands for attention, touching, and food. But society opposes the self-centred id, which is why one of the first words a child usually learns is "no."

To avoid frustration, a child must learn to approach the world realistically. This is done through the **ego** (Latin for "I"), which is *a person's conscious efforts to balance innate pleasure-seeking drives with the demands of society*. The ego arises as we gain awareness of

our distinct existence and face the fact that we cannot have everything we want.

In the human personality, **superego** (Latin for "above or beyond the ego") is *the cultural values and norms internalized by an individual*. The superego operates as our conscience, telling us *why* we cannot have everything we want. The superego begins to form as a child becomes aware of parental demands and matures as the child comes to understand that everyone's behaviour should take account of cultural norms.

Personality Development

To the id-centred child, the world is a jumble of physical sensations that bring either pleasure or pain. As the superego develops, however, the child learns the moral concepts of right and wrong. Initially, in other words, children can feel good only in a physical way (as when being held and cuddled), but after three or four years they feel good or bad according to how they judge their behaviour against cultural norms (doing "the right thing").

The id and the superego remain in conflict, but in a well-adjusted person the ego manages these opposing forces. If conflicts are not resolved during childhood, they may surface as personality disorders later on.

Culture, in the form of superego, *represses* selfish demands, forcing people to look beyond their own desires. Often the competing demands of self and society result in a compromise Freud called *sublimation*, which changes selfish drives into socially acceptable behaviour. For example, marriage makes the satisfaction of sexual urges socially acceptable, and competitive sports are an outlet for aggression.

○ **CRITICAL REVIEW** In Freud's time, few people were ready to accept sex as a basic drive. Some critics have charged that Freud's work presents humans in male terms and devalues women (Donovan & Littenberg, 1982). Freud's theories are also difficult to test scientifically. But Freud influenced everyone who later studied human personality. Of special importance to sociology are his ideas that we internalize social norms and that childhood experiences have a lasting impact on personality.

○ **CHECK YOUR LEARNING** What are the three elements in Freud's model of personality? What does each one mean?

Jean Piaget's Theory of Cognitive Development

The Swiss psychologist Jean Piaget (1896–1980) studied *human cognition*, how people think and understand. As Piaget watched his own three children grow, he wondered not just what they knew but how they made sense of the world. Piaget went on to identify four stages of cognitive development.

sensorimotor stage		preoperational stage		concrete operational stage		formal operational stage
Piaget's term for the level of human development at which individuals experience the world only through their senses	→	Piaget's term for the level of human development at which individuals first use language and other symbols	→	Piaget's term for the level of human development at which individuals first see causal connections in their surroundings	→	Piaget's term for the level of human development at which individuals think abstractly and critically

The Sensorimotor Stage

Stage one is the **sensorimotor stage**, *the level of human development at which individuals experience the world only through their senses*. For about the first two years of life, infants know the world only by touching, tasting, smelling, looking, and listening. "Knowing" to very young children amounts to what their senses tell them.

The Preoperational Stage

At about age two, children enter the **preoperational stage**, *the level of human development at which individuals first use language and other symbols*. Now children begin to think about the world using their imagination. But "pre-op" children between about ages two and six attach meanings only to specific experiences and objects. They can identify a toy as their "favourite" but cannot describe what *types* of toys they like.

Lacking abstract concepts, a child cannot judge size, weight, or volume. In one of his best-known experiments, Piaget placed two identical glasses containing equal amounts of water on a table. He asked several five- and six-year-olds whether the amount in each was the same. They nodded that it was. The children then watched Piaget take one of the glasses and pour its contents into a taller, narrower glass, raising the level of the water. He asked again whether each glass held the same amount. The typical five- or six-year-old now insisted that the taller glass held more water. By about age seven, children are able to think more abstractly and realize that the amount of water stays the same.

The Concrete Operational Stage

Next comes the **concrete operational stage**, *the level of human development at which individuals first see causal connections in their surroundings*. Between the ages of 7 and 11, children focus on how and why things happen. In addition, they attach more than one symbol to an event or object. If, for example, you say to a child of five, "Today is Wednesday," she may respond, "No, it's my birthday!" indicating that she can use just one symbol at a time. But an older child at the concrete operational stage would be able to respond, "Yes, and it's also my birthday."

The Formal Operational Stage

The last step in Piaget's model is the **formal operational stage**, *the level of human development at which individuals think abstractly and critically*. At about age 12, young people begin to reason in the abstract rather than think only of concrete situations. For example, if you ask a child of seven, "What would you like to be when you grow up?", you will get a concrete response such as "a teacher." But most teenagers can consider the question more abstractly and may respond, "I would like a job that helps others." As they gain the capacity for abstract thought, young people also learn to understand metaphors. Hearing the phrase *A penny for your thoughts* may lead a child to ask for a coin, but a teenager will recognize a gentle invitation to intimacy.

CRITICAL REVIEW Freud saw human beings as passively torn by opposing forces of biology and culture. Piaget saw the mind as active and creative. He saw the ability to engage the world unfolding in stages as the result of both biological maturation and social experience.

But do people in all societies pass through all four of Piaget's stages? Living in a traditional society that changes slowly probably limits the capacity for abstract and critical thought. Even in North American society, perhaps 30 percent of people never reach the formal operational stage (Kohlberg & Gilligan, 1971).

CHECK YOUR LEARNING What are Piaget's four stages of cognitive development? What does his theory teach us about socialization?

Lawrence Kohlberg's Theory of Moral Development

Lawrence Kohlberg (1981) built on Piaget's work to study *moral reasoning*, how people come to judge situations as right or wrong. Here again, development occurs in stages.

Young children who experience the world in terms of pain and pleasure (Piaget's sensorimotor stage) are at the *preconventional* level of moral development. At first, "rightness" amounts to "what feels good to me." For example, a child may reach for something on a table that looks shiny, which is the reason why parents of young children have to "childproof" their homes.

The *conventional* level, Kohlberg's second stage, appears by the teens (corresponding to Piaget's final, formal operational stage). At this point, young people lose some of their selfishness as they learn to define right and wrong in terms of what pleases parents and conforms to cultural norms. At this stage, individuals also become aware of not just action but also intention. They may realize, for example, that stealing food for hungry children is not the same as stealing an iPod to sell for pocket change.

In Kohlberg's final stage of moral development, the *postconventional* level, people move beyond their society's norms to consider abstract ethical principles. As they think about ideas such as liberty, freedom, or justice, they may argue that what is lawful still may not be right. When the South African civil rights activist Nelson Mandela challenged white rule in the mid-1960s (the apartheid system of government at the time), he violated his country's segregation laws to call attention to the injustice of those laws.

CRITICAL REVIEW Like the work of Piaget, Kohlberg's model explains moral development in terms of distinct stages. But whether this model applies to people in all societies remains unclear. Further, many people in Canada apparently never reach the postconventional level of moral reasoning, although exactly why is still an open question.

looking-glass self Cooley's term for a self-image based on how we think others see us

self Mead's term for the part of an individual's personality composed of self-awareness and self-image

Another problem with Kohlberg's research is that all of his subjects were boys. He committed a common research error, described in Chapter 1 ("Sociology: Perspective, Theory, and Method"), by generalizing the results of male subjects to all people. This problem led a colleague, Carol Gilligan, to investigate how gender affects moral reasoning.

○ **CHECK YOUR LEARNING** What are Kohlberg's three stages of moral development? What does his theory teach us about socialization?

Carol Gilligan's Theory of Gender and Moral Development

Carol Gilligan (1982) set out to compare the moral development of girls and boys and concluded that the two sexes use different standards of rightness. Boys, she claims, have a *justice perspective*, relying on formal rules to define right and wrong. Girls, by contrast, have a *care and responsibility perspective*, judging a situation with an eye toward personal relationships and loyalties. For example, as boys see it, stealing is wrong because it breaks the law. Girls are more likely to wonder why someone would steal and to be sympathetic toward someone who steals, say, to feed her family.

Kohlberg treats rule-based male reasoning as morally superior to the person-based female perspective. Gilligan notes that impersonal rules have long governed men's lives in the workplace, but personal relationships are more relevant to women's lives as mothers and caregivers. Why, then, Gilligan asks, should we set up male standards as the norms by which to judge everyone?

○ **CRITICAL REVIEW** Gilligan's work sharpens our understanding of both human development and gender issues in research. Yet the question remains, does nature or nurture account for the differences between females and males? In Gilligan's view, cultural conditioning is at work, a view that finds support in other research. For example, sociologist Nancy Chodorow (1994) claims that children grow up in homes in which, typically, mothers do much more nurturing than fathers. As girls learn to identify with mothers, they become more concerned with care and responsibility to others. By contrast, boys become more like fathers, who are often away from the home, and they may develop more detached personalities and a greater concern for abstract rules. Traditional assumptions of the moral reasoning of females and males are being contested as more women organize their lives around the workplace and more men organize their lives around the home (Fox, 2010).

○ **CHECK YOUR LEARNING** According to Gilligan, how do boys and girls differ in their approach to understanding right and wrong?

Charles Horton Cooley's Theory of the Looking-Glass Self

Charles Horton Cooley (1864–1929) was a sociologist who worked in the symbolic-interactionist tradition. Cooley believed that human beings are essentially social in nature and that a major way in which they discover the world around them is through interaction with others. His major contribution to the study of human socialization is his concept of the **looking-glass self**, meaning *a self-image based on how we think others see us* (Cooley, 1964, orig. 1902). In effect, others are a mirror (which people used to call a "looking glass") in which we see ourselves. What we think of ourselves, then, depends on how we think others see us. For example, if we think others see us as clever, we will think of ourselves in the same way. But if we feel that they think of us as clumsy, then that is how we will see ourselves.

George Herbert Mead's Theory of the Social Self

A contemporary of Cooley, sociologist George Herbert Mead (1863–1931) expanded Cooley's concept of the looking-glass self and developed a sociological theory of *social behaviourism* to explain how social experience develops an individual's personality (Mead, 1962, orig. 1934).

The Self

Mead's central concept is the **self**, *the part of an individual's personality composed of self-awareness and self-image*. Mead's genius lay in seeing the self as the product of social experience.

First, said Mead, *the self develops only with social experience*. The self is not part of the body and does not exist at birth. Mead rejected the psychological idea that personality is guided by biological drives (as Freud asserted) or even by biological maturation (as Piaget claimed). For Mead, self develops only as the individual interacts with others. Without interaction, as we see in cases of isolated children, the body grows but no self emerges.

Second, Mead explained, *social experience is the exchange of symbols*. Only people use words, a wave of the hand, or a smile to create meaning. We can train a dog using reward and punishment, but the dog attaches no meaning to its actions. By contrast, human beings find meaning in action by imagining people's underlying intentions. In short, a dog responds to *what you do*, but a human responds to *what you have in mind* as you do it. You can train a dog to go to the hallway and bring back an umbrella. But without understanding intention, if the dog cannot find the umbrella, it is incapable of the *human* response: to look for a raincoat instead.

Third, Mead continues, *understanding intention requires imagining a situation from the other's point of view*. Using symbols, we imagine ourselves in another person's shoes and see ourselves as that person does. This capacity allows us to anticipate how others will

significant others people, such as parents, who have special importance for socialization

generalized other Mead's term for widespread cultural norms and values we use as a reference in evaluating ourselves

respond to us even before we act. A simple toss of a ball, for example, requires stepping outside yourself to imagine how the other person will catch your throw. All symbolic interaction, then, involves seeing ourselves as others see us, a process Mead called *taking the role of the other* in a process similar to what Cooley described as the looking-glass self.

The I and the Me

Mead's fourth point is that *by taking the role of the other, we become self-aware.* Another way of saying this is that the self has two parts. One part of the self operates as subject, being active and spontaneous. Mead called the subjective side of the self the "I" (the subjective form of the personal pronoun). The other part of the self works as an object, the way we imagine others see us. Mead called the objective side of the self the "me" (the objective form of the personal pronoun). All social experience has both components: We initiate action (the I-phase, or subjective side, of the self) and we evaluate the action based on how others respond to us (the me-phase, or objective side, of the self).

Development of the Self

According to Mead, the key to developing the self is learning to take the role of the other. With limited social experience, infants can do this only through *imitation*. They mimic the behaviour of other people without understanding the underlying intention, and so at this point they have no self.

As children learn to use language and other symbols, the self emerges in the form of *play*. Play involves assuming roles modelled on **significant others**, *people, such as parents, who have special importance for socialization.* Playing "mommy" or "daddy" begins to teach children to imagine the world from a parent's point of view.

Gradually, children learn to take the roles of several others at once. This skill allows them to move from simple play (such as playing catch) involving one other person to complex *games* (such as baseball) involving many others. By about age seven, most children have the social experience needed to engage in team sports.

Figure 3–1 on page 70 charts the progression from imitation to play to games. But there is a final stage in the development of the self. A game involves dealing with a limited number of other people in just one situation. Everyday life demands that we see ourselves in terms of cultural norms as *any* member of our society might. Mead used the term **generalized other** to refer to *widespread cultural norms and values we use as a reference in evaluating ourselves.*

As life goes on, the self continues to change along with our social experiences. But no matter how much the world shapes us, we always remain creative beings able to react to the world around us. Thus, Mead concluded, we play a key role in our own socialization.

George Herbert Mead wrote: "No hard-and-fast line can be drawn between our own selves and the selves of others." The painting *Manyness* by Rimma Gerlovina and Valeriy Gerlovin conveys this important truth. Although we tend to think of ourselves as unique individuals, each person's characteristics develop in an ongoing process of interaction with others.

Rimma Gerlovina and Valeriy Gerlovin, *Manyness,* 1990. © the artists, New City, N.Y.

CRITICAL REVIEW Cooley's and Mead's work explores the essence of social experience itself. In the symbolic interaction of human beings, they believed they had found the root of both self and society.

Their views are completely social, allowing no biological element at all. This is a problem for followers of Freud (who said our drives are rooted in the body) and Piaget (whose stages of development are tied to biological maturity).

Be careful not to confuse Mead's concepts of the I and the me with Freud's id and superego. For Freud, the id originates in our biology, but Mead rejected any biological element of self (although he never clearly spelled out the origin of the I). In addition, the id and the superego are locked in continual combat, but the I and the me work co-operatively together (Meltzer, 1978).

CHECK YOUR LEARNING Explain the meaning and importance of Mead's concepts of the I and the me. What did Mead mean by "taking the role of the other"? Why is this process so important to socialization?

We now take a closer look at the important agents of socialization.

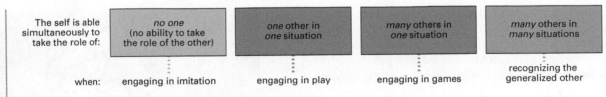

| The self is able simultaneously to take the role of: | *no one* (no ability to take the role of the other) | *one* other in *one* situation | *many* others in *one* situation | *many* others in *many* situations |

when: engaging in imitation   engaging in play   engaging in games   recognizing the generalized other

FIGURE 3–1 **Building on Social Experience**

George Herbert Mead described the development of the self as a process of gaining social experience. That is, the self develops as we expand our capacity to take the role of the other.

Agents of Socialization

Every social experience we have affects us in at least a small way. However, several familiar settings have special importance to the socialization process. Among them are the family, the school, the peer group, and the mass media.

The Family

The family affects socialization in many ways. For most people, the family may be the most important socializing agent of all.

Nurture in Early Childhood

Responsibility for the care of infants, who are totally dependent on others, typically falls on parents and other family members. For several years—at least until children begin school—the family has the job of teaching children skills, values, and beliefs. Overall, research suggests, nothing is more likely to produce a happy, well-adjusted child than a loving family (Gibbs, 2001).

Not all family learning results from intentional teaching by parents. Children also learn from the type of environment adults create. Whether children learn to see themselves as strong or weak, smart or stupid, loved or simply tolerated—and as Canadian researcher Clyde Hertzman (2010) suggests, whether they see the world as trustworthy or dangerous—depends largely on the quality of the surroundings provided by parents and other caregivers. Hertzman and colleagues (2001) have gathered a wide range of scientific evidence to support the idea that what happens to children during their early years is important to lifelong health and well-being. Research suggests that this is also the case for many street-involved youth (Benoit, Jansson, & Anderson, 2007; Ensign & Bell, 2004).

Race, Ethnicity, and Class

The family also gives children a social identity and, in part, social identity involves race and ethnicity. Racial and ethnic identity is complex because, as Chapter 11 ("Race and Ethnicity") explains, societies define these concepts in different ways. Approximately 2 percent of the population of Canada, 2.4 percent in the United States, and 0.6 percent in Britain now self-identify as mixed race, and inter-ethnic unions are

increasing (Aspinall, 2003). In addition, in the 2006 Canadian census, almost 13 million people (about 40 percent) said that they consider themselves to be in two or more ethnic categories, and almost 6 million more chose *Canadian* as their single ethnic origin. Table 3–1 on page 71 shows the most frequently listed ethnic categories in Canada.

Social class, like race, plays a large part in shaping a child's personality. Whether born into families of high or low social position, children gradually come to realize that their family's social standing affects how others see them and, in time, how they come to see themselves.

In addition, research shows that the class position of parents affects not just how much money parents have to spend on their children but also what parents expect of them (Ellison, Bartkowski, & Segal, 1996). When people were asked to pick from a list of traits they thought most desirable in a child, people at all social class levels chose hard work and helping others as the most important personal qualities. However, people with lower class standing were nearly twice as likely as people in the upper classes to say that obedience and popularity are important personal traits. Similarly, people of higher social class position are more likely to encourage imagination and creativity in their children (NORC, 2009). Canadian children from the lowest social class are twice as likely to have conduct disorders as children from the highest social class, although the reason for this is not well understood (Stevenson, 1999).

What accounts for the difference? Melvin Kohn (1977) explains that people of lower social standing usually have only limited education and hold jobs that involve performing routine tasks under close supervision. Expecting that their children will grow up to take similar positions, they encourage obedience and may even use physical punishment such as spanking to get it. Because well-off parents generally have had more schooling, they usually have jobs that demand imagination and creativity, so they try to inspire the same qualities in their children. Consciously or not, all parents act in ways that encourage their children to follow in their footsteps.

Wealthier parents typically provide their children with an extensive program of leisure activities, including sports, vacation travel, and music lessons. These enrichment activities—far less available to children growing up in low-income families—build

TABLE 3–1 Most Frequently Mentioned Ethnic Origins, Canada, 2006

Ethnic Origins	Total Responses	Percentage of Population Declaring Being Only	Percentage of Population Declaring as One of Several
Canadian	10 066 290	18.4%	13.8%
English	6 570 015	4.4%	16.7%
French	4 941 210	3.9%	11.9%
Scottish	4 719 850	1.8%	13.3%
Irish	4 354 155	1.6%	12.4%
German	3 179 425	2.1%	8.0%
Italian	1 445 335	2.4%	2.3%
Chinese	1 346 510	3.6%	0.7%
North American Indian	1 253 615	1.6%	2.4%
Ukrainian	1 209 085	1.0%	2.9%
Dutch	1 035 965	1.0%	2.3%
Polish	984 565	0.9%	2.3%
East Indian	962 665	2.5%	0.6%
Russian	500 600	0.3%	1.3%
Welsh	440 965	0.1%	1.3%
Filipino	436 190	1.0%	0.4%
Norwegian	432 515	0.1%	1.2%
Portuguese	410 850	0.8%	0.5%
Metis	409 065	0.2%	1.1%
Swedish	334 765	0.1%	1.0%
Spanish	325 730	0.2%	0.8%
American	316 350	0.1%	0.9%
Hungarian	315 510	0.3%	0.7%
Jewish	315 120	0.4%	0.6%
Greek	242 685	0.5%	0.3%
Jamaican	231 110	0.4%	0.3%
Danish	200 035	0.1%	0.5%
Austrian	194 255	0.1%	0.5%
Romanian	192 170	0.3%	0.4%
Vietnamese	180 125	0.4%	0.1%
Belgian	168 910	0.1%	0.4%
Lebanese	165 150	0.3%	0.2%
Québécois	146 585	0.3%	0.2%
Korean	146 550	0.4%	0.0%
Swiss	137 775	0.1%	0.4%
Finnish	131 040	0.1%	0.3%
Pakistani	124 730	0.3%	0.1%
Iranian	121 510	0.3%	0.1%
Croatian	110 880	0.2%	0.2%
Sri Lankan	103 625	0.3%	0.1%
Haitian	102 430	0.3%	0.1%
Japanese	98 900	0.2%	0.1%
Czech	98 090	0.1%	0.2%
Acadian	96 145	0.1%	0.2%
Icelandic	88 875	0.0%	0.3%
Serbian	72 690	0.1%	0.1%
Inuit	65 885	0.1%	0.1%
Slovak	64 145	0.1%	0.1%
Mexican	61 505	0.1%	0.1%
Black	61 430	0.1%	0.1%
Guyanese	61 085	0.1%	0.1%
Salvadorean	59 145	0.1%	0.1%
Total responses	**52 573 810**	**18 319 475**	**34 254 240**
Total population	**31 241 030**	**59%**	**41%**

Source: Statistics Canada (2007b).

cultural capital, which advances learning and creates a sense of confidence in these children that they will be successful throughout their lives (Lareau, 2002). But there is no conclusive evidence that poverty or affluence is directly related to the quality of parenting that children receive. Research shows that neither rich nor poor Canadians have a monopoly on child-rearing skills. Rather, children with behaviour problems and low academic achievement come from different economic backgrounds, as do children who perform well socially and academically (Bertrand, McCain, Mustard, & Williams, 1999). Regardless of class background, Bernd Baldus and Verna Tribe (1992) argue that by grade 6 (average age 11 years) most children use social inequality as a criterion to order the world around them. Further, grade 6 students have by this age learned to acquire cognitive and affective predispositions causing them to think that less economically advantaged persons are likely to be unsuccessful in life or to engage in morally questionable behaviour.

Social class also affects how long the process of growing up takes, as the Seeing Sociology in Everyday Life box on page 73 explains.

The School

Schooling enlarges children's social world to include people with backgrounds different from their own. It is only as they encounter people who differ from themselves that children come to understand the importance of factors, such as race and social position. As they do, they are likely to cluster together in playgroups made up of their own class, race, and gender.

These young people come to Tokyo's Yoyogi Park on Sundays to dress up and have their picture taken.

Gender

Schools join with families in socializing children into gender roles. Studies show that, at school, boys engage in more physical activities and spend more time outdoors and girls are more likely to help teachers with various housekeeping chores. Boys also engage in more aggressive behaviour in the classroom, where girls are typically quieter and better behaved (Best, 1983; Jordan & Cowan, 1995). Gender differences continue through post-secondary education (see Chapter 14, "Education, Health, and Medicine"). While gender decisions are changing, women still tend to major in the arts, humanities, or social sciences, while men gravitate toward economics, engineering and computer science, or the natural sciences. Moreover, even for women who enter the traditionally male-dominated professions, such as medicine and law, gender stratification persists in regard to both choice of specialty and income (Brooks, Jarman, & Blackburn, 2003; Hagan & Kay, 1995; Reskin & Padavic, 1994; Riska & Wegar, 1993).

What Children Learn

Schooling is not the same for children living in rich and poor communities. As Chapter 14 ("Education, Health, and Medicine") explains, children from well-off families typically have a far richer experience in school than children whose families are poor.

What children learn in school goes beyond the formally planned lessons. Schools informally teach many things, which together may be called the *hidden curriculum*. Activities such as spelling bees, for example, teach children not only how to spell and think on their feet but also that society divides the population into "winners" and "losers." Sports help students develop their strength and skills and also teach children important lessons in co-operation and competition.

For most children, school is also their first experience with bureaucracy. The school day is based on impersonal rules and a strict time schedule. Not surprisingly, these are also the traits of the large organizations that will employ them later in life.

The Peer Group

December 16, Yoyogi Park, Tokyo. The young people who come here on Sundays to get dressed up and have their picture taken can't be the same young people that we see in the obligatory school uniforms in the mornings and afternoons during the week. We learn later that they put on their elaborate makeup and change into their costumes in the bathroom at the Harajuku subway station around the corner. By 6:00 P.M., they have all changed back into their regular clothes and taken the subway home again. Are they rebelling or just having fun with their friends? Perhaps it is both.

By the time they enter school, children have also discovered the **peer group**, *a social group whose members have interests, social position, and age in common*. Unlike the family and the school, the peer group allows children to escape the direct supervision of adults. Among their peers, children learn how to form relationships on their own. Peer groups also offer the chance to discuss interests that adults may not share (such as clothes and popular music) or permit (such as drugs and sex).

It is not surprising, then, that parents express concern about who their children's friends are. In a rapidly changing society, peer groups have great influence, and the attitudes of young and old may be different enough to form a "generation gap." The importance of peer groups typically peaks during adolescence, when young people begin to break away from their families and think of themselves as adults. Relentless teasing by peers—girls as well as boys—can result in brutal beatings and even murder (such as in the 1997 case of 14-year-old Reena Virk of Victoria, British Columbia) or in the suicide of affected youths who are unable to withstand the taunting and other forms of abuse (Alphonso, 2000). The problem is that there is no single cause of bullying at our nation's schools. In addition, youth tend to condone bullying and even to join in, rather than to speak out against it (Artz, 1998; Hymel, Rocke Henderson, & Bonanno, 2005; Moretti, Jackson, & Odgers, 2004).

Even during adolescence, however, parental influence on children remains strong. Peers may affect short-term interests such as music or television shows, but parents have greater influence on long-term goals such as going to college or university (Davies & Kandel, 1981). Research shows that parents continue to have an influence on adolescents' physical activity, and efforts to increase physical activity among teens should focus on increasing

Only one out of six people in their late twenties lived with their parents in the mid-1980s.

As a result of the economic downturn, about one out of four people in their late twenties now live with their parents.

SEEING SOCIOLOGY IN EVERYDAY LIFE

Are We Grown Up Yet? Defining Adulthood

SOLLY: (*seeing several friends walking down the dorm hallway, just returned from dinner*) Yo, guys! Jeremy's 18 today. We're going down to the Box Car to celebrate.

MATT: (*shaking his head*) Dunno, dude. I got a lab to finish up. It's just another birthday.

SOLLY: Not just any birthday, my friend. He's 18—an *adult!*

MATT: (*sarcastically*) If turning 18 would make me an adult, I wouldn't still be clueless about what I want to do with my life!

Are you an adult or still an adolescent? Does turning 18 make you a "grown-up"? According to the sociologist Tom Smith (2003), in our society, no one factor announces the onset of adulthood. In fact, the results of his survey—using a representative sample of 1398 people over the age of 18—suggest that many factors play a part in our decision to consider a young person as "grown up."

According to the survey, the single most important transition in claiming adult standing in North America today is the completion of schooling. But other factors are also important: Smith's respondents linked adult standing to taking on a full-time job, gaining the ability to support a family financially, no longer living with parents, and finally marrying and becoming a parent. In other words, almost everyone in Canada thinks that a person who has done *all* of these things is fully "grown up."

The age of leaving the parental home is rising in Canada. In 1986, only 16 percent of those aged 25 to 29 lived with their parents. In 2006, this number was 26 percent—one out of four. (See Figure 3–2.) At what age is this transition likely to be completed? On average, somewhere between ages 25 and 27. But such an average masks important differences based on factors related to social class. People who do not attend college or university (more common among people growing up in lower-income families) typically finish school before age 20, and a full-time job, independent living, marriage, and parenthood may follow within a year or two. Those from more privileged backgrounds are likely to attend college or university and may go on to graduate or professional school, delaying the process of becoming an adult for as long as 10 years, past the age of 30.

Only one out of six people in their late twenties lived with their parents in the mid-1980s.

As a result of the economic downturn, about one out of four people in their late twenties now live with their parents.

WHAT DO YOU THINK?

1. Do you consider yourself an adult? At what age did your adulthood begin?

2. Consider a woman whose children are grown, who has recently divorced, and who is now going to university to earn a degree

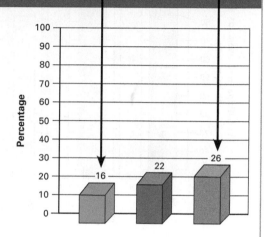

FIGURE 3–2 **Percentage of 25- to 29-Year-Olds Living in Parental Home, Canada**

Source: Statistics Canada (2011d).

so she can find a job. Is she likely to feel that she is suddenly not quite "grown up" now that she is back in school? Why or why not?

3. How does the research described in this box show that adulthood is a socially defined concept rather than a biological stage of life?

levels of family cohesion, parental engagement, parent-child communication, and adolescent self-esteem (Ornelas, Perreira, & Ayala, 2007).

Finally, any neighbourhood or school is made up of many peer groups. As Chapter 5 ("Groups and Organizations") explains, individuals tend to view their own group in positive terms and put down other groups. In addition, people are influenced by peer groups they would like to join, a process sociologists call **anticipatory socialization**, *learning that helps a person achieve a desired position.* In school, for example, young people may copy the styles and slang of a group they hope will accept them. Later in life, a young lawyer who hopes to move up may conform to the attitudes and behaviour of the firm's partners to be accepted.

The Mass Media

August 30, Isle of Coll, off the west coast of Scotland. The last time we visited this remote island, there was no electricity and most people spoke the ancient Gaelic language. Now that a power cable comes from the mainland, homes have lights, appliances, television, and the internet! Almost with the flip of a switch, this tiny place has been thrust into the modern world. It is no surprise that traditions are fast disappearing and a rising share of the population is now mainlanders who ferry over with their cars to spend time in their vacation homes. And everyone now speaks English.

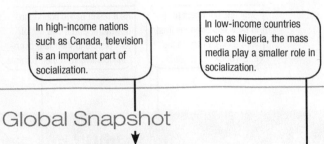

Global Snapshot

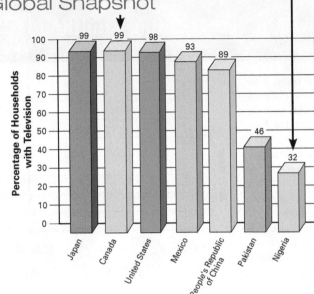

FIGURE 3–3 Television Ownership in Global Perspective

Television is popular in high- and middle-income countries, where almost every household owns at least one TV set.

Sources: U.S. Census Bureau (2008a) and International Telecommunication Union (2008).

The **mass media** are *the means for delivering impersonal communications to a vast audience.* The term *media* (plural of *medium*) comes from the Latin word for "middle," suggesting that the media connect people. *Mass* media resulted as communications technology (first newspapers and then radio, television, films, and the internet) spread information on a massive scale. The mass media are important not only because they are so powerful but also because their influence is likely to differ from that of the family, the local school, and the peer group. In short, the mass media introduce people to ideas and images that are new and different.

In North America, television, introduced in the 1930s, quickly became the dominant medium after World War II. Today, 99 percent of Canadian households have at least one TV set, and a majority have three or more. As Figure 3–3 indicates, Canada has one of the highest rates of television ownership in the world.

The Extent of Television Viewing

Just how "glued to the tube" are we? Some categories of people watch television more than others, of course. Generally, minorities, older people, and people with lower incomes spend the most time watching TV.

The latest statistics show that Canadian viewers watched television an average of 21.4 hours each week in 2004. Virtually everyone in Canada watches television, but not equally: Women, French-speaking Quebecers, and residents of the Atlantic provinces watched more television than other Canadians. Years before children learn to read, television watching is a regular routine. Children aged 2 to 11 watch more than 14 hours each week. This is so despite research that suggests that television makes children more passive and less likely to use their imagination (American Psychological Association, 1993; Fellman, 1995; Singer & Singer, 1983). Teens aged 12 to 17 spent 12.9 hours a week in front of the TV in 2004, two hours less than in 2003 and almost three hours less than five years previously (Statistics Canada, 2006b). On the other hand, internet use in households with children under age 18 has risen substantially, from 50 percent in 1999 to 81 percent in 2004 (Statistics Canada, 2006c). The number of hours of viewing tends to increase in later adulthood, exceeding 30 hours per week for those aged 60 and over (Statistics Canada, 2002h).

Television and Politics

The comedian Fred Allen once quipped that we call television a "medium" because it is "rarely well done." For a variety of reasons, television (as well as other mass media) provokes plenty of criticism. Some liberal critics argue that for most of television's history, racial and ethnic minorities have been invisible or have been shown only in stereotypical roles (such as minorities playing servants or Southeast Asians playing new immigrants). In recent years, however, minorities have moved closer to centre stage on television. There are now far more ethnic minority actors on prime-time North American television than there were a generation ago, and they play a far wider range of characters (Fetto, 2003; Lichter & Amundson, 1997). Some argue that the number of people from minority groups who appear in the mass media has increased mainly because advertisers recognize the marketing advantages of appealing to these large segments of North American society (Wilson & Gutiérrez, 1985). In Canada, the popularity of such shows as *This Hour Has 22 Minutes* is a case in point, placing at centre stage representatives from Canada's poorest province to poke fun at our national quirks.

On the other side of the fence, conservative critics charge that the television and film industries are dominated by a liberal "cultural elite." In recent years, they claim, "politically correct" media have advanced liberal causes, including feminism and gay rights (B. Goldberg, 2002; Rothman, Powers, & Rothman, 1993). But not everyone agrees, and some counter that the popularity of Fox News, home to Sean Hannity, Bill O'Reilly, Glenn Beck, and other conservative commentators, suggests that television programming offers "spin" from both sides of the political spectrum.

Television and Violence

In 1996, the American Medical Association (AMA) issued the startling statement that violence in television and films had reached such a high level that it posed a hazard to our health. More recently, a study found a strong link between aggressive behaviour and the amount of time elementary school children spend watching television and using video games (Robinson et al., 2001). The public is concerned about this issue: Three-fourths of North American adults have either walked out of a movie or turned off television because of too much violence. About two-thirds of parents say that they are "very concerned" that their children are exposed to too much media violence. There may be reason for this concern: Almost two-thirds of television programs contain violence, and in most such scenes violent characters show no remorse and are not punished (Rideout, 2007).

Like the American television industry, the Canadian industry has moved to control television viewing of violent programming, especially by children. Both countries have adopted a rating system for programs. The Canadian Association of Broadcasters has a "violence code," which it uses to evaluate particular programs for violent content. The voluntary code bans the broadcast of shows containing gratuitous violence of any type or shows that condone, encourage, or glamorize violence. As far as children are concerned, the code establishes a cut-off time of 9:00 p.m., prior to which violent programming aimed at adult viewers may not be broadcast.

In 1997, the television industry adopted a rating system for programs. But we are left to wonder whether watching violent programming harms people as much as critics say. More important, why do the mass media contain so much violence in the first place?

Television and other mass media have enriched our lives with entertaining and educational programming. The media also increase our exposure to other cultures and provoke discussion of current issues. At the same time, the power of the media—especially television—to shape how we think remains controversial.

Of course, the effects of mass media on how we grow up and how we understand the world around us also include new computer technology. Evidence suggests that the rate of technological change is increasing, with new forms of computer-based communication introduced all the time. Seeing Sociology in the News on page 76 takes a look at how the internet can serve as a vehicle for "cyberbullying" among young people.

○ **CRITICAL REVIEW** This section shows that socialization is complex, with many factors shaping our personalities as we grow. In addition, these factors do not always work together, with children learning things from peer groups and the mass media that may conflict with what they learn at home.

Beyond family, school, peer groups, and the mass media, other spheres of life also play a part in social learning. For most people in Canada, these include religious organizations, the workplace, the military, and social clubs. In the end, socialization is not a simple learning process but a complex balancing act as we absorb information from a variety of sources. In the process of sorting and weighing all of the information we receive, we form our own distinctive personalities.

○ **CHECK YOUR LEARNING** Identify all of the major agents of socialization discussed in this section. What are some of the unique ways in which each helps us develop our individual personalities?

Socialization and the Life Course

Although childhood has special importance in the socialization process, learning continues throughout our lives. An overview of the life course reveals how society organizes human experience according to age—namely, the stages of life we know as childhood, adolescence, adulthood, and old age.

Childhood

The next time you go shopping for athletic shoes, check where the shoes on display are made. Most are manufactured in countries such as Taiwan and Indonesia where wages are far lower than they are in Canada. What is not stated anywhere on the shoes is that many are made by children who spend their days working in factories instead of going to school. More than 160 million of the world's children work, half of them full time, and almost half of these boys and girls do work that is dangerous to their physical and mental health. For their efforts, they earn very little—typically, about 50 cents an hour (International Labour Organization, 2006; U.S. Bureau of International Labor Affairs, 2008). Global Map 3–1 on page 77 shows that child labour is most common in the nations of Africa and Asia.

The idea of children working long days in factories bothers people who live in high-income nations because we think of *childhood*—roughly the first 12 years of life—as a carefree time of learning and play. In fact, as the historian Philippe Ariès (1965) explains, the whole idea of "childhood" is fairly new. In the Middle Ages, children of four or five were treated like adults and expected to fend for themselves.

We support our view of childhood by pointing out that youngsters are biologically immature. But a look back in time and around the world shows that the concept of childhood is grounded not in biology but in culture (LaRossa & Reitzes, 2001). In high-income countries today, not everyone has to work, so childhood is extended to allow time for young people to learn the skills they will need in a high-technology workplace.

Because childhood in Canada lasts such a long time, some people worry when children seem to be growing up too fast. In part, this "hurried child" syndrome results from changes in the family—including high divorce rates and both parents in the labour force—that leave children with less supervision. In addition, "adult"

The Vancouver Sun

Vancouver the Cyberbullying Capital of Canada

BY GILLIAN SHAW
May 17, 2011

Vancouver is the cyberbullying capital of Canada according to the results of a survey released today by Norton Canada.

The statistics in the Norton study suggest that children and teens in Vancouver are more likely to be involved in online bullying than children in the other four major cities across Canada that were part of the survey.

Among parents with children aged eight to 18, some 40 per cent of Vancouver parents reported their child had been involved in online bullying, compared to 25 per cent of parents across Canada. Toronto comes second to Vancouver, with 31 per cent of parents there reporting that they have cyberbullying kids.

Close to three out of four said their child was a victim, while 16 per cent said their child was the bully. Eighteen per cent said their child witnessed a cyberbullying incident.

Among the Vancouver parents, 17 per cent said their children are guilty of online bullying, putting Vancouver only second to Calgary at 22 per cent. Toronto was third at 15 per cent, Montreal fourth at 11 per cent, followed by Halifax at eight per cent.

The majority of Vancouver parents ignore the prohibition on many social media web sites that's supposed to stop kids under of 13 [sic]

from joining. Some 55 per cent of parents here say they're fine with their kids joining such sites as long as they are supervised.

The survey found girls are more likely to be bullied online than boys and social media channels are the communications weapons of choice for cyberbullies. Social networks account for 63 per cent of the online bullying, compared to 25 per cent for email and 19 per cent by phone.

"The connectivity and immediacy of social networking sites has adults and children alike tethered to the online world as a means of communicating," said Lynn Hargrove, director of consumer solutions for Norton Canada said in a release. "Words said online have a different impact than words exchanged on a playground, because online messages and posts have the potential to live on for an indefinite amount of time."

Tweens—those eight to 12 years of age—are somewhat more likely to be involved in online bullying.

While parents used to be able to monitor their kids' online activities by keeping their computers in the kitchen, the family room or another spot where they could keep an eye on them, the rise of mobile Internet access has lessened that control. Cyberbullying via cell phones was the most common among kids aged 13 and 14.

More than 50 per cent of the parents surveyed said they use online monitoring software to keep tabs on their children's Internet use and 42 per cent

check the browser history when their kids are surfing to see where they've been online.

The statistics came from an online survey with a random sample of 507 men and women in Calgary, Halifax, Montreal, Toronto and Vancouver, who have a child between the ages of 8-18. The respondents are members of the Impulse Research proprietary online panel and the survey was conducted last February. The survey has a margin of error of +/–3 per cent at the 95 per cent level of confidence.

WHAT DO YOU THINK?

1. Have you or one of your friends ever been exposed to cyberbulling? If yes, was the impact any different from being bullied in person?

2. In your view, is cyberbullying a growing problem in Canada's major cities?

3. Do young people who cyberbully have a different demographic profile than those who bully in face-to-face interactions?

4. Do you think that parents should limit their child's access to new technologies such as cellphones to reduce aggressive behaviour over the internet? What else can parents do to curb cyberbullying?

Source: Vancouver the Cyberbullying Capital of Canada, by Gillian Shaw, *The Vancouver Sun*, May 17, 2011. Material reprinted with the express permission of: **The Vancouver Sun,** a division of Postmedia Network Inc."

---

programming on television, in films, and on the internet carries grown-up concerns such as sex, drugs, and violence into young people's lives. Today's 10- to 12-year-olds, says one executive of a children's television channel, have about the same interests and experiences typical of 12- to 14-year-olds a generation ago (K.S. Hymowitz, 1998). Perhaps this is why today's children, compared to kids 50 years ago, have higher levels of stress and anxiety (Gorman, 2000).

Adolescence

At the same time that industrialization created childhood as a distinct stage of life, adolescence emerged as a buffer between childhood and adulthood. We generally link *adolescence*, or the teenage years, with emotional and social turmoil as young people develop their own identities.

Again, we are tempted to attribute teenage rebelliousness and confusion to the biological changes of puberty. But it really comes from cultural inconsistency. For example, the mass media glorify sex

and schools hand out condoms, even as many parents urge restraint. Consider, too, that it is legal for an 18-year-old to sell sex in all provinces of Canada but there are only three provinces where he or she can legally buy alcohol at that age. In short, adolescence is a time of social contradictions, when people are no longer children but not yet adults.

Like all stages of life, adolescence varies according to social background. Most young people from working-class families move right from high school to the adult world of work and parenting. Such men and women are typically considered adults by the time they reach age 20 (Tanner, Krahn, & Hartnagel, 1995). Wealthier teens, however, have the resources to attend college or university and perhaps graduate school, thereby stretching adolescence to the late twenties and even the thirties (T.W. Smith, 2003). The Thinking About Diversity box on page 79 provides an example of how class, age, and gender shape the life course transitions of Canadian youth.

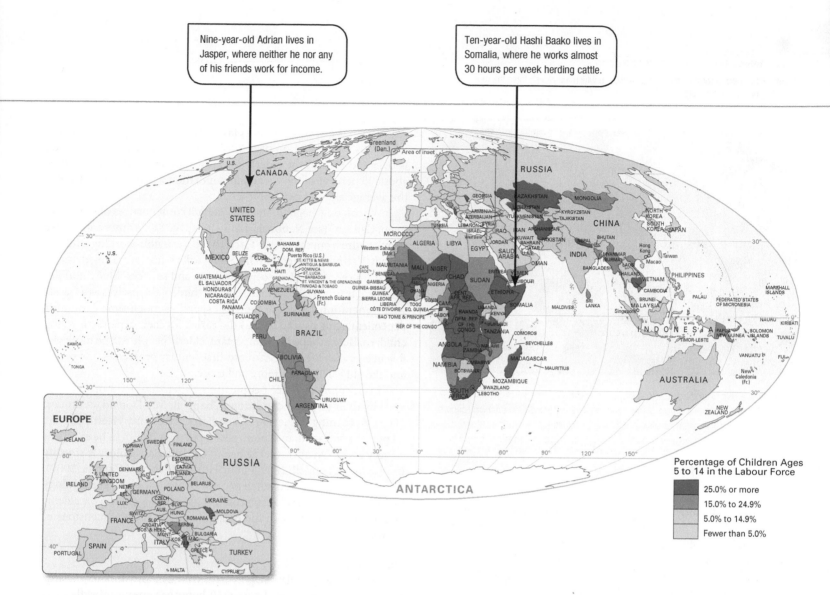

Nine-year-old Adrian lives in Jasper, where neither he nor any of his friends work for income.

Ten-year-old Hashi Baako lives in Somalia, where he works almost 30 hours per week herding cattle.

Percentage of Children Ages 5 to 14 in the Labour Force

- 25.0% or more
- 15.0% to 24.9%
- 5.0% to 14.9%
- Fewer than 5.0%

Window on the World

GLOBAL MAP 3–1 Child Labour in Global Perspective

Industrialization extends childhood and discourages children from work and other activities considered suitable only for adults. This is why child labour is uncommon in Canada and other high-income countries. In lower-income nations of the world, however, children are a vital economic asset, and they typically begin working as soon as they are able. How would childhood in, say, the African nations of Chad or Somalia differ from that in Canada?

Sources: World Bank (2010), and UNICEF (2011).

Adulthood

If stages of the life course were based on biological changes, it would be easy to define *adulthood*. Regardless of exactly when it begins, adulthood is the time of life when most accomplishments take place, including pursuing a career and raising a family. Personalities are largely formed by then, although dramatic change in a person's environment—such as unemployment, divorce, or serious illness—can cause significant changes to the self.

During early adulthood—until about age 40—young adults learn to manage day-to-day affairs for themselves, often juggling

conflicting priorities: parents, partner, children, schooling, work, and leisure activities. Women are especially likely to try to "do it all" because our culture gives them major responsibility for child rearing and household chores even if they have demanding jobs outside the home. Women in Canada find themselves occupied by an unending series of "family shifts" (Eichler, 1997) that results in little leisure and in chronic sleep deprivation. It should be noted, however, that the participation of partners in sharing home responsibilities (Fox, 2010) and whether women have access to public services such as quality child care (available in France and Sweden, for example) have been

Many of us experienced adolescence as a difficult stage of life. The popular Canadian television show *Degrassi High Next Generation* follows a group of students with challenging lives, including low self esteem, early history of abuse and neglect, peer difficulties, experimentation with sex and drugs.

shown to significantly reduce women's second shift of unpaid caring work in the home (Baker, 1995; Benoit & Hallgrimsdottir, 2011).

In middle adulthood—roughly between ages 40 and 65—people sense that their life circumstances are pretty well set. They also become more aware of the fragility of health, which the young typically take for granted (Kobayashi, 2010). Women who have devoted many years to raising a family can find middle adulthood emotionally trying. Children grow up and require less attention, and husbands become absorbed in their careers, leaving some women with spaces in their lives that are difficult to fill. Many women who divorce during middle adulthood also face serious financial problems (Weitzman, 1985, 1996) and social isolation (Kobayashi, Cloutier-Fisher, & Roth, 2009). For all of these reasons, an increasing number of women in middle adulthood decide to return to school and seek new careers.

For everyone, growing older means facing physical decline, a prospect our culture makes especially painful for women. Because good looks are considered more important for women, the appearance of wrinkles and greying hair can be traumatic. Men have their own particular difficulties as they grow older. Some must admit that they are never going to reach earlier career goals. Others realize that the price of career success has been neglect of family or personal health. Social isolation is also a major concern for some (Kobayashi et al., 2009).

Old Age

Old age—the later years of adulthood and the final stage of life— begins around the mid-sixties. With people living longer, the elderly

population is growing nearly as fast as the Canadian population as a whole. As Figure 3–4 on page 80 shows, about one person in seven is over age 65, and the elderly now outnumber teenagers. By 2031, about 25 percent of the Canadian population will be 65 or older and the average age will be almost 45.

We can only begin to imagine the full consequences of the "greying of Canada" (see National Map 3–1 on page 81). As more and more people retire from the labour force, the share of non-working adults— already 10 times greater than in 1900—will go up, increasing demand for health care and other social products and services. Many middle-aged people (especially women) already think of themselves as a "sandwich generation," because they will spend as much time caring for dependent aging parents as they did caring for their dependent young children. But perhaps most important, elderly people will be more visible in everyday life. As the twenty-first century progresses, the young and the old will interact more and more.

Even so, most older people are neither disabled nor discouraged by their physical condition (Chappell, MacDonald, & Stones, 2005). According to the 2009 Canadian Community Health Survey, 44 percent of Canadian seniors perceived their health to be excellent or very good. On average, the health of Canadian seniors is steadily improving (Chappell, 2009; Public Health Agency of Canada, 2009).

The aging of the Canadian population is the focus of **gerontology** (*geron* in Greek means "old person"), *the study of aging and the elderly*. Gerontologists study both the physical and the social dimensions of growing old.

Aging and Biology

For most of our population, grey hair, wrinkles, and declining energy begin in middle age. After about age 50, bones become more brittle, injuries take longer to heal, and the risks of chronic illnesses (such as arthritis and diabetes) and life-threatening conditions (such as heart disease and cancer) rise steadily. Sensory abilities—taste, sight, touch, smell, and especially hearing—become less sharp with age (Metz & Miner, 1998; Treas, 1995).

Aging and Culture

Culture shapes how we understand growing old. In low-income countries, old age gives people great influence and respect because elders control the most land and have wisdom gained over the course of a lifetime. For these reasons, a pre-industrial society usually takes the form of a **gerontocracy**, *a form of social organization in which the elderly have the most wealth, power, and prestige.*

Industrialization lessens the social standing of the elderly, giving more wealth, power, and prestige to younger people. This trend seems to be continuing: The average age of today's corporate executives, which was 59 in 1980, was just 54 in 2008 (Spencer Stuart, 2008). In an industrial society, older people typically live apart from their grown children, and rapid social change makes much of what seniors know obsolete, at least from the point of view of

THINKING ABOUT DIVERSITY: AGE, CLASS, & GENDER

Street Youth: A Fast Track to Adulthood

If you went to a public high school in Canada with a few hundred students or more, there was likely someone in your school who did not have a home to go to every night. How do you think this homeless individual's life differed from your own and that of your other classmates, other than not having a regular bed to sleep in? Cecilia Benoit and Mikael Jansson, two of the authors of this book, have conducted studies with street-involved youth in Victoria, British Columbia, for almost a decade and find that the behaviours that many see as the exuberance of university students, including experimenting with drugs, jobs, partners, and living situations, are normative for street-involved youth of a younger age. Why might this be?

When considering the characteristics of these two groups of young people, we notice important differences in regard to access to resources. For example, street-involved youth tend to come from families that are less well off, grant less social support to young people, and experience more change in family structure. These differences have important consequences because they mean that street-involved youth

experiment with a less secure safety net and therefore the consequences of making a mistake are much worse for them. It is also more difficult for them to phone home when they need a place to stay, when they've broken up with a partner, or when they've misused drugs.

Street-involved youth enter adulthood faster than other youth in the general population, but without supports and resources. When we con-

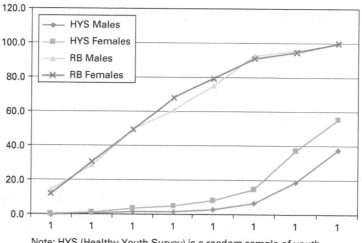

Percentage of Youth Having Lived Alone for a Month or Longer, by Gender and Study

Legend:
- HYS Males
- HYS Females
- RB Males
- RB Females

Note: HYS (Healthy Youth Survey) is a random sample of youth. RB (Risky Business?) is a sample of street-involved youth.

sider solutions for these young people, we need to think about their needs as similar to those of youth who enter adulthood at a later age. Both groups need social support, consistency, and access to financial resources. Focusing on only one element, such as homelessness or addiction, is not enough.

The needs of street-involved youth must be met at their non-normative stage, as if they are older than their chronological age, and they need an environment that respects their individuality and talents and willingly grants them access to crucial services.

WHAT DO YOU THINK?

1. Can you construct a formal definition of "homeless" and "street-involved"?

2. According to this definition, have you ever been homeless? How many street-involved people do you know?

3. How do you think we can reduce the number of street-involved youth in Canada?

Sources: Arnett (2005, 2006); Benoit, Jansson, Hallgrimsdottir, and Roth (2008); Nelson and Barry (2005), and Schulenberg, Merline, Johnston, O'Malley, and Bachman (2005).

---

younger people. A problem common to industrial societies, then, is **ageism**, *prejudice and discrimination against older people.*

> November 1, approaching Kandy, Sri Lanka. Our little van struggles up the steep mountain incline. Breaks in the lush vegetation offer spectacular views that interrupt our conversation about growing old. "Then there are no old-age homes in your country?" I ask. "In Colombo and other cities, I am sure," our driver responds, "but not many. We are not like you Americans." "And how is that?" I ask, stiffening a bit. His eyes remain fixed on the road: "We would not leave our fathers and mothers to live alone."

Not surprisingly, growing old in Canada is challenging. When we're young, becoming older means taking on new roles and

responsibilities. In old age, the opposite happens as people leave behind roles that have given them identity, pleasure, and prestige. When people retire from familiar work routines, some find restful recreation or new activities, but others lose their sense of self-worth and suffer outright boredom.

Aging and Income

Reaching old age means living with less income. But today, the Canadian elderly population is doing better than ever. The rate of poverty among the elderly, as measured by Statistics Canada's low income cut-off, has declined from about 21 percent in 1980 to 5.8 in 2008 (Statistics Canada, 2011c). A generation ago, old age carried the highest risk of poverty; today, seniors are much less likely to live below the poverty line than are adolescents.

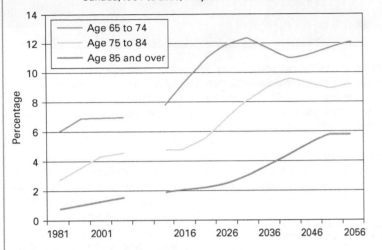

Percentage of the Total Population Composed of Seniors, by Age Group, Canada,1981 to 2005, Projections from 2011 to 2056

FIGURE 3–4 **The Greying of the Canadian Population**

Source: Statistics Canada (2007f).

What changed? An increasing share of older couples earned double incomes during their working years, which helped them save more. In addition, better health allows older people to continue to work for income. Government programs have become more generous, so that almost half of all government spending now goes to programs that assist the elderly even as spending on children has remained more or less flat. But the recent economic downturn has cancelled out many of these advantages, as people have lost some of the pension income they were counting on and more of today's workers are not receiving pension benefits at all. Many retirees live with fixed incomes, so inflation tends to affect them more severely than it does younger working people. Women and visible minorities are especially likely to find that growing old means growing poorer (Milligan, 2007; Statistics Canada, 2000m).

If many seniors are struggling, they are doing better than many younger people. From 1980 to 2005, senior Canadian men living alone increased their income by 64 percent, while senior women living alone increased theirs by 46 percent, which was many times higher than people under age 35 (Statistics Canada, 2008a). A reasonable question, then, is whether we should continue to favour the oldest members of our society and risk slighting younger members, who now suffer most from poverty.

Death and Dying

Throughout most of human history, low living standards and limited medical technology meant that death, caused most often by disease or accident, could come at any stage of life. Today, however, men have a life expectancy of 78.0 years while women are expected to live

82.7 years, a mere 4.7 years difference, the lowest since the end of World War II (Statistics Canada, 2008b).

After observing many dying people, the psychologist Elisabeth Kübler-Ross (1969) described death as an orderly transition involving five distinct stages. Typically, a person first reacts to the prospect of dying with *denial*, perhaps to be expected in a culture that doesn't like to talk about death. The second phase is *anger* as the person facing death sees it as a gross injustice. Third, anger gives way to *negotiation* as the person imagines it might be possible to avoid death by striking a bargain with God. The fourth stage, *resignation*, is often accompanied by psychological depression. Finally, a complete adjustment to death requires *acceptance*. At this point, no longer paralyzed by fear and anxiety, the person whose life is ending sets out to make the most of whatever time remains.

As older people become a larger share of the Canadian population, we can expect our culture to become more comfortable with the idea of death. In recent years, for example, people in Canada and in other high-income nations have been discussing death more openly, and the trend is toward viewing dying as preferable to prolonged suffering. More couples are taking steps to prepare for death with legal and financial planning; this openness may help ease the pain of the surviving spouse or partner, a consideration for women who, more often than not, outlive their husbands.

The Life Course: Patterns and Variations

This brief examination of the life course points to two major conclusions. First, although each stage of life reflects the biological process of aging, the life course is largely a social construction. For this reason, people in different societies may experience a stage of life quite differently or not at all. Second, in any society, the stages of the life course present certain problems and transitions that involve learning something new and, in many cases, unlearning familiar routines.

Societies organize the life course according to age, but other forces such as class, race, ethnicity, and gender also shape people's lives. Thus the general patterns described in this chapter apply somewhat differently to various categories of people.

People's life experiences also vary, depending on when, in the history of a society, they are born. A **cohort** is *a category of people with something in common, usually their age*. Because members of a particular age cohort are generally influenced by the same economic and cultural trends, they tend to develop similar attitudes and values. Women and men born in the late 1940s and 1950s grew up during a period of economic expansion that gave them a sense of optimism. Today's college and university students, who have grown up in an age of economic uncertainty, are less confident about the future.

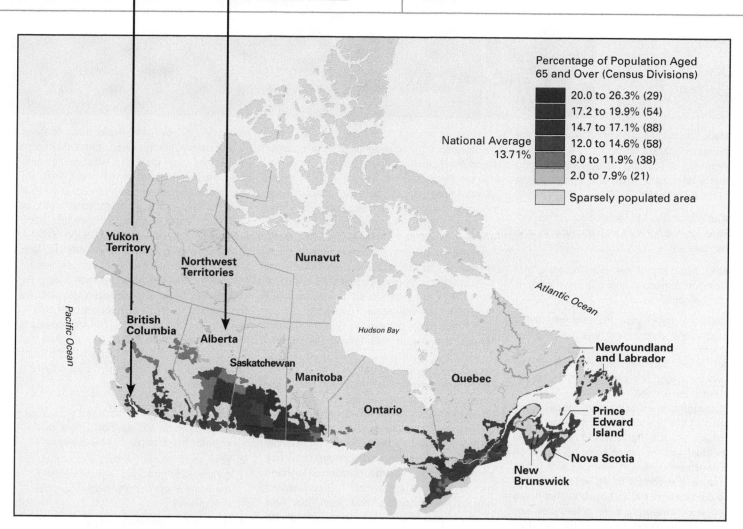

Don and Carol Poy (both in their seventies) live in Qualicum Beach, where 41% of the 8500 residents are at least 65 years old.

June Brentnall, 65, is one of the few seniors who live in Fort McMurray, where 98% of the population is below age 65.

total institution a setting in which people are isolated from the rest of society and controlled by an administrative staff

resocialization radically changing an inmate's personality by carefully controlling the environment

Percentage of Population Aged 65 and Over (Census Divisions)

National Average 13.71%

- 20.0 to 26.3% (29)
- 17.2 to 19.9% (54)
- 14.7 to 17.1% (88)
- 12.0 to 14.6% (58)
- 8.0 to 11.9% (38)
- 2.0 to 7.9% (21)
- Sparsely populated area

Seeing Ourselves

NATIONAL MAP 3–1 **Aging across Canada, 2006**

The aging of the population is largely a southern phenomenon. Even though we associate Victoria, British Columbia, with the phrase *newlyweds and nearly deads*, the map shows that the concentration of those over age 65 is also high in the Prairies and north of Toronto. Which do you think primarily determines this pattern: social forces or individual choices?

Source: Calculated based on Statistics Canada (2011e).

Resocialization: Total Institutions

A final type of socialization, experienced by more than 2 million people in North America at any one time, involves being confined—often against their will—in prisons or mental hospitals. This is the special world of the **total institution**, *a setting in which people are isolated from the rest of society and controlled by an administrative staff.*

According to Erving Goffman (1961), total institutions have three important characteristics. First, staff members supervise all aspects of daily life, including where residents (often called "inmates") eat, sleep, and work. Second, life in a total institution is controlled and standardized, with the same food, uniforms, and activities for everyone. Third, formal rules dictate when, where, and how inmates perform their daily routines.

The purpose of such rigid routines is **resocialization**, *radically changing an inmate's personality by carefully controlling*

Are We Free within Society?

MIKE: Sociology is a good course. Since my professor started telling us to look at our lives with a sociological eye, I'm realizing that a lot of who, what, and where I am is because of society.

KIM: (*teasingly*) Oh, so society is responsible for making you so smart and witty and handsome?

MIKE: No, that's all me. But I'm seeing that being at university and playing hockey is maybe not all me.

What do you think? How free are we, really? Throughout this chapter, we have stressed one key theme: Society—through its agents (family, school, peers, and the mass media)—shapes how we think, feel, and act. If this is so, then in what sense are we free?

Sociologists speak with many voices when addressing this question. One response is that individuals are not free of society—in fact, as social creatures, we never could be. But if we are condemned to live in a society with power over us, it is important to do what we can to make our home as just as possible. That is, we should work to lessen class differences and other barriers to opportunity for visible minorities and women.

Another approach is that we are free because society can never dictate our dreams. North American history—right from early settlement to the present—is one story after another of individuals pursuing personal goals in spite of great challenges. This argument says that individual efforts rather than progressive government social policies result in the greatest freedom for citizens. This sentiment is much stronger in the United States than Canada but even in our country many people believe that we can change our lives around or achieve great things if we just worked hard enough.

We find both attitudes in George Herbert Mead's analysis of socialization. Mead recognized that society makes demands on us, sometimes setting itself before us as a barrier. But he also reminded us that human beings are spontaneous and creative, capable of continually acting back—individually and collectively—on society. Thus Mead noted the power of society while still affirming the human capacity to evaluate, to criticize, and ultimately to choose and to change. A large number of children around the world are trapped in circumstances beyond their choosing, and often face lives of abuse and neglect. But some—though not all—manage to survive and sometimes flourish,

emotionally, socially, and intellectually. In these more positive life histories, certain children with a deep inner drive and initiative also tend to be helped by significant others who are willing to lend economic and emotional support on a sustained basis. As Leadbeater and Way (2007) note about inner-city female youth, some are able to resist dominant stereotypes of them as sexually promiscuous, impoverished, and uneducated; create new positive identities for themselves; and take control of their lives.

In the end, we are socialized into who we become as human beings yet also are able to change the world around us. The anthropologist Margaret Mead once mused, Never doubt that a small group of thoughtful, committed citizens can change the world; indeed, it's the only thing that ever has.

CONTINUE THE DEBATE . . .

1. Do you think our society affords more freedom to males than to females? Why or why not?

2. What about modern, industrial countries compared to traditional, agrarian nations: Are some of the world's people more free than others?

3. How does an understanding of sociology enhance personal freedom? Why?

the environment. Prisons and mental hospitals physically isolate inmates behind fences, barred windows, and locked doors and control their access to the telephone, computers, mail, and visitors. The institution becomes their entire world, making it easier for the staff to bring about personality change—or at least obedience—in the inmate.

Resocialization is a two-part process. First, the staff breaks down a new inmate's existing identity. For example, an inmate must surrender personal possessions, including clothing and grooming articles used to maintain a distinctive appearance. Instead, the staff provides standard-issue clothes so that everyone looks alike. The staff subjects new inmates to "mortifications of self," which can include searches, medical examinations, head shaving, fingerprinting, and assignment of a serial number. Once inside the walls, individuals also give up their privacy as guards routinely inspect their living quarters.

In the second part of the resocialization process, the staff tries to build a new self in the inmate through a system of rewards and punishments. Having a book to read, watching television, or making a telephone call may seem like minor pleasures to the outsider, but in the rigid environment of the total institution, the opportunity to gain such simple privileges can be a powerful motivation to conform. The length of confinement typically depends on how well the inmate co-operates with the staff.

Total institutions affect people in different ways. Some inmates may end up "rehabilitated" or "recovered," but others may change little, and still others may become hostile or bitter. Over a long period of time, living in a rigidly controlled environment can leave some *institutionalized*, without the capacity for independent living.

But what about the rest of us? Does socialization crush our individuality or empower us to reach our creative potential? The Controversy & Debate box takes a closer look at this vital question.

CHAPTER 3 SOCIALIZATION: FROM INFANCY TO OLD AGE

WHEN DO WE GROW UP AND BECOME ADULTS? As this chapter explains, many factors come into play in the process of moving from one stage of the life course to another. In global perspective, what makes our society unusual is that there is no one event that clearly tells everyone (and us, too) that the milestone of adulthood has been reached. We have important events that say, for example, when someone completes high school (graduation ceremony) or gets married (wedding ceremony). Look at the photos below. In each case, what do we learn about how the society defines the transition from one stage of life to another?

Among the Hamer people in the Omo Valley of Ethiopia, young boys must undergo a test to mark their transition to manhood. Usually the event is triggered by the boy's expressing a desire to marry. In this ritual, witnessed by everyone in his society, the boy must jump over a line of bulls selected by the girl's family. If he succeeds in doing this three times, he is declared a man and the wedding can take place (marking the girl's transition to womanhood). Does our society have any ceremony or event similar to this to mark the transition to adulthood?

These young men and women in Seoul, South Korea, are participating in a Confucian ceremony to mark their becoming adults. This ritual, which takes place on the twentieth birthday, defines young people as full members of the community and also reminds them of all of the responsibilities they are now expected to fulfill. If we had such a ritual in Canada, at what age would it take place? Would a person's social class affect the timing of this ritual?

HINT: Societies differ in how they structure the life course, including which stages of life are defined as important, what years of life various stages correspond to, and how clearly movement from one stage to another is marked. Given our cultural emphasis on individual choice and freedom, many people tend to say, "You're only as old as you feel" and let people decide these things for themselves. When it comes to reaching adulthood, our society is not very clear—the Seeing Sociology in Everyday Life box on page 73 points out many factors that figure into becoming an adult. So there is no widespread "adult ritual" as we see in the photos. Keep in mind that, for us, class matters a lot in this process, with young people of higher social standing staying in school and delaying full adulthood until well into their twenties or even their thirties. Finally, in these tough economic times, the share of young people in their twenties living with parents goes way up, which can delay adulthood for an entire cohort.

Applying Sociology in Everyday Life

1. Across Canada, many families plan elaborate parties to celebrate a daughter's or son's graduation from high school. In what respect is this a ritual that marks reaching adulthood? How does social class affect whether people define this event as the beginning of adulthood?

2. In Canada, when does the stage of life we call "old age" begin? Is there an event that marks the transition to old age? Does social class play a part in this process? If so, how?

3. Watch several hours of prime-time programming on network or cable television. Keep track of every time any element of violence is shown and calculate the number of violent scenes per hour. On the basis of observing a small and unrepresentative sample of programs, what are your conclusions?

CHAPTER 3 Socialization: From Infancy to Old Age

Social Experience: The Key to Our Humanity

SOCIALIZATION is a lifelong process.
- Socialization develops our humanity as well as our particular personalities.
- The importance of socialization is seen in the fact that extended periods of social isolation result in permanent damage (cases of Anna and Genie).

`p. 64`

Socialization is a matter of **NURTURE** rather than **NATURE**.
- A century ago, most people thought human behaviour resulted from biological instinct.
- For us as human beings, it is our nature to nurture.

`pp. 64–65`

socialization (p. 64) the lifelong social experience by which people develop their human potential and learn culture

personality (p. 64) a person's fairly consistent patterns of acting, thinking, and feeling

Understanding Socialization

SIGMUND FREUD's model of the human personality has three parts:
- **id:** innate, pleasure-seeking human drives
- **superego:** the demands of society in the form of internalized values and norms
- **ego:** our efforts to balance innate, pleasure-seeking drives and the demands of society

`p. 66`

LAWRENCE KOHLBERG applied Piaget's approach to stages of moral development:
- We first judge rightness in preconventional terms, according to our individual needs.
- Next, conventional moral reasoning takes account of parental attitudes and cultural norms.
- Finally, postconventional reasoning allows us to criticize society itself.

`p. 67`

CHARLES HORTON COOLEY used the term **looking-glass self** to explain that we see ourselves as we imagine others see us.

`p. 68`

JEAN PIAGET believed that human development involves both biological maturation and gaining social experience. He identified four stages of cognitive development:
- The **sensorimotor stage** involves knowing the world only through the senses.
- The **preoperational stage** involves starting to use language and other symbols.
- The **concrete operational stage** allows individuals to understand causal connections.
- The **formal operational stage** involves abstract and critical thought.

`pp. 66–67`

CAROL GILLIGAN found that gender plays an important part in moral development, with males relying more on abstract standards of rightness and females relying more on the effects of actions on relationships.

`p. 68`

According to **GEORGE HERBERT MEAD**:
- The **self** is part of our personality and includes self-awareness and self-image.
- The self develops only as a result of social experience.
- Social experience involves the exchange of symbols.
- Social interaction depends on understanding the intention of another, which requires taking the role of the other.
- Human action is partly spontaneous (the I) and partly in response to others (the me).
- We gain social experience through imitation, play, games, and understanding the generalized other.

`pp. 68–69`

id (p. 66) Freud's term for the human being's basic drives

ego (p. 66) Freud's term for a person's conscious efforts to balance innate pleasure-seeking drives with the demands of society

superego (p. 66) Freud's term for the cultural values and norms internalized by an individual

sensorimotor stage (p. 67) Piaget's term for the level of human development at which individuals experience the world only through their senses

preoperational stage (p. 67) Piaget's term for the level of human development at which individuals first use language and other symbols

concrete operational stage (p. 67) Piaget's term for the level of human development at which individuals first see causal connections in their surroundings

formal operational stage (p. 67) Piaget's term for the level of human development at which individuals think abstractly and critically

looking-glass self (p. 68) Cooley's term for a self-image based on how we think others see us

self (p. 68) Mead's term for the part of an individual's personality composed of self-awareness and self-image

significant others (p. 69) people, such as parents, who have special importance for socialization

generalized other (p. 69) Mead's term for widespread cultural norms and values we use as a reference in evaluating ourselves

Agents of Socialization

The **FAMILY** is usually the first setting of socialization.

- Family has the greatest impact on attitudes and behaviour.
- A family's social position, including race and social class, shapes a child's personality.
- Ideas about gender are learned first in the family.

pp. 70–71

SCHOOLS give most children their first experience with bureaucracy and impersonal evaluation.

- Schools teach knowledge and skills needed for later life.
- Schools expose children to greater social diversity.
- Schools reinforce ideas about gender.

pp. 71–72

peer group (p. 72) a social group whose members have interests, social position, and age in common

anticipatory socialization (p. 73) learning that helps a person achieve a desired position

mass media (p. 74) the means for delivering impersonal communications to a vast audience

The **PEER GROUP** helps shape attitudes and behaviour.

- The peer group takes on great importance during adolescence.
- The peer group frees young people from adult supervision.

pp. 72–73

The **MASS MEDIA** have a huge impact on socialization in modern, high-income societies.

- The average North American child spends about 6.5 hours per day watching television and playing video games—as much time as spent attending school and interacting with parents.
- The mass media often reinforce stereotypes about gender and race.
- The mass media expose people to a great deal of violence.

pp. 73–75

Socialization and the Life Course

The concept of **CHILDHOOD** is grounded not in biology but in culture. In high-income countries, childhood is extended.

pp. 75–76

The emotional and social turmoil of **ADOLESCENCE** results from cultural inconsistency in defining people who are not children but not yet adults. Adolescence varies by social class.

pp. 76–77

gerontology (p. 78) the study of aging and the elderly

gerontocracy (p. 79) a form of social organization in which the elderly have the most wealth, power, and prestige

ageism (p. 79) prejudice and discrimination against older people

cohort (p. 80) a category of people with something in common, usually their age

ADULTHOOD is the stage of life when most accomplishments take place. Although personality is now formed, it continues to change with new life experiences.

pp. 77–78

OLD AGE is defined as much by culture as by biology.

- In high-income countries, old age is a time of disengagement and loss of social importance.
- The "greying of Canada" means that our country's average age is going up.

pp. 78–80

Acceptance of **DEATH AND DYING** is part of socialization for the elderly. This process typically involves five stages: denial, anger, negotiation, resignation, and acceptance.

p. 80

✓ *Every stage of life is socially constructed in ways that vary from society to society (pp. 80–81).*

Resocialization: Total Institutions

TOTAL INSTITUTIONS include prisons, mental hospitals, and monasteries.

- Staff members supervise all aspects of life.
- Life is standardized, with all inmates following set rules and routines.

p. 81

RESOCIALIZATION is a two-part process:

- breaking down inmates' existing identity
- building a new self through a system of rewards and punishments

pp. 81–82

total institution (p. 81) a setting in which people are isolated from the rest of society and controlled by an administrative staff

resocialization (p. 81) radically changing an inmate's personality by carefully controlling the environment

MySocLab

Visit MySocLab at www.mysoclab.com to access a variety of online resources that will help you to prepare for tests and to apply your knowledge, including

- an eText
- videos
- self-grading quizzes
- glossary flashcards

4 Social Interaction in Everyday Life

- What makes something funny?
- How do we create reality in our face-to-face interactions?
- Why do employers try to control their workers' feelings on the job as well as their behaviour?

This chapter takes a micro-level look at society, examining patterns of everyday social interaction. First, the chapter identifies important social structures, including status and role. Then the chapter explains how we construct reality in social interaction. Finally, it applies the lessons learned to three everyday experiences: emotion, gender, and humour.

Harold and Sybil are on their way to another couple's home in an unfamiliar area of their city. For the last 20 minutes, as Sybil sees it, they have been driving in circles, searching in vain for Mortimer Street.

"Look, Harold," says Sybil. "There are some people up ahead. Let's ask for directions."

Harold, gripping the wheel ever more tightly, begins muttering under his breath. "I know where I am. I don't want to waste time talking to strangers. Just let me get us there."

"I'm sure you know where you are, Harold," Sybil responds, looking straight ahead. "But I don't think you know where you're going."

Harold and Sybil are lost in more ways than one: Not only can't they find where their friends live, but they also cannot understand why they are growing angrier with each other with each passing minute.

What's going on? Like most men, Harold cannot stand getting lost. The longer he drives around, the more incompetent he feels. Sybil can't understand why Harold doesn't pull over to ask someone the way to Mortimer Street. If she were driving, she thinks to herself, they would already be comfortably settled in with their friends.

Why don't many men like to ask for directions? Because men value their independence, they are uncomfortable asking for any type of help and are reluctant to accept it. To ask another person for assistance is the same as saying, "You know something I don't know." If it takes Harold a few more minutes to find Mortimer Street on his own—and to keep his sense of being in control—he thinks that's the way to go.

Women are more in tune with others and strive for connectedness. From Sybil's point of view, asking for help is right because sharing information builds social bonds and at the same time gets the job done. Asking for directions seems as natural to her as searching on his own is to Harold. Obviously, getting lost is sure to create conflict for Harold and Sybil as long as neither one of them understands the other's point of view.

Such everyday social patterns are the focus of this chapter. The central concept is **social interaction**, *the process by which people act and react in relation to others.* We begin by presenting the rules and building blocks of everyday experience and then explore the almost magical way in which face-to-face interaction creates the reality in which we live.

Social Structure: A Guide to Everyday Living

September 8, Åbo, Finland. It is shortly before 8:00 A.M. when we arrive at Folkhälsans Daghem (daycare centre) for the first time. We help our daughter discard her outside wear and change from sneakers to slippers at the space already labelled with her name. The other children are washing their hands—part of the arrival routine—and, eager to fit into her new environment, our daughter follows suit. Seated at two small square tables are a dozen or so children aged three to six, peacefully eating their breakfast with their non-parental caregivers. As Canadians, we used to attend to our daughter's dietary needs at daycare ourselves—packed lunches and a snack. The communal arrangement seems very strange (and appealing) to us. We are all the more amazed to learn that Finnish law requires that all daycare children be given a daily breakfast, hot lunch, and afternoon snack free of charge! When we pick our daughter up at the end of the day, we notice that she is the last one there at 4:30 P.M. Eager to fit in ourselves, we soon adjust our daily schedule and start to pick our daughter up around 4:00 P.M., as the other parents do.

Members of every society rely on social structure to make sense out of daily situations. As our family's introduction to the daycare system in Finland suggests, what is taken for granted in one society can seem unfamiliar and strange in another. Let's take a closer look at the ways in which society organizes everyday life.

social interaction (p. 87) the process by which people act and react in relation to others

status a social position that a person holds

ascribed status a social position a person receives at birth or takes on involuntarily later in life

achieved status a social position a person takes on voluntarily that reflects personal ability and effort

status set all of the statuses a person holds at a given time

master status a status that has special importance for social identity, often shaping a person's entire life

We celebrate athletes such as Brian McKeever not only because in 2010 he became the first Canadian athlete to be named to both Paralympic and Olympic teams and went on to win three golds at the 2010 Paralympics, but also because of challenges in his life resulting from legal blindness.

Status

In every society, people build their lives using the idea of **status**, *a social position that a person holds.* In everyday use, the word *status* generally refers to "prestige," as when a bank president is said to have more "status" than a bank teller. But sociologically speaking, both "president" and "teller" are two statuses, or positions, within the bank occupational structure.

Status is part of our social identity and defines our relationships to others. As Georg Simmel (1950:307, orig. 1902), one of the founders of sociology, pointed out, before we can deal with anyone, we need to know who the person is.

Each of us holds many statuses at once. The term **status set** refers to *all of the statuses a person holds at a given time.* A teenage girl may be a daughter to her parents, a sister to her brother, a student at her school, and a goalie on her soccer team.

Status sets change over the life course. A child grows up to become a parent, a student graduates to become a lawyer, a goalie becomes a coach, and a single person marries to become a partner, sometimes becoming single again as a result of death or divorce. Joining an organization or finding a job enlarges our status set; retirement or withdrawing from activities makes it smaller. Over a lifetime, people gain and lose dozens of statuses.

Ascribed and Achieved Status

Sociologists classify statuses in terms of how people attain them. An **ascribed status** is *a social position a person receives at birth or takes on involuntarily later in life.* Examples of ascribed statuses are being a son, a Canadian, an Aboriginal, or a widower. Ascribed statuses are matters about which we have little or no choice.

By contrast, an **achieved status** refers to *a social position a person takes on voluntarily that reflects personal ability and effort.* Examples of achieved statuses in Canada are being an honour student, NHL hockey player, rap artist, computer programmer, or drug dealer.

In the real world, of course, most statuses involve a combination of ascription and achievement. That is, people's ascribed statuses influence the statuses they achieve. People who share the ascribed benefit of being born into relatively well-off families, for example, are more likely to achieve the status of lawyer. By the same token, many less desirable statuses, such as homeless person, drug addict, HIV-positive person, or recipient of social welfare, are more easily achieved by people who were born into poverty.

Master Status

Some statuses matter more than others. A **master status** is *a status that has special importance for social identity, often shaping a person's entire life.* For most people, a job is a master status because it reveals a great deal about social background, education, and income. In a few cases, a person's name is a master status; being an Eaton, a Trudeau, or a Bronfman is enough by itself to push an individual into the Canadian limelight.

A master status can be negative as well as positive. Consider serious illness. Sometimes people, even lifelong friends, avoid cancer patients or people with AIDS because of their illnesses (Flowers et al., 2006; Nancarrow Clarke & Nancarrow Clarke, 1999). As another example, the fact that all societies limit opportunities for women makes gender a master status, especially when it intersects with sexual transmitted infections and other chronic illnesses (Nack, 2002).

Sometimes a physical disability can serve as a master status to the point that we dehumanize people by seeing them only in terms of their disability (Darling & Bryant, 2001; Nosek, Hughes, Swedlund, Taylor, & Swank, 2003; Taub, McLorg, & Fanflik, 2004). The Thinking about Diversity box shows how.

THINKING ABOUT DIVERSITY: RACE, CLASS, AND GENDER

Physical Disability as a Master Status

Physical disability works in much the same way as class, gender, or race in defining people in the eyes of others. In the following interviews, two women explain how a physical disability can become a master status—a trait that overshadows everything else about them. The first voice is of 29-year-old Donna Finch, who lives with her husband and son and holds a master's degree in social work. She is also blind.

> Most people don't expect handicapped people to grow up; they are always supposed to be children. . . . You aren't supposed to date; you aren't supposed to have a job; somehow you're just supposed to disappear. I'm not saying this is true of anyone else, but in my own case I think I was more intellectually mature than most children, and more emotionally immature. I'd say that not until the last four or five years have I felt really whole.

Rose Helman is an elderly woman who has recently retired. She suffers from spinal meningitis and is also blind.

> You ask me if people are really different today than in the '20s and '30s. Not too much. They are still fearful of the handicapped. I don't know if fearful is the right word, but uncomfortable at least. But I can understand it somewhat; it happened to me. I once asked a man to tell me which staircase to use to get from the subway out to the street. He started giving me

directions that were confusing, and I said, "Do you mind taking me?" He said, "Not at all." He grabbed me on the side with my dog on it, so I asked him to take my other arm. And he said, "I'm sorry, I have no other arm." And I said, "That's all right, I'll hold onto the jacket." It felt funny hanging onto the sleeve without the arm in it.

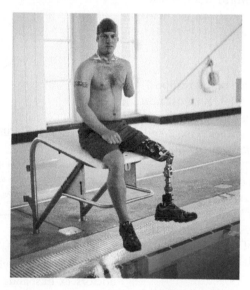

Modern technology means that most soldiers who lose limbs in war now survive. How do you think the loss of an arm or a leg affects a person's social identity and sense of self?

Some stigmatized individuals manage their identity through acts of resistance; that is, they "artfully dodge or constructively challenge stigmatizing processes" (Link & Phelan, 2001:378). The Canadian Federation of the Blind, a voluntary organization whose members work to fight the social and economic inequality of blind people in Canada, has developed a variety of strategies to educate the general public and employers about the societal barriers to attaining meaningful employment for legally blind adults and to assist governments to develop social policies to rectify the problem (McCreath, 2011).

WHAT DO YOU THINK?

1. Have you ever had an illness or disability that became a master status? If so, how did others react?

2. How might such a master status affect someone's personality?

3. Can being very fat or very thin serve as a master status? Why or why not?

4. What are some factors that may increase success in resisting a negative master status?

Source: Based on Orlansky and Heward (1981).

Role

A second important social structure is **role**, *behaviour expected of someone who holds a particular status*. A person *holds* a status and *performs* a role (Linton, 1937b). For example, holding the status of student leads you to perform the role of attending classes and completing assignments.

Both statuses and roles vary by culture. In Canada, the status "uncle" refers to a brother of either mother or father; in Vietnam and Sweden, however, the word for "uncle" is different when referring to the mother's or father's side of the family, and the two men have different responsibilities. In every society, actual role performance varies according to a person's unique personality, although some societies such as Canada permit more individual expression than others.

Because we hold many statuses at once in our status set, everyday life is a mix of many roles. Robert Merton (1968) introduced the term **role set** to identify *a number of roles attached to a single status*.

Figure 4–1 on page 90 shows four statuses of one person, each linked to a different role set. First, as a professor, this woman interacts with students (the teacher role) and other academics (the colleague role). Second, as a researcher, she gathers and analyzes data (the fieldwork role) that she uses in her publications (the author role). Third, the same woman holds the status of "wife," with a marital role

role conflict conflict among the roles connected to two or more statuses

role strain tension among the roles connected to a single status

(such as confidante and sexual partner) toward her spouse, with whom she shares a domestic role toward the household. Fourth, she holds the status of "mother," with routine responsibilities for her children (the maternal role) as well as involvement in their school and other organizations (the civic role).

A global perspective shows us that the roles people use to define their lives differ from society to society. In low-income countries, people spend fewer years as students and family roles typically last longer and are very important to social identity. In high-income countries, people spend more years as students and family roles may or may not be very important to social identity. Another dimension of difference involves housework. As Global Map 4–1 on page 91 shows, especially in lower-income nations of the world, doing housework is an important role that still falls more heavily on women's shoulders (Enemark, 2006).

Role Conflict and Role Strain

People in complex, high-income countries juggle many responsibilities demanded by their various statuses and roles. As most new parents soon learn, being a parent and working outside the home both involve physically and emotionally draining roles (Fox, 2009). Sociologists thus recognize **role conflict** as *conflict among the roles connected to two or more statuses.*

We experience role conflict when we find ourselves pulled in various directions as we try to respond to the many statuses we hold. One response to role conflict is deciding that "something has to go." More than one politician, for example, has decided not to run for office because of the conflicting demands of a hectic campaign schedule and family life. In other cases, people delay or avoid having children to stay on the "fast track" for career success.

Even roles linked to a single status can make competing demands on us. **Role strain** is *tension among the roles connected to a single status.* A university professor may enjoy being friendly with students. At the same time, however, the professor must maintain the personal distance needed to evaluate students objectively and fairly. In short, performing the roles of even a single status can be something of a balancing act.

One strategy for minimizing role conflict is separating parts of our lives so that we perform roles for one status at one time and in one place and carry out roles for another status in a completely different setting (Nippert-Eng, 1995). A familiar example of this is deciding to "leave the job at work" before heading home to the family or, perhaps more relevant for Canadian women these days, "leaving the family at home" while at their job (McDaniel, 2002).

Role Exit

After she left the life of a Catholic nun to become a university sociologist, Helen Rose Fuchs Ebaugh began to study her own experience of *role exit*, the process by which people disengage from important

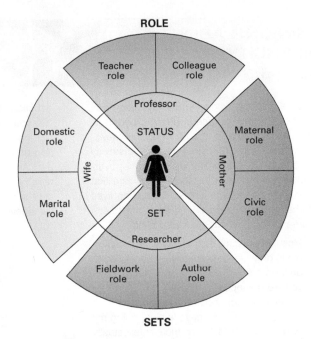

ROLE

FIGURE 4–1 Status Set and Role Sets

A status set includes all of the statuses a person holds at a given time. The status set defines *who we are* in society. The many roles linked to each status define *what we do.*

North Wind Picture Archives

social roles. In studying a range of "exes," including ex-nuns, ex-doctors, ex-husbands, and ex-alcoholics, Ebaugh saw a pattern in the process of becoming an "ex."

According to Ebaugh (1988), the process begins as people come to doubt their ability to continue in a certain role. As they imagine alternative roles, they ultimately reach a tipping point when they decide to pursue a new life. Even at this point, however, a past role can continue to influence their lives. Exes carry with them a self-image shaped by an earlier role, which can interfere with building a new sense of self. For example, an ex-nun may hesitate to wear stylish clothing and makeup.

Exes must also rebuild relationships with people who knew them in their earlier life. Learning new social skills is another challenge. For example, Ebaugh reports, ex-nuns who enter the dating scene after decades in the church are often surprised to learn that today's sexual norms are very different from those they knew when they were teenagers. Exiting a role is made more complicated if that role is seen by society as deviant, such as the role of sex worker. Saunders (2007) argues that national policies that reinforce "exiting" through compulsory rehabilitation and the criminalization of sex work make leaving the role very difficult for those involved.

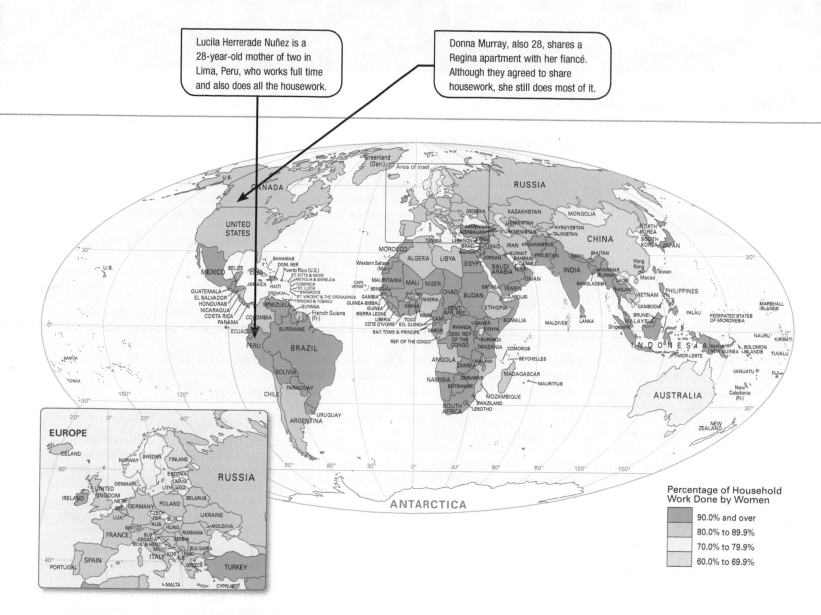

Lucila Herrerade Nuñez is a 28-year-old mother of two in Lima, Peru, who works full time and also does all the housework.

Donna Murray, also 28, shares a Regina apartment with her fiancé. Although they agreed to share housework, she still does most of it.

Percentage of Household Work Done by Women

- 90.0% and over
- 80.0% to 89.9%
- 70.0% to 79.9%
- 60.0% to 69.9%

Window on the World

GLOBAL MAP 4–1 **Housework in Global Perspective**

Throughout the world, housework is a major part of women's routines and identities. This is especially true in low- and middle-income societies of Latin America, Africa, and Asia, where women's work does not generally bring in a wage or salary. But our society also defines housework and child care as "feminine" activities, even though a majority of Canadian women work in the paid economy.

The Social Construction of Reality

In 1917, the Italian playwright Luigi Pirandello wrote a play titled *The Pleasure of Honesty*, about a character named Angelo Baldovino, a brilliant man with a checkered past. Baldovino enters the fashionable home of the Renni family and introduces himself in a peculiar way:

Inevitably we construct ourselves. Let me explain. I enter this house and immediately I become what I have to become, what I can become: I construct myself. That is, I present myself to you in a form suitable to the relationship I wish to achieve with you. And, of course, you do the same with me. (act 1, scene 1)

Baldovino suggests that although behaviour is guided by status and role, we have considerable ability to shape what happens from

The Toronto Star

For Teenagers, Body-to-Body Contact Says It All

FRANCINE KOPUN
September 12, 2009

Hugging is the new hello, if you're a teenager.

It's also good-bye, nice to see you, good job, let's chat and, even, hey, it's recess.

"Basically, when you become a teenager, you just hug everyone," says Casey Malvern, 13, a student at Lakeside Public School in Ajax. . .

Girls hug each other and they hug boys. The boys hug girls. Some guys say they hug their guy friends—but not at Upper Canada College, a private day and boarding school for boys.

"I hug girls but I don't hug guys—maybe a man-pat," says Ben Fickling, 14, a student at UCC. To demonstrate, he grabs his friend's right hand and shakes it and they bump their right shoulders together.

The most popular hug is the side-squeeze: Teenagers stand beside each other; they extend their arms to the side and move in for a cheek-to-cheek hug. This may sometimes be accompanied by squealing.

"It's like saying, 'Hi,'" says Sara Jasion, 13, of All Saints Catholic School in Mississauga.

The surprise hug, usually from behind, is designed to generate screams.

Then there's the boyfriend-girlfriend hug, which, everybody agrees, is different because it lasts longer and can involve kissing.

There even appear to be regional differences. According to Mackenzie Pazos and her friends at Joan of Arc High School in Barrie, guys are supposed to put their arms around a girl's waist to hug them and girls are supposed to put their arms around a guy's neck.

"If a guy doesn't, they get a hard time, like, 'Oh, you can't hug,'" Pazos says.

Hugging has become such a concern at some U.S. schools that it has been banned amid fears of allegations of harassment or improper touching. Spokeswomen for the Toronto District School Board and the Toronto Catholic Separate School Board said they were unaware of any schools that have banned hugging. . .

But even without a ban, teachers are keeping a wary eye and a quiver of jokes to pry students apart.

"I would like daylight between you! A ribbon of daylight would be nice," Kate Dickson, English teacher and vice-principal of student services and admissions, tells her students at SOLA, the School of Liberal Arts. There are 95 students at the Toronto school in Grades 9 to 12.

Dickson says the trend has been building. "Kids are feeling that they have to hug. It has become the new social imperative. I'm becoming wary of it.". . .

"People shouldn't have to touch one another if they don't feel like it."

Dickson and others attribute the trend in part to the fact that teenagers are becoming more comfortable with their bodies and express themselves with an ease and openness unfamiliar to most North American adults. Most of it is innocent, they agree. . .

Dave Davis, principal of Bronte College of Canada, a private school in Mississauga, agrees hugging has become much more popular over the past few years.

"It's definitely a common sight in the school. There's no question about it. It's kind of nice to see."

Social worker and family therapist Gary Direnfeld sees the phenomenon as a backlash against the proliferation of "no-touch" policies that followed in the wake of horrifying revelations of child sexual abuse in the 1990s.

Schools, churches and groups for youth, like Scouts Canada, issued detailed guidelines governing physical contact between adults and their young charges. "A handshake is generally acceptable; a hug is sometimes acceptable; and an embrace is usually unacceptable," according to the Scouts Canada code of conduct.

Teachers complain that they can't even hug young children when they cry.

Direnfeld thinks the hugging between teenagers may have sprung up in reaction to that. He says it's not inherently inappropriate contact.

"Teenagers will naturally be exploring their social relationships. This is part of the adolescent norm to be touching each other," says Direnfeld, who also hosts the television show *Newlywed, Nearly Dead?*, on Slice Television. "But, sometimes, we as adults worry ourselves that where there's smoke, there's fire. It's silly on our part" . . .

WHAT DO YOU THINK?

1. The handshake of the adult world has been replaced by the hug of the teenage world. Can you think of other everyday life gestures that differ from one generation to another? Explain.

2. Have you ever felt "not hip" for not hugging someone? If so, explain what happened.

3. Why do you think many older people consider hugging (or other physical touching) "dangerous territory," while younger people seem more casual about it?

4. Why, in your view, is the movement to ban hugging in schools widespread in the United States but not Canada?

Source: Adapted from "For Teenagers, Body-To-Body Contact Says It All,'" by Francine Kopun, *The Toronto Star*, on September 12, 2009. Reprinted with permission—Torstar Syndication Services.

moment to moment. In other words, "reality" is not as fixed as we may think.

The **social construction of reality** is *the process by which people creatively shape reality through social interaction*. This idea is the foundation of the symbolic-interaction approach, described in Chapter 1 ("Sociology: Perspective, Theory, and Method"). As Baldovino's remark suggests, quite a bit of "reality" remains unclear in everyone's mind, especially in unfamiliar situations. So we present ourselves in terms that suit the setting and our purposes, and as others do the same, reality takes shape.

Social interaction, then, is a complex negotiation that builds reality. Most everyday situations involve at least some agreement about what's going on. But how people see events depends on their different backgrounds, interests, and intentions. One example of changing patterns in everyday interaction involves greeting another person. Seeing Sociology in the News takes a look at how young people have embraced hugging as a form of greeting, replacing the handshakes that are common among their parents.

social construction of reality (p. 92) the process by which people creatively shape reality through social interaction

Thomas theorem W.I. Thomas's claim that situations defined as real are real in their consequences

ethnomethodology Harold Garfinkel's term for the study of the way people make sense of their everyday surroundings

Flirting is an everyday experience in reality construction. Each person offers information to the other and hints at romantic interest. Yet the interaction proceeds with a tentative and often humorous air so that either individual can withdraw at any time without further obligation.

"Street Smarts"

What people commonly call "street smarts" is actually a form of constructing reality. In his autobiography, *Down These Mean Streets*, Piri Thomas recalls moving to a new apartment in Spanish Harlem. Returning home one evening, young Piri found himself cut off by Waneko, the leader of the local street gang, who was flanked by a dozen others.

"Whatta ya say, Mr. Johnny Gringo," drawled Waneko.

Think man, I told myself, think your way out of a stomping. Make it good. "I hear you 104th Street coolies are supposed to have heart," I said. "I don't know this for sure. You know there's a lot of streets where a whole 'click' is made out of punks who can't fight one guy unless they all jump him for the stomp." I hoped this would push Waneko into giving me a fair one. His expression didn't change.

"Maybe we don't look at it that way."

Crazy, man, I cheer inwardly, the cabron is falling into my setup. . . . "I wasn't talking to you," I said. "Where I come from, the pres is president 'cause he got heart when it comes to dealing."

Waneko was starting to look uneasy. He had bit on my worm and felt like a sucker fish. His boys were now light on me. They were no

longer so much interested in stomping me as seeing the outcome between Waneko and me. "Yeah," was his reply. . . .

I knew I'd won. Sure, I'd have to fight; but one guy, not ten or fifteen. If I lost, I might still get stomped, and if I won I might get stomped. I took care of this with my next sentence. "I don't know you or your boys," I said, "but they look cool to me. They don't feature as punks."

I had left him out purposely when I said "they."

Now his boys were in a separate class. I had cut him off. He would have to fight me on his own, to prove his heart to himself, to his boys, and most important, to his turf. He got away from the stoop and asked, "Fair one, Gringo?" (Thomas, 1967:56–57)

This situation reveals the drama—sometimes subtle, sometimes savage—by which human beings creatively build everyday reality. Of course, not everyone enters a situation with equal power. Should a police officer on patrol have come upon the fight that took place between Piri and Waneko, both young men might have ended up in jail.

The Thomas Theorem

By using his wits and fighting with Waneko until they both tired, Piri Thomas won acceptance by the gang. What took place that evening in Spanish Harlem is an example of the **Thomas theorem**, named after W.I. Thomas and Dorothy Thomas (1928; Thomas, 1966:301, orig. 1931): *Situations that are defined as real are real in their consequences.*

Applied to social interaction, the Thomas theorem means that although reality is "soft" as it is being shaped, it can become "hard" in its effects. In the situation just described, local gang members saw Piri Thomas act in a worthy way, so in their eyes he *became* worthy.

Ethnomethodology

Most of the time, we take social reality for granted. To become more aware of the social world we help create, Harold Garfinkel (1967) came up with **ethnomethodology**, *the study of the way people make sense of their everyday surroundings.* This approach begins by pointing out that everyday behaviour rests on a number of assumptions. For instance, when you ask someone the simple question "How are you?" you usually want to know how someone is doing in general, but you may be wondering how a person is dealing with a specific physical, mental, spiritual, or financial challenge. However, as Canadians, we tend to assume that people are not really interested in the details about these things. Upon arrival in Canada from Sweden, one of the authors soon learned that Canadians asked "How are you?" out of politeness, not because they wanted to listen to an honest answer of how he was feeling.

One good way to investigate the assumptions we make about everyday reality is to break the rules. For example, the next time

People build reality from their surrounding culture. Yet because cultural systems are marked by diversity and even outright conflict, reality construction always involves tensions and choices. Turkey is a nation with a mostly Muslim population, but it has also embraced Western culture. Here, women confront starkly different definitions of what is "feminine."

Staton R. Winter, *The New York Times*.

Erving Goffman (1922–1982), born in the small town of Manville, Alberta, to Jewish immigrants from Ukraine, was one of the most important North American sociologists of the twentieth century. A Canadian Jew of short stature who researched topics at the margins of the discipline at the time, Goffman had a keen sense of the dynamics of social interaction. He relied on careful observation to capture the drama of everyday life, rather than on adherence to the formal scientific method (Treviño, 2003).

someone asks "How are you?" offer details from your last physical examination or explain all of the good and bad things that have happened since you woke up that morning and see how the person reacts.

The results are predictable, because we all have some idea of what the "rules" of everyday interaction are. The person will most likely become confused or irritated by your unexpected behaviour—a reaction that helps us see not only what the rules are but how important they are to everyday reality.

Reality Building: Class and Culture

People do not build everyday experience from nothing. In part, how we act or what we see in our surroundings depends on our interests. Scanning the sky on a starry night, for example, lovers discover romance, whereas scientists see hydrogen atoms fusing into helium. Social background also directs what we see, so that residents of, say, Hull, Quebec, experience the world somewhat differently than most people living across the river in Ottawa, Ontario.

In global perspective, the construction of reality is even more variable. Consider these everyday situations: People waiting for a bus in London typically "queue up" in a straight line; people in Winnipeg, on the other hand, are rarely so orderly. The law in Saudi Arabia forbids women to drive cars, a constraint unheard of in Canada. Significant events also shape reality: Fear of crime

in the big cities of the United States is considerably greater than it is elsewhere—including London, Paris, Rome, Calcutta, Helsinki, and Hong Kong—and this sense of public danger shapes the daily realities of a large number of U.S. citizens. Comparatively high private ownership of handguns, for example, illustrates how fear of violence and losing wealth can prompt people to purchase a gun for protection.

The point is that people build reality from the surrounding culture. Chapter 2 ("Culture") explains how people the world over find different meanings in specific gestures, so inexperienced travellers can find themselves building an unexpected and unwelcome reality. Similarly, in a study of popular culture, JoEllen Shively (1992) screened westerns—films set in the American West—to men of European descent and to Aboriginal men. The men in both categories claimed to enjoy the films, but for different reasons. White men interpreted the films as praising rugged people striking

dramaturgical analysis Erving Goffman's term for the study of social interaction in terms of theatrical performance

presentation of self Erving Goffman's term for a person's efforts to create specific impressions in the minds of others

non-verbal communication communication using body movements, gestures, and facial expressions rather than speech

out for the frontier and conquering the forces of nature. Aboriginal men saw in the same films a celebration of land and nature. Given their different cultures, it is as if people in the two categories saw two different films.

Films also have an effect on the reality we all experience. The 2010 film *My Name is Khan*, for example, about a Muslim man with Asperger syndrome, is one in a series of recent films that have changed people's awareness of the struggle of coping with mental disorders.

Dramaturgical Analysis: The "Presentation of Self"

Erving Goffman explained how people live their lives much like actors performing on a stage. If we imagine ourselves as directors observing what goes on in the theatre of everyday life, we are engaging in what Goffman called **dramaturgical analysis**, *the study of social interaction in terms of theatrical performance.*

Dramaturgical analysis offers a fresh look at the concepts of status and role. A status is like a part in a play, and a role is a script, supplying dialogue and action for the characters. Goffman described each person's performance as the **presentation of self**, *a person's efforts to create specific impressions in the minds of others.* This process, sometimes called *impression management*, begins with the idea of personal performance (Goffman, 1959, 1967).

Performances

As we present ourselves in everyday situations, we reveal information to others both consciously and unconsciously. Our performances include the way we dress (in theatrical terms, our costume), the objects we carry (props), and our tone of voice and the way we carry ourselves (our demeanour). In addition, we vary our performances according to where we happen to be (the set). We may joke loudly in a restaurant, for example, but lower our voices when entering a synagogue, mosque, or church. People design settings—such as homes, offices, and corner pubs—to bring about desired reactions in others.

An Application: The Doctor's Office

Consider how the operation of a doctor's office conveys important information to an audience of patients. The fact that medical doctors enjoy high prestige and power in Canada is clear upon entering a doctor's office. First, the doctor is nowhere to be seen. Instead, in what Goffman describes as the "front region" of the setting, the patient encounters a receptionist, who works as a gatekeeper, deciding whether and when the patient can meet the doctor. A simple glance around the doctor's waiting room, with patients (often impatiently) waiting to be invited into the inner sanctum, leaves little doubt that the doctor and staff are in charge.

The "back region" is composed of the examination rooms as well as the doctor's private office. Once inside the office, the patient can see a wide range of props, such as medical books and framed degrees, that give the impression that the doctor has the specialized knowledge necessary to call the shots. The doctor is usually seated behind a desk—the larger and grander the desk, the greater the statement of power—and the patient is given only a chair.

The doctor's appearance and manner offer still more information. The usual white lab coat (costume) may have the practical function of keeping clothes from becoming dirty, but its social function is to let others know the physician's status at a glance. A stethoscope around the neck and a black medical bag in hand (more props) have the same purpose. The doctor uses highly technical language that is often mystifying to the patient, again emphasizing that the doctor is in charge. Finally, patients use the title "doctor," but they, in turn, are often addressed only by their first names, which further shows the doctor's dominant position. The overall message of a doctor's performance is clear: "I will help you, but you must allow me to take charge."

Non-verbal Communication

The novelist William Sansom describes the performance of a character named Mr. Preedy, an English vacationer on a beach in Spain:

> He took care to avoid catching anyone's eye. First, he had to make it clear to those potential companions of his holiday that they were of no concern to him whatsoever. He stared through them, round them, over them—eyes lost in space. The beach might have been empty. If by chance a ball was thrown his way, he looked surprised; then let a smile of amusement light his face (Kindly Preedy), looked around dazed to see that there were people on the beach, tossed it back with a smile to himself and not a smile *at* the people. . . .
>
> [He] then gathered together his beach-wrap and bag into a neat sand-resistant pile (Methodical and Sensible Preedy), rose slowly to stretch his huge frame (Big-Cat Preedy), and tossed aside his sandals (Carefree Preedy, after all). (1956:230–31)

Without saying a single word, Mr. Preedy offers a great deal of information about himself to anyone watching him. This is the process of **non-verbal communication**, *communication using body movements, gestures, and facial expressions rather than speech.*

Many parts of the body can be used to generate *body language*, that is, to convey information to others. Facial expressions are the most significant form of body language. Smiling, for example, shows pleasure, although we distinguish among the deliberate smile of Kindly Preedy on the beach, a spontaneous smile of joy at seeing a friend, a pained smile of embarrassment, and the full, unrestrained smile of self-satisfaction we often associate with winning some important contest.

Eye contact is another crucial element of non-verbal communication. Generally, we use eye contact to invite social interaction. Someone across the room "catches our eye," sparking a conversation. Avoiding another's eyes, by contrast, discourages communication. Hands also speak for us. Common hand gestures within our culture convey, among other things, an insult, a request for a ride, an invitation for someone to join us, or a demand that others stop in their tracks. Gestures also add meaning to spoken words. For example, pointing in a threatening way gives greater emphasis to a word of warning, shrugging the shoulders adds an air of indifference to the phrase "I don't know," and rapidly waving the arms lends urgency to the single word "Hurry!"

Body Language and Deception

As any actor knows, it is very difficult to pull off a perfect performance in front of others. In everyday life, unintended body language can contradict our planned meaning: A teenage boy explains why he is getting home so late, for example, but his mother doubts his words because he avoids looking her in the eye; the movie star on a television talk show claims that her recent flop at the box office is "no big deal," but the nervous swing of her leg suggests otherwise. Because non-verbal communication is hard to control, it provides clues to deception, in much the same way that changes in breathing, pulse rate, perspiration, and blood pressure recorded on a lie detector suggest that a person is lying.

Recognizing dishonest performances is difficult because no single bodily gesture tells us for sure that someone is lying. But because any performance involves so many bits of body language, few people can keep up a lie without some slip-up, raising the suspicions of a careful observer. Therefore, the key to detecting lies is to view the whole performance with an eye for inconsistencies.

Gender and Performances

Compared to men, women are more likely to be socialized to respond to others, and thus they tend to be more sensitive than men to non-verbal communication (Butler, 1997; van Sterkenburg & Knoppers, 2004). In fact, research shows that gender is a central element in personal performances (Drudy & Chathain, 2002).

Demeanour

Demeanour—the way we act and carry ourselves—is a clue to social power. Simply put, powerful people enjoy more personal freedom in how they act. Off-colour remarks, swearing, or putting one's feet on the desk may be acceptable for the boss but rarely for employees. Similarly, powerful people can interrupt others, but less powerful people are expected to show respect through silence (Henley, Hamilton, & Thorne, 1992; C. Johnson, 1994; Smith-Lovin & Brody, 1989).

Because women generally occupy positions of less power, demeanour is a gender issue as well. As Chapter 10 ("Gender

This photo of Canada's Supreme Court consists of the Chief Justice of Canada and eight puisne judges appointed by the Governor in Council. Historically, male judges dominated the Supreme Court but increasingly women judges are gaining entry into this powerful office.

Stratification") explains, more than 50 percent of all employed women in Canada are employed in a small number of "feminine" occupations—teaching, nursing, health-related occupations, and clerical service work—all of which are under the control of supervisors (in many cases, males). Women, then, learn to craft their personal performances more carefully than men and defer to men more often in everyday interaction.

Use of Space

How much space does a personal performance require? Our culture has traditionally measured femininity by how *little* space women occupy—the standard of "daintiness"—and masculinity by how *much* territory a man controls—the standard of "turf" (Henley, Hamilton, & Thorne, 1992). The next time you write an exam or are at a movie, observe how men and women are sitting. Males typically spread their legs while sitting or casually stretch out an arm over the back of the seat, while females are more likely to cross their legs and keep their arms close to their bodies. Why? Power plays a key role here; the more power you have, the more space you use. Compared with men, women are more likely to craft their personal performances during leisure time as well as while performing their jobs. They are called on to "manage their hearts" by conjuring up and displaying surface and sometimes deep feelings of caring for those they serve (Hochschild, 1983). Women and other socially disadvantaged groups are also more likely to embody their stress and unease (Krieger, 2005; Lennon, 1987) and to speak through their bodies about the unease they feel because of the work they do (Lock, 1993; Scheper-Hughes, 1993; Van Wolputte, 2004).

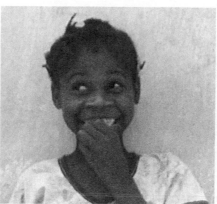

Hand gestures vary widely from one culture to another. Yet people everywhere chuckle, grin, or smirk to indicate that they don't take another person's performance seriously. Therefore, the world over, people who cannot restrain their mirth tactfully cover their faces.

For both sexes, **personal space** is *the surrounding area over which a person makes some claim to privacy*. In Canada and the United States, people generally stay about a metre apart when speaking; throughout the Middle East, by contrast, people stand much closer. But just about everywhere, men (with their greater social power) often intrude into women's personal space. If a woman moves into a man's personal space, however, he is likely to take it as a sign of sexual interest.

Smiling, Staring, and Touching

Eye contact encourages interaction. In conversations with the opposite sex, women tend to hold eye contact more than men. But men have their own brand of eye contact: staring. When men stare at women, they are claiming social dominance and defining women as sexual objects.

Although it often shows pleasure, smiling can also be a sign of trying to please someone or of submission. In a male-dominated world, it is not surprising that women smile more than men (Henley, Hamilton, & Thorne, 1992).

Finally, mutual touching suggests intimacy and caring, as between parents and their toddler or between two lovers. Apart from such close relationships, however, touching is generally something men do to women (but rarely, in our culture, to other men, though as noted earlier about cross-sex and same-sex hugging, this may be changing). A male doctor touches the shoulder of his female nurse as they examine a report, a young man touches the back of his woman friend as he guides her across the street, or a male instructor touches the arms of young women as he teaches them to ski. In such examples, the intent of the touching may be harmless and may bring little response, but it amounts to a subtle ritual by which men claim dominance over women.

Idealization

People behave the way they do for many, often complex reasons. Even so, Goffman suggests, we construct performances to *idealize* our intentions. That is, we try to convince others (and perhaps ourselves) that our actions reflect ideal cultural standards rather than selfish motives.

Idealization is easily illustrated by returning to the world of doctors and patients. In a hospital, doctors engage in a performance known as "making rounds." Upon entering a patient's room, the doctor often stops at the foot of the bed and silently examines the patient's chart. Afterwards, doctor and patient talk briefly. In ideal terms, this routine represents a personal visit to check on a patient's condition.

In reality, the picture is not so perfect. A doctor may see dozens of patients a day and remember little about many of them. Reading the chart is a chance to recall the patient's name and medical problems, but revealing the impersonality of the patient's care would undermine the cultural ideal of the doctor as deeply concerned about the welfare of others.

Doctors, professors, and other professionals typically idealize their motives for entering their chosen careers. They are quick to describe their work as "making a contribution to science," "serving the community," or even "answering a call from God." Rarely do people admit the more common, less honourable motives: the income, power, prestige, and leisure time that these occupations provide.

We all use idealization to some degree. When was the last time you smiled and made polite remarks to someone you did not like? Such little lies ease our way through social interactions. Even when we suspect that others are putting on an act, we are unlikely to challenge their performance, for reasons that we shall examine next.

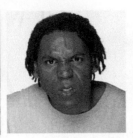

To most people in Canada, these expressions convey anger, fear, disgust, happiness, surprise, and sadness. But do people elsewhere in the world define them in the same way? Research suggests that all human beings experience the same basic emotions and display them to others in the same basic ways. But culture plays a part by specifying the situations that trigger one emotion or another.

Embarrassment and Tact

The famous speaker giving a campus lecture keeps mispronouncing the university's name; the visiting ambassador rises from the table to speak, unaware of the napkin that still hangs from his neck; the president becomes ill at a state dinner. As carefully as people may craft their performances, slip-ups of all kinds happen. The result is *embarrassment*, or discomfort after a spoiled performance. Goffman describes embarrassment as "losing face."

Embarrassment is an ever-present danger because idealized performances typically contain some deception. In addition, most performances involve juggling so many elements that one thoughtless moment can shatter the intended impression.

A curious fact is that an audience often overlooks flaws in a performance, allowing the actor to avoid embarrassment. If we do point out a misstep ("Excuse me, but your fly is open"), we do it quietly and only to help someone avoid even greater loss of face. In Hans Christian Andersen's classic fable "The Emperor's New Clothes," the child who blurts out the truth, that the emperor is parading about naked, is scolded for being rude.

Often members of an audience actually help the performer recover from a flawed performance. *Tact* is helping someone "save face." After hearing a supposed expert make an embarrassingly inaccurate remark, for example, we might ignore the comment, as if it had never been spoken. Or with mild laughter we could treat what was said as a joke. Or we could simply respond, "I'm sure you didn't mean that," hearing the statement but not allowing it to destroy the performance.

Why is tact so common? Embarrassment creates discomfort not only for the actor but also for everyone else. Just as the entire audience feels uneasy when an actor forgets a line, people who observe the awkward behaviour of others are reminded of how fragile their own performances often are. Socially constructed reality thus functions like a dam holding back a sea of chaos. Should one person's performance spring a leak, others tactfully help make repairs. After all, everyone lends a hand in building reality, and no one wants it suddenly swept away.

In sum, Goffman's research shows that although behaviour is spontaneous in some respects, it is more patterned than we like to think. Almost 400 years ago, William Shakespeare captured this idea in lines that still ring true:

> All the world's a stage,
> And all the men and women merely players:
> They have their exits and their entrances;
> And one man in his time plays many parts.
> (*As You Like It*, act 2, scene 7)

Interaction in Everyday Life: Three Applications

The final sections of this chapter illustrate the major elements of social interaction by focusing on three important dimensions of everyday life: emotions, language, and humour.

Emotions: The Social Construction of Feeling

Emotions, more commonly called *feelings*, are an important dimension of everyday life. Indeed, what we *do* often matters less than how we *feel* about it. Emotions seem very personal because they are "inside." Even so, just as society guides our behaviour, it guides our emotional life.

The Biological Side of Emotions

Studying the social interaction of men and women all over the world, Paul Ekman (1980a, 1980b) reported that people everywhere express six basic emotions: happiness, sadness, anger, fear, disgust, and surprise. In addition, Ekman found that people in every society use much the same facial expressions to show these emotions. To help us understand this universal problem, Ekman explains that some emotional responses seem to be "wired" into human beings; that is,

Managing Feelings: Women's Abortion Experiences

LIZ: I just *can't* be pregnant! There's no way I can deal with a baby at this point in my life! I'm going to see my doctor tomorrow about an abortion.

JEN: I can't believe you'd do that, Liz! How are you going to feel in a couple of years when you think of what that *child* would be doing if you'd let it live?

Few issues today generate as much emotion as abortion. In a study of women's abortion experiences, the sociologist Jennifer Keys (2010) discovered emotional scripts or "feeling rules" that guide how women feel about ending a pregnancy.

Keys explains that different emotional scripts arise from the political controversy surrounding abortion. The anti-abortion movement defines abortion as a personal tragedy, the "killing of an unborn child." Given this definition, which is illustrated in Jen's comment above, women who end a pregnancy through abortion are doing something very wrong and can expect to feel grief, guilt, and regret. So intense are these feelings, according to supporters of this position, that such women often suffer from "post-abortion syndrome."

Those who take the pro-choice position have an opposing view of abortion. From this point of view, illustrated by Liz's comment above, the woman's problem is the *unwanted pregnancy*; abortion is an acceptable medical solution. Therefore, the emotion to be expected in a woman who ends a pregnancy is not guilt but relief.

In her research, Keys conducted in-depth interviews with 40 women who had recently had abortions and found that all of them used such scripts to "frame" their situation in an anti-abortion or pro-choice manner. In part, this construction of reality reflects the woman's own attitude about abortion. In addition, however, women's partners and friends typically encouraged specific feelings about the event. Ivy, one young woman in the study, had a close friend who was also pregnant. "Congratulations!" she exclaimed when she learned of Ivy's condition. "We're going to be having babies together!" Such a statement established one "feeling rule"—having a baby is *good*—which sent the message to Ivy that her planned abortion should trigger guilt. Working in the other direction, Jo's partner was horrified at the news that she was pregnant. Doubting his own ability to be a father, he blurted out, "I would rather put a gun to my head than have this baby!" His panic not only defined having the child as a mistake but also alarmed Jo. Clearly, her partner's reaction made the decision to end the pregnancy a matter of relief from a terrible problem.

Medical personnel also play a part in the process of reality construction by using specific

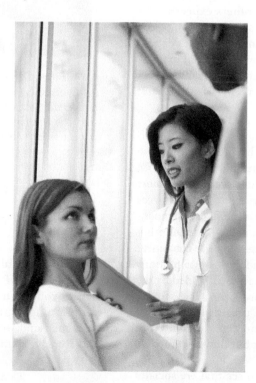

The words that doctors and nurses use guide whether a woman having an abortion defines the experience in positive or negative terms.

terms. Nurses and doctors who talk about "the baby" encourage the anti-abortion framing of abortion and provoke grief and guilt. On the other hand, those who use language such as "pregnancy tissue," "fetus," or "the contents of the uterus" encourage the pro-choice framing of abortion as a simple medical procedure that leads to relief. Olivia began using the phrase "products of conception," which she picked up from her doctor. Denise spoke of her procedure as "taking the extra cells out of my body. Yeah, I did feel some guilt when I thought that this was the beginning of life, but my body is full of life—you have lots of cells in you."

After the procedure, most women reported actively trying to manage their feelings. Explained Ivy, "I never used the word 'baby.' I kept saying to myself that it was not formed yet. There was nothing there yet. I kept that in my mind." On the other hand, Keys found that all of the women in her study who had undergone abortions but nevertheless leaned toward the anti-abortion position did use the term *baby*. When interviewed, Gina explained, "I do think of it as a baby. The truth is that I ended my baby's life and I should not have done that. Thinking that makes me feel guilty. But—considering what I did—maybe I *should* feel guilty." Believing that what she had done was wrong, in other words, Gina actively called out the feeling of guilt—in part, Keys concluded, to punish herself.

WHAT DO YOU THINK?

1. In your own words, explain "emotional scripts" or "feeling rules."
2. Can you apply the idea of "scripting feelings" to the experience of getting married?
3. In light of this discussion, to what extent is it correct to say that our feelings are not as personal as we may think they are?

Source: Keys, 2010.

they are biologically programmed in our facial features, muscles, and central nervous system.

Why? Over centuries of evolution, emotions developed in the human species because they serve a social purpose: supporting group life. Emotions are powerful forces that allow us to overcome our individualism and build connections with others. Thus the capacity for emotion arose in our ancestors along with the capacity for culture (Turner, 2000).

The Cultural Side of Emotions

But culture does play an important role in guiding human emotions. First, Ekman explains, culture defines *what triggers* an emotion. Whether people define the departure of an old friend as joyous (causing happiness), insulting (arousing anger), a loss (creating sadness), or mystical (causing surprise and awe) has a lot to do with the culture. Second, culture provides rules for the *display* of emotions. For example, most people in Canada express emotions more freely with family members than with others in the workplace. Similarly, we expect children to express emotions to parents, although parents tend to be more reserved with their children. Third, culture guides how we *value* emotions. Some societies encourage the expression of emotion, while others expect members to control their feelings and maintain a "stiff upper lip." Gender also plays a part; traditionally, at least, many cultures expect women to show emotions while condemning emotional expression by men as a sign of weakness. In some cultures, of course, this pattern is less pronounced or even reversed (Brody, 1999; Lee, 1999).

Emotions on the Job

In Canada, most people are freer to express their feelings at home than on the job. This is because, as Arlie Russell Hochschild (1979, 1983) explains, the typical corporation or other place of business does indeed try to control not only the behaviour of its employees but also their emotions. Take the case of an airline flight attendant who offers passengers a drink, a snack, and a smile. Do you think that this smile might convey real pleasure at serving the customer? It may. But Hochschild's study of flight attendants points to a different conclusion: The smile is an emotional script demanded by the airline as the right way to do the job. Therefore, from Hochschild's research we see an added dimension of the "presentation of self" described by Erving Goffman. Not only do our everyday life presentations to others involve surface acting but they also involve the "deep acting" of emotions.

With these patterns in mind, it is easy to see that we socially construct our emotions as part of our everyday reality, a process sociologists call *emotion management*. The Controversy & Debate box on page 99 relates the very different emotions displayed by women who decide to have an abortion, depending on their personal view of terminating a pregnancy.

Many of us think emotions are simply part of our biological makeup. While there is a biological foundation to human emotion, sociologists have demonstrated that what triggers an emotion—as well as when, where, and to whom the emotion is displayed—is shaped by culture. For example, many occupations not only regulate a worker's on-the-job behaviour but also expect workers to display a particular emotion, as in the case of the always-smiling airline flight attendant. Can you think of other jobs that regulate emotions in this way?

Language: The Social Construction of Gender

As Chapter 2 ("Culture") explains, language is the thread that weaves members of a society in the symbolic web we call culture. Language conveys not only a surface message but also deeper levels of meaning. One important level involves gender. Language defines men and women differently in terms of both power and value (Henley, Hamilton, & Thorne, 1992; Thorne, Kramarae, & Henley, 1983).

Language and Power

A young man proudly rides his new motorcycle up his friend's driveway and asks, "Isn't she a beauty?" On the surface, the question has little to do with gender. Yet why does he use the pronoun *she* rather than *he* or *it* to refer to his prized possession?

The answer is that language helps men establish control over their surroundings. That is, a man attaches a female pronoun to a motorcycle (or car, boat, or other object) because doing so reflects *ownership*. Perhaps this is also why, in Canada and elsewhere, traditionally a woman who marries takes the last name of her husband. But many women today are asserting their independence by keeping their own name or combining the two family names. Thus, language and power are shaped by social context (Bourdieu, 1993).

Language and Value

Typically, the English language treats as masculine whatever has greater value, force, or significance. For instance, the adjective *virtuous*, meaning "morally worthy" or "excellent," is derived from the Latin word *vir*, meaning "man." On the other hand, the adjective *hysterical*, meaning "emotionally out of control," comes from the Greek word *hyster*, meaning "uterus."

In many familiar ways, language also confers a different value on the two sexes. Traditional masculine terms such as *king* or *lord* have a positive meaning, while comparable terms, such as *queen*, *madam*, or *dame*, can have negative meanings. Similarly, the use of the suffixes *-ess* and *-ette* to indicate femininity usually devalues the words to which they are added. For example, a *major* has higher standing than a *majorette*, as does a *host* in relation to a *hostess* or a *master* to a *mistress*. Thus language both mirrors social attitudes and helps perpetuate them.

Given the importance of gender to social interaction in everyday life, perhaps we should not be surprised that women and men sometimes have trouble communicating with each other.

Reality Play: The Social Construction of Humour

Humour plays an important part in everyday life. Everyone laughs at a joke, but few people think about what makes something funny. Even professors include humour in their performances: Did you hear the one about the two students who slept through their exam because they had been partying too late? They told their professor that they got a flat tire on their way back from visiting their parents in the nearby town. Both were delighted to accept the offer of their considerate professor to write a makeup exam the next day, and went home to study hard that evening. However, they were both a little confused when—seated in two different rooms—they noticed that their exam paper had only one question. Their feeling of confusion was replaced by another feeling when they read the question: "Which tire?"

Although everyone laughs at a joke, few people think about what makes something funny or why humour is a part of people's lives all around the world. We can apply many of the ideas developed

Because humour involves challenging established social conventions, comedians have typically been "outsiders" of some sort. Rick Mercer, originally from "The Rock" (Newfoundland and Labrador), is among the many comics starring on radio and television who use their cultural roots to poke fun at themselves and their audiences. Mercer's *Talking to Americans* shows that some people have a need to speak even when they don't understand the question.

in this chapter to explain how, when we use humour, we "play with reality."

The Foundation of Humour

Humour is produced by the social construction of reality; specifically, it arises as people create and contrast two different realities. Generally, one reality is *conventional*, that is, what people in a specific situation expect. The other reality is *unconventional*, an unexpected violation of cultural patterns. In short, humour arises from the contradictions, ambiguities, and double meanings found in differing definitions of the same situation.

Note how this principle works in one of Woody Allen's lines: "I'm not afraid to die; I just don't want to be there when it happens." Or take the old Czech folk saying: "All mushrooms are edible—but some only once." In these examples, the first thought represents a conventional notion; the second half, however, interjects an unconventional—even absurd—meaning that collides with what we are led to expect.

This same pattern holds true for virtually all humour. Rick Mercer's New Year's resolution to "not stop drinking altogether but to explore light beer as a lunchtime beverage" ends up being not much of a resolution after all.

There are countless ways to mix realities and thereby generate humour. Contrasting realities emerge from statements that contradict themselves, such as "Nostalgia is not what it used to be"; statements that repeat themselves, such as Yogi Berra's line "It's *déjà vu* all over again"; or statements that mix up words, such as Oscar Wilde's line "Work is the curse of the drinking class." Even switching around syllables does the trick, as in the case of the country song "I'd Rather Have a Bottle in Front of Me than a Frontal Lobotomy."

You can also build a joke the other way around, leading the audience to expect an unconventional answer and then delivering a very ordinary one. When a reporter asked the famous criminal Willy Sutton why he robbed banks, for example, he replied dryly, "Because that's where the money is." Regardless of how a joke is constructed, the greater the opposition or difference between the two definitions of reality, the greater the humour.

When telling jokes, the comedian uses various strategies to strengthen this opposition and make the joke funnier. One common technique is to present the first, conventional remark in conversation with another actor but then turn toward the audience or the camera to deliver the second, unexpected line. In a Marx Brothers movie, Groucho remarks, "Outside of a dog, a book is a man's best friend." Then, raising his voice and turning to the camera, he adds, "And *inside* of a dog, it's too dark to read!" Such "changing channels" emphasizes the difference between the conventional and unconventional realities. Following the same logic, many stand-up comedians also "reset" the audience to conventional expectations by adding "But seriously, folks, . . ." between jokes. Monty Python comedian John Cleese did this with his trademark line, "And now for something completely different."

Comedians pay careful attention to their performances—the precise words they use and the timing with which they deliver their lines. A joke is well told if the comic times the lines to create the sharpest possible opposition between the realities; in a careless performance, the joke falls flat. Because the key to humour lies in the collision of realities, we can see why the climax of a joke is termed the "*punch* line."

The Dynamics of Humour: "Getting It"

After hearing a joke, did you ever say, "I don't get it"? To "get" humour, members of an audience must understand the two realities involved well enough to appreciate their difference.

But comics may make getting the joke harder still by leaving out some important information. In other words, the audience must pay attention to the *stated* elements of the joke and fill in the missing pieces on their own. As a simple case, consider Rick

Mercer's comment on the New Democratic Party (NDP) in Canada: "I wanted to work in a political campaign and went with them because, essentially, they'd take anyone." Here, "getting" the joke depends on realizing that the NDP had, until the 2011 federal election, a marginal status in Canada and was therefore not attractive to many volunteers. Or take one of W.C. Fields's lines: "Some weasel took the cork out of my lunch!" "What a lunch!" we think to ourselves to "finish" the joke.

Here is an even more complex joke: What do you get if you cross an insomniac, a dyslexic, and an agnostic? Answer: A person who stays up all night wondering if there is a dog. To get this one, you must know that insomnia is an inability to sleep, that dyslexia causes a person to reverse letters in words, and that an agnostic doubts the existence of God.

Why would a comedian require the audience to make this sort of effort to understand a joke? Our enjoyment of a joke is increased by the pleasure of figuring out all of the pieces needed to "get it." In addition, "getting" the joke makes you an "insider" compared to those who don't get it. We have all experienced the frustration of not getting a joke: fear of being judged stupid, coupled with a sense of being excluded from a pleasure shared by others. Sometimes someone may tactfully explain a joke so the other person doesn't feel left out. But as the old saying goes, if a joke has to be explained, it isn't very funny.

The Topics of Humour

All over the world, people smile and laugh, making humour a universal element of human culture. But because the world's people live in different cultures, humour rarely travels well.

October 1, Kobe, Japan. Can you share a joke with people who live halfway around the world? At dinner, I ask two Japanese college women to tell me a joke. "You know 'crayon'?" Asako asks. I nod. "How do you ask for a crayon in Japanese?" I respond that I have no idea. She laughs out loud as she says what sounds like "crayon crayon." Her companion Mayumi laughs too. My wife and I sit awkwardly, straight-faced. Asako relieves some of our embarrassment by explaining that the Japanese word for "give me" is kureyo, which sounds like "crayon." I force a smile.

What is humorous to the Japanese, then, may be lost on the Finns, Iraqis, or Canadians. To some degree, too, the social diversity of our own country means that people will find humour in different situations. People in Atlantic Canada and the Prairies have their own brands of humour, as do the French and English, 15- and 40-year-olds, investment bankers and construction workers. Aboriginal people and those from visible minority groups also make jokes that get back at people in more advantaged positions.

But for everyone, topics that lend themselves to double meanings or controversy generate humour. For example, in Canada, the first jokes many of us learned as children concerned bodily functions kids are not supposed to talk about. The mere mention of "unmentionable acts" or certain parts of the body can dissolve young faces in laughter.

Are there jokes that can break through the cultural barrier? Yes, but they must touch on universal human experiences such as, say, turning on a friend:

> I think of a number of jokes, but none seems likely to work. Understanding jokes is difficult for people who know little about our culture. Is there something more universal? Inspiration: "Two men are walking in the woods and come upon a huge bear. One guy leans over and tightens up the laces on his running shoes. 'Jake,' says the other, 'what are you doing? You can't outrun that bear!' 'I don't have to outrun the bear,' responds Jake. 'I just have to outrun you!'" Smiles all around.

The controversy found in humour often walks a fine line between what is funny and what is "sick." During the Middle Ages, people used the word *humours* (derived from the Latin *humidus*, meaning "moist") to mean a balance of bodily fluids that regulated a person's health. Researchers today document the power of humour to reduce stress and improve health. One recent study of cancer patients, for example, found that the greater a patient's sense of humour, the greater the odds of surviving the disease. Such findings confirm the old saying "Laughter is the best medicine" (Bakalar, 2005; Sven Svebak, cited in M. Elias, 2007). At the extreme, however, people who always take conventional reality lightly risk being defined as deviant or even mentally ill (a common stereotype shows insane people laughing uncontrollably, and for a long time mental hospitals were known as "funny farms").

Then, too, every social group considers certain topics too sensitive for humorous treatment. If you joke about such things, you risk criticism for telling a "sick" joke (and being labelled "sick" yourself). People's religious beliefs, tragic accidents, or appalling crimes are some of the subjects of "sick" jokes or no jokes at all. Even years later, there have been no jokes about the victims of the September 11, 2001, terrorist attacks.

The Functions of Humour

Humour is found everywhere because it works as a safety valve for potentially disruptive statements and ideas. Put another way, humour provides an acceptable way to discuss a sensitive topic without appearing to be serious or being offensive. Having said something controversial, people often use humour to defuse the situation by simply stating, "I didn't mean anything by what I said—it was just a joke!"

People also use humour to relieve tension in uncomfortable situations. One study of medical examinations found that most

Dave Thomas and Rick Moranis portrayed the stereotypical Canadian hosers Bob and Doug McKenzie in a skit that premiered on *SCTV* in 1980. The comedy is based in making fun of ourselves. But do you think that we would find the same skit funny if it was on an American show with American actors? When people in a category (especially those who have historically been dominant) make fun of people in another category, their humour can easily seem like a "put-down."

patients try to joke with doctors to ease their own nervousness (Baker et al., 1997).

Humour and Conflict

Humour holds the potential to liberate those who laugh, but it can also be used to put down other people. Men who tell jokes about women, for example, are typically expressing some measure of hostility toward them. Similarly, jokes about gay people reveal tensions about sexual orientation. Real conflict can be masked by humour when people choose not to bring the conflict out into the open (Primeggia & Varacalli, 1990).

In turn, disadvantaged people, of course, also make fun of the powerful. Canadian women have long joked about Canadian men, just as French Canadians portray Anglos in humorous ways and poor people poke fun at the rich. Throughout the world, people also target their leaders with humour, and officials in some countries take such jokes seriously enough to arrest those who do not show proper respect (Speier, 1998).

In sum, humour is much more important than we may think. It is a means of mental escape from a conventional world that is not entirely to our liking (Flaherty, 1984, 1990; Yoels & Clair, 1995). This fact helps explain why so many of North American comedians come from the ranks of historically marginalized peoples, including Jews and African-Americans. As long as we maintain a sense of humour, we assert our freedom and are never prisoners of reality. By putting a smile on our faces, we change ourselves and the world just a little and for the better.

CHAPTER 4 SOCIAL INTERACTION IN EVERYDAY LIFE

HOW DO WE ALL CONSTRUCT THE REALITY WE EXPERIENCE? This chapter suggests that Shakespeare may have had it right when he said: "All the world's a stage." And, if so, the internet may be the latest and greatest stage so far. When we use websites such as Facebook, as Goffman explains, we present ourselves as we want others to see us. Everything we write about ourselves as well as how we arrange our page creates an impression in the mind of anyone interested in "checking us out." Take a look at the page shown below, paying careful attention to all of the details. What is the young man explicitly saying about himself? What can you read "between the lines"? That is, what information can you identify that he may be trying to conceal or at least purposely not be mentioning? How honest do you think his "presentation of self" is? Why? Do a similar analysis of the young woman's profile shown on the right.

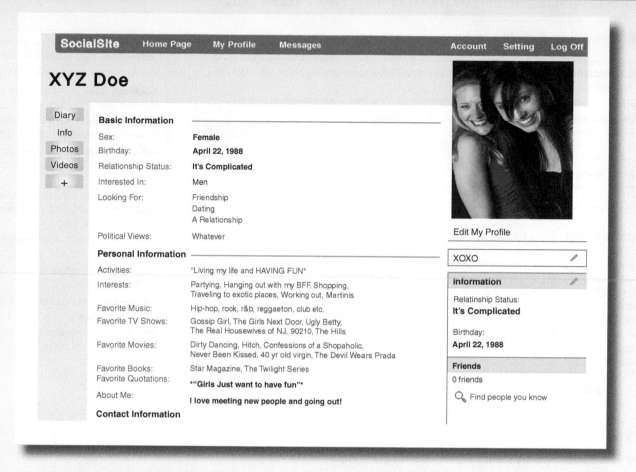

HINT Just about every element of a presentation conveys information about us to others, so all information found on a website like this one is significant. Some information is intentional—for example, what people write about themselves and the photos they choose to post. Other information may be unintentional but is nevertheless picked up by the careful viewer, who may be noting the following things:

- The length and tone of the person's profile (Is it a long-winded list of talents and accomplishments or humorous and modest?)
- The language used (Poor grammar may be a clue to educational level.)
- What hour of the day or night the person wrote the material (A person creating his or her profile at 11:00 P.M. on a Saturday may not be quite the party person he or she describes himself or herself to be.)

Applying Sociology in Everyday Life

1. Identify five important ways in which you present yourself to others, including, for example, the way you decorate your dorm room, apartment, or house; the way you dress; and the way you behave in the classroom. In each case, think about what you are trying to say about yourself. Have your presentations changed in recent years? If so, how, and why?

2. During one full day, every time somebody asks, "How are you?" or "How's it goin'?" stop and actually give a complete, truthful answer.

What happens when you respond to a polite question in an honest way? Listen to how people respond, and also watch their body language. What can you conclude?

3. Stroll around downtown or at a local mall. Pay attention to how many women and men you find at each location. From your observations, are there stores that are "gendered" so that there are "female spaces" and "male spaces"? How and why are spaces "gendered"?

CHAPTER 4 — Social Interaction in Everyday Life

Social Structure: A Guide to Everyday Living

SOCIAL STRUCTURE refers to social patterns that guide our behaviour in everyday life. The building blocks of social structure are
- **STATUS**—a social position that is part of our social identity and that defines our relationships to others
- **ROLE**—the action expected of a person who holds a particular status

pp. 87–90

✓ A person holds a status and performs a role.

A status can be either an

- **ASCRIBED STATUS,** which is involuntary (for example, being a teenager, an orphan, or an Aboriginal person), or an
- **ACHIEVED STATUS,** which is earned (for example, being an honours student, a pilot, or a thief).

p. 88

A **MASTER STATUS,** which can be either ascribed or achieved, has special importance for a person's identity (for example, being blind, a doctor, or a Trudeau).

p. 88

ROLE CONFLICT results from tension among roles linked to two or more statuses (for example, a woman who juggles her responsibilities as a mother and a corporate CEO).

p. 90

ROLE STRAIN results from tension among roles linked to a single status (for example, the professor who enjoys personal interaction with students but at the same time knows that social distance is necessary to evaluate students fairly).

p. 90

social interaction (p. 87) the process by which people act and react in relation to others

status (p. 88) a social position that a person holds

status set (p. 88) all of the statuses a person holds at a given time

ascribed status (p. 88) a social position a person receives at birth or takes on involuntarily later in life

achieved status (p. 88) a social position a person takes on voluntarily that reflects personal ability and effort

master status (p. 88) a status that has special importance for social identity, often shaping a person's entire life

role (p. 89) behaviour expected of someone who holds a particular status

role set (p. 89) a number of roles attached to a single status

role conflict (p. 90) conflict among the roles connected to two or more statuses

role strain (p. 90) tension among the roles connected to a single status

✓ A person's status set changes over the life course (p. 88).

✓ The role sets attached to a single status vary from society to society around the world (pp. 89–90).

The Social Construction of Reality

Through **SOCIAL INTERACTION** , we construct the reality we experience.
- For example, two people interacting both try to shape the reality of their situation.

p. 92

The **THOMAS THEOREM** says that the reality people construct in their interaction has real consequences for the future.
- For example, a teacher who believes a certain student to be intellectually gifted may well encourage exceptional academic performance.

p. 93

ETHNOMETHODOLOGY is a strategy to reveal the assumptions people have about their social world.
- We can expose these assumptions by intentionally breaking the "rules" of social interaction and observing the reactions of other people.

pp. 93–94

Both **CULTURE** and **SOCIAL CLASS** shape the reality people construct.
- For example, a "short walk" for someone from Montreal is a few city blocks, but for a peasant in Latin America it could be a few kilometres.

pp. 94–95

social construction of reality (p. 92) the process by which people creatively shape reality through social interaction

Thomas theorem (p. 93) W.I. Thomas's claim that situations defined as real are real in their consequences

ethnomethodology (p. 93) Harold Garfinkel's term for the study of the way people make sense of their everyday surroundings

✓ Through the social construction of reality, people creatively shape their social world (pp. 92–95).

Dramaturgical Analysis: The "Presentation of Self"

DRAMATURGICAL ANALYSIS explores social interaction in terms of theatrical performance: A status operates as a part in a play and a role is a script.

p. 95

PERFORMANCES are the way we present ourselves to others.
- Performances are both conscious (intentional action) and unconscious (non-verbal communication).
- Performances include costume (the way we dress), props (objects we carry), and demeanour (tone of voice and the way we carry ourselves).

pp. 95–96

GENDER affects performances because men typically have greater social power than women. Gender differences involve demeanour, use of space, and staring, smiling, and touching.

pp. 96–97

dramaturgical analysis (p. 95) Erving Goffman's term for the study of social interaction in terms of theatrical performance

presentation of self (p. 95) Erving Goffman's term for a person's efforts to create specific impressions in the minds of others

non-verbal communication (p. 95) communication using body movements, gestures, and facial expressions rather than speech

personal space (p. 97) the surrounding area over which a person makes some claim to privacy

DEMEANOUR— With greater social power, men have more freedom in how they act.
- USE OF SPACE—Men typically command more space than women.
- STARING and TOUCHING are generally done by men to women.
- SMILING, as a way to please another, is more commonly done by women.

pp. 96–97

IDEALIZATION of performances means we try to convince others that our actions reflect ideal culture rather than selfish motives.

pp. 97–98

EMBARRASSMENT is the "loss of face" in a performance. People use **TACT** to help others "save face."

p. 98

Interaction in Everyday Life: Three Applications

EMOTIONS: The Social Construction of **FEELING** The same basic emotions are biologically programmed into all human beings, but culture guides what triggers emotions, how people display emotions, and how people value emotions. In everyday life, the presentation of self involves managing emotions as well as behaviour.

pp. 98–100

LANGUAGE: The Social Construction of **GENDER** Gender is an important element of everyday interaction. Language defines women and men as different types of people, reflecting the fact that society attaches greater power and value to what is viewed as masculine.

pp. 100–02

REALITY PLAY: The Social Construction of **HUMOUR** Humour results from the difference between conventional and unconventional definitions of a situation. Because humour is a part of culture, people around the world find different situations funny.

pp. 102–04

MySocLab

Visit MySocLab at www.mysoclab.com to access a variety of online resources that will help you to prepare for tests and to apply your knowledge, including
- an eText
- videos
- self-grading quizzes
- glossary flashcards

5 Groups and Organizations

- How do groups affect how we behave?

- Why can "who you know" be as important as "what you know"?

- In what ways have large business organizations changed in recent decades?

This chapter analyzes social groups, both small and large, highlighting the differences between them. Then the focus shifts to formal organizations that carry out various tasks in our modern society and provide most of us with jobs.

With the workday over, Rey and Flor pushed through the doors of the local McDonald's restaurant. "Man, am I hungry," announced Rey, heading right into line. "Look at all the meat I'm gonna eat." But Flor, a recent immigrant from a small village in the Philippines, is surveying the room with a sociological eye. "There is much more than food to see here. This place is all about Canada!"

And so it is, as we shall see. But back in 1948, when the story of McDonald's began, people in Pasadena, California, paid little attention to the opening of a new restaurant by brothers Maurice and Richard McDonald. The McDonald brothers' basic concept, which was soon called "fast food," was to serve meals quickly and cheaply to large numbers of people. The brothers trained employees to do highly specialized jobs: One person grilled hamburgers while others "dressed" them, made french fries, whipped up milkshakes, and handed the food to the customers in assembly-line fashion.

As the years went by, the McDonald brothers prospered, and they opened several more restaurants, including one in San Bernardino. It was there, in 1954, that Ray Kroc, a travelling blender and mixer salesman, paid them a visit.

Kroc was fascinated by the efficiency of the McDonald brothers' system and saw the potential for expanding into a nationwide chain of fast-food restaurants. The three launched the plan as partners. Soon Kroc bought out the McDonalds (who returned to running their original restaurant) and went on to become one of the greatest success stories of all time. Today, McDonald's is one of the mostly widely known brand names in the world, with 32 000 restaurants serving 58 million people daily throughout Canada and in 117 other countries.

The success of McDonald's points to more than just the popularity of hamburgers and french fries. The organizational principles that guide this company are coming to dominate social life in Canada and elsewhere. As Flor correctly observed, this one small business not only transformed the restaurant industry but also changed our way of life.

We begin this chapter by looking at *social groups*, the clusters of people with whom we interact in our daily lives. As you will learn, the scope of group life expanded greatly during the twentieth century. From a world of families, local neighbourhoods, and small businesses, our society now relies on the operation of huge corporations and other bureaucracies that sociologists describe as *formal organizations*. Understanding this expansion of social life and appreciating what it means for us as individuals are the main objectives of this chapter.

Social Groups

Almost everyone wants a sense of belonging, which is the essence of group life. A **social group** is *two or more people who identify with and interact with one another*. Human beings come together as couples, families, circles of friends, sport teams, churches, clubs, businesses, neighbourhoods, and corporations. Whatever the form, groups contain people with shared experiences, loyalties, and interests. While keeping their individuality, members of social groups also think of themselves as a special "we."

Not every collection of individuals forms a group. People with a status in common, such as "punk rocker," "civil servant," "East Asian," or "Nova Scotian," are not a group but a *category*. Though they know that others hold the same status, most are strangers to one another. Similarly, students sitting in a large stadium interact to a very limited extent. Such a loosely formed collection of people in one place is a *crowd* rather than a group.

However, the right circumstances can quickly turn a crowd into a group. Events from terrorist attacks to a policeman at Osgoode Law School in Toronto saying that "women should avoid dressing like sluts in order not to be victimized" can make people bond quickly with strangers.

Primary and Secondary Groups

People often greet one another with a smile and a simple "Hi! How are you?" The response is usually "Fine, thanks. How about you?" This answer is often more scripted than sincere. Explaining how you are *really* doing might make people feel so awkward that they would beat a hasty retreat.

social group (p. 109) two or more people who identify with and interact with one another

primary group a small social group whose members share personal and lasting relationships

secondary group a large and impersonal social group whose members pursue a specific goal or activity

As human beings, we live our lives as members of groups. Such groups may be large or small, temporary or long-lasting, and can be based on kinship, cultural heritage, or some shared interest.

Social groups are of two types, based on their members' degree of genuine personal concern for one another. According to sociologist Charles Horton Cooley (introduced in Chapter 3, p. 68), a **primary group** is *a small social group whose members share personal and lasting relationships*. Joined by *primary relationships*, people spend a great deal of time together, engage in a wide range of activities, and feel that they know one another pretty well. In short, they show real concern for one another. Cooley called personal and tightly integrated groups "primary" because they are among the first groups we experience in life. While family and friends have primary importance in the socialization process, shaping our attitudes, behaviour, and social identity, sociologists agree that the family is every society's most important primary group.

Members of primary groups help one another in many ways, but they generally think of their group as an end in itself rather than as a means to other ends. In other words, we tend to think that family and friendship link people who "belong together." Members of a primary group also tend to view each other as unique and irreplaceable. Especially in the family, we are bound to others by emotion and loyalty. Brothers and sisters may not always get along, but they always remain "family."

In contrast to the primary group, the **secondary group** is *a large and impersonal social group whose members pursue a specific goal or activity*. In most respects, secondary groups have characteristics opposite those of primary groups. *Secondary relationships* involve weak emotional ties and little personal knowledge of one another. Many

secondary groups exist for only a short time, beginning and ending without particular significance. Students enrolled in the same course at a large university or people walking together on a "slut walk[1]"—people who may or may not see one another after the semester or the walk ends—are examples of secondary groups.

Secondary groups include many more people than primary groups. For example, dozens or even hundreds of people may work for the same company, yet most of them pay only passing attention to one another. Sometimes the passage of time transforms a group from secondary to primary, as with co-workers who share an office for many years and develop closer relationships. But generally, members of a secondary group do not think of themselves as "we." Secondary ties need not be hostile or cold, of course. Interactions among students, co-workers, sports team members, and business associates are often quite pleasant even if they are impersonal.

Unlike members of primary groups, who display a *personal orientation*, people in secondary groups have a *goal orientation*. Primary group members define each other according to *who* they are in terms of family ties or personal qualities, but people in secondary groups look to one another for *what* they are—that is, what they can do for each other. In secondary groups, we tend to "keep score," aware of what we give others and what we receive in return. This goal orientation means that secondary group members usually remain formal and polite. It is in a secondary relationship, therefore, that we ask the question "How are you?" without expecting a truthful answer.

The Summing Up table on page 111 reviews the characteristics of primary and secondary groups. Keep in mind that these traits define two types of groups in ideal terms; most real groups contain elements of both. For example, a women's group on a university campus may be quite large (and therefore secondary), but its members may identify strongly with one another and provide a lot of mutual support (making it seem primary).

Are some regions of Canada more primary in character than others? Many people think that small towns and rural areas emphasize primary relationships and that large cities are characterized by secondary ties. This generalization holds some truth, but some urban neighbourhoods, especially those populated by people of a single ethnic or religious category, can be very tightly knit.

The internet may be helping Canadians to redefine their social interactions and even to start new relationships via the web. Almost 90 percent of Canadian teenagers have used the internet to participate in an online social activity (Ipsos Reid, 2008c). Other studies show that Canadians are increasingly using the internet to remain in contact with family and friends (Zamaria & Fletcher, 2008).

---

[1]The social movement began in Toronto after a male police officer told a group of female university students to stop "dressing like sluts" if they didn't want to be raped. The movement caused women to take to the streets and spread to cities around the world, demonstrating their anger with being treated as sexual objects and intimidated into sexual conformity.

SUMMING UP		
Primary Groups and Secondary Groups		
	Primary Group ◄————————►	**Secondary Group**
Quality of relationships	Personal orientation	Goal orientation
Duration of relationships	Usually long term	Variable; often short term
Breadth of relationships	Broad; usually involving many activities	Narrow; usually involving few activities
Perception of relationships	Ends in themselves	Means to an end
Examples	Families, circles of friends	Co-workers, political organizations

Group Leadership

How do groups operate? One important element of group dynamics is leadership. Although a small circle of friends may have no leader at all, most large secondary groups place leaders in a formal chain of command.

Two Leadership Roles

Groups typically benefit from two kinds of leadership. **Instrumental leadership** refers to *group leadership that focuses on the completion of tasks*. Members look to instrumental leaders to make plans, give orders, and get things done. **Expressive leadership**, by contrast, is *group leadership that focuses on the group's well-being*. Expressive leaders take less of an interest in achieving goals and focus on promoting the well-being of members and minimizing tension and conflict among members.

Because they concentrate on performance, instrumental leaders usually have formal, secondary relationships with other members. These leaders give orders and reward or punish people according to how much they contribute to the group's efforts. Expressive leaders build more personal, primary ties. They offer sympathy to members going through tough times, keep the group united, and lighten serious moments with humour. Typically, successful instrumental leaders enjoy more *respect* from members and expressive leaders generally receive more personal *affection*.

Three Leadership Styles

Sociologists also describe leadership in terms of its decision-making style. *Authoritarian leadership* focuses on instrumental concerns, takes personal charge of decision making, and demands that group members obey orders. Although this leadership style may win little affection from the group, a fast-acting authoritarian leader is appreciated in a crisis.

Democratic leadership is more expressive, making a point of including everyone in the decision-making process. Although less successful in a crisis situation, when there is little time for discussion, democratic leaders generally draw on the ideas of all members to develop creative solutions to problems.

Laissez-faire leadership allows the group to function more or less on its own (*laissez-faire* in French means "leave it alone"). This style is typically the least effective in promoting group goals (Eagly, Johannesen-Schmidt, & van Engen, 2003; Ridgeway, 1983; White & Lippitt, 1953).

In the earliest types of societies, the same person combined several elements of leadership. In patriarchal societies, such as nineteenth- and early twentieth-century Canada, conventional cultural norms bestowed authoritarian leadership on men. As family "breadwinners" and "heads," men assumed primary responsibility for bringing in family income, made major decisions, and disciplined children, a responsibility that was strongly endorsed by the Canadian government of the time (Benoit, 2000a; Christie, 2000). Women were assigned a democratic leadership role, with the expectation that they would lend family members emotional support and maintain peaceful family relationships. Greater equality between men and women has blended the gender-based distinction between authoritarian and democratic leadership. Yet recent research shows that women's leadership styles still tend to be more democratic than men's, which is possibly due to female leaders' continuing struggle for legitimacy if they attempt to lead in an authoritarian manner (Eagly & Johannesen-Schmidt, 2001).

Group Conformity

Groups influence the behaviour of their members, often promoting conformity. "Fitting in" provides a secure feeling of belonging, but at the extreme, group pressure can be unpleasant and even dangerous. Interestingly, as experiments by Solomon Asch and Stanley Milgram showed, even strangers can encourage group conformity.

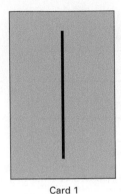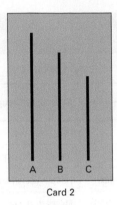

Card 1 Card 2

FIGURE 5–1 Cards Used in Asch's Experiment in Group Conformity

In Asch's experiment, subjects were asked to match the line on Card 1 to one of the lines on Card 2. Many subjects agreed with the wrong answers given by others in their group.

Source: Asch (1952).

Asch's Research

Solomon Asch (1952) recruited students for what he told them was a study of visual perception. Before the experiment began, he explained to all but one member of a small group that their real purpose was to put pressure on the remaining person. Placing six to eight students around a table, Asch showed them a "standard" line, as drawn on Card 1 in Figure 5–1, and asked them to match it to one of the three lines on Card 2.

Anyone with normal vision can see that the line marked "A" on Card 2 is the correct choice. Initially, as planned, everyone made the matches correctly. But then Asch's secret accomplices began answering incorrectly, leaving the uninformed student (seated at the table so as to answer next to last) bewildered and uncomfortable.

What happened? Asch found that one-third of all subjects chose to conform by answering incorrectly. Apparently, many of us are willing to compromise our own judgment to avoid the discomfort of being different, even from people we do not know.

Milgram's Research

Stanley Milgram, a former student of Solomon Asch's, conducted conformity experiments of his own. In Milgram's controversial study (1963, 1965; A.G. Miller, 1986), a researcher explained to male recruits that they would be taking part in a study of how punishment affects learning. One by one, he assigned them to the role of teacher and placed another person—actually an accomplice of Milgram's—in a connecting room to pose as a learner.

The teacher watched as the learner sat down in what looked like an electric chair. The researcher applied electrode paste to one of the learner's wrists, explaining that this would "prevent blisters and burns." The researcher then attached an electrode to the wrist and secured the leather straps, explaining that they would "prevent excessive movement while the learner was being shocked." Although the shocks would be painful, the researcher reassured the teacher that they would cause "no permanent tissue damage."

The researcher then led the teacher back into the adjoining room, pointing out that the "electric chair" was connected to a "shock generator," actually a phony but realistic-looking piece of equipment with a label that read "Shock Generator, Type ZLB, Dyson Instrument Company, Waltham, Mass." On the front was a dial that supposedly regulated electric current from 15 volts (labelled "Slight Shock") to 300 volts ("Intense Shock") to 450 volts ("Danger: Severe Shock").

Seated in front of the "shock generator," the teacher was told to read aloud pairs of words. Then the teacher was to repeat the first word of each pair and wait for the learner to recall the second word. Whenever the learner failed to answer correctly, the teacher was told to apply an electric shock.

The researcher directed the teacher to begin at the lowest level (15 volts) and to increase the shock by 15 volts every time the learner made a mistake. And so the teacher did. At 75, 90, and 105 volts, the teacher heard moans from the learner; at 120 volts, shouts of pain; by 270 volts, screams; at 315 volts, pounding on the wall; after that, dead silence. Only a few of the 40 subjects assigned to the role of teacher during the initial research even questioned the procedure before reaching the dangerous level of 300 volts, and 26 of the subjects—almost two-thirds—went all the way to the potentially lethal 450 volts. Even Milgram was surprised at how readily people obeyed authority figures.

Milgram (1964) then modified his research to see whether ordinary people—not authority figures—could pressure strangers to administer electrical shocks, in the same way that Asch's groups had pressured individuals to match lines incorrectly.

This time, Milgram formed a group of three teachers, two of whom were his accomplices. Each of the teachers was to suggest a shock level when the learner made an error; the rule was that the group would then administer the *lowest* of the three suggested levels. This arrangement gave the person who was not in on the experiment the power to deliver a lesser shock regardless of what the others said.

The accomplices suggested increasing the shock level with each error the learner made, putting pressure on the third person to do the same. The subjects in these groups applied voltages three to four times higher than those applied by subjects acting alone. Thus Milgram's research suggests that people are likely to follow the directions not only of legitimate authority figures but also of groups of ordinary individuals, even if doing so means harming another person.

A perceived security threat from demonstrators led to police groupthink behaviour during the G20 meeting in Toronto in 2010.

Janis's "Groupthink"

Experts also cave in to group pressure, says Irving Janis (1972, 1989). Janis argues that a number of U.S. foreign policy blunders, including the failure to foresee the Japanese attack on Pearl Harbor during World War II and the country's ill-fated involvement in the Vietnam War, resulted from group conformity among the highest-ranking American political leaders. A Canadian example of group conformity among political leaders happened in December 2010, when provincial and federal politicians spent millions, allegedly for the G20 meeting in Toronto even though the expenditures were totally unrelated.

Common sense tells us that group discussion improves decision making. Janis counters that group members often seek agreement that closes off other points of view. Janis called this process **groupthink**, *the tendency of group members to conform, resulting in a narrow view of some issue.*

A classic example of groupthink resulted in the disastrous American invasion of the Bay of Pigs in Cuba in 1961. Looking back, Arthur Schlesinger Jr., an adviser to President John F. Kennedy at the time, confessed feeling guilty "for having kept so quiet during those crucial discussions in the Cabinet Room," adding that the group discouraged anyone from challenging what, in hindsight, Schlesinger considered "nonsense" (quoted in Janis, 1972:30, 40). Groupthink may also have been a factor in the American invasion of Iraq in 2003, when American leaders were led to believe—erroneously—that Iraq had stockpiles of weapons of mass destruction. Interestingly, many of the United States' foreign allies, including Canada, did not support either of these two decisions.

Reference Groups

How do we assess our own attitudes and behaviour? Frequently, we use a **reference group**, *a social group that serves as a point of reference in making evaluations and decisions.*

A young man who imagines his family's response to a woman he is dating is using his family as a reference group. A supervisor who tries to predict her employees' reaction to a new vacation policy is using them in the same way. As these examples suggest, reference groups can be primary or secondary. In either case, our need to conform shows how others' attitudes affect us.

We also use groups we do *not* belong to for reference. Being well prepared for a job interview means showing up dressed the way people in that company dress for work. Conforming to groups we do not belong to is a strategy to win acceptance and illustrates the process of *anticipatory socialization*, described in Chapter 3 ("Socialization: From Infancy to Old Age").

Stouffer's Research

Samuel Stouffer and his colleagues (1949) conducted a classic study of reference groups during World War II. Researchers asked soldiers to rate their own, or any competent soldier's, chances of promotion in their army unit. You might guess that soldiers serving in outfits with high promotion rates would be optimistic about advancement. Yet Stouffer's research pointed to the opposite conclusion: Soldiers in army units with low promotion rates were actually more positive about their chances to move ahead.

The key to understanding Stouffer's results lies in the groups against which soldiers measured themselves. Those assigned to units with lower promotion rates looked around them and saw people making no more headway than they were. Although they had not been promoted, neither had many others, so they did not feel deprived. However, soldiers in units with higher promotion rates could think of many people who had been promoted sooner or more often than they had. With such people in mind, even soldiers who had been promoted themselves were likely to feel shortchanged.

The point is that we do not make judgments about ourselves in isolation, nor do we compare ourselves with just anyone. Regardless of our situation in *absolute* terms, we form a subjective sense of our well-being by looking at ourselves *relative* to specific reference groups (Merton, 1968; Mirowsky, 1987).

In-Groups and Out-Groups

Each of us favours some groups over others, whether because of political outlook, social prestige, or just manner of dress. On some university campuses, for example, left-leaning student activists may look down on fraternity members, whom they view as conservative; fraternity members, in turn, may snub the "nerds" who work too

in-group a social group toward which a member feels respect and loyalty

out-group a social group toward which a person feels a sense of competition or opposition

dyad a social group with two members

triad a social group with three members

hard. People in just about every social setting make similar positive and negative evaluations of members of other groups.

Such judgments illustrate another key element of group dynamics: the opposition of in-groups and out-groups. An **in-group** is *a social group toward which a member feels respect and loyalty*. An **out-group**, by contrast, is *a social group toward which a person feels a sense of competition or opposition*. In-groups and out-groups are based on the idea that "we" have valued traits that "they" lack.

Tensions between groups sharpen the groups' boundaries and give people a clearer social identity. However, members of in-groups generally hold overly positive views of themselves and unfairly negative views of various out-groups.

Power also plays a part in intergroup relations. A powerful in-group can define others as a lower-status out-group. Historically, colonial settler populations in countries such as Canada and Australia viewed the original Aboriginal inhabitants as an out-group and subordinated them socially, politically, and economically. Internalizing these negative attitudes, Aboriginal peoples have struggled to overcome negative self-images (Kaplan-Myrth, 2005). In this way, in-groups and out-groups foster loyalty but also generate conflict (Bobo & Hutchings, 1996; Tajfel, 1982).

Group Size

The next time you go to a party, try to arrive first. If you do, you will be able to observe some fascinating group dynamics. Until about six people enter the room, every person who arrives usually joins in a single conversation. As more people arrive, the group divides into two or more clusters, and it divides again and again as the party grows. This process shows that group size plays a crucial role in how group members interact.

To understand why, note the mathematical number of relationships possible among two to seven people. As shown in Figure 5–2, two people form a single relationship; adding a third person results in three relationships; a fourth person yields six. Increasing the number of people further boosts the number of relationships much more rapidly because every new individual can interact with everyone already there. Thus by the time seven people join one conversation, 21 "channels" connect them. With so many open channels, at this point the group usually divides into smaller conversation groups.

The Dyad

The German sociologist Georg Simmel (1858–1918) explored the dynamics in the smallest social groups. Simmel (1950, orig. 1902) used the term **dyad** (Greek for "pair") to designate *a social group with two members*. Simmel explained that social interaction in a dyad is typically more intense than in larger groups because neither member must share the other's attention with anyone else. In Canada, love affairs, marriages, and the closest friendships are dyadic.

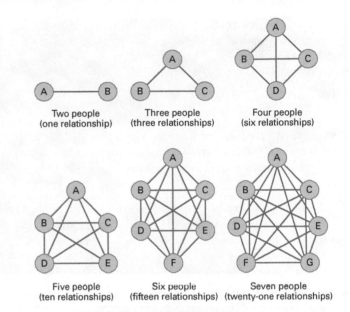

FIGURE 5–2 Group Size and Relationships

As the number of people in a group increases, the number of relationships that link them increases much faster. By the time six or seven people share a conversation, the group usually divides into two. Why are relationships in smaller groups typically more intense?

But like a stool with only two legs, dyads are unstable. Both members of a dyad must work to keep the relationship going; if either withdraws, the group collapses. To make marriage more stable, society supports the marital dyad with legal, economic, and often religious ties.

The Triad

Simmel also studied the **triad**, *a social group with three members*. A triad contains three relationships, each of which unites two of the three people. A triad is more stable than a dyad because one member can act as a mediator if relations between the other two become strained. This analysis of group dynamics helps explain why members of a dyad (say, intimate partners having conflict) often seek out a third person (such as a therapist) to discuss tensions between them.

On the other hand, two of the three can pair up to press their views on the third, or two may intensify their relationship, leaving the other feeling left out. For example, when two of the three members of a triad develop a romantic interest in each other, they will come to understand the meaning of the old saying, "Two's company, three's a crowd."

As groups grow beyond three people, they become more stable and capable of withstanding the loss of one or more members. At the same time, increases in group size reduce the intense interaction possible in only the smallest groups. This is why larger groups are based less on personal attachments and more on formal rules and regulations.

Social Diversity: Race, Class, and Gender

Race, ethnicity, class, and gender each play a part in group dynamics. Peter Blau (1977; Blau, Blum, & Schwartz, 1982; South & Messner, 1986) points out three ways in which social diversity influences intergroup contact:

1. **Large groups turn inward.** Blau explains that the larger a group is, the more likely its members are to concentrate relationships among themselves. Say that a university is trying to enhance social diversity by increasing the number of international students. These students may add a dimension of difference, but as their numbers rise they become more likely to form their own social group. Thus efforts to promote social diversity may have the unintended effect of promoting separatism.

2. **Heterogeneous groups turn outward.** If you look at the various ethnic groups in your community, you are likely to find that those with a longer history in Canada are more heterogeneous and more likely to interact with others than are recent arrivals. Immigrants to Canada tend to settle in our major cities. This is one reason that residents of Montreal and Vancouver have more intergroup contact than residents of small towns and outports, which comprise people of only one or a few types.

3. **Physical boundaries create social boundaries.** To the extent that a social group is physically segregated from others (by having its own dorm or dining area, for example), its members are less likely to interact with other people. Military families in Canada and elsewhere serve as an example. As Deborah Harrison and Lucie Laliberté (1994:21) point out, "[T]he military is a portable total institution that isolates its members from civilians. . . . As in the case of other total institutions, isolation from civilians facilitates control." One result has been concealment of abuse and violence by dominant members of the in-group against those with less power (Harrison, 2006).

Networks

A **network** is *a web of weak social ties.* Think of a network as a "fuzzy" group containing people who come into occasional contact but lack a sense of boundaries and belonging. If you think of a *group* as a "circle of friends," think of a *network* as a "social web" expanding outward, often reaching great distances and including large numbers of people.

The triad, illustrated by Jonathan Green's painting *Friends*, includes three people. A triad is more stable than a dyad because conflict between any two persons can be mediated by the third member. Even so, should the relationship between any two become more intense in a positive sense, those two are likely to exclude the third.

Jonathan Green, *Friends*, 1992. Oil on masonite, 14 in. x 11 in. © Jonathan Green. http://www.jonathangreenstudios.com

The largest network of all is the World Wide Web. But the internet has expanded much more in some global regions than in others. Global Map 5–1 on page 116 shows that internet use is high in high-income countries and far less common in low-income nations.

Some networks come close to being groups, as in the case of university friends who stay in touch years after graduation by email and telephone. More commonly, however, a network includes people we know of or who know of us but with whom we interact rarely, if at all. As one woman known as a community organizer puts it, "I get calls at home, [and] someone says, 'Are you Roseann Navarro? Somebody told me to call you. I have this problem . . .'" (Kaminer, 1984:94).

Network ties often give us the sense that we live in a "small world." In a classic experiment, Stanley Milgram (1967; Watts, 1999)

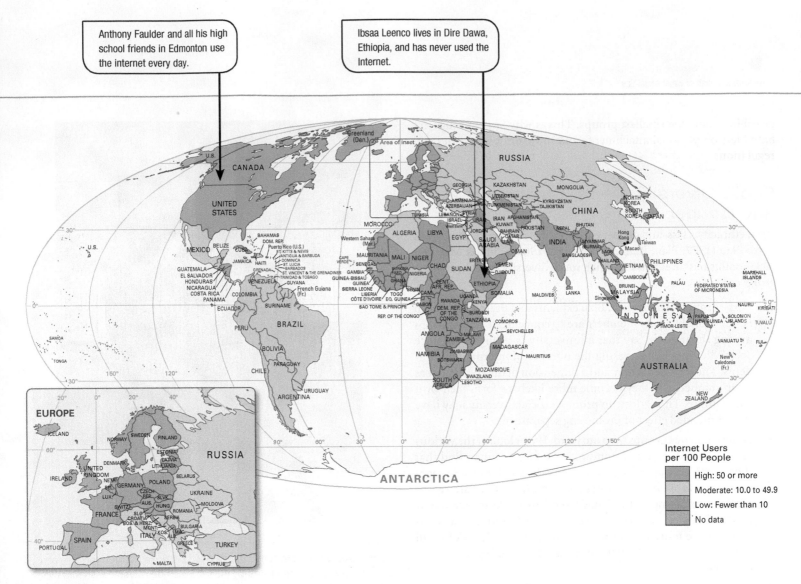

Window on the World

GLOBAL MAP 5–1 **Internet Users in Global Perspective**

This map shows how the Information Revolution has affected countries around the world. In most high-income nations, at least one-third of the population uses the internet. By contrast, only a small share of people in low-income nations does so. What effect does this pattern have on people's access to information? What does this mean for the future in terms of global inequality?

Source: International Telecommunication Union (2010).

gave letters to subjects in Kansas and Nebraska intended for specific people in Boston who were unknown to the original subjects. No addresses were given, and the subjects in the study were told to send the letters to others they knew personally who might know the target people. Milgram found that the target people received the letters with, on average, six people passing them on. This result led Milgram to claim that everyone is connected to everyone else by "six degrees of separation." Later research, however, has cast doubt on Milgram's claim. Examining Milgram's original data, Judith

Kleinfeld noted that most of Milgram's letters (240 out of 300) never arrived at all (Wildavsky, 2002). Most of those that did reach their destination had been given to people who were wealthy, a fact that led Kleinfeld to conclude that rich people are better connected across the country than ordinary men and women.

Network ties may be weak, but they can be a powerful resource. For immigrants trying to become established in a new community, business people seeking to expand their operations, or new university and college graduates looking for a job, *whom* you know often is

formal organizations a large secondary group organized to achieve its goals efficiently

just as important as *what* you know (Hagan, 1998; Petersen, Saporta, & Seidel, 2000).

Networks are based on people's educational institutions, clubs, neighbourhoods, political parties, religious organizations, and personal interests. Obviously, some networks are made up of people with more wealth, power, and prestige than others; that explains the importance of being "well connected." The networks of more privileged categories of people—such as the members of the prestigious Royal Society of Canada—are a valuable form of "social capital," which is more likely to lead people in these categories to higher-paying jobs (Green, Tigges, & Diaz, 1999; Lin, Cook, & Burt, 2001).

Some people also have denser networks than others; that is, they are connected to more people. Typically, the largest social networks include people who are young, well educated, and living in large cities (Fernandez & Weinberg, 1997; Podolny & Baron, 1997). Some researchers go further; rather than studying geographical communities, such as neighbourhoods, they study social networks or ties that members use to gain resources, and call these "communities" (Chen & Wellman, 2009; Wellman, 1999).

Gender also shapes networks. Although the networks of men and women are typically of the same size, women include more relatives (and more women) in their networks, and men include more co-workers (and more men). Women's ties, therefore, may not be quite as powerful as typical "old boy" networks. But research suggests that as gender equality increases, the networks of men and women are becoming more alike (Reskin & McBrier, 2000; Torres & Huffman, 2002).

Formal Organizations

As noted earlier, a century ago, most people lived in small groups of family, friends, and neighbours. Today, our lives revolve more and more around **formal organizations**, *large secondary groups organized to achieve their goals efficiently.* Formal organizations such as corporations and government agencies differ from small primary groups in their impersonality and their formally planned atmosphere.

When you think about it, organizing the more than 34.4 million members of Canadian society is truly remarkable, whether it involves paving roads, collecting taxes, schooling children, or delivering the mail. To carry out most of these tasks, we rely on large formal organizations.

Types of Formal Organizations

Amitai Etzioni (1975) identified three types of formal organizations, distinguished by the reasons people participate in them: utilitarian organizations, normative organizations, and coercive organizations.

Utilitarian Organizations

Just about everyone who works for income belongs to a *utilitarian organization*, one that pays people for their efforts. Becoming part

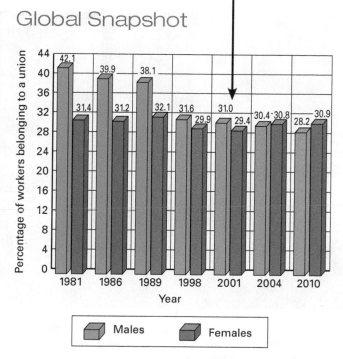

Until the early 2000s males were more likely than females to belong to a union.

Global Snapshot

FIGURE 5–3   Union Membership, Canada, 1981–2010

Source: Morrisette, Schellenberg, & Johnson (2005); Uppal (2010).

of a utilitarian organization—a business, government agency, or school system, for example—is usually a matter of individual choice, although most people must join one or another such organization to make a living. Figure 5–3 shows that union membership declined by almost 30 percent for Canadian males between 1981 (42.1 percent) and 2010 (28.2 percent), while union membership remained relatively constant for females.

Normative Organizations

People join *normative organizations* not for income but to pursue some goal they think is morally worthwhile. Sometimes called *voluntary associations*, these include community service groups (such as the Canadian International Development Agency [CIDA], the Lions Club, the Status of Women Canada, the Red Cross, or the whites-only organization Stormfront), political parties, and religious organizations. In global perspective, people in Canada and other high-income countries are most likely to join voluntary associations. A recent Canadian survey found that young people (aged 15 to 24) had the highest participation in volunteering (58% compared to 46% of all respondents) (Hall, Lasby, Ayer, & Gibbons, 2009; see also Curtis, Baer, & Grabb, 2001; Schofer & Fourcade-Gourinchas, 2001).

tradition values and beliefs passed from generation to generation

rationality a way of thinking that emphasizes deliberate, matter-of-fact calculation of the most efficient way to accomplish a particular task

rationalization of society the historical change from tradition to rationality as the main type of human thought

bureaucracy an organizational model rationally designed to perform tasks efficiently

Weber described the operation of the ideal bureaucracy as rational and highly efficient. In real life, actual large organizations often operate very differently from Weber's model, as can be seen on the television show *The Office*.

pre-industrial societies they were trying to rule had traditional cultures. **Tradition**, according to the German sociologist Max Weber, consists of *values and beliefs passed from generation to generation*. Tradition makes a society conservative, Weber explained, because it limits an organization's efficiency and ability to change.

By contrast, Weber described the modern world view as **rationality**, *a way of thinking that emphasizes deliberate, matter-of-fact calculation of the most efficient way to accomplish a particular task*. A rational world view pays little attention to the past and is open to any changes that might get the job done better or more quickly.

The rise of the "organizational society" rests on what Weber called the **rationalization of society**, *the historical change from tradition to rationality as the main type of human thought*. Modern society, he claimed, becomes "disenchanted" as sentimental ties give way to a rational focus on science, complex technology, and the organizational structure called bureaucracy.

Coercive Organizations

Coercive organizations have involuntary memberships. People are forced to join these organizations as a form of punishment (prisons) or treatment (some psychiatric hospitals). Coercive organizations have special physical features, such as locked doors and barred windows, and are supervised by security personnel. They isolate people (whom they label "inmates" or "patients") for a period of time to radically change their attitudes and behaviour. Recall from Chapter 3 ("Socialization: From Infancy to Old Age") the power of a total institution to change a person's sense of self.

It is possible for a single formal organization to fall into *all* of these categories from the point of view of different individuals. For example, a mental hospital serves as a coercive organization for a patient, a utilitarian organization for a psychiatrist, and a normative organization for a hospital volunteer.

Origins of Formal Organizations

Formal organizations date back thousands of years. Elites who controlled early empires relied on government officials to collect taxes, undertake military campaigns, and build monumental structures, from the Great Wall of China to the pyramids of Egypt.

However, early organizations had two limitations. First, they lacked the technology to travel over large distances, to communicate quickly, and to gather and store information. Second, the

Characteristics of Bureaucracy

Bureaucracy is *an organizational model rationally designed to perform tasks efficiently*. Bureaucratic officials regularly create and revise policy to increase efficiency. To appreciate the power and scope of bureaucratic organization, consider that a phone in the 67 percent of Canadian households that have a traditional land line plus the cellphone owned by 78 percent of Canadian households can connect within seconds to any other phone in a home, a business, an automobile, or even a hiker's backpack on a remote trail in the Rocky Mountains. Such instant communication is beyond the imagination of people who lived in the ancient world.

Our telephone system depends on technology such as electricity, fibre optics, and computers. But the system could not exist without the organizational capacity to keep track of every telephone call—recording which phone called which other phone, when, and for how long—and presenting all of this information to millions of telephone users in the form of a monthly bill (Statistics Canada, 2011f).

What specific traits promote organizational efficiency? Max Weber (1978, orig. 1921) identified six key elements of the ideal bureaucratic organization:

1. **Specialization.** Our ancestors spent most of their time looking for food and finding shelter. Bureaucracy, by contrast, assigns individuals highly specialized jobs.

SUMMING UP		
Small Groups and Formal Organizations		
	Small Groups	**Formal Organizations**
Activities	Much the same for all members	Distinct and highly specialized
Hierarchy	Often informal or non-existent	Clearly defined according to position
Norms	General norms, informally applied	Clearly defined rules and regulations
Membership criteria	Variable; often based on personal affection or kinship	Technical competence to carry out assigned tasks
Relationships	Variable and typically primary	Typically secondary, with selective primary ties
Communications	Typically casual and face to face	Typically formal and in writing
Focus	Person oriented	Task oriented

2. **Hierarchy of offices.** Bureaucracies arrange workers in a vertical ranking. Each person is thus supervised by someone "higher up" in the organization while in turn supervising others in lower positions. Usually, with few people at the top and many at the bottom, bureaucratic organizations take the form of a pyramid.

3. **Rules and regulations.** Rationally enacted rules and regulations guide a bureaucracy's operation. Ideally, a bureaucracy seeks to operate in a completely predictable way.

4. **Technical competence.** Bureaucratic officials have the technical competence to carry out their duties. Bureaucracies typically hire new members according to set standards and then monitor their performance. Such impersonal evaluation contrasts with the ancient custom of favouring relatives, whatever their talents, over strangers.

5. **Impersonality.** Bureaucracy puts rules ahead of personal whim so that both clients and workers are all treated in the same way. From this impersonal approach comes the commonplace image of the "faceless bureaucrat."

6. **Formal, written communications.** It is often said that the heart of bureaucracy is not people but paperwork. Rather than casual, face-to-face talk, bureaucracy depends on formal, written memos and reports, which accumulate in vast files.

Bureaucratic organization promotes efficiency by carefully hiring workers and limiting the unpredictable effects of personal taste and opinion. The Summing Up table reviews the differences between small social groups and large formal organizations.

Organizational Environment

All organizations exist in the larger world. How well any organization performs depends not only on its own goals and policies but also on the **organizational environment**, *factors outside an organization that affect its operation.* These factors include technology, economic and political trends, current events, the available workforce, population patterns, and other organizations.

Modern organizations are shaped by *technology,* including copiers, telephones, and computer equipment. Computers give employees access to more information and people than ever before. At the same time, computer technology allows managers to closely monitor the activities of workers (Markoff, 1991).

Economic and political trends affect organizations. All organizations are helped or hurt by periodic economic growth or recession. Most industries also face competition from abroad as well as changes in laws—such as new environmental standards—at home.

Current events can have significant effects even on organizations that are far away. Events such as the rise in energy prices that followed the 2010 *Deepwater Horizon* oil spill in the Gulf of Mexico, the uprisings in Egypt and Libya in 2011, and the 2011 federal election that gave majority power to Stephen Harper and the Conservative Party affected the operation of both government and business organizations.

Population patterns also affect organizations. The average age, typical level of education, social diversity, and size of a local community determine the available workforce and sometimes the market for an organization's products or services.

Other organizations also contribute to the organizational environment. To be competitive, a hospital in Canada must keep open lines of communication with provincial medical, nursing, and allied workers' professional associations and unions, abide by federal laws governing the health care system, and work with regional health boards attempting to balance increasing public demands for quality health services and limited annual budgets (Armstrong & Armstrong, 1996, 2002; Segall & Fries, 2011).

The Informal Side of Bureaucracy

Weber's ideal bureaucracy deliberately regulates every activity. In real-life organizations, however, human beings are creative (and stubborn) enough to resist bureaucratic regulation. Informality may amount to cutting corners on the job at times, but it can also provide the flexibility needed for an organization to adapt and be successful.

In part, informality comes from the personalities of organizational leaders. Studies of Canadian and American corporations document that the qualities and quirks of individuals—including personal charisma, interpersonal skills, and the ability to recognize problems—can have a great effect on organizational performance (Baron, Hannan, & Burton, 1999; Halberstam, 1986; Zhang & Bruning, 2011). Authoritarian, democratic, and laissez-faire types of leadership (described earlier in this chapter) reflect individual personality as much as any organizational plan. Then, too, in the "real world" of organizations, leaders sometimes seek to benefit personally through abuse of organizational power. Many of the corporate leaders of banks and insurance companies that collapsed during the North American financial meltdown of 2008 walked away with multi-million-dollar "golden parachutes." More commonly, leaders take credit for the efforts of the people who work for them. For example, the responsibilities—and authority—of many secretaries and other front-line service workers are far greater than their official job titles and salaries suggest (Drew, Mills, & Gassaway, 2007).

Communication offers another example of organizational informality. Memos and other written documents are the formal way to spread information through the organization. Typically, however, people create informal networks, or "grapevines," that spread information quickly, if not always accurately. Grapevines, using word of mouth and email, are particularly important to rank-and-file workers because higher-ups often try to keep important information from them.

The spread of email has "flattened" organizations somewhat, allowing even the lowest-ranking employee to bypass immediate superiors to communicate directly with the organization's leader or all fellow employees at once. Some organizations consider such "open channel" communication unwelcome and limit the use of email. Leaders may also seek to protect themselves from a flood of messages each day. Microsoft Corporation founder Bill Gates, who supposedly has the email address billg@microsoft.com, is unlikely to be the first person who reads messages sent to that address. Using new information technology together with age-old human ingenuity, members of formal organizations often find ways to personalize their work and surroundings. Such efforts suggest that we should take a closer look at some of the problems of bureaucracy.

Problems of Bureaucracy

We rely on bureaucracy to manage everyday life efficiently, but many people are uneasy about large organizations gaining too much influence. Bureaucracy can dehumanize and manipulate us, and some say it poses a threat to political democracy. These dangers are discussed in the following sections.

Bureaucratic Alienation

Max Weber held up bureaucracy as a model of productivity. Yet Weber was keenly aware of bureaucracy's potential to *dehumanize* the people it is supposed to serve. The impersonality that fosters efficiency also keeps officials and clients from responding to each other's unique personal needs. Typically, officials treat each client impersonally as a standard "case." Sometimes the tendency toward dehumanization goes too far, as in 2008 when the U.S. Army accidentally sent letters to family members of soldiers killed in Iraq and Afghanistan, addressing the recipients as "John Doe" ("Army Apologizes," 2009).

Formal organizations create *alienation*, according to Weber, by reducing the human being to "a small cog in a ceaselessly moving mechanism" (1978:988, orig. 1921). Although formal organizations are designed to benefit humanity, Weber feared that people might well end up serving formal organizations.

Bureaucratic Inefficiency and Ritualism

Inefficiency, the failure of a formal organization to carry out the work it exists to perform, is a familiar problem. Anyone who has ever tried to complain to Canada Post about a lost or damaged package, to obtain a refund for a coupon attached to a purchased item, or to convince a librarian that an overdue book has already been returned knows that bureaucracies sometimes can be maddeningly unresponsive. According to one report, government agencies responsible for buying equipment for staff can take up to three years to process a request for a new computer. This ensures that by the time the computer arrives, it is already out of date (Gwynne & Dickerson, 1997). While, as noted above, new technology has greatly expanded networking in today's world, especially among younger people who typically make use of Facebook, MySpace, Bebo, Friendster, and other popular social networking websites, things may be less effective once in cyberspace. Information we post may end up being read by almost anyone, which can cause some serious problems, especially if it is partial or, worse, inaccurate. The Seeing Sociology in the News box on page 122 takes a closer look.

People sometimes describe inefficiency by saying that an organization has too much "red tape," meaning that important work does not get done. The term *red tape* is derived from the ribbon used by slow-working eighteenth-century English administrators to wrap official parcels and records (Shipley, 1985).

To Robert Merton (1968), red tape amounts to a new twist on the familiar concept of group conformity. He coined the term **bureaucratic ritualism** to describe *focusing on rules and regulations to the point of undermining an organization's goals*. In short, rules and regulations should be a means to an end, not an end in themselves that takes the focus away from the organization's stated goals. A new bureaucracy—the Red Tape Reduction Commission— was created in January 2011 by Prime Minister Stephen Harper to reduce the costs to business resulting from burdensome federal regulatory requirements.

Bureaucratic Inertia

If bureaucrats sometimes have little reason to work very hard, they have every reason to protect their jobs. Thus officials typically work to keep their organization going even when its goal has been realized. As Max Weber put it, "Once fully established, bureaucracy is among the social structures which are hardest to destroy" (1978:987, orig. 1921).

Bureaucratic inertia refers to *the tendency of bureaucratic organizations to perpetuate themselves*. Formal organizations tend to take on a life of their own beyond their formal objectives. This can be done, for example, by the organization taking on a broad range of work to attract a more diverse clientele. Another example is the transition that spy and military agencies have undergone since the Cold War ended: The Canadian Security Intelligence Service (CSIS) now protects us from international terrorism and economic espionage rather than from communists. Similarly, the North Atlantic Treaty Organization (NATO) now focuses on peacekeeping and humanitarian missions, and the organization includes the Czech Republic, Hungary, and Poland as member nations rather than as the foes that NATO was originally created to defend against.

Oligarchy

Early in the twentieth century, Robert Michels (1876–1936) pointed out the link between bureaucracy and political **oligarchy**, *the rule of the many by the few* (1949, orig. 1911). According to what Michels called the "iron law of oligarchy," the pyramid shape of bureaucracy places a few leaders in charge of the resources of the entire organization.

Weber believed that a strict hierarchy of responsibility resulted in high organizational efficiency. But Michels countered that hierarchy also weakens democracy because officials can and often do use their access to information, resources, and the media to promote their own personal interests.

Furthermore, bureaucracy helps distance officials from the public, as when the corporate president or public official is "unavailable for comment" to the local press or when the Prime Minister's Office withholds documents from Parliament claiming "executive privilege." Oligarchy, then, thrives in the hierarchical structure of bureaucracy and reduces the accountability of leaders to the people (Tolson, 1995).

Political competition, term limits, a system of checks and balances, and the law prevent the Canadian government from becoming an out-and-out oligarchy. Even so, in Canadian political races, candidates who have the visibility, power, and money that come with already being in office enjoy a significant advantage. To illustrate, consider Canada's 2011 federal election. Even with spending limits and a non-partisan system for drawing districts, the system still favoured incumbents, as 83 percent were re-elected. The situation is even worse in the United States, where in recent congressional elections as few as 6 percent of incumbents running for re-election were defeated by their challengers (Center for Responsive Politics, 2009).

The Evolution of Formal Organizations

The problems of bureaucracy—especially the alienation it produces and its tendency toward oligarchy—stem from two organizational traits: hierarchy and rigidity. To Weber, bureaucracy is a top-down system: Rules and regulations made at the top guide every part of people's work down the chain of command. A century ago in North America, Weber's ideas took hold in an organizational model called *scientific management*. We take a look at this model and then examine three challenges over the course of the twentieth century that gradually have led to a new model: the *flexible organization*.

Scientific Management

Frederick Winslow Taylor (1911) had a simple message: Most businesses were sadly inefficient. Managers had little idea of how to increase their business's output, and workers relied on the same tired

ABC News

Professor Suspended after Joke about Killing Students on Facebook

BY DALIA FAHMY
March 3, 2010

The list of Facebook faux-pas just grew longer.

Gloria Gadsden, a sociology professor at East Stroudsburg University in Pennsylvania, says she was suspended last week after updating her Facebook status with complaints about work that alluded to violence.

In January, she wrote: "Does anyone know where I can find a very discreet hitman? Yes, it's been that kind of day." Then in February: "had a good day today. DIDN'T want to kill even one student. :-). Now Friday was a different story."

Gadsden says she posted the comments in jest, on a profile she thought could only be seen by friends and family. She says officials were notified of the posts by a student—even though she says she had no students in her "friend" list.

"I was just having a bad day, and I was venting to family and friends," says Gadsden, who says she didn't realize her comments could be read by the public after Facebook relaxed its privacy standards in December. "My friends and family knew I was being facetious. They knew I wasn't targeting anyone."

Nevertheless, university officials were unhappy about the allusions to violence in the posts, she says, and in a meeting with her even mentioned the recent shooting spree by a disgruntled biologist at the University Alabama-Huntsville.

"Given the climate of security concerns in academia, the university has an obligation to take all threats seriously and act accordingly," Marilyn Wells, ESU's interim provost and vice president for academic affairs, told *The Chronicle of Higher Education* last week. Wells and other university officials did not return calls from ABC News seeking comment.

Workers have been getting in trouble often over their online vents. Not only do employers want to control their online image as closely as they can, but they are also vulnerable, like anybody else, to hurt pride.

"When you badmouth your boss and the boss is hearing, whether you're doing it online or at the coffee maker, the boss isn't going to be happy," says Jonathan Ezor, assistant professor of law and technology at Touro Law Center in Huntington, New York. "The fact that it's online makes it more easily findable and have a broader potential impact."

The comments that provoke employers into action usually contain obscenities or exaggerations that could hurt relations with customers.

Last year, for example, Dan Leone, a stadium worker for the Philadelphia Eagles, was fired after he reacted with an online obscenity to news that one of the Eagles' star players was leaving to join the Denver Broncos.

"Dan is [deleted] devastated about Dawkins signing with Denver. Dam Eagles R Retarted," was the comment that cost Leone his job.

Although he later apologized and tried to get his job back, his employer wouldn't budge. . . .

In the U.K., Virgin Atlantic Airlines fired thirteen cabin crew members after they made fun of passengers in their postings and quipped about defective engines.

The discount airline, owned by Sir Richard Branson, told *The Guardian* at the time that the postings were "totally inappropriate" and "brought the company into disrepute."

Social media mavens can even get in trouble before they've been hired. Remember the case of the Cisco fatty that went viral last year?

One Twitter user posted an update last year saying "Cisco just offered me a job! Now I have to weigh the utility of a fatty paycheck against the daily commute to San Jose and hating the work."

A Cisco employee responded, "Who is the hiring manager? I'm sure they would love to know that you will hate the work. We here at Cisco are versed in the Web."

Needless to say, the applicant did not end up working at Cisco.

Several Web sites, such as JobVent.com, have sprung up in recent years to make it easier for employees to vent their job frustrations online. There's even a website called IhateDell.net that allows employees (and customers) to air their complaints about the computer maker.

In some cases, online postings by disgruntled employees can seriously damage a company's bottom line. Just ask Domino's Pizza.

Domino's sales dropped last year after an employee posed for five YouTube videos. In one, he stuffed cheese up his nose and put it into a sandwich. In another, he sneezed into a cheese steak sandwich.

Once the poser and the photographer—also a Domino's employee—were identified, they were fired and sued by Dominos.

In this case, the transgression seemed very clear. But employees often complain that their online posts are only used as excuses to fire them.

Gadsden, the professor from East Stroudsburg, says that university officials have been discriminating against her ever since she wrote an essay in *The Chronicle of Higher Education* saying universities don't do enough to retain minority faculty. . . .

"Their reaction (to the posts) was exaggerated," says Gadsden, noting that she was not given a warning or a chance to correct her actions before she was suspended.

WHAT DO YOU THINK?

1. Do you have a Facebook page? If so, whom do you allow to view it? Could something like what happened to Professor Gadsden or others mentioned in this article happen to you?

2. Is "badmouthing" your boss online more serious than verbal gossip among co-workers? Why or why not?

3. Do you think the university was justified in suspending Professor Gadsden? Do you think it would happen at a Canadian university?

Source: "Professor Suspended After Joke About Killing Students on Facebook" by Dalia Fahmy. ABC News, March 3, 2010. Copyright © 2010 ABC News Internet Ventures.

scientific management the application of scientific principles to the operation of a business or other large organization

skills of earlier generations. To increase efficiency, Taylor explained, business should apply the principles of modern science. **Scientific management**, then, is *the application of scientific principles to the operation of a business or other large organization.*

Scientific management involves three steps. First, managers carefully observe the job performed by each worker, identifying all operations involved and measuring the time needed for each. Second, managers analyze their data, trying to discover ways for workers to perform each job more efficiently. For example, managers may decide to give workers different tools or to reposition various work operations within the factory. Third, management provides guidance and incentives for workers to do their jobs more efficiently. If a factory worker moves 20 tonnes of pig iron in one day, for example, management would show the worker how to do the job more efficiently and then provide higher wages as the worker's productivity rises. Taylor concluded that if scientific principles were applied to all steps of the production process, companies would become more profitable, workers would earn higher wages, and consumers would pay lower prices.

A century ago, the auto pioneer Henry Ford put it this way: "Save ten steps a day for each of 12,000 employees, and you will have saved fifty miles of wasted motion and misspent energy" (Allen & Hyman, 1999:209). In the early 1900s, Ford Motor Company and many other businesses followed Taylor's lead and experienced dramatic improvements in efficiency.

The successful application of scientific management suggested that decision-making power in the workplace should rest with the owners and executives, who paid little attention to the ideas of their workers. As the decades passed, however, formal organizations faced important challenges involving gender, rising competition from abroad, and the changing nature of work itself. We now take a brief look at each of these challenges and how they prompted organizations to change.

The First Challenge: Gender

In the 1960s, critics pointed out that big businesses and other organizations were inefficient—and also unfair—in their hiring practices. Rather than hiring on the basis of competence, as Weber had proposed, they routinely excluded women and other minorities. As a result, in the early 1960s, the vast majority of managers—just under 90 percent—were white men (Benoit, 2000a).

Patterns of Privilege and Exclusion

By 1987, 30 percent of managerial positions in Canada were held by women, and by 2009 the figure had risen to 37 percent. Therefore, even today, Canadian men still hold 63 percent of managerial jobs across the country. Moreover, all of this growth in women's presence in management occurred in the early part of this period. Further, women who hold managerial positions tend to be

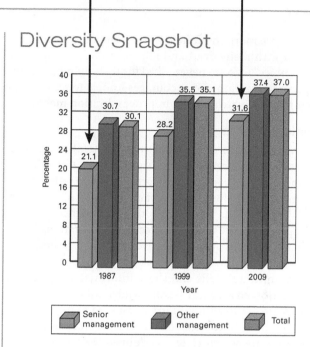

> Only about one-third of senior managers are women, despite dramatic improvements over the last three decades.

Diversity Snapshot

FIGURE 5–4 Women as a Percentage of Total Canadians Employed in Management Positions

Source: Data from Statistics Canada (2010a).

clustered in lower-level managerial positions. As Figure 5–4 shows, in 2009 women comprised only 32 percent of senior managers (Statistics Canada, 2010a). The 2010 Catalyst Census: Financial Post 500 Women Senior Officers and Top Earners does not show much improvement. According to the report, only 17.7 percent of senior posts in Financial Post 500 companies were held by women, a minor increase from 16.9 percent in 2008. Additionally, women corporate officers had increased their percentage of the top earner positions in 2010 to 6.2 percent from 5.6 percent in 2008. Meanwhile, more than 30 percent of companies had zero women senior officers (Mulligan-Ferry, Soares, Combopiano, Cullen & Riker, 2011).

Rosabeth Moss Kanter (1977; Kanter & Stein, 1979) points out that excluding women and minorities from the workplace ignores the talents of more than half of the population. Furthermore, under-represented people in an organization often feel like socially isolated out-groups: uncomfortably visible, taken less seriously, and with fewer chances for promotion. Sometimes what passes for "merit" or good work in an organization is simply being of the right social category (Castilla, 2008).

Opening up an organization so that change and advancement happen more often, Kanter claims, improves everyone's on-the-job performance by motivating employees to become "fast-trackers" who work harder and are more committed to the company. By contrast, an organization with many dead-end jobs turns workers into less productive "zombies" who are never asked for their opinion on anything. An open organization also encourages leaders to seek out the ideas of all employees, which usually improves decision making.

The "Female Advantage"

Some organizational researchers argue that women bring special management skills that strengthen an organization. According to Deborah Tannen (1994), women have a greater "information focus" and more readily ask questions to understand an issue. Men, by contrast, have an "image focus" that makes them wonder how asking questions in a particular situation will affect their reputation.

In another study of women executives, Sally Helgesen (1990) found three other gender-linked patterns. First, women place greater value on communication skills and share information more than men do. Second, women are more flexible leaders who typically give their employees greater freedom. Third, compared to men, women tend to emphasize the interconnectedness of all organizational operations. These patterns, which Helgesen dubbed the *female advantage*, help make companies more flexible and democratic. Some argue that women's more democratic leadership style makes them better leaders, at least in the business world (Sharpe, 2000).

In sum, one challenge to conventional bureaucracy is to become more open and flexible in order to take advantage of the experience, ideas, and creativity of everybody, regardless of gender. The result goes right to the bottom line: greater profits.

The Second Challenge: The Japanese Work Organization

In 1980, the corporate world in North America was shaken to discover that the most popular automobile model sold was not a Chevrolet, Ford, or Plymouth but the Honda Accord, made in Japan. And the trend continued: In 2008, the Japanese corporation Toyota passed General Motors to become the largest carmaker in the world (Fowler, 2008). Ironically, as late as the 1950s, the label "Made in Japan" generally indicated that a product was cheap and poorly made. But times have changed. The success of the Japanese auto industry, as well as companies making electronics, cameras, and many other products, has drawn attention to the "Japanese work organization." How has so small a country been able to challenge the world's economic powerhouse?

December 9, Kyoto (8:05 A.M.). After five minutes of collective warmup, the 25 workers on the construction project next to our hotel stand in four lines. For five minutes they stand listening to something. What is it? Are they listening to the work plan for today or are they listening to an inspirational speaker? So many things are different here, even as most things are familiar.

Japanese organizations reflect that nation's strong collective spirit. In contrast to the Canadian emphasis on rugged individualism, the Japanese value co-operation. In effect, formal organizations in Japan are more like large primary groups. A generation ago, William Ouchi (1981) highlighted differences between formal organizations in Japan and North America. First, Japanese companies hired new workers in groups, giving everyone the same salary and responsibilities. Second, many Japanese companies hired workers for life, fostering a strong sense of loyalty. Third, with the idea that employees would spend their entire careers there, many Japanese organizations trained workers in all phases of their operations. Fourth, although Japanese corporate leaders took ultimate responsibility for their organizations' performance, they involved workers in "quality circles" to discuss decisions that affected them. Fifth, Japanese companies played a large role in the lives of workers, providing home mortgages, sponsoring recreational activities, and scheduling social events. Together, such policies encouraged much more loyalty among members of Japanese organizations than was the case in their North American counterparts (Lowe, 2000).

Not everything has worked out well for Japanese corporations. Around 1990, the Japanese economy entered a downward trend that has persisted for two decades. During this downturn, many Japanese companies changed their policies, no longer offering workers jobs for life or many of the other benefits noted by Ouchi. Japanese society is also aging—with a large share of the population over age 65 and not working—and this pattern is likely to slow economic growth in the future.

For the widely admired Toyota corporation, 2010 turned out to be a year when trouble started. Having expanded its operations to become the world's largest auto company, Toyota was forced to announce recalls of millions of its vehicles because of mechanical problems, suggesting that one consequence of its rapid growth was the loss of some of the company's focus on what had been the key to its success all along: quality (Saporito, 2010). Then in March 11, 2011, an 8.9 magnitude earthquake and devastating tsunami resulted in thousands of deaths and crippled car manufacturers. Some argue that great efficiencies are also causing tenuous supply chains with many sole-source suppliers, which can have grave economic consequences if these chains are interrupted.

The Third Challenge: The Changing Nature of Work

Beyond rising global competition and the need to provide equal opportunity for all, pressure to modify conventional work organizations is also coming from changes in the nature of work itself. Over the past few decades, the economies of Canada and other high-income countries have moved from industrial to post-industrial production. Rather than working in factories using heavy machinery to make *things*, more

During the last 50 years in most high-income countries, women have moved into management positions throughout the corporate world. While some men initially opposed women's presence in the executive office, it is now clear that women bring particular strengths to the job, including leadership flexibility and communication skills. Thus, some analysts speak of women offering a "female advantage."

people today are using computers and other electronic technology to create or process *information*. A post-industrial society, then, is characterized by information-based organizations.

Frederick Taylor developed his concept of scientific management at a time when most jobs involved tasks that, though often backbreaking, were routine. Workers shovelled coal, poured liquid iron into moulds, welded body panels to automobiles on an assembly line, or shot hot rivets into steel girders to build skyscrapers. In addition, a large part of the labour force in Taylor's day was made up of immigrants, most of whom had little schooling and many of whom knew little English. The routine nature of industrial jobs, coupled with the limited skills of the labour force, led Taylor to treat work as a series of fixed tasks set down by management and followed by employees.

Many of today's information age jobs are very different: The work of designers, artists, consultants, writers, editors, composers, programmers, business owners, and others now demands creativity and imagination. What does this mean for formal organizations? Here are several ways in which today's organizations differ from those of a century ago:

1. **Creative freedom.** As one Hewlett-Packard executive put it, "From their first day of work here, people are given important responsibilities and are encouraged to grow" (Brooks, 2000:128). Today's organizations treat employees with information age skills as a vital resource. Executives can set

production goals but cannot dictate how to accomplish tasks that require imagination and discovery. This gives highly skilled workers *creative freedom*, which means they are subject to less day-to-day supervision as long as they generate good results in the long run.

2. **Competitive work teams.** Many organizations allow several groups of employees to work on a problem and offer the greatest rewards to the group that comes up with the best solution. Competitive work teams—a strategy first used by Japanese organizations—draw out the creative contributions of everyone and at the same time reduce the alienation often found in conventional organizations (Maddox, 1994; Yeatts, 1994).

3. **A flatter organization.** By spreading responsibility for creative problem solving throughout the workforce, organizations take on a flatter shape. That is, the pyramid shape of conventional bureaucracy is replaced by an organizational form with fewer levels in the chain of command, as shown in Figure 5–5 on page 126.

4. **Greater flexibility.** The typical industrial age organization was a rigid structure guided from the top. Such organizations may accomplish a good deal of work, but they are not especially creative or able to respond quickly to changes in their larger environment. The ideal model in the information age is a *more open* and *flexible* organization that both generates new ideas and adapts quickly to the rapidly changing global marketplace.

What does this all mean for organizations? As David Brooks puts it, "The machine is no longer held up as the standard that healthy organizations should emulate. Now, it's the ecosystem" (2000:128). Today's "smart" companies seek out intelligent, creative people (AOL calls its main buildings "creative centres") and nurture the growth of their talents.

Keep in mind, however, that many of today's jobs do not involve creative work at all. More correctly, the post-industrial economy has created two very different types of work: high-skill creative work and low-skill service work. Work in the fast-food industry, for example, is routine and highly supervised and thus has much more in common with the factory work of a century ago than with the creative teamwork typical of today's information organizations. Therefore, at the same time that some organizations have taken on a flatter, more flexible form, others continue to use a rigid chain of command.

The "McDonaldization" of Society

As noted in the opening to this chapter, McDonald's has enjoyed enormous success, now operating more than 32 000 restaurants in Canada and around the world. Japan has more than 3700 Golden

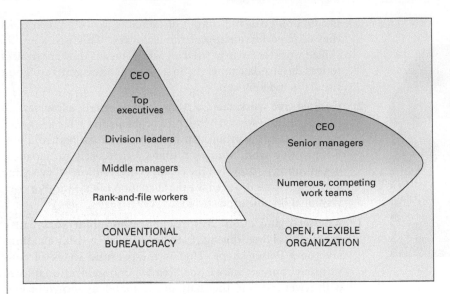

FIGURE 5–5 Two Organizational Models

The conventional model of bureaucratic organizations has a pyramid shape, with a clear chain of command. Orders flow from the top down, and reports of performance flow from the bottom up. Such organizations have extensive rules and regulations, and their workers have highly specialized jobs. More open and flexible organizations have a flatter shape, more like a football. With fewer levels in the hierarchy, responsibility for generating ideas and making decisions is shared throughout the organization. Many workers do their jobs in teams and have a broad knowledge of the entire organization's operation.

Arches, and the world's largest McDonald's is found in China's capital, Beijing.

McDonald's is far more than a restaurant chain; it is a cultural symbol. People around the world associate McDonald's with North America. One poll found that 98 percent of U.S. schoolchildren could identify Ronald McDonald, making him as well known as Santa Claus.

Even more important, the organizational principles that underlie McDonald's are coming to dominate our entire society. Our culture is becoming "McDonaldized,"[2] a clever way of saying that we model many aspects of life on the approach taken by the restaurant chain: Parents buy toys at worldwide chain stores that all carry identical merchandise; we drop in at a convenient shop for a 10-minute drive-through oil change; face-to-face communication is being replaced more and more with electronic methods such as voice mail, email, and instant messaging; more vacations take the form of resorts and tour packages; television packages the news into 10-second sound bites; university admissions officers size up applicants they have never met by glancing at their GPAs; and professors assign ghostwritten textbooks[3] and evaluate students by using tests that publishing companies mass-produce for them.

Can you tell what all these developments have in common?

Four Principles

According to George Ritzer (1993), the McDonaldization of society involves four basic organizational principles:

1. **Efficiency.** Ray Kroc, the marketing genius behind the expansion of McDonald's, set out to serve a hamburger, french fries, and a milkshake to a customer in 50 seconds. Today, one of the company's most popular items is the Egg McMuffin, an entire breakfast packaged into a single sandwich. In the restaurant, customers pick up their meals at a counter, dispose of their own trash, and stack their own trays as they walk out the door or, better still, drive away from the pickup window taking whatever mess they make with them. Such efficiency is now central to our way of life. We tend to think that anything done quickly is, for that reason alone, good.

2. **Predictability.** An efficient organization wants to make everything it does as predictable as possible. McDonald's prepares all food using set formulas. Company policies guide the performance of every job.

3. **Uniformity.** The first McDonald's operating manual declared the weight of a regular raw hamburger to be 1.6 ounces, its size to be 3.875 inches across, and its fat content to be 19 percent. A slice of cheese weighs exactly half an ounce, and french fries are cut precisely 9/32 inch thick.

    Think about how many of the objects we see every day around the home, the workplace, and the campus are designed and mass-produced uniformly according to a standard plan. Not just our environment but our everyday life

---

[2]The term *McDonaldization* was coined by Jim Hightower (1975); much of this discussion is based on the work of George Ritzer (1993, 1998, 2000) and Eric Schlosser (2002).

[3]A number of popular sociology textbooks were not written by the person whose name appears on the cover. This book is not one of them.

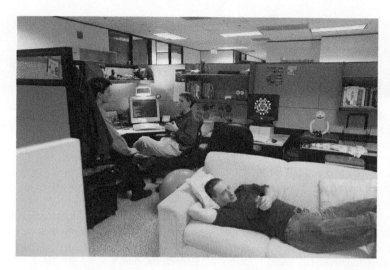

The best of today's information age jobs—including working at Google, the popular search engine website—allow people a lot of personal freedom as long as they produce good ideas. At the same time, many other jobs, such as working the counter at McDonald's, involve the same routines and strict supervision found in factories a century ago.

experiences—from travelling the nation's highways to sitting at home viewing national TV shows—are more standardized than ever before.

Almost anywhere in the world, a person can walk into a McDonald's restaurant and buy the same sandwiches, drinks, and desserts prepared in the same way.[4] Uniformity results from a highly rational system that specifies every action and leaves nothing to chance.

4. **Control.** The most unreliable element in the McDonald's system is human beings. After all, people have their good and bad days, and they sometimes let their minds wander or decide to do something in a different way. To minimize the unpredictable human element, McDonald's has automated its equipment to cook food at a fixed temperature for a set length of time. Even the cash registers at McDonald's are keyed to pictures of the menu items so that ringing up a customer's order is as simple as possible.

[4]As McDonald's has "gone global," a few products have been added or changed according to local tastes. For example, in Uruguay, customers enjoy the McHuevo (a hamburger with a poached egg on top); Norwegians can buy McLaks (grilled salmon sandwiches); the Dutch favour the Groenteburger (vegetable burger); in Thailand, McDonald's serves Samurai pork burgers; the Japanese can purchase a Chicken Tatsuta Sandwich (chicken seasoned with soy and ginger); Filipinos eat McSpaghetti (spaghetti with tomato sauce and bits of hot dog); and in India, where Hindus eat no beef, McDonald's sells a vegetarian Maharaja Mac (Sullivan, 1995).

Similarly, automatic teller machines are replacing banks, highly automated bakeries produce bread while people stand back and watch, and chickens and eggs (or is it eggs and chickens?) emerge from automated hatcheries. In supermarkets, laser scanners at self-checkouts are phasing out human checkers. Much of our shopping now occurs in malls, where everything from temperature and humidity to the kinds of stores and products sold are subject to continuous control and supervision (Ide & Cordell, 1994).

Can Rationality Be Irrational?

There is no doubt about the popularity or efficiency of McDonald's. But there is another side to the story.

Max Weber was alarmed at the increasing rationalization of the world, fearing that formal organizations would cage our imaginations and crush the human spirit. As he saw it, rational systems are efficient but dehumanizing. McDonaldization bears him out. Each of the principles we have just discussed limits human creativity, choice, and freedom. Echoing Weber, Ritzer reaches the conclusion that "the ultimate irrationality of McDonaldization is that people could lose control over the system and it would come to control us" (1993:145). Perhaps even McDonald's understands the limits of rationalization: The company has now expanded its offerings of more upscale foods, such as premium roasted coffee and salad selections that are more sophisticated, fresh, and healthful (Philadelphia, 2002).

CONTROVERSY & DEBATE

Computer Technology, Large Organizations, and the Assault on Privacy

JAKE: I'm doing MySpace. It's really cool.

DUNCAN: Why do you want to put your whole life out there for everyone to see?

JAKE: I'm famous, man!

DUNCAN: Famous? Ha! You're throwing away whatever privacy you have left.

Jake completes a page on MySpace.com, which includes his name and academic location, email address, photo, biography, and current personal interests. It can be accessed by billions of people around the world.

Late for a meeting with a new client, Sarah drives her car through a yellow light as it turns red at a main intersection. A computer linked to a pair of cameras notes the violation and takes one picture of her licence plate and another of her sitting in the driver's seat. Seven days later, she receives a summons to appear in traffic court.

Julio looks through his mail and finds a letter from a Toronto data services company telling him that he is one of about 145 000 people whose name, address, social insurance number, and credit file have recently been sold to criminals posing as business people. With this information, these crooks can obtain credit cards or take out loans in his name.

These are all cases showing that today's organizations—which know more about us than ever before and more than most of us even realize—pose a growing threat to personal privacy. Large organizations are necessary for today's society to operate. In some cases, organizations using information about us may actually be helpful. But cases of identity theft are on the rise, and personal privacy is on the decline.

In the past, small-town life gave people little privacy. But at least if people knew something about you, you were just as likely to know something about them. Today, unknown people "out there" can access information about each of us all the time without our learning about it.

In part, the loss of privacy is a result of more and more complex computer technology. Are you aware that every email you send and every web site you visit leaves a record in one or more computers? Most of these records can be retrieved by people you don't know, as well as by employers and other public officials.

Another part of today's loss of privacy reflects the number and size of formal organizations. As explained in this chapter, large organizations tend to treat people impersonally, and they have a huge appetite for information. Mix large organizations with ever more complex computer technology, and it is no wonder that most people in Canada are concerned about who knows what about them and what people are doing with this information.

For decades, the level of personal privacy in our country has been declining. When the government first began issuing driver's licences, for example, they generated files for every licensed driver. Today, officials can send this information at the touch of a button not only to the police but also to many other organizations. Similarly, Canada Revenue Agency and federal and provincial social services agencies collect

The Future of Organizations: Opposing Trends

Early in the twentieth century, ever-larger organizations arose in Canada, most taking on the bureaucratic form described by Max Weber. In many respects, these organizations were like armies led by powerful generals who issued orders to their captains and lieutenants. Ordinary soldiers, working in the factories, did as they were told.

With the emergence of the post-industrial economy after 1950, as well as rising competition from abroad, many organizations evolved toward the flatter, more flexible model that encourages communication and creativity. Such "intelligent organizations" (Brooks, 2000; Pinchot & Pinchot, 1993) have become more productive than ever. Just as important, for highly skilled people who enjoy creative freedom, these organizations create less of the alienation that so worried Weber.

But this is only half the story. Although the post-industrial economy created many highly skilled jobs, it created even more routine service jobs, such as those offered by McDonald's. Fast-food companies now represent the largest pool of low-wage labour, aside from migrant workers (Schlosser, 2002). Work of this kind, which Ritzer

extensive information. Business organizations now do much the same thing, although, as these examples show, people may not be aware that their choices and activities end up in a company's database. Most people find credit cards a great convenience—the Canadian population now holds almost 50 million of them—but few people stop to think that credit card purchases automatically generate records that can end up almost anywhere.

Then there are the small cameras found not only at traffic intersections but also in stores, public buildings, and parking garages and across university and college campuses. The number of surveillance cameras that monitor our movements rapidly increases with each passing year. So-called security cameras may increase public safety in some ways—say, by discouraging a mugger or even a terrorist—at the cost of the little privacy we have left (Hier, 2010; Walby, 2005).

Of course, some legal protections remain. The federal government and all but two prov-inces (Prince Edward Island and Newfoundland and Labrador) have enacted laws giving citizens rights to examine and correct records kept on them by these governments. These governments also limit the collection, use, and disclosure of personal information between government agencies, but the fact is that many private as well as public organizations now have information about us. Experts estimate that 90 percent of U.S. households are profiled in databases somewhere, and estimates for Canadian households are likely to be similar. In both countries there is public concern that current laws simply do not address the extent of the privacy problem. In the last 10 years, the internet revolution has made the problem of personal privacy more serious than ever before (Crowley, 2002).

WHAT DO YOU THINK?

1. Do you believe that our concern about national security is destroying privacy? How can the loss of privacy threaten our security?

2. Do you use websites such as MySpace? Why do you think so many young people are eager to spread personal information in this way?

3. Have you checked your credit history recently? Do you know how to reduce the chances of having your identity stolen? (If not, one place to start is http://stopidentitytheft.ca/).

Sources: Wright (1998), "Online Privacy" (2000), Rosen (2000), Hamilton (2001), Heymann (2002), O'Harrow (2005), Bruxelles (2009), Walby (2005), and Hier (2010).

terms *McJobs*, offers few of the benefits that today's highly skilled workers enjoy. On the contrary, the automated routines that define work in the fast-food industry, telemarketing, and similar fields are not very different from those that Frederick Taylor described a century ago.

Today, the organizational flexibility that gives better-off workers more freedom carries, for rank-and-file employees, the ever-present threat of "downsizing" (Sennett, 1998). Organizations facing global competition are eager to attract creative employees, but they are just as eager to cut costs by eliminating as many routine jobs as possible. The net result is that some people are better off than ever while others worry about holding their jobs and struggle to make ends meet—a trend that we will explore in detail in Chapter 8 ("Social Stratification").

Our organizations remain the envy of the world for their productive efficiency. Indeed, there are few places on Earth where the mail arrives as quickly and dependably as it does in this country. But we should remember that the future is far brighter for some people than for others. In addition, as the Controversy & Debate box explains, formal organizations pose a mounting threat to our privacy, something to keep in mind as we envision our organizational future.

CHAPTER 5 GROUPS AND ORGANIZATIONS

TO WHAT EXTENT IS THE CONCEPT OF MCDONALDIZATION A PART OF OUR EVERYDAY LIVES? This chapter explains that since the opening of the first McDonald's restaurant in 1948, the principles that underlie the fast-food industry—efficiency, predictability, uniformity, and control—have spread to many aspects of our everyday lives. Here is a chance to identify aspects of McDonaldization in several familiar routines. In each of the two photos below, can you identify specific elements of McDonaldization? That is, in what ways does the organizational pattern or the technology involved increase efficiency, predictability, uniformity, and control? In the photo below, what elements do you see that are clearly not McDonaldization? Why?

Small, privately owned stores like this one were once the rule in Canada. But the number of "mom and pop" businesses is declining as "big box" discount stores expand. Why are small stores disappearing? What social qualities of these stores are we losing in the process?

At checkout counters in many supermarkets and large discount stores, the customer lifts each product through a laser scanner linked to a computer to identify what the product is and what it costs. The customer then inserts a credit or debit card to pay for the purchase and proceeds to bag the items.

HINT This process, which is described as the "McDonaldization of society," has made our lives easier in some ways, but it has also made our society ever more impersonal, gradually diminishing our range of human contact. Also, although this organizational pattern is intended to serve human needs, it may end up doing the opposite by forcing people to live according to the demands of machines. Max Weber feared that our future would be an overly rational world in which we all might lose much of our humanity.

Applying Sociology in Everyday Life

1. Have colleges and universities been affected by the process called McDonaldization? Do large, anonymous lecture courses qualify as an example? Why? What other examples of McDonaldization can you identify on your campus?

2. Visit any large public building with an elevator. Observe groups of people as they approach the elevator, and enter the elevator with them. Watch their behaviour: What happens to conversations as the elevator doors close? Where do people fix their eyes? Can you explain these patterns?

3. Using campus publications or your school's webpage (and some assistance from an instructor), try to draw an organizational pyramid for your college or university. Show the key offices and how they supervise and report to one another.

MAKING THE GRADE

Social Groups

SOCIAL GROUPS are two or more people who identify with and interact with one another.
p. 109

A **PRIMARY GROUP** is small, personal, and lasting (examples include family and close friends).
pp. 110–11

A **SECONDARY GROUP** is large, impersonal, goal-oriented, and often of shorter duration (examples include a college class or a corporation).
pp. 110–11

See the Summing Up table on page 111.

Elements of Group Dynamics

GROUP LEADERSHIP
- Instrumental leadership focuses on completing tasks.
- Expressive leadership focuses on a group's well-being.
- Authoritarian leadership is a "take charge" style that demands obedience; democratic leadership includes everyone in decision making; laissez-faire leadership lets the group function mostly on its own.
p. 111

GROUP CONFORMITY
- The Asch, Milgram, and Janis research shows that group members often seek agreement and may pressure one another toward conformity.
- Individuals use reference groups—including both in-groups and out-groups—to form attitudes and make evaluations.
pp. 111–14

GROUP SIZE AND DIVERSITY
- Georg Simmel described the dyad as intense but unstable; the triad, he said, is more stable but can dissolve into a dyad by excluding one member.
- Peter Blau claimed that larger groups turn inward, socially diverse groups turn outward, and physically segregated groups turn inward.
pp. 114–15

NETWORKS are relational webs that link people with little common identity and limited interaction. Being "well connected" in networks is a valuable type of social capital.
pp. 115–17

Formal Organizations

FORMAL ORGANIZATIONS are large secondary groups organized to achieve their goals efficiently.
p. 117

UTILITARIAN ORGANIZATIONS pay people for their efforts (examples include businesses and government agencies).
p. 117

NORMATIVE ORGANIZATIONS have goals that people consider worthwhile (examples include voluntary associations such as the Scotts Canada).
p. 117

COERCIVE ORGANIZATIONS are organizations that people are forced to join (examples include prisons and mental hospitals).
p. 118

---

social group (p.109) two or more people who identify with and interact with one another

primary group (p. 110) a small social group whose members share personal and lasting relationships

secondary group (p. 110) a large and impersonal social group whose members pursue a specific goal or activity

instrumental leadership (p. 111) group leadership that focuses on the completion of tasks

expressive leadership (p. 111) group leadership that focuses on the group's well-being

groupthink (p. 113) the tendency of group members to conform, resulting in a narrow view of some issue

reference group (p. 113) a social group that serves as a point of reference in making evaluations and decisions

in-group (p. 114) a social group toward which a member feels respect and loyalty

out-group (p. 114) a social group toward which a person feels a sense of competition or opposition

dyad (p. 114) a social group with two members

triad (p. 114) a social group with three members

network (p. 115) a web of weak social ties

formal organization (p. 117) a large secondary group organized to achieve its goals efficiently

tradition (p. 118) values and beliefs passed from generation to generation

rationality (p. 118) a way of thinking that emphasizes deliberate, matter-of-fact calculation of the most efficient way to accomplish a particular task

rationalization of society (p. 118) the historical change from tradition to rationality as the main type of human thought

Formal Organizations (continued)

All formal organizations operate in an **ORGANIZATIONAL ENVIRONMENT** that is influenced by

- technology
- economic and political trends
- current events
- population patterns
- other organizations

p. 119

See the Summing Up table on page 119.

bureaucracy (p. 118) an organizational model rationally designed to perform tasks efficiently

organizational environment (p. 119) factors outside an organization that affect its operation

bureaucratic ritualism (p. 121) a focus on rules and regulations to the point of undermining an organization's goals

bureaucratic inertia (p. 121) the tendency of bureaucratic organizations to perpetuate themselves

oligarchy (p. 121) the rule of the many by the few

scientific management (p. 123) the application of scientific principles to the operation of a business or other large organization

Modern Formal Organizations: Bureaucracy

BUREAUCRACY, which Max Weber saw as the dominant type of organization in modern societies, is based on

- specialization
- hierarchy of offices
- rules and regulations
- technical competence
- impersonality
- formal, written communication

pp. 118–19

PROBLEMS OF BUREAUCRACY include

- bureaucratic alienation
- bureaucratic inefficiency and ritualism
- bureaucratic inertia
- oligarchy

pp. 120–22

The Evolution of Formal Organizations

CONVENTIONAL BUREAUCRACY

MORE OPEN, FLEXIBLE ORGANIZATIONS

In the early 1900s, Frederick Taylor's **SCIENTIFIC MANAGEMENT** applied scientific principles to increase productivity.

p. 123

In the 1960s, Rosabeth Moss Kanter proposed that opening up organizations for all employees, especially women and other minorities, increased organizational efficiency.

pp. 123–24

In the 1980s, global competition drew attention to the Japanese work organization's collective orientation.

pp. 124–25

The Changing Nature of Work

Recently, the rise of a post-industrial economy has created two very different types of work:

- highly skilled and creative work (examples include designers, consultants, programmers, and executives)
- low-skilled service work associated with the "McDonaldization" of society, based on efficiency, uniformity, and control (examples include jobs in fast-food restaurants and telemarketing)

pp. 125–28

MySocLab

Visit MySocLab at www.mysoclab.com to access a variety of online resources that will help you to prepare for tests and to apply your knowledge, including

- **an eText**
- **videos**
- **self-grading quizzes**
- **glossary flashcards**

6 Sexuality and Society

- What was the sexual revolution, and how did it change Canadian society?

- Why do societies try to control people's sexual behaviour?

- How does sexuality play a part in social inequality?

This chapter explains how society shapes human sexuality and also how sexuality figures into our everyday lives. Although sexuality is biological, society (including culture and patterns of inequality) shapes how we experience sexuality.

Pam Goodman walks along the hallway with her friends Jennifer Delosier and Cindy Thomas. The three young women are high school students in a small prairie town.

"What's happening after school?" Pam asks.

"Dunno," replies Jennifer. "Maybe Todd is coming over."

"Got the picture," adds Cindy. "We're so gone."

"Shut up!" Pam stammers, smiling. "I hardly know Todd." The three girls break into laughter.

It is no surprise that young people spend a lot of time thinking and talking about sex. But as the sociologist Peter Bearman discovered, sex involves more than just talk. Bearman and two colleagues (Bearman, Moody, & Stovel, 2004) conducted confidential interviews with 832 high school students, learning that 573 (69 percent of the students) had had at least one "sexual and romantic relationship" during the previous 18 months. So most, but not all, of these students were sexually active.

Bearman wanted to learn about sexual activity to understand the problem of sexually transmitted infections (STIs) among young people. Why are the rates of STIs so high? And why can there be sudden "outbreaks" of infection that involve dozens of young people in a community?

To find the answers to these questions, Bearman and colleagues asked the students to identify their sexual partners (promising, of course, not to reveal any confidential information). This information allowed them to trace connections between individual students in terms of sexual activity and produced a surprising pattern: Sexually active students were linked to each other through common partners much more than anyone might have expected. In all, common partners linked half of the sexually active students, as shown in the diagram.

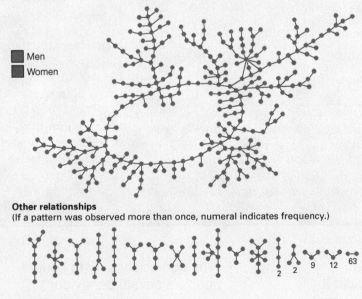

Other relationships
(If a pattern was observed more than once, numeral indicates frequency.)

Source: Bearman, Moody, & Stovel (2004).

sex the biological distinction between females and males

primary sex characteristics the genitals, organs used for reproduction

secondary sex characteristics bodily development, apart from the genitals, that distinguishes biologically mature females and males

We claim that beauty is in the eye of the beholder, which suggests the importance of culture in setting standards of attractiveness. All of the people pictured here—from Arizona, New Zealand, and South Africa—are considered beautiful by members of their own society. At the same time, sociobiologists point out that in every society on Earth, people are attracted to youthfulness. The reason, as sociobiologists see it, is that attractiveness underlies our choices about reproduction, which is most readily accomplished in early adulthood.

Awareness of the connections among people can help us understand how STIs spread from one infected person to another in a short period of time. Bearman's study also shows that research can teach us a great deal about human sexuality, which is an important dimension of social life. You will also see that sexual attitudes and behaviour have changed dramatically over the past century in Canada.

Understanding Sexuality

How many of your thoughts and actions every day have something to do with sexuality? If you are like most people, the answer is "quite a lot," because sexuality is about much more than just having sex. Sexuality is a theme found almost everywhere—in sports, on campus, in the workplace, and especially in the mass media. There is also a sex industry that includes pornography and prostitution, both of which are multi-billion-dollar businesses in this country. The bottom line is that sexuality is an important part of how we think about ourselves as well as how others think about us. For this reason, there are few areas of social life in which sexuality does not play some part.

Nevertheless, Canadian culture has long treated sex as taboo; even today, many people avoid talking about it. As a result, although sex can produce much pleasure, it also causes confusion, anxiety, and sometimes outright fear. Even scientists long considered sex off limits as a topic to study. It was not until the middle of the twentieth century that researchers turned their attention to this vital dimension of social life. Since then, as this chapter explains, we have discovered a great deal about human sexuality.

Sex: A Biological Issue

Sex refers to *the biological distinction between females and males.* From a biological point of view, sex is the way humans reproduce. A female ovum and a male sperm, each containing 23 chromosomes (biological codes that guide physical development), combine to form an embryo. To one of these pairs of chromosomes, which determines the child's sex, the mother contributes an X chromosome and the father contributes either an X or a Y. An X from the father produces a female (XX) embryo; a Y from the father produces a male (XY) embryo. A child's sex is thus determined biologically at the moment of conception.

The sex of an embryo guides its development. If the embryo is male, the growth of testicular tissue starts to produce large amounts of testosterone, a hormone that triggers the development of male genitals (sex organs). If little testosterone is present, the embryo develops female genitals.

Sex and the Body

Some differences in the body set males and females apart. Right from birth, the two sexes have different **primary sex characteristics**, namely, *the genitals, organs used for reproduction.* At puberty, as people reach sexual maturity, additional sex differentiation takes place. At this point, people develop **secondary sex characteristics**, *bodily development, apart from the genitals, that distinguishes biologically mature females and males.* Sexually mature females have wider hips for giving birth, milk-producing breasts for nurturing infants, and soft, fatty tissue that provides a reserve supply of nutrition during pregnancy and breastfeeding. Sexually mature males typically develop more muscle in the upper body, more extensive body hair, and deeper voices. Of

intersexual people people whose bodies (including genitals) have both female and male characteristics

transsexuals people who feel they are one sex even though biologically they are the other

Chaz Bono, on the left, is the only child of entertainers Sonny Bono and Cher. Born Chastity Bono, she "came out" as a lesbian in the 1990s and became a gay rights advocate. In 2010, Chaz legally changed his name after completing a female-to-male gender transition.

course, these are general differences; some males are smaller and have less body hair and higher voices than some females.

Keep in mind that sex is not the same thing as gender. *Gender* is an element of culture and refers to the personal traits and patterns of behaviour (including responsibilities, opportunities, and privileges) that a culture attaches to being female or male. Chapter 10 ("Gender Stratification") explains that gender is an important dimension of social inequality.

Intersexual People

Sex is not always as clear-cut as has been just described. The term **intersexual people** refers to *people whose bodies (including genitals) have both female and male characteristics*. Intersexuality is both natural and very rare, involving well below 1 percent of a society's population. An older term for intersexual people is *hermaphrodite* (a word derived from Hermaphroditus, the child of the mythological Greek gods Hermes and Aphrodite, who embodied both sexes). A true hermaphrodite has both a female ovary and a male testis.

However, our culture demands that sex be clear-cut, a fact evident in the requirement that parents record the sex of their child at birth as either female or male. In Canada, some people respond to intersexual people with confusion or even disgust. But attitudes in other cultures are quite different: The Pokot of eastern Africa, for example, pay little attention to what they consider a simple biological error, and the Navajo look on intersexual people with awe, seeing in them the full potential of both the female and the male (Geertz, 1975).

Transsexuals

Transsexuals are *people who feel they are one sex even though biologically they are the other*. Estimates suggest that 1 or 2 of every 1000 people who are born have experienced the feeling of being trapped in a body of the wrong sex and a desire to be the other sex. Sometimes called transgender people, many begin to disregard conventional ideas about how females and males should look and behave. Some also go one step further and undergo *gender reassignment*, surgical alteration of their genitals, which is usually accompanied by hormone treatments. This medical process is complex and takes months or even years, but it helps many people gain a joyful sense of finally becoming on the outside who they feel they are on the inside (Gagné, Tewksbury, & McGaughey, 1997; Olyslager & Conway, 2007).

Sex: A Cultural Issue

Sexuality has a biological foundation. But like all other elements of human behaviour, sexuality is also very much a cultural issue. Biology may explain some animals' mating rituals, but humans have no similar biological program. Although there is a biological "sex drive" in the sense that people find sex pleasurable and may seek to engage in sexual activity, our biology does not dictate any specific ways of being sexual any more than our desire to eat dictates any particular foods or table manners.

Cultural Variation

Almost every sexual practice shows considerable variation from one society to another. In his pioneering study of human sexuality in North America, Alfred Kinsey and his colleagues (1948) found that most couples reported having intercourse in a single position: face to face, with the woman on the bottom and the man on top. Halfway around the world, in the South Seas, most couples *never* have sex in this way. In fact, when the people of the South Seas learned of this practice from Western missionaries, they poked fun at it as the strange "missionary position."

Even the simple practice of displaying affection varies from society to society. Most people in Canada kiss in public, but the Chinese kiss only in private. The French kiss publicly, often twice (once on each cheek), and Belgians kiss three times (starting on either cheek). The Maori of New Zealand rub noses, and most people in Nigeria don't kiss at all.

Modesty, too, is culturally variable. If a woman stepping into a bath is disturbed, what body parts does she cover? Helen Colton

incest taboo a norm forbidding sexual relations or marriage between certain relatives

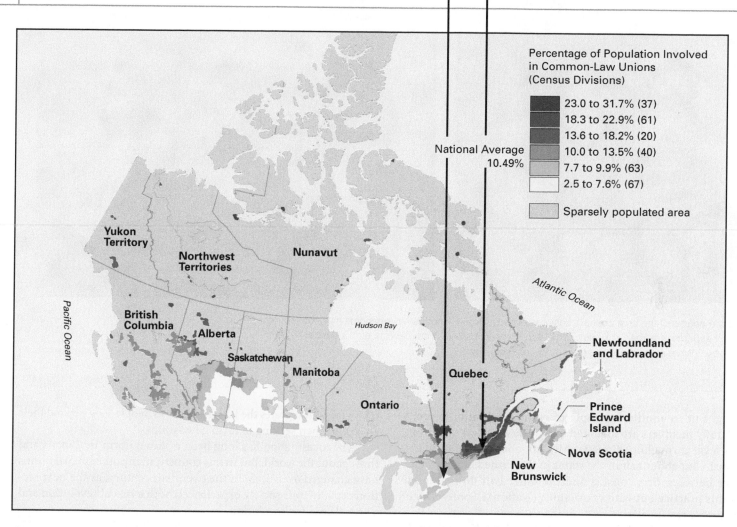

Mario and Maria Cabano married shortly before Mario came to Canada when he was 18 years old. Maria came to Canada two years later.

Marie Clare ad Anthony Barri in Saint-Colomban have lived together in a common law relationship for 35 years.

Percentage of Population Involved in Common-Law Unions (Census Divisions)

23.0 to 31.7% (37)
18.3 to 22.9% (61)
13.6 to 18.2% (20)
10.0 to 13.5% (40)
7.7 to 9.9% (63)
2.5 to 7.6% (67)

Sparsely populated area

National Average 10.49%

Seeing Ourselves

NATIONAL MAP 6–1 **Common-Law Living Arrangements across Canada, 2006**

About 10 percent of people in Canada over the age of 15 live in a common-law relationship. There are marked differences across Canada, primarily by rural or urban status, but there are also marked differences differences between Quebec and the other provinces.

Source: Statistics Canada (2011j).

(1983) reports that an Islamic woman covers her face, a Laotian woman covers her breasts, a Samoan woman covers her navel, a Sumatran woman covers her knees, and a European woman covers her breasts with one hand and her genital area with the other.

Around the world, some societies restrict sexuality and others are more permissive. In China, for example, societal norms so closely regulate sexuality that few people have sexual intercourse before they marry. In Canada, at least in recent decades, intercourse prior to marriage has become the norm, and some people choose to have sex even without strong commitment. As National Map 6–1

indicates, Canadians in different parts of Canada have different attitudes about living together before marriage.

The Incest Taboo

When it comes to sex, do all societies agree on anything? The answer is yes. One cultural universal—an element found in every society the world over—is the **incest taboo,** *a norm forbidding sexual relations or marriage between certain relatives.* In Canada, the law, reflecting cultural mores, prohibits close relatives (including brothers and sisters, parents and children) from having sex or

Over the course of the past century, social attitudes in North America have become more accepting of most aspects of human sexuality. What do you see as some of the benefits of this greater openness? What are some of the negative consequences?

marrying. But in another example of cultural variation, exactly which family members are included in a society's incest taboo varies. It is legal throughout Canada, Mexico, and Europe to marry your cousin but about half of the states in the United States outlaw marriage between first cousins and the other half do not; a few permit this practice but with restrictions (National Conference of State Legislatures, 2009).

Some societies (such as the North American Navajo) apply incest taboos only to the mother and others on her side of the family. There are also societies on record (including ancient Peru and Egypt) that have approved brother-sister marriages among the nobility as a strategy to keep power within a single family (Murdock, 1965, orig. 1949).

Why does some form of incest taboo exist everywhere? Part of the reason is biology: Reproduction between close relatives of any species increases the odds of producing offspring with mental or physical problems. But why, of all living species, do only humans observe an incest taboo? This fact suggests that controlling sexuality between close relatives is a necessary element of *social* organization. For one thing, the incest taboo limits sexual competition in families by restricting sex to spouses (ruling out, for example, sex between parent and child). Second, because family ties define people's rights and obligations to one another, reproduction between close relatives would hopelessly confuse kinship; if a mother and son had a daughter, would the child consider the male a father or a brother? Third, by requiring people to marry outside their immediate families, the

incest taboo integrates the larger society as people look beyond their close kin when seeking to form new families.

The incest taboo has long been a sexual norm in Canada and throughout the world. But in this country, many other sexual norms have changed over time. In the twentieth century, as the next section explains, our society experienced both a sexual revolution and a sexual counter-revolution.

Sexual Attitudes in Canada

What do people in Canada think about sex? Our culture's attitudes toward sexuality have always been somewhat contradictory. Early immigrants demanded strict conformity in attitudes and behaviour, and they imposed severe punishment for any sexual misconduct, even if it took place in the privacy of the home. Later on, most European immigrants arrived with rigid ideas about "correct" sexuality, typically limiting sex to reproduction within marriage. Some regulation of sexual activity has continued ever since. Until 1969, for example, section 179 of the Criminal Code of Canada stated the following: "Everyone is guilty of an indictable offence and liable to two years' imprisonment who knowingly, without lawful excuse or justification, offers to sell, advertises, publishes an advertisement of or has for sale or disposal any medicine, drug or article intended or represented as a means of preventing conception or causing abortion" (quoted in McLaren & McLaren, 1986:19). Today, section 159(1) of the Criminal Code states that "every person who engages in an act of anal intercourse is guilty of an indictable offence and liable to imprisonment for a term not exceeding ten years or is guilty of an offence punishable on summary conviction." It wasn't until 1969 that an exception clause was written into the latter law, stating that the subsection does not apply to acts that take place in private—defined as there being only two people present in a private space—between consenting adults.

But this is just one side of the story. As Chapter 2 ("Culture") explains, our culture is individualistic—many of us believe that people should be free to do pretty much as they wish, as long as they cause no direct harm to others. The idea that what people do in the privacy of their own homes is no one else's business makes sex a matter of individual freedom and personal choice. One of Canada's former prime ministers, the late Pierre Elliott Trudeau, while still serving as the minister of justice, said as much in what is perhaps his most famous statement while in public office: "[T]he state has no business in the bedrooms of the nation."

When it comes to sexuality, is Canada restrictive or permissive? The answer is both. On one hand, many Canadians still view sexual conduct as an important indicator of personal morality. On the other hand, sex has become more and more a part of popular culture carried by the mass media; one recent report concluded that the number of scenes in television shows with sexual content doubled in a mere 10 years (Kunkel et al., 2005). Within this complex framework, we turn now to changes in sexual attitudes and behaviour that have occurred over the course of the past century.

The Sexual Revolution

Over the past century, Canada witnessed profound changes in sexual attitudes and practices. The first indications of this change came in the 1920s as thousands of people migrated from farms and small towns to rapidly growing cities. There, living apart from their families and meeting new people in the workplace, young men and women enjoyed considerable sexual freedom, one reason that decade became known as the "Roaring Twenties."

In the 1930s and 1940s, the Great Depression and World War II slowed the rate of change. But in the postwar period, after 1945, Alfred Kinsey set the stage for what later came to be known as the *sexual revolution*. In 1948, Kinsey and his colleagues published their first study of sexuality in the United States, and it raised eyebrows there as well as in Canada and Europe. The uproar resulted mostly from the fact that scientists were actually studying sex, a topic many people were uneasy talking about even in the privacy of their homes.

Kinsey also had some very interesting things to say. His two books (Kinsey, Pomeroy, & Martin, 1948, 1953) became bestsellers because they revealed that people, on average, were far less conventional in sexual matters than most had thought. These books encouraged a new openness toward sexuality, which helped set the sexual revolution in motion.

In the late 1960s, the sexual revolution truly came of age. Youth culture dominated public life, and expressions such as "sex, drugs, and rock-and-roll" and "if it feels good, do it!" summed up the new, freer attitude toward sex. The baby boom generation, born between 1946 and 1964, became the first cohort in Canadian history to grow up with the idea that sex was part of people's lives, whether they were married or not.

New technology also played a part in the sexual revolution. The birth control pill, introduced in 1960, not only prevented pregnancy but also made having sex more convenient. Unlike a condom or a diaphragm, which has to be applied at the time of intercourse, the pill could be taken like a daily vitamin supplement. Now women as well as men could engage in sex without any special preparation.

Because women were historically subject to greater sexual regulation than men, the sexual revolution had special significance for them. Society's traditional "double standard" allows (and even encourages) men to be sexually active but expects women to be virgins until marriage and faithful to their husbands afterwards. Canadian surveys since the mid-1990s show that females aged 15 to 19 are considerably less likely than their male counterparts to have had multiple sex partners in the last year, as shown in Figure 6–1(A) on page 140. But as Figure 6–1(B) shows, in the mid-1990s, females in this age group were more likely to ever have had sex than their male peers. More recent data from 2005 show no difference between males and females. The reasons for this equality between males and females is unclear but what is clear is that young males and females are delaying having sex today as compared to 15 years ago, when 11 percent of males and 13 percent of females had sex before age 15. By 2005, 8 percent of both males and females said they had had sex so before turning 15 (Rotermann, 2008).

Greater openness about sexuality develops as societies become richer and the opportunities for women increase. With these facts in mind, look for a pattern in the global use of birth control shown in Global Map 6–1 on page 141.

The Sexual Counter-revolution

The sexual revolution made sex a topic of everyday discussion and sexual activity more a matter of individual choice. However, by 1980, the climate of sexual freedom that had marked the late 1960s and 1970s was criticized by some people as evidence of moral decline, and the *sexual counter-revolution* began.

Politically speaking, the sexual counter-revolution was a conservative call for a return to "family values" and a change from sexual freedom back toward what critics saw as the sexual responsibility valued by earlier generations. Critics of the sexual revolution objected not just to the idea of "free love" but also to trends such as cohabitation (living together without being married) and unmarried couples having children.

Looking back, the sexual counter-revolution did not greatly change the idea that people should decide for themselves when and

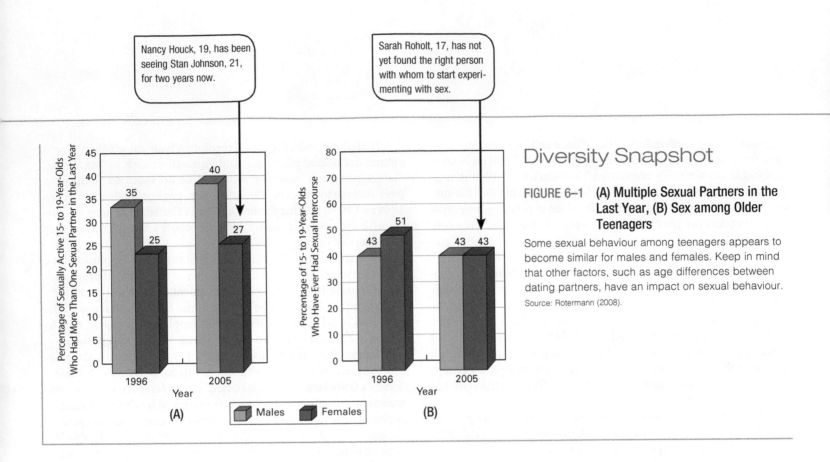

Diversity Snapshot

FIGURE 6–1 **(A) Multiple Sexual Partners in the Last Year, (B) Sex among Older Teenagers**

Some sexual behaviour among teenagers appears to become similar for males and females. Keep in mind that other factors, such as age differences between dating partners, have an impact on sexual behaviour.

Source: Rotermann (2008).

with whom to have a sexual relationship. But whether for moral reasons or because of concerns about STIs, more people began choosing to limit their number of sexual partners or to not have sex at all.

Is the sexual revolution over? It is true that people are making more careful decisions about sexuality. But as the rest of this chapter explains, the ongoing sexual revolution is evident in the fact that there is now greater acceptance of premarital sex as well as increasing tolerance for various sexual orientations.

Premarital Sex

In light of the sexual revolution and the sexual counter-revolution, how much has sexual behaviour in Canada really changed? One interesting trend involves premarital sex—sexual intercourse before marriage—among young people.

Consider first what North Americans *say* about premarital intercourse. Public opinion in North America is far more accepting of premarital sex today than was the case a generation ago, but American society clearly remains more divided on this issue than does Canadian society. While only about 52 percent of people in the US recently polled say premarital sex is "not wrong at all" (NORC, 2009), some 87 percent of Canadians surveyed had no qualms about sexual relations before marriage (Angus Reid, 2009a). As shown in Table 6–1 on page 142, Canadians increasingly find other social behaviours morally acceptable, including contraception, divorce, abortion, and having a baby outside of marriage.

Now let's look at what young people *do*. For women, there has been marked change over time. The Kinsey studies reported that for

people born in the early 1900s, about 50 percent of men but just 6 percent of women had premarital sexual intercourse before age 19. Studies of baby boomers, born after World War II, show a slight increase in premarital sex among men but a large increase—to about one-third—among women. The most recent studies show that by the time they are seniors in high school, slightly more than half of young men and women have had premarital sexual intercourse. In addition, sexual experience among high school students who are sexually active is limited—only 15 percent of students report four or more sexual partners. These statistics have remained much the same for the past 20 years (Centers for Disease Control and Prevention, 2008; Laumann et al., 1994:323–24, Yabroff, 2008). In fact, as shown in Figure 6–1, Canadian teens appear to be initiating sexual intercourse a bit later than the generation before and there is a small drop in the number of sex partners teens are reporting compared to a decade and a half ago (Boyce, 2004; Boyce et al., 2003; Maticka-Tyndale, 2008; Rotermann, 2008). Recent research shows that romantic love between young people can help fill the emotional gaps during the transition to adulthood, and it may act as a barrier to delinquent behaviour, including involvement in crime (McCarthy & Casey, 2008).

A common belief is that an even larger share of young people engages in oral sex. This choice reflects the fact that this practice avoids the risk of pregnancy; in addition, many young people see oral sex as something less than "going all the way." Recent research suggests that the percentage of young people who have had oral sex is greater than the percentage who have had intercourse, but only by about 10 percent. Therefore, claims in the mass media of an "oral sex epidemic" among young people are almost certainly

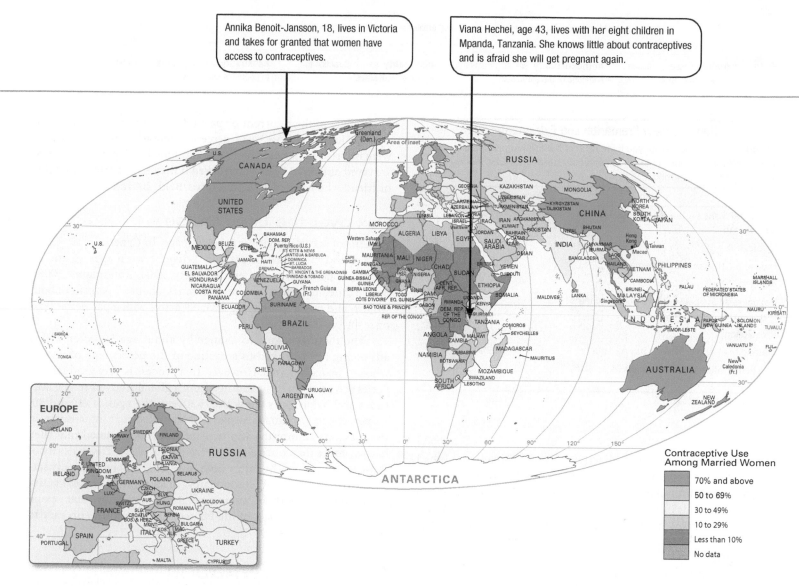

Annika Benoit-Jansson, 18, lives in Victoria and takes for granted that women have access to contraceptives.

Viana Hechei, age 43, lives with her eight children in Mpanda, Tanzania. She knows little about contraceptives and is afraid she will get pregnant again.

Contraceptive Use Among Married Women

- 70% and above
- 50 to 69%
- 30 to 49%
- 10 to 29%
- Less than 10%
- No data

Window on the World

GLOBAL MAP 6–1 **Contraceptive Use in Global Perspective**

The map shows the percentage of married women using modern contraception methods (such as barrier methods, contraceptive pill, implants, injectables, intrauterine devices, or sterilization). In general, how do high-income nations differ from low-income nations? Can you explain this difference?

Sources: Data from United Nations (2008) and Population Reference Bureau (2011).

exaggerated. We should also keep in mind that "over the last 30 to 40 years oral sex has become a normative aspect of the adult sexual script and this trend has been followed by youth" (Maticka-Tyndale, 2008:86).

Finally, a significant minority of young people choose abstinence (not having sexual intercourse). Many also choose not to have oral sex, which, like intercourse, can transmit infection. Even so, research confirms the fact that premarital sex is widely accepted among young people today and it would be wise to have a more progressive sex education policy that acknowledges the reality of most youth's lives (McCarthy & Grodsky, 2011).

Sex between Adults

Judging from the mass media, Canadians are very active sexually. But do popular images reflect reality? According to a poll by the Angus Reid Group (1998e), the frequency of sexual activity varies widely in the Canadian population. In response to the question "How many times a month do you have sex?" the pattern breaks down like this: while, on average, Canadians have sex 6.2 times per month, the average is 7.5 times for Atlantic Canadians, 8.9 times for adults aged 18 to 34, 12.0 times for those living with a partner, and 7.3 times for high-income Canadians (defined as those with household incomes over $55 000). In short, no single pattern accurately describes sexual activity in Canada today.

sexual orientation a person's romantic and emotional attraction to another person

heterosexuality sexual attraction to someone of the other sex

homosexuality sexual attraction to someone of the same sex

bisexuality sexual attraction to people of both sexes

asexuality a lack of sexual attraction to people of either sex

TABLE 6–1 How We View Premarital and Extramarital Sex

"Regardless of whether or not you think each of the following issues should be legal, please indicate whether you personally believe they are morally acceptable or morally wrong."

	Morally Acceptable
Sexual relations between an unmarried man and woman	87%
Divorce	84%
Having a baby outside of marriage	79%
Abortion	66%
Sexual relations between two people of the same sex	66%
Prostitution	42%
Married men and/or women having an affair	15%
Polygamy, when one spouse has more than one partner at the same time	12%

Source: Angus Reid (2009a).

We also know that sexual activity among Canadian adults is lower today (64 percent) than it was in 1984 (75 percent). But precisely why Newfoundlanders, for example, are deemed the "champions" in the nation's bedrooms (77 percent sexual activity) and British Columbians hold the unenviable position as the country's "sexual slackers" (56 percent) remains a mystery (Angus Reid Group, 1998e).

Despite the widespread image of "swinging singles" promoted on television shows such as *Sex and the City*, it is married people who have sex with partners the most. In addition, married people report the highest level of satisfaction—both physical and emotional—with their partners (Laumann et al., 1994).

Extramarital Sex

What about married people having sex outside of marriage? This practice, commonly called "adultery" (sociologists prefer the more neutral term *extramarital sex*), is widely condemned in most countries, including Canada. Table 6–1 shows that only 15 percent of Canadians think that "married men and/or women having an affair" is morally acceptable. Likewise, 90 percent of U.S. adults consider a married person's having sex with someone other than the marital partner to be "always wrong" or "almost always wrong" (NORC, 2009:339). The norm of sexual fidelity within marriage has been and remains a strong element of North American culture.

But actual behaviour falls short of the cultural ideal. A national Canadian survey shows that nearly 10 percent of married or common-law Canadians surveyed stated that they have had an extramarital affair while in their current or past relationship. Furthermore, the number jumps to close to 17 percent when asked if someone they were married to has ever had an affair. Finally, 61 percent of those surveyed answered "yes" when asked if they have a family member or friend who has had an affair (Ipsos-Reid, 2001a).

Sex over the Life Course

Patterns of sexual activity change with age. In Canada, most young women and men become sexually active between ages 16 and 21 (Boyce, 2004; McCreary Centre Society, 2004; Rotermann, 2008). By the time they reach their mid-twenties, about 90 percent of both women and men report being sexually active with a partner at least once during the past year.

The picture begins to change by about age 50, after which advancing age is linked to a decline in the percentage of people who are sexually active. However, this process is very gradual and varies across countries. Findings from a global study of sexual attitudes and behaviours show that between the ages of 40 and 80, 73 percent of Canadians surveyed had had sexual intercourse in the previous 12 months and two-thirds of them stated that they had sex more than once a week (Pfizer Inc., 2002). The majority of those surveyed said they were both physically and emotionally satisfied with their sexual relationships. In short, while sexual activity does decline with advancing age, these data show that sexual activity is a normal part of life for most older adults, contrary to popular stereotypes.

Sexual Orientation

In recent decades, public opinion about sexual orientation has shown a remarkable change. **Sexual orientation** is *a person's romantic and emotional attraction to another person*. The norm in all human societies is **heterosexuality** (*hetero* is Greek for "the other of two"), meaning *sexual attraction to someone of the other sex*. Yet in every society, a certain share of people experience **homosexuality** (*homo* is Greek for "the same"), *sexual attraction to someone of the same sex*. Keep in mind that people do not necessarily fall into just one of these categories; they may have varying degrees of attraction to both sexes.

The idea that sexual orientation is often not clear-cut points to the existence of a third category: **bisexuality**, *sexual attraction to people of both sexes*. Some bisexual people are *attracted* equally to males and females; many others are attracted more strongly to one sex than the other. Finally, **asexuality** is *a lack of sexual attraction to people of either sex*. Figure 6–2 places each of these sexual orientations in relation to the others.

It is important to remember that sexual *attraction* is not the same thing as sexual *behaviour*. Many people have experienced some attraction to someone of the same sex, but far fewer ever actually engage in same-sex behaviour. This is in large part because our culture discourages such actions.

In Canada and around the world, heterosexuality is the norm because, biologically speaking, heterosexual relations permit human reproduction. Even so, most societies tolerate homosexuality. Among the ancient Greeks, upper-class men considered homosexuality the highest form of relationship, partly because they looked down on women as intellectually inferior. As men saw it, heterosexuality was necessary only so they could have children, and "real" men preferred homosexual relations (Ford & Beach, 1951; Greenberg, 1988; Kluckhohn, 1948).

What Gives Us a Sexual Orientation?

The question of how people come to have a particular sexual orientation is strongly debated. The arguments cluster into two general positions: sexual orientation as a product of society and sexual orientation as a product of biology.

Sexual Orientation: A Product of Society

This approach argues that people in any society attach meanings to sexual activity, and these meanings differ from place to place and over time. As Michel Foucault (1990, orig. 1978) points out, for example, there was no distinct category of people called "homosexuals" until a century ago, when scientists and eventually the public as a whole began defining people that way. Throughout history, many people no doubt had what we would call "homosexual experiences." But neither they nor others saw in this behaviour the basis for any special identity.

Anthropological studies show that patterns of homosexuality differ greatly from one society to another. In Siberia, for example, the Chukchee Eskimo perform a ritual during which one man dresses as a woman and does a woman's work. The Sambia, who dwell in the Eastern Highlands of New Guinea, have a ritual in which young boys perform oral sex on older men in the belief that eating semen will make them more masculine. In southeastern Mexico, a region in which religions recognize gods who are both female and male, the local culture defines people not only as female and male but also as *muxes* ("MOO-shayss"), a third sexual category. *Muxes* are men who dress and act as women, some only on ritual occasions, some all the time. The Thinking about Diversity box on page 144 takes a closer look. Such diversity of sexual expression around the world shows that sexual expression is socially constructed (Blackwood & Wieringa, 1999; Gave, 2005; Lacey, 2008; Rosenberg, 2008).

Sexual Orientation: A Product of Biology

A growing body of research suggests that sexual orientation is innate, or rooted in human biology, in much the same way that people are born right-handed or left-handed. Arguing this position, Simon

Diversity Snapshot

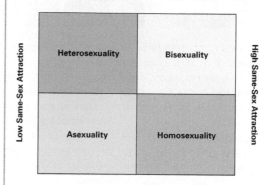

FIGURE 6–2 Four Sexual Orientations

A person's levels of same-sex attraction and opposite-sex attraction are two distinct dimensions that combine in various ways to produce four major sexual orientations.

Source: Adapted from Storms (1980).

LeVay (1993) links sexual orientation to the structure of a person's brain. LeVay studied the brains of both homosexual and heterosexual men and found a small but important difference in the size of the hypothalamus, a part of the brain that regulates hormones. Such an anatomical difference, he claims, plays a part in shaping sexual orientation.

Genetics may also influence sexual orientation. One study of 44 pairs of brothers, all homosexual, found that 33 pairs had a distinctive genetic pattern involving the X chromosome. Moreover, the gay brothers had an unusually high number of gay male relatives—but only on their mother's side. Such evidence leads some researchers to think there may be a "gay gene" located on the X chromosome (Hamer & Copeland, 1994).

CRITICAL REVIEW Mounting evidence supports the conclusion that sexual orientation is rooted in biology, although the best guess at present is that both nature and nurture play a part. Remember that sexual orientation is not a matter of neat categories. Most people who think of themselves as homosexual have had one or more heterosexual experiences, just as many people who think of themselves as heterosexual have had one or more homosexual experiences. Explaining sexual orientation, then, is not easy.

There is also a political issue here with great importance for gay men and lesbians. To the extent that sexual orientation is based in biology, homosexuals have no more choice about their sexual orientation than they do about their skin colour. If this is

A Third Gender: The *Muxes* of Mexico

Alejandro Taledo, 16 years old, stands on a street corner in Juchitán, a small town in the state of Oaxaca, in southeastern Mexico. Called Alex by her friends, she has finished a day of selling flowers with her mother and now waits for a bus to ride home for dinner.

As you may know, Alejandro is commonly a boy's name. In fact, this young Mexican was born a boy. But several years ago, Alex decided that, whatever her sex, she felt she was a girl and she decided to live according to her own feelings.

In this community, she is not alone. Juchitán and the surrounding region are well known not only for beautiful black pottery and delicious food but also for the large number of gays, lesbians, and transgender people who live there. At first glance, this fact may surprise people who think of Mexico as a traditional country, especially when it comes to gender and sexuality. In Mexico, the stereotype goes, men control the lives of women, especially their sexuality. But like all stereotypes, this one misses some important facts. Nationally, Mexico has become more tolerant of diverse sexual expression. In 2009, Mexico City, the nation's capital, began recognizing same-sex marriages. And nowhere is tolerance for sexual orientation greater than it is in the region around Juchitán.

There, transgender people are called *muxes* (pronounced "MOO-shayss"), which is based on the Spanish word *mujer*, meaning "woman." *Muxes* are considered neither male nor female but of a third gender. Some *muxes* wear women's clothing and act almost entirely in a feminine way. Others adopt a feminine look and behaviour only on

special occasions. One of the most popular events is the region's grand celebration, which is held every November and is attended by more than 2000 *muxes* and their families. A highlight of this event is a competition for the title of "transvestite of the year."

The acceptance of transgender people in central Mexico has its roots in the culture that existed before the Spanish arrived. At that time, anyone with ambiguous gender was viewed as especially wise and talented. The region's history includes accounts of Aztec priests and Mayan gods who cross-dressed or were considered to be both male and female. In the sixteenth century, the coming of the Spanish colonists and the influence of the Catholic Church reduced much of this gender tolerance. But acceptance of mixed sexual identity continues today in this region, where many people hold so tightly to their traditions that they speak only their ancient Zapotec language rather than Spanish.

And so it is in Juchitán that *muxes* are respected, accepted, and even celebrated. *Muxes* are successful in business and take leadership roles in the church and in politics. Most important, they are commonly accepted by friends and family alike. Alejandro lives with her parents and five siblings and helps her mother both selling flowers on the streets and at home. Her father, Victor Martinez Jimenez, is a local construction worker who speaks only Zapotec. He still refers to Alex as "him" but says "it was God who sent him, and why would I reject him? He helps his mother very much. Why would I get mad?" Alex's mother, Rosa Taledo Vicente, adds, "Every family considers it a blessing to have one gay son. While daughters marry and leave home, a *muxe* cares for his parents in their old age."

WHAT DO YOU THINK?

1. Do you think that Canadian society is tolerant of people wishing to combine masculine and feminine dress and behaviour? Why or why not?

2. *Muxes* are people who were born biologically male. How do you think the local people in this story would feel about women who wanted to dress and act like men? Would you expect equal tolerance for such people? Why or why not?

3. How do you personally feel about the existence of a third category of sexual identity? Explain your views.

Sources: Gave (2005), Lacey (2008), and Rosenberg (2008).

so, shouldn't gay men and lesbians expect the same legal protection from discrimination as, for example, Aboriginal Canadians?

○ **CHECK YOUR LEARNING** What evidence supports the position that sexual behaviour is constructed by society? That sexual orientation is rooted in biology?

How Many Gay People Are There?

What share of our population is gay? This is a hard question to answer because, as noted, sexual orientation is not a matter of neat categories. In addition, people are not always willing to discuss their sexuality with strangers or even family members. Alfred

Kinsey estimated that about 4 percent of males and 2 percent of females have an exclusively same-sex orientation, although he pointed out that most people experience same-sex attraction at some point in their lives.

Some social scientists put the gay share of the population at 10 percent. But research surveys show that how homosexuality is defined makes a big difference in the results (Mosher, Chandra, & Jones, 2005). In one study, just 6 percent of men and 11 percent of women between the ages of 15 and 44 reported engaging in homosexual activity *at some time in their lives*. At the same time, just 2.3 percent of men and 1.3 percent of women defined themselves as "partly" or "entirely" homosexual (Laumann et al., 1994). In recent American surveys, about 1.8 percent of men and 2.8 percent of women described themselves as bisexual. But bisexual experiences appear to be more common among younger people, especially while they live on college and university campuses (Laumann et al., 1994; Mosher, Chandra, & Jones, 2005). Many bisexuals do not think of themselves as either gay or straight, and their behaviour reflects elements of both gay and straight living.

Though there are no comparable Canadian studies on the number of gay and bisexual people, the results are likely to be about the same. A total of 34 200 couples identified themselves in the 2001 Census of Canada as belonging to a same-sex intimate union, which is 0.5 percent of all marital and common-law unions in the country. The 2006 Census enumerated 45 300 same-sex couples, which is a slight increase of 0.6 percent of all marital and common-law unions in Canada (Statistics Canada, 2009a). Figure 6–3 on page 146 shows the number of same-sex and opposite-sex Canadian families based on the percentage of people who label their sexual identity as either homosexual or bisexual.

The Gay Rights Movement

In the long term, the public attitude toward homosexuality is moving toward greater acceptance. In a national Canadian opinion poll (April 1998), for example, the majority in all provinces (64 percent of the population) agreed that "human rights legislation in Canada should protect gays and lesbians from discrimination based on their sexual orientation" (Angus Reid Group, 1998b). This is an increase in support from a previous poll (May/June 1996), which found less public support on other gay rights issues. On the issue of same-sex spousal benefits, a majority (55 percent) of those polled said they believe that "the partners of homosexual employees should be entitled to the same spousal benefits as an employer provides to the partners of heterosexual employees," with 41 percent opposed. There was lower public support for legally recognizing same-sex marriages. When asked the question "[D]o you think homosexual couples who wish to marry should or should not qualify for legal recognition of the marriage?", 47 percent opposed and 49 percent supported the recognition. A follow-up 2003 poll found that a slim majority—

Gay parades are now a common feature in most Canadian cities despite resistance in the past by some elected officials in places like Fredericton, Hamilton, and Kelowna.

54 percent—agreed with legal recognition of same-sex marriages (Ipsos-Reid, 2003d).

In 2003, the Ontario Court of Appeal issued the first certificate of marriage to a gay couple in Canada. Since this historic moment, it is estimated that more than 10 000 marriage licences have been issued to same-sex couples in Canada. Opinion polls show that Canadians have become increasingly supportive of gay "equal" marriage. A poll conducted by Environics Research Group (2006) asked those surveyed "whether they support equal marriage" and "whether the Conservative government should re-open the issue and have another vote or whether the issue is settled and there should not be another vote." Results show that nearly two-thirds of respondents were in favour of equal marriage and 62 percent of the respondents considered the matter settled and were thus opposed to reopening the issue and having an open vote in Parliament. A 2009 Angus Reid poll found that the level of support for same-sex unions remains the same and that 66 percent of Canadians believe that sexual relations between two people of the same sex is morally acceptable (Angus Reid, 2009c). Figure 6–4 on page 146 shows that attitudes about homosexuality have changed dramatically over the last 30 years.

In large measure, this change in public attitude was brought about by the gay rights movement, which arose in the middle of the twentieth century. Until that time, most people in Canada did not discuss homosexuality, and it was common for organizations (including the federal government and the armed forces) to fire anyone who was accused of being gay. Mental health

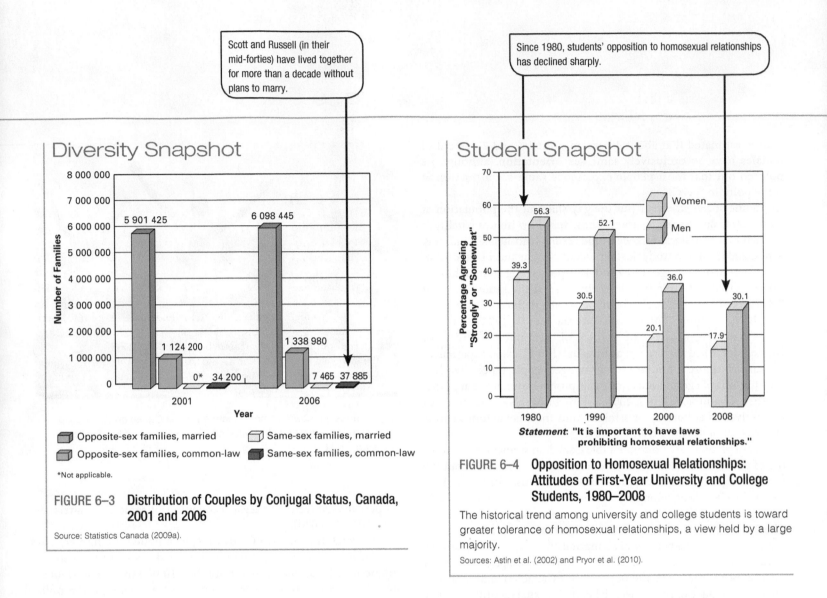

Scott and Russell (in their mid-forties) have lived together for more than a decade without plans to marry.

Since 1980, students' opposition to homosexual relationships has declined sharply.

Diversity Snapshot

FIGURE 6–3 **Distribution of Couples by Conjugal Status, Canada, 2001 and 2006**

Source: Statistics Canada (2009a).

*Not applicable.

Opposite-sex families, married
Opposite-sex families, common-law
Same-sex families, married
Same-sex families, common-law

Student Snapshot

Statement: "It is important to have laws prohibiting homosexual relationships."

FIGURE 6–4 **Opposition to Homosexual Relationships: Attitudes of First-Year University and College Students, 1980–2008**

The historical trend among university and college students is toward greater tolerance of homosexual relationships, a view held by a large majority.

Sources: Astin et al. (2002) and Pryor et al. (2010).

professionals also took a hard line, describing homosexuals as "sick" and sometimes placing them in mental hospitals, where it was hoped they might be "cured." It is no surprise that most lesbians and gay men remained "in the closet," closely guarding the secret of their sexual orientation. But the gay rights movement gained strength in the 1960s. One early milestone for the movement occurred in 1973, when the American Psychiatric Association declared that homosexuality was not an illness but simply "a form of sexual behaviour."

The gay rights movement also began using the term **homophobia** to describe *discomfort over close personal interaction with people thought to be gay, lesbian, or bisexual* (Weinberg, 1973). Concepts such as homophobia (literally, "fear of sameness"), and more recently "heterosexism" and "heteronormativity," turn the tables on society. Instead of asking "What's wrong with gay people?" the question becomes "What's wrong with people who can't accept a different sexual orientation?" (Martindale, 1998).

As another indication of the growing tolerance of same-sex relationships, in recent years an increasing number of high schools have had requests from gay and lesbian students that they be allowed to

bring a same-sex date to the senior prom. In many cases, this request sparks a controversy, as Seeing Sociology in the News explains.

Sexual Issues and Controversies

Sexuality lies at the heart of a number of controversies in Canada today. Here we take a look at four key issues: teen pregnancy, pornography, prostitution, and sexual violence.

Teen Pregnancy

Because of the risk of pregnancy, engaging in sexual activities—especially having intercourse—demands a high level of responsibility. Teenagers may be biologically mature enough to conceive, but many are not emotionally secure enough to appreciate the consequences of their actions.

In 2001, the annual teenage pregnancy rate in Canada fell to 30.6 pregnancies for every 1000 women under the age of 20 (Statistics Canada, 2004b). The teen pregnancy rate in Canada has continued

Gay Activist Student Marc Hall Drops Court Case, Leaving Catholic School Board without Chance for V

BY LIFESITENEWS.COM
June 29, 2005

OSHAWA, ON, June 29, 2005 (LifeSiteNews .com)—In 2002 Marc Hall was, using the words of Durham school board chair Mary Ann Martin, "the centre of the gay universe". The 17-year-old high school student burst onto the international scene when he demanded that his Catholic high school allow him to bring his 21-year-old boyfriend to the prom. When the school board refused to acquiesce, standing firmly behind the moral convictions of the Catholic faith to which the board adheres, he pursued legal action.

After costing the Durham school board well over $150,000 in legal fees, Marc was given what he demanded. An unprecedented court injunction was issued which ordered the school board not only to allow Hall to bring his homosexual partner to the prom, but also forbade the school from canceling the event to avoid violating the precepts of the Catholic faith.

David Corbett, Hall's legal council [sic], also gained from the anti-Catholic action, being promoted to the Ontario Superior Court shortly after winning the injunction.

But as an injunction ultimately holds little permanent legal weight, Hall also launched a $100,000 lawsuit against the school board. But now, after mainstream news media across the world have elevated him as a hero of the gay community, and after the school board has paid hundreds of thousands in legal fees, and the CBC shot and aired a made-for-TV movie about Halls [sic] fight for 'justice', Hall has announced his decision not to pursue the case to its conclusion.

"Marc is interested in these issues," said Andrew Pinto, Hall's current legal council, "but he realized it was not realistic for him to be personally involved in an issue that is actually one of philosophical and legal, moral and religious rights."

Durham school board chair Mary Ann Martin, however, isn't convinced that this is at all the reason for dropping the case. "My personal opinion is that the prom issue was just a stepping stone towards same-sex marriage and now that [gay rights activists] got the coverage that they wanted at the time, Mark's story has just fallen off to the side," said Martin. She pointed out that one of the main reasons Hall has chosen to drop the case is a lack of funding to pay for legal council. This wasn't a problem in 2002 when Hall had the whole gay-rights community backing him up. "They have dropped him like a hotcake," said Martin.

"And the thing was that [the Durham Catholic school board] wanted to continue and go to court," said Martin, lamenting this recent decision and what it means for the school board. In 2002, "The media didn't even understand that the injunction was not the trial itself, it was part of the case, that the case had never really been settled. We won't have the opportunity to go before the courts. We're being deprived of that."

In fact, Justice Shaughnessy, the judge who allowed Hall to drop the case, predicted that in all likelihood the school board would have been successful had the case proceeded to its conclusion. "The one good thing that came out of this was the endorsement by Shaughnessy," said Martin. "He believed that we probably would have been successful in court."

Phil Horgan, president of the Catholic Civil Rights League (CCRL) pointed out that the damage has already been done in the eyes of public opinion, and that it isn't likely to be corrected. "At the end of the day, although Justice Shaughnessy has cautioned any long-term precedent value of the initial decision, I would not expect same-sex advocates to highlight this recent finding in future discussion on this," said Horgan. "They'll talk about the 2002 deliberations, but not those of 2005."

"The school board has been denied the ability to defend its constitutionally protected denominational rights," said Horgan of Hall's recent decision.

WHAT DO YOU THINK?

1. Did your high school ever experience controversy about bringing same-sex dates to the prom or other events? Explain.

2. Do you think Marc Hall wanted to become a symbol of gay rights or did he simply want to go to his school's prom? Explain.

3. Why do you think Hall dropped the lawsuit against the Durham school board?

4. What about you? Would you take a public stand in a case like this? Explain.

Source: Gay Activist Student Marc Hall Drops Court Case, Leaving Catholic School Board Without Chance For V. Source: LifeSiteNews.com, June 29, 2005, http://www. lifesitenews.com/news/archive/ldn/2005/jun/05062905. Permission of LifeSiteNews.com.

See also Grace and Wells (2005) and Wells (2008).

to fall, and is in fact dropping faster than in the United States and England. Between 1996 and 2006, Canada's teen pregnancy rate fell by 36.9 percent, compared to a 25.0 percent decline in the United States and a 4.75 percent dip in England and Wales (Bielski, 2010). These outcomes are an indication of a greater awareness among Canadian youth about how to prevent pregnancy and delay parenting, as well as their ready access to contraception and abortion (McKay & Barrett, 2010). However, research shows that inequities persist in our country, including among rural and very young teens who have less access to sexual and reproductive health care (Shoveller et al., 2007). Furthermore, access to abortion remains limited or out of reach in some regions of the country (Maticka-Tyndale, 2008).

The situation is much different in the United States. Surveys show that there are almost 750 000 teen pregnancies in the United States each year, most of them unplanned (Alan Guttmacher Institute, 2006; Ventura et al., 2009). The rate of births to teenage women in the United States is higher than that of all other high-income countries and is twice the rate in Canada (Darroch et al., 2001; Population Reference Bureau, 2010).

homophobia (p. 146) discomfort over close personal interaction with people thought to be gay, lesbian, or bisexual

pornography sexually explicit material intended to cause sexual arousal

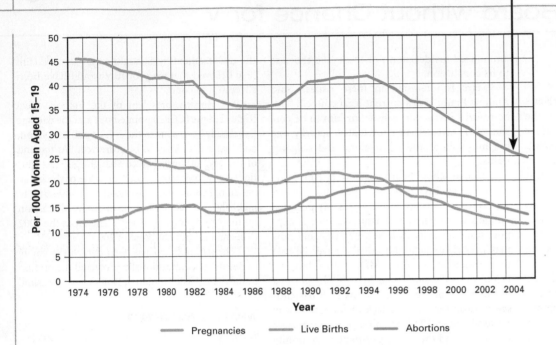

Delaying sexual activity is part of the reason why women today (and their partners) are less likely to become pregnant.

Student Snapshot

FIGURE 6–5 Teenage Pregnancies, Abortions, Live Births, Canada, 1974–2005

Source: Statistics Canada (2011g, 2011h, 2011i, 2011j).

Did the sexual revolution raise the rate of teenage pregnancy? Perhaps surprisingly, the answer is no. The rate of pregnancy among teens in 1950 was higher than it is today, partly because people then married at a younger age. In addition, because abortion was against the law, many pregnancies led to quick marriages. As a result, there were many pregnant teenagers, but most were married. Figure 6–5 shows that the number of pregnant teens today has fallen, but the vast majority of these women are unmarried.

Pornography

Pornography is *sexually explicit material intended to cause sexual arousal.* But what is and is not pornographic has long been a matter of debate. Recognizing that people view the portrayal of sexuality differently, the Supreme Court of Canada gives local communities the power to decide for themselves what violates "community standards" of decency and lacks any redeeming social value.

Child pornography is a very different matter, however. Section 163.1 of the Criminal Code states that "every person who possesses any child pornography is guilty of either a) an indictable offence and liable to imprisonment for a term not exceeding five years; or b) an offence punishable on summary conviction." Yet enforcement of even this law has proven to be difficult. In 1999, the British Columbia Court of Appeal struck down subsection 4 of section 163.1 of the Criminal Code, which makes the possession of child pornography a criminal offence, because the subsection

contravened the Charter of Rights and Freedoms. In January 2000, the Supreme Court of Canada heard arguments in an appeal of this B.C. court decision. During a retrial in March 2002, the presiding judge concluded that the written document of the accused, which consisted of 17 short stories describing man-boy and boy-boy sex—including sadism, masochism, and fellatio—was "artistic" and thus not in violation of child pornography law. However, the accused was found guilty of the lesser offence of possessing child pornography and given a minimal sentence of house arrest for four months.

Supreme Court decisions aside, pornography and erotica are popular in Canada: X-rated internet sites and videos, "900" telephone numbers for sexual conversations, and a host of sexually explicit movies and magazines together constitute a multi-billion-dollar-a-year industry. One-third of Canadians report having watched X-rated movies, and 20 percent of Canadians say that they read erotic literature or magazines (Angus Reid Group, 1998e). The figure is rising as Canadians consume more and more pornography from thousands of sites on the web.

Yet pornography has its critics. Some claim that pornography is a power issue because it endorses the cultural ideal of men as the legitimate controllers of both sexuality and women (MacKinnon, 1987). While it is difficult to document a scientific cause-and-effect relationship between what people view and how they act, research does support the idea that pornography makes men think of women as objects rather than as people (Attorney General's Commission on

Pornography, 1986; Malamuth & Donnerstein, 1984). The public share a concern about pornography and violence, with many lay people, as well as feminist researchers, holding the opinion that pornography encourages people to commit rape (Russell, 1998).

Canadians' moral compass with regards to pornography is also linked to their income. In a recent online survey of a representative national sample of Canadian adults, just over half (54%) of respondents in the higher-income bracket found pornography morally acceptable, which was much less the case for those in the middle-income (41%) and lower-income brackets (37%) (Angus Reid, 2009c).

Prostitution

Prostitution is *the selling of sexual services*. Often called the "world's oldest profession," prostitution has existed throughout recorded history. One Canadian survey found that 4 percent of male respondents admitted having paid for sexual favours one or more times (Peat Marwick, 1984). A more recent poll found that an even smaller number—2 percent—of Canadians have ever visited an erotic massage parlour, hired a sex worker, or used an escort service (Angus Reid Group, 1998e). Even so, to the extent that people think of sex as an expression of interpersonal intimacy, they find the idea of sex for money disturbing. Even in this regard, however, there are no cross-cultural universals.

Prostitution is actually not illegal in Canada. Rather, sex workers in Canada are arrested, prosecuted, and sometimes convicted not because they sell sex for money but because they "communicate" in a public place for the purpose of engaging in prostitution (Hackler, 1999; Shaver, 1993). Meanwhile, in Sweden, a recent law makes it legal for sex workers to sell sex but illegal for "johns" (customers) to purchase it (Boethus, 1999). The common belief in Canada is that "sex workers" or "sex industry workers" (less stigmatizing terms than *prostitutes*) are almost always female rather than male and are more culpable and blameworthy than their customers. Regulatory strategies are much more likely to concentrate on women who sell sex rather than on their male customers, because of the assumption that most customers are "square johns who would not otherwise fall afoul with the law, while prostitutes are members of a criminal underclass whose lifestyle involves various types of law breaking" (Lowman, 1990:63–64). Consequently, as it is socially constructed and legally enforced, prostitution in Canada remains biased against women and in favour of men (Boritch, 1997; Shaver, 1993).

Around the world, prostitution shows tremendous variation: sex workers in the Netherlands and Germany not only have legal rights to work but also pay taxes and collect social benefits that accompany most legitimate jobs. In Queensland and Victoria, Australia, brothels may operate legally if their owners and operators are licensed by state-level government and if the town approves the brothel premises under town planning guidelines. The Prostitution

Reform Act 2003 was passed in New Zealand with the main aim of decriminalizing most aspects of sex industry work at the national level and enhancing the working conditions and health and safety of legal adult residents working in the sex industry (Abel, Fitzgerald, & Healy, 2010). On the other hand, in low-income countries where patriarchy is strong and traditional cultural norms limit women's ability to earn a living, prostitution may be the only option available to women in terms of providing for their own and their children's survival. Global Map 6–2 on page 150 shows where in the world prostitution is most widespread.

Types of Prostitution

Most sex workers are women (estimates range from 70 to 80 percent), but they fall into different categories. Call girls (and, more rarely, call boys) are elite sex workers who are typically young, attractive, and well educated and who arrange their own "dates" with clients via telephone. The classified pages of any large city newspaper contain numerous ads for "escort services," through which women (and sometimes men) offer both companionship and sex for a fee. A middle category of sex workers is located in "massage parlours" and brothels, which are under the control of managers. These sex workers have less choice about their clients, receive less money for their services, and are allowed to keep no more than half of what they earn. At the bottom of the sex worker hierarchy are streetwalkers, women and men who "work the streets" of large cities. Some female streetwalkers are under the control of male pimps who take most of their earnings. Many streetwalkers fall victim to violence from pimps' managers and clients (Davidson, 1998; Gordon & Snyder, 1989).

Canadian research shows that sex workers located in off-street "escort agencies" tend to enjoy safer, more stable, and more lucrative work conditions than do their counterparts working on the street (Brock, 1998; Lewis & Maticka-Tyndale, 1999; Lowman & Fraser, 1995). Other research on off-street and on-street sex work supports this general finding but also shows that, in the absence of even minimum work standards, workers in escort agencies and massage parlours and other indoor employment venues have no legal avenue to protect themselves when subject to exploitation by their employers (Benoit & Millar, 2001; Phillips & Benoit, 2005).

Most, but not all, sex workers offer heterosexual services. Some gays also trade sex for money. Researchers report that many gay sex workers have suffered rejection by family and friends because of their sexual orientation (Boyer, 1989; Kruks, 1991; Weisberg, 1985). Research on transgender sex workers in San Francisco's Tenderloin area suggests that they face a similar situation of discrimination and rejection because of their sexual orientation (Weinberg, Shaver, & Williams, 2000).

A Victimless Crime?

Prostitution is against the law in many countries, but many people consider it a victimless crime (see Chapter 7, "Deviance"). Consequently,

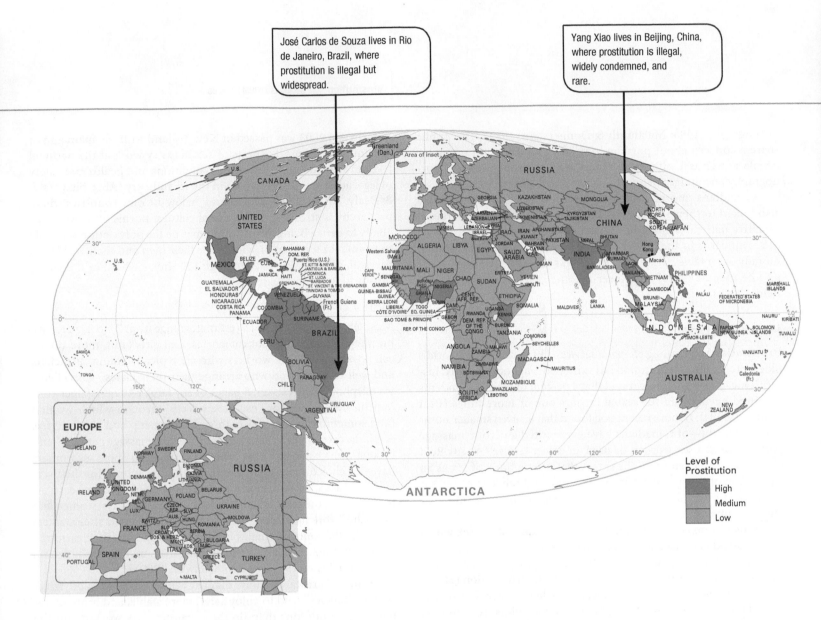

Generally speaking, prostitution is widespread in societies where women have low standing. Officially, at least, the People's Republic of China boasts of gender equality, including the elimination of "vice" such as prostitution, which oppresses women. By contrast, in much of Latin America, where patriarchy is strong, prostitution is common. In many Islamic societies, patriarchy is also strong, but religion is a counterbalance, so prostitution is limited. Western, high-income nations have a moderate amount of prostitution.

José Carlos de Souza lives in Rio de Janeiro, Brazil, where prostitution is illegal but widespread.

Yang Xiao lives in Beijing, China, where prostitution is illegal, widely condemned, and rare.

Level of Prostitution

High

Medium

Low

Window on the World

GLOBAL MAP 6–2 Prostitution in Global Perspective

Generally speaking, prostitution is widespread in societies where women have low standing. Officially, at least, the People's Republic of China boasts of gender equality, including the elimination of "vice" such as prostitution, which oppresses women. By contrast, in much of Latin America, where patriarchy is strong, prostitution is common. In many Islamic societies, patriarchy is also strong, but religion is a counterbalance, so prostitution is limited. Western, high-income nations have a moderate amount of prostitution.

Sources: Mackay (2000).

instead of enforcing prostitution laws all the time, police stage only occasional crackdowns. This policy reflects a desire to control prostitution while assuming that nothing will totally eliminate it.

Is selling sex a victimless crime that hurts no one? Certainly, many people take this position, arguing that prostitution should be viewed as an occupation, as simply a way to make a living (Elias, Bullough, Elias, & Elders, 1998; Scambler & Scambler, 1997). Further, because of difficulties in getting jobs that provide a decent wage for marginalized people, in particular working-class female single parents, sex work represents a viable choice from their perspective (Chapkis, 1997). However, because prostitution is a semi-illegal and illegitimate occupation in Canada, it is very difficult for sex workers to receive the same benefits and rights as other workers, such as sick leave, health insurance, social insurance, or workers' compensation (Lewis & Maticka-Tyndale, 1999; Lowman & Fraser, 1995; Shaver, 1993).

Challenging the Prostitution Laws in Canada

Canadians place a premium on the importance of personal safety and health. To this end we have instituted a universal health care system and a variety of social, legal, and economic policies designed to ensure the health and safety of all members of Canadian society. Sadly, members of some of Canada's most stigmatized and vulnerable populations have fallen through this safety net. Many women, men, and transgender individuals working in the most unregulated and impoverished environments of the sex industry not only suffer from comparatively poor physical, emotional, and mental health but also experience an elevated risk of violence, victimization, and premature death. Violence against people working in the sex industry has become an even more salient social problem in light of the sentencing of Robert Pickton in 2007 for the multiple murders of Vancouver's Downtown Eastside "missing women," the majority of whom have been identified as Aboriginal and all of whom were involved in sex work. While research shows that street-based sex workers are at greatest risk of sexual assault and homicide (Du Mont & McGregor, 2004; Lowman, 1998), other forms of systematic racial, sexual, and gender-based violence—ranging from emotional abuse to dangerous working conditions—which are exacerbated by social and legal stigma, have been found to be embedded in the structural organization of many other segments of the sex industry (Church &

Henderson, 2001; Lewis et al., 2005; Watts & Zimmerman, 2002).

Canadian federal prostitution laws have long been seen by many academics, sex worker rights advocates, and health and social service providers as one of the most significant contributing factors in the violence and victimization experienced by sex workers (Benoit & Shaver, 2006; Lowman, 1998). The September 2010 landmark ruling by Ontario Superior Court Justice Susan Himel, which struck down these laws for endangering the lives of sex workers, not only supports this belief but has also been celebrated by some as a major step forward since it opens up a space for the development of policy and legislation that can better meet the health and safety needs of those involved in Canada's sex industry. A moratorium was granted for the federal government

to organize an appeal of the ruling; which party ultimately will be successful remains uncertain. The deeper sociological question is what forms of policy and legislation will be most effective in helping to prevent violence and victimization and in supporting the diverse health and safety needs of people involved in this industry. Should the context of selling and buying sex continue to be criminalized, or should Canada change its prostitution laws and legalize off-street sex work, as is currently the case in many European countries such as the Netherlands and Germany? Alternatively, should Canada decriminalize the industry, as New Zealand did in 2003? A final strategy would be for Canada to decriminalize the selling of sex but continue to criminalize the buying of sex, which is the current law in Sweden.

CONTINUE THE DEBATE . . .

1. Should Canada change its prostitution laws?

2. If changed, in which direction do you think legal policy should go and why?

3. Apart from legal changes, what else should be done to reduce violence and victimization of people in the sex industry?

Sources: Benoit and Shaver (2006); Church and Henderson (2001); Du Mont and McGregor (2004); Globe and Mail (2010, September 28); Lewis, Maticka-Tyndale, Shaver, and Schramm (2005); Lowman (1998); Surratt, Inciardi, Kurtz, and Kiley (2004); and Watts and Zimmerman (2002).

The issue of violence among sex workers has recently gained media attention after the multiple murders of women involved in street-based sex work in Vancouver's Downtown Eastside. Subsequently, on September 28, 2010, Ontario Superior Court Justice Susan Himel found three crucial sections of the Criminal Code of Canada unconstitutional and struck them down because "the law as it stands is currently contributing to danger faced by

prostitutes."[1] See the Controversy & Debate box for a discussion of this issue. An Angus Reid (2009b) survey conducted following this court case asked a representative sample of Canadian adults how strongly they supported or opposed allowing sex workers to work indoors or

[1]*Bedford v. Canada*, 07-CV-329807 PD1 ONSC 4264 (2010, p. 130). Retrieved from http://www.canlii.org/en/on/onsc/doc/2010/2010onsc4264/2010onsc4264.html

SEEING SOCIOLOGY
IN EVERYDAY LIFE

When Sex Is Only Sex: The Campus Culture of "Hooking Up"

BRYNNE: My mom told me once that she didn't have SEX with my dad until after they were engaged.

KATY: I guess times really have changed!

Have you ever been in a sexual situation and not been sure of the right thing to do? Most colleges and universities highlight two important rules. First, sexual activity must take place only when both participants have given clear statements of consent. The consent principle is what makes "having sex" different from date rape. Second, no one should knowingly expose a partner to a sexually transmitted infection, especially when the partner is unaware of the danger.

These rules are very important, but they say little about the larger issue of what sex *means*. For example, when is it "right" to have a sexual relationship? How well do you have to know the other person? If you do have sex, are you obligated to see the person again?

Two generations ago, there were informal rules for campus sex. Dating was part of the courtship process. That is, "going out" was a way in which women and men evaluated each other as possible marriage partners while they sharpened their own sense of what they wanted in a mate. Because, on average, marriage took place when people were in their early twenties, many college and university students became engaged

and married while they were still completing their post-secondary education. In this cultural climate, sex became part of a relationship along with commitment—a serious interest in the other person as a possible marriage partner.

Today, the sexual culture of the campus is very different. Partly because people now marry or cohabit much later, the culture of courtship has declined dramatically. About three-fourths of women in a recent national survey point to a new campus pattern, the culture of "hooking up." What exactly is hooking up? Most describe it in words like these: "When a girl and a guy get together for a physical encounter—anything from kissing to having sex—and don't necessarily expect anything further."

Student responses to the survey suggest that "hookups" have three characteristics. First, most couples who hook up know little about each other. Second, a typical hookup involves people who have been drinking alcohol, usually at a campus party. Third, most women are critical of the culture of hooking up and express little satisfaction with these encounters. Certainly, some women (and men) who hook up simply walk away, happy to have enjoyed a sexual experience free of further obligation. But given the powerful emotions that sex can unleash, hooking up often leaves someone wondering what to expect next. "Will you call me tomorrow?" "Will I see you again?"

The survey asked women who had experienced a recent hookup to report how they felt about the experience a day later. A majority of respondents said they felt "awkward," about half felt "disappointed" and "confused," and one in four felt "exploited." Clearly, for many people, sex is more than a physical encounter. Further, because today's campus is very sensitive to charges of sexual exploitation, there is a need for clearer standards of fair play.

WHAT DO YOU THINK?

1. How extensive is hooking up on your campus? Are you aware of differences in these encounters among heterosexuals and among homosexuals?

2. What do you see as the advantages of sex without commitment? What are the disadvantages of this kind of relationship? Are men and women likely to answer these questions differently? Explain.

3. Do you think that college and university students need more guidance about sexual issues? If so, who should provide this guidance?

Source: Based in part on Marquardt and Glenn (2001).

in brothels. Overall, 60 percent of respondents gave moderate or strong support to allowing indoor sex work, while 30 percent were opposed. Seventy-one percent of men would allow sex work indoors or in brothels, compared to 50 percent of women, and respondents become more liberal in their attitudes the further west they live. These results show that Canadians are becoming less supportive of criminalization of prostitution, but that significant gender and regional differences remain.

Sexual Violence: Rape and Date Rape

Ideally, sexual activity occurs within a loving relationship between consenting adults. In reality, however, sex can sometimes be twisted by hatred and violence. Here we consider two types of sexual violence: rape and date rape.

Rape

Although some people think that rape is motivated only by a desire for sex, it is actually an expression of power, a violent act that uses sex to hurt, humiliate, or control another person. Data from the Canadian Centre for Justice Statistics indicate that 6 percent of females who reported being victims of a violent crime in Canada in 2008 were victims of sexual assault, and that 92 percent of the victims of sexual violence were women (Vaillancourt, 2010). Remember that these crime statistics reflect only the reported cases; it is estimated that 91 percent of sexual assaults are not reported (Brennan & Taylor-Butts, 2008). The actual incidence of sexual assault is therefore much higher. *Sexual assault* is a comprehensive term referring to non-consensual sexual activity ranging from sexual touching, kissing, and sexual intercourse to sexual violence against a person's will. While men constitute 15 percent of sexual assault victims, women and children make up a disproportionate share. In 2007, 58 percent of all victims of sexual assault reported to the police in Canada were children and youth under 18 years of age, with children under the age of 12 making up 25 percent (Brennan & Taylor-Butts, 2008).

Date Rape

A common myth is that rape involves strangers. In reality, however, only about one-third of all rapes fit this pattern. Two of every three rapes involve people who know each other—more often than not, pretty well—and these crimes usually take place in familiar surroundings, such as the home or a college or university campus. The terms *date rape* and *acquaintance rape* refer to forcible sexual violence against women by men they know (Brennan & Taylor-Butts, 2008; Laumann et al., 1994).

A second myth, often linked specifically to date rape, is the idea that a woman who has been raped must have done something to encourage the man and make him think she wanted to have sex. Perhaps the victim agreed to go out with the offender. Maybe she even invited him to her room. But, of course, such actions no more justify rape than they would any other kind of physical assault.

Although rape is a physical attack, it also leaves emotional and psychological scars. Beyond the brutality of being physically violated, rape by an acquaintance affects a victim's ability to trust others. Psychological scars are especially serious among the two-thirds of sexual assault victims who are under age 18 and even more so among the one-third who are under age 12. The home is no refuge from rape: One-third of all victims under age 18 are attacked by their own fathers or stepfathers (Snyder, 2000).

How common is date rape? Recent surveys in the United States have found that about 10 percent of all teens and 20 percent of high school girls report having been victims of sexual or physical violence inflicted by the boys they were dating (Centers for Disease Control and Prevention, 2008; Teenage Research Unlimited, 2008). It is estimated that 20 to 25 percent of women will be victims of sexual assault at some point during their university careers (Decker, Silverman, & Raj, 2005).

Nowhere has the issue of date rape been more widely discussed than on university and college campuses, where the danger of date rape is high. The collegiate environment promotes easy friendships and encourages trust. At the same time, many young students have much to learn about relationships and about themselves. As the Seeing Sociology in Everyday Life box explains, although campus life encourages communication, it provides few social norms to help guide young people's sexual experiences. To counter the problem, many schools now actively address myths about rape. In addition, greater attention is now focused on the use of alcohol, which increases the likelihood of sexual violence.

The control of women's sexuality is a common theme throughout human history. During the Middle Ages, Europeans devised the "chastity belt"—a metal device locked about a woman's groin that prevented sexual intercourse (and probably interfered with other bodily functions as well). While such devices are all but unknown today, the social control of sexuality continues. Can you point to examples?

Theoretical Analysis of Sexuality

Applying sociology's various theoretical approaches gives us a better understanding of human sexuality. The following sections discuss the three major approaches. The Applying Theory table on page 154 highlights the key insights of each approach.

Structural-Functional Analysis

The structural-functional approach explains the contribution of any social pattern to the overall operation of society. Because sexuality can have such important consequences, society regulates this type of behaviour.

The Need to Regulate Sexuality

From a biological point of view, sex allows our species to reproduce. But culture and social institutions regulate *with whom* and *when* people reproduce. For example, most societies condemn married people who have sex with someone other than a spouse. To allow the forces of sexual passion to go unchecked would threaten family life, especially the raising of children.

APPLYING THEORY

Sexuality

	Structural-Functional Approach	Symbolic-Interaction Approach	Social-Conflict/Feminist Approach
What is the level of analysis?	Macro level	Micro level	Macro level
What is the importance of sexuality for society?	Society depends on sexuality for reproduction. Society uses the incest taboo and other norms to control sexuality in order to maintain social order.	Sexual practices vary among the many cultures of the world. Some societies allow individuals more freedom than others in matters of sexual behaviour.	Sexuality is linked to social inequality. Canadian society regulates women's sexuality more than men's, which is part of the larger pattern of men dominating women.
Has sexuality changed over time? How?	Yes. As advances in birth control technology separate sex from reproduction, societies relax some controls on sexuality.	Yes. The meanings people attach to virginity and other sexual matters are all socially constructed and subject to change.	Yes and no. Some sexual standards have relaxed over time, but society still defines women in sexual terms, just as homosexual people are harmed by society's heterosexual bias.

The fact that the incest taboo exists everywhere shows clearly that no society permits a completely free choice of sexual partners. Reproduction by family members other than married partners would break down the kinship system and hopelessly confuse human relationships.

Historically, the social control of sexuality was strong, mostly because sex often led to childbirth. We see these controls at work in the old-fashioned distinction between "legitimate" reproduction (within marriage) and "illegitimate" reproduction (outside marriage). But once a society develops the technology to control births, its sexual norms become more permissive. This occurred in Canada and other high-income countries, when over the course of the twentieth century sex moved beyond its basic reproductive function and became mainly a form of intimacy and even recreation (Giddens, 1992).

Latent Functions: The Case of Prostitution

Previously we saw why critics see prostitution as harmful. But does it have latent functions that help explain why this institution is so widespread? According to Kingsley Davis (1971), prostitution is one way to meet the sexual needs of a large number of people who do not have ready access to sex, including soldiers, travellers, disabled people, and those who are not physically attractive enough or are too poor to attract a romantic partner (Lowman & Atchison, 2006).

CRITICAL REVIEW The structural-functional approach helps us appreciate the important role sexuality plays in the organization of society. The incest taboo and other cultural norms suggest that society has always paid attention to who has sex with whom and, especially, who reproduces with whom.

Functional analysis sometimes ignores gender; when Kingsley Davis wrote of the benefits of prostitution for society, he was really talking about the benefits to *men*. As some researchers have noted, men favour prostitution because they want sex without the "trouble" of a relationship—that is, "Men don't pay for sex; they pay so they can leave" (Miracle, Miracle, & Baumeister, 2003:421).

In addition, the fact that sexual patterns change over time, just as they differ around the world, is ignored by this perspective. To appreciate the varied and changeable nature of sexuality, we now turn to the symbolic-interaction approach.

CHECK YOUR LEARNING Compared to traditional societies, why do modern societies give people more choice about matters involving sexuality?

Symbolic-Interaction Analysis

The symbolic-interaction approach highlights how as people interact, they construct everyday reality. As explained in Chapter 4

("Social Interaction in Everyday Life"), different people construct different realities, so the views of one group or society may well differ from those of another. In the same way, our understanding of sexuality can and does change over time, just as it differs from one society to another.

The Social Construction of Sexuality

Almost all social patterns involving sexuality saw a lot of change over the course of the past century. One good illustration is the changing importance of virginity. A century ago, our society's norm—for women, at least—was virginity before marriage. This norm was strong because there was no effective means of birth control available, and virginity was the only assurance a man had that his bride-to-be was not carrying another man's child. Today, because we have gone a long way toward separating sex from reproduction, the virginity norm has weakened considerably.

Another example of our society's construction of sexuality involves young people. A century ago, childhood was a time of innocence in sexual matters. In recent decades, however, thinking has changed. Although few people encourage sexual activity between children, most people believe that children should be educated about sex so they can make intelligent choices about their behaviour as they grow older.

Global Comparisons

Around the world, different societies attach different meanings to sexuality. For example, Ruth Benedict (1938), an anthropologist who spent years learning the ways of life of the Melanesian people of southeastern New Guinea, reported that adults paid little attention when young children engaged in sexual experimentation with one another. Parents in Melanesia shrugged off such activity because before puberty, sex cannot lead to reproduction. Is it likely that most parents in Canada would respond the same way?

Sexual practices also vary from culture to culture. Circumcision of infant boys (the practice of removing all or part of the foreskin of the penis) is common in Canada and the United States but rare in most other parts of the world, including European countries. A practice sometimes referred to as female circumcision (removal of the clitoris) is rare in Canada and the United States but common in parts of Africa and the Middle East (Crossette, 1995; Huffman, 2000). (For more about this practice, more accurately called *female genital mutilation*, see the Thinking about Diversity box on page 268).

○ **CRITICAL REVIEW** The strength of the symbolic-interaction approach lies in revealing the socially constructed character of familiar social patterns. Understanding that people "construct" sexuality, we can better appreciate the variety of sexual attitudes and practices found over the course of history and around the world.

One limitation of this approach is that not all sexual practices are so variable. Men everywhere have always been more likely to see women in sexual terms than the other way around. Some broader social structure must be at work in a pattern that is this widespread, as we shall see in the following section on the social-conflict approach.

○ **CHECK YOUR LEARNING** What evidence can you provide showing that human sexuality is socially constructed?

Social-Conflict and Feminist Analysis

As you have seen in earlier chapters, the social-conflict approach highlights dimensions of inequality. This approach reveals how sexuality both reflects patterns of social inequality and helps perpetuate them. Feminism, a social-conflict approach focusing on gender inequality, links sexuality to the domination of women by men.

Sexuality: Reflecting Social Inequality

Recall our discussion of prostitution, a practice about which Canadians are deeply divided. Enforcement of prostitution laws is uneven at best, especially when it comes to who is and is not likely to be arrested. Gender bias is evident here: Although two people are involved, the record shows that police are far more likely to arrest (less powerful) female sex workers than (more powerful) male clients. Class inequality, too, is involved: It is street-level sex workers—those usually with the least income and most likely to be Aboriginals—who face the highest risk of arrest (Lowman, 2000; Saint James & Alexander, 2004). A feminist approach also leads us to ask whether as many women would be involved in prostitution in the first place if they had economic opportunities equal to those of men.

More generally, which categories of people in Canadian society are most likely to be defined in terms of their sexuality? The answer, once again, is those with less power: women compared to men, visible minorities compared to whites, and gays and lesbians compared to heterosexuals. In this way, sexuality, a natural part of human life, is used by society to define some people as less worthy.

Sexuality: Creating Social Inequality

Social-conflict theorists, especially feminists, point to sexuality as the root of inequality between women and men. Defining women in sexual terms devalues them from full human beings to objects of men's interest and attention. Is it any wonder that the word *pornography* comes from the Greek word *porne*, meaning "harlot" or "prostitute"?

If men define women in sexual terms, it is easy to see pornography—almost all of which is consumed by males—as a power issue. Because pornography typically shows women focused on pleasing men, it supports the idea that men have power over women.

queer theory a body of research findings that challenges the heterosexual bias in North American society

heterosexism a view that labels anyone who is not heterosexual as "queer"

From a social-conflict point of view, sexuality is not so much a "natural" part of our humanity as it is a socially constructed pattern of behaviour. Sexuality plays an important part in social inequality: By defining women in sexual terms, men devalue them as objects. Would you consider the behaviour shown here to be "natural" or socially directed? Why?

Some radical critics doubt that this element of power can ever be removed from heterosexual relations (Dworkin, 1987). Most social-conflict theorists do not reject heterosexuality, but they do agree that sexuality can and does degrade women and other minority groups. Our culture often describes sexuality in terms of sport (men "scoring" with women) and violence ("slamming," "banging," and "hitting on," for example, are verbs used for both fighting and sex).

Queer Theory

Social-conflict theory has taken aim not only at the domination of women by men but also at heterosexuals dominating homosexuals.

In recent years, as many lesbians and gay men have sought public acceptance, a gay voice has risen in sociology. The term **queer theory** refers to *a body of research findings that challenges the heterosexual bias in North American society.*

Queer theory begins with the claim that our society is characterized by **heterosexism**, *a view that labels anyone who is not heterosexual as "queer."* Our heterosexual culture victimizes a wide range of people, including gay men, lesbians, bisexuals, transsexuals, and even asexual people. Furthermore, although most people agree that bias against women (sexism) and people of colour (racism) is wrong, heterosexism is widely tolerated and sometimes well within the law. For example, U.S. military forces cannot legally discharge a female soldier for "acting like a woman" because that would be a clear case of gender discrimination. But until 2011, when the policy was changed, as long as it was "Don't ask, don't tell", the military forces could discharge her form homosexuality if she was a sexually active lesbian.

Heterosexism is also part of everyday culture (Land & Kitzinger, 2005). When we describe something as "sexy," for example, don't we really mean that it's attractive to *heterosexuals*?

CRITICAL REVIEW The social-conflict approach shows how sexuality is both a cause and an effect of inequality. In particular, it helps us understand men's power over women and heterosexual people's domination of homosexual people.

At the same time, this approach overlooks the fact that many people do not see sexuality as a power issue. On the contrary, many couples enjoy a vital sexual relationship that deepens their commitment to one another. In addition, the social-conflict approach pays little attention to steps our society has made toward reducing inequality. Today's men are less likely to describe women as sex objects than they were a few decades ago. One of the most important issues in the workplace today is ensuring that all employees remain free from sexual harassment. Rising public concern (see Chapter 10, "Gender Stratification") has reduced sex abuse in the workplace. There is also ample evidence that the gay rights movement has won greater opportunities and social acceptance for gay people.

CHECK YOUR LEARNING How does sexuality play a part in creating social inequality?

CHAPTER 6 SEXUALITY AND SOCIETY

HOW DO THE MASS MEDIA PLAY INTO OUR SOCIETY'S VIEWS OF HUMAN SEXUALITY? Far from it being a "natural" or simply "biological" concept, cultures around the world attach all sorts of meanings to human sexuality. The photos below show how the mass media—in this case, popular magazines—reflect our own culture's ideas about sexuality. In each case, can you "decode" the magazine cover and explain its messages? To what extent do you think the messages are true?

Magazines like this one are found at the checkout lines of just about every supermarket and discount store in Canada. Looking just at the cover, what can you conclude about women's sexuality in our society?

Messages about sexuality are directed to men as well as to women. Here is a recent issue of *GQ*. What messages about masculinity can you find? Do you see any evidence of heterosexual bias?

HINT: The messages we get from mass media sources like these tell us not only about sexuality but also about what sort of people we ought to be. The message of hegemonic femininity places a lot of importance on sexuality for women, putting pressure on women to look good to men and to define life success in terms of attracting men with their sexuality. Similarly, the message of hegemonic masculinity portrays men as successful, sophisticated, in charge, and, of course, able to attract desirable women. When the mass media endorse sexuality, it is almost always according to the norm of heterosexuality.

Applying Sociology in Everyday Life

1. Looking at the *Marie Claire* cover, what evidence of heterosexual bias do you see? Explain.
2. Contact your school's student services office and ask for information about the extent of sexual violence on your campus. Do people typically report such crimes? What policies and procedures does your school have to respond to sexual violence?
3. Use the campus library and internet sources to learn more about the experiences of women and men involved in sex work. As you learn more, decide whether you think prostitution should be considered a "victimless crime."

MAKING THE GRADE

CHAPTER 6   Sexuality and Society

Understanding Sexuality

SEX is biological, referring to bodily differences between females and males.
p. 135

GENDER is cultural, referring to behaviour, power, and privileges a society attaches to being female or male.
pp. 135–36

sex (p. 135) the biological distinction between females and males

primary sex characteristics (p. 135) the genitals, organs used for reproduction

secondary sex characteristics (p. 135) bodily development, apart from the genitals, that distinguishes biologically mature females and males

intersexual people (p. 136) people whose bodies (including genitals) have both female and male characteristics

transsexuals (p. 136) people who feel they are one sex even though biologically they are the other

incest taboo (p. 137) a norm forbidding sexual relations or marriage between certain relatives

Sexuality is a **BIOLOGICAL ISSUE.**
- Sex is determined at conception as a male sperm joins a female ovum.
- Males and females have different genitals (primary sex characteristics) and bodily development (secondary sex characteristics).
- Intersexual people (hermaphrodites) have some combination of male and female genitalia.
- Transsexual people feel they are one sex although biologically they are the other.
pp. 135–36

Sexuality is a **CULTURAL ISSUE.**
- For humans, sex is a matter of cultural meaning and personal choice rather than biological programming.
- Sexual practices vary considerably from one society to another (examples include kissing, ideas about modesty, and standards of beauty).
- The incest taboo exists in all societies because regulating sexuality, especially reproduction, is a necessary element of social organization. Specific taboos vary from one society to another.
pp. 136–38

✓ Sexuality is a theme found throughout most areas of social life in Canada (p. 135).

Sexual Attitudes in Canada

The **SEXUAL REVOLUTION**, which peaked in the 1960s and 1970s, drew sexuality into the open. Baby boomers were the first generation to grow up with the idea that sex was a normal part of social life.
p. 139

The **SEXUAL COUNTER-REVOLUTION**, which was evident by 1980, aimed criticism at "permissiveness" and urged a return to more traditional "family values."
p. 139

Beginning with the work of Alfred Kinsey, researchers have studied sexual behaviour and reached many interesting conclusions:
- Premarital sexual intercourse became more common during the twentieth century.
- The majority of young men and women in Canada have intercourse between the ages of 16 and 18 years.
- Canadians have sex about six times per month, but the rate varies across age groups and geographical regions.
- Extramarital sex is widely condemned; just 15 percent of Canadians agree that married men or women having an affair is morally acceptable.
pp. 139–42

Sexual Orientation

SEXUAL ORIENTATION is a person's romantic or emotional attraction to another person. Four sexual orientations are
- heterosexuality
- homosexuality
- bisexuality
- asexuality
p. 142

The 2006 Census of Canada enumerated 45 300 same-sex couples.
p. 145

Most research supports the claim that sexual orientation is rooted in biology in much the same way as is being right-handed or left-handed.
p. 143

Sexual orientation is not a matter of neat categories because many people who think of themselves as heterosexual have homosexual experiences; the reverse is also true.

pp. 144–45

The gay rights movement helped change public attitudes toward greater acceptance of homosexuality. Still, 44 percent of Canadian adults say homosexuality is morally unacceptable.

pp. 145–46

sexual orientation (p. 142) a person's romantic and emotional attraction to another person

heterosexuality (p. 142) sexual attraction to someone of the other sex

homosexuality (p. 142) sexual attraction to someone of the same sex

bisexuality (p. 142) sexual attraction to people of both sexes

asexuality (p. 142) a lack of sexual attraction to people of either sex

homophobia (p. 146) discomfort over close personal interaction with people thought to be gay, lesbian, or bisexual

Sexual Issues and Controversies

TEEN PREGNANCY Between 1996 and 2006, Canada's teen pregnancy rate fell by 36.9 percent, indicating a greater awareness among Canadian youth about how to prevent pregnancy and delay parenting, as well as their ready access to contraception and abortion.

pp. 146–48

PORNOGRAPHY The law allows local communities to set standards of decency. Conservatives condemn pornography on moral grounds; liberals view pornography as a power issue, condemning it as demeaning to women.

pp. 148–49

PROSTITUTION The selling of sexual services is illegal almost everywhere in the United States but not in Canada, and its legality varies greatly across the globe. Many people view prostitution as a victimless crime, while others view it as the best alternative for economically disadvantaged people and thus believe it should be decriminalized.

pp. 149–52

SEXUAL VIOLENCE Rapes are violent crimes in which victims and offenders typically know one another. It is estimated that 20 to 25 percent of women will be victims of sexual assault at some point during their university careers.

pp. 152–54

pornography (p. 148) sexually explicit material intended to cause sexual arousal

prostitution (p. 149) the selling of sexual services

Theoretical Analysis of Sexuality

The **STRUCTURAL-FUNCTIONAL APPROACH** highlights society's need to regulate sexual activity and especially reproduction. One universal norm is the incest taboo, which keeps family relations clear.

p. 154

The **SYMBOLIC-INTERACTION APPROACH** emphasizes the various meanings people attach to sexuality. The social construction of sexuality can be seen in sexual differences between societies and in changing sexual patterns over time.

pp. 155

queer theory (p. 156) a body of research findings that challenges the heterosexual bias in North American society

heterosexism (p. 156) a view that labels anyone who is not heterosexual as "queer"

The **SOCIAL-CONFLICT/FEMINIST APPROACH** links sexuality to social inequality. Feminist theory claims that men dominate women by devaluing them to the level of sexual objects. Queer theory claims that our society has a heterosexual bias, defining anything different as "queer."

pp. 155–56

MySocLab

Visit MySocLab at www.mysoclab.com to access a variety of online resources that will help you to prepare for tests and to apply your knowledge, including

- an eText
- videos
- self-grading quizzes
- glossary flashcards

7 Deviance

- Why does every society have deviance?

- How does *who* and *what* are defined as deviant reflect social inequality?

- What effect has punishment had in reducing crime in Canada?

This chapter investigates how society encourages both conformity and deviance, and it provides an introduction to crime and the criminal justice system.

"Timmy[1] is a lifer who spent several decades in prison. Having begun his prison sentence as a teenager, he missed out on the usual rituals associated with growing into adulthood; instead, he became an adult in prison and institutional life was his reality. After release, he struggled to cope and to find his place in society. It wasn't easy and little things 'tripped him up'; eloquently demonstrating this metaphor, he once said that he kept stumbling over the sidewalk because there were 'no curbs in prison'" (Munn, 2011:1).

There are currently nearly 5000 Canadians serving life sentences who are serving a minimum of 10 years in prison before becoming eligible for parole (Olotu et al., 2009). Most lifers will eventually be released into the community and will be expected to become active members of Canadian society.

"But readjustment after longterm prison is no easy feat (C. Jones, 2007). Most have nowhere to go and no way to get there. They often have no valid identification, which is needed to find a place to live and a job. They likely have no money to buy the clothes they need to go out and start looking. In addition, they have to learn to become self-reliant: 'Once you leave the halfway house, then you have to take care of yourself. . . . I have to do my own cooking. I have to do my own laundry. I have to clean my room, apartment . . . You have to become reliant on yourself and it's not easy when you've had people telling you what to do for x amount of years.' (F.G.)" (Munn, 2011:9).

This chapter explores issues involving crime and criminals, asking not only how our criminal justice system handles offenders but also why societies develop standards of right and wrong in the first place. As you will see, the law is simply one part of a complex system of social control: Society teaches us all to conform, at least most of the time, to countless rules. We begin our investigation by defining several basic concepts.

What Is Deviance?

Deviance is *the recognized violation of cultural norms.* Norms guide virtually all human activities, so the concept of deviance is quite broad. One category of deviance is **crime**, *the violation of a society's formally enacted criminal law.* Even criminal deviance spans a wide range, from minor traffic violations to sexual assault and murder.

Most familiar examples of nonconformity are negative instances of rule breaking, such as stealing from a campus bookstore, assaulting a fellow student, or driving while intoxicated. But we also define especially righteous people—students who speak up too much in class or people who are overly enthusiastic about the latest electronic gadgets—as deviant, even if we give them a measure of respect. What all deviant actions or attitudes, whether negative or positive, have in common is some element of *difference* that causes us to think of another person as an "outsider" (Becker, 1966).

Not all deviance involves action or even choice. The very *existence* of some categories of people can be troublesome to others.

To the young, elderly people may seem hopelessly "out of touch," and to some non-Aboriginals, the mere presence of an Aboriginal person may cause discomfort. Able-bodied people often view people with disabilities as an out-group, just as rich people may shun the poor for falling short of their high-class standards.

Social Control

All of us are subject to **social control**, *attempts by society to regulate people's thoughts and behaviour.* Often this process is informal, as when parents praise or scold their children or when friends make fun of a classmate's choice of music. Cases of serious deviance, however, may bring action by the **criminal justice system**, *the organizations—police, courts, and prison officials—that respond to alleged violations of the law.*

How a society defines deviance, *who* is branded as deviant, and *what* people decide to do about deviance all have to do with the way a society is organized. Only gradually, however, have people come to understand that the roots of deviance are deep in society, as the chapter now explains.

The Biological Context

Chapter 3 ("Socialization: From Infancy to Old Age") explained that, a century ago, most people understood—or, more correctly, misunderstood—human behaviour to be the result of biological instincts. Early interest in criminality therefore focused on biological causes. In 1876, Cesare Lombroso (1835–1909), an Italian physician who

---

[1]To protect anonymity and confidentiality, all names used in this article are pseudonyms chosen by the men.

deviance (p. 161) the recognized violation of cultural norms

crime (p. 161) the violation of a society's formally enacted criminal law

social control (p. 161) attempts by society to regulate people's thoughts and behaviour

criminal justice system (p. 161) the organizations—police, courts, and prison officials—that respond to alleged violations of the law

Deviance is always a matter of difference. Deviance emerges in everyday life as we encounter people whose appearance or behaviour differs from what we consider "normal." Who is the "deviant" in this photograph? From whose point of view?

worked in prisons, theorized that criminals stand out physically, with low foreheads, prominent jaws and cheekbones, protruding ears, hairy bodies, and unusually long arms. All in all, Lombroso claimed that criminals look like our apelike ancestors.

Had Lombroso looked more carefully, he would have found the physical features he linked to criminality throughout the entire population. We now know that no physical traits distinguish criminals from non-criminals.

In the middle of the twentieth century, William Sheldon took a different approach, suggesting that body structure may predict criminality (Sheldon, Hartl, & McDermott, 1949). He cross-checked hundreds of young men for body type and criminal history and concluded that delinquency was most common among boys with muscular, athletic builds. Sheldon Glueck and Eleanor Glueck (1950) confirmed that conclusion but cautioned that a powerful build does not necessarily *cause* or even *predict* criminality. Parents, they suggested, tend to be somewhat distant from powerfully built sons, who in turn grow up to show less sensitivity toward others. In a self-fulfilling prophecy, people who expect muscular boys to be bullies may act in ways that bring about the aggressive behaviour they expect.

Today, genetics research seeks possible links between biology and crime. In 2003, scientists at the University of Wisconsin reported results of a 25-year study of crime among 400 boys. The researchers collected DNA samples from each boy and noted any history of trouble with the law. The researchers concluded that genetic factors (especially defective genes that, say, make too much of an enzyme) together with environmental factors (especially abuse early in life) were strong predictors of adult crime and violence. They noted, too, that these factors together were a better predictor of crime than either one alone (Lemonick, 2003; Pinker, 2003).

CRITICAL REVIEW Biological theories offer a limited explanation of crime. The best guess at present is that biological traits in combination with environmental factors explain some serious crime. Most of the actions we define as deviant are carried out by people who are physically quite normal.

In addition, because a biological approach looks at the individual, it offers no insight into how some kinds of behaviours come to be defined as deviant in the first place. Therefore, although there is much to learn about how human biology may affect behaviour, research currently puts far greater emphasis on social influences.

CHECK YOUR LEARNING What does biological research add to our understanding of crime? What are the limitations of this approach?

Personality Factors

Like biological theories, psychological explanations of deviance focus on individual abnormality. Some personality traits are inherited, but most psychologists think personality is shaped primarily by social experience. Deviance, then, is viewed as the result of "unsuccessful" socialization.

Classic research by Walter Reckless and Simon Dinitz (1967) illustrates the psychological approach. Reckless and Dinitz began by asking teachers to categorize 12-year-old male students as either likely or unlikely to get into trouble with the law. They then interviewed both the boys and their mothers to assess each boy's self-concept and how he related to others. Analyzing their results, the researchers found that the "good boys" displayed a strong conscience (what Freud called superego), could handle frustration, and identified with cultural norms and values. The "bad boys," by contrast, had a weaker conscience, displayed little tolerance for frustration, and felt out of step with conventional culture.

As we might expect, the "good boys" went on to have fewer run-ins with the police than the "bad boys." Because all of the boys lived in areas where delinquency was widespread, the investigators attributed staying out of trouble to a personality that controlled deviant impulses. Based on this conclusion, Reckless and Dinitz called their analysis *containment theory.*

○ **CRITICAL REVIEW** Psychologists have shown that personality patterns have some connection to deviance. Some serious criminals are psychopaths who do not feel guilt or shame, have no fear of punishment, and have little sympathy for the people they harm (Herpertz & Sass, 2000). However, as noted in the case of biological factors, most serious crimes are committed by people whose psychological profiles are normal.

Both biological and psychological research views deviance as a trait of individuals. The reason these approaches have limited value in explaining deviance is that wrongdoing has more to do with the organization of society. We now turn to a sociological approach, which explores where ideas of right and wrong come from, why people define some rule breakers but not others as deviant, and what role power plays in this process.

○ **CHECK YOUR LEARNING** Why do biological and psychological analyses not explain deviance very well?

The Social Foundations of Deviance

Although we tend to view deviance as the free choice or personal failings of individuals, all behaviour—deviance as well as conformity—is shaped by society. Three social foundations of deviance identified here will be detailed later in this chapter:

1. **Deviance varies according to cultural norms.** No thought or action is inherently deviant; it becomes deviant only in relation to particular norms. In Saskatchewan, for example, it is illegal for businesses to offer both striptease and drinking; exotic dancing is fine, as is drinking, but the two must not occur together. Moreover, in some Canadian cities it is legal to play music on the sidewalk and to beg for money, while street musicians and panhandlers in other cities risk being fined or imprisoned. The Criminal Code of Canada lays out what types of gaming activities are illegal in Canada, and the provinces are assigned responsibility to operate, license, and regulate legal forms of gaming, including internet casinos—the "wild west" of gaming. Some countries have moved to license online gaming, while others have increased criminalization (CBC News, 2003). The new Distracted Driving Legislation in Alberta bans "engaging in personal grooming or hygiene" while driving, while other provinces allow people to comb their hair while driving.

Why is it that street-corner gambling like this is usually against the law but playing the same games in a fancy casino is not?

Further, Killarney, Manitoba, has a curfew for people under the age of 15, who can be fined $250 if they in a public space later than 1 A.M. Many cities and towns have different bylaws about activities such as operating escort agencies, camping in downtown parks, panhandling, vehicle parking, and public nudity.

Around the world, deviance is even more diverse. Albania outlaws any public display of religious faith, such as "crossing" oneself; Cuba bans citizens from owning personal computers; Vietnam can prosecute citizens for meeting with foreigners; Malaysia does not allow tight-fitting jeans for women; Saudi Arabia bans the sale of red flowers on Valentine's Day; Iran does not allow women to wear makeup and forbids the playing of rap music (Chopra, 2008).

2. **People become deviant as others define them that way.** Everyone violates cultural norms at one time or another. For example, have you ever walked around talking to yourself or "borrowed" a pen from your workplace? Whether such behaviour defines us as mentally ill or criminal depends on how others perceive, define, and respond to it.

3. **Both norms and the way people define rule breaking involve social power.** The law, claimed Karl Marx, is the means by which powerful people protect their interests. A homeless person who stands on a street corner speaking out against the government risks arrest for disturbing the peace; a mayoral candidate doing exactly the same thing during an election campaign gets police protection. In short, norms and how we apply them reflect social inequality.

Fidel Castro erected this billboard in Havana across the street from the United States Special Interest Building. This was in response to a ticker display on the building showing news headlines from around the world.

The Functions of Deviance: Structural-Functional Analysis

The key insight of the structural-functional approach is that deviance is a necessary element of social organization. This point was made a century ago by Emile Durkheim.

Durkheim's Basic Insight

In his pioneering study of deviance, Emile Durkheim (1964a, orig. 1893; 1964b, orig. 1895) made the surprising statement that there is nothing abnormal about deviance. In fact, it performs four essential functions:

1. **Deviance affirms cultural values and norms.** As moral creatures, people must prefer some attitudes and behaviours to others. But any definition of virtue rests on an opposing idea of vice: There can be no good without evil and no justice without crime. Deviance is needed to define and support morality.

2. **Responding to deviance clarifies moral boundaries.** By defining some individuals as deviant, people draw a boundary between right and wrong. For example, colleges and universities mark the line between academic honesty and deviance by disciplining students who cheat on exams.

3. **Responding to deviance brings people together.** People typically react to serious deviance with shared outrage. In doing so, Durkheim explained, they reaffirm the moral ties that bind them. For example, after the September 11, 2001, terrorist attacks, people across the United States were joined by a common desire to protect their country and bring the perpetrators to justice.

4. **Deviance encourages social change.** Deviant people push a society's moral boundaries, suggesting alternatives to the status quo and encouraging change. Today's deviance, declared Durkheim, can become tomorrow's morality (1964b:71, orig. 1895). For example, rock and roll, condemned as immoral in the 1950s, became a mainstream, multi-billion-dollar industry just a few years later. In recent decades, hip-hop music has followed the same path toward respectability.

An Illustration: The Puritans of Massachusetts Bay

Kai Erikson's classic study of the Puritans of Massachusetts Bay brings Durkheim's theory to life. Erikson (2005b, orig. 1966) shows that even the Puritans, a disciplined and highly religious group, created deviance to clarify their moral boundaries. In fact, Durkheim may well have had the Puritans in mind when he wrote:

> Imagine a society of saints, a perfect cloister of exemplary individuals. Crimes, properly so called, will there be unknown; but faults which appear [insignificant] to the layman will create there the same scandal that the ordinary offense does in ordinary consciousness. . . . For the same reason, the perfect and upright man judges his smallest failings with a severity that the majority reserve for acts more truly in the nature of an offense. (1964b:68–69, orig. 1895)

Deviance is thus not a matter of a few "bad apples" but a necessary condition of "good" social living.

Deviance may be found in every society, but the *kind* of deviance that people generate depends on the moral issues they seek to clarify. The Puritans, for example, experienced a number of "crime waves," including the well-known outbreak of witchcraft in 1692. With each response, the Puritans answered questions about the range of proper beliefs by celebrating some of their members and condemning others as deviant.

Erikson discovered that although the offences changed, the proportion of the population the Puritans defined as deviant remained steady over time. This stability, he concluded, confirms Durkheim's claim that society creates deviants to mark its changing moral boundaries. In other words, by constantly defining a small number of people as deviant, the Puritans maintained the moral shape of their society.

Merton's Strain Theory

Some deviance may be necessary for a society to function, but Robert Merton (1938, 1968) argued that too much deviance results from particular social arrangements. Specifically, the extent and kind of deviance depend on whether a society provides the *means* (such as schooling and job opportunities) to achieve cultural *goals* (such as financial success).

Conformity lies in pursuing cultural goals through approved means. Thus the Canadian "success story" is someone who gains wealth and prestige through talent, schooling, and hard work. But not everyone who wants conventional success has the opportunity to attain it. For example, people living in poverty may see little hope of becoming successful if they play by the rules. According to Merton, the strain between our culture's emphasis on wealth and the lack of opportunities to get rich may encourage some people, especially the poor, to engage in stealing, drug dealing, and other forms of street crime. Merton called this type of deviance *innovation*—using unconventional means (street crime) rather than conventional means (hard work at a "straight" job) to achieve a culturally approved goal (wealth).

The inability to reach a cultural goal may also prompt another type of deviance that Merton calls *ritualism*. For example, people who believe they cannot achieve the cultural goal of becoming rich may stick rigidly to the rules (the conventional means) in order at least to feel respectable.

A third response to the inability to succeed is *retreatism*: rejecting both cultural goals and means so that one in effect "drops out." People dealing with problematic alcohol or drug use and others who are without a secure home sometimes retreat from society. The deviance of retreatists lies in their unconventional lifestyles and, perhaps more seriously, in what seems to be their willingness to live this way.

The fourth response to failure is *rebellion*. Like retreatists, rebels such as radical "survivalists" reject both the cultural definition of success and the conventional means of achieving it but go one step further by forming a counterculture supporting alternatives to the existing social order.

Deviant Subcultures

Richard Cloward and Lloyd Ohlin (1966) extended Merton's theory, proposing that crime results not simply from limited legitimate (legal) opportunity but also from readily accessible illegitimate (illegal) opportunity. In short, deviance or conformity depends on the *relative opportunity structure* that frames a person's life.

The life of Al Capone, a notorious gangster, illustrates Cloward and Ohlin's theory. As a son of poor immigrants, Capone faced barriers of poverty and ethnic prejudice, which lowered his odds of achieving success in conventional terms. Yet as a young man during the Prohibition era (the early decades of the twentieth century, when alcoholic beverages were banned in Canada, the United States, and a number of European countries), Capone found in his neighbourhood people who could teach him how to sell alcohol illegally—a source of illegitimate opportunity. Where the structure of opportunity favours criminal activity, Cloward and Ohlin predict the development of *criminal subcultures*, such as Capone's criminal organization or today's inner-city street gangs.

But what happens when people are unable to find *any* opportunities, legal or illegal? Then deviance may take one of two forms. One is *conflict subcultures*, such as armed street gangs that regularly engage in violence, ignited by frustration and a desire for respect. Another possible outcome is the development of *retreatist subcultures*, in which deviants drop out and often engage in problematic alcohol or other drug use.

Albert Cohen (1971, orig. 1955) suggests that criminality is most common among lower-class youths because they have the least opportunity to achieve success by conventional means. Neglected by society, they seek self-respect by creating a deviant subculture that defines as worthy the traits these youths do have. Being feared on the street may win few points with society as a whole, but it may satisfy a youth's desire to "be somebody" in a local neighbourhood.

Walter Miller (1970, orig. 1958) adds that deviant subcultures are characterized by (1) *trouble*, arising from frequent conflict with teachers and police; (2) *toughness*, the value placed on physical size, strength, and agility, especially among males; (3) *smartness*, the ability to succeed on the streets, to outsmart or "con" others; (4) *a need for excitement*, the search for thrills, risk, or danger; (5) *a belief in fate*, a sense that people lack control over their own lives; and (6) *a desire for freedom*, often expressed as anger toward authority figures.

Finally, Elijah Anderson (1994, 2002; Kubrin, 2005) explains that in poor urban neighbourhoods, most people manage to conform to conventional ("decent") values. Yet faced every day with neighbourhood crime and violence, indifference or even hostility from police, and sometimes even neglect from their own parents, some young men decide to live by the "street code." To show that he can survive on the street, a young man displays "nerve," a willingness to stand up to any threat. Following this street code, the young man believes that even a violent death is better than being "dissed" (disrespected) by others. Some manage to escape the dangers, but the risk of ending up in jail—or worse—is very high for these young men, who have been pushed to the margins of our society.

labelling theory the idea that deviance and conformity result not so much from what people do as from how others respond to those actions

Young people cut off from legitimate opportunity often form subcultures that many people view as deviant. Gang subcultures, including tattoos on the fingers, are one way people gain a sense of belonging and respect denied to them by the larger culture.

CRITICAL REVIEW Durkheim made an important contribution by pointing out the functions of deviance. However, there is evidence that a community does not always come together in reaction to crime; sometimes fear of crime drives people to withdraw from public life (Liska & Warner, 1991; Warr & Ellison, 2000).

Merton's strain theory also has been criticized for explaining some kinds of deviance (stealing, for example) better than others (crimes of passion or mental illness). Furthermore, not everyone seeks success in conventional terms of wealth, as strain theory suggests.

The general argument of Cloward and Ohlin, Cohen, and Miller—that deviance reflects the opportunity structure of society—has been confirmed by later research (Allan & Steffensmeier, 1989; Uggen, 1999). However, these theories fall short by assuming that everyone shares the same cultural standards for judging right and wrong. If we define crime as including not just burglary and auto theft but also fraud and other crimes carried out by corporate executives and Wall Street tycoons, many more high-income people will be counted among criminals. There is evidence that people of all social backgrounds have become more casual about breaking the rules, as the Seeing Sociology in Everyday Life box explains.

Finally, all structural-functional theories suggest that everyone who breaks the rules will be labelled deviant. However, becoming deviant is actually a highly complex process, as the next section explains.

CHECK YOUR LEARNING Why do you think many of the theories just discussed seem to say that crime is more common among people with lower social standing?

Deviant subcultures affect specific segments of the population. At the same time, as the economy rises and falls, the level of criminal activity typically goes up and down. Hard times, in short, tend to encourage widespread anxiety and a belief that we have to look out for ourselves any way we can. The Seeing Sociology in the News box on page 168 offers a recent chapter in this very old story.

Labelling Deviance: Symbolic-Interaction Analysis

The symbolic-interaction approach explains how people come to see deviance in everyday situations. From this point of view, definitions of deviance and conformity are surprisingly flexible.

Labelling Theory

The central contribution of symbolic-interaction analysis is **labelling theory**, *the idea that deviance and conformity result not so much from what people do as from how others respond to those actions*. Labelling theory stresses the relativity of deviance, meaning that people may define the same behaviour in any number of ways.

Consider these situations: A college student takes a sweater off the back of a roommate's chair and packs it for a weekend trip, a married woman at a convention in a distant city has sex with an old boyfriend, and an advertising company that is a major campaign contributor to a political party receives a large federal advertising contract. We might define the first situation as carelessness, borrowing, or theft. The consequences of the second situation depend largely on whether the woman's behaviour becomes known at home. In the third situation, is the advertising company the best contractor or was it chosen merely to pay off a political debt? The social construction of reality is a highly variable process of detection, definition, and response.

Primary and Secondary Deviance

Edwin Lemert (1951, 1972) observed that some norm violations—say, skipping school or underage drinking—may provoke some reaction from others, but this process has little effect on a person's self-concept. Lemert calls such passing episodes *primary deviance*.

But what happens if people take notice of someone's deviance and really make something of it? After an audience has defined some action as primary deviance, the individual may begin to change, taking on a deviant identity by talking, acting, or dressing in a different way, rejecting the people who are critical, and repeatedly breaking the rules. Lemert (1951:77) calls this change of self-concept *secondary deviance*. He explains that "when a person begins to employ . . . deviant behavior as a means of defense, attack, or adjustment to the . . . problems created by societal reaction . . . , deviance [becomes]

stigma a powerfully negative label that greatly changes a person's self-concept and social identity

Deviant (Sub)Culture: Has It Become Okay to Do Wrong?

It's been a bad few years for the idea of playing by the rules. First Auditor General Sheila Fraser reported that senior civil servants broke rules when they awarded advertising contracts to Montreal advertising agencies. Then we learned that the executives of not just one but many corporations were guilty of fraud and outright stealing. Perhaps worst of all, the Roman Catholic Church, which many hold up as a model of moral behaviour, became embroiled in a scandal of its own. In this case, hundreds of priests across Canada, the United States, Europe, and Latin America are said to have sexually abused parishioners (most of them teens and children) over many decades while church officials busied themselves covering up the crimes. Hundreds of priests have been removed from their duties pending investigations of abuse.

Plenty of people are offering explanations for this widespread pattern of wrongdoing. Some suggest that the pressure to win in the highly competitive corporate world—by whatever means necessary—can be overwhelming. As one analyst put it, "You can get away with your embezzlements and your lies, but you can never get away with *failing*."

Such thinking helps explain the wrongdoing among many CEOs in the corporate world, but

Do you consider cheating in school to be wrong? Would you turn in someone you saw cheat? Why or why not?

it offers little insight into the problem of abusive priests. In some ways, at least, wrongdoing seems to have become a way of life for just about everybody. For example, the Auditor General has estimated that Canadians are more

and more willing to evade taxes by engaging in the underground economy, particularly in the construction industry. The music industry claims that it has lost a vast amount of money because of illegal piracy of recordings, a practice especially common among young people. And surveys of high school students reveal that 75 percent admit to having cheated on a test at least once during the past year.

Emile Durkheim considered society to be a moral system, built on a set of rules about what people should and should not do. Years earlier, another French thinker named Blaise Pascal made the opposite claim that "cheating is the foundation of society." Today, which of the two statements is closer to the truth?

WHAT DO YOU THINK?

1. In your opinion, how widespread is wrongdoing in Canadian society today?

2. Do you think the people whose actions are described in this box consider what they are doing as wrong? Why or why not?

3. What are the reasons for this apparent increase in dishonesty?

Source: Based on "Our Cheating Hearts" (2002).

secondary." For example, say that people have begun describing a young man as an "alcohol abuser," which establishes primary deviance. These people may then exclude him from their friendship network. His response may be to become bitter toward them, start drinking even more, and seek the company of others who approve of his drinking. These actions mark the beginning of secondary deviance, a deeper deviant identity.

Stigma

Secondary deviance marks the start of what Canadian sociologist Erving Goffman (1963) called a *deviant career*. As people develop a deeper commitment to their deviant behaviour, they typically acquire a **stigma**, *a powerfully negative label that greatly changes a person's self-concept and social identity*.

Weiss and Ramakrishna (2001) contribute to our understanding of stigma by adding that stigma is not just a label but is

"a social process or related personal experience characterized by exclusion, rejection, blame, or devaluation that results from experience or reasonable anticipation of an adverse social judgment about a person or group." Stigma operates as a master status (see Chapter 4, "Social Interaction in Everyday Life"), overpowering other dimensions of identity so that a person is discredited in the minds of others and consequently becomes socially isolated and may suffer depression and other ill effects (Corrigan, 2004; Corrigan, Kuwabara, & O'Shaughnessy, 2009; Link & Phelan, 1995). Sometimes an entire community stigmatizes a person through what Harold Garfinkel (1956) calls a degradation ceremony. A criminal prosecution is one example, operating much like a high school graduation ceremony in reverse: A person stands before the community to be labelled in a negative rather than a positive way.

San Francisco Chronicle

Ex-Employees Turn to Cyber Crime after Layoffs

BY ALEJANDRO MARTINEZ-CABRERA
April 8, 2010

SAN FRANCISCO—When a slumping economy and historically high unemployment rates dropped the ax on the country's workforce and left the survivors wondering if—or when—they'd be next, law enforcers and security experts braced themselves for what they considered would be an almost inevitable rise in data breaches and high-tech crimes. And they were right.

National unemployment rates peaked in October at 10.1 percent and remained at 9.7 percent during the first two months of the year. Local law enforcers say the inability to find gainful employment has been a recurrent motivation behind new cases of identity theft and software piracy that drop on their desks almost daily.

"We're constantly coming across people who typically we wouldn't see and wouldn't engage in this criminal behavior if the economy was better. They see it as a way out," said Detective Sgt. Ken Taylor of California's Silicon Valley high-tech crimes task force Rapid Enforcement Allied Computer Team.

In one recent case under investigation, Taylor said, an unemployed San Mateo, California, woman in her twenties was detained with a large number of re-encoded credit cards in her possession. She said she was using them to buy food.

And a Fremont, California, man who had been recently laid off was arrested in February for selling pirated copies of a $2,500 Adobe design program for $150 on Craigslist. Task force members could look at cases of workers-turned-software-pirates all day every day, Taylor said.

According to cyber-security researchers, corporations across all industries have been dealing with a steadily growing number of internal data breaches since the financial meltdown.

A Verizon data-loss report noted that individuals with insider knowledge of organizations accounted for 20 percent of all breaches last year, and that number has been increasing as economic malaises drag on, said Chris Novak, managing principal of Verizon Business's Global Investigative Response Team.

Even though external attacks made up the bulk of the breaches, the report found that each internal incident compromised on average 100,000 individual pieces of sensitive information—at least 60,000 pieces more than external hacks.

Researchers say that anyone from top-level executives and IT personnel to low-level support employees can have access to data that can be sold illegally. A 2009 survey of almost 1,000 laid-off individuals found that 59 percent admitted keeping company data after leaving the business, according to the Ponemon Institute, a privacy research center in Traverse City, Michigan.

In fact, data breach originators are "moving from being just the administrators and super-type users to your everyday users," Novak said.

"When data breaches are caused by administrators or super users, it's a big deal and the organization loses a great deal of information," he said. "When they come from average users, they're smaller pinpricks but can drag on longer and cost the company more in the long run."

Stolen data can range from employees' health care records or clients' credit card numbers to merger and acquisition plans, confidential agreements or valuable source code, said Rick Kam, president and co-founder of data breach prevention firm ID Experts.

Thieves can easily sell the information to cyber-criminal rings or use it as a bargaining chip to get a job with their former employer's competitors. According to the Ponemon Institute study, 67 percent of respondents said they would use "their former company's confidential, sensitive or proprietary information to leverage a new job."

"The issue of identity theft is all about opportunity," Kam said. "And our first instinct is to protect ourselves."

In one case handled by Kam's company six months ago, a disgruntled man went as far as trying to extort his former employer, a large health care provider, by threatening to release thousands of sensitive patient records that would have triggered an avalanche of lawsuits.

Those who remain employed but fear being the next to go can also grow alienated or resentful toward their companies and may be tempted to steal corporate data, said Kevin Rowney, director of breach response at Symantec.

"It's a common trend in economic history. Rising stress creates the circumstances that motivate people to go into financial fraud," Rowney said. "Employees in this economy feel it's every man for himself."

WHAT DO YOU THINK?

1. In what way does this article show that crime is not just a personal behaviour but also a societal issue?

2. If anxiety and a sense that "it's every man for himself" breed crime, can you think of ways in which we can generate a stronger sense of community and collective responsibility? What would you suggest?

3. If you were a courtroom judge, would you be inclined to show leniency toward someone who engaged in cyber crime because the person was facing economic challenges? Why or why not?

Source: "Ex-Employees Turn to Cyber Crime after Layoffs" by Alejandro Martinez-Cabrera, *San Francisco Chronicle*, April 8, 2010. Permission of the San Francisco Chronicle.

Retrospective and Projective Labelling

Once people stigmatize a person as deviant, they may engage in *retrospective labelling*, a reinterpretation of the person's past in light of some present deviance (Scheff, 1984). For example, after discovering that a priest has sexually molested a child, others rethink his past, perhaps offering comments such as "He always did want to be around young children." Retrospective labelling, which distorts a person's biography by being highly selective, typically deepens a deviant identity.

Similarly, people may engage in *projective labelling* of a stigmatized person, using a deviant identity to predict the person's future actions. Regarding the priest, people might say, "He's going to keep at it until he's caught." The more people in someone's social world think such things and act accordingly, the more these definitions affect the individual's self-concept, and the greater the chance that the predictions will come true.

Labelling Difference as Deviance

Is a man without a home who refuses to allow police to take him to a city shelter on a cold night simply trying to live independently, or is he "crazy"? People have a tendency to treat behaviour that irritates or threatens them not simply as "different" but as deviance or even mental illness.

The psychiatrist Thomas Szasz (1961, 1970, 2003, 2004) claims that people are too quick to apply the label of mental illness to conditions that simply amount to differences we don't like. The only way to avoid this troubling practice, Szasz concludes, is to stop using the idea of mental illness entirely. The world is full of people whose differences in thought or action may irritate us, but such differences are not grounds for defining someone as mentally ill. Such labelling, Szasz says, simply enforces conformity to the standards of people powerful enough to impose their will on others.

Most mental health professionals reject the idea that mental illness does not exist. But they agree that it is important to think carefully about how we define "difference." First, people who are mentally ill are no more to blame for their condition than people who suffer from cancer or some other physical problem. Therefore, having a mental or physical illness is no grounds for a person being labelled "deviant." Second, people (especially those without the medical knowledge to diagnose mental illness) should avoid applying such labels just to make others conform to their own standards of behaviour.

The Medicalization of Deviance

Labelling theory, particularly the ideas of Szasz and Goffman, helps explain an important shift in the way our society understands deviance. Over the past 50 years, the growing influence of psychiatry and medicine has led to the **medicalization of deviance**, *the transformation of moral and legal deviance into a medical condition.*

Medicalization amounts to swapping one set of labels for another. In moral terms, we judge people or their behaviour as either "bad" or "good." However, the scientific objectivity of medicine passes no moral judgment, instead using clinical diagnoses such as "sick" or "well."

To illustrate this idea, until the mid-twentieth century, most people viewed alcoholics as morally weak people easily tempted by the pleasure of drink. Gradually, however, medical specialists redefined alcoholism so that most people now consider it an illness, leading us to define alcoholics as "sick" rather than "bad." In the same way, obesity, problematic drug use, child abuse, sexual promiscuity, and other behaviours that used to be strictly moral matters are widely defined today as illnesses for which people need help rather than punishment.

The Difference Labels Make

Whether we define deviance as a moral or a medical issue has three consequences. First, it affects *who responds* to deviance. An offence against common morality typically brings a reaction from members of the community or the police. A medical label, however, places the situation under the control of clinical specialists, including counsellors, psychiatrists, and physicians.

A second issue is *how people respond* to deviance. A moral approach defines deviants as offenders subject to punishment. Medically, however, they are patients who need treatment. Punishment is designed to fit the crime, but treatment programs are tailored to the patient and may involve any therapy that a specialist thinks might prevent future illness.

Third, and most important, the two labels differ on the issue of *the competence of the deviant person.* From a moral standpoint, whether we are right or wrong, at least we are responsible for our own behaviour. Once we are defined as sick, however, we are seen as unable to control (or if "mentally ill," even to understand) our actions. People who are labelled incompetent are subject to treatment, often against their will. For this reason alone, defining deviance in medical terms should be done with extreme caution.

Sutherland's Differential Association Theory

Learning any social pattern, whether conventional or deviant, is a process that takes place in groups. According to Edwin Sutherland (1940), a person's tendency toward conformity or deviance depends on the amount of contact with others who encourage or reject conventional behaviour. This is Sutherland's theory of *differential association.*

A number of studies confirm the idea that young people are more likely to engage in delinquent behaviour if they believe that members of their peer group encourage such activity (Akers et al., 1979; Dishion & Owen, 2002; Miller & Matthews, 2001). One recent investigation focused on sexual activity among grade 8 students. Two strong predictors of such behaviour in young girls were having a boyfriend who encouraged sexual relations and having girlfriends they believed would approve of such activity. Similarly, boys were encouraged to become sexually active by friends who rewarded them with high status in the peer group (Little & Rankin, 2001). However, ability to resist peer influence increases as youth move through adolescence. Gender differences are most evident during mid-adolescence, when girls are more successful in resisting peer influences than male counterparts (Fergusson et al., 2007; Sumter et al., 2009).

Hirschi's Control Theory

The sociologist Travis Hirschi (1969; Gottfredson & Hirschi, 1995) developed *control theory*, which states that social control depends on people's anticipating the consequences of their behaviour. Hirschi assumes that everyone finds at least some deviance tempting. But the thought of a ruined career keeps most people from breaking the

In 2010, Amy Bishop, a biology professor with a Harvard Ph.D., was denied tenure by her colleagues at her university. Soon after, she took a gun to a campus faculty meeting and killed three colleagues, wounding three others. What effect does the social standing of the offender have in our assessment of her as "crazy" or "sick" as opposed to simply "evil"?

All social groups teach their members skills and attitudes that encourage certain behaviour. In recent years, discussion on university and college campuses has focused on the dangers of binge drinking, which results in several deaths each year among young people in Canada. How much of a problem is binge drinking on your campus?

rules; for some, just imagining the reactions of family and friends is enough. On the other hand, people who think that they have little to lose from deviance are likely to become rule breakers.

Specifically, Hirschi links conformity to four different types of social control:

1. **Attachment.** Strong social attachments encourage conformity. Weak family, peer, and school relationships leave people freer to engage in deviance.

2. **Opportunity.** The greater a person's access to legitimate opportunity, the greater the advantages of conformity. By contrast, someone with little confidence in future success is more likely to drift toward deviance.

3. **Involvement.** Extensive involvement in legitimate activities—such as holding a job, going to school, or playing sports—inhibits deviance (Langbein & Bess, 2002). By contrast, people who simply "hang out" waiting for something to happen have the time and energy to engage in deviant activity.

4. **Belief.** Strong beliefs in conventional morality and respect for authority figures restrain tendencies toward deviance. By contrast, people with a weak conscience (and who are left unsupervised) are more open to temptation (Stack, Wasserman, & Kern, 2004).

Hirschi's analysis calls to mind our earlier discussions of the causes of deviant behaviour. Here again, a person's relative social privilege and family and community environment affect the risk of deviant behaviour (Hagan & Foster, 2006; Hope, Grasmick, & Pointon, 2003; Loury, 2002).

CRITICAL REVIEW The various symbolic-interaction theories all see deviance as a process. Labelling theory links deviance not to action but to the *reaction* of others. Thus some people are defined as deviant but others who think or behave in the same way are not. The concepts of secondary deviance, deviant career, and stigma show how being labelled deviant can become a lasting self-concept.

Yet labelling theory has several limitations. First, because it takes a highly relative view of deviance, labelling theory ignores the fact that some kinds of behaviour—such as murder—are condemned just about everywhere. Therefore, labelling theory is most usefully applied to less serious issues, such as sexual promiscuity or mental illness. Second, research on the consequences of deviant labelling does not clearly show whether it produces further deviance or discourages it (Sherman & Smith, 1992; Smith & Gartin, 1989). Third, not everyone resists being labelled as deviant; some people actively seek it (Vold & Bernard, 1986). For example, people engage in civil disobedience and willingly subject themselves to arrest to call attention to social injustice.

But why do society's norms and laws define certain kinds of activities as deviant in the first place? This important question is addressed by social-conflict analysis, the focus of the next section.

○ **CHECK YOUR LEARNING** Clearly define primary deviance, secondary deviance, deviant career, and stigma.

Deviance and Inequality: Social-Conflict Analysis

The social-conflict approach links deviance to social inequality. That is, who or what is labelled "deviant" depends on which categories of people hold power in a society.

Deviance and Power

Alexander Liazos (1972) points out that the people we tend to define as deviants—the ones we dismiss as "nuts" and "sluts"—are typically not those who are bad or harmful as much as they are *powerless*. Bag ladies and unemployed men on street corners, not corporate polluters or international arms dealers, carry the stigma of deviance.

Social-conflict theory explains this pattern in three ways. First, all norms—especially the laws of any society—generally reflect the interests of the rich and powerful. People who threaten the wealthy are likely to be labelled deviant, whether it's by taking people's property ("common thieves") or advocating a more egalitarian society ("political radicals"). Karl Marx, a major architect of the social-conflict approach, argued that the law and all social institutions support the interests of the rich. Or as Richard Quinney puts it, "Capitalist justice is by the capitalist class, for the capitalist class, and against the working class" (1977:3).

Second, even if their behaviour is called into question, the powerful have the resources to resist deviant labels. The majority of the corporate executives who were involved in the corporate scandals of recent years were not arrested, and only a small number ever went to jail.

Third, the widespread belief that norms and laws are "just" and "good" masks their political character. For this reason, although we may condemn the unequal application of the law, most of us give little thought to whether the laws themselves are really fair or not.

Deviance and Capitalism

In the Marxist tradition, Steven Spitzer (1980) argues that deviant labels are applied to people who interfere with the operation of capitalism. First, because capitalism is based on private control of property, people who threaten the property of others—especially the poor who steal from the rich—are prime candidates for being labelled deviant. Conversely, the rich who take advantage of the poor are less likely to be labelled deviant. For example, landlords who charge poor tenants high rents and evict those who cannot pay are not considered criminals; they are simply "doing business."

Justice John Gomery headed the commission investigating the government's sponsorship program and advertising activities. The final report was released in 2006. Jean Brault (who ran Groupaction), Paul Coffin (who ran another advertising company that benefited from the program), and Chuck Guité (who ran the program for Public Works) all received criminal convictions for their parts in the program.

Second, because capitalism depends on productive labour, people who cannot or will not work risk being labelled deviant. Many members of our society think people who are out of work, even through no fault of their own, are somehow deviant.

Third, because the operation of the capitalist system depends on respect for authority figures, people who resist authority are likely to be labelled deviant. Examples are children who skip school or talk back to parents or teachers and adults who do not co-operate with employers or police.

Fourth, anyone who directly challenges the capitalist status quo is likely to be defined as deviant. Such has been the case with labour organizers, radical environmentalists, civil rights and antiwar activists, and feminists.

On the other side of the coin, society positively labels whatever supports the operation of capitalism. For example, winning athletes enjoy celebrity status because they make money and express the values of individual achievement and competition, both vital to capitalism. Also, Spitzer notes, we condemn using drugs of escape (marijuana, psychedelics, heroin, and crack) as deviant but promote drugs (such as alcohol and caffeine) that encourage adjustment to the status quo.

The capitalist system also tries to control people who do not fit into the system. The elderly, people with mental or physical disabilities, and Robert Merton's "retreatists" (people addicted to alcohol or other drugs) represent a "costly yet relatively harmless burden" to society. Such people, claims Spitzer, are subject to control by

white-collar crime crime committed by people of high social position in the course of their occupations

corporate crime the illegal actions of a corporation or people acting on its behalf

organized crime a business supplying illegal goods or services

social welfare agencies. But people who openly challenge the capitalist system, including the inner-city "underclass" and revolutionaries—Merton's "innovators" and "rebels"—are controlled by the criminal justice system or—in times of crisis such as the 1970 Front de liberation du Québec crisis, the 1990 Oka Crisis in Quebec, the 1995 Ipperwash standoff in Ontario, and the 1997 APEC summit in Vancouver—by military forces (De Lint, 2005).

Note that both the social welfare and the criminal justice systems blame individuals, not the system, for social problems. Welfare recipients are considered unworthy freeloaders, poor people who rage at their plight are labelled rioters, anyone who actively challenges the government is branded a radical or a communist, and those who attempt to gain illegally what they will never get legally are rounded up as common criminals.

White-Collar Crime

St. Paul, Alberta, was known in the mid-1990s as the town of Bre-X millionaires because of the proportionately large number of people there who had invested in the gold company. The only problem was that Bre-X was a fraud and many of those who had been wealthy on paper lost all of the money they had invested when it was discovered that the $6 billion company had become so valuable based only on some mining ore samples that had been tampered with.

Bre-X's management engaged in **white-collar crime**, defined by Edwin Sutherland in 1940 as *crime committed by people of high social position in the course of their occupations*. White-collar crime does not involve violence and rarely brings police with guns drawn to the scene. Rather, white-collar criminals use their powerful offices illegally to enrich themselves or others, often causing significant public harm in the process. For this reason, sociologists sometimes call white-collar offences "crime in the suites" as opposed to "crime in the streets."

The most common white-collar crimes are bank embezzlement, business fraud, bribery, and violating antitrust laws that require businesses to be competitive. Sutherland (1940) explains that such white-collar offences typically end up in a civil hearing rather than in a criminal courtroom. *Civil law* regulates business dealings between private parties; *criminal law* defines a person's moral responsibilities to society. In practice, someone who loses a civil case pays for damage or injury but is not labelled a criminal. Furthermore, corporate officials are protected by the fact that most charges of white-collar crime target the organization rather than individuals.

In the rare cases that white-collar criminals are charged and convicted, the odds are that they will not go to jail. Advertising executive Paul Coffin pleaded guilty to defrauding the government of about $1.5 million as his part of the Liberal party sponsorship scandal. In 2005, he received a sentence of two years' house arrest, although this sentence was later overturned on appeal and replaced by a jail sentence of 18 months. Nobody has been convicted in relation to the Bre-X affair.

As some analysts see it, until courts impose more prison terms, we should expect white-collar crime to remain widespread (Shover & Hochstetler, 2006).

Corporate Crime

Sometimes whole companies, not just individuals, break the law. **Corporate crime** consists of *the illegal actions of a corporation or people acting on its behalf*.

Corporate crime ranges from knowingly selling faulty or dangerous products to deliberately polluting the environment (Derber, 2004). The collapse of a number of corporations in recent years, linked to criminal conduct on the part of company officials, has cost tens of thousands of people their jobs and their pensions.

In addition, companies often violate safety regulations, resulting in injury or death. In May 2011, the operators of a mushroom farm outside Vancouver pleaded guilty in the deaths of three farm workers who died in a small shed when they were overcome by the toxic fumes from a broken pipe. Only 18 months earlier, three farm workers died on a British Columbia highway when the overloaded van in which they were taken to and from work crashed. The death toll for all job-related hazards in Canada is about five per workday, and most at risk are older workers and workers in mining, logging, and fishing (Sharpe & Hardt, 2006). Mining hazards are even worse in countries with fewer economic resources, such as China (BBC News, 2005).

Organized Crime

Organized crime is *a business supplying illegal goods or services*. Sometimes crime organizations force people to do business with them, as when a gang extorts money from shopkeepers for "protection." In most cases, however, organized crime involves selling illegal goods and services—often sex, drugs, or gambling—to willing buyers.

Organized crime has flourished in Canada and other high-income countries for more than a century. The scope of its operations expanded among immigrants who found that this society was not willing to share its opportunities with them. Thus some ambitious minorities (such as Al Capone, mentioned earlier) made their own success, especially during Prohibition, when the government banned the production and sale of alcohol.

The Italian Mafia is a well-known example of organized crime. But other criminal organizations involve African-Americans, Chinese, Colombians, Cubans, Haitians, Nigerians, and Russians, as well as others of almost every racial and ethnic category. Organized crime today involves a wide range of activities, from selling illegal drugs to sex trafficking to credit card fraud to selling false identification papers to illegal immigrants (Federal Bureau of Investigation, 2008; Valdez, 1997).

hate crime a criminal act against a person or a person's property by an offender motivated by racial or other bias

APPLYING THEORY

Deviance

	Structural-Functional Approach	Symbolic-Interaction Approach	Social-Conflict Approach
What is the level of analysis?	Macro level	Micro level	Macro level
What is deviance? What part does it play in society?	Deviance is a basic part of social organization. By defining deviance, society sets its moral boundaries.	Deviance is part of socially constructed reality that emerges in interaction. Deviance comes into being as individuals label something deviant.	Deviance results from social inequality. Norms, including laws, reflect the interests of powerful members of society.
What is important about deviance?	Deviance is universal: It exists in all societies.	Deviance is variable: Any act or person may or may not be labelled deviant.	Deviance is political: People with little power are at high risk of being labelled deviant.

In Canada, the vicious scope of organized crime garnered public attention in spring of 2006 when eight members of the Bandidos motorcycle gang were murdered by other members of the gang, apparently for wanting to join the Hells Angels motorcycle gang. In the late 1990s, some 150 people died as a result of fighting between these archrival motorcycle gangs (Beltrame & Branswell, 2000; Canadian Press Newswire, 2000).

CRITICAL REVIEW According to social-conflict theory, a capitalist society's inequality in wealth and power shapes its laws and how they are applied. The criminal justice and social welfare systems thus act as political agents, controlling categories of people who are a threat to the capitalist system.

Like other approaches to deviance, social-conflict theory has its critics. First, this approach implies that laws and other cultural norms are created directly by the rich and powerful. At the very least, this is an oversimplification because the law also protects workers, consumers, and the environment, sometimes opposing the interests of corporations and the rich.

Second, social-conflict analysis argues that criminality springs up only to the extent that a society treats its members unequally. However, as Durkheim noted, deviance exists in all societies, whatever the economic system and their degree of inequality.

The various sociological explanations for crime and other types of deviance are summarized in the Applying Theory table.

CHECK YOUR LEARNING Define white-collar crime, corporate crime, and organized crime.

Deviance, Race, and Gender

What people consider deviant reflects the relative power and privilege of different categories of people. The following sections offer two examples: how racial and ethnic hostility motivates hate crimes and how gender is linked to deviance.

Hate Crimes

A **hate crime** is *a criminal act against a person or a person's property by an offender motivated by racial or other bias.* A hate crime may express hostility toward someone based on race, religion, ancestry, sexual orientation, or physical disability (Dauvergne, Scrim, & Brennan, 2008; Perry, 2001). Hate crimes increased by one-third between 2007 and 2008. The results indicate that hate crimes—face to face and via the internet—have increased for the main targeted groupings (Perry, 2003). Those who contend with multiple stigmas—such as visible minority and Muslim gay men—are especially likely to become victims of hate-motivated violence. Canadian police services reported 1036 hate crimes in 2008, with 55 percent of those reported motivated by race or ethnicity. Of all race-based attacks, Blacks were targeted 40 percent of the time. Jews were targeted in two-thirds of all religious hate crimes (Statistics Canada, 2010b). Yet hate crimes can happen to anyone: In 2008, 4 percent of hate crimes reported by Statistics Canada were against Caucasians (Statistics Canada, 2010b).

In 2010, two brothers from Nova Scotia erected a large cross (2.5 metres tall) on the front lawn of an interracial couple in their neighbourhood and then set the cross on fire. The targeted family reported that there was a noose around the cross and that the

THINKING ABOUT
DIVERSITY: RACE,
CLASS, & GENDER

Hate Crime Laws: Do They Punish Actions or Attitudes?

Just after 2:00 A.M. on November 17, 2001, in a corner of Vancouver's Stanley Park where gays commonly meet, local resident Aaron Webster was brutally killed. His assailants were a group of five young males, also from the city, who told reporters that they "wanted to get into a fight."

Three years later, 22-year-old Ryan Cran, who was considered to be the ringleader of the group, was found guilty of manslaughter in Webster's beating death. In Cran's sentencing in February 2005, British Columbia Supreme Court Justice Mary Humphries said the attack on Webster was "random, cowardly, and terrifying" but an individual act—not a hate crime. The gay community and members of Webster's family argued otherwise, categorizing the murder as caused by hatred of gay people and pointing out the need for a stiffer sentence.

As this case illustrates, hate crime laws punish a crime more severely if the offender is motivated by bias against some category of

people. Supporters make three arguments in favour of hate crime legislation. First, the offender's intentions are always important in weighing criminal responsibility, so considering hatred as an intention is nothing new. Second, a crime motivated by bias against homosexuals or other groups who experience discrimination inflames the public mood more than a crime carried out, say, for money. Third, victims of hate crimes typically suffer more serious injuries than victims of crimes with other motives.

Critics counter that while some hate crime cases involve hard-core homophobia or racism, most are impulsive acts by young people. Hate crime laws allow courts to sentence offenders not just for their actions but also for their attitudes. As Harvard University law professor Alan Dershowitz cautions, "As much as I hate bigotry, I fear much more the Court attempting to control the minds of citizens." In short, according to critics, hate crime laws

open the door to punishing beliefs rather than behaviour.

In the case of Aaron Webster, the British Columbia Supreme Court decided against the hate crime ruling and instead punished Cran for his actual behaviour rather than his beliefs about homosexuals.

WHAT DO YOU THINK?

1. Do you think that crimes motivated by hate are more harmful than those motivated by, say, greed? Why or why not?

2. On balance, do you favour or oppose hate crime laws? Why?

Sources: Terry, Don. "In Crackdown on Bias, a New Tool." From The New York Times, June 12, 1993. © 1993. The New York Times. All rights reserved. Used by permission and protected by the Copyright Laws of the United States. The printing, copying, redistribution, or retransmission of this Content without express written permission is prohibited; and Sullivan, Andrew. Lecture delivered at Kenyon College, April 4, 2002. Permission of Wylie Agency.

brothers made racial remarks. The case was brought to court and became a benchmark for hate crimes involving cross burning. One brother was sentenced to 4 months in jail for inciting racial hatred and 6 months in jail for criminal harassment, in addition to 2.5 years of probation and 50 hours of community service. The other brother received two months in jail for inciting racial hatred and criminal harassment and 2.5 years of probation (CBC News, 2010). Many Canadians are gratified that the criminal justice system has taken a strong stand against crimes motivated by hatred. But opponents charge that such laws, which increase the penalty for a crime based on the attitudes of the offender, amount to punishing "politically incorrect" thoughts. The Thinking about Diversity box takes a closer look at the issue of hate crime laws.

The Feminist Perspective: Deviance and Gender

Virtually every society in the world tries to control the behaviour of women more than that of men. Historically, our own society has centred women's lives around the home. In Canada, even today, women's opportunities in the workplace, in politics, in athletics, and in the military are more limited than are men's. In some other parts of the world, the constraints on women are greater still. In Saudi Arabia, women cannot vote or legally operate motor vehicles; in Iran, women who expose their hair or wear makeup in public can be whipped; and

not long ago, a Nigerian court convicted a divorced woman of bearing a child out of wedlock and sentenced her to death by stoning; her life was later spared out of concern for her child (Eboh, 2002).

Gender also figures into the theories about deviance noted earlier. For example, Robert Merton's strain theory defines cultural goals in terms of financial success. Traditionally, at least, this goal has had more to do with the lives of men, because women have been socialized to define success in terms of relationships, particularly marriage and motherhood (E.B. Leonard, 1982). A more woman-focused theory might recognize the "strain" that results from the cultural ideal of equality clashing with the reality of gender-based inequality.

According to labelling theory, gender influences how we define deviance because people commonly use different standards to judge the behaviour of females and males. Further, because society puts men in positions of power over women, men often escape direct responsibility for actions that victimize women. In the past, at least, men who sexually harassed or assaulted women were labelled only mildly deviant and sometimes escaped punishment entirely.

By contrast, women who are victimized may have to convince others—even members of a jury—that they are not to blame for their own sexual harassment or assault. The ruling by the Ontario Court of Justice in favour of "Jane Doe," who sued Toronto Police Services for negligence in their handling of a serial rape case, illustrates this

crimes against the person (violent crimes) crimes that direct violence or the threat of violence against others

crimes against property (property crimes) crimes that involve theft of money or property belonging to others

victimless crimes violations of law in which there are no obvious victims

Violent crime is much more likely to involve victims and offenders who are males rather than females. While Paul Bernardo was convicted of two murders, Karla Homolka negotiated a lesser sentence before her full involvement in the murders was discovered.

point. Ms. Doe alleged that the police should have done more to warn women in her neighbourhood about the rapist. It took 12 years before the court finally ruled that Ms. Doe's rights under the Canadian Charter of Rights and Freedoms had been violated because the police failed to give her equal protection under the law. This example confirms what research tells us: Whether people define a situation as deviance—and, if so, whose deviance it is—depends on the gender of both the audience and the actors (King & Clayson, 1988)

Finally, despite its focus on inequality, much social-conflict analysis does not address the issue of gender. If economic disadvantage is a primary cause of crime, as conflict theory suggests, why do women (whose economic position is much worse than men's) commit far *fewer* crimes than men?

Crime

Crime is the violation of criminal laws enacted by a locality, province or territory, or the federal government. All crimes are composed of two distinct elements: the *act* itself (or in some cases, a failure to do what the law requires) and *criminal intent* (in legal terminology, *mens rea*, or "guilty mind"). Intent is a matter of degree, ranging from wilful conduct to negligence. Someone who is negligent does not set out deliberately to hurt anyone but acts (or fails to act) in a way that results in harm. Prosecutors weigh the degree of intent in determining whether, for example, to charge someone with first-degree murder, second-degree murder, or negligent manslaughter. Alternatively, they may consider a killing justifiable, as in self-defence.

The Canadian Centre for Justice Statistics provides summary reports on the basis of its Uniform Crime Reporting (UCR) survey.

Statistics Canada originally designed the UCR survey with the agreement of, and help from, the Canadian Association of Chiefs of Police. Implemented in 1962, the aggregate UCR survey gathers crime statistics reported by police departments across the country. It is important to keep in mind that these statistics are based only on "recorded crimes"—that is, crimes reported to the police in Canada—and not on all crimes actually committed (see National Map 7–1 on page 176 on the severity of crime in our country).

Crimes against the person, also referred to as *violent crimes*, are *crimes that direct violence or the threat of violence against others*. Violent crimes include murder and manslaughter (legally defined as "the willful killing of one human being by another"), aggravated assault ("an unlawful attack by one person on another for the purpose of inflicting severe or aggravated bodily injury"), sexual assault (includes unwanted sexual touching, sexual attack with or without a weapon, etc.), and robbery ("taking or attempting to take anything of value from the care, custody, or control of a person or persons, by force or threat of force or violence and/or putting the victim in fear").

Crimes against property, also referred to as *property crimes*, are *crimes that involve theft of money or property belonging to others*. Property crimes include burglary ("the unlawful entry of a structure to commit a [serious crime] or a theft"), larceny-theft ("the unlawful taking, carrying, leading, or riding away of property from the possession of another"), motor vehicle theft ("the theft or attempted theft of a motor vehicle"), and arson ("any willful or malicious burning or attempt to burn the personal property of another").

A third category of Criminal Code offences—traffic and others—include **victimless crimes**, *violations of law in which there are no obvious victims*. Also called *crimes without complaint*, they include illegal drug use, prostitution, and gambling. The term *victimless crime* is misleading, however. How victimless is a crime when young drug users embark on a life of crime to support their drug habit? What about a pregnant woman who, by smoking crack, permanently harms her baby? Or a gambler who loses the money needed to support himself and his family? Perhaps it is more correct to say that people who commit such crimes are both offenders and victims.

Because public opinion about such activities varies considerably, the laws regulating victimless crimes differ from place to place. For example, prostitution—the exchange of money for sex—is not illegal in Canada (see Chapter 6, "Sexuality and Society"). Nonetheless, a person can be charged who "in a public place . . . communicates . . . for the purpose of engaging in prostitution. . . ." This law is often more heavily enforced when residents of a neighbourhood complain about prostitution (HIV/AIDS Legal Network, 2005; Statistics Canada, 1997g).

Criminal Statistics

Statistics gathered by police show crime rates rising from the early 1960s to 1991, but declining over the past two decades.

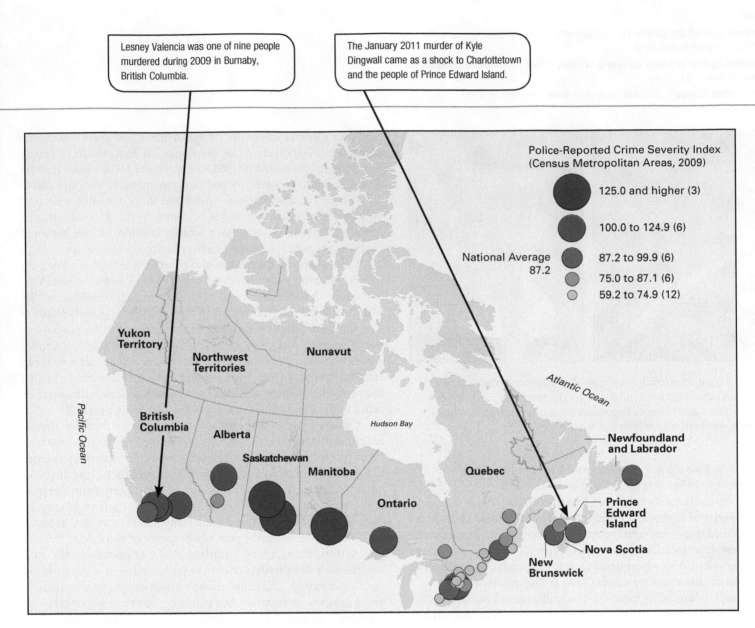

Lesney Valencia was one of nine people murdered during 2009 in Burnaby, British Columbia.

The January 2011 murder of Kyle Dingwall came as a shock to Charlottetown and the people of Prince Edward Island.

Police-Reported Crime Severity Index (Census Metropolitan Areas, 2009)

- 125.0 and higher (3)
- 100.0 to 124.9 (6)
- National Average 87.2
- 87.2 to 99.9 (6)
- 75.0 to 87.1 (6)
- 59.2 to 74.9 (12)

Seeing Ourselves

NATIONAL MAP 7–1 **The Severity of Crime across Canada**

The crime severity index is based on the volume of crime and the severity of the crime reported to the police. The severity of the crime is estimated based on the sentence assigned by the courts for various crimes. This means that the impact of a murder on the index is greater than that of the theft of a bicycle, even though both would have the same impact on the total crime rate.

Source: Dauvergne and Turner (2010).

Even so, police tallied nearly 2.2 million crimes in 2009, about 43 000 fewer than in 2008 (Sauvé, 2005). Figure 7–1 shows the crime rates for violent crimes and property crimes in Canada from 1962 to 2007.

Always read crime statistics with caution, however, because they include only crimes known to the police. Almost all murders are reported, but other assaults—especially between people who know one another—often are not. Police records include an even smaller proportion of property crimes, especially when the losses are small.

Researchers check official crime statistics by conducting *victimization surveys*, in which they ask a representative sample of people about their experiences with crime. Victimization surveys carried out in 2008 showed that the actual number of serious crimes was more than twice as high as police reports indicate (Rand, 2009).

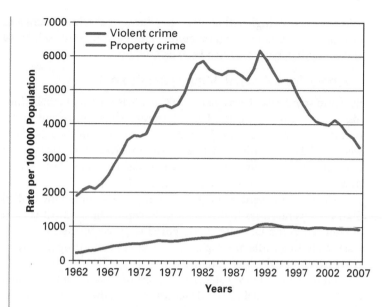

FIGURE 7–1 Crime Rates in Canada, 1962–2007

The graphs show that crime has been decreasing in Canada since the early 1990s.

Source: Dauvergne (2008).

The Street Criminal: A Profile

Using various government crime reports, we can draw a general description of the categories of people most likely to be arrested for crimes.

Gender

Although each sex makes up roughly half of the population, police arrested males in 79 percent of all crime arrests in 2005; the other 21 percent of arrests involved women. In other words, men are arrested for crimes more than three-quarters as often as women are (1080 versus 4193 per 100 000 population). This gender crime rate difference occurred across all crime categories. Only in regard to prostitution were rates comparatively equal (19 females and 20 males per 100 000 population in 2005), which is likely because both sex workers and clients are considered to be breaking the law (Kong & AuCoin, 2008).

It may be that law enforcement officials are reluctant to define women as criminals. In global perspective, the greatest gender difference in crime rates occurs in societies that most severely limit the opportunities of women. While still quite low compared to male youth, the rate of serious violent crime among female youth has more than doubled since 1986, increasing from 60 per 100 000 to 132 per 100 000 in 2005. The rate has also grown for female adults, from 25 to 46 per 100 000 (Kong & AuCoin, 2008).

Age

Official crime rates rise sharply during adolescence, peak in the late teens, and fall as people get older. In 2009, age-specific rates for those accused of crime were highest among 15- to 22-year-olds, with the peak age at 17 years (Statistics Canada, 2010c). On the other hand, the youth crime rate dropped by 2 percent in 2007, following a 3 percent increase the year before. Violent crimes committed by this population remained stable, and there were drops in most non-violent offences in 2007.

Social Class

Canadian police do not assess the social class of arrested persons, so no statistical data of the kind given for age and gender are available. But research has long indicated that street crime is more widespread among people of lower social position (Thornberry & Farnsworth, 1982; Wolfgang, Thornberry, & Figlio, 1987).

Yet the connection between class and crime is more complicated than it appears on the surface. For one thing, many people see the poor as less worthy than the rich, whose wealth and power confer "respectability" (Elias, 1986; Tittle, Villemez, & Smith, 1978). And although crime—especially violent crime—is a serious problem in the poorest inner-city communities of Canada and other countries, most of these crimes are committed by a few hard-core offenders. The majority of people in inner-city neighbourhoods have no criminal record at all (Elliott & Ageton, 1980; Harries, 1990; Wolfgang, Figlio, & Sellin, 1972).

The connection between social standing and criminality also depends on the type of crime. If we expand our definition of crime beyond street offences to include white-collar crime, the "common criminal" suddenly looks much more affluent and may live in a $100 million home.

Race and Ethnicity

In multicultural societies such as Canada, both race and ethnicity are strongly correlated to crime rates, although the reasons are many and complex. Official U.S. statistics indicate that 69.2 percent of arrests for index crimes in 2008 involved white people. However, arrests of African-Americans are higher in proportion to their share of the general population. African-Americans make up 12.8 percent of the American population but account for 30.1 percent of the arrests for property crimes (versus 67.4 percent for whites) and 39.4 percent of arrests for violent crimes (versus 58.3 percent for whites) (Federal Bureau of Investigation, 2009).

Firm conclusions about Canada are not as easy to come by because our police do not collect data on race and ethnicity, a situation that researchers have criticized (Closs & McKenna, 2006; Wortley & Marshall, 2005). However, the available evidence points to two conclusions. First, visible ethnic minorities tend to be underrepresented in arrest data and prison populations. Second, Aboriginals and Black people constitute two exceptions and are overrepresented.

Aboriginals are dramatically overrepresented in Canada's correctional facilities: In 1998–1999, Aboriginal persons made up 17 percent of admissions to provincial or territorial sentenced custody, even though they account for only 2 percent of the Canadian population (Thomas, 2000). By 2006, the percentage had risen to 24 percent.

Similarly, research in the Metro Toronto area on self-declared "Black," "white," and "Chinese" male residents shows that Black males were almost twice as likely as white males to have been stopped by the police sometime in the previous two years. As well, the percentage of Black males who reported having been stopped *twice* (29 percent) is greater than the percentage of white males who reported having been stopped *once* (25 percent) (The Commission on Systematic Racism in the Ontario Criminal Justice System, 1995; quoted in James, 1998). A more recent study on the total number of traffic stops made by the police in Kingston, Ontario, showed that the Black male residents of Kingston between the ages of 15 and 24 were three times more likely to be stopped and questioned by the police than people from other racial backgrounds (Wortley & Marshall, 2005).

What accounts for the disproportionate number of arrests among various ethnic groups? Two factors come into play. First, prejudice related to race prompts white police to arrest Aboriginal people more readily (Schissel, 1993). Second, Aboriginal status in Canada closely relates to social standing, which, as we have already explained, affects the likelihood of engaging in street crimes. Poor people living in the midst of affluence come to see society as unjust and thus are more likely to turn to crime (Anderson, 1994; Blau & Blau, 1982).

Prejudice prompts predominately white police to arrest Black and Aboriginal people more often and leads citizens to report them more willingly; as a result, people of Aboriginal background or people of colour are overly criminalized (Chiricos, McEntire, & Gertz, 2001; Demuth & Steffensmeier, 2004; Quillian & Pager, 2001).

Remember that the official crime index does not include arrests for offences ranging from drunk driving to white-collar violations. This omission contributes to the view of the typical criminal as a person who is Aboriginal or Black. If we broaden our definition of crime to include drunk driving, business fraud, embezzlement, stock swindles, and cheating on income tax returns, the proportion of white criminals rises dramatically.

Keep in mind, too, that categories of people with high arrest rates are also at higher risk of being victims of crime. In the United States, for example, African-Americans are six times as likely as white people to die as a result of homicide (Heron et al., 2009; Rogers et al., 2001). In Canada, Aboriginal people are more likely than non-Aboriginal people to report being victimized. In 2009, 37 percent of Aboriginal people self-reported being the victim of a crime, compared to 26 percent of non-Aboriginals (Perreault, 2011).

Finally, some categories of the population have unusually low rates of arrest. People of Asian descent are very unlikely to be arrested. As Chapter 11 ("Race and Ethnicity") explains, Asian Canadians enjoy higher-than-average educational achievement and income. Also, Asian immigrant culture emphasizes family solidarity and discipline, both of which keep criminality down.

Crime in Global Perspective

By world standards, the crime rate in Canada is not very high, including when compared to the United States. Although recent crime trends are downward in the United States as well as in Canada, there were 16 272 murders in the United States in 2008, which amounts to one murder every half-hour. In large cities such as New York, a week never goes by without someone being killed.

The rate of violent crime (but not property crime) in the United States is several times higher than in Europe. The contrast is even greater when the U.S rate is compared to those in the nations of Asia, including India and Japan, where violent and property crime rates are among the lowest in the world.

Elliott Currie (1985) suggests that crime arises from a cultural emphasis on individual economic success, often at the expense of strong families and neighbourhoods. The United States also has extraordinary cultural diversity—a result of centuries of immigration—that can lead to conflict. In addition, economic inequality is higher in that country than in most other high-income nations. U.S. society's relatively weak social fabric, combined with considerable frustration among the poor, increases the level of criminal behaviour.

Another factor contributing to violence in the United States is extensive private ownership of guns. About two-thirds of murder victims in the United States die from shootings. The U.S. rate of handgun homicides is about five times higher than in Canada, with our strict limits to handgun ownership (Federal Bureau of Investigation, 2009; Statistics Canada, 2009).

Surveys show that about one-third of U.S. households have at least one gun. In fact, there are more guns (about 283 million) than adults in our neighbour to the south, and 40 percent of these weapons are handguns, which are commonly used in violent crimes. In large part, gun ownership reflects people's fear of crime, yet easy availability of guns in that country makes crime more deadly (Brady Campaign, 2008; NORC, 2009).

Supporters of gun control in the United States claim that restricting gun ownership would reduce the number of murders. They point out that the number of murders each year in Canada, where the law prevents most of us from owning guns, is about the same as the annual number of murders in just the cities of New York and Newark combined. But as critics of gun control point out, laws regulating gun ownership do not keep guns out of the hands of criminals, who almost always obtain guns illegally. They also claim that gun control is not a magic bullet in the war on crime: The number of people in the United States killed each year by knives alone is three times the number of Canadians killed by weapons of all kinds (Federal Bureau of Investigation, 2009; Munroe, 2007; Statistics Canada, 2009; Wright, 1995).

By the end of 2008, gun sales to private citizens in the United States were up sharply, reflecting fears on the part of many gun owners that the Obama administration would act to curtail gun ownership. Changes in American law may or may not occur in the next few years, but debate over the consequences of widespread gun ownership will continue (Potter, 2008).

December 24–25, travelling through Peru. In Lima, Peru's capital city, the concern with crime is obvious. Almost every house is fortified with gates, barbed wire, or broken glass embedded in cement at the top of a wall. Private security forces are everywhere in the rich areas along the coast, where we find the embassies, the expensive hotels, and the international airport.

The picture is very different as we pass through small villages high in the Andes to the east. The same families have lived in these communities for generations, and people know one another. No gates or fences here. And we've seen only one police car all afternoon.

Crime rates are high in some of the largest cities of the world, such as Manila, Philippines, and São Paulo, Brazil, which have rapid population growth and millions of desperately poor people. Outside of big cities, however, the traditional character of low-income societies and their strong family structure allow local communities to control crime informally.

Some types of crime have always been multinational, such as terrorism, espionage, and arms dealing. But today, the globalization we are experiencing on many fronts also extends to crime. A case in point is the illegal drug trade. In part, the problem of illegal drugs in countries such as Canada is a *demand* issue. That is, the demand for cocaine and other drugs is strong, with high rates of addiction and many young people who are willing to risk arrest or even violent death for a chance to get rich in the drug trade. But the *supply* side of the issue is just as important. In the South American nation of Colombia, at least 20 percent of the people depend on cocaine production for their livelihood. Not only is cocaine Colombia's most profitable export, but it outsells all other exports combined, including coffee. Clearly, then, drug dealing and many other crimes are closely related to social conditions both in this country and elsewhere.

Different countries have different strategies for dealing with crime. The use of capital punishment (the death penalty) is one example. According to Amnesty International (2010), five nations account for 93 percent of the world's executions carried out by governments. Global Map 7–1 on page 180 shows which countries currently use capital punishment. The global trend is toward abolishing the death penalty: Amnesty International (2010) reports that since 1985, more than 60 nations have ended this practice.

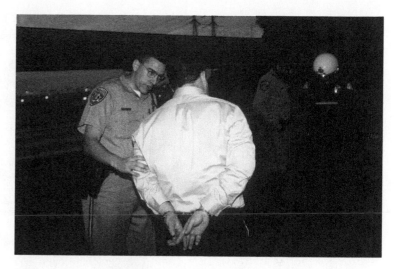

Police must be allowed discretion if they are to effectively handle the many different situations they face every day. At the same time, it is important to treat people fairly. Here, we see a police officer deciding whether to charge a motorist for driving while drunk. What factors do you think enter into this decision?

The Canadian Criminal Justice System

The criminal justice system is a society's formal response to crime. We will briefly examine the key elements of the Canadian criminal justice system: police, the courts, and the system of punishment and corrections. First, however, we must understand an important principle that underlies the entire system: the idea of due process.

Basic Principles

Canada's criminal justice system is built on a number of important principles, including:

1. **Presumption of Innocence.** The Canadian justice system is founded on the presumption of innocence until proven guilty. The Crown counsel thus has to prove beyond a reasonable doubt that the accused person actually committed the crime.

2. **Due Process.** Closely tied to the principle of presumption of innocence, due process is the principle that the government must conduct a thorough examination of the facts of each case and respect all of the legal rights a person is entitled to under the law.

3. **Independent Judiciary.** A person accused of a crime has the right to judicial independence—i.e., to have their court case adjudicated by detached and unbiased judges, without external intrusion of any sort.

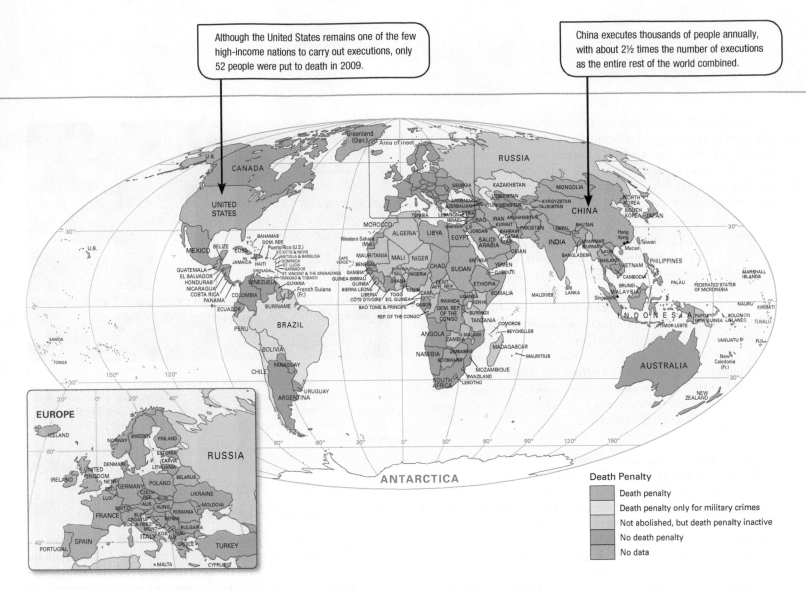

Although the United States remains one of the few high-income nations to carry out executions, only 52 people were put to death in 2009.

China executes thousands of people annually, with about 2½ times the number of executions as the entire rest of the world combined.

Death Penalty

Death penalty

Death penalty only for military crimes

Not abolished, but death penalty inactive

No death penalty

No data

Window on the World

GLOBAL MAP 7–1 **Capital Punishment in Global Perspective**

The map identifies 58 countries in which the law allows the death penalty for ordinary crimes; in 9 more, the death penalty is reserved for exceptional crimes under military law or during times of war. The death penalty does not exist in 95 countries; in 35 more, although the death penalty remains in law, no execution has taken place in more than 10 years. Compare high-income and low-income nations: What general pattern do you see? In what way are the United States and Japan exceptions to this pattern?

Source: Amnesty International (2011).

4. **Openness and Accessibility of Court.** Trials must be as open and accessible as possible to help ensure that the accused and the public have confidence that the justice system works as it should and that everyone involved is treated justly.

5. **Equality Before the Law.** As discussed in Chapter 2 ("Culture"), all Canadian residents are treated equally under the Canadian Charter of Rights and Freedoms. The charter includes a number of legal rights, including the right to life, liberty, and security of the person, the right to be secure against unreasonable search

and seizure, and the right not to be arbitrarily arrested (see http://www.canlii.org/en/ca/const/const1982.html for a full list charter rights and freedoms).

The fundamental principles of the Canadian Criminal Justice System limit the power of government, with an eye toward our country's cultural support of individual rights and freedoms. Deciding exactly how far government can go makes up much of the work of the judicial system, especially the Supreme Court of Canada, which guarantees that the government acts in accordance with our Constitution.

Four Justifications for Punishment

retribution an act of moral vengeance by which society makes the offender suffer as much as the suffering caused by the crime

deterrence the attempt to discourage criminality through the use of punishment

rehabilitation (p. 182) a program for reforming the offender to prevent later offences

societal protection (p. 182) rendering an offender incapable of further offences temporarily through imprisonment or permanently by execution

Police

The police generally serve as the point of contact between a population and the criminal justice system. In principle, the police maintain public order by enforcing the law. Of course, there is only so much that 69 299 full-time police officers across Canada can do to monitor the activities of more than 34 million people. As a result, the police use a great deal of personal judgment in deciding which situations warrant their attention and how to handle them. Police also face danger on a daily basis. Between 1961 and 2009, 133 police officers were murdered in the line of duty (Dunn, 2010). This is in sharp contrast to the situation in the United States, where more than 100 American police officers are killed in the line of duty each year.

Given these facts, how do police officers carry out their duties? In a study of police behaviour in five cities, Douglas Smith and Christy Visher (1981; Smith, 1987) concluded that because they must act swiftly, police quickly size up situations in terms of six factors. First, the more serious they think the situation is, the more likely they are to make an arrest. Second, police take account of the victim's wishes in deciding whether to make an arrest. Third, the odds of arrest go up the more unco-operative a suspect is. Fourth, police are more likely to take into custody someone they have arrested before, presumably because this suggests guilt. Fifth, the presence of bystanders increases the chances of arrest. According to Smith and Visher, the presence of observers prompts police to take stronger control of a situation, if only to move the encounter from the street (the suspect's turf) to the police department (where law officers have the edge). Sixth, all else being equal, police are more likely to arrest visible minorities and Aboriginals, perceiving them as either more dangerous or more likely to be guilty.

Courts

After arrest, a court determines a suspect's guilt or innocence. In principle, Canadian courts rely on an adversarial process involving lawyers—one representing the defendant and another representing the state—in the presence of a judge who monitors legal procedures.

In practice, however, about 90 percent of criminal cases are resolved before court appearance through **plea bargaining**, *a legal negotiation in which a prosecutor reduces a charge in exchange for a defendant's guilty plea.* For example, the Crown may offer a defendant charged with burglary a lesser charge, perhaps possession of burglary tools, in exchange for a guilty plea.

Plea bargaining is widespread because it spares the system the time and expense of trials. A trial is usually unnecessary if there is little disagreement as to the facts of the case. Moreover, because of the high number of cases entering the system, prosecutors could not possibly bring every case to trial even if they wanted to. By quickly resolving most of their work, then, the courts can devote their resources to the most important cases.

But plea bargaining pressures defendants (who are presumed innocent) to plead guilty. A person can exercise his or her right to a trial, but only at the risk of receiving a more severe sentence if found guilty. Furthermore, low-income defendants must often rely on a crown attorney—typically an overworked and underpaid lawyer who may devote little time to even the most serious cases (Novak, 1999).

On the other hand, plea bargaining sometimes allows individuals to receive inadequate sentences if further facts against them are discovered after agreement with the Crown prosecutor is finalized. There is near universal condemnation of the plea bargain that the Crown prosecutor negotiated with Karla Homolka in exchange for her testimony against Paul Bernardo because of the additional facts that emerged against Homolka during the trial against her husband.

In short, plea bargaining may be efficient, but it undercuts both the adversarial process and the rights of defendants.

Punishment

In 2009, a man with a long criminal record who was out on bail on charges of raping a child walked into a coffee shop in Parkland, Washington, and shot and killed four uniformed police officers as they were doing "paperwork" on their laptops. Two days later, a massive manhunt ended when the man was killed in a confrontation with another police officer (MSNBC, 2009).

Such cases force us to wonder about the reasons that drive some people to deadly violence and also to ask how a society should respond to such acts. In the case of the Parkland shootings, the crime was resolved through gunfire. But typically, of course, a suspect is apprehended and put on trial. If found guilty, the next step is punishment.

What does a society gain through the punishment of wrongdoers? Scholars give four basic answers, which are described in the following sections: retribution, deterrence, rehabilitation, and societal protection.

Retribution

The oldest justification for punishment is to satisfy a society's need for **retribution**, *an act of moral vengeance by which society makes the offender suffer as much as the suffering caused by the crime.* Retribution rests on the view that society exists in a moral balance. When criminality upsets this balance, punishment in equal measure restores the moral order, as suggested in the ancient code calling for "an eye for an eye, a tooth for a tooth."

In the Middle Ages, most people viewed crime as sin—an offence against God as well as society—that required a harsh response. Although critics point out that retribution does little to reform the offender, many people today still consider vengeance reason enough for punishment.

Deterrence

A second justification for punishment is **deterrence**, *the attempt to discourage criminality through the use of punishment.* Deterrence is

plea bargaining (p. 181) a legal negotiation in which a prosecutor reduces a charge in exchange for a defendant's guilty plea

SUMMING UP

Four Justifications for Punishment

Retribution	The oldest justification for punishment.
	Punishment is society's revenge for a moral wrong.
	In principle, punishment should be equal in severity to the crime itself.
Deterrence	An early modern approach.
	Crime is considered social disruption, which society acts to control.
	People are viewed as rational and self-interested; deterrence works because the pain of punishment outweighs the pleasure of crime.
Rehabilitation	A modern strategy linked to the development of social sciences.
	Crime and other deviance are viewed as the result of social problems (such as poverty) or personal problems (such as mental illness).
	Social conditions are improved; treatment is tailored to the offender's condition.
Societal protection	A modern approach easier to carry out than rehabilitation.
	Even if society is unable or unwilling to rehabilitate offenders or reform social conditions, people are protected by the imprisonment or execution of the offender.

based on the eighteenth-century Enlightenment idea that, as calculating and rational creatures, humans will not break the law if they think that the pain of the punishment will outweigh the pleasure of the crime.

Deterrence emerged as a reform measure in response to harsh punishments based on retribution. Why put someone to death for stealing if theft can be discouraged by a prison sentence? As the concept of deterrence gained acceptance in industrial societies, execution and physical mutilation of criminals were replaced by milder forms of punishment such as imprisonment.

Rehabilitation

The third justification for punishment, **rehabilitation**, is *a program for reforming the offender to prevent later offences.* Rehabilitation arose along with the social sciences in the nineteenth century. Since then, sociologists have claimed that crime and other deviance spring from a social environment marked by poverty or lack of parental supervision. Logically, then, if offenders learn to be deviant, they can also learn to obey the rules; the key is controlling the environment. *Reformatories* or *houses of correction* provided a controlled setting where people could learn proper behaviour (recall the description of total institutions in Chapter 3, "Socialization: From Infancy to Old Age").

Like deterrence, rehabilitation motivates the offender to conform. In contrast to deterrence and retribution, which simply make the offender suffer, rehabilitation encourages constructive improvement. Unlike retribution, which demands that the punishment fit the crime, rehabilitation tailors treatment to each offender. Thus

identical crimes would prompt similar acts of retribution but different rehabilitation programs.

Societal Protection

A final justification for punishment is **societal protection**, *rendering an offender incapable of further offences temporarily through imprisonment or permanently by execution.* Like deterrence, societal protection is a rational approach to punishment intended to protect society from crime. The reason why there are more than 31 000 adults in Canadian prisons is partly a reflection of the widespread attitude that we should "get criminals off the streets." Remember that this number represents only about 20 percent of the total number under the supervision of the correctional system—about 66 percent of the grand total are on probation and the remainder serve a conditional sentence or are on conditional release (Beattie, 2005).

In 2007–2008, on a given day, 36 330 adults and 2018 youth aged 12 to 17 were in custody in Canada, for a total of 38 348 inmates or about 108 per 100 000 population. Even though the incarceration rate in Canada has decreased 18 percent from 131 per 100 000 in 1996, this is higher than the rates in most Western European countries but much lower than in the United States, where some 2.4 million people were in prison in 2010. This large prison population reflects both tougher public attitudes toward crime in the United States and an increasing number of arrests for drug-related crimes. As Figure 7–2 shows, the United States now imprisons a larger share of its population than any other country in the world (Pew Center on the States, 2008; Sentencing Project, 2008b; U.S. Bureau of Justice Statistics, 2010).

Global Snapshot

The United States has the dubious distinction of having the highest incarceration rate in the world.

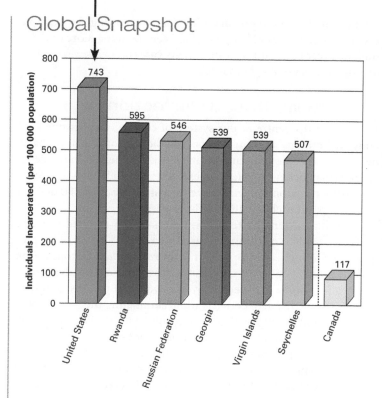

FIGURE 7–2   Nations with the Highest Incarceration Rates

Note: Figures are for different years but are the most recent available as of 2011.

Source: International Centre for Prison Studies (2011).

To increase the power of punishment to deter crime, capital punishment was long carried out in public. The 1902 hanging in Hull, Quebec, of Stanislaus Lacroix, a logger who killed his wife and a neighbour, is believed to be the last public execution in Canada. Now that the mass media report on executions across the United States, states carry out capital punishment behind closed doors.

CRITICAL REVIEW   The Summing Up table on page 182 reviews the four justifications for punishment. However, an accurate assessment of the consequences of punishment is no simple task.

The value of retribution lies in Durkheim's claim that punishing the deviant person increases society's moral awareness. For this reason, punishment was traditionally a public event. Although the last public execution in Canada is believed to have taken place in 1902 in Hull, Quebec, today's mass media ensure public awareness of executions carried out inside prison walls in countries where the practice is still legal (Kittrie, 1971).

Does punishment deter crime? Despite our extensive use of punishment, our society has a high rate of **criminal recidivism**, *later offences by people previously convicted of crimes*. After being released, about half of those convicted of a Criminal Code offence are convicted of a new offence within three years, and some studies suggest that almost four out of five offenders are eventually convicted again (DeFina & Arvanites, 2002; Langan & Levin, 2002). So does punishment really deter crime? Fewer than half of all crimes are known to police and, of these, only about one in five results in an arrest. Most crimes, therefore, go unpunished, leading us to conclude, perhaps, that the old saying "crime doesn't pay" may not be entirely true.

Prisons provide short-term societal protection by keeping offenders off the streets, but they do little to reshape attitudes or behaviour in the long term (Carlson, 1976; Wright, 1994). Perhaps rehabilitation is an unrealistic expectation, because according to Sutherland's theory of differential association, locking up criminals together for years probably strengthens criminal attitudes and skills. Imprisonment also breaks whatever social ties inmates may have in the outside world, which, following Hirschi's control theory, makes inmates likely to commit more crimes upon release.

CHECK YOUR LEARNING   What are society's four justifications for punishment? Does sending offenders to prison accomplish each of them? How?

The Death Penalty

Perhaps the most controversial issue involving punishment is the death penalty. From 1993 through 2009, more than 3500 people were sentenced to death in U.S. courts; 1000 executions were carried out. In 36 U.S. states, the law allows the state to execute offenders convicted of very serious crimes such as first-degree murder. But while a majority of states do permit capital punishment, only a few states are likely to carry out executions. Across the United States, half of the 3207 people on death row at the end of 2008 were in just four states: California, Texas, Florida, and Pennsylvania (U.S. Bureau of Justice Statistics, 2010).

Opponents of capital punishment point to research suggesting that the death penalty has limited value as a crime deterrent. Countries such as Canada, where the death penalty has been abolished, have not seen a rise in the number of murders. Critics also point out that the United States is the only high-income nation that routinely executes offenders. As public concern about the death penalty has increased, the use of capital punishment declined from as many as 98 executions in 1999 to 37 in 2008 but rose again to 52 in 2009.

Public opinion surveys reveal that the share of American adults who claim to support the death penalty as a punishment for murder remains high (62 percent) and has been fairly stable over time (NORC, 2009:214). American college students hold about the same attitudes as everyone else, with about two-thirds of first-year students expressing support for the death penalty (Pryor et al., 2008). Canadian surveys find our population more divided. According to an EKOS poll conducted in March 2010, Canadians are about evenly split on the issue of whether to revive the death penalty: 46 percent of those surveyed were opposed to bringing back capital punishment while 40 percent thought such a move was a good idea. These results were similar to those from a poll conducted in June 2000, when there was an almost even split on the issue (CBC News, 2010).

But judges, criminal prosecutors, and members of trial juries are less and less likely to call for the death penalty. One reason is that because the crime rate has come down in recent years, the public now has less fear of crime and is less interested in applying the most severe punishment.

A second reason is public concern that the death penalty may be applied unjustly. The analysis of DNA evidence—a recent advance—from old crime scenes has shown that many people were wrongly convicted of a crime. Across the United States, between 1975 and 2010, at least 137 people who had been sentenced to death were released from death row after DNA evidence demonstrated their innocence. Such findings were one reason that, in 2000, the governor of Illinois stated he could no longer support the death penalty, leading him to commute the death sentences of every person on that state's death row (Death Penalty Information Center, 2010; Levine, 2003).

A third reason for the decline in the use of the death penalty is that judges and juries in Canada and most other countries, and including those in many U.S. states, are now permitted to sentence serious offenders to life in prison without the possibility of parole. Such punishment offers to protect society from dangerous criminals who can be "put away" forever without requiring an execution.

Fourth and finally, prosecuting capital cases is very costly. Death penalty cases require more legal work and demand superior defence lawyers, often at public expense. In addition, such cases commonly include testimony by various paid "experts," including physicians and psychiatrists, which also runs up the costs of trial. Then there is the cost of the many appeals that almost always follow a conviction leading to a sentence of death. When all of these factors are put together, the cost of a death penalty case typically exceeds the cost of

sending an offender to prison for life. One accounting, for example, reveals that the state of New Jersey has been spending more than $10 million a year prosecuting death penalty cases that have yet to result in a single execution (Thomas & Brant, 2007).

Community-Based Corrections

Prison is at the centre of our system of corrections. Prisons keep convicted criminals off the streets. The thought of prison probably deters many people from committing serious crime. But the evidence suggests that locking people up does little to rehabilitate most offenders. Further, prisons are expensive; it costs more than $80 000 per year to support each inmate in federal prison.

A recent alternative to prison that has been adopted in many parts of Canada is **community-based corrections**, *correctional programs operating within society at large rather than behind prison walls*. Community-based corrections have three main advantages: They reduce costs, they reduce overcrowding in prisons, and they allow for supervision of convicts while eliminating the hardships of prison life and the stigma that accompanies going to jail. In general, the idea of community-based corrections is not so much to punish as to reform; such programs are therefore usually offered to individuals who have committed less serious offences and who appear to be good prospects for avoiding future criminal violations (Inciardi, 2000).

Probation

One form of community-based corrections is *probation*, a policy of permitting a convicted offender to remain in the community under conditions imposed by a court, including regular supervision. Courts may require that a probationer receive counselling, attend a drug treatment program, hold a job, avoid associating with "known criminals," or anything else a judge thinks is appropriate. Typically, a probationer must check in with an officer of the court (the probation officer) on a regular schedule to make sure the guidelines are being followed. Should the probationer fail to live up to the conditions set by the court or commit a new offence, the court may revoke probation and send the offender to jail.

Parole

Parole is a policy of releasing inmates from prison to serve the remainder of their sentences in the local community under the supervision of a parole officer. Although courts may sometimes sentence an offender to prison without the possibility of parole, most other inmates become eligible for parole after serving a certain portion of their sentence. At this time, a parole board evaluates the risks and benefits of an inmate's early release from prison. If parole is granted, the parole board then monitors the offender's conduct until the sentence is completed. Should the offender not comply with the conditions of parole or be arrested for another crime, the board can revoke parole, returning the offender to prison to complete the original sentence.

Violent Crime Is Down—but Why?

DUANE: I'm a criminal justice major, and I want to be a police officer. Crime is a huge problem in Canada, and police are what keeps the crime rate low.

SANDY: I'm a sociology major. As for combating crime, I'm not sure it's quite that simple. . . .

During the 1980s, crime rates shot upward and there seemed to be no solution to the problem. In the 1990s, something good and unexpected happened: Serious crime rates began to fall until, by 2000, they were at levels not seen in more than a generation. Why? Researchers point to several reasons:

1. **A reduction in the youth population.** It was noted earlier that young people (particularly males) are responsible for much violent crime. Between 1990 and 2000, the share of the population aged 15 to 24 dropped significantly.

2. **Changes in policing.** Much of the drop in crime (as well as the earlier rise in crime) has taken place in large cities. Many cities have adopted a policy of community policing, which means that police are concerned not just with making arrests but also with preventing crime before it happens. Officers get to know the areas they patrol and frequently stop young people for jaywalking or other minor infractions so they can check them for other things. In addition, there are more police working in Canada today. The

One reason that crime has gone down is that there are nearly 40 000 people incarcerated in this country. This has caused severe overcrowding of facilities such as this prison in Saskatchewan.

number of police officers in Canada increased 3 percent between 1991 and 1996, another 6 percent by 2001, and 4 percent in 2006 (Statistics Canada, 2006d; Taylor-Butts, 2004).

3. **A better economy.** The Canadian economy boomed during the 1990s. With unemployment down, more people were working, reducing the likelihood that some would turn to crime out of economic desperation. The logic here is simple: More jobs, fewer crimes. By the same token, the recent economic downturn has slowed the downward crime trend.

4. **The declining drug trade.** Many analysts think that the most important factor in reducing rates of violent crime is the decline of crack cocaine. Crack came on the scene around 1985, and violence spread, especially in the inner cities, as young people—facing few legitimate job opportunities and increasingly armed with guns—became part of a booming drug trade.

By the early 1990s, however, the popularity of crack had begun to fall as people saw the damage the drug was causing to entire communities. This realization, coupled with steady economic improvement and stiffer sentences for drug offences, helped bring about the turnaround in violent crime.

The current picture looks better relative to what it was a decade or two ago. But one researcher cautions: "It looks better, but only because the early 1990s were so bad. So let's not fool ourselves into thinking everything is resolved. It's not."

WHAT DO YOU THINK?

1. Do you support the policy of community policing? Why or why not?

2. What do you see as the pros and cons of building more prisons?

3. Of all the factors mentioned here, which do you think is the most important in crime control? Which is least important? Why?

Sources: Winship & Berrien (1999), Donahue & Levitt (2000), Rosenfeld (2002), Liptak (2008), and Mitchell (2008).

CRITICAL REVIEW Evaluations of probation and parole have been mixed. There is little question that community-based programs are much less expensive than conventional imprisonment; they also free up room in prisons for people who commit more serious crimes. Yet research suggests that although probation seems to work for some people, it does not significantly reduce criminal recidivism. Similarly, parole is useful to prison officials as a means to encourage good behaviour among prison inmates who hope for early release. Yet levels of crime among those released on parole are so high that a number of U.S. states have ended their parole programs entirely (Inciardi, 2000).

Such evaluations point to a sobering truth: By itself, the criminal justice system cannot eliminate crime. As the Controversy & Debate box explains, although police, courts, and prisons do affect crime rates, crime and other deviance are not just the acts of "bad people" but reflect the operation of society itself.

CHECK YOUR LEARNING What are three types of community-based corrections? What are their advantages?

CHAPTER 7 DEVIANCE

WHY DO MOST OF US—AT LEAST MOST OF THE TIME—OBEY THE RULES? As this chapter explains, every society is a system of social control that encourages conformity to certain norms and discourages deviance or norm breaking. One way society does this is through the construction of heroes and villains. Heroes, of course, are people we are supposed to look up to and use as role models. Villains are people we look down on and whose example we reject. Organizations of all types create heroes that serve as guides to everyday behaviour. In each case below, who is being made into a hero? Why? What are the values or behaviours we are encouraged to copy in our own lives?

Religious organizations, too, use heroes to encourage certain behaviour and beliefs. The Catholic Church has defined the Virgin Mary and more than 10 000 other men and women as "saints." For what reasons might someone be honoured in this way? What do saints do for the rest of us?

Most sports have a "hall of fame." A larger-than-life-sized statue of the legendary slugger Babe Ruth attracts these children on their visit to the Baseball Hall of Fame. What are the qualities that make an athlete "legendary"? Isn't it more than just how far someone hits a ball?

HINT: A society without heroes and villains would be one in which no one cared how people think or act. Societies create heroes as role models that are supposed to inspire us to be more like them. Societies create heroes by emphasizing one aspect of someone's life and ignoring many other things. For example, Babe Ruth was a great ball player, but his private life was sometimes less than inspiring. Perhaps this is why the Catholic Church never considers anyone a candidate for sainthood until after—usually long after—the person has died.

Applying Sociology in Everyday Life

1. Do athletic teams, fraternities and sororities, and even people in a university classroom create heroes and villains? Explain how and why.

2. Identity theft is a new type of crime that victimizes thousands of Canadians each year. Research this phenomenon and explain how this offence differs from property crime that takes place "on the street." (Consider differences in the crime, the offenders, and the victims.)

3. Watch an episode of a real-action police show such as *Cops*. Based on what you see, how would you profile the people who commit crimes?

MAKING THE GRADE

What Is Deviance?

DEVIANCE refers to norm violations ranging from minor infractions, such as bad manners, to major infractions, such as serious violence.

p. 161

deviance (p. 161) the recognized violation of cultural norms

crime (p. 161) the violation of a society's formally enacted criminal law

social control (p. 161) attempts by society to regulate people's thoughts and behaviour

criminal justice system (p. 161) the organizations—police, courts, and prison officials—that respond to alleged violations of the law

Theories of Deviance

BIOLOGICAL THEORIES

- focus on individual abnormality
- explain human behaviour as the result of biological instincts

LOMBROSO claimed criminals have apelike physical traits; later research links criminal behaviour to certain body types and genetics.

pp. 161–62

PSYCHOLOGICAL THEORIES

- focus on individual abnormality
- see deviance as the result of "unsuccessful socialization"

RECKLESS AND DINITZ'S CONTAINMENT THEORY links delinquency to weak conscience.

pp. 162–63

✓ Biological and psychological theories provide a limited understanding of crime and other deviance because most violations are carried out by people who are normal (pp. 161–63).

SOCIOLOGICAL THEORIES view all behaviour—deviant as well as conforming—as products of society. Sociologists point out that

- what is deviant varies from place to place according to cultural norms
- behaviour and individuals become deviant as others define them that way
- what and who a society defines as deviant reflect who has social power and who does not

p. 163

labelling theory (p. 166) the idea that deviance and conformity result not so much from what people do as from how others respond to those actions

stigma (p. 167) a powerfully negative label that greatly changes a person's self-concept and social identity

medicalization of deviance (p. 169) the transformation of moral and legal deviance into a medical condition

white-collar crime (p. 172) crime committed by people of high social position in the course of their occupations

corporate crime (p. 172) the illegal actions of a corporation or people acting on its behalf

organized crime (p. 172) a business supplying illegal goods or services

hate crime (p. 173) a criminal act against a person or a person's property by an offender motivated by racial or other bias

Theoretical Analysis of Deviance

The Functions of Deviance: Structural-Functional Analysis

Durkheim claimed that deviance is a normal element of society that

- affirms cultural norms and values
- clarifies moral boundaries
- brings people together
- encourages social change

p. 164

Merton's **strain theory** explains deviance in terms of a society's cultural goals and the means available to achieve them.
Deviant subcultures are discussed by Cloward and Ohlin, Cohen, Miller, and Anderson.

pp. 165–66

Labelling Theory: Symbolic-Interaction Analysis

Labelling theory claims that deviance depends less on what someone does than on how others react to that behaviour. If people respond to primary deviance by stigmatizing a person, secondary deviance and a deviant career may result.

pp. 166–68

The **medicalization of deviance** is the transformation of moral and legal deviance into a medical condition. In practice, this means a change in labels, replacing "good" and "bad" with "sick" and "well."

p. 169

Sutherland's **differential association theory** links deviance to how much others encourage or discourage such behaviour.

p. 169

Hirschi's **control theory** states that imagining the possible consequences of deviance often discourages such behaviour. People who are well integrated into society are less likely to engage in deviant behaviour.

pp. 169–70

See the Applying Theory table on page 173.

Deviance and Inequality: Social-Conflict Analysis

Based on Karl Marx's ideas, social-conflict theory holds that laws and other norms operate to protect the interests of powerful members of any society.

- **White-collar offences** are committed by people of high social position as part of their jobs. Sutherland claimed such offences are rarely prosecuted and are most likely to end up in civil rather than criminal court.
- **Corporate crime** refers to illegal actions by a corporation or people acting on its behalf. Although corporate crimes cause considerable public harm, most cases of corporate crime go unpunished.
- **Organized crime** has a long history in Canada and many other countries, especially among categories of people with few legitimate opportunities.

pp. 172–73

Deviance, Race, and Gender

- What people consider deviant reflects the relative power and privilege of different categories of people.
- **Hate crimes** are crimes motivated by racial or other bias; they target people with disadvantages based on race, gender, or sexual orientation.
- In Canada and elsewhere, societies control the behaviour of women more closely than that of men.

pp. 173–75

Crime

CRIME is the violation of criminal laws enacted by municipal, provincial or territorial, or federal governments. There are two major categories of serious crime:

- crimes against the person (violent crime), including murder, aggravated assault, forcible rape, and robbery
- crimes against property (property crime), including burglary, larceny-theft, auto theft, and arson

p. 175

PATTERNS OF CRIME IN CANADA

- Official statistics show that arrest rates peak in late adolescence and drop steadily with advancing age.
- About 65% of people arrested for property crimes and 82% of people arrested for violent crimes are male.
- Street crime is more common among people of lower social position. Including white-collar and corporate crime makes class differences in criminality smaller.
- More whites than Aboriginals and Blacks are arrested for street crimes. However, more visible minorities and Aboriginals are arrested than whites in relation to their population size. Asian Canadians have a lower-than-average rate of arrest.
- The Canadian crime rate is not very high compared to many other countries, including the United States.

pp. 176–79

crimes against the person (p. 175) crimes that direct violence or the threat of violence against others; also known as *violent crimes*

crimes against property (p. 175) crimes that involve theft of money or property belonging to others; also known as *property crimes*

victimless crimes (p. 175) violations of law in which there are no obvious victims

plea bargaining (p. 180) a legal negotiation in which a prosecutor reduces a charge in exchange for a defendant's guilty plea

retribution (p. 181) an act of moral vengeance by which society makes the offender suffer as much as the suffering caused by the crime

deterrence (p. 181) the attempt to discourage criminality through the use of punishment

rehabilitation (p. 181) a program for reforming the offender to prevent later offences

societal protection (p. 181) rendering an offender incapable of further offences temporarily through imprisonment or permanently by execution

criminal recidivism (p. 182) later offences by people previously convicted of crimes

community-based corrections (p. 184) correctional programs operating within society at large rather than behind prison walls

The Canadian Criminal Justice System

Police

The police maintain public order by enforcing the law.

- Police use personal discretion in deciding whether and how to handle a situation.
- Research suggests that police are more likely to make an arrest if the offence is serious, if bystanders are present, or if the suspect is a Black or Aboriginal male.

p. 180

Courts

Courts rely on an adversarial process in which lawyers—one representing the defendant and one representing the state—present their cases in the presence of a judge who monitors legal procedures.

- In practice, Canadian courts resolve most cases through plea bargaining. Though efficient, this method puts less powerful people at a disadvantage.

pp. 180–81

Punishment

There are four justifications for punishment:
- retribution
- rehabilitation
- deterrence
- societal protection

pp. 181–82

The **death penalty** is banned in Canada and other high-income countries except the United States. The long-term trend is toward fewer executions there, as around the world.

pp. 182–84

Community-based corrections include probation and parole. These programs lower the cost of supervising people convicted of crimes and reduce prison overcrowding but have not been shown to reduce recidivism.

p. 184

See the Summing Up table on page 182.

MySocLab

Visit MySocLab at www.mysoclab.com to access a variety of online resources that will help you to prepare for tests and to apply your knowledge, including

- an eText
- videos
- self-grading quizzes
- glossary flashcards

8 Social Stratification

- What is social stratification?
- Why does social inequality exist?
- How do social classes in Canada differ from one another?

This chapter introduces the central concept of social stratification, which is important because our social standing affects almost everything about our lives. While making comparisons to other societies, the chapter surveys social stratification in Canada, identifying important measures of inequality and describing the Canadian class system.

On April 10, 1912, the ocean liner *Titanic* slipped away from the docks of Southampton, England, on its first voyage across the North Atlantic to New York. A proud symbol of the new industrial age, the towering ship carried 2300 men, women, and children, some of them enjoying more luxury than most travellers today could imagine. Many poor immigrants crowded the lower decks, journeying to what they hoped would be a better life in North America.

Two days out, the crew received reports of icebergs in the area but paid little notice. Then, near midnight, as the ship steamed swiftly westward, a stunned lookout reported a massive shape rising out of the dark ocean directly ahead. Moments later, the *Titanic* collided with a huge iceberg, as tall as the ship itself, that split open its side as if the grand vessel were a giant tin can.

Seawater flooded into the vessel's lower levels, pulling the ship down by the bow. Within 25 minutes of impact, people were rushing for the lifeboats. By 2:00 A.M., the bow was completely submerged, and the stern rose high above the water. Clinging to the deck, quietly observed by those in lifeboats, hundreds of helpless passengers and crew solemnly passed their final minutes before the ship disappeared into the frigid Atlantic (Lord, 1976).

The tragic loss of more than 1600 lives made news around the world. Looking back on this terrible event with a sociological eye, we see that some categories of passengers had much better odds of survival than others. In keeping with that era's traditional ideas about gender, women and children boarded the lifeboats first, with the result that 80 percent of those who died were men. Class was also a factor in who survived and who did not. More than 60 percent of the passengers travelling on first-class tickets were saved because they were on the upper decks, where warnings were sounded first and lifeboats were accessible. Only 36 percent of the second-class passengers survived, and of the third-class passengers on the lower decks, only 24 percent escaped drowning. On board the *Titanic*, class meant more than the quality of accommodations; it was a matter of life or death.

The fate of the passengers on the *Titanic* dramatically illustrates how social inequality affects the way people live—and sometimes whether they live at all. This chapter explores the important concept of social stratification and examines social inequality in Canada.

What Is Social Stratification?

Every society is marked by inequality, with some people having more money, schooling, health, and power than others. **Social stratification**, defined as *a system by which a society ranks categories of people in a hierarchy*, is based on four important principles:

1. Social stratification is a trait of society, not simply a reflection of individual differences. Many of us think of social standing in terms of personal talent and effort and, as a result, we often exaggerate the extent to which we control our own fate. Did a higher percentage of the first-class passengers on the *Titanic* survive because they were better swimmers than second- and third-class passengers? No. They did better because of their privileged position on the ship. Similarly, children born into wealthy families are more likely than children born into poverty to enjoy good health, do well in school, succeed in a career, and live a long life. Neither the rich nor the poor are responsible for creating social stratification, yet this system shapes the lives of us all.

2. Social stratification carries over from generation to generation. We have only to look at how parents pass their social position on to their children to understand that stratification is a trait of societies rather than individuals. Some individuals, especially in industrial societies, do experience **social mobility**, *a change in position within the social hierarchy*. Social mobility may be upward or downward. We celebrate the achievements of rare individuals such as Céline Dion and Wayne Gretzky, who rose from modest beginnings to fame and fortune. Some people also move downward in the social hierarchy because of business setbacks, unemployment, or illness. More often people move *horizontally*; they switch one job for another at about the same social level. The social standing of most people remains much the same over their lifetimes.

social stratification (p. 190) a system by which a society ranks categories of people in a hierarchy

social mobility (p. 190) a change in position within the social hierarchy

3. Social stratification is universal but variable. Social stratification is found everywhere. Yet *what* is unequal and *how* unequal it is vary from one society to another. In some societies, inequality is mostly a matter of prestige; in others, wealth or power is the key element of difference. In addition, some societies contain more inequality than others.

4. Social stratification involves not just inequality but beliefs as well. Any system of inequality not only gives some people more than others but also defines these arrangements as fair. Like the *what* of social inequality, the explanations of *why* people should be unequal differ from society to society.

Caste and Class Systems

When comparing societies in terms of inequality, sociologists distinguish between *closed systems*, which allow little change in social position, and *open systems*, which permit much more social mobility. Closed systems are called *caste systems*, and more open systems are called *class systems*.

In rural India, the traditional caste system still shapes people's lives. This girl is a member of the "untouchables," a category below the four basic castes. She and her family are clothes washers, people who clean material "polluted" by blood or human waste. Such work is defined as unclean for people of higher caste position.

The Caste System

A **caste system** is *social stratification based on ascription, or birth.* A pure caste system is closed because birth alone determines a person's entire future, with little or no social mobility based on individual effort. People live out their lives in the rigid categories into which they were born, without the possibility for change for the better or worse.

An Illustration: India

Many of the world's agrarian societies are caste systems. Although India's economy is growing rapidly, much of the population still lives in traditional villages, where the caste system is part of everyday life. The traditional Indian system includes four major castes (or *varnas*, from a Sanskrit word that means "colour"): Brahmin, Kshatriya, Vaishya, and Sudra. On the local level, however, each of these is composed of hundreds of subcaste groups (*jatis*).

From birth, caste position determines the direction of a person's life. First, with the exception of farming, which is open to everyone, families in each caste perform one type of work, as priests, soldiers, barbers, leather workers, sweepers, and so on.

Second, a caste system demands that people marry others of the same ranking. If people were to have "mixed" marriages with members of other castes, what rank would their children hold? Sociologists call this pattern of marrying within a social category *endogamous* marriage (*endo-* stems from the Greek word for "within"). According to tradition—this practice is now rare and found only in remote rural areas—Indian parents select their children's marriage partners, often before the children reach their teens.

Third, caste guides everyday life by keeping people in the company of "their own kind." Norms reinforce this practice by teaching, for instance, that a "purer" person of a higher caste position is "polluted" by contact with someone of lower standing.

Fourth, caste systems rest on powerful cultural beliefs. Indian culture is built on the Hindu tradition that doing the caste's life work and accepting an arranged marriage are moral duties.

Caste and Agrarian Life

Caste systems are typical of agrarian societies because agriculture demands a lifelong routine of hard work. By teaching a sense of moral duty, a caste system ensures that people are disciplined for a lifetime of work and are willing to perform the same jobs as their parents. Thus the caste system has hung on in rural India more than 70 years after being formally outlawed. People living in the industrial cities of India have many more choices about work and marriage partners than people in rural areas.

Another country dominated by caste is South Africa, although the racial system of *apartheid* is no longer legal and now in decline. The Thinking Globally box on page 192 takes a closer look.

The Class System

Because a modern economy must attract people to work in many occupations other than farming, it depends on developing people's talents in diverse fields. This process of schooling and specialization gives rise to a **class system**, *social stratification based on both birth and individual achievement.*

meritocracy social stratification based on personal merit

caste system (p. 191) social stratification based on ascription, or birth

class system (p. 191) social stratification based on both birth and individual achievement

THINKING GLOBALLY

Race as Caste: A Report from South Africa

DON: I've been reading about racial caste in South Africa. I'm glad that's over.

MIKE: But racial inequality is far from over. . . .

At the southern tip of the African continent lies South Africa, a country a little bit larger than Ontario but smaller than Quebec with a population of about 50 million. For 300 years, the native Africans who lived there were ruled by white people, first by the Dutch traders and farmers who settled there in the mid-seventeenth century and then by the British, who colonized the area early in the nineteenth century. By the early 1900s, the British had taken over the entire country, naming it the Union of South Africa.

In 1961, the nation declared its independence from Britain, calling itself the Republic of South Africa, but freedom for the Black majority was still decades away. To ensure their political control over the Black population, whites instituted the policy of *apartheid*, or racial separation. Apartheid, written into law in 1948, denied Blacks national citizenship, ownership of land, and any voice in the nation's government. As a lower caste, Blacks received little schooling and performed menial, low-paying jobs. White people with even average wealth had at least one Black household servant.

The members of the white minority claimed that apartheid protected their cultural traditions from the influence of people they considered inferior. When Blacks resisted apartheid, whites used brutal military repression to maintain their power. Even so, steady resistance—especially from younger Blacks, who demanded a political voice and economic opportunity—gradually forced the country to change. Criticism from other industrial nations added to the pressure. By the mid-1980s, the tide began to turn as the South African government granted limited political rights to people of mixed race and Asian ancestry. Next came the right of all people to form labour unions, to enter occupations once limited to whites, and to own property. Officials also repealed apartheid laws that separated the races in public places.

The pace of change increased in 1990 with the release from prison of Nelson Mandela, who led the fight against apartheid. In 1994, the first national election open to all races made Mandela president, ending centuries of white minority rule.

Despite this dramatic political change, social stratification in South Africa is still based on race. Even with the right to own property, one-fourth of Black South Africans have no work, and half of the population lives below the poverty line. The worst off are some 7 million *ukuhleleleka*, which means "marginal people" in the Xhosa language. Soweto-by-the-Sea may sound like a summer getaway, but it is a shantytown, home to hundreds of thousands of people crammed into shacks made of packing cases, corrugated metal, cardboard, and other discarded materials. Recent years have seen some signs of prosperity. But for most families, there is no electricity for lights or refrigeration. Without plumbing, the majority of people use buckets to haul sewage. The community's women line up to take a turn at various water taps that each serves more than 1000 people. Jobs are hard to come by, and those who do find work are lucky to earn $250 a month.

South Africa's current president, Jacob Zuma, who was elected in 2009, leads a nation still crippled by its history of racial caste. Tourism is up and holds the promise of an economic boom in years to come, but the country can break from the past only by providing real opportunity to all of its people.

WHAT DO YOU THINK?

1. How has race been a form of caste in South Africa?

2. Although apartheid is no longer law, why does racial inequality continue to shape South African society?

3. Does race operate as an element of caste in Canada? Explain your answer.

Sources: Mabry & Masland (1999), Murphy (2002), and Perry (2009).

Class systems are more open than caste systems, so people who gain schooling and skills may experience social mobility. As a result, class distinctions become blurred and even blood relatives may have different social standings. Categorizing people according to their colour, sex, or social background comes to be seen as wrong in modern societies as all people gain political rights and, in principle, equal standing before the law. In addition, work is no longer fixed at birth but involves some personal choice. Greater individuality also translates into more personal freedom in the process of selecting a marital partner.

Meritocracy

The concept of **meritocracy** refers to *social stratification based on personal merit*. Because industrial societies need to develop a broad range of abilities beyond farming, stratification is based not just on the accident of birth but also on *merit* (from a Latin word meaning "earned"), which includes a person's knowledge, abilities, and effort. A rough measure of merit is the importance of a person's job and how well it is done. To increase meritocracy, industrial societies expand equality of opportunity and teach people to expect unequal rewards based on individual performance.

In a pure meritocracy, which has never existed, social position would depend entirely on a person's ability and effort. Such a system would have ongoing social mobility, blurring social categories as individuals continuously move up or down in the system, depending on their latest performance.

Caste societies define merit in different terms, emphasizing loyalty to the system—that is, dutifully performing whatever job comes with the social position a person has at birth. Because they assign jobs before anyone can know anything about a person's talents or interests, caste systems waste human potential. On the other hand, because caste systems clearly assign everyone a "place" in society and a specific type of work, they are very orderly. A need for some amount of order is the reason that even industrial and post-industrial societies keep some elements of caste—such as letting wealth pass from generation to generation—rather than becoming complete meritocracies. A pure meritocracy, with individuals moving up and down the social ranking all the time, would pull apart families and other social groupings. After all, economic performance is not everything: Would we want to evaluate our family members solely on how successful they are in their jobs outside of the home? Probably not. Class systems in industrial societies move toward meritocracy to promote productivity and efficiency; but at the same time, they keep caste elements, such as family, to maintain order and social unity.

One of the major events of the twentieth century was the socialist revolution in Russia, which led to the creation of the Soviet Union. Following the ideas of Karl Marx, the popular uprising overthrew a feudal aristocracy, as depicted in the 1920 painting *Bolshevik* by Boris Mikhailovich Kustodiev.

Status Consistency

Status consistency is *the degree of uniformity in a person's social standing across various dimensions of social inequality*. A caste system has little social mobility and high status consistency, so the typical person has the same relative standing with regard to wealth, power, and prestige as everyone else in the same caste. However, the greater mobility of class systems produces less status consistency. In Canada, most college and university professors with advanced degrees enjoy high social prestige but earn relatively modest incomes. Low status consistency means that it is much harder to define people's social position. Therefore, *classes* are much harder to define than *castes*.

Caste and Class: The United Kingdom

The mix of meritocracy and caste in class systems is well illustrated by the United Kingdom (Great Britain—composed of England, Wales, and Scotland—and Northern Ireland), an industrial nation with a long agrarian history.

Aristocratic England

In the Middle Ages, England had a system of aristocracy that resembled a caste. The aristocracy included the leading members of the church, who were thought to speak with the authority of God. Some clergy were local priests, who were not members of the aristocracy and who lived simple lives. But the highest church officials lived in palaces and presided over an organization that owned much land, which was the major source of wealth. Church leaders, who were typically referred to as the *first estate* in France and other European countries, also had a great deal of power to shape the political events of the day.

The rest of the aristocracy, which in France and other European countries was called the *second estate*, was a hereditary nobility that made up barely 5 percent of the population. The royal family—the king and queen at the top of the power structure—as well as lesser nobles (including several hundred families headed by men titled as dukes, earls, and barons) together owned most of the nation's land. Most of the men and women within the aristocracy were wealthy because of their land, and they had many servants for their homes as well as ordinary farmers to work their fields. With all of their work done for them by others, members of the aristocracy had no occupation and thought that engaging in any work for income was beneath them. They used their time to develop skills in horseback riding and warfare and to cultivate refined tastes in art, music, and literature.

To prevent their vast landholdings from being divided by heirs when they died, aristocrats devised the law of *primogeniture* (from the Latin meaning "first-born"), which required that all property pass to the oldest son or other male relation. Younger sons had to find other means of support. Some of these men became leaders in the church, where they would live as well as they were used to, and helped tie together the church and the state by having members of the same families running both. Other younger sons within the aristocracy became military officers or judges or took up other professions considered honourable for gentlemen. In an age when no woman could inherit her father's property and few women had the opportunity to earn a living on their own, a noble daughter depended for her security on marrying well.

Below the high clergy and the rest of the aristocracy, the vast majority of men and women were called *commoners* or, in France and other European countries, the *third estate*. Most commoners were serfs working land owned by nobles or the church. Unlike members of the aristocracy, most commoners had little schooling and were illiterate.

As the Industrial Revolution expanded England's economy, some commoners living in cities made enough money to challenge the nobility. More emphasis on meritocracy, the growing importance of money, and the expansion of schooling and legal rights eventually blurred the differences between aristocrats and commoners and gave rise to a class system.

Perhaps it is a sign of the times that these days, traditional titles are put up for sale by aristocrats who need money. In 1996, for example, Earl Spencer—the brother of Princess Diana—sold one of his titles, Lord of Wimbledon, to raise the $300 000 he needed to redo the plumbing in one of his large homes (McKee, 1996).

The United Kingdom Today

The United Kingdom has a class system today, but caste elements of the past are still evident. A small number of British families still hold considerable inherited wealth and enjoy high prestige, schooling at excellent universities, and substantial political influence. A traditional monarch, Queen Elizabeth II, is the United Kingdom's head of state, and Parliament's House of Lords is composed of "peers," about half of whom are of noble birth. However, control of government has passed to the House of Commons, where the prime minister and other ministers typically reach their positions by achievement—winning an election—rather than by birth.

Lower in the class hierarchy, roughly one-fourth of the British people fall into the middle class. Some earn comfortable incomes from professions and businesses and are likely to have investments in the form of stocks and bonds. Below the middle class, perhaps half of all Britons consider themselves "working class," earning modest incomes through manual labour. The remaining one-fourth of the British people make up the lower class, those with low incomes who lack steady work or who work full time but are paid too little to live comfortably. Most lower-class Britons live in the nation's northern and western regions, which have been plagued by closings of mines and factories.

The British mix of caste elements and meritocracy has produced a highly stratified society with some opportunity to move upward or downward, much the same as exists in Canada (Corak, 2006b). Historically, British society has been somewhat more castelike than is the case in Canada, a fact reflected in the importance attached to linguistic accent. Distinctive patterns of speech develop when people are set off from one another over several generations. People in Canada treat accent as a clue to where a person lives or grew up (we can easily differentiate a person who has lived her whole life in an outport of Newfoundland from a Bay Street lawyer who has lived her whole life in Toronto). In the United Kingdom, however, accent is more a mark of social class (upper-class people speak "the King's English" but most people speak "like commoners"). So different are these two accents that the British seem to be, as the saying goes, "a single people divided by a common language."

Classless Societies? The Former Soviet Union

Nowhere in the world do we find a society without some degree of social inequality. Yet some nations have claimed to be classless.

The Russian Revolution

The Union of Soviet Socialist Republics (USSR), one of the two military superpowers in the mid- to late twentieth century, was born out of a revolution in Russia in 1917. The Russian Revolution ended the feudal estate system ruled by a hereditary nobility and transferred most farms, factories, and other productive property from private ownership to state control. Following the lead of Karl Marx, who believed that private ownership of property was the source of social stratification, Soviet leaders boasted of becoming a classless society.

Critics, however, pointed out that, based on their jobs, the Soviet people were actually stratified into four unequal categories. At the top were high government officials, known as *apparatchiks*. Next came the Soviet intelligentsia, including lower government officials, professors, scientists, physicians, and engineers. Below them were manual workers and, at the lowest level, the rural peasantry.

In reality, the Soviet Union was not classless at all, and political power was concentrated in only a small percentage of the population. But putting factories, farms, colleges, and hospitals under state control did create greater economic equality (although with sharp differences in power) than in capitalist societies such as Canada.

The Modern Russian Federation

In 1985, Mikhail Gorbachev came to power with a new economic program known as *perestroika* ("restructuring"). Gorbachev saw that although the Soviet system had significantly reduced economic inequality, overall living standards lagged far behind those of other industrial nations. Gorbachev tried to generate economic growth by reducing the centralized control of the economy, which had proved to be inefficient.

Gorbachev's economic reforms turned into one of the most dramatic social movements in history. People throughout Eastern Europe blamed their poverty and lack of basic freedoms on the repressive ruling class of Communist party officials. Beginning in 1989, people throughout Eastern Europe toppled their socialist governments and, in 1991, the Soviet Union itself collapsed, with its largest republic remaking itself as the Russian Federation.

The Soviet Union's story shows that social inequality involves more than economic resources. Soviet society may not have had the extremes of wealth and poverty found in the United Kingdom and Canada. But an elite class existed all the same, based on political power rather than wealth.

What about social mobility in so-called classless societies? In the twentieth century, there was as much upward social mobility in the Soviet Union as in the United Kingdom or Canada. Rapidly expanding industry and government drew many poor rural peasants into factories and offices. This trend illustrates what sociologists call **structural social mobility**, *a shift in the social position of large numbers of people due more to changes in society itself than to individual efforts.*

> December 20, Tallinn, Estonia. Tallinn is located only 90 minutes across the Baltic Sea from Helsinki, Finland. Yet the visual contrast between the two capital cities—apart from the common winter snow—is so great that we wonder if we have not docked in a distant land. As we walk the cobblestone streets of the medieval part of the city with our tour guide—a retired schoolteacher whose fixed pension is so low that she is forced to supplement her income by entertaining visitors such as ourselves—we marvel at the Christmas decorations in the numerous shops and restaurants. The snow starts to fall while we are enjoying a nice meal in a warmly lit restaurant off the main square. It is nearly 11:00 P.M. before we make our way back to our hotel, and on our way we notice that work crews are starting to shovel the snow away from the square. We are surprised to notice a woman who appears to be well into her seventies working beside a man a decade or two younger. They are both bundled up in large overcoats to help fend off the bitter cold while they sweep. . . . We see first-hand what happens when the pensions that people have worked 40 or more years to earn are suddenly eliminated. Independence, it seems, has not resulted in material wealth for all of Tallinn's population.

During the 1990s, structural social mobility in the Russian Federation turned downward as that country experienced something similar to the Great Depression of the 1930s in Canada. One indicator is that the average lifespan for men dropped by eight years and for women by two years. Many factors contributed to this decline, including Russia's poor health care system, but the Russian people clearly have suffered in the turbulent period of economic change that began in 1991 (Bohlen, 1998; Gerber & Hout, 1998; Mason, 2004).

The hope was that, in the long run, closing inefficient state industries would improve the nation's economic performance. The economy has expanded, but living standards have fallen and millions of Russians face hard times. The few people who made huge fortunes have seen much of their new wealth vanish in the recent recession. This fact, along with more government control over the Russian economy, has caused economic inequality to decline. At the same time, however, many people wonder what a return to a more socialist society will mean for their living standards and political freedoms (Wendle, 2009; Zuckerman, 2006).

China: Emerging Social Classes

Sweeping political and economic change has affected not just the Russian Federation but also the People's Republic of China. After the Communist revolution in 1949, the state took control of all farms, factories, and other productive property. Communist party leader Mao Zedong declared all work to be equally important, so officially, social classes no longer existed.

The new program greatly reduced economic inequality. But as in the Soviet Union, social differences remained. The country was ruled by a political elite with enormous power and considerable privilege; below them were managers of large factories and skilled professionals; next came industrial workers; at the bottom were rural peasants, who were not even allowed to leave their villages to migrate to cities.

Further economic change came in 1978, when Mao died and Deng Xiaoping became China's leader. The state gradually loosened its hold on the economy, allowing a new class of business owners to emerge. Communist party leaders remain in control of the country, and some have prospered as they have joined the ranks of the small but wealthy elite who control new, privately run industries. China's economy has experienced rapid growth, and the nation has now moved into the middle-income category. Much of this new prosperity has been concentrated in coastal areas where living standards have soared far above those in China's rural interior.

Since the late 1990s, the booming cities along China's coast have become home to many thousands of people made rich by the expanding economy. In addition, these cities have attracted more than 100 million young migrants from rural areas in search of better jobs and a better life. Many more have wanted to move to the booming cities, but the government still restricts movement, which has the effect of slowing upward social mobility. For those who have been able to move, the jobs that are available are generally better than the work that people knew before. But many of these new jobs are dangerous, and most pay wages that barely meet the higher costs of living in the city, so the majority of the migrants remain poor. To make matters worse, the weakening global economy has caused

Global Snapshot

Inequality in Canada is less extreme than in the United States but still relatively high compared to the Nordic countries such as Sweden.

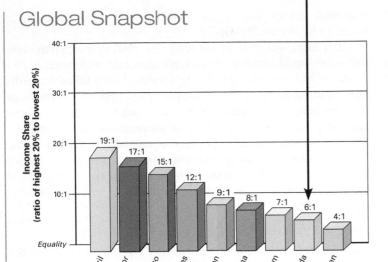

FIGURE 8–1 Economic Inequality in Selected Countries, 2008

Many low- and middle-income, and some high-income, countries have greater economic inequality than Canada. But our country has more economic inequality than many north European high-income nations.

These data are the most recent available, representing income share for various years between 1998 and 2008.

Sources: U.S. Census Bureau (2010a) and World Bank (2010).

many Chinese factories to lay off workers or even to shut down. As a result, beginning in 2008, some people began to migrate from cities back to the countryside—a case of downward social mobility (Atlas, 2007; Chang, 2008; Powell, 2008; Wu & Treiman, 2007).

A new category in China's social hierarchy consists of the *hai gui*, a term derived from words meaning "returned from overseas" or "sea turtles." The ranks of the "sea turtles" are increasing by tens of thousands each year as young men and women return from educations in other countries, in many cases with degrees and diplomas from Canada. These young people, most of whom were from privileged families to begin with, typically return to China to find many opportunities and soon become very influential (Liu & Hewitt, 2008).

In China, a new class system is emerging: a mix of the old political hierarchy and a new business hierarchy. Economic inequality in China has increased as members of the new business elite have become millionaires and even billionaires; as Figure 8–1 shows, it is now greater than in Canada and the United Kingdom but not as high as in the United States. With so much change in China, patterns of social stratification are likely to remain in flux for some time to come (Bian, 2002).

Ideology: The Power behind Stratification

How do societies persist without sharing their resources more equally? The highly stratified British aristocracy lasted for centuries, and for 2000 years people in India accepted the idea that they should be privileged or poor based on the accident of birth.

A major reason that social hierarchies endure is **ideology**, *cultural beliefs that justify particular social arrangements, including patterns of inequality.* A belief—for example, the idea that the rich are smart and the poor are lazy—is ideological to the extent that it supports inequality by defining it as fair.

Plato and Marx on Ideology

According to the ancient Greek philosopher Plato (427–347 BCE), every culture considers some type of inequality fair. Although Karl Marx understood this, he was far more critical of inequality than Plato. Marx criticized capitalist societies for defending wealth and power in the hands of a few as a "law of the marketplace." Capitalist law, he continued, defines the right to own property, which encourages money to remain within the same families from one generation to the next. In short, Marx concluded, culture and institutions combine to support a society's elite, which is why established hierarchies last such a long time.

Historical Patterns of Ideology

Ideology changes along with a society's economy and technology. Because agrarian societies depend on most of their people performing a lifetime of labour, they develop caste systems that make carrying out the duties of a person's social position or "station" a moral responsibility. With the rise of industrial capitalism, an ideology of meritocracy arises, defining wealth and power as prizes to be won by the individuals who perform the best. This change means that the poor—often given charity under feudalism—are looked down on as personally undeserving. This harsh view is linked to the ideas of Herbert Spencer, as explained in the Thinking about Diversity box.

History shows how difficult it is to change social stratification. However, challenges to the status quo always arise. Traditional ideas about "a woman's place," for example, have given way to economic opportunity for women in societies today. The continuing progress toward racial equality in South Africa is another case of widespread rejection of the ideology of apartheid.

The Functions of Social Stratification

Why does social stratification exist at all? According to the structural-functional approach, social stratification plays a vital part in the operation of society. This argument was presented many years ago by Kingsley Davis and Wilbert Moore (1945).

THINKING ABOUT DIVERSITY: RACE, CLASS, & GENDER

The Meaning of Class: Is Getting Rich "the Survival of the Fittest"?

JAKE: "My dad is amazing. He's really smart!"
FRANK: "You mean he's rich. He owns I don't know how many businesses."
JAKE: "Do you think people get rich without being smart?"

It's a question we all wonder about. How much is our social position a matter of intelligence? What about hard work? Being born to the "right family"? Even "dumb luck"?

More than in most societies, in Canada we link social standing to personal abilities including intelligence. This idea goes back a long time. We have all heard the words "the survival of the fittest," which describes our society as a competitive jungle in which the "best" survive and the rest fall behind. The phrase was coined by one of sociology's pioneers, Herbert Spencer (1820–1903), whose ideas about social inequality are still widespread today.

Spencer, who lived in England, eagerly followed the work of the natural scientist Charles Darwin (1809–1882). Darwin's theory of biological evolution held that a species changes physically over many generations as it adapts to the natural environment. Spencer incorrectly applied Darwin's theory to the operation of society, which does not operate according to biological principles. In Spencer's distorted view, society became the "jungle," with the "fittest" people rising to wealth and the "failures" sinking into miserable poverty.

As wrong as they were, it is no surprise that Spencer's views were popular among the rising industrialists of the day. John D. Rockefeller (1839–1937), who made a vast fortune building the oil industry, recited Spencer's "social gospel" to young children in Sunday school. As Rockefeller saw it, the growth of giant corporations—and the astounding wealth of their owners—was merely the result of the survival of the fittest, a basic fact of nature. Neither Spencer nor Rockefeller had much sympathy for the poor, seeing poverty as evidence of individuals' failing to measure up in a competitive world. Spencer opposed social welfare programs because he thought they penalized society's "best" people (through taxes) and rewarded its "worst" members (through welfare benefits). By incorrectly using Darwin's theory, the rich could turn their backs on everyone else, assuming that inequality was inevitable and somehow "natural."

Today, sociologists point out that our society is far from a meritocracy, as Spencer claimed. And it is not the case that companies or individuals who generate a lot of money necessarily benefit society. The people who made hundreds of millions of dollars selling complicated economic instruments called derivatives on Bay Street that nobody understood certainly ended up hurting just about everyone. But Spencer's view that the "fittest" rise to the top remains widespread in our very unequal and individualistic culture.

WHAT DO YOU THINK?

1. How much do you think inequality in our society can correctly be described as "the survival of the fittest"? Why?

2. Why do you think Spencer's ideas are still popular in Canada today?

3. Is how much you earn a good measure of your importance to society? Why or why not?

The Davis-Moore Thesis

The **Davis-Moore thesis** states that *social stratification has beneficial consequences for the operation of society.* How else, ask Davis and Moore, can we explain the fact that some form of social stratification has been found in every society?

Davis and Moore note that modern societies have hundreds of occupational positions of varying importance. Certain jobs—say, washing cars or answering a telephone—are fairly easy and can be performed by almost anyone. Other jobs—such as designing a new generation of computers or transplanting human organs—are very difficult and demand the scarce talents of people with extensive and expensive training.

Inequality in Canada is less extreme than in the United States but still relatively high compared to many nations in Northern Europe.

Therefore, Davis and Moore explain, the greater the functional importance of a position, the more rewards a society attaches to it. This strategy promotes productivity and efficiency because rewarding important work with income, prestige, power, or leisure encourages people to do these things and to work better, longer, and harder. In short, unequal rewards (which are what social stratification is) benefit society as a whole.

Davis and Moore claim that any society could be egalitarian, but only to the extent that people are willing to let *anyone* perform *any* job. Equality also demands that someone who performs a job poorly be rewarded just as much as someone who performs the job well. Such a system clearly offers little incentive for people to try their best, reducing the society's productive efficiency.

capitalists people who own and operate factories and other businesses in pursuit of profits

proletarians people who sell their labour for wages

The Davis-Moore thesis suggests the reason stratification exists; it does not state precisely what rewards a society should give to any occupational position or how unequal rewards should be. It merely points out that positions a society considers crucial must offer enough rewards to draw talented people away from less important work.

CRITICAL REVIEW Although the Davis-Moore thesis is an important contribution to understanding social stratification, it has provoked criticism. Melvin Tumin (1953) wondered, first of all, how we assess the importance of a particular occupation. Perhaps the high rewards our society gives to physicians result partly from deliberate efforts by medical schools to limit the supply of physicians and thereby increase the demand for their services.

Furthermore, do rewards actually reflect the contribution someone makes to society? With an estimated income averaging more than $75 million per year, Céline Dion earns more in two days than the prime minister of Canada earns all year. Would anyone argue that the work of Céline Dion is more important than leading a country? And what about members of the Canadian military being trained to serve in Afghanistan? Although they face the daily risk of combat, a new soldier begins basic training with an annual salary of $31 000 plus benefits. And what about the heads of the big financial firms on Bay Street?

It seems reasonable to conclude that these corporate leaders made some bad decisions, yet their salaries were astronomical. Even after finishing its worst year ever, with losses of $27 billion, Merrill Lynch paid bonuses of more than $1 million to each of more than 700 employees. The top people in the financial industry made out even better. In 2007, James Dimon, head of JPMorgan Chase, had earnings of more than $55 million; the same year, Lloyd Blankfein, head of Goldman Sachs, made more than $70 million—an amount it would take a typical Canadian solider more than 3000 years to earn. Do corporate executives deserve such megasalaries for their contributions to society?

Second, Tumin claimed that Davis and Moore ignore how the caste elements of social stratification can *prevent* the development of individual talent. Born to privilege, rich children have opportunities to develop their abilities, which is something many gifted poor children never have.

Third, living in a society that places so much importance on money, we tend to overestimate the importance of high-paying work; how do stockbrokers or people who trade international currencies really contribute to society? For the same reason, it is difficult for us to see the importance of work not oriented toward making money, such as parenting, creative writing, playing in a symphony, or just being a good friend to someone in need (Packard, 2002).

Finally, by suggesting that social stratification benefits all of society, the Davis-Moore thesis ignores how social inequality promotes conflict and can even provoke revolution. This criticism leads to the social-conflict approach, which provides a very different explanation for social inequality.

CHECK YOUR LEARNING State the Davis-Moore thesis in your own words. What are Tumin's criticisms of this thesis?

Stratification and Conflict

Social-conflict analysis argues that rather than benefiting society as a whole, social stratification benefits some people and disadvantages others. This analysis draws heavily on the ideas of Karl Marx, with contributions from Max Weber.

Karl Marx: Class Conflict

As Marx saw it, the Industrial Revolution promised humanity a society free from want. Yet during Marx's lifetime, the capitalist economy had done little to improve the lives of most people. Marx set out to explain a glaring contradiction: how, in a society so rich, so many could be so poor.

In Marx's view, social stratification is rooted in people's relationship to the means of production. People either own productive property (such as factories and businesses) or sell their labour to others. In feudal Europe, the aristocracy and the church owned the productive land; the peasants toiled as farmers. Under industrial capitalism, the aristocracy was replaced by **capitalists** (sometimes called the *bourgeoisie*, a French word meaning "town dwellers"), *people who own and operate factories and other businesses in pursuit of profits*. Peasants became the **proletarians**, *people who sell their labour for wages*. Capitalists and proletarians have opposing interests and are separated by a vast gulf of wealth and power, making class conflict inevitable.

Marx lived during the nineteenth century, a time when a small number of industrialists in the United States were amassing great fortunes. Andrew Carnegie, J.P. Morgan, and John Jacob Astor (one of the few rich passengers to drown on the *Titanic*) lived in fabulous mansions that were filled with priceless works of art and staffed by dozens of servants. Even by today's standards, their incomes were staggering. For example, Carnegie earned more than $20 million in 1900 (roughly $530 million in today's dollars), when the average worker earned roughly $500 a year (Baltzell, 1964; Williamson, 2010).

In time, Marx believed, the working majority would overthrow the capitalists once and for all. Capitalism would bring about its own downfall, Marx reasoned, because it makes workers poorer and poorer and gives them little control over what they

alienation the experience of isolation and misery resulting from powerlessness

blue-collar occupations lower-prestige jobs that involve mostly manual labour

white-collar occupations higher-prestige jobs that involve mostly mental activity

make or how they make it. Under capitalism, work produces only **alienation**, *the experience of isolation and misery resulting from powerlessness.*

To replace capitalism, Marx imagined a *socialist* system that would meet the needs of all rather than just the needs of the elite few: "The proletarians have nothing to lose but their chains. They have a world to win" (Marx & Engels, 1972:362, orig. 1848).

CRITICAL REVIEW Marx has had enormous influence on sociological thinking. But his revolutionary ideas, calling for the overthrow of capitalist society, also make his work highly controversial.

One of the strongest criticisms of the Marxist approach is that it ignores a central idea of the Davis-Moore thesis: that a system of unequal rewards is needed to place people in the right jobs and to motivate people to work hard. Marx separated reward from performance; his egalitarian ideal was based on the principle "from each according to ability, to each according to need" (Marx & Engels, 1972:388, orig. 1848). However, failure to reward individual performance may be precisely what caused the low productivity of the former Soviet Union and other socialist economies around the world. Defenders respond to such criticism by asking why we assume that humanity is inherently selfish rather than social; individual rewards are not the only way to motivate people to perform their social roles (Clark, 1991).

A second problem is that the revolutionary change Marx predicted has failed to happen, at least in advanced capitalist societies. The next section explains why.

CHECK YOUR LEARNING How does Marx's view of social stratification differ from the Davis-Moore thesis?

Oprah Winfrey consistently earns more than $200 million a year and enjoys fame to match her fortune. Guided by the Davis-Moore thesis, why would societies reward some people so much more than others? How would Karl Marx answer this question differently?

Why No Marxist Revolution?

Despite Marx's prediction, capitalism is still thriving. Why have industrial workers not overthrown capitalism? Ralf Dahrendorf (1959) suggested four reasons:

1. Fragmentation of the capitalist class. Today, millions of stockholders, rather than single families, own most large companies. Day-to-day corporate operations are in the hands of a large class of managers, who may or may not be major stockholders. With stock so widely held—about 50 percent of North American households own stocks—more and more people have a direct stake in the capitalist system (U.S. Census Bureau, 2010).

2. A higher standard of living. As Chapter 12 ("Economics and Politics") explains, a century ago, most Canadian workers were in factories or on farms in **blue-collar occupations**, *lower-prestige jobs that involve mostly manual labour.* Today, most workers are in **white-collar occupations**, *higher-prestige jobs that involve mostly mental activity.* These jobs are in sales, customer support, management, and other service fields. Most of today's white-collar workers do not think of themselves as an "industrial proletariat." Just as important, the average income in Canada rose almost tenfold over the course of the twentieth century, even allowing for inflation, and the number of hours in the workweek decreased. Most workers today are far better off than workers were a century ago, an example of structural social mobility. One result of this rising standard of living is that more people support the status quo.

3. More worker organizations. Workers today have the right to form labour unions that make demands of management,

socio-economic status (SES) a composite ranking based on various dimensions of social inequality

During the Great Depression of the 1930s, "tent cities" that were home to desperately poor people could be found in much of Canada. The Depression came to an end, but poverty persisted. The recent recession and the growing social inequality between classes in Canada have sparked a resurgence of tent cities in many Canadian cities, including this one—on the waterfront at the foot of Cherry St. How would structural-functional analysis explain such poverty? What about the social-conflict approach?

backed by threats of work slowdowns and strikes. As a result, labour disputes are settled without threatening the capitalist system.

4. Greater legal protections. Over the past century, new laws made the workplace safer, and employment insurance, disability protection, and Old Age Security now provide workers with greater financial security.

A Counterpoint

First, wealth remains highly concentrated, with much of the privately controlled corporate stock in the hands of a small proportion of our population. Second, many of today's white-collar jobs offer no more income, security, or satisfaction than factory work did a century ago (Lowe, 2000; Reid, 1996). Third, many benefits enjoyed by today's workers came about through the class conflict Marx described, and workers still struggle to hold on to what they have. Fourth, although workers have gained legal protections, the law has not helped ordinary people use the legal system as effectively as the rich. Therefore, social-conflict theorists conclude, the absence of a socialist revolution in high-income countries does not disprove Marx's analysis of capitalism.

Max Weber: Class, Status, and Power

Max Weber agreed with Karl Marx that social stratification causes social conflict, but he viewed Marx's two-class model as too simple.

Instead, he viewed social stratification as involving three distinct dimensions of inequality.

The first dimension, economic inequality—the issue so important to Marx—Weber called *class* position. Weber did not think of classes as well-defined categories but as a continuum ranging from high to low. Weber's second dimension is *status*, or social prestige, and the third is *power*.

Weber's Socio-economic Status Hierarchy

Marx viewed prestige and power as simple reflections of economic position and did not treat them as distinct dimensions of inequality. But Weber noted that status consistency in modern societies is often quite low: A local government official may exercise great power yet have little wealth or social prestige.

Weber, then, characterizes stratification in industrial societies as a multi-dimensional ranking rather than a hierarchy of clearly defined classes. In line with Weber's thinking, sociologists use the term **socio-economic status (SES)** to refer to *a composite ranking based on various dimensions of social inequality.*

Inequality in History

Weber observed that each of his three dimensions of social inequality stands out at a different time in the history of human societies. Status or social prestige is the main dimension of difference in agrarian societies, taking the form of honour. Members of these societies gain prestige by conforming to cultural norms that apply to their particular rank.

Industrialization and the development of capitalism eliminate traditional rankings based on birth but create striking financial inequality. Thus in an industrial society, the crucial difference between people is the economic dimension of class.

Over time, industrial societies witness the growth of a bureaucratic state. Bigger government and the spread of all types of other organizations make power more important in the stratification system. Especially in socialist societies, where government regulates many aspects of life, high-ranking officials become the new ruling elite.

This historical analysis points to a final difference between Weber and Marx. Marx thought societies could eliminate social stratification by abolishing private ownership of productive property. Weber doubted that overthrowing capitalism would significantly lessen social stratification. It might reduce economic differences, he reasoned, but socialism would increase inequality by expanding government and concentrating power in the hands of a political elite. The popular uprisings against socialist bureaucracies in Eastern Europe and the former Soviet Union show that discontent can be generated by socialist political elites and thus support Weber's position.

APPLYING THEORY

Social Stratification

	Structural-Functional Approach	Social-Conflict Approach	Symbolic-Interaction Approach
What is the level of analysis?	Macro level	Macro level	Micro level
What is social stratification?	Stratification is a system of unequal rewards that benefits society as a whole.	Stratification is a division of a society's resources that benefits some people and harms others.	Stratification is a factor that guides people's interactions in everyday life.
What is the reason for our social position?	Social position reflects personal talents and abilities in a competitive economy.	Social position reflects the way society divides resources.	The products we consume all say something about social position.
Are unequal rewards fair?	Yes. Unequal rewards boost economic production by encouraging people to work harder and try new ideas. Linking greater rewards to more important work is widely accepted.	No. Unequal rewards only serve to divide society, creating "haves" and "have-nots." There is widespread opposition to social inequality.	Maybe. People may or may not define inequality as fair. People may view their social position as a measure of self-worth, justifying inequality in terms of personal differences.

CRITICAL REVIEW Weber's multi-dimensional view of social stratification greatly influenced sociologists and made the concept of socio-economic status hierarchy popular. But critics (particularly those who favour Marx's ideas) argue that although social class boundaries may have blurred, industrial and post-industrial nations still show striking patterns of social inequality.

As will be explained shortly, economic inequality has increased recently in Canada. Although some people favour Weber's multi-dimensional hierarchy, others think, in light of this trend, that Marx's view of the rich versus the poor is closer to the truth.

CHECK YOUR LEARNING What are Weber's three dimensions of social inequality? According to Weber, which of them would you expect to be most important in Canada? Why?

Stratification and Interaction

Because social stratification has to do with the way an entire society is organized, sociologists (Marx and Weber included) typically treat it as a macro-level issue. But a micro-level analysis of social stratification is also important because people's social standing affects their everyday interactions. The Applying Theory table summarizes the contributions of three theoretical approaches to social stratification.

In most communities, people interact primarily with others of about the same social standing. This pattern begins with the fact that due to social stratification, people tend to live with others like themselves. In larger public spaces, such as a large shopping mall, we often see couples or groups made up of individuals whose appearance and shopping habits are similar. At the same time, people with very different social standing commonly keep their distance from one another. Well-dressed people walking down the street on their way to an expensive restaurant, for example, may move across the sidewalk or even cross the street to avoid getting close to others they think are homeless people. The Seeing Sociology in Everyday Life box on page 202 gives another example of how differences in social class position can affect interaction.

Finally, just about everyone realizes that the way we dress, the car we drive (or the bus we ride), and even the food and drink we order at the campus snack bar say something about our budget and personal tastes. Sociologists use the term **conspicuous consumption** to refer to *buying and using products because of the "statement" they make about social position.* Ignoring the water fountain in favour of paying for bottled water tells people that you have extra money to spend. And no one needs a $100 000 automobile to get around, of course, but driving up in such a vehicle says "I have arrived" in more ways than one.

When Class Gets Personal: Picking (with) Your Friends

The sound of banjo music drifted across the field late one summer afternoon. I laid my brush down, climbed over the fence I had been painting, and walked toward the sound of the music to see what was going on. That's how I met my neighbour Max, a retired factory worker who lived just up the road. Max was a pretty good "picker," and within an hour I was back on his porch with my guitar. I called Howard, a friend who teaches at the university, and he showed up a little while later, six-string in hand. The three of us jammed for a couple of hours, smiling all the while.

The next morning, I was mowing the grass in front of the house when Max came walking down the road. I turned off the lawnmower as he came down the driveway. "Hi, Max," I said. "Thanks for having us over last night. I really had fun."

"Don't mention it," Max responded. Then he shook his head a little and added, "Ya know, I was thinkin' after you guys left. I mean, it was really somethin' how you guys looked like you were having a great time. With somebody like me!"

"Well, yeah," I replied, not sure what he meant. "You sure played better than we did."

Max looked down at the ground, embarrassed by the compliment. Then he added, "What I mean is that you guys were having a good time with somebody like *me.* You're both professors, right? *Doctors,* even. . ."

WHAT DO YOU THINK?

1. Why do you think Max felt that two university teachers would not enjoy spending time with him?

2. How does his reaction suggest that people take social position personally?

3. Can you think of a similar experience you have had with someone of a different social position?

○ **CRITICAL REVIEW** A micro-level analysis of social stratification helps us see patterns of social inequality in our everyday lives. At the same time, the limitation of this approach is that it has little to say about how and why broad patterns of social inequality exist, which was the focus of the structural-functional and social-conflict approaches.

○ **CHECK YOUR LEARNING** Point to several ways in which social stratification shapes the way people of different social positions behave in the course of a typical day.

Stratification and Technology: A Global Perspective

We can weave together a number of observations made in this chapter by considering the relationship between a society's technology and its type of social stratification. This analysis draws on Gerhard Lenski's model of socio-cultural evolution discussed in Chapter 2 ("Culture").

Hunting and Gathering Societies

With simple technology, hunters and gatherers produce only what is necessary for day-to-day living. Some people may produce more than others, but the group's survival depends on all sharing what they have. Thus no categories of people are better off than others.

Horticultural, Pastoral, and Agrarian Societies

As technological advances create a surplus, social inequality increases. In horticultural and pastoral societies, a small elite controls most of the surplus. Larger-scale agriculture is more productive still, and striking inequality—as great as at any time in history—places the nobility in an almost godlike position over the masses.

Industrial Societies

Industrialization pushes inequality downward. Prompted by the need to develop people's talents, meritocracy takes hold and weakens the power of traditional elites. Industrial productivity also raises the living standards of the historically poor majority. Specialized work demands schooling for all, sharply reducing illiteracy. A literate population demands a greater voice in political decision making, reducing social inequality and lessening men's domination of women.

Over time, even wealth becomes somewhat less concentrated (contradicting Marx's prediction). In the 1920s, the richest 1 percent of North American families owned about 40 percent of all wealth, a figure that fell to 30 percent by the 1980s as taxes—with higher tax rates for people with higher incomes—paid for new government programs benefiting the poor (Beeghley, 1989; U.S. House of Representatives, 1991; Williamson & Lindert, 1980). Such trends help explain why Marxist revolutions occurred in *agrarian* societies, such as Russia (1917), Cuba (1959), and Nicaragua (1979), where social inequality is most pronounced, rather than in *industrial* societies as Marx predicted. However, wealth inequality turned upward again after 1990 and is once again about the same as it was in the 1920s (Keister, 2000; Wolff, 2007). With the goal of reducing this trend, some governments have expressed their intention to raise federal income tax rates on high-income individuals.

The Kuznets Curve

In human history, then, technological advances first increase but then moderate the intensity of social stratification. Greater inequality is functional for agrarian societies, but industrial societies benefit from a more equal system. This historical trend, recognized by the Nobel Prize–winning economist Simon Kuznets (1955, 1966), is illustrated by the Kuznets curve, shown in Figure 8–2.

Social inequality around the world generally supports the Kuznets curve. Global Map 8–1 on page 204 shows that high-income nations that have passed through the industrial era (including Canada, the United States, and the nations of Western Europe) have somewhat less income inequality than nations in which a larger share of the labour force remains in farming (as is common in Latin America and Africa). At the same time, it is important to remember that income inequality reflects not just technological development but also a society's political and economic priorities. Income inequality in Canada may have declined during much of the last century, but this country still has more economic inequality than Japan and countries throughout Europe.

Another criticism of the Kuznets curve is that it was developed by comparing societies at different levels of economic development (using what sociologists call "cross-sectional data"). Such data do not tell us about the future of any one society. In Canada, recent trends showing increases in economic inequality suggest that the Kuznets curve may require serious revision—represented by the broken line in Figure 8–2. The fact that American society is now experiencing greater economic inequality suggests that the long-term trend may differ from what Kuznets projected half a century ago.

Inequality in Canada

Canada, like the United States, differs from most European nations and Japan in never having had a titled nobility. With the significant exception of our racial history, we have never known a caste system that rigidly ranks categories of people.

Even so, Canadian society is highly stratified. Not only do the rich have most of the money, but they also receive the most schooling, enjoy the best health, and consume the most goods and services.

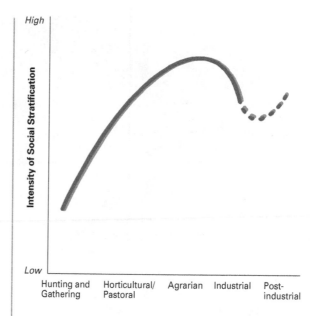

FIGURE 8–2   Social Stratification and Technological Development: The Kuznets Curve

The Kuznets curve shows that greater technological sophistication generally is accompanied by more pronounced social stratification. The trend reverses itself as industrial societies relax rigid, castelike distinctions in favour of greater opportunity and equality under the law. Political rights are more widely extended, and there is even some levelling of economic differences. However, the emergence of post-industrial society has brought an upturn in economic inequality, as indicated by the broken line added by the author.

Sources: Drawn by the author based on Kuznets (1955) and Lenski (1966).

Such privilege contrasts sharply with the poverty of millions of women and men who worry about paying next month's rent or a dentist's bill for their teenage son or daughter. Many people think of Canada as a "middle-class society" in which people are more or less alike. But is this really the case?

Income, Wealth, and Power

One important dimension of economic inequality is **income,** *earnings from work or investments*. Statistics Canada reports that the average income of families (two people or more) declined in 2009 to $78 500 from $80 700 in 2008 (Statistics Canada, 2011). The first part of Figure 8–3 (on page 205) shows the distribution of income among all families in the country in 2009. The second and third parts of Figure 8–3 illustrate Canadian family income after transfer payments (federal and provincial payments to families and individuals) and taxes. Despite the important equalizing effect

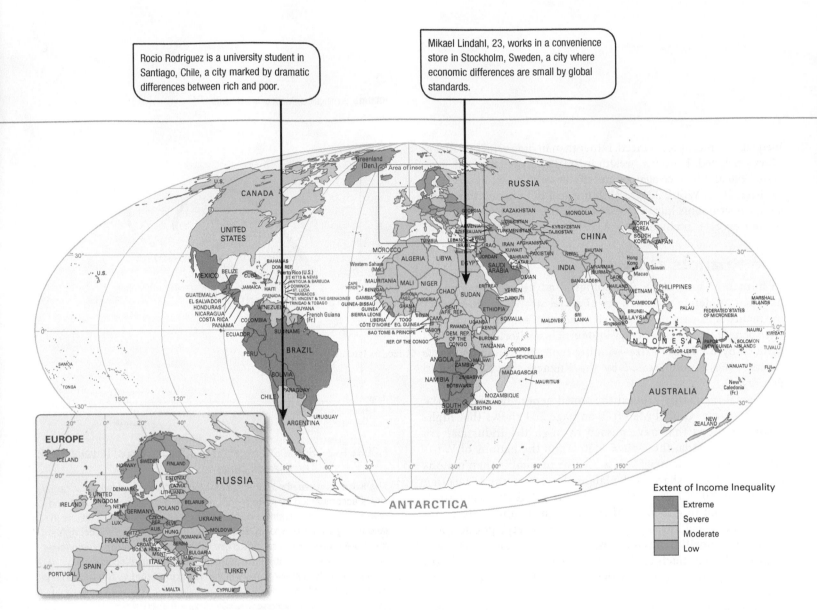

Rocio Rodriguez is a university student in Santiago, Chile, a city marked by dramatic differences between rich and poor.

Mikael Lindahl, 23, works in a convenience store in Stockholm, Sweden, a city where economic differences are small by global standards.

Extent of Income Inequality

- Extreme
- Severe
- Moderate
- Low

Window on the World

GLOBAL MAP 8–1 Income Inequality in Global Perspective

Societies throughout the world differ in the rigidity and extent of their social stratification and their overall standard of living. This map highlights income inequality. Generally speaking, the United States stands out among high-income nations, such as Canada, Great Britain, Sweden, Japan, and Australia, as having greater income inequality. The less economically developed countries of Latin America and Africa, including Colombia, Brazil, and the Central African Republic, as well as much of the Arab world, exhibit the most pronounced inequality of income. Is this pattern consistent with the Kuznets curve?

Source: Based on Gini coefficients obtained from World Bank (2010) and Central Intelligence Agency (2010).

of transfer payments and taxes, large differences remain between Canadian families earning the most and those earning the least. Before taxes and transfer payments, the 20 percent of families with the highest income received $19 in income for every $1 received by the 20 percent with the lowest income. After taxes and transfer payments, the richest 20 percent of families in 2009 received $5.60 for every $1 received by the 20 percent with the lowest income. Put another way, families with the lowest 20 percent of incomes earned, on average, $26 500 while the 20 percent of families on the other end of the continuum earned an average of $149 400 after taxes and transfer payments (Statistics Canada, 2011l). The data also indicate that income inequality has started to increase. Until 1995, the ratio had held fairly constant, with the 20 percent of families with the highest income getting about $5 for every $1 received by those 20 percent of families with the lowest income (Statistics Canada, 2011).

wealth the total value of money and other assets, minus outstanding debts

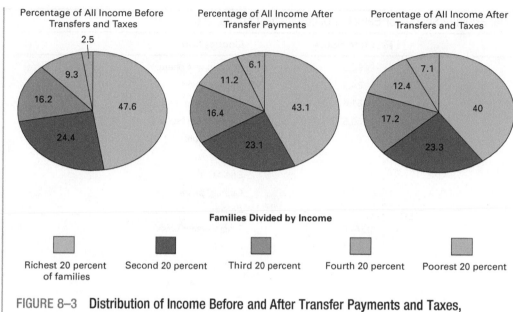

FIGURE 8–3 **Distribution of Income Before and After Transfer Payments and Taxes, Canada, 2009**

Source: Statistics Canada (2011l).

TABLE 8–1 **Canadian Census Family Income, 2005**

Highest paid . . .	Annually earns more than . . .	Lowest paid . . .	Annually earns less than
10%	$142 000	50%	$63 866
20%	$110 000	40%	$52 000
30%	$90 000	30%	$43 000
40%	$76 000	20%	$33 000
50%	$63 866	10%	$23 000

Source: Statistics Canada (2011m).

Table 8–1 takes a closer look at the 2005 income data from the 2006 census.[1] The distribution is after transfer payments. The highest-paid 10 percent of Canadian families earned more than $142 000 in 2005, while the lowest-paid 10 percent earned less than $23 000. In short, while a small number of people have very high incomes, the majority make do with far less.

Income is only one part of a person's or family's **wealth**, *the total value of money and other assets, minus outstanding debts.*

Wealth—including stocks, bonds, and real estate—is distributed even more unequally than income.

The richest 5 percent of Canadian families have wealth valued at more than $600 000, excluding pension plans and household articles. In contrast, the poorest 5 percent of Canadian families have a negative wealth valued at $5700; that is, they actually live in debt (Morissette, Zhang, & Drolet, 2002a). In total, it is estimated that the wealthiest 5 percent of families control more than 40 percent of all wealth in Canada (Davies, 1993, quoted in Morissette, Zhang and Drolet, 2002b.)

The wealth of average people is not only less than that of the rich but also different in kind. Most people's wealth centres on a home and a car—property that generates no income—but the greater wealth of the rich is mostly in the form of stocks and other income-producing investments.

In Canada, wealth is an important source of power. The small proportion of families that controls most of the country's wealth also has the ability to shape the agenda of the entire society. As explained in Chapter 12 ("Economics and Politics"), some sociologists argue that such concentrated wealth weakens democracy because the political system primarily serves the interests of the super-rich.

In addition to generating income, work is also an important source of prestige. We commonly evaluate each other according to the kind of work we do, giving greater respect to those who do what we consider to be more important work and less respect to those with more modest jobs.

[1]Statistics Canada reports both mean and median incomes for families ("two or more persons related by blood, marriage, or adoption"). In 2009, mean family income (after transfers and taxes) was $74 700, higher than median family income ($63 800) because high-income families pull up the mean but not the median.

TABLE 8–2 Occupational Prestige Scores for Selected Occupations, Canada, 2005

Occupation	Prestige Score	Occupation	Prestige Score
Physician	90.5	Power crane operator	57.6
University professor	84.3	Oil field worker	57.5
Registered nurse	81.6	Private in the army	57.5
Physicist	80.6	Construction labourer	57.4
High school teacher	80.3	Farm labourer	56.9
Police officer	78.6	Mail carrier	56.7
Chemist	77.7	Bricklayer	56.2
Architect	77.3	Catholic priest	56.1
Psychologist	76.7	Sculptor	55.9
Mathematician	74.8	Tractor-trailer driver	53.8
Lawyer	73.1	Bank teller	53
Sociologist	73	Quarry worker	53
Social worker	71.4	Butcher in a store	52.7
Bank manager	69	Supervisor of survey interviewers	52.4
Accountant	68.9	House painter	51.6
Economist	68.4	Logger	51.2
Electrician	67.9	Coal miner	50.7
Building contractor	67.2	Beauty salon operator	49
Dental hygienist	66.4	Flagperson on a road construction site	48.8
Child-care provider in a private home	65.1	Apprentice bricklayer	48.4
Professional forester	64.1	Waitress in a restaurant	48.3
Member of Canadian Senate	63.5	Garbage collector	47.9
Member of Canadian House of Commons	63.3	Cod fisherman	47.6
Librarian	63.2	Service station manager	47.5
Plumber	62.9	Sewing machine operator	45.3
Professionally trained librarian	62.3	Shipping clerk	43.7
Owner of a coffee shop	61.4	Lunchroom operator	43.3
House carpenter	61.1	Bartender	43.1
Funeral director	60.9	Taxicab driver	41.5
Tool and die maker	60.3	Stockroom attendant	40.4
Welder	60.2	Fruit packer in a cannery	40.1
Protestant minister	60.1	Bill collector	38.1
Automobile mechanic	59.8	Used car salesman	37.1
User support technician	58.9	Telemarketer	32.8
Cook in a restaurant	58.6	Someone who lives on social assistance	22.1
Survey research director	58.4		

Source: Goyder (2009).

Sociologists measure the relative social prestige of various occupations (Goyder, 2009). Table 8–2 shows that people give high prestige to occupations, such as medicine, law, and engineering, that require extensive training and generate high income. By contrast, less prestigious work—as a waitress or janitor, for example—not only pays less but requires less ability and schooling. We used to believe that occupational prestige rankings were much the same in all high-income nations (Lin & Xie, 1988) and relatively constant over time. In 2005, Canadian sociologist John Goyder replicated a study of occupational prestige conducted 40 years earlier and found that blue-collar occupations had gained the most prestige over the intervening years while many white-collar occupations had lost prestige. It is illustrative that child-care providers and firefighters gained the most prestige while members of Parliament, senators, Catholic priests, and lawyers lost the most.

In any society, high-prestige occupations go to privileged categories of people. In Table 8–2, for example, the highest-ranking occupations are dominated by men. Similarly, many of the lowest-prestige jobs are commonly performed by minorities.

Schooling

Industrial societies have expanded opportunities for schooling, with 60 percent of Canadians aged 25 to 64 having acquired a post-secondary education certificate, diploma, or degree. But it is important to note an important change in the recent decade with women taking more advantage of post-secondary schooling than men. Among 45- to 54-year-olds, women make up only 44 percent of those who have graduated from a university. Among 25- to 34-year-olds, by contrast, women make up 58 percent of those who have graduated (Statistics Canada, 2008c).

Schooling affects both occupational choice and income. Table 8–3 shows that the amount of income earned increases with the level of education achieved. Schooling also is related to whether you have a paid job at all. Table 8–3 shows that people with less education are more likely to be unemployed than those with more education (with the exception of those who have completed post-bachelor training). Most (but not all) of the better-paying, white-collar jobs listed in Table 8–2 require a post-secondary degree or other advanced study. Most blue-collar jobs, which bring lower income and less prestige, require less schooling.

Ancestry, Race, and Gender

A class system rewards individual talent and effort. But nothing affects one's social standing as much as birth into a particular family. Ancestry has a strong bearing on future schooling, occupation, and income. Research suggests that at least half of the richest

TABLE 8–3   Education, Income, and Work, 25- to 35-Year-Olds

	Median Income (2005)	Unemployment Rate (2006)
Post-bachelor	$50 444	5.7%
Bachelor's degree	$46 118	4.9%
University below bachelor's degree	$38 559	6.1%
College diploma	$36 686	5.4%
Trade or apprenticeship	$34 505	6.9%
High school	$32 260	7.5%
Less than high school	$28 832	12.2%

Note: Income data are based on full-year 2005 income of people working full time, full year. The unemployment rate refers to the week before the census date of May 16, 2006.

Source: Statistics Canada (2008d, 2008e).

individuals in the United States—those with hundreds of millions of dollars in wealth—derived their fortunes mostly from inheritance (Queenan, 1989; Thurow, 1987). The situation is much the same in Canada (Brym & Fox, 1989; Clement, 1975; Olsen, 1980; Porter, 1965). By the same token, inherited poverty just as surely shapes the future of others.

Race and ethnicity, too, are closely linked to social position in Canada. While the median 2005 employment income for those who worked full-time for the whole year was $41 401, recent immigrant men who had some employment income earned only 63 cents for each dollar received by Canadian-born men; recent immigrant women earned a mere 56 cents (Statistics Canada, 2008e). Aboriginal people are even more disadvantaged (Statistics Canada, 2009b). The larger proportion of young workers among visible minorities and Aboriginals accounts for some of this income disparity. Varying levels of education of these three populations can also be used to help us understand some of the disadvantage of Aboriginal workers. Visible minorities are more disadvantaged than these income data indicate because they tend to have a higher level of education than other Canadians, which should result in a higher income. A detailed examination of how race and ethnicity affect social standing is presented in Chapter 11 ("Race and Ethnicity").

Of course, both men and women are found in families at every social level. Yet, on average, women have less income, wealth, and occupational prestige than men. Among single-parent families, those headed by a woman are more than twice as likely to be poor as those headed by a man. Chapter 10 ("Gender Stratification") examines the link between gender and social stratification.

People often distinguish between the "new rich" and families with "old money." Men and women who suddenly begin to earn high incomes tend to spend their money on status symbols because they enjoy the new thrill of high-roller living and they want others to know of their success. Those who grow up surrounded by wealth, by contrast, are used to a privileged way of life and are quieter about it. Thus the conspicuous consumption of the lower-upper class (*left*) can differ dramatically from the more private pursuits and understatement of the upper-upper class (*right*).

Social Classes in Canada

As noted earlier, rankings in a caste system are rigid and obvious to all. Defining the social categories in a more fluid class system, however, is not so easy. Followers of Karl Marx see two major social classes: capitalists and proletarians. Other sociologists find as many as six classes (Warner & Lunt, 1941) or even seven (Coleman & Rainwater, 1978). Still others side with Max Weber, believing that people form not clear-cut classes but a multi-dimensional status hierarchy.

Defining classes in Canada is difficult because of the relatively low level of status consistency. Especially toward the middle of the hierarchy, people's social position on one dimension may not be the same as their standing on another. For example, a government official may have the power to administer a multi-million-dollar budget yet earn only a modest personal income. Similarly, many members of the clergy enjoy ample prestige but only moderate power and low pay. Or consider the casino poker player who wins little respect but makes a lot of money.

Finally, the social mobility characteristic of class systems—again, most pronounced near the middle—means that social position may change during a person's lifetime, further blurring class boundaries. With these issues in mind, we can examine four general rankings: the upper class, the middle class, the working class, and the lower class.

The Upper Class

Families in the upper class—5 percent of the Canadian population—earn at least $135 000, and many earn 10 times that much. As a general rule, the more a family's income comes from inherited wealth in the form of shares of stock and bonds, real estate, and other investments, the stronger a family's claim to being upper class.

In 2003, *The Globe and Mail* estimated that there were 180 000 people in Canada with more than $1 million in the bank (Willis & MacDonald, 2003). In a different category are the estimated 7600 families who have assets exceeding $10 million, not including real estate. In 2009, *Forbes* listed 20 Canadian families or individuals worth more than US$1 billion (*Forbes*, 2009). David Thomson and family, of Thomson Reuters, topped the list of the richest persons in Canada and ranked as the thirteenth-richest in the world. The upper class are Karl Marx's "capitalists"—those who own most of the means of production and, thus, most of the nation's private wealth. Many upper-class people work as top executives in large corporations and as senior government officials. Historically, though less so today, the upper class has comprised white Anglo-Saxon Protestants (WASPs) (Clement, 1975; Porter, 1965).

Upper-Uppers

The *upper-upper class*, sometimes called "blue bloods" or simply "society," includes less than 1 percent of the Canadian population.

Membership is almost always the result of birth, as suggested by the joke that the easiest way to become an upper-upper is to be born one. Most of these families possess enormous wealth that is mostly inherited. For this reason, members of the upper-upper class are said to have "old money."

Set apart by their wealth, members of the upper-upper class live in exclusive neighbourhoods such as Westmount in Montreal, Forest Hill in Toronto, or the Uplands in Victoria. Their children typically attend private schools with others of similar background and complete their formal education at high-prestige universities. In the historical pattern of European aristocrats, they study liberal arts rather than vocational skills. Women of the upper-upper class often do volunteer work for charitable organizations; while helping the larger community, these activities also build networks that increase this elite's power (Ostrander, 1980, 1984).

Lower-Uppers

Most upper-class people actually fall into the *lower-upper class*. The Queen of England is in the upper-upper class based not on her fortune of $660 million but on her family tree. J.K. Rowling, author of the Harry Potter books, is worth even more—about $1 billion—but this woman (who was once on welfare) is a member of the lower-upper class. The major difference is that members of the lower-upper class are the "working rich": the primary source of their income is earnings, not inherited wealth. Although these "new rich" families—who make up 3 or 4 percent of the Canadian population—generally live in expensive neighbourhoods, most do not gain entry into the clubs and associations of "old money" families.

Compared to high-income people, low-income people are half as likely to report good health and, on average, live about seven fewer years. The toll of low income—played out in inadequate nutrition, little medical care, and high stress—is easy to see on the faces of the poor, who look old before their time.

The Middle Class

Made up of 40 to 45 percent of the Canadian population, the large middle class has a tremendous influence on our culture. Television and movies usually show middle-class people, and most commercial advertising is directed at these average consumers. The middle class contains far more ethnic and racial diversity than the upper class.

Upper-Middles

The top third in this category are referred to as the *upper-middle class*, based on their above-average income, in the range of $90 000 to $135 000 a year. Such income allows upper-middle-class families to accumulate property: a comfortable house in a fairly expensive area, several automobiles, and investments. Most upper-middle-class children go on to university or college, and postgraduate degrees are common. Many go on to high-prestige occupations as physicians, engineers, lawyers, accountants, or business executives.

Lacking the power of the richest people to influence national or international events, upper-middles often play an important role in local political affairs.

Average-Middles

The rest of the middle class falls close to the centre of the Canadian class structure. *Average-middles* typically work in less prestigious white-collar occupations as bank tellers, middle managers, or sales clerks, or in highly skilled blue-collar jobs such as electrical work and carpentry. Family income falls between $55 000 and $90 000 a year, which is roughly the national average.

The Working Class

About one-third of the population is in the working class (sometimes called the *lower-middle class*). In Marxist terms, the working class forms the core of the industrial proletariat. The blue-collar jobs held by members of the working class generally yield a family

SEEING SOCIOLOGY IN EVERYDAY LIFE

Nickel and Dimed: On (Not) Getting By in America

All of us know people who work at low-wage jobs as waitresses at diners, clerks at drive-throughs, or sales associates at discount stores such as Walmart. We see such people just about every day. Many of us actually *are* such people. In Canada and the United States, "common sense" tells us that the jobs people have and the amount of money they make reflect their personal abilities as well as their willingness to work hard.

U.S. sociologist, Barbara Ehrenreich (2001) had her doubts. To find out what the world of low-wage work is really like, the successful journalist and author decided to leave her comfortable upper-middle-class life to live and work in the world of low-wage jobs. She began by taking a job as a waitress for $2.43 an hour plus tips. Right away, she found out she had to work much harder than she ever imagined. By the end of a shift, she was exhausted, but after sharing tips with the kitchen staff, she averaged less than $6.00 an hour. This was barely above the national minimum wage at the time and provided just enough income to pay the rent on her tiny apartment, buy food, and cover other basic expenses. She had

to hope that she didn't get sick, because the job did not provide health insurance and she couldn't afford to pay for a visit to a doctor's office (one worry counterparts do not face in Canada).

After working for more than a year at a number of other low-wage jobs, including cleaning motels and working on the floor of a Walmart store, she had rejected quite a bit of "common sense." First, she now knew that tens of millions of people with low-wage jobs work very hard every day. If you don't think so, Ehrenreich says, take on one of these jobs for yourself. Second, these jobs require not only hard work (imagine thoroughly cleaning three motel rooms every hour all day long) but also special skills and real intelligence (try waiting on 10 tables in a restaurant at the same time and keeping everybody happy). She found that the people she worked with were, on average, just as smart, clever, and funny as others she knew who wrote books for a living or taught at a college or university.

Why, then, do we think of low-wage workers as lazy or as having less ability? It surprised Ehrenreich to learn that many low-wage workers

felt this way about themselves. In a society that teaches us to believe that personal ability is everything, we learn to size people up by their job. Ehrenreich discovered that many low-wage workers, subject to constant supervision, random drug tests, and other rigid rules that usually come with such jobs, end up feeling unworthy, even to the point of not trying for anything better. Such beliefs, she concludes, help support a society of extreme inequality in which some people live very well because of the low wages paid to the rest.

WHAT DO YOU THINK?

1. Have you ever held a low-wage job? If so, would you say you worked hard? What was your pay? Were there any benefits?

2. Ehrenreich claims that most well-off people are dependent on low-wage workers. What does she mean by this?

3. How much of a chance do most people with jobs at Wendy's or Walmart have to enrol in college or university and work toward a different career? Explain.

---

income of between $25 000 and $55 000 a year, somewhat below the national average.

Working-class families have little or no wealth and are vulnerable to financial problems caused by unemployment or illness.

Many working-class jobs provide little personal satisfaction—they require discipline but rarely imagination—and place workers under constant supervision. These jobs also offer fewer benefits, such as pension plans. About half of working-class families own their homes, usually in lower-cost neighbourhoods. College or university becomes a reality for only about one-third of working-class children.

The Lower Class

The remaining 20 percent of our population make up the lower class. Low income makes their lives insecure and difficult. Many belong to the so-called "working poor." They are just slightly better off than unemployed people, holding low-prestige jobs that provide little satisfaction and minimal income. Barely half manage

to complete high school, and fewer than one in three ever reach college or university. In the Seeing Sociology in Everyday Life box above, one sociologist describes the experience of trying to survive day to day doing low-wage work.

Society segregates the lower class, especially when the poor are racial or ethnic minorities. Only some lower-class families own their own home, typically in the least desirable neighbourhoods. Although poor neighbourhoods are found in our inner cities, lower-class families also live in rural areas.

The Difference Class Makes

Health

Health is closely related to social standing. Children born into poor families are more likely to die from disease, neglect, accidents, or violence during their first year of life than children born into privileged families. Among adults, people with the lowest incomes are five times more likely than those from the highest income groups to describe their health as only fair or poor. Moreover, on average, richer people live longer because they eat more nutritious food, live in safer and less stressful environments, and receive better medical care (Diderichsen et al., 2001; Statistics Canada, 1999d; Wilkinson, 2005).

Values and Attitudes

Some cultural values vary from class to class. The "old rich" have an unusually strong sense of family history because their position is based on wealth passed down from generation to generation. Secure in their birthright privileges, upper-uppers also favour understated manners and tastes, whereas many "new rich" people practise *conspicuous consumption*, using homes, cars, and even airplanes as *status symbols* to make a statement about their social position.

Affluent people with greater education and financial security are also more tolerant of controversial behaviour such as homosexuality. Working-class people, who grow up in an atmosphere of greater supervision and discipline and are less likely to attend college or university, tend to be less tolerant (Baltzell, 1979, orig. 1958; Lareau, 2002; NORC, 2007).

Politics

Political affiliations also flow along class lines. By and large, more privileged people support the Conservative or Liberal parties, while less advantaged people favour the NDP. But issue by issue, the pattern is more complex. A desire to protect wealth prompts well-off people to take a more conservative approach to economic issues, favouring, for example, lower taxes. But on social matters—such as abortion and gay rights—highly educated, more affluent people are more liberal. People of lower social standing, on the other hand, tend to be economic liberals, favouring government social programs, but support a more conservative social agenda (Angus Reid Group, 1996e, 1998b; Ipsos-Reid, 2003e).

Social class has a great deal to do with an individual's self-concept. People with higher social standing experience more confidence in everyday interaction for the simple reason that others tend to view them as having greater importance. The Thinking about Diversity box on page 212 describes the challenges faced by one young woman from a poor family attending a college or university where most students are from elite families.

Family and Gender

Social class also shapes family life. Generally, lower-class families are somewhat larger than middle-class families because of earlier marriage and less use of birth control. Another family pattern is that working-class parents encourage children to conform to conventional norms and respect authority figures. Parents of higher social standing pass on a different "cultural capital" to their children, teaching them

to express their individuality and imagination more freely (Kohn, 1977; Lareau, 2002; McLeod, 1995).

The more money a family has, the more opportunities parents have to develop their children's talents and abilities According to some calculations, the cost of raising a child in Canada to age 18 is more than $150 000 (Scott, 1996). Given the large amount of money involved, it stands to reason that only those families with the highest incomes can afford to pay for such luxuries as private schools. Privilege leads to privilege as family life reproduces the class structure in each generation.

Class also shapes our world of relationships. In a classic study of married life, Elizabeth Bott (1971, orig. 1957) found that most working-class couples divide their responsibilities according to traditional gender roles; middle-class couples, by contrast, are more egalitarian, sharing more activities and expressing greater intimacy. More recently, Karen Walker (1995) discovered that working-class friendships typically serve as sources of material assistance; middle-class friendships are likely to involve shared interests and leisure pursuits.

Social Mobility

Ours is a dynamic society marked by quite a bit of social movement. Earning a university or college degree, landing a higher-paying job, or marrying someone who has a good income contributes to *upward social mobility*; dropping out of school, losing a job, or becoming divorced (especially for women) may result in *downward social mobility*.

Over the long term, though, social mobility is not so much a matter of individual changes as changes in society itself. In the first half of the twentieth century, for example, industrialization expanded the Canadian economy, pushing up living standards. Even people who were not good swimmers rode the rising tide of prosperity. More recently, the "outsourcing" of jobs and the closing of factories and other business operations has brought downward structural social mobility, dealing economic setbacks to many people in the United States and to a lesser extent in Canada. The economic downturn that hit hard in 2008 and 2009 reduced the income and economic opportunities of millions of people.

Sociologists distinguish between shorter- and longer-term changes in social position. **Intragenerational social mobility** is *a change in social position occurring during a person's lifetime* (*intra* is Latin for "within"). **Intergenerational social mobility**, *upward or downward social mobility of children in relation to their parents*, is important because it reveals long-term changes in society that affect everyone (*inter* is Latin for "between").

Myth versus Reality

In few societies do people think about "getting ahead" as much as they do in Canada and the United States. But is there as much social mobility in our country as we like to think?

The Power of Class: A Low-Income Student Asks, "Am I as Good as You?"

Marcella grew up without the privileges that most other students on the campus of this private, liberal arts college take for granted. During her senior year, she and I talked at length about her college experiences and why social class presented a huge challenge to her. Marcella is not her real name; she wishes to remain anonymous. I have summarized what she has said about her college life in the story that follows.

When I came here, I entered a new world. I found myself in a strange and dangerous place. All around me were people with habits and ideas I did not understand. A thousand times, I thought to myself, I hope all of you will realize that there are other worlds out there and that I am from one of them. Will you accept me?

I am a child of poverty, a young woman raised in a world of want and violence. I am now on the campus of an elite college. I may have a new identity as a college student. But my old life is still going on in my head. I have not been able to change how I think of myself.

Do you want to find out more about me? Learn more about the power of social class to shape how we feel about ourselves? Here is what I want to say to you.

When I was growing up, I envied most of you. You lived in a middle-class bubble, a world that held you, protected you, and comforted you. Not me. While your parents were discussing current events, planning family trips, and looking out for you, my father and mother were screaming at each other. I will never be able to forget summer nights when I lay in my bed, sticky with sweat, biting my fingernails as a telephone crashed against the wall that separated my room from theirs. My father was drunk and out of control; my mother ducked just in time.

Your fathers and mothers work in office buildings. They have good jobs, as doctors, lawyers, and architects; they are corporate managers; they run small businesses. Your mothers and fathers are people who matter. My mom takes the bus to a hospital where she works for $10 an hour cleaning up after people. She spends her shift doing what she is told. My dad? Who knows. He was a deadbeat, a drunk, a drug addict. I don't know if he still is or not. I haven't heard from him in eight years.

You grew up in a neighbourhood and probably lived for many years in one house. My family lived in low-cost rental housing. We moved a lot. When there was no money for rent, we packed up our stuff and moved to a new place. It seemed like we were always running away from something.

You grew up with books, with trips to the library, with parents who read to you. You learned how to speak well and have an impressive vocabulary. I never heard a bedtime story, and I had maybe one inspiring teacher. Most of what I know I had to learn on my own. Maybe that's why I always feel like I am trying to catch up to you.

You know how to use forks, knives, and spoons the right way. You know how to eat Chinese food and what to order at a Thai restaurant. You have favourite Italian dishes. You know how to order wine. You know about German beers, Danish cheeses, and French sauces. Me? I grew up having Thanksgiving dinner on paper plates, eating turkey served by social service volunteers. When you ask me to go with you to some special restaurant, I make some excuse and stay home. I can't afford it. I am afraid you will find out how little I know about things you take for granted.

How did I ever get to this college? I remember one of my teachers telling me that I "have promise." The college admission office accepted me. But I am not sure why. I was given a scholarship that covers most of my tuition. That solved one big problem, and now I am here. But sometimes I am not sure I will stay. I have to study more than many of you to learn things you already know. I have to work two part-time jobs to make the money I needed to buy a used computer, clothes, and the occasional pizza at the corner place where many of you spend so much time.

It's amazing to me that I am here. I realize how lucky I am. But now that I am here, I realize that the road is so much longer than I thought it would be. Getting to this college was only part of the journey. The scholarship was only part of the answer. The biggest challenge for me is what goes on every day—the thousands of ways in which you live a life that I still don't really understand, the thousands of things that I won't know or that I will do wrong that will blow my cover, and show me up for the fraud I am.

WHAT DO YOU THINK?

1. How does this story show that social class involves much more than how much money a person has?

2. Why does Marcella worry that other people will think she is a "fraud"? If you could speak to her about this fear, what would you say?

3. Have you ever had similar feelings about being less important than—or better than—someone else based on social class position? Explain.

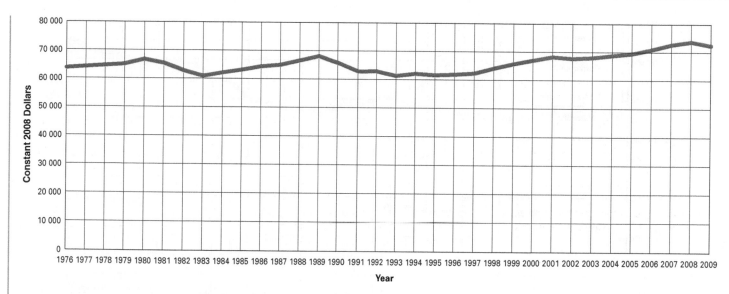

FIGURE 8-4 Median Annual Income, Canadian Families, 1976–2009

Average Canadian family income peaked in 1980 and 1989 and has grown since 1998 (in 2009 dollars, adjusted for inflation).

Source: Statistics Canada (2011n).

One recent American study of intergenerational mobility shows that about 32 percent of men had the same type of work as their fathers, 37 percent were upwardly mobile (for example, a son born to a father with a blue-collar job ends up doing white-collar work), and 32 percent were downwardly mobile (for example, the father has a white-collar job and the son does blue-collar work). Among women, 46 percent were upwardly mobile, 28 percent were downwardly mobile, and 27 percent showed no change compared to their fathers (Beller & Hout, 2006). Other countries fare better than the United States, including Canada. A recent OECD (2010) study of mobility in earnings, wages, and education across generations indicates that mobility is comparatively low in the United States, the United Kingdom, France, and southern European countries, and higher in Canada, Australia, and the Nordic countries.

Horizontal social mobility—changing jobs at the same class level—is even more common. Overall, about 80 percent of children show some type of social mobility in relation to their parents (Beller & Hout, 2006; Hout, 1998).

Research points to four general conclusions about social mobility in North America:

1. Social mobility over the course of the past century has been fairly high. A high level of mobility is what we would expect in an industrial class system.

2. Within a single generation, social mobility is usually small. Most young families increase their income over time as they gain education and skills. In 2005, median earnings of economic families in which at least one partner, or the parent, was aged 15 to 64 years was $63 715 (Statistics Canada, 2008e). Yet only a few people move from "rags to riches" (the way J.K. Rowling did) or lose a lot of money (a number of rock stars who make it big have little money left a few years later). Most social mobility involves small movement within one class level rather than large movement between classes.

3. The long-term trend in social mobility has been upward. Industrialization, which greatly expanded the Canadian economy, and the growth of white-collar work over the course of the twentieth century have raised living standards.

4. Social mobility since the 1970s has been uneven. Real income (adjusted for inflation) rose during the twentieth century until the 1970s. Since then, as shown in Figure 8–4, real income has risen and fallen, with overall smaller gains than was the case before 1970. Most recently, the economic recession that began in 2007 resulted in downward social mobility for many families. But general historical trends do not show the experiences of different categories of people, as the next section explains.

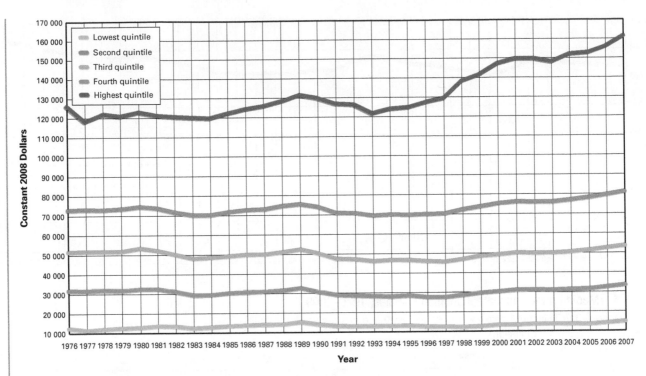

FIGURE 8–5 Average Annual Income, Canadian Families, 1976–2007 (in 2007 dollars, adjusted for inflation)

The gap between high-income and low-income families is wider today than it was in 1976.

Source: Statistics Canada (2011o).

Mobility by Income Level

Figure 8–5 shows how Canadian families at different income levels made out between 1976 and 2007. Well-to-do families (the highest 20 percent, but not all of the same families over the entire period) saw their incomes jump 58 percent, from an average of $126 100 in 1976 to $161 400 in 2007. People in the middle of the population saw almost no gains during these three decades. The 20 percent with the lowest income saw their incomes increase 19 percent from $12 500 to $14 800 (adjusted for inflation). In addition to these changes over time, income varies regionally. National Map 8-1 illustrates this variation.

Mobility: Race, Ethnicity, and Gender

White people in Canada have always been in a more privileged position than people of Aboriginal and visible minority backgrounds. There was a slight decrease in the income gap percentage differences between Aboriginal and non-Aboriginal Canadians from 2000 to 2005, but the gap remains large and chronic unemployment persists among our Aboriginal peoples

(Statistics Canada, 2009b). Moreover, between 1980 and 2005, recent immigrants, who tend to be of visible minority backgrounds yet have a higher level of education than others in Canada, actually lost ground relative to their Canadian-born counterparts (Statistics Canada, 2008f).

Feminists point out that, historically, women have had less chance for upward mobility than men because most working women hold clerical jobs (such as secretary) and service positions (such as food server) that offer few opportunities for advancement.

Over time, however, the median earnings gap between women and men has been narrowing. Women working full time in 1978 earned 62 percent as much as men working full time; by 2008, women's median earnings was 76 percent as much (Statistics Canada, 2010d).

Mobility and Marriage

Research points to the conclusion that marriage has an important effect on social standing. In a study of women and men in their forties, Jay Zagorsky (2006) found that people who marry and stay married accumulate about twice as much wealth as people who remain

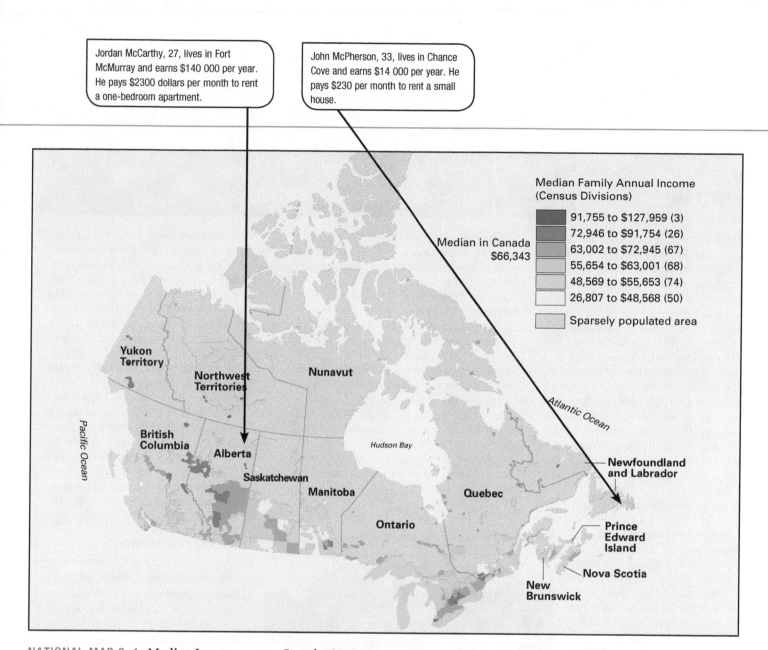

Jordan McCarthy, 27, lives in Fort McMurray and earns $140 000 per year. He pays $2300 dollars per month to rent a one-bedroom apartment.

John McPherson, 33, lives in Chance Cove and earns $14 000 per year. He pays $230 per month to rent a small house.

Median Family Annual Income (Census Divisions)

Median in Canada $66,343

	91,755 to $127,959 (3)
	72,946 to $91,754 (26)
	63,002 to $72,945 (67)
	55,654 to $63,001 (68)
	48,569 to $55,653 (74)
	26,807 to $48,568 (50)
	Sparsely populated area

NATIONAL MAP 8–1 Median Income across Canada, 2005

The map shows the median family income in each of the 288 census divisions across Canada. While 50 percent of Canadian families earned less than $66 343 in 2005, there were 50 census divisions where the median income was less than $48 600. At the other end of the continuum, there are very high-income areas in Alberta, the Northwest Territories and west of Toronto. What is the income level where you live? How can you tell what the income level of an area is?

Source: Statistics Canada (2011p).

single or who divorce. Reasons for this difference include the fact that couples who live together typically enjoy double incomes and also pay only half of the bills they would have if they were single and living in separate households.

It is also likely that compared to single people, married men and women work harder in their jobs and save more money. Why? Primarily because they are working not just for themselves but to support children and spouses who are counting on them.

Just as marriage pushes social standing upward, divorce usually makes social position go down. Couples who divorce take on the costs of supporting two households, which leaves them with less money for savings or other investment. After divorce, women are hurt more than men because typically the man earns more. Many women who divorce lose not only most of their income but also benefits such as health care and insurance coverage (Weitzman, 1996).

As CEOs Get Richer, the Great Mansions Return

I (John Macionis) grew up in Elkins Park, Pennsylvania, an older Philadelphia suburb that is a mostly middle-class community, although like most of suburbia, some neighbourhoods boast bigger houses than others. What made Elkins Park special was that a century ago, a handful of great mansions were built by early industrialists. Back then, all there was to the town was these great "estates," separated by fields and meadows. By about 1940, however, most of this land had been split off into lots for the homes of newer middle-class suburbanites. The great mansions suddenly seemed out of place, with heirs disagreeing over who should live there and how to pay the rising property taxes. As a result, many of the great mansions were sold, the buildings were taken down, and the land was subdivided.

In the 1960s, when I was a teenager, a short bike ride could take me past the Breyer estate (built by the founder of the ice cream company, now the township police building), the Curtis estate (built by a magazine publisher and transformed into a community park), and the Wanamaker estate (built by the founder of a large department store, now the site of high-rise apartments). Probably the grandest of them all was the Wiedner estate, modelled after a French chateau, complete with doorknobs and window pulls covered in gold; it now stands empty.

In their day, these structures were not just home to a family and many servants; they were also monuments to a time when

the rich were, well, *really* rich. By contrast, the community that emerged on the grounds once owned by these rich families is middle class, with modest homes on small lots.

But did the so-called Gilded Age of great wealth disappear forever? No. By the 1980s, a new wave of great mansions was being built. Take the architect Thierry Despont, who designs huge houses for the super-rich. One of Despont's "smaller" homes might be 20 000 square feet (about 10 times the size of the average North American house), and they go all the way up to 60 000 square feet (as big as any of the Elkins Park mansions built a century ago and almost the size of the White House). These megahomes have kitchens as large as college classrooms, exercise rooms, indoor swimming pools, and even indoor tennis courts (Krugman, 2002).

Megahouses are being built by newly rich chief executive officers (CEOs) of large corporations. Although CEOs have always made more money than most people, recent years have seen executive compensation soar. Between 1970 and 2008, the average North American family saw only a modest increase in income (about 26 percent after inflation is taken into account). During the same period, the average compensation for the 100 highest-paid CEOs skyrocketed from $1.3 million (about 40 times the earnings of an average worker at that time) to $29.7 million (equal to 494 times the compensation of today's average worker). Richer still, the 20 highest-earning investment fund managers in 2008 (a terrible year for the stock market) had, on average, $465 million *each* in income, earning more in 10 minutes than an average worker made all year (Corporate Library, 2010; Story, 2009; U.S. Census Bureau, 2010).

WHAT DO YOU THINK?

1. Do you consider increasing economic inequality a problem? Why or why not?

2. How many times more than an average worker should a CEO earn? Explain your answer.

3. Does very high CEO pay help or hurt stockholders? What about the general public? Explain your reasoning.

The North American Dream: Still a Reality?

The expectation of upward social mobility is deeply rooted in North American culture. Through much of our history, the economy has grown steadily, raising living standards. Today, at least for some people, this dream is alive and well. In 2006, more than half a million Canadians earned more than $100 000 and just over one-third earned more than $150 000. Looking at the data over time, 3.4 percent of full-time, full-year earners received $100 000 or

more in 1980 (in 2005 constant dollars). This proportion had almost doubled to 6.5 percent in 2005. Similarly, in 2005, about 2.2 percent of full-time, full-year earners received $150 000 or more, which was an increase from 1.0 percent in 1980 (Statistics Canada, 2009c).

Yet not all indicators are so positive. Note these disturbing trends:

1. For many workers, earnings have stalled or worsened. Median earnings of Canadian workers in full-time, full-year employment remained stalled over the past 25 years, showing only a minor

relative poverty the lack of resources of some people in relation to those who have more

absolute poverty a lack of resources that is life-threatening

feminization of poverty (p. 219) the trend of women making up an increasing proportion of the poor

increase from $41 348 in 1980 to $41 401 in 2005 (in 2005 constant dollars). During this time period, median earnings among those in the bottom one-fifth of the distribution actually fell 20.6 percent. Median earnings among those in the middle 20 percent remained still (Statistics Canada, 2008f).

2. More jobs offer little income. The expanding global economy has moved many industrial jobs overseas, reducing the availability of high-paying factory work here in Canada. At the same time, the expansion of our service economy means that more of today's jobs—in fast-food restaurants or large discount stores—offer relatively low wages.

3. Young people are remaining at home. Currently, more than half of young people aged 18 to 24, unable to support a household, are still living with their parents. Since 1975, the average age at first marriage has moved upward four years (to 25.9 years for women and 28.1 years for men).

Over the past generation, more people have become rich, and the rich have become richer; as the Seeing Sociology in Everyday Life box on page 216 explains, the highest-paid corporate executives have enjoyed a runaway rise in their earnings. But at the same time, the increasing share of low-paying jobs has brought downward mobility for many families, feeding the fear that the chance to enjoy a middle-class lifestyle is slipping away.

For years, the mass media have presented the North American dream as alive and well in "reality" shows such as *Canadian Idol*, which is based on the idea that talent and effort can make anyone rich and famous. More recently, as Seeing Sociology in the News on pages 218–19 explains, television shows are presenting a more pessimistic view of people's chances to get ahead.

The Global Economy and the Canadian Structure

Underlying the shifts in the North American class structure over recent decades is global economic change. Much of the industrial production that gave Canadian workers high-paying jobs a generation ago has been moved overseas, where wages are cheaper. With less industry at home, Canada now serves as a vast consumer market for industrial goods such as cars, stereos, cameras, and computers made in China, Japan, South Korea, and elsewhere.

High-paying jobs in manufacturing are on a long-term decline. Between 2002 and 2007 alone, there was a decline of 241 000 workers in manufacturing (Statistics Canada, 2008g). In terms of real manufacturing output, Canada ranked the worst among 16 high-income countries in 2009, with real output declining at an average rate of 0.3 percent per year (U.S. Bureau of Labor Statistics, 2010). In their place, the economy offers service work, which pays far less. Traditionally high-paying corporations now employ fewer people than the

expanding chains such as McDonald's, and fast-food clerks make only a fraction of what steelworkers earn.

The global reorganization of work has not been bad news for everyone. The global economy is driving upward social mobility for educated people who specialize in law, finance, marketing, and computer technology. Even allowing for the downturn in 2008 and 2009, the global economic expansion also helped push up the stock market more than tenfold between 1980 and 2010, reaping profits for families with money to invest.

But the same trend has hurt many average workers, who have lost their factory jobs and now perform low-wage service work. In addition, many companies (General Motors and Ford are recent examples) have downsized—cutting the ranks of their workforce—in an attempt to stay competitive in world markets. As a result, although the majority of all families today contain two or more people in the labour force—more than twice the share in 1950—many families are working harder than ever before simply to hold on to what they have (Nelson, 1998; Sennett, 1998; Statistics Canada, 2008f).

Poverty in Canada

Social stratification creates both "haves" and "have-nots." All systems of social inequality create poverty, or at least **relative poverty**, *the lack of resources of some people in relation to those who have more*. A more serious but preventable problem is **absolute poverty**, *a lack of resources that is life-threatening*.

As Chapter 9 ("Global Stratification") explains, about 1.4 billion human beings around the world—one person in five—are at risk of absolute poverty. Even in affluent Canada, families go hungry, sleep in parked cars or on the streets, and suffer from poor health simply because they are poor.

The Extent of Poverty

According to this measure, a family has an income below the low income cut-off (LICO) if it spends more than 63 percent of its after-tax income on the necessities of food, clothing, and shelter, including corrections for different family sizes and the cost of living in particular communities. For example, in 2005, a family of four living in a large urban area (more than 500 000 people) with an after-tax income below $32 556 lived below the LICO. Similarly, this same family would have to have a before-tax income above $38 610 to be living above the LICO (Statistics Canada, 2006an).

In 2009, the government classified 3.2 million men, women, and children—9.6 percent of the Canadian population—as poor.[2] In 2009, about 1.3 million unattached individuals had income below the after-tax LICO, consistent with 2008 data.

---

[2]These statistics refer to after-tax income. The proportion of the population living below LICO before taxes and transfers is considerably higher, as Figure 8–5 on page 214 shows.

Postmedia News

As the Economy Turns the Corner, Young Canadians Face Downsized "Dream"

BY ANDREW MAYEDA
September 4, 2010

OTTAWA – When Blaine Higgs graduated with an engineering degree from the University of New Brunswick in the late 1970s, it didn't take him long to land a job with the company that would be his employer for the next 32 years.

The job with Irving Oil, one of the pillars in the empire of the province's powerful Irving family, gave him the stability to settle down with his high school sweetheart in the Saint John area, only a few hours' drive from Forest City, the village by the Maine border where he grew up.

As Higgs climbed the corporate ladder, he and his wife Marcia bought a house and raised four daughters. Last year, he retired with a company pension that should keep them secure for the rest of their lives.

So it is with some concern that he watches his eldest daughter, Lindsey, struggle to establish herself in the Canadian job market, despite being fluently bilingual, having a wealth of international experience, and boasting a bachelor's degree in political studies from Queen's University and a master's degree from Carleton University's Norman Paterson School of International Affairs.

After moving to Toronto last year from Tanzania, where she was doing development work for an NGO, it took her about a year to finally find a contract position with an organization that helps children in developing countries.

"When I came back, I thought I'd try living in Toronto for a while, and didn't really understand how difficult it would be to find something," said Lindsey, 27. "The year was very tough—hard on my self-esteem, hard on my sense of where I was going, career-wise. Now, I'm happy with the work I'm doing, but again, it's contract work."

Her experience isn't uncommon among her generation. As the economy recovers from the first recession in nearly two decades, many young Canadians are finding it more difficult to attain the same comfortable standard of living—complete with stable job, nice house, and reliable pension—that their parents enjoyed.

With the economy expected to grow more slowly than it did in the boom years before the financial crisis, many are having to downgrade their expectations.

If there's a silver lining, it's that the recession didn't turn out as bad as some expected in the fall of 2008, when the global financial crisis erupted. Compared with the recessions of the early 1980s and early 1990s, employment fell faster in the early months of the latest downturn but stabilized earlier, according to Statistics Canada.

At the end of July, employment had climbed back to just 90 200 jobs short of its pre-recession peak. Moreover, the damage here hasn't been nearly as severe as in the United States, where nearly seven 7 million jobs have been lost since late 2007 and the unemployment rate stands at 9.5 per cent, compared with eight per cent in Canada.

The ongoing fragility of the American housing market, and renewed fears of a "double-dip" recession south of the border, has prompted several publications, including the *New York Times*, to ponder whether the "American dream" is slipping out of reach. Is the Canadian version of that dream fading too?

Even though the recovery is underway, times are still tough for many Canadians. Certain groups were hit especially hard during the recession, including workers in the manufacturing and construction sectors, low-income individuals, families with young children, recent immigrants and young people. As of July, youth employment in Canada stood at 14.1 per cent.

To make matters worse, the average Canadian student finishes their undergraduate degree nearly $27,000 in debt, more than double the average 20 years ago. Under such conditions, some young jobseekers are being forced to put off goals, such as buying a house, getting married and having kids.

The recession marked the end of what some economists call the Great Moderation, one of the longest, most prosperous booms in modern history. Between the early '90s and the global financial crisis in 2008, Canada and other developed countries enjoyed strong economic growth and low unemployment rates.

Tame inflation allowed central bankers to keep interest rates low, setting the stage for even relatively low-income earners to become

Who Are the Poor?

Although no single description fits all poor people, poverty is greater among certain categories of the Canadian population. Where these categories overlap, the problem is especially serious.

Age

A generation ago, the elderly were at greatest risk for poverty, but no longer. From 21 percent in 1980, the poverty rate for seniors over the age of 65 plummeted to 4.8 percent in 2007 (Collin & Jensen, 2009). The poverty rate of the elderly has fallen because of better retirement programs from private employers and government. Still, almost 201 000 seniors had a low income in 2009 (Statistics Canada, 2009).

Today, the burden of poverty falls most heavily on children. About 634 000 children younger than age 18 (9.5 percent of the total) lived in low-income families in 2009, similar to the year before but lower than in the decade before (Statistics Canada, 2011k).

Race and Ethnicity

Recent data show that the poverty rates for visible minorities are much higher than the national average. In 2001, the 26 percent poverty rate for visible minority groups was twice that of the national average of 12.9 percent (Statistics Canada, 2003ak). The 2006 census found that immigrants who had arrived in the preceding five years and who were in economic families had a low-income rate of 32.6 percent in 2005; visible

homeowners and take advantage of the seemingly inexorable rise of housing prices.

The entire edifice rested on a global trade system in which export powerhouses, such as China, and oil-rich nations, such as Saudi Arabia, reinvested their massive trade surpluses in the United States, keeping the American dollar strong and enabling U.S. consumers to continue their credit-fuelled spending binge.

But now that system appears to be unravelling, and growth in the U.S. and other advanced economies is expected to be moderate in the next few years.

Although Canada finds itself in a better position than many rich countries, few forecasters expect the economy to return anytime soon to the heady growth rates of the early 2000s. Powerful demographic forces are also coming into play that will constrain Canada's economic potential. . .

"In Canada, we've known this demographic challenge is coming. We know that it's going to slow labour input, we've known that the potential growth rate will slow, but it seems like we don't want to really deal with it," said Kevin Page, who as Canada's parliamentary budget officer has been sounding the alarm about the long-term pressures that the greying population will put on the country's finances.

Canadian consumers could be in store for a serious reality check. . .

"In the last 10 years, we've seen a huge increase in consumer confidence, without an increase in capability," said Tal. "A wake-up call is overdue."

That wake-up call could be especially jarring for 20-somethings launching their careers. . .

Members of the Millennial generation, born in 1980 or later, certainly have ambitious career expectations. According to a study published earlier this year, that generation expects salaries to start at just under $43,000 and climb to just under $70,000 within five years of graduation.

The actual salary averages of people at those two stages of their careers are just under $33,000 and slightly less than $45,000, notes one of the study's co-authors, Sean Lyons.

In addition to good pay and rapid career advancement, Millennials expect to find an employer whose "values" match their own and that provides a "nurturing" work environment where they can make friends and have fun.

Lyons says many baby boomers, born between the end of the Second World War and the mid-1960s, tend to find such expectations unrealistic. But he notes that Millennials have been encouraged, often by their own parents, to aim high.

"They don't see these things as mutually exclusive," said Lyons, an associate professor at the University of Guelph. "They've been told, time and again, that baby boomers are going to retire and there's going to be so many jobs that people are going to be bidding for you."

Page says Canada's changing demographics will put an increasing strain on federal finances, as slowing growth curbs tax revenues and spending rises in areas such as health care and elderly benefits. He foresees a major political battle in 2014, when the federal government's deal with the provinces on health-care transfers expires.

And he sees a rise in "intergenerational" tension across the country, unless politicians tackle the problem soon.

"We have to make changes. We do not have a fiscal structure in this country that's sustainable."

WHAT DO YOU THINK?

1. Do you think the current economic recovery will last and times will soon get better for Canadians?

2. Why is the Millennial generation, born in 1980 or later, so ambitious career-wise compared to the previous generation?

3. Do you feel that, if you work hard and follow the rules, you can achieve the Canadian version of the American dream? Explain your personal views on this question.

Source: As the Economy Turns the Corner, Young Canadians Face Downsized "Dream," by Andrew Mayeda, September 04, 2010, Postmedia News. Material reprinted with the express permission of: Postmedia News, a division of Postmedia Network Inc.

minorities who were unattached had a low-income rate of 58.3 percent. The respective rates of low income among their non-immigrant counterparts were 6.9 percent for economic families and 26.3 percent for unattached individuals (Collin & Jensen, 2009). The situation is even worse for Aboriginals, with a poverty rate of 31 percent, or almost one in three (Statistics Canada, 2003bu). Among Canadians of Aboriginal identity living in private households, 18.7 percent who live in economic families and 42.8 percent who live alone experienced low income in 2005. Aboriginal people in urban areas are more likely to experience low income (Collin & Jensen, 2009).

Gender and Family Patterns

Of all poor people, 54 percent are female and 46 percent are male. This disparity reflects the fact that women who head households bear the brunt of poverty: 36 percent of children who live in female lone-parent families live in poverty, and almost 40 percent of all children who live in poverty live with a lone mother.

The term **feminization of poverty** describes *the trend of women making up an increasing proportion of the poor.* Analyzing differences between males and females, we notice that females have higher poverty rates than males in all age groups over 15 years of age (Statistics Canada, 2003al). In 2007, 9.4 percent of females were living on a low income compared to 9 percent for males, indicating a narrowing of the gap over the last few decades. Once women have fallen into poverty, they also tend to remain poor for a longer period of time than men do. Between 2002 and 2007, 5.6 percent of females experienced poverty for four to six years, compared to 4.6 percent of males (Collin & Jensen, 2009).

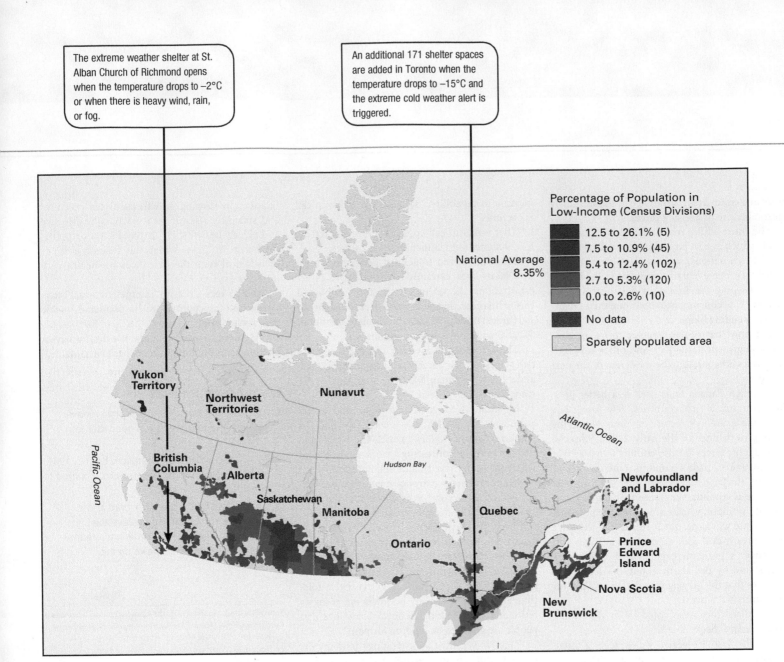

The extreme weather shelter at St. Alban Church of Richmond opens when the temperature drops to –2°C or when there is heavy wind, rain, or fog.

An additional 171 shelter spaces are added in Toronto when the temperature drops to –15°C and the extreme cold weather alert is triggered.

Percentage of Population in Low-Income (Census Divisions)

National Average 8.35%

12.5 to 26.1% (5)
7.5 to 10.9% (45)
5.4 to 12.4% (102)
2.7 to 5.3% (120)
0.0 to 2.6% (10)

No data

Sparsely populated area

Seeing Ourselves

NATIONAL MAP 8–2   **Poverty across Canada**

The map shows the extent of poverty in different regions of Canada. There is a relatively high percentage in some of our largest urban centres but also in rural areas on the prairies and in eastern Canada. What is the poverty level where you live? Do you think that a high poverty level always coincides with a low median income level?

Source: Statistics Canada (2011q).

Urban and Rural Poverty

The greatest number of poor people today live in our country's largest cities: 41 percent of the total number of people living below the poverty line in 2001 lived in Toronto, Montreal, or Vancouver (at the time, 34 percent of Canada's total population lived in these three cities). The 2006 census reported similar findings (Statistics Canada, 2010d). These data also show that the incidence of poverty is higher in urban areas than in rural areas, which is a phenomenon that has emerged in the last 20 years; before that time, the

proportion living below the LICO was higher in rural areas. National Map 8–2 provides a picture of the shape of the housing where people live in different parts of Canada.

Explaining Poverty

For one of the richest nations on Earth to contain millions of poor people raises serious questions. It is true, as some analysts remind us, that most poor people in Canada are far better off than the poor in other countries: For example, health care and education are publicly funded here. Nevertheless, poverty harms the overall well-being of millions of people in this country.

Why is there poverty in the first place? We will examine two opposing explanations that lead to a lively and important political debate.

One View: Blame the Poor

One view holds that *the poor are primarily responsible for their own poverty.* Throughout the nation's history, people have placed a high cultural value on self-reliance, convinced that a person's social standing is mostly a matter of individual talent and effort. According to this view, society offers plenty of opportunities to anyone who is able and willing to take advantage of them, and the poor are people who cannot or will not work because of a lack of skills, schooling, or motivation.

In his study of Latin American cities, the anthropologist Oscar Lewis (1961) concluded that the poor become trapped in a *culture of poverty*, a lower-class subculture that can destroy people's ambition to improve their lives. Socialized in poor families, children become resigned to their situation, producing a self-perpetuating cycle of poverty.

Another View: Blame Society

A different position, argued by the sociologist William Julius Wilson (1996a, 1996b; see also Mouw, 2000), holds that *society is primarily responsible for poverty.* Wilson points to the loss of jobs in our inner cities as the primary cause of poverty, claiming that there is simply not enough work to support families. Wilson sees any apparent lack of trying on the part of the poor as a result of little opportunity rather than as a cause of poverty. From Wilson's point of view, Lewis's analysis amounts to *blaming the victim*, that is, saying that victims are responsible for their own suffering (Ryan, 1976). To combat poverty and reduce the need for welfare, Wilson argues, the government should fund jobs and provide affordable child care for low-income mothers and fathers.

> **CRITICAL REVIEW** Both sides have evidence to support their positions. One observation is that almost half of young people in the United States who are born to low-income parents become low-income adults themselves. The results for the United Kingdom were 4 in 10, and 1 in 3 for Canada (Corak, 2006a). Such a fact seems to support the argument that poverty is intergenerational and the poor are at least in part the blame for their position.

> **CHECK YOUR LEARNING** Explain the view that the poor should take responsibility for poverty and the view that society is responsible for poverty. Which is closer to your own view?

The Working Poor

The reasons that people do not work are more in step with the "blame society" position. Middle-class women may be able to combine working and child rearing, but this is much harder for poor women who cannot afford child care, and few employers provide child-care programs for their employees. Moreover, as William Julius Wilson explains, many people are idle not because they are avoiding work but because there are not enough jobs. In short, most poor people in Canada find few opportunities and alternatives to improve their lives (Duncan, 1999; Edin & Lein, 1996; Pease & Martin, 1997; Popkin, 1990; Schiller, 1994; Wilson, 1996a).

But not all poor people are jobless, and the working poor command the sympathy and support of people on both sides of the poverty debate. In 2007, just under 6 percent of working families in which the main income recipient had 910 hours or more of paid work that year lived on a low income. While this was a decline from 7.3 percent in 2006, in 2007 working poor families still accounted for 31 percent of all low-income families (Collin & Jensen, 2009). It is clear, then, that many poor families remained poor despite employment. A key cause for "working poverty" is that even two people working 40 hours per week, 52 weeks per year, cannot keep a family of four above the poverty line if they live in an urban area with a population of more than 500 000 and make only minimum wage, which in 2004 ranged from $5.90 per hour in Newfoundland and Labrador to $8.50 in Nunavut.

To sum up, individual ability and personal initiative do play a part in shaping everyone's social position. However, the weight of sociological evidence points toward society—not individual character traits—as the primary source of poverty. Society must be at fault because the poor are categories of people—female heads of families, Aboriginal people, and people isolated from the larger society in inner-city neighbourhoods—who face special barriers and limited opportunities.

Understanding this important social issue can help us decide how our society should respond to the problem of poverty, as well as the problem of homelessness discussed next.

Homelessness

Many low-income people in Canada cannot afford even basic housing. There is no precise count of homeless people, but experts estimate that in 2011 there were 150 000 homeless living on the streets in cities across Canada (Salvation Army, 2011).

The familiar stereotypes of homeless people—men sleeping in doorways and women carrying everything they own in shopping bags—have been replaced by the "new homeless": some thrown out of work because of plant closings, people forced out of apartments by rent increases, and others who cannot meet mortgage or rent payments because of low wages or no work at all. Today, no stereotype paints a complete picture of the homeless.

But virtually all homeless people have one thing in common: poverty. For that reason, the approaches already used in explaining

Many young disadvantaged people are faced with little opportunity to improve their lives. Does this explain high substance abuse levels in some communities?

poverty also apply to homelessness. One side of the debate places responsibility on personal traits of the homeless themselves. One-third of homeless people are substance abusers, and one-fourth are mentally ill. Perhaps we should not be surprised that a fraction of 1 percent of our population, for one reason or another, is unable to cope with our complex and highly competitive society (Bassuk, 1984; Whitman, 1989).

On the other side of the debate, advocates assert that homelessness results from societal factors, including unemployment, a lack of low-income housing, and the increasing number of low-income jobs (Bohannan, 1991; Hagan & McCarthy, 1997; Kozol,

1988; Schutt, 1989). Supporters of this position point out that one-third of all homeless people are entire families, and that children are the fastest-growing subcategory among the homeless. Others call attention to the myth that the homeless people are "just like you and me." In fact, a 2009 survey of residents at Salvation Army shelters revealed that nearly 25 percent of the shelter population have jobs—but are still unable to make ends meet (Salvation Army, 2011).

No one disputes that a large proportion of homeless people are personally impaired to some degree, although it is difficult to untangle how much is cause and how much effect. But structural changes in the Canadian economy, the closing down of mental institutions in recent decades, and limited government support for lower-income people have all certainly contributed to homelessness.

Class, Welfare, Politics, and Values

We have reviewed many facts about social inequality. In the end, however, our opinions about wealth and poverty depend not just on facts but also on our politics and values. As we might expect, the idea that social standing reflects personal merit is popular among well-off people; the opposing idea, that government should spread wealth more equally, finds favour among those who are less well off (NORC, 2009). In Canada, our cultural emphasis on individual responsibility encourages us to see successful people as personally worthy and to view poor people as personally falling short. Such attitudes go a long way toward explaining why our society spends much more than most other high-income nations on education (to promote opportunity) but much less on public assistance programs (which directly support the poor).

Most members of our society are willing to accept a high level of income inequality, and many hold a harsh view of the poor. To the extent that we define poor people as undeserving, we look on public assistance programs as at best a waste of money and at worst a substitute for personal initiative.

Finally, the drama of social stratification extends far beyond the borders of Canada. The most striking social inequality is found not by looking inside one country but by comparing living standards in various parts of the world. In Chapter 9, we broaden our focus by investigating global stratification.

CHAPTER 8 SOCIAL STRATIFICATION

HOW DO WE UNDERSTAND INEQUALITY IN OUR SOCIETY? This chapter sketches the class structure of Canada and also explains how factors such as race are linked to social standing. You already know, for example, that the rate of poverty is double for new immigrants, the majority of whom have visible minority backgrounds, and you have also learned that they earn about two-thirds as much as other Canadians. But affluent people—here, we'll define "affluence" as a family earning more than $50 000 a year—come in all colours. Here's a chance to test your sociological thinking by answering several questions about how race affects being affluent. Look at each of the statements below: Does the statement reflect reality or is it a myth?

Q

1. In Canada, all affluent people are white. Reality or myth?
2. People in visible minority families do not work as hard as members of other Canadian families. Reality or myth?
3. When you are rich, colour doesn't matter. Reality or myth?

A

1. Of course, this is a myth. But when it comes to being affluent, race does matter: About one-quarter of recent immigrants are in this income group in comparison with one-third of the total Canadian population.
2. Myth. On average, affluent visible minority families are more likely to rely on multiple incomes (that is, they have more people working) than their white counterparts. In addition, affluent white families receive more unearned income—that is, income from investments.
3. Myth. Visible minority Canadians still face social barriers based on their race, just as rich whites benefit from the privileges linked to their colour.

Applying Sociology in Everyday Life

1. Identify three ways in which social stratification is evident in the everyday lives of students on your campus. In each case, explain exactly what is unequal and what difference it makes. Do you think that individual talent or family background is more important in creating these social differences?

2. Sit down with parents, grandparents, or other relatives and assess the social position of your family over the last three generations. Has social mobility taken place? How much? Why?

3. During an evening of television viewing, assess the social class level of the characters you see on various shows. In each case, explain why you assign someone a particular social position. Do you find many clearly upper-class people? Middle-class people? Working-class people? Poor people? Describe the patterns you find.

MAKING THE GRADE

CHAPTER 8 Social Stratification

What Is Social Stratification?

SOCIAL STRATIFICATION is a system by which a society ranks categories of people in a hierarchy, so that some people have more money, power, and prestige than others. Social stratification

- is a trait of society, not simply a reflection of individual differences
- carries over from one generation to the next
- is supported by a system of cultural beliefs that defines certain kinds of inequality as just
- takes two general forms: caste systems and class systems

pp. 190–91

CASTE SYSTEMS

- are based on birth (ascription)
- permit little or no social mobility
- shape a person's entire life, including occupation and marriage
- are common in traditional, agrarian societies

p. 191

CLASS SYSTEMS

- are based on both birth (ascription) and **meritocracy** (individual achievement)
- permit some social mobility
- are common in modern industrial and post-industrial societies

pp. 191–95

social stratification (p. 190) a system by which a society ranks categories of people in a hierarchy

social mobility (p. 190) a change in position within the social hierarchy

caste system (p. 191) social stratification based on ascription, or birth

class system (p. 191) social stratification based on both birth and individual achievement

meritocracy (p. 192) social stratification based on personal merit

status consistency (p. 193) the degree of uniformity in a person's social standing across various dimensions of social inequality

structural social mobility (p. 195) a shift in the social position of large numbers of people due more to changes in society itself than to individual efforts

ideology (p. 196) cultural beliefs that justify particular social arrangements, including patterns of inequality

The Functions of Social Stratification

The **STRUCTURAL-FUNCTIONAL APPROACH** points to ways social stratification helps society operate.

- The **Davis-Moore thesis** states that social stratification is universal because of its functional consequences.
- In caste systems, people are rewarded for performing the duties of their position at birth.
- In class systems, unequal rewards attract the ablest people to the most important jobs and encourage effort.

pp. 196–98

The **SOCIAL-CONFLICT APPROACH** claims that stratification divides societies into classes, benefiting some categories of people at the expense of others and causing social conflict.

- Karl Marx claimed that capitalism places economic production under the ownership of capitalists, who exploit the proletarians who sell their labour for wages.
- Max Weber identified three distinct dimensions of social stratification: economic class, social status or prestige, and power. Conflict exists between people at various positions on a multi-dimensional hierarchy of socio-economic status (SES).

pp. 198–201

The **SYMBOLIC-INTERACTION APPROACH**, a micro-level analysis, explains that we size people up by looking for clues to their social standing. Conspicuous consumption refers to buying and displaying products that make a "statement" about one's position in the social class system. Most people tend to socialize with others whose social standing is similar to their own.

pp. 201–02

Davis-Moore thesis (p. 197) the functional analysis claiming that social stratification has beneficial consequences for the operation of society

capitalists (p. 198) people who own and operate factories and other businesses in pursuit of profits

proletarians (p. 198) people who sell their labour for wages

alienation (p. 199) the experience of isolation and misery resulting from powerlessness

blue-collar occupations (p. 199) lower-prestige jobs that involve mostly manual labour

white-collar occupations (p. 199) higher-prestige jobs that involve mostly mental activity

socio-economic status (SES) (p. 200) a composite ranking based on various dimensions of social inequality

conspicuous consumption (p. 201) buying and using products because of the "statement" they make about social position

See the Applying Theory table on page 201.

Social Stratification and Technology: A Global Perspective

Hunting and Gathering → **Horticultural and Pastoral** → **Agrarian** → **Industrial** → **Post-industrial**

- Gerhard Lenski explains that advancing technology initially increases social stratification, which is most intense in agrarian societies.

p. 202

- Industrialization reverses the trend, reducing social stratification.

pp. 202–03

- In post-industrial societies, social stratification again increases.

p. 203

See the Kuznets curve (Figure 8–2 on page 203).

Inequality in Canada

SOCIAL STRATIFICATION involves many dimensions:

- Income: After taxes and transfer payments, the richest 20 percent of families in 2009 received $5.60 for every $1 received by the 20 percent with the lowest income.
- Wealth: The total value of all assets minus debts, wealth is distributed more unequally than income, with the richest 5 percent of families holding 40 percent of all wealth.
- Power: Income and wealth are important sources of power.
- Prestige: Work generates not only income but also prestige. White-collar jobs generally offer more income and prestige than blue-collar jobs. Many lower-prestige jobs are performed by women and people of colour.
- Family ancestry, race and ethnicity, and gender all affect social standing.

pp. 203–07

income (p. 203) earnings from work or investments

wealth (p. 205) the total value of money and other assets, minus outstanding debts

Social Classes in Canada

UPPER CLASS—5 percent of the population. Most members of the upper-upper class, or "old rich," inherited their wealth; the lower-upper class, or "new rich," work at high-paying jobs.
MIDDLE CLASS—40 to 45 percent of the population. People in the upper-middle class have significant wealth; average-middles have less prestige and do white-collar work, and most attend college or university.
WORKING CLASS—30 to 35 percent of the population. People in the lower-middle class do blue-collar work; only about one-third of children attend college or university.
LOWER CLASS—20 percent of the population. Most people in the lower class lack financial security because of low income; many live below the poverty line; half do not complete high school.

pp. 208–10

intragenerational social mobility (p. 211) a change in social position occurring during a person's lifetime

intergenerational social mobility (p. 211) upward or downward social mobility of children in relation to their parents

- People with higher social standing generally have better health, hold certain values and political attitudes, and pass on advantages in the form of "cultural capital" to their children.
- Social mobility is common in Canada, as it is in other high-income countries, but typically only small changes occur from one generation to the next.
- Because of the expansion of the global economy, the richest families now earn more than ever; families near the bottom of the class system have seen only small increases.

pp. 210–17

relative poverty (p. 217) the lack of resources of some people in relation to those who have more

absolute poverty (p. 217) a lack of resources that is life-threatening

feminization of poverty (p. 218) the trend of women making up an increasing proportion of the poor

Poverty in Canada

POVERTY PROFILE
- The government classified 9.6 percent of the Canadian population as poor.
- About 634 000 children younger than age 18 (9.5 percent of total) lived in low-income families in 2009.
- Poverty rates for visible minorities and Aboriginals are much higher than the national average.
- The "feminization of poverty" means that more poor families are headed by women.
- About 31 percent of all low-income families are the "working poor" who are employed at least part time but do not earn enough to lift a family of four above the poverty line.
- It is estimated that there are currently 150 000 homeless living on the streets in cities across Canada.

pp. 217–18, 220–21

EXPLANATIONS OF POVERTY
- Blame individuals: The culture of poverty thesis states that poverty is caused by shortcomings in the poor themselves (Oscar Lewis).
- Blame society: Poverty is caused by society's unequal distribution of wealth and lack of good jobs (William Julius Wilson).

pp. 218–20

MySocLab

Visit MySocLab at www.mysoclab.com to access a variety of online resources that will help you to prepare for tests and to apply your knowledge, including
- an eText
- videos
- self-grading quizzes
- glossary flashcards

9 Global Stratification

- What share of the world's people live in absolute poverty?

- Why are some of the world's countries so rich and others so poor?

- Are high-income nations making global poverty better or worse? How?

This chapter shifts the focus from inequality within Canada to inequality in the world as a whole. The chapter begins by describing global inequality and then provides two theoretical models that explain global stratification.

More than a thousand workers were busily sewing together polo shirts on the fourth floor of the garment factory in Narsingdi, a small town about 50 kilometres northeast of Bangladesh's capital city of Dhaka. The thumping of hundreds of sewing machines produced a steady roar throughout the long working day.

But in an instant everything changed when an electric gun used to shoot spot remover onto stained fabric gave off a spark, which ignited the flammable liquid. Suddenly, a work table burst into flames. People rushed to smother the fire with shirts, but there was no stopping the blaze: In a room filled with combustible materials, the flames spread quickly.

The workers scrambled toward the narrow staircase that led to the street. At the bottom, however, the human wave pouring down the steep steps collided with a folding metal gate across the doorway that was kept locked to prevent workers from leaving during working hours. Panicked, the people turned, only to be pushed back by the hundreds behind them. In a single terrifying minute of screaming voices, thrusting legs, and pounding hearts, dozens were crushed and trampled. By the time the gates were opened and the fire was put out, 52 garment workers lay dead.

Garment factories like this one are big business in Bangladesh, where clothing accounts for 75 percent of the country's total economic exports. Half of these garments end up in stores in North America. The reason so much of the clothing we buy is made in low-income countries like Bangladesh is simple economics—Bangladeshi garment workers labour for as many as 12 hours a day, often 7 days a week, and most earn the minimum wage of only $25 a month—as little as 12 cents an hour, which is just a few percent of what a garment worker makes in Canada.

Tanveer Chowdhury manages this garment factory, which his family owns. Speaking to reporters, he complained bitterly about the tragedy. "This fire has cost me $586 373, and that does not include $70 000 for machinery and $20 000 for furniture. I made commitments to meet deadlines, and I still have the deadlines. I am now paying for air freight at $10 a dozen when I should be shipping by sea at 87 cents a dozen."

There was one other cost Chowdhury did not mention. To compensate families for the loss of their loved ones in the fire, the factory eventually agreed to pay $1952 per person. In Bangladesh, life—like labour—is cheap (based on Bearak, 2001, Bajaj, 2010, and World Bank, 2010).

Garment workers in Bangladesh are part of the roughly 1.4 billion of the world's people who work hard every day and yet remain poor. As this chapter explains, although poverty is a reality in Canada and other nations, the greatest social inequality is not *within* nations but *between* them (Chen & Ravallion, 2008; Goesling, 2001). We can understand the full dimensions of poverty only by exploring **global stratification**, *patterns of social inequality in the world as a whole.*

Global Stratification: An Overview

Chapter 8 ("Social Stratification") described inequality in Canada. In global perspective, however, social stratification is far greater. The left pie chart in Figure 9–1 (on page 228) divides the world's total income by quintiles (fifths) of the population. Recall from

global stratification (p. 226) patterns of social inequality in the world as a whole

high-income countries (p. 228) nations with the highest overall standards of living

middle-income countries (p. 228) nations with a standard of living about average for the world as a whole

low-income countries (p. 228) nations with a low standard of living in which most people are poor

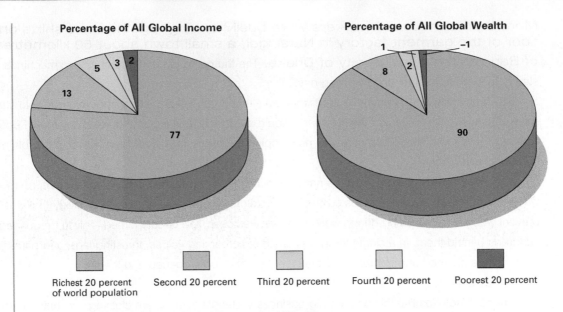

Percentage of All Global Income

Percentage of All Global Wealth

Richest 20 percent of world population — Second 20 percent — Third 20 percent — Fourth 20 percent — Poorest 20 percent

FIGURE 9–1   Distribution of Global Income and Wealth

Global income is very unequal, with the richest 20 percent of the world's people earning almost 40 times as much as the poorest 20 percent. Global wealth is even more unequally divided, with the richest 20 percent owning 85 percent of private wealth and the poorest half of the world's people having barely anything at all.

Sources: Milanovic (2009) and Davies et al. (2010).

Chapter 8 that the richest 20 percent of the Canadian population with the highest incomes earns about 48 percent of the national income (see Figure 8–3 on page 205). The richest 20 percent of the global population, however, receives about 77 percent of world income. At the other extreme, the poorest 20 percent of the Canadian population earns about 2.5 percent of our national income; the poorest fifth of the world's people similarly struggles to survive on just 2 percent of global income (Milanovic, 2008). Remember that Figure 8–3 also shows the impact of progressive taxation and government support to low-income earners. Because of these policies, the 20 percent of the Canadian population with the lowest income earns a little more than 7 percent of the national income after transfer payment and taxes.

In terms of wealth, as the pie chart at the right in Figure 9–1 shows, global inequality is even greater. A rough estimate is that the richest 20 percent of the world's adults own about 85 percent of the planet's wealth. According to the most recent estimates from 2000, about half of all wealth is owned by less than 5 percent of the world's adult population; about 30 percent is owned by the richest 1 percent. On the other hand, the poorest half of the world's adults owned less than 2 percent of all global wealth. In terms of dollars, half of the world's adults have less than $8700 in total wealth,

far less than the $45 800 in wealth for the typical Canadian adult (Davies et al., 2010). Note that the amounts for income and wealth presented here are based on figures adjusted for the different costs of goods and services in different countries. This adjustment has a great impact on relative income and wealth. A traveller experiences this when noting that a Canadian dollar is worth more in Phnom Penh than in Saskatoon.

Because some countries are so much richer than others, even people in Canada with income below the government's poverty line live far better than the majority of people on the planet. The average person in a wealthy nation such as Canada is extremely well off by world standards. Any one of the world's richest people (in 2009, the world's three richest people—Bill Gates and Warren Buffett in the United States and Carlos Slim Helu in Mexico— were *each* worth more than $35 billion) has more personal wealth than the total economic output of the world's 34 poorest *countries* (Kroll, Miller, & Serafin, 2009; United Nations Development Programme, 2008).

A Word about Terminology

Classifying the 214 nations on Earth into categories ignores many striking differences. These nations have rich and varied histories,

Japan (*above, left*) is among the world's high-income countries, in which industrial technology and economic expansion have produced material prosperity. The presence of market forces is evident in this view of downtown Tokyo. India (*above, right*) has recently become one of the world's middle-income countries. An increasing number of motor vehicles fill city streets. Ethiopia (*left*) is among the world's low-income countries. As the photograph suggests, these nations have limited economic development and rapidly increasing populations. The result is widespread poverty.

speak different languages, and take pride in their distinctive cultures. However, various models have been developed that classify countries in order to study global stratification (U.S. Department of State, 2008).

One global model, developed after World War II, labelled the rich, industrial countries the "First World"; the less industrialized, socialist countries the "Second World"; and the non-industrialized, poor countries the "Third World." But the "three worlds" model is less useful today. For one thing, it was a product of Cold War politics, when the capitalist West (the First World) faced off against the socialist East (the Second World) while other nations (the Third World) remained more or less on the sidelines. But the sweeping changes in Eastern Europe and the collapse of the Soviet Union in the early 1990s mean that a distinctive Second World no longer exists.

Another problem is that the "three worlds" model lumped together more than 100 countries as the Third World. In reality, some better-off nations of the Third World (such as Chile in South America) have 13 times the per-person productivity seen in the poorest countries of the world (such as Ethiopia in East Africa).

These facts call for a modestly revised system of classification. The 69 **high-income countries** are defined as the *nations with the highest overall standards of living*. These nations have a per capita gross national income (GNI) greater than $18 000. The world's 101 **middle-income countries** are not as rich; they are *nations with a standard of living about average for the world as a whole*. Their per capita GNI is less than $18 000 but greater than $2000. The remaining 43 **low-income countries** are *nations with a low standard of living in which most people are poor*. In these nations, per capita GNI is less than $2000.

When natural disasters strike high-income nations, property damage may be great, but the loss of life is relatively low. For example, the 2010 earthquake in Chile (*left*) forced people from damaged homes but the death toll for the entire nation was about 400. By contrast, when another earthquake hit Haiti in 2010 (*right*), less well-built structures came tumbling down, resulting in more than 100 000 deaths.

This model has two advantages over the "three worlds" system. First, it focuses on economic development rather than political system (capitalist or socialist). Second, it gives a better picture of the relative economic development of various countries because it does not lump together all lower-income nations into a single "Third World."

When ranking countries, keep in mind that there is social stratification within every nation. In Bangladesh, for example, members of the Chowdhury family, who own the garment factory described in the chapter-opening story, earn as much as $1 million per year, which is several thousand times more than one of their workers earns. The full extent of global inequality is even greater, because the wealthiest people in high-income countries such as Canada live worlds apart from the poorest people in low-income countries such as Bangladesh, Haiti, and Sudan.

High-Income Countries

In nations where the Industrial Revolution first took place more than two centuries ago, productivity increased more than a hundredfold. To understand the power of industrial and computer technology, consider that any one of the high-income nations of Europe (such as the United Kingdom, France, Germany, or Italy) is more productive than the whole continent of Africa south of the Sahara, where industrialization and internet connections are limited.

Global Map 9–1 on page 231 shows that the high-income nations of the world include Canada, the United States, the nations of Western Europe, Israel, Saudi Arabia, Singapore, Hong Kong (part of the People's Republic of China), Japan, South Korea, the Russian Federation, Australia, and New Zealand.

These countries cover roughly 39 percent of Earth's land area, including parts of five continents, and lie mostly in the Northern Hemisphere. In 2010, the population of these nations was about 1.2 billion, or about 18 percent of the world's people. About three-fourths of the people in high-income countries live in or near cities (Population Reference Bureau, 2010; World Bank, 2011a, 2011c).

Significant cultural differences exist among high-income countries; for example, the nations of Europe recognize more than 30 official languages. But these societies all produce enough economic goods and services to enable their people to lead comfortable material lives. Per capita annual income (that is, average income per person per year) ranges from about $18 000 annually (in the Russian Federation and Poland) to more than $50 000 annually (in Kuwait and Norway). In fact, the people who live in high-income countries enjoy 60 percent of the world's total income (World Bank, 2011b).

Keep in mind that high-income countries have many low-income people. The Thinking about Diversity box on page 232 profiles the striking poverty that exists in *las colonias* along the southern border of the United States.

Production in high-income nations is capital-intensive. This means that it is based on the use of factories, big machinery, and advanced technology. Most of the largest corporations that design and market computers, as well as most computer users, are located in high-income countries. In addition, high-income countries also control the world's financial markets, so daily events on the stock exchanges of Toronto, New York, London, Frankfurt, and Tokyo affect people throughout the world. In short, high-income nations are very productive because of their advanced technology and also because they control the global economy.

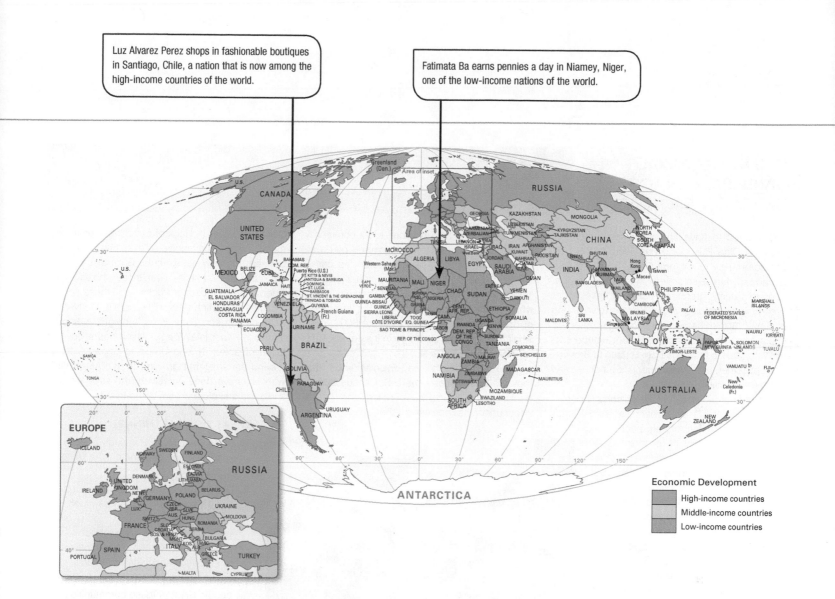

Luz Alvarez Perez shops in fashionable boutiques in Santiago, Chile, a nation that is now among the high-income countries of the world.

Fatimata Ba earns pennies a day in Niamey, Niger, one of the low-income nations of the world.

Economic Development
- High-income countries
- Middle-income countries
- Low-income countries

Window on the World

GLOBAL MAP 9–1 Economic Development in Global Perspective

In high-income countries—including Canada, the United States, the nations of Western Europe, Israel, Saudi Arabia, Australia, the Russian Federation, and Japan—a highly productive economy provides people, on average, with material plenty. Middle-income countries—including most of Latin and South America and Asia—are less economically productive, with a standard of living about average for the world as a whole but far below that of Canada. These nations also have a significant share of poor people who are barely able to feed and house themselves. In the low-income countries of the world, poverty is severe and widespread. Although small numbers of elites live very well in the poorest nations, most people struggle to survive on a small fraction of the income common in Canada.

Note: Data for this map are provided by the World Bank. Each country's economic productivity is measured in terms of its gross national income (GNI), which is the total value of all the goods and services produced by a country's economy within its borders in a given year plus income from other countries minus income sent to other countries. Dividing each country's GNI by the country's population gives us the per capita (per-person) GNI and allows us to compare the economic performance of countries of different population sizes. High-income countries have a per capita GNI of more than $18 000. Many are far richer than this, however; the figure for Canada is $37 410 and more than $45 000 for the United States. Middle-income countries have a per capita GNI ranging from $2000 to $18 000. Low-income countries have a per capita GNI of less than $2000. Figures used here reflect the United Nations' "purchasing power parities" (PPP) system, which is an estimate of what people can buy using their income in the local economy.

Source: Data from United Nations Development Programme (2010).

Las Colonias: "America's Third World"

"We wanted to have something for ourselves," explains Olga Ruiz, who has lived in the border community of College Park, Texas, for two decades. There is no college in College Park, nor does this dusty stretch of rural land have sewer lines or even running water. Yet this town is one of some 1800 settlements that have sprouted up in southern Texas along the 2000-kilometre border with Mexico that runs from El Paso to Brownsville. Together, these settlements are home to an estimated 1 million people.

Many people speak of *las colonias* (Spanish for "the colonies") as "America's Third World" because these desperately poor communities look much like their counterparts in Mexico or in many other middle- or low-income nations. But almost all of the people living in the *colonias* are Latino, 85 percent of them are legal residents, and more than half are U.S. citizens.

Anastacia Ledesma, 72 years old, moved to a *colonia* called Sparks more than 40 years ago. Born in Mexico, Ledesma married a Texas man, and together they paid $200 for a quarter-acre lot in a new border community. For months, they camped out on their land. Step by step, however, they invested their labour and their money to build a modest

house. Not until 1995 did their small community get running water—a service promised by developers years earlier. After the water line came, things changed more than they had expected. "When we got water," recalls Ledesma, "that's when so many people came in." The population of Sparks quickly doubled to about 3000, overwhelming the water supply so that sometimes the faucet does not run at all.

The residents of the *colonias* know that they are poor. Indeed, the U.S. Census Bureau declared the county surrounding one border community the poorest in the United States.

Concerned over the lack of basic services in so many of these communities, Texas officials have banned any new settlements. But most of the people who move here—even those who start off sleeping in their cars or trucks—see these communities as the first step on the path to the North American dream. Oscar Solis, a neighbourhood leader in Panorama Village, which has a population of about 150, is proud to show visitors around the small but growing town. "All of this work we have done ourselves," he says with a smile, "to make our dream come true."

WHAT DO YOU THINK?

1. Are you surprised that such poverty exists in a rich country like the United States? Why or why not?

2. Does Canada have similar communities where poverty rates look much like communities in many middle- or low-income nations? How about Vancouver's Downtown Eastside and many of our Aboriginal communities?

3. To what extent do you think the people living in these communities will have their "dreams come true"? Explain your answer.

Source: Based on Schaffer (2002).

Middle-Income Countries

Middle-income countries have per capita annual incomes ranging from $2000 to $18 000. Typically, 55 to 60 percent of the people in middle-income countries live in or near cities, and industrial jobs are common. The remaining 40 to 45 percent of the people live in rural areas, where most are poor and lack access to schools, medical care, adequate housing, and even safe drinking water.

Looking at Global Map 9–1, we see that 101 of the world's nations fall in the middle-income category. At the high end are Lithuania and Latvia (Europe), Mexico (North America), and Argentina, (South America), where annual income is greater than $14 000. At the low end are Nicaragua (Latin America), Congo (Africa), Laos and Vietnam (Asia), with less than $3000 annually in per capita income.

One cluster of middle-income nations used to be part of the Second World. These countries, found in Eastern Europe and Western Asia, had mostly socialist economies until popular revolts between 1989 and 1991 swept their governments aside. Since then, these nations have introduced more free-market economies. These middle-income countries include Belarus and Ukraine, as well as Kazakhstan, Georgia, and Turkmenistan.

Other middle-income countries include countries in South America and Namibia and Angola in Africa. Both India and the People's Republic of China have entered the middle-income category, which now includes much of Asia.

Taken together, middle-income countries span roughly 46 percent of the world's land area and are home to about 4.6 billion people, or about 68 percent of humanity. Some very large countries (such as China) are far less crowded than others (such as El Salvador), but compared to high-income countries, these societies are densely populated (Population Reference Bureau, 2010; World Bank, 2009).

Low-Income Countries

Low-income countries, where most people are very poor, are mostly agrarian societies with some industry. Forty-three low-income nations, identified on Global Map 9–1, are spread across Central and East Africa and Asia. Low-income countries cover 15 percent of the planet's land area and are home to 14 percent of its people. Population density is generally high, although it is greater in Asian countries (such as Bangladesh and Pakistan) than in Central African nations (such as Chad and the Democratic Republic of the Congo).

In low-income countries, about one-third of the people live in cities; most inhabit villages and farms as their ancestors have done for centuries. In fact, half of the world's people are farmers, most of whom follow cultural traditions. With limited industrial technology, they cannot be very productive—one reason that many endure severe poverty. Hunger, disease, and unsafe housing shape the lives of the world's poorest people.

Those of us who live in high-income nations such as Canada find it hard to understand the scope of human need in much of the world. From time to time, televised pictures of famine in countries such as Ethiopia and Bangladesh give us shocking glimpses into the poverty that makes every day a life-and-death struggle for many people in low-income nations. Behind these images lie cultural, historical, and economic forces that we will explore in the remainder of this chapter.

Global Wealth and Poverty

October 14, Manila, Philippines. What caught my eye was how clean she was—a girl no more than seven or eight years old, wearing a freshly laundered dress and with her hair carefully combed. She followed us with her eyes: Camera-toting North Americans stand out here, in one of the poorest neighbourhoods in the entire world.

Fed by methane from the decomposing garbage, the fires never go out on Smokey Mountain, the vast garbage dump on the north side of Manila. Smoke covers the hills of refuse like a thick fog. But Smokey Mountain is more than a dump; it is a neighbourhood that is home to thousands of people. It is hard to imagine a setting more hostile to human life. Amid the smoke and the squalor, men and women do what they can to survive. They pick plastic bags from the garbage and wash them in the river, and they collect cardboard boxes or anything else they can sell. What chance do their children have, coming from families that earn only a few hundred dollars a year, with hardly any opportunity for schooling, year after

year, breathing this foul air? Against this backdrop of human tragedy, one lovely little girl has put on a fresh dress and gone out to play.

Now our taxi driver threads his way through heavy traffic as we head for the other side of Manila. The change is amazing: The smoke and smell of the dump give way to neighbourhoods that could be in Halifax or Victoria. A cluster of yachts floats on the bay in the distance. No more rutted streets; now we glide quietly along wide boulevards lined with trees and filled with expensive European cars. We pass shopping plazas, upscale hotels, and high-rise office buildings. Every block or so we see the gated entrance to an exclusive residential community with security guards standing watch. Here, in large, air-conditioned homes, the rich of Manila live—and many of the poor work.

Low-income nations are home to some rich and many poor people. The fact that most people live with incomes of a few hundred dollars a year means that the burden of poverty is far greater than among the poor of Canada. This is not to suggest that Canadian poverty is a minor problem. In so rich a country, too little food, substandard housing, and tens of thousands who are homeless—many of whom are children—amount to a national tragedy (Hwang, 2001).

The Severity of Poverty

Poverty in low-income countries is more severe than it is in high-income countries. A key reason that quality of life differs so much around the world is that economic productivity is lowest in precisely the regions where population growth is highest. Figure 9–2 on page 234 shows the proportion of world population and global income for countries at each level of economic development. High-income countries are by far the most advantaged, with 60 percent of global income supporting just 18 percent of humanity. In middle-income nations, 68 percent of the world's people earn 39 percent of global income. This leaves 14 percent of the planet's population with just 1.5 percent of global income (World Bank, 2011a, 2011b). For every dollar received by an individual in a low-income country, someone in a high-income nation takes home $30.

Table 9–1 on page 234 shows the extent of wealth and well-being in specific countries around the world. The first column of figures gives the GNI for a number of high-, middle-, and low-income countries. The United States, a large industrial nation, had a 2010 GNI of more than $14 trillion; Japan's GNI that same year approached $4.5 trillion and Canada's GNI was $1.3 trillion. A comparison of GNI figures shows that the world's richest nations are thousands of times more productive than the poorest countries.

The second column of figures in Table 9–1 divides GNI by the entire population size to give an estimate of what people can buy using their income in the local economy. The per capita GNI for the richest high-income countries, including Norway, Canada, and the United States, is very high, exceeding $35 000. For middle-income

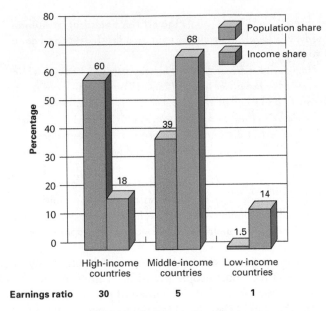

FIGURE 9–2 The Relative Share of Income and Population by Level of Economic Development

For every dollar earned by people in low-income countries, people in high-income countries earn $60.

Source: Estimated based on data from World Bank (2011a, 2011b).

TABLE 9–1	Wealth and Well-Being in Global Perspective, 2009		
Country Name	**Gross National Income (PPP $ billions)**	**GNI per Capita (PPP $)**	**Quality of Life Index**
High-Income			
Norway	265	54 880	0.876
Australia	836	38 210	0.864
Canada	1262	37 410	0.812
United States	14 011	45 640	0.799
United Kingdom	2302	37 230	0.766
Korea, Rep.	1331	27 310	0.731
Russian Federation	2604	18 350	0.636
Middle-Income			
Eastern Europe			
Romania	311	14 460	0.675
Bulgaria	97	12 750	0.659
Ukraine	284	6180	0.652
Albania	26	8300	0.627
Latin America			
Uruguay	43	12 900	0.642
Mexico	1514	14 100	0.593
Brazil	1976	10 200	0.509
Asia			
China	9170	6890	0.511
Vietnam	244	2790	0.478
India	3758	3250	0.365
Middle East			
Syrian Arab Republic	97	4620	0.467
Egypt, Arab Rep.	471	5680	0.449
Africa			
Tunisia	81	7810	0.511
South Africa	496	10 050	0.411
Namibia	14	6350	0.338
Nigeria	321	2070	0.246
Angola	96	5190	0.242
Low-Income			
Asia			
Bangladesh	251	1550	0.331
Nepal	35	1180	0.292
Africa			
Tanzania	57	1350	0.285
Ethiopia	77	930	0.216
Mozambique	20	880	0.155
World	71 845	10 604.097	0.489

*These data are based on the United Nations' purchasing power parity (PPP) calculations, which avoid currency rate distortion by showing the local purchasing power of incomes in each domestic currency.

Sources: World Bank (2009, 2011b, 2011d) and United Nations Development Programme (2009).

countries, such as Nigeria, Mexico, and Romania, the figures range from less than $3000 in Nigeria to more than $14 000 in Mexico and Romania. In the world's low-income countries, per capita GNI is just a few hundred dollars. In Nepal or Ethiopia, a typical person labours all year to make what the average worker in Canada earns in a week.

The last column of Table 9–1 is a measure of quality of life in the various nations. This index, calculated by the United Nations, combines income, education (extent of adult literacy and average years of schooling), and longevity (how long people typically live) and adjusts for inequality in a country to arrive at a number reflecting the quality of life of the average person. Index values are decimals that fall between extremes of 1 (highest) and 0 (lowest). By this calculation, Norwegians enjoy the highest quality of life (.876), with Canadians close behind (.812). At the other extreme, people in the African nation of Mozambique have the lowest quality of life (.155).

Relative versus Absolute Poverty

The distinction between relative and absolute poverty, made in Chapter 8 ("Social Stratification"), has an important application to global inequality. People living in high-income countries generally focus on *relative poverty*, meaning that some people lack resources that are taken for granted by others. By definition, relative poverty exists in every society, rich or poor.

Millions of children fend for themselves every day on city streets in low- and middle-income countries where many fall victim to disease, drug abuse, and violence. What do you think must be done to put an end to scenes like this one in Kolkata, India?

risk of disease (Chen & Ravallion, 2008; United Nations Food and Agriculture Organization, 2010).

The typical adult in a high-income nation such as Canada consumes about 3500 calories a day, which is actually too much and leads to obesity and related health problems. The typical adult in a low-income country not only does more physical labour but consumes just 2500 calories a day. The result is undernourishment: too little food or not enough of the right kinds of food.

In the 10 minutes it takes to read this section of the chapter, about 100 people in the world who are sick and weakened from hunger will die. This amounts to about 25 000 people a day, or 9 million people each year. Clearly, easing world hunger is one of the most serious challenges facing humanity today.

Poverty and Children

Death comes early in poor societies, where families lack adequate food, safe drinking water, secure housing, and access to health care. In the world's low- and middle-income nations, one-third of all children do not receive enough nutrition to be healthy (Levinson & Bassett, 2007).

Poor children live in poor families, and many share in the struggle to get through each day. Organizations fighting child poverty estimate that at least 100 million city children in poor countries beg, steal, sell sex, or work for drug gangs to provide income for their families. Such a life almost always means dropping out of school and puts children at high risk of disease and violence. Many girls, with little or no access to medical assistance, become pregnant, a case of children who cannot support themselves having children of their own.

Analysts also estimate that millions of children in low- and middle-income countries leave their families altogether, sleeping and living on the streets as best they can or perhaps trying to migrate to Canada and other high-income countries. Roughly half of all street children are found in Latin American cities such as Mexico City and Rio de Janeiro, where half of all children grow up in poverty. Many people in Canada know these cities as exotic travel destinations, but they are also home to thousands of children living in makeshift huts, under bridges, or in alleyways (Collymore, 2002; Leopold, 2007; United Nations Development Programme, 2000).

In cities around the world, officials engage in "urban cleansing," rounding up street children in an effort to make the city more attractive to visitors. As Seeing Sociology in the News on page 236 explains, these efforts are especially common when cities host major events such as the World Cup in soccer.

Poverty and Women

In high-income societies, a lot of the work that women do is undervalued, underpaid, or not paid at all. In low- and middle-income societies, women face even greater disadvantages. Most of the people who

More important in global perspective, however, is *absolute poverty*, a lack of resources that is life-threatening. Human beings in absolute poverty lack the nutrition necessary for health and long-term survival. To be sure, some absolute poverty exists in Canada. But such immediately life-threatening poverty strikes only a small proportion of the Canadian population; in low-income countries, by contrast, one-third or even half of the people are in desperate need.

Because absolute poverty is deadly, one global indicator of this problem is the median age at death. In high-income countries, more than two-thirds of all people die after the age of 70, but in low-income countries, more than a third of all deaths occur among children under the age of 14. In the world's poorest low-income nations, half of all children never live to the age of 10 (World Health Organization, 2008c).

The Extent of Poverty

Poverty in low-income countries is more widespread than it is in high-income nations such as Canada. Chapter 8 ("Social Stratification") noted that the Canadian government officially classifies 9.6 percent of the population as poor. In low-income countries, however, most people live no better than the poor in Canada, and many are far worse off. The high death rates among children in Africa indicate that absolute poverty is greatest there, where 30 percent of the population is malnourished. In the world as a whole, at any given time, 13 percent of the people—more than 1 billion—suffer from chronic hunger, which leaves them less able to work and puts them at high

The Sun

The Child Catchers

BY SHARON HENRY
March 27, 2010

DURBAN, South Africa—It has just gone 10 A.M. and the searing South African sun is beating down, forcing city dwellers to seek shade under newly planted palm trees.

Only the many teams of workmen preparing Durban for the gaze of World Cup visitors must continue their heavy toil in temperatures exceeding 30°C.

With seventy-six days to go before the eyes of the world fall upon this city, time is running out.

Above the whirr of drills and heavy-duty diggers, a different and more harrowing sound begins to emerge from behind the wire mesh covering the windows of a parked police van.

On closer inspection, tiny fingers can be seen reaching out desperately through the holes, as the voices inside beg for help.

"Please, please come. We will die in this heat," a small voice pleads before collapsing into pitiful sobs.

Shockingly, the van contains eight street children aged nine to fifteen.

In the build-up to the biggest football show on earth, these helpless youngsters are being rounded up each day by police and dumped miles outside Durban in a bid to keep the city looking pristine.

To an extent it is a pointless exercise, as the children simply embark on the 24-hour trek back to Durban as soon as they are dumped.

To the outside world, they appear in desperate need of rehabilitation. But to Durban Municipal Police they are unsightly vermin in need of urgent removal.

The Sun witnessed the police's heavy-handed tactics firsthand, less than a day after arriving in Durban last week.

Sun photographer Marc Giddings was detained and interrogated by police for more than two hours after taking pictures of children locked in the back of a van without food or water.

Inside the city's Metropolitan police station, he was shocked to discover a poster on display entitled "Operation Beach Clean-Up."

It blatantly revealed police tactics in the build-up to the World Cup. Street children were listed alongside vagrants and debris on a register of rubbish to be removed from the city centre. . . .

Later we traced one of the girls who had been detained in the police truck.

Her harrowing story reveals a different side to the sun-and-surf South Africa that its government officials would like World Cup fans to buy into.

It is more in tune with official figures that show one in four South Africans are jobless and live daily on less than 84p [C$1.30].

Nobuhle Sishi is still only fifteen but she has lived on the streets of Durban for two years. . . .

She said, "Life was always very difficult for us because we are very poor and Mum and Dad's drinking meant we all had to fend for ourselves and raise each other. And there was a lot of violence that we all witnessed daily.

"But the hardest thing for me was when I was raped by someone in our village when I was just thirteen. After that I just felt I had to get away—anywhere was better than being at home."

Nobuhle sprinted away barefoot from her family home—a corrugated iron shack—and hitched twenty miles into Durban, where other street children told her to make her home in the Emagghumeri area.

She said, "At first I thought it would be a better life but I soon realised the truth. At night, I had just a small blanket to sleep under and I was regularly beaten up and abused by men."

Shockingly, Nobuhle has been raped a further five times on the streets. It is estimated that 500,000 rapes are committed annually in South Africa and 52 people are murdered every day.

Nobuhle added, "Who would seriously choose a life on the streets? The only way to survive it is by sniffing pots of glue that dull every feeling. But I have seen the terrible effects it has had on my friends, crippling their joints so they can no longer walk."

Recalling the round-up witnessed by *The Sun*, Nobuhle said, "The police pulled up in a van and dragged us into it from across the street.

"Then they beat us with sticks and sprayed pepper in our faces until our chests felt like they were on fire. On this occasion we were driven to the police station and kept with adult criminals in the back of the van while the sun was beating down on us.

"At other times, the police drive us round the city all day before taking us out to townships far away and dumping us.

"Sometimes it takes us a whole night and day to walk back to the city, and then the whole round-up process begins again the next day. It has been getting more and more frequent in recent weeks."

As a temporary measure, the street charity Umthombo has rescued Nobuhle and taken her back to her family home, where social workers are monitoring her progress.

They say she will be safer there during the period of intense pre–World Cup police activity.

But Nobuhle said, "I don't know how long I will be able to stay. . . . All I wish for is a space. . . where I can go to school. I would like to learn computers and become a teacher so I can help other children to avoid a life of misery." . . .

WHAT DO YOU THINK?

1. Does it surprise you that, in cities around the world, officials "clean up" evidence of poverty, especially when events attract the eyes of the world? Can you point to other examples of this pattern? How about during the XXI Olympic Winter Games in Vancouver, British Columbia?

2. How would you respond to the existence of street children in cities such as Durban?

3. Do you think that street children are the problem or are they a symptom of larger problems in a society? Explain.

Source: "The Child Catchers" by Sharon Henry from *The Sun*, March 27, 2010, copyright © 2010 *The Sun*. Reprinted by permission of News International Trading Ltd., nisyndication.com

work under poor or even dangerous conditions in sweatshops like the one described in the opening to this chapter are girls and women.

To make matters worse, in many low- and middle-income nations, tradition keeps women out of many jobs. In Bangladesh, for example, women work in garment factories because that nation's conservative Muslim religious norms bar them from most other paid work and limit their opportunities for advanced schooling (Bearak, 2001). Traditional norms also give women primary responsibility for child rearing and maintaining the household. As a result, many of the world's girls and women are overworked and underpaid or receive no remuneration for their substantial efforts. One United Nations study (UNICEF, 2004) concluded that, worldwide, females perform 66 percent of all work and produce 50 percent of all food but earn just 10 percent of all income and own only 1 percent of all wealth. It is no surprise, then, that about 70 percent of the world's 1.4 billion people living near absolute poverty are females (Moghadam, 2005; UNICEF, 2004).

Finally, most girls and women in low-income and many middle-income countries receive inadequate reproductive health care. Limited access to birth control keeps mothers at home with their children, keeps the birth rate high, and limits the economic production of the country. In addition, the world's poorest women typically give birth without help from trained health care personnel. Figure 9–3 draws a stark contrast between low- and high-income countries in this regard.

Slavery

Low- and middle-income countries have many problems in addition to hunger, including illiteracy, warfare, and slavery. The British Empire, including what then comprised Canada at the time, banned slavery in 1833, followed by the United States in 1865. But slavery is a reality for at least 12 million men, women, and children, and as many as 200 million people (about 3 percent of humanity) live today in conditions that come close to slavery (Anti-Slavery International, 2008; U.S. Department of Labor, 2009c).

Anti-Slavery International (ASI) describes four types of slavery. First is *chattel slavery*, in which one person owns another. In spite of the fact that this practice is against the law almost everywhere, about 27 million people fall into this category. The buying and selling of slaves still takes place in many countries in Asia, the Middle East, and especially Africa. The Thinking Globally box on page 238 describes the reality of one slave's life in the African nation of Mauritania.

A second, more common form of bondage is *child slavery*, in which desperately poor families let their children take to the streets to do what they can to survive. The International Labour Organization estimates that more than 200 million children are at work, at least 8 million of whom are in forced and hazardous forms of labour. In 2009, more than 100 goods that Canadians consume

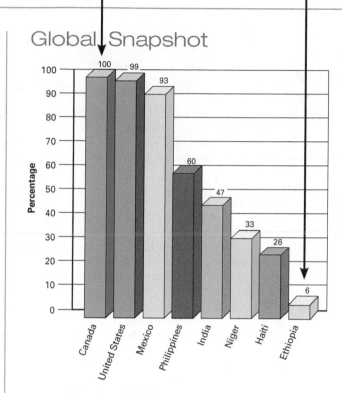

Compared to a woman in Canada, an Ethiopian woman is far less likely to give birth with the help of health professionals and is much more likely to die in childbirth.

Global Snapshot

FIGURE 9–3 Percentage of Births Attended by Skilled Health Staff

In Canada, most women give birth with the help of medical professionals or certified midwives and nurse practitioners, but this is usually not the case in low-income nations.

Source: World Bank (2009).

routinely—including cotton, sugarcane, tobacco, and coffee—were produced in more than 50 nations with forced labour, mostly by children.

Third, *debt bondage* is the practice by which employers hold workers captive by paying them too little to meet their debts. In this case, workers receive a wage, but it is too small to cover the food and housing provided by the employer; for practical purposes, they are enslaved. Many sweatshop workers in low-income nations fall into this category.

Fourth, *servile forms of marriage* may also amount to slavery. In India, Thailand, and some African nations, families marry off women against their will. Many end up as slaves to their husband's family; some are forced into sex work against their will.

One additional form of slavery is *human trafficking*, the movement of men, women, and children from one place to another for the purpose of performing forced labour. In many cases, women or men are brought to a new country on the promise of a job and then find themselves held captive, forced to become labourers with few rights. In other cases, "parents" adopt children from another

Fatma Mint Mamadou is a young woman living in North Africa's Islamic Republic of Mauritania. Asked her age, she pauses, smiles, and shakes her head. She has no idea when she was born. Nor can she read or write. What she knows is tending camels, herding sheep, hauling bags of water, sweeping, and serving tea to her owners. This young woman is one of perhaps 90 000 slaves in Mauritania.

In the central region of this nation, having very dark skin almost always means being a slave to an Arab owner. Fatma accepts her situation; she has known nothing else. She explains in a matter-of-fact voice that she is a slave, like her mother before her and her grandmother before that. "Just as God created a camel to be a camel," she shrugs, "he created me to be a slave."

Fatma, her mother, and her brothers and sisters live together in a squatter settlement on the edge of Nouakchott, Mauritania's capital city. Their home is a 3-by-4-metre hut they built from wood scraps and other materials taken from construction sites. The roof is nothing more than a piece of cloth; there is no plumbing or furniture. The nearest water comes from a well a kilometre and a half down the road.

In this region, slavery began more than 500 years ago, about the time Columbus sailed west toward the Americas. As Arab and Berber tribes moved across the African continent spreading Islam, they raided local villages and made slaves of the people, a practice that was continued for dozens of generations. In 1905, the French colonial rulers of Mauritania banned slavery. After the nation gained independence in 1961, the new government reaffirmed the ban. However, slavery was not officially abolished until 1981, and even then it was not made a crime. In 2007, the nation passed legislation making the practice of slavery punishable by up to 10 years in prison, and the government now provides monetary compensation to victims of slavery. But the new laws have done little to change strong traditions. The sad truth is that people like Fatma still have no idea of the concept of "freedom to choose."

The next question is more personal: "Are you and other girls ever raped?" Again, Fatma hesitates. With no hint of emotion, she responds, "Of course, in the night the men come to breed us. Is that what you mean by rape?"

WHAT DO YOU THINK?

1. How does tradition play a part in keeping people in slavery?

2. What might explain the fact that the world still tolerates slavery?

3. Explain the connection between slavery and poverty.

Source: Based on Burkett (1997).

---

country and then force them to work in sweatshops. Such activity is big business: Next to trading in guns and drugs, trading in people brings the greatest profits to organized crime around the world (Orhant, 2002).

In 1948, the United Nations issued the Universal Declaration of Human Rights, which states, "No one shall be held in slavery or servitude; slavery and the slave trade shall be prohibited in all their forms." Unfortunately, more than six decades later, this social evil still exists.

Explanations of Global Poverty

What accounts for severe and widespread poverty in much of the world? The rest of this chapter provides answers to this question using the following facts about low-and middle-income societies:

1. **Technology.** About one-quarter of people in low-income countries farm the land using human muscles or animal power. With such limited energy sources, agricultural production is modest.

2. **Population growth.** As Chapter 15 ("Population, Urbanization, and Environment") explains, the poorest countries have the world's highest birth rates. Despite the death toll from poverty, the populations of many countries in Africa double their numbers every 25 years. In sub-Saharan Africa, 43 percent of the people are under the age of 15. With such a large share of the population just entering the child-bearing years, the wave of population growth will continue to roll into the future. For example, in recent years, the population of Uganda has swelled by more than 3 percent annually, so even with economic development, living standards have fallen (Population Reference Bureau, 2009).

3. **Cultural patterns.** Most low-income and many middle-income countries are usually traditional. People who hold on to long-established ways of life resist change—even change that promises a richer material life.

4. **Social stratification.** Low-income and many middle-income nations distribute their wealth very unequally. Chapter 8 ("Social Stratification") explained that social inequality is greater in agrarian societies than in industrial societies. In Brazil, for example, 75 percent of all farmland is owned by just 4 percent of the people (Bergamo & Camarotti, 1996; Galano, 1998).

colonialism the process by which some nations enrich themselves through political and economic control of other nations

neocolonialism a new form of global power relationships that involves not direct political control but economic exploitation by multinational corporations

multinational corporation a large business that operates in many countries

modernization theory a model of economic and social development that explains global inequality in terms of technological and cultural differences between nations

5. **Gender inequality.** Extreme gender inequality in most low-income and many middle-income nations keeps girls and women from well-paying jobs, and instead rewards having many children. An expanding population, in turn, slows economic development. Many analysts conclude that raising living standards in much of the world depends on improving the social standing of women.

6. **Global power relationships.** A final cause of global poverty lies in the relationships between the nations of the world. Historically, wealth flowed from less-advantaged societies to more-advantaged nations through **colonialism**, *the process by which some nations enrich themselves through political and economic control of other nations.* The countries of Western Europe colonized much of Latin America beginning roughly 500 years ago. Such global exploitation allowed some nations to develop economically at the expense of other nations.

Although 130 former colonies gained their independence during the twentieth century, exploitation continues through **neocolonialism**, *a new form of global power relationships that involves not direct political control but economic exploitation by multinational corporations.* A **multinational corporation** is *a large business that operates in many countries.* Corporate leaders can impose their will on countries in which they do business to create favourable economic conditions, just as colonizers did in the past (Bonanno, Constance, & Lorenz, 2000).

Global Stratification: Theoretical Analysis

There are two major explanations for the unequal distribution of the world's wealth and power: *modernization theory* and *dependency theory.* Each theory suggests a different solution to the suffering of hungry and exploitation of people in much of the world.

Modernization Theory

Modernization theory is *a model of economic and social development that explains global inequality in terms of technological and cultural differences between nations.* Modernization theory, which follows the structural-functional approach, emerged in the 1950s, a time when U.S. society was fascinated with new developments in technology. To showcase the power of protective technology and also to counter the growing influence of the Soviet Union and socialism in much of the world, North American policy-makers drafted a market-based foreign policy that has been with us ever since (Bauer, 1981; Berger, 1986; Firebaugh, 1996; Firebaugh & Sandu, 1998; Rostow, 1960, 1978).

Historical Perspective

Until a few centuries ago, the entire world was poor. Because poverty has been the norm throughout human history, modernization theory proposes that it is *affluence* that demands an explanation.

Affluence came within reach of a growing share of people in Western Europe during the late Middle Ages as world exploration and trade expanded. Soon the Industrial Revolution was under way, transforming first Western Europe and then North America. Industrial technology, together with the spirit of capitalism, created new wealth as never before. At first, this new wealth benefited only a few individuals. But industrial technology was so productive that gradually the living standards of even the poorest people began to improve. Absolute poverty, which had plagued humanity throughout history, was finally in decline.

In high-income countries where the Industrial Revolution began, the standard of living jumped at least fourfold during the twentieth century. As middle-income nations in Asia and Latin America have industrialized, they too have become richer. But with limited industrial technology, low-income countries have changed much less.

The Importance of Culture

Why didn't the Industrial Revolution sweep away poverty the world over? Modernization theory points out that not every society wants to adopt new technology. Doing so takes a cultural environment that emphasizes the benefits of innovation as well as material wealth.

Modernization theory identifies *tradition* as the greatest barrier to economic development. A reverence for the past may discourage people from adopting new technologies that would raise their living standards. Even today, many people—from the Amish in North America to traditional Islamic people in the Middle East to the Semai of Malaysia—oppose new technology because they see it as a threat to their family relationships, customs, and religious beliefs.

Max Weber (1958, orig. 1904–05) found that at the end of the Middle Ages, Western Europe's cultural environment favoured change. As Chapter 13 ("Family and Religion") explains, the Protestant Reformation reshaped traditional Catholic beliefs to generate a progress-oriented way of life. Wealth—looked on with suspicion by the Roman Catholic Church—became a sign of personal virtue, and the growing importance of individualism steadily replaced the traditional emphasis on family and community. These new cultural patterns laid the groundwork for the Industrial Revolution.

Rostow's Stages of Modernization

Modernization theory holds that the door to affluence is open to all. As technological advances spread around the world, all societies should

In high-income nations such as Canada, most parents expect their children to enjoy years of childhood, largely free from the responsibilities of adult life. This is not the case in many nations across Latin America, Africa, and Asia. Poor families depend on whatever income their children can earn, and many children as young as six or seven work full days weaving or performing other kinds of manual labour. Child labour lies behind the low prices of many products imported for sale in this country.

gradually industrialize. According to Walt Rostow (1960, 1978), modernization occurs in four stages:

1. **Traditional stage.** Socialized to honour the past, people in traditional societies cannot easily imagine that life can or should be any different. They therefore build their lives around families and local communities, following well-worn paths that allow little individual freedom or change. Life is often spiritually rich but lacking in material goods.

   A century ago, much of the world was in this initial stage of economic development. Nations such as Bangladesh, Niger, and Somalia are still at the traditional stage and remain poor. Even in countries such as India that have recently joined the ranks of middle-income nations, certain elements of the population have remained highly traditional. The Seeing Sociology in Everyday Life box takes a look at traditional life in India.

2. **Takeoff stage.** As a society shakes off the grip of tradition, people start to use their talents and imagination, sparking economic growth. A market emerges as people produce goods not just for their own use but to trade with others for profit. Greater individualism, a willingness to take risks, and a desire for material goods also take hold, often at the expense of family ties and time-honoured norms and values.

   Great Britain reached takeoff by about 1800, the United States by 1820. Thailand, a middle-income country in eastern Asia, is now in this stage. Such development is typically speeded by progressive influences from rich nations, including foreign aid, the availability of advanced technology and investment capital, and opportunities for schooling abroad.

3. **Drive to technological maturity.** As this stage begins, "growth" is a widely accepted idea that fuels a society's pursuit of higher living standards. A diversified economy drives a population eager to enjoy the benefits of industrial technology. At the same time, people begin to realize (and sometimes regret) that industrialization is weakening traditional family and local community life. Great Britain entered this stage by about 1840, the United States by 1860, and Canada in the early twentieth century. Today, Mexico, the U.S. territory of Puerto Rico, and South Korea are among the nations driving to technological maturity.

   At this stage of development, absolute poverty is greatly reduced. Cities swell with people who have left rural villages in search of economic opportunity. Specialization gives rise to the wide range of jobs that we find in our economy today. An increasing focus on work makes relationships less personal. Growing individualism generates social movements demanding greater political rights. Societies approaching technological maturity also provide basic schooling for all of their people and advanced training for some. The newly educated consider tradition "backward" and push for further change. The social position of women steadily approaches that of men.

4. **High mass consumption.** Economic development steadily raises living standards as mass production stimulates mass consumption. Simply put, people soon learn to "need" the expanding selection of goods that their society produces. The United States, Japan, Canada, Australia, and the nations of Western Europe entered this stage of development by 1900. Reaching this level of economic prosperity today are two

SEEING SOCIOLOGY
IN EVERYDAY LIFE

"Happy Poverty" in India: Making Sense of a Strange Idea

Although India has become a middle-income nation, its per capita GNI is only $3250, less than one-tenth that in Canada. For this reason, India is home to more than one-quarter of the world's hungry people.

But most North Americans do not easily understand the reality of poverty in India. Many of the country's 1.2 billion people live in conditions far worse than those our society labels "poor." A traveller's first experience of Indian life can be shocking. Chennai (formerly known as Madras), for example, one of India's largest cities with 7 million inhabitants, seems chaotic to the outsider, with streets choked by motorbikes, trucks, carts pulled by oxen, and waves of people. Along the roadway, vendors sit on burlap cloths selling fruits, vegetables, and cooked food while people a few yards away work, talk, bathe, and sleep.

Although some people live well, Chennai is dotted by more than 1000 shanty settlements, home to half a million rural village people who have come to the city in search of a better life. Shantytowns are clusters of huts built with branches, leaves, and pieces of discarded cardboard and tin. These dwellings offer little privacy and lack refrigeration, running water, and bathrooms. A visitor from Canada may feel uneasy in such an area, knowing

that the poorest sections of our own inner cities seethe with frustration and sometimes explode with violence.

But India's people understand poverty differently than we do. No restless young men hang out at the corner, no drug dealers work the streets, and there is little danger of violence. In Canada, poverty often means anger and isolation; in India, even shantytowns are organized around strong families—children, parents, and often grandparents—who offer a smile of welcome to a stranger.

For traditional people in India, life is shaped by *dharma*, the Hindu concept of duty and destiny that teaches people to accept their fate, whatever

it may be. Mother Teresa, a Catholic nun who worked among the poorest of India's people, went to the heart of the cultural differences: "Americans have angry poverty," she explained. "In India, there is worse poverty, but it is a happy poverty."

Perhaps we should not describe anyone who clings to the edge of survival as happy. But poverty in India is eased by the strength and support of families and communities, a sense that life has a purpose, and a world view that encourages each person to accept whatever life offers. As a result, a visitor may come away from a first encounter with Indian poverty rather confused: "How can people be so poor and yet seem content, active, and *joyful*?"

WHAT DO YOU THINK?

1. What did Mother Teresa mean when she said that in India there is "happy poverty"?

2. How might a visit to an Indian shantytown change the way you think of being "rich"?

3. Do you know of any poor people in Canada who have attitudes toward poverty similar to these people in India? What would make people seem to accept their poverty?

former British colonies in eastern Asia: Hong Kong (now part of the People's Republic of China) and Singapore (independent since 1965).

The Role of High-Income Nations

Modernization theory claims that high-income countries play four important roles in global economic development:

1. **Controlling population.** Because population growth is greatest in the poorest low-income societies, rising population can overtake economic advances. High-income nations can help limit population growth by exporting birth control technology and promoting its use. Once economic development is under way, birth rates should decline, as they have in industrialized nations,

because children are no longer an economic asset and now cost a great deal of money to raise.

2. **Increasing food production.** High-income nations can export sophisticated farming methods to low-income nations to help increase their agricultural yields. Such techniques, collectively referred to as the Green Revolution, include new hybrid seeds, modern irrigation methods, chemical fertilizers, and pesticides for insect control.

3. **Introducing industrial technology.** Rich nations can encourage economic growth in poor societies by introducing machinery and information technology, which raise productivity. Industrialization also shifts the labour force from farming to skilled industrial and service jobs.

dependency theory a model of economic and social development that explains global inequality in terms of the historical exploitation of poor, low-income nations by wealthier, high-income ones

4. **Providing foreign aid.** Investment capital from rich nations can boost the prospects of low-income societies striving to reach Rostow's takeoff stage. Foreign aid can raise farm output by making it possible for these countries to buy more fertilizer and build irrigation projects. In addition, financial and technical assistance to construct power plants and factories improves industrial output. Each year, North America provides about $29 billion in foreign aid to low- and middle-income countries (U.S. Census Bureau, 2010).

CRITICAL REVIEW Modernization theory has many influential supporters among social scientists (Berger, 1986; Firebaugh, 1996; Firebaugh & Sandu, 1998; Moore, 1977, 1979; Parsons, 1966). For decades, it has shaped the foreign policy of Canada, the United States, and other high-income nations. Supporters point to rapid economic development in Asia—especially in South Korea, Taiwan, Singapore, Hong Kong, and China—as proof that the affluence created in Western Europe and North America is within the reach of all countries.

But modernization theory faces criticism from socialist countries (and left-leaning analysts in the West) as little more than a defence of capitalism. Its most serious flaw, according to critics, is that modernization has simply not occurred in many low-income countries. The United Nations reported that living standards in a number of nations, including Haiti and Nicaragua in Latin America and Sudan, Ghana, and Rwanda in Africa, are actually lower today than they were in 1960 (United Nations Development Programme, 2009).

A second criticism of modernization theory is that it fails to recognize how high-income nations, which benefit from the status quo, often block the path to development for some less-affluent countries. Centuries ago, powerful countries industrialized from a position of global strength. Can we expect poor countries today to do so from a position of global weakness?

Third, modernization theory treats high-, middle-, and low-income societies as separate worlds, ignoring the fact that the global economy affects all nations. Many countries in Latin America and Asia are still struggling to overcome the harm caused by colonization, which boosted the fortunes of Europe.

Fourth, modernization theory holds up the world's wealthiest countries as the standard for judging the rest of humanity, revealing an ethnocentric bias. We need to remember that our Western idea of "progress" has caused us to rush headlong into a competitive, materialistic way of life, which uses up the world's scarce resources and damages the natural environment.

Fifth and finally, modernization theory suggests that the causes of global poverty lie almost entirely within the less-wealthy societies themselves. Critics see this analysis as little more than blaming the victims for their own problems. Instead, they argue, an analysis of global inequality should focus just as much on the behaviour of more-advantaged nations as it does on the behaviour of less-advantaged ones and also on the global economic system.

Concerns such as these reflect a second major approach to understanding global inequality: dependency theory.

CHECK YOUR LEARNING State the main ideas of modernization theory, including Rostow's four stages of economic development. Point to strengths and weaknesses of this theory.

Dependency Theory

Dependency theory is *a model of economic and social development that explains global inequality in terms of the historical exploitation of poor, low-income nations by wealthier, high-income ones.* This analysis, which follows the social-conflict approach, puts primary responsibility for global poverty on high-income nations, which for centuries have systematically impoverished low-income countries and made them dependent on the high-income ones. This destructive process continues today.

Historical Perspective

Everyone agrees that before the Industrial Revolution, there was little affluence in the world. However, dependency theory asserts that people living in less-wealthy countries were actually better off economically in the past than their descendants are now. André Gunder Frank (1975), a noted supporter of this theory, argues that the colonial process that helped develop high-income nations also *underdeveloped* less wealthy societies.

Dependency theory is based on the idea that the economic positions of today's nations are linked and cannot be understood apart from one another. Low- and middle-income nations are not simply lagging behind high-income ones on the "path of progress"; rather, the prosperity of the most wealthy high-income countries came largely at the expense of less wealthy ones. In short, some nations became rich only because others became poor. Both are the result of the global economic system that began to take shape five centuries ago.

The Importance of Colonialism

Late in the fifteenth century, Europeans began surveying the Americas to the west, Africa to the south, and Asia to the east in order to establish colonies. They were so successful that, a century ago, Great Britain controlled about one-fourth of the world's land, boasting that "the sun never sets on the British Empire." The United States, itself originally a patchwork of small British colonies on the eastern seaboard of North America, soon pushed across the continent, purchased Alaska, and gained control of Haiti, Puerto Rico, Guam, the Philippines, the Hawaiian Islands, and Guantanamo Bay in Cuba.

As colonialism spread, there emerged a brutal form of human exploitation—the international slave trade—from about

Wallerstein's Capitalist World Economy

Immanuel Wallerstein (1974, 1979, 1983, 1984) explains global stratification using a model of the "capitalist world economy." Wallerstein's term *world economy* suggests that the prosperity of some nations and the poverty and dependency of other countries result from a global economic system. He traces the roots of the global economy to the beginning of colonization more than 500 years ago, when Europeans began gathering wealth from the rest of the world. Because the global economy is based in high-income countries, it is capitalist in character.[1]

Wallerstein calls the wealthy high-income nations the *core* of the world economy. Colonialism enriched this core by funnelling raw materials from around the world to Western Europe, where they fuelled the Industrial Revolution. Today, multinational corporations operate profitably worldwide, channelling wealth to North America, Western Europe, Australia, and Japan.

Low-income countries are the *periphery* of the global economy. Drawn into the world economy by colonial exploitation, these nations continue to support wealthy high-income ones by providing inexpensive labour and a vast market for industrial products. The remaining countries are the *semiperiphery* of the world economy. They include middle-income countries such as India and Brazil that have closer ties to the global economic core.

According to Wallerstein, the world economy benefits high-income societies (by generating profits for them) and harms the rest of the world (by causing poverty). The world economy thus makes economically disadvantaged nations dependent on advantaged ones. This dependency involves three factors:

1. **Narrow, export-oriented economies.** Low-income nations produce only a few crops for export to wealthier countries. Examples include coffee and fruits from Latin American nations, oil from Nigeria, hardwoods from the Philippines, and palm oil from Malaysia. Today's multinational corporations buy raw materials cheaply in low-income societies and transport them to core (advantaged middle- and high-income) nations, where factories process them for profitable sale. Thus low-income nations develop few industries of their own.

2. **Lack of industrial capacity.** Without an industrial base, low-income societies face a double bind: They count on economically advantaged nations to buy their inexpensive raw materials, and they must then try to buy from these nations whatever expensive manufactured goods they can afford. In a classic example of this dependency, British colonialists encouraged the people of India to raise cotton but prevented them from weaving their own cloth. Instead, the British shipped

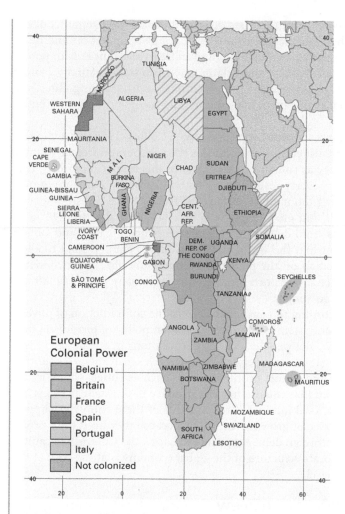

FIGURE 9–4 Africa's Colonial History

For more than a century, most of Africa was colonized by North European nations, with France dominating in the northwestern region of the continent and Great Britain dominating in the east and south.

1500 until 1850. Even as the world was turning away from slavery, Europeans took control of most of the African continent, as Figure 9–4 shows, and dominated most of the continent until the early 1960s.

Formal colonialism has almost disappeared from the world. However, according to dependency theory, political liberation has not translated into economic independence. Far from it—the economic relationship between wealthy high-income and poorer low- and middle-income nations continues the colonial pattern of domination. This *neocolonialism* is the heart of the capitalist world economy.

---

[1] This discussion also draws on A.G. Frank (1980, 1981), Delacroix and Ragin (1981), Bergesen (1983), Dixon and Boswell (1996), and Kentor (1998).

How does modernization theory view investment by global corporations such as Coca-Cola in low-income nations such as Mozambique? How does the view of dependency theory differ?

Indian cotton to English textile mills in Birmingham and Manchester, manufactured the cloth, and shipped finished goods back to India, where the very people who harvested the cotton bought the garments.

Dependency theorists claim that the Green Revolution—widely praised by modernization theorists—works the same way. Less-advantaged low- and middle-income countries sell cheap raw materials to more-advantaged nations and then try to buy expensive fertilizers, pesticides, and machinery in return. Typically, these countries profit from this exchange more than less-advantaged nations do.

3. **Foreign debt.** Unequal trade patterns have plunged low-income countries into debt. Collectively, these nations of the world owe high-income countries some $3 trillion; hundreds of billions of dollars are owed to North America alone. Such staggering debt paralyzes a country, causing high unemployment and rampant inflation (World Bank, 2010).

The Role of High-Income Nations

Modernization theory and dependency theory assign very different roles to high-income nations. Modernization theory holds that these societies *produce wealth* through capital investment and new technology. Dependency theory views global inequality in terms of how countries *distribute wealth*, arguing that wealthy high-income nations have *overdeveloped* themselves as they have *underdeveloped* the rest of the world.

Dependency theorists dismiss the idea that programs developed by high-income countries to control population and boost agricultural and industrial output raise living standards in poorer countries. Instead, they claim, such programs actually benefit already wealthy high-income nations and the ruling elites, not the poor majority, in low- and middle-income countries (Kentor, 2001).

Frances Moore Lappé and Joseph Collins (1986) maintain that the capitalist culture of North America encourages people to think of poverty as somehow inevitable. In this line of reasoning, they explain, poverty results from "natural" processes, including people having too many children, and from natural disasters such as droughts. But global poverty is far from inevitable; in their view, it results from deliberate government policies. Lappé and Collins point out that the world already produces enough food to allow every person on the planet to become quite fat. In fact, most of Africa actually exports food, even though many people in African nations go hungry.

According to Lappé and Collins, the contradiction of poverty amid plenty stems from the rich-nation policy of producing food for profit, not people. That is, corporations in advantaged high-income nations co-operate with elites in less-advantaged countries to grow and export profitable crops such as coffee, which means using land that could otherwise produce basics such as beans and corn for local families. Governments of these countries support the practice of growing for export because they need food profits to repay foreign debt. According to Lappé and Collins, the capitalist corporate structure of the global economy is at the core of this vicious circle.

CRITICAL REVIEW The main idea of dependency theory is that no nation becomes rich or poor in isolation because a single global economy shapes the future of all nations. Pointing to continuing poverty in Latin America, Africa, and Asia, dependency theorists claim that development simply cannot proceed under the constraints now imposed by powerful high-income countries. Rather, they call for radical reform of the entire world economy so that it operates in the interests of the majority of people.

Critics charge that dependency wrongly treats wealth as if no one gets richer without someone else getting poorer. Farmers, small business owners, and corporations can and do create new wealth through hard work and imaginative use of new technology. After all, they point out, the entire world's wealth has increased sixfold since 1950.

Second, dependency theory is wrong in blaming high-income nations for global poverty because many of the world's poorest countries (such as Ethiopia) have had little colonial contact. On the contrary, a long history of trade with high-income countries has dramatically improved the economies of nations including Sri Lanka, Singapore, and Hong Kong (all former British colonies), as well as South Korea and Japan. In short, say the critics, most evidence shows that foreign investment encourages economic growth, as modernization theory claims, and not economic decline, as dependency theory holds (Firebaugh, 1992; Vogel, 1991).

Third, critics call dependency theory simplistic for pointing the finger at a single factor—the capitalist market system—as the cause of global inequality (Worsley, 1990). Dependency theory views less wealthy societies as passive victims and ignores factors inside these countries that contribute to their economic problems. Sociologists have long recognized the vital role of culture in shaping people's willingness to embrace or resist change. Under the rule of the ultratraditional Muslim Taliban, for example, Afghanistan became economically isolated, and its living standards sank to among the lowest in the world. Is it reasonable to blame high-income, capitalist societies for that country's stagnation?

Nor can high-income societies be held responsible for the reckless behaviour of foreign leaders whose corruption and militarism impoverish their countries. Examples include the regimes of Ferdinand Marcos in the Philippines, François Duvalier in Haiti, Manuel Noriega in Panama, Mobutu Sese Seko in Zaire (today's Democratic Republic of the Congo), and Saddam Hussein in Iraq. Some leaders even use food supplies as a weapon in internal political struggles, leaving the masses starving, as in the African nations of Ethiopia, Sudan, and Somalia. Likewise, many countries throughout the world have done little to improve the status of women or to control population growth.

Fourth, critics say that dependency theory is wrong to claim that global trade always makes high-income nations richer and low-income nations poorer. For example, in 2008, the United States had a trade deficit of $821 billion, meaning that this nation imports that much more goods than it sells abroad. The United States' single greatest debt was to China, whose profitable trade has now pushed that country into the ranks of the world's middle-income nations (U.S. Census Bureau, 2009).

Fifth, critics fault dependency theory for offering only vague solutions to global poverty. Most dependency theorists urge low-income nations to end all contact with high-income countries, and some call for nationalizing foreign-owned industries. In other words, dependency theory is really an argument for some sort of world socialism. In light of the difficulties socialist countries (even better-off socialist countries such as Russia) have had in meeting the needs of their own people, critics ask, should we really expect such a system to rescue the entire world from poverty?

Although the world continues to grow richer, billions of people are being left behind. This shantytown in Lagos, Nigeria, is typical of many cities in low-income countries. What can you say about the quality of life in such a place?

The Applying Theory table on page 246 summarizes the main arguments of modernization theory and dependency theory.

CHECK YOUR LEARNING State the main ideas of dependency theory. What are several strengths and weaknesses of this theory?

Global Stratification: Looking Ahead

Among the most important trends of recent decades is the development of a global economy. In North America, rising production and sales abroad bring profits to many corporations and their stockholders, especially those who already have substantial wealth. At the same time, the global economy has moved manufacturing jobs abroad, closing factories in this country and hurting many average workers. The net result: greater economic polarization in countries such as Canada and the United States.

People who support the global economy claim that the expansion of trade results in benefits for all countries involved. For this reason, they endorse policies such as the North American Free Trade Agreement (NAFTA) signed by Canada, the United States, and Mexico, which took effect in 1994. Critics of expanding globalization make other claims: Manufacturing jobs are being lost in Canada and the United States, and more manufacturing now takes

Global Poverty

	Modernization Theory	Dependency Theory
Which theoretical approach is applied?	Structural-functional approach	Social-conflict approach
How did global poverty come about?	The whole world was poor until some countries developed industrial technology, which allowed mass production and created affluence.	Colonialism moved wealth from some countries to others, making some nations poor as it made other nations rich.
What are the main causes of global poverty today?	Traditional culture and a lack of productive technology.	Neocolonialism—the operation of multinational corporations in the global, capitalist economy.
Are rich countries part of the problem or part of the solution?	Rich countries are part of the solution, contributing new technology, advanced schooling, and foreign aid.	Rich countries are part of the problem, making poor countries economically dependent and in debt.

place abroad in factories (including Mexico) where workers are paid little and few laws ensure workplace safety. In addition, other critics of expanding globalization point to the ever-greater stresses that our economy places on the natural environment.

But perhaps the greatest concern is the vast economic inequality that exists between the world's countries. The concentration of wealth in high-income countries, coupled with increasing inequality within middle-income countries and grinding poverty in low-income nations, may well be the biggest problem facing humanity in the twenty-first century.

Both modernization theory and dependency theory offer some understanding of this urgent problem. In evaluating these theories, we must consider empirical evidence. Over the course of the twentieth century, living standards rose in most of the world. Even the economic output of the poorest 25 percent of the world's people increased four-fold during those 100 years. As a result, the number of people living on less than $1.25 per day fell from about 1.9 billion in 1981 to about 1.4 billion in 2005 (Chen & Ravallion, 2008). In short, most people around the world are better off than ever before in *absolute* terms.

The greatest reduction in poverty has taken place in Asia, a region generally regarded as an economic success story. In 1981, almost 80 percent of global $1.25-per-day poverty was in East Asia; by 2005, that figure had fallen to 17 percent. Since then, two very large Asian countries—India and China—have joined the ranks of the middle-income nations. The economic growth in India and China has been so great that, in the last two decades, global economic inequality has actually decreased as economic prosperity has spread from Europe and North America to Asia (Bussollo et al., 2007; Chen & Ravallion, 2008; Davies et al., 2008; Sala-i-Martin, 2002).

Latin America represents a mixed case. In the 1970s, this world region enjoyed significant economic growth; during the 1980s and 1990s, however, there was little overall improvement. The share of the global $1.25-per-day poverty was slightly higher in 2005 (3 percent) than it was in 1981 (2 percent) (Chen & Ravallion, 2008).

In Africa, about half of the nations are showing economic growth greater than in the past. In many countries, however, especially those south of the Sahara, the extent of extreme

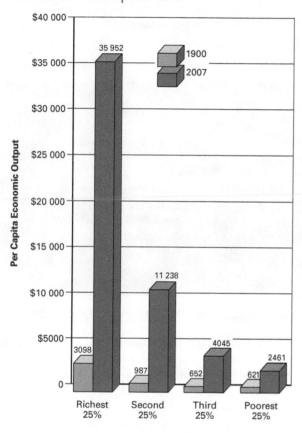

Global Snapshot

Per Capita Economic Output

- $40 000
- $35 000 — 35 952
- $30 000
- $25 000
- $20 000
- $15 000
- $10 000 — 11 238
- $5000
- 0

1900
2007

Richest 25%: 3098
Second 25%: 987
Third 25%: 4045
Poorest 25%: 621, 2461

FIGURE 9–5 The World's Increasing Economic Inequality

The gap between the richest and poorest people in the world is nearly three times as big as it was a century ago.

Source: United Nations Development Programme (2009).

poverty has become worse. In 1981, sub-Saharan Africa accounted for 11 percent of $1.25-per-day poverty; by 2005, this share had risen to 28 percent (Chen & Ravallion, 2008; Sala-i-Martin, 2002).

Overall, then, most people are doing better than in the past. However, richer people in the world are moving ahead much faster than poor people, so that the world's *relative* poverty has been increasing (United Nations Development Programme, 2009). In 2007, the gap between the rich and the poor in the world was almost three times as big as it was in 1900. Figure 9–5 shows that the poorest of the world's people are being left behind.

Recent trends suggest the need to look critically at both modernization theory and dependency theory. The fact that governments have played a large role in the economic growth that has occurred in Asia and elsewhere challenges modernization theory and its free-market approach to development. On the other hand, since the upheavals in the former Soviet Union and Eastern Europe, a global re-evaluation of socialism has also been taking place. Because socialist nations have a record of poor economic performance and political repression, many low-income nations are unwilling to follow the advice of dependency theory and place economic development entirely under government control.

Although the world's future is uncertain, we have learned a great deal about global stratification. One major insight, offered by modernization theory, is that poverty is partly a *problem of technology*. A higher standard of living for a growing world population depends on the ability of low-income nations to raise their agricultural and industrial productivity. A second insight, derived from dependency theory, is that global inequality is also a *political issue*. Even with higher productivity, the human community must address crucial questions concerning the distribution of resources, both within societies and around the globe.

Although economic development raises living standards, it also places greater strains on the natural environment. As middle-income nations such as India and China—with a combined population of 2.5 billion—become more affluent, their people will consume more energy and other natural resources (China has recently passed Japan to become the second-largest consumer of oil, behind the United States, which is one reason that oil prices have been rising). High- and middle-income nations, in which people consume more, also produce more solid waste and create more pollution.

Finally, the vast gulf that separates the world's richest and poorest people puts everyone at greater risk of war and terrorism as the poorest people challenge the social arrangements that threaten their existence (Lindauer & Weerapana, 2002). In the long run, it is probably true that we can achieve peace on this planet only by ensuring that all of the world's people enjoy a significant measure of dignity and security.

CHAPTER 9 GLOBAL STRATIFICATION

HOW MUCH SOCIAL INEQUALITY CAN WE FIND IF WE LOOK AROUND THE WORLD? This chapter explains that a global perspective reveals even more social stratification than we find here in Canada. Around the world, an increasing number of people in lower-income countries are travelling to higher-income nations in search of jobs. As "guest workers," they perform low-wage work that the country's own more well-off citizens do not wish to do. In such cases, the rich and poor truly live "worlds apart."

With so little income, many guest workers sleep six to a small room. How do you think living in a strange country, with few legal rights, affects these workers' ability to improve their working conditions?

Many guest workers come to Dubai from India to take jobs building this country's new high-rise hotels and business towers. Workers labour about 12 hours a day but earn only between $50 and $175 a month—typically, twice what people can earn at home. Do you think the chance to take a job like this in a foreign country is an opportunity or a form of exploitation?

> **HINT:** Dubai's recent building boom has been accomplished using the labour of about 1 million guest workers, who actually make up about 85 percent of the population of the United Arab Emirates. Recent years have seen a rising level of social unrest, including labour strikes, which has led to some improvements in working and living conditions and better health care. But guest workers have no legal rights to form labour unions, nor do they have any chance to gain citizenship.

Applying Sociology in Everyday Life

1. What comparisons can you make between the pattern of guest workers coming to places such as Dubai in the Middle East and workers coming to Canada from the Philippines?
2. Page through several issues of any current news magazine or travel magazine to find any stories or advertising mentioning lower-income countries (selling, say, coffee from Colombia or exotic vacations to India). What picture of life in low-income countries does the advertising present? In light of what you have learned in this chapter, how accurate does this image seem to you?

3. Millions of students from abroad study on Canadian and American campuses. Find a woman and a man on your campus who were raised in a low-income country. After explaining that you have been studying global inequality, ask if they would be willing to share information about what life is like back home. If they are, ask about stratification in general, as well as their own social position in their home country.

CHAPTER 9   Global Stratification

Global Stratification: An Overview

HIGH-INCOME COUNTRIES

- contain 18% of the world's people
- receive 60% of global income
- have a high standard of living based on advanced technology
- produce enough economic goods to enable their people to lead comfortable lives
- include 69 nations, among them Canada, the United States, the nations of Western Europe, Israel, Saudi Arabia, the Russian Federation, Japan, South Korea, and Australia

pp. 229–31

MIDDLE-INCOME COUNTRIES

- contain 68% of the world's people
- receive 39% of global income
- have a standard of living about average for the world as a whole
- include 101 nations, among them the nations of Eastern Europe, Peru, Brazil, Namibia, Egypt, Indonesia, India, and the People's Republic of China

pp. 231–32

LOW-INCOME COUNTRIES

- contain 14% of the world's people
- receive 1% of global income
- have a low standard of living because of limited industrial technology
- include 43 nations, generally in Central and East Africa and Asia, among them Chad, the Democratic Republic of the Congo, Ethiopia, Bangladesh, and Pakistan

p. 232

See Global Map 9–1 on page 230.

✓ Although poverty is a reality in Canada and other high-income nations, the greatest social inequality is not within nations but between them.

global stratification (p. 226) patterns of social inequality in the world as a whole

high-income countries (p. 228) nations with the highest overall standards of living

middle-income countries (p. 228) nations with a standard of living about average for the world as a whole

low-income countries (p. 228) nations with a low standard of living in which most people are poor

Global Wealth and Poverty

All societies contain **RELATIVE POVERTY**, but low-income nations face widespread **ABSOLUTE POVERTY** that is life-threatening.

- Worldwide, about 1 billion people are at risk due to poor nutrition.
- About 9 million people, most of them children, die each year from diseases caused by poverty.
- Throughout the world, women are more likely than men to be poor. Gender bias is strongest in low-income societies.
- As many as 200 million men, women, and children (about 3% of humanity) live in conditions that can be described as slavery.

pp. 232–37

FACTORS CAUSING POVERTY

- Lack of technology limits production.
- High birth rates produce rapid population increase.
- Traditional cultural patterns make people resist change.
- Extreme social inequality distributes wealth very unequally.
- Extreme gender inequality limits the opportunities of women.
- Colonialism allowed some nations to exploit other nations; neocolonialism continues today.

pp. 237–38

colonialism (p. 238) the process by which some nations enrich themselves through political and economic control of other nations

neocolonialism (p. 238) a new form of global power relationships that involves not direct political control but economic exploitation by multinational corporations

multinational corporation (p. 238) a large business that operates in many countries

Global Stratification: Theoretical Analysis

MODERNIZATION THEORY maintains that nations achieve affluence by developing advanced technology. This process depends on a culture that encourages innovation and change toward higher living standards. Walt Rostow identified four stages of development:

- *Traditional stage*—People's lives are built around families and local communities. (Example: Bangladesh)
- *Takeoff stage*—A market emerges as people produce goods not just for their own use but to trade with others for profit. (Example: Thailand)
- *Drive to technological maturity*—The ideas of economic growth and higher living standards gain widespread support; schooling is widely available; the social standing of women improves. (Example: Mexico)
- *High mass consumption*—Advanced technology fuels mass production and mass consumption as people now "need" countless goods. (Example: Canada)

`pp. 238–41`

modernization theory (p. 238) a model of economic and social development that explains global inequality in terms of technological and cultural differences between nations

dependency theory (p. 242) a model of economic and social development that explains global inequality in terms of the historical exploitation of poor, low-income nations by wealthier, high-income ones

MODERNIZATION THEORY CLAIMS

- High-income nations can help middle- and low-income nations by providing technology to control population size, increase food production, and expand industrial and information economy output and by providing foreign aid to pay for new economic development.
- Rapid economic development in Asia shows that affluence is within reach of other nations of the world.

`pp. 241–42`

CRITICS CLAIM

- High-income nations do little to help less-advantaged countries and benefit from the status quo. Low living standards in much of Africa and South America result from the policies of high-income nations.
- Because high-income nations, including Canada, control the global economy, many low-income nations struggle to support their people and cannot follow the path to development taken by high-income countries centuries ago.

`p. 242`

DEPENDENCY THEORY maintains that global wealth and poverty were created by the colonial process beginning 500 years ago that overdeveloped high-income nations and underdeveloped low-income nations. This capitalist process continues today in the form of neocolonialism—economic exploitation of less-advantaged nations by multinational corporations.
Immanuel Wallerstein's model of the capitalist world economy identified three categories of nations:

- *Core*—the world's high-income countries, which are home to multinational corporations
- *Semiperiphery*—the world's middle-income countries, with ties to core nations
- *Periphery*—the world's low-income countries, which provide low-cost labour and a vast market for industrial products

`pp. 242–43`

DEPENDENCY THEORY CLAIMS

- Three key factors—export-oriented economies, a lack of industrial capacity, and foreign debt—make poor countries dependent on rich nations and prevent their economic development.
- Radical reform of the entire world economy is needed so that it operates in the interests of the majority of people.

`pp. 243–44`

CRITICS CLAIM

- Dependency theory overlooks the sixfold increase in global wealth since 1950 and the fact that the world's poorest low-income countries have had weak, not strong, ties to high-income countries.
- High-income nations are not responsible for cultural patterns or political corruption that block economic development in many middle- and low-income nations.

`pp. 244–45`

See the Applying Theory table on page 246.

MySocLab

Visit MySocLab at www.mysoclab.com to access a variety of online resources that will help you to prepare for tests and to apply your knowledge, including
- **an eText**
- **videos**
- **self-grading quizzes**
- **glossary flashcards**

10 Gender Stratification

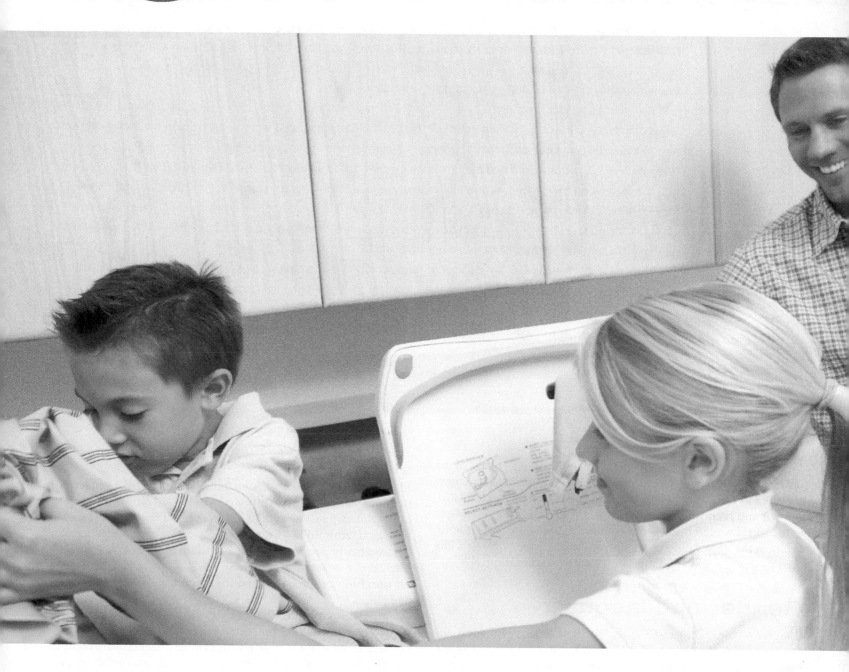

- How is gender a creation of society?

- What differences does gender make in people's lives?

- Why is gender an important dimension of social stratification?

This chapter examines gender—the meaning that societies attach to being female or male—and explains why gender is an important dimension of social stratification.

"We went to the Manitoba Legislature asking for plain, common justice, an old-fashioned square deal, and in reply to that we got hat-lifting. I felt that when a man offers hat-lifting when we ask for justice we should tell him to keep his hat right on. I will go further and say that we should tell him not only to keep his hat on but to pull it right down over his face."

So wrote Nellie McClung in her book *In These Times*, which tells the story of her struggle to gain equal rights for women in the public realm. Born in Ontario in 1873, McClung migrated west as a child with her family, first settling in Manitoba and later, as an adult, moving to Alberta and British Columbia. By the time she was 40, she had given birth to five children and had become a well-known public speaker for women's rights. Back then, in much of Canada, women could not own property or keep their wages if they were married; they could not draft a will; they were barred from filing lawsuits in a court, including seeking custody of their own children; they could not attend university; and they legally could be beaten by their husbands as long as the stick used was no wider than a thumb (the origin of today's phrase "the rule of thumb").

Nor could women express their disapproval of such conditions. In this "free country," many more decades would pass before all Canadian women gained the right to vote. At that time, most people considered such a proposal absurd and outrageous. Toronto journalist Goldwin Smith argued that giving women the right to vote would lead to "national emasculation." Smith also protested the right of women to enter universities (Prentice et al., 1996:221).

Much has changed in the 140 years since McClung's birth. Many of the proposals that she and other early feminists made are now accepted as a matter of basic fairness. But as this chapter explains, women and men still lead different lives in Canada and elsewhere in the world, and in many respects men still dominate. This chapter explores the importance of gender, and explains how gender, like class position, is a major dimension of social stratification.

Gender and Inequality

Chapter 6 ("Sexuality and Society") explained that biological differences divide the human population into categories of female and male. **Gender** refers to *the personal traits and social positions that members of a society attach to being female or male*. Gender, then, is a dimension of social organization, shaping how we interact with others and even how we think about ourselves. More importantly, gender also involves *hierarchy*, placing men and women in different positions in terms of power, wealth, and other resources. This is why sociologists speak of **gender stratification**, *the unequal distribution of wealth, power, and privilege between men and women*. In short, gender affects the opportunities and constraints we face throughout our lives.

Male-Female Differences

Many people think there is something "natural" about gender distinctions because biology does make one sex different from the other. But we must be careful not to think of social differences in biological terms. In 1848, for example, women were denied the vote because many people assumed that women did not have enough intelligence or interest in politics. Such attitudes had nothing to do with biology; they reflected the *cultural patterns* of that time and place.

Another example is athletic performance. In 1925, most people—both women and men—believed that the best women runners could never compete with men in a marathon. Today, as Figure 10–1 shows, the gender gap has greatly narrowed, and the best women runners routinely post better times than the fastest men of decades past. Here again, most of the differences between men and women turn out to be socially created.

Differences in physical ability between the sexes do exist. On average, males are 10 percent taller than women, 20 percent heavier, and 30 percent stronger, especially in the upper body (Ehrenreich, 1999). On the other hand, women outperform men in the ultimate game of life itself: Life expectancy for men in 2007 was 78.3, while among women it was 83 years (Statistics Canada, 2011r).

gender (p. 252) the personal traits and social positions that members of a society attach to being female or male

gender stratification (p. 252) the unequal distribution of wealth, power, and privilege between men and women

In adolescence, males show greater mathematical ability, whereas adolescent females excel in verbal skills, a difference that reflects both biology and socialization (College Board, 2009; Lewin, 2008). While North American culture contains strong gendered beliefs that the sexes differ in their experience and expression of specific emotions, sociological research shows there is little connection between men's and women's feelings and expressive behaviour and gender-linked cultural beliefs about emotion (Simon & Nath, 2004). Research does not point to any overall differences in intelligence between males and females.

Biologically, then, men and women differ in limited ways, with neither one naturally superior. But culture can define the two sexes differently, as the global study of gender described in the next section shows.

Gender in Global Perspective

The best way to see how gender is based in culture is by comparing one society to another. Three important studies highlight just how different "masculine" and "feminine" can be.

The Israeli Kibbutz

In Israel, collective Jewish settlements are called *kibbutzim*. The *kibbutz* (the singular form of the word) has been an important setting for gender research because gender equality is one of its stated goals; men and women share in both work and decision making.

In recent decades, kibbutzim have become less collective and thus less distinctive organizations. But for much of their history, both sexes shared most everyday jobs. Many men joined women in taking care of children, and women joined men in repairing buildings and providing armed security. Both sexes made everyday decisions for the group. Girls and boys were raised in the same way; in many cases, young children were raised together in dormitories away from parents. Women and men in the kibbutzim achieved remarkable (although not complete) social equality, evidence that culture defines what is feminine and what is masculine.

Margaret Mead's Research

The anthropologist Margaret Mead carried out groundbreaking research on gender. If gender is based in the biological differences between men and women, she reasoned, people everywhere should define "feminine" and "masculine" in the same way; if gender is cultural, these concepts should vary.

Mead (1963, orig. 1935) studied three societies in New Guinea. In the mountainous home of the Arapesh, Mead observed men and women with remarkably similar attitudes and behaviour. Both sexes, she reported, were co-operative and sensitive to others—in short, what our culture would label "feminine."

Moving south, Mead studied the Mundugumor, whose headhunting and cannibalism stood in striking contrast to the gentle ways of the Arapesh. In this culture, both sexes were typically selfish and aggressive, traits we define as "masculine."

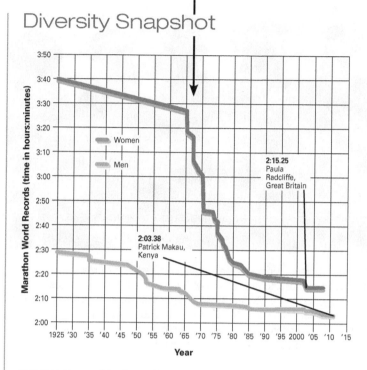

The women's movement of the 1960s encouraged women to show their true abilities.

Diversity Snapshot

FIGURE 10–1 Men's and Women's Athletic Performance

Do men naturally outperform women in athletic competition? The answer is not obvious. Early in the twentieth century, men outpaced women by more than an hour in marathon races. But as opportunities for women in athletics have increased, women have been closing the performance gap. Only 11 minutes separate the current world marathon records for women (set in 2003) and for men (set in 2008).

Source: Marathonguide.com (2011).

Finally, travelling west to the Tchambuli, Mead discovered a culture that, like our own, defined females and males differently. But, Mead reported, the Tchambuli *reversed* many of our ideas of gender: Females were dominant and rational, and males were submissive, emotional, and nurturing toward children. Based on her observations, Mead concluded that culture is the key to gender distinctions because what one society defines as masculine another may see as feminine.

Some critics view Mead's findings as "too neat," as if she saw in these societies just the patterns she was looking for. Deborah Gewertz (1981) challenged what she called Mead's "reversal hypothesis," pointing out that Tchambuli males are really the more aggressive sex. Gewertz explains that Mead visited the Tchambuli (who themselves spell their name Chambri) during the 1930s, after they had lost much of their property in tribal wars, and observed men rebuilding their homes, a temporary role for Chambri men.

matriarchy a form of social organization in which females dominate males

patriarchy a form of social organization in which males dominate females

sexism the belief that one sex is innately superior to the other

In every society, people assume that certain jobs, patterns of behaviour, and ways of dressing are "naturally" feminine while others are just as obviously masculine. But in global perspective, we see remarkable variety in such social definitions. These men, Wodaabe pastoral nomads who live in the African nation of Niger, are proud to engage in a display of beauty most people in our society would consider feminine.

George Murdock's Research

In a broader study of more than 200 pre-industrial societies, George Murdock (1937) found some global agreement on which tasks are feminine and which are masculine. Hunting and warfare, Murdock observed, generally fall to men, and home-centred tasks such as cooking and child care tend to be women's work. With their simple technology, pre-industrial societies apparently assign roles reflecting men's and women's physical characteristics. With their greater size and strength, men hunt game and protect the group; because women bear children, they do most of the work in the home.

Beyond this general pattern, Murdock found much variety. Consider agriculture: Women did the farming in about the same number of societies as men; in most societies, the two sexes divided this work. When it came to many other tasks, from building shelters to tattooing the body, Murdock found that pre-industrial societies were as likely to turn to one sex as the other.

○ **CRITICAL REVIEW** Global comparisons show that, overall, societies do not consistently define tasks as feminine or masculine. With industrialization, the importance of muscle power declines, further reducing gender differences (Nolan & Lenski, 2007). In sum, gender is too variable to be a simple expression of biology; what it means to be female and male is mostly a creation of society.

○ **CHECK YOUR LEARNING** By comparing many cultures, what do we learn about the origin of gender differences?

Patriarchy and Sexism

Conceptions of gender vary, and there is evidence of societies in which women have greater power than men. One example is the Musuo, a very small society in southwestern China's Yunnan province, in which women control most property, select their sexual partners, and make most decisions about everyday life. The Musuo appear to be a case of **matriarchy** ("rule by mothers"), *a form of social organization in which females dominate males*, which has only rarely been documented in human history.

The pattern found almost everywhere in the world is **patriarchy** ("rule by fathers"), *a form of social organization in which males dominate females.* Global Map 10–1 shows the great variation in the relative power and privilege of women that exists from country to country. According to the United Nations' gender development index, Australia, Iceland, and Norway give women the highest social standing; by contrast, women in the Central African Republic, Sierra Leone, Mali, Afghanistan, and Niger have the lowest social standing compared with men. Of the world's 194 nations, Canada was ranked sixteenth in terms of gender equality in 2008 (United Nations Development Programme, 2009).

The justification for patriarchy is **sexism**, *the belief that one sex is innately superior to the other.* Sexism is not just a matter of individual attitudes; it is built into the institutions of our society. *Institutional sexism* is found throughout the economy, with women highly concentrated in low-paying jobs. Similarly, the legal system has long excused violence against women, especially on the part of boyfriends, husbands, and fathers.

The Costs of Sexism

Sexism limits the talents and the ambitions of the half of the human population who are women. Although men benefit in some respects from sexism, their privilege comes at a high price. Masculinity in our culture encourages men to engage in many high-risk behaviours: using tobacco and alcohol, playing dangerous sports, and even driving recklessly. As Marilyn French (1985) argues, patriarchy drives men to relentlessly seek control, not only of women but also of themselves and their world. Thus masculinity is linked not only to accidents but also to suicide, violence, and stress-related diseases. The *Type A personality*—marked by chronic impatience, driving ambition, competitiveness, and free-floating hostility—is one cause of heart disease and an almost perfect match with the behaviour our culture considers masculine (Ehrenreich, 1983).

However, as Elianne Riska (2002) argues, at issue was a certain type of white middle-class masculinity that had up to then served as the norm for all male behaviour—the hard-working, achievement-oriented white middle-class male breadwinner making his way in a highly competitive, capitalist society. Riska (2000) traces the decline of the notion of the Type A man in the late 1970s and the development of a new psychological construct—the "hardy" man.

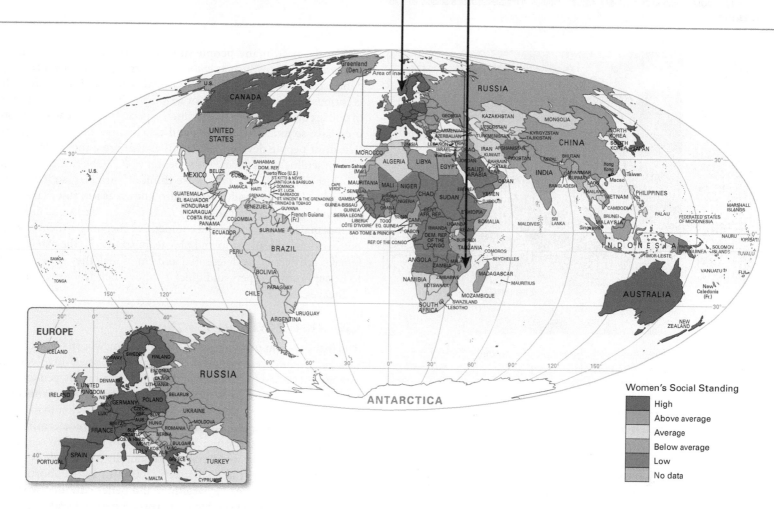

Astrid Brügger, age 19, lives in Norway; like most girls growing up in high-income nations, she enjoys most of the rights and opportunities available to men.

Jendayi Gattuso, age 20, lives in Mozambique, a low-income nation that limits the rights and opportunities of women.

Women's Social Standing
- High
- Above average
- Average
- Below average
- Low
- No data

Window on the World

GLOBAL MAP 10–1 **Women's Power in Global Perspective**

Women's social standing in relation to men's varies around the world. In general, women live better in high-income countries than in middle- and low-income countries. Even so, some nations stand out: In Denmark, Sweden, Switzerland, and Norway, women come closest to social equality with men.

Source: United Nations Development Programme (2010).

According to Suzanne Kobasa (1979:3), "persons who experience high degrees of stress without falling ill have a personality structure differentiating them from persons who become sick under stress." In contrast to Type A man, who was driven by a seemingly irrational passion to reach extrinsic goals and rewards, the hardy man is constructed as one who is driven by intrinsic motivation. Riska (2002) notes that both the Type A personality and the hardy personality provide individualized explanations for differences in the health of middle-class men in capitalist societies. These models need to be tested with diverse groups of men and women from different social positions and cultural backgrounds. Such research on the social patterning of health within and across the genders would help us better understand the link between social conditions and individual well-being.

Must Patriarchy Go On?

In pre-industrial societies, women have little control over pregnancy and childbirth, which limits the scope of their lives. In those same societies, men's greater height and physical strength are valued resources that give them power. But industrialization, including birth

Sex is a biological distinction that develops prior to birth. Gender is the meaning that a society attaches to being female or male. Gender differences are a matter of power, because what is defined as masculine typically has more importance than what is defined as feminine. Infants begin to learn the importance of gender by the way parents treat them. Do you think this child is a girl or a boy? Why?

control technology, increases people's choices about how to live. In societies like our own, biological differences offer little justification for patriarchy.

But males are dominant in many areas of life in Canada and elsewhere. Does this mean that patriarchy is inevitable? Some researchers claim that biological factors such as differences in hormones and slight differences in brain structure "wire" the sexes with different motivations and behaviours—especially aggressiveness in males—making patriarchy difficult or perhaps even impossible to change (S. Goldberg, 1974; Popenoe, 1993b; Rossi, 1985; Udry, 2000). However, most sociologists believe that gender is socially constructed and *can* be changed (West, 2002). The fact that no society has completely eliminated patriarchy does not mean that we must remain prisoners of the past.

To understand why patriarchy continues today, we next examine how gender is rooted and reproduced in society, a process that begins in childhood and continues throughout our lives.

Gender and Socialization

From birth until death, gender shapes human feelings, thoughts, and actions. Children quickly learn that their society considers females and males different kinds of people; by about age three, they begin to think of themselves in these terms.

In the past, many people in Canada traditionally described women using terms such as *emotional, passive,* and *co-operative.* By contrast, men were described as *rational, active,* and *competitive.* It is curious that we were taught for so long to think of gender in terms of one sex being opposite to the other, especially because women and men have so much in common and also because research suggests that most people develop personalities that are a mix of feminine and masculine traits (Bem, 1993; Benoit et al., 2009; Krieger, 2003).

Just as gender affects how we think of ourselves, so it teaches us how to behave. **Gender roles** (also known as **sex roles**) are *attitudes and activities that a society links to each sex.* A culture that defines males as ambitious and competitive encourages them to seek out positions of leadership and play team sports. To the extent that females are defined as deferential and emotional, they are expected to be supportive helpers and quick to show their feelings (Johnson & Greaves, 2007).

Gender and the Family

The first question people usually ask about a newborn—"Is it a boy or a girl?"—has great importance because the answer involves not just sex but the likely direction of the child's life. In fact, gender is at work even before a child is born because, especially in lower-income nations, parents hope their first-born will be a boy rather than a girl. In countries such as China and India, new sex predetermination techniques such as ultrasound are reported to be used to reinforce anti-female prejudice, resulting in unnaturally low female-to-male ratios at birth (Jha et al., 2006; Sen, 2003). In India, abortion of female fetuses is higher for wealthier and better educated women, challenging the prediction that modernization would lead to a more balanced cultural preference for either gender (Jha et al., 2011).

Soon after birth, family members welcome infants into the "pink world" of girls or the "blue world" of boys (Bernard, 1981). People even send gender messages in the way they handle infants. One researcher at an English university presented an infant dressed as either a boy or a girl to a number of women; her subjects handled the "female" child tenderly, with frequent hugs and caresses, while treating the "male" child more aggressively, often lifting him up high in the air or bouncing him on a knee (Bonner, 1984; Tavris & Wade, 2001). The lesson is clear: The female world revolves around co-operation and emotion, and the male world puts a premium on independence and action.

Gender and the Peer Group

About the time they enter school, children begin to move outside the family and make friends with others of the same age. Considerable research points to the fact that young children tend to form single-sex playgroups (Martin & Fabes, 2001).

Peer groups teach additional lessons about gender. After spending a year watching children at play, Janet Lever (1978) concluded that boys favour team sports with complex rules and clear objectives such as scoring runs or making touchdowns. Such games nearly always have winners and losers, reinforcing masculine traits of aggression and control.

Girls, too, play team sports. But, Lever explains, girls also play hopscotch, jump rope, or simply talk, sing, or dance. These activities have few rules, and rarely is victory the ultimate goal. Instead of teaching girls to be competitive, Lever explains, female peer groups promote the interpersonal skills of communication and co-operation, presumably the basis for girls' future roles as wives and mothers.

The games we play offer important lessons for our later lives. Lever's observations recall Carol Gilligan's gender-based theory of moral reasoning, discussed in Chapter 3 ("Socialization: From Infancy to Old Age"). Boys, Gilligan (1982) claims, reason according to abstract principles. For them, "rightness" amounts to "playing by the rules." By contrast, girls consider morality a matter of responsibility to others. Recent research on sports among adolescents and emergent adults extend these earlier findings. While sports such as rugby continue to be an important site for the construction of gender and the embodiment of unequal gender relations (Light & Kirk, 2000), three different types of gender-role conflict emerged; however, similar to previous findings, athletics use a variety of strategies to deal with gender-role conflict (Fallon & Jome, 2007).

Gender and Schooling

Gender shapes our interests and beliefs about our own abilities, guiding areas of study and, eventually, career choices (Correll, 2001). In high school, more girls than boys learn secretarial skills and take vocational classes such as cosmetology and food services. Classes in woodworking and auto mechanics attract mostly young men.

Women have now become a majority (59 percent) of the students on college and university campuses across Canada. As their numbers have increased, women have become well represented in many fields of study that once excluded them, including mathematics, chemistry, and biology. But men still predominate in many fields, including engineering, physics, and philosophy, and women cluster in the fine arts (including music, dance, and drama) as well as in the social sciences (including anthropology and sociology). Newer areas of study are also gender-typed: More men than women take computer science, and courses in gender studies enrol mostly women. This is a pattern for many high-income countries. Research in Italy largely confirms these findings: While the gender gap in the relational and economic fields has declined because of women's transfer to these areas, in the technical and scientific fields a substantial gender gap persists in recent cohorts (Triventi, 2010).

Gender and the Mass Media

Since television captured the public imagination in the early 1950s, white males have held centre stage; racial and ethnic minorities were all but absent from television until the early 1970s. And when both sexes appeared on camera, men generally played the brilliant detectives, fearless explorers, and skilled surgeons. Women played

In our society, the mass media have enormous influence on our attitudes and behaviour, and what we see shapes our views of gender. In the 2009 film *Twilight*, we see a strong, "take charge" male playing against a more passive female. Do you think the mass media create these gender patterns? Or it is more correct to say that they reproduce them? Is there another option?

the less capable characters, often unnecessary except for the sexual interest they added to the story.

Historically, advertisements have shown women in the home, cheerfully using cleaning products, serving food, trying out appliances, and modelling clothes. Men predominate in ads for cars, travel, banking services, industrial companies, and alcoholic beverages. The authoritative voice-over—the voice that describes a product on television and radio—is almost always male (D.M. Davis, 1993).

A careful study of gender in advertising reveals that men usually appear taller than women, implying male superiority. Women, by contrast, are more frequently presented lying down (on sofas and beds) or, like children, seated on the floor. Men's facial expressions and behaviour give off an air of competence and imply dominance; women often appear childlike, submissive, and sexual. Men focus on the products being advertised, and women often focus on the men (Cortese, 1999; Goffman, 1979).

Finally, advertising perpetuates what Naomi Wolf (1990) calls the "beauty myth." The Seeing Sociology in Everyday Life box on page 260 takes a closer look at how this myth affects both women and men.

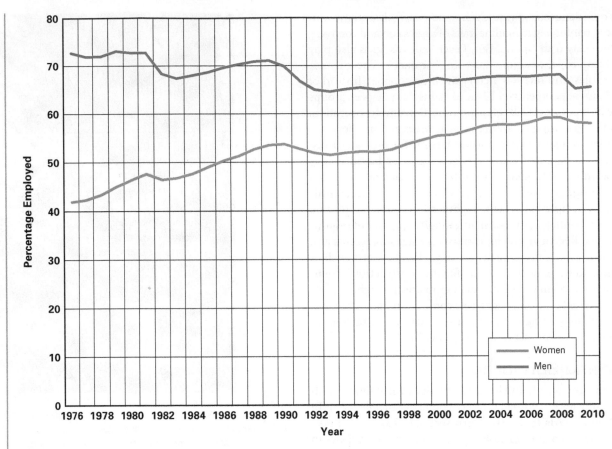

FIGURE 10–2   Percentage of Employed Women and Men Aged 15 and Older, 1976 to 2010

Source: Statistics Canada (2011s, 2011t).

Gender and Social Stratification

Gender involves more than how people think and act. It is also about how society is organized, how our lives are affected by social hierarchy. The reality of gender stratification can be seen in just about every aspect of our everyday lives (Huffman, 1999). We look, first, to the world of working women and men.

Working Women and Men

In 1891, just 11.4 percent of females in Canada were engaged in paid employment. In 2010, 57.9 percent of women aged 15 and over worked for income, and just less than three-fourths of working women did so full time (Statistics Canada, 2010a, 2011t). The traditional view that earning an income is a "man's role" no longer holds true, as Figure 10–2 shows.

Factors that have changed the Canadian labour force include the decline of farming, the growth of cities, a shrinking family size,

and a rising divorce rate. Thus, Canada and other industrial societies today consider women working for income to be the rule rather than the exception. In fact, 80 percent of Canadian women with a partner and a child under the age of 16 living at home are employed. In total, women represent 47.9 percent of all those employed in Canada (Statistics Canada, 2010a).

Gender and Occupations

Although women are closing the gap with men as far as working for income is concerned, the work done by the two sexes remains very different. The Canada 2006 Census reports a high concentration of women in two types of jobs. Clerical and administrative support work draws 24 percent of working women, most of whom are secretaries or other office workers. These are called "pink-collar jobs" because 75 percent are filled by women. Another 29 percent of employed women perform sales and service work. Most of these jobs are in the food service industries, child care, and health care.

Table 10–1 shows the small changes in the gender balance (and imbalance!) of different occupations in Canada between 1987 and 2006. The improvement in the managerial ranks is impressive but still only about one-third of managers are female. Teaching has become even more dominated by women, with almost two-thirds of all teachers being female. Among nurses (87%) and clerical (75%) and sales (57%) workers, there has been very little change over these 20 years (Statistics Canada, 2007c).

Men dominate in the trades, transport, and construction, as well as in professionals employed in the natural sciences, engineering, and mathematics. In 2006, 78 percent of professionals in these occupations were men, a figure almost the same as it was in 1987 when men held 80 percent of these positions. Given the low female university enrolments in these fields at present, it is unlikely that female representation in these occupations will increase any time soon.

On the positive side, women have increased their representation in some other traditionally masculine fields in the last few decades. Women made up just over 50 percent of business and finance professionals in 2006, a substantial increase from 38 percent in 1987. There has also been substantial growth in the number of women in medical and health-related fields: In 2006, they comprised 55 percent of all doctors and dentists, up from 43 percent two decades ago. In 1987, women made up 61 percent of professionals employed in social sciences or religion; in 2006, the figure was 70 percent. In 2006, women comprised 36 percent of all those employed in managerial positions, which is a 6 percent increase from 1987 (Statistics Canada, 2007c).

Among managers, however, women tend to be better represented at lower levels rather than more senior levels. In 2006, women made up only 26 percent of senior managers, compared to 37 percent of managers at other levels (Statistics Canada, 2007c). This finding parallels results from recent international studies. According to one survey, just 15 of the *Fortune* 500 companies have a woman as their chief executive officer, and just 15 percent of the seats on corporate boards of directors are held by women. In 2009, the highest-paid female CEO in the United States had the same total compensation as the ninth-highest-paid male CEO. Increasing the leadership role of women in the business world is not just a matter of fairness; research into the earnings of the United States' 500 largest corporations showed that the companies with more women on the board also are the most profitable (Catalyst, 2010; Dickler, 2007; *Fortune,* 2010; Graybow, 2007; Loomis, 2007; U.S. Department of Labor, 2009a).

Overall, although more women now work for pay and some women have made significant inroads into traditionally male-dominated occupations, by and large they still remain segregated in the labour force in jobs at the middle and low end of the pay scale, usually supervised by men and with limited opportunity for advancement (Benoit, 2000a; Charles, 1992; Krahn & Lowe, 1998).

Gender stratification in everyday life is easy to see: Female nurses assist male physicians, female secretaries serve male

TABLE 10–1 Percentage of Canadian Women in Occupational Categories, 1987 and 2006

Occupations		1987 % Women (of all employed in occupation)	2006 % Women (of all employed in occupation)
Managerial			
	Senior management	21.0	26.3
	Other management	30.7	36.9
	Total management	30.1	36.3
Professional			
	Business and finance	38.3	51.6
	Natural sciences, engineering, mathematics	19.6	22.0
	Social sciences, religion	61.4	71.3
	Teaching	52.3	63.9
	Doctors, dentists, other health	43.1	55.3
	Nursing, therapy, other health-related	87.1	87.4
	Artistic, literary, recreational	48.4	54.1
	Total professional	50.4	55.9
	Clerical and administrative	73.9	75.0
	Sales and service	55.2	56.8
	Primary*	19.7	20.5
	Trades, transport, and construction	5.2	6.5
	Processing, manufacturing, and utilities	32.4	31.1

*Primary means occupations in the primary industries, including agriculture, mining, logging, and fishing.
Source: Statistics Canada (2007c).

executives, and female flight attendants are under the command of male airline pilots. In any field, the greater a job's income and prestige, the more likely it is to be held by a man. For example, in 2005, women represented 71.5 percent of elementary and secondary school educators, 54.7 percent of college teachers, and 40.5 percent of university teachers. In 2008, across Canada's 92 colleges and universities, only 15 pecent had female presidents (AUCC, 2008; Statistics Canada, 2006e).

How are women kept out of certain jobs? By defining some kinds of work as "men's work," society defines women as less competent than men. In a study of coal miners, Suzanne Tallichet (2000) found that most men considered it "unnatural" for women to work in the mines. Women who did so were defined as deviant and subject to

The Beauty Myth

BETH: "I can't eat lunch. I need to be sure I can get into that black dress for tonight."

SARAH: "Maybe eating is more important than looking good for Tom."

BETH: "That's easy for you to say. You're a size 2 and Jake adores you!"

The Duchess of Windsor once remarked, "A woman can never be too rich or too thin." The first half of her observation may apply to men as well, but certainly not the second half. After all, the vast majority of ads placed by the $15 billion per year North American cosmetics industry and the $20 billion diet industry target women.

According to Naomi Wolf (1990), certain cultural patterns create a "beauty myth" that is damaging to women. The beauty myth arises, first, because society teaches women to measure their worth in terms of physical appearance. Yet the standards of beauty embodied by the *Playboy* centrefold or the 100-pound fashion model are out of reach for most women.

The way society teaches women to prize relationships with men, whom they presumably attract with their beauty, also contributes to the beauty myth. Striving for beauty not only drives women to be extremely disciplined but also forces them to be highly attentive and responsive to men. In short, beauty-minded women try to please men and avoid challenging male power.

Belief in the beauty myth is one reason why so many young women are focused on body image, particularly being as thin as possible, often to the point of endangering their health. During the past several decades, the share of young women who develop an eating disorder such as anorexia nervosa (dieting to the point of starvation) or bulimia (binge eating followed by vomiting) has risen dramatically.

The beauty myth affects males as well: Historically, cosmetic surgery was viewed solely as a woman's domain. Males now make up 14 percent of all cosmetic surgery patients in North America, seeking a range of surgery options to make them feel young and beautiful. These include pectoral muscle implants, calf implants, tummy tucks, and facelifts, procedures that, as with women's cosmetic surgery, make major demands on the wallet (Rudy, 2006).

In sum, there can be little doubt that the idea of beauty is important in everyday life. The question is whether beauty is still gendered. According to Davis (2002), the idea that there will soon be gender equality in this realm because of men's increasing option to go under the knife to beautify themselves is suspect, and cosmetic surgery will remain mainly a practice undertaken by women.

WHAT DO YOU THINK?

1. What, exactly, is the myth surrounding beauty?
2. How does the beauty myth apply differently to men and women?
3. Do you agree that the great importance attached to beauty for women and increasingly for men is a problem? Why or why not?

Sources: Based on Wolf (1990), Davis (2002), and Rudy (2006).

---

labelling as "sexually loose" or as lesbians. Such labelling made these women outcasts, presented a challenge to holding the job, and made advancement all but impossible.

In the corporate world, too, the higher in the company we look, the fewer women we find. You hardly ever hear anyone say out loud that women don't belong at the top levels of a company. But many people seem to feel this way, which can prevent women from being promoted. Sociologists describe this barrier as a *glass ceiling* that is not easy to see but blocks women's careers all the same (Benokraitis & Feagin, 1995). In a recent survey of 3000 members of the Institute of Leadership and Management in the United Kingdom, 73 percent of female respondents felt that barriers still existed for women seeking senior management and board-level positions. Just over one-third of men surveyed stated that a glass ceiling exists (Snowdon, 2011).

One challenge to male domination in the workplace comes from women who are entrepreneurs. In 2006, there were more than 800 000 self-employed woman in Canada, and this is expected to increase to 1 million Canadian women in the next decade. This involves almost a tripling of the number of self-employed women in Canada in the past three decades. By starting their own businesses, women have shown that they can make opportunities for themselves apart from large, male-dominated companies (CIBC, 2005; Statistics Canada, 2007c).

Of course, gender stratification shapes the workforce not only in Canada but in other nations as well. The Seeing Sociology in the News box provides a close look at Japan, a nation where, traditionally, patriarchy has been very strong, but where evidence of change is now beginning to appear.

Gender, Income, and Wealth

In 2008, the median earnings for women working full time were $44 700, and men working full time earned $62 600. This means that for every dollar earned by men, women earned about 71.3 cents (Statistics Canada, 2007c). These earnings differences are greatest among older workers because older working women typically have less education and less seniority than older working men. Earnings differences are smaller among younger workers because younger men and women tend to have similar schooling and work experience.

The main reason women earn less is the *type* of work they do: largely clerical and service jobs. In effect, jobs and gender interact.

CNN.com

Women on Board: Breaking the "Bamboo Ceiling"

BY KYUNG LAH
April 22, 2010

TOKYO—Change a few circumstances in her life and Sakie Fukushima says she would have been a housewife. She was raised to be a good Japanese wife and homemaker, after all. That's what was expected of women of her generation—to sit behind their men, make their bentos, iron their shirts and watch them rise to lead Japan's economy.

Life did not go as Fukushima expected.

Sixty-year-old Fukushima is one of Japan's most powerful executives, sitting on the board of both U.S. and Japanese-based multinational companies. The fact that she is a female in one of the most male-dominated business cultures is a stunning backstory in one woman's remarkable ascent through the so-called "bamboo ceiling." Bamboo bends, and unlike glass, never breaks. But Fukushima managed to crack through, by working for a U.S. company.

"I was lucky to be in a place where the hard work was appreciated," said Fukushima, of her corporate beginnings at Korn-Ferry International. The American company saw her sales output, the highest in the Asia-Pacific region, as the reason for promotion.

An American mentor and her supportive husband urged Fukushima to push beyond her Japanese cultural expectations.

"If I was to work for a Japanese company, a large Japanese company, I don't think I would have come this far."

The World Economic Forum's Global Gender Gap Index ranks Japan 101 out of 134 countries. Part of the reason for the low ranking is that just 1.4 percent of Japanese executives are women.

What that has meant for women in the workplace is they are pushed to traditionally female roles: secretary and store clerk. It is a dismal reality for the world's second-largest economy, said Beth Brooke, Ernst and Young's Global vice chairwoman and a *Forbes* Magazine 100 most powerful woman.

"Japan is a very homogeneous society. So on the spectrum of diversity, not just gender, it is more difficult to embrace diversity because it's not a terribly diverse culture to begin with."

Ironically, Brooke believes the global economic slowdown and Japan's aging population is a chance to rediscover the people underutilized in the workforce.

"I think we have an opportunity to change the conversation here. Whether you're a country or a company, you need growth. Japan has an enormous opportunity, frankly, to see the opportunity to spark innovation through a gender lens of diversity. I think gender diversity is a big part of the solution."

Fukushima agreed, as she celebrates her recent appointment to the Bridgestone Corporation board. She is the first female to be elected to the Japanese company's boardroom.

"Experimenting is the best way to say it," said Fukushima, describing Japan's corporate sentiment toward women. "They know they have to have

diversity but they don't know how to do it and how to use it effectively. As a result of increasing competition outside of Japan from China and Korea, the Japanese business community has realized it has to change. They can't rely on the past successful model of the 1970s and '80s. They will have to increase diversity, change the way of doing business in order to compete."

Fukushima's new colleague, Bridgestone Americas, Inc. CEO and President Gary Garfield, said he is encouraged that his company in Japan is catching up to other global companies.

He calls having a female on the board a no-brainer. His advice to Japanese companies: "Just branch out and do it. They'll be stronger for it. I think they'll be better companies for it."

WHAT DO YOU THINK?

1. What does the article say about why Japan has such strong gender stratification?

2. Are there reasons to think that Japan's future will be different from its past? What are they?

3. Does the "glass ceiling" in North America differ from the "bamboo ceiling" in Japan? If so, how?

Source: Courtesy of CNN.

People still perceive jobs with less clout as "women's work," just as people devalue certain work simply because it is performed by women (Cohen & Huffman, 2003; England, Hermsen, & Cotter, 2000).

In recent decades, supporters of gender equality have proposed a policy of "comparable worth," paying people not according to the historical double standard but according to the level of skill and responsibility involved in the work. Several nations, including Canada, Great Britain, and Australia, have adopted comparable worth policies. Dedication to the pay equity principle was tested in the summer of 1998 when the Canadian Human Rights Tribunal determined that female federal workers were owed an estimated $5 billion. The federal government found itself torn between supporting the pay equity principle and dealing with the cost of doing so (Greenspoon, 1998). Finally, on October 29, 1999, the Public Service Alliance of Canada and the federal government came

to an agreement to implement the Canadian Human Rights Tribunal's decision. Comparative worth policies have found limited acceptance in the United States. As a result, it is estimated that women in the United States lose as much as $1 billion in income annually.

A second cause of gender-based income inequality has to do with society's view of the family. Both men and women have children, of course, but our culture gives more of the responsibility of parenting to women. Pregnancy and raising small children keep many younger women out of the labour force at a time when their male peers are making significant career advancements. When women workers return to the labour force, they have less job experience and seniority than their male counterparts (Drolet, 2001; Stier, 1996; Sussman & Yssaad, 2005; Waldfogel, 1997). Variation does exist across high-income countries, however. Countries with "women-friendly" parental

Women in Canada still spend almost an hour per day longer on housework than men do.

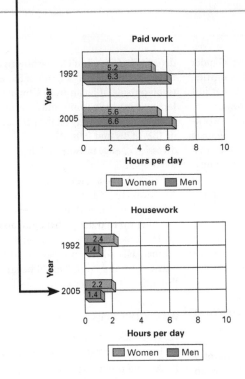

FIGURE 10–3 Time Allocation of Employed Women and Men in Two-Income Families, Canada, 1992 and 2005

Source: Marshall (2006).

leaves and benefits and publicly funded child-care programs lessen the cost of child-bearing for female workers (Benoit, 2000b; Beaujot, 2006; Leira, 2000). Canada's year-long parental and maternity leave policy moves the country closer to the Nordic norm of at least one year of paid leave for parents with their newborns.

In addition, women who choose to have children may be unable or unwilling to take on fast-paced jobs that tie up their evenings and weekends. To avoid role strain, they may take jobs that offer shorter commuting distances, more flexible hours, and employer-provided child-care services. For example, research shows that having babies alters the career paths of female academics (Mason & Goulden, 2004; Sussman & Yssaad, 2005). Women pursuing both a career and a family are torn between their dual responsibilities in ways that men are not. One study found that almost half of women in competitive jobs took time off to have children, compared to about 12 percent of men (Hewlett & Luce, 2005). Role conflict is also experienced by women on campus, where one study concluded that young female professors with at least one child were at least 20 percent less likely to have tenure than comparable men in the same field (Shea, 2002).

The two factors noted so far—type of work and family responsibilities—account for about two-thirds of the earnings difference between women and men. A third factor—discrimination against women—accounts for most of the remainder (Fuller & Schoenberger, 1991). Drolet (2001) found that gender differences in the opportunity to supervise and perform certain tasks accounted for about 5 percent of the gender wage gap in Canada. Because overt discrimination is illegal, it is practised in subtle ways. Women on their way up the corporate ladder often run into the glass ceiling described earlier; company officials may deny its existence, but it effectively prevents many women from rising above middle management.

For all of these reasons, then, women earn less than men in all major occupational categories. This disparity varies from job to job, but a significant gender wage gap remains.

Housework: Women's "Second Shift"

In Canada, housework has always presented a cultural contradiction: We claim that it is essential for family life, but people get little reward for doing it (Bernard, 1981). Here, as around the world, taking care of the home and children has been considered "women's work" (see Global Map 4–1 on page 91). As women have entered the labour force, the amount of housework women do has gone down, but the *share* done by women has stayed the same. Figure 10–3 shows corresponding changes in the number of hours per day spent on housework by females (–2 hours, 12 minutes) and males (+1 hour, 6 minutes) between 1992 and 2005. Nevertheless, in 2005, employed women living with an employed male partner put in an average of 2.2 hours of housework per day. Her male partner put in an average of 1.4 hours of housework per day, or almost an hour less than his female counterpart. Men are also more likely than women to do zero hours of housework, as National Maps 10–1 and 10–2 on pages 263 and 264 show. Nevertheless, the latest data suggest a gender convergence in the time Canadian families spend on paid and unpaid work (Marshall, 2006).

Gender and Education

In the past, our society considered schooling to be irrelevant for women because women's lives revolved around the home. But times have changed. By 1997, women earned 59 percent of all associate and bachelor's degrees and first professional degrees (Statistics Canada, 2000h); this remained about the same in 2000 (Statistics Canada, 2003be) and 2006 (Statistics Canada, 2009d).

In the mid-1990s, for the first time, women were earning half of postgraduate degrees, which are often a springboard to high-prestige jobs. For all areas of study in 1997, women earned 51 percent of master's degrees and 36 percent of all doctorates. In 2001–2002, the proportions awarded to women at master's (51 percent) and doctoral levels (46 percent) were higher than ever before, and men outnumbered women only at the doctoral level (Statistics Canada, 2003be, 2006au).

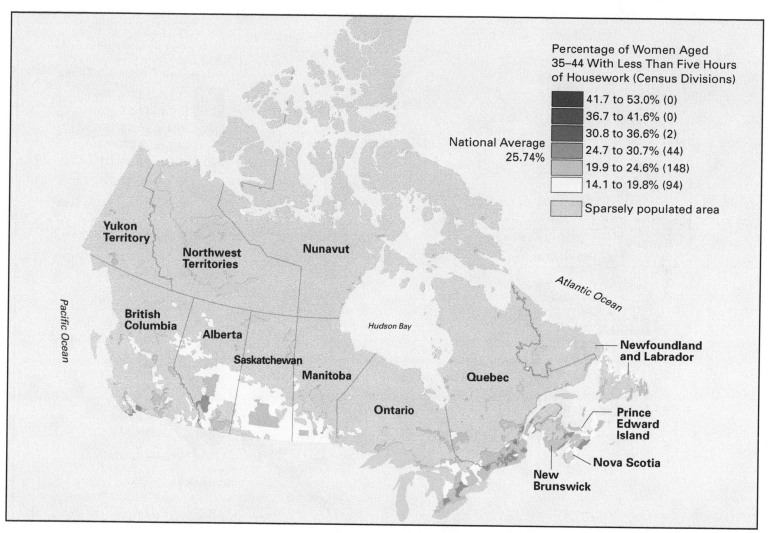

Percentage of Women Aged 35–44 With Less Than Five Hours of Housework (Census Divisions)

41.7 to 53.0% (0)
36.7 to 41.6% (0)
30.8 to 36.6% (2)
24.7 to 30.7% (44)
19.9 to 24.6% (148)
14.1 to 19.8% (94)

Sparsely populated area

National Average 25.74%

Seeing Ourselves

NATIONAL MAP 10–1   Housework by Women, Canada, 2006

This map shows that it is rare for women to do less than five hours of housework per week. Only in Quebec City and Montreal do more than 30.8 percent of women fall in this category. In contrast, relatively few women living on the prairies, particularly those living outside of large cities, tend to spend more than five hours on housework.

Source: Statistics Canada (2006).

College and university doors have opened to women, and differences in men's and women's majors are becoming smaller. In 1972–1973, for example, women made up just 3 percent of students in engineering and applied sciences. In 2001–2002, women received 24 percent of all degrees in these fields. Women's enrolment in mathematics and physical sciences had increased from 19 to 30 percent of all graduates (Statistics Canada, 2000h, 2003be, 2006au).

According to the 2004–2005 Survey of Earned Doctorates, nearly half (46 percent) of doctorate holders are women, up from

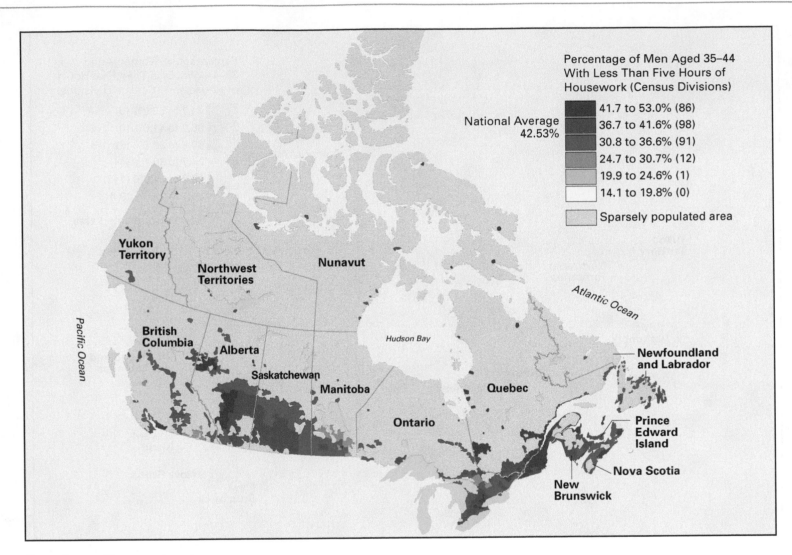

Percentage of Men Aged 35–44 With Less Than Five Hours of Housework (Census Divisions)

National Average 42.53%

- 41.7 to 53.0% (86)
- 36.7 to 41.6% (98)
- 30.8 to 36.6% (91)
- 24.7 to 30.7% (12)
- 19.9 to 24.6% (1)
- 14.1 to 19.8% (0)
- Sparsely populated area

Seeing Ourselves

NATIONAL MAP 10–2   Housework by Men, Canada, 2006

The contrast between National Maps 10–1 and 10–2 is very sharp. Almost half of all men in Canada spend less than five hours per week on housework, and only in one small area in northern Labrador are there less than 25 percent of men who do so. What trends do you see in these maps? People in Quebec tend to spend less time on housework than people in other areas as do people in urban regions. We might expect that in those areas where more men tend to to housework, women would do less, but that does not seem to be the case. Why do you think that is?

Source: Calculated based on data in Statistics Canada (2011u).

minority any category of people distinguished by physical or cultural difference that a society sets apart and subordinates

intersection theory (p. 266) analysis of the interplay of race, class, and gender, often resulting in multiple dimensions of disadvantage

43 percent in 2003–2004. The proportion of women who hold a doctorate degree has grown considerably in traditionally male-dominated fields. Nevertheless, women with a doctorate are still a minority in these fields and, as noted above, this is unlikely to change dramatically in the coming years because of the relatively low enrolments of females at the undergraduate level (Statistics Canada, 2008h).

Gender and Politics

A century ago, virtually no women held elected office in any industrial country, including Canada. In fact, women were legally barred from voting in national elections until 1918 in our country, and it was not until more than a decade later that they were permitted to sit in the Canadian Senate (Prentice et al., 1996). Women in most countries were legally barred from voting in national elections until the early decades of last century. By 2003, this picture of gender exclusion in the political life of industrial countries had changed, but not as much as one might imagine. Table 10–2 shows that there have been significant gains for women, primarily in Nordic countries, but limited progress in many other high-income countries. Several low-income countries are also doing very well in this respect.

In global perspective, although women are half the Earth's population, the median representation is just 16.6 percent of seats in the 180 parliaments with available data. Although this represents a small increase from 50 years ago, only in the two countries of Rwanda (56.3 percent) and Sweden (45 percent) does the share of parliamentary seats held by women approximate their share of the population (Inter-Parliamentary Union, 2011).

Nevertheless, a small number of Canadian female politicians have achieved national prominence, as in the cases of Kim Campbell, who, in 1993, served as Canada's first female prime minister, and Alexa McDonough, who served as the national New Democratic Party leader from 1997 to 2003. Nevertheless, in 2006, our provincial premiers and territorial leaders, as well as our prime minister, were a completely male cast. In 2011, two provinces were headed by women (Newfoundland and Labrador and British Columbia) and women occupied 25 percent of the 308 seats in the House of Commons. Green Party leader Elizabeth May made history in the May 2001 federal election by winning her party's first ever seat in the House of Commons. She is also the only female federal leader on Parliament Hill.

Are Women a Minority?

A **minority** is *any category of people distinguished by physical or cultural difference that a society sets apart and subordinates.* Given the clear economic disadvantage of being a woman in our society, it

TABLE 10–2	Women in National Parliaments, Lower or Single House, 2011, Selected Countries	
Rank	**Country**	**% Women**
1	Rwanda	56.3
3	Sweden	45.0
8	Norway	39.6
9	Netherlands	39.3
14	Argentina	38.5
21	Germany	32.8
30	Austria	27.9
32	Afghanistan	27.7
41	Canada	24.7
52	Pakistan	22.2
56	United Kingdom	22.0
61	China	21.3
68	Nicaragua	20.7
73	Israel	19.2
77	France	18.9
85	Greece	17.3
87	USA	16.8
97	Ireland	15.1
121	Syria	12.4
126	Haiti	11.1
132	Morocco	10.5
140	Kenya	9.8
147	Brazil	8.6
154	Algeria	7.7
160	Somalia	6.8
165	Myanmar	4.3
175	Bahrain	2.5
178	Saudi Arabia	0.0

Source: Inter-Parliamentary Union (2011) and calculations by the authors.

seems reasonable to say that women are a minority in Canada even though they outnumber men.[1]

Even so, most white women do not think of themselves in this way (Lengermann & Wallace, 1985). This is partly because, unlike racial minorities (including Aboriginal Canadians) and

---

[1]Sociologists use the term *minority* instead of *minority group* because, as explained in Chapter 5 ("Groups and Organizations"), women make up a *category*, not a group. People in a category share a status or identity but generally do not know one another or interact.

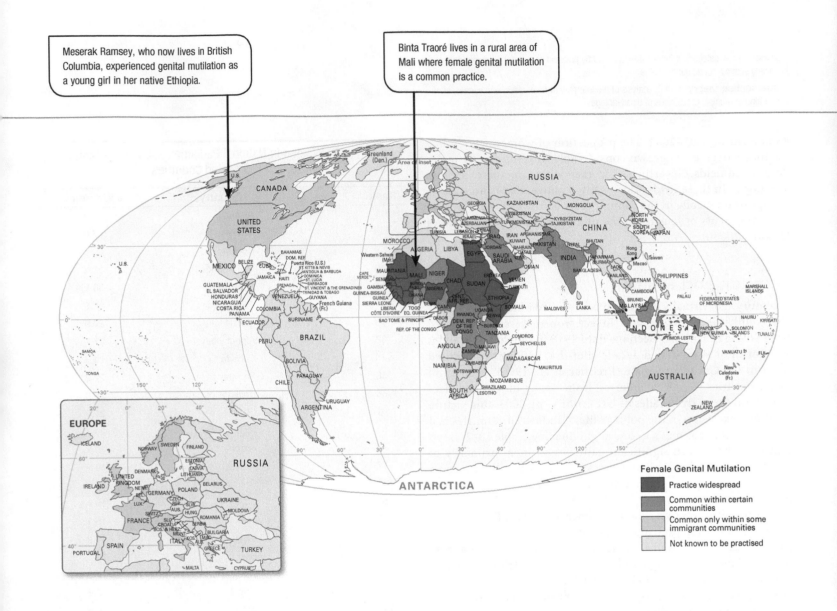

Meserak Ramsey, who now lives in British Columbia, experienced genital mutilation as a young girl in her native Ethiopia.

Binta Traoré lives in a rural area of Mali where female genital mutilation is a common practice.

Female Genital Mutilation

- Practice widespread
- Common within certain communities
- Common only within some immigrant communities
- Not known to be practised

Window on the World

GLOBAL MAP 10–2 Female Genital Mutilation in Global Perspective

Female genital mutilation is known to be performed in at least 28 countries around the world. Across Africa, the practice is common and affects a majority of girls in the eastern African nations of Sudan, Ethiopia, and Somalia. In several Asian nations, including India, the practice is limited to a few ethnic minorities. In the United States, Canada, several European nations, and Australia, there are reports of the practice among some immigrants.

Sources: Seager (2003), World Health Organization (2008), UNICEF (2009), and Population Reference Bureau (2010).

ethnic minorities (say, Haitian Canadians), white women are well represented at all levels of the class structure, including the very top.

Bear in mind, however, that at every class level, women typically have less income, wealth, education, and power than men. Patriarchy makes women depend on men—first their fathers and later their husbands—for their social standing (Bernard, 1981).

Minority Women: Intersection Theory

If women are defined as a minority, what about minority women? Are they doubly handicapped? This question lies at the heart of **intersection theory**, *analysis of the interplay of race, class, and gender, often resulting in multiple dimensions of disadvantage.* Research shows that disadvantages linked to race and gender often combine to produce especially low social standing for some people (Hankivsky et al., 2010; Hankivsky & Cormier, 2009; Ovadia, 2001).

We can demonstrate this with some income comparisons. As noted earlier, Canadian women working full time, full year earn just over 70 percent of the earnings of a male involved in full-time, full-year employment. The situation for visible minority and Aboriginal women working full time, full year is even bleaker: The former has earnings at just 64 percent of Canadian men's and the latter has earnings at just 46 percent (Lambert, 2010).

These data confirm that although gender has a powerful effect on our lives, it never operates alone. Class position, race and ethnicity, and gender form a multi-layered system of disadvantage for some and privilege for others (Arat-Koc, 1989; Benoit et al., 2009; Ginsburg & Tsing, 1990; Ng, 1993; St. Jean & Feagin, 1998; Veenstra, 2011).

Violence against Women

The phrase *rule of thumb* entered our language about 150 years ago when common decency of the day demanded that a man not beat his wife with a stick thicker than his thumb. Even today, a great deal of "manly" violence is directed against women. A Statistics Canada study found that 54 percent of Canadian women reported having experienced at least one instance of unwanted sexual attention (Statistics Canada, 1993b). While men also can be victims of sexual assault, 85 percent of all victims are female, indicating a strong association between gender and this type of violent activity (Statistics Canada, 2000m).

More recent data from 2004 show that the rate of spousal assault also varies among women. The incidence of spousal assault against Aboriginal women in the previous five years was three times higher than that of spousal assault reported by non-Aboriginal women (Statistics Canada, 2005). Aboriginal women were also much more likely than non-Aboriginal women to report more harsh forms of violence (Statistics Canada, 2006f).

Violence toward women also occurs in casual relationships. As noted in Chapter 6 ("Sexuality and Society"), most rapes involve men known to and often trusted by their victims.

Dianne Herman (2001) argues that the extent of sexual abuse shows that the tendency toward sexual violence is built into our way of life. All forms of violence against women—from the catcalls that intimidate women on city streets to a pinch in a crowded subway to physical assaults that occur at home—express what she calls a "rape culture" of men trying to dominate women. Feminists explain that sexual violence is fundamentally about *power*, not sex, and therefore should be understood as a dimension of gender stratification.

In global perspective, violence against women is built into other cultures in many different ways. One case in point is the practice of female genital mutilation or reinfibulation, a painful and often

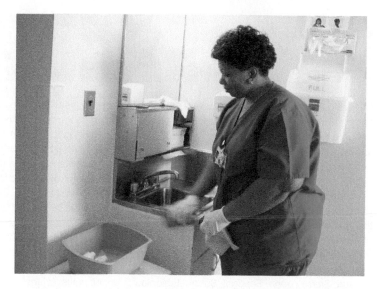

The basic insight of intersection theory is that various dimensions of social stratification—including race and gender—can add up to great disadvantages for some categories of people, including women working as maids. How would you explain the fact that some categories of people are much more likely to end up in low-paying jobs like this one?

dangerous surgical procedure that is performed in more than two dozen countries and is also known to occur in the United States, as shown in Global Map 10–2 on page 266. The practice is considered a form of child assault in Canada and prohibited under the Criminal Code. Some provincial and territorial colleges of physicians have also come out against the practice of female genital mutilation and made official statements advising physicians to refuse requests to perform the operation (Health Canada, 1999). However, this does not mean that the practice has ceased among some ethnic groups. The Thinking about Diversity box on page 268 describes an instance of female genital mutilation that took place in California and asks whether this practice, which some people defend as promoting "morality," amounts to a case of violence against women.

Violence against Men

If our way of life encourages violence against women, it may encourage even more violence against men. As noted in Chapter 7 ("Deviance"), in just under 80 percent of cases in which a police officer makes an arrest for all crime categories except for prostitution, the offender is a male. In addition, victims of violent crime are just as likely to be males as females. Adult females accounted for just over half (about 152 000 of the 298 000 victims) of violent incidents reported to the police in Canada 2008, while some 146 000 victims were males over 18 years (Statistics Canada, 2008i).

sexual harassment comments, gestures, or physical contacts of a sexual nature that are deliberate, repeated, and unwelcome

THINKING ABOUT DIVERSITY: RACE, CLASS, AND GENDER

Female Genital Mutilation: Violence in the Name of Morality

Meserak Ramsey, a woman born in Ethiopia and now working as a nurse in California, paid a visit to an old friend's home. Soon after arriving, she noticed her friend's 18-month-old daughter huddled in the corner of a room in obvious distress. "What's wrong with her?" she asked.

Ramsey was shocked when the woman said her daughter had recently had a clitoridectomy, the surgical removal of the clitoris. This type of female genital mutilation—performed by a midwife, a tribal practitioner, or a doctor and typically without anaesthesia—is common in Nigeria, Sierra Leone, Senegal, Sudan, Ethiopia, Somalia, and Egypt and is known to be practised in certain cultural groups in other nations around the world. It is illegal in the United States as well as in Canada.

Among members of highly patriarchal societies, husbands demand that their wives be virgins at marriage and remain sexually faithful thereafter. The point of female genital mutilation is to eliminate sexual feeling, which, people assume, makes the girl less likely to violate sexual norms and thus be more desirable to men. In about one-fifth of all cases, an even more severe procedure, called infibulation, is performed, in which the entire external genital area is removed and the surfaces are stitched together, leaving only a small hole for urination and menstruation. Before marriage, a husband has the right to open the wound and ensure himself of his bride's virginity.

How many women have undergone female genital mutilation? Worldwide, estimates place the number at more than 100 million (World Health Organization, 2008a). In the United States, hundreds or even thousands of such procedures are performed every year. In most cases, immigrant mothers and grandmothers who have themselves been mutilated insist that young girls in their family follow their example. Indeed, many immigrant women demand the procedure *because* their daughters now live in the United States, where sexual mores are more lax. "I don't have to worry about her now," the girl's mother explained to Meserak Ramsey. "She'll be a good girl."

Medically, the consequences of female genital mutilation include more than loss of sexual pleasure. Pain is intense and can last for years. There is also the danger of infection, infertility, and even death. Ramsey knows the anguish all too well: She herself underwent genital mutilation as a young girl. She is one of the lucky ones who has had few medical problems since. But the extent of her suffering is suggested by this story:

She invited a young couple to stay at her home. Late at night, she heard the woman's cries and burst into their room to investigate, only to learn that the couple was making love and the woman had just had an orgasm. "I didn't understand," Ramsey recalls. "I thought that there must be something wrong with American girls. But now I know that there is something wrong with me." Or with a system that inflicts such injury in the name of traditional morality.

WHAT DO YOU THINK?

1. Is female genital mutilation a medical procedure or a means of social control? Explain your answer.

2. Can you think of other examples of physical mutilation imposed on women? What are they?

3. What do you think should be done about the practice of female genital mutilation in places where it is widespread? Do you think respect for human rights should override respect for cultural differences in this case?

Sources: Crossette (1995) and Boyle, Songora, & Foss (2001).

Our culture tends to define masculinity in terms of aggression and violence. "Real men" work and play hard, speed on the highways, and let nothing stand in their way. A higher crime rate is one result. But even when no laws are broken, men's lives involve more stress and isolation than women's lives, which is one reason why the suicide rate for men is four times higher than for women (Heron et al., 2009). In addition, as noted earlier, men live, on average, about five fewer years than women.

Violence is not simply a matter of choices made by individuals. It is built into our very way of life, with resulting harm to both men and women. In short, the way any culture constructs gender plays an important part in how violent or peaceful that society will be.

Sexual Harassment

Sexual harassment refers to *comments, gestures, or physical contacts of a sexual nature that are deliberate, repeated, and unwelcome.* During the 1990s, sexual harassment became an issue of national importance that rewrote the rules for workplace interaction between women and men.

Most (but not all) victims of sexual harassment are women (Statistics Canada, 2008i). The reason for this is that, first, our culture

In recent decades, our society has recognized sexual harassment as an important problem. As a result, at least officially, unwelcome sexual attention is no longer tolerated in the workplace. To what extent do you think sexual comments, off-colour jokes, and unnecessary touching still take place on the job?

encourages men to be sexually assertive and to view women in sexual terms. As a result, social interaction between men and women in the workplace, on campus, and elsewhere can easily take on sexual overtones. Second, most people in positions of power—including business executives, doctors, bureau chiefs, assembly line supervisors, professors, and military officers—are men who oversee the work of women. Surveys carried out in widely different work settings show that about 5 percent of women claim that they have been harassed on the job in the last year and about half of women say that they receive unwanted sexual attention (NORC, 2009).

Sexual harassment is sometimes obvious and direct: A supervisor may ask for sexual favours from an employee and make threats if the advances are refused. Courts have declared that such *quid pro quo* sexual harassment (the Latin phrase means "one thing in return for another") is a violation of civil rights.

More often, however, the problem of unwelcome sexual attention is a matter of subtle behaviour—sexual teasing, off-colour jokes, comments about someone's looks—that may or may not be intended to harass anyone. But based on the *effect* standard, which is favoured by many feminists, such actions add up to creating a *hostile environment* for women in the workplace. Incidents of this kind are far more complex because they involve different perceptions of the same behaviour. For example, a man may think that repeatedly complimenting a co-worker on her appearance is simply being friendly. The co-worker, on the other hand, may believe that

the man is thinking of her in sexual terms and is not taking her work seriously, an attitude that could harm her job performance and prospects for advancement.

Pornography

Chapter 6 ("Sexuality and Society") defined *pornography* as sexually explicit material that causes sexual arousal. However, people take different views of exactly what is or is not pornographic; the law gives local communities the power to define whether sexually explicit material violates "community standards of decency" and lacks "any redeeming social value."

Traditionally, people have raised concerns about pornography as a *moral* issue. But pornography also plays a part in gender stratification. From this point of view, pornography is really a *power* issue because most pornography dehumanizes women, treating them as the playthings of men.

In addition, there is widespread concern that pornography encourages violence against women by portraying them as weak and undeserving of respect. Men show contempt for women defined in this way by striking out against them. A 2007 survey found that 54 percent of Canadian adults find pornography "morally unacceptable" (Angus Reid, 2009c).

Like sexual harassment, pornography raises complex and sometimes conflicting concerns. Despite the fact that some material may offend just about everyone, many people defend the rights of free speech and artistic expression. Nevertheless, pressure to restrict pornography has increased in recent decades, reflecting both the long-standing concern that pornography weakens morality and the more recent concern that it is demeaning and threatening to women.

Theoretical Analysis of Gender

Why does gender exist in all known societies? Sociology's macro-level approaches—the structural-functional and social-conflict approaches—address the central place of gender in social organization. In addition, the symbolic-interaction approach helps us see the importance of gender in everyday life. The Applying Theory table on page 270 summarizes the important insights offered by each of these approaches.

Structural-Functional Analysis

The structural-functional approach views society as a complex system of many separate but integrated parts. From this point of view, gender serves as a means to organize social life.

As Chapter 2 ("Culture") explained, the earliest hunting and gathering societies had little power over biology. Lacking effective

Gender

	Structural-Functional Approach	Symbolic-Interaction Approach	Social-Conflict Approach
What is the level of analysis?	Macro level	MIcro level	Macro level
What does gender mean?	Parsons described gender in terms of two complementary patterns of behaviour: masculine and feminine.	Numerous sociologists have shown that gender is part of the reality that guides social interaction in everyday situations.	Engels described gender in terms of the power of one sex over the other.
Is gender helpful or harmful?	Helpful. Gender gives men and women distinctive roles and responsibilities that help society operate smoothly. Gender builds social unity as men and women come together to form families.	Hard to say; gender is both helpful and harmful. In everyday life, gender is one of the factors that helps us relate to one another. At the same time, gender shapes human behaviour, placing men in control of social situations. Men tend to initiate most interactions, while women typically act in a more deferential manner.	Harmful. Gender limits people's personal development. Gender divides society by giving power to men to control the lives of women. Capitalism makes patriarchy stronger.

birth control, women could do little to prevent pregnancy, and the responsibilities of child care kept them close to home. At the same time, men's greater strength made them better suited for warfare and hunting. Over the centuries, this sex-based division of labour became institutionalized and largely taken for granted (Freedman, 2002; Lengermann & Wallace, 1985).

Industrial technology opens up a much greater range of cultural possibilities. With human muscle power no longer the main energy source, the physical strength of men becomes less important. In addition, the ability to control reproduction gives women greater choices about how to live. Modern societies relax traditional gender roles as the societies become more meritocratic because rigid roles waste an enormous amount of human talent. Yet change comes slowly because gender is deeply rooted in culture.

Talcott Parsons: Gender and Complementarity

As Talcott Parsons (1942, 1951, 1954) observed, gender helps integrate society, at least in its traditional form. Gender forms a *complementary* set of roles that links women and men into family units and gives each sex responsibility for carrying out important tasks. Women take the lead in managing the day-to-day life of the household and raising children. Men connect the family to the larger world as they participate in the labour force.

Thus gender plays an important part in socialization. Society teaches boys—presumably destined for the labour force—to be rational, self-assured, and competitive. Parsons called this complex of traits *instrumental* qualities. To prepare girls for child rearing, socialization stresses *expressive* qualities, such as emotional responsiveness and sensitivity to others.

Society encourages gender conformity by instilling in men and women a fear that straying too far from accepted standards of masculinity or femininity will cause rejection by the opposite sex. In simple terms, women learn to reject non-masculine men as sexually unattractive, and men learn to reject unfeminine women. In sum, gender integrates society both structurally (in terms of what we do) and morally (in terms of what we believe).

○ **CRITICAL REVIEW** Influential in the 1950s, this approach has lost much of its standing today. First, structural-functionalism assumes a singular vision of society that is not shared by everyone. For example, historically, many women have worked outside the home because of economic necessity, a fact not reflected in Parsons's conventional, middle-class view of social life. Second, Parsons's analysis ignores the personal strains and social costs of rigid gender roles. Third, in the eyes of those seeking sexual equality, Parsons's gender "complementarity" amounts to little more than women submitting to male domination.

○ **CHECK YOUR LEARNING** In Parsons's analysis, what functions does gender perform for society?

Symbolic-Interaction Analysis

The symbolic-interaction approach takes a micro-level view of society, focusing on face-to-face interaction in everyday life. As suggested in Chapter 4 ("Social Interaction in Everyday Life"), gender affects everyday interaction in a number of ways.

Gender and Everyday Life

If you watch women and men interacting, you will probably notice that women typically engage in more eye contact than men do. Why? Holding eye contact is a way of encouraging the conversation to continue; in addition, looking directly at someone clearly shows the other person that you are paying attention.

This pattern is an example of sex roles, defined earlier as the way a society defines how women and men should think and behave. To understand such patterns, consider the fact that people with more power tend to take charge of social encounters. When men and women engage one another, as they do in families and in the workplace, it is men who typically initiate the interaction. That is, men speak first, set the topics of discussion, and control the outcomes. With less power, women are expected to be more *deferential*, meaning that they show respect for others of higher social position. In many cases, this means that women (just like children or others with less power) spend more time being silent and also encouraging men (or others with more power) not just with eye contact but by smiling or nodding in agreement. As a technique to control a conversation, men often interrupt others, just as they typically feel less need to ask the opinions of other people, especially those with less power (Henley, Hamilton, & Thorne, 1992; Ridgeway & Smith-Lovin, 1999; Tannen, 1990, 1994).

○ **CRITICAL REVIEW** The strength of the symbolic-interaction approach is helping us see how gender plays a part in shaping almost all of our everyday experiences. Because our society defines men (and everything that is defined as masculine) as having more value than women (and what is defined as feminine), just about every familiar social encounter is "gendered," so that men and women interact in distinctive and unequal ways.

The symbolic-interaction approach suggests that individuals socially construct the reality they experience as they interact every day, using gender as one element of their personal "performances." Gender can be a useful guide to how we behave.

Yet gender, as a structural dimension of society, is beyond the immediate control of any of us as individuals and also gives some people power over others. Therefore, patterns of everyday social interaction reflect our society's gender stratification. Everyday interaction also helps reinforce this inequality. For example, to the extent that fathers take the lead in family discussions, the entire family learns to expect men to "display leadership" and "show their wisdom"; to the extent that mothers let them take the lead, the family learns to expect women to be deferential to men.

A limitation of the symbolic-interaction approach is that by focusing on situational social experience, it says little about the broad patterns of inequality that set the rules for our everyday lives. To understand the roots of gender stratification, we have to "look up" to see more closely how society makes men and women unequal. We will do this using the social-conflict approach.

○ **CHECK YOUR LEARNING** Point to several ways that gender shapes the everyday face-to-face interactions of individuals.

Social-Conflict Analysis

From a social-conflict point of view, gender involves differences not just in behaviour but in power as well. Consider the striking similarity between the way traditional ideas about gender benefit men and the way oppression of racial and ethnic minorities benefits white people. Conventional ideas about gender do not make society operate smoothly; on the contrary, they create division and tension, with men seeking to protect their privileges as women challenge the status quo.

As earlier chapters noted, the social-conflict approach draws heavily on the ideas of Karl Marx. Yet as far as gender is concerned, Marx was a product of his times, and his writings focused almost entirely on men. However, his friend and collaborator Friedrich Engels did develop a theory of gender stratification.

Friedrich Engels: Gender and Class

Looking back through history, Engels saw that in hunting and gathering societies, the activities of women and men, though different, had equal importance. A successful hunt brought men great prestige, but the vegetation gathered by women provided most of a group's food supply. As technological advances led to a productive surplus, social equality and communal sharing gave way to private property and ultimately to a class hierarchy. At this point, men gained significant power over women. With surplus wealth to pass on to heirs, upper-class men needed to be sure that their sons were their own, which led them to control the sexuality of women. The desire to control property brought about monogamous marriage and the family. Women were taught

In the 1950s, Talcott Parsons proposed that sociologists interpret gender as a matter of *differences*. As he saw it, masculine men and feminine women formed strong families and made for an orderly society. In recent decades, however, social-conflict theory has reinterpreted gender as a matter of *inequality*. From this point of view, Canadian society places men in a position of dominance over women.

NASCAR racing has always been a masculine world. But Danica Patrick has made a name for herself as an outstanding driver. At the same time, she has made much of her income from trading on her good looks, including the 2009 *Sports Illustrated* swimsuit edition. Are men as likely to do the same? Why or why not?

to remain virgins until marriage, to remain faithful to their husbands thereafter, and to build their lives around bearing and raising one man's children.

According to Engels (1902, orig. 1884), capitalism makes male domination even stronger. First, capitalism creates more wealth, which gives greater power to men as income earners and owners of property. Second, an expanding capitalist economy depends on turning people, especially women, into consumers who seek personal fulfillment by buying and using products. Third, society assigns women the task of maintaining the home to free men to work in factories. The double exploitation of capitalism, as Engels saw it, lies in paying low wages for male labour and paying women no wages at all.

CRITICAL REVIEW Social-conflict analysis is strongly critical of conventional ideas about gender, claiming that society would be better off if we minimized or even did away with this dimension of social structure. That is, this approach regards conventional families, which traditionalists claim are personally and socially positive, as a social evil. A problem with social-conflict analysis, then, is that it minimizes the extent to which women and men live together co-operatively and often happily in families. A second problem lies in the assertion that capitalism is the basis of gender stratification. In fact, agrarian societies are typically more patriarchal than industrial-capitalist societies. Although socialist nations, including the People's Republic of China and the former Soviet Union, did move women into the labour force, by and large they provided women with very low pay in sex-segregated jobs (Haney, 2002; Rosendahl, 1997).

CHECK YOUR LEARNING According to Engels, how does gender support social inequality in a capitalist class system?

Feminism

Feminism is *support of social equality for women and men, in opposition to patriarchy and sexism*. The first wave of feminism in North America began in the 1840s as women opposed to slavery, including Elizabeth Cady Stanton and Lucretia Mott, drew parallels between the oppression of Black and other minorities. Their main objective was obtaining the right to vote, which was finally achieved in 1918 in Canada and 1920 in the United States. But other disadvantages persisted, causing a second wave of feminism to arise in the 1960s that continues today.

Basic Feminist Ideas

Feminism views the everyday lives of women and men through the lens of gender. How we think of ourselves (gender identity), how we act (gender roles), and our social standing as women or men (gender stratification) are all rooted in the operation of society.

Although feminists disagree about many things, most support five general principles:

1. **Working to increase equality.** Feminist thinking is political; it relates ideas to action. Feminism is critical of the status quo, pushing for change toward social equality for women and men.

2. **Expanding human choice.** Feminists argue that cultural ideas about gender divide the full range of human qualities into two opposing and limiting spheres: the female world of emotion and co-operation and the male world of rationality and competition. As an alternative, feminists propose a "reintegration of humanity" by which all individuals develop all human traits (French, 1985).

3. **Eliminating gender stratification.** Feminism opposes laws and cultural norms that limit the education, income, and job opportunities of women. For this reason, feminists have long supported the passage of Canada's Charter of Rights and Freedoms, which guarantees women and other disadvantaged groups equality and equal protection under the law, and the Canadian Human Rights Act, which prohibits discrimination based on sex, among other characteristics.

4. **Ending sexual violence.** Today's women's movement seeks to eliminate sexual violence. Feminists argue that patriarchy distorts relationships between women and men, encouraging violence against women in the form of rape, domestic abuse, sexual harassment, and pornography (Dworkin, 1987; Freedman, 2002).

5. **Promoting sexual freedom.** Finally, feminism advocates women's control over their sexuality and reproduction. Feminists support the free availability of birth control information. As Figure 10–4 shows, about three-quarters of married Canadian women of child-bearing age use contraception; the use of contraceptives is far less common in many lower-income nations. Most feminists also support a woman's right to choose whether to have children or to end a pregnancy, rather than allowing men—husbands, physicians, and legislators—to control their reproduction. Many feminists also support gay people's efforts

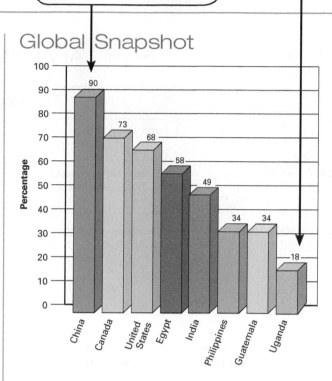

Global Snapshot

FIGURE 10–4 Use of Contraception by Married Women of Child-Bearing Age

In Canada, most married women of child-bearing age use contraception. In many lower-income countries, however, most women do not have the opportunity to make this choice.

Source: Population Reference Bureau (2009).

to end prejudice and discrimination in a largely heterosexual culture (Armstrong, 2002; Ferree & Hess, 1995).

Types of Feminism

Although feminists agree on the importance of gender equality, they disagree on how to achieve it: through liberal feminism, socialist feminism, or radical feminism (Armstrong, 2002; Ferree & Hess, 1995; Freedman, 2002; Stacey, 1983; Vogel, 1983). The Applying Theory table on page 274 highlights key arguments made by each type of feminist thinking.

Liberal Feminism

Liberal feminism is rooted in classic liberal thinking that individuals should be free to develop their own talents and pursue their own interests. Liberal feminists accept the basic organization of our society but seek to expand the rights and opportunities of women; they look to the passage of the Charter of Rights and Freedoms as an important step to achieving this goal. Liberal feminists also support reproductive freedom for all women. They respect the family as a

Feminism

	Liberal Feminism	Socialist Feminism	Radical Feminism
Does it accept the basic order of society?	Yes. Liberal feminism seeks change only to ensure equality of opportunity.	No. Socialist feminism supports an end to social classes and to family gender roles that encourage "domestic slavery."	No. Radical feminism supports an end to the family system.
How do women improve their social standing?	Individually, according to personal ability and effort.	Collectively, through socialist revolution.	Collectively, by working to eliminate gender itself.

social institution but seek changes in society, including more widely available maternity and paternity leave and child care for parents who work.

Given their beliefs in the rights of individuals, liberal feminists think that women should advance according to their individual efforts and merit, rather than by working collectively for change. Both women and men, through personal achievement, are capable of improving their lives, as long as society removes legal and cultural barriers.

Socialist Feminism

Socialist feminism evolved from the ideas of Karl Marx and Friedrich Engels. From this point of view, capitalism increases patriarchy by concentrating wealth and power in the hands of a small number of men. Socialist feminists do not think the reforms supported by liberal feminists go far enough. They believe that the family form fostered by capitalism must change in order to replace "domestic slavery" with some collective means of carrying out housework and child care. Replacing the traditional family can come about only through a socialist revolution that creates a state-centred economy to meet the needs of all.

Radical Feminism

Like socialist feminism, *radical feminism* finds liberal feminism inadequate. Radical feminists believe that patriarchy is so firmly entrenched that even a socialist revolution would not end it. Instead, reaching the goal of gender equality means that society must eliminate gender itself.

Feminism is one type of social-conflict approach to understanding gender.

Opposition to Feminism

Because feminism calls for significant change, it has always been controversial. Figure 10–5 shows a downward trend in opposition to feminism among college students after 1970. Note, however, that little change has occurred in recent years and that more men than women express anti-feminist attitudes.

Feminism provokes criticism and resistance from both men and women who hold conventional ideas about gender. Some men oppose sexual equality for the same reasons that many white people have historically opposed social equality for Aboriginal people and visible minorities: They do not want to give up their privileges. Other men and women, including those who are neither rich nor powerful, distrust a social movement (especially its radical expressions) that attacks the traditional family and rejects patterns that have guided male-female relations for centuries. Canadians belonging to the Real Women of Canada promote their organization as Canada's "alternative women's movement," which represents the concerns of women homemakers and emphasizes the family as society's most important institution.

Men who have been socialized to value strength and dominance may feel uneasy about feminist ideals of men as gentle and warm (Doyle, 1983). Similarly, some women whose lives centre on their husbands and children may think that feminism does not value the social roles that give meaning to their lives. In general, opposition

Student Snapshot

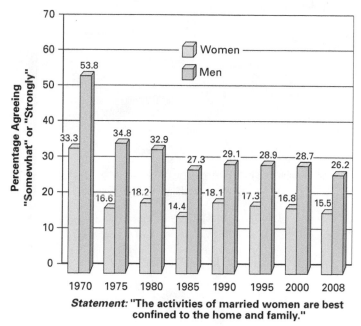

Percentage Agreeing "Somewhat" or "Strongly"

Women
Men

1970: 53.8, 33.3
1975: 16.6, 34.8
1980: 18.2, 32.9
1985: 14.4, 27.3
1990: 18.1, 29.1
1995: 17.3, 28.9
2000: 16.8, 28.7
2008: 15.5, 26.2

Statement: "The activities of married women are best confined to the home and family."

FIGURE 10–5   **Opposition to Feminism among First-Year College Students, 1970–2008**

The share of college students expressing anti-feminist views declined after 1970. Men are still more likely than women to hold such attitudes.

Sources: Astin et al. (2002) and Pryor et al. (2009).

to feminism is greatest among women who have the least education and those who do not work outside the home (Ferree & Hess, 1995; Marshall, 1985).

Resistance to feminism is also found within academic circles. Some sociologists charge that feminism ignores a growing body of evidence that men and women do think and act in somewhat different ways, which may make complete gender equality impossible. Furthermore, say critics, with its drive to increase women's presence in the workplace, feminism undervalues the crucial and unique contribution women make to the development of children, especially in the first years of life (Baydar & Brooks-Gunn, 1991; Gibbs, 2001; Popenoe, 1993b).

Finally, there is the question of *how* women should go about improving their social standing. A large majority of adults in Canada think that women should have equal rights, but many

also say that women should advance individually, according to their training and abilities.

For these reasons, most opposition to feminism is directed toward its socialist and radical forms, while support for liberal feminism is widespread. In addition, we are seeing an unmistakable trend toward gender equality, with more and more Canadian women participating in the labour force and an increasing number of male partners sharing responsibilities in the home. While gender equality in family and working life is more apparent in dual-career marriages of professional men and women (Hertz, 1986), pro-feminist men argue that their gender can be taught that both masculine and feminine identities are changing and that many of the choices open to them conflict with archaic masculine values (Morra & Smith, 1998).

Gender: Looking Ahead

Predictions about the future are no more than educated guesses. Just as economists disagree about the likely inflation rate a year from now, sociologists can offer only general observations about the likely future of gender and society.

Change so far has been remarkable. A century ago, women were second-class citizens, without access to many jobs, barred from public office, and with no right to vote. Although women remain socially disadvantaged, the movement toward equality has surged ahead. Two-thirds of people entering the workforce in the 1990s were women, and in 2000, for the first time, a majority of families had both husband and wife in the paid labour force. Today's economy depends a great deal on the earnings of women. In addition, as recent research shows, one-third of married or common-law men in Canada have partners who earn more than they do (Statistics Canada, 2006g).

Many factors have contributed to this transformation. Perhaps most important, industrialization and advances in computer technology have shifted the nature of work from physically demanding tasks that favoured male strength to jobs that require thought and imagination. This change puts women and men on an even footing. Also, because birth control technology has given us greater control over reproduction, women's lives are less constrained by unwanted pregnancies.

Many women and men have deliberately pursued social equality. For example, sexual harassment complaints in the workplace are taken much more seriously today than they were a generation ago. As more women assume positions of power in the corporate and political worlds, social changes in the twenty-first century may be as great as those that have already taken place.

CHAPTER 10 GENDER STRATIFICATION

CAN YOU SPOT "GENDER MESSAGES" IN THE WORLD AROUND YOU? As this chapter makes clear, gender is one of the basic organizing principles of everyday life. Most of the places we go and most of the activities we engage in as part of our daily routines are "gendered," meaning that they are defined as either more masculine or more feminine. In the work force gender reflects in both wages and profession. Take a look at the photos below. In each case, can you explain how gender is at work?

Based on what you have read about gender roles, who would you assume is the doctor in this photo? Why do you make that assumption?

According to Statistics Canada in 2006, only 6.5% of women were employed in trades, transport, and construction. Do you see support for these statistics in the enrolment for these programs on your campus?

HINT: As this chapter explained, men dominate the trades, transport and construction, as well as professionals employed in the natural sciences, engineering, and mathematics. Clerical and administrative support positions are called "pink-collar jobs" because 75 percent are filled by women.

Applying Sociology in Everyday Life

1. Look through some recent magazines and select three advertisements that involve gender. In each case, provide analysis of how gender is used in the ad.

2. Watch several hours of children's television programming on a Saturday morning. Notice the advertising, which mostly sells toys and breakfast cereal. Keep track of what share of toys is "gendered"—that is, aimed at one sex or the other. What traits do you associate with toys intended for boys and those intended for girls?

3. Do some research on the history of women's issues in your province or territory. When was the first woman sent to Parliament? What laws once existed that restricted the work women could do? Do any such laws exist today? What share of political officials today are women?

MAKING THE GRADE

CHAPTER 10 Gender Stratification

Gender and Inequality

GENDER refers to the meaning a culture attaches to being female or male.

- Evidence that gender is rooted in culture includes global comparisons by Margaret Mead and others showing how societies define what is feminine and masculine in various ways.
- Gender is not only about difference: Because societies give more power and other resources to men than to women, gender is an important dimension of social stratification. **Sexism** is built into the operation of social institutions.
- Although some degree of **patriarchy** is found almost everywhere, it varies throughout history and from society to society.

pp. 252–56

Gender and Socialization

Through the socialization process, gender becomes part of our personalities (**gender identity**) and our actions (**gender identity**). All of the major agents of socialization—family, peer groups, schools, and the mass media—reinforce cultural definitions of what is feminine and masculine.

pp. 256–57

gender (p. 252) the personal traits and social positions that members of a society attach to being female or male

gender stratification (p. 252) the unequal distribution of wealth, power, and privilege between men and women

matriarchy (p. 254) a form of social organization in which females dominate males

patriarchy (p. 254) a form of social organization in which males dominate females

sexism (p. 254) the belief that one sex is innately superior to the other

gender roles (sex roles) (p. 256) attitudes and activities that a society links to each sex

Gender and Social Stratification

Gender stratification shapes
THE WORKPLACE:

- A majority of women are now in the paid labour force, but more than 50 percent hold clerical, administrative assistant, or sales and service jobs.
- Comparing full-time Canadian workers, women earn 71.3% of what men earn.
- This gender difference in earnings results from differences in jobs, differences in family responsibilities, and discrimination.

pp. 258–62

Gender stratification shapes
FAMILY LIFE:

- Most unpaid housework is performed by women, whether or not they hold jobs outside the home.
- Pregnancy and raising small children keep many women out of the labour force at a time when their male peers are making important career gains.

p. 262

Gender stratification shapes
EDUCATION:

- Women now earn 59 percent of all associate's and bachelor's degrees.
- Women make up more than 50 percent of students with master's degrees, nearly half of doctorate holders, and are an increasing share of graduates in professions traditionally dominated by men, including medicine and business administration.

pp. 262–63

minority (p. 265) any category of people distinguished by physical or cultural difference that a society sets apart and subordinates

intersection theory (p. 266) analysis of the interplay of race, class, and gender, often resulting in multiple dimensions of disadvantage

sexual harassment (p. 268) comments, gestures, or physical contacts of a sexual nature that are deliberate, repeated, and unwelcome

Gender stratification shapes
POLITICS:

- Until a century ago, almost no women held elected office in Canada.
- In recent decades, the number of women in politics has increased significantly.
- Even so, the vast majority of elected officials, especially at the national level, are men.

p. 265

INTERSECTION THEORY
investigates the intersection of race, class, and gender, factors that combine to cause special disadvantages to some categories of people.

- Aboriginal and visible minority women encounter greater social disadvantages than white women and earn much less than white men.
- Because all women have a distinctive social identity and are disadvantaged, they are a minority, although most white women do not think of themselves this way.

pp. 266–67

VIOLENCE AGAINST WOMEN AND MEN is a widespread problem that is linked to how a society defines gender. Related issues include

- **sexual harassment**, which mostly victimizes women because our culture encourages men to be assertive and to see women in sexual terms.
- **pornography**, which portrays women as sexual objects. Many see pornography as a moral issue; because pornography dehumanizes women, it is also a power issue.

pp. 267–69

Theoretical Analysis of Gender

The **STRUCTURAL-FUNCTIONAL APPROACH** suggests that

- in pre-industrial societies, distinctive roles for males and females reflect biological differences between the sexes.
- in industrial societies, marked gender inequality becomes dysfunctional and gradually decreases.

Talcott Parsons described gender differences in terms of complementary roles that promote the social integration of families and society as a whole.

pp. 269–71

The **SYMBOLIC-INTERACTION APPROACH** suggests that

- individuals use gender as one element of their personal performances as they socially construct reality through everyday interactions.
- gender plays a part in shaping almost all of our everyday experiences.

Because our society defines men as having more value than women, the sex roles that define how women and men should behave place men in control of social situations; women play a more deferential role.

p. 271

The **SOCIAL-CONFLICT APPROACH** suggests that

- gender is an important dimension of social inequality and social conflict.
- gender inequality benefits men and disadvantages women.

Friedrich Engels tied gender stratification to the rise of private property and a class hierarchy. Marriage and the family are strategies by which men control their property through control of the sexuality of women. Capitalism exploits everyone by paying men low wages and assigning women the task of maintaining the home.

pp. 271–72

See the Applying Theory table on page 270.

Feminism

FEMINISM

- endorses the social equality of women and men and opposes patriarchy and sexism.
- seeks to eliminate violence against women.
- advocates giving women control over their reproduction.

There are three types of feminism:

- Liberal feminism seeks equal opportunity for both sexes within the existing society.
- Socialist feminism claims that gender equality will come about by replacing capitalism with socialism.
- Radical feminism seeks to eliminate the concept of gender itself and to create an egalitarian and gender-free society.

Today, only a minority of Canadians oppose feminism. Most opposition is directed toward socialist and radical feminism. Support for liberal feminism is widespread.

pp. 271–75

feminism (p. 272) support of social equality for women and men, in opposition to patriarchy and sexism

See the Applying Theory table on page 274.

MySocLab

Visit MySocLab at www.mysoclab.com to access a variety of online resources that will help you to prepare for tests and to apply your knowledge, including

- **an eText**
- **videos**
- **self-grading quizzes**
- **glossary flashcards**

11 Race and Ethnicity

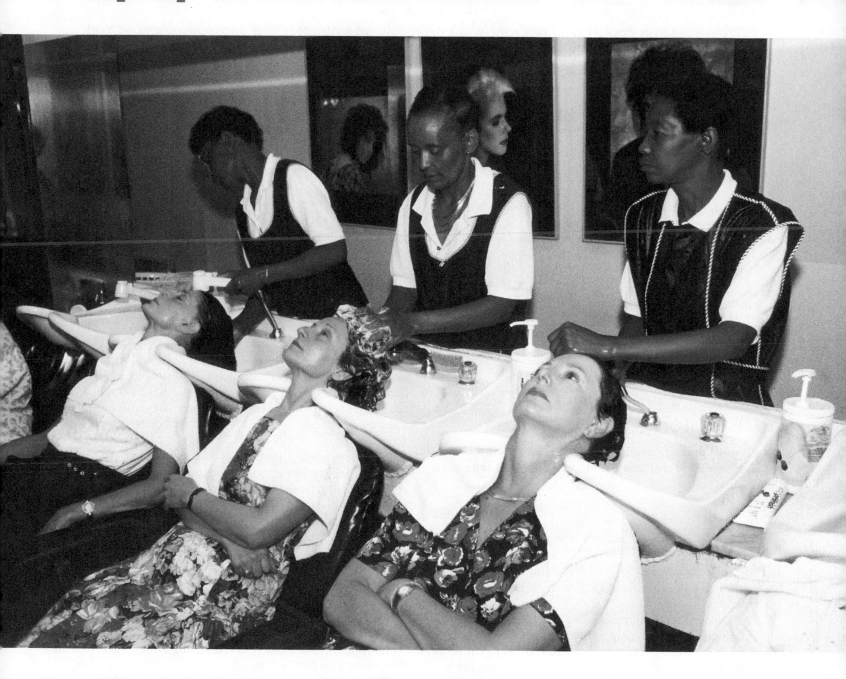

- What are race and ethnicity, and how are they created by society?

- Why does Canada have so much racial and ethnic diversity?

- How are race and ethnicity important dimensions of social inequality today?

This chapter explains how race and ethnicity are created by society. Both race and ethnicity are not only matters of difference but also dimensions of social inequality.

On a cool November morning in Toronto, an instructor in a sociology class at York University is leading a small-group discussion of race and ethnicity. He explains that the meaning of both concepts is far less clear than most people think. Then he asks, "How do you describe yourself?"

Eva Rodriguez leans forward in her chair and is quick to respond. "Who am I? Or should I say what am I? This is hard for me to answer. Most people think of race as black and white. But it's not. I have both black and white ancestry in me, but you know what? I don't think of myself in that way. I don't think of myself in terms of race at all. It would be better to call me Puerto Rican or Hispanic. Personally, I prefer the term 'Latina.' Calling myself Latina says I have mixed racial heritage, and that's what I am. I wish more people understood that race is not clear-cut."

This chapter examines the meaning of race and ethnicity. There are now millions of people in Canada who, like Eva Rodriguez, do not think of themselves in terms of a single category but as having a mix of ancestry.

The Social Meaning of Race and Ethnicity

As the story that opened this chapter suggests, people often confuse "race" and "ethnicity." For this reason, we begin with some basic definitions.

Race

A **race** is *a socially constructed category of people who share biologically transmitted traits that members of a society consider important.* People may classify one another racially on the basis of physical characteristics such as skin colour, facial features, hair texture, and body shape.

Racial diversity appeared among our human ancestors as the result of living in different geographic regions of the world. In regions of intense heat, people developed darker skin (from the natural pigment melanin), which offers protection from the sun; in moderate climates, people developed lighter skin. Such traits are literally only skin deep because human beings the world over are members of a single biological species.

The striking variety of racial traits found today is also the product of migration; genetic characteristics once common to a single place are now found in many lands. Especially pronounced is the racial mix in the Middle East (that is, western Asia), historically a crossroads of migration. Greater racial uniformity characterizes more isolated peoples such as the island-dwelling Japanese. But every population has some genetic mixture, and increasing contact ensures even more racial blending of physical characteristics in the future.

Although we often think of race in terms of biological elements, race is a socially constructed concept. It is true that human beings differ in any number of ways involving physical traits, but a "race" comes into being only when the members of a society decide that some particular physical trait (such as skin colour or eye shape) actually *matters.*

Because race is a matter of social definitions, it is a highly variable concept. For example, the members of American society consider racial differences more important than people of many other countries. They also tend to "see" three racial categories: typically, Black, white, and Asian. Canadians commonly see Aboriginal, Asian, white, and Black. Other societies identify many more categories. People in Brazil, for instance, distinguish between *branca* (white), *parda* (brown), *morena* (brunette), *mulata* (mulatto), *preta* (black), and *amarela* (yellow) (Inciardi, Surratt, & Telles, 2000).

In addition, race may be defined differently by various categories of people within a society. Research shows that white people in North America "see" Black people as having darker skin colour than Black people do (Hill, 2002).

The meaning and importance of race not only differ from place to place but also change over time. Back in 1900, for example, it was common in Canada to consider people of Irish, Italian, or Jewish ancestry as "non-white." By 1950, however, this was no longer the case, and such people today are considered part of the "white" category (Brodkin, 2007; Loveman, 1999).

Today, Statistics Canada presents data on visible minorities rather than on race and allows people to describe themselves using more than one racial category, allowing one or more choices among

race (p. 280) a socially constructed category of people who share biologically transmitted traits that members of a society consider important

The range of biological variation in human beings is far greater than any system of racial classification allows. This fact is made obvious by trying to place all of the people pictured here into simple racial categories.

more than 10 options and "other." As Table 11–1 on page 282 shows, our society officially recognizes a wide range of multiracial people.

Racial Types

Scientists invented the concept of race more than a century ago as they tried to organize the world's physical diversity into three racial types. They called people with relatively light skin and fine hair *Caucasoid*, people with darker skin and coarse hair *Negroid*, and people with yellow or brown skin and distinctive folds on the eyelids *Mongoloid*.

Sociologists consider such terms misleading at best and harmful at worst. For one thing, no society contains biologically "pure" people. The skin colour of people we might call "Caucasoid" (or "Indo-European," "Caucasian," or, more commonly, "white") ranges from very light (typical in Scandinavia) to very dark (in southern India). The same variation exists among so-called "Negroids" ("Africans" or, more commonly, "Black" people) and "Mongoloids" ("Asians"). In fact, many "white" people (say, in southern India) actually have darker skin than many "Black" people (the Aborigines of Australia). Overall, the three racial categories differ in just 6 percent of their genes, and there is

actually more genetic variation *within* each category than *between* categories. This means that two people in the European nation of Sweden, randomly selected, are likely to have at least as much genetic difference as a Swede and a person in the African nation of Senegal (American Sociological Association, 2003; California Newsreel, 2003; Harris & Sim, 2002).

So just how important is race? From a biological point of view, knowing people's racial category allows us to predict almost nothing about them. Why, then, do societies make so much of race? Such categories allow societies to rank people in a hierarchy, giving some people more money, power, and prestige than others and allowing some people to feel that they are inherently "better" than others.

Because race may matter so much, some societies construct racial categories in extreme ways. Throughout much of the twentieth century, for example, many southern U.S. states labelled as "coloured" anyone with as little as one thirty-second African ancestry (that is, one African-American great-great-great-grandparent). Today, American law allows parents to declare the race of a child (or not) as they wish. Even so, most members of American society are still very sensitive to people's racial backgrounds.

TABLE 11–1 Visible Minority Categories, Age 15 and Over, Canada, 2006

Visible Minority Category	Number of People
Chinese	1 005 635
South Asian	957 645
Black	562 135
Filipino	320 915
Latin American	244 330
Southeast Asian	184 575
Arab	195 900
West Asian	125 855
Korean	114 615
Japanese	66 400
Visible minority, Other	57 115
Multiple categories	87 565
Not a visible minority	21 741 525

Source: Statistics Canada (2008j).

A Trend toward Mixture

The population of Canada is quite mixed. Over many generations and throughout the Americas, the genetic traits of Negroid Africans, Caucasoid Europeans, and Mongoloid Native Americans (whose ancestors came from Asia) have intermingled. Many "Black" people therefore have a significant Caucasoid ancestry, many "white" people have some Negroid genes, and many "Aboriginals" have either or sometimes both. In short, whatever people may think, race is no black-and-white issue.

Ninety-eight percent of Canadians who declare themselves as belonging to a visible minority group tend to identify with only one group, even though there may many races in their background. But twice as many second-generation Canadians declare multiple visible minority categories when compared to first-generation Canadians (Statistics Canada, 2008j).

Ethnicity

Ethnicity is *a shared cultural heritage.* People define themselves—or others—as members of an *ethnic category* based on common ancestors, language, and religion that give them a distinctive social identity. Canada is a multi-ethnic society in which English and French are the "official languages," yet many people speak other languages at home, including Mandarin, Cantonese, Hindi, Thai, Italian, German, Spanish, or Swedish. Keep in mind that race is constructed from *biological* traits and ethnicity is constructed from *cultural* traits. Of course, the two may go hand in hand. For example, Japanese Canadians have distinctive physical traits and, for those who maintain a traditional way of life, a distinctive culture as well. Table 11–2

TABLE 11–2 Largest Ethnic Groups, Canada, 2006

Ethnic group	Number of responses	Single response	One of several responses
Canadian	10 066 290	18.4%	13.8%
English	6 570 015	4.4%	16.7%
French	4 941 210	3.9%	11.9%
Scottish	4 719 850	1.8%	13.3%
Irish	4 354 155	1.6%	12.4%
German	3 179 425	2.1%	8.0%
Italian	1 445 330	2.4%	2.3%
Chinese	1 346 510	3.6%	0.7%
North American Indian	1 253 620	1.6%	2.4%
Ukrainian	1 209 090	1.0%	2.9%
Dutch (Netherlands)	1 035 965	1.0%	2.3%
Polish	984 565	0.9%	2.3%
East Indian	962 670	2.5%	0.6%
Russian	500 600	0.3%	1.3%
Welsh	440 960	0.1%	1.3%
Filipino	436 195	1.0%	0.4%
Norwegian	432 515	0.1%	1.2%
Portuguese	410 850	0.8%	0.5%
Metis	409 065	0.2%	1.1%
Swedish	334 765	0.1%	1.0%
Spanish	325 730	0.2%	0.8%
American	316 350	0.1%	0.9%
Hungarian (Magyar)	315 510	0.3%	0.7%
Jewish	315 120	0.4%	0.6%
Greek	242 685	0.5%	0.3%
Jamaican	231 110	0.4%	0.3%
Danish	200 035	0.1%	0.5%
Austrian	194 255	0.1%	0.5%
Romanian	192 170	0.3%	0.4%
Vietnamese	180 130	0.4%	0.1%
Belgian	168 915	0.1%	0.4%
Lebanese	165 150	0.3%	0.2%
Québécois	146 590	0.3%	0.2%
Korean	146 545	0.4%	0.0%
Swiss	137 775	0.1%	0.4%
Finnish	131 045	0.1%	0.3%
Pakistani	124 730	0.3%	0.1%

(Continued)

minority any category of people distinguished by physical or cultural difference that a society sets apart and subordinates

TABLE 11–2 *(Continued)*

Ethnic group	Number of responses	Single response	One of several responses
Iranian	121 505	0.3%	0.1%
Croatian	110 880	0.2%	0.2%
Sri Lankan	103 625	0.3%	0.1%
Haitian	102 430	0.3%	0.1%
Japanese	98 905	0.2%	0.1%
Czech	98 090	0.1%	0.2%
Acadian	96 145	0.1%	0.2%
Icelandic	88 875	0.0%	0.3%
Serbian	72 690	0.1%	0.1%
Inuit	65 885	0.1%	0.1%
Total Responses	52 573 830	18 319 460	34 254 260
Total Population	31 241 030	58.6%	41.4%

Source: Statistics Canada (2008l).

presents the broad sweep of ethnic diversity in Canada, as recorded by the 2006 census.

On an individual level, people either play up or play down their ethnicity, depending on whether they want to fit in or stand apart from the surrounding society: Immigrants may drop their cultural traditions over time or, like many people of Aboriginal background in recent years, try to revive their heritage (Dickason, 1992; Nagel, 1994; Spencer, 1994). For most people, ethnicity is a more complex issue than race because they identify with several ethnic backgrounds. The golf star Tiger Woods, for example, describes himself as one-eighth American Indian, one-fourth Thai, one-fourth Chinese, one-eighth white, and one-fourth Black (White, 1997).

Minorities

March 3, Toronto, Ontario. Spending several hours waiting at an airport in any major city in Canada presents a lesson in contrasts: The majority of the unionized airline staff are white; the majority of the employees who serve the food and clean are visible minorities.

As defined in Chapter 10 ("Gender Stratification"), a **minority** is *any category of people distinguished by physical or cultural difference that a society sets apart and subordinates.* Minority standing can be based on race, ethnicity, or both; many people define themselves as multiracial. In the 2006 Census, 41.4 percent of the

Canadian population defined themselves with two or more of the 200-plus racial categories (up by 15 percent from 2001) (Statistics Canada, 2006h).

The 1996 census was the first in which "Canadian" was included in the examples accompanying the question on ethnicity. In that year, 18.7 percent of the population stated "Canadian" as their only ethnic origin and another 12.2 percent included it in among up to six permissible ethnic origins. In the 2001 census, almost 40 percent of Canadians marked "Canadian" as one of their ethnicities or their only one. In the 2006 census, 10.1 million people, or 32.2 percent of the total population, made this choice. While "Canadian" remained the most frequently reported ethnic origin in 2006, the absolute number of people checking this category actually declined from 2001.

Table 11–2 also illustrates the ethnic diversity of Canada. If the first category, "Canadian," is disregarded, the lengthy list of sole ethnicities covers only 35 percent of the Canadian population in 2001. In addition to the 206 specific ethnic backgrounds listed in the census summary tables—down to the smallest, Dinka (500 people)—there are 17 other ethnic categories that list those "not included elsewhere" (n.i.e.). Nevertheless, the numerical dominance of the British (7.5 percent), and the French (6.7 percent) is declining over time. In 2006, 6.2 percent claim Chinese ethnicity among all Canadians who claim only one ethnic background.

Minorities have two important characteristics. First, they share a *distinct identity*, which may be based on physical or cultural traits. Second, minorities experience *subordination*. As the rest of this chapter shows, Canadian minorities typically have lower income, lower occupational prestige, and limited schooling. Class, race, and ethnicity, as well as gender, are overlapping and reinforcing dimensions of social stratification.

Of course, not all members of a minority category are disadvantaged. For example, some Aboriginals are quite wealthy; other Aboriginals are celebrated academic, professional, and artistic leaders. But even job success rarely allows individuals to escape their minority standing (Benjamin, 1991; Shields & Wheatley Price, 2000). As described in Chapter 4 ("Social Interaction in Everyday Life"), race or ethnicity often serves as a master status that overshadows personal accomplishments.

As noted, minorities usually—but not always—make up a small proportion of a society's population. For example, Black South Africans are disadvantaged even though they are a numerical majority in their country. In Canada, women make up slightly more than half of the population but are still struggling for the opportunities and privileges enjoyed by men. National Map 11–1 on page 284 shows the percentage of visible minorities in different parts of Canada.

The Thinking about Diversity box on page 285 describes the struggles of recent Latin American immigrants to North America.

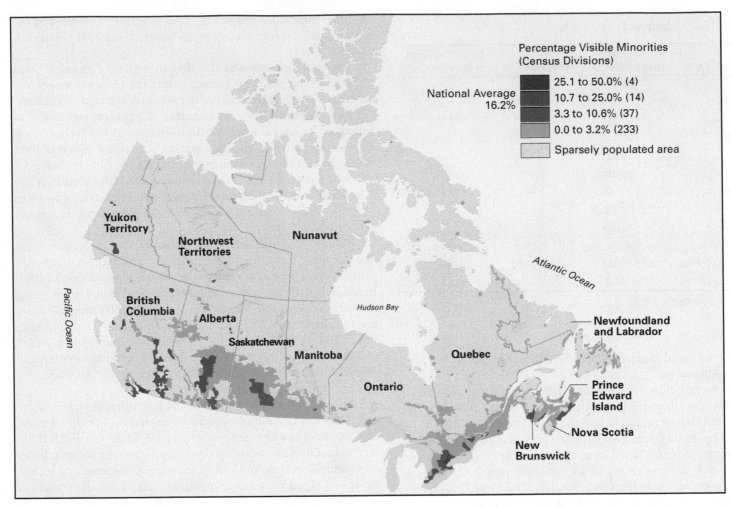

Seeing Ourselves

NATIONAL MAP 11–1   Visible Minorities in Canada, 2006

This map shows that there are only 18 census divisions in Canada where visible minorities make up 10.7 percent or more of the population. Only a few census divisions exceed the national average of 16.2 percent. Why do you think there are so few visible minorities in most of Canada?

Source: Calculated based on data in Statistics Canada (2011v).

Prejudice and Stereotypes

November 19, Jerusalem, Israel. We are driving along the edge of this historical city, a holy place to Jews, Christians, and Muslims, when Razi, our taxi driver, spots a small group of Falasha—Ethiopian Jews—on a street corner. "Those people over there," he begins, "they are different. They don't drive cars. They don't want to improve themselves. Even when our country offers them schooling, they don't take it." He shakes his head at the Ethiopians and drives on.

Prejudice is *a rigid and unfair generalization about an entire category of people.* Prejudice is unfair because *all* people in some category are described as the same, based on little or no direct evidence. Prejudice may target people of a particular social class, sex, sexual orientation, age, political affiliation, race, or ethnicity.

stereotype a simplified description applied to every person in some category

THINKING ABOUT DIVERSITY: RACE, CLASS, AND GENDER

Hard Work: The Immigrant Life in North America

On Saturday, June 10, 2006, British Columbia's minister for transportation, Kevin Falcon, celebrated the start of the tunnel-boring operation for the new rapid transit line linking Vancouver airport with other parts of the city. The boring machine—Sweet Leilani—was so sophisticated that it required specialized staffing from Costa Rica, Peru, and Colombia. The only problem was that these workers were paid as little as $3.47 per hour, a lot less than the legislated minimum wage in British Columbia. Less than a month later, a majority of the foreign workers had voted to become unionized.

As each driver pulls into the yard, the foreman asks, "How much?" Most of the people in the trucks offer $5 an hour. Cespedes automatically responds, "$7.25; the going rate is $7.25 for an hour's hard work." Sometimes he convinces people to pay that much, but usually not. The workers, who come from Mexico, El Salvador, and Guatemala, know that dozens of them will end up with no work at all this day. Most accept $5 or $6 an hour because they know that when the day is over, $50 is better than nothing.

Canada today is confronting a unique problem: it no longer has enough workers, especially those in construction and the trades. Employers crying out for temporary workers argue that Canada should beef up its guest worker program and make it easier to recruit immigrants. On the other hand, critics (including trade unions) argue that guest workers depress wages for Canadian workers and worsen working conditions. At the same time, some Canadian unions have begun to support guest workers struggling to unionize.

The hard truth is that immigrants to Canada and the United States do the jobs that no one else wants. Immigrants represent the bottom level of our national economy, working in restaurants and hotels, on construction crews, and in private homes cooking, cleaning, and caring for children. Across North America, about half of all housekeepers, household cooks, tailors, and restaurant waiters are men or women born abroad. Few immigrants make much more than the minimum wage and—unless they gain landed immigrant or citizenship status—are unlikely to receive any health or pension benefits.

Like the United States and Britain, Canada has not signed a UN Convention that protects the rights of migrant workers.

WHAT DO YOU THINK?

1. In what ways do you or members of your family depend on the low-paid labour of immigrants?

2. Do you think there is anything wrong with paying someone the current minimum wage for hard work? Why or why not?

3. Do you think that guest workers to Canada should have the right to become permanent residents and eventually citizens?

Sources: Wong, Lloyd and Trumper, Ricardo. "Canada's Guestworkers: Racialized, Gendered and Flexible," 151–170, in *Race and Racism in 21st Century Canada: Continuity, Complexity, and Change*, Edited by Sean P. Hier and B. Singh Bolaria. University of Toronto Press, Higher Education Division © 2007. Reprinted with permission of the publisher; and From *The Washington Post*, © [July 13, 1998] *The Washington Post* All rights reserved. Used by permission and protected by the Copyright Laws of the United States. The printing, copying, redistribution, or retransmission of the Material without express written permission is prohibited.

Prejudices are *prejudgments* that can be either positive or negative. Our positive prejudices exaggerate the virtues of people like ourselves, and our negative prejudices condemn those who are different from us. Negative prejudice can be expressed as anything from mild dislike to outright hostility. Because such attitudes are rooted in culture, everyone has at least some prejudice.

Prejudice often takes the form of a **stereotype** (*stereo* is derived from a Greek word meaning "solid"), which is *a simplified description applied to every person in some category*. Many white people hold stereotypical views of minorities. Stereotyping is especially harmful to minorities in the workplace. If company officials see minority workers only in terms of a stereotype, they will make assumptions about their abilities, steer them toward certain jobs, and limit their access to better opportunities (R.L. Kaufman, 2002).

Minorities, too, stereotype whites and also other minorities (Cummings & Lambert, 1997; Smith, 1996). Surveys show, for example, that more African-Americans than whites express the belief that Asians engage in unfair business practices and that more Asians than whites criticize Hispanics for having too many children (Perlmutter, 2002).

Measuring Prejudice: The Social Distance Scale

One measure of prejudice is *social distance*, how closely people are willing to interact with members of some category. In the 1920s, Emory Bogardus developed the *social distance scale* shown in Figure 11-1 on page 286. Bogardus (1925) asked students at colleges and universities in the United States how closely they were willing to interact with people in 30 racial and ethnic categories. People express the greatest social distance (most negative prejudice) by declaring that some category of people should be barred from the country entirely (point 7 in the figure); at the other extreme, people express the least social distance (most social acceptance) by saying they would accept a member of some category into their family through marriage (point 1).

Bogardus (1925, 1967; Owen, Elsner, & McFaul, 1977) found that people felt much more social distance from some categories than from others. In general, students in his surveys expressed the most social distance from Hispanics, African-Americans, Asians,

Student Snapshot

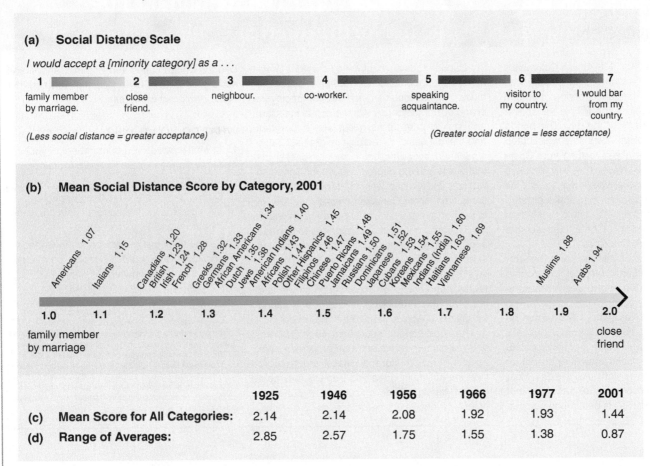

(a) Social Distance Scale

I would accept a [minority category] as a . . .

1	2	3	4	5	6	7
family member by marriage.	close friend.	neighbour.	co-worker.	speaking acquaintance.	visitor to my country.	I would bar from my country.

(Less social distance = greater acceptance)   *(Greater social distance = less acceptance)*

(b) Mean Social Distance Score by Category, 2001

Americans 1.07 · Italians 1.15 · Canadians 1.20 · British 1.23 · Irish 1.24 · French 1.28 · Greeks 1.32 · Germans 1.33 · African Americans 1.34 · Dutch 1.35 · Jews 1.38 · American Indians 1.40 · Africans 1.43 · Polish 1.44 · Other Hispanics 1.45 · Filipinos 1.46 · Chinese 1.47 · Puerto Ricans 1.48 · Jamaicans 1.49 · Russians 1.50 · Dominicans 1.51 · Japanese 1.52 · Cubans 1.53 · Koreans 1.54 · Mexicans 1.55 · Indians (India) 1.60 · Haitians 1.63 · Vietnamese 1.69 · Muslims 1.88 · Arabs 1.94

Scale: 1.0 · 1.1 · 1.2 · 1.3 · 1.4 · 1.5 · 1.6 · 1.7 · 1.8 · 1.9 · 2.0

1.0 family member by marriage — 2.0 close friend

	1925	1946	1956	1966	1977	2001
(c) Mean Score for All Categories:	2.14	2.14	2.08	1.92	1.93	1.44
(d) Range of Averages:	2.85	2.57	1.75	1.55	1.38	0.87

FIGURE 11–1 **Bogardus Social Distance Research**

The social distance scale is a good way to measure prejudice. Part (a) illustrates the complete social distance scale, from least social distance at the far left to greatest social distance at the far right. Part (b) shows the mean (average) social distance score received by each category of people in 2001. Part (c) presents the overall mean score (the average of the scores received by all racial and ethnic categories) in specific years. These scores have fallen from 2.14 in 1925 to 1.44 in 2001, showing that students express less social distance from minorities today than they did in the past. Part (d) shows the range of averages, the difference between the highest and lowest scores in given years (in 2001, for instance, it was 0.87, the difference between the high score of 1.94 for Arabs and the low score of 1.07 for Americans). This figure has also become smaller since 1925, indicating that today's students tend to see fewer differences between various categories of people.

Source: Parrillo & Donoghue (2005).

and Turks by indicating that they would accept such people as co-workers but not as neighbours, close friends, or family members. People expressed the least social distance from those from northern and western Europe, including English and Scottish people, and also Canadians, indicating that they were willing to include them in their families by marriage.

What patterns of social distance do we find among college and university students today? A recent study using the same social

racism the belief that one racial category is innately superior or inferior to another

scapegoat a person or category of people, typically with little power, whom other people unfairly blame for their own troubles

distance scale[1] reported three major findings (Parrillo & Donoghue, 2005):

1. **Student opinion shows a trend toward greater social acceptance.** Today's students express less social distance from all minorities than students did decades ago. Figure 11–1 shows that the mean (average) score on the social distance scale declined from 2.14 in 1925 to 1.93 in 1977 and to 1.44 in 2001. Respondents (81 percent of whom were white) showed notably greater acceptance of African-Americans, a category of people that moved up from near the bottom in 1925 to the top one-third in 2001.

2. **People see less difference between various minorities.** The earliest studies found the difference between the highest- and lowest-ranked minorities (the range of averages) equal to almost three points on the scale. As the figure shows, the most recent research produced a range of averages of less than one point, indicating that today's students tend to see fewer differences between various categories of people.

3. **The terrorist attacks of September 11, 2001, may have reduced social acceptance of Arabs and Muslims.** The most recent study was conducted just a few weeks after September 11, 2001. Perhaps the fact that the 19 men who attacked the U.S. World Trade Center and the Pentagon were Arabs and Muslims is part of the reason that students ranked these categories last on the social distance scale. However, not a single student gave Arabs or Muslims a 7, indicating that they should be barred from the country. On the contrary, the 2001 mean scores (1.94 for Arabs and 1.88 for Muslims) show higher social acceptance than students in 1977 expressed toward 18 of the 30 categories of people studied.

Racism

A powerful and harmful form of prejudice, **racism** is *the belief that one racial category is innately superior or inferior to another.* Racism has existed throughout world history. Despite their many achievements, the ancient Greeks, the peoples of India, and the Chinese all considered people unlike themselves inferior.

Canadian historical records also contain racism: we should not forget that Canada has a long history of oppression. The practice of slavery is recorded among many of the fishing communities of the Pacific Northwest coast predating European contact (Donald, 1997). Racism was also practised in British North America prior to Canadian Confederation, and officially ended

---

[1]Parrillo and Donoghue dropped seven of the categories used by Bogardus (Armenians, Czechs, Finns, Norwegians, Scots, Swedes, and Turks), claiming that they were no longer visible minorities. They added nine new categories (Africans, Arabs, Cubans, Dominicans, Haitians, Jamaicans, Muslims, Puerto Ricans, and Vietnamese), claiming that these are visible minorities today. This change probably encouraged higher social distance scores, making the trend toward decreasing social distance all the more significant.

only in 1834 (Brand, 1992; Ponting, 1994; Prentice et al., 1996). More recently, evidence has been found of the interplay between racism, sexism, and immigration in our country (Etowa et al., 2007; Iacovetta, 1995; Ng, 1993; Ng & Das Gupta, 1993; Williams, Neighbors, & Jackson, 2003).

Racism remains a serious social problem, as some people still argue that certain racial and ethnic categories are smarter than others. The Seeing Sociology in Everyday Life box on page 288 explains that these common-sense stereotypes fail to recognize that racial differences in mental abilities result from environment rather than from biology.

Theories of Prejudice

Where does prejudice come from? Social scientists provide several answers to this vexing question, focusing on frustration, personality, culture, and social conflict.

Scapegoat Theory

Scapegoat theory holds that prejudice springs from frustration among people who are themselves disadvantaged (Dollard et al., 1939). Take the case of a white woman who is frustrated by her low-paying job in a textile factory. Directing her hostility at the powerful factory owners carries the obvious risk of being fired; therefore, she may blame her low pay on the presence of minority co-workers. Her prejudice does not improve her situation, but it is a relatively safe way to express anger, and it may give her the comforting feeling that at least she is superior to someone.

A **scapegoat**, then, is *a person or category of people, typically with little power, whom other people unfairly blame for their own troubles.* Because they have little power and thus are usually "safe targets," minorities often are used as scapegoats.

Authoritarian Personality Theory

Theodor Adorno and his colleagues (1950) considered extreme prejudice a personality trait of certain individuals. This conclusion is supported by research indicating that people who show strong prejudice toward one minority are usually intolerant of all minorities. These *authoritarian personalities* rigidly conform to conventional cultural values and see moral issues as clear-cut matters of right and wrong. According to Adorno, people who grow up developing authoritarian personalities also view society as naturally competitive, with "better" people (like themselves) dominating those who are weaker (all minorities).

Adorno and colleagues also found the opposite pattern to be true: People who express tolerance toward one minority are likely to be accepting of all. Such people tend to be more flexible in their moral judgments and treat all people as equals.

Adorno thought that people with little education and those raised by cold and demanding parents tend to develop authoritarian personalities. Filled with anger and anxiety as children, they grow into hostile and aggressive adults who seek out scapegoats.

discrimination (p. 289) unequal treatment of various categories of people

institutional prejudice and discrimination (p. 289) bias built into the operation of society's institutions

---

SEEING SOCIOLOGY IN EVERYDAY LIFE — Does Race Affect Intelligence?

As we go through an average day, we encounter people of various racial and ethnic categories. We also deal with people who are very intelligent as well as those whose abilities are more modest. But is there a connection between race or ethnicity and intelligence?

Are Asians smarter than white people? Is the typical white person more intelligent than the average Black person? Throughout the history of Canada, we have painted one category of people as intellectually more gifted than another. Moreover, people have used such thinking to justify the privileges of the allegedly superior category and even to bar supposedly inferior people from entering this country.

So what do we know about intelligence? Scientists know that people, as individuals, differ in mental abilities. The distribution of human intelligence forms a "bell curve." A person's *intelligence quotient* (IQ) is calculated as the person's mental age in years, as measured by a test, divided by the person's actual age in years, with the result multiplied by 100. An eight-year-old who performs like a ten-year-old has an IQ of $10 \div 8 = 1.25 \times 100 = 125$. Average performance is defined as an IQ of 100.

In a controversial study of intelligence and social inequality, Richard Herrnstein and Charles Murray (1994) claim that race is related to measures of intelligence. More specifically, they say that the average IQ for people of European ancestry is 100, for people of East Asian ancestry is 103, and for people of African ancestry is 90.

Such assertions go against our democratic and egalitarian beliefs that no racial type is nat-urally better than another. Because these findings can increase prejudice, critics argue that intelligence tests are not valid and even that the concept of intelligence has little real meaning.

Most social scientists believe that IQ tests do measure something important that we think of as intelligence, and they agree that *individuals* vary in intellectual aptitude. But they reject the idea that any *category* of people, on average, is naturally smarter than any other. So how do we explain the overall differences in IQ scores by race?

Thomas Sowell (1994, 1995) explains that most of this difference results not from biology but from environment. In some skilful sociological detective work, Sowell traced IQ scores for various racial and ethnic categories throughout the twentieth century. He found that, on average, early-twentieth-century immigrants from European nations such as Poland, Lithuania, Italy, and Greece, as well as from Asian countries including China and Japan, scored 10 to 15 points below the U.S. average. But by the end of the twentieth century, people in these same categories had IQ scores that were average or above average. Among Italian Americans, for example, average IQ jumped almost 10 points; among Polish Americans and Chinese Americans, the increase was almost 20 points.

Because genetic changes occur over thousands of years and most people in these categories marry others like themselves, biological factors cannot explain such a rapid rise in IQ scores. The only reasonable explanation is changing cultural patterns. The descendants of early immigrants improved their intellectual performance as their standard of living rose and their opportunity for schooling increased.

Sowell found that much the same was true of African-Americans. Historically, the average IQ score of African-Americans living in the North has been about 10 points higher than the average score of those living in the South. Among the descendants of African-Americans who migrated from the South to the North after 1940, IQ scores went up, just as they did for descendants of European and Asian immigrants. Thus environmental factors appear to be critical in explaining differences in IQ among various categories of people.

According to Sowell, these test score differences tell us that *cultural patterns matter*. Asians who score high on tests are no smarter than other people, but they have been raised to value learning and pursue excellence. For their part, African-Americans are no less intelligent than anyone else, but they carry a legacy of disadvantage that can undermine self-confidence and discourage achievement.

WHAT DO YOU THINK?

1. If IQ scores reflect people's environment, are they valid measures of intelligence? Could they be harmful?

2. According to Thomas Sowell, why do some racial and ethnic categories show dramatic short-term gains in average IQ scores?

3. Do you think that parents and schools influence a child's IQ score? If so, how?

Culture Theory

A third theory claims that although extreme prejudice is found in certain people, some prejudice is found in everyone. Why? Because prejudice is part of the culture in which we all live and learn. The Bogardus social distance studies help prove the point. Bogardus found that students across the country had mostly the same attitudes toward specific racial and ethnic categories, feeling closer to some and more distant from others.

More evidence that prejudice is rooted in culture is the fact that minorities express the same attitudes as white people toward catego-ries other than their own. Such patterns suggest that individuals hold prejudices because we live in a "culture of prejudice" that has taught us to view certain categories of people as "better" or "worse" than others.

Do we live in a "culture of prejudice"? The Seeing Sociology in the News box explains that minority job-seekers, especially those with good training, have reason to think that the answer may be yes.

Conflict Theory

A fourth explanation proposes that prejudice is used as a tool by powerful people not only to justify privilege for themselves but also

The Vancouver Sun

Discrimination to Blame for Prosperity Gap

BY DEREK ABMA, POSTMEDIA NEWS
March 21, 2011

Visible minorities are still facing issues regarding pay equity and access to opportunities. A report released today says non-whites in Canada earned 81.4 cents for every dollar made by white people, according to the last census in 2006. . . .

Visible minorities were also found to have a higher unemployment rate of 8.6 percent in 2006—referred to in the study as "the heyday of the economic boom"—compared to 6.2 percent for white Canadians.

That was despite visible minorities being more willing to work, an assumption based on data showing 67.3 per cent of the non-white population was in the labour force compared to 66.7 percent of whites.

"The distribution of work tells a disturbing story," said Grace-Edward Galabuzi, a board member with the Canadian Centre for Policy Alternatives and professor of politics at Ryerson University in Toronto. "Equal access to opportunity eludes many racialized Canadians."

The study said Canada's economy grew 13.1 per cent from 2000 to 2005. But at the same time, the average income of white Canadians, adjusted for inflation, grew 2.7 percent, and racial minorities actually saw a 0.2 percent slide in average pay.

Sheila Block, director of economic analysis at the Wellesley Institute, said the prosperity gap between whites and non-whites in Canada is largely the result of racial discrimination.

"It's an issue that's in some ways inconsistent with how we perceive our society," she said. "But it's there and it's something that we have to have a public discussion about and address."

Block said public policy, including regulations that are more stringent in enforcing racial equality in the workplace, is something that should be looked at.

It is sometimes said that non-minorities are already hard-pressed to find work in areas where equity rules apply, particularly in government. However, Block pointed out that the study showed minorities are under-represented in public administration and other industries that are among the more high-paying and stable sources of employment in this country.

While racial minorities made up 16.2 percent of the country's population in 2006, they filled just 8.1 percent of public administration jobs, the data shows.

Block added that Canada's economy will suffer if minorities continue to face barriers to the labour market. This is due to rising retirements as baby boomers age, low birthrates and continued reliance on immigration to fulfil roles in the job market.

"We really need to fully use the talents and skills of all Canadians," she said.

WHAT DO YOU THINK?

1. Based on the article, what evidence do you find of outright prejudice against visible minorities? What evidence do you find of subtle prejudice?

2. One might wonder if what seems to be racial prejudice is simply a bad job market for everyone. What do you find in the article that suggests that this is not the case?

3. Sometimes people don't intend to discriminate racially but want to employ someone who is a "cultural fit." Explain this pattern. Have you ever experienced anything like this?

Adapted from the original article "Discrimination to Blame for Prosperity Gap: Study. Non-Whites Earn Less Than Whites," by Derek Abma © Copyright (c) Postmedia News, March 21, 2011. Material reprinted with the express permission of: *The Vancouver Sun*, a division of Postmedia Network Inc."

to oppress others. Oil companies in northern Canada who look down on immigrant workers, for example, can get away with paying the immigrants low wages for hard work. Similarly, all elites benefit when prejudice divides workers along racial and ethnic lines and discourages them from working together to advance their common interests (Geschwender, 1978; Olzak, 1989; Rothenberg, 2008).

According to another conflict-based argument, made by Shelby Steele (1990), minorities themselves encourage *race consciousness* (which is sometimes called "identity politics") to win greater power and privileges. Because of their historical disadvantage, minorities claim that they are victims entitled to special consideration based on their race. Although this strategy may bring short-term gains, Steele cautions that such thinking often sparks a backlash from whites or others who oppose "special treatment" on the basis of race or ethnicity.

Discrimination

Closely related to prejudice is **discrimination**, *unequal treatment of various categories of people*. Prejudice refers to *attitudes*; discrimination is a matter of *action*. Like prejudice, discrimination can be either positive (providing special advantages) or negative (creating obstacles) and ranges from subtle to extreme.

Institutional Prejudice and Discrimination

We typically think of prejudice and discrimination as the hateful ideas or actions of specific people. But Stokely Carmichael and Charles Hamilton (1967) point out that far greater harm results from **institutional prejudice and discrimination**, *bias built into the operation of society's institutions*, including schools, hospitals, law enforcement, and the workplace. For example, researchers have shown that banks reject home mortgage applications from minorities at a higher rate—or charge higher rates for the same mortgage—compared to white applicants, even when income and quality of neighbourhood are held constant (Blanton, 2007; Gotham, 1998).

According to Carmichael and Hamilton, people are slow to condemn or even recognize institutional prejudice and discrimination because it often involves respected public officials and long-established traditions. One example of institutional discrimination in Canada was the previously mentioned Indian Act and its harsh rules

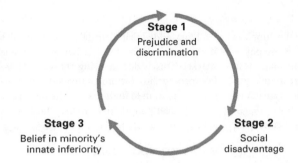

Stage 1
Prejudice and discrimination

Stage 3
Belief in minority's innate inferiority

Stage 2
Social disadvantage

Stage 1: Prejudice and discrimination begin, often as an expression of ethnocentrism or an attempt to justify economic exploitation.

Stage 2: As a result of prejudice and discrimination, a minority is socially disadvantaged, occupying a low position in the system of social stratification.

Stage 3: This social disadvantage is then interpreted not as the result of earlier prejudice and discrimination but as evidence that the minority is innately inferior, unleashing renewed prejudice and discrimination by which the cycle repeats itself.

FIGURE 11–2 **Prejudice and Discrimination: The Vicious Circle**

Prejudice and discrimination can form a vicious circle, perpetuating themselves.

Prejudice and Discrimination: The Vicious Circle

Prejudice and discrimination reinforce each other. The Thomas theorem, discussed in Chapter 4 ("Social Interaction in Everyday Life"), offers a simple explanation of this fact: *Situations that are defined as real become real in their consequences* (Thomas, 1966:301, orig. 1931; Thomas & Thomas, 1928).

As Thomas recognized, stereotypes become real to people who believe them and sometimes even to those victimized by them. Prejudice on the part of white people toward visible minority and Aboriginal peoples does not produce *innate* inferiority, but it can produce *social* inferiority, pushing minorities into low-paying jobs, inferior schools, and racially segregated housing or residential schools. Then, as white people interpret that social disadvantage as evidence that non-whites do not measure up, they unleash a new round of prejudice and discrimination, giving rise to a vicious circle in which each perpetuates the other, as shown in Figure 11–2.

Majority and Minority: Patterns of Interaction

Social scientists describe interaction between majority and minority members of a society in terms of four models: pluralism, assimilation, segregation, and genocide.

Pluralism

Pluralism is *a state in which people of all races and ethnicities are distinct but have equal social standing.* In other words, people who differ in appearance or social heritage all share resources roughly equally.

Canada is pluralistic to the extent that all people have equal standing under the law. In addition, large cities contain countless "ethnic villages" where people proudly display the traditions of their immigrant ancestors. These include Chinatowns found in Victoria, Vancouver, and Toronto; the Jewish area around Avenue du Parc in Montreal; and the Portuguese neighbourhoods around Dundas Street West in Toronto (Zucchi, 2007).

But Canada is not really pluralistic, for three reasons. First, although many people appreciate their cultural heritage, only a small proportion want to live with others exactly like themselves. Second, our tolerance for social diversity goes only so far. One reaction to the growing proportion of minorities in Canada, for example, is the rise of white supremacist groups in many Canadian cities. Third, as we shall see later in this chapter, it is simply a fact that people of various colours and cultures have unequal social standing.

Assimilation

Many people traditionally have viewed Canada as a "mosaic" in which disparate cultural groups join together to create a tolerant and peaceful

toward Aboriginal people (Jamieson, 1986; Ponting & Kiely, 1997). The Act specifically discriminated against Aboriginal women. If a Status Indian woman married a non–Status Indian man, she lost her legal status and was denied rights and benefits under the Indian Act. This meant that many women and children of subsequent generations were culturally alienated from their traditional communities. According to Jeffries (1992:92–93),

> The government's treatment of women under the *Indian Act* was particularly devastating and tantamount to cultural genocide, because women were responsible for maintaining culture. If a woman chose to marry a non-Indian man, she was removed from the government's list of registered Indians . . . Upon marriage, the woman could no longer live in the community in which she was born, nor could she participate in any matters respecting the community. The final insult was upon death: neither she nor any of her children could be buried in a family plot on band land.

With the passage of Bill C-31 in 1985, this patriarchal principle was finally revoked. Yet Aboriginal women's access to land and housing remains problematic to this day (Benoit & Carroll, 1995). Since provincial divorce laws do not hold on reserves, Aboriginal women are at risk of losing all common property after separation or divorce.

●
miscegenation biological reproduction by partners of different racial categories

Most Canadian cities today have distinct ethnic enclaves. Some people see this as a positive trend, arguing that it validates the uniqueness of ethnic cultures. Others argue the opposite, viewing ethnic enclaves as indicative of the ghettoization of marginalized groups in our society (Zucchi, 2007).

multicultural society. Rather than everyone joining as equals in some new cultural pattern, however, minorities typically adopt the traits of the dominant culture established by the earliest settlers. Why? As an avenue to upward social mobility and to escape the prejudice and discrimination directed against more visible foreigners. Sociologists use the term **assimilation** to describe *the process by which minorities gradually adopt patterns of the dominant culture.* Assimilation involves changing styles of dress, values, religion, language, and friends.

The amount of assimilation varies by category. For example, Swedes have assimilated more than Italians, the Dutch more than Dominicans, Germans more than the Japanese. Multiculturalists oppose making assimilation a goal, because it suggests that minorities are "the problem" and it defines them (rather than majority people) as the ones who need to do all of the changing.

Note that assimilation involves changes in ethnicity but not in race. For example, many descendants of Japanese immigrants have discarded their ethnic traditions but retain their racial identity. For racial traits to diminish over generations, **miscegenation**, or *biological reproduction by partners of different racial categories*, must occur. Interracial marriage is becoming more common. In 2006, about 300 000 Canadians were in mixed marriages or common-law relationships, which is an increase of almost 30 percent since 2001. Still, only 3.9 percent of all couples in 2006 were in mixed unions (Milan, Maheux & Chui, 2010).

Segregation

Segregation is *the physical and social separation of categories of people.* Sometimes minorities, especially religious orders such as the Amish, voluntarily segregate themselves. Usually, however, majorities segregate minorities by excluding them. Neighbourhoods,

schools, occupations, hospitals, and even cemeteries may be segregated. Pluralism encourages cultural distinctiveness without disadvantage; segregation enforces separation that harms a minority.

Racial segregation has a long history in Canada, as mentioned above, starting with the segregation of Aboriginal peoples on reserves. Apart from the internment of Japanese Canadians during World War II (Kogawa, 1981; Omatsu, 1992), *de jure* (Latin meaning "by law") discrimination in Canada has been relatively rare, in contrast, for example, with the United States. However, *de facto* ("in fact") segregation continues to this day.

Research by Balakrishnan and Hou (1995) has documented the concentration of different groups in Canada's urban centres. The authors found that visible minorities and Jewish people tend to live in specific areas of a city rather than being dispersed throughout. This contrasts with the British, Germans, and French, who are relatively evenly distributed (the British in Montreal are an exception to this general pattern).

Balakrishnan and Hou also documented the changing nature of residential segregation. First, even though the composition of the immigration stream to Canada has changed in recent decades—a larger proportion of today's immigrants are from Asia—the authors found that the distribution of Asians in urban areas is not changing. Balakrishnan and Hou attributed this to the fact that the selective nature of immigration policy has led to immigrants being highly skilled and therefore not choosing to live in the traditional low-income areas of our cities. Second, the authors pointed out, a certain amount of residential segregation comes from families and individuals choosing to live together rather than being forced into ethnic ghettos. The Jewish population is a case in point. Even though this population is above average in income and education—factors that historically imply freedom of choice—Jews are also among the most segregated ethnic groups in Canada.

Research from the United States shows that, across that country, whites (especially those with young children) continue to avoid neighbourhoods where African-Americans live (Emerson, Yancey, & Chai, 2001; Krysan, 2002). At the extreme, Douglas Massey and Nancy Denton (1989) documented the *hypersegregation* of poor African-Americans in some inner cities. Hypersegregation means having little contact of any kind with people beyond the local community. Hypersegregation is the daily experience of about 20 percent of poor African-Americans and is a pattern found in about 25 large U.S. cities (Wilkes & Iceland, 2004).

Genocide

Genocide is *the systematic killing of one category of people by another.* This deadly form of racism and ethnocentrism violates nearly every recognized moral standard, yet it has occurred time and again in human history.

Genocide was common in the history of contact between Europeans and the original inhabitants of the Americas. From the sixteenth century on, the Spanish, Portuguese, English, French, and Dutch forcibly colonized vast empires. Although most native people died from diseases brought by Europeans, against which they had no natural defences, many who opposed the colonizers were killed deliberately (Matthiessen, 1984; Sale, 1990).

Genocide also occurred in the twentieth century. Beginning in 1915, more than 1 million Armenians were killed by the Ottoman Empire. Likewise, unimaginable horror befell European Jews during Adolf Hitler's reign of terror. During the Holocaust that lasted from about 1935 to 1945, the Nazis murdered more than 6 million Jewish men, women, and children, along with gay people, Gypsies, and people with handicaps. The Soviet dictator Josef Stalin murdered on an even greater scale, killing some 30 million real and imagined enemies during decades of violent rule. Between 1975 and 1980, Pol Pot's Communist regime in Cambodia butchered all "capitalists," which included anyone able to speak a Western language. In all, some 2 million people (one-fourth of the population) perished in the Cambodian "killing fields."

Tragically, genocide continues in the modern world. Recent examples include Hutus killing Tutsis in the African nation of Rwanda, Serbs killing Bosnians in the Balkans of Eastern Europe, and the killing of hundreds of thousands of people in the Darfur region of Sudan.

These four patterns of minority-majority contact have all been played out in Canada. Although many people proudly point to patterns of pluralism and assimilation, it is also important to recognize the degree to which Canadian society has been built on segregation from one end of the country to the other (Black Canadians in Eastern Canada and Japanese Canadians in British Columbia) and genocide (of Aboriginal Canadians). The remainder of this chapter examines how these four patterns have shaped the past and present social standing of major racial and ethnic categories in Canada.

Race and Ethnicity in Canada

Like all people who have nothing, I lived on dreams. I burned my way through stone walls to get to America.

Nu, I got to America.

Ten hours I pushed a machine in a shirtwaist factory, when I was yet lucky to get work.

And always my head was drying up with saving and pinching and worrying to send home a little from the little I earned.

Where are my dreams that were so real to me in the old country?

These words by Jewish immigrant Anzia Yezierska (quoted in Frager, 1992:10) capture the dreams and subsequent disappointments of many European immigrants who made the difficult journey across the Atlantic to find work in the emerging cities of the New World—including "Little York" (Toronto) in Upper Canada and

There has recently been a resurgence in Aboriginals' pride in their heritage. Do you think that this resurgence is because of, or despite, being a minority group?

"Ville-Marie" (Montreal) in Lower Canada. As the following history of Canada's racial and ethnic minorities reveals, our nation's golden door has opened more widely for some than for others.

Canada's Aboriginal Peoples

Some 30 000 years before Columbus "discovered" the Americas, migrating peoples crossed a land bridge from Asia to North America where the Bering Strait (off the coast of Alaska) lies today. Gradually, they made their way throughout North and South America.

When the first Europeans arrived late in the fifteenth century, Native Americans numbered in the millions. But by the beginning of the twentieth century, after relentless subjugation and even acts of genocide, the "vanishing Americans" numbered a mere 250 000 (Dobyns, 1966; Tyler, 1973).

It was Christopher Columbus (1446–1506) who first referred to Native Americans as "Indians"; when he landed in the Bahama Islands in the Caribbean, he mistakenly thought he had reached India. Columbus found the indigenous people to be passive and peaceful, in stark contrast with the more materialistic and competitive Europeans (Matthiessen, 1984; Sale, 1990). Yet even as Europeans seized the land of Native Americans, they demeaned their victims as thieves and murderers to justify their actions (Josephy, 1982; Unruh, 1979).

TABLE 11–3 Aboriginal Population, Canada, 2006

	Total Aboriginal Population	% of Population	% of Aboriginals
Canada	172 790	3.8	100.0
Newfoundland and Labrador	23 450	4.7	2.0
Prince Edward Island	1730	1.3	0.1
Nova Scotia	24 175	2.7	2.1
New Brunswick	17 655	2.5	1.5
Quebec	108 430	1.5	9.2
Ontario	242 495	2.0	20.7
Manitoba	175 395	15.5	15.0
Saskatchewan	141 890	14.9	12.1
Alberta	188 365	5.8	16.1
British Columbia	196 075	4.8	16.7
Yukon Territory	7580	25.1	0.6
Northwest Territories	20 635	50.3	1.8
Nunavut	24 920	85.0	2.1

Source: Statistics Canada (2011w).

At the beginning of the eighteenth century there were about 10 Aboriginal people for every European settler in Canada; by 1881, there were about 40 Europeans for every Aboriginal person (Jaffe, 1992). This was not primarily because of a natural increase of European immigrants, however. Traders and later settlers to British North America and New France (later renamed Upper and Lower Canada) brought with them not only trade items but also racist attitudes toward the non-Christian "savages" who resided in the New World. The Europeans were even prepared to use their superior military power to subdue any Aboriginal peoples unwilling to be colonized.

Europeans also brought with them deadly diseases. Smallpox and other epidemic diseases (including measles, influenza, and tuberculosis) had killed many Europeans in the previous centuries. However, for the Aboriginal peoples of the New World, these contagions were "virgin soil epidemics," ravaging hitherto unexposed populations without any built-up immunity to soften the impact (Cohen, 1989). These "diseases of civilization," along with the ill effects of adulterated whisky, reduced the Aboriginal population of British Columbia, for example, by nearly two-thirds before the end of the 1800s (Jaffe, 1992). So marginalized were Canada's Aboriginal peoples that they were not entitled to vote alongside non-Aboriginal Canadian citizens until 1960.

In 2006, 1 172 790 Canadians identified themselves as Aboriginal persons: North American Indian (First Nations people), Metis, or Inuit. There has been a substantial increase in Canada's Aboriginal population in recent decades: Between 1996 and 2006, it grew by 45 percent, nearly six times faster than the 8 percent rate of growth for non-Aboriginal Canadians (Statistics Canada, 2008s). Table 11–3 shows the geographic distribution of Canada's Aboriginal peoples.

Despite their growing number, Aboriginal peoples in Canada continue to earn far below the median average income for Canadians. Aboriginal peoples also are more likely to live in single-parent families, and they record higher rates of unemployment and have lower rates of school attendance. Their health status is also bleak when compared with that of the country's non-Aboriginal population. Aboriginal peoples have higher tuberculosis and suicide rates, and much shorter life expectancies, than their non-Aboriginal counterparts (Health Canada, 2009; Statistics Canada, 1995b).

Like other racial and ethnic minorities in Canada, Aboriginal peoples have recently reasserted pride in their cultural heritage. Some are finally resolving negotiations over territorial lands. Yet, as discussed in the Controversy & Debate box on page 294, not all Canadians are comfortable with special rights for Aboriginal groups, such as the Nisga'a of British Columbia.

British Canadians

British Canadians—sometimes referred to as White Anglo-Saxon Protestants (WASPs)—were not the first people to inhabit Canada, but they came to dominate this nation once European settlement began. Most British Canadians are of English descent, but this category also includes Scots, Irish, and Welsh. On the 2006 census, as shown in Table 11–2, among the most frequently cited British origins was English (6.6 million), Scottish (4.7 million), and Irish (4.4 million).

Historically, British immigrants were highly skilled and motivated by what we now call the "Protestant work ethic." Because of their number and power, British Canadians (with the possible exception of Irish Catholics) were not subject to the prejudice and discrimination experienced by other categories of immigrants. The historical dominance of British Canadians has been so great that, as noted earlier, others have sought to become more like them.

And the British cultural legacy still stands: English remained, until recent decades, Canada's only official language, and it still dominates the country's media and electronic communication systems. The Canadian legal and political systems, too, reflect their British origins.

French Canadians

The French explorers arrived in Canada in the sixteenth century, initially involving themselves in fishing and fur trading. Eventually, more French immigrated in search of a better life in "New France." By 1760, there were about 70 000 inhabitants of the colony, with approximately the same number of women as men (Prentice et al., 1996:37). When Acadia (now Nova Scotia) passed from French to British hands in 1713, men and women from that region were either deported to France or resettled in the northeastern regions of what

Should Certain Groups in Canada Enjoy Special Rights?

"We are all governed by one law, the constitution, and that most fundamental of laws states that existing Aboriginal rights are recognized and affirmed . . . Critics . . . who oppose special rights per se oppose the constitution, and they should take their quarrel elsewhere."—Hamar Foster, Professor, University of Victoria, Victoria, British Columbia

Foster was commenting on final treaty negotiations among the federal government, the provincial government of British Columbia, and the Nisga'a people of the Nass Valley in the northwestern area of the province, which resulted in a number of benefits for this Aboriginal group, including an estimated $448 million. Other gains for the Nisga'a include the right to elect their own government, with authority to make laws in several key provincial jurisdictions, including those regarding land use, culture, and employment.

Such "special rights" accompanying the groundbreaking treaty (which, it is worth noting, had been pursued by the Nisga'a people for six generations) ignited a heated debate in the province, as well as across the country. People questioned whether any group—Aboriginal or otherwise—should have legal rights that are different from those of other Canadian citizens. Some critics of the deal argued that it entrenches inequality in Canadian society since the Treaty gives the Nisga'a "special" rights based solely on race. Critics called for a province-wide referendum to let the public decide whether the treaty should become law. Others, sympathetic to the Nisga'a people's historical struggle, welcomed the agreement as a compromise that was finally acceptable to the Nisga'a. Such a compromise, argued proponents, would allow the Nisga'a to get on with tackling the high unemployment and other problems affecting their people. Supporters pointed out as well that the Nisga'a had given up other (similarly special) rights they previously held under the Indian Act.

Highlights of Nisga'a Treaty

Land. The Nisga'a receive 1930 square kilometres of Crown land and title to 62 square kilometres of land currently designated as Indian reserves. Nisga'a lands do not include private property held by non-Natives or agricultural leases. Provincial laws continue to apply to several parcels of land owned by non-Natives that will be surrounded by Nisga'a lands.

Self-government. Elections for a central Nisga'a government and four village governments must be held no later than six months after the treaty comes into force. Only Nisga'a can vote for the Nisga'a government, which will adopt a constitution recognizing the rights and freedoms of its citizens.

The Nisga'a government can make laws on Nisga'a citizenship, language, culture, property, public order, safety, employment, traffic, child and family services, health services, policing, and correctional and court services.

Non-Nisga'a Canadians can participate in elected bodies that directly affect them by making representations and seeking elections to public agencies such as the health board. Local laws affecting everything from traffic to garbage collection will apply to non-Nisga'a within Nisga'a lands, but most laws will apply only to Nisga'a citizens.

Nisga'a continue to be Aboriginal peoples under the Constitution and are entitled to the same rights as other Canadian citizens. The Charter of Rights and Freedoms and all federal and provincial laws continue to apply to Nisga'a people. However, Nisga'a people will no longer be exempt from sales and income taxes.

Resources. Ownership of all forests within Nisga'a lands, and all mineral, oil, and other subsurface resources, will be transferred to the Nisga'a, who can set conditions for their use. Current forest licences will remain in effect for five years. Nisga'a management standards must meet or exceed provincial standards.

Public access to Nisga'a lands for hunting, fishing, and recreation will be provided, although the Nisga'a government may make laws regulating public access for public safety or environmental reasons.

Nisga'a people will be guaranteed 26 percent of the Nass River allowable catch for salmon, and will be allowed to sell their salmon. Any federal commercial or recreational ban on fishing will also apply to the Nisga'a.

Key geographic features will be renamed with Nisga'a names and important cultural sites will be designated as heritage sites. The treaty states that it is the final settlement of Nisga'a Aboriginal rights.

Canadians continue to debate the treaty, asking what the outcome will be if Nisga'a treaty rights conflict with the rights of other Canadians. Indian and Northern Affairs Canada (2008) answers this way:

"Everyone on Nisga'a Lands will continue to enjoy the same rights and freedoms under the Canadian Charter of Rights and Freedoms. Everyone will continue to be subject to the Criminal Code of Canada. The Treaty addresses the relationships of Nisga'a laws with the laws of Canada and B.C. and identifies the specific areas in which Nisga'a law will prevail. In addition, the Nisga'a Government will be required to consult individuals who are not Nisga'a citizens living on Nisga'a Lands about decisions that directly and significantly affect them. These people will also be able to participate in elected bodies that deal with issues that have a direct and significant effect on their lives. The means of participation can include opportunities to make representations, to vote for, or seek election to, Nisga'a public institutions and to have the same means of appeal as Nisga'a citizens."

CONTINUE THE DEBATE . . .

1. What is your interpretation of the Nisga'a treaty? Is it right that the treaty bestows special rights on a group of people?

2. Should other Aboriginal groups in Canada also be able to claim "special legal rights" to the land and resources of their forebears? Why or why not?

3. How can sociology play a part in understanding this and other debates over Aboriginal land claims?

Source: Adapted from Matas and McInnes (1998) and Indian and Northern Affairs Canada (2008).

The Quebec language law—Bill 101—was upheld in April 2000, when the Quebec superior court ruled that French had to be the predominant language on commercial signs. A spray can quickly changes the familiar stop sign into a political message.

was then "British North America." In the aftermath of the Seven Years' War (1756–1763), Canada fell under British colonial rule. Though the French retained some control over their own language, religion, and legal institutions, English Canada gained control over economic, political, and social matters.

To some extent, this remains the case even today. The historical legacy of the "two solitudes"—French and English—joined in an uneasy political union resulted in the so-called Quiet Revolution of the 1960s in Quebec. At its most intense, the Quiet Revolution involved the use of radical terrorism as a political weapon against the English (Rocher, 1990). And though the province has undergone substantial change in subsequent decades, in many respects French Quebec and English Canada can still be said to be "two nations warring in the bosom of the same state" (Guindon, 1990:30).

In the 2006 census, 4.9 million Canadians claimed at least partial French ancestry, up from 4.7 million in 2001 (Statistics Canada, 2011v).

Unlike the economy of earlier times when English merchants and traders were in control, the Quebec economy today is mainly under the control of francophone entrepreneurs. Politics has also changed significantly. During the 1990s, two French political parties controlled the majority of seats in the province, with the Parti Québécois holding

power in the Quebec Legislature (the National Assembly) and a new separatist party—the Bloc Québécois—leading the separatist cause at the federal level for a while as the official opposition. The razor-thin defeat of the separatists in the Quebec referendum of 1995 (by a mere 1 percent of the vote) opened the eyes of other Canadians to the very real possibility of the breakup of the country. Since then, however, the separatist parties have suffered setbacks at both the provincial and the federal levels.

During Canada's thirty-ninth general election held on January 23, 2006, the Bloc Québécois lost support. Although it captured 51 of Quebec's 75 seats (only three fewer than in 2004), its share of the vote declined from 49 percent in 2004 to 42 percent; a sizable group of Quebecers moved late in the campaign to the surging Conservatives, who won a minority government in Parliament. Continuing this trend, in the most recent general election (May 2, 2011), the Bloc Québécois lost official party status for the first time since its first election, winning just 4 seats in Quebec. The majority of its former seats went to the New Democratic Party, indicating a major change in the province regarding the important issues of the day: jobs, social security, and social justice rather than separation from Canada.

Meanwhile, many English-speaking Canadian parents have, in the past few decades, enrolled their children in French-immersion school programs, and the civil service has become increasingly staffed with bilingual francophones. Yet many issues remain unresolved regarding the future of Quebec or, indeed, of French Canadians in Canada. These issues include the "French-only" sign law, the requirement that new immigrants to the province educate their children in French, and the insistence that the lands claimed by the Aboriginal peoples of the province's North be included in the territory proposed for a sovereign Quebec.

Canada's Other Immigrants

As previously noted, Canada is a country of founding peoples, but also one of immigrants. Four distinct historical eras can be distinguished when investigating international migration to the country (Gee, 1990). As mentioned above, the French were the original immigrants to the part of the New World that would later be called "Canada." The French immigrants eventually established the colony of New France between 1608 and 1760. During the nineteenth century, a new wave of immigrants came, mainly from Britain, in two population flows: the United Empire Loyalists came from the American colonies, fleeing the American independence movement; and immigrants came directly from the British Isles. Smaller numbers of other Europeans also immigrated to Canada during this time, including Germans, Scandinavians, and Eastern Europeans.

The last decades of the nineteenth century and the first decades of the early twentieth century saw the arrival of the largest wave of immigrants to the country up to that point. Their numbers ranged from 3.7 to 4.6 million (Kalbach & McVey, 1979). Among them were 15 000 Chinese who were permitted to come to Canada as a cheap

On December 7, 1941, Japan attacked Pearl Harbor and Hong Kong. Just weeks later, the Canadian federal government, under the War Measures Act, demanded the evacuation of all Japanese Canadians residing within about 160 kilometres of the Pacific Coast. Although apparently relocated for reasons of national security, no Japanese Canadian was ever charged with disloyalty to the country. In all, 20 000 men, women, and children of Japanese descent were forced to leave their homes for camps in the interior of British Columbia and farms in Alberta and Manitoba.

Source: William Lyon Mackenzie King Collection/National Archives of Canada/C-24452.

source of labour for the construction of the transcontinental railroad. Between 1886 and 1923, Canada barred all Asians from settling permanently in the country and imposed a "head tax" on all Chinese wishing to immigrate. The initial head tax was $50, later $100, and finally, in 1904, $500, a very large sum at the time. The head tax on Chinese immigrants was not lifted until 1947. Everyone seemed to line up against the Chinese, as captured in a popular phrase of the time that a person "didn't have a Chinaman's chance" (Sung, 1967).

The head tax and generally racist attitude of many Canadians toward the Chinese created domestic hardship, because in Canada (and similarly in the United States) Chinese men outnumbered Chinese women (Hsu, 1971; Lai, 1980; Prentice et al., 1996). For the relatively few Chinese women who managed to enter the country, the situation was far from friendly. Below, a woman of Chinese background recalls her life in Nanaimo, British Columbia, in the early decades of this century:

> When I went to school in Nanaimo in the 1920s we had to go to a segregated school. In those days there was still segregation for the "Others." We had to go to a special school because we were not white . . . We had to walk past the better schools, which were only for the white people or westerners, to go to this "ward" school that housed all the Indians, the ethnic people, or "Others" (quoted in Yee, 1992:235–6).

With the relaxation of Canadian immigration laws after 1947, and the more open immigration policies of recent decades, Chinese immigrants to Canada have received a warmer, if not wholehearted, welcome.

The Chinese were not the only immigrants to enter the country during the early part of the twentieth century, however. Many immigrants came from the United States, some from Britain and other parts of Europe, and others from as far away as India.

The last wave of immigrants to Canada arrived in the post–World War II period—more than 5 million of them—many from middle- and low-income countries around the globe. Canada does not have a quota system in place regarding how many immigrants may enter the country annually. The current regulations emphasize "economic immigration"—that is, the preferred immigrants ideally possess the particular skills and disposable capital to establish themselves economically after migration.

The 2006 census showed that almost 6.2 million people were born outside Canada, up from 5.6 million in 2001 (Natural Resources Canada, 2009a). The majority of the foreign-born population (86.8 percent) live in three provinces: Ontario, Quebec and British Columbia. The composition of the immigration stream is changing substantially. Recent newcomers born in Asia (as well as in the Middle East) made up the largest proportion (58.3 percent), a similar pattern as in 2001. People from Europe made up the second largest group (16.1 percent) of new immigrants. An additional 10.8 percent originated from Central and South America and the Caribbean, an increase from 8.9 percent in 2001, and a similar percentage of immigrants were born in Africa.

Nearly three-quarters of the immigrant population since 1981 are members of a visible minority group. It is to this category that we now turn.

Visible Minorities

The Canadian Employment Equity Act defines visible minorities as "persons, other than Aboriginal peoples, who are non-Caucasian in race or non-white in colour." Based on this definition the following ethnic groups are designated as visible minorities in Canada: Chinese, South Asians, Blacks, Arabs and West Asians, Filipinos, Southeast Asians, Latin Americans, Japanese, Koreans, and Pacific Islanders. In 2006, there were 5 068 100 individuals who belonged to the visible minority population, comprising 16.2 percent of the total population in Canada, an increase from 13.4 percent of the total population in 2001 (Statistics Canada, 2008k).

As with the Chinese immigrants who immigrated a century earlier, Canada's visible minorities tend to live in the larger metropolitan areas (95.9 percent). Toronto, Vancouver, Montreal, Calgary, Ottawa-Gatineau, Edmonton, and Winnipeg each had at least 100 000 visible minorities in 2006. As shown in National Map 11–1 on page 284, in 2006 the majority of visible minorities resided in

TABLE 11–4	Income and Education, Aboriginal and Visible Minority Full-Time, Full-Year Workers Aged 25 to 44, Canada, 2006		
	All Canadians	**Aboriginals**	**Visible Minorities**
Average income	$48 832	$39 896	$43 567
Percentage with post-secondary diploma or degree	28.4%	11.9%	41.6%
Average income of those with a post-secondary diploma or degree	$65 296	$55 340	$54 468

Source: Statistics Canada (2008m, 2008n).

Although sometimes portrayed as a successful "model minority," Canadians with Asian ancestry are highly diverse and, like other categories of people, include both rich and poor. These young people contend with many of the same patterns of prejudice and discrimination familiar to members of other minorities.

either Toronto or Vancouver (42.9 percent and 41.7 percent, respectively) (Natural Resources Canada, 2009b).

Even as the concentration of visible minorities in our largest urban areas is predicted to remain at 75 percent, the proportions of the populations within these cities are expected to change dramatically over the next decade. By 2017, the majority of the populations of Toronto and Vancouver are expected to be members of a visible minority (Belanger & Malenfant, 2005a).

It is clear that the total integration of visible minorities into Canadian society is not complete, since visible minorities are more likely to hold university degrees yet visible minority individuals have, on average, lower incomes than the average for all Canadians, as shown in Table 11–4. Yet the educational aspirations of visible minority students are consistently higher than those of other students. The differences between visible minority and non–visible minority students are particularly strong in the face of adversity, when parents have low income and no post-secondary education (Taylor & Krahn, 2005).

Race and Ethnicity: Looking Ahead

Canada has been, and will remain, a land of immigrants. Immigration has brought striking cultural diversity and tales of success, hope, and struggle told in hundreds of languages.

For those who came to this country during the second wave of immigration that peaked around 1910, the next generations brought gradual economic gains and at least some cultural assimilation. The government also granted basic freedoms that earlier had been denied, including citizenship and the right to vote and hold public office.

A third wave of immigration began after World War II, and swelled as immigration laws were relaxed in the 1960s. Since 1990, more than 225 000 people have come to Canada each year on average, twice the number that arrived during the "Great Immigration" a century ago (although newcomers now enter a country with a much larger population). Most contemporary immigrants come not from Europe but from middle- and low-income countries.

Many new arrivals face much the same prejudice and discrimination that were directed toward the country's Aboriginal peoples, as well as toward earlier generations of immigrants. Indeed, recent years have witnessed rising hostility toward foreigners (sometimes called *xenophobia*, a word with Greek roots meaning "fear of what is strange"). This is especially the case in the United States, where, in 1994, California voters passed Proposition 187, which mandates a cut-off in social services (including schooling) to illegal immigrants. The rise of neo-Nazi groups in Canada in the 1990s, and indeed across many high-income countries, suggests that the United States is not alone in its fear of foreigners.

Even so, like Canada's Aboriginal peoples, who are enjoying a cultural revival, many new immigrants now try to join Canadian society while maintaining their traditional cultures. Some have also built racial and ethnic enclaves to keep their ethnic traditions and celebrations alive for the next generation. Others have been more open to joining the Canadian mainstream, adhering to the traditional hope of their predecessors—that racial and ethnic diversity, while a dimension of difference, will not be viewed as a badge of inferiority.

CHAPTER 11 RACE AND ETHNICITY

IS OUR SOCIETY BECOMING MORE ACCEPTING OF RACIALLY AND ETHNI-CALLY MIXED COUPLES AND FRIENDSHIP GROUPS? As the social distance research presented in this chapter shows, today's college and university students express greater acceptance of social diversity. Look at the two photos of social gatherings. What evidence of greater acceptance do you see? In your opinion, does this evidence mean that our society has really changed? Why or why not?

At today's dance clubs, racial and ethnic mixing has become the rule. How accurately does this image reflect everyday life? Do you think young people differ from older people in their degree of social tolerance? Explain.

Young adults gathered at the local soda shop to dance in the 1950s, when the civil rights movement was just getting under way. Based on what you have read in this chapter, how does this reflect what U.S. society was like fifty years ago in terms of racial segregation? Do you think Canadian society was any different in the 1950s?

HINT: On the face of it, today's television shows suggest far greater racial and ethnic tolerance than was true in the 1950s, when we rarely saw images of people of different categories interacting with one another. The social distance research noted in this chapter also supports the idea that tolerance is increasing. Being more racially inclusive is also a smart business policy, in light of the increasing economic resources of various minority categories of the Canadian population.

Applying Sociology in Everyday Life

1. Thinking about your own campus, can you point to ways in which race does not matter in students' lives? In what ways does race still matter? On balance, how important is race today?

2. Does your college or university take account of race and ethnicity in its admissions policies? How about special policies for Aboriginals? Ask to speak with an admissions officer to see what you can learn about your school's use of race and ethnicity in admissions.

Ask whether there is a "legacy" policy that favours children of parents who attended the school.

3. Give several of your friends or family members a quick quiz, asking them what share of the Canadian population is white, Aboriginal, Black, Hispanic, and Asian (see Table 11–1 on page 282). You will probably find that most white people exaggerate the size of the Aboriginal population. Why do you think this is so?

MAKING THE GRADE

CHAPTER 11 Race and Ethnicity

The Social Meaning of Race and Ethnicity

RACE refers to socially constructed categories based on biological traits that a society defines as important.

- The meaning and importance of race vary from place to place and over time.
- Societies use racial categories to rank people in a hierarchy, giving some people more money, power, and prestige than others.
- In the past, scientists created three broad categories—Caucasoids, Mongoloids, and Negroids—but there are no biologically pure races.

pp. 280–82

ETHNICITY refers to socially constructed categories based on cultural traits that a society defines as important.

- Ethnicity reflects common ancestors, language, and religion.
- The importance of ethnicity varies from place to place and over time.
- People choose to play up or play down their ethnicity.

pp. 282–83

race (p. 280) a socially constructed category of people who share biologically transmitted traits that members of a society consider important

ethnicity (p. 282) a shared cultural heritage

minority (p. 283) any category of people distinguished by physical or cultural difference that a society sets apart and subordinates

✓ Minorities are people of various racial and ethnic categories who are visually distinctive and disadvantaged by a society (p. 283).

Prejudice and Stereotypes

PREJUDICE is a rigid and unfair generalization about a category of people.

- The social distance scale is one measure of prejudice.
- One type of prejudice is the **STEREOTYPE,** a simplified description applied to every person in some category.
- **RACISM,** a very destructive type of prejudice, asserts that one race is innately superior or inferior to another.

pp. 284–87

There are four **THEORIES OF PREJUDICE:**

- **Scapegoat theory** claims that prejudice results from frustration among people who are disadvantaged.
- **Authoritarian personality theory** (Adorno) claims that prejudice is a personality trait of certain individuals, especially those with little education and those raised by cold and demanding parents.
- **Culture theory** (Bogardus) claims that prejudice is rooted in culture; we learn to feel greater social distance from some categories of people.
- **Conflict theory** claims that prejudice is a tool used by powerful people to divide and control the population.

pp. 287–89

prejudice (p. 284) a rigid and unfair generalization about an entire category of people

stereotype (p. 285) a simplified description applied to every person in some category

racism (p. 287) the belief that one racial category is innately superior or inferior to another

scapegoat (p. 287) a person or category of people, typically with little power, whom other people unfairly blame for their own troubles

Discrimination

DISCRIMINATION is treating various categories of people unequally.

- Prejudice refers to attitudes; discrimination involves actions.
- Institutional prejudice and discrimination is bias built into the operation of society's institutions, including schools, hospitals, the police, and the workplace.
- Prejudice and discrimination perpetuate themselves in a vicious circle, resulting in social disadvantage that fuels additional prejudice and discrimination.

pp. 289–90

discrimination (p. 289) unequal treatment of various categories of people

institutional prejudice and discrimination (p. 289) bias built into the operation of society's institutions

Majority and Minority: Patterns of Interaction

PLURALISM requires that racial and ethnic categories, although distinct, have roughly equal social standing.

- Canadian society is pluralistic in that all people in Canada, regardless of race or ethnicity, have equal standing under the law.
- Canadian society is not pluralistic in that all racial and ethnic categories do not have equal *social* standing.

p. 290

ASSIMILATION is the process by which minorities gradually adopt the patterns of the dominant culture.

- Assimilation involves changes in dress, language, religion, values, and friends.
- Assimilation is a strategy to escape prejudice and discrimination and to achieve upward social mobility.
- Some categories of people have assimilated more than others.

pp. 290–91

299

SEGREGATION is the physical and social separation of categories of people.

- Although some segregation is voluntary (for example, the Amish), majorities usually segregate minorities by excluding them from neighbourhoods, schools, and occupations.
- De jure segregation is segregation by law; de facto segregation describes settings that contain only people of one category.
- Hypersegregation means having little social contact with people beyond the local community.

p. 291

GENOCIDE is the systematic killing of one category of people by another.

- Historical examples of genocide include the extermination of Jews by the Nazis and the killing of Western-leaning people in Cambodia by Pol Pot.
- Recent examples of genocide include Hutus killing Tutsis in the African nation of Rwanda, Serbs killing Bosnians in the Balkans of Eastern Europe, and the systematic killing in the Darfur region of Sudan.

pp. 291–92

pluralism (p. 290) a state in which people of all races and ethnicities are distinct but have equal social standing

assimilation (p. 291) the process by which minorities gradually adopt patterns of the dominant culture

miscegenation (p. 291) biological reproduction by partners of different racial categories

segregation (p. 291) the physical and social separation of categories of people

genocide (p. 291) the systematic killing of one category of people by another

Race and Ethnicity in Canada

ABORIGINAL PEOPLES, the earliest human inhabitants of the Americas, have endured genocide, segregation, and forced assimilation. Today, the social standing of Aboriginal peoples is well below the national average.

pp. 292–93

FRENCH CANADIANS were the other major European group to settle in Canada. Canada eventually fell under British colonial rule. Though the French retained some control over their own language, religion, and legal institutions, English Canada gained control over economic, political, and social matters. The historical legacy of the "two solitudes"—French and English— to some extent continues to this day.

pp. 293–95

VISIBLE MINORITIES The Canadian Employment Equity Act defines visible minorities as "persons, other than Aboriginal peoples, who are non-Caucasian in race or non-white in colour." In 2006, there were 5 068 100 individuals who belonged to the visible minority population, comprising 16.2 percent of the total population in Canada.

pp. 296–97

BRITISH CANADIANS—sometimes referred to as White Anglo-Saxon Protestants (WASPs)—were among the original European settlers of Canada, and many continue to enjoy high social position today.

p. 293

OTHER IMMIGRANTS
Canada is also a country of immigrants from many other areas of the world. The 2006 census showed that almost 6.2 million people in Canada were born outside the country, up from 5.6 million in 2001.

pp. 295–96

MySocLab

Visit MySocLab at www.mysoclab.com to access a variety of online resources that will help you to prepare for tests and to apply your knowledge, including

- an eText
- videos
- self-grading quizzes
- glossary flashcards

12 Economics and Politics

- What is a social institution?

- How does change in the economy reshape society?

- Why do some critics say Canada is not really a democracy?

Here's a quick quiz about the North American economy. (Hint: All six questions have the same correct answer.)

- Which business do 170 million people in North America visit each week?
- Which business sells the products of more than 61 000 companies?
- Which North American company, on average, opens a new or remodelled store every day?
- Which North American company buys more than $18 billion worth of goods each year from China, which, if the company were a country, would be China's seventh-largest trading partner?
- Which North American company created 33 000 new jobs in the United States (and another 30 000 in other countries) in 2008?
- Which single company actually grew in size during the recent economic downturn?

The answer, of course, is Walmart, the global discount store chain founded by Sam Walton, who opened his first store in Arkansas in 1962. In 2009, Walmart announced revenues of well over $400 billion in annual sales through more than 4200 stores in North America and 3615 stores in other countries from Brazil to China, making it the second-largest corporation in North America.

But not everyone is pleased with the expansion of Walmart. Across North America, many people have joined a social movement to keep Walmart out of their local communities, fearing the loss of local businesses and, in some cases, local culture. Critics claim that the merchandising giant pays low wages, keeps out unions, and sells many products made in sweatshops abroad. In 2005, the Walmart store in Jonquière, Quebec, closed six months after the workers voted to have their interests represented by United Food and Commercial Workers union. In 2010, the U.S. federal court ruled that Walmart would go to trial to defend itself against claims of sex discrimination made by female employees (A. Clark, 2010; Saporito, 2003; Walmart, 2009; Walsh, 2007).

This chapter explores the economy and the closely related institution of politics. A number of very large corporations, including Walmart, are at the centre of the Canadian economy, raising questions about just how the economy operates, whose interests it ought to serve, and to what extent big business shapes the political life of our country.

Economics and politics are **social institutions,** *major spheres of social life or societal subsystems organized to meet human needs.* The two chapters that follow consider other social institutions: Chapter 13 focuses on family and religion, and Chapter 14 highlights education, health, and medicine. These discussions explain how social institutions have changed over the course of history, describe how they operate today, and point out controversies that are likely to shape them tomorrow.

The Economy: Historical Overview

The **economy** is *the social institution that organizes a society's production, distribution, and consumption of goods and services.* The economy operates, for better or worse, in a generally predictable manner. *Goods* are commodities ranging from necessities (such as food, clothing, and shelter) to luxury items (such as cars, swimming pools, and yachts). *Services* are activities that benefit people (including the work of priests, physicians, teachers, and computer software specialists). Three times in the past, technological revolutions reorganized the economy and, in the process, transformed social life.

The Agricultural Revolution

As Chapter 2 ("Culture") explained, the earliest societies were made up of hunters and gatherers living off the land. In these technologically simple societies, there was no distinct economy; producing and consuming were part of family life.

Harnessing animals to plows around 5000 years ago permitted the development of agriculture, which was 50 times more productive than hunting and gathering. The resulting surpluses meant that not everyone had to produce food, so many people took on other specialized work: making tools, raising animals, and building dwellings. Soon towns sprang up, linked by networks of traders dealing in food, animals, and other goods. These four factors—agricultural

social institution (p. 302) a major sphere of social life or societal subsystem organized to meet human needs

economy (p. 302) the social institution that organizes a society's production, distribution, and consumption of goods and services

post-industrial economy a productive system based on service work and high technology

technology, specialized work, permanent settlements, and trade—made the economy a distinct social institution.

The Industrial Revolution

By the mid-eighteenth century, a second technological revolution was under way, starting in England and spreading to Canada, the United States, and elsewhere. Industrialization changed the economy in five fundamental ways:

1. **New sources of energy.** Throughout history, "energy" had meant the muscle power of people or animals. Then, in 1765, the English inventor James Watt introduced the steam engine. A hundred times more powerful than animal muscles, early steam engines soon drove heavy machinery.

2. **Centralization of work in factories.** Steam-powered machinery moved work from homes to factories, centralized workplaces that housed the machines.

3. **Manufacturing and mass production.** Before the Industrial Revolution, most people grew or gathered raw materials such as grain, wood, or wool. In an industrial economy, the focus shifts so that most people turn raw materials into a wide range of finished products such as furniture and clothing.

4. **Specialization.** Centuries ago, people worked at home making products from start to finish. In the factory, a labourer repeats a single task over and over, making only a small contribution to the finished product.

5. **Wage labour.** Instead of working for themselves, factory workers became wage labourers working for strangers, who often cared less for them than for the machines they operated.

The Industrial Revolution gradually raised the standard of living as countless new products fuelled an expanding marketplace. Yet the benefits of industrial technology were shared very unequally, especially at the beginning. Some factory owners made huge fortunes, while the majority of industrial workers lived close to poverty. Children, too, worked in factories or in coal mines for pennies a day. As time went on, workers formed labour unions to represent their interests collectively to factory owners. In the twentieth century, new laws banned child labour, set minimum wage levels, improved workplace safety, and extended schooling and political rights to a larger segment of the population (Krahn & Lowe, 2002).

The Information Revolution and Post-industrial Society

By about 1950, the nature of production was changing once again. Canada was creating a **post-industrial economy,** *a productive system based on service work and high technology.* Automated machinery

As societies industrialize, a smaller and smaller share of the labour force works in agriculture. In Canada, much of what agricultural work remains is performed by immigrants from lower-income nations.

(and, later, robotics) reduced the role of human labour in factory production and expanded the ranks of clerical workers and managers. The post-industrial era is marked by a shift from industrial work to service work.

Driving this economic change is a third technological breakthrough: the computer. Just as the Industrial Revolution did two-and-a-half centuries ago, the Information Revolution has introduced new kinds of products and new forms of communication and has changed the character of work. There have been three significant changes:

1. **From tangible products to ideas.** The industrial era was defined by the production of goods; in the post-industrial era, people work with symbols. Computer programmers, writers, financial analysts, advertising executives, architects, editors, and various types of consultants make up more of the labour force in the information age.

2. **From mechanical skills to literacy skills.** The Industrial Revolution required mechanical skills, but the Information Revolution requires literacy skills: speaking and writing well and, of course, knowing how to use a computer. People able to communicate effectively are likely to do well; people without these skills face fewer opportunities.

3. **From factories to almost anywhere.** Industrial technology drew workers to factories located near power sources, but computer technology allows people to work almost anywhere. Laptop and wireless computers and cellphones now turn the home, car, or even an airplane into a "virtual office." What this means for everyday life is that new information technology blurs the line between our lives at work and at home.

primary sector the part of the economy that draws raw materials from the natural environment

secondary sector the part of the economy that transforms raw materials into manufactured goods

tertiary sector the part of the economy that involves services rather than goods

global economy economic activity that crosses national borders

Global Snapshot

In high-income nations such as Canada, almost three out of four jobs are in the tertiary or service sector of the economy.

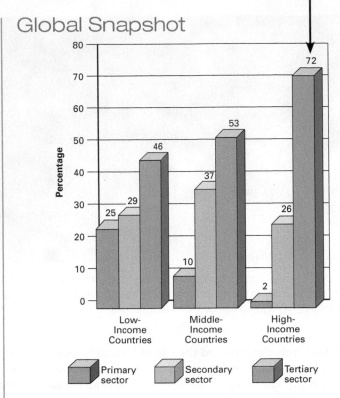

FIGURE 12–1 **The Size of Economic Sectors, by National Income Level**

As countries become richer, the primary sector becomes a smaller part of the economy and the tertiary or service sector becomes larger.

Source: Estimates based on World Bank (2009).

Sectors of the Economy

The three revolutions just described reflect a shifting balance among the three sectors of a society's economy. The **primary sector** is *the part of the economy that draws raw materials from the natural environment.* The primary sector—agriculture, raising animals, fishing, forestry, and mining—is largest in low-income nations. Figure 12–1 shows that 25 percent of the economic output of low-income countries is in the primary sector, compared with 10 percent of economic activity among middle-income nations and just 2 percent in high-income countries such as Canada.

The **secondary sector** is *the part of the economy that transforms raw materials into manufactured goods.* This sector expands quickly as societies industrialize. It includes operations such as refining petroleum into gasoline and turning metals into tools and automobiles. The globalization of industry means that just about all the world's countries have a significant share of

workers employed in the secondary sector. Figure 12–1 shows that the secondary sector now accounts for a greater share of economic output in middle-income nations than it does in high-income countries.

The **tertiary sector** is *the part of the economy that involves services rather than goods.* The tertiary sector grows with industrialization, accounting for 46 percent of economic output in low-income countries, 53 percent in middle-income countries, and 72 percent in high-income countries. About 80 percent of the Canadian labour force is employed in service work, including secretarial and clerical jobs and work in food service, sales, law, health care, advertising, and teaching (Industry Canada, 2009).

The Global Economy

New information technology is drawing people around the world together and creating a **global economy,** *economic activity that crosses national borders.* The development of a global economy has five major consequences.

First, we see a global division of labour: Different regions of the world specialize in one sector of economic activity. As Global Map 12–1 shows, agriculture represents about half of the total economic output of the world's poorest countries. Most of the economic output of high-income countries, including Canada, is in the service sector. In short, the world's poorest nations specialize in producing raw materials, and the richest nations specialize in the production of services.

Second, an increasing number of products pass through more than one nation. Look no further than your morning coffee: The beans may have been grown in Colombia and transported to Halifax on a freighter that was registered in Liberia, made in a shipyard in Japan using steel from Korea, and fuelled by oil from Venezuela.

Third, national governments no longer control the economic activity that takes place within their borders. In fact, governments cannot even accurately regulate the value of their national currencies because dollars, euros, pounds sterling, and yen are traded around the clock in the financial markets of Toronto, New York, London, and Tokyo.

A fourth consequence of the global economy is that a small number of businesses operating internationally now control a vast share of the world's economic activity. Using the latest available data, the 1500 largest multinational companies account for half of the world's economic output (DeCarlo, 2009; World Bank, 2010).

Fifth and finally, the globalization of the economy raises concerns about the rights and opportunities of workers. Critics of this trend claim that Canada, the United States, and other high-income countries are losing jobs—especially factory jobs—to low-income nations. This means that workers here face lower wages and higher

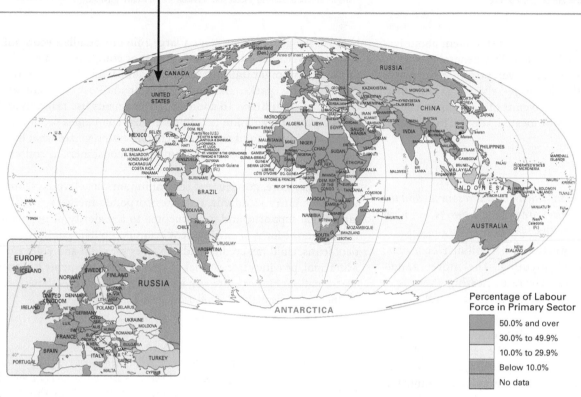

Sandra Johanson is a hygiene technician on a corporate-owned farm in Saskatchewan. She is one of the relatively few people in Canada working in agriculture.

Percentage of Labour Force in Primary Sector

- 50.0% and over
- 30.0% to 49.9%
- 10.0% to 29.9%
- Below 10.0%
- No data

Window on the World

GLOBAL MAP 12–1   Agricultural Employment in Global Perspective

The primary sector of the economy is largest in the nations that are least developed. In the poor countries of Africa and Asia, up to half of all workers are farmers. This picture is altogether different in the world's most economically developed countries—including Canada, the United States, Great Britain, and Australia—which have a mere 2 percent of their labour force in agriculture.

Source: Data from International Labour Organization (2010).

unemployment. At the same time, many workers abroad are paid extremely low wages. As a result, say critics, the global expansion of capitalism threatens the well-being of workers throughout the world.

The world is still divided into 194 politically distinct nations. But the rising level of international economic activity makes nationhood less significant than it was even a decade ago.

Economic Systems: Paths to Justice

December 12, Hanoi, Vietnam. Walking through the bustling Old Quarters is an unsettling experience for anyone who came of age in the 1960s. People like me need to remember that Vietnam is a country, not a war, and that nearly 50 years have passed.

Hanoi is now a boomtown where you can buy every convenience available in Canada—it is just much cheaper here. As we stroll past the many stores selling a few genuine (among the many "genuine" copies of) North Face backpacks we spot a waterproof canoe bag with the Mountain Equipment Co-op (MEC) logo.

There is heavy irony here: After decades of manufacturing bags under the Serratus name, MEC is now selling cheaper (and probably better) bags made in Vietnam. This is part of the reason that Hanoi, and Vietnam, is booming and much wealthier than it used to be.

We don't buy the MEC bag, but we spend the evening discussing the consequences of buying MEC bags made in Vietnam versus those made in Canada. We all agree that opinions formed at home in Victoria take on a different meaning when considered from a Vietnamese perspective.

capitalism an economic system in which natural resources and the means of producing goods and services are privately owned

socialism an economic system in which natural resources and the means of producing goods and services are collectively owned

Every society's economic system makes a statement about justice by determining who is entitled to what. Two general economic models are capitalism and socialism. However, no nation anywhere in the world has an economy that is completely one or the other; rather, capitalism and socialism are two ends of a continuum along which all real-world economies can be located. We will look at each of these models in turn.

Capitalism

Capitalism is *an economic system in which natural resources and the means of producing goods and services are privately owned.* An ideal capitalist economy has three distinctive features:

1. **Private ownership of property.** In a capitalist economy, individuals can own almost anything. The more capitalist an economy is, the more private ownership there is of wealth-producing property such as factories, real estate, and natural resources.

2. **Pursuit of personal profit.** A capitalist society seeks to create profit and wealth. The profit motive is the reason people take new jobs, open new businesses, or try to improve products. Making money is considered the natural way of economic life. Just as important, the Scottish philosopher Adam Smith (1723–1790) claimed that as individuals pursue their self-interest, the entire society prospers (1937, orig. 1776).

3. **Competition and consumer choice.** A purely capitalist economy is a free-market system with no government interference (sometimes called a *laissez-faire economy*, from the French words meaning "leave it alone"). Adam Smith stated that a freely competitive economy regulates itself by the "invisible hand" of the law of supply and demand.

Consumers guide a market economy, Smith explained, by selecting the goods and services offering the greatest value. As producers compete for the customer's business, they provide the highest-quality goods at the lowest possible prices. In Smith's time-honoured phrase, from narrow self-interest comes "the greatest good for the greatest number of people." Government control of an economy, on the other hand, distorts market forces by reducing the quantity and quality of goods, shortchanging consumers in the process.

Justice in a capitalist system amounts to freedom of the marketplace, where anyone can produce, invest, buy, and sell according to individual self-interest. The increasing popularity of Walmart, described in the opening to this chapter, reflects the fact that the company's customers think they get a lot for their money when shopping there.

Canada is considered a capitalist nation because most businesses are privately owned. However, it is not completely capitalist because the government plays a large role in Canadian economic affairs. Government itself owns—in part or completely—a number of productive organizations, including almost all of this country's schools, roads, parks, and museums; Canada Post; Via Rail; and the Canadian military. In addition, governments use taxation and other forms of regulation to influence what companies produce, to control the quality and cost of merchandise, to regulate what businesses import and export, and to motivate consumers to conserve natural resources.

Furthermore, government sets minimum wage levels, enforces workplace safety standards, regulates corporate mergers, provides farm price supports, and gives income to a majority of people in Canada in the form of employment insurance, public pensions, student loans, child tax credits, and subsidies for child and elder care. Municipal, provincial, territorial, and federal governments together are the nation's biggest employer, with 17.4 percent of the labour force on their payrolls in 2007 (Statistics Canada, 2008p).

Socialism

Socialism is *an economic system in which natural resources and the means of producing goods and services are collectively owned.* In its ideal form, a socialist economy rejects each of the three characteristics of capitalism just described in favour of three opposite features:

1. **Collective ownership of property.** A socialist economy limits rights to private property, especially property used to generate income. Government controls such property and makes housing and other goods available to all, not just to the people with the most money.

2. **Pursuit of collective goals.** The individualistic pursuit of profit goes against the collective orientation of socialism. What capitalism celebrates as the "entrepreneurial spirit," socialism condemns as greed; individuals are urged to work for the common good of all.

3. **Government control of the economy.** Socialism rejects capitalism's laissez-faire approach in favour of a *centrally controlled* or *command economy* operated by the government. Commercial advertising thus plays little role in socialist economies.

Justice in a socialist context means not competing to gain wealth but meeting everyone's basic needs in a roughly equal manner. From a socialist point of view, the common capitalist practice of giving workers as little in wages and benefits as possible to boost company earnings is unjust because it puts profits before people.

North Korea and more than two dozen other nations in Asia, Africa, and Latin America model their economies on socialism,

welfare capitalism an economic and political system that combines a mostly market-based economy with extensive social welfare programs

state capitalism an economic and political system in which companies are privately owned but co-operate closely with the government

Capitalism still thrives in Hong Kong (*left*), evident in streets choked with advertising and shoppers. Socialism is more the rule in China's capital, Beijing (*right*), a city dominated by government buildings rather than a downtown business district.

placing almost all wealth-generating property under state control (Miller, Holmes, & Kim, 2010). The extent of world socialism declined during the 1990s as countries in Eastern Europe and the former Soviet Union geared their economies toward a market system. More recently, however, voters in Bolivia, Venezuela, Ecuador, and other nations in South America have elected leaders who are moving the national economies in a socialist direction.

Welfare Capitalism and State Capitalism

Most of the nations in Western Europe—especially Sweden, Denmark, and Italy—have market-based economies but also offer broad social welfare programs. Analysts call this third type of economic system **welfare capitalism,** *an economic and political system that combines a mostly market-based economy with extensive social welfare programs.*

Under welfare capitalism, a nation's government owns some of the largest industries and services, such as transportation, the mass media, and health care. In Sweden and Italy, about 12 percent of economic production is *nationalized*, or under state control. Most industry is left in private hands, but all economic activity is subject to extensive government regulation. High taxation (aimed especially at the rich) funds a wide range of social welfare programs, including universal health care and child care, that benefit the entire population (CQ Press, 2010; Olsen, 1996).

Another alternative is **state capitalism,** *an economic and political system in which companies are privately owned but co-operate closely with the government.* State capitalism is the rule in the nations

along the Pacific Rim. Japan, South Korea, and Singapore are all capitalist countries, but their governments work in partnership with large companies, supplying financial assistance and controlling foreign imports to help their businesses compete in world markets (Gerlach, 1992).

Relative Advantages of Capitalism and Socialism

Which economic system works best? Comparing economic models is difficult because all nations mix capitalism and socialism to varying degrees. In addition, nations differ in cultural attitudes toward work, access to natural resources, levels of technological development, and patterns of trade. Despite such complicating factors, some crude comparisons are revealing.

Economic Productivity

One key dimension of economic performance is productivity. A commonly used measure of economic output is *gross domestic product* (GDP), the total value of all goods and services produced within the nation's borders each year. Per capita (per-person) GDP allows us to compare the economic performance of nations of different population sizes.

The output of mostly capitalist countries in the late 1980s—before the end of socialist economies in the Soviet Union and Eastern Europe—varied somewhat but averaged about $13 500 per person. The comparable figure for the mostly socialist former Soviet Union and nations of Eastern Europe was about $5000. This means that the capitalist countries outproduced the socialist nations by a ratio of

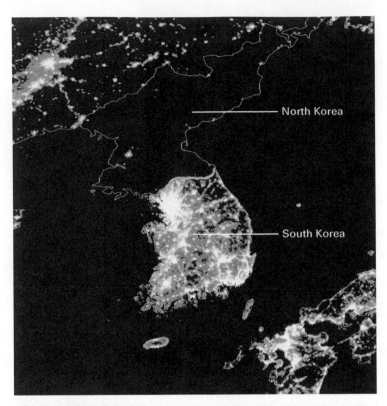

Directly comparing the economic performance of capitalism and socialism is difficult because nations differ in many ways. But a satellite image of socialist North Korea and capitalist South Korea at night shows the dramatically different electrical output of the two nations, one indication of economic activity.

2.7 to 1 (United Nations Development Programme, 1990). A recent comparison of socialist North Korea (per capita GDP of $1800) and capitalist South Korea ($24 801) provides an even sharper contrast (Central Intelligence Agency, 2010; United Nations Development Programme, 2009).

Economic Equality

The distribution of resources within the population is another important measure of how well an economic system works. A comparative study of Europe in the mid-1970s, when that region was split between mostly capitalist and mostly socialist countries, compared the earnings of the richest 5 percent of the population and the poorest 5 percent (Wiles, 1977). Societies with mostly capitalist economies had an income ratio of about 10 to 1; the figure for socialist countries was 5 to 1. In other words, capitalist economies tend to support a higher average economic output but with greater income inequality. Said another way, socialist economies create more economic equality but provide a lower overall level of productivity.

Personal Freedom

One additional consideration in evaluating capitalism and socialism is the personal freedom each system gives its people. Capitalism emphasizes the *freedom to pursue self-interest* and depends on the ability of producers and consumers to interact with little interference by the state. Socialism, by contrast, emphasizes *freedom from basic want*. The goal of equality requires the state to regulate the economy, which in turn limits personal choices and opportunities for citizens.

Can a single society offer both political freedom and economic equality? In capitalist Canada, our political system offers many personal freedoms, but the economy generates a fair bit of inequality, and freedom is not worth as much to a poor person as to a rich one. By contrast, North Korea or Cuba has considerable economic equality, but people cannot speak out or travel freely within or outside of the country. Perhaps the closest any countries have come to "having it all" is Denmark—the Thinking Globally box takes a closer look.

Changes in Socialist and Capitalist Countries

In 1989 and 1990, the nations of Eastern Europe, which had been seized by the former Soviet Union at the end of World War II, overthrew their socialist regimes. These nations—including the former German Democratic Republic (East Germany), the Czech Republic, Slovakia, Hungary, Romania, and Bulgaria—are all moving toward capitalist market systems after decades of state-controlled economies. At the end of 1991, the Soviet Union itself formally dissolved, and many of its former republics introduced some free-market principles into their economies. Within a decade, three-fourths of former Soviet government enterprises were partly or entirely in private hands (Montaigne, 2001).

There were many reasons for these sweeping changes. First, the capitalist economies far outproduced their socialist counterparts. The socialist economies were successful in achieving economic equality, but living standards were low compared with those of Western Europe. Second, Soviet socialism was heavy-handed, rigidly controlling the media and restricting individual freedoms. In other words, socialism did away with *economic* elites, as Karl Marx predicted, but as Max Weber foresaw, socialism increased the power of *political* elites.

So far, the market reforms in Eastern Europe are proceeding unevenly. Some nations (Czech Republic, Slovakia, Poland, and the Baltic states of Latvia, Estonia, and Lithuania) are doing relatively well. But other countries (Romania, Bulgaria, and the Russian Federation) have been buffeted by price increases and falling living standards. Officials hope that expanding production will gradually bring a turnaround. However, the introduction of a market economy has brought with it an increase in economic inequality (Ignatius, 2008; World Bank, 2008).

THINKING GLOBALLY

Want Equality and Freedom? Try Denmark

Denmark is located in northwestern Europe, has about 5.5 million people, and is a little smaller than Nova Scotia. This country is a good example of the economic and political system called welfare capitalism, in which a market economy is mixed with broad government programs that provide for the welfare of all Danish people.

Most Danes consider life in their country to be very good. There is a high standard of living—Denmark and Canada both have a per-person GDP of about $37 800. However, Canada has almost 50 percent more income inequality than Denmark (the United States has almost twice as much). Denmark's unemployment rate for 2010 was 6 percent, lower than the 8.3 percent in Canada (OECD, 2011b).

Low inequality and low unemployment are largely the result of government regulation of the Danish economy. Taxes in Denmark are the highest in the world, with most people paying about 40 percent of their income in taxes and those earning over $70 000 paying more than 50 percent (people in Quebec pay close to 30 percent, while most people in Canada pay less than 25 percent at that income level). That's in addition to a sales tax of 25 percent on everything people buy. These high taxes increase economic equality (by taking more taxes from the rich and giving more benefits to the poor) and they also allow the government to fund social welfare programs that provide benefits to everyone. For example, every Danish citizen is entitled to government-funded schooling and government-funded health care, and each worker receives at least five weeks of paid vacation leave each year. People who lose their jobs receive about 90 percent of their prior income from the government for up to four years.

Many people—especially the Danes themselves—feel that Denmark offers an ideal mix of political freedom (Danes have extensive political rights and elect their leaders) and economic security (all citizens benefit from extensive government services and programs).

WHAT DO YOU THINK?

1. What evidence of less income inequality might you expect to see in Denmark if you were to visit that country?

2. Would you be willing to pay most of your income in taxes if the government provided you with benefits such as schooling and health care? Why or why not?

3. Do you think most people in Canada would like to have our society become more like Denmark? Why or why not?

Sources: Fox (2007) and OECD (2011a, 2011b).

A number of countries, primarily in South America, have recently been heading in a more socialist direction. In 2005, the people of Bolivia elected Evo Morales, a former farmer, union leader, and activist, as their new president, over a wealthy business leader who was educated abroad. This election placed Bolivia in a group of South American nations—including Ecuador, Venezuela, Brazil, Chile, and Uruguay—that are moving toward more socialist economies. The reasons for the shift toward socialism vary from country to country, but the common element is economic inequality. In Bolivia, for example, the economy has grown in recent decades, but most of the benefits have gone to a wealthy business elite. By contrast, more than half of the country's people remain very poor (Howden, 2005).

Work in the Post-industrial Canadian Economy

Economic change is occurring not just in the socialist world but also in Canada. The latest census for which data are available showed that, in 2006, there were approximately 17.15 million people in the labour force, representing approximately two-thirds of those aged 16 and over. A larger share of men (72.3 percent) than women (61.6 percent) were participating in the labour force, although the gap is closing (Human Resources and Skills Development Canada, 2006). Women now account for 47.9 percent of the Canadian workforce, up from 37 percent in 1976 (Ministry of Industry, 2007). In 2006, Aboriginals aged 16 and over had a participation rate of 63 percent. The percentage for visible minority groups was 61.5 percent (Human Resources and Skills Development Canada, 2006).

The Changing Workplace

In 1911, 40 percent of Canadian workers had jobs in the primary sector. In 2010, just 4 percent were part of this economy. Figure 12–2 on page 310 illustrates the shrinking role of the primary sector in the Canadian economy.

Similarly, a century ago, industrialization swelled the ranks of workers in the manufacturing sector. By the mid-1900s, however, a white-collar revolution was gaining momentum. More than 90 percent of new jobs are in the service sector, and close to 80 percent of the labour force perform service work.

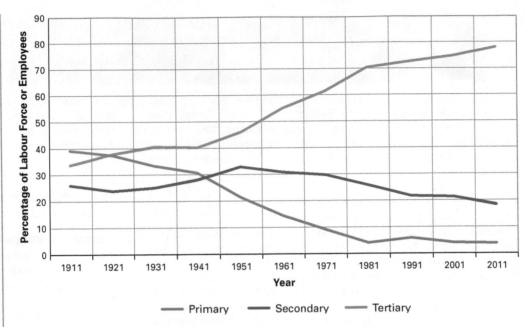

Primary — Secondary — Tertiary

FIGURE 12–2   The Changing Pattern of Work in Canada, 1900–2010

Compared to a century ago, when the economy involved a larger share of factory and farm work, making a living in Canada now involves mostly white-collar service jobs.

Source: Estimated based on data in Bowlby (2001); Leacy (1999); CANSIM Tables D137024–D137028, D137032, D137051, D137052, D137056, D137059–D137061, D137067; and Statistics Canada (2011x, 2011y, 2011z, 2011aa, 2011ab, 2011ac, 2011ad).

As Chapter 8 ("Social Stratification") explained, much service work—including sales, clerical positions, and work in hospitals and restaurants—pays much less than older factory jobs. This means that many jobs in the post-industrial era provide only a modest standard of living. Women and other minorities, as well as many young people just starting their working careers, are the most likely to have jobs doing low-paying service work (Greenhouse, 2006; Kalleberg, Reskin, & Hudson, 2000).

Labour Unions

The changing Canadian economy has seen a shift in the role of *labour unions*, organizations that seek to improve wages and working conditions. During the Great Depression of the 1930s, Canadian union membership increased to more than one-third of non-farm workers by 1950. Then it fell slightly during the 1960s, but increased during the 1970s to return to the 1950 level, where it has stabilized (Marshall, 2000). In 2010, the unionized rate for the total employed workforce in Canada was 29.6 percent (Uppal, 2010).

Canada has a middling position in regard to union rates. While unions in the United States (7.2 percent) and Japan (18 percent)

claim a smaller share of workers than our country, union membership is between 20 and 40 percent in much of Europe, and it reaches a high of 71 percent in Sweden (OECD, 2010; Swank, 2002; Visser, 2006).

The decline in union membership in countries such as Japan and the United States reflects the shrinking industrial sector of the economy. Newer service jobs—such as sales jobs at retailers like Walmart, described in the opening to this chapter—are unlikely to be unionized. Citing low wages and worker complaints, unions are trying to organize Walmart employees, but the Walmart store in Jonquière, Quebec, closed six months after the workers voted to have their interests represented by United Food and Commercial Workers union. The weak economy in Japan and the United States in the past few years has given unions a short-term boost. The Obama administration is supporting new laws that may make it easier for workers to form unions. But long-term gains probably depend on the ability of unions, including those located in Canada, to adapt to the new global economy. Union members in Canada and elsewhere, accustomed to seeing foreign workers as "the enemy," will have to build new international alliances (Allen, 2009; Dalmia, 2008; Rousseau, 2002).

In a society such as ours, with so many different types of work, no one career attracts the interest of more than a small share of today's students.

profession a prestigious white-collar occupation that requires extensive formal education

Student Snapshot

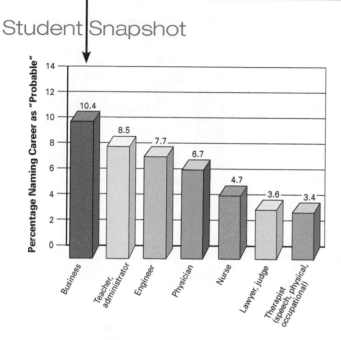

FIGURE 12–3   **The Careers Most Commonly Named as Probable by First-Year University and College Students, 2009**

Today's university and college students expect to enter careers that pay well and carry high prestige.

Source: Pryor et al. (2010).

Professions

All kinds of jobs today are called *professional*; there are professional tennis players, professional housecleaners, and even professional exterminators. As distinct from an *amateur* (from the Latin for "lover," meaning one who acts out of love for the activity itself), a professional performs some task to earn a living. But what exactly is a profession?

A **profession** is *a prestigious white-collar occupation that requires extensive formal education*. People performing this kind of work make a *profession*, or public declaration, of their willingness to work according to certain principles. Professions include the ministry, medicine, law, academia, and fields such as architecture, accountancy, and social work. An occupation is considered a profession to the extent that it demonstrates four basic characteristics (Goode, 1960; Ritzer & Walczak, 1990):

1. **Theoretical knowledge.** Professionals have a theoretical understanding of their field rather than mere technical training. Anyone can master first-aid skills, for example, but doctors have a theoretical understanding of human health. This means that although playing tennis, cleaning houses, and

exterminating insects may be important, they do not really qualify as professions.

2. **Self-regulating practice.** The typical professional is self-employed, "in private practice" rather than working for a company. Professionals oversee their own work and observe a code of ethics.

3. **Authority over clients.** Because of their expertise, professionals are sought out by clients, who value their advice and follow their directions.

4. **Community orientation rather than self-interest.** The traditional professing of duty states an intention to serve the community rather than merely to seek income.

In almost all cases, professional work requires not just a university or college degree but a graduate degree. Not surprisingly, professions are well represented among the jobs that beginning university and college students say they hope to get after graduation, as shown in Figure 12–3.

Many occupations that do not qualify as true professions nonetheless seek to *professionalize* their services. Claiming professional standing usually begins by renaming the work to suggest special, theoretical knowledge, moving the field away from its original, lesser reputation. Stockroom workers become "inventory supply managers" and exterminators are reborn as "insect control specialists."

Interested parties may also form a professional association that certifies their skills. The organization then licenses its members, writes a code of ethics, and emphasizes the work's importance in the community. To win public acceptance, a professional association may also establish schools or other training facilities and perhaps start a professional journal. Not all occupations try to claim professional status. Some *paraprofessionals*, including paralegals and medical technicians, have specialized skills but lack the extensive theoretical education required of full professionals.

Self-Employment

Self-employment—earning a living without being on the payroll of a large organization—was once common in Canada. About 80 percent of the labour force was self-employed in 1800, compared with just 16 percent of workers in 2009. The relative decline has been steady in recent years as the number of self-employed Canadians has increased by 11 percent, compared to an increase of 17 percent for the overall labour force.

Lawyers, physicians, architects, and other professionals are well represented among the ranks of the self-employed in Canada. But most self-employed workers are small business owners, plumbers, farmers, carpenters, freelance writers and editors, artists, and long-distance truck drivers. In all, the self-employed are more likely to have blue-collar than white-collar jobs.

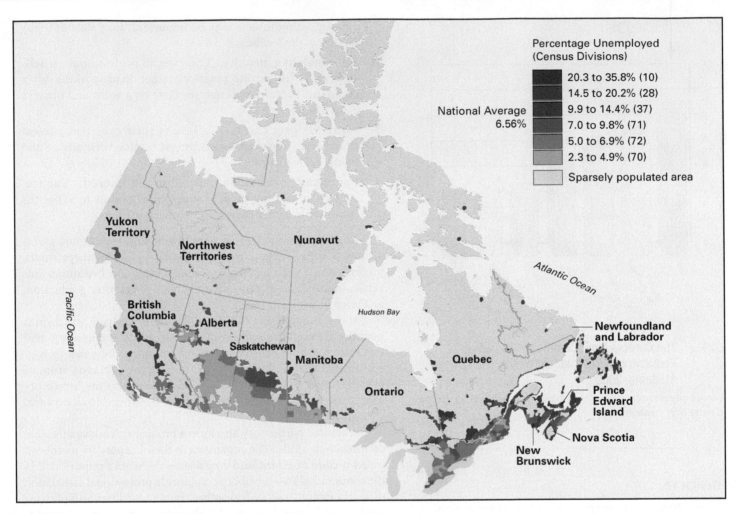

Seeing Ourselves

NATIONAL MAP 12–1   Unemployment Rates across Canada

The 2006 census reported an unemployment rate of 6.6 percent for all of Canada. As in the 2001 census, the highest level of unemployment was in Newfoundland, where several census divisions had unemployment rates over 30 percent. The depiction of the unemployment rate on this map makes us think of the structural causes and consequences of unemployment. Do you usually consider structural or personal factors when you try to understand the unemployment that exists where you live?

Source: Statistics Canada (2011ae).

Women own one-third of this nation's small businesses, a share that increased steadily from 1976 (26 percent) to 1998 (36 percent) but has since levelled out (Industry Canada, 2011a). A 2004 survey showed that the degree of female ownership varied by industry, with accommodation and food services industries having the highest share. Yet in every industry the percentage of female-owned businesses lags behind that of male-owned businesses (Industry Canada, 2011b).

Unemployment and Underemployment

Every society has some level of unemployment. For one thing, few young people entering the labour force find a job right away; workers may leave their jobs to seek new work or to stay at home raising children; others may be on strike or suffer from long-term illnesses; and still others lack the skills to perform useful work.

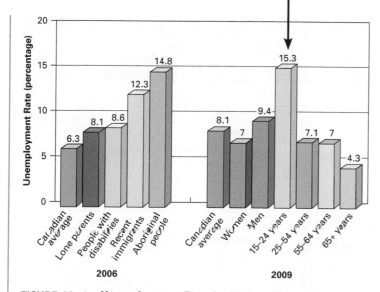

Darlene Drako, 19, was laid off three months into her first job after graduating from high school

FIGURE 12–4 **Unemployment Rate for Various Categories of Adults, Canada, Various Years**

Source: Human Resources and Skills Development Canada (2011).

But unemployment is not just an individual problem; it is also caused by the economy. Jobs disappear as occupations become obsolete and companies change the way they operate. Since 1980, the largest Canadian businesses and different levels of government have eliminated thousands of jobs in manufacturing and the public service.

As National Map 12–1 shows, some regions of Canada, particularly the east coast and the Prairies, had high unemployment in 2006; in some places, the unemployment rate was more than three times the national rate (Statistics Canada, 2011ae).

Figure 12–4 shows that the unemployment rate in 2009 for Canadian men (9.4 percent) is substantially higher than for women (7.0 percent). The rate for recent immigrants (12.3 percent) was higher than for other Canadians, as was the rate for Aboriginal people (14.8 percent) (Human Resources and Skills Development Canada, 2011).

Underemployment is also a problem for millions of workers. In an era of corporate bankruptcy, the failure of large banks, and downsizing by companies throughout the North American economy, millions of workers—the lucky ones who still have their jobs—have been left with lower salaries, fewer benefits such as health insurance, and disappearing pensions. Rising global competition, weaker worker organizations, and economic recession have combined to allow many people to keep their jobs only by agreeing to cutbacks in pay or to the loss of other benefits (Clark, 2002; Gutierrez, 2007; McGeehan, 2009).

Workplace Diversity: Race and Gender

In the past, white men were the mainstay of the Canadian labour force. However, the nation's proportion of minorities is rising rapidly. The visible minority and Aboriginal populations are increasing faster than other Canadians.

Such dramatic changes are likely to affect Canadian society in countless ways. Not only will more and more workers be women and minorities, but the workplace will have to develop programs and policies that meet the needs of a socially diverse workforce and also encourage everyone to work together effectively and respectfully. The Thinking about Diversity box on page 314 takes a closer look at some of the issues involved in our changing workplace.

In addition, in 2010, 19.4 percent of employed Canadians worked part-time, defined as less than 35 hours a week; 27.4 percent of Canadian women in the paid workforce worked part-time at their main job, compared with 12.1 percent of employed men. Although most say they are satisfied with this arrangement, when viewed cross-nationally Canada has one of the highest shares of involuntary part-time workers (27.6 percent) as a percentage of part-time work (OECD, 2011c). As the North American economy struggles to climb out of the recent recession, it is likely that many workers are working less than what they desire. Many other adults are out of work and looking for a job or are "discouraged workers" who have given up entirely.

New Information Technology and Work

July 2, Edmonton, Alberta. The manager of the local hardware store scans the bar codes of a bagful of items. "The computer doesn't just total the costs," she explains. "It also keeps track of inventory, places orders with the warehouse, and decides which products to continue to sell and which to drop." "Sounds like what you used to do, Maureen," I respond with a smile. "Yep," she nods, with no smile at all.

Another workplace issue is the increasing role of computers and other new information technology. The Information Revolution is changing what people do in a number of ways (Rule & Brantley, 1992; Vallas & Beck, 1996):

1. **Computers are deskilling labour.** Just as industrial machines replaced the master craftsworkers of an earlier era, computers now threaten the skills of managers. More business operations are based not on executive decisions but on computer modelling. In other words, a machine decides whether to place an order, stock a dress in a certain size and colour, or approve a loan application.

2. **Computers are making work more abstract.** Most industrial workers have a hands-on relationship with their product. Post-industrial workers use symbols to perform abstract

THINKING ABOUT DIVERSITY: RACE, CLASS, & GENDER

Twenty-First Century Diversity: Changes in the Workplace

An upward trend in the Canadian visible minority population is changing the workplace. The share of visible minorities employed in Canada increased from 4.7 percent in 1981 to about 15 percent in 2006 (Statistics Canada, 2003t, 2008o). As shown in Chapter 10 ("Gender Stratification"), over this time period, the proportion of women employed markedly increased, while a significantly lower proportion of men were employed than was the case 25 years before.

Welcoming social diversity means, first, recruiting talented workers of both sexes and all racial and cultural backgrounds. But developing the potential of all employees requires meeting the needs of women and other minorities, which may not be the same as those of white men. For example, child care at the workplace is a big issue for working mothers with small children.

Second, businesses must develop effective ways to deal with tension that arises from social differences. They will have to work harder to ensure that workers are treated equally and respectfully, which means having zero tolerance for racial or sexual harassment.

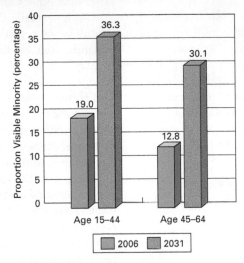

Proportion of Visible Minority Canadians, Aged 15 through 64, 2006 and 2031

Looking ahead, the share of visible minorities in the Canadian labour force will more than double between 2006 and 2031.

Source: Statistics Canada (2010e).

Third, companies will have to rethink current promotion practices. At present, 72 percent of the directors of *Fortune* 100 companies are white men; 28 percent are women or other minorities (Executive Leadership Council, 2008). As noted in Chapter 11 ("Race and Ethnicity"), visible minorities, which today comprise 15.4 percent of the labour force, and Aboriginals are even less likely than women to have managerial jobs, especially at the top levels. In sum, "glass ceilings" that limit the advancement of skilled workers not only discourage effort but also deprive companies of their largest source of talent: women and other minorities.

WHAT DO YOU THINK?

1. What underlying factors are increasing the social diversity of the Canadian workplace?

2. In what specific ways do you think businesses should support minority workers?

3. In what other settings (such as schools) is social diversity becoming more important? Why?

---

tasks, such as making a company more profitable or making software more user-friendly.

3. **Computers limit workplace interaction.** Spending time at computer terminals, workers become isolated from one another.

4. **Computers increase employers' control of workers.** Computers allow supervisors to check employees' output continuously, whether they work at keyboard terminals or on assembly lines.

5. **Computers allow companies to relocate work.** Because computer technology allows information to flow almost anywhere instantly, the symbolic work in today's economy may not take place where we might think. We have all had the experience of calling a business (for instance, a hotel or a bookstore) located in our own town only to find out that we are talking to a person at a computer workstation thousands of kilometres away. Computer technology provides the means to outsource many jobs—especially service work—to other places where wages may be lower.

Perhaps in the wake of widespread failures on Bay Street, there will be a trend away from allowing computers to manage risk, putting responsibility for business decisions back in the hands of people (Kivant, 2008). Or perhaps both computers and people have flaws that will always prevent us from living in a perfect world. But the rapidly increasing reliance on computers in business reminds us that new technology is never socially neutral. It changes the relationships between people in the workplace, shapes the way we work, and often alters the balance of power between employers and employees. Understandably, then, people welcome some aspects of the Information Revolution and oppose others.

Corporations

At the core of today's capitalist economy is the **corporation,** *an organization with a legal existence, including rights and liabilities, separate from that of its members.* Incorporating makes an organization a legal entity, able to enter into contracts and own property. Of the more than

corporation (p. 314) an organization with a legal existence, including rights and liabilities, separate from that of its members

monopoly the domination of a market by a single producer

oligopoly the domination of a market by a few producers

30 million businesses in North America, about 6 million are incorporated (U.S. Census Bureau, 2009). Incorporating protects the wealth of owners from lawsuits that result from business debts or harm to consumers; it can also mean a lower tax rate on the company's profits.

Economic Concentration

Most corporations are small, with assets of less than $500 000, so it is the largest corporations that dominate our nation's economy. In 2006, the U.S. government listed 2568 corporations with assets exceeding $2.5 billion, representing 80 percent of all corporate assets in that country (Internal Revenue Service, 2009). Similar trends have also been observed in Canada (Ministry of Industry, 2003).

America's largest corporation, measured in terms of sales, is Exxon Mobil, with 2009 revenue of more than $440 billion. Second in line is Walmart, with annual sales of more than $400 billion.

Conglomerates and Corporate Linkages

Economic concentration creates *conglomerates*, giant corporations composed of many smaller corporations. Conglomerates form as corporations enter new markets, spin off new companies, or merge with other companies. For example, PepsiCo is a conglomerate that includes Pepsi-Cola, Frito-Lay, Gatorade, Tropicana, and Quaker.

Many conglomerates are linked because they own each other's stock, the result being worldwide corporate alliances of staggering size. Until 2009, General Motors, for example, owned Opel (Germany), Vauxhall (Great Britain), Saab (Sweden), and a share of Daewoo (South Korea) and had partnerships with Suzuki and Toyota (Japan). Similarly, Ford owned Volvo (Sweden) and still maintains a small interest in Aston Martin (Great Britain) and Mazda (Japan).

Corporations are also linked through *interlocking directorates*, networks of people who serve as directors of many corporations (Kono et al., 1998; Weidenbaum, 1995). These boardroom connections provide access to valuable information about other companies' products and marketing strategies. While perfectly legal, such linkages encourage illegal activity, such as price fixing, as companies share information about their pricing policies.

Corporations: Are They Competitive?

According to the capitalist model, businesses operate independently in a competitive market. But in light of the extensive linkages that exist between them, it is obvious that large corporations do not operate independently. Also, a few large corporations dominate many markets, so they are not truly competitive.

The law forbids any company from establishing a **monopoly**, *domination of a market by a single producer*, because with no competition such a company could simply charge whatever it wanted for its products. But **oligopoly**, *domination of a market by a few producers*,

Canada is now a "post-industrial" society: Industry involves just over 25 percent of the labour force, while the service sector involves nearly 75 percent of workers. How does this transformation change the nature as well as the location of work?

is both legal and common. Oligopoly arises because the huge investment needed to enter a major market, such as the auto industry, is beyond the reach of all but the biggest companies. In addition, true competition involves risk, which big business tries to avoid.

Federal governments seek to regulate corporations in order to protect the public interest. Yet as corporate scandals have shown—most recently, involving the housing mortgage business and the collapse of so many banks—regulation is often too little too late, resulting in harm to millions of people. Government is also the corporate world's single biggest customer, and sometimes steps in to support many struggling corporations with multi-billion-dollar bailout programs. Especially during tough economic times, the public tends to support a greater role for the government in the economy (Sachs, 2009).

Corporations and the Global Economy

Corporations have grown so large that they now account for most of the world's economic output. The biggest corporations are based in the United States, Japan, and Western Europe, but their marketplace is the entire world.

Global corporations know that low-income countries contain most of the world's people and resources. In addition, labour costs there are attractively low: A manufacturing worker in Mexico, who earns about $2.88 an hour, labours for more than a week to earn about what a worker in Japan (who averages about $19.68 an hour) or the United States ($24.03 an hour) or Canada ($22.85) earns in a single day (U.S. Department of Labor, 2009a).

The Market: Does the "Invisible Hand" Look Out for Us or Pick Our Pockets?

The market or government planning? Governments rely on one or the other to determine the products and services companies will produce and what people will consume. So important is this question that the answer has much to do with how nations define themselves, choose their allies, and identify their enemies.

Historically, Canadian society and, to an even greater extent, American society has relied on the "invisible hand" of the market to make economic decisions. Market dynamics move prices up or down according to the supply of products and buyer demand. The market thus links the efforts of countless people, each of whom—to restate Adam Smith's insight—is motivated only by self-interest. Defenders of the market system—including the economists Milton Friedman and Rose Friedman (1980)—claim that a more or less freely operating market system is the key to North America's high standard of living.

But others point to the contributions that governments make to the economy of countries such as Canada and the United States. First, governments must step in to carry out tasks that no private company could do as well, such as defending the country against enemies abroad or terrorists at home. Governments (in partnership with private companies) also play a key role in building and maintaining public projects such as roads, utilities, schools, libraries, and museums.

The Friedmans counter that, whatever the task, governments usually end up being very inefficient. They claim that, for most people, the least satisfying goods and services available today—public schools, the postal service, and passenger railroad service—are government operated. The products we enjoy most—household appliances, computers and other electronics, and fashionable clothes—are products of the market. The Friedmans and other supporters of free markets believe that minimal state regulation serves the public interest best.

But supporters of government intervention in the economy make other arguments. First, they claim that the market has incentives to produce only what is profitable. Few private companies set out to meet the needs of poor people because, by definition, poor people have little money to spend.

Second, the market has certain self-destructive tendencies that only the government can curb. In 1890, for example, the U.S. government passed the Sherman Antitrust Act to break up the monopolies that controlled the nation's oil and steel production. In the decades since then—and especially after President Franklin Roosevelt's New Deal of the 1930s—the U.S. government has taken a strong regulatory role to control inflation (by setting interest rates), enhance the well-being of workers (by imposing workplace safety standards), and benefit consumers (by setting standards for product quality). Canada's federal and provincial governments have taken similar measures in recent decades.

Third, because the market magnifies social inequality, the government must step in on the side of social justice. Since capitalist economies concentrate income and wealth in the hands of a few, it is necessary for government to tax the rich at a higher rate to ensure that wealth reaches more of the population.

Does the market's "invisible hand" look out for us or pick our pockets? Although most people in Canada continue to favour a free market, they also support government intervention that benefits the public. In recent years, public confidence in corporations has fallen, and confidence in the federal government has gone up. Government's job is not only to ensure national security but also to maintain economic stability. The Harper government's $60 billion stimulus package to create employment during the recent recession is a case in point.

In the decades to come, we should expect to see people in Canada, and around the world, continue to debate the best balance of market forces and government decision making.

WHAT DO YOU THINK?

1. Do you agree or disagree with the statement that "the government is best that governs least"? Why?

2. Do you think people support less government control of the economy in good times and more government control in bad times? Why or why not?

3. In what ways has the Harper government expanded the role of government in the Canadian economy? What about in the auto industry?

As Chapter 9 ("Global Stratification") explained, the impact of multinational corporations on low-income countries is controversial. Modernization theorists claim that multinational corporations, by unleashing the great productivity of capitalism, raise living standards in poor nations, offering tax revenues, capital investment, new jobs, and advanced technology that together accelerate economic growth (Berger, 1986; Firebaugh & Beck, 1994; Firebaugh & Sandu, 1998). Dependency theorists respond that multinationals in fact make global inequality worse by blocking the development of local industries and by pushing low-income countries to produce goods for export rather than food and other products for local people. From this standpoint, multinationals make poor nations increasingly dependent on rich nations (Dixon & Boswell, 1996; Kentor, 1998; Wallerstein, 1979).

In short, modernization theory praises the market as the key to progress and affluence for all of the world's people. Dependency theory takes a different position, calling for replacing markets with government-based economic policies. The Controversy & Debate box takes a closer look at the issue of market versus government economies.

politics the social institution that distributes power, sets a society's goals, and makes decisions

power the ability to achieve desired ends despite resistance from others

government a formal organization that directs the political life of a society

authority power that people perceive as legitimate rather than coercive

routinization of charisma (p. 318) the transformation of charismatic authority into some combination of traditional and bureaucratic authority

monarchy (p. 318) a political system in which a single family rules from generation to generation

The Economy: Looking Ahead

Social institutions are a society's ways of meeting people's needs. But as we have seen, the Canadian economy only partly succeeds in this mission. As the years go by, our economy experiences alternating periods of expansion and recession. And in both good times and bad, our economy provides for some people much better than for others.

One important trend that underlies change in the economy is the Information Revolution. First, the share of the Canadian labour force engaged in manufacturing is less than half of what it was in 1960; service work, especially computer-related jobs, makes up the difference. For industrial workers, the post-industrial economy has brought unemployment and declining wages. Our society must face up to the challenge of providing millions of men and women with the language and computer skills they need to succeed in the modern economy. Yet in recent years, millions of people in "good" service jobs have found themselves out of work. In addition, there are regional differences in the economic outlook: National Map 12–1 on page 312 shows which regions have the highest unemployment rates. A second transformation of recent years is the expansion of the global economy. Two centuries ago, the ups and downs people experienced reflected events and trends in their own town. One century ago, communities were economically linked so that one town's prosperity depended on producing goods demanded by people elsewhere in the country. Today, we have to look beyond the national economy because, for example, the historical rise in the cost of gasoline at our local gas station has as much to do with increasing demand for oil around the world, especially in India and China, as it does with local or national trends in Canada. As both producers and consumers, we are now subject to factors and forces that are both distant and unseen.

Finally, analysts around the world are rethinking conventional economic models. The global economy shows that socialism is less productive than capitalism, one important reason behind the collapse of socialist regimes in Eastern Europe and the Soviet Union. But capitalism has its own problems, including high levels of inequality and a steady stream of corporate scandal—two important reasons that the economy now operates with significant government regulation.

What will be the long-term effects of all these changes? Two conclusions seem certain. First, the economic future of Canada, the United States, and other nations will be played out in a global arena. The new post-industrial economy in Canada has emerged as more industrial production has moved to other nations. Second, it is imperative that we address the urgent challenges of global inequality and population increase. Whether the world reduces or enlarges the gap between rich and poor societies may well steer our planet toward peace or war.

Politics: Historical Overview

There is a close link between economics and **politics** (also known as the "polity"), *the social institution that distributes power, sets a society's goals, and makes decisions.* Early in the twentieth century, Max Weber (1978, orig. 1921) defined **power** as *the ability to achieve desired ends despite resistance from others.* The use of power is the business of **government,** *a formal organization that directs the political life of a society.* Governments typically claim to help people, but at the same time governments demand that people obey the rules. Yet, as Weber noted, most governments do not openly threaten their people. Most of the time, people respect (or at least accept) their society's political system.

No government, Weber explained, is likely to keep its power for very long if compliance comes only from the threat of brute force, because there could never be enough police to watch everyone—and who would watch the police? Every government therefore tries to make itself seem legitimate in the eyes of the public.

This brings us to the concept of **authority,** *power that people perceive as legitimate rather than coercive.* A society's source of authority depends on its economy. According to Weber, pre-industrial societies rely on *traditional authority*, power legitimized by respect for long-established cultural patterns. Woven into a society's collective memory, traditional authority may seem almost sacred. Chinese emperors in centuries past were legitimized by tradition, as were the nobles in medieval Europe.

Traditional authority declines as societies industrialize. For example, royal families still exist in 10 European nations, but the democratic cultures of countries such as the United Kingdom, Sweden, and Denmark have shifted power to commoners elected to office. Weber explained that the expansion of rational bureaucracy is the modern foundation of authority. *Rational-legal authority* (sometimes called *bureaucratic authority*) is power legitimized by rationally enacted law.

Traditional authority is tied to family; rational-legal authority flows from offices in governments. A traditional monarch passes power on to heirs; a modern prime minister takes office and gives up power according to law.

Weber described one additional type of authority that has surfaced throughout history. *Charismatic authority* is power legitimized by the extraordinary personal qualities—the *charisma*—of a leader. Unlike its traditional and rational-legal counterparts, charismatic authority depends less on a person's ancestry or office and more on personality. Followers see in charismatic leaders some special, perhaps even divine, power. Examples of charismatic leaders include Jesus of Nazareth; Nazi Germany's Adolf Hitler; India's liberator, Mahatma Gandhi; and civil rights leaders Martin Luther King, Jr. and Nelson Mandela. All charismatic leaders aim to radically transform society, which explains why they are almost always controversial and why few of them die of old age.

In early 2010, Google users placed flowers and candles outside the company's headquarters in Beijing after government leaders demanded that the internet giant accept state censorship. Rather than comply with government demands, Google chose to close down its operations within China, although it continued to operate in Hong Kong. If you were a company leader, would you support this principled action or would you agree to state censorship in order to gain access to the vast Chinese market?

Because charismatic authority flows from a single individual, the leader's death creates a crisis. The survival of a charismatic movement, Weber explained, requires the **routinization of charisma:** *the transformation of charismatic authority into some combination of traditional and bureaucratic authority.* After the death of Jesus, for example, followers institutionalized his teachings in a church, built on tradition and bureaucracy. Routinized in this way, Christianity has lasted 2000 years.

Politics in Global Perspective

The world's political systems differ in countless ways. Generally, however, they fall into four categories: monarchy, democracy, authoritarianism, and totalitarianism.

Monarchy

Monarchy (with Latin and Greek roots meaning "one ruler") is *a political system in which a single family rules from generation to generation.* Monarchy is commonly found in agrarian societies; for example, the Bible tells of great kings such as David and Solomon. In the world today, 27 nations have royal families; most trace their ancestry back centuries. In Weber's analysis, then, monarchy is legitimized by tradition.

During the Middle Ages, *absolute monarchs* in much of the world claimed a monopoly of power based on divine right (or God's will). In some nations—including Oman, Saudi Arabia, and Swaziland—monarchs (not necessarily with divine support) still exercise virtually absolute control over their people.

With industrialization, however, monarchs gradually pass from the scene in favour of elected officials. All of the European societies with royal families today are *constitutional monarchies*, meaning that their monarchs are little more than symbolic heads of state; actual governing is the responsibility of elected officials, led by a prime minister and guided by a constitution. In these countries, nobility *reigns*, but elected officials actually *rule*.

Democracy

The historical trend throughout most of the world has been toward **democracy,** *a political system that gives power to the people as a whole.* Because it is unrealistic to expect all citizens to be involved in governing, our system is in fact a *representative democracy*, which puts authority in the hands of leaders who from time to time compete for office in elections.

Most high-income countries of the world, including those that still have royal families, claim to be democratic. Industrialization and democracy go together because both require a literate populace. Also, with industrialization, the traditional legitimization of power in a monarchy gives way to rational-legal authority. Thus democracy and rational-legal authority are linked just like monarchy and traditional authority are.

But high-income countries such as Canada are not truly democratic, for two reasons. First, there is the problem of bureaucracy. The number of people employed at the various levels of government in Canada (federal, provincial, territorial, and municipal) is nearly 1 million strong. Most of the officials who run the government are never elected by anyone and do not have to answer directly to the people.

The second problem involves economic inequality: Rich people have far more political power than poor people. Most of our political leaders have been wealthy men and women, and in politics, "money talks." Though many of Canada's elected leaders do not come from wealthy families, many have substantial personal wealth. Moreover, Canadian politicians are privileged by their education, with two-thirds of them having some background in law. The current prime minister,

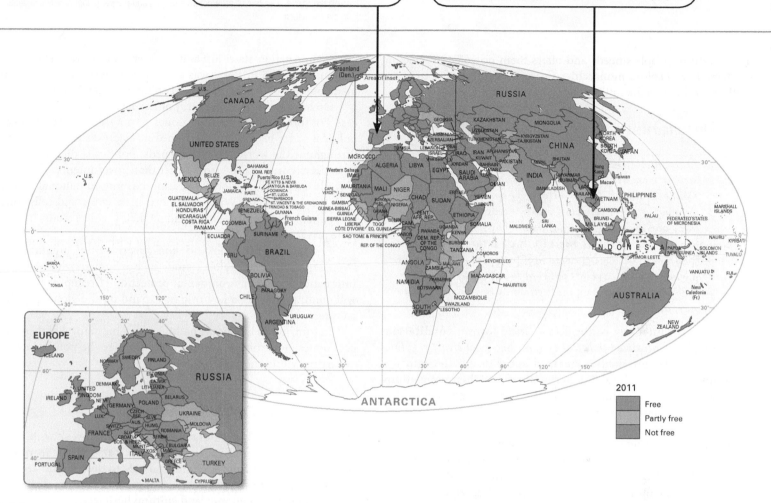

Rosa Canellas Perez lives in Madrid, the capital of Spain, a high-income nation with extensive political freedom.

Nguyen Hung Anh lives near Hanoi, Vietnam, a middle-income nation that restricts political freedom and closely monitors the movements, actions, and speech of its people.

2011
Free
Partly free
Not free

Window on the World

GLOBAL MAP 12–2 **Political Freedom in Global Perspective**

In 2009, a total of 89 of the world's 194 nations at that time, containing 46 percent of all people, were politically "free"; that is, they offered their citizens extensive political rights and civil liberties. Another 58 countries, which included 20 percent of the world's people, were "partly free," with more limited rights and liberties. The remaining 47 nations, home to 34 percent of humanity, fall into the category of "not free." In these countries, government sharply restricts individual initiative. While there have been some setbacks in recent years, between 1989 and 2009, democracy made significant gains, largely in Latin America and Eastern Europe. In Asia, India (containing 1.1 billion people) returned to the "free" category in 1999. In 2000, Mexico joined the ranks of nations considered "free" for the first time.

Source: Freedom House (2011).

Stephen Harper, has a master's degree in economics. Given the even greater resources of billion-dollar corporations, how well does our "democratic" system listen to the voices of "average people"?

Still, democratic nations do provide many rights and freedoms. Global Map 12–2 shows one assessment of political freedom around the world. According to Freedom House, an organization that tracks political trends, 89 of the world's nations (with 46 percent of the global population) were "free,"

respecting many civil liberties, in 2009. This represents a gain for democracy: Just 85 nations were free a decade earlier (Freedom House, 2010).

Authoritarianism

Some governments prevent their people from having any voice in politics. **Authoritarianism** is *a political system that denies the people participation in government.* An authoritarian government is

totalitarianism a highly centralized political system that extensively regulates people's lives

welfare state a system of government agencies and programs that provides benefits to the population

indifferent to people's needs and offers them no voice in selecting leaders. The absolute monarchies in Saudi Arabia and Oman are authoritarian, as is the military junta in Ethiopia.

Totalitarianism

October 30, Beijing, China. Several Canadian students are sitting around a computer in the lounge of a Chinese university dormitory. They are taking turns running internet searches on keywords such as democracy and Amnesty International. They soon realize that China's government filters the results of internet searches, permitting only officially approved sites to appear. One Chinese student who is watching points out that things could be worse—in North Korea, she explains, most students have no access to computers at all.

The most intensely controlled political form is **totalitarianism,** *a highly centralized political system that extensively regulates people's lives.* Totalitarianism emerged in the twentieth century as governments gained the ability to rigidly control their populations. The Vietnamese government closely monitors the activities of all of its citizens. Similarly, the government of North Korea uses surveillance equipment and powerful computers to control its people by collecting and storing information about them.

Although some totalitarian governments claim to represent the will of the people, most seek to bend people to the will of the government. As the term *totalitarian* implies, such governments have a *total* concentration of power, allowing no organized opposition. Denying the people the right to assemble and controlling access to information, these governments create an atmosphere of isolation and fear. In the former Soviet Union, for example, most citizens had no access to telephone directories, copiers, fax machines, or accurate city maps.

Socialization in totalitarian societies is highly political, seeking obedience and commitment to the system. In North Korea, one of the world's strictest totalitarian states, pictures of leaders and political messages are everywhere, reminding citizens that they owe total allegiance to the state. Government-controlled schools and mass media present only official versions of events.

Totalitarian governments span the political spectrum from fascist (including Nazi Germany) to communist (such as North Korea). In all cases, however, one party claims total control of the society and permits no opposition.

A Global Political System?

Is globalization changing politics in the same way that it is changing the economy? On one level, the answer is no. Although most of today's economic activity is international, the world remains divided into nation-states just as it has been for centuries. The United Nations (founded in 1945) was a small step toward global government, but its political role in world affairs has been limited.

On another level, however, politics has become a global process. For some analysts, multinational corporations represent a new political order because of their enormous power to shape events throughout the world. In other words, politics is dissolving into business as corporations grow larger than governments.

Also, the Information Revolution has moved national politics onto the world stage. With email, text messaging, and cellphones everywhere, few countries can conduct their political affairs in complete privacy.

Finally, several thousand *non-governmental organizations* (NGOs) seek to advance global issues, such as human rights (Amnesty International) and environmental protection (Greenpeace). NGOs will continue to play a key role in expanding the global political culture.

In sum, just as individual nations are losing control of their own economies, governments cannot fully manage the political events occurring within their borders.

Politics in Canada

In contrast to the United States' revolutionary break with Great Britain, Canada's political independence came about through a peaceful transition from monarchical rule to democratic decision making. Our nation's political development reflects its distinctive history, capitalist economy, and cultural heritage.

Canadian Culture and the Rise of the Welfare State

Our cultural emphasis on individualism is reflected in the Canadian Human Rights Act and the Charter of Rights and Freedoms, both of which make explicit that all individuals have an equal right to make the lives for themselves that they are able to and wish to achieve. In making the best lives for themselves, some people in Canada—and many more in the United States, no doubt—share the sentiment of nineteenth-century philosopher and poet Ralph Waldo Emerson: "The government that governs best is the government that governs least." Yet many other Canadians view the government in a more positive light, agreeing to pay higher taxes to support quality public services.

What is clear is that our government has grown into a vast and complex **welfare state**, *a system of government agencies and programs that provide benefits to the population.* Government benefits begin even before birth (through prenatal nutrition programs, coverage of midwives' and physicians' fees, and patients' hospital stays) and continue into old age (through public pensions). Some programs

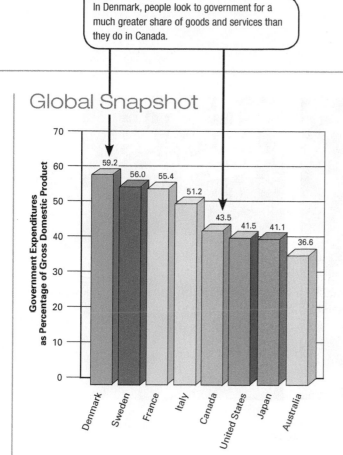

Global Snapshot

FIGURE 12–5 The Size of Government, 2010

Government activity accounts for a smaller share of economic output in the United States than in Canada and most other high-income countries.

Source: OECD (2010d).

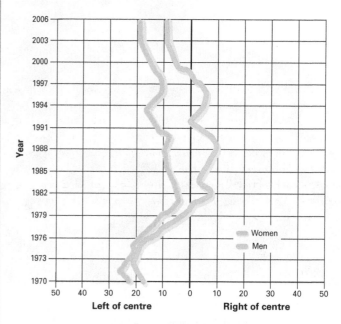

Student Snapshot

FIGURE 12–6 Left-Right Political Identification of University and College Students, 1970–2006

Student attitudes moved to the right after 1970 and shifted to the left in the late 1990s. Female students tend to be more liberal than their male counterparts.

Sources: Astin et al. (2002), Sax et al. (2003), and Pryor et al. (2008).

are especially important to the poor, who are not well served by our capitalist economic system; nevertheless, students, farmers, homeowners, small business operators, veterans, performing artists, and even giant corporations also get various subsidies and supports. In fact, virtually all Canadian adults look to the government to fund their health care services as well as public education programs for their children, and a majority of us also look to government for at least part of our income (Bartlett & Steele, 1998; Benoit, 2000a; Caplow et al., 1982; Devine, 1985; Myles, 1996).

Today's welfare state is the result of a gradual increase in the size and scope of government. At the time of Confederation in 1867, in most communities the presence of the federal government amounted to little more than a flag. Since then, the federal budget has steadily risen, reaching $212 billion in 2005–2006.

As much as government has expanded in this country, the Canadian welfare state, though larger than that of our neighbour to the south, is still smaller than in many other industrial nations. Figure 12–5 shows that government is larger in most of Europe, especially in Scandinavian countries such as Denmark and Sweden.

The Political Spectrum

Who supports a bigger welfare state? Who wants to cut it back? Answers to such questions reveal attitudes that form the *political spectrum*, which ranges from the extremely liberal on the left to the extremely conservative on the right. In the United States, about one-fourth of adults fall on the liberal or "left" side, and one-third say they are conservative, placing themselves on the political "right." The remaining 40 percent claim to be moderates, in the political "middle" (NORC, 2009:189). Figure 12–6 shows how this pattern has changed among young people over time. Canadian researchers draw a parallel between Canada's Conservative Party and America's Democratic Party, which places most Canadians to the political left of their neighbours to the south (Adams, 2009). The political spectrum helps us understand the ways in which people think about the economy. *Economic issues* focus on economic inequality. On economic issues, liberals support extensive government regulation of the economy and a larger welfare state to reduce income inequality. Economic conservatives want to limit

Lower-income people have more pressing financial needs and so they tend to focus on economic issues, such as the level of the minimum wage. Higher-income people, by contrast, provide support for many social issues, such as animal rights.

the hand of government in the economy and allow market forces more freedom.

The political spectrum can also be applied to *social issues*, which are moral questions about how people ought to live. Social issues include abortion, the death penalty, gay rights, and the treatment of minorities. Members of the New Democratic Party tend to support equal rights and opportunities for all categories of people, view abortion as a matter of individual choice, and oppose the death penalty because it has been unfairly applied to minorities. The "family values" agenda of the Conservatives supports traditional gender roles and opposes gay marriage, affirmative action, and other "special programs" for minorities. Conservatives tend to condemn abortion and prostitution as morally wrong and support the death penalty as a just response to the most serious crimes. Liberal members tend to adopt a middle ground on most social issues, focusing on extending choice rather than favouring a single solution.

Until a few decades ago, there were two major political parties in Canada: Progressive Conservatives ("Tories") and Liberals ("Grits"). A third party, the New Democratic Party, usually but not always campaigned for political office along the lines described above. But Canada's political spectrum has changed recently, with a number of newer political parties competing for the public's attention and, ultimately, their votes. These include the comparatively conservative Canadian Alliance Party (formerly the Reform Party),

almost exclusively based in Western Canada, which merged with the Conservatives; and the provincial Parti Québécois and federal Bloc Québécois, French parties based in Quebec. Both continuity and change in the political power matrix could be seen in the 2006 federal election. Stephen Harper's Conservative Party won a minority government with 124 seats. The last time this party was in office was in 1993. The second-largest number of seats (104) was won by the former reigning party, the Liberal Party. The Bloc Québécois (51 seats) picked up support from the Liberal Party, as did the New Democrats with 29 seats. Canadians clearly wanted a change from the Liberal Party, cautiously choosing the Conservative Party to take the lead under the helm of Stephen Harper.

In the 2011 federal election, major changes occurred for most parties. The Conservative Party not only remained in power, but also increased its status to a majority government (166 seats). The Liberal Party won the fewest seats in their history (34 seats), and party leader Michael Ignatieff was defeated in his riding. The Bloc Québécois (4 seats) lost official party status for the first time since their first election, and party leader Gilles Duceppe was also defeated in his riding. The New Democratic Party won the largest number of seats in their history (103 seats) and became the Official Opposition. Green Party leader Elizabeth May won the first ever elected seat for the Green Party in Canada and, indeed, in North America, but the party lost votes overall.

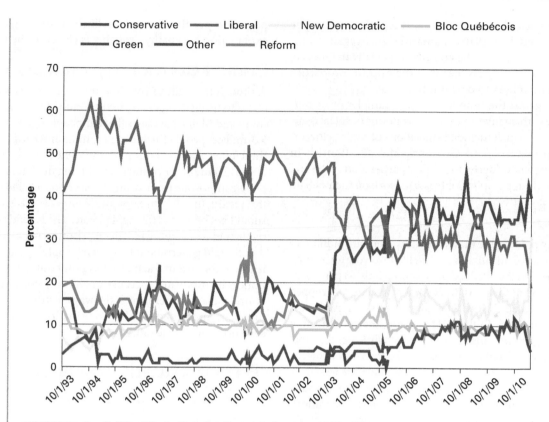

FIGURE 12–7   Political Party Popular Support, Canada, 1993–2011

Note: October 1993; June 1997; November 27, 2000; June 28, 2004; January 23, 2006; October 14, 2008; and May 5, 2011 are based on election results.

Sources: Angus Reid Group (1995, 1996b, 1997c, 1998c, 2000b); Ipsos-Reid (2001c to 2001h, 2002a to 2002e, 2003g to 2003j, 2004a to 2004c, 2005a to 2005m, 2006a to 2006j, 2007a to 2007j, 2008a to 2008l, 2009a to 2009i, 2010a to 2010l, 2011a, 2011b).

Party Identification

Because many people hold mixed political attitudes, with liberal views on some issues and conservative stands on others, party identification in Canada has tended to be weak historically. Figure 12–7 shows, however, that from the early 1990s until 2006, the Liberal Party enjoyed remarkable support from Canadians. During this time, the Liberals enjoyed popular support that dropped below 40 percent only during the 1997 and 2000 elections; its support dipped to 30 percent in 2006. Meanwhile, the Conservative Party (made up of the former Alliance [Reform] Party and Progressive Conservatives) gained in popular support from 20 percent in 2000 to 30 percent in 2006 to 39.6 percent in 2011.

Although more than 8 in every 10 people polled preferred one party over another, most were not strongly committed to their party of choice. But most individuals do not hold views entirely consistent with either party of preference. With wealth to protect, well-to-do people generally hold conservative views on economic issues.

Yet their extensive schooling and secure social standing encourage them to adopt liberal attitudes on many social issues. Individuals of low social position exhibit the opposite pattern, tending toward social democratic views on economic policy and embracing a socially conservative agenda (Erikson, Luttbeg, & Tedin, 1980; Humphries, 1984; McBroom & Reed, 1990; Nunn, Crocket, & Williams, 1978; Syzmanski, 1983).

Special-Interest Groups

In the wake of events such as school shootings across North America, public support for gun control has been rising. In 1995, the Canadian government passed Bill C-68, which radically changed firearms legislation. The keystone of the law is universal firearms registration. The Canadian Association of Police Chiefs has been a strong supporter of the legislation, arguing that it will improve police safety across the country. Yet members of the National Firearms Association and its supporters have steadily worked

pluralist model an analysis of politics that sees power as spread among many competing interest groups

power-elite model an analysis of politics that sees power as concentrated among the rich

in opposition to the legislation. In 2011, the majority Harper government introduced Bill 19 to dismantle gun registration. Despite strong opposition across the country, especially in Quebec, this legislation is expected to pass, because the opposition parties do not have enough members to defeat it in a vote.

Groups for and against the "gun lobby" are examples of *special-interest groups*, people with an interest in some economic or social issue. Special-interest groups—which include associations of senior citizens, farmers, fireworks producers, and environmentalists—flourish in nations such as Canada, where loyalty to political parties tends to be low. Many special-interest groups employ lobbyists to work on their behalf.

Voter Apathy

It is a disturbing fact of political life that many Canadians are indifferent about voting. In fact, Canadian citizens are less likely to vote today than they were a century ago. In the 2000 federal election, only 63 percent of eligible voters showed up at the polls. In 2004, the percentage dropped even further, to 60.9 percent. More Canadian voters—65 percent— went to the ballot box in 2006. In the 2011 election, the voter turnout dropped again, to 61.4 percent. This turnout is generally lower than that in almost all other industrialized nations except for the United States.

Who is and is not likely to vote? Canadian women are less likely to cast a ballot than men. Seniors are more likely to vote than young people. White people are more likely to vote than are visible minorities, and Aboriginals are the least likely of all to vote. Generally speaking, people with a bigger stake in society—homeowners, parents with children at home, people with good jobs and extensive schooling— are most likely to vote. Income matters, too: people with incomes in the top 20 percent are much more likely to vote than are people with incomes in the bottom 20 percent (Bennett, 1991; DeLuca, 1998; Fetto, 1999; Hackey, 1992; Lewis, McCracken, & Hunt, 1994). See National Map 12–2 for voting patterns in different regions of Canada.

Some non-voting is, of course, to be expected. At any given time, many people are sick or disabled; many more are away from home, having made no arrangement to submit an absentee ballot. Others forget to reregister after moving to a new neighbourhood. Moreover, registering and voting depend on the ability to read and write, which discourages Canadian adults who have limited literacy skills. Electoral reforms made it possible for homeless people to vote in the 2000 federal election, a privilege that was previously denied them because they had no fixed address.

Conservatives suggest that apathy amounts to *indifference* to politics because most people are, by and large, content with their lives. Liberals, and especially political radicals, counter that apathy reflects *alienation* from politics: People are so deeply dissatisfied with society that they doubt elections will make any real difference. Yet, as noted above, there is a link between income and voting: Higher income is associated with greater likelihood of voting (Pammet & LeDuc, 2003). The fact that it is the disadvantaged and powerless people who are least likely to vote suggests that the liberal explanation for apathy probably is closer to the truth.

Should Convicted Criminals Vote?

Although the right to vote is at the very foundation of our country's claim to being democratic, in the United States, all states except Vermont and Maine have laws that bar people in jail from voting. Overall, 5.3 million people (including 1.4 million African-American men) in the United States do not have the right to vote (Sentencing Project, 2008a). Many other countries, including the United Kingdom, restrict people in prisons from voting in elections. Canada is an exception in this regard. In 2002, the Supreme Court of Canada ruled that prisoners should not be denied the right to vote. The federal election in 2004 was the first in which those in federal prison were permitted to cast a vote.

Should government take away people's political rights as a punishment for criminal acts? Critics point out that this practice may be politically motivated, because preventing convicted criminals from voting makes a difference in the way elections turn out because prisoners are more likely to be from the lower classes, which tend to support more left-leaning parties (Uggen & Manza, 2002).

Theoretical Analysis of Power in Society

Sociologists have long debated how power is spread throughout the Canadian population. Power is a very difficult topic to study because decision making is complex and often takes place behind closed doors. Despite this difficulty, researchers have developed three competing models of power in Canada and other high-income countries.

The Pluralist Model: The People Rule

The **pluralist model,** closely linked to structural-functional theory, is *an analysis of politics that sees power as spread among many competing interest groups.* Pluralists claim, first, that politics is an arena of negotiation. No single organization can expect to achieve all of its goals. Organizations therefore operate as *veto groups*, realizing some goals but mostly keeping opponents from achieving all of theirs. The political process relies heavily on creating alliances and compromises among numerous interest groups so that policies gain wide support. In short, pluralists see power as spread widely throughout society, with all people having at least some voice in the political system (Dahl, 1961, 1982; Rothman & Black, 1998).

The Power-Elite Model: A Few People Rule

The **power-elite model,** based on social-conflict theory, is *an analysis of politics that sees power as concentrated among the rich.* The term *power elite* was coined by C. Wright Mills (1956), a social-conflict

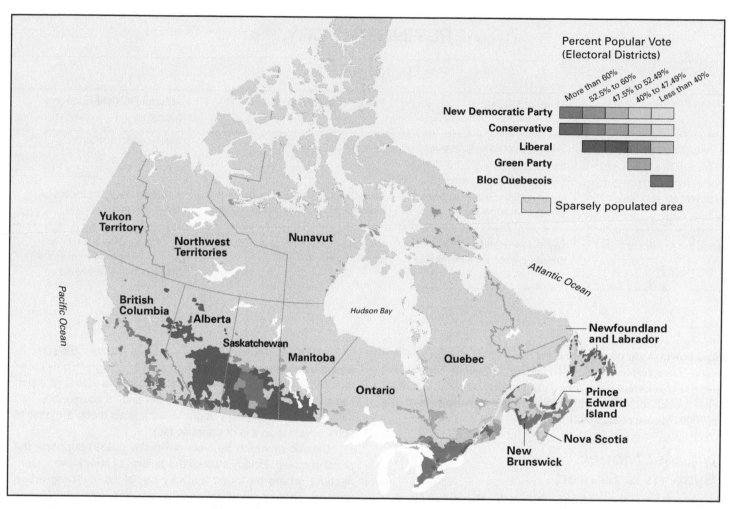

Seeing Ourselves

NATIONAL MAP 12–2   Votes in the 2011 Federal Election, Canada

The strong vote for the Conservative Party in the 2011 federal election is clear on this map, where more than 50 percent of votes cast in the Prairie provinces supported the right-of-centre conservative candidates. Of course, the percentages in British Columbia and Ontario are not much lower. The strength of the left-of-centre New Democratic Party in Quebec is also apparent on this map. Why do you think there was such strong support for the NDP in Quebec in the 2011 election?

Source: Adapted from Elections Canada (2011).

theorist who argued that the upper class holds most of society's wealth, prestige, and power.

Mills claimed that members of the power elite are in charge of the three major sectors of societies: the economy, the government, and the military. Elites in this privileged category move easily from one sector to another, Mills continued, consolidating power as they go. Wallace Clement (1975) argues this point about

the Canadian elite, concluding that the corporate elite control both the economy and the mass media, and also have a major influence over politics. Cases in point are Canadian corporate giants that include Bell Canada, Rogers, Shaw Communications, and Vidéotron.

Power-elite theorists say that countries such as Canada and the United States are not democracies because the concentration of

Marxist political-economy model an analysis that explains politics in terms of the operation of a society's economic system

political revolution (p. 327) the overthrow of one political system to establish another

APPLYING THEORY

Politics

	Pluralist Model	Power-Elite Model	Marxist Political-Economy Model
Which theoretical approach is applied?	Structural-functional approach	Social-conflict approach	Social-conflict approach
How is power spread throughout society?	Power is spread widely so that all groups have some voice.	Power is concentrated in the hands of business, political, and military leaders.	Power is directed by the operation of the capitalist economy.
Is Canada a democracy?	Yes. Power is spread widely enough to make the country a democracy.	No. Power is too concentrated for the country to be a democracy.	No. The capitalist economy sets political decision making, so the country is not a democracy.

wealth and power is simply too great for the average person's voice to be heard. They reject the pluralist idea that various centres of power serve as checks and balances on one another; according to the power-elite model, those at the top face no real opposition (Bartlett & Steele, 2000; Moore et al., 2002).

The Marxist Model: The System Is Biased

A third approach to understanding politics is the **Marxist political-economy model,** *an analysis that explains politics in terms of the operation of a society's economic system.* Like the power-elite model, the Marxist approach rejects the idea that Canada is a political democracy. But the power-elite model focuses on the enormous wealth and power of certain individuals; the Marxist model goes further and sees bias rooted in the nation's institutions, especially its economy. Karl Marx believed that a society's economic system (capitalist or socialist) shapes its political system. Therefore, power elites do not simply appear out of nowhere; they are creations of the capitalist economy.

From this point of view, reforming the political system—by, say, limiting the amount of money that rich people can contribute to political candidates—is unlikely to bring about true democracy. The problem does not lie in the people who exercise great power or the people who don't vote; the problem is the system itself— what Marxists call the "political economy of capitalism." In other words, as long as Canada has a predominantly capitalist economy, the majority of people will be shut out of politics, just as they are exploited in the workplace.

CRITICAL REVIEW The Applying Theory table summarizes the three models of the political system of high-income countries. Which model is most accurate? Over the years, research has shown support for each one. In the end, of course, how you think our political system ought to work is as much a matter of political values as it is of scientific fact.

Classic research by Nelson Polsby (1959) supports the pluralist model. Polsby studied the politics of New Haven, Connecticut, where he found that key decisions involving urban renewal, choosing political candidates, and running the city's schools were made by different groups. Polsby concluded that in New Haven, no one group—not even the upper class—ruled all of the others.

Robert Lynd and Helen Lynd (1937) studied Muncie, Indiana (which they called "Middletown," to suggest that it was a typical city), and documented the fortune amassed by a single family, the Balls, from its business producing glass jars. Their findings support the power-elite position. The Lynds showed how the Ball family dominated the city's life, pointing to that family's name on a local bank, university, hospital, and department store. In Muncie, according to the Lynds, the power elite boiled down to more or less a single family. In Canada, such influence of wealth is observable in the province of New Brunswick, where the McCain and Irving families seem omnipotent.

From the Marxist perspective, the point is not which individuals make decisions. Rather, as Alexander Liazos (1982:13) explains, "The basic tenets of capitalist society shape everyone's life: the inequalities of social classes and the importance of profits over people." As long as the basic institutions of society are organized to meet the needs of the few rather than the many, Liazos concludes, a democratic society is impossible.

Clearly, the political system in Canada gives almost everyone the right to participate in politics through elections. But as the power-elite and Marxist models point out, at the very least, the Canadian political system is far less democratic than most people think. Most citizens have the right to vote, but the major political parties and their candidates typically support only the positions that are acceptable to the most powerful segments of society and in tune with the operation of our capitalist economy.

Whatever the reasons, many people in Canada appear to be losing confidence in their leaders. Canadians want more government transparency and greater accountability (Pammet & LeDuc, 2003).

○ **CHECK YOUR LEARNING** What is the main argument of the pluralist model of power? What about the power-elite model? The Marxist political-economy model?

Power beyond the Rules

Politics is always a matter of disagreement over a society's goals and the means to achieve them. A political system tries to settle controversy within a system of rules. But political activity sometimes breaks the rules or even tries to do away with the entire system.

Revolution

Political revolution is *the overthrow of one political system to establish another.* Revolution goes beyond *reform*, or change within a system, and even beyond a *coup d'état* (in French, literally, "blow to the state"), as when one leader topples another. Revolution involves change in the type of system itself.

No political system is immune to revolution, nor does revolution produce any one type of government. The U.S. Revolutionary War (1775–1776) replaced colonial rule by the British monarchy with a representative democracy. French revolutionaries in 1789 also overthrew a monarch, only to set the stage for the return of monarchy in the person of Napoleon. In 1917, the Russian Revolution replaced a monarchy with a socialist government built on the ideas of Karl Marx. In 1991, a second Russian revolution dismantled the socialist Soviet Union, and the nation was reborn as 15 independent republics, the largest of which—known as the Russian Federation—has moved closer to a market system with a somewhat greater political voice for its people.

Despite their striking variety, revolutions share a number of traits (Skocpol, 1979; Tilly, 1986; de Tocqueville, 1955, orig. 1856):

1. **Rising expectations.** Common sense suggests that revolution is more likely when people are severely deprived, but history shows that most revolutions occur when people's lives are improving. Rising expectations, rather than bitterness and despair, make revolution more likely.

Not all terrorism is the work of individuals or groups. Since 1950, China has sought to maintain control of Tibet by force. This Tibetan refugee displays instruments of torture used against him by officials of the Chinese government.

2. **Unresponsive government.** Revolution becomes more likely when a government is unwilling to reform itself, especially when demands for change being made by powerful segments of society are ignored.

3. **Radical leadership by intellectuals.** The English philosopher Thomas Hobbes (1588–1679) claimed that intellectuals provide the justification for revolution and universities are often at the centre of political change. Students played a key role in China's pro-democracy movement and in the uprisings in Eastern Europe.

4. **Establishing a new legitimacy.** Overthrowing a political system is not easy, but ensuring a revolution's long-term success is harder still. Some revolutionary movements are held together merely by hatred of the past regime and fall apart once new leaders are installed. Revolutionaries must also guard against counter-revolutionary drives led by overthrown leaders. This explains the speed and ruthlessness with which victorious revolutionaries typically dispose of former leaders.

Scientific research cannot declare that a revolution is good or bad. That judgment depends on the personal values of the citizenry, and the full consequences of such an upheaval become evident only after many years.

Terrorism

On September 11, 2001, terrorists hijacked four commercial airliners; one crashed in a wooded area, but the other three crashed into public buildings full of people. The attack killed more than 3000 innocent people (representing 68 nations, including Canada), injured many

terrorism acts of violence or the threat of violence used as a political strategy by an individual or a group

war organized, armed conflict among the people of two or more nations, directed by their governments

thousands more, completely destroyed the twin towers of the World Trade Center in New York City, and seriously damaged the Pentagon in Washington, DC. Not since the attack on Pearl Harbor at the outbreak of World War II had the United States suffered such a blow. This event was the most serious terrorist act ever recorded in that country.

Terrorism refers to *acts of violence or the threat of violence used as a political strategy by an individual or a group*. Like revolution, terrorism is a political act beyond the rules of established political systems. According to Paul Johnson (1981), terrorism has four distinguishing characteristics.

First, terrorists try to paint violence as a legitimate political tactic, despite the fact that such acts are condemned by virtually every nation. Terrorists also bypass (or are excluded from) established channels of political negotiation. Therefore, terrorism is a weak organization's strategy against a stronger enemy. The 1970 Front de liberation du Québec kidnapping and subsequent murder of then Quebec labour minister Pierre Laporte was strongly condemned in all of Canada. At the same time, it served as a wake-up call for Canadians outside Quebec to the bitterness many Québécois feel about their position in Canada. Likewise, attacks against the U.S. embassies in Tanzania and Kenya in 1998 and the *U.S.S. Cole* in 2000 may have been morally wrong because they harmed innocent people, but they did raise the profile of organizations with grievances against the United States.

Second, terrorism is used not just by groups but also by governments against their own people. *State terrorism* is the use of violence, generally without support of law, by government officials. State terrorism is lawful in some authoritarian and totalitarian states, which survive by creating widespread fear and intimidation. Saddam Hussein, for example, relied on secret police and state terror to protect his power in Iraq.

Third, democratic societies reject terrorism in principle, but they are especially vulnerable to terrorists because they give broad civil liberties to their people and have less extensive police networks. In contrast, totalitarian regimes make widespread use of state terrorism, but their vast police power gives individuals few opportunities for acts of terror against the government.

Fourth and finally, terrorism is always a matter of definition. Governments claim the right to maintain order, even by force, and may label opposition groups who use violence as "terrorists." Political differences may explain why one person's "terrorist" is another's "freedom fighter" (Jenkins, 2003).

Although hostage taking and outright killing provoke popular anger, taking action against terrorists is difficult. Most terrorist groups have no formal connection to any established state, so identifying the parties responsible may be all but impossible. In addition, a military response may risk confrontation with other governments. Yet as the terrorism expert Brian Jenkins warns, a failure to respond "encourages other terrorist groups, who begin to realize that this can be a pretty cheap way to wage war" (quoted in Whitaker, 1985:29).

War and Peace

Perhaps the most critical political issue is **war,** *organized, armed conflict among the people of two or more nations, directed by their governments*. War is as old as humanity, but understanding it is crucial today because we now have weapons that can destroy the entire planet.

At almost any moment during the twentieth century, nations somewhere in the world were engaged in violent conflict. In the "Great War" (World War I) alone, 56 500 Canadian soldiers lost their lives, and many more were injured. Other deadly conflicts since then took the lives of countless Canadians and people from all corners of the globe. To take another example, the United States has participated in 11 major wars. From the Revolutionary War to the War in Iraq, more than 1.3 million American men and women have been killed in armed conflicts. Domestic and international wars continue to be waged at this time around the world, eating up a substantial portion of national budgets that could otherwise be used for more constructive purposes.

The Causes of War

Wars occur so often that we may think there is something natural about armed conflict. But there is no evidence that human beings must wage war under any particular circumstances. On the contrary, governments around the world usually have to force their people to go to war.

Like other forms of social behaviour, warfare is a product of society that is more common in some places than in others. The Semai of Malaysia, among the most peace-loving of the world's peoples, rarely resort to violence. In contrast, the Yąnomamö (see the box on page 38) are quick to wage war.

If society holds the key to war or peace, under what circumstances do humans go to war? Quincy Wright (1987) cites five factors that promote war:

1. **Perceived threats.** Nations mobilize in response to a perceived threat to their people, territory, or culture. Leaders justified the U.S.-led military campaign against Iraq, for example, by stressing the threat that Saddam Hussein posed to neighbouring countries and also to the United States. However, Paul Martin, who was Canadian prime minister when the war started, decided not to support the U.S.-led campaign.

2. **Social problems.** When internal problems cause widespread frustration at home, a nation's leaders may try to divert public attention by attacking an external "enemy" as a form of scapegoating. Some analysts think the lack of development toward democratic

military-industrial complex (p. 330) the close association of the federal government, the military, and defence industries

rule in the People's Republic of China, for example, led to hostility toward Vietnam, Tibet, and the former Soviet Union.

3. **Political objectives.** Poor nations, such as Vietnam, have used wars to end foreign domination. Powerful countries such as the United States may benefit from periodic shows of force to increase global political standing.

4. **Moral objectives.** Nations rarely claim that they are going to war to gain wealth and power. Instead, their leaders infuse military campaigns with moral urgency. By calling the 2003 invasion of Iraq "Operation Iraqi Freedom," American leaders portrayed the mission as a morally justified war of liberation from an evil tyrant.

5. **The absence of alternatives.** A fifth factor promoting war is the lack of alternatives. Although the goal of the United Nations is to maintain international peace by finding alternatives to war, the organization has had limited success in preventing conflict between nations.

Social Class, Gender, and the Military

In World War II, three out of every four men in their late teens and twenties served in the military, either voluntarily or by being *drafted*—called to service. Only those who were ruled ineligible because of some physical or mental problem performed no military service. Today, by contrast, there is no draft, and fighting is done by a volunteer military. But not every member of our society is equally likely to volunteer.

One recent study concluded that the military has few young people who are rich and few who are very poor. Rather, working-class people, males in particular, look to the Canadian military for a job, to become eligible for money to use for higher education, or simply to get out of the small town where they grew up (Wait, 2002).

Throughout our nation's history, women have been a part of the Canadian military. In recent decades, however, women have taken on greater importance in the armed forces. For one thing, the share of women is on the rise, now standing at about 15 percent of the Canadian Forces. Just as important, although regulations continue to keep many military women out of harm's way, more women are now engaging in combat. The Seeing Sociology in the News box on pages 330–31 takes a closer look at the changes under way in Canada and, more recently, in the United States.

Is Terrorism a New Kind of War?

People speak of terrorism as a new kind of war. War has historically followed certain patterns: It is played out according to basic rules, the warring parties are known to each other, and the objectives of the warring parties—which generally involve control of territory—are clearly stated.

One reason to pursue peace is the rising toll of death and mutilation caused by millions of land mines placed in the ground during wartime and left there afterwards. Civilians—many of them children—maimed by land mines receive treatment in this clinic in Kabul, Afghanistan.

Terrorism breaks from these patterns. The identity of terrorist individuals and organizations may not be known, those involved may deny responsibility, and their goals may be unclear. The 2001 terrorist attacks against the United States were not attempts to defeat the nation militarily or to secure territory. They were carried out by people representing not a country but a cause, one not well understood in the United States. In short, they were expressions of anger and hate intended to create widespread fear.

Conventional warfare is symmetrical, with two nations sending armies into battle. By contrast, terrorism is a new kind of war: an asymmetrical conflict in which a small number of attackers use terror and their own willingness to die as a means to level the playing field against a much more powerful enemy. Although the terrorists may be ruthless, the nation under attack must use caution in its response to terrorism because little may be known about the identity and location of the parties responsible.

The Costs and Causes of Militarism

The cost of armed conflict extends far beyond battlefield casualties. Together, the world's nations spend more than $1.4 trillion annually for military-related purposes. Spending this much diverts resources from the desperate struggle for survival by hundreds of millions of poor people.

Defence is the U.S. government's second biggest expenditure (after Social Security), accounting for about 20 percent of all federal spending, which amounted to more than $700 billion in 2010. The United States has emerged as the world's single military superpower, accounting for about 42 percent of the world's military spending. Put another way, the United States spends nearly as much on the military as the rest of the world's nations combined (Stockholm International Peace Research Institute, 2009; U.S. Office of Management and Budget, 2010).

Seeing SOCIOLOGY in the NEWS

The Star

U.S. May Allow Women into Combat—A Move Canada Made Decades Ago

BY MARCIA KAYE
January 30, 2011

Now that the U.S. Senate has voted to do away with the ban on openly gay troops, the focus is suddenly swerving to another group that has long been the target of discrimination in the American military: Women.

The U.S. defence department bans women from serving in on-the-ground combat units, such as the infantry, armour and special forces. This may surprise those who thought the 1997 Hollywood movie *G.I. Jane*—remember the bald, foul-mouthed machine-gun-toting Demi Moore who liked to "blow s— up"?—was based on a real story. (It wasn't.)

It may also surprise some Canadians—and likely many Americans—that Canada has allowed women into all military trades, including combat arms, for 22 years. The only exception was submarine service, a final bastion that fell in 2001. About a dozen other countries also allow women into active ground combat roles, including Sweden, Norway, Switzerland, France, Germany, Serbia, New Zealand and Israel.

But the United States doesn't. At least, that's the official policy. The reality is that it's happening anyway. In Iraq and Afghanistan, officers don't formally "assign" women to combat units; they "attach" them, which skirts the policy while exposing the women to the same dangers as the men.

American women can patrol perilous areas as military police, but not as infantry. Female officers can lead men into battle, but aren't supposed to serve alongside them. The sad irony is that in modern-day wars, where battles take place on street corners and in marketplaces, the combat ban doesn't shield women at all—except from job titles, personal satisfaction and future promotions that ensue directly from officially documented combat experience.

That's why the Military Leadership Diversity Commission, which Congress set up in 2009, will be sending a report to President Barack Obama this spring recommending the ban be lifted "to create a level playing field for all qualified service members."

"It's about time, isn't it?" says an exasperated Lt. Col. (retired) Shirley Robinson, who served 30 years in the Canadian military.

As cofounder of the Association for Women's Equity in the Canadian Forces, Robinson was instrumental in helping to change the similar policy in Canada in 1989.

Robinson says she knows exactly what the critics are going to argue in the U.S. because she heard it all in Canada back in the 1980s, when she acted as a consultant to human-rights lawyers. "We heard all the stereotypes and all the myths they could dream up," she says.

One of those staunch opponents is the Michigan-based Center for Military Readiness, the same independent advocacy organization (whose president is a woman, Elaine Donnelly) that fought to keep the ban on gays in the armed forces.

It's now using similar reasoning regarding women, arguing the push toward diversity will undermine combat effectiveness. As its website says, "The armed forces should not be used for political purposes or social experiments that needlessly elevate risks, detract from readiness, or degrade American cultural values."

But Mary Anne Baker, a retired U.S. colonel now living in Haymarket, Virginia, doesn't buy

---

For decades, military spending went up because of the *arms race* between the United States and the former Soviet Union, which dropped out of the race after its collapse in 1991. But some analysts (who support power-elite theory) link high military spending to the domination of U.S. society by a **military-industrial complex,** *the close association of the federal government, the military, and defence industries.* The roots of militarism, then, lie not just in external threats but also in institutional structures at home (Barnes, 2002b; Marullo, 1987).

A final reason for continuing militarism is regional conflict. In the 1990s, localized wars broke out in Bosnia, Chechnya, and Zambia and long-standing conflict continues between Israel and the Palestinians. Even limited wars have the potential to grow and involve other countries, including Canada's involvement in Afghanistan. India and Pakistan—both nuclear powers—moved to the brink of war in 2002 and then pulled back. In 2003, the announcement by North Korea that it, too, had nuclear weapons raised tensions in Asia. Iran continues to pursue nuclear technology, raising fears that this nation may soon have an atomic bomb.

Nuclear Weapons

Despite the easing of superpower tensions, the world still contains more than 8000 operational nuclear warheads, representing a destructive power of several tonnes of TNT for every person on the planet. If even a small fraction of this stockpile is used in war, life as we know it would end. Albert Einstein, whose genius contributed to the development of nuclear weapons, reflected, "The unleashed power of the atom has changed everything save our modes of thinking and we thus drift toward unparalleled catastrophe" ("Atomic Education," 1946). In short, nuclear weapons make full-scale war unthinkable in a world not yet capable of peace.

The United States, the Russian Federation, Great Britain, France, the People's Republic of China, Israel, India, Pakistan, and probably North Korea all have nuclear weapons. A few nations stopped the development of nuclear weapons; Argentina and Brazil halted work in 1990 and South Africa dismantled its arsenal in 1991. But by 2015 there could be 10 new nations in the

it. "Your morale, good order and discipline are managed by your leaders," she says. Baker was permitted to work as a field artillery officer during the Cold War because of the perceived safer distance involved in delivering nuclear weapons, compared to rockets or cannon fire. She believes all combat positions should be open to women.

Not that there is likely to be a flood of combat-seeking women, judging by the Canadian experience.

In Canada today, only about 250 women serve in the combat trades, out of a total 13,000 combat personnel. That puts female representation at less than 2 percent. Women make up 10 percent of personnel deployed on international operations, and 15 percent of the combined Regular Force and Primary Reserve . . .

Robinson says during the Canadian policy debates, the generals at the top understood a ban on women in combat contravened both the Canadian Human Rights Act and the Charter of Rights and Freedoms, which prohibit gender discrimination. The biggest opponents, Robinson says, were the lower ranks—the regular male soldiers. "They were digging their heels in like mad.

They weren't going to have any women in their battalions," she says.

Why not? One of the biggest arguments Robinson heard, and still hears today, is that we shouldn't be exposing military women to danger by allowing them to serve in combat-related positions. But that's an artificial distinction in a war situation where the traditional "front line" no longer exists.

"Today you're not safe if you're a cook, or working at the Tim Hortons (in Kandahar)," Robinson says. "If you're driving along in a vehicle that gets blown up, that's combat.". . .

Shirley Robinson, the retired lieutenant colonel, agrees that motherhood probably doesn't mix well with combat work (she has no children), adding it should be up to individual women to make those decisions. But she insists anyone in the Armed Forces—combat or noncombat—who expects to have a "normal life" while still in the military is dreaming.

"If you're in the Armed Forces your first priority is to your country, not your family," she says. "And that's true for men, as well as women."

WHAT DO YOU THINK?

1. Do you consider allowing women to take part in combat operations to be a step forward for women? Why or why not?

2. Would you support a policy that allowed women to take all military assignments, including combat branches? Why or why not?

3. Apart from danger and parenthood, what other arguments might be made to keep women out of combat work?

Source: Adapted from "U.S. May Allow Women into Combat—A Move Canada Made Decades Ago," by Marcia Kaye, The Star, January 30, 2011. Permission of Marcia Kaye.

"nuclear club," and as many as 50 countries by 2025 (Grier, 2006). Such a trend makes any regional conflict very dangerous to the entire planet.

Mass Media and War

The 2003 U.S.-led invasion of Iraq was the first war in which television crews travelled with troops, reporting as the campaign unfolded. The mass media provided ongoing and detailed reports of events; cable television made available live coverage of the war 24 hours a day, 7 days a week.

Media outlets "frame" the news according to their own politics. Those media outlets that were critical of the war—especially the Arab news channel Al-Jazeera—tended to report the slow pace of the conflict, the casualties to the allied forces, and the deaths and injuries suffered by Iraqi civilians, all of which was information that would increase pressure to end the war. Media outlets that were supportive of the war—including most news organizations in the United States—tended to report the rapid pace of the war and the casualties to Iraqi

forces and to downplay any harm to Iraqi civilians as minimal and unintended. In short, the power of the mass media to provide selective information to a worldwide audience means that television and other media may be almost as important to the outcome of a conflict as the military forces that are doing the actual fighting.

Pursuing Peace

How can the world reduce the dangers of war? Here are the most recent approaches to peace:

1. **Deterrence.** The logic of the arms race holds that security comes from a "balance of terror" between the superpowers. The principle of *mutual assured destruction* (MAD) means that a nation launching a first strike against another will face greater retaliation. This deterrence policy kept the peace for almost 50 years during the Cold War. Yet it encouraged an enormous arms race and cannot control nuclear proliferation, which represents a growing threat to peace. Deterrence also does little to stop terrorism or to prevent wars that

Islam and Freedom: A "Democracy Gap"?

As the United States, Britain, and the other participating allies launched the war in Iraq, their respective heads of state spoke hopefully of liberating the Iraqi people and holding up a democratic Iraq as an example to the rest of the Islamic world.

But does the Middle East really need democracy? Is democracy a goal that is sought—and equated with freedom—everywhere? The answer is not entirely clear because nations have unique political histories and "freedom" means different things in different cultural settings.

Political freedom is a basic element of all democracies. Freedom House, an organization that monitors political freedom around the world, tracks people's right to vote, to express ideas freely, and to move about without undue interference from government. It reports that the region of the world with the least political freedom stretches from Africa through the Middle East to Asia (look back at Global Map 12–2 on page 319).

Many of the nations that Freedom House characterizes as "not free" have populations that are largely Islamic. According to the Pew Forum on Religion and Public Life in 2008, 50 of the world's 194 nations had an Islamic majority population. Just 9 of these countries had democratic governments (18 percent). Of the 144 nations without a majority Islamic population, 109 (76 percent) had democratic governments. In other words, countries without Islamic majorities are four times more likely to have democratic governments than countries with Islamic majorities. Freedom House concludes that countries with Islamic majority populations display a "democracy gap."

This relative lack of political democracy was found in all world regions that have Islamic-majority nations—in Africa, central Europe, the Middle East, and Asia. The pattern is especially strong among the 16 Islamic-majority states in the Middle East and North Africa that are ethnically Arabic: Not one is an electoral democracy.

What explains this "democracy gap"? Freedom House points to four factors. First, Islamic-majority countries are typically less developed economically, with widespread poverty and limited schooling for their people. Second, these countries have cultural traditions that provide women with few economic, educational, or political opportunities. Third, while most countries limit the power of religious elites in government, and some even require a "separation of church and state," Islamic-majority nations support giving Islamic leaders political power. In two recent cases—Iran and Afghanistan under the Taliban—Islamic leaders have had formal control of government; in many more countries, religious leaders exert considerable influence on political outcomes.

Fourth and finally, the enormous wealth that comes from Middle Eastern oil plays a part in preventing democratic government. In Iraq, Saudi Arabia, Kuwait, Qatar, the United Arab Emirates, and other nations, this resource has provided astounding riches to a small number of families, money they can use to shore up their political control. In addition, oil wealth permits elites to build airports and other modern facilities without encouraging broader economic development that would raise the living standards of the majority. For all of these reasons, Freedom House concludes that the road to democracy for Islamic-majority nations is likely to be long. But today's patterns may not predict those of tomorrow. In 1950, very few Catholic-majority countries (mostly in Europe and Latin America) had democratic governments. Today, however, most of these nations are democratic. Note too that 40 percent of the world's Muslims—who live in Nigeria, Turkey, Bangladesh, India, Indonesia, Canada, and the United States—already live under democratic governments. But perhaps the best indicator that change is already under way is that by the end of 2009, Freedom House had added two more countries with Islamic majorities (Indonesia and Mali) to the list of "free" nations of the world.

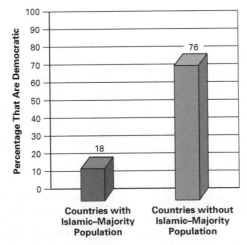

Democracy and Islam

Today, democratic government is much less common in countries with Islamic-majority populations. Fifty years ago, the same was true of countries with Catholic-majority populations.

WHAT DO YOU THINK?

1. Is the United States right or wrong in trying to bring about a democratic political system in Iraq? Explain your answer.

2. Do you expect to see greater democracy in Islamic-majority countries 50 years from now? Why or why not?

3. Can you point to several reasons that Muslims might object to the kind of political system we call "democracy"? Explain.

Sources: Karatnycky (2002), Pew Forum on Religion and Public Life (2008b), and Freedom House (2010).

are started by a stronger nation (such as the United States) against a weaker foe (such as the Taliban government in Afghanistan or Saddam Hussein's Iraq).

2. **High-technology defence.** If technology created the weapons, perhaps it can also protect us from them; such is the claim of the *strategic defence initiative* (SDI). Under SDI, satellites and ground installations would destroy enemy missiles soon after they were launched. In a survey shortly after the 2001 terrorist attacks, two-thirds of American adults supported SDI ("Female Opinion," 2002; Thompson & Waller, 2001). However, critics, many of them Canadians, claim that the system, which they refer to as "Star Wars," would be, at best, a leaky umbrella. Others worry that building such a system will spark another massive arms race. In 2009, the Obama administration stated that as part of its Ballistic Missile Defense System, the United States was expanding land- and sea-based missile defence systems in the Persian Gulf but not in Eastern Europe.

3. **Diplomacy and disarmament.** Some analysts believe that the best road to peace is diplomacy rather than technology (Dedrick & Yinger, 1990). Teams of diplomats working together can increase security by reducing, rather than building, weapons stockpiles.

   But disarmament has limitations. No nation wants to be weakened by eliminating its defences. Successful diplomacy depends on everyone involved sharing responsibility for a common problem (Fisher & Ury, 1988). Although the United States and the Russian Federation continue to negotiate arms reduction agreements, the world now faces threats from other nations such as North Korea and Iran.

4. **Resolving underlying conflict.** In the end, reducing the dangers of war may depend on resolving underlying conflicts by promoting a more just world. Poverty, hunger, and illiteracy are all root causes of war. Perhaps the world needs to reconsider the wisdom of spending thousands of times as much money on militarism as we do on efforts to find peaceful solutions (Kaplan & Schaffer, 2001; Sivard, 1988).

Politics: Looking Ahead

Just as economies are changing, so are political systems. Several problems and trends are likely to be important in the decades to come.

One troublesome problem in Canada is inconsistency between our democratic ideals and our low turnout at the polls. Perhaps, as conservative pluralist theorists say, many people do not bother to vote because they are content with their lives. On the other hand, the liberal power-elite theorists may be right when they say that people withdraw from a system that concentrates so much wealth and power in the hands of a few people. Or perhaps, as radical Marxist critics claim, people find that our political system offers little real choice, limiting options and policies to those that support our capitalist economy. In any case, the current high level of apathy and distrust in our nation's government reflect a widespread desire for political change.

A second issue is the global rethinking of political models. The Cold War between the United States and the Soviet Union encouraged people to think of politics in terms of two opposing models, capitalism and socialism. Today, however, people are more likely to consider a broader range of political systems that link government to the economy in various ways. Welfare capitalism, as found in Sweden and Denmark, or state capitalism, as found in South Korea and Japan, are just two possibilities. The Thinking Globally box takes a look at the debate over the chances for the emergence of democratic governments in the world's Islamic countries.

Third, we still face the danger of war in many parts of the world. Even as the United States and the Russian Federation dismantle some warheads, vast stockpiles of nuclear weapons remain, and nuclear technology continues to spread around the world. In addition, new superpowers are likely to arise (the People's Republic of China and India are likely candidates), just as regional conflicts and terrorism are likely to continue. We can only hope (and vote!) for leaders who will work toward finding non-violent solutions to the age-old problems that provoke war, thereby putting us on the road to world peace.

CHAPTER 12 ECONOMICS AND POLITICS

HOW IMPORTANT ARE YOU TO THE POLITICAL PROCESS? Historically, as this chapter explains, young people have been less likely than older people to take part in politics. But, as a study of the 2008 U.S. presidential election suggests, that trend may be changing in the United States.

Tom Morello, guitarist for Rage Against the Machine and other bands, has made political activism a central part of his career as a musician, speaking for various left-of-centre causes. Can you identify other celebrities who have tried to shape public opinion?

Brigette DePape, a 21-year-old graduate from the University of Ottawa and a Senate page, was fired shortly after the 2011 election for holding a "Stop Harper" sign during the government's throne speech. Knowing that the Conservative government would remain in power for the next four years, DePape stated to CTV News (2011), "This is the only way we're going to see real change" and encouraged other young people to take part in similar acts of "civil disobedience."

HINT: In the 2008 U.S. presidential campaign, thousands of young people served as volunteers for both major political candidates, telephoning voters or walking door to door in an effort to increase public interest, raise money, and get people to the polls on election day. Many celebrities—including musicians and members of the Hollywood entertainment scene—spoke out in favour of a candidate, most of them favouring the Democratic Party. Barack Obama was different— the first African-American who had a genuine chance at winning the presidency. Largely because so many young people—as well as previously disenfranchised minority groups—came out to support him, he was victorious.

The opposite was the case in the 2011 Canadian federal election. Many young people complained that they had to choose among three white men and that the likely leader, Stephen Harper, was not promising to bring about positive change for Canadian youth. As a result, most young people did not show up at the polls. This does not mean they failed to protest, however.

Applying Sociology in Everyday Life

1. Freedom House, an organization that studies civil rights and political liberty around the world, publishes an annual report titled "Freedom in the World." Find a copy in the library, or examine global trends and the political profile of any country on the web at www.freedomhouse.org.

2. Visit a discount store such as Walmart or Kmart and do a little "fieldwork" in an area of the store that interests you. Pick 10 products and see where they are made. Do the results support the existence of a global economy?

MAKING THE GRADE

Economics and Politics

The Economy: Historical Overview

The **ECONOMY** is the major social institution through which a society produces, distributes, and consumes goods and services.

- In technologically simple societies, economic activity is simply part of family life.
- The Agricultural Revolution (5000 years ago) made the economy a distinct social institution based on agricultural technology, specialized work, permanent settlements, and trade.
- The Industrial Revolution (beginning around 1750) expanded the economy based on new sources of energy and specialized work in factories that turned raw materials into finished products.
- The post-industrial economy is based on a shift to service work and computer technology.

pp. 302–03

✓ Today's expanding global economy produces and consumes products and services with little regard for national borders. The world's 1500 largest corporations account for half of the world's economic output (p. 304).

PRIMARY SECTOR
- draws raw materials from the natural environment
- is of greatest importance (25 percent of the economy) in low-income nations

p. 304

SECONDARY SECTOR
- transforms raw materials into manufactured goods
- is a significant share (26 to 37 percent) of the economy in low-, middle-, and high-income nations

p. 304

TERTIARY SECTOR
- produces services rather than goods
- is the largest sector (46 to 72 percent) in low-, middle-, and high-income countries

p. 304

Economic Systems: Paths to Justice

CAPITALISM
is based on private ownership of property and the pursuit of profit in a competitive marketplace. Capitalism results in
- greater productivity
- a higher overall standard of living
- greater income inequality
- freedom to act according to self-interest

SOCIALISM
is grounded in collective ownership of productive property through government control of the economy. Socialism results in
- less productivity
- a lower overall standard of living
- less income inequality
- freedom from basic want

pp. 305–09

Work in the Post-industrial Canadian Economy

JOBS
- Agricultural work represents about 1.5 percent of jobs.
- Blue-collar, industrial work has declined to just over 20 percent of jobs.
- White-collar, service work has increased to 78 percent of jobs.

pp. 309–11

SELF-EMPLOYMENT
- 17 percent of Canadian workers are self-employed.
- Many professionals fall into this category, but most self-employed people have blue-collar jobs.

pp. 311–12

UNEMPLOYMENT
- Unemployment has many causes, including the operation of the economy itself.
- In 2010, 8.3 percent of the country's labour force was unemployed.
- At highest risk for unemployment are young people, visible minorities, and Aboriginal people.

pp. 312–13

Corporations

CORPORATIONS form the core of the Canadian economy.
- The largest corporations, which are conglomerates, account for most corporate assets and profits.
- Many large corporations operate as multinationals, producing and distributing products in nations around the world.

pp. 314–16

social institution (p. 302) a major sphere of social life or societal subsystem organized to meet human needs

economy (p. 302) the social institution that organizes a society's production, distribution, and consumption of goods and services

post-industrial economy (p. 303) a productive system based on service work and high technology

primary sector (p. 304) the part of the economy that draws raw materials from the natural environment

secondary sector (p. 304) the part of the economy that transforms raw materials into manufactured goods

tertiary sector (p. 304) the part of the economy that involves services rather than goods

global economy (p. 304) economic activity that crosses national borders

capitalism (p. 306) an economic system in which natural resources and the means of producing goods and services are privately owned

socialism (p. 306) an economic system in which natural resources and the means of producing goods and services are collectively owned

welfare capitalism (p. 307) an economic and political system that combines a mostly market-based economy with extensive social welfare programs

state capitalism (p. 307) an economic and political system in which companies are privately owned but co-operate closely with the government

profession (p. 311) a prestigious white-collar occupation that requires extensive formal education

corporation (p. 314) an organization with a legal existence, including rights and liabilities, separate from that of its members

monopoly (p. 315) the domination of a market by a single producer

oligopoly (p. 315) the domination of a market by a few producers

politics (p. 317) the social institution that distributes power, sets a society's goals, and makes decisions

power (p. 317) the ability to achieve desired ends despite resistance from others

government (p. 317) a formal organization that directs the political life of a society

authority (p. 317) power that people perceive as legitimate rather than coercive

routinization of charisma (p. 318) the transformation of charismatic authority into some combination of traditional and bureaucratic authority

Politics: Historical Overview

POLITICS is the major social institution by which a society distributes power and organizes decision making. Max Weber claimed that raw power is transformed into legitimate authority in three ways:

- Pre-industrial societies rely on tradition to transform power into authority. Traditional authority is closely linked to kinship.
- As societies industrialize, tradition gives way to rationality. *Rational-legal authority* underlies the operation of bureaucratic offices as well as the law.
- At any time, however, some individuals transform power into authority through charisma. *Charismatic authority* is linked to extraordinary personal qualities (as found in Jesus of Nazareth, Adolf Hitler, and Mahatma Gandhi).

p. 317

monarchy (p. 318) a political system in which a single family rules from generation to generation

democracy (p. 318) a political system that gives power to the people as a whole

authoritarianism (p. 318) a political system that denies the people participation in government

totalitarianism (p. 320) a highly centralized political system that extensively regulates people's lives

Politics in Global Perspective

MONARCHY is common in agrarian societies; leadership is based on kinship.

p. 318

DEMOCRACY is common in modern societies; leadership is linked to elective office.

pp. 318–19

AUTHORITARIANISM is any political system that denies the people participation in government.

pp. 319–20

TOTALITARIANISM concentrates all political power in one centralized leadership.

p. 320

✓ *The world is divided into 194 politically independent nation-states. A political trend, however, is the growing wealth and power of multinational corporations. In an age of computers and other new information technology, governments can no longer control the flow of information across their borders (p. 320).*

welfare state (p. 320) a system of government agencies and programs that provides benefits to the population

pluralist model (p. 324) an analysis of politics that sees power as spread among many competing interest groups

power-elite model (p. 324) an analysis of politics that sees power as concentrated among the rich

Marxist political-economy model (p. 326) an analysis that explains politics in terms of the operation of a society's economic system

Politics in Canada

The Canadian government has expanded over the past two centuries. The *welfare state* in Canada is larger than in the United States but smaller than in most European countries.

pp. 320–21

The *political spectrum*, from the liberal left to the conservative right, involves attitudes on both economic issues and social issues.

pp. 321–22

Special-interest groups advance the political aims of specific segments of the population.

pp. 323–24

Voter apathy runs high in Canada: Only 61.4 percent of eligible voters went to the polls in the 2011 federal election.

p. 324

Theoretical Analysis of Power in Society

The **PLURALIST** model claims that political power is spread widely in Canada.

p. 324

The **POWER-ELITE** model claims that power is concentrated in a small, wealthy segment of the population.

pp. 324–26

The **MARXIST POLITICAL-ECONOMY** model claims that our political agenda is determined by a capitalist economy, so true democracy is impossible.

pp. 326–27

See the Applying Theory table on page 326.

political revolution (p. 327) the overthrow of one political system to establish another

terrorism (p. 328) acts of violence or the threat of violence used as a political strategy by an individual or a group

war (p. 328) organized, armed conflict among the people of two or more nations, directed by their governments

military-industrial complex (p. 330) the close association of the federal government, the military, and defence industries

Power beyond the Rules

- **REVOLUTION** radically transforms a political system.
- **TERRORISM** employs violence in the pursuit of political goals and is used by a group against a much more powerful enemy.

pp. 327–28

War and Peace

- The development and spread of nuclear weapons have increased the threat of global catastrophe.
- World peace ultimately depends on resolving the tensions and conflicts that fuel militarism.

pp. 328–33

MySocLab

Visit MySocLab at www.mysoclab.com to access a variety of online resources that will help you to prepare for tests and to apply your knowledge, including

- an eText
- videos
- self-grading quizzes
- glossary flashcards

13 Family and Religion

- What is a family?

- How is religion linked to social inequality?

- Why are both family and religion changing in today's world?

This chapter explores the importance of the family for society and also analyzes the meaning and importance of religion, another major social institution, which is based on the concept of the sacred.

Rosa Yniguez is one of seven children who grew up in Jalisco, Mexico, in a world in which families worked hard, went to church regularly, and were proud of having many children. Rosa remembers friends of her parents who had a clock in their living room with a picture of each of their 12 children where the numbers on the clock face would be.

Now 35 years old, Rosa is living in San Francisco, attends a local Catholic church, and works as a cashier in a department store. In some respects, she has carried on her parents' traditions—but not in every way. Recalling her childhood, she says, "In Mexico, many of the families I knew had six, eight, ten children. Sometimes more. But I came to this country to get ahead. That is simply impossible with too many kids." As a result of her desire to keep her job and make a better life for her family, Rosa has decided to have no more than the three children she has now.

A tradition of having large families has helped make Hispanics the largest racial or ethnic minority in the United States and a substantial minority in Canada. But today, more and more Latinas are making the same decision as Rosa Yniguez and opting to have fewer children. Studies show that the birth rate for all immigrant women has been dropping for at least the past 10 years (Navarro, 2004; Statistics Canada, 2008k; U.S. Census Bureau, 2008a).

Families have been with us for a very long time. But as this story indicates, Canadian families are changing in response to a number of factors, including the desire of women to have more career options and to provide better lives for their children. In fact, the family is changing faster than any other social institution (Bianchi & Spain, 1996; Charles et al., 2008; Fox, 2001).

Religion is changing, too, as membership in long-established denominations is declining and new religious organizations are flourishing. This chapter examines family and religion, which are closely linked as society's *symbolic institutions.* Both the family and religion help set standards of morality, maintain traditions, and join people together. Focusing on Canada and making comparisons to other countries, we will examine why many people consider family and religion the foundations of society while others predict—and may even encourage—the decline of both institutions.

Family: Basic Concepts

The **family** is *a social institution found in all societies that unites people in co-operative groups to care for one another, including any children.* Family ties also reflect **kinship**, *a social bond based on common ancestry, marriage, or adoption.* All societies contain families, but exactly who people call their kin has varied through history and varies today from one culture to another. Here and in other countries, families form around **marriage**, *a legal relationship, usually involving economic co-operation, sexual activity, and child-bearing.*

Today, some people object to defining only married couples or parents and children as families because it endorses a narrow standard of how to live. Because some business and government programs still use this conventional definition, many unmarried but committed partners of the same or opposite sex are excluded from family health care and other benefits. However, organizations are gradually coming to recognize as families people with or without legal or blood ties who feel they belong together and define themselves as a family.

Like many European countries today, Canada has now joined the international trend toward acceptance of a wider definition of "family" (Beaujot, 2000; Fox & Luxton, 2001; Jenson, 2004), though this has not yet occurred south of the border. Statistics Canada no longer employs the traditional notion of family when collecting data on the Canadian "census family," which is currently defined to include "a married couple (with or without children of either or both spouses); a couple living common-law (with or without children of either or both partners); a lone parent of any marital status, with at least one child living in the same dwelling" (Statistics Canada, 2011af). Until the 2001 census, when a question on "sexual orientation" was added, sociologists in Canada did not have access to accurate national data on gay families; the 2001 census was the first to provide data on same-sex partnerships. In 2001, a total of 34 200 couples—0.5 percent of all couples in Canada—identified themselves as same-sex common-law couples (Statistics Canada, 2002a). The figure for 2006 was 45 300 same-sex couples (Statistics Canada, 2009a).

family (p. 338) a social institution found in all societies that unites people in co-operative groups to care for one another, including any children

kinship (p. 338) a social bond based on common ancestry, marriage, or adoption

extended family a family composed of parents and children as well as other kin; also known as a *consanguine family*

nuclear family a family composed of one or two parents and their children; also known as a *conjugal family*

marriage (p. 338) a legal relationship, usually involving economic co-operation, sexual activity, and child-bearing

endogamy marriage between people of the same social category

exogamy marriage between people of different social categories

monogamy marriage that unites two partners

polygamy marriage that unites a person with two or more spouses

Family: Global Variations

In pre-industrial societies, people take a broad view of family ties, recognizing the **extended family**, *a family composed of parents and children as well as other kin*. This group is also called the *consanguine family* because it includes everyone with "shared blood." With industrialization, however, increasing social mobility and geographic migration give rise to the **nuclear family**, *a family composed of one or two parents and their children*. The nuclear family is also called the *conjugal family*, meaning "based on marriage." Although many people in our society live in extended families, far more live in nuclear families.

Marriage Patterns

Cultural norms—and often laws—identify people as suitable or unsuitable marriage partners. Some norms promote **endogamy**, *marriage between people of the same social category*. Endogamy limits marriage prospects to others of the same age, village, race, ethnicity, religion, or social class. By contrast, **exogamy** is *marriage between people of different social categories*. In rural India, for example, a person is expected to marry someone from the same caste (endogamy) but from a different village (exogamy). The reason for endogamy is that people of similar position pass along their standing to their children, maintaining the traditional social hierarchy. Exogamy, on the other hand, links distant communities and encourages the spread of culture.

In higher-income nations, laws permit only **monogamy** (from the Greek, meaning "one union"), *marriage that unites two partners*. Global Map 13–1 on page 340 shows that monogamy is the rule throughout the Americas and Europe. But many lower-income countries, especially in Africa and southern Asia, permit **polygamy** (Greek, "many unions"), *marriage that unites a person with two or more spouses*. Polygamy has two forms. By far the more common is *polygyny* (Greek, "many women"), a form of marriage that unites one man and two or more women. For example, Islamic nations in the Middle East and Africa permit men up to four wives. Even so, most Islamic families are monogamous because few men can afford to support several wives and even more children. *Polyandry* (Greek, "many men") unites one woman and two or more men. This extremely rare pattern exists in Tibet, a mountainous land where agriculture is difficult. There, polyandry discourages the division of land into parcels too small to support a family and divides the work of farming among many men.

Most of the world's societies at some time have permitted more than one marital pattern. Even so, most marriages have been monogamous (Murdock, 1965, orig. 1949). The historical preference for monogamy reflects two facts of life: Supporting several spouses is very expensive, and the number of men and women in most societies is roughly equal. Monogamy is also the dominant marriage pattern

What does the modern family look like? If we look to the mass media, this is a difficult question to answer. In the television series *Modern Family*, Jay Pritchett's family includes his much younger new wife, his stepson Manny, his daughter Claire (who is married with three children), and his son Mitchell (who, with his gay partner, has an adopted Vietnamese daughter). How would you define "the family"?

in Canada. However, there is a polygamist colony commune called "Bountiful," a community of approximately 1000 people just outside Creston in southeast British Columbia. This fundamentalist group broke away from the U.S.-based Mormon church or, officially, the Church of Jesus Christ of Latter-day Saints, in 1886 when the Mormon church disavowed polygamy. Polygamy is illegal in British Columbia, but until recently the government has adopted a hands-off approach to the community because the guarantee of freedom of religion in the Charter of Rights and Freedoms protects church members from the law. There is currently a Supreme Court challenge underway that may result in Canada enforcing the criminal code banning the practice of polygamy in Bountiful and similar communities.

Residential Patterns

Just as societies regulate mate selection, they also designate where a couple may live. In pre-industrial societies, most newlyweds live with one set of parents who offer protection and assistance. Most often married couples live with or near the husband's family, an arrangement called *patrilocality* (Greek, "place of the father"). But some societies, including the North American Iroquois, favour *matrilocality* ("place of the mother"), in which couples live with or near the wife's family.

Industrial societies show yet another pattern. Finances permitting, they favour *neolocality* (Greek, "new place"), in which a married couple lives apart from both sets of parents.

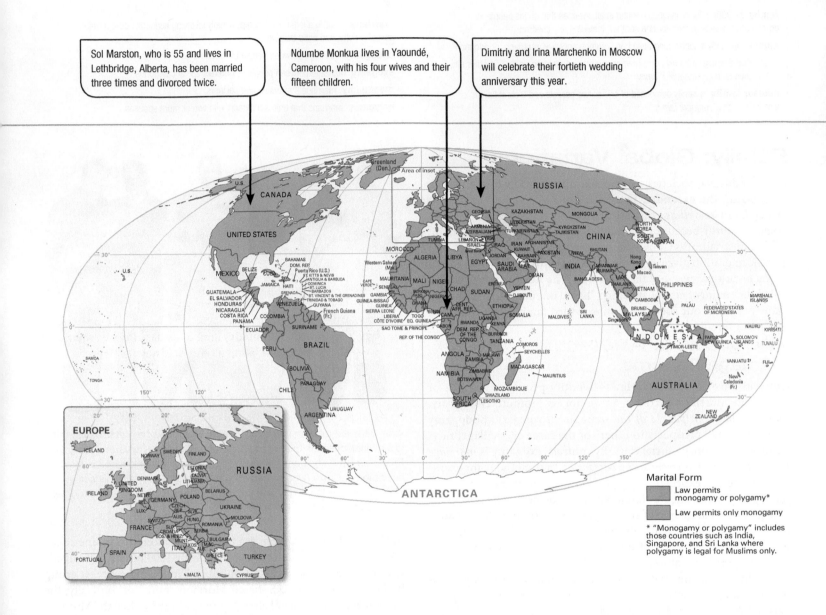

Sol Marston, who is 55 and lives in Lethbridge, Alberta, has been married three times and divorced twice.

Ndumbe Monkua lives in Yaoundé, Cameroon, with his four wives and their fifteen children.

Dimitriy and Irina Marchenko in Moscow will celebrate their fortieth wedding anniversary this year.

Marital Form

Law permits monogamy or polygamy*

Law permits only monogamy

* "Monogamy or polygamy" includes those countries such as India, Singapore, and Sri Lanka where polygamy is legal for Muslims only.

Window on the World

GLOBAL MAP 13–1   **Marital Form in Global Perspective**

Monogamy is the only legal form of marriage throughout the Western Hemisphere and in much of the rest of the world. In most African nations and in southern Asia, however, polygamy is permitted by law. In many cases, this practice reflects the influence of Islam, a religion that allows a man to have up to four wives. Even so, most marriages in these countries are monogamous, primarily for financial reasons.

Patterns of Descent

Descent refers to *the system by which members of a society trace kinship over generations.* Most pre-industrial societies trace kinship through either the father's side or the mother's side of the family. *Patrilineal descent*, the more common pattern, traces kinship through males, so that fathers pass property on to their sons. Patrilineal descent characterizes most pastoral and agrarian societies, in which men produce the most valued resources. *Matrilineal descent*, by which people define only the mother's side as kin and property passes from mothers to daughters, is found in horticultural societies where women are the main food producers.

Industrial societies with greater gender equality recognize *bilateral descent* ("two-sided descent"), a system tracing descent through both men and women. In this pattern, children include people on both the father's side and the mother's side among their relatives.

descent (p. 340) the system by which members of a society trace kinship over generations

incest taboo a norm forbidding sexual relations or marriage between certain relatives

Patterns of Authority

Worldwide, the family patterns discussed so far—polygyny, patrilocality, and patrilineal descent—are dominant and reflect the global pattern of patriarchy. In high-income countries such as Canada, men are still typically heads of households, and most Canadian parents give children their father's last name. However, more egalitarian families are evolving, especially as the share of women in the labour force goes up. Nevertheless, while children now more commonly take both of their parents' last names, children very rarely use only their mother's last name when both parents are married and living together.

Theoretical Analysis of Families

As in earlier chapters, the various theoretical approaches offer a range of insights about families.

Functions of Family: Structural-Functional Analysis

According to the structural-functional approach, the family performs many vital tasks. For this reason, the family is sometimes called the "backbone of society."

1. **Socialization.** As noted in Chapter 3 ("Socialization: From Infancy to Old Age"), the family is the first and most important setting for child rearing. Ideally, parents help children develop into well-integrated and contributing members of society. Of course, family socialization continues throughout the life cycle. Adults change within marriage and, as any parent knows, mothers and fathers learn as much from their children as their children learn from them.

2. **Regulation of sexual activity.** Every culture regulates sexual activity in the interest of maintaining kinship organization and property rights. As discussed in Chapter 6 ("Sexuality and Society"), the **incest taboo** is *a norm forbidding sexual relations or marriage between certain relatives.* Although the incest taboo exists in every society, exactly which relatives cannot marry varies from one culture to another (Murdock, 1965, orig. 1949).

   Reproduction between close relatives of any species can result in mental and physical damage to offspring. Yet only humans observe an incest taboo, suggesting that the key reason for controlling incest is social. Why? First, the incest taboo limits sexual competition in families by restricting sex to spouses. Second, because kinship defines people's

rights and obligations toward one another, reproduction between close relatives would hopelessly confuse kinship ties and threaten the social order. Third, forcing people to marry beyond their immediate families ties together the larger society.

3. **Social placement.** Families are not needed for people to reproduce biologically, but they do help maintain social organization. Parents pass on their own social identity—in terms of race, ethnicity, religion, and social class—to their children at birth.

4. **Material and emotional security.** Many people view the family as a "haven in a heartless world," offering physical protection, emotional support, and financial assistance. Perhaps this is why people living in families tend to be happier, healthier, and wealthier than people living alone (Goldstein & Kenney, 2001; U.S. Census Bureau, 2009).

○ **CRITICAL REVIEW** Structural-functional analysis explains why society, at least as we know it, is built on families. But this approach glosses over the diversity of Canadian family life and ignores how other social institutions (such as government) could meet at least some of the same human needs. Finally, structural-functionalism overlooks the negative aspects of family life, including patriarchy and family violence.

○ **CHECK YOUR LEARNING** What four important functions does the family provide for society?

Often, we experience modern society as cold and impersonal. In this context, the family can be a haven in a heartless world. Not every family lives up to this promise, of course, but people in families do live happier and longer lives than those who live alone.

Inequality and Family: Social-Conflict and Feminist Analysis

Like the structural-functional approach, the social-conflict approach, which includes feminist analysis, considers the family central to our way of life. But instead of focusing on ways that kinship benefits society, this approach points out how family perpetuates social inequality.

1. **Property and inheritance.** Friedrich Engels (1902, orig. 1884) traced the origin of the family to men's need (especially in the higher classes) to identify heirs so that they could hand down property to their sons. Families thus concentrate wealth and reproduce the class structure in each new generation.

2. **Patriarchy.** Feminists link the family to patriarchy. To know who their heirs are, men must control the sexuality of women. Families therefore transform women into the sexual and economic property of men. A century ago in Canada, most wives' earnings belonged to their husbands. Today, women still bear most of the responsibility for child rearing and housework (Benoit & Hallgrimsdottir, 2011; England, 2001; Stapinski, 1998).

3. **Race and ethnicity.** Racial and ethnic categories persist over generations only to the degree that people marry others like themselves. Endogamous marriage supports racial and ethnic inequality (Lynn & Todoroff, 1998; Mandell & Duffy, 2000, 2004).

○ **CRITICAL REVIEW** Social-conflict and feminist analysis shows another side of family life: its role in social stratification. Friedrich Engels criticized the family as part and parcel of capitalism. But non-capitalist societies also have families (and family problems). The family may be linked to social inequality, as Engels argued, but it carries out societal functions not easily accomplished by other means.

○ **CHECK YOUR LEARNING** Point to three ways in which families support social inequality.

Constructing Family Life: Micro-Level Analysis

Both the structural-functional and social-conflict approaches view the family as a structural system. By contrast, micro-level analysis explores how individuals shape and experience family life.

The Symbolic-Interaction Approach

Ideally, family living offers an opportunity for *intimacy*, a word with Latin roots that mean "sharing fear." As family members share many activities and establish trust, they build emotional bonds. Of course, the fact that parents act as authority figures often limits their closeness with younger children. Only as young people approach adulthood do kinship ties open up to include sharing confidences with greater intimacy (Macionis, 1978).

The Social-Exchange Approach

Social-exchange analysis, another micro-level approach, describes courtship and marriage as forms of negotiation (Blau, 1964). Dating allows each person to assess the advantages and disadvantages of a potential spouse. In essence, exchange analysts suggest, people "shop around" to make the best "deal" they can.

In patriarchal societies, gender roles dictate the elements of exchange: Men bring wealth and power to the marriage marketplace, and women bring beauty. The importance of beauty explains women's traditional concern with their appearance and sensitivity about revealing their age. But as women have joined the labour force, they have become less dependent on men to support them, and so the terms of exchange are converging for men and women.

○ **CRITICAL REVIEW** Micro-level analysis balances structural-functional and social-conflict visions of the family as an institutional system. Both the symbolic-interaction and social-exchange approaches focus on the individual experience of family life. However, micro-level analysis misses the bigger picture: The experience of family life is similar for people in the same social and economic categories. The Applying Theory table summarizes what we learn from the three theoretical approaches to family life.

○ **CHECK YOUR LEARNING** How does a micro-level approach to understanding family differ from a macro-level approach?

Stages of Family Life

Members of our society recognize several distinct stages of family life across the life course.

Courtship and Romantic Love

November 17, Victoria, British Columbia. It is a typical late-autumn Saturday in the city. We are at the Interfaith Chapel attending the marriage of Jan and Nathan. Both are in their early twenties and beaming at their new status. On the surface, there is nothing at all unusual about the young couple. Their relationship is based on romantic love rather than an arrangement struck between their parents or extended families, a practice still common in parts of the world. However, the new couple is different in at least one respect. Signifying the expanding role of the internet in both Canada and England (where Nathan comes from), the couple's courtship (which spanned several months) took place online. According to Jan, by the time she actually met Nathan in person, they were already planning their marriage.

APPLYING THEORY

Family

	Structural-Functional Approach	Social-Conflict and Feminist Approaches	Symbolic-Interaction and Social-Exchange Approaches
What is the level of analysis?	Macro level	Macro level	Micro level
What is the importance of family for society?	The family performs vital tasks, including socializing the young and providing emotional and financial support for members.	The family perpetuates social inequality by handing down wealth from one generation to the next.	The symbolic-interaction approach explains that the reality of family life is constructed by members in their interaction.
	The family helps regulate sexual activity.	The family supports patriarchy as well as racial and ethnic inequality.	The social-exchange approach shows that courtship typically brings together people who offer the same level of advantages.

In rural areas of low- and middle-income countries throughout the world, most people consider courtship too important to be left to the young. *Arranged marriages* are alliances between two extended families of similar social standing and usually involve an exchange not just of children but also of wealth and favours. Romantic love has little to do with marriage, and parents may make such arrangements when their children are very young. A century ago in Sri Lanka and India, half of all girls married before age 15 (Mace & Mace, 1960; Mayo, 1927). As the Thinking Globally box on page 344 explains, child marriage still occurs in some parts of the world today.

Industrialization both erodes the importance of extended families and weakens traditions. As young people begin the process of choosing their own mate, dating sharpens courtship skills and allows sexual experimentation. Marriage is delayed until young people complete their education and gain the experience needed to select a suitable partner.

Our culture celebrates *romantic love*—affection and sexual passion toward another person—as the basis for marriage. We find it hard to imagine marriage without love, and popular culture, from fairy tales such as *Cinderella* to today's television sitcoms and dramas, portrays love as the key to a successful marriage.

Our society's emphasis on romantic love motivates young people to "leave the nest" to form families of their own; physical passion may also help a new couple through difficult adjustments in living together (Goode, 1959). On the other hand, because feelings change over time, romantic love is a less stable foundation for marriage than social and economic considerations, one reason that the divorce rate is much higher in Canada than in nations where societal traditions are a stronger guide in the choice of a partner. Responding to concern about the possibility of eventual separation, an increasing share of couples in Canada, the United States, and many other high-income countries now includes creating a prenuptial agreement as part of their wedding preparations. The Seeing Sociology in the News box on page 346 provides details.

But even in our country, sociologists point out, society aims Cupid's arrow more than we like to think. Most people fall in love with others of the same race who are close in age and of similar social class. Our society "arranges" marriages by encouraging **homogamy** (literally, "like marrying like"), *marriage between people with the same social characteristics.*

The extent of homogamy is greater for some categories of our population (such as younger people and immigrants from traditional societies) than for others (older people and those who do not live according to strict traditions).

Settling In: Ideal and Real Marriage

Our culture gives young people an idealized, "happily ever after" picture of marriage. Such optimism can lead to disappointment, especially for women, who are taught that marriage is the key to personal happiness. Also, romantic love involves a lot of fantasy: We fall in love with others not always as they are but as we want them to be.

Sexuality, too, can be a source of disappointment. In the romantic haze of falling in love, people may see marriage as an endless sexual honeymoon, only to face the sobering realization that sex eventually becomes a less-than-all-consuming passion. Although

Early to Wed: A Report from Rural India

Sumitra Jogi cries as her wedding is about to begin. Are they tears of joy? Not exactly. This "bride" is an 18-month-old squirming in the arms of her mother. The groom? A boy of seven.

In a remote village in India's western state of Rajasthan, the two families gather at midnight to celebrate a traditional wedding ritual. It is May 2, in Hindu tradition an especially good day to marry. Sumitra's father smiles as the ceremony begins; her mother cradles the infant, who has fallen asleep. The groom, wearing a special costume and a red and gold turban on his head, gently reaches up and grasps the baby's hand. Then, as the ceremony ends, the young boy leads the child and mother around the wedding fire three-and-a-half times while the audience beams at the couple's first steps together as husband and wife.

Child weddings are illegal in India, but traditions are strong in rural regions, and laws against child marriage are hard to enforce. As a result, thousands of children marry each year. "In rural Rajasthan," explains one social worker, "all of the girls

are married by age 14. These are poor, illiterate families, and they don't want to keep girls past their first menstrual cycle."

For now, Sumitra Jogi will remain with her parents. But in 8 or 10 years, a second ceremony

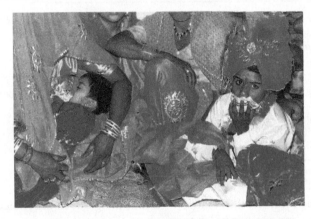

The 18-month-old girl on the left is breastfeeding during her wedding ceremony in a small village in the state of Rajasthan, India; her new husband is seven years old. Although outlawed, such arranged marriages involving children are still known to take place in traditional, remote areas of India.

will send her to live with her husband's family, and her married life will begin.

If the reality of marriage is years in the future, why do families push their children to marry at such an early age? Parents of girls know that the younger the bride, the smaller the dowry they must offer to the groom's family. Also, when girls marry this young, there is no question about their virginity, which raises their value on the marriage market. No one in these situations thinks about love or the fact that the children are too young to understand what is taking place (J.W. Anderson, 1995).

WHAT DO YOU THINK?

1. Why are arranged marriages common in very traditional communities?

2. List several advantages and disadvantages of arranged marriages from the point of view of the families involved.

3. Can you point to ways in which mate selection in Canada is "arranged" by society?

the frequency of marital sex does decline over time, about two in three married people report that they are satisfied with the sexual dimension of their relationship. In general, couples with the best sexual relationships experience the most satisfaction in their marriages. Sex may not be the key to marital happiness, but more often than not, good sex and good relationships go together (Laumann et al., 1994; Smith, 2006).

Infidelity—sexual activity outside marriage—is another area where the reality of marriage does not match our cultural ideal. Most Canadian adults do not approve of sex outside of marriage, but many have difficulty discussing infidelity—in thought and in action—with their spouse. In a 2003 poll on marriage in Canada, 23 percent of married Canadians said that they had not mentioned to their spouse an attraction to another person, 16 percent of those surveyed had not discussed with their spouses doubts about their marriage, 9 percent had not mentioned using the internet to view risqué material, and 4 percent had avoided discussing an extramarital

affair (Ipsos-Reid 2003a). These findings are not surprising given that Canadians strongly disapprove of married men and women having an affair. The approval rate was 17 percent in 2007 and dropped to 15 percent in 2009 (Angus Reid Global Monitor, 2009).

Child Rearing

Despite the demands children make on us, a majority of adults in one international poll—including the majority surveyed in Canada (60 percent)—identified raising children as one of life's great joys (The Gallup Organization, 1997). Today, however, few people in Canada, similar to their counterparts in a number of other countries, want more than a few children. This is a change from two centuries ago, when eight children was the Canadian average!

Big families pay off in pre-industrial societies because children supply needed labour. People therefore regard having children as a wife's duty, and in the absence of effective birth control, child-bearing

"Son, you're all grown up now. You owe me two
hundred and fourteen thousand dollars."

© *The New Yorker* Collection, 1983, Robert Weber, from cartoonbank.com.
All rights reserved.

is a regular event. Of course, a high death rate in pre-industrial societies prevents many children from reaching adulthood; as late as 1900, one-third of children in Canada died by age 10.

Economically speaking, industrialization transforms children from an asset to a liability. It now costs middle-class parents almost $300 000 to raise one child, including university or college tuition (Lino & Carlson, 2010). No wonder the Canadian average steadily dropped during the twentieth century to one child per family (Statistics Canada, 2007d)!

The trend toward smaller families is most pronounced in high-income nations. The picture differs in low-income regions in Latin America, Asia, and especially Africa, where many women have few alternatives to bearing children. In many African nations, as a glance back at Global Map 1–1 on page 3 shows, between four and six children is still the norm.

Parenting is a very expensive, lifelong commitment. As our society has given people greater choice about family life, more adults have decided to delay becoming couples and having children. Among young adults aged 20 to 24, only 17.9 percent were part of

a couple in 2006, down from 19.6 percent in 2001 and 28.4 percent in 1986. Among individuals in their late twenties, 48.5 percent lived as part of a couple in 2006, compared to 51.1 percent in 2001 and 62.3 percent in 1986 (Statistics Canada, 2009a).

About two-thirds of parents in Canada claim that they would like to devote more of their time to child rearing (Statistics Canada, 1999f). For many families, including Rosa Yniguez's family described in the opening to this chapter, having fewer children is an important step toward resolving the tension between work and parenting (Fox, 2001; Gilbert, 2005).

Children of working parents spend most of the day at school. But after school, more than 20 percent of our children aged 6 to 12 are "latchkey kids" who spend time alone at home unsupervised (Child and Family Canada, 2003; Vandivere et al., 2003).

Most Northern European countries provide generous family leaves and benefits, as well as public child care, to help ease the conflict between family and work (Baker, 1995). Changes in the Canadian Employment Insurance Act have brought the length of family leave (12 months as of January 2001) within the range of that found in the Nordic countries. However, the Canadian leave is accompanied by low benefits (55 percent of previous wages), compared to Nordic counties (Benoit, 2000a). Even worse off are American parents. Congress took a small step toward easing the conflict between family and job responsibilities by passing the Family and Medical Leave Act in 1993. This law allows up to 90 days of unpaid leave from work for a new child or a serious family emergency. Still, most parents in the United States have to juggle parental and occupational responsibilities, and there are direct economic consequences because the U.S. family leave has no monetary benefit unless parents belong to employer-sponsored parental programs.

Recent research shows that the countries with the highest participation rates of fathers in parental leave are those with nontransferable leave programs (i.e., if the father does not take the leave, the couple loses it) and high wage replacement rates, such as in the Nordic countries. Sweden currently has a father's parental leave participation rate of 90 percent, while participation in Norway is 89 percent and in Iceland is 84 percent (Moss & O'Brien, 2006). One in five fathers claims parental leave benefits in Canada (Beaupré & Cloutier, 2007; Marshall, 2008). In 2006, Quebec introduced its own Parental Insurance Plan, which set aside a five-week nontransferable leave for fathers. Data show that 56 percent of eligible fathers in Quebec claimed benefits for an average of seven weeks, compared with 11 percent of non-Quebec fathers (Statistics Canada, 2008q). Reasons behind these cross-national and intra-country differences include the fact that males are generally higher earners than females, and families may be reluctant for the father to claim parental leave because of the greater financial load (Anxo et al., 2007).

Traditionalists in the "family values" debate charge that many mothers work at the expense of their children, who receive less parenting. Progressives reply that such criticism unfairly blames women for wanting the same opportunities that men have long enjoyed.

Financial Times

UK court upholds prenuptial deal for heiress

BY JANE CROFT, LAW COURTS CORRESPONDENT

Published: October 20 2010 11:07 | Last updated: November 6, 2010 15:27

Prenuptial agreements should be upheld in certain divorce settlements, the UK's highest court has ruled, in a decision that will help wealthy individuals protect their assets and avoid big pay-outs.

The Supreme Court decided by eight justices to one to uphold a prenuptial agreement signed by Katrin Radmacher, a German paper industry heiress worth more than £100m, which was being challenged by Nicolas Granatino, her French ex-husband and former investment banker at JPMorgan.

The ruling will hearten wealthy people living in London who might be embroiled in "big money" divorces and had faced the prospect that prenuptial deals signed in their native countries would not be upheld in England.

Prenuptial deals, which specify the division of real estate and personal property such as family heirlooms, have not been legally binding in England and Wales, unlike in the US or in most of the rest of Europe.

This ruling brings England closer to the rest of Europe but stops short of making prenuptial deals legally binding as the fairness of the agreements will be assessed by judges on a case-by-case basis.

Joe Vaitilingam, partner at Hughes Fowler Carruthers, the law firm, said this "modern judgment for a modern age" should "deter gold diggers".

Ms Radmacher and Mr Granatino married in 1998 after signing a prenuptial agreement four months earlier, waiving their rights to claim against each other's wealth if they split.

The couple, who have two children, separated in 2006, and in spite of their agreement, the High Court awarded a £5.85m lump sum to Mr Granatino.

The Court of Appeal overturned the ruling in July, awarding him £1m ($1.6m) plus £2.5m for a house after ruling for the first time that prenuptial deals ought to be taken into account when deciding on divorce settlements.

The Supreme Court has upheld this decision, saying that in the right case, prenuptial agreements can have decisive or compelling weight.

Lord Phillips, court president, said the majority of justices "hold that in this case the agreement was freely entered into and that both the husband and wife fully appreciated its implications".

Ms Radmacher said: "I'm delighted Britain has upheld fairness. It is important to me that no one else should have to go through this."

But some family lawyers said the ruling meant there was a danger that vulnerable parties, usually women, could be coerced into signing unfair prenuptial deals.

Wednesday's ruling is likely to reduce the number of legal challenges by ex-husbands to huge divorce settlements – often running into tens of millions of pounds – awarded by English judges to their former wives.

It will mean that the super-rich will be able to protect their wealth more easily.

Scores of divorce cases involving prenuptial agreements had been put on hold awaiting this decision.

Michael Gouriet, partner in the family law team at Withers said: "It would have been incredibly difficult and politically embarrassing for the English Supreme Court to dismiss a valid European prenuptial agreement out of hand, in effect saying that the English law knew better than the German."

Ms Radmacher's lawyers argued to the Supreme Court this year that she was worried that she could be targeted for her wealth and would not have married Mr Granatino without a prenuptial agreement.

London has had a reputation as the "divorce capital of the world", with huge pay-outs for ex-wives such as the £48m awarded to Beverley Charman after 28 years of marriage to John Charman, the insurance magnate, and the £24m awarded to Heather Mills on her divorce from Sir Paul McCartney.

The English courts have upheld since 2000 the case of White v White which made it clear that the starting point for any divorce should be an equal split of assets.

Mr Granatino admitted that he willingly entered into the prenuptial deal but said he did not know the extent of his wife's wealth and did not receive independent legal advice.

His lawyers also pointed out their circumstances when they split in 2006 were very different from when they met at members' only Tramp nightclub in Mayfair, when Ms Radmacher was running a fashion store in central London.

Mr Granatino had since quit his City job to study for an Oxford university doctorate and has started patenting biochemical processes.

Court documents showed that Mrs Radmacher accepted that if her former husband, who has just completed his doctorate and is looking for a research post, failed in his appeal, he faced "financial ruin".

Richard Todd QC, acting for Ms Radmacher, argued in the Supreme Court that Mr Granatino could expect to inherit millions from his parents, who are tax exiles worth up to £30m, and could easily give up academia and return to investment banking if he really was struggling financially.

The Law Commission is now examining whether the law should be changed to recognise prenuptial deals but will not make recommendations until 2012.

WHAT DO YOU THINK?

1. What are some of the reasons that more people are including a prenuptial agreement in their wedding plans?

2. To what extent can partners set terms for their marriage that regulate things other than money, such as personal behaviour?

3. If you were getting married in the near future, would you wish to have both partners sign a prenuptial agreement? Why or why not?

Source: UK court upholds prenuptial deal for heiress, By Jane Croft, Law Courts Correspondent, October 20 2010, *Financial Times*. Permission of the Financial Times Ltd.

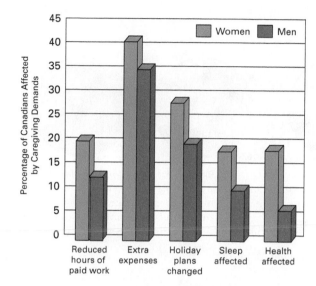

FIGURE 13–1 Consequences of Informal Caregiving to Seniors

Source: Habtu and Popovic (2006).

The Family in Later Life

Increasing life expectancy in Canada and across high-income countries means that couples who stay married do so for a longer time. By age 60, most have completed the task of raising children. At this point, marriage brings a return to living with only a spouse.

Like the birth of children, their departure—creating an "empty nest"—requires adjustments, although a marriage often becomes closer and more satisfying. Years of living together may lessen a couple's sexual passion, but understanding and commitment often increase.

Personal contact with children usually continues because most older adults live near at least one of their grown children. In 2006, 209 900 Canadian children (3.8 percent) aged 14 and under lived with their grandparents. About 0.5 percent of this age group (28 200 children aged 14 and under) resided with one or both grandparents where no parents or middle generation was present. A term often applied to these families is *skip-generation families* (Statistics Canada, 2007e.)

The other side of the coin is that adults in midlife now provide more care for aging parents. Many of the "baby boomers"—who are now between 40 and 60 years old—are called the "sandwich generation" because they have children under age 18 living at home as well as caring responsibilities for one or more of their own parents (Habtu & Popovic, 2006; Lund, 1993). While Canadian women and men are equally likely to find themselves in the role of caring for an older adult while still caring for a child, Figure 13–1 shows that women are more likely to be negatively affected by the ensuing changes to their professional and personal lives.

The final and surely the most difficult transition in married life comes with the death of a spouse. Wives typically outlive husbands because of their greater life expectancy and the fact that women usually marry men several years older than themselves. Wives can thus expect to spend some years as widows. The challenge of living alone after the death of a spouse is especially great for men, who usually have fewer friends than widows and may lack housekeeping skills.

Canadian Families: Class, Race, and Gender

Dimensions of inequality—social class, ethnicity, race, and gender—are powerful forces that shape marriage and family life. This discussion addresses each of these factors in turn, but bear in mind that they overlap in our lives.

Social Class

Social class determines a family's financial security and range of opportunities. Interviewing working-class women, Lillian Rubin (1976) found that wives thought a good husband was a man who held a steady job, did not drink too much, and was not violent. Rubin's middle-class respondents, by contrast, never mentioned such things; these women simply *assumed* that a husband would provide a safe and secure home. Their ideal husband was a man with whom they could communicate easily and share feelings and experiences.

While times have changed, it remains the case still today that what women (and men) hope for in marriage—and what they end up with—is linked to their social class. Much the same holds for children: Boys and girls lucky enough to be born into more affluent families enjoy better mental and physical health, develop more self-confidence, and go on to greater achievement than children born to poor parents (Duncan et al., 1998; Hertzman, 1999; Kohen et al., 2002; McLeod & Shanahan, 1993). A case is point is participating regularly in organized sport or lessons, with 17 to 25 percent of Canadian youth not doing so. Low household income is one of the strongest determinants of lack of participation (Brooker & Hyman, 2010).

Ethnicity and Race

Ethnicity and race, too, shape families. Analysis of Aboriginal and visible minority families must begin with the stark reality of economic disadvantage. Despite upward mobility over the generations, the incidence of low income among families of visible minorities is still significantly above the Canadian average (Statistics Canada, 2006au). In 2005, the low-income rate among non-Aboriginal Canadian children under 15 years was 12.9 percent; the figure for Aboriginal children of the same age was 27.5 percent (Tait, 2008). Likewise, immigrants who are members of visible minorities—even those who have been in Canada for an extended period of time—are at much

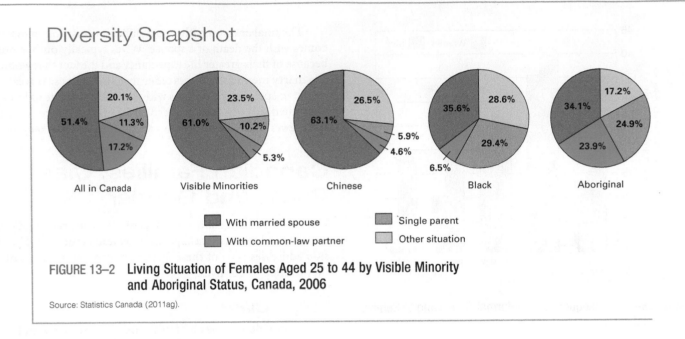

Diversity Snapshot

All in Canada
- 20.1%
- 11.3%
- 17.2%
- 51.4%

Visible Minorities
- 23.5%
- 10.2%
- 5.3%
- 61.0%

Chinese
- 26.5%
- 5.9%
- 4.6%
- 63.1%

Black
- 28.6%
- 29.4%
- 6.5%
- 35.6%

Aboriginal
- 17.2%
- 24.9%
- 23.9%
- 34.1%

Legend:
- With married spouse
- With common-law partner
- Single parent
- Other situation

FIGURE 13–2 Living Situation of Females Aged 25 to 44 by Visible Minority and Aboriginal Status, Canada, 2006

Source: Statistics Canada (2011ag).

greater risk of poverty than other immigrants. In a 2004 study, 86 percent of recent immigrants with low income were members of a visible minority group (Boris, 2004).

Many Aboriginals and some visible minority groups are also more likely to be single parents. In 2006, among females aged 25 to 44, Black women (29 percent) and Aboriginal women (25 percent) were more than twice as likely to be single parents compared to other women in Canada (11 percent). Among Chinese women, on the other hand, the incidence of lone parenthood is very low, as illustrated in Figure 13–2 (Statistics Canada, 2011ag).

Gender

The sociologist Jessie Bernard (1982) says that every marriage is actually two different relationships: the woman's marriage and the man's marriage. The reason is that few marriages have two equal partners. Although patriarchy has diminished, many people still expect husbands to be older and taller than their wives and to have more important, better-paid jobs.

Why, then, do many people think that marriage benefits women more than men? The positive stereotype of the carefree bachelor contrasts sharply with the negative image of the lonely spinster, suggesting that women are fulfilled only through being wives and mothers.

However, Bernard points out, married women actually have poorer mental health, less happiness, and more passive attitudes toward life than single women do. Married men, on the other hand, generally live longer, are mentally better off, and report being happier than single men. These differences suggest why, after divorce, men are more eager than women to find a new partner.

Bernard concludes that there is no better assurance of long life, health, and happiness for a man than having a woman devote her life to taking care of him and providing the security of a well-ordered home. She is quick to add that marriage *could* be healthful for women if husbands did not dominate wives and expect them to do almost all of the housework. Survey responses confirm that couples rank "sharing household chores" as one of the most important factors that contribute to a successful marriage (Eichler, 1997; Leira, 1992; Pew Research Center, 2007a). Another structural force affecting gender relationship in families is the renegotiation of gender roles during the transition to parenthood. As Fox (2010:7) describes, the postpartum period offers a rare opportunity to examine how gender differences and divisions are negotiated and thereby created, strengthened, and sometimes contested in subsequent life course transitions. The gender patterns established in this period may be formative and have indelible effects on the organization of family life and health. A particular area of focus for feminist scholars is the impact of an often renegotiated division of labour on women's economic options and physical and mental health.

Transitions and Problems in Family Life

The newspaper columnist Ann Landers once remarked that 1 marriage in 20 is wonderful, 5 in 20 are good, 10 in 20 are tolerable, and the remaining 4 are "pure hell." Families can be a source of joy, but the reality of family life can also fall short of the ideal.

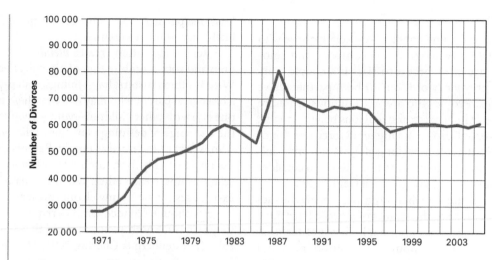

FIGURE 13–3   Divorces in Canada, 1970–2005

Source: Statistics Canada (2011ah, 2011ai).

Divorce

Our society strongly supports marriage. A survey of Canadians found that getting married at some point in their lives is "very important" (47 percent) or "somewhat important" (33 percent) to them (Bibby, 2004). In another study, nearly all young people between ages 15 and 19 years surveyed planned to get married, and most of them said they expected to spend the rest of their lives with their future partner (Bibby, 2009).

But while about 9 out of 10 people in Canada at some point "tie the knot," many of today's marriages unravel. Figure 13–3 shows an increase in the Canadian divorce rate that started in the late 1960s (when the divorce laws were liberalized) and peaked in 1987 (when restrictions were eased on marital dissolutions). Demographers estimate that if the divorce rate remained as high as it was in 1987, 50.6 percent of marriages would end in divorce by the thirtieth wedding anniversary. The divorce rate gradually levelled off and the estimated number of marriages ending in divorce before the thirtieth anniversary decreased to 40 percent in 1995 and to 34.8 percent in 1997, but climbed to 37.7 percent in 2000. In 2003, the rate was 221 divorces per 100 000 population, a decrease of 3 percent (Statistics Canada, 2006au; Statistics Canada, 2011aj).

The United States has the highest divorce rate in the world; it is about one-and-a-half times higher than in Canada and Japan and four times higher than in Italy and Ireland (European Union, 2010; OECD, 2010).

Causes of Divorce

The high Canadian divorce rate has many causes (Etzioni, 1993; Furstenberg & Cherlin, 1991; Greenspan, 2001; Luxton, 2001; Popenoe, 1999):

1. **Individualism is on the rise.** Today's family members spend less time together. We have become more individualistic, more concerned with our own personal happiness and earning income than with the happiness and well-being of our partners and children.

2. **Romantic love fades.** Because our culture bases marriage on romantic love, relationships may fail as sexual passion fades. Many people end a marriage in favour of a new relationship that promises renewed excitement and romance.

3. **Women are less dependent on men.** Women's increasing participation in the labour force has reduced wives' financial dependency on their husbands. Thus women find it easier to leave unhappy marriages.

4. **Many of today's marriages are stressful.** With both partners working outside the home in most cases, people have less time and energy for family life. This makes raising children harder than ever. Children do stabilize some marriages, but divorce is most common during the early years of marriage when many couples have young children.

5. **Divorce has become socially acceptable.** Divorce no longer carries the powerful stigma it did just a few generations ago. Family and friends are now less likely to discourage couples in conflict from divorcing.

6. **Legally, a divorce is easier to get.** In the past, courts required divorcing couples to demonstrate that one or both were guilty of behaviour such as adultery or physical abuse. Today, all provinces allow divorce if a couple simply states that the marriage has failed. Concern about easy divorce, voiced by many Canadians, has led some to advocate rewriting the marriage laws.

family violence emotional, physical, or sexual abuse of one family member by another

Who Divorces?

At greatest risk of divorce are young couples—especially those who marry after a brief courtship—who tend to lack money and emotional maturity. The chance of divorce also rises if a couple marries after an unexpected pregnancy or if one or both partners have substance abuse problems. People who are not religious are more likely to divorce than those who have strong religious beliefs. Finally, people whose parents divorced also have a higher divorce rate themselves. Research suggests that a role modelling effect is at work: Children who see parents go through divorce are more likely to consider divorce themselves (Amato, 2001; Pew Research Center, 2008).

Divorce is also more common when both partners have successful careers, perhaps because of the strains of a two-career marriage but also because financially secure people may not feel that they have to remain in an unhappy home. In addition, men and women who divorce once are more likely to divorce again, probably because high-risk factors follow them from one marriage to another.

Divorce and Children

In previous decades, the vast majority of Canadian mothers gained custody of children and, because fathers typically earn more income, the well-being of children was often dependent on fathers making court-ordered child support payments (Statistics Canada, 1998k). In recent years, however, this trend has changed. In 2003 mothers were awarded sole custody of fewer than half (48 percent) of the dependent Canadian children for whom custody was determined through divorce proceedings. This is down from 75.8 percent in 1988. A similar downward trend also occurred with husbands. Custody of a child or dependant was awarded to the husband in only 8 percent of cases in 2003, a drop from a peak of 15 percent in 1986. The other big change is that, in 2004, 46.5 percent of dependent children for whom custody was awarded had custody given jointly to the husband and wife, a continuation of a 15-year trend of steady increases in joint custody arrangements (Statistics Canada, 2008t).

While all of the reasons may not be clear, recent research indicates that children living in post-divorce custodial households have higher incidences of behavioural or emotional problems than children living with both of their biological parents (Strohschein, 2005; Williams, 2002). Other research shows that children adapt better when their father remains an active parent, even if he is not residing in the same household (Allard et al., 2005). This involves non-residential fathers who are more than "Sunday daddies" and instead relate to their children as fully engaged parents who provide emotional and other support and take an active role in discipline (Ambert, 2009).

Remarriage and Blended Families

Four out of five people who divorce remarry, most within five years. Nationwide, about half of all marriages are now remarriages for at least one partner. Men, who benefit more from wedlock, are more likely than women to remarry.

Remarriage often creates *blended families*, composed of children and some combination of biological parents and step-parents. With brothers, sisters, half-siblings, a step-parent—not to mention a biological parent who may live elsewhere and be married to someone else with other children—young people in blended families face the challenge of defining many new relationships and deciding just who is part of the nuclear family. Parents often have trouble defining responsibility for household work among people unsure of their relationships to each other. When the custody of children is an issue, ex-spouses can be an unwelcome presence for people in a new marriage. Although blended families require a great deal of adjustment, they also offer both young and old the chance to relax rigid family roles (Furstenberg & Cherlin, 2001; McLanahan, 2002).

Family Violence

The ideal family is a source of pleasure and support. However, the disturbing reality of many homes is **family violence**, *emotional, physical, or sexual abuse of one family member by another*. The sociologist Richard J. Gelles calls the family "the most violent group in society with the exception of the police and the military" (quoted in Roesch, 1984:75).

Violence against Women and Men

Family brutality often goes unreported to police, but results from the 1999 General Social Survey estimate that nearly 700 000 women who are married, in common-law relationships, or in contact with their former partners were exposed to spousal violence over the five-year period predating the survey. Data from 2001 indicate that the number of cases reported to police departments has been increasing, although there are also suggestions that victims are now more willing to report incidents to police than earlier victims were (Statistics Canada, 2000m, 2003m). In 2004, women were the victims of 51 percent of violent crimes reported to a sample of police forces; during that year, women committed 17 percent of violent crimes in Canada (Statistics Canada, 2006au).

But men, too, are victims of spousal violence (Straus, 1993). In the 1999 and 2004 General Surveys on Victimization, men were victims at a rate similar to that of women (7 percent for men compared to 8 percent for women in 1999, and 6 percent for each in 2004). However, women (25 percent) are much more likely than are men (10 percent) to be severely abused by their partners. Women were also more likely to be victims of repeat spousal violence (57 percent of women versus 50 percent of men in 2004). Further, women who are victims of spousal abuse are more likely than men in comparable situations to incur a physical injury: 44 percent of women versus 19 percent of men. Finally, though the overall rate is decreasing, women are at a much greater risk of spousal homicide than men.

Divorce may be a solution for a couple in an unhappy marriage, but it can be a problem for children who experience the withdrawal of a parent from their social world. In what ways can divorce be harmful to children? Is there a positive side to divorce? How might separating parents better prepare their children for the transition of parental divorce?

This is especially the case for women in common-law unions. In other words, women are much more likely to be killed by a family member than men are: While only 4 percent of male homicide victims were murdered by a spouse or ex-spouse in 2004, the rate for female homicide victims of spouses or ex-spouses was 37 percent (Statistics Canada, 2006au). Overall, Canadian women are still more likely to be hurt by a family member than to be mugged or raped by a stranger or injured in an automobile accident (Statistics Canada, 2000m). Males are also 3.5 times more likely to be accused of spousal homicide or attempted homicide (repeat offenders) than females; males were also more likely to be chronic offenders. The vast majority of females who killed or attempted to kill their husbands did so without any previous attempt. The opposite was the case for the majority of males (Canadian Centre for Justice Statistics, 2007).

Historically, the law defined wives as the property of husbands, so that no man could be charged with raping his wife. In the past, too, the law regarded domestic violence as a private family matter, giving victims few options. Now, even without separation or divorce, a woman can at least obtain court protection from an abusive spouse. Bill C-126, known as the Anti-Stalking Law, prohibits an ex-partner

from following or otherwise threatening a woman (Statistics Canada, 1995a). Further, communities across North America have established domestic abuse shelters that provide counselling as well as temporary housing for women and children driven from their homes by domestic violence. While in 1975 there were only 15 shelters for abused women and children across the country, by 2004 this number had increased to more than 500 (Statistics Canada, 2005a). On the other hand, there still are no shelters for men and their children leaving abusive relationships (Modrcin, 1998).

Violence against Children

Family violence also victimizes children. Family members caused crimes against children in 37 percent of cases involving physical assaults and in 43 percent of cases involving sexual assaults (Statistics Canada, 2003m). Child abuse is most common among the youngest and most vulnerable children and females while males were more likely to be victims of physical abuse (Straus & Gelles, 1986; Van Biema, 1994). According to the 2005 Homicide Survey, nearly 4 in 10 child and youth victims of family violence sustained a physical injury. More than one-third of the 60 homicides committed against children and youth under the age of 18 across Canada in 2005 were carried out by family members (Canadian Centre for Justice Statistics, 2007).

Most child abusers are men; in 1996, fathers were the perpetrators of 73 percent of the reported physical assaults against children and 98 percent of the sexual assaults (Statistics Canada, 1998j). These men do not conform to a simple stereotype, but most abusers do share one trait: They were abused themselves as children. Researchers have found that violent behaviour in close relationships is learned; in families, then, violence begets violence (Browning & Laumann, 1997; Gwartney-Gibbs, Stockard, & Bohmer, 1987; Widom, 1996).

Alternative Family Forms

The majority of Canadian families in the mid-twentieth century were composed of a married couple who raised children. But in recent decades, our society has displayed significant diversity in family forms.

One-Parent Families

Lone parents represented 15.9 percent of all census families in 2006, which is just slightly higher than the 15.7 percent in 2001, suggesting a levelling out (Statistics Canada, 2007e). One-parent families—81 percent of which in 2006 were headed by lone mothers, or four out of every five such families—may result from divorce, death, or the decision of an unmarried woman to have a child. Men headed the remainder of the one-parent families (19.9 percent). One-parent families headed by men increased 14.6 percent between 2001 and 2006, more than double the growth of one-parent families headed by women (Statistics Canada, 2007e).

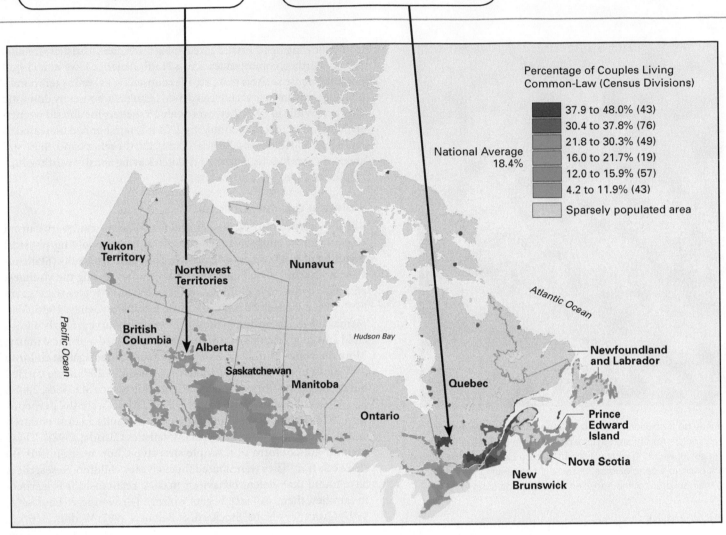

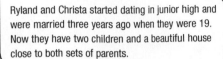

Ryland and Christa started dating in junior high and were married three years ago when they were 19. Now they have two children and a beautiful house close to both sets of parents.

Louise and Andre are both in their 60s and are thinking about getting married now after having lived together for 36 years.

Percentage of Couples Living Common-Law (Census Divisions)

	37.9 to 48.0% (43)
	30.4 to 37.8% (76)
	21.8 to 30.3% (49)
	16.0 to 21.7% (19)
	12.0 to 15.9% (57)
	4.2 to 11.9% (43)
	Sparsely populated area

National Average 18.4%

Seeing Ourselves

NATIONAL MAP 13–1 **Cohabitation across Canada**

Even though more than 18 percent of all couples live in common-law relationships in Canada, this percentage varies greatly across the country. One might think that it would be couples in urban areas leading the way in this trend. But as the map shows, it is Quebec and the rural areas in other parts of Canada that are at the forefront in this trend. The lowest rate of cohabitation, on the other hand, occurs in Southern Manitoba and in York, just outside of Toronto. What do you think explains the patterns you see in this map? Perhaps it is easier to explain why Quebec has a high rate than to explain the high rate in the rural areas.

Source: Estimated based on data in Statistics Canada (2011ak).

Many one-parent families are multi-generational, with single parents (most of whom are mothers) turning to their own parents (again, often mothers) for support. In countries such as Canada and the United States, then, the rise in single parenting is tied to both a declining role for fathers and a growing importance for grandparents. By contrast, in countries such as Sweden and Finland, the increasing role of the welfare state in providing social services, such as public child care, significantly increases single parenthood (Macionis & Plummer, 1997:476–77).

Much research points to the conclusion that growing up in a one-parent family usually disadvantages children. According to some studies, a father and a mother each make a distinctive contribution to a child's social development, so it is unrealistic to expect a single parent to do as good a job. To make matters worse, most North

In recent years, the proportion of young people who cohabit—that is, live together without being married—has risen sharply. This trend contributes to the debate over what is and is not a family: Do you consider a cohabiting couple a family? Why or why not?

American families with one parent—especially if that parent is a woman—contend with poverty. On average, children growing up in a one-parent family start out poorer, gain less schooling, and end up with lower incomes as adults. Such children are also more likely to be single parents themselves (Astone & McLanahan, 1991; Biblarz & Raftery, 1993; Duncan et al., 1998; Li & Wojtkiewicz, 1992; Popenoe, 1993a; Shapiro & Schrof, 1995; Wallerstein & Blakeslee, 1989; Webster, Orbuch, & House, 1995; Weisner & Eiduson, 1986; Wu, 1996). Other research suggests, however, that single parenting itself is not the problem, and that one caring parent is much better for a child than two uncaring ones. Further, in countries where the state has reduced poverty among one-parent families, children in these families appear to do as well as their counterparts in two-parent families (Sainsbury, 1996).

Given the instability of common-law relationships, it is interesting to note that countries vary wildly in regard to their moral views on children being born outside marriage; views diverge especially in regard to the growing trend in Canada and other high-income countries of never-married women having children (in 2006, 29.5 percent of Canadian female lone parents were of this type; Statistics Canada, 2007e).

Cohabitation

Cohabitation is *the sharing of a household by an unmarried couple.* The prevalence of cohabiting couples in Canada increased substantially over the past two decades, from a low of 6 percent in 1981 to 14 percent of all families in 2001 and 15.5 percent in 2006 (Statistics Canada, 2007e). Nearly half of such unions involve children, sometimes born within the common-law union itself or otherwise from a former relationship. In the last 20 years, the proportions of common-law couples who both were parents (from 2.7 percent to 6.8 percent between 1986 and 2006) and who both had no children (from 4.5 percent to 8.7 percent between 1986 and 2006) increased (Statistics Canada, 2007e).

In global perspective, cohabitation as a long-term form of family life, with or without children, is common in Sweden and other Scandinavian countries but it is rare in more traditional (especially Roman Catholic) nations such as Italy. National Map 13–1 illustrates the high proportion of cohabitation in Quebec, where 30 percent of all couples live in such a union, a rate similar to that in Sweden (Statistics Canada, 2002a; Turcotte & Bélanger, 1998). Cohabitation is gaining in popularity in Canada, and as this trend continues it may influence the future number of one-parent families because common-law unions have a higher probability of dissolution than do formal marriages (Wu, 2000). According to one Statistics Canada study (2000d), women whose first marriage ended in divorce tend to enter a new union, but are likely to opt for a common-law arrangement rather than marriage. The same holds true for women whose first union was common-law: They are also likely to form a new relationship but tend to continue to live common-law. So, while marriage may be less popular, conjugal unions continue to be popular among Canadians.

Gay and Lesbian Couples

In 1989, Denmark became the first country to permit registered partnerships with the benefits of marriage for same-sex couples. Since then, more than 15 countries, including Norway (1993), Sweden (1994), Iceland (1996), Finland (2001), the United Kingdom (2004), and Australia (2008) have followed suit. However, apart from Canada (2005), only six countries have extended marriage—in name as well as in practice—to same-sex couples: the Netherlands (2001), Belgium (2003), Spain (2005), South Africa (2006), Norway (2008), and Sweden (2009).

In the United States, Massachusetts became the first state to legalize same-sex marriage in 2004. As of 2012, Iowa, Vermont, New York, Connecticut, New Hampshire, and Washington, D.C. have also changed their laws to allow same-sex marriage. Several other states, including California, permit same-sex civil unions or domestic partnerships with varying similarities to the rights of marriage.

In 1999, the Supreme Court of Canada held that same-sex couples must be granted essentially the same rights as married couples.

Gay couples can legally marry in Canada. Some are raising children from previous heterosexual unions, and some have adopted children.

In 2003, the Court of Appeal of Ontario held that homosexuals have a right to get married. The federal government decided not to appeal this and similar cases, and instead instituted legislation to the same effect. The federal government was forced to act after a series of court rulings struck down provincial marriage laws. Courts in Ontario, Quebec, and British Columbia have ruled that the exclusion of gays and lesbians unjustifiably violates equality rights. Gays and lesbians were allowed to marry immediately after the Ontario verdict, and did so, as a result of a new right denied to them throughout most of human history. Other changes have taken place as well. A bill in 2000 extended full federal tax and social benefits to same-sex couples, and some provincial benefit plans and employers have recognized same-sex unions in their private insurance plans. In 2000, British Columbia changed a variety of provincial statutes to grant same-sex couples the same rights and obligations as common-law couples. The Conservative federal government elected in 2006 stated it would introduce a free vote in Parliament to repeal the same-sex marriage laws. However, this has not happened and, at the time of writing, the state of gay marriage in Canada remains the same. Meanwhile, the number of same-sex couples has increased; between 2001 and 2006, their number grew by 32.6 percent, compared to a 5.9 percent increase for opposite-sex couples (Statistics Canada, 2007e).

Some same-sex couples are conceiving using donated sperm (for lesbian couples) or a surrogate (for gay male couples), while others are rasing offspring from pervious heterosexual unions or taking the adoption route. Clearly, gay parenting challenges many traditional notions about the family. It also indicates that many gay and lesbian couples derive the same rewards from child rearing as do "straight" couples (Bell, Weinberg, & Kiefer-Hammersmith, 1981; Gross, 1991; Henry, 1993; Herman, 1994; Pressley & Andrews, 1992).

Singlehood

Because most people in Canada marry at some point in their lives, we tend to see singlehood as a transitory stage of life that ends with marriage. In recent decades, however, more people have deliberately chosen to live alone. In the early 1950s, only 1 household in 12 consisted of a single person. This proportion had risen to one in four by 2001. In 2006, there were actually more unmarried Canadians aged 15 and older than married Canadians (Statistics Canada, 2007e).

The figure for unmarried women was almost 1.7 million, or 13.7 percent of the total female population 15 years of age and older. Most striking is the surging number of single young women. In 1960, approximately one in four Canadian women aged 20 to 24 were single; by 2001, the proportion had soared to 88.5 percent (Statistics Canada, 2003l). Underlying this trend is women's greater participation in the labour force. Women who are economically secure view a husband as a matter of choice rather than a financial necessity (Edwards, 2000).

Women aged 65 and over also are now much more likely to live alone—in fact, twice as likely as their male counterparts. In large part this is because women tend to survive their husbands and to subsequently remain unmarried (Statistics Canada, 2007e).

New Reproductive Technologies and Family

Medical advances involving new reproductive technologies are also changing families. In 1978, England's Louise Brown became the world's first "test-tube baby"; since then, tens of thousands of children have been conceived outside the womb.

Test-tube babies are the product of *in vitro fertilization*, in which doctors unite a woman's egg and a man's sperm "in glass" (usually not a test tube but a shallow dish) rather than in a woman's body. Doctors then either implant the resulting embryo in the womb of the woman who is to bear the child or freeze it for implantation at a later time.

Modern reproductive technologies allow some couples who cannot conceive normally to have children. These techniques may also eventually help reduce the incidence of birth defects. Genetic screening of sperm and eggs would allow medical specialists to increase the odds for the birth of a healthy baby. But new reproductive technologies also raise difficult and troubling questions: When one woman carries an embryo developed from the egg of another, who is the mother? When a couple divorces, which spouse is entitled to use, or destroy, their frozen embryos? Should parents use genetic screening to select the traits of their child? Such questions remind us that technology changes faster than our ability to understand the consequences of its use.

CONTROVERSY & DEBATE

Ectogenesis and the Mother as Machine

Ectogenesis, sometimes referred to as "genesis outside the womb," refers to the process of fertilizing an ovum and then developing it in an artificial womb outside a woman's body (Colman, 2004). Direct ectogenesis on humans is not currently permitted but scientists have been testing the procedure on animals. Recent pioneering ectogenetic research by Dr. Hung-Ching Liu at Cornell University in the United States and Dr. Yoshinori Kuwabara at Juntendo University in Japan suggests that Huxley's "brave new world" is close at hand. In 1997, Kuwabara developed an artificial womb made from a plastic box filled with amniotic fluid that was used to bring goat fetuses to term after they were taken from their mothers' wombs. The offspring developed complications due to respiratory problems and later died, but the experiment itself was deemed a major breakthrough. Liu has refined a procedure that allows an egg to be fertilized through in vitro fertilization and then implanted into an artificial uterus made of cells from a human uterus. Authorities intervened after six days of gestation because of legal restrictions, but had they not done so, it is highly likely that the fertilized eggs would have matured in the artificial womb and produced full-term newborns. Biomedical science thus promises a not-too-distant future when human ectogenesis will be a viable option.

Yet, as with other complex developments in new reproductive technologies, the societal implications of ectogenesis

have caused heated debate among ethicists and social scientists. One cause for concern has been its impact on reproductive rights for women and men. Ethicists, including Peter Singer and Deane Wells (2006), make their case in support of the procedure, arguing that ectogenesis could be regulated in the same way as other reproductive technologies and holds the possibility of sidestepping the abortion debate and enhancing reproductive equality between women and men. Radical feminists such as Shulamith Firestone (1970) have contended that ectogenesis could be a powerful tool to eliminate the fundamental biological inequality between women and men: physical pregnancy and childbirth. Firestone argued that eliminating biological differences between the genders was a fundamental prerequisite for gender equality

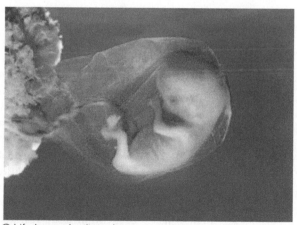

© Life Issues Institute, Inc.

in family life (Najand, 2010). Other researchers are less convinced that technological developments such as ectogenesis will have the desired long-range societal impact of gender equality in families. The evidence is clear that gender equality is premised not only on equal partnership in the home but also on the social context of other crucial factors, including access to postpartum support, child care, employment, wage equity, and health and social services (Saul, 2003). Irina Aristarkhova (2005) argues that feminist scholars need to challenge head-on the dichotomy between "mother" and "machine" that underlies the ectogenetic desire (the desire for reproduction external to the maternal body) among philosophers and scientists to enable a positive and ethical understanding of the maternal body within society.

CONTINUE THE DEBATE . . .

1. What, exactly, are the social implications of ectogenesis?

2. How does this new technology apply differently to men and women?

3. Do you agree that "genesis outside the womb" is an ethical problem as well as a social problem? Why or why not?

4. In your opinion, should we support research on human ectogenesis?

Sources: Aristarkhova (2005), Colman (2004), Firestone (1970), Najand (2010), Saul (2003), and Singer and Wells (2006).

The Controversy & Debate box discusses the ethical dilemma surrounding a recent new reproductive technology: ectogenesis, or "genesis outside the womb."

Families: Looking Ahead

Family life in Canada will continue to change in years to come, and with change comes controversy. Advocates of "traditional family values" line up against those who support greater personal choice.

Sociologists cannot predict the outcome of this debate, but based on ongoing research on family patterns, we can suggest five likely future trends.

First, the divorce rate is likely to remain high, even in the face of evidence that marital breakups put children at higher risk of poverty. Today's marriages are about as durable as they were a century ago, when many were cut short by death. The difference is that now more couples *choose* to end marriages that fail to meet their expectations. Although the divorce rate has declined since 1980, it is unlikely that

profane included as an ordinary element of everyday life

sacred set apart as extraordinary, inspiring awe and reverence

religion a social institution involving beliefs and practices based on recognizing the sacred

we will ever return to the low rates that marked the early decades of the twentieth century.

Second, family life in the future will be more diverse. Cohabiting couples, one-parent families, gay and lesbian families, and blended families are all on the rise. Most families are still based on marriage, and most married couples still have children. But the diversity of family forms implies a trend toward more personal choice.

Third, men will play a limited role in child rearing. In the 1950s, a decade many people consider the "golden age" of families, men began to withdraw from active parenting (Snell, 1990; Stacey, 1990). In recent years, a counter-trend has become evident, with some older, highly educated fathers making the choice to stay at home with young children, many using computer technology to continue their work. In non-earner parent stay-at-home families (18 percent of all families) in 2009, 12 percent (or nearly one in eight) had stay-at-home dads, compared to just 1 percent in 1976 (Statistics Canada, 2010f). But we should not overestimate the importance of this trend because the stay-at-home dad still represents only a small minority of all fathers of young children. The bigger picture is that the high divorce rate in Canada, the continuing high rate of single motherhood, and the low involvement of fathers with their children after divorce are weakening children's ties to fathers and increasing children's risk of poverty.

Fourth, families will continue to feel the effects of economic changes. In many homes, both household partners work, increasing income but reducing marriage and family to the interaction of weary men and women trying to fit a little "quality time" with their children into an already full schedule. The long-term effects of the two-career couple on families as we have known them are likely to be mixed.

Fifth and finally, the importance of new reproductive technologies will increase. Ethical concerns about whether what *can* be done *should* be done will surely slow these developments, but new reproductive technologies will continue to alter the traditional experience of parenthood.

Despite the changes and controversies that have shaken the family in Canada, most people in our society still report being happy in their roles as partners and parents. Marriage and family life will likely remain a foundation of our society for generations to come, while family types become increasingly more diverse.

Religion: Basic Concepts

Like family, religion plays an important part in human society. Families have long used religious rituals to celebrate birth, recognize adulthood, and mourn the dead.

The French sociologist Emile Durkheim stated that religion involves "things that surpass the limits of our knowledge" (1965:62, orig. 1915). As human beings, we regard most objects, events, and experiences as **profane** (from Latin, meaning "outside the temple"),

Religion is founded on the concept of the sacred: that which is set apart as extraordinary and which demands our submission. Bowing, kneeling, or prostrating oneself are all ways of symbolically surrendering to a higher power. This monk is performing an act of "prostration circumambulation," a complicated way of saying that he falls flat on the ground every few steps as he moves around a holy shrine. In this way, he expresses his complete surrender to his faith.

included as an ordinary part of everyday life. But we also consider some things **sacred**, *set apart as extraordinary, inspiring awe and reverence*. Setting the sacred apart from the profane is the essence of all religious belief. **Religion**, then, is *a social institution involving beliefs and practices based on recognizing the sacred*.

There is great diversity in matters of faith, and nothing is sacred to everyone on Earth. Although people regard most books as profane, Jews believe that the Torah (containing the first five books of the Hebrew Bible, also known as the Old Testament) is sacred, in the same way that Christians revere the Old and New Testaments of the Bible and Muslims exalt the Qur'an (Koran).

But no matter how a community of believers draws religious lines, Durkheim (1965:62, orig. 1915) explained, people understand profane things in terms of their everyday usefulness: We log on to the internet with our computer or turn a key to start our car. What is sacred we reverently set apart from daily life, giving it a "forbidden" or "holy" aura. For example, Muslims remove their shoes before entering a mosque to avoid defiling a sacred place with soles that have touched the profane ground outside.

The sacred is embodied in *ritual*, or formal ceremonial behaviour. Holy Communion is the central ritual of Christianity; to the Christian faithful, the wafer and wine consumed during Communion are treated not in a profane way as food but as the sacred symbols of the body and blood of Jesus Christ.

faith belief based on conviction rather than on scientific evidence

totem an object in the natural world collectively defined as sacred

Because religion deals with ideas that transcend everyday experience, neither common sense nor sociology can prove or disprove religious doctrine. Religion is a matter of **faith**, *belief based on conviction rather than on scientific evidence*. The New Testament of the Bible defines faith as "the conviction of things not seen" (Hebrews 11:1) and urges Christians to "walk by faith, not by sight" (2 Corinthians 5:7).

Some people with strong religious beliefs may be disturbed by the thought of sociologists turning a scientific eye on what they hold sacred. However, sociological study is no threat to anyone's faith. Sociologists study religion just as they study family, to understand religious experiences around the world and how religion is tied to other social institutions. They make no judgments about whether a specific religion is "right" or "wrong." Sociological analysis takes a more worldly approach, seeking to understand what religions have in common and how they differ as well as how religious activity affects society as a whole.

Theoretical Analysis of Religion

Sociologists apply the major theoretical approaches to the study of religion just as they do to any other topic. Each provides distinctive insights about the ways religion shapes social life.

Functions of Religion: Structural-Functional Analysis

According to Emile Durkheim (1965, orig. 1915), society has a life and power of its own beyond the life of any individual. In a sense, society itself is godlike, shaping the lives of its members and living on beyond them. Practising religion, people everywhere celebrate the awesome power of their society.

No wonder people around the world transform everyday objects into sacred symbols of their collective life. Members of technologically simple societies do this with a **totem**, *an object in the natural world collectively defined as sacred*. The totem—perhaps an animal or an elaborate work of art—becomes the centrepiece of ritual and symbolizes the power of collective life over the individual. In our society, the flag is a quasi-religious totem that is not to be used in a profane way (say, as clothing) or allowed to touch the ground.

Durkheim identified three major functions of religion that contribute to the operation of society:

1 **Social cohesion.** Religion unites people through shared symbolism, values, and norms. Religious thought and ritual establish rules of fair play, organizing our social life.

2 **Social control.** Society uses religious ideas to promote conformity. By defining God as a "judge," many religions encourage people to obey cultural norms. Religion can also be used to back up political systems. In medieval Europe, for example, monarchs claimed to rule by "divine right." Even today, our

leaders publicly ask for God's blessing, implying that their efforts are right and just.

3 **Providing meaning and purpose.** Religious belief offers the comforting sense that our lives serve some greater purpose. Strengthened by such beliefs, people are less likely to despair in the face of change or even tragedy. For this reason, we mark major life transitions—including birth, marriage, and death—with religious observances.

○ **CRITICAL REVIEW** In Durkheim's structural-functional analysis, religion represents the collective life that helps hold society together. The major weakness of this approach is that it downplays religion's dysfunctions, especially the fact that strongly held beliefs can generate social conflict. Terrorists have claimed that God supports their actions, and nations march to war under the banner of their God. Looking around the world, few people would deny that religious beliefs have provoked more violence in the world than differences of social class.

○ **CHECK YOUR LEARNING** What are Durkheim's three functions of religion for society?

Constructing the Sacred: Symbolic-Interaction Analysis

From a symbolic-interaction point of view, religion (like all of society) is socially constructed (although perhaps with divine inspiration). Through various rituals—from daily prayer to annual events such as Easter, Passover, or Ramadan—people sharpen the distinction between the sacred and the profane. Furthermore, says Peter Berger (1967:35–36), placing our small, brief lives within some "cosmic frame of reference" gives us the appearance of "ultimate security and permanence."

Marriage is a good example. If two people look on marriage as a simple contract, they can walk away whenever they want. Their bond makes much stronger claims on them when it is defined as holy matrimony, which is surely one reason for the lower divorce rate among people with strong religious beliefs. More generally, whenever humans face uncertainty or life-threatening situations—such as illness, natural disaster, terrorist attack, or war—we find comfort in our sacred symbols.

○ **CRITICAL REVIEW** Using the symbolic-interaction approach, religion gives everyday life sacred meaning. Berger adds that the sacred's ability to give meaning and stability to society depends on ignoring the fact that it is socially constructed. After all, how much strength could we gain from sacred beliefs if we saw them merely as strategies for coping with tragedy? Also, this micro-level view ignores religion's link to social inequality, to which we turn next.

○ **CHECK YOUR LEARNING** Following Berger's thinking, why would religious people have a low divorce rate?

Reverend Lois Mike, a mother of four children, was the first Inuit female priest in the 4 million square kilometres that make up the Anglican Church of Canada's Arctic Diocese.

Inequality and Religion: Social-Conflict Analysis

The social-conflict approach highlights religion's support of social inequality. Religion, proclaimed Karl Marx, serves elites by legitimizing the status quo and diverting people's attention from social inequities.

Today, the British monarch is the formal head of the Church of England, illustrating the close ties between religious and political elites. In practical terms, working for political change may mean opposing the church and, by implication, opposing God. Religion also encourages people to accept the social problems of this world while they look hopefully to a "better world to come." In a well-known statement, Marx dismissed religion as "the sigh of the oppressed creature, the sentiment of a heartless world, and the soul of soulless conditions. It is the opium of the people" (1964:27, orig. 1848).

Religion and social inequality are also linked through gender because virtually all of the world's major religions are patriarchal. For example, the Qur'an, the sacred text of Islam, gives men social dominance over women by defining gender roles: "Men are in charge of women. . . . Hence good women are obedient. . . . As for those whose rebelliousness you fear, admonish them, banish them from your bed, and scourge [punish] them" (Qur'an 4:34, quoted in Kaufman, 1976:163).

Christianity, the major religion in the Western Hemisphere, has also supported patriarchy throughout history. Although Christians revere Mary, the mother of Jesus, the New Testament contains the following passages:

> A man . . . is the image and glory of God; but woman is the glory of man. For man was not made from woman, but woman from man. Neither was man created for woman, but woman for man. (1 Corinthians 11:7–9)

> As in all the churches of the saints, the women should keep silence in the churches. For they are not permitted to speak, but should be subordinate, as even the law says. If there is anything they desire to know, let them ask their husbands at home. For it is shameful for a woman to speak in church. (1 Corinthians 14:33–35)

> Wives, be subject to your husbands, as to the Lord. For the husband is the head of the wife as Christ is the head of the church. . . . As the church is subject to Christ, so let wives also be subject in everything to their husbands. (Ephesians 5:22–24)

Judaism has also traditionally supported patriarchy. Male Orthodox Jews recite the following prayer each day:

> Blessed art thou, O Lord our God, King of the Universe, that I was not born a gentile.
> Blessed art thou, O Lord our God, King of the Universe, that I was not born a slave.
> Blessed art thou, O Lord our God, King of the Universe, that I was not born a woman.

Despite patriarchal traditions, most religions now have women in leadership roles, and many are introducing more gender-neutral language in hymnals and prayer books. Such changes involve not just organizational patterns but also conceptions of God. The theologian Mary Daly puts the matter bluntly: "If God is male, then male is God" (cited in Woodward, 1989:58).

CRITICAL REVIEW Social-conflict analysis emphasizes the power of religion to support social inequality. Yet religion also promotes change toward equality. For example, nineteenth-century religious groups in North America played an important role in the movement to abolish slavery. In the 1950s and 1960s, religious organizations and their leaders were at the core of the civil rights movement. In the 1960s and 1970s, many clergy actively opposed the Vietnam War, and today many support any number of progressive causes such as feminism, gay rights, and the rights of Aboriginal peoples.

The Applying Theory table summarizes the three theoretical approaches to understanding religion.

CHECK YOUR LEARNING How does religion help maintain class inequality and gender stratification?

liberation theology the combining of Christian principles with political activism, often Marxist in character

APPLYING THEORY

Religion

	Structural-Functional Approach	Symbolic-Interaction Approach	Social-Conflict Approach
What is the level of analysis?	Macro level	Micro level	Macro level
What is the importance of religion for society?	Religion performs vital tasks, including uniting people and controlling behaviour.	Religion strengthens marriage by giving it (and family life) sacred meaning.	Religion supports social inequality by claiming that the social order is just.
	Religion gives life meaning and purpose.	People often turn to sacred symbols for comfort when facing danger and uncertainty.	Religion turns attention from problems in this world to a "better world to come."

Religion and Social Change

Religion can be the conservative force portrayed by Karl Marx. But at some points in history, as Max Weber (1958, orig. 1904–1905) explained, religion has promoted dramatic social change.

Max Weber: Protestantism and Capitalism

Weber believed that particular religious ideas set into motion a wave of change that brought about the industrialization of Western Europe. The rise of industrial capitalism was encouraged by Calvinism, a movement within the Protestant Reformation.

Central to the religious thought of John Calvin (1509–1564) is the doctrine of *predestination*: An all-knowing, all-powerful God has selected some people for salvation while condemning most to eternal damnation. Each person's fate, sealed before birth and known only to God, is either eternal glory or endless hellfire.

Driven by anxiety over their fate, Calvinists understandably looked for signs of God's favour in this world and came to see prosperity as a sign of divine blessing. Religious conviction and a rigid devotion to duty thus led Calvinists to work hard, and many amassed great wealth. But money was not for selfish spending or even for sharing with the poor, whose plight they saw as a mark of God's rejection. As agents for God's work on Earth, Calvinists believed that they could best fulfill their "calling" by reinvesting profits and achieving ever-greater success in the process.

All the while, the Calvinists lived thrifty lives and embraced technological advances, thereby laying the groundwork for the rise of industrial capitalism. In time, the religious fervour that motivated early Calvinists weakened, resulting in a profane "Protestant work ethic." To Max Weber, industrial capitalism itself was a "disenchanted" religion, further showing the power of religion to change the shape of society.

Liberation Theology

Historically, Christianity has reached out to suffering and oppressed people, urging all to strengthen their faith in a better life to come. In recent decades, however, some church leaders and theologians have taken a decidedly political approach and endorsed **liberation theology**, *the combining of Christian principles with political activism, often Marxist in character.*

This social movement started in the late 1960s in Latin America's Roman Catholic Church. Today, Christian activists continue to help people in poor nations liberate themselves from abysmal poverty. Their message is simple: Social oppression runs counter to Christian morality, so as a matter of faith and justice, Christians must promote greater social equality.

Pope Benedict XVI, like Pope John Paul II before him, condemns liberation theology for distorting church doctrine with left-wing politics. Nevertheless, the liberation theology movement has gained strength in the poorest countries of Latin America, where

church a religious organization that is well integrated into the larger society

state church a church formally linked to the state

denomination a church, independent of the state, that recognizes religious pluralism

sect a religious organization that stands apart from the larger society

Patriarchy is found in all of the world's major religions, including Christianity, Judaism, and Islam. Male dominance can be seen in restrictions that limit religious leadership to men and also in regulations that prohibit women from worshipping along with men.

many people's Christian faith drives them to improve conditions for the world's poor (Neuhouser, 1989; J.E. Williams, 2002).

Types of Religious Organizations

Sociologists categorize the hundreds of different religious organizations in Canada along a continuum with *churches* at one end and *sects* at the other. We can describe any religious organization in relation to these two ideal types by placing it on the church-sect continuum.

Church

Drawing on the ideas of his teacher Max Weber, Ernst Troeltsch (1931) defined a **church** as *a religious organization that is well integrated into the larger society.* Churchlike organizations typically persist for centuries and include generations of the same families. Churches have well-established rules and regulations and expect leaders to be formally trained and ordained.

Though concerned with the sacred, a church accepts the ways of the profane world. Church members conceive of God in intellectual terms (say, as a force for good) and favour abstract moral standards ("Do unto others as you would have them do unto you"). By teaching morality in safely abstract terms, church leaders avoid social controversy. For example, many churches celebrate the unity of all peoples but say little about their own lack of social diversity.

By downplaying this type of conflict, a church makes peace with the status quo (Troeltsch, 1931).

A church may operate with or apart from the state. A **state church** is *a church formally linked to the state.* For centuries, Roman Catholicism was the official religion of the Roman Empire, and Confucianism was the official religion in China until the early twentieth century. Today, the Anglican church is the official church of England, and Islam is the official religion of Pakistan and Iran. State churches count everyone in a society as a member, which sharply limits tolerance of religious differences.

A **denomination** is *a church, independent of the state, that recognizes religious pluralism.* Denominations exist in nations, including Canada, that formally separate church and state. Our country has dozens of Christian denominations, including Catholics, Baptists, Episcopalians, Methodists, and Lutherans, as well as various branches of Judaism, Islam, and other traditions. Although members of a denomination hold to their own beliefs, they recognize the right of others to have different beliefs.

Sect

Unlike a church, which tries to fit into the larger society, a **sect** is *a religious organization that stands apart from the larger society.* Sect members have rigid religious convictions and deny the beliefs of others. In extreme cases, members of a sect may withdraw completely from society to practise their faith without interference. The Amish and Hutterite communities of Canada have long isolated themselves from modern life. Because North American culture generally considers religious tolerance a virtue, members of sects are sometimes accused of being narrow-minded in insisting that they alone follow the true religion (Kraybill, 1994; P.W. Williams, 2002).

In organizational terms, sects are less formal than churches. Sect members may be highly spontaneous and emotional in worship, compared to members of churches, who tend to listen passively to their leaders. Sects also reject the intellectualized religion of churches, stressing instead the personal experience of divine power. Rodney Stark (1985:314) contrasts a church's vision of a distant God ("Our Father, who art in Heaven") with a sect's more immediate God ("Lord, bless this poor sinner kneeling before you now").

Churches and sects also have different patterns of leadership. The more churchlike an organization, the more likely that its leaders are formally trained and ordained. Sectlike organizations, which celebrate the personal presence of God, expect their leaders to show divine inspiration in the form of **charisma** (from Greek, meaning "divine favour"), *extraordinary personal qualities that can infuse people with emotion and turn them into followers.*

Sects generally form as breakaway groups from established religious organizations (Stark & Bainbridge, 1979). Their psychic

charisma (p. 361) extraordinary personal qualities that can infuse people with emotion and turn them into followers

cult a religious organization that is largely outside a society's cultural traditions

intensity and informal structure make them less stable than churches, and many sects form only to disappear soon after. The sects that do endure typically become more like churches, with declining emphasis on charismatic leadership as they become more bureaucratic.

To sustain their membership, many sects actively recruit (*proselytize*) new members. Sects value highly the experience of *conversion*, or religious rebirth. For example, Jehovah's Witnesses go door to door to share their faith with others in the hope of attracting new members.

Finally, churches and sects differ in their social composition. Because they are more closely tied to the world, well-established churches tend to include people of high social standing. Sects attract more disadvantaged people. A sect's openness to new members and promise of salvation and personal fulfillment appeal to people who feel they are social outsiders.

Cult

A **cult** is *a religious organization that is largely outside a society's cultural traditions*. Most sects spin off from a conventional religious organization. However, a cult typically forms around a highly charismatic leader who offers a compelling message of a new and very different way of life. Researchers have counted as many as 5000 cults in the United States and an unknown number in Canada (Marquand & Wood, 1997).

Because some cult principles or practices are unconventional, many people view cults as deviant or even evil. The suicides of 39 members of California's Heaven's Gate cult in 1997—people who claimed that dying was the doorway to a higher existence, perhaps in the company of aliens from outer space—confirmed the negative image the public holds of many cults. Also in 1997, the charred bodies of five people were found inside a house in Saint Casimir, Quebec. The three women and two men were members of the Solar Temple, an international cult professing the belief that such ritualized suicides lead to rebirth on a planet known as "Sirius." In short, say some scholars, calling a religious community a "cult" amounts to dismissing its members as crazy (Gleick, 1997; Shupe, 1995).

This charge is unfair because there is nothing basically wrong with this kind of religious organization. Many religions—Christianity, Islam, and Judaism included—began as cults. Of course, few cults exist for very long. One reason is that they are even more at odds with the larger society than sects. Many cults demand that members not only accept their teaching but also adopt a radically new lifestyle. This is why people sometimes accuse cults of brainwashing their members, although research suggests that most people who join cults suffer no psychological harm (Kilbourne, 1983; P.W. Williams, 2002).

Animism is widespread in traditional societies, whose members live respectfully within the natural world on which they depend for their survival. Animists see a divine presence not just in themselves but in everything around them. Their example has inspired "New Age" spirituality, described on pages 365–66.

Religion in History

Like family, religion is a part of every known society. Also like family, religion shows marked variation over time and from place to place.

Early hunters and gatherers embraced **animism** (from the Latin, meaning "breath of life"), *the belief that elements of the natural world are conscious life forms that affect humanity*. Animists view forests, oceans, mountains, and the wind as spiritual forces. Many

animism the belief that elements of the natural world are conscious life forms that affect humanity

religiosity the importance of religion in a person's life

Native American societies are animistic, which accounts for their reverence for the natural environment.

Belief in a single divine power responsible for creating the world arose with pastoral and horticultural societies, which first appeared 10 000 to 12 000 years ago. The conception of God as a "shepherd" arose because Judaism, Christianity, and Islam all had their beginnings among pastoral peoples.

Religion becomes more important in agrarian societies. The central role of religion in social life is seen in the huge cathedrals that dominated the towns of medieval Europe.

The Industrial Revolution introduced the growing importance of science to everyday life. More and more, people looked to physicians and scientists for the knowledge and comfort they used to get from priests. However, religion persists in industrial societies because science is powerless to address issues of ultimate meaning in human life. In other words, *how* this world works is a matter for scientists, but *why* we and the rest of the universe exist is a question of faith.

Religion in Canada

Compared to other high-income nations, as Figure 13–4 suggests, Canada is a relatively religious country (Inglehart & Welzel, 2010). But measuring the strength of religion in our society turns out to be difficult, as the following section explains. Research shows that changes are under way but also confirms the ongoing role of religion in social life (Bibby, 1993, 2002; Bibby & Brinkeroff, 1994; Collins, 1982; Dawson, 1996; Greeley, 1989; Hadaway, Marler, & Chaves, 1993; Woodward, 1992).

Religious Commitment

Religiosity is *the importance of religion in a person's life.* According to the General Social Survey conducted in 2004, about 81 percent of Canadian adults identify with a particular religion.

As Table 13–1 shows, Protestants and Catholics are projected to remain the largest religious groups for the foreseeable future (Mata, 2010). At the national level, the largest religious group remains Catholic; 40 percent of Canadians identify with this religion and their membership has slightly increased over the decade. While Protestant denominations still comprised the second-largest major religious group in 2011, their numbers have declined along with their representation in the population from 35 percent in 1991 to 26 percent in 2011.

Most of the decline in Protestant denominations during the decade took place within the largest six denominations, such as the Anglican church and the United Church, with Baptists being the only group bucking this downward trend. The largest increases in religious affiliations occurred among faiths such as Islam,

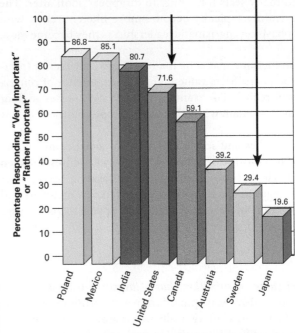

> In general, people in higher-income countries, including Canada, are less religious than those in lower-income nations. The U.S. population is an important exception to this pattern.

Global Snapshot

Survey Question: **"How important is religion in your life?"**

FIGURE 13–4   Religiosity in Global Perspective

Religion is stronger in the United States than in many other high-income nations. Canada holds a middling position. Sweden and Japan are comparatively unreligious.

Source: World Values Survey (2010).

Hinduism, Sikhism, and Buddhism, reflecting the increasing numbers of immigrants from regions outside of Europe, in particular Asia and the Middle East.

By global standards, people in Canada and the United States are relatively religious; more so, for example, than Australians, Norwegians, Swedes and Japanese. Just how religious we are, however, depends on precisely how one operationalizes this concept. Almost 20 percent of Canadians in 2004 reported "no religion," a substantial increase from 1985, when the figure was 12 percent, and 1971, when a mere 1 percent reported not having any religion (Clark & Schellenberg, 2006).

Moreover, even among those reporting a religious affiliation, an increasing number of Canadians report that they have not attended any religious services in the previous year. In total, 43 percent of Canadian adults in 2004 reported either having no religious affiliation or having one but not attending religious service. Further, there is a notable regional pattern regarding people

TABLE 13–1 Religions in Canada, 2006 to 2031 (millions)

	Catholic	Protestant	Orthodox	Other Christian	Muslim	Jewish	Buddhist	Hindu	Sikh	Other Non-Christian	No Religion
2006	13.8	9.0	0.6	1.0	0.9	0.3	0.4	0.4	0.4	0.1	5.7
2011	14.2	9.0	0.6	1.2	1.2	0.4	0.4	0.5	0.5	0.1	6.3
2016	14.6	9.0	0.7	1.4	1.6	0.4	0.5	0.6	0.6	0.1	7.0
2021	14.9	9.0	0.8	1.6	2.0	0.4	0.5	0.8	0.7	0.2	7.6
2026	15.2	9.0	0.9	1.8	2.4	0.4	0.6	0.9	0.8	0.2	8.2
2031	15.4	9.0	1.0	1.9	2.9	0.4	0.6	1.0	0.9	0.2	8.8

Source: Mata (2010).

who report a religious affiliation and/or attend religious services regularly (Figure 13–5 on page 364). People from Quebec were the most likely to report religious affiliation, but also to report not attending religious services. People from British Columbia were most likely to not attend religious services over the time period, while residents of Atlantic Canada were least likely to not attend religious services (Clark & Schellenberg, 2006).

Keep in mind, too, that people probably claim to be more religious than they really are. One team of researchers, which recently tallied actual church attendance in Ashtabula County in northeast Ohio, concluded that twice as many people said they attended church on a given Sunday as really did so. Strong religious values in American society encouraged a "desirability" effect in the reporting of church attendance (Campbell & Curtis, 1994). In actuality, it is estimated that no more than 20 percent of the Canadian population actually attend worship services regularly, while another 58 percent attend at least once a year (Bibby, 2002). Finally, religiosity varies among denominations. In Canada, weekly attendance at religious services has declined significantly for both Catholics and Protestants since World War II, although in the past decade attendance has increased slightly among fundamentalist Protestant sects, a phenomenon that is much more pronounced in the United States.

Yet in his book *Restless Gods: The Renaissance of Religion in Canada* (2002), well-known sociologist of religion Reginald Bibby maintains that there is a significant rejuvenation of religion currently under way in Canada, both inside and outside the churches. Bibby notes that the vast majority of Canadians are continuing to look to religion for answers to the "the big questions" about the meaning of life, birth, suffering, and life after death, and a large number of them talk to and say that they have experienced God. Clearly, the question "How religious are we?" yields no easy answers.

Religion: Class, Ethnicity, and Visible Minority Status

Religious affiliation is related to a number of other factors. We shall consider three: social class, ethnicity, and visible minority status.

Social Class

Protestants of European background have traditionally occupied a privileged place in Canadian society, while Catholics—the majority from French backgrounds and residing in the poorer regions of the country, such as Quebec and the Atlantic provinces—have tended to be of more moderate social standing (Porter, 1965). Yet circumstances have changed recently: Quebec society has become more secularized, and the population has experienced increased upward mobility, while at the same time the increasing religious diversity of Canadian society has challenged the once-dominant Protestant majority.

Ethnicity

Throughout the world, religion is closely allied with ethnicity, largely because one religion may predominate in a single region or society. The Arab cultures of the Middle East, for example, are mostly Islamic; Hinduism is tightly fused with the culture of India. Christianity and Judaism diverge from this pattern; while these religions are primarily Western, followers live in nations around the world (Riis, 1998).

The link between religion and ethnicity also comes through in Canada. Our society encompasses Anglo-Saxon Protestants, Irish Catholics, Russian Jews, and Greek Orthodox. This fusion of nationality and religion derives from an influx of immigrants from countries with a single major religion. Still, nearly every Canadian ethnic group incorporates at least some religious diversity. People of English ancestry, for instance, may be Protestants, Roman Catholics, Jews, or affiliated with some other religion.

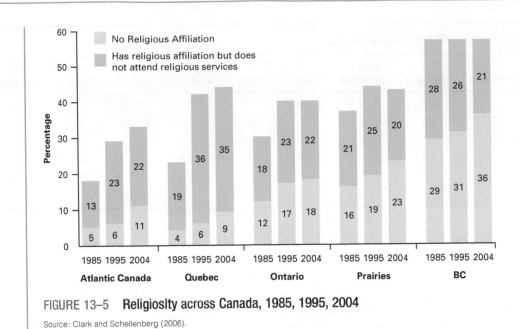

FIGURE 13–5 **Religiosity across Canada, 1985, 1995, 2004**

Source: Clark and Schellenberg (2006).

Visible Minority Status

Historically, the church has been central to the spiritual—and also political—lives of Blacks living in Canada and the United States. Transported to the Western Hemisphere, most people of African descent became Christians—the dominant religion in the Americas—but they blended Christian belief and practice with elements of African tribal religions. Guided by this multicultural religious heritage, many people of colour participate in religious rituals that are—by European standards—both spontaneous and emotional (Frazier, 1965; Roberts, 1980).

As Black people migrated from the rural South to the industrial cities of the North, and some as far afield as eastern Canada, the church played a key role in addressing problems of dislocation, poverty, and prejudice. Further, Black churches have provided an important avenue of achievement for talented men and women. Ralph Abernathy, Martin Luther King, Jr., and Jesse Jackson all gained world recognition as religious leaders.

Religiosity also varies by immigrant status. Compared with people born in Canada, immigrants who migrated to Canada between 1982 and 2001 have a high degree of religiosity (41 percent versus 26 percent). Immigrants coming from South Asia (e.g., India and Pakistan), Southeast Asia (e.g., the Philippines), and the Caribbean and Central and South America report the highest religiosity while the lowest level of religiosity is found among immigrants from East Asia (e.g., China and Japan) and Western, Northern, and Eastern Europe (Clark & Schellenberg, 2006).

Religion in a Changing Society

Like family life, religion is also changing in Canada. In the following sections, we look at two major aspects of change: changing affiliations over time and the process of secularization.

Changing Affiliation

A lot of change is going on in the world of religion. Membership in established, mainstream churches such as the Episcopalian and Presbyterian denominations has fallen dramatically. At the same time, other religious categories, from the New Age spiritual movement to conservative fundamentalist organizations, have increased in popularity.

Many people are moving from one religious organization to another. A recent survey in the United States by the Pew Forum on Religion and Public Life (2008b) reveals that 44 percent of adults report having switched religious affiliation at some point in their lives. The pattern of being born and raised with a religious affiliation one keeps throughout one's life is no longer the case.

Such personal changes mean that religious organizations experience a pattern of people coming and going. For some time, for example, Catholics have represented almost one-fourth of the American adult population. But this fairly stable statistic hides the fact that about one-third of all people raised Catholic have left

secularization the historical decline in the importance of the supernatural and the sacred

civil religion a quasi-religious loyalty linking individuals in a basically secular society

the church. At the same time, about the same number of people—including many immigrants—have joined this church. A more extreme example is the Jehovah's Witnesses: Two-thirds of the people raised in this church have left, but their numbers have been more than replaced by converts recruited by members who travel from door to door spreading their message.

Secularization

If people are less connected to the religious organization of their childhood, should we conclude that religion is getting weaker? Investigating this question brings us to the concept of **secularization**, *the historical decline in the importance of the supernatural and the sacred*. Secularization (from a Latin word for "worldly," meaning literally "of the present age") is commonly associated with modern, technologically advanced societies in which science is the major way of understanding.

Today, we are more likely to experience the transitions of birth, illness, and death in the presence of physicians (people with scientific knowledge) than church leaders (whose knowledge is based on faith). This shift alone suggests that religion's importance for our everyday lives has declined. Harvey Cox (1971:3, orig. 1965) explains:

> The world looks less and less to religious rules and rituals for its morality or its meanings. For some [people] religion provides a hobby, for others a mark of national or ethnic identification, for still others an aesthetic delight. For fewer and fewer does it provide an inclusive and commanding system of personal and cosmic values and explanations?

If Cox is right, should we expect religion to disappear someday? Most sociologists say no. More correctly, some dimensions of religion (such as belief in life after death) may have declined, but others (such as religious affiliation) have increased, especially for certain minority groups (Bibby, 2002). We should also be attentive to variation over time and differences across age groups. As Figure 13–5 shows, there has been an increase in the percentage of Canadians reporting no religious affiliation between 1985 and 2004. However, while between 1985 and 1995 religious non-attendance rates of Canadians expressing a religious affiliation increased across all age groups, in 2004 there was a slight decrease in non-attendance across all age groups apart from those over 60 years (Clark & Schellenberg, 2006).

Moreover, people are of two minds about whether secularization is good or bad. Conservatives see any weakening of religion as a mark of moral decline. Progressives view secularization as liberation from the all-encompassing beliefs of the past, so people can choose what to believe. Secularization has also brought many traditional religious practices (such as ordaining only men) into line with widespread social attitudes (such as that of gender equality).

New Age "seekers" are people in pursuit of spiritual growth, often using the age-old technique of meditation. The goal of this activity is to quiet the mind so that by moving away from everyday concerns, one can hear an inner, divine voice. Countless people attest to the spiritual value of meditation; it has also been linked to improved physical health.

According to the secularization thesis, religion should weaken in high-income nations as people enjoy higher living standards and greater security. A global perspective shows that this thesis holds for the nations of Western Europe, where most measures of religiosity have declined and are now low. In Canada, religious affiliation has declined somewhat and at the same time become increasingly diversified. In contrast, the United States, the richest country of all, is an exception; religion remains quite strong there.

Civil Religion

One dimension of secularization is what Robert Bellah (1975) calls **civil religion**, *a quasi-religious loyalty binding individuals in a basically secular society*. In other words, formal religion may lose power, but citizenship has its own religious qualities. Most people in the United States consider their way of life a force for moral good in the world. Some Canadians express similar sentiments. Many people also find religious qualities in political movements, whether liberal or conservative (Williams & Demerath, 1991).

Civil religion involves a range of rituals, from standing to sing the national anthem at sporting events to waving the flag at public parades. At all such events, the Canadian flag serves as a sacred symbol of our national identity, and we expect people to treat it with respect.

"New Age" Seekers: Spirituality without Formal Religion

December 29, Machu Picchu, Peru. We are ending the first day exploring this magnificent city built by the Inca people at the top of the Andes Mountains.

Lucas, a local shaman, or religious leader, is leading a group of 12 members of our tour group in a ceremony of thanks. He kneels on the dirt floor of the small stone building and reverently places offerings—corn and beans, sugar, plants of all colours, and even bits of gold and silver—in front of him as gifts to Mother Earth as he prays for harmony, joy, and the will to do good for one another. His words and the magic of the setting make the ceremony a very powerful experience.

In recent decades, an increasing number of people have sought spiritual development outside of established religious organizations. This trend has led some analysts to conclude that Canada is becoming a *post-denominational society.* In simple terms, more people seem to be spiritual seekers, believing in a vital spiritual dimension to human existence that they pursue more or less separately from any formal denomination.

What exactly is the difference between this "New Age" focus on spirituality and a traditional concern with religion? As one analysis puts it, spirituality is

the search for . . . a religion of the heart, not the head. It . . . downplays doctrine and dogma, and revels in direct experience of the divine— whether it's called the "holy spirit" or "divine consciousness" or "true self." It's practical and personal, more about stress reduction than salvation, more therapeutic than theological. It's about feeling good rather than being good. It's as much about the body as the soul. (Cimino & Lattin, 1999:62)

Millions of people across North America today take part in New Age spirituality. Hank Wesselman (2001:39–42), an anthropologist and spiritual teacher, identifies five core values that define this approach:

1. **Seekers believe in a higher power.** There exists a higher power, a vital force that is within all things and all people. Each of us, then, is partly divine, just as the divine spirit exists in the world around us.

2. **Seekers believe we're all connected.** Everything and everyone is interconnected as part the universal divine pattern that seekers call spirit.

3. **Seekers believe in a spirit world.** The physical world is not all there is; a more important spiritual reality (or "spirit world") also exists.

4. **Seekers want to experience the spirit world.** Spiritual development means gaining the ability to experience the spirit world. Many seekers come to understand that helpers and teachers who dwell in the spirit world can and do touch their lives.

5. **Seekers pursue transcendence.** Various techniques (such as yoga, meditation, and prayer) give people an increasing ability to rise

above the immediate physical world (the experience of "transcendence"), which seekers believe to be the larger purpose of life.

From a traditional point of view, this New Age concern with spirituality may seem more like psychology than religion. Perhaps it would be fair to say that New Age spirituality combines elements of rationality (an emphasis on individualism as well as tolerance and pluralism) with a spiritual focus (search for meaning beyond our everyday concerns). It is this combination that makes New Age seeking particularly popular in the modern world (Besecke, 2003, 2005; Tucker, 2002).

Religious Revival: "Good Old-Time Religion"

At the same time that New Age spirituality is flourishing, a great deal of change has been going on in the world of organized religion. Membership in established, mainstream churches has plummeted. The largest decline occurred among Presbyterians, whose numbers fell 36 percent in the 1990s. Pentecostals recorded the second-largest drop in membership, falling 15 percent across the decade. The number of United Church adherents declined 8 percent, Anglicans declined 7 percent, and Lutherans declined 5 percent. During the same period, affiliation with other religious organizations (including Evangelical Missionary Church, Hutterites, Adventists, and Christian and Missionary Alliance) has risen just as dramatically. Since the 1950s, weekly attendance at conservative evangelical churches in Canada has increased from 700 000 to 1.5 million (Bibby, 2002).

These opposing trends suggest that secularization itself may be self-limiting: As churchlike organizations become worldlier, many people leave them in favour of sectlike communities that offer a more intense religious experience (Hout, Greeley, & Wilde, 2001; Iannaccone, 1994; Jacquet & Jones, 1991; Roof & McKinney, 1987; Warner, 1993).

One striking religious trend today is the growth of **fundamentalism**, *a conservative religious doctrine that opposes intellectualism and worldly accommodation in favour of restoring traditional, otherworldly religion.* In the United States, fundamentalism has made the greatest gains among Protestants. Southern Baptists, for example, are the largest Protestant religious community in the United States. But fundamentalist groups have also grown among Roman Catholics, Jews, and Muslims.

Religious "fundamentalism" such as that of the Fundamentalist Church of Jesus Christ of Latter-day Saints has mainly emerged in parts of Alberta and British Columbia, reflecting the somewhat moralistic social values (for example, anti–gay rights, traditional gender roles) and conservative political views articulated more often in Alberta and B.C. than in other provinces. Yet the flavour of conservative Protestantism found there tends to be less evangelical and all-encompassing than the religious fundamentalism south of the Canadian border (Dawson, 1998).

In response to what they see as the growing influence of science and the weakening of the conventional family, religious fundamentalists defend what they call "traditional values." As they see it, liberal churches are simply too open to compromise and change. Religious fundamentalism is distinctive in five ways (Hunter, 1983, 1985, 1987):

1. **Fundamentalists take the words of sacred texts literally.** Fundamentalists insist on a literal reading of sacred texts such as the Bible to counter what they see as excessive intellectualism among more liberal religious organizations. For example, fundamentalist Christians believe that God created the world in seven days precisely as described in the biblical book of Genesis.

2. **Fundamentalists reject religious pluralism.** Fundamentalists believe that tolerance and relativism water down personal faith. Therefore, they maintain that their religious beliefs are true and other beliefs are not.

3. **Fundamentalists pursue the personal experience of God's presence.** In contrast to the worldliness and intellectualism of other religious organizations, fundamentalists encourage a return to "good old-time religion" and spiritual revival. Among fundamentalist Christians, being "born again" and having a personal relationship with Jesus Christ should be evident in a person's everyday life.

4. **Fundamentalists oppose "secular humanism."** Fundamentalists think accommodation to the changing world weakens religious faith. They reject "secular humanism," our society's tendency to look to scientific experts rather than God for guidance about how to live. There is nothing new in this tension between science and religion, as the Controversy & Debate box on page 368 explains.

5. **Many fundamentalists endorse conservative political goals.** Although fundamentalism tends to back away from worldly concerns, some fundamentalist leaders (including the Christian fundamentalists Jerry Falwell, Pat Robertson, and Gary Bauer) have entered politics to oppose the "liberal agenda," which includes feminism and gay rights. Fundamentalists oppose abortion, same-sex marriage, and liberal bias in the media; they support the traditional two-parent family, seek a return of prayer in schools, and criticize the mass media for approaching stories from a liberal viewpoint (Manza & Brooks, 1997; Rozell, Wilcox, & Green, 1998; Thomma, 1997).

Some people regard fundamentalism as judgmental, rigid, and self-righteous. But many believers find in fundamentalism, with its greater religious certainty and emphasis on experiencing God's presence, an appealing alternative to the more intellectual, tolerant, and worldly "mainstream" denominations (Marquand, 1997).

Which religious organizations are fundamentalist? In recent years, the world has become aware of an extreme form of fundamentalist Islam that supports violence directed against Western culture. In North America, the term is most commonly applied to conservative Christian organizations in the evangelical tradition, including Pentecostals, Southern Baptists, Seventh-Day Adventists, and the Assemblies of God. Several national religious movements, including Promise Keepers (a men's organization) and Chosen Women, have a fundamentalist orientation. In national surveys, 31 percent of American adults describe their religious upbringing as "fundamentalist," 41 percent claim a "moderate" religious upbringing, and 24 percent cite a "liberal" background (NORC, 2009:243). Canada differs from the United States in this regard, with just less than 3 percent of the population claiming membership in "other Christian" groups

In contrast to local congregations of years past, some religious organizations, especially fundamentalist ones, have become *electronic churches* dominated by "prime-time preachers" (Hadden & Swain, 1981). It has made James Dobson, Joel Osteen, Billy and Franklin Graham, Robert Schuller, and other "televangelists" more famous in the United States than all but a few clergy in the past. Perhaps 5 percent of the American television audience (about 10 million people) are regular viewers of religious television, and 20 percent (about 40 million) watch some religious programming every week (NORC, 2009:474). Again, the data from Canada show a different trend: Canadians appear to have much smaller appetites than do their southern neighbours for viewing evangelical services on television. One explanation is that aggressive marketing of religion by sectarian competitors is much more advanced in the United States than in other countries, including Canada and Britain (Bibby, 1987; Dawson, 1998).

Religion: Looking Ahead

The popularity of media ministries, the growth of religious fundamentalism, new forms of spirituality, and the connection of millions of people to mainstream churches show that religion will remain a major part of modern society for decades to come. High levels of immigration from South Asia, Southeast Asia, and the Caribbean and Central and South America should intensify as well as diversify the religious character of Canadian society in the twenty-first century (Clark and Schellenberg, 2006; Yang & Ebaugh, 2001).

The world is becoming more complex, and social change seems to move at a faster pace than our capacity to make sense of it all. But rather than weakening religion, this process fires the religious imagination. As new technology gives us the power to alter, sustain, and even create life, we face increasingly difficult moral questions. Against this backdrop of uncertainty, it is little wonder that many people look to their faith for guidance and hope.

Does Science Threaten Religion?

CIHAN: I think someday science will prove religion to be false.

RASHEED: I don't think science and religion are talking about the same thing at all.

About 400 years ago, the Italian physicist and astronomer Galileo (1564–1642) helped launch the Scientific Revolution with a series of startling discoveries. Dropping objects from the Leaning Tower of Pisa, he discovered some of the laws of gravity; making his own telescope, he observed the solar system and found that Earth orbited the sun, not the other way around.

For his trouble, Galileo was challenged by the Roman Catholic Church, which had preached for centuries that Earth stood motionless at the centre of the universe. Galileo only made matters worse by responding that religious leaders had no business talking about matters of science. Before long, he found his work banned and himself under house arrest.

As Galileo's treatment shows, right from the start, science has had an uneasy relationship with religion. In the nineteenth century, the two clashed again over the issue of creation. Charles Darwin's masterwork, *On the Origin of Species*, states that humanity evolved from lower forms of life over the course of a billion years—a theory that seems to fly in the face of the biblical account of creation found in Genesis, which states that "God created the heavens and the earth," introducing living things on the third day and, on the fifth and sixth days, animals, including human beings fashioned in God's own image.

But a middle ground is emerging, which acknowledges that the Bible is a book of truths *inspired* by God without being correct in a literal, scientific sense. That is, science and religion are two different ways of understanding that answer different questions. Both Galileo and Darwin devoted their lives to investigating *how* the natural world works. Yet only religion can address *why* we and the natural world exist in the first place.

The more scientists discover about the origins of the universe, the more overwhelming the entire process appears. Indeed, as one scientist recently noted, the mathematical odds that some cosmic "Big Bang" 12 billion years ago created the universe and led to the formation of life on Earth as we know it today are utterly infinitesimal—surely much smaller than the chance of one person winning a lottery for 20 weeks in a row. Doesn't such a scientific fact point to the operation of an intelligent and purposeful power underlying our creation? Can't one be both a scientific investigator and a religious believer?

In 1992, a Vatican commission concluded that the church's silencing of Galileo was wrong. Today, most scientific and religious leaders agree that science and religion represent important but different truths. Many also believe that in today's rush to scientific discovery, our world has never been more in need of the moral guidance provided by religion.

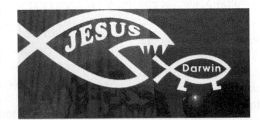

Today—almost four centuries after Galileo was silenced—many people still debate the apparently conflicting claims of science and religion. Almost one-third of American adults believe that the Bible is the literal word of God, and many of them reject any scientific findings that run counter to it (NORC, 2009:250). In 2005, all eight members of the school board in Dover, Pennsylvania, were voted out of office after they took a stand that many townspeople saw as weakening the teaching of evolution; at the same time, the Kansas state school board ordered the teaching of evolution to include its weaknesses and limitations from a religious point of view ("Much Ado about Evolution," 2005). In 2008, the province of Quebec made it mandatory for students in private, religious, and public schools to take the controversial "ERC" (Ethics, Religion and Culture) classes. The regulation has been challenged and the Supreme Court of Canada is currently hearing arguments over the mandatory teaching. A decision is pending.

WHAT DO YOU THINK?

1. Why do you think some scientific people reject religious accounts of human creation? Why do some religious people reject scientific accounts?

2. Do you think that the sociological study of religion should also include the study of science as a belief system? Why or why not?

3. Do you think that ethics in scientific research should be given priority in Canadian universities? Why or why not?

Sources: Gould (1981), Huchingson (1994), Applebome (1996), and Greeley (2008).

CHAPTER 13 FAMILY AND RELIGION

HOW RELIGIOUS IS OUR SOCIETY? Compared to other high-income nations, Canada holds a middling position regarding the level of religious belief and activity. We consider ourselves to be a modern, secular society, yet as this chapter explains, many Canadians claim a religious affiliation. Civil religion is also evident in many aspects of our everyday lives. Look at the photos below: Can you point to elements of civil religion in each of these familiar situations?

On Thanksgiving Day, many families across Canada gather to share a special dinner and give thanks for their good fortune. What religious or quasi-religious elements are part of a typical Thanksgiving celebration?

In recent decades, competitive sport competitions have emerged as important annual events. What elements of civil religion can you find in the Grey Cup and Stanley Cup finals?

HINT: As this chapter explains, civil religion is a quasi-religious loyalty linking members of a mostly secular society. Important events that qualify as civil religion are not formally religious but are typically defined as holidays (a word derived from "holy days"); involve gatherings of family, neighbours, and friends; and include ritual activities and the sharing of specific foods and beverages.

Applying Sociology in Everyday Life

1. Make a list of other events, activities, and pastimes that might be considered examples of civil religion. (Start off with election day; what about soccer and hockey?) Are there any local university or college events or rituals that might be included? In each case, explain the religious element that you see and the way the event or activity affects members of a community.

2. Is religion in Canada getting weaker? To evaluate the claim that our society is undergoing secularization, go to the library or local newspaper office and obtain an issue of your local newspaper published 50 years ago and, if possible, one published 100 years ago. Compare the amount of attention given to religious issues then and now. What pattern do you see?

3. Parents and grandparents can be a wonderful source of information about changes in marriage and family. Ask them at what ages they married, what their married lives have been like, and what changes in family life today stand out to them. Compare the answers of people of different generations—how are they different?

CHAPTER 13 Family and Religion

Family: Basic Concepts

All societies are built on kinship. The **FAMILY** varies across cultures and over time:

- In industrialized societies such as Canada, marriage is monogamous.
- Many pre-industrial societies permit polygamy, of which there are two types: polygyny and polyandry.
- In global perspective, patrilocality is most common, but industrial societies favour neolocality and a few societies have matrilocal residence.
- Industrial societies use bilateral descent; pre-industrial societies are either patrilineal or matrilineal.

pp. 338–41

Theoretical Analysis of Families

The **STRUCTURAL-FUNCTIONAL APPROACH** identifies major family functions: socialization of the young, regulation of sexual activity, social placement, and providing material and emotional support.

p. 341

The **SOCIAL-CONFLICT AND FEMINIST APPROACHES** explore how the family perpetuates social inequality by transmitting divisions based on class, ethnicity, race, and gender.

p. 342

The **SYMBOLIC-INTERACTION AND SOCIAL-EXCHANGE APPROACHES** highlight the variety of family life as experienced by various family members.

p. 342

See the Applying Theory table on page 343.

Stages of Family Life

COURTSHIP AND ROMANTIC LOVE

- Courtship based on romantic love is central to mate selection in Canada.
- Arranged marriages are common in pre-industrial societies.

pp. 342–44

CHILD REARING

- Family size has decreased over time as industrialization increases the costs of raising children.
- Fewer children are born as more women go to school and join the labour force.

pp. 344–45

THE FAMILY IN LATER LIFE

- Many middle-aged couples care for aging parents, and many older couples are active grandparents.
- The final transition in marriage begins with the death of a spouse.

p. 347

✓ Most spouses have similar social background with regard to class and race, but over the last century ethnicity has mattered less and less (pp. 347-49).

Transitions and Problems in Family Life

- Just less than 4 in 10 of today's marriages will end in **DIVORCE**. Remarriage creates blended families that include children from previous marriages.
- **FAMILY VIOLENCE** is a widespread problem. Most adults who abuse family members were themselves abused as children.

pp. 348–51

Alternative Family Forms

Family life is becoming more varied:

- One-parent families, cohabitation, gay and lesbian couples, and singlehood have become more common in recent years.

- Same-sex marriage are lawful in Canada but not in many other countries. Many gays and lesbians form long-lasting relationships and, increasingly, are becoming parents.

pp. 351–54

New Reproductive Technologies

- Although ethically controversial, new reproductive technologies are changing conventional ideas of parenthood.

pp. 354–55

Religion: Basic Concepts

- **RELIGION** is a major social institution based on setting the sacred apart from the profane.
- Religion is grounded in faith rather than scientific evidence, and people express their religious beliefs through various rituals.

pp. 356–57

family (p. 339) a social institution found in all societies that unites people in co-operative groups to care for one another, including any children

kinship (p. 339) a social bond based on common ancestry, marriage, or adoption

marriage (p. 339) a legal relationship, usually involving economic co-operation, sexual activity, and child-bearing

extended family (p. 339) a family composed of parents and children as well as other kin; also known as a *consanguine family*

nuclear family (p. 339) a family composed of one or two parents and their children; also known as a *conjugal family*

endogamy (p. 339) marriage between people of the same social category

exogamy (p. 339) marriage between people of different social categories

monogamy (p. 339) marriage that unites two partners

polygamy (p. 339) marriage that unites a person with two or more spouses

descent (p. 340) the system by which members of a society trace kinship over generations

incest taboo (p. 341) a norm forbidding sexual relations or marriage between certain relatives

homogamy (p. 343) marriage between people with the same social characteristics

family violence (p. 350) emotional, physical, or sexual abuse of one family member by another

cohabitation (p. 353) the sharing of a household by an unmarried couple

profane (p. 356) included as an ordinary element of everyday life

sacred (p. 356) set apart as extraordinary, inspiring awe and reverence

religion (p. 356 a social institution involving beliefs and practices based on recognizing the sacred

faith (p. 357) belief based on conviction rather than on scientific evidence

Theoretical Analysis of Religion

- The **STRUCTURAL-FUNCTIONAL APPROACH** suggests that religion unites people, promotes cohesion, and gives meaning and purpose to life; through religion, we celebrate the power of our society (Emile Durkheim).
- The **SYMBOLIC-INTERACTION APPROACH** explains that we socially construct religious beliefs; we are especially likely to seek religious meaning when faced with life's uncertainties and disruptions (Peter Berger).
- The **SOCIAL-CONFLICT APPROACH** claims that religion justifies the status quo. In this way, religion supports inequality and discourages change toward a more just and equal society (Karl Marx).

pp. 357–59

See the Applying Theory table on page 359.

Religion and Social Change

- Max Weber argued, in opposition to Marx, that religion can encourage social change. He showed how Calvinist beliefs promoted the rise of industrial capitalism.
- **LIBERATION THEOLOGY**, a fusion of Christian principles and political activism, tries to encourage social change.

p. 359

Types of Religious Organizations

- **CHURCHES** are religious organizations well integrated into their society. Churches fall into two categories: state churches and denominations.
- **SECTS** are the result of religious division and are marked by charismatic leadership and members' suspicion of the larger society.
- **CULTS** are religious organizations based on new and unconventional beliefs and practices.

pp. 361-62

Religion in Canada

Canada is a moderately religious society. How researchers operationalize "religiosity" affects how "religious" our people seem to be:

- 19 percent of Canadians reported "no religion" in 2004, a substantial increase from 1985, when the figure was 12 percent, and 1971, when a mere 1 percent reported not having any religion.
- 81 percent of adults reported belonging to a religion in 2004.
- 43 percent reported either having no religious affiliation or having one but not attending religious service.

pp. 362–63

Religious affiliation is tied to social class, ethnicity, and race:

- On average, Episcopalians, Presbyterians, and Jews enjoy high standing; lower social standing is typical of Baptists, Lutherans, and members of sects.
- Religion is often linked to ethnic background because many immigrants to Canada are from countries that have a major religion (e.g., most Irish are Catholic).

pp. 363–64

Religion in a Changing Society

- In Canada, while some indicators of religiosity (such as membership in mainstream churches) have declined, others (such as membership in sects) have increased.
- **SECULARIZATION** is a decline in the importance of the supernatural and the sacred.
- Today, **CIVIL RELIGION** takes the form of a quasi-religious patriotism that ties people to their society.
- Spiritual seekers are part of the "New Age" movement, which pursues spiritual development outside conventional religious organizations.
- **FUNDAMENTALISM** opposes religious accommodation to the world, interprets religious texts literally, and rejects religious diversity.

pp. 364–67

totem (p. 357) an object in the natural world collectively defined as sacred

liberation theology (p. 359) the combining of Christian principles with political activism, often Marxist in character

church (p. 360) a religious organization that is well integrated into the larger society

state church (p. 360) a church formally linked to the state

denomination (p. 360) a church, independent of the state, that recognizes religious pluralism

sect (p. 358) a religious organization that stands apart from the larger society

charisma (p. 361) extraordinary personal qualities that can infuse people with emotion and turn them into followers

cult (p. 360) a religious organization that is largely outside a society's cultural traditions

animism (p. 362) the belief that elements of the natural world are conscious life forms that affect humanity

religiosity (p. 362) the importance of religion in a person's life

secularization (p. 365) the historical decline in the importance of the supernatural and the sacred

civil religion (p. 365) a quasi-religious loyalty binding individuals in a basically secular society

fundamentalism (p. 366) a conservative religious doctrine that opposes intellectualism and worldly accommodation in favour of restoring traditional, otherworldly religion

MySocLab

Visit MySocLab at www.mysoclab.com to access a variety of online resources that will help you to prepare for tests and to apply your knowledge, including
- an eText
- videos
- self-grading quizzes
- glossary flashcards

14 Education, Health, and Medicine

- Why do people in low-income nations have little access to schooling and health care?

- How are schooling and health linked to social inequality in Canada?

- What changes in schooling and health have taken place in Canada in recent generations?

This chapter explains the operation of education and health care, two major social institutions that emerge in modern societies. The discussion offers both a global perspective and a focus on Canada.

When Lisa Addison was growing up, she always smiled when her teachers said she was smart and should go to college. "I liked hearing that," she recalls. "But I didn't know what to do about it. No one in my family had ever gone to college. I didn't know what courses to take in high school. I had no idea of how to apply to a college. How would I pay for it? What would it be like if I got there?"

Uncertain about her future, Addison found herself "kind of goofing off in school." After finishing high school, she took a job as a waitress and as a kitchen helper in a catering company. One day she realized that 15 years had gone by and her dream of going to college seemed further away than ever.

But at the age of 38, Addison made the decision to go back to school. It was hard to give up a steady paycheque. But she was looking for more: "I don't want to do this kind of work for the rest of my life. I *am* smart. I can do better. At this point, I am ready for college."

Addison took a giant step through the door of her local community college and, with the help of career counsellors, set her sights on an associate's degree in business. She is now almost finished with this two-year program, and she plans to transfer to a four-year university to complete a bachelor's degree. Then she hopes to go back into the food service industry—but this time as a manager at higher pay (Toppo & DeBarros, 2005).

Education is a social institution that has particular importance to people looking to advance their careers. This chapter explains *why* schooling is more important than ever for success in Canada today and also describes *who* benefits most from schooling. The second half of the chapter examines *health* and the social institution of *medicine*. Good health, like good schooling, is distributed unequally throughout our society's population. In addition, like education, the practice of medicine reveals striking differences from society to society.

Education: A Global Survey

Education is the *social institution through which society provides its members with important knowledge, including basic facts, job skills, and cultural norms and values.* Education takes many forms, from informal family discussions around the dinner table to lectures and labs at large universities. In high-income nations, education depends largely on **schooling**, *formal instruction under the direction of specially trained teachers.*

Schooling and Economic Development

The extent of schooling in any society is tied to its level of economic development. In low- and middle-income countries, which are home to most of the world's people, families and local communities teach young people important knowledge and skills. Formal schooling, especially learning that is not directly connected to survival, is available mainly to wealthy people who can afford to pursue personal enrichment. The word *school* is from a Greek root that means "leisure." In ancient Greece, famous teachers such as Plato, Socrates, and Aristotle taught aristocratic, upper-class men who had plenty of spare time. The same was true in ancient China, where the famous philosopher K'ung Fu-tzu (Confucius) shared his wisdom with just a privileged few.

> December 30, the Cuzco region, Peru. High in the Andes Mountains of Peru, families send their children to the local school. But "local" can mean 5 kilometres away or more, and there are no buses, so these children, almost all from poor families, walk an hour or more each way. Schooling is required by law, but in the rural highlands some parents prefer to keep their children at home where they can help with the farming and livestock.

Today, schooling in low-income countries reflects the national culture. In Iran, for example, schooling is closely tied to Islam. Similarly, schooling in Bangladesh (Asia), Zimbabwe (Africa), and Nicaragua (Latin America) has been shaped by the distinctive cultural traditions of these nations.

All low-income countries have one trait in common when it comes to schooling: There is not very much of it. In the poorest nations (including several in Central Africa), more than one-fourth of all children never get to school (World Bank, 2010); worldwide, one-third of all children never make it as far as the secondary grades. As a result, about one-sixth of the world's people cannot read or write.

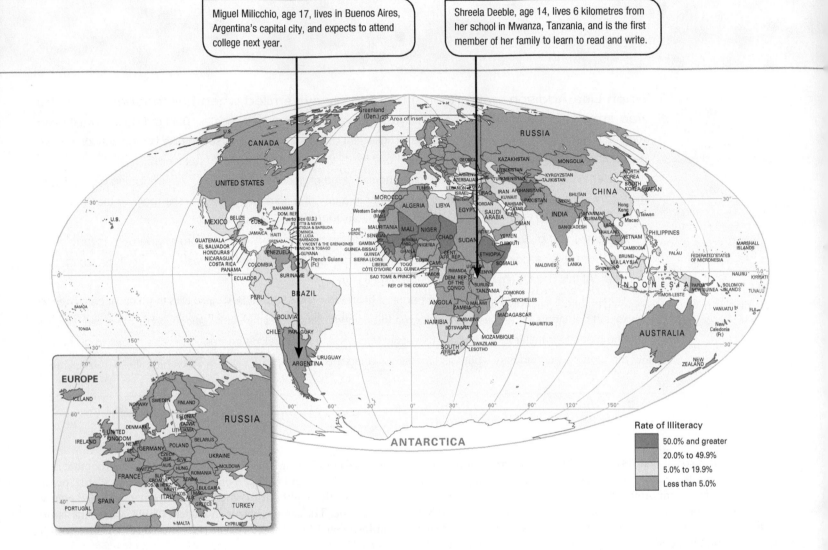

Miguel Milicchio, age 17, lives in Buenos Aires, Argentina's capital city, and expects to attend college next year.

Shreela Deeble, age 14, lives 6 kilometres from her school in Mwanza, Tanzania, and is the first member of her family to learn to read and write.

Rate of Illiteracy

- 50.0% and greater
- 20.0% to 49.9%
- 5.0% to 19.9%
- Less than 5.0%

Window on the World

GLOBAL MAP 14–1   Illiteracy in Global Perspective

Reading and writing skills are widespread in high-income countries, where illiteracy rates generally are below 5 percent. In much of Latin America, however, illiteracy is more common, one consequence of limited economic development. In 14 nations—most of them in Africa—illiteracy is the rule rather than the exception; there people rely on the oral tradition of face-to-face communication rather than the written word.

Source: World Bank (2011e).

Global Map 14–1 shows the extent of illiteracy around the world, and the national comparisons in the text illustrate the link between schooling and economic development.

Schooling in India

India has recently become a middle-income country, but people there still earn only about 6 percent of the average North American income, and most poor families depend on the earnings of children.

Even though India has outlawed child labour, many children continue to work in factories—weaving rugs or making handicrafts—up to 60 hours a week, which greatly limits their opportunities for schooling.

Today, 90 percent of children in India complete primary school, typically in crowded schoolrooms where one teacher may face as many as 60 children, twice as many as in the average Canadian public school classroom. Almost 60 percent go on to secondary

education (p. 373) the social institution through which society provides its members with important knowledge, including basic facts, job skills, and cultural norms and values

schooling (p. 373) formal instruction under the direction of specially trained teachers

education, and very few enter college or university. As a result, 34 percent of India's people are unable to read and write (UNESCO Institute of Statistics, 2009).

Patriarchy also shapes Indian education. Indian parents are joyful at the birth of a boy because he and his future wife will both contribute income to the family. But there are economic costs to raising a girl: Parents must provide a dowry (a gift of wealth to the groom's family) and, after her marriage, a daughter's work benefits her husband's family. Therefore, many Indians see less reason to invest in the schooling of girls, which is why only 52 percent of girls (compared to 61 percent of boys) reach the secondary grades. So what do the girls do while the boys are in school? Most of the children working in Indian factories are girls—a family's way of benefiting from their daughters while they can (UNESCO Institute of Statistics, 2009).

Schooling in Japan

September 30, Kobe, Japan. Compared to people in Canada, the Japanese are particularly orderly. Young boys and girls on their way to school stand out with their uniforms, their arms filled with books, and a look of seriousness and purpose on their faces.

Schooling has not always been part of the Japanese way of life. Before industrialization brought mandatory education in 1872, only a privileged few attended school. Today, Japan's educational system is widely praised for training some of the world's highest achievers.

The early grades concentrate on transmitting Japanese traditions, especially a sense of obligation to family. Starting in their early teens, students take a series of rigorous and highly competitive examinations. These written tests, which are like the Scholastic Assessment Tests (SATs) in the United States, decide the future of all Japanese students.

More men and women graduate from high school in Japan (97 percent) than in Canada (87 percent). But competitive examinations in Japan, among other factors, mean that fewer students complete a college or university degree when compared to many other high-income countries. In 2007, 25 percent of Canadians aged 25 to 64 had received a university degree or a university certificate above a bachelor's, surpassing 23 other OECD nations, including Japan. Norway led the way with 32 percent, followed by the United States (31 percent). Understandably, then, Japanese students take these examinations very seriously, and about half attend cram schools to prepare for them.

Japanese schooling produces impressive results. In a number of fields, notably mathematics and science, young Japanese students outperform students in most other high-income nations, including the United States but not Canada, Hong Kong, and Finland.

Schooling in the United States

The United States was among the first countries to set a goal of mass education. By 1850, about half of the young people between the ages of 5 and 19 were enrolled in school. By 1918, all states had passed *mandatory education laws* requiring children to attend school until the age of 16 or completion of grade 8. The country reached a milestone in the mid-1960s, when for the first time a majority of American adults had high school diplomas. In 2009, 86.7 percent of adults have high school educations, and 29.5 percent have a four-year college degree. The United States is ranked behind only Norway in terms of the share of adults who have earned a university degree (OECD, 2009).

Schooling in the United States also tries to promote *equal opportunity*. National surveys show that most people think that schooling is crucial to personal success, and a majority believe that everyone has the chance to get an education consistent with personal ability and talent (NORC, 2009). However, this opinion expresses cultural ideals rather than reality. A century ago, for example, women were all but excluded from higher education; even today, most people who attend college and university come from families with above-average incomes.

Schooling in Canada

As in the United States and Japan, the educational system in Canada has been shaped by past patriarchal traditions and cultural norms. The result is a mixture of public schools, elite private schools, and publicly funded Roman Catholic schools. At the same time, a strong belief in social equality in regard to literacy and basic schooling has prevailed—a tradition, in fact, that predates the emergence of the modern education system as we have come to know it (Harrigan, 1990). Yet throughout the twentieth century, educational participation was influenced by gender, geographic location, and social class. And to some extent, it can be argued that this remains the case even today.

Nevertheless, formal education for children of all social backgrounds has changed enormously since the mid-nineteenth century in our country. Prior to this time, education for most children— apart from those of the elite—was informal and unorganized (Prentice, 1977). Even by the turn of the twentieth century, school attendance remained sporadic, and most students—boys and girls in equal proportions—dropped out after grade 3 (Baldus & Kassam, 1996; Harrigan, 1990). This was especially true for rural children. Further, school teachers were often ill-trained and poorly paid, typically receiving lower wages than day labourers of the time. Prejudice restricted females from public teaching until the second half of the nineteenth century and, even thereafter, conditions were hardly equal between the sexes. For example, when Martha Hamm Lewis entered teachers' training school in the mid-nineteenth century in New Brunswick, her principal required that she "enter the classroom ten minutes before the male students, sit alone at the back of the room, always wear a veil, leave the classroom five minutes before the end of the lesson and leave the building without speaking to any of the young men" (MacLellan, 1972:6, cited in Wilson, 1996:99).

The early public schools in Canada did not champion class equality despite proclaiming an egalitarian ideology. Rather, they served to reproduce the existing social class system and to teach its validity to students in order to minimize conflict between the social classes (Curtis, 1988:370–371). Likewise, the early school books of Upper Canada (later to be called Ontario) were "infused with a hefty dose of class interest" (Baldus & Kassam, 1996:328), with their authors aiming mainly to curtail insubordination stemming from the "lower orders."

As the twentieth century unfolded, women came to dominate the teaching profession, the quality of instruction greatly improved, and national legislation was passed requiring that children of both sexes across Canada remain in school until at least their mid-teens. Increasingly, most groups embraced publicly funded education as a minimum requirement for future success in a modern industrial society.

Today, about 5.1 million students were enrolled in publicly funded elementary and secondary schools in Canada during the academic year 2007–2008, a slight drop from the previous year (Statistics Canada, 2011al). Many students continue their educations. Enrolment in Canadian universities for 2008–2009 was 1.1 million students, and in colleges it was 605 300; Canada has approximately 95 public and private not-for-profit universities and university degree–level colleges and 80 community colleges (Statistics Canada, 2010g). Table 14–1 shows that Canadians have made great strides in educational attainment, accelerating the trend that has slowly emerged over the last century or so. The increase for females is particularly impressive, as noted in Chapter 8 ("Social Stratification"). According to the 2006 census, 60 percent of Canadians aged 25 to 64 have acquired a post-secondary education certificate, diploma, or degree. Among 45- to 54-year-olds, women make up only 44 percent of those who have graduated from a university. Among 25- to 34-year-olds, however, women make up 58 percent of all those who have graduated (Statistics Canada, 2008g).

In 2005–2006, Canadian provincial and federal governments spent an estimated $76 billion on education—16 percent of total public expenditures—making it the second-largest item of public expenditure after health. This was 6.1 percent of the gross domestic product (GDP) spent on education, which is more than the average of 5.7 percent for OECD countries. In 2006, Canada and the United States allocated the largest share of their education budgets to higher education (OECD, 2010a). Canada also compares well internationally in regard to educational attainment. Our percentage of adults with post-secondary education is among the highest in the world. In 2008, Canada had the highest proportion of post-secondary graduates (49 percent) in the 25 to 64 age group among member OECD countries (OECD, 2010a).

TABLE 14–1 Educational Achievement in Canada, Men and Women Aged 25 to 34, 2006

	Men	Women
Less than high school	12.7%	9.2%
High school certificate	25.0%	20.2%
Apprenticeship or trade	13.0%	8.0%
College or university certificate, diploma, or degree	49.3%	62.7%

Source : Statistics Canada (2011am).

The Functions of Schooling

Structural-functional analysis focuses on ways in which schooling supports the operation and stability of society:

1. **Socialization.** Technologically simple societies look to families to transmit a way of life from one generation to the next. As societies gain complex technology, they turn to trained teachers to pass on specialized knowledge that adults will need for their future jobs.

2. **Cultural innovation.** Faculty at colleges and universities invent culture as well as pass it along to students. Especially at centres of higher education, scholars conduct research that leads to discoveries and changes our way of life.

3. **Social integration.** Schools mould a diverse population into one society sharing norms and values. This is one reason why provinces enacted mandatory education laws a century ago when immigration became very high. In light of the ethnic diversity of many urban areas today, schooling continues to serve this purpose.

4. **Social placement.** Schools identify talent and match instruction to ability. Schooling increases meritocracy by rewarding talent and hard work regardless of social background and provides a path to upward social mobility.

5. **Latent functions.** Schooling serves several less widely recognized functions. It provides child care for the growing number of parents who work outside the home. In addition, it occupies thousands of young people in their twenties who would otherwise be competing for limited opportunities in the job market. High schools, colleges, and universities also bring together people of marriageable age. Finally, school networks can be a valuable career resource throughout life.

In many low-income nations, children are as likely to work as they are to attend school, and girls receive less schooling than boys. But the doors to schooling are now opening to more girls and women. These young women are studying nursing at Somalia University in downtown Mogadishu.

How good are you as a student? The answer is that you are as good as you and your teachers think you are. The television show *Glee* demonstrates how, with the help of an inspiring teacher, students can accomplish more than they expect.

○ **CRITICAL REVIEW** Structural-functional analysis stresses ways in which formal education supports the operation of a modern society. However, this approach overlooks the fact that the classroom behaviour of teachers and students can vary from one setting to another, a focus of the symbolic-interaction approach discussed next. In addition, structural-functional analysis says little about many problems of our educational system and how schooling helps reproduce the class structure in each generation, which is the focus of the social-conflict approach, covered in the final theoretical section on schooling.

○ **CHECK YOUR LEARNING** Identify five functions of schooling for the operation of society.

Schooling and Social Interaction

The basic idea of the symbolic-interaction approach is that people create the reality they experience in their day-to-day interactions. We use this approach to explain how stereotypes can shape what goes on in the classroom.

The Self-Fulfilling Prophecy

Chapter 4 ("Social Interaction in Everyday Life") presented the Thomas theorem, which states that situations people define as real become real in their consequences. Put another way, people who

expect others to act in certain ways often encourage that very behaviour. In doing so, people set up a *self-fulfilling prophecy*.

Jane Elliott, an elementary school teacher in the all-white community of Riceville, Iowa, carried out a simple experiment that showed how a self-fulfilling prophecy can take place in the classroom. In 1968, Elliott was teaching a grade 4 class when Martin Luther King, Jr. was murdered. Her students were puzzled and asked why a national hero had been brutally shot. Elliott responded by asking her white students what they thought about people of colour and was stunned to learn that they held many powerful negative stereotypes.

To show the class the harmful effects of such stereotypes, Elliott performed a classroom experiment. She found that almost all of the children in her class had either blue eyes or brown eyes. She told the class that children with brown eyes were smarter and worked harder than children with blue eyes. To be sure that everyone could easily tell which category a child fell into, a piece of brown or blue cloth was pinned to each student's collar.

Elliott recalls the effect of this "lesson" on the way students behaved: "It was just horrifying how quickly they became what I told them they were." Within half an hour, Elliott continued, a blue-eyed girl named Carol had changed from a "brilliant, carefree, excited

Sociological research has documented the fact that young people living in low-income communities suffer in school because of large class sizes, poor-quality teaching, and insufficient budgets for technology and other instructional materials. In countries such as Canada and the United States, where people believe that schools should give everyone a chance to develop talents and abilities, should such inequalities exist?

little girl to a frightened, timid, uncertain, almost-person." Not surprisingly, in the hours that followed, the brown-eyed students came to life, speaking up more and performing better than they had before. The prophecy had been fulfilled: Because the brown-eyed children thought they were superior, they became superior in their classroom performance; they also became "arrogant, ugly, and domineering" toward the blue-eyed children. For their part, the blue-eyed children began underperforming, becoming the inferior people they believed themselves to be.

At the end of the day, Elliott explained to the students what they had experienced. She applied the lesson to race, pointing out that if white children thought they were superior to Black children, they would expect to do better in school, just as many children of colour who live in the shadow of the same stereotypes would underperform in school. The children also realized that the society that teaches these stereotypes, as well as the hate that often accompanies them, encourages the kind of violence that ended the life of Martin Luther King, Jr. (Kral, 2000).

CRITICAL REVIEW The symbolic-interaction approach explains how we all build reality in our everyday interactions with others. When school officials define some students as "gifted," for example, we can expect teachers to treat them differently and expect the students themselves to behave differently as a result of having been labelled in this way. If students and teachers come to believe that one race is academically superior to another, the behaviour that follows may be a self-fulfilling prophecy.

One limitation of this approach is that people do not just make up such beliefs about superiority and inferiority. Rather,

these beliefs are built into a society's system of social inequality, which brings us to the social-conflict approach.

CHECK YOUR LEARNING How can the labels that schools place on some students affect the students' actual performance and the reactions of others?

Schooling and Social Inequality

Social-conflict analysis challenges the structural-functional idea that schooling develops everyone's talents and abilities. Instead, this approach emphasizes three ways in which schooling causes and perpetuates social inequality:

1. **Social control.** As Samuel Bowles and Herbert Gintis (1976) see it, the demand for public education in the late nineteenth century was based on capitalist factory owners' need for an obedient and disciplined workforce. Once in school, immigrants learned not only the English language but also the importance of following orders.

2. **Standardized testing.** Critics claim that the assessment tests widely used by schools reflect our society's dominant culture, placing minority students at a disadvantage. By defining majority students as smarter, standardized tests unfairly transform privilege into personal merit (Crouse & Trusheim, 1988; Putka, 1990). Scott McLean (1997) argues that even the very notion of an individual assessment measure, as well as our detailed statistical

system for recording students' academic performance, holds little meaning among Inuit in the Canadian Arctic.

3. **Tracking.** Despite controversy over standardized tests, many North American schools use them for **tracking**, *assigning students to different types of educational programs*, such as college preparatory classes, general education, and vocational and technical training. Tracking supposedly helps teachers meet each student's individual abilities and interests. However, the education critic Jonathan Kozol (1992) considers tracking one of the "savage inequalities" in the North American school system. Most students from privileged backgrounds get into higher tracks, where they receive the best the school can offer. Students from disadvantaged backgrounds end up in lower tracks, where teachers stress memorization and put little focus on creativity (Bowles & Gintis, 1976; Gamoran, 1992; Kilgore, 1991; Oakes, 1985). As a result of such criticisms, some Canadian schools have destreamed their educational programs in recent years. Yet a variety of groups have opposed destreaming—including school boards, teachers, and middle-class parents; the latter worry that, without different tracks, their university-bound children will not have the required skills to compete successfully at university.

Public and Private Education

Across Canada, virtually all elementary and secondary school students continue to attend public schools. In 1998–1999, only 297 798 students out of a total school population of 5 369 716 attended a private educational institution (Statistics Canada, 2001c). According to the Canadian Council on Learning (2006), the growth of private schooling has continued to rise slightly across the country.

When examined over time, private school enrolment in Canada shows a very gradual climb, from an all-time low in 1971 of only 2.41 percent to 4 percent of elementary and secondary students in 1981–1982. However, in the mid-1980s, private school enrolment dropped noticeably, owing in part to a decision by the Ontario government to publicly fund Catholic secondary education for students in grades 11, 12, and 13. Such students were subsequently excluded from private school student rolls. More recently, private school enrolment numbers have begun to climb slowly again—about 5.6 percent of elementary and secondary students were enrolled in private schools in 1999—reflecting some Canadian parents' growing dissatisfaction with the quality of public school education for their children (Maxwell & Maxwell, 1995; Statistics Canada, 2003d).

Two earlier Angus Reid polls attempted to capture Canadians' views on Canadian schools. These polls found, among other things, that 39 percent of respondents would seriously consider sending their child to a private school with an annual tuition fee of $5000 per student (Angus Reid, 1996a) and that more than 60 percent thought students in private schools "receive much better education

than public school students" (Angus Reid, 1999b). When it comes to using taxpayer money to fund *religious* private schools, however, Canadians are more divided. A 2009 Angus Reid poll showed that 51 percent of Canadians are against funding private Christian schools. The level of opposition to taxpayer funding is much higher (68 to 75 percent) for other religions (Geddes, 2009).

The Canadian Association of Independent Schools (CAIS) is an association for elite private schools across the country. Its membership comprises 74 "independent" (non-public) schools that enrol about 35 000 private school students (a little more than 10 percent of the total private school enrolment). According to Mary Percival Maxwell and James Maxwell (1995:335), "[d]espite their small numbers these schools have played a crucial role in the social reproduction of the upper classes . . . [and] their graduates are disproportionately represented in the various institutional elites."

More than half of CAIS private schools were established prior to 1920; 22 of them were founded in the nineteenth century. The original-member CAIS schools were not only exclusive along class lines; most were open only to a single sex, a policy that was reinforced by the sponsoring religious denomination. Before World War I, upper-class Canadian families were likely to send both their daughters and sons to board at elite private schools. Worsening economic circumstances in subsequent decades meant that many could no longer afford private educations for both daughters and sons. Instead, families tended to commit their reduced resources to their sons' private school educations and send their daughters to less expensive local schools. As a result, by 1993, there remained only 16 private girls' schools (Maxwell & Maxwell, 1995). Yet even the single-sex private schools for boys have been forced to change with the times. During the 1970s, declining enrolment forced many of them to go "co-ed." At the same time, the ethnic makeup of these schools has become more diverse, reflecting the more heterogeneous ethnic makeup of the upper and upper-middle classes in present-day Canadian society. Despite their changing student populations, Canada's elite private schools continue to prepare their students for leadership positions in the various elites of the larger society, which does not differ significantly from what sociologists have observed in earlier generations (Clement, 1975; Newman, 1975; Porter, 1965).

Public school financing does not differ very much across Canada, owing to the country's relative success in redistributing wealth through income tax (Oreopoulos, 2006). Nevertheless, Canadian data indicate that the provinces vary substantially in the number of years of education of the adult population. In 2001, in three Canadian provinces—Newfoundland and Labrador, Manitoba, and New Brunswick—and one territory—Nunavut—more than half of their working populations had completed only high school or less. The remainder of the provinces and territories had more than 50 percent of their working populations with some post-secondary education (Statistics Canada, 2003c).

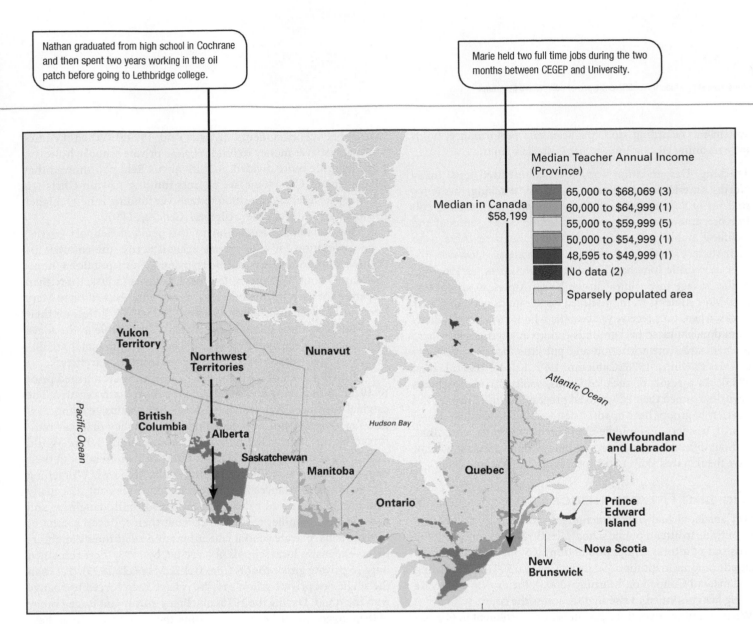

Nathan graduated from high school in Cochrane and then spent two years working in the oil patch before going to Lethbridge college.

Marie held two full time jobs during the two months between CEGEP and University.

Median Teacher Annual Income (Province)

Median in Canada $58,199

	65,000 to $68,069 (3)
	60,000 to $64,999 (1)
	55,000 to $59,999 (5)
	50,000 to $54,999 (1)
	48,595 to $49,999 (1)
	No data (2)
	Sparsely populated area

Seeing Ourselves

NATIONAL MAP 14–1   Teachers' Salaries across Canada

In 2005, the median employment income for high school teachers in Canada who worked full time for the whole year was $58 199. The map shows the median income for all provinces and one territory; incomes range from a high of $76 817 in Norfolk, Ontario, to a low of $43 491 in Rimouski, Quebec. Looking at the map, what pattern do you see? What do high-salary (and low-salary) regions have in common?

Source: Statistics Canada (2011an).

Even if schools were exactly the same everywhere, students whose families value and encourage learning would still perform better since success in school is correlated with parents encouraging reading at home, buying books or borrowing them from public libraries, and enrolling children in extracurricular activities (de Brouker & Lavalleé, 1998).

But even public schools are not all the same. Differences in funding between rich and poor communities result in unequal resources; this means that children in more affluent areas receive a better education than children in low-income communities. National Map 14–1 shows one key dimension of difference: Median teacher salaries vary by about $25 000 in regional comparisons.

At the local level, differences in school funding can be dramatic. Blanshard Elementary is in one of Victoria's poorest neighbourhoods, where 37 percent of families earn less than $30 000 per year, and the school looks the part, with large classes and a building in obvious need

THINKING ABOUT
DIVERSITY: RACE,
CLASS, & GENDER

Schooling in the United States: Savage Inequality

"Public School 261? Head down Jerome Avenue and look for the mortician's office." Off for a day studying the New York City schools, Jonathan Kozol parks his car and walks toward PS 261. Finding PS 261 is not easy because the school has no sign. In fact, the building is a former roller rink and doesn't look much like a school at all.

The principal explains that this is in a minority area of the North Bronx, so the population of PS 261 is 90 percent African-American and Hispanic. Officially, the school should serve 900 students, but it actually enrols 1300. The rules say class size should not exceed 32, but Kozol observes that it sometimes approaches 40. Because the school has just one small cafeteria, the children must eat in three shifts. After lunch, with no place to play, students squirm in their seats until they are told to return to their classrooms. Only one classroom in the entire school has a window to the world outside.

Toward the end of the day, Kozol remarks to a teacher about the overcrowding and the poor condition of the building. She sums up her thoughts: "I had an awful room last year. In the winter, it was 56 degrees. In the summer, it was up to 90." "Do the children ever comment on the building?" Kozol asks. "They don't say," she responds, "but they know. All these kids see TV. They know what suburban schools are like. Then they look around them at their school. They don't

comment on it, but you see it in their eyes. They understand."

Several months later, Kozol visits PS 24, in the affluent Riverdale section of New York City. This school is set back from the road, beyond a lawn planted with magnolia and dogwood trees, which are now in full bloom. On one side of the building is a playground for the youngest children; behind the school are playing fields for the older kids. Many people pay the high price of a house in Riverdale because the local schools have such an excellent reputation. There are 825 children here; most are white and a few are Asian, Hispanic, or African-American. The building is in good repair. It has a large library and even a planetarium. All of the classrooms have windows with bright curtains.

Entering one of the many classes for gifted students, Kozol asks the children what they are

doing today. A young girl answers confidently, "My name is Laurie, and we're doing problem solving." A tall, good-natured boy continues, "I'm David. One thing that we do is logical thinking. Some problems, we find, have more than one good answer." Kozol asks if such reasoning is innate or if it is something a child learns. Susan, whose smile reveals her braces, responds, "You know some things to start with when you enter school. But we learn some things that other children don't. We learn certain things that other children don't know because we're *taught* them."

WHAT DO YOU THINK?

1. Do you think such savage inequality in schooling exists in Canada? How about in the schooling situation of Aboriginal students living on our reserves?

2. Are there differences between schools in your city or town? Explain.

3. Why is there so little public concern about schooling inequality?

4. What changes would our society have to make to eliminate schooling inequality? Would you support such changes? Why or why not?

Source: Adapted from Kozol (1991:85–88, 92–96).

of repair. Uplands Elementary, by contrast, is found in one of Victoria's most affluent communities, where only 12 percent of families earn less than $30 000 per year. The teachers are keen and the facilities are state-of-the-art. The Thinking about Diversity box above shows the effects of funding differences in the everyday lives of students.

Because school funding is most often based on the collection of local property taxes, schools in more affluent areas will offer better schooling than schools in poor communities. This difference also benefits whites over visible minorities, which is why some districts started a policy of *bussing*, transporting students to achieve racial balance and equal opportunity in schools (Logan, Oakley, & Stowell, 2008).

Not everyone thinks that money is the key to good schooling. A classic report by a research team headed by James Coleman (1966) confirmed that schools in low-income communities and with mostly minority populations suffer problems ranging from large class size to

insufficient libraries and too few science labs. But the Coleman report cautioned that more money by itself will not magically improve schooling. More important are the co-operative efforts of teachers, parents, and the students themselves.

In other words, even if school funding were exactly the same everywhere (as in Alberta), students who benefit from more *cultural capital*—that is, those whose families value schooling, read to their children, and encourage the development of imagination—would still perform better. In short, we should not expect schools alone to overcome marked social inequality (Israel, Beaulieu, & Hartless, 2001; Schneider et al., 1998).

Further research confirms the difference that the home environment makes in a student's school performance. A research team studied the rate at which school-age children gain skills in reading and mathematics (Downey, von Hippel, & Broh, 2004). Because Canadian

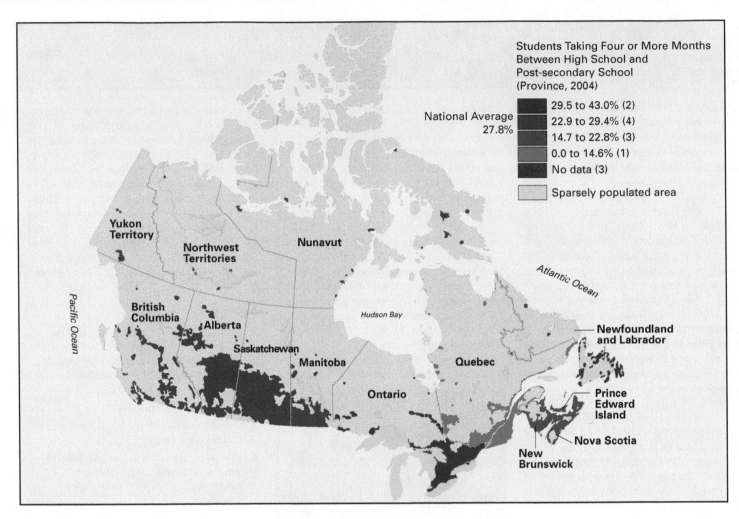

Seeing Ourselves

NATIONAL MAP 14–2   **Proportion of Students Following Various Pathways after High School, by Province, 2004**

Generally speaking, a gapper pathway is most common in Ontario and provinces west and less common in Quebec and provinces east. However, in Newfoundland and Labrador the pattern is the reverse. How would you explain this?

Source: Hango (2008).

Note: Data are based on those aged 22 to 24.

children go to school for six to seven hours a day, five days a week, and do not attend school during summer months, the researchers calculate that children spend only about 13 percent of their waking hours in school. During the school year, high-income children learn somewhat more quickly than low-income children, but the learning gap is far greater during the summer season when children are not in school. The researchers conclude that when it comes to student performance, schools matter, but the home and local environment matter more.

Put another way, schools close some of the learning gap that is created by differences in family resources, but they do not "level the playing field" between rich and poor children the way we like to think they do.

Access to Higher Education

Schooling is the main path to high-paying jobs, but 29.4 percent of young Canadians—known as "gappers"—delay their post-secondary studies for at least four months after graduating from high school

(Canadian Council on Learning, 2008). By age 20, two in ten high school graduates had not enrolled in a college, university, or trade school (Tomkowicz & Bushnik, 2003). National Map 14–2 shows the proportion of students following various pathways after high school, by province. Young people often take time off between high school and post-secondary education for pragmatic reasons, such as the desire to have a break from school or to travel. However, the most important reason is the need to save up enough money to pay for their post-secondary studies. Aboriginal youth, Anglophones, youth from Ontario, and youth whose parents have lower levels of education take the longest time between completing high school and entering post-secondary education (Bozick & DeLuca, 2005; Hango, 2008). There are long-range consequences for taking time off before pursuing post-secondary education; once employed, gappers have higher incomes initially but non-gappers, once employed, catch up quickly and eventually make higher incomes (Canadian Council on Learning, 2008).

In short, while more young people in Canada are accessing higher education today than ever before, those from less privileged family backgrounds are not increasing their participation nearly to the extent that their more privileged friends are (Bouchard & Zhao, 2000; Lowe & Krahn, 2000; Statistics Canada, 2005b, 2008u). On average, undergraduate students in Canadian universities and colleges paid $5138 in tuition fees in 2010–2011 compared with $4942 a year earlier (Statistics Canada, 2010g). Government funding as a portion of overall institutional revenues has declined steadily for the past 20 years, forcing universities and colleges to look for additional funding from student tuition fees and, to a lesser extent, from the private sector. In 1986–1987, 81 percent of university operating revenue came from government funding and 16 percent came from student fees. By 2000–2001, government's share of university funding had decreased to 61 percent, whereas revenues from student fees had grown to 34 percent (Robertson, 2003). At the same time, however, post-secondary students have gained from increased public expenditure on scholarships and bursaries, including most recently the Millennium Scholarship Fund (MSF). However, while there was an increase in expenditure on scholarships and bursaries in the recent decades, federal government investment has now levelled out.

The amount owing by those who take out student loans is also increasing. Students from the graduating class of 1995 who received student loans owed on average $11 000 at graduation—a whopping 39 percent increase over the class of 1990 and 59 percent over the class of 1986 (Statistics Canada, 2003f). It is little wonder that the financial burdens of higher education discourage many young people from less privileged backgrounds from attending.

Over the past 25 years, educational attainment for Aboriginal people aged 20 to 25 has also generally improved. The fact remains, however, that Aboriginal people still lag behind other

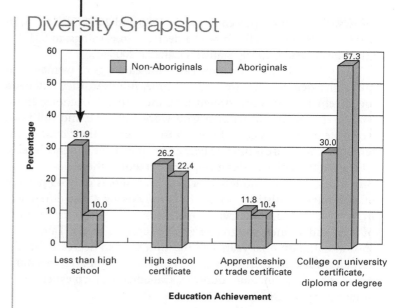

Almost a third of Aboriginal Canadians finish their formal education before completing high school.

Diversity Snapshot

FIGURE 14–1   **Aboriginals and Non-Aboriginals, Aged 25 to 34, by Education Achievement, Canada, 2006**

Source: Statistics Canada (2011ao).

Canadians in regard to post-secondary degrees or diplomas (see Figure 14–1). In 2006, 41 percent of the Aboriginal population had post-secondary certification but a mere 8 percent had attained a university degree (Statistics Canada, 2011al). On a more positive note, new immigrants to Canada actually attain more education than do their Canadian-born counterparts. This is partly explained by the higher educational levels of recent immigrants when compared with those of the Canadian-born population (Statistics Canada, 2011al).

For those who do complete post-secondary education, rewards include not just intellectual and personal growth but also increased opportunities for secure employment and higher income. This is especially the case for women. In 2010, almost three-quarters of women (71.4 percent) but only about two-thirds of men (64.5 percent) aged 25 to 44 had completed post-secondary education. This is in contrast to the group age 65 and over, in which only 32.7 percent of women and 42.6 percent of men had completed post-secondary education (Statistics Canada, 2011al). In 2010, women with university degrees who worked full time, full year earned $53 400, up from $48 260 in 2000 and up more than 10 percent since 1968. This was the largest increase in earnings across the educational groupings for both men and women. Earnings for women with some secondary school but who had not completed their high school education increased much more slowly—up 4.1 percent between 1980 and 2000 to $24 914. In 2003, this group actually showed a decrease in earnings, to $22 900 (Statistics Canada, 2003g; Statistics Canada, 2006au).

Despite this dramatic increase in the earnings of women with university degrees who worked full time, full year, they still get a lower return on this investment than men. In 2003, among 25- to 34-year-old men and women who work full time and full year, women earn only 78 cents for every $1 earned by their male counterparts. This figure is inflated because women have a higher level of education than men in this group—61 percent of these women have earned a certificate, diploma, or degree, whereas only 45 percent of men have (Statistics Canada, 2003h). Looking at the differences in income by education level, the differences between the earnings of men and women are greater at all education levels. Table 14–2 shows that additional years of education tend to decrease the discrepancy for Canadian women. Nevertheless, compared to a number of other high-income countries, Canadian women experience a large wage gap (OECD, 2010b).

Privilege and Personal Merit

If attending college or university is a rite of passage for rich men and women, as social-conflict analysis suggests, then *schooling transforms social privilege into personal merit.* But given our cultural emphasis on individualism, we tend to see credentials as badges of ability rather than as symbols of family affluence (Sennett & Cobb, 1973).

When we congratulate the new graduate, we rarely recognize the resources—in terms of both money and cultural capital—that made this achievement possible. Yet young people from families with annual incomes exceeding $200 000 average more than 375 points higher on the SAT exam than those whose families earn less than $20 000 a year (College Board, 2009). The richer students are thus more likely to get into college and university; once there, they are also more likely to complete their studies and get a degree. In a *credential society* such as ours, which evaluates people on the basis of their schooling, companies hire those with the best education. This process ends up helping people who are already advantaged and hurting those who are already disadvantaged (Collins, 1979).

○ **CRITICAL REVIEW** Social-conflict analysis links formal education to social inequality to show how schooling transforms privilege into personal worthiness and disadvantage into personal deficiency. However, the social-conflict approach overlooks the extent to which schooling provides upward mobility for talented women and men from all backgrounds. In addition, despite claims that schooling supports the status quo, today's college and university curricula challenge social inequality on many fronts.

○ **CHECK YOUR LEARNING** Explain several ways in which education is linked to social inequality.

TABLE 14–2 **Women's Earnings as a Percentage of Men's Earnings, Ages 35 to 44, by Education, Selected Countries**

	Below Upper Secondary Education	Upper Secondary and Post-Secondary Non-Tertiary Education	Tertiary Education	All Levels of Education
Australia	88	87	80	88
Luxembourg	85	76	73	79
Germany	69	86	76	79
Hungary	83	86	57	79
Sweden	94	77	72	78
Denmark	68	83	72	78
Greece	61	78	68	77
Finland	78	76	72	77
New Zealand	78	76	74	77
Italy	71	81	52	77
United Kingdom	82	69	77	76
Canada	68	70	76	75
Norway	74	72	68	74
Austria	71	76	73	73
Slovak Republic	71	72	61	68
Czech Republic	72	73	67	66
Korea	66	58	84	59

Note: Data are for 2008 or most recent available.

Source: OECD (2010a).

The Applying Theory table on page 386 sums up what the theoretical approaches show us about education.

Problems in the Schools

An intense debate revolves around schooling in Canada. Because we expect schools to do so much—to equalize opportunity, instill discipline, and fire the individual imagination—few people think that public schools are doing an excellent job; about two-thirds of Canadians think that high school graduates do not have strong reading and writing skills, and the same proportion do not think that our high schools do a good job of preparing students for today's workforce (Angus Reid Group, 1999b).

Discipline and Violence

When many of today's older teachers think back to their own student days, school "problems" consisted of talking out of turn, chewing gum, breaking the dress code, or cutting class. But today's schools are also grappling with drug and alcohol abuse, teenage pregnancy, and outright violence.

While Canadians are used to hearing about violence in the United States, our collective conscience was shocked by the 1999 fatal shooting at the W.R. Myers school in Taber, Alberta. Moreover, in a survey conducted just prior to the shooting, one-third of Canadian teenagers under 18 believed that violence had increased in their school over the last five years (Angus Reid Group, 1999a).

Student Passivity

If some schools are plagued by violence, many more are filled with students who are bored. Some of the blame for their passivity can be placed on the fact that electronic devices, from television to iPods, now claim far more of young people's time than school, parents, and community activities. But schools must share the blame because the educational system itself encourages student passivity (Coleman, Hoffer, & Kilgore, 1981).

These are Cree students attending the Lac la Ronge mission school in Saskatchewan. Several hundred thousand aboriginal students attended schools run by the Anglican church between 1820 and 1969. In 1993, the Archbishop Michael Peers issued a formal apology for the physical, sexual, cultural, and emotional abuse many of the aboriginal students suffered in these schools.

Bureaucracy

The small, personal schools that served local communities a century ago have evolved into huge education factories. Theodore Sizer (1984:207–09) identified five ways in which large, bureaucratic schools undermine education:

1. **Rigid uniformity.** Bureaucratic schools run by outside specialists (such as provincial education officials) generally ignore the cultural character of local communities and the personal needs of their children.

2. **Numerical ratings.** School officials define success in terms of numerical attendance rates and dropout rates, and teachers "teach to the tests," hoping to raise test scores. Overlooked in the process are dimensions of schooling that are difficult to quantify, such as creativity and enthusiasm.

3. **Rigid expectations.** Officials expect 15-year-olds to be in grade 10 and those in grade 11 to score at a certain level on a standardized verbal achievement test. Rarely are exceptionally bright and motivated students permitted to graduate early. Likewise, poor performers are pushed from grade to grade, doomed to fail year after year.

4. **Specialization.** High school students learn French from one teacher, receive guidance from another, and are coached in

sports by still others. Students shuffle between 50-minute periods throughout the school day. As a result, no school official comes to know the child well.

5. **Little individual responsibility.** Highly bureaucratic schools do not empower students to learn on their own. Similarly, teachers have little say in how they teach their classes; any change in the pace of learning or other deviation from the set curriculum risks disrupting the system.

Of course, with 5.1 million schoolchildren in Canada, schools have to be bureaucratic to get the job done. But Sizer recommends that we "humanize" schools by eliminating rigid scheduling, reducing class size, and training teachers more broadly to make them more involved in the lives of their students. Overall, as James Coleman (1993) has suggested, schools should be less "administratively driven" and more "output-driven." Perhaps this transformation could begin by ensuring that graduation from high school depends on what students have learned rather than on how many years they have spent in the building.

Higher Education: The Silent Classroom

Passivity is also common among college and university students (Gimenez, 1989). Sociologists rarely study the college or university classroom—a curious fact considering how much time they spend

Education

	Structural-Functional Approach	Symbolic-Interaction Approach	Social-Conflict Approach
What is the level of analysis?	Macro level	Macro level	Macro level
What is the importance of education for society?	Schooling performs many vital tasks for the operation of society, including socializing the young and encouraging discovery and invention to improve our lives. Schooling helps unite a diverse society by teaching shared norms and values.	How teachers define their students—as well as how students think of themselves—can become real to everyone and affect students' educational performance.	Schooling maintains social inequality through unequal schooling for rich and poor. Within individual schools, tracking provides privileged children with a better education than poor children.

there. One exception was a study of a co-educational university where David Karp and William Yoels (1976) found that, even in small classes, only a few students speak up. Thus passivity is a classroom norm, and students even become irritated if one among them is especially talkative.

According to Karp and Yoels, most students think that classroom passivity is their own fault. But as anyone who watches young people outside of class knows, they are usually active and vocal. It is clearly the schools that teach students to be passive and to view instructors as experts who serve up "knowledge" and "truth." Students see their proper role as quietly listening and taking notes. As a result, the researchers estimate, just 10 percent of college class time is used for discussion.

Faculty can bring students to life in their classrooms by making use of four teaching strategies: (1) calling on students by name when they volunteer, (2) positively reinforcing student participation, (3) asking analytical rather than factual questions and giving students time to answer, and (4) asking for student opinions even when no one volunteers a response (Auster & MacRone, 1994).

Dropping Out

If many students are passive in class, others are not there at all. The problem of *dropping out*—quitting before earning a high school diploma—leaves young people (many of whom are disadvantaged to begin with) unprepared for the world of work and at high risk of poverty.

There has been a notable reduction in the Canadian high school dropout rates in the last decade. Nevertheless, in 1999, 12 percent of 20-year-olds had not completed their secondary education and,

equally disturbing, the boys' rate was 1.5 times higher than that of girls. By 2009–2010, while the overall dropout rate had fallen to 8.5 percent, it was 10.3 percent for males but only 6.6 percent for females. Check out the Sociology in Everyday Life box on page 389 for further information about why males are less likely to be seen on university and college campuses.

Dropout rates for Aboriginal youth remain high (22.6 percent in 2009–2010). Immigrant and visible minority youth have comparatively low dropout rates (6.2 percent in 2009–2010) and also go on to attain more university education than Canadian-born youth. However, as noted in Chapter 11 ("Race and Ethnicity"), immigrant and visible minority youth get a lower return on education when trying to enter the labour market (Statistics Canada, 2010i).

Many of the problems students have during their high school years follow them to college and university. Those who had difficulty attending, passing, and attaining high grades in high school are much more likely to drop out of post-secondary school than their colleagues who did not have these difficulties in high school (Bowlby, 2005; Butlin, 2000; Canadian Council on Learning, 2006).

Academic Standards

In Canada, as in many other countries, fears have been growing about the standard of education. According to a Conference Board of Canada report in 2000, Canada's position as one of the strongest economic nations in the world is "at risk because of the high secondary-school dropout rate, as well as a short supply of skilled labour and high public debt (Conference Board of Canada, 2000). A more recent report stated

The Barriers Come Down: Distance Education Is the Way for Many

MACLEAN'S
December 15, 2008

In the current economic climate, continuing education is an imperative. Not only will the stimulation help to keep your mind active, but the new skills and credentials you acquire will make your resume shine in a competitive job market. Engagement as a life-long learner demonstrates a creative responsiveness to change, helping you to identify new opportunities and add value wherever you go.

Tamie Perryment did most of the work for her Bachelor of Arts degree between 11 p.m. and 2 a.m. from the comfort of her home sofa. The Edmonton-based woman's four children were aged 4 to 10 when she began her degree, and she also worked part-time as a teaching assistant.

The demands of family, work and school may sound exhausting, but Perryment loved it! "I'm an over-achiever who gets bored easily. School was stimulating and gave me something to work on that was just for me," she comments. Perryment graduated from Edmonton's Athabasca University with her BA in 1993 and in 2000 started a master's program in conflict analysis and management at Victoria-based Royal Roads University (RRU). The course work was mostly done online, with one month per year of in-class learning.

A big fan of online distance learning, Perryment says the experience was in no way isolating. The online discussions were mature, thoughtful and reflective, and the coaching (or teaching) was to a high standard, she says. "Overall, I found it a very positive way to learn."

Athabasca is part of a consortium of Canadian universities that have banded together under the rubric Canadian Virtual University (CVU). They offer a wide range of online and distance education degrees, diplomas and certificates in both French and English. With 12 participating universities from every region in Canada, students can choose from over 2,500 courses and 350 programs. Credits are awarded by the university that offers the course.

CVU's executive director, Vicky Busch, says the consortium offers many benefits to students, including the ability to mix and match courses for degree completion and one-stop access to a much wider array of courses than they would find at any single member school. "Some students even begin their degree online, and since the first two years of a program are generally transferable anywhere, may choose to complete the degree on campus at the university of their choosing."

Over 120,000 students took courses from CVU partner universities last year and there is consistent growth in both graduate and undergraduate enrolment and programs offered. New programs include a Doctor of Business Administration from Athabasca and a Bachelor of Arts in Police Studies from Memorial University in Newfoundland. Niche programs include a Certificate in Crime Prevention from Cape Breton University. Nursing programs are very popular, especially a Bachelor of Nursing degree for graduates of practical nursing programs, as is social work.

Maureen MacDonald is dean of continuing studies at the University of Victoria (not a CVU participant), which is active in online and distance learning, with over 2,000 registrations a year in its continuing studies distance education programs. "The job market continues to change and upgrading skills may help people remain more employable or adapt to the changing market. For example, distance education courses, certificates and diplomas are perfect for people with arts or science degrees who find themselves working in the business world. They may want to know more about business administration or technology but don't necessarily want or need a full degree in business. A certificate program, with job-related skills, can really enhance their value to their employer or enable them to move around within the job market."

Lyn Jakimchuk is a University of Victoria continuing education student. After completing a teaching degree and working as an elementary school teacher for four years, Jakimchuk realized that she wanted to explore other options. "I love learning and teaching but I wasn't in the right place for me. I didn't want to jump into a masters program and I was looking for an educational upgrade that would qualify me to teach in the adult learning sector."

The Certificate in Adult and Continuing Education was a perfect fit for Jakimchuk. "I like it because it is so flexible. I can take courses in the classroom or online and I have up to five years to complete it. I can continue working and meet my family responsibilities. The courses and workshops have enhanced my skills and abilities as an instructor in a deep and meaningful way, and I also enjoy the face-to-face and online networking with other students from across Canada and from many walks of life."

A different take on online learning will soon be available at Toronto's Seneca College. Seneca's Managed E-Lab offers a campus-based place for students engaged in government-sponsored re-training programs, such as Second Career, to work on online courses even though they may not have a computer, Internet access or a quiet place to study.

"The lab will be open from 9 a.m. to 8 p.m. and while students will have to physically attend, it gives them a lot of flexibility in terms of when they do so," says Susan Savoie, dean, Faculty of Continuing Education and Training. "We can support up to 10 students at any given time and staff will be available to help them get familiar with the technology. It's a great way to begin a second career and we have a lot of diploma and certificate programs available for them to choose from."

WHAT DO YOU THINK?

1. According to the article, what are some of the reasons for the recent increase in distance education?

2. What are the personal goals that are driving adults to register in online courses to obtain an additional degree? Have you taken online courses in high school or at the post-secondary level? If yes, what did you think about the experience?

3. What categories of people may decide to take a Sociology 101 class online? What categories of people would have difficulty doing this?

Source: *Maclean's Magazine*, December 15, 2008, p.41.
Courtesy of Paddy Kamen.

functional illiteracy a lack of the reading and writing skills needed for everyday living.

medicine the social institution that focuses on fighting disease and improving health

health a state of complete physical, mental, and social well-being

For all categories of people in Canada, dropping out of school greatly reduces the chances to get a good job and earn a secure income.

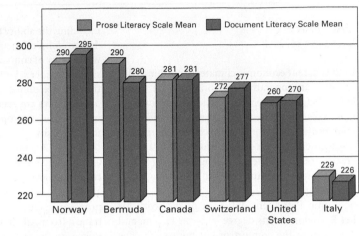

FIGURE 14–2 Adult Literacy and Life Skills Survey

Source: Adadpted from Statistics Canada and OECD (2005).

that, while our education system has improved to an "A" grade, with a ranking of second among 17 peer countries, and our graduation rate has significantly improved, we need to improve our graduate education and our adult literacy rate (Conference Board of Canada, 2011). Similar fears surround the extent of **functional illiteracy**, *a lack of the reading and writing skills needed for everyday living* (Coulombe, Tremblay, & Marchand, 2004).

Results from the 2003 Adult Literacy and Life Skills Survey (Statistics Canada and OECD, 2005) confirmed earlier 1994 findings: Many older Canadians have difficulty coping with the unfamiliar literacy and numeracy demands of employment and daily living. Depending on the country surveyed, 33 to 66 percent of adults did not attain the third of five skill levels, the minimum that educators consider needed to deal with our post-industrial knowledge society. As shown in Figure 14–2, Canadian adults compare well to adults in other nations on literacy performance measures.

Schooling: Looking Ahead

Despite the fact that Canada leads the world in sending people to post-secondary schools, and that our high school dropout rates have improved, the public school system still struggles with serious problems, including comparative lower success rates for males and Aboriginals, problems that have their roots in the larger society. Thus, during the next decades we cannot expect schools by themselves to provide high-quality education. Schools will only improve to the extent that students, teachers, parents, and local communities commit to educational excellence. In short, educational problems are social problems that extend across the life course, and there is no quick fix.

For much of the twentieth century, there were just two models for education in Canada: public schools run by the government and private schools operated by non-governmental organizations. In the last decade, however, many new ideas about schooling have come on the scene, including schooling for profit and a wide range of "choice" programs (Finn & Gau, 1998). In the decades ahead, we will likely see some significant changes in mass education guided, in part, by social science research pointing out the consequences of different strategies.

Another factor that will continue to shape schools is new information technology. Today almost all schools—and many daycare centres—use computers for instruction. Computers prompt students to be more active and allow them to progress at their own pace. Even so, computers have their limitations; they can never replace the personal insight or imagination of a motivated human teacher. Nor will technology solve the problems—including violence and rigid bureaucracy—that plague our schools. What we need is a broad plan for social change that re-ignites this country's early ambition to provide quality universal schooling to all—a goal that has so far eluded us.

Health and Medicine

Another institution that expands greatly in modern societies is **medicine**, *the social institution that focuses on fighting disease and improving health.* In ideal terms, according to the World Health Organization (1946:3), **health** is *a state of complete physical, mental, and social well-being.* This definition underscores the important fact that health is as much a social as a biological issue.

The Twenty-First-Century Campus: Where Are the Men?

MEG: I mean, where are the men on this campus? Seems like they're hard to find.

TRICIA: Does it matter? I'd rather focus on my work anyway.

MARK: But, hey, it's really cool for us guys!

A century or so ago, the campuses of colleges and universities across North America may as well have hung out a sign that read "Men Only." Almost all of the students and faculty were male. There were a small number of women's colleges, but many more schools—including some of the most prestigious universities, including University of Toronto, McGill, Yale, Harvard, and Princeton—barred women outright.

Since then, women have won greater social equality. By 1980, the number of women enrolled at North American universities and colleges finally matched the number of men.

In a surprising trend, however, the share of women on campus has continued to increase. As a result, in 2008, men accounted for only 42 percent of all Canadian undergraduates and 43 percent of all American undergraduates. Meg DeLong noticed the gender imbalance right away when she moved into her dorm at her new university; she soon learned that just 39 percent of her first-year classmates were men. In some classes there were few men, and

women usually dominated discussions. Outside of class, DeLong and many other women soon complained that having so few men on campus hurt their social life. Not surprisingly, most of the men felt otherwise (Fonda, 2000).

What accounts for the shifting gender balance on North American campuses? One theory is that young men are drawn away from college or university by the lure of jobs, especially in high technology. This pattern is sometimes termed the "Bill Gates syndrome," after the Microsoft founder, who dropped out of higher education and soon became the world's richest person. In addition, analysts point to an anti-intellectual male culture. Young women are drawn to learning and seek to do well in school, but young men attach less importance to studying. Rightly or wrongly, more men seem to think that they can get a good job without investing years of their lives and a considerable amount of money in getting a university or college degree.

The gender gap is evident in all racial and ethnic categories and at all class levels. Among Canadian Aboriginals on campus, only 42 percent are men; among African-Americans on U.S. campuses, only 36 percent are men. The lower the income level, the greater the gender gap in post-secondary attendance.

Many educators are concerned about a lack of men on campus. In an effort to attract more balanced enrolments, some North American academic institutions are adopting what amounts to affirmative action programs for males. But courts in several jurisdictions have ruled that such policies are illegal. Many colleges and universities are therefore turning to more active recruitment; admissions officers are paying special attention to male applicants and stressing an institution's strength in mathematics and science—areas traditionally popular with men. In the same way that colleges and universities across the country are striving to increase their share of Aboriginal and visible minority students, the hope is that they can also succeed in attracting a larger share of men.

WHAT DO YOU THINK?

1. Among high school students, are males less concerned than females about academic achievement? Why or why not?

2. Is there a gender imbalance on your campus? Does it create problems? If so, what problems? For whom?

3. What programs or policies do you think might increase the number of men going to higher education?

Health and Society

Society affects people's health in four major ways:

1. **Cultural patterns define health.** Standards of health vary from culture to culture. A century ago, yaws, a contagious skin disease, was so common in sub-Saharan Africa that people there considered it normal (Dubos, 1980). In many areas of Canada and the United States, a rich diet is so common that most adults consider overeating to be normal and are now overweight. "Health," therefore, is sometimes a matter of having the same conditions or diseases as one's neighbours (Pinhey, Rubinstein, & Colfax, 1997).

What people see as healthful also reflects what they think is morally good. Members of our society (especially men) think that a competitive way of life is "healthy" because it fits our cultural mores, but stress contributes to heart disease and many other illnesses. People who object to homosexuality on moral grounds often call it "sick," even though it is natural from a biological point of view. Thus ideas about health act as a form of social control, encouraging conformity to cultural norms.

2. **Cultural standards of health change over time.** Early in the twentieth century, some doctors warned women not to go to college or university because higher education strained the female brain. Others claimed that masturbation was a threat to

Educators have long debated the proper manner in which to school children with disabilities. On the one hand, such children may benefit from distinctive facilities and specially trained teachers. On the other hand, they are less likely to be stigmatized as "different" if included in regular classroom settings. What do you consider to be the ramifications of the "special education" versus "inclusive education" debate for the classroom experience of all children, not only those who have disabilities?

health. We now know that both of these ideas are false. Fifty years ago, on the other hand, few doctors understood the dangers of cigarette smoking or too much sun exposure, practices that we now recognize as serious health risks. Even patterns of basic hygiene change over time. Today, most people in Canada bathe or shower every day; this is three times as often as 50 years ago (Gillespie, 2000).

3. **A society's technology affects people's health.** In low-income nations, infectious diseases are widespread because of malnutrition and poor sanitation. As industrialization raises living standards, people become healthier. But industrial technology also creates new threats to health. As Chapter 15 ("Population, Urbanization, and Environment") explains, high-income societies endanger health by overtaxing the world's resources and creating pollution.

4. **Social inequality affects people's health.** All societies distribute resources unequally. Overall, the rich have far better physical, mental, and emotional health than the poor.

Health: A Global Survey

Because health is closely linked to social life, human well-being has improved over the long course of history as societies developed more advanced technology. Differences in societal development are also the cause of striking differences in health around the world today.

Health in Low-Income Countries

With only simple technology, our ancestors could do little to improve health. Hunters and gatherers faced frequent food shortages, which sometimes forced mothers to abandon their children. Those lucky enough to survive infancy were still vulnerable to injury and illness, so half died by age 20 and few lived to 40 (Nolan & Lenski, 2007; Scupin, 2000).

As agricultural societies developed, food became more plentiful. Yet social inequality also increased, so that elites enjoyed better health than peasants and slaves, who lived in crowded, unsanitary shelters and often went hungry. In the growing cities of medieval Europe, human waste and refuse piled up in the streets, spreading infectious diseases, and plagues periodically wiped out entire towns (Mumford, 1961).

In much of the world, poverty cuts decades off the life expectancy found in high-income countries. In low-income nations of sub-Saharan Africa, for example, people have a life expectancy of barely 50, and in the poorest countries most people die before reaching their teens.

The World Health Organization reports that 1 billion people around the world—one person in six—suffer from serious illness due to poverty. Poor sanitation and malnutrition kill people of all ages. In a classic vicious circle, poverty breeds disease, which reduces people's ability to work, increasing poverty. When medical technology is used to control infectious disease, the populations of poor nations soar. But without enough resources to provide for the current population, low-income societies can ill afford population increases. Therefore, programs that lower death rates in these countries will succeed only if they are coupled with programs that reduce birth rates.

 November 1, Central India. Poverty is not just a matter of what you have; it shapes what you are. Most of the people we see in the villages here have never had the benefit of a doctor's or dentist's services. The result is easy to see: People look old before their time.

social epidemiology the study of how health and disease are distributed throughout a society's population.

Health in High-Income Countries

By 1800, as the Industrial Revolution took hold, factory jobs in cities attracted people from the countryside. Cities quickly became overcrowded, causing serious sanitation problems. Factories fouled the air with smoke, and workplace accidents were common.

Gradually, industrialization raised living standards, providing better nutrition and safer housing for most people, so that after about 1850 health began to improve. Also around this time, medical advances began to control infectious diseases. In 1854, a researcher named John Snow mapped the street addresses of London's cholera victims and found that they had all drunk water from the same well. Not long afterwards, scientists linked cholera to a specific bacterium and developed a vaccine against the deadly disease. Armed with scientific knowledge, early environmentalists campaigned against common practices such as discharging raw sewage into rivers used for drinking water. By the early twentieth century, death rates from infectious diseases had fallen sharply.

Table 14–3 shows that the leading killers in Nigeria—infectious diseases—account for few deaths in Canada today. It is now chronic illnesses, such as heart disease, cancer, and stroke, that cause most deaths in Canada, usually in old age.

Health in Canada

Because Canada is a high-income nation, health is generally good by world standards. Still, some categories of people have much better health than others.

Who Is Healthy? Age, Gender, Class, and Race

Social epidemiology is *the study of how health and disease are distributed throughout a society's population.* Social epidemiologists examine the origin and spread of epidemic diseases and try to understand how people's health is tied to their physical and social environments. This difference can be examined through the lens of age, gender, social class, and race.

The trend in Canada and other high-incomes countries is toward a higher level of health for all people, but recent analysis shows that differences persist between high- and low-income earners (Feinstein, 1993; Wilkinson & Marmot, 2003). One study showed that men in the richest 20 percent of neighbourhoods lived five years longer than men in the poorest 20 percent of neighbourhoods in Canada in 1996. The analysis shows that while the top 80 percent of neighbourhoods have almost achieved the goal of equal health for all, the bottom 20 percent remain far behind (Frohlich, Ross & Richmond, 2006; Wilkins, Berthelot, & Ng, 2002). Regarding health outcomes, the rates of diabetes and heart disease among the poorest 20 percent of

TABLE 14–3 Leading Causes of Death, Canada and Nigeria, 2002	
Nigeria	**Canada**
HIV/AIDS	Ischemic heart disease
Lower respiratory infections	Trachea, bronchus, and lung cancers
Malaria	Cerebrovascular disease
Diarrheal diseases	Alzheimer's disease and other dementias
Measles	Chronic obstructive pulmonary disease
Perinatal conditions	Colon and rectum cancers
Tuberculosis	Diabetes mellitus
Cerebrovascular disease	Lower respiratory infections
Ischemic heart disease	Breast cancer
Whooping cough	Lymphomas, multiple myeloma

Sources: World Health Organization (2006a, 2006b).

the population were more than double the rates among the richest 20 percent in 2008. After 20 years of decline, both inequality and poverty rates have increased in Canada in the past decade and they are now higher than the OECD average (OECD, 2008).

Age and Gender

Death is now rare among young people. Still, young people do fall victim to accidents and, more recently, to acquired immune deficiency syndrome (AIDS).

Throughout the life course, women have better health than men. First, females are less likely than males to die before or immediately after birth. Then, as socialization into gender roles proceeds, males become more aggressive and individualistic, resulting in higher rates of accidents, violence, and suicide. Yet women are more likely than men to report poor mental health (Annandale & Hunt, 2000). Studies report that the lifetime prevalence of major depression is twice the amount for adult women compared to adult men, and women are also more prone to experience stress caused by life events (Stephens, Dulberg, & Joubert, 1999). A number of explanations have been suggested for this pattern, including socializing practices and structural differences between the genders in work and family roles (Sachs-Ericsson & Ciarlo, 2000). Women are twice as likely as men to be given a diagnosis of unipolar depression, anxiety, panic disorder, or agoraphobia, and three times as likely to be diagnosed as having a histrionic personality and borderline personality disorder. Men, on the other hand, receive a diagnosis of alcohol abuse at the ratio of 5:1, anti-social personality disorder at 3:1, and obsessive-compulsive personality disorder at 2:1. These findings suggest that mental health problems are influenced by gender roles and, in fact, that certain diagnoses are gender specific (Benoit et al., 2009).

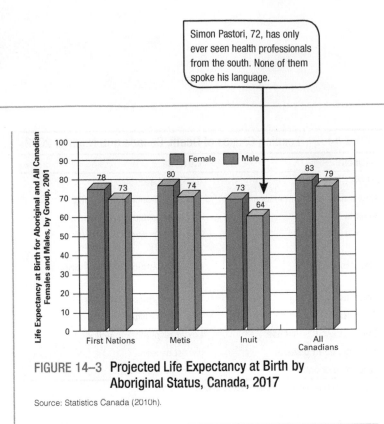

Simon Pastori, 72, has only ever seen health professionals from the south. None of them spoke his language.

eating disorder an intense form of dieting or other unhealthy method of weight control driven by the desire to be very thin

FIGURE 14–3 **Projected Life Expectancy at Birth by Aboriginal Status, Canada, 2017**

Source: Statistics Canada (2010h).

Social Class and Race

Infant mortality—the death rate among children under one year of age—is twice as high for Aboriginal children in Canada as for other children born to privilege. Although the health of the richest children in this country is the best in the world, our poorest children are as vulnerable to disease as those in low-income nations such as Lebanon and Vietnam.

Health, race, and ethnicity are also linked. Because Aboriginal Canadians are much more likely than other Canadians to be poor, they are more likely to die in infancy and to have a shorter life expectancy, as Figure 14–3 shows. Sex complicates this picture because females outlive males in each racial category. See the Thinking about Diversity box for a discussion of masculinity and its threat to health.

Cigarette Smoking

Cigarette smoking tops the list of preventable health hazards in Canada. Only after World War I did smoking become popular in this country. Despite growing evidence of its dangers, smoking remained fashionable until around a generation ago. Today, however, an increasing number of people consider smoking a mild form of social deviance, and an increasing number of provinces have banned smoking in public buildings (Niesse, 2007).

The popularity of cigarettes peaked in 1960, when almost 45 percent of Canadian adults smoked. By 2008, 24.4 percent of males and 18.5 percent of females aged 12 or older smoked cigarettes either daily or occasionally. This was about 3.4 million males and 2.6 million females (Statistics Canada, 2010j). Quitting is difficult because cigarette smoke contains nicotine, a physically addictive drug. And many people smoke to cope with stress: Divorced and separated people are likely to smoke, as are lower-income people, the unemployed, and people in the armed forces. While more Canadian men than women smoke, cigarettes (the only form of tobacco use popular among women) have taken a toll on women's health. By the early 1990s, lung cancer surpassed breast cancer as a cause of death among Canadian women.

In 2003 alone, it was predicted that 21 100 new cases of lung cancer would be diagnosed and 18 880 people in Canada would die of lung cancer. Lung cancer is the leading cause of death due to cancer in Canada. Cigarette smoking causes about 30 percent of cancer deaths in Canada and about 85 percent of lung cancer (Cancer Society of Canada, 2008).

Smokers also suffer more often from minor illnesses such as flu, and pregnant women who smoke increase the likelihood of spontaneous abortion, prenatal death, and low-birth-weight babies. Even non-smokers exposed to cigarette smoke have a high risk of smoking-related diseases.

Tobacco is an $89 billion industry in North America. In 1997, the tobacco industry admitted that cigarette smoking is harmful to health and agreed to stop marketing cigarettes to young people. Despite the anti-smoking trend in North America, the percentage of college and university students who smoke has now passed 30 percent and continues to rise (College Tobacco Prevention Resource, 2006; U.S. Department of Health and Human Services, 2010). In addition, the use of chewing tobacco, also a threat to health, is increasing among the young.

The tobacco industry has increased marketing abroad, where there is less regulation of tobacco products. In many countries, especially in Asia, a large majority of men smoke. Worldwide, more than 1 billion adults (about 25 percent of the total) smoke, consuming some 6 trillion cigarettes annually, and smoking is on the rise. One result of the rise in global smoking is that cancer is likely to overtake heart disease as the world's number one killer in the next year or two (Stobbe, 2008; World Health Organization, 2009). The harm that comes from cigarette smoking is real. But the good news is that about 10 years after quitting, an ex-smoker's health is about as good as that of someone who never smoked at all.

Health and the Body

Since the early 1980s, sociologists have developed a strong research agenda to study the relationship between health and the body, adding to research by geneticists and psychologists, among others (Shillings, 2005). One focus has been on the root causes of eating disorders. An **eating disorder** is *an intense form of dieting or other unhealthy method of weight control driven by the desire to be very thin.* One eating disorder, *anorexia nervosa*, is characterized by dieting to the point of starvation; another is *bulimia*, which involves binge eating

Masculinity: A Threat to Health?

JEFF: Cindy! If you don't get out of there in 10 seconds, I'm gonna break the door down!

CINDY: Chill out, bro! I have as much right to be in the bathroom as you do. I'm not finished.

JEFF: Are you going to take *all day*?

CINDY: Why are you guys always in such a hurry?

Doctors call it "coronary-prone behaviour." Psychologists call it "Type A personality." Sociologists recognize it as our culture's idea of masculinity. This combination of attitudes and behaviour, common among men in our society, includes chronic impatience ("Get outta my way!"), uncontrolled ambition ("I've gotta have it. I *need* that!"), and free-floating hostility ("Why are people *such idiots?*").

This pattern, although normal from a cultural point of view, is one major reason why men who are driven to succeed are at high risk of heart disease. By acting out the Type A personality, we may get the job done, but we set in motion complex biochemical processes that are very hard on the human heart.

Here are a few questions to help you determine your own degree of risk (or that of someone important to you):

1. Do you believe that you have to be aggressive to succeed? Do nice guys finish last? For your heart's sake, try to remove hostility from your life. Here's a place to start: Eliminate profanity from your speech. Try to replace aggression with compassion, which can be surprisingly effective in dealing with other people. Medically speaking, substituting compassion and humour for irritation and aggravation will improve your health.

2. How well do you handle uncertainty and opposition? Do you lose patience with other people ("Why won't the waiter take my order?" "This jerk just doesn't get it!")? We all like to know what's going on, and we want others to go along with us. But the world often doesn't work that way. Accepting uncertainty and opposition makes us more mature and certainly healthier.

3. Are you uncomfortable showing positive emotions? Many men think that giving and accepting love—from women, from children, and from other men—is a sign of weakness. But the medical truth is that love supports health and anger damages it.

As human beings, we have a great deal of choice about how we live. Think about the choices you make, and reflect on how our society's idea of masculinity often makes us hard on others (including those we love) and, just as important, hard on ourselves.

WHAT DO YOU THINK?

1. What aspects of masculinity are harmful to health?

2. Why are so many people unaware of how masculinity can be harmful to health?

3. How can sociology play a part in changing men's health for the better?

Sources: Friedman and Rosenman (1974) and M.P. Levine (1990).

---

followed by induced vomiting to avoid weight gain. Eating disorders are chronic conditions that are linked to a combination of genetic, psychological, and sociological determinants. Some research on identical twins suggests that there is a genetic predisposition to having an eating disorder. Other studies have linked eating disorders and depression. Sociologists have contributed to this research by studying the demographic variation of the phenomenon in populations and the social environmental factors, including market factors, that reinforce eating disorders (Jacobs, 2003).

Eating disorders involve gender, race, and class: 95 percent of people who suffer from anorexia nervosa or bulimia are women, most of them from white, affluent families. For women, North American culture equates slimness with being successful and attractive to men. Conversely, we tend to stereotype overweight women (and to a lesser extent men) as lazy, sloppy, and even stupid (A.E. Becker, 1999; M. Levine, 1987).

Research shows that most college- and university-age women believe that "guys like thin girls," that being thin is crucial to physical attractiveness, and that they are not as thin as men would like. In fact, most college-age women actually want to be thinner than most college-age men want them to be. Because few women are able to meet our culture's unrealistic standards of beauty, many women develop a low self-image. Our idealized image of beauty leads many young women to diet to the point of risking their health and even their lives.

For their part, most men display far less dissatisfaction with their own body shape (Fallon & Rozin, 1985), though some research into young men has related body image dissatisfaction to unhealthy body-building practices, including the use of anabolic steroids (Canadian Centre for Drug-Free Sport, 1993).

Whatever the cause of eating disorders, the fact remains that North Americans are rapidly increasing their body size. During the past two decades, the prevalence of obesity has increased significantly in North America. Obesity is defined in terms of a *body mass index* (BMI) greater than 30.0, which means that persons are at least 14 kilograms (30 pounds) over their healthy weight.

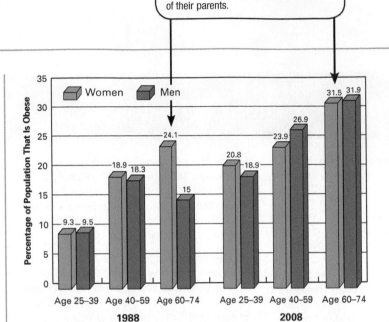

Since their youth, Sam and Dorothy Stone have both been much heavier than either of their parents.

FIGURE 14–4 Obesity in Canada, Men and Women, 1988 and 2008

The graph shows the increase in medically defined obesity rates for men and women in Canada over time, and variations by age.
Note: 1988 refers to 1986 to 1992; 2008 refers to 2007 to 2009.

Source: Shields, Carroll, and Ogden (2011).

If you like this table then this is the source:

http://www.cdc.gov/nchs/data/databriefs/db56.htm

http://www.cdc.gov/nchs/data/databriefs/db56.pdf

Figure 14–4 shows the change in obesity rates over time and by gender and age in Canada. According to Health Canada, from 2007 to 2009, 24.1 percent of Canadian adults were obese, based on measured data (the prevalence rate in the United States was 34.4 percent). Among Canadian men, the prevalence of obesity was 24.3 percent, while the rate for Canadian women was just below 23.9 percent (Statistics Canada, 2011ap).

Being overweight can limit physical activity and raises the risk of a number of serious diseases, including heart disease, stroke, and diabetes. The cost of treating diseases caused by obesity plus the cost of lost days at work because of such illnesses is more than $150 billion every year in North America. Most seriously, more than 112 000 people die each year from diseases related to being overweight (Centers for Disease Control and Prevention, 2007; Ferraro & Kelley-Moore, 2003; R. Stein, 2005).

What are the social causes of obesity? One factor is that we live in a society in which more and more people have jobs that keep them sitting in front of computer screens rather than engaging in the type of physical labour that was common a century ago. Even when we are not on the job, most of the work around the house is done by machines (or other people). Children spend more of their time sitting as well, watching television or playing video games.

Then, of course, there is diet. The typical person in North America is eating more salty, sugary, and fatty foods than ever before (Wells & Buzby, 2008). And meals are getting larger: The U.S. Department of Agriculture reported that, in 2000, the typical American adult consumed an additional 64 kilograms (140 pounds) of food each year than was true a decade earlier. Comparing old and new editions of cookbooks, recipes that used to say they would feed six now say they will feed four. The odds of being overweight go up among people with lower incomes partly because they may lack the education to make healthy choices and partly because stores in low-income communities offer a greater selection of low-cost, high-fat snack foods and fewer inexpensive healthful fruits and vegetables. As well, those with lower incomes may lack an affordable way to exercise (Hellmich, 2002). Some sociologists also argue that the food industry contributes to the obesity epidemic by bombarding the public with misleading messages about diet and activity, a market strategy not unlike consumer marketing strategies endorsed by the tobacco industry (Kwan, 2008).

Sexually Transmitted Infections

Sexual activity, though both pleasurable and vital to the continuation of our species, can transmit more than 50 types of *sexually transmitted infections* (STIs). Because our culture associates sex with sin, some people regard STIs not only as illnesses but also as marks of immorality.

STIs grabbed national attention during the "sexual revolution" of the 1960s, when infection rates rose dramatically as people became sexually active at younger ages and had a greater number of partners. This means that STIs are an exception to the general decline in infectious diseases over the course of the past century. By the late 1980s, the rising danger of STIs, especially AIDS, generated a sexual counter-revolution as people moved away from casual sex (Kain, 1987; Laumann et al., 1994). The following sections briefly describe several common STIs.

Gonorrhea and Syphilis

After a steady and dramatic decline in gonorrhea rates since the early 1980s, an increase was reported in 2009 (33.1 per 100 000), up from 28.9 per 100 000 in 2004 and 23.5 per 100 000 in 2002 (Public Health Agency of Canada, 2006, 2011a). Syphilis rates have followed a similar pattern of significant decline over time, though the pattern has reversed in the recent period for both males and females and is especially noticeable among the country's poorer populations, such as residents of Vancouver's Downtown Eastside. Thus, the national rate had remained between 0.4 and 0.6 per 100 000 throughout the 1990s, but rose to 4.0 per 100 000 in 2006 and increased again to 5.0 per 100 000 in 2009 (Health Canada, 2002). Both STIs can easily be cured with antibiotics such as penicillin. Thus, neither is currently a major health problem in Canada (Public Health Agency of Canada, 2011b).

Genital Herpes

Genital herpes is not a reportable STI in Canada. It is estimated, however, that the prevalence rate is about one in five in the adult population (Steben & Sacks, 1997). Though far less serious than gonorrhea and syphilis, herpes is incurable. People with genital herpes may not have any symptoms, or they may experience periodic, painful blisters on the genitals accompanied by fever and headache. Although it is not fatal to adults, women with active genital herpes can transmit the disease during a vaginal delivery, and it can be deadly to newborns.

AIDS

The most serious of all STIs is acquired immune deficiency syndrome (AIDS). Identified in 1981, it is incurable and almost always fatal. AIDS is caused by the human immunodeficiency virus (HIV), which attacks white blood cells, weakening the immune system. AIDS thus makes a person vulnerable to a wide range of other diseases that eventually cause death.

At the end of 1999, a total of 49 800 people were living with HIV infection in Canada. Of these, about one-third—approximately 15 000 infected individuals—were not aware of their health condition, and an estimated 15 000 to 17 000 individuals had died by the end of 1999 (adjusted for underreporting and delayed reporting) (Health Canada, 2003c). According to the Public Health Agency of Canada (2011c), there were an estimated 65 000 people living with HIV in 2008. The rate of increase is also growing: approximately 2300 to 4300 new HIV infections occurred in 2008, compared with 2200 to 4200 in 2005.

Globally, HIV infects some 33 million people—half of them under age 25—and the number continues to rise. The global death toll now exceeds 25 million, with less than 1 percent of all deaths occurring in North America in 2008. Global Map 14–2 on page 396 shows that sub-Saharan Africa has the highest HIV infection rate and accounts for 68 percent of all world cases. A United Nations study found that across much of sub-Saharan Africa, 15-year-olds face a fifty-fifty chance of becoming infected with HIV. The risk is especially high for girls, not only because HIV is transmitted more easily from men to women but also because many African cultures encourage women to be submissive to men. According to some analysts, the AIDS crisis now threatens the political and economic security of Africa, which affects the entire world (Ashford, 2002; UNAIDS, 2008b).

Upon infection, people with HIV display no symptoms at all, so most are unaware of their condition. Symptoms of AIDS may not appear for a year or longer, during which time an infected person may infect others. Within five years, one-third of infected people who have gone untreated develop full-blown AIDS; half develop AIDS within 10 years; and almost all become sick within 20 years. In low-income countries, the progression of the illness

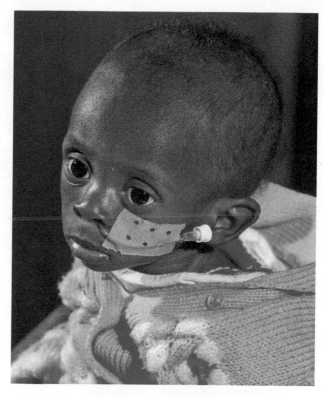

In the African nation of Kenya, about 300 people die from AIDS every day. In parts of sub-Saharan Africa, the epidemic is so great that half of all children will eventually become infected with HIV. This infant from Manyemen, Cameroon, who already has AIDS, is fighting for his life.

is much more rapid, with many people dying within a few years of becoming infected.

HIV is infectious but not contagious. This means that HIV is transmitted from person to person through blood, semen, or breast milk but not through casual contact such as shaking hands, hugging, sharing towels or dishes, swimming together, or even coughing and sneezing. The risk of transmitting AIDS through saliva (as in kissing) is extremely low. The risk of transmitting HIV through sexual activity is greatly reduced by the use of latex condoms. However, abstinence or an exclusive relationship with an uninfected person is the only sure way to avoid infection.

Specific behaviours place people at high risk for HIV infection. The first is *anal sex*, which can cause rectal bleeding, allowing easy transmission of HIV from one person to another. The fact that many men who have sex with other men (MSM) engage in anal sex helps explain why these categories of people accounted for 58 percent of AIDS cases in Canada in 2002 (Public Health Agency of Canada, 2004).

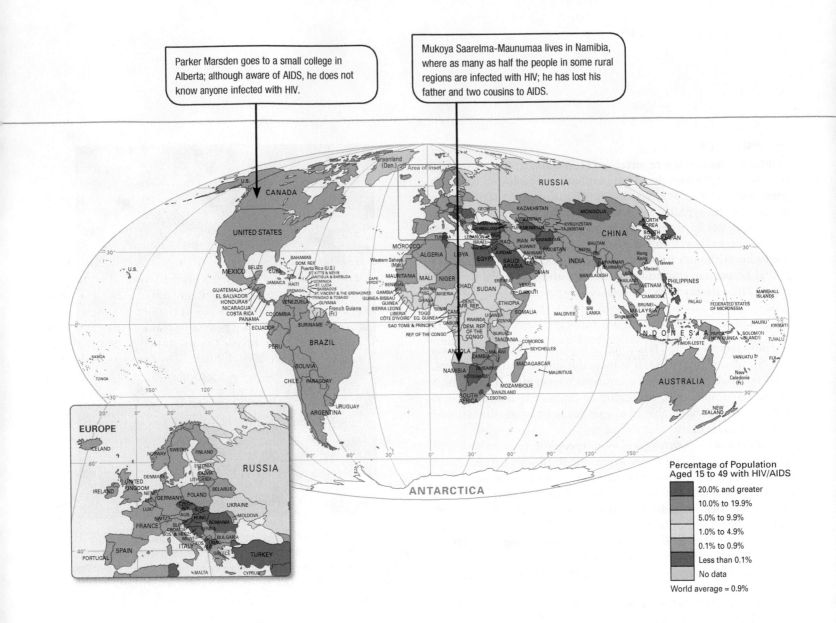

Parker Marsden goes to a small college in Alberta; although aware of AIDS, he does not know anyone infected with HIV.

Mukoya Saarelma-Maunumaa lives in Namibia, where as many as half the people in some rural regions are infected with HIV; he has lost his father and two cousins to AIDS.

Percentage of Population Aged 15 to 49 with HIV/AIDS

- 20.0% and greater
- 10.0% to 19.9%
- 5.0% to 9.9%
- 1.0% to 4.9%
- 0.1% to 0.9%
- Less than 0.1%
- No data

World average = 0.9%

Window on the World

GLOBAL MAP 14–2 HIV/AIDS Infection of Adults in Global Perspective

Sixty-eight percent of all global HIV infections are in sub-Saharan Africa. In Swaziland, one-fourth of people between the ages of 15 and 49 are infected with HIV/AIDS. This very high infection rate reflects the prevalence of other sexually transmitted infections and infrequent use of condoms, two factors that promote transmission of HIV. South and Southeast Asia account for about 13 percent of global HIV infections. In Thailand, 1.4 percent of people aged 15 to 49 are now infected. All of North and South America taken together account for 9 percent of global HIV infections. In North America, less than 1 percent of people aged 15 to 49 are infected. The incidence of infection in Muslim nations is extremely low by world standards.

Source: Population Reference Bureau (2010) and UNAIDS (2011).

Sharing needles used to inject drugs is a second high-risk behaviour. Sex with an intravenous drug user is also very risky. Because intravenous drug use is more common among poor people and Aboriginals in Canada, AIDS is now becoming a disease of the socially disadvantaged.

Using any drug, including alcohol, also increases the risk of being infected with HIV to the extent that it impairs judgment. In other words, even people who understand what places them at risk of infection may act less responsibly once they are under the influence of alcohol, marijuana, or some other drug.

euthanasia assisting in the death of a person suffering from an incurable disease ; also known as *mercy killing*

While only 14 percent of the people with AIDS in Canada in 1999 were women, the figure had increased to 20 percent in 2004, and there is an increasing trend toward positive HIV reports among heterosexuals (Health Canada, 2003d). Heterosexual activity does transmit HIV (27 percent in 2005), and the danger rises with the number of sexual partners, especially if they fall into high-risk categories. In fact, worldwide, heterosexual relations are the primary means of HIV transmission, accounting for two-thirds of all infections.

The Canadian government initially responded slowly to the AIDS crisis, largely because gays and intravenous drug users are widely viewed as deviant. But funding for AIDS research, including from the country's primary health funding agency (the Canadian Institutes of Health Research), has increased dramatically in recent years, and researchers have identified some drugs, including protease inhibitors, that suppress the symptoms of the disease. Canada has also approved on a trial basis the safe injection site in Vancouver, British Columbia. The facility opened its doors in 2003 and is the first of its kind in North America. A study published in the *New England Journal of Medicine* shows that drug users who use Vancouver's safe injection site are more likely to enter detox and other treatment facilities (Kerr et al., 2005). Other research has shown that the safe injection site has helped to increase public order and reduce needle sharing in Vancouver's Downtown Eastside (Wood et al., 2004). But educational programs remain the most effective weapon against AIDS because prevention is the only way to stop a disease that has no cure.

Ethical Issues Surrounding Death

Now that technological advances are giving human beings the power to draw the line separating life and death, we must decide how and when to do so. In other words, questions about the use of medical technology have added an ethical dimension to health and illness.

When Does Death Occur?

Common sense suggests that life ends when breathing and heartbeat stop. But the ability to revive or replace a heart and artificially sustain respiration makes this definition of death obsolete. So medical and legal experts now define death as an *irreversible* state involving no response to stimulation, no movement or breathing, no reflexes, and no indication of brain activity (D.G. Jones, 1998; Ladd, 1979; Wall, 1980).

Do people have a right to die? Today, medical personnel, family members, and patients themselves bear the agonizing burden of deciding when a terminally ill person should die. Among the most difficult cases are the 10 000 people in Canada in a permanent vegetative state who cannot express their own desires about life and death. Generally speaking, the first duty of doctors and hospitals is to protect a patient's life. Even so, a mentally competent person in the process of dying can refuse medical treatment or even nutrition (either at the time or, in advance, through a document called a "living will").

Mercy killing is the common term for **euthanasia**, *assisting in the death of a person suffering from an incurable disease*. Euthanasia (from Greek, meaning "a good death") poses an ethical dilemma, as it is considered by some to be an act of kindness and by others to be a form of killing.

Whether there is a "right to die" is one of today's most difficult issues. All people with incurable diseases have a right to refuse treatment that could prolong their lives. But whether a doctor should be allowed to help bring about death is at the heart of today's debate. Though Parliament no longer views attempted suicide as a crime in Canada, it is still against the Criminal Code to assist a suicide. Still, many people in Canada are terminally ill, and some do express a wish for assistance to end their life. Such was the case for British Columbia resident Sue Rodriguez, who took her case all the way to the Supreme Court in 1993. The court did not rule in her favour, though Rodriguez ultimately got her wish through the assistance of an anonymous physician. A sympathetic former member of Parliament, Svend Robinson, was also at her side. A special prosecutor later ruled against charging either party with wrongdoing.

Supporters of *active* euthanasia—allowing a dying person to enlist the services of a doctor to bring on a quick death—argue that there are circumstances (such as when a dying person suffers from great pain) that make death preferable to life. Critics counter that permitting active euthanasia invites abuse. They fear that patients will feel pressure to end their lives to spare family members the burden of caring for them and avoid the high costs of hospitalization. Research in the Netherlands, where physician-assisted suicide is legal, indicates that about one-fifth of all such deaths have occurred without a patient explicitly requesting to die (Gillon, 1999).

In Canada, Saskatchewan farmer Robert Latimer has been in and out of court for the carbon-monoxide poisoning of his disabled daughter, Tracy, in 1993. She had a severe case of cerebral palsy and Latimer maintains he acted "out of love" and that he had no choice but to kill her because she had had enough. The Saskatchewan Court of Appeal ruled in November 1998 that Latimer had to return to prison to serve his life sentence, with no opportunity for parole for 10 years. Latimer's lawyers appealed the case to the Supreme Court of Canada but lost. Latimer served his 10-year sentence for ending his daughter's life and was granted full parole on December 8, 2010. The Canadian public remain torn over the case.

A 2010 Angus Reid poll reported that 85 percent of Canadians believe that legalizing euthanasia would allow suffering people to ease their pain and establish clearer regulations for doctors regarding end-of-life decisions. In addition, two-thirds of Canadians agreed that legalizing euthanasia would not send the message that the lives of the sick or disabled are less valuable (Angus Reid Global Monitor, 2010). Therefore, the right-to-die debate is sure to continue.

The Medical Establishment

Throughout most of human history, health care was the responsibility of individuals and their families. Medicine emerges as a social institution only as societies become more productive and people take on specialized work.

Members of agrarian societies today still turn to traditional health practitioners, including acupuncturists and herbalists. In industrial societies, medical care falls to specially trained and licensed professionals, from anaesthesiologists to X-ray technicians. The medical establishment of modern, industrial societies took form over the past 200 years.

The Rise of Scientific Medicine

In pre-Confederation Canada, herbalists, druggists, barbers, midwives, and ministers practised the healing arts. But not all were effective. Unsanitary instruments, lack of anaesthesia, and simple ignorance made surgery a terrible ordeal, and doctors probably killed as many people as they saved.

In 1795, the first Medical Act attempted to regulate the practices of "physic and surgery" in Upper Canada by making it illegal for untrained healers to practise medicine without licences; only those with university degrees were exempted. The impracticality of the ruling soon became apparent, and the small degree-holding segment of the medical profession was left vulnerable to public critics. The original Medical Act was repealed in 1806, and traditional healers, including midwives, remained immune from the licensing laws of the Ontario Medical Board for the next half-century. In 1866, however, the government changed the law so that practitioners of midwifery and other healing arts, such as naturopathy, required medical degrees. That meant the predominantly male medical profession in the province enjoyed a legal monopoly over the birthing chamber by the time of Confederation in 1867 (Benoit, 1998b). No female physicians were licensed in Ontario until the 1880s, and owing to continuing patriarchal traditions, few women entered this profession for many decades thereafter. Although some "traditionalist" physicians opposed this turn of events embraced by their "radical" colleagues and called instead for formal training and legalization of lay healers, their efforts proved unsuccessful (Biggs, 1983).

The Canadian Medical Association (CMA), founded in 1867, also symbolized the growing acceptance of a scientific model of medicine. The CMA widely publicized the successes of its members in identifying the causes of life-threatening diseases—bacteria and viruses—and developing vaccines to prevent them. Still, other approaches to health care, such as regulating nutrition, also had defenders. But the CMA responded boldly—some thought arrogantly—to these alternative approaches to health care, trumpeting the superiority of its practitioners.

The influential Flexner Report of 1910 highlighted the abysmal situation of Canadian (and American) medical education, reporting that 90 percent of all physicians at the time received their training from profit-making schools, which offered few or no resources for authentic clinical training. Abraham Flexner recommended the elimination of all "diploma mills" and the tightening of education and licensing standards for North American physicians. Traditional healers, as well as Black and female physicians, became easy targets for the reformed medical profession.

The Flexner Report effectively led to the closing down of schools teaching other methods of healing (herbal medicine, homeopathy, etc.), limiting the practice of medicine to those with medical science degrees. These developments awarded medical doctors the primary role in the health care of the population, and gave social legitimacy to *scientific medicine*—the social institution that focuses on combating disease and improving health. In the process, both the prestige and the income of physicians rose dramatically; today, doctors in Canada are among the highest-paid workers in the country.

Practitioners of other approaches (such as naturopathy, midwifery, and chiropractic medicine) for a time held on to their traditional practices, but these practitioners were relegated to the fringe of the medical profession. However, chiropractic services have in the past decade gained partial coverage under some provincial health care systems. More recently, midwifery has also gained coverage under most territorial and provincial health care systems and the process is under way in the other regions (Bourgeault, Benoit, & Davis-Floyd, 2004; DeVries et al., 2001; Wrede, Benoit, & Einarsdottir, 2008). Scientific medicine, taught in expensive, urban medical schools, also changed the social profile of doctors. As the CMA standards took hold, most physicians came from privileged backgrounds and practised in cities. Furthermore, as mentioned above, women had figured prominently in many fields of healing denigrated by the CMA. Some early medical schools did train women but, owing to the Flexner Report and declining financial resources, most of these schools soon closed. Only in recent decades have women increased their representation in the medical profession. In 1998, women accounted for 28 percent of Canada's practising physicians, up from 25 percent in 1993 (Canadian Institute for Health Information, 2000). In 2004, women made up 55 percent of all doctors in Canada (Statistics Canada, 2006au).

Yet female physicians in our country tend to remain clustered in the lower-ranking medical specialties, separated by a glass ceiling from their male colleagues in top administrative and specialty posts.

Holistic Medicine

The scientific model of medicine has been tempered by the introduction of **holistic medicine**, *an approach to health care that emphasizes the prevention of illness and takes into account a person's entire physical and social environment*. Holistic practitioners agree on the need for drugs, surgery, artificial organs, and high technology, but they emphasize treating the whole person rather than just symptoms and focus

The profession of surgery has existed only for several centuries. Before that, barbers offered their services to the very sick, often cutting the skin to "bleed" a patient. Of course, this "treatment" was rarely effective, but it did produce plenty of bloody bandages, which practitioners hung out to dry. This practice identifies the origin of the red and white barber poles we see today.

Jan Sanders von Hemessen (c. 1504–1566), *The Surgeon,* oil on panel. Prado, Madrid, Spain/Giraudon/Bridgeman Art Library.

on health rather than disease. There are three foundations of holistic health care (Gordon, 1980; Patterson, 1998):

1. **Treat patients as people.** Holistic practitioners are concerned not only with symptoms but also with how people's environment and lifestyle affect health. Holistic practitioners extend the bounds of conventional medicine, taking an active role in fighting poverty, environmental pollution, and other dangers to public health.

2. **Encourage responsibility, not dependency.** A scientific approach to medicine puts doctors in charge of health, and patients are to follow doctors' orders. Holistic medicine tries to shift some responsibility for health from doctor to patient by emphasizing health-promoting behaviour. Holistic medicine favours an *active approach to health* rather than a *reactive approach to illness.*

3. **Provide personal treatment.** Scientific medicine treats patients in impersonal offices and hospitals, both disease-centred settings. Holistic practitioners favour, as much as possible, a personal and relaxed environment such as the home.

In sum, holistic care does not oppose scientific medicine but shifts the emphasis from treating disease to achieving the greatest well-being for everyone. Recently, the College of Family Physicians of Canada

(2009) issued a discussion paper that built on changes elsewhere and introduced the concept of "medical home" as part of its efforts to renew primary health care across the country. Underlying the concept of medical home is a patient-centred approach to care that draws on principles of holistic medicine.

Paying for Health Care: A Global Survey

As medicine has come to rely on advanced technology, the costs of medical care in industrial societies have skyrocketed. Countries throughout the world have adopted different strategies to meet these costs.

> March 14, Vinales, Cuba. We have difficulty finding the hospital because there are no big signs on the modest whitewashed building. Finally, we enter the large open area and encounter a friendly, efficient nurse who beckons us into an examination room. Annika has felt weak ever since we left Victoria for Havana and was not able to ride her touring bike more than a few kilometres yesterday. We explain our story in English to the Spanish-speaking doctor assigned to us; it's a challenge, but gestures and goodwill come to our aid. The hospital is spotless but crumbling. A slow leak has made a hole in the ceiling; water drops into a bucket. The X-ray machine looks as if it is hand-cranked. But, 90 minutes later, we walk out of the hospital with a firm diagnosis of pneumonia, an X-ray to take back home to our family doctor, and prescriptions for two kinds of antibiotics. To our amazement, the Cuban doctor attending our daughter declined any payment, shaking her head in seeming disbelief that we should even ask about the cost. After picking up the medicine in the local pharmacy we have spent the equivalent of $1.35! We wonder if we could have been helped so quickly and efficiently on a Saturday morning back in Canada and know that the cost of the medicine would have been much higher at home. Why did we bother to get travellers' health insurance?

People's Republic of China

A poor, agrarian society in the process of industrializing, the People's Republic of China faces the immense task of providing for the health of more than 1.3 billion people. China has experimented with private medicine, but the government controls most health care.

China's "barefoot doctors," roughly comparable to paramedics or nurse practitioners in Canada, used to bring some modern methods of health care to peasants in rural villages, though this rural system has declined significantly in recent decades. Traditional healing arts, involving acupuncture and medicinal herbs, are still widely practised in rural and urban areas. In addition, the Chinese approach to health is based on a holistic concern for the interplay of mind and

socialized medicine a medical care system in which the government owns and operates most medical facilities and employs most physicians

direct-fee system a medical care system in which patients pay directly for the services of physicians and hospitals

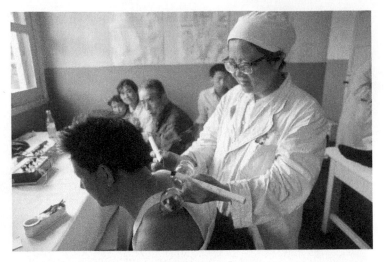

Traditional healers work to improve people's health throughout the world. This patient is receiving a traditional needle therapy in Suining, a city in China's Sichuan province. Do you think people in Canada are accepting of traditional healing practices? Why or why not?

body (Kaptchuk, 1985; Sidel & Sidel, 1982b). In 2009, the government announced a series of reforms, with the promise of universal, safe, affordable, and effective basic health care by 2020. Success will depend on the investment that actually takes place and the emphasis placed on building a comprehensive primary care system that will be free to all citizens, including economic migrants (OECD, 2010c).

Russian Federation

The Russian Federation is struggling to transform a state-dominated economy into more of a market system. For this reason, health care in this country is also in transition. Nevertheless, the idea that everyone has a right to basic health care remains widespread.

As in China, people in the Russian Federation do not choose a doctor but report to a local government health facility. Physicians there have much lower incomes than physicians in Canada, earning about the same salary as skilled industrial workers (Canadian doctors earn roughly five times as much as Canadian industrial workers). Also, about 70 percent of Russia's doctors are women, compared to 55 percent in Canada. Yet Russian female physicians receive comparatively low wages and have poorer working conditions than women doctors in high-income countries.

In recent years, the Russian Federation has suffered setbacks in health, due in part to a falling standard of living. Rising demand for medical care has strained a bureaucratic system that at best provides highly standardized and impersonal care. The optimistic view is that as living standards rise, the quality of medical service will improve. In Russia's uncertain times, what does seem clear is that inequalities in medical care will increase (Landsberg, 1998; Mason, 2004; Specter, 1995; Zuckerman, 2006).

Sweden

In 1891, Sweden began a compulsory, comprehensive system of government health care. Citizens pay for this program with their taxes, which are among the highest in the world. Typically, physicians are government employees and most hospitals are government-managed. Sweden's system is called **socialized medicine**, *a medical care system in which the government owns and operates most medical facilities and employs most physicians.*

Great Britain

In 1948, Great Britain also established socialized medicine by creating a dual system of health services. All British citizens are entitled to care provided by the National Health Service, but those who can afford it can also go to doctors and hospitals that operate privately.

Japan

Physicians in Japan operate privately, but a combination of government programs and private insurance pays medical costs. As shown in Figure 14–5, the Japanese approach medical care much like the Europeans, with most medical expenses paid through the government.

The United States

Even after the historic passage of the new health care bill in 2010, the United States stands alone among high-income nations in having no universal, government-operated program of health care. The United States has a **direct-fee system**, *a medical care system in which patients pay directly for the services of physicians and hospitals.* Europeans look to government to fund 70 to nearly 90 percent of health care costs (paid for through taxation), but the U.S. government pays just 42 percent of the country's health costs (U.S. Department of Health and Human Services, 2010).

In the United States, rich people can buy the best medical care in the world, but poor people are worse off than their counterparts in Europe. This difference translates into relatively high death rates among both infants and adults in the United States compared with many European countries (Population Reference Bureau, 2010).

Several states, including Maine, Vermont, and Massachusetts, have enacted programs that provide health care to everyone. Why does the United States have no national program that provides universal care? First, because its culture stresses self-reliance, it has limited the scope of government programs. Second, at least until recently, political support for a national medical program has not been strong, even among labour unions, which have concentrated on winning medical care benefits from employers. Third, the American Medical Association and the insurance industry have strongly and consistently opposed national medical care.

Medical expenditures in the United States have increased dramatically, from $12 billion in 1950 to more than $2 trillion in 2008 (U.S. Department of Health and Human Services, 2010).

This amounts to more than $7600 per person, more than any other nation spends for health care, including Canada.

The Canadian Health Care System

Since 1972, Canada has had a single-payer model of health care that provides care to all Canadians. Like a vast insurance company, the Canadian government pays doctors and hospitals according to a set schedule of fees. Canada's "medicare" system is predominantly a publicly financed, privately delivered health care system. The system provides access to universal comprehensive coverage for hospital and in-patient and out-patient services that are deemed necessary by a physician. While the administration and delivery of health services is the responsibility of each individual province or territory, the system is a national one to the extent that all areas of the country are expected to adhere to national principles. The federal government sets and administers national principles, or standards, for the health care system under the 1984 Canada Health Act (the standards are universality, accessibility, portability, comprehensive coverage, and public administration). The federal government also helps to finance provincial health care services through monetary transfers.

Therefore, Canada does not have a system of "socialized health care," such as that of Sweden, where the government is the principal employer of doctors. Most Canadian physicians are instead private practitioners who work in independent or group practices and enjoy a high degree of autonomy. Private physicians are mainly paid on a fee-for-service basis and submit their service claims directly to the provincial health insurance plan for payment (Blishen, 1991; Segall & Chappell, 2000). Non-hospital dental care, many drugs, ambulance transport, private hospital beds, and other health services not covered by provincial health plans are either privately financed through employee benefit plans or paid for by individual Canadians. Total spending on health care in Canada was more than $191 billion in 2010, increasing an estimated $9.5 billion (5.2 percent) from 2009. This means that the total health expenditure per capita in 2010 was approximately $5614. Health care spending in 2010 was about 11.7 percent of GDP (CIHI, 2010a).

As shown in Figure 14–5, non-insured private health costs made up 32 percent of total health care costs in Canada in 2010. All other G7 countries in 2008, except for Australia (at 68 percent) and the United States (at 48.6 percent), had greater public financing of health care than Canada (The World Bank, 2010).

In sum, despite the many benefits of the Canadian health care system, there are problems that need to be addressed. Compared with the systems of other countries, including that of our neighbour to the south, the Canadian health care system makes less use of state-of-the-art technology. Some critics also point out that it responds slowly to people's needs, often requiring those facing major surgery to wait months or even a year for attention (Grant, 1984; Rosenthal, 1991; Vayda & Deber, 1984). Further, recent government cutbacks in health care funding have

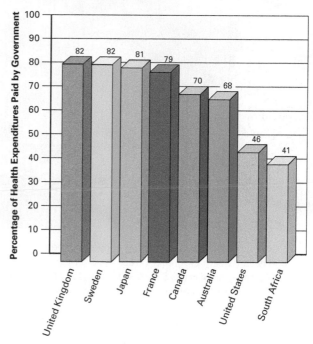

Global Snapshot

FIGURE 14–5 **Extent of Socialized Medicine in Selected Countries, 2006**

The governments of most high-income countries pay a greater share of their people's medical costs than the U.S. government does.
Source: World Bank (2010).

caused concern among Canadians that their much-admired health care system is in crisis. In fact, an Ipsos-Reid poll (2000a) reported that most people in Canada—along with people in 16 other nations—felt that the government should spend more on health care.

One government-commissioned review of the health care system, established in 1994 and known as the National Forum on Health, solicited opinions from the public and health providers on the way forward for coming decades. The final report, *Canada Health Action: Building on the Legacy*, noted that the country is not confronting a health care crisis as such, yet the health care system is under significant stress. Though underfunding was not singled out as a main cause, the report noted the need for better strategies in spending public tax dollars on health care, as well as the need to focus attention on the underlying determinants of health.

A more recent 2002 report—*Building on Values: The Future of Health Care in Canada*, by the Commission on the Future of Health Care in Canada headed by former premier of Saskatchewan Roy Romanow—made similar recommendations. The Commission's mandate was to review the country's health care system, engage Canadians in a national dialogue on its future, and make

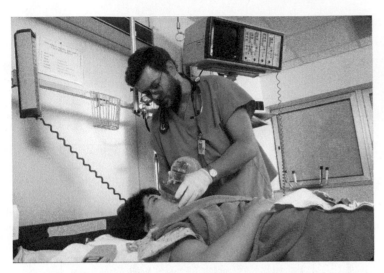

Throughout Canada, there is a serious shortage of nurses. One strategy for filling the need is for nursing programs to recruit more men into this profession. In 2009, nearly all RNs (93.8 percent) in the Canadian workforce were female; this figure has not changed much in the last half-decade.

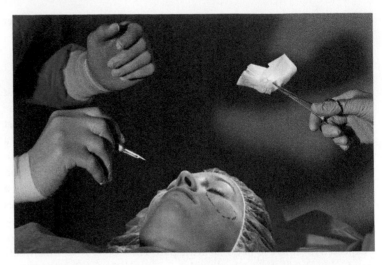

Definitions of health are based on cultural standards, including ideas about beauty. Every year, millions of people undergo cosmetic surgery to bring their appearance into line with societal definitions of how people ought to look.

recommendations to improve the system's quality and sustainability. The report was based on comprehensive, broad-based public consultations that included 21 days of public hearings, televised in-studio policy debates with health care experts, 12 policy dialogues at Canadian universities, a forum on Aboriginal health, and deliberative dialogue sessions with Canadian citizens in 12 cities across Canada. In addition, more than 30 000 Canadians took part in the Commission's two consultation surveys. The results reinforce the findings of early reports on health care in Canada, which found that Canadians want to keep the core principles of the medicare model that accorded with their strongly held values of universality, equal access, solidarity, and fairness. On the other hand, they also stated very strongly that the present employment of health care resources does not match their values of efficiency and accountability.

The proposal to create a national accountability system for Canadian health care was one recommendation to help solve such weaknesses. Some of the provinces, on the other hand, do not agree with this recommendation, because they would like more control over the health care in their province. This old battle between Ottawa and the provincial capitals is unlikely to be resolved in the near future given that the stakes are perceived to be very high due to the large proportion of governmental budgets spent on health care.

The Nursing Shortage

The Canadian Nurses Association (2009) forecasted a shortage of about 78 000 nurses in 2011; that number is expected to increase to 113 000 in 2016.

Two often-cited reasons for the unfilled jobs for nurses relate to population changes: The last decades have seen a major increase in chronic illnesses in Canada, as well as the aging of the population. Both have placed an increased demand on the Canadian health care system for services, and much of this increased demand involves the need for professional nursing services.

Another cause of the shortage is that fewer people are entering the nursing profession. During the last decade, enrolment in nursing programs has dropped by one-third, even as the need for nurses (driven by the aging of the Canadian population) goes up. Why this decline? One factor is that today's young women have a wide range of job choices, and fewer are drawn to the traditionally female occupation of nursing. This fact is evident in the rising median age of working nurses, which is now 43 years. Another is that many of today's nurses are unhappy with their working conditions, citing heavy patient loads, too much required overtime, a stressful working environment, and a lack of recognition and respect from supervisors, doctors, and hospital managers. In fact, one recent survey found that a majority of working nurses say they would not recommend the field to others, and more registered nurses are leaving the field for other jobs (Bourgeault & Wrede, 2008).

A positive sign is that the nursing shortage is bringing change to this profession. Salaries for certified nurse anaesthetists are rising, although slowly. Some hospitals and doctors are also offering signing bonuses in an effort to attract new nurses. In addition, nursing programs are trying harder to recruit a more diverse population, seeking more minorities (which are currently underrepresented) and, especially, more men (who currently make up only about 6.7 percent of registered nurses) (CIHI, 2010b).

Theoretical Analysis of Health and Medicine

Each of the theoretical approaches in sociology helps us organize and understand facts and issues concerning human health.

Structural-Functional Analysis: Role Theory

Talcott Parsons (1951) viewed medicine as society's strategy to keep its members healthy. Parsons considered illness dysfunctional because it reduces people's abilities to perform their roles.

The Sick Role

Society responds to illness not only by providing medical care but also by allowing people a **sick role**, *patterns of behaviour defined as appropriate for people who are ill*. According to Parsons, the sick role releases people from everyday obligations such as going to work or attending classes. However, people cannot simply claim to be ill; they must "look the part" and, in serious cases, get the help of a medical expert. After assuming the sick role, the patient must want to get better and must do whatever is needed to regain good health, including co-operating with health professionals.

The Physician's Role

Physicians evaluate people's claims of sickness and help restore the sick to normal routines. To do this, physicians use their specialized knowledge and expect patients to follow "doctor's orders" to complete treatment.

○ **CRITICAL REVIEW** Parsons's analysis links illness and medicine to the broader organization of society. Others have extended the concept of the sick role to some non-illness situations such as pregnancy (Myers & Grasmick, 1989).

One limitation of the sick role concept is that it applies to acute conditions (such as the flu or a broken leg) better than to chronic illnesses (such as heart disease), which may not be reversible. In addition, a sick person's ability to assume the sick role (to take time off from work to regain health) depends on the person's resources. Finally, illness is not completely dysfunctional; it can have some positive consequences. Many people who experience a serious illness consider it an opportunity to re-evaluate their lives and gain a better sense of what is truly important to them (Ehrenreich, 2001; D.G. Myers, 2000).

○ **CHECK YOUR LEARNING** Define the sick role. How does turning illness into a role in this way help society operate?

Symbolic-Interaction Analysis: The Meaning of Health

Using the symbolic-interaction approach, society is less a grand system than a complex and changing reality. In this view, health and medical care are socially constructed by people in everyday interaction.

The Social Construction of Illness

If both health and illness are socially constructed, people in a poor society may view malnutrition as normal. Similarly, many members of our own society give little thought to the harmful effects of a rich diet.

Our response to illness is based also on social definitions that may or may not square with medical facts. People with AIDS may be forced to deal with prejudice that has no medical basis. Likewise, students may pay no attention to symptoms of illness on the eve of vacation but head for the infirmary hours before a midterm examination with a case of the sniffles. In short, health is less an objective fact than a negotiated outcome.

How people define a medical situation may actually affect how they feel. Medical experts marvel at *psychosomatic* disorders (a fusion of the Greek words for "mind" and "body"), when state of mind guides physical sensations (Hamrick, Anspaugh, & Ezell, 1986). Applying the Thomas theorem (presented in Chapter 4, "Social Interaction in Everyday Life"), we can say that once health or illness is defined as real, it can become real in its consequences.

The Social Construction of Treatment

Also in Chapter 4, we used Erving Goffman's dramaturgical approach to explain how doctors tailor their physical surroundings (their office) and their behaviour (the "presentation of self") so that others see them as competent and in charge.

The sociologist Joan Emerson (1970) further illustrates this process of reality construction in her analysis of the gynecological examination carried out by a male doctor. The situation could be seriously misinterpreted because a man touching a woman's genitals is conventionally viewed as a sexual act and possibly an assault.

To ensure that the situation is defined as impersonal and professional, medical personnel wear uniforms and the examination room is furnished with nothing but medical equipment. The doctor's manner is designed to make the patient feel that, to him, examining the genital area is no different from treating any other part of the body. A female nurse is usually present during the examination, not only to assist the physician but also to avoid any impression that a man and woman are "alone together."

Managing situational definitions is rarely taught in medical schools. This oversight is unfortunate, because as Emerson's analysis shows, understanding how medical personnel construct reality in the examination room is as important as mastering the medical skills needed for treatment. One recent

APPLYING THEORY

Health

	Structural-Functional Approach	Symbolic-Interaction Approach	Social-Conflict Approach
What is the level of analysis?	Macro level	Micro level	Macro level
How is health related to society?	Illness is dysfunctional for society because it prevents people from carrying out their daily roles. The sick role releases people who are ill from responsibilities while they try to get well.	Societies define "health" and "illness" differently according to their living standards. How people define their own health affects how they actually feel (psychosomatic conditions).	Health is linked to social inequality, with rich people having more access to care than poor people. Capitalist medical care places the drive for profits over the needs of people, treating symptoms rather than addressing poverty and sexism as causes of illness.

study found that physicians who were weak in social skills, even if they were well trained medically, were much more likely to be the targets of complaints and lawsuits filed by patients (Tamblyn, 2008).

The Social Construction of Personal Identity

A final insight provided by the symbolic-interaction approach is how surgery can affect people's social identity. The reason that medical procedures can have a major effect on how we think of ourselves is that our culture places great symbolic importance on some organs and other parts of our bodies. People who lose a limb (say, in military combat) typically experience serious doubts about being "as much of a person" as before. The effects of surgery can be important even when there is no obvious change in physical appearance. For example, Jean Elson (2004) points out that one out of three women in the United States eventually has her uterus surgically removed in a procedure known as a *hysterectomy*. In interviews with women who had undergone the procedure, Elson found that the typical woman faced serious self-doubt about gender identity—asking, in other words, "Am I still a woman?" Only 10 percent of hysterectomies are for cancer; most are for pain, bleeding, or cysts—serious conditions but not so dangerous that other types of treatment might be considered. Perhaps, Elson points out, doctors would be more willing to consider alternative treatment if they were aware of how symbolically important the loss of the uterus is to many women.

Many women who undergo breast surgery have much the same reaction, doubting their own feminine identity and worrying that men will no longer find them attractive. For men to understand the significance of such medical procedures, it is only necessary to imagine how a male might react to the surgical loss of any or all of his genitals.

CRITICAL REVIEW The symbolic-interaction approach reveals that what people view as healthful or harmful depends on a host of factors that are not, strictly speaking, medical. This approach also shows that in any medical procedure, both patient and medical staff engage in a subtle process of reality construction. Finally, this approach has helped us understand the symbolic importance of limbs and other bodily organs; the loss of any part of the body—through accident or elective surgery—can have important consequences for personal identity.

By directing attention to the meanings people attach to health or illness, the symbolic-interaction approach draws criticism for implying that there are no objective standards of well-being. Certain physical conditions do indeed cause specific changes in people, regardless of how we may view those conditions. For example, people who lack sufficient nutrition and safe water suffer from their unhealthy environment, whether they define their surroundings as normal or not.

A recent study shows that the share of beginning college or university students who describe their physical health as "above average" is lower today than it was in 1985. Do you think this trend reflects changing perceptions or a real decline in health (due, say, to eating more unhealthy food)? The study also found that more women than men see their health as below average. Can you offer any possible reasons?

CHECK YOUR LEARNING Explain what it means to say that both health and the treatment of illness are socially constructed.

The Genetic Crystal Ball: Do We Really Want to Look?

FELISHA: Before I get married, I want my partner to have a genetic screening. It's like buying a house or a car—you should check it out before you sign on the line.

EVA: Do you expect to get a warranty, too?

The discovery of deoxyribonucleic acid, or DNA, was one of the greatest medical breakthroughs of all time. The spiralling DNA molecule is found in every cell of the human body and contains the blueprint for making each one of us human as well as different from every other person.

Your body is composed of roughly 100 trillion cells, most of which contain a nucleus of 23 pairs of chromosomes (one of each pair comes from each parent). Each chromosome is packed with DNA in segments called genes. Genes guide the production of proteins, the building blocks of the human body.

If genetics sounds complicated (and it is), the social implications of genetic knowledge are even more complex. Scientists discovered the structure of the DNA molecule in 1952, but it wasn't until 2000 that scientists had mapped most of the human genome. Charting our genetic landscape will help us understand how each bit of DNA shapes our being.

But many people urge caution in such research, warning that genetic information can easily be abused. At its worst, genetic mapping opens the door to Nazi-like efforts to breed a "super race." In 1994, the People's Republic of China began to use genetic information to regulate marriage and childbirth with the purpose of avoiding "new births of inferior quality."

All over the world, many parents will want to use genetic testing to predict the health (or even the eye colour) of their future children. What if they want to abort a fetus because it falls short of their standards? When genetic manipulations become possible, should parents be able to create "designer children"?

But do we really want to turn the key to understanding life itself? And what do we do with this knowledge once we have it? Research has already identified genetic abnormalities that cause many diseases, including sickle-cell anemia, muscular dystrophy, Huntington's disease, cystic fibrosis, and some forms of cancer. Gazing into a person's genetic "crystal ball," doctors may be able to manipulate segments of DNA to prevent diseases before they appear.

Then there is the issue of "genetic privacy." Can a woman request a genetic evaluation of her fiancé before agreeing to marry? Can life insurance companies demand genetic testing before issuing policies? Should employers be allowed to screen job applicants to weed out those whose future illnesses may drain their company's health care funds? Clearly, what is scientifically possible is not always morally desirable. Society is already struggling with questions about the proper use of our expanding knowledge of human genetics. Such ethical dilemmas will multiply as genetic research moves forward in the years to come.

WHAT DO YOU THINK?

1. Traditional wedding vows join couples "in sickness and in health." Do people have a right to know the future health prospects of a partner before marriage? Why or why not?

2. Should parents be permitted to genetically "design" their children? Why or why not?

3. Should genetic research companies be allowed to patent their discoveries so they can profit from the results, or should this information be made available to everyone? Explain your answer.

Sources: D. Thompson (1999) and Golden and Lemonick (2000).

Social-Conflict and Feminist Analysis

Social-conflict analysis points out the connection between health and social inequality. Some analysts, taking a cue from Karl Marx, tie medicine to the operation of capitalism. In addition, feminists link medicine to sexism and gender stratification. Most attention has gone to three main issues: access to medical care, the effects of the profit motive, and the politics of medicine.

Access to Care

Health is important to everyone. But by requiring individuals to pay directly for medical care, capitalist societies allow the richest people to have the best health. The access problem is more serious in the United States than in most other high-income nations because that country does not have a universal medical care system.

Conflict theorists argue that capitalism provides excellent health care for the rich but at the expense of the rest of the population. Most of the 46 million people in the United States who lack any health care coverage at present have moderate to low incomes. The same is the case in middle- and low-income countries around the globe without comprehensive health care systems.

The Profit Motive

Some social-conflict analysts go further, arguing that the real problem is not access to medical care but capitalist medicine itself. The profit motive turns doctors, hospitals, and the pharmaceutical industry into multi-billion-dollar corporations. The drive for higher profits encourages unnecessary tests and surgery and a reliance on expensive drugs rather than focusing on improving people's lifestyles and living conditions.

Of more than 25 million surgical operations performed in North America each year, three-fourths are elective, meaning that they are intended to promote long-term health and are not prompted by a medical emergency. Of course, any medical procedure or use of drugs is risky and harms between 5 and 10 percent of patients. Therefore, social-conflict theorists argue that surgery reflects not just the medical needs of patients but also the financial interests of surgeons and hospitals (Cowley, 1995; Nuland, 1999).

Finally, say conflict theorists, our society is too tolerant of doctors having a direct financial interest in the tests and procedures they order for their patients (Pear & Eckholm, 1991). Health care should be motivated by a concern for people, not profits.

Medicine as Politics

Although science declares itself to be politically neutral, scientific medicine often takes sides on significant social issues. For example, throughout most of the twentieth century, the Canadian medical establishment mounted a strong and sustained campaign against the legalization and public funding of midwives, although the World Health Organization recommends midwives as essential health care providers for women. Moreover, the history of medicine shows that racial and sexual discrimination have been supported by "scientific" opinions (Leavitt, 1984). Consider the diagnosis of "hysteria," a term that has its origins in the Greek word *hyster*, meaning "uterus." In choosing this word to describe a wild, emotional state, the medical profession suggested that being a woman is somehow the same as being irrational.

CRITICAL REVIEW Social-conflict analysis provides still another view of the relationships among health, medicine, and society. According to this approach, social inequality is the reason why some people have better health than others.

The most common objection to the conflict approach is that it minimizes the advances in health brought about by scientific medicine and higher living standards. Though there is plenty of room for improvement, health indicators for our population as a whole rose steadily over the course of the twentieth century, and they compare well with those in other high-income nations.

CHECK YOUR LEARNING How are health and medical care linked to social classes, capitalism, and gender stratification?

Sociology's three major theoretical approaches, summed up in the Applying Theory table on page 404, explain why health and medicine are social issues.

But advancing technology will not solve every health problem. On the contrary, as the Controversy & Debate box on page 405 explains, today's advancing technology is raising new questions and concerns.

The famous French scientist Louis Pasteur (1822–1895), who spent much of his life studying how bacteria cause disease, said just before he died that health depends less on bacteria than on the social environment in which the bacteria are found (Gordon, 1980:7). Explaining Pasteur's insight is sociology's contribution to human health.

Health and Medicine: Looking Ahead

In the early 1900s, deaths from infectious diseases such as diphtheria and measles were widespread. Because scientists had not yet developed penicillin and other antibiotics, even a simple infection from a minor wound was sometimes life-threatening. Today, a century later, most members of our society take good health and long life for granted. It seems reasonable to expect improvements in the health of Canadians to continue throughout the twenty-first century.

Another encouraging trend is that more people are taking responsibility for their own health (Lelonde, 1974; Segall & Chappell, 2000). Every one of us can live better and longer if we avoid tobacco, eat sensibly and in moderation, and exercise regularly.

Yet health problems will continue to plague Canadian society in the decades to come. The changing social profile of people with AIDS—which increasingly afflicts youth, the poor, Aboriginals, women, and the marginalized—reminds us that Canada has much to do to improve the health of disadvantaged members of our society. Even those among us who do not easily embrace the notion of serving as "our brother's keeper" should recognize our moral obligation to guarantee everyone the security of health care.

Finally, we find that health problems are far greater in low-income nations than in Canada. The good news is that life expectancy for the world as a whole has been rising—from 48 years in 1950 to 69 years today—and the biggest gains have been in poor-resourced countries (Population Reference Bureau, 2010). But in much of Latin America, Asia, and especially Africa, hundreds of millions of adults and children lack not only basic health care but adequate food and safe water as well. Improving the health of the world's poorest people is a critical challenge in the years to come.

CHAPTER 14 EDUCATION, HEALTH, AND MEDICINE

HOW DOES SOCIETY AFFECT PATTERNS OF HEALTH? Certain occupations put people at higher-than-average risk of accident or death. One example is coal mining, which has long been one of the deadliest jobs. Although the death toll from mining accidents in Canada has gone down over time, even miners who manage to avoid mine collapses or explosions typically suffer harm from years of breathing coal dust. Look at the photos below: How do they link health to a way of life?

Crews on fishing boats such as this one spend months at a time battling high seas and often frigid temperatures. As documented on the television show *The Deadliest Catch*, it is a rare and fortunate fishing season that brings no death or serious injury. What other jobs threaten the health and well-being of Canadian workers?

The worst mining disaster in Canadian history occurred in 1914, when 189 miners lost their lives. This photo was taken after an explosion ripped through a coal mine in Hillcrest, Alberta. About 80 workers died annually over a three-year period ending in 2009 in jobs that involve mining, quarrying, and petroleum production. What social patterns (think about class, gender, and other factors) can you see in the history of mining and health?

HINT: Among the most dangerous jobs in Canada are farming (dangers come from using power equipment), mining, timber cutting, truck driving, and constructing tall buildings. Many members of the military also face danger on a daily basis. In general, people in the working class are at greater risk than middle-class people, who typically work in offices; men also predominate in the most dangerous jobs. In Canada, about 1000 workplace fatalities and well over 300 000 lost-time workplace injuries occur annually.

Applying Sociology in Everyday Life

1. Think about the effects of schooling on health. In what ways does getting a university or college degree (and perhaps a graduate or professional degree) improve a person's likelihood of leading a healthy life?

2. Visit a secondary school near your school or home. Does it have a tracking policy? If so, find out how it works. How much importance does a student's family background have in making a tracking assignment?

3. Given the importance of sexuality in our thinking about women in Canada (and how they think about themselves), how do you think medical procedures such as mastectomy (surgical removal of part or all of a breast) affect women's personal and social identity? (To learn more about these experiences, see Elson, 2004.)

MAKING THE GRADE

CHAPTER 14   Education, Health, and Medicine

Education: A Global Survey

EDUCATION is the major social institution for transmitting knowledge and skills, as well as teaching cultural norms and values.
- In pre-industrial societies, education occurs informally within the family.
- Industrial societies develop formal systems of schooling to educate their children.

pp. 373–76

education (p. 373) the social institution through which society provides its members with important knowledge, including basic facts, job skills, and cultural norms and values

schooling (p. 373) formal instruction under the direction of specially trained teachers

Theoretical Analysis of Schooling

The **STRUCTURAL-FUNCTIONAL APPROACH** highlights major functions of schooling, including socialization, cultural innovation, social integration, and the placement of people in the social hierarchy.
- Latent functions of schooling include providing child care and building social networks.

pp. 376–77

The **SYMBOLIC-INTERACTION APPROACH** helps us understand that stereotypes can have important consequences for how people act. If students think they are academically superior, they are likely to perform better; students who think they are inferior are likely to perform less well.

pp. 377–78

tracking (p. 379) assigning students to different types of educational programs

The **SOCIAL-CONFLICT APPROACH** links schooling to the hierarchy involving class, race, and gender.
- Formal education serves as a means of generating conformity to produce obedient adult workers.
- Standardized achievement tests have been criticized as culturally biased tools that may lead to labelling less privileged students as personally deficient.
- Tracking has been challenged by critics as a program that gives privileged youngsters a richer education.
- The great majority of young people in Canada attend provincially funded public schools. A small proportion of students—usually the most well-to-do—attend elite private schools.
- Largely due to the high cost of higher education, by age 20, two in ten high school graduates have not enrolled in a college, university, or trade school.

pp. 378–84

See the Applying Theory table on page 386.

Problems in the Schools

- Violence permeates many schools, especially in poor neighbourhoods.
- The bureaucratic character of schools fosters student passivity and high dropout rates.
- Declining academic standards are reflected in the functional illiteracy of a significant proportion of high school graduates and in grade inflation.

pp. 384–88

functional illiteracy (p. 388) a lack of the reading and writing skills needed for everyday living

Health and Medicine

HEALTH is a social issue because personal well-being depends on a society's level of technology and its distribution of resources. A society's culture shapes definitions of health.

p. 388–90

medicine (p. 388) the social institution that focuses on fighting disease and improving health

health (p. 388) a state of complete physical, mental, and social well-being

Health: A Global Survey

HEALTH VARIES OVER TIME:
- With industrialization, health improved dramatically in Western Europe and North America in the nineteenth century.
- A century ago, infectious diseases were leading killers; today, most people in Canada die in old age of chronic illnesses such as heart disease, cancer, or stroke.

p.390

HEALTH VARIES AROUND THE WORLD:
- Poor-resourced nations suffer from inadequate sanitation, hunger, and other problems linked to poverty.
- Life expectancy in low-income nations is about 25 years less than in Canada; in the poorest nations, half of the children do not survive to adulthood.

pp. 390–91

Health in Canada

HEALTH FACTS

- Throughout the life course, women have better health than men, and people of high social position enjoy better health than the poor.
- There is a seven-year gap in life expectancy between Canada's Aboriginal population and other Canadians.

pp. 391–92

CURRENT ISSUES in Canadian health care include

- cigarette smoking, which is the greatest preventable cause of death
- eating disorders and obesity
- the increase in sexually transmitted infections
- ethical dilemmas associated with advancing medical technology and the right to die

pp. 392–97

social epidemiology (p. 391) the study of how health and disease are distributed throughout a society's population

eating disorder (p. 392) an intense form of dieting or other unhealthy method of weight control driven by the desire to be very thin

euthanasia (p. 397) assisting in the death of a person suffering from an incurable disease; also known as *mercy killing*

The Medical Establishment

THE RISE OF SCIENTIFIC MEDICINE

- Health care was historically a family concern but with industrialization became the responsibility of trained specialists.
- The model of scientific medicine is the foundation of the Canadian medical establishment.

pp. 398–99

PAYING FOR HEALTH CARE: A GLOBAL SURVEY

- Socialist societies define medical care as a right; governments offer basic care equally to everyone.
- Capitalist societies view medical care as a commodity to be purchased, although most capitalist governments help pay for medical care through socialized medicine or national health insurance.

pp. 399–401

PAYING FOR HEALTH CARE: CANADA

- All Canadians have access to government health insurance.
- There is a primary health care renewal movement currently under way cross the country.

pp. 401–403

holistic medicine (p. 398) an approach to health care that emphasizes the prevention of illness and takes into account a person's entire physical and social environment

socialized medicine (p. 400) a health care system in which the government owns and operates most medical facilities and employs most physicians

direct-fee system (p. 400) a health care system in which patients pay directly for the services of physicians and hospitals

Theoretical Analysis of Health and Medicine

The **STRUCTURAL-FUNCTIONAL APPROACH** considers illness dysfunctional because it reduces people's abilities to perform their roles (Talcott Parsons). Society responds to illness by defining roles:

- The sick role excuses the ill person from routine social responsibilities.
- The physician's role is to use specialized knowledge to take charge of the patient's recovery.

p. 403

The **SYMBOLIC-INTERACTION APPROACH** investigates how health and medical care are socially constructed by people in everyday interaction:

- Our response to illness is not always based on medical facts.
- How people define a medical situation may affect how they feel.

pp. 403–04

The **SOCIAL-CONFLICT AND FEMINIST APPROACHES** focus on the unequal distribution of health and medical care. They criticize the medical establishment for

- its overreliance on drugs and surgery.
- the dominance of the profit motive.
- an overemphasis on the biological rather than the social causes of illness.

pp. 405–06

sick role (p. 403) patterns of behaviour defined as appropriate for people who are ill

See the Applying Theory table on page 404.

MySocLab

Visit MySocLab at www.mysoclab.com to access a variety of online resources that will help you to prepare for tests and to apply your knowledge, including

- an eText
- videos
- self-grading quizzes
- glossary flashcards

15 Population, Urbanization, and Environment

- How is the state of the natural environment a social issue?

- Why should we worry about the rapid rate of global population increase?

- What makes city and rural living different?

This chapter explores three related dimensions of social change: population dynamics, urbanization, and increasing threats to the natural environment.

Two hundred years ago, Captain Vancouver first charted the Burrard Inlet. One hundred years later, Vancouver was home to fewer than 50 000 people. Today, with a population of more than 2 million, and as the city has expanded outward, commuting for an hour to work is commonplace.

Growth like this prompted experts to coin the term *urban sprawl.* Such uncontrolled growth is the result of more and more people, all of whom want bigger houses, as well as the conveniences offered by roads, schools, recreation facilities, and, of course, superstores and shopping malls. No doubt, most people in Canada see growth like this as good—the product of prosperity.

But is it that simple? This chapter examines three closely related processes: population increase, urbanization, and the state of the natural environment. As we shall see, population has soared during the past two centuries—in Canada and also around the world—and cities everywhere have grown rapidly. We shall consider how these changes have altered the shape of societies and what they mean for the future of the planet. We begin with population.

Demography: The Study of Population

When humans first began to cultivate plants some 12 000 years ago, Earth's entire *Homo sapiens* population was about 5 million, or about the number of people living in Toronto today. Very slow growth pushed the total in 1 CE to perhaps 300 million, or a little less than 10 times the population of Canada today.

Starting around 1750, world population began to spike upward. We are currently adding nearly 83 million people to the planet each year; the world now holds 7 billion people.

The causes and consequences of this drama are the focus of **demography**, *the study of human population.* Demography (from the Greek, meaning "description of people") is a cousin of sociology that analyzes the size and composition of a population and studies how and why people move from place to place. Demographers not only collect statistics but also raise important questions about the effects of population growth and suggest how it might be controlled. The following sections present basic demographic concepts.

Fertility

The study of human population begins with how many people are born. **Fertility** is *the incidence of child-bearing in a country's population.* During a woman's child-bearing years, from the onset of menstruation (typically in the early teens) to menopause (usually in the late forties), she is capable of bearing more than 20 children. But *fecundity,* or maximum possible child-bearing, is sharply reduced by cultural norms, finances, and personal choice.

Demographers describe fertility using the **crude birth rate**, *the number of live births in a given year for every 1000 people in a population.* To calculate a crude birth rate, divide the number of live births in a year by the total population and multiply the result by 1000. In Canada, in 2010, there were 382 027 births in a population of 34 108 752, yielding a crude birth rate of 11.2 (Statistics Canada, 2011aq, 2011ar).

> *January 18, Coshocton County, Ohio. Having just finished off the mountains of meat and potatoes that make up a typical Amish meal, our group of college students has gathered in the living room of Jacob and Anna Raber, members of this rural Amish community. Anna, a mother of four, is telling us about Amish life. "Most of the women I know have 5 or 6 children," she says with a smile, "but certainly not everybody—some have 11 or 12!"*

A country's birth rate is described as "crude" because it is based on the entire population, not just women in their child-bearing years. In addition, this measure ignores differences among various categories of the population: Fertility among the Amish, for example, is quite high, and fertility among Asians Canadians is low. But the measure is easy to calculate and allows rough comparisons of the fertility of one country or region to others. Part (a) of Figure 15–1 shows that, compared to the rest of the world, the crude birth rate of North Americans is low.

Mortality

Population size also reflects **mortality**, *the incidence of death in a country's population.* To measure mortality, demographers use the **crude death rate**, *the number of deaths in a given year for every 1000 people in a population.* This time, we take the number of deaths in a year, divide by the total population, and multiply the result by 1000. In 2010, there were 250 810 deaths in the Canadian population of 34 108 752, yielding a crude death rate of 7.4 (Statistics Canada, 2011ar, 2011as). Part (a) of Figure 15–1 shows that, in global context, this rate is about average.

demography (p. 411) the study of human population

fertility (p. 411) the incidence of child-bearing in a country's population

crude birth rate (p. 411) the number of live births in a given year for every 1000 people in a population

mortality (p. 411) the incidence of death in a country's population

crude death rate (p. 411) the number of deaths in a given year for every 1000 people in a population

infant mortality rate the number of deaths among infants under one year of age for each 1000 live births in a given year

life expectancy the average lifespan of a country's population

migration the movement of people into and out of a specified territory

Global Snapshot

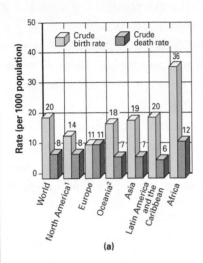
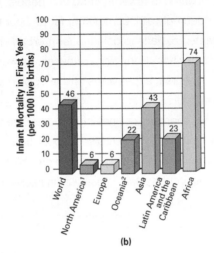
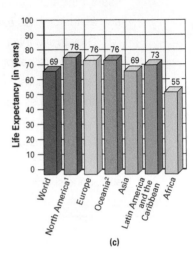

(a)   (b)   (c)

FIGURE 15–1   (a) Crude Birth Rates and Crude Death Rates, (b) Infant Mortality Rates, and (c) Life Expectancy around the World, 2009

By world standards, North America has a low birth rate, an average death rate, a very low infant mortality rate, and high life expectancy.

[1] Canada and the United States.

[2] Australia, New Zealand, and South Pacific Islands.

Source: Population Reference Bureau (2009).

A third useful demographic measure is the **infant mortality rate**, *the number of deaths among infants under one year of age for each 1000 live births in a given year*. To compute infant mortality, divide the number of deaths of children under one year of age by the number of live births during the same year and multiply the result by 1000. In 2007, there were 1881 infant deaths and 367 864 live births in Canada (Statistics Canada, 2011at, 2011au). Dividing the first number by the second and multiplying the result by 1000 yields an infant mortality rate of 5.11. Part (b) of Figure 15–1 indicates that, by world standards, North American infant mortality is very low.

But remember the differences among various categories of people. For example, Aboriginals, who are twice as likely as non-Aboriginals to live below the poverty line, have an infant mortality rate almost twice as high as the national rate.

Low infant mortality greatly raises **life expectancy**, *the average lifespan of a country's population*. According to the most recent Statistics Canada estimates, males born in Canada can expect to live 78.3 years and females can look forward to 83.0 years (Statistics Canada, 2011av, 2011aw). As part (c) of Figure 15–1 shows, life expectancy for North Americans is 23 years greater than that typical of the low-income countries of Africa.

Migration

Population size is also affected by **migration**, *the movement of people into and out of a specified territory*. Movement into nations, or *immigration*, is calculated as the number of people entering a nation area for every 1000 people in the population. Movement out of a nation, or *emigration*, is measured as the number leaving for every 1000 people. Both types of migration usually occur at the same time, of course, and the difference between the immigration rate and the emigration rate is called the *net migration rate*.

All nations also experience internal migration—that is, movement within their borders, from one region to another. We use the terms *in-migration* and *out-migration* to describe this movement. Most internal migration consists of short-distance moves. Fewer than 1 million Canadians moved across a provincial or territorial border between 1996 and 2001, out of the 11.7 million (one in four) Canadians who moved during this time period (Statistics Canada, 2008r).

Migration is sometimes voluntary, as when people leave a small town to move to a larger city. In such cases, "push-pull" factors are usually at work: A lack of jobs "pushes" people to move, and more opportunity elsewhere "pulls" people to someplace new. The lack of

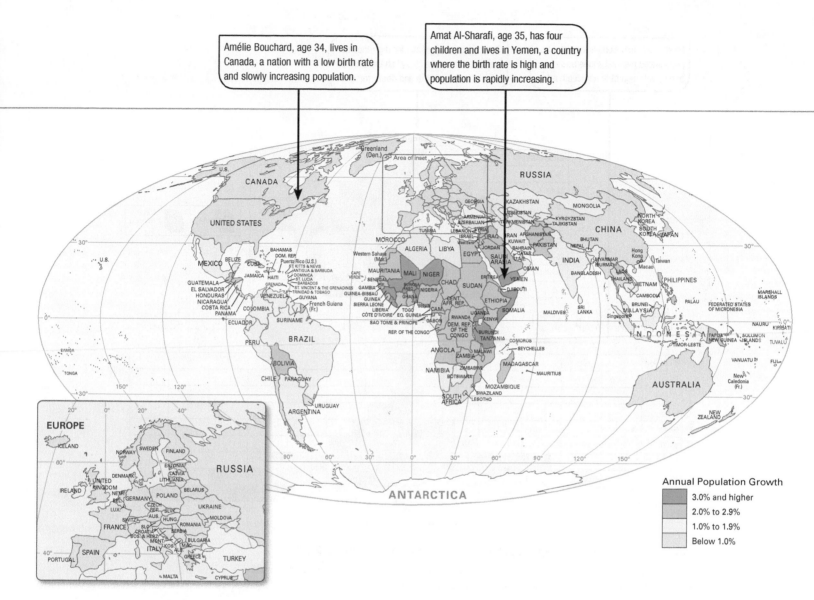

Amélie Bouchard, age 34, lives in Canada, a nation with a low birth rate and slowly increasing population.

Amat Al-Sharafi, age 35, has four children and lives in Yemen, a country where the birth rate is high and population is rapidly increasing.

Annual Population Growth

- 3.0% and higher
- 2.0% to 2.9%
- 1.0% to 1.9%
- Below 1.0%

Window on the World

GLOBAL MAP 15–1 **Population Growth in Global Perspective**

The richest countries of the world—including Canada, the United States, and the nations of Europe—have growth rates below 1 percent. The nations of Latin America and Asia typically have growth rates around 1.5 percent, a rate that doubles a population in 47 years. Africa has an overall growth rate of 2.4 percent (despite only small increases in countries with a high rate of AIDS), which cuts the doubling time to 29 years. In global perspective, we see that a society's standard of living is closely related to its rate of population growth: Population is rising fastest in the world regions that can least afford to support more people.

Source: U.S. Census Bureau (2011).

jobs for Newfoundlanders in the last few decades stimulated out-migration to Fort McMurray, Alberta. It is estimated that Newfoundland migrants make up 17 percent of that city's population today, the largest groups after Albertans. Migration can also be involuntary, such as the forced transport of 10 million Africans to the Western Hemisphere as slaves or when Hurricane Katrina caused tens of thousands of people to flee New Orleans.

Population Growth

Fertility, mortality, and migration all affect the size of a society's population. In general, well-resourced nations (such as Canada) grow almost as much from immigration as from natural increase; poorer nations (such as Pakistan) grow almost entirely from natural increase.

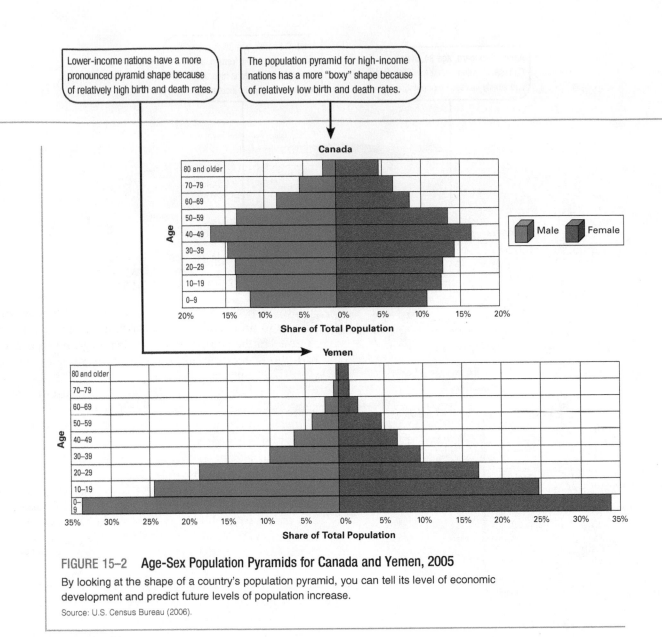

FIGURE 15–2 Age-Sex Population Pyramids for Canada and Yemen, 2005

By looking at the shape of a country's population pyramid, you can tell its level of economic development and predict future levels of population increase.

Source: U.S. Census Bureau (2006).

To calculate a population's *natural growth rate*, demographers subtract the crude death rate from the crude birth rate. The natural growth rate of the Canadian population in 2010 was 3.8 per 1000 (the crude birth rate of 11.2 minus the crude death rate of 7.4), or about 0.4 percent annual growth.

Global Map 15–1 on page 413 shows that population growth in Canada and other high-income nations is well below the world average of 1.2 percent. Earth's low-growth continents are Europe (currently posting no growth) and North America (increasing by 0.6 percent). Near the global average are Oceania (1.1 percent), Asia (1.2 percent), and Latin America (1.4 percent). The highest-growth region of the world is Africa (2.4 percent).

A handy rule for estimating population growth is to divide a society's population growth into the number 70; this yields the *doubling time* in years. Thus an annual growth rate of 2 percent (found in parts of Latin America) doubles a population in 35 years, and a 3 percent growth rate (found in some countries in Africa) drops the

doubling time to just 23 years. The rapid population growth of the poorest countries is deeply troubling because these countries can barely support the populations they have now.

Population Composition

Demographers also study the makeup of a society's population at a given point in time. One variable is the **sex ratio**, *the number of males for every 100 females in a nation's population.* In 2010, the sex ratio in Canada was 98, or 99 males for every 100 females. Sex ratios are ordinarily below 100 because, on average, women outlive men. Because the area around Cape Breton, Nova Scotia, has an aging population, its sex ratio is 91, or 91 males for every 100 females. In India, however, the sex ratio is 108 because parents value sons more than daughters and may either abort a female fetus or, after birth, give more care to a male infant, raising the odds that a female child will die.

A more complex measure is the **age-sex pyramid**, *a graphic representation of the age and sex of a population.* Figure 15–2 presents

sex ratio (p. 414) the number of males for every 100 females in a nation's population

age-sex pyramid (p. 414) a graphic representation of the age and sex of a population

This street scene in Kolkata (Calcutta), India, conveys the vision of the future found in the work of Thomas Robert Malthus, who feared that population increase would overwhelm the world's resources. Can you explain why Malthus had such a serious concern about population? How is demographic transition theory a more hopeful analysis?

natural growth is many times higher than the Canadian rate. This illustrates what demographers call *demographic momentum*—even with a sharp reduction in the number of children per family, the large number of people in their child-bearing years ensures a large number of births.

History and Theory of Population Growth

In the past, people wanted large families because human labour was the key to productivity. In addition, until rubber condoms were invented in the mid-1800s, preventing pregnancy was uncertain at best. But high death rates from infectious diseases put a constant brake on population growth.

A major demographic shift began about 1750 as the world's population turned upward, reaching the 1 billion mark by 1800. This milestone (which took all of human history to reach) was matched barely a century later in 1930, when a second billion people were added to the planet. In other words, not only was population increasing, but the *rate* of growth was accelerating. Global population reached 3 billion by 1962 (just 32 years later) and 4 billion by 1974 (only 12 years later). The rate of world population increase has slowed recently, but the planet passed the 5 billion mark in 1987 and the 6 billion mark in 1999 and now stands at 7 billion. In no previous century did the world's population even double. In the twentieth century, it *quadrupled*.

Currently, the world is gaining almost 83 million people each year; 98 percent of this increase is in low-income countries. Experts predict that Earth's population will be more than 9 billion in 2050 (United Nations Population Division, 2010). Given the world's troubles feeding its present population, such an increase is a matter of urgent concern.

Malthusian Theory

The sudden population growth 250 years ago sparked the development of demography. Thomas Robert Malthus (1766–1834), an English economist and clergyman, warned that rapid population increase would lead to social chaos. Malthus (1926, orig. 1798) calculated that population would increase in what mathematicians call a *geometric progression*, illustrated by the series of numbers 2, 4, 8, 16, 32, and so on. At such a rate, Malthus concluded, world population would soon soar out of control.

Food production would also increase, Malthus explained, but only in an *arithmetic progression* (as in the series 2, 3, 4, 5, 6, and so on) because even with new agricultural technology, farmland is limited. Thus Malthus presented a troubling vision of the future: people reproducing beyond what the planet could feed, leading ultimately to widespread starvation and war over what resources were left.

the age-sex pyramids for Canada and Yemen. Higher death rates as people age give these figures a rough pyramid shape. In the Canadian pyramid, the bulge near the middle reflects the high birth rates during the "baby boom" from the mid-1940s to the mid-1960s. The contraction for people in their twenties and thirties reflects the subsequent "baby bust" when the number of births declined from a high of 479 000 in 1959 to 343 000 in 1973.

Comparison of the Canadian and Yemeni age-sex pyramids shows different demographic trends. The age-sex pyramid for Yemen, like that of other nations with high fertility, is wide at the bottom because the number of births increases every year. Yemen, in short, is a much younger population. With a larger share of females still in their child-bearing years, Yemen's crude birth rate is, understandably, considerably higher than our own, and its annual rate of

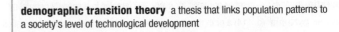

demographic transition theory a thesis that links population patterns to a society's level of technological development

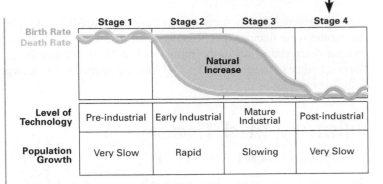

Canada is in this historical stage, with both a low birth rate and a low death rate.

	Stage 1	Stage 2	Stage 3	Stage 4
Birth Rate Death Rate		Natural Increase		
Level of Technology	Pre-industrial	Early Industrial	Mature Industrial	Post-industrial
Population Growth	Very Slow	Rapid	Slowing	Very Slow

FIGURE 15–3   Demographic Transition Theory

Demographic transition theory links population change to a society's level of technological development.

Malthus recognized that artificial birth control or abstaining from sex might change his prediction. But he considered one morally wrong and the other impractical. Famine and war therefore stalked humanity in Malthus's mind, and he was justly known as "the dismal parson."

○ **CRITICAL REVIEW**   Fortunately, Malthus's prediction was flawed. First, by 1850, the European birth rate began to drop, partly because, with industrialization, children were becoming an economic liability rather than an asset and partly because people began using artificial birth control. Second, Malthus underestimated human ingenuity: Modern irrigation techniques, fertilizers, and pesticides have increased farm production far more than he could have imagined.

Some people criticized Malthus for ignoring the role of social inequality in world abundance and famine. For example, Karl Marx (1967, orig. 1867) objected to his view of suffering as a "law of nature" rather than the curse of capitalism. More recently, "critical demographers" have claimed that saying poverty is caused by a high birth rate in low-income countries amounts to blaming the victims. On the contrary, they see global inequality as the real issue (Horton, 1999; Kuumba, 1999).

Still, Malthus offers an important lesson. Habitable land, clean water, and fresh air are limited resources, and increased economic productivity has taken a heavy toll on the natural environment. In addition, medical advances have lowered death rates, pushing up world population. In principle, of course, no level of population growth can go on forever. People everywhere must become aware of the dangers of population increase.

○ **CHECK YOUR LEARNING**   What did Malthus predict about human population increase? About food production? What was his overall conclusion?

Demographic Transition Theory

A more complex analysis of population change is **demographic transition theory**, *a thesis that links population patterns to a society's level of technological development.* Figure 15–3 shows the demographic consequences at four levels of technological development. Pre-industrial, agrarian societies (Stage 1) have high birth rates because of the economic value of children and the absence of birth control. Death rates are also high because of low living standards and limited medical technology. Outbreaks of disease cancel out births, so population rises and falls with only a modest overall increase. This was the case for thousands of years in Europe before the Industrial Revolution.

Stage 2, the onset of industrialization, brings a demographic transition as death rates fall because of greater food supplies and scientific medicine. But birth rates remain high, resulting in rapid population growth. It was during Europe's Stage 2 that Malthus formulated his ideas, which accounts for his pessimistic view of the future. The world's poorest countries today are in this high-growth stage.

In Stage 3, a mature industrial economy, the birth rate drops, curbing population growth once again. Fertility falls because most children survive to adulthood, so fewer are needed, and because high living standards make raising children expensive. In short, affluence transforms children from economic assets into economic liabilities. Smaller families, made possible by effective birth control, are also favoured by women working outside the home. As birth rates follow death rates downward, population growth slows further.

Stage 4 corresponds to a post-industrial economy in which the demographic transition is complete. The birth rate keeps falling, partly because dual-income couples gradually become the norm and partly because the cost of raising and schooling children continues to increase. This trend, coupled with steady death rates, means that population grows only very slowly or even decreases. This is the case today in Japan, Europe, Canada, and the United States.

○ **CRITICAL REVIEW**   Demographic transition theory suggests that the key to population control lies in technology. Instead of the runaway population increase feared by Malthus, this theory sees technology slowing growth and spreading material plenty.

Demographic transition theory is linked to modernization theory, one approach to global development discussed in Chapter 9 ("Global Stratification"). Modernization theorists are optimistic that low-income countries will solve their population problems as they industrialize. But critics, notably dependency theorists, strongly disagree. Unless there is a redistribution of global resources, they maintain, our planet will become increasingly divided into affluent "haves," enjoying low population growth, and poor "have-nots," struggling in vain to feed more and more people.

○ **CHECK YOUR LEARNING**   Explain the four stages of demographic transition theory.

zero population growth the rate of reproduction that maintains population at a steady level

Global Population Today: A Brief Survey

What can we say about population in today's world? Drawing on the discussion so far, we can identify important patterns and reach several conclusions.

The Low-Growth North

When the Industrial Revolution began in the Northern Hemisphere, population growth in Western Europe and North America was a high 3 percent annually. But in the centuries since, the growth rate has steadily declined, and in 1970 it fell below 1 percent. As our post-industrial society settles into Stage 4, the Canadian birth rate of 1.66 in 2007 is below the replacement level of 2.1 children per woman, a point that demographers call **zero population growth**, *the rate of reproduction that maintains population at a steady level.* More than 70 nations, almost all of them rich, are at or below the point of zero population growth.

Among the factors that serve to hold down population in these post-industrial societies are the high proportion of men and women in the labour force, the rising costs of raising children, trends toward later marriage and singlehood, and the widespread use of contraceptives and abortion.

In high-income nations, then, population increase is not the pressing problem that it is in poor countries. On the contrary, many governments in high-income countries are concerned about a future problem of *underpopulation* because declining population size may be difficult to reverse and also because the swelling ranks of the elderly will have fewer and fewer young people to look to for support (Kent & Mather, 2002; United Nations Population Division, 2009).

The High-Growth South

Population is a critical problem in low-income nations of the Southern Hemisphere. No nation in the world lacks industrial technology entirely; demographic transition theory's Stage 1 applies only to remote rural areas of low-income nations. But much of Latin America, Africa, and Asia is at Stage 2, with mixed agrarian and industrial economies. Advanced medical technology, supplied by well-resourced societies, has sharply reduced death rates, but birth rates remain high. This is why low-income societies now account for two-thirds of Earth's people and 98 percent of global population increase.

In inadequately resourced countries around the world, birth rates have fallen from an average of about six children per woman in 1950 to three or four today. But fertility this high will only intensify global poverty. That is why leaders in the battle against global poverty point to the importance of reducing fertility rates in low-income nations. Notice, too, that a key element in controlling world population growth is improving the status of women. Why? Because of this simple truth: Give women more life choices and they will have fewer children. History has shown that women

Fertility in Canada has fallen during the past century and is now quite low. But some categories of the Canadian population have much higher fertility rates. One example is the Mennonites, a religious society that lives in rural areas of Ontario. It is common for Mennonite couples to have five, six, or more children. Why do you think the Mennonites favour large families?

who are free to decide when and where to marry, who bear children as a matter of choice, and who have access to education and to good jobs will limit their own fertility (Axinn & Barber, 2001; Roudi-Fahimi & Kent, 2007).

The Demographic Divide

High- and low-income nations display very different population dynamics, a gap that is sometimes called the *demographic divide.* In Italy, a high-income, very-low-growth nation, women average just more than one child in their lifetimes. Such a low birth rate means that the number of annual births is actually less than the number of deaths. This means that, at the moment, Italy is actually *losing* population. Looking ahead to 2050 and even assuming some gains from immigration, Italy's population is projected to be about the same as it is today. The share of elderly people in Italy—now 20 percent—will only increase as time goes on.

Look at how different the patterns are in a low-income nation such as the Democratic Republic of the Congo in Central Africa. There, women still have an average of six to seven children, so even with a high mortality rate this nation's population will triple by 2050. The share of elderly people is extremely low—about 3 percent—and half of the country's people are below the age of 15. With such a high growth rate, it is no surprise that the problem of poverty is bad and getting worse: About three-fourths of the people are undernourished (Population Reference Bureau, 2009).

In sum, a demographic divide now separates higher-income countries with low birth rates and aging populations from lower-income countries with high birth rates and very young populations. Just as humanity has devised ways to reduce deaths around the world, so it must now bring down population growth, especially in

THINKING ABOUT DIVERSITY: RACE, CLASS, & GENDER

What's Happened to the Girls? China's One-Child Policy

The parents had argued for hours. But the man was determined and the woman was exhausted. The father wrestled the sleeping baby girl from the mother's arms. The decision was now made; the girl had to go. The father put several extra layers of clothing on his daughter and lay the newborn girl in a cardboard box lined with blankets. Next to her, he placed a small bottle of milk. He walked off into the dark night toward the distant village, leaving behind the sobbing of his beloved wife—the baby's mother—who cried out, "Please, I beg you, bring back my baby!"

Yet in her heart, she too knew that this must be done. Half an hour later, the father arrived in the village and found his way to the local school. For the last time, he kissed his daughter good-bye. He set her makeshift crib on the steps of the school's front entrance, knowing that when dawn broke in an hour or so, she would be found and cared for. With tears in his eyes, he said a quick prayer to his ancestors to keep the baby safe from harm. Then he turned and again disappeared into the night, knowing that he would never see or hear from her again.

This story may be heartbreaking, but it is one that has occurred tens of thousands of times in China. What would prompt parents to give up a child? Why would a father abandon his daughter in a public place? The answer lies in China's population control policy and the nation's cultural traditions.

Back in the 1970s, the high Chinese birth rate was fuelling an extremely rapid population increase. Government leaders could see that the country's economic development depended on controlling population growth. As a result, they passed a law stating that a family can have only one child. Families who follow the one-child policy can expect rewards such as a better job, a higher salary, and maybe even a larger apartment. On the other hand, parents who violate the law by having a second child face a stiff fine, and their second child may not be eligible for educational and health care benefits.

The government actively promotes the one-child message in the mass media, in popular songs, and in the schools. But education is not the government's only tactic—enforcement officials can be found in most neighbourhoods and workplaces. Most Chinese willingly comply with the policy, praising it as good for the country. Those who do not must face the consequences.

Modern China is determined to control population increase. But China is also a country steeped in a tradition of male dominance. If government rules permit only one child, most families would prefer a boy. Why? Parents see boys as a better investment because sons will carry on the family name and must care for their aging parents. On the other hand, girls will end up caring for their husbands' parents, leading most Chinese to see raising daughters as a waste of precious resources. The Chinese government has expanded women's rights and opportunities, but patriarchal traditions are deeply rooted in the country's history and, as is true everywhere, attitudes change slowly.

Around the world, the one-child policy has attracted both praise and condemnation. On the positive side, analysts agree that it has succeeded in its goal of reducing the rate of population increase. This trend, in turn, has helped raise living standards and lifted China to the ranks of middle-income nations. Many one-child families are happy with the added income from women who now work outside the home, and parents now have more to spend on a child's schooling.

But the one-child policy also has a dark side, shown in the story that began this box. Since the law was passed, as many as 1 million girls have "disappeared." In some cases, parents who learn that the woman is carrying a female fetus may choose abortion so they can "try again." In other cases, family members decide to kill a female infant soon after birth. In still other cases, girls survive but are never recorded in the birth statistics so that they grow up as "non-citizens" who can never go to school or receive treatment at a local health clinic. Finally, some parents, like those described earlier, give up or abandon their daughter in the hope that the child may find a home elsewhere.

China's one-child policy has certainly held population increase in check. But it has had a dramatic toll on the female population of China. In one recent year, the nation's birth records showed almost 1 million fewer girls than boys. The Chinese population is now about 250 million lower than it would have been without the one-child policy, but it is also steadily becoming more and more male.

WHAT DO YOU THINK?

1. Point to the reasons why China's one-child policy has attracted praise and also blame. On balance, do you think this is a good policy? Can you think of a better way to control population? Explain.

2. What about cases where parents think they can afford additional children? Should family size be a couple's decision? Or does government have a responsibility to look out for the entire country's well-being?

3. Do you now understand why almost all of the babies that North American parents adopt from China are girls?

Sources: Gu et al. (2007), Hesketh & Lu (2005), and Yardley (2008).

poor countries where projections suggest a future as bleak as that imagined by Thomas Malthus centuries ago.

China stands out as a nation that has taken a strong stand on reducing the rate of population increase. That country's one-child policy, enacted in the 1970s, has reduced China's potential population by about 250 million. Yet, as the Thinking about Diversity box above explains, this policy has been controversial.

In much of the world today, mortality is falling. To limit population increase, the world—especially poor nations—must control births as successfully as it is fending off deaths.

Urbanization:
The Growth of Cities

October 8, Hong Kong. The cable train grinds to the top of Victoria Peak, where we behold one of the world's most spectacular vistas: the city of Hong Kong at night. A million bright, colourful lights ring the harbour as ships, ferries, and traditional Chinese junks churn by. Few cities match Hong Kong for sheer energy: This small city is as economically productive as British Columbia, Alberta, and Saskatchewan combined or the nation of Finland. We could sit here for hours entranced by the spectacle of Hong Kong.

Throughout most of human history, the sights and sounds of great cities such as Hong Kong, New York, and Paris were simply unimaginable. Our distant ancestors lived in small, nomadic groups, moving from place to place as they depleted vegetation or hunted migratory game. The small settlements that marked the emergence of civilization in the Middle East some 12 000 years ago held only a small fraction of Earth's people. Today, the largest three or four cities of the world hold as many people as the entire planet did back then.

Urbanization is *the concentration of population into cities*. Urbanization both redistributes population within a society and transforms many patterns of social life. We will trace these changes in terms of three urban revolutions: the emergence of cities beginning 10 000 years ago, the development of industrial cities after 1750, and the explosive growth of cities in poor countries today.

The Evolution of Cities

Cities are a relatively new development in human history. Only about 12 000 years ago did our ancestors begin founding permanent settlements, which paved the way for the *first urban revolution*.

The First Cities

Hunting and gathering forced people to move all the time; however, once our ancestors discovered how to domesticate animals and cultivate crops, they were able to stay in one place. Raising their own food also created a material surplus, which freed some people from food production and allowed them to build shelters, make tools, weave cloth, and take part in religious rituals. The emergence of cities led to both specialization and higher living standards.

The first city that we know of was Jericho, which lies to the north of the Dead Sea in what is now the West Bank. When first settled 10 000 years ago, it was home to only 600 people. But as the centuries passed, cities grew to tens of thousands of people and became the centres of vast empires. By 3000 BCE , Egyptian cities flourished, as did cities in China about 2000 BCE and in Central and South America about 1500 BCE. In North America, however, only

a few Native American societies formed settlements; widespread urbanization did not take place until the arrival of European settlers in the seventeenth century.

Pre-industrial European Cities

European cities date back some 5000 years to the Greeks and, later, the Romans, both of whom formed great empires and founded cities across Europe, including Vienna, Paris, and London. With the fall of the Roman Empire, the so-called Dark Ages began as people withdrew within defensive walled settlements and warlords battled for territory. Only in the eleventh century did Europe become more peaceful; trade flourished once again, allowing cities to grow.

Medieval cities were quite different from those familiar to us today. Beneath towering cathedrals, the narrow, winding streets of London, Brussels, and Florence teemed with merchants, artisans, priests, peddlers, jugglers, nobles, and servants. Occupational groups such as bakers, carpenters, and metalworkers clustered in distinct sections or "quarters." Ethnicity also defined communities as people sought to keep out those who differed from themselves. The term *ghetto* (from the Italian word *borghetto*, meaning "outside the city walls") was first used to describe the neighbourhood into which the Jews of Venice were segregated.

Industrial European Cities

As the Middle Ages came to a close, steadily increasing commerce enriched a new urban middle class called the *bourgeoisie* (French, meaning "townspeople"). Earning more and more money, the bourgeoisie soon rivalled the hereditary nobility.

By about 1750, the Industrial Revolution triggered a *second urban revolution*, first in Europe and then in North America. The tremendous productive power of factories caused cities to grow bigger than ever before. London, the largest European city, reached 550 000 people by 1700 and exploded to 6.5 million by 1900 (Chandler & Fox, 1974; A.F. Weber, 1963, orig. 1899).

Cities not only grew but changed shape as well. Older winding streets gave way to broad, straight boulevards to handle the increasing flow of commercial traffic. Steam and electric trolleys soon crisscrossed the expanding cities. Because land was now a commodity to be bought and sold, developers divided cities into regular-sized lots (Mumford, 1961). The centre of the city was no longer the cathedral but a bustling central business district filled with banks, retail stores, and tall office buildings.

With a new focus on business, cities became ever more crowded and impersonal. Crime rates rose. Especially at the outset, a few industrialists lived in grand style, but most men, women, and children barely survived by working in factories.

Organized efforts by workers eventually brought improvements to the workplace, better housing, and the right to vote. Public services such as water, sewer systems, and electricity further improved urban

metropolis a large city that socially and economically dominates an urban area

suburbs urban areas beyond the political boundaries of a city

living. Today, some urbanites still live in poverty, but a rising standard of living has partly fulfilled the city's historical promise of a better life.

The Growth of North American Cities

As noted, most of the Native Americans who inhabited North America for thousands of years before the arrival of Europeans were migratory people who formed few permanent settlements. The spread of villages and towns came after European colonization.

Colonial Settlement, 1565–1800

In 1565, the Spanish built a settlement at St. Augustine, Florida, and in 1607 the English founded Jamestown, Virginia. However, the first lasting settlement came in 1624 when the Dutch established New Amsterdam, later called New York. These settlements preceded those in Canada. For example, the first European did not reach the site that was to become Toronto until 1615.

New York, Boston (founded by the English in 1630), and Quebec City (where there was merely a trading post in 1608) started out as tiny villages in a vast wilderness. They resembled medieval towns in Europe, with narrow, winding streets that still curve through lower Manhattan, downtown Boston, and parts of Quebec City.

But economic growth soon transformed these quiet villages into thriving towns with wide streets usually laid out in a grid pattern. Montreal (founded in 1642) had grown to about 18 000 by the end of the eighteenth century, while Captain Vancouver had just explored and charted the Burrard Inlet in 1792. As the century closed, Canada was still an overwhelmingly rural society.

Urban Expansion: 1800–1860

Early in the nineteenth century, towns sprang up along the transportation routes that opened the Canadian West. First, the cities along the major waterways connected to the Great Lakes emerged. By 1851, Quebec City had a population of 52 000, whereas the younger city of Montreal had already grown to 57 000.

Progress was slow away from the waterways of the Great Lakes. It was only in 1860, for example, that New Westminster (now part of the Greater Vancouver Area) became the first incorporated municipality west of Ontario. It was not until the completion of the Canadian Pacific Railway in 1885 that urbanization spread to the western provinces.

The Metropolitan Era: 1860–1950

Industrialization also gave an enormous boost to urbanization, as factories strained to produce goods. Now waves of people fled the countryside for cities in hopes of obtaining better jobs. Soon after, tens of millions of immigrants—mostly from Europe—joined the surge to the cities to form a culturally diverse urban mix.

At the time of Canadian Confederation in 1867, less than 20 percent of the population lived in urban areas. By 1951, this proportion had grown to 63 percent. Individual cities grew accordingly. By 1911, the supremacy of Montreal and Toronto (with populations of 470 000 and 377 000, respectively) was well established. The next-largest cities were Winnipeg (136 000) and Vancouver (100 000). These were still small cities compared to New York, which had already passed the 4 million mark. Such growth marked the era of the **metropolis** (from Greek words meaning "mother city"), *a large city that socially and economically dominates an urban area.* Metropolises became the economic centres of Canada.

Industrial technology further changed the physical shape of cities, pushing buildings well above the three or four storeys common to this point. By the 1880s, steel girders and mechanical elevators raised structures more than 10 storeys high. Railroads and highways drew cities outward. By 1931, pushing upward and outward, cities were home to a majority of the Canadian population.

Urban Decentralization: 1950–Present

The industrial metropolis reached its peak about 1950. Since then, something of a turnaround—termed *urban decentralization*—has occurred as people have deserted downtown areas for outlying **suburbs**, *urban areas beyond the political boundaries of a city* (Balakrishnan & Jarvis, 1991). Thus the centres of the largest cities have actually experienced population decreases in the past few decades. Instead of densely packed central cities, the urban landscape has evolved into sprawling regions. Nevertheless, Canada remains a country dotted with population centres located in a vast expanse of sparsely populated land, as National Map 15–1 illustrates.

Suburbs and Urban Decline

Imitating European nobility, some of the rich had always kept houses in the city as well as country homes beyond the city limits. But not until after World War II did ordinary people find a suburban home within their reach. With more and more cars, new four-lane highways, affordable mortgages, and inexpensive tract homes, suburbs grew as never before. By 1981, most of the population in Canada's largest cities lived in suburbs outside the central city (McVey, Jr., & Kalbach, 1995).

Decentralization was not good news for everyone, however. Rapid suburban growth threw cities into financial chaos. Population decline meant reduced tax revenues. Further, cities that lost affluent people to the suburbs were left with the burden of providing expensive social programs to the poor who stayed behind.

Urban critic Paul Goldberger (2002) points out that the decline of central cities has led to a decline in the importance of public space. Inner-city decay has been particularly dramatic in the United States, where deteriorating city centres have become synonymous with slum housing, crime, drugs, unemployment, poverty, and minority populations. There are similarities in Canada, Vancouver's Downtown Eastside being the most dramatic. However, marginalized populations

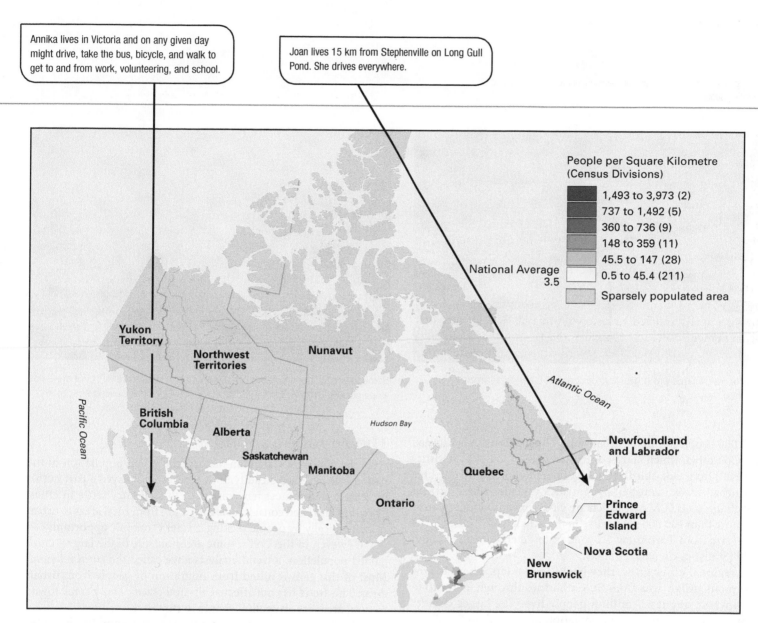

Annika lives in Victoria and on any given day might drive, take the bus, bicycle, and walk to get to and from work, volunteering, and school.

Joan lives 15 km from Stephenville on Long Gull Pond. She drives everywhere.

People per Square Kilometre (Census Divisions)

- 1,493 to 3,973 (2)
- 737 to 1,492 (5)
- 360 to 736 (9)
- 148 to 359 (11)
- 45.5 to 147 (28)
- 0.5 to 45.4 (211)
- Sparsely populated area

National Average 3.5

Seeing Ourselves

NATIONAL MAP 15–1   **Population Density, Canada, 2006**

The map illustrates how sparsely populated Canada is. Looking only at the population data, we see that Canada is an urban country, with most people living in urban centres. But as this map shows, from a geographical perspective these urban centres can also be thought of as exceptions. Chances are very good that you will spend all of your life living in urban areas. How will your life be different as a result of this?

Source: Statistics Canada (2011ax).

are not as concentrated in other Canadian cities as they are in the cities of our neighbour to the south.

Canadian inner cities have fared better in large part because of early adoption of urban renewal policies. Under this program, provincial and local governments have paid for the rebuilding of many inner cities; Montreal started this as early as 1966 (Wolfe, 1992). Affordable housing and effective public transportation in Canada's large and middle-sized cities have recently emerged as

major problems for city planners (Bunting, Filion, & Walks, 2004; Filion, McSpurren, & Appleby, 2006).

Megalopolis: The Regional City

Another result of urban decentralization is urban regions. Statistics Canada recognizes 111 regional cities, which are called *census agglomerations* (CAs)—towns and surrounding areas where more

megalopolis a vast urban region containing a number of cities and their surrounding suburbs

Commuter traffic jams are a growing concern in Canada's large metropolitan areas.

Some towns in spectacular settings have grown dramatically. There are times when people living in Banff, Alberta, cannot even find a parking space.

than 10 000 people live in the urban core. The smallest CA is Kitimat, British Columbia, which had a population of 8987 in 2006 (Statistics Canada, 2011ax). One-third of Canada's population lives in the three largest urban areas identified by Statistics Canada—the 27 *census metropolitan areas* (CMAs), which are cities and surrounding areas where more than 100 000 people live in the urban core. These CMAs range in size from Toronto at 5.1 million to Peterborough at about 117 000 (Statistics Canada, 2011ax).

As regional cities grow, they begin to overlap. There is now a continuous urban area from St. Catharines through Toronto to Oshawa where about 6.7 million people live. The larger Greater Golden Horseshoe Area has a population of more than 8 million, which represents over half of the population of Ontario and about 20 percent of Canada's population (Statistics Canada, 2010k). On an even larger scale, along the U.S. East Coast a 650-kilometre supercity stretches from New England to Virginia. In the early 1960s, the French geographer Jean Gottmann (1961) coined the term **megalopolis** to designate *a vast urban region containing a number of cities and their surrounding suburbs.*

Edge Cities

Urban decentralization has also created *edge cities*, business centres some distance from the old downtowns. Edge cities—a mix of corporate office buildings, shopping malls, hotels, and entertainment complexes—differ from suburbs, which contain mostly homes. The population of suburbs peaks at night, but the population of edge cities peaks during the workday.

As part of expanding urban regions, most edge cities have no clear physical boundaries, although some do have names (including Oshawa outside Toronto and Surrey outside Vancouver).

The Rural Rebound

Over the course of Canadian history, the urban population of the nation has increased steadily. Immigration has played a part in this increase because most newcomers to this country settle in cities. There has also been considerable migration from rural areas to urban places, typically by people seeking greater economic opportunity.

However, in the 1990s, some areas outside of the largest cities gained population, a trend analysts have called the *rural rebound.* Most of this gain resulted from migration of people from urban areas. This trend has not affected all rural places: Many small towns in rural areas are struggling simply to stay alive.

The greatest gains have come to rural communities that offer scenic and recreational attractions, such as lakes, mountains, and ski areas. People are drawn not only to the natural beauty of rural communities but also to their slower pace: less traffic, a lower crime rate, and cleaner air. Looking ahead to National Map 16-1 on page 443, it is easy to identify some of these areas. Standing out is the whole area between Vancouver and Calgary, and also "cottage country" north of Toronto.

Urbanism as a Way of Life

Early sociologists in Europe and North America focused their attention on the rise of cities. We briefly examine their accounts of urbanism as a way of life.

Ferdinand Tönnies: *Gemeinschaft* and *Gesellschaft*

In the nineteenth century, the German sociologist Ferdinand Tönnies (1855–1937) studied how life in the new industrial

Gemeinschaft a type of social organization in which people are closely tied by kinship and tradition

Gesellschaft a type of social organization in which people come together only on the basis of individual self-interest

metropolis differed from life in rural villages. From this contrast, he developed two concepts that have become a lasting part of sociology's terminology.

Tönnies (1963, orig. 1887) used the German word *Gemeinschaft* ("community") to refer to *a type of social organization in which people are closely tied by kinship and tradition.* The Gemeinschaft of the rural village, Tönnies explained, joins people in what amounts to a single primary group.

By and large, argued Tönnies, *Gemeinschaft* is absent in the modern city. On the contrary, urbanization creates *Gesellschaft* ("association"), *a type of social organization in which people come together only on the basis of individual self-interest.* In the *Gesellschaft* way of life, individuals are motivated by their own needs rather than by a desire to help improve the well-being of everyone. By and large, city dwellers have little sense of community or common identity and look to other people mainly when they need something. Tönnies saw in urbanization the weakening of close, long-lasting social relations in favour of the brief and impersonal ties or secondary relationships typical of business.

Emile Durkheim: Mechanical and Organic Solidarity

The French sociologist Emile Durkheim agreed with much of Tönnies's thinking about cities. However, Durkheim countered that urbanites do not lack social bonds; they simply organize social life differently than rural people do.

Durkheim described traditional, rural life as *mechanical solidarity*, social bonds based on common sentiments and shared moral values. With its emphasis on tradition, Durkheim's concept of mechanical solidarity bears a strong similarity to Tönnies's *Gemeinschaft*. Urbanization erodes mechanical solidarity, Durkheim explained, but it also generates a new type of bonding, which he called *organic solidarity*, social bonds based on specialization and interdependence. This concept, which parallels Tönnies's *Gesellschaft*, reveals an important difference between the two thinkers. Both felt that the growth of industrial cities weakened tradition, but Durkheim optimistically pointed to a new kind of solidarity. Where societies had been built on *likeness*, Durkheim now saw social life based on *difference*.

For Durkheim, urban society offers more individual choice, moral tolerance, and personal privacy than people find in rural villages. In sum, Durkheim thought that something is lost in the process of urbanization, but much is gained.

Georg Simmel: The Blasé Urbanite

The German sociologist Georg Simmel (1858–1918) offered a micro-level analysis of cities, studying how urban life shapes individual experience. According to Simmel, individuals see the city as a crush of people, objects, and events. To prevent being overwhelmed by all of this stimulation, urbanites develop a *blasé attitude*, tuning out much of what goes on around them. Such detachment does not mean that city dwellers lack compassion for others; they simply keep their distance as a survival strategy so that they can focus their time and energy on the people and things that really matter to them.

The Chicago School: Robert Park and Louis Wirth

Sociologists in North America soon joined the study of rapidly growing cities. Robert Park (1864–1944), a leader of the first North American sociology program at the University of Chicago, sought to add a street-level perspective by getting out and studying real cities. As he said of himself, "I suspect that I have actually covered more ground, tramping about in cities in different parts of the world, than any other living man" (1950:viii). Walking the streets, Park found the city to be an organized mosaic of distinctive ethnic communities, commercial centres, and industrial districts. Over time, he observed, these "natural areas" develop and change in relation to one another. To Park, the city was a living organism—a human kaleidoscope.

Another major figure in the Chicago School of urban sociology was Louis Wirth (1897–1952). Wirth (1938) is best known for blending the ideas of Tönnies, Durkheim, Simmel, and Park into a comprehensive theory of urban life.

Wirth began by defining the city as a setting with a large, dense, and socially diverse population. These traits result in an impersonal, superficial, and transitory way of life for city dwellers. Living among millions of others, urbanites come into contact with many more people than residents of rural areas. Thus when city people take notice of others at all, they usually know them not in terms of *who they are* but *what they do*—as, for instance, the bus driver, the pharmacist, or the grocery store clerk. These specialized urban relationships are sometimes pleasant for all concerned, but we should remember that self-interest rather than friendship is the main reason behind the interaction.

The impersonal nature of urban relationships, together with the great social diversity found in cities today, makes city dwellers more tolerant than rural villagers. Rural communities often jealously enforce their narrow traditions, but the heterogeneous population of a city rarely shares any single code of moral conduct (T.C. Wilson, 1985, 1995).

CRITICAL REVIEW In both Europe and North America, early sociologists presented a mixed view of urban living. Rapid urbanization troubled Tönnies and Wirth, who saw personal ties and traditional morality lost in the anonymous rush of the city. Durkheim and Park emphasized urbanism's positive face, pointing to more personal freedom and greater personal choice.

One problem with all of these views is that they paint urbanism in broad strokes that overlook the effects of class, race, and

Peasant Dance (above, c. 1565), by Pieter Breughel the Elder, conveys the essential unity of rural life forged by generations of kinship and neighbourhood. By contrast, Lily Furedi's *Subway* (right) communicates the impersonality common to urban areas. Taken together, these paintings capture Tönnies's distinction between *Gemeinschaft* and *Gesellschaft*.

Pieter Breughel the Elder (c. 1525/30–1569), *Peasant Dance*, c. 1565, Kunsthistorisches Museum, Vienna/Superstock. Lily Furedi, American. *Subway*. Oil on canvas, 99 x 123 cm. National Collection of Fine Arts, Washington, D.C./Smithsonian Institute.

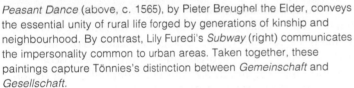

gender. There are many kinds of urbanites—rich and poor, Black and white, Anglo and Aboriginal, women and men—all of whom are leading distinctive lives (Gans, 1968). Indeed, as the Thinking about Diversity box explains, the share of visible minorities in the largest Canadian cities is expected to continue growing sharply in the next decade. We see social diversity most clearly in cities, where various categories of people are large enough to form visible communities (Macionis & Parrillo, 2007).

CHECK YOUR LEARNING Of these urban sociologists—Tönnies, Durkheim, Park, and Wirth—which were more positive about urban life? Which were more negative? In each case, explain why.

Urban Ecology

Sociologists (especially members of the Chicago School) developed **urban ecology**, *the study of the link between the physical and social dimensions of cities.* For example, why are cities located where they are? The first cities emerged in fertile regions where the ecology favoured raising crops. Pre-industrial people, concerned with defence, built their cities on mountains (ancient Athens was perched on an outcropping of rock) or surrounded by water (Paris and

Mexico City were built on islands). With the Industrial Revolution, economic considerations placed all major North American cities near rivers and natural harbours that facilitated trade.

Urban ecologists also study the physical design of cities. In 1925, Ernest W. Burgess, a student and colleague of Robert Park, described land use in Chicago in terms of *concentric zones*. City centres, Burgess observed, are business districts bordered by a ring of factories, followed by residential rings with housing that becomes more expensive the farther it is from the noise and pollution of the city's centre.

Homer Hoyt (1939) refined Burgess's observations, noting that distinctive districts sometimes form *wedge-shaped sectors*. For example, one fashionable area may develop next to another, or an industrial district may extend outward from a city's centre along a train or trolley line.

Chauncy Harris and Edward Ullman (1945) added yet another insight: As cities decentralize, they lose their single-centre form in favour of a *multi-centred model*. As cities grow, residential areas, industrial parks, and shopping districts typically push away from one another. Few people want to live close to industrial areas, for example, so the city becomes a mosaic of distinct districts.

Social area analysis investigates what people in particular neighbourhoods have in common. Three factors seem to explain most of the variation in neighbourhood types: family patterns, social class, and race and ethnicity (Johnston, 1976; Shevky & Bell, 1955). Families with children look for areas with large apartments or single-family homes and good schools. The rich seek high-prestige neighbourhoods, often in the central city near cultural attractions.

THINKING ABOUT DIVERSITY: RACE, CLASS, & GENDER

Minorities Now a Majority in the Largest Canadian Cities

According to the results of the 2006 census, 20 percent of Canadians—one in five—are foreign born. In 2006, 39 percent of Canadian residents aged 15 and over were foreign born or had one parent who was born abroad. It is predicted that, by 2031, just about a half (46 percent) will be foreign born or have a foreign-born parent (Statistics Canada, 2010k). As well, by 2031, the prediction is that almost half (47 percent) of second-generation Canadians will belong to a visible minority group, which is almost double the 2006 proportion at 24 percent (Statistics Canada, 2010k).

Why the change? By far, the most important reason is the increase in immigration and the large proportion of immigrants who are visible minorities; recall from Chapter 11 that 8 of 10 immigrants to Canada since 1980 have arrived from Asia. Contributing factors for the increase are the younger age structure of the visible minority population (younger populations have more children) and the slightly higher fertility rates.

There will be dramatic differences in the proportions of visible minorities in different parts of Canada. The greatest increase in the size and proportion of the visible minority population will be evident in Toronto and Vancouver, where visible minorities are expected to be a numerical majority by 2017—up from 40-plus percent of the population in 2006. Montreal is an interesting contrast because, with only 13 percent, it has relatively few visible minority persons.

The differences in the proportions of visible minorities in rural and urban areas are reflected in provincial differences also, with British Columbia and Ontario having the highest proportions of visible minorities. By 2017, it is expected that about one in three people in these two provinces will belong to a visible minority group.

Political officials and other policy-makers examine these figures closely. Clearly, the future vitality of the largest Canadian cities depends on meeting the needs of and taking advantage of the contributions of their swelling minority populations.

WHAT DO YOU THINK?

1. Why are the visible minority populations of large Canadian cities increasing?

2. Why are there relatively few visible minority persons in Montreal?

3. What positive changes does a numerical majority of visible minorities bring to a city?

4. What challenges does a numerical majority of visible minorities bring to a city?

Source: Based on Bélanger & Malenfant (2005a, 2005b).

People with a common race or ethnic heritage cluster in distinctive communities.

Brian Berry and Philip Rees (1969) tied together many of these insights. They explained that distinct family types tend to settle in the concentric zones described by Burgess. Specifically, households with few children tend to cluster toward the city's centre, and those with more children live farther away. Social class differences are primarily responsible for the sector-shaped districts described by Hoyt; the rich occupy one "side of the tracks" and the poor the other. And racial and ethnic neighbourhoods are found at various places throughout the city, consistent with Harris and Ullman's multi-centred model.

Urban Political Economy

In the late 1960s, many large North American cities were rocked by major riots. As public awareness of racial and economic inequality increased, some analysts turned away from the ecological approach to a social-conflict understanding of city life. The *urban political-economy model* applies Karl Marx's analysis of conflict in the workplace to conflict in the city (Lindstrom, 1995).

Political economists disagree with the ecological approach, which sees the city as a natural organism with particular districts and neighbourhoods developing according to an internal logic. They claim that city life is defined by people with power: corporate leaders and political officials. Capitalism, which transforms the city into real estate traded for profit and concentrates wealth in the hands of the few, is the key to understanding city life. From this point of view, for example, the development of the West Edmonton Mall and the resulting decline in downtown Edmonton can be understood only by an analysis that includes the close relationship that the developer (the Ghermezian family) had with provincial and municipal politicians.

CRITICAL REVIEW The fact that our largest Canadian cities appear to be in crisis—with pockets of deep poverty, high crime rates, and homelessness—seems to favour the political-economy view over the urban ecology approach. But one criticism applies to both: they focus on Canadian cities during a limited period of history. Much of what we know about industrial cities does not apply to pre-industrial towns in our own past or the rapidly growing cities in many low-income nations today. It

ecology the study of the interaction of living organisms and the natural environment

natural environment Earth's surface and atmosphere, including living organisms, air, water, soil, and other resources necessary to sustain life

ecosystem a system composed of the interaction of all living organisms and their natural environment

is unlikely that any single model of cities can account for the full range of urban diversity found in the world today.

CHECK YOUR LEARNING In your own words, explain what the urban ecology theories and the urban political-economy theory teach us about cities.

Urbanization in Low-Income Countries

November 16, Cairo, Egypt. People call the vast Muslim cemetery in Old Cairo the "City of the Dead." In truth, it is very much alive: Tens of thousands of squatters have moved into the mausoleums, making this place an eerie mix of life and death. Children run across the stone floors, clotheslines stretch between the monuments, and an occasional television antenna protrudes from a tomb roof. With Cairo gaining 1000 people a day, families live where they can.

Twice in its history, the world has experienced a revolutionary expansion of cities. The first urban revolution began about 8000 BCE with the first urban settlements and continued until permanent settlements were in place on several continents. About 1750, the second urban revolution took off; it lasted for two centuries as the Industrial Revolution spurred rapid growth of cities in Europe and North America.

A third urban revolution is now under way. Today, 75 percent of people in high-income countries are already city dwellers. But extraordinary urban growth is occurring in low-income nations. In 1950, about 25 percent of the people in poor countries lived in cities. In 2008, the world became mostly urban for the first time in history, with more than half of humanity living in cities (Population Reference Bureau, 2009).

Not only are more people urban, but cities are also getting bigger. In 1950, only seven cities in the world had populations over 5 million, and only two of these were in low-income countries. By 2007, 49 cities had passed this mark, and two-thirds of them were in less-resourced nations (Brockerhoff, 2000; United Nations Population Division, 2008).

This third urban revolution is the result of many low-income nations entering the high-growth Stage 2 of demographic transition theory. Falling death rates have fuelled population increases in Latin America, Asia, and especially Africa. For urban areas, the rate of increase is *twice as high* because in addition to natural increase, millions of people leave the countryside each year in search of jobs, health care, education, and conveniences such as running water and electricity. As cities grow, so do suburbs.

Cities do offer more opportunities than rural areas, but they provide no quick fix for the problems of escalating population and grinding poverty. Many cities in less-resourced nations—including Mexico City, Egypt's Cairo, India's Kolkata (formerly Calcutta), and Manila in the Philippines—are simply unable to meet the basic needs of much of their population. All of these cities are surrounded by wretched shantytowns, settlements of makeshift homes built from discarded materials. As noted in Chapter 9 ("Global Stratification"), even city dumps are home to thousands of poor people, who pick through the waste hoping to find enough to eat or sell to make it through another day.

Environment and Society

The human species has prospered, rapidly expanding over the entire planet. An increasing share of the global population now lives in large, complex settlements that offer the promise of a better life than that found in rural villages.

But these advances have come at a high price. Never before in history have human beings placed such demands on the planet. This disturbing development leads us to focus on the interplay of the natural environment and society. Like demography, **ecology** is another cousin of sociology, formally defined as *the study of the interaction of living organisms and the natural environment*. Ecology rests on the research of natural scientists as well as social scientists. We will focus on the aspects of ecology that involve familiar sociological concepts and issues.

The **natural environment** is *Earth's surface and atmosphere, including living organisms, air, water, soil, and other resources necessary to sustain life*. Like every other species, humans depend on the natural environment to survive. Yet with our capacity for culture, humans stand apart from other species; we alone take deliberate action to remake the world according to our own interests and desires, for better and for worse.

Why is the environment of interest to sociologists? Environmental problems, from pollution to global warming, do not arise from the natural world operating on its own. Such problems result from the choices and actions of human beings, making them *social* problems.

The Global Dimension

The study of the natural environment requires a global perspective. The reason is simple: Regardless of political divisions between nations, the planet is a single **ecosystem**, which encompasses *the interaction of all living organisms and their natural environment*.

The Greek meaning of *eco* is "house," reminding us that this planet is our home and that all living things and their natural environment are interrelated. A change in any part of the natural environment sends ripples through the entire global ecosystem.

Consider, from an ecological point of view, our national love of eating hamburgers. People in North America (and, increasingly, around the world) have created a huge demand for beef, which has greatly expanded ranching in Brazil, Costa Rica, and other Latin American nations. To produce the lean meat sought by fast-food corporations, cattle in Latin America feed on grass, which uses a great deal of land. Latin American ranchers clear the land for grazing by cutting down thousands of square miles of forests each year. These tropical forests are vital to maintaining Earth's atmosphere. Deforestation ends up threatening everyone, including the people in North America enjoying their hamburgers (N. Myers, 1984a).

Technology and the Environmental Deficit

Sociologists point to a simple formula: $I = PAT$, where environmental impact (I) reflects a society's population (P), its level of affluence (A), and its level of technology (T). Members of simpler societies—the hunters and gatherers described in Chapter 2 ("Culture")—hardly affect the environment because they are few in number, are poor, and have only simple technology. Nature affects all aspects of their lives as they follow the migration of game, watch the rhythm of the seasons, and suffer from natural catastrophes such as fires, floods, droughts, and storms.

Societies at intermediate stages of socio-cultural evolution have a somewhat greater capacity to affect the environment. But the environmental impact of horticulture (small-scale farming), pastoralism (the herding of animals), and even agriculture (the use of animal-drawn plows) is limited because people still rely on muscle power for producing food and other goods.

Human control of the natural environment increased dramatically with the changes brought about by the Industrial Revolution. Muscle power gave way to engines that burn fossil fuels: coal at first and then oil. The use of such machinery affects the environment in two ways: It consumes more natural resources and releases more pollutants into the atmosphere. Even more important, humans armed with industrial technology are able to bend nature to their will, tunnelling through mountains, damming rivers, irrigating deserts, and drilling for oil in the arctic wilderness and on the ocean floor. This explains why people in rich nations, who represent just 23 percent of humanity, account for half of the world's energy use (World Bank, 2009).

Not only do industrial societies use more energy, but they produce 100 times more goods than agrarian societies do. Higher living standards are good in some ways, but they increase the problems of solid waste (because people ultimately throw away most of what they produce) and pollution (industrial production generates smoke and other toxic substances).

From the start, people recognized the material benefits of industrial technology. But only a century later did they begin to see

The most important insight sociology offers about our physical world is that environmental problems do not simply "happen." Rather, the state of the natural environment reflects the ways in which social life is organized—how people live and what they think is important. Moreover, the greater the technological power of a society, the greater that society's ability to threaten the natural environment.

its long-term effects on the natural environment. Today, we realize that the technological power to make our lives better can also put the lives of future generations at risk, and there is a national debate about how to address this issue. The Seeing Sociology in the News box on page 428 describes recent efforts to "green" our high schools as a way of addressing environmental issues.

Evidence is mounting that we are running up an **environmental deficit**, *profound long-term harm to the natural environment caused by humanity's focus on short-term material affluence* (Bormann, 1990). The concept of environmental deficit is important for three reasons. First, it reminds us that environmental concerns are *sociological*, reflecting societies' priorities about how people should live. Second, it suggests that much environmental damage—to the air, land, and water—is *unintended*. By focusing on the short-term benefits of, say, cutting down forests, strip mining, or using throwaway packaging, we fail to see the long-term environmental effects. Third, in some respects, the environmental deficit is *reversible*. Inasmuch as societies have created environmental problems, societies can undo many of them.

Culture: Growth and Limits

Whether we recognize environmental dangers and decide to do something about them is a cultural matter. Thus along with technology, culture has powerful environmental consequences.

Metro Canada

School Grants Encourage Green Living

BY BEN KNIGHT

June 13, 2011—Small ideas can lead to big changes. That's why WWF-Canada has teamed up with Loblaw to offer Green CommUnity School Grants to students and schools who want to help build a cleaner, greener world.

"We developed the program to tap into the excitement, passion and sense of community that comes with schools," says Christina Topp, WWF VP of marketing and communications, "to drive everyday change in the school environment, and in the broader community."

Composting, gardening, solar energy, recycling programs—any innovative idea from any school, anywhere in Canada, can receive up to $5,000 in financial backing.

"We've been doing this program for two years, and it's great fun to look at the applications," says Topp. "Bike recycling programs, and gardens, and worm recycling. It's phenomenal."

Grants have been awarded to large inner-city schools, tiny one-room schoolhouses, and almost every kind of classroom in between.

"You'll have students doing everything from biodiversity and natural projects outside to solar panels, to creating bio-fuel buses," Topp enthuses. "Whatever the problem is, they're thinking about it and coming up with solutions."

Peggy Hornell, senior director of community investment at Loblaw, says the program arose from one of the supermarket chain's ongoing environmental efforts.

From schools to sponsors, this simple, open-ended program is impressing and delighting everyone involved.

"There is certainly room for expansion," Topp concludes.

"But kids—if we get them to adopt green ways of living from childhood—we don't need to change behaviours. It just becomes the every-day way they live."

In 2011, the Green CommUnity School Grants Program received more than 550 applications from across the country. Twenty-eight projects were chosen, including one from Pasadena Elementary in Newfoundland and Labrador.

"Our province has challenged citizens to 'Get to Half,'" says Carla Brake, who teaches at Pasadena Elementary, in Pasadena, Newfoundland. "Our school certainly has a ways to go to cut waste by 50 percent."

But they're working on it. Last year, they initiated a recycling program and planted a vegetable garden. This year they'll start composting. With funds from the grant, the school will buy worms and containers.

But Pasadena Elementary grant project isn't called "Naturalizing our School, Inside and Out" for nothing. To complement the recycling and composting going on indoors, the school has a range of outdoor initiatives in mind. "We want to start a naturalization plan," Brake says. "We'll be creating a nature trail around our school grounds, completing an outdoor classroom, planting a flower bed around our school welcome sign and identifying plants."

Brake says the school is aware initiatives like this take planning and coordination, and they've started on that. "We've already compiled a list of volunteers and are ready to dig down to business!" While the school has also been pulling together resources, "the grant will provide the necessary funds to carry out and finish the project," says Brake.

The grant will also mean the school can participate in Plant Watch, Environment Canada's program to track the response of plants to climate change. "Some classes will be reporting to Plant Watch, while others will be assigned composting duties," says Brake. "We hope to involve the entire school population in one way or another."

WHAT DO YOU THINK?

1. Do you think that many people consider environmental issues to be the concern mainly of adults? Explain.

2. Would you make an environmental study part of the curriculum of every school in the country? Why or why not?

3. What specific strategies or policies would you suggest to encourage greater environmental understanding on the part of this country's young people?

Sources: Courtesy of Ben Knight and Metro News, at: http://www.metronews.ca/london/life/article/887117—school-grants-encourage-green-living, and WWF-Canada, at: http://wwf.ca/takeaction/greencommunity_recipients.cfm

The Logic of Growth

When you turn on the television news, you might hear a story like this: "The government reported bad economic news today, with the economy growing by only half a percent during the first quarter of the year." If you stop to think about it, our culture defines an economy that isn't growing as "stagnant" (which is bad) and an economy that is getting smaller as a recession or a "depression" (which is *very* bad). What is "good" is *growth*—the economy getting bigger and bigger. More cars, bigger homes, more income, more spending—the idea of *more* is at the heart of our cultural definition of living well (McKibben, 2007).

One of the reasons we define growth in positive terms is that we value *material comfort*, believing that money and the things it buys improve our lives. We also believe in the idea of *progress*, thinking that the future will be better than the present. In addition, we look to *science* to make our lives easier and more rewarding. In simpler terms, "having things is good," "life gets better," and "people are clever." Taken together, such cultural values form the *logic of growth*.

An optimistic view of the world, the logic of growth holds that more powerful technology has improved our lives and that new discoveries will continue to do so in the future. Throughout the history of Canada and other high-income nations, the logic of growth has been the driving force behind settling the wilderness, building towns and roads, and pursuing material affluence.

However, "progress" can lead to unexpected problems, including strain on the environment. The logic of growth responds by arguing that people (especially scientists and other technology experts) will find a way out of any problem placed in our path. If, for example, the world runs short of oil, scientists will come up with hydrogen, solar, or nuclear engines or some as yet unknown technology to meet the world's energy needs.

Environmentalists counter that the logic of growth is flawed because it assumes that natural resources such as clean air, fresh water, and fertile soil will always be plentiful. We can and will exhaust these *finite* resources if we continue to pursue growth at any cost. Echoing Malthus, environmentalists warn that if we call on the planet to support increasing numbers of people, we will surely destroy the environment—and ourselves—in the process.

The Limits to Growth

If we cannot invent our way out of the problems created by the logic of growth, perhaps we need another way of thinking about the world. Environmentalists therefore counter that growth must have limits. Stated simply, the *limits-to-growth thesis* is that humanity must put in place policies to control the growth of population, production, and the use of resources in order to avoid environmental collapse.

In *The Limits to Growth*, a controversial book that played a large part in launching the environmental movement, Donella Meadows and her colleagues (1972) used a computer model to calculate the planet's available resources, rates of population growth, amount of land available for cultivation, levels of industrial and food production, and amount of pollutants released into the atmosphere. The model reflects changes that have occurred since 1900 and projects forward to the end of the twenty-first century. The authors concede that such long-range predictions are speculative, and some critics think they are plain wrong (Simon, 1981).

But right or wrong, the conclusions of the study call for serious consideration. The authors claim that we are quickly consuming Earth's finite resources. Supplies of oil, natural gas, and other energy sources are declining and will continue to drop, a little faster or more slowly depending on the conservation policies of rich nations and the speed with which other nations such as India and China continue to industrialize. Within the next 100 years, resources will run out, crippling industrial output and causing a decline in food production.

This limits-to-growth theory shares Malthus's pessimism about the future. People who accept it doubt that current patterns of life are sustainable for even another century. Perhaps we can all learn to live with less. This may not be as hard as you might think: Research shows, for example, that as material consumption has gone up in recent decades, there has been no increase in levels of personal happiness (Myers, 2000). In the end, environmentalists warn, either make fundamental changes in how we live, placing less strain on

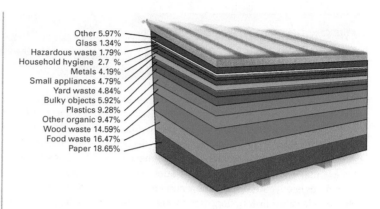

FIGURE 15–4 Composition of Vancouver's Trash, 2004

Source: TRI Technology Resources Inc. (2005).

the natural environment, or widespread hunger and conflict will force change on us.

Solid Waste: The Disposable Society

Across Canada, people generate a massive amount of solid waste *each and every day*. Figure 15–4 shows the composition of Vancouver's trash.

As a rich nation of people who value convenience, Canada has become a *disposable society*. We consume more products than virtually any other nation, and many of these products have throwaway packaging. For example, fast food is served in cardboard, plastic, and Styrofoam containers that we throw away within minutes. But countless other products, from film to fish hooks, are elaborately packaged to make them more attractive to the customer and to discourage tampering and theft.

Manufacturers market soft drinks, beer, and fruit juices in aluminum cans, glass jars, and plastic containers, which not only use up finite resources but also create mountains of solid waste. Countless items are intentionally designed to be disposable: pens, razors, flashlights, batteries, even cameras. Other goods, from light bulbs to automobiles, are designed to have a limited useful life, after which they become unwanted junk. As Paul Connett (1991) points out, even the words we use to describe what we throw away—*waste, trash, refuse, garbage, rubbish*—show how little we value what we cannot immediately use. But this was not always the case, as the Seeing Sociology in Everyday Life box on page 430 explains.

Living in a rich society, the average person in North America consumes hundreds of times more energy, plastics, lumber, and other resources than someone living in a low-income nation such as Bangladesh or Tanzania (and nearly twice as much as someone living in many other high-income countries such as Japan or Sweden). This high level of consumption means not only that we in Canada

Why Grandma Macionis Had No Trash

Grandma Macionis, we always used to say, never threw away anything. She was born and raised in Lithuania—the "old country"—where growing up in a poor village shaped her in ways that never changed, even after she came to North America as a young woman and settled in Philadelphia.

In her later years, when I knew her, I remember the family travelling together to her house to celebrate her birthday. We never knew what to get Grandma because although she didn't have all that much, she never seemed to need anything. She lived a simple life and had simple clothes and showed little interest in "fancy things." She used everything until it wore out. Her kitchen knives, for example, were worn narrow from decades of sharpening. And she hardly ever threw anything away—she recycled all her garbage as compost for her vegetable garden.

After opening a birthday present, she would carefully save the box, wrapping paper, and ribbon, which meant as much to her as whatever gift they surrounded. We all expected her to save every bit of whatever she was given, smiling to each other as we watched her put

everything away, knowing she would find a way to use it all again and again.

As strange as Grandma sometimes seemed to her grandchildren, she was a product of her culture. A century ago, there was little "trash." If a pair of socks wore thin, people mended them, probably more than once. When they were beyond repair, they were used as rags for clean-

Grandma Macionis, in the 1970s, with the first author.

ing or sewn, along with other old clothing, into a quilt. For her, everything had value, if not in one way, then in another.

During the twentieth century, as women joined men working outside of the home, income went up and families began buying more and more "time-saving" products. Before long, few people cared about the home recycling that Grandma practised. Soon cities sent crews from block to block to pick up truckloads of discarded material. The era of "trash" had begun.

WHAT DO YOU THINK?

1. Just as Grandma Macionis was a product of her culture, so are we. What cultural values make people today demand time-saving products and "convenience" packaging?

2. Do you recycle drink containers, paper, or other materials? Why or why not?

3. In what ways does this box demonstrate that the state of the natural environment is a social issue?

---

use a disproportionate share of the planet's natural resources but also that we generate most of the world's refuse.

We like to say that we "throw things away." But 80 percent of our solid waste never "goes away." Rather, it ends up in landfills, which are, literally, filling up. Material in landfills also can pollute groundwater. The city of Toronto is trying to deal with this issue. After running out of space in its own landfills, it tried to ship garbage 600 kilometres north by rail to the abandoned Adams Lake mine, close to the community of Kirkland Lake. Fierce opposition led to the garbage being shipped to the Green Lane landfill near St. Thomas, Ontario. However, the controversy erupts again whenever an accident occurs that involves one of the hundreds of trucks that daily drive back and forth. In addition, what goes into landfills all too often stays there, sometimes for centuries. Tens of millions of tires, diapers, and other items that we bury in landfills each year do not decompose and will be an unwelcome legacy for future generations.

Environmentalists argue that we should address the problem of solid waste by doing what many of our grandparents did: turn "waste" into a resource. One way to do this is through *recycling*, reusing resources we would otherwise throw away. Recycling is an accepted practice in Japan and many other nations, and it is becoming more common in Canada and the United States, where we now reuse about 33 percent of waste materials. The share is increasing as more municipalities pass laws requiring reuse of certain materials such as glass bottles and aluminum cans and as the business of recycling becomes more profitable.

Water and Air

Oceans, lakes, and streams are the lifeblood of the global ecosystem. Humans depend on water for drinking, bathing, cooling, cooking, recreation, and a host of other activities.

According to what scientists call the *hydrologic cycle*, the planet naturally recycles water and refreshes the land. The process begins as heat from the sun causes Earth's water, 97 percent of which is in the oceans, to evaporate and form clouds. Because water evaporates at lower temperatures than most pollutants, the water vapour that rises from the seas is relatively pure, leaving various contaminants behind. Water then falls to the Earth as rain, which drains into streams and rivers and finally returns to the sea. Two major concerns about water, then, are supply and pollution.

Water Supply

Less than one-tenth of 1 percent of Earth's water is suitable for drinking. It is not surprising, then, that for thousands of years water rights have figured prominently in laws around the world. Today, some regions of the world, especially the tropics, enjoy plentiful fresh water, using only a small share of the available supply. High demand, coupled with modest reserves, makes water supply a matter of concern in much of North America and Asia, where people look to rivers rather than rainfall for their water. In China, deep aquifers are dropping rapidly. In the Middle East, water supply is reaching a critical level. Iran is rationing water in its capital city. In Egypt, people can consume just one-sixth as much water from the Nile River today as in 1900. Across northern Africa and the Middle East, as many as 1 billion people may lack the water they need for irrigation and drinking by 2025 ("China Faces Water Shortage," 2001; International Development Research Center, 2006).

Rising population and the development of more complex technology have greatly increased the world's appetite for water. The global consumption of water (now estimated at almost 4000 cubic kilometres, or 140 trillion cubic feet, per year) has doubled since 1950 and is rising steadily. As a result, even in parts of the world that receive plenty of rainfall, people are using groundwater faster than it can be replenished naturally. In the Tamil Nadu region of southern India, for example, people are drawing so much groundwater that the local water table has fallen 30 metres over the past several decades. Mexico City—which has sprawled to some 3600 square kilometres—has pumped so much water from its underground aquifer that the city has sunk 10 metres in the past century and continues to drop about 5 centimetres per year. Closer to home, the Colorado River often does not reach the ocean, in part because so much water is used for irrigation. While we in Canada have access to a disproportionate share of the world's fresh water, we seem to realize the importance of our resource: Whenever water exports have been proposed, Canadians are up in arms in opposition.

In light of such developments, we must face the reality that water is a valuable and finite resource. Greater conservation of water by individuals (the average person in North America consumes 3 million gallons in a lifetime) is part of the answer. However, households around the world account for just 10 percent of water use. We need to reduce water consumption by industry, which uses 20 percent of the global total, and farming, which consumes 70 percent of the total for irrigation.

Water is vital to life, and it is also in short supply. The state of Gujarat, in Western India, has experienced a decade-long drought. In the village of Natwarghad, people crowd together, lowering pots into the local well, taking what little water is left.

Perhaps new irrigation technology will reduce demand for water in the future. But here again, we see how population increase, as well as economic growth, strains our ecosystem (Population Action International, 2000; Postel, 1993; United Nations World Water Assessment Programme, 2009; U.S. Geological Survey, 2009).

Water Pollution

In large cities from Mexico City to Cairo to Shanghai, many people have no choice but to drink contaminated water. Infectious diseases such as typhoid, cholera, and dysentery, all caused by waterborne microorganisms, spread rapidly through these populations. In addition to ensuring ample *supplies* of water, we must protect the *quality* of water.

Water quality in Canada is generally good by global standards. However, even here the problem of water pollution is growing steadily, as in the case of the raw sewage from Halifax, St. John's, and Victoria that goes straight into the ocean. Decades of heavy pollution of the Great Lakes, and of countless streams and rivers across the country, has seriously threatened plant and fish life, and for some species has resulted in extinction.

A special problem is *acid rain*—rain made acidic by air pollution—which destroys plant and animal life. Acid rain (or snow) begins with power plants burning fossil fuels (oil and coal) to generate electricity; this burning process releases sulphuric and nitrous oxides into the air. As the wind sweeps these gases into the atmosphere, they react with the air to form sulphuric and nitric acids, which turns atmospheric moisture acidic.

This is a clear case of one type of pollution causing another: Air pollution (from smokestacks) ends up contaminating water (in lakes and streams that collect acid rain). Acid rain is truly a global

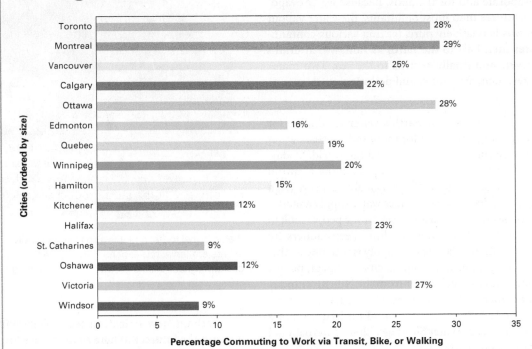

FIGURE 15–5 **Commuting to Work by Walking, Bike, or Transit, Percentage of People, Canada, 2006**

Most Canadians drive to work rather than taking public transit, riding along as a passenger, or using human-powered modes of transportation. The largest urban areas in Canada have a relatively high percentage of people who walk, bike, or use transit to get to work, while the percentages in smaller centres are lower. Why do you think Ottawa, Edmonton, Victoria, and Halifax appear to differ a little from this general pattern?

Note: Data are for the 15 largest Census Metropolitan Areas.
Source: Statistics Canada (2011ay).

phenomenon because the regions that suffer the harmful effects may be thousands of kilometres from the source of the pollution. For instance, British power plants have caused acid rain that has devastated forests and fish in Norway and Sweden, 1600 kilometres to the northeast. Similarly, U.S. smokestacks have been accused of poisoning the forests in Eastern Canada.

Air Pollution

Because we are surrounded by air, most people in Canada are more aware of air pollution than contaminated water. One of the unexpected consequences of industrial technology—especially the factory and the motor vehicle—has been a decline in air quality. In 1950, exhaust fumes from automobiles shrouded cities such as Vancouver, where the air is trapped between the wind from the ocean and the postcard-pretty mountains. In London, factory smokestacks, automobiles, and

coal fires used to heat households all added up to what was probably the worst urban air quality of the last century. What some British jokingly called "pea soup" was, in reality, a deadly mix of pollution: During five days in 1952, an especially thick haze that hung over London killed 4000 people (Clarke, 1984).

Air quality improved in the final decades of the twentieth century. High-income nations passed laws that banned high-pollution heating, including the coal fires that choked London. In addition, scientists devised ways to make factories and motor vehicles operate much more cleanly. It is fortunate that the cleanest of today's automobiles emit only a small percentage of the pollutants released by the typical car in 1960 because most Canadians prefer to travel by car. Figure 15–5 shows that even in the largest urban areas, where public transit is well developed, workers prefer their cars to less polluting modes of transportation.

rainforests regions of dense forestation, most of which circle the globe close to the equator

global warming a rise in Earth's average temperature due to an increasing concentration of carbon dioxide in the atmosphere

If people in high-income countries can breathe a bit more easily than they once did, those living in low-income societies face problems of air pollution that are becoming more serious. One reason is that people in these regions still rely on wood, coal, peat, or other "dirty" fuels to cook their food and heat their homes. In addition, nations eager to encourage short-term industrial development may pay little attention to the longer-term dangers of air pollution. As a result, many cities in Latin America, Eastern Europe, and Asia are plagued by air pollution as bad as London's pea soup back in the 1950s.

The Rainforests

Rainforests are *regions of dense forestation, most of which circle the globe close to the equator.* The largest tropical rainforests are in South America (notably Brazil), west-central Africa, and Southeast Asia. In all, the world's rainforests cover some 1.5 billion acres, or 4.5 percent of Earth's total land surface (United Nations Environment Programme, 2009).

Like other global resources, rainforests are falling victim to the needs and appetites of the surging world population. As noted earlier, to meet the demand for beef, ranchers in Latin America burn forested areas to increase their supply of grazing land. We are also losing rainforests to the hardwood trade. People in high-income nations pay high prices for mahogany and other woods because, as environmentalist Norman Myers (1984c:88) puts it, they have "a penchant for parquet floors, fine furniture, fancy panelling, weekend yachts, and high-grade coffins." Under such economic pressure, the world's rainforests are now just half their original size, and they continue to shrink by about 1 percent (170 000 square kilometres) annually. Unless we stop this loss, the rainforests will vanish before the end of the twenty-first century and with them will disappear protection for the Earth's biodiversity and climate.

Global Warming

Why are rainforests so important to our natural environment? One reason is that they cleanse the atmosphere of carbon dioxide (CO_2). Since the beginning of the Industrial Revolution, the amount of CO_2 produced by humans (mostly from factories and automobiles) has risen sharply. Much of this CO_2 is absorbed by the oceans. But plants also take in CO_2 and in the process expel oxygen. This is why the rainforests—our largest concentration of plant life—are vital to maintaining the chemical balance of the atmosphere.

The problem is that production of CO_2 is rising while the amount of plant life on Earth is shrinking. To make matters worse, rainforests are being destroyed mostly by burning, which releases even more CO_2 into the atmosphere. Experts estimate that the atmospheric concentration of CO_2 is now 40 percent higher than it was 150 years ago (Gore, 2006; National Oceanic and Atmospheric Administration, 2010; United Nations Environment Programme, 2009).

High above Earth, CO_2 acts like the glass roof of a greenhouse, letting heat from the sun pass through to the surface while preventing much of it from radiating away from the planet. The result of this *greenhouse effect*, say ecologists, is **global warming**, *a rise in Earth's average temperature due to an increasing concentration of carbon dioxide in the atmosphere.* Over the past century, the global temperature has risen about 0.5°C (to an average of 14.5°C). Scientists warn that it could rise by 3°C to 6°C during this century. Already, the polar ice caps are melting, and scientists predict that increasing temperatures could melt so much ice that the sea level would rise to cover low-lying land all around the world. Were this to happen, water would cover all of Bangladesh, for example, and much of coastal Canada. On the other hand, the Canadian Prairies, currently one of the most productive agricultural regions in the world, probably would become arid.

Some scientists point out that we cannot be sure of the consequences of global warming. Others point to the fact that global temperature changes have been taking place throughout history, perhaps having little or nothing to do with rainforests. A few are optimistic, suggesting that higher concentrations of CO_2 in the atmosphere may speed up plant growth (because plants thrive on this gas), and this increase may correct the imbalance and nudge Earth's temperature downward once again. But the consensus of scientists is clear: Global warming is a serious problem that threatens the future for all of us (Gore, 2006; International Panel on Climate Change, 2007; Kerr, 2005; National Oceanic and Atmospheric Administration, 2010).

Declining Biodiversity

Our planet is home to as many as 30 million species of animals, plants, and micro-organisms. As rainforests are cleared and humans extend their control over nature, several dozen unique species of plants and animals cease to exist each day.

But given the vast number of living species, why should we be concerned about the loss of a few? Environmentalists give four reasons. First, our planet's biodiversity provides a varied source of human food. Using agricultural high technology, scientists can cross familiar crops with more exotic plant life, making food more bountiful and more resistant to insects and disease. Thus biodiversity helps feed our planet's rapidly increasing population.

Second, Earth's biodiversity is a vital genetic resource used by medical and pharmaceutical researchers to provide hundreds of new compounds each year that cure disease and improve our lives. For example, children in Canada now have a good chance of surviving leukemia, a disease that was almost a sure killer two generations ago, because of a compound derived from a tropical flower called the rosy periwinkle. The oral birth control pill, used by tens of millions of women in this country, is another product of plant research, this one involving the Mexican forest yam.

Third, with the loss of any species of life—whether it is the ancient Kootenay River white sturgeon, the magnificent California

environmental racism patterns of development that expose poor people, especially minorities, to environmental hazards

ecologically sustainable culture a way of life that meets the needs of the present generation without threatening the environmental legacy of future generations

condor, the famed Chinese panda, the spotted owl, or even a single species of ant—the beauty and complexity of our natural environment are diminished. And there are clear warning signs: Three-fourths of the world's 10 000 species of birds are declining in number.

Finally, unlike pollution, the extinction of any species is irreversible and final. An important ethical question, then, is whether people living today have the right to impoverish the world for those who will live tomorrow (Brown et al., 1993; N. Myers, 1991; Wilson, 1991).

Environmental Racism

Environmental problems threaten us all. But most environmental issues harm some people more than others. Conflict theory has given birth to the concept of **environmental racism**, *patterns of development that expose poor people, especially minorities, to environmental hazards.* Historically, factories that spew pollution have stood near neighbourhoods housing the poor and people of colour. Why? In part, the poor themselves were drawn to factories in search of work, and their low incomes often meant they could afford housing only in undesirable neighbourhoods. Sometimes the only housing that fit their budgets stood in the very shadow of the plants and mills where they worked.

Looking Ahead: Toward a Sustainable Society and World

The demographic analysis presented in this chapter points to some disturbing trends. We see, first, that our planet's population has reached record levels because birth rates remain high in poor nations and death rates have fallen just about everywhere. Reducing fertility will remain a pressing issue throughout this century. Even with some recent decline in the rate of population increase, the nightmare of Thomas Malthus is still a real possibility, as the Controversy & Debate box explains.

Further, population growth remains greatest in the least-resourced countries of the world, which cannot support their present populations, much less their future ones. Supporting 83 million additional people on our planet each year, 81 million of whom are in poor societies, will take a global commitment to provide not only food but also housing, schools, and employment. The well-being of the entire world may ultimately depend on resolving the economic and social problems of bridging the widening gulf between "have" and "have-not" nations.

If human ingenuity created the threats to our environment we now face, can humans also solve these problems? In recent years, a number of designs for small, environmentally friendly cars show the promise of new technology. But do such innovations go far enough? Will we have to make more basic changes to our way of life to ensure human survival in the centuries to come?

Urbanization is continuing, especially in poor countries. People have always sought out cities in the hope of finding a better life. But the sheer numbers of people who live in the emerging global supercities, including Mexico City, São Paulo (Brazil), Kinshasa (Democratic Republic of the Congo), Mumbai (India), and Manila (Philippines), have created urban problems on a massive scale.

Throughout the world, humanity is facing a serious environmental challenge. Part of this problem is population increase, which is greatest in poor societies. But part of the problem is the high levels of consumption in rich nations such as our own. By increasing the planet's environmental deficit, our present way of life is borrowing against the well-being of our children and their children. Globally, members of high-income societies, who currently consume so much of Earth's resources, are mortgaging the future security of the poor countries of the world.

The answer, in principle, is to create an **ecologically sustainable culture**, *a way of life that meets the needs of the present generation without threatening the environmental legacy of future generations.* Sustainable living depends on three strategies.

First, we need to *bring population growth under control.* The current population of 7 billion is already straining the natural environment. Clearly, the higher the world population climbs, the more difficult environmental problems will become. Even if the recent slowing of population growth continues, the world will have 9 billion people by 2050. Few analysts think that Earth can support this many people; most argue that we must hold the line at about 7 billion, and some argue that we must *decrease* population in the coming decades (Smail, 2010).

A second strategy is to *conserve finite resources.* This means meeting our needs with a responsible eye toward the future by using resources efficiently, seeking alternative sources of energy, and, in some cases, learning to live with less.

A third strategy is to *reduce waste.* Whenever possible, simply using less is the best solution. Learning to live with less will not come easily, but keep in mind that as our society has consumed more and more in recent decades, people have not become any happier (Myers, 2000). Recycling programs, too, are part of the answer, and recycling can make everyone part of the solution to our environmental problems.

In the end, making all three of these strategies work depends on a more basic change in the way we think about ourselves and our world. Our *egocentric* outlook sets our own interests as standards for how to live; a sustainable environment demands an *ecocentric* outlook that helps us see that the present is tied to the future and that everyone must work together. Most nations in the

Apocalypse: Will People Overwhelm the Planet?

NUSHAWN: I'm telling you, there are too many people already! Where is everyone going to live?

TABITHA: Have you ever been to Saskatchewan? Or the Yukon? There's plenty of empty space out there.

MARCO: Maybe now. But I'm not so sure there'll be all that room for our children—or their children . . .

Are you worried about the world's rapidly increasing population? Think about this: By the time you finish reading this box, more than 1000 people will have been added to our planet. By this time tomorrow, global population will have risen by more than 200 000. Currently, as the table shows, there are four births for every two deaths on the planet, pushing the world's population upward by almost 83 million people annually. Put another way, global population growth amounts to adding another Germany to the world each year.

It is no wonder that many demographers and environmentalists are deeply concerned about the future. Earth has an unprecedented population: The 2.8 billion people we have added since 1974 alone exceed the planet's total in 1900. Might Thomas Malthus—who predicted that overpopulation would push the world into war and suffering—be right after all? Lester Brown and other *neo-Malthusians* predict a coming apocalypse if we do not change our ways. Brown (1995) admits that Malthus failed to imagine how much technology (especially fertilizers and plant genetics) could boost the planet's agricultural output. But he maintains that Earth's rising population is rapidly outstripping its finite resources. Families in many poor countries can find little firewood, members of rich countries are depleting the oil reserves, and everyone is draining our supply of clean water and poisoning the planet with waste. Some analysts argue that we have already passed Earth's "carrying capacity" for population and that we need to hold the line or even reduce global population to ensure our long-term survival.

But other analysts, the *anti-Malthusians*, sharply disagree. Julian Simon (1995) points out that two centuries after Malthus predicted catastrophe, Earth supports almost six times as many people who, on average, live longer, healthier lives than ever before. With more advanced technology, people have devised ways to increase productivity and limit population increase. As Simon sees it, this is cause for celebration. Human ingenuity has consistently proved the doomsayers wrong, and Simon is betting that it will continue to do so.

WHAT DO YOU THINK?

1. Where do you place your bet? Do you think Earth can support 8 or 10 billion people? Explain your reasoning.

2. Almost all current population growth is in low-income countries. What does this mean for the future of high-income nations? For the future of those with fewer resources?

3. What should people in high-income countries do to ensure the future of children everywhere?

Sources: Brown (1995), Scanlon (2001), Simon (1995), and Smail (2010).

Global Population Increase, 2009

	Births	Deaths	Net Increase
Per year	138 949 000	56 083 000	82 866 000
Per month	11 579 083	4 673 583	6 905 500
Per day	380 682	155 652	227 030
Per hour	15 862	6402	9460
Per minute	264	107	158
Per second	4.4	1.8	2.6

southern half of the world are unable to meet the basic needs of their people. At the same time, most countries in the northern half of the world are using more resources than Earth can sustain over time. The changes needed to create a sustainable ecosystem will not come easily, and they will be costly. But the price of *not* responding to the growing environmental deficit will certainly be greater (Brown et al., 1993; Gore, 2006; Population Action International, 2000).

Finally, consider that the great dinosaurs dominated this planet for some 160 million years and then perished forever. Humanity is far younger, having existed for a mere 250 000 years. Compared to the rather dim-witted dinosaurs, our species has the gift of great intelligence. But how will we use this ability? What are the chances that humans will continue to flourish 160 million years—or even 160 years—from now? The answer depends on the choices made by just one of the 30 million species living on Earth: human beings.

CHAPTER 15 POPULATION, URBANIZATION, AND ENVIRONMENT

WHY IS THE ENVIRONMENT A SOCIAL ISSUE? As this chapter explains, the state of the natural environment depends on how society is organized, especially the importance a culture attaches to consumption and economic growth.

We learn to see economic expansion as natural and good. When the economy stays the same for a number of months, we say we are experiencing "stagnation." How do we define a period when the economy gets smaller, as happened during the fall of 2008?

What would it take to convince members of our society that smaller (rather than bigger) might be better? Why do we seem to prefer not just bigger cars but bigger homes and more and more material possessions?

HINT: If expansion is "good times," then contraction is a "recession" or perhaps even a "depression." Such a world view means that it is normal—or even desirable—to live in a way that increases stress on the natural environment. Sustainability, an idea that is especially important as world population increases, depends on learning to live with what we have or maybe even learning to live with less. Although many people seem to think so, they really don't require a 2700-kilogram SUV to move around urban areas. Actually, they may not require a car at all. This new way of thinking requires that we do not define social standing and personal success in terms of what we own and what we consume. Can you imagine a society like that? What would it be like?

Applying Sociology in Everyday Life

1. Here is an illustration of the problem of runaway growth (Milbrath, 1989:10): "A pond has a single water lily growing on it. The lily doubles in size each day. In thirty days, it covers the entire pond. On which day does it cover half the pond?" When you realize the answer, discuss the implications of this example for population increase.

2. Draw a mental map of a city familiar to you with as much detail of specific places, districts, roads, and transportation facilities as you can. Compare your map to a real one or, better yet, a map drawn by someone else. Try to account for the differences.

3. As an interesting exercise, carry a trash bag around for a single day and collect everything you throw away. Most people are surprised to find that the average person in North America discards close to 2.25 kilograms (5 pounds) of paper, metal, plastic, and other materials daily (over a lifetime, that's about 50 tonnes).

MAKING THE GRADE

CHAPTER 15 — Population, Urbanization, and Environment

Demography: The Study of Population

✓ *Demography analyzes the size and composition of a population and how and why people move from place to place. Demographers collect data and study several factors that affect population (p. 411).*

FERTILITY
- Fertility is the incidence of child-bearing in a country's population.
- Demographers describe fertility by using the **CRUDE BIRTH RATE.**

p. 411

MORTALITY
- Mortality is the incidence of death in a country's population.
- Demographers measure mortality using both the **CRUDE DEATH RATE** and the **INFANT MORTALITY RATE.**

pp. 411–12

MIGRATION
- The **NET MIGRATION RATE** is the difference between the in-migration rate and the out-migration rate.

pp. 412–13

POPULATION GROWTH
In general, high-income nations grow as much from immigration as from natural increase; nations with fewer resources grow almost entirely from natural increase.

pp. 413–14

POPULATION COMPOSITION
Demographers use **AGE-SEX PYRAMIDS** to show graphically the composition of a population and to project population trends.

pp. 414–15

demography (p. 411) the study of human population

fertility (p. 411) the incidence of child-bearing in a country's population

crude birth rate (p. 411) the number of live births in a given year for every 1000 people in a population

mortality (p. 411) the incidence of death in a country's population

crude death rate (p. 411) the number of deaths in a given year for every 1000 people in a population

infant mortality rate (p. 412) the number of deaths among infants under one year of age for each 1000 live births in a given year

life expectancy (p. 412) the average lifespan of a country's population

migration (p. 412) the movement of people into and out of a specified territory

sex ratio (p. 414) the number of males for every 100 females in a nation's population

age-sex pyramid (p. 414) a graphic representation of the age and sex of a population

History and Theory of Population Growth

- Historically, world population grew slowly because high birth rates were offset by high death rates.
- About 1750, a demographic transition began as world population rose sharply, mostly because of falling death rates.
- In the late 1700s, Thomas Robert Malthus warned that population growth would outpace food production, resulting in social calamity.
- **DEMOGRAPHIC TRANSITION THEORY** contends that technological advances gradually slow population increase.
- World population is expected to exceed 9 billion by 2050.

pp. 415–16

demographic transition theory (p. 416) a thesis that links population patterns to a society's level of technological development

zero population growth (p. 417) the rate of reproduction that maintains population at a steady level

✓ *Currently, the world is gaining 83 million people each year, with 98 percent of this increase taking place in low-income countries (p. 415).*

Urbanization: The Growth of Cities

The **FIRST URBAN REVOLUTION** began with the appearance of cities about 10 000 years ago.
- By about 2000 years ago, cities had emerged in most regions of the world except North America and Antarctica.
- Pre-industrial cities have low buildings; narrow, winding streets; and personal social ties.

p. 419

A **SECOND URBAN REVOLUTION** began about 1750 as the Industrial Revolution propelled rapid urban growth in Europe.
- The physical form of cities changed as planners created wide, regular streets to allow for more trade.
- The emphasis on commerce, as well as the increasing size of cities, made urban life more impersonal.

pp. 419–20

urbanization (p. 419) the concentration of population into cities

metropolis (p. 420) a large city that socially and economically dominates an urban area

suburbs (p. 420) urban areas beyond the political boundaries of a city

megalopolis (p. 422) a vast urban region containing a number of cities and their surrounding suburbs

IN CANADA, urbanization has been going on for more than 400 years and continues today.
- Urbanization came to North America with European colonists.
- By 1850, hundreds of new cities had been founded from coast to coast.
- By 1920, a majority of North Americans lived in urban areas.
- Since 1950, the decentralization of cities has resulted in the growth of suburbs and edge cities and a rebound in rural population.

pp. 420–21

Urbanism as a Way of Life

✓ *Rapid urbanization during the nineteenth century led early sociologists to study the differences between rural and urban life. These early sociologists included, in Europe, Tönnies, Durkheim, and Simmel, and in North America, Park and Wirth.*

FERDINAND TÖNNIES built his analysis on the concepts of *Gemeinschaft and Gesellschaft.*

- *Gemeinschaft*, typical of the rural village, joins people in what amounts to a single primary group.
- *Gesellschaft*, typical of the modern city, describes individuals motivated by their own needs rather than the well-being of the community.

pp. 422–23

EMILE DURKHEIM agreed with much of Tönnies's thinking but claimed that urbanites do not lack social bonds; the basis of social solidarity simply differs in the two settings.

- **Mechanical Solidarity** involves social bonds based on common sentiments and shared moral values. This type of social solidarity is typical of traditional, rural life.
- **Organic Solidarity** arises from social bonds based on specialization and interdependence. This type of social solidarity is typical of modern, urban life.

p. 423

GEORG SIMMEL claimed that the overstimulation of city life produced a blasé attitude in urbanites.

p. 423

ROBERT PARK, at the University of Chicago, claimed that cities permit greater social freedom.

p. 423

LOUIS WIRTH saw large, dense, heterogeneous populations creating an impersonal and self-interested, though tolerant, way of life.

p. 423

Gemeinschaft (p. 423) a type of social organization in which people are closely tied by kinship and tradition

Gesellschaft (p. 423) a type of social organization in which people come together only on the basis of individual self-interest

urban ecology (p. 424) the study of the link between the physical and social dimensions of cities

Urbanization in Low-Income Nations

- The world's first urban revolution took place about 8000 BCE with the first urban settlements.
- The second urban revolution took place after 1750 in Europe and North America with the Industrial Revolution.
- A third urban revolution is now occurring in poor countries. Today, most of the world's largest cities are found in nations with fewer resources.

p. 426

Environment and Society

The state of the **ENVIRONMENT** is a social issue because it reflects how human beings organize social life.

- Societies increase the environmental deficit by focusing on short-term benefits and ignoring the long-term consequences brought on by their way of life.
- The more complex a society's technology, the greater its capacity to alter the natural environment.

pp. 426–27

- The logic-of-growth thesis supports economic development, claiming that people can solve environmental problems as they arise.
- The limits-to-growth thesis states that societies must curb development to prevent eventual environmental collapse.

pp. 427–29

ecology (p. 426) the study of the interaction of living organisms and the natural environment

natural environment (p. 426) Earth's surface and atmosphere, including living organisms, air, water, soil, and other resources necessary to sustain life

ecosystem (p. 426) a system composed of the interaction of all living organisms and their natural environment

environmental deficit (p. 427) profound long-term harm to the natural environment caused by humanity's focus on short-term material affluence

rainforests (p. 433) regions of dense forestation, most of which circle the globe close to the equator

global warming (p. 433) a rise in Earth's average temperature due to an increasing concentration of carbon dioxide in the atmosphere

environmental racism (p. 434) patterns of development that expose poor people, especially minorities, to environmental hazards

ecologically sustainable culture (p. 434) a way of life that meets the needs of the present generation without threatening the environmental legacy of future generations

ENVIRONMENTAL ISSUES include

- Disposing of solid waste: More than half of what we throw away ends up in landfills, which are filling up and which can pollute groundwater under Earth's surface.
- Protecting the quality of water and air: The supply of clean water is already low in some parts of the world. Industrial technology has caused a decline in air quality.
- Protecting the rainforests: Rainforests help remove carbon dioxide from the atmosphere and are home to a large share of this planet's living species. Under pressure from development, the world's rainforests are now half their original size and are shrinking by about 1 percent annually.
- Global warming: Increasing levels of carbon dioxide in the atmosphere are causing the average temperature of the planet to rise, melting the ice caps and bringing other dramatic changes to the natural environment.
- Environmental racism: Conflict theory has drawn attention to the fact that the poor, especially minorities, suffer most from environmental hazards.

pp. 429–34

MySocLab

Visit MySocLab at www.mysoclab.com to access a variety of online resources that will help you to prepare for tests and to apply your knowledge, including
- an eText
- videos
- self-grading quizzes
- glossary flashcards

16 Social Change: Modern and Postmodern Societies

- Why do societies change?

- What do sociologists say is good and bad about today's society?

- How do social movements both encourage and resist social change?

The five-storey red brick apartment building at 253 East Tenth Street has been standing for more than a century. In 1900, one of the 20 small apartments in the building was occupied by 39-year-old Julius Streicher; Christine Streicher, age 33; and their four young children. The Streichers were immigrants, both having come in 1885 from their native Germany.

The Streichers probably considered themselves successful. Julius operated a small clothing shop a few blocks from his apartment; Christine stayed at home, raised the children, and did housework. Like most people in the country at that time, neither Julius nor Christine had graduated from high school, and they worked for 10 to 12 hours a day, 6 days a week. Their income—average for that time—was about $35 a month, or about $425 per year. (In today's dollars, that would be slightly more than $11 000, which would put the family well below the poverty line.) They spent almost half of their income for food; most of the rest went for rent.

Today, Dorothy Sabo resides at 253 East Tenth Street, living alone in the same apartment where the Streichers spent much of their lives. Now 87, she is retired from a career teaching art at a nearby museum. In many respects, Sabo's life has been far easier than the life the Streichers knew. For one thing, when the Streichers lived there, the building had no electricity (people used kerosene lamps and candles) and no running water (Christine Streicher spent most of every Monday doing laundry using water she carried from a public fountain at the end of the block). There were no telephones, no television, and of course no computers. Today, Dorothy Sabo takes such conveniences for granted. Although she is hardly rich, her pension and social security amount to several times as much (in constant dollars) as the Streichers earned.

Sabo has her own worries. She is concerned about the environment and often speaks out about global warming. But a century ago, if the Streichers and their neighbours were concerned about "the environment," they probably would have meant the smell coming up from the street. At a time when motor vehicles were just beginning to appear in their city, carriages, trucks, and trolleys were all pulled by horses—thousands of them. These animals dumped 60 000 gallons of urine and 2.5 million pounds of manure on the streets each and every day—an offensive mixture churned and splashed by countless wheels onto everything and everyone within a stone's throw of the streets (Simon & Cannon, 2001).

It is difficult for most people today to imagine how different life was a century ago. Not only was life much harder then, but it was also much shorter. Statistical records show that life expectancy was just 46 years for U.S. men and 48 years for U.S. women, compared to about 75 and 80 years today, respectively (Xu, Kochanek, & Tejada-Vera, 2009). The figures for Canadian men and women at the turn of the twentieth century were similar: 50 years for women and 47 years for men (Martel & Bélanger, 2000). For Canadians born in 2005 to 2007, the life expectancy is now 83 years for females and 78 years for males (Statistics Canada, 2010l).

Over the course of the past century, much has changed for the better. Yet as this chapter explains, social change is not all positive. Change has negative consequences too, causing unexpected new problems. Early sociologists had a mixed assessment of *modernity*, changes brought about by the Industrial Revolution. Likewise, today's sociologists point to both good and bad aspects of *postmodernity*, the transformations caused by the Information Revolution and the post-industrial economy. One thing is clear: For better or worse, the rate of change has never been faster than it is now.

What Is Social Change?

In earlier chapters, we examined relatively fixed or *static* social patterns, including status and role, social stratification, and social institutions. We also looked at the *dynamic* forces that have shaped our way of life, ranging from innovations in technology to the growth of bureaucracy and the expansion of cities. These are all dimensions of **social change**, *the transformation of culture and social institutions over time*. This complex process has four major characteristics:

1. **Social change happens all the time.** People used to say that the only sure things in life were "death and taxes." Yet our thoughts about death have changed dramatically as life expectancy in Canada has nearly doubled in the past century. A century ago, Canadians paid little or no taxes on their earnings; taxation increased dramatically over the course of the twentieth century, along with the size and scope of government. In short, just about everything in life, even the "sure things," is subject to the twists and turns of change.

   Still, some societies change faster than others. As Chapter 2 ("Culture") explained, hunting and gathering societies change quite slowly; members of technologically complex societies, by contrast, can witness significant change within a single lifetime.

   It is also true that in any society, some cultural elements change faster than others. William Ogburn's theory of *cultural lag* (see Chapter 2) asserts that material culture (that is, things) changes faster than nonmaterial culture (ideas and attitudes). For example, genetic techtnology that allows scientists to alter and perhaps even create life has developed more rapidly than our ethical standards for deciding when and how to use the technology.

2. **Social change is sometimes intentional but often unplanned.** Industrial societies actively promote many kinds of change. Scientists seek more efficient forms of energy, and advertisers try to convince us that we cannot live without the latest electronic gadget. Yet rarely can anyone envision all of the consequences of changes as they are set in motion.

   Back in 1900, when the country still relied on horses for transportation, people looked ahead to motor vehicles that would take a single day to carry them distances that used to take weeks or months. But no one could see how much the mobility provided by automobiles would alter life in Canada and other industrial societies, scattering family members, threatening the environment, and reshaping cities and suburbs. Nor could automotive pioneers have predicted the more than 3000 deaths that occur as a result of car accidents each year in Canada alone (National Highway Traffic Safety Administration, 2009).

3. **Social change is controversial.** The history of the automobile shows that social change brings both good and bad consequences. Cars brought an end to the muck of urine and manure on city streets, but they spewed carbon monoxide into the air. In the same contradictory way, capitalists benefited from greater production and profits made possible by the Industrial

These young men are performing in a hip-hop dance marathon in Hong Kong. Hip-hop music, dress style, and dancing have become popular in Asia, a clear case of cultural diffusion. Social change occurs as cultural patterns move from place to place, but people in different societies don't always attach the same meanings to these patterns. How might Chinese youth understand hip hop differently from the young Black North Americans who originated it?

Revolution at the same time that workers pushed back against the machines that they feared would make their skills obsolete.

Today, as in the past, people disagree about how we ought to live and what we should welcome as "progress." We see this disagreement every day in the changing patterns of social interaction between Aboriginal people and non-Aboriginal people, visible minorities and other Canadians, women and men, and homosexuals and heterosexuals that are celebrated by some people and opposed by others.

4. **Some changes matter more than others.** Some changes (such as clothing fads) have only passing significance; others (such as the invention of computers) may change the world. Will the Information Revolution turn out to be as important as the Industrial Revolution? Like the automobile and television, computers have both positive and negative effects, providing new kinds of jobs while eliminating old ones, isolating people in offices while linking people in global electronic networks, offering vast amounts of information while threatening personal privacy.

Causes of Social Change

Social change has many causes. In a world linked by sophisticated communication and transportation technology, change in one place often sets off change elsewhere.

social movement an organized activity that encourages or discourages social change

Culture and Change

Chapter 2 ("Culture") identified three important sources of cultural change. First, *invention* produces new objects, ideas, and social patterns. Rocket propulsion research, which began in the 1940s, has produced sophisticated spacecraft that can reach toward the stars. Today we take such technology for granted; during the present century, a significant number of people may well have an opportunity to travel in space.

Second, *discovery* occurs when people take notice of existing elements of the world. For example, medical advances offer a growing understanding of the human body. Beyond their direct effects on human health, medical discoveries have extended life expectancy, setting in motion the "greying" of Canadian society (see Chapter 3, "Socialization: From Infancy to Old Age").

Third, *diffusion* creates change as products, people, and information spread from one society to another. Ralph Linton (1937a) recognized that many familiar aspects of our culture came from other lands. For example, the cloth used to make our clothing was developed in Asia, the clocks we see all around us were invented in Europe, and the coins we carry in our pockets were devised in what is now Turkey.

In general, material things change more quickly than cultural ideas. For example, breakthroughs such as the science of cloning occur faster than our understanding of when—and even whether—they are morally desirable.

Conflict and Change

Inequality and conflict within a society also produce change. Karl Marx saw class conflict as the engine that drives societies from one historical era to another. In industrial-capitalist societies, he maintained, the struggle between capitalists and workers pushes society toward a socialist system of production.

In the more than 125 years since Marx's death, this model has proved simplistic. Yet Marx correctly foresaw that social conflict arising from inequality (involving not just class but also race and gender) would force changes in every society, including our own, to improve the lives of working people.

Ideas and Change

Max Weber also contributed to our understanding of social change. Although Weber acknowledged that conflict could bring about change, he traced the roots of most social changes to ideas. For example, people with charisma (Martin Luther King, Jr. and Mother Teresa are examples) can carry a message that changes the world.

Weber highlighted the importance of ideas by revealing how the religious beliefs of early Protestants set the stage for the spread of industrial capitalism (see Chapter 13, "Family and Religion"). The fact that industrial capitalism developed primarily in areas of Western Europe where the Protestant work ethic was strong proved to Weber (1958, orig. 1904–05) the power of ideas to bring about change.

Demographic Change

Population patterns also play a part in social change. The typical Canadian household was twice as large in 1900 (5 people) as it is today (2.5 people). Women are having fewer children, and more people are living alone. Change is also taking place as our population grows older. As Chapter 3 ("Socialization: From Infancy to Old Age") explained, 14.4 percent of the Canadian population was over age 65 in 2011, three times the proportion in 1900. By 2031, seniors will account for 22.8 percent of the country's total population (Statistics Canada, 2011ba). Medical research and health care services already focus extensively on the elderly, and life will change in countless other ways as homes and household products are redesigned to meet the needs of growing numbers of older consumers.

Migration within and among societies is another demographic factor that promotes change. Between 1870 and 1930, millions of immigrants entered industrial cities. Thousands more from rural areas joined the rush. As a result, farm communities declined, metropolises expanded, and Canada for the first time became a predominantly urban nation. Similar changes are taking place today as people moving from Moncton to Prince George mix with new immigrants from Latin America, Asia, and India.

Where in Canada have demographic changes been greatest, and where have they been less pronounced? National Map 16–1 on page 443 provides one answer, showing areas of Canada that have grown and declined recently.

Social Movements and Change

A final cause of social change lies in the efforts of people like us. People commonly band together to form a **social movement**, *an organized activity that encourages or discourages social change.* Our nation's history includes all kinds of social movements, from the drive against slavery and the vote for women and other minorities to today's organizations supporting or opposing special rights for Aboriginal people, abortion, gay rights, and the death penalty.

Social movements are about connecting people who share some political goal. Computer technology, including smartphones and social networking internet sites, has made it possible for people to connect as never before. The Seeing Sociology in the News box on page 444 takes a closer look at the power of networking sites such as Facebook to support effective social movements.

Types of Social Movements

Researchers classify social movements according to the type of change they seek (Aberle, 1966; Blumer, 1969; Cameron, 1966). One variable asks: Who is changed? Some movements target selected people and others try to change everyone. A second variable asks: How much change? Some movements seek only limited change in our

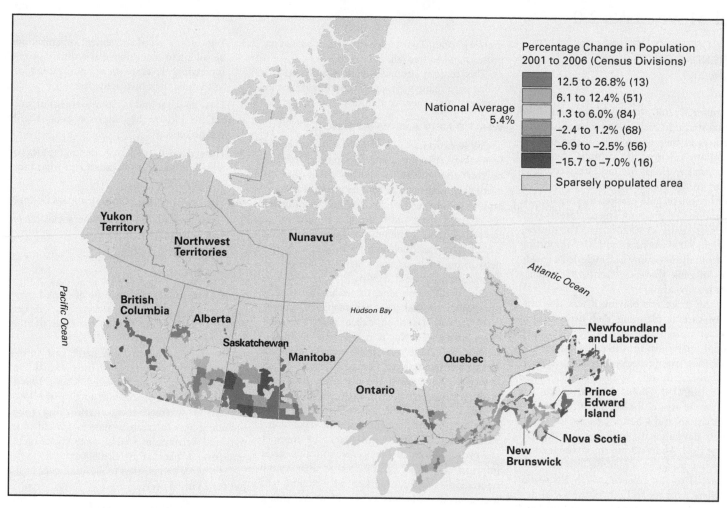

Seeing Ourselves

NATIONAL MAP 16–1   **Population Change, Canada, 2001 to 2006**

Between 2001 and 2006, the high growth rates in central Alberta and around Toronto, Ottawa, and Montreal stand out. Large areas of Saskatchewan and the Maritime provinces saw declines that started long before 2001. How well do these changes reflect the moves you have made during your lifetime? How do you think these changes (and your moves) have affected the communities you moved to and from?

Source: Statistics Canada (2011bb).

lives; others pursue a radical transformation of society. Combining these variables results in four types of social movements, as shown in Figure 16–1 (on page 445).

Alterative social movements are the least threatening to the status quo because they seek limited change in only part of the population. Their aim is to help certain people *alter* their lives. Promise Keepers is one example of an alterative social movement; it

encourages men to live more spiritual lives and be more supportive of their families.

Redemptive social movements also target specific individuals, but they seek more radical change. Their aim is to help certain people *redeem* their lives. For example, Alcoholics Anonymous is an organization that helps people with problematic alcohol consumption achieve a sober life.

The Nation

Social Movements 2.0

BY TIM COSTELLO, JEREMY BRECHER
AND BRENDAN SMITH
January 16, 2009

On September 27, 2007, the world experienced its first virtual strike. In response to a wage dispute, IBM workers in Italy organized a picket outside their company's "corporate campus" based in the 3-D virtual world of Second Life. According to a report in the *Guardian*, workers "marched and waved banners, gate-crashed a [virtual] staff meeting and forced the company to close its [virtual] business center to visitors. . . . The protest, by more than 9,000 workers and 1,850 supporting 'avatars' from thirty countries," included a rowdy collection of pink triangles, "sentient" bananas and other bizarro avatars.

While the strike was playful, it was also buttressed by careful planning and organization. Workers set up a strike task force, developed educational materials in three languages and held more than twenty worker strategy meetings. The hard work paid off. According to Christine Revkin of the UNI Global Union, which was involved in the strike, the online protest led to new negotiations and a better deal for the workers. Twenty days after the initial protest the Italian CEO of IBM, Andrea Pontremoli, resigned . . .

Stories like this offer a glimpse into the powerful potential of the emerging Web 2.0 world, a place where workers and others use social networking tools to quickly reach across national and workplace borders, outflank bosses and politicians and wield collective power. But right now, the type of virtual solidarity seen in the IBM strike remains more promise than reality. People are willing to sign petitions, donate money, trade information and join in political discussions online, but translating these activities into solidarity built on trust and a willingness to take economic or physical risk on another's behalf is exceedingly rare.

As a result, political action online has been largely relegated to electoral politics and tepid humanitarianism: it's been great for raising money for tsunami relief and mobilizing voters, but pretty flaccid when it comes to wielding social movement power. (One exception is organizing around highly repressive regimes, where workers, students and others have successfully used mobile phones, Twitter, etc. to organize escalating protests and to free jailed activists.)

This tension around the pros and cons of online organizing has spurred a healthy debate in the social movement community . . .

WHAT'S NEW AND WHAT'S NOT

Social networking is not new and not about technology. It's not about MySpace, Facebook or YouTube; instead it's about what all of us do every day: kindle and expand networks of friends, family, co-workers, etc. In the political context it's about finding and building communities of interest, linking common struggles and acting collectively. Facebook and other online social networking tools are just a new way for people engage in this age-old activity.

But at the same time, the online universe is not simply another place for people to congregate, circulate a petition, debate politics or mail out a newsletter. Nor is it simply a new technology like cable television—merely bringing more channels into the home. Instead, the web is increasingly looking like the invention of the printing press, which radically changed the lives of even those who could not read, by spurring the Protestant reformation and scientific revolution.

During the past several years, the Internet has evolved from its first generation as a static information portal (e.g. websites) to what is now referred to as Web 2.0, marked by the explosion of user-generated and interactive content. According to Clay Shirky, author of *Here Comes Everybody: The Power of Organizing Without Organizations* and one of the best chroniclers of the social implications of Web 2.0, this communications revolution promises to be the "largest increase in human expressive capability in history." . . .

WHAT WE DON'T KNOW

These rapid changes raise more questions than they answer. Here are eight that we've been grappling with:

1. What does it mean when individuals begin organizing outside and without the help of traditional organizations?

2. It's easy and cheap for organizations to bring people together into a swarm or smart mob, but what do you do with them then?

3. Will offline social movement organizations be willing to cede control as ordinary people increasingly leverage social networking tools to channel their own activities?

4. How do labor and social movement organizations address the dangers associated with online action?

5. How do we track the demographics of who's online and who's not and what tools they are using?

6. How do we present complex ideas online?

7. How does offline and online social movement building fit together?

8. How can social movements wield real power online?

None of these questions will be answered overnight, but it is in our interest to engage this new terrain and figure out how to use these swirling forces to our advantage.

So where to we go from here? Last spring, encouraged by the success of their virtual IBM strike, labor organizers launched "Union Island" on Second Life, a space built to help the labor movement leverage social networking tools, including how to create avatars and build more dynamic websites, as well as swap tricks of the trade over a "beer" at the virtual bar.

Maybe we can all start by heading over to the bar for a virtual beer.

WHAT DO YOU THINK?

1. According to the article, why are Facebook and other computer-based networking systems becoming a "core component for social movements"?

2. Do you think that the use of Facebook for political purposes will help the global union movement? Why or why not?

3. Have you ever used Facebook or a similar networking site as part of an effort to organize a political demonstration or other social movement activity? Explain.

Source: Courtesy of Brendan Smith.

claims making the process of trying to convince the public and public officials of the importance of joining a social movement to address a particular issue

relative deprivation a perceived disadvantage arising from some specific comparison

How Much Change?

	Limited	Radical
Specific Individuals	Alterative Social Movement	Redemptive Social Movement
Everyone	Reformative Social Movement	Revolutionary Social Movement

Who Is Changed?

FIGURE 16–1   Four Types of Social Movements

There are four types of social movements, reflecting who is changed and how great the change is.

Source: Based on Aberle (1966).

One example of a new social movement is the worldwide effort to eliminate land mines. Years after hostilities cease, these mines remain in place and take a staggering toll in civilian lives. At a protest in Berlin, Germany, a mountain of shoes stands as a memorial to the tens of thousands who have been crippled or died as a result of stepping on buried mines.

Reformative social movements aim for only limited change but target everyone. The environmental movement seeks to interest everyone in protecting the natural environment.

Revolutionary social movements are the most extreme of all, working for major transformation of an entire society. Sometimes pursuing specific goals, sometimes spinning utopian dreams, these social movements, including both the left-wing Communist party (pushing for government control of the entire economy) and right-wing militia groups (seeking the destruction of "big government") seek to radically change our way of life.

Claims Making

In 1981, the Centers for Disease Control and Prevention began to track a strange disease that was killing people, most of them homosexual men. The disease came to be known as AIDS (acquired immune deficiency syndrome). Although AIDS was clearly a deadly disease, it was given little public or media attention. Only about five years later did the public begin to take notice of the rising number of deaths and start to think of AIDS as a serious social threat.

The change in public thinking was the result of **claims making**, *the process of trying to convince the public and public officials of the importance of joining a social movement to address a particular issue.* In other words, for a social movement to form, some issue has to be defined as a problem that demands public attention. Usually, claims making begins with a small number of people. In the case of AIDS, the gay community in large cities (notably Toronto, Vancouver, San Francisco, and New York) mobilized to convince people of the dangers posed by this deadly disease. Over time, if the mass media give the issue attention and public officials speak out on behalf of the problem, it is likely that the social movement will gain strength.

Considerable public attention has now been given to AIDS, and there is ongoing research aimed at finding a cure. The process of claims making goes on all the time for dozens of issues. Today, for example, a movement to ban the use of cellphones in automobiles has pointed to the thousands of automobile accidents each year related to the use of phones while driving; as of 2011, six provinces had passed or were in the process of passing laws banning the use of hand-held phones, and debate continues in other provinces (Macionis, 2010; McVeigh, Welch, & Bjarnason, 2003).

Explaining Social Movements

Sociologists have developed several explanations of social movements. *Deprivation theory* holds that social movements arise among people who feel deprived of something, such as income, safe working conditions, or political rights. Whether you feel deprived or not, of course, depends on what you expect in life. Thus people band together in response to **relative deprivation**, *a perceived disadvantage arising from some specific comparison.* This concept helps explain why movements for change surface in both good and bad times: It is not people's absolute standing that counts but how they perceive their situation in relation to the situations of others (J.C. Davies, 1962; Merton, 1968).

Mass-society theory, a second explanation, argues that social movements attract socially isolated people who join a movement to gain a sense of identity and purpose. From this point of view, social movements have a personal as well as a political agenda (Melucci, 1989).

Resource mobilization theory, a third theoretical scheme, links the success of any social movement to the resources that are available

disaster an event, generally unexpected, that causes extensive harm to people and damage to property

Sociologists classify disasters into three types. The 2010 earthquake in Haiti, which claimed several hundred thousand lives, is an example of a natural disaster. The 2010 oil spill in the Gulf of Mexico is an example of a technological disaster. The slaughter of hundreds of thousands of people and the displacement of millions more from their homes in the Darfur region of Sudan since 2003 is an example of an intentional disaster.

to it, including money, human labour, and the mass media. Because most social movements begin small, they must look beyond themselves to mobilize the resources required for success (Packer, 2003; Passy & Giugni, 2001; Valocchi, 1996; Zhao, 1998).

Fourth, *culture theory* points out that social movements depend not only on money and other material resources but also on cultural symbols. People must have a shared understanding of injustice in the world before they will mobilize to bring about change. In addition, specific symbols (such as photographs of the World Trade Center towers engulfed in flames after the September 11, 2001, terrorist attacks) helped mobilize people to support the military campaigns in Afghanistan and Iraq (McAdam, McCarthy, & Zald, 1996; J.E. Williams, 2002).

Fifth, *new social movements theory* points out the distinctive character of recent social movements in post-industrial societies. Rather than being local matters, these movements are typically national or international in scope, and most focus on quality-of-life issues, such as the natural environment, world peace, or animal rights, rather than more traditional economic issues. This broader scope of contemporary social movements results from closer ties between governments and between ordinary people around the world, who are now linked by the mass media and new information technology (Jenkins & Wallace, 1996; Kriesi, 1989; Pakulski, 1993).

Sixth and finally, *political economy theory* is a Marxist approach that claims that social movements arise in opposition to the capitalist economic system, which fails to meet the needs of the majority of people. Despite great economic productivity, North American society is in crisis, with millions of people unable to find good jobs, living below the poverty line, and (in the United States) struggling to survive without health insurance. Social movements arise as workers organize to demand higher wages, citizens rally for a health policy that protects everyone, and people march in opposition to spending billions to fund wars while ignoring basic needs at home (Buechler, 2000).

Stages in Social Movements

Social movements typically unfold in four stages: emergence, coalescence, bureaucratization, and decline. The *emergence* of social movements occurs as people begin to think that all is not well. Some, such as gay rights and women's movements, are born of widespread dissatisfaction. Others emerge as a small group tries to mobilize the population, as when gay activists raised public concern about AIDS.

Coalescence takes place when a social movement defines itself and develops a strategy for attracting new members and "going public." Leaders determine policies and decide on tactics, which may include demonstrations or rallies to attract media attention.

A Never-Ending Atomic Disaster

It was just after dawn on March 1, 1954, and the air was already warm on Utrik Island, a small bit of coral and volcanic rock in the South Pacific that is one of the Marshall Islands. The island was home to 159 people, who lived by fishing much as their ancestors had done for centuries. The population knew only a little about the outside world—a missionary from the United States taught the local children, and the island had been occupied by the Japanese and then the Americans in World War II.

At 6:45 A.M., the western sky suddenly lit up brighter than anyone had ever seen, and seconds later, a rumble like a massive earthquake rolled across the island. The Utrik people did not know what was happening. Their world, at least as they had known it, had changed forever.

About 160 miles to the west, on one of the islands of the Bikini atoll, the United States military had just detonated an atomic bomb, a huge device with 1000 times the power of the bomb used at the end of World War II to destroy the Japanese city of Hiroshima. The enormous blast sent a massive cloud of dust and radiation into the atmosphere and the island disappeared. The military stated that the winds were expected to take the cloud north into an open area of the ocean, but it blew east instead. At 100 miles, the radiation cloud had engulfed a Japanese fishing boat ironically called the *Lucky Dragon*, exposing the 23 people on board. At 150 miles, the cloud had passed Rongelap and then Rongelik, the permanent home of scores of islanders and the temporary home of 28 American weather observers. At 275 miles, finally, the deadly cloud reached Utrik.

The cloud was made up of coral and rock dust from the Bikini atoll. The dust fell softly on Utrik Island, and the children, who remembered pictures of snow from tracts left by the missionaries, ran out to play in the white powder that was piling up everywhere. No one realized that it was contaminated with deadly radiation.

Three-and-one-half days later, the military landed planes on Utrik Island and informed the people that they would have to leave immediately, taking nothing with them. For three months, the island people were held at another military base, and then they were returned home.

Many of the people who were on the island that fateful morning died young, typically from cancer or other diseases associated with radiation exposure. But even today, those who survived consider themselves and their island poisoned by the radiation, and they believe that the poison will never go away. The radiation may or may not still be in their bodies, but it has worked its way deep into their culture. More than half a century after the bomb exploded, people still talked about the morning that "everything changed." The damage from this disaster turns out to be much more than medical—it was a social transformation that left the people with a deep belief that they are all sick, that life will never be the same, and that the people who live on the other side of the world could have prevented the disaster but did not.

WHAT DO YOU THINK?

1. In what sense is a disaster like this one never really over?

2. In what ways did the atomic bomb test change the culture of the Utrik people?

3. What does this account lead us to expect about the long-term consequences of other disasters, such as the 1982 sinking of the *Ocean Ranger* in the Grand Banks area of Newfoundland that caused 84 crew members to drown?

Source: Based on Erikson (2011).

As it gains members and resources, a social movement may undergo *bureaucratization*. As a movement becomes established, it depends less on the charisma and talents of a few leaders and more on a professional staff, which increases the chances for the movement's long-term survival.

Finally, social movements *decline* as resources dry up, the group faces overwhelming opposition, or members achieve their goals and lose interest. Some well-established organizations outlive their original causes and move on to new crusades; others lose touch with the idea of changing society and choose instead to become part of the "system" (Miller, 1983; Piven & Cloward, 1977).

Disasters: Unexpected Change

Sometimes change results from events that are both unexpected and unwelcome. A **disaster** is *an event, generally unexpected, that causes extensive harm to people and damage to property*. Disasters are of three types. Floods, earthquakes, forest fires, and hurricanes (such as Hurricane Katrina, which devastated the Gulf Coast in 2005) are examples of *natural disasters* (Erikson, 2005a). A second type is the *technological disaster*, which is widely regarded as an *accident* but is more accurately the result of our inability to control technology (Erikson, 2005a). The nuclear accident at the Chernobyl power plant in Ukraine in 1986 and the spilling of millions of gallons of oil in the Gulf of Mexico in 2010 were technological disasters. A third type is the *intentional disaster*, in which one or more organized groups deliberately harm others. War, terrorist attacks, and the genocide that took place in Yugoslavia (1992–1995), Rwanda (2000), and the Darfur region of Sudan (2003–2010) are examples of intentional disasters.

The full scope of the harm caused by disasters may become evident only many years after the event. The Thinking Globally box on page 447 describes a technological disaster that is still affecting people and their descendants more than half a century after it took place.

Kai Erikson (1976, 1994, 2005a) has investigated disasters of all types and has reached three major conclusions about the social consequences of disasters. First, we all know that disasters harm people and destroy property, but what most people don't realize is that disasters also cause social damage by disrupting human community. When a dam burst and sent a mountain of water down West Virginia's Buffalo Creek in 1972, it killed 125 people, destroyed 1000 homes, and left 4000 people homeless. After the waters had gone and help was streaming into the area, the people were paralyzed not only by the loss of family members and friends but also by the loss of their way of life. Even four decades later, they have been unable to rebuild the community life they once knew. We can know when disasters start, Erikson points out, but we cannot know when they will end.

Second, Erikson explains that the social damage is more serious when an event involves some toxic substance, as is common with technological disasters. As the case of radiation falling on Utrik Island shows us, people feel "poisoned" when they have been exposed to a dangerous substance that they fear and over which they have no control. People in Ukraine felt much the same way after the 1986 explosion and radiation leak at the Chernobyl nuclear plant.

Third, the social damage is most serious when the disaster is caused by the actions of other people. This can happen through negligence or carelessness (as in technological disasters) or through wilful action (intentional disasters). Our belief that "other people will do us no harm" is a foundation of social life, Erikson claims. But when others act carelessly (as in the case of an oil spill) or intentionally in ways that harm us (as in the case of genocide in Darfur), survivors typically lose their trust in others to a degree that may never go away.

Modernity

A central concept in the study of social change is **modernity**, *social patterns resulting from industrialization*. In everyday terms, *modernity* (its Latin root means "lately") refers to the present in relation to the past. Sociologists use this catch-all concept to describe the many social patterns set in motion by the Industrial Revolution, which began in

TABLE 16–1 Canada: A Century of Change

	1900	2000
National population	5 million	31 million
Share living in cities	40%	80%
Life expectancy	46 years (men), 48 years (women)	78 years (men), 83 years (women)
Median age	23	39
Average household income	$8000 (in 2000 dollars)	$60 000 (in 2000 dollars)
Share of income spent on food	43%	10%
Share of homes with flush toilets	10%	98%
Average number of cars	1 car for every 2000 households	1.5 cars/trucks for every household
Divorce rate	about 1 in 20 marriages	about 8 in 20 marriages
Average litres of petroleum products consumed	100 per person per year	4000 per person per year

Western Europe in the 1750s. **Modernization**, then, is *the process of social change begun by industrialization*. Table 16–1 provides a summary of change in Canada over the course of the twentieth century.

Peter Berger (1977) identified four major characteristics of modernization:

1. **The decline of small, traditional communities.** Modernity involves "the progressive weakening, if not destruction, of the . . . relatively cohesive communities in which human beings have found solidarity and meaning throughout most of history" (1977:72). For thousands of years, in the camps of hunters and gatherers and in the rural villages of Europe and North America, people lived in small communities where life revolved around family and neighbourhood. Such traditional worlds gave each person a well-defined place that, although limiting range of choice, offered a strong sense of identity, belonging, and purpose.

   Small, isolated communities still exist in Canada, of course, but they are home to only a tiny percentage of our nation's people. These days, their isolation is only geographic: Except among those who are extremely poor, cars, telephones, television, and computers give rural families the pulse of the larger society and connect them to the entire world.

2. **The expansion of personal choice.** People in traditional, pre-industrial societies view their lives as shaped by forces beyond human control—gods, spirits, fate. As the power of

tradition weakens, people come to see their lives as an unending series of options, a process Berger calls *individualization*. For instance, many people in Canada choose a particular "lifestyle" (sometimes adopting one after another), showing an openness to change. Indeed, it is a common belief that people *should* take control of their lives.

3. **Increasing social diversity.** In pre-industrial societies, strong family ties and powerful religious beliefs enforce conformity and discourage diversity and change. Modernization promotes a more rational, scientific world view as tradition loses its hold and people gain more individual choice. The growth of cities, the expansion of impersonal bureaucracy, and the social mix of people from various backgrounds combine to encourage diverse beliefs and behaviour.

4. **Orientation toward the future and a growing awareness of time.** Premodern people focus on the past; people in modern societies think more about the future. Modern people are not only forward-looking but also optimistic that new inventions and discoveries will improve their lives.

Modern people organize daily routines down to the very minute. With the introduction of clocks in the late Middle Ages, Europeans began to think not in terms of sunlight and seasons but in terms of hours and minutes. Focused on personal gain, modern people demand precise measurement of time and are likely to agree that "time is money." Berger points out that one good indicator of a society's degree of modernization is the share of people who keep track of time by continually glancing at their wristwatches (or, nowadays, their cellphones).

Finally, recall that modernization touched off the development of sociology itself. As Chapter 1 ("Sociology: Perspective, Theory, and Method") explained, the discipline originated in the wake of the Industrial Revolution in Western Europe at a point when social change was proceeding rapidly. Early European and North American sociologists tried to analyze the rise of modern society and its consequences, both good and bad, for human beings.

Ferdinand Tönnies: The Loss of Community

The German sociologist Ferdinand Tönnies produced a lasting account of modernization in his theory of *Gemeinschaft* and *Gesellschaft* (see Chapter 15, "Population, Urbanization, and Environment"). Like Peter Berger, whose work he influenced, Tönnies (1963, orig. 1887) viewed modernization as the progressive loss of *Gemeinschaft*, or human community. As Tönnies saw it, the Industrial Revolution weakened the social fabric of family and tradition by introducing a businesslike emphasis on facts, efficiency, and money. European and North American societies gradually became rootless and impersonal as people came to associate with one another mostly on the basis of self-interest—the state Tönnies termed *Gesellschaft*.

Early in the twentieth century, at least some parts of Canada could be described using Tönnies's concept of *Gemeinschaft*. Families that had lived for many generations in small villages and towns were bound together into a hard-working and slowly changing way of life. Telephones (invented in 1876) were rare; not until 1915 could one place a coast-to-coast call. Living without television (introduced commercially in 1933 and not widespread until after 1950), families entertained themselves, often gathering with friends in the evening to share stories, sorrows, or song. Lacking rapid transportation (Henry Ford's assembly line began in 1908, but cars became common only after World War II), many people knew little of the world beyond their hometown.

Inevitable tensions and conflicts divided these communities of the past. But according to Tönnies, the traditional spirit of *Gemeinschaft* meant that people were "essentially united in spite of all separating factors" (1963:65, orig. 1887).

Modernity turns society inside out so that, as Tönnies put it, people are "essentially separated in spite of uniting factors" (1963:65, orig. 1887). This is the world of *Gesellschaft*, where, especially in large cities, most people live among strangers and ignore the people they pass on the street. Trust is hard to come by in a mobile and anonymous society in which people put their personal needs ahead of group loyalty and a majority of adults believe "you can't be too careful" in dealing with people (NORC, 2009:1811). No wonder researchers conclude that even as we have become more affluent, the social health of modern societies has declined (Myers, 2000).

CRITICAL REVIEW Tönnies's theory of *Gemeinschaft* and *Gesellschaft* is the most widely cited model of modernization. The theory's strength lies in its synthesis of various dimensions of change: growing population, the rise of cities, and increasingly impersonal interaction. But modern life, though often impersonal, still has some degree of *Gemeinschaft*. Even in a world of strangers, modern friendships can be strong and lasting. In addition, some analysts think that Tönnies favoured—perhaps even romanticized—traditional societies while overlooking bonds of family and friendship that continue to flourish in modern societies.

CHECK YOUR LEARNING As types of social organization, how do *Gemeinschaft* and *Gesellschaft* differ?

Emile Durkheim: The Division of Labour

The French sociologist Emile Durkheim shared Tönnies's interest in the important social changes that resulted from the Industrial Revolution. For Durkheim (1964a, orig. 1893), modernization was marked by an increasing **division of labour**, or *specialized economic activity*. Every member of a traditional society performs more or

division of labour (p. 449) specialized economic activity

anomie a condition in which society provides little moral guidance to individuals

In traditional societies, such as Amish and Hutterite communities in Canada and United States, everyone does much the same work. These societies are held together by strong moral beliefs. Modern societies, illustrated by urban areas in this country, are held together by a system of production in which people perform specialized work and rely on one another.

less the same activities; modern societies function by having people perform highly specific jobs.

Durkheim explained that pre-industrial societies are held together by *mechanical solidarity*, or shared moral sentiments (see Chapter 15). Members of such societies view everyone as basically alike, doing the same work and belonging together. Durkheim's concept of mechanical solidarity is virtually the same as Tönnies's *Gemeinschaft*.

With modernization, the division of labour (job specialization) becomes more and more pronounced. To Durkheim, this change means less mechanical solidarity but more of another kind of tie: *organic solidarity*, mutual dependency between people engaged in specialized work. Put simply, modern societies are held together not by likeness but by difference: All of us must depend on others to meet most of our needs. Organic solidarity corresponds to Tönnies's concept of *Gesellschaft*.

Despite obvious similarities in their thinking, Durkheim and Tönnies viewed modernity somewhat differently. To Tönnies, modern *Gesellschaft* amounted to the loss of social solidarity because people lose the "natural" and "organic" bonds of the rural village, leaving only the "artificial" and "mechanical" ties of the big city. Durkheim had a different view of modernity, even reversing Tönnies's language to bring home the point. Durkheim labelled modern society "organic," arguing that modern society is no less natural than any other, and he described traditional societies as "mechanical" because they are so regimented. Durkheim viewed modernization not so much as a loss of community as a change from community based on bonds of likeness (kinship and neighbourhood) to community based on economic interdependence (the division of labour). Durkheim's view of modernity is thus both more complex and more positive than Tönnies's view.

CRITICAL REVIEW Durkheim's work, which resembles that of Tönnies, is a highly influential analysis of modernity. Of the two, Durkheim was more optimistic; still, he feared that modern societies might become so diverse that they would collapse into **anomie**, *a condition in which society provides little moral guidance to individuals.* Living with weak moral norms, modern people can become egocentric, placing their own needs above those of others and finding little purpose in life.

The suicide rate, which Durkheim considered a good index of anomie, did in fact increase in North America over the course of the twentieth century, and the vast majority of adults report that they see moral questions not in clear terms of right and wrong but as confusing "shades of gray" (NORC, 2009:478). Yet shared norms and values seem strong enough to give most people a sense of meaning and purpose. Whatever the hazards of anomie, most people value the personal freedom modern society gives us.

CHECK YOUR LEARNING Define mechanical solidarity and organic solidarity. In his view of the modern world, what makes Durkheim more optimistic than Tönnies?

Max Weber: Rationalization

For Max Weber, modernity meant replacing a traditional world view with a rational way of thinking. In pre-industrial societies, tradition acts as a constant brake on social change. To traditional people, "truth" is roughly the same as "what has always been" (1978:36, orig. 1921). To modern people, however, "truth" is the result of rational calculation. Because they value efficiency and have little reverence for the past, modern people adopt social patterns that allow them to achieve their goals.

Max Weber maintained that the distinctive character of modern society was its rational world view. Virtually all of Weber's work on modernity centred on types of people he considered typical of their age: the scientist, the capitalist, and the bureaucrat. Each is rational to the core: The scientist is committed to the orderly discovery of truth, the capitalist to the orderly pursuit of profit, and the bureaucrat to orderly conformity to a system of rules.

Echoing Tönnies's and Durkheim's claim that industrialization weakens tradition, Weber characterized modern society as "disenchanted." The unquestioned truths of an earlier time had been challenged by rational thinking. In short, said Weber, modern society turns away from the gods just as it turns away from the past. Throughout his life, Weber studied various modern "types"—the scientist, the capitalist, the bureaucrat—all of whom share the forward-looking, rational, and detached world view that he believed was coming to dominate humanity.

CRITICAL REVIEW Compared with Tönnies and especially Durkheim, Weber was very critical of modern society. He knew that science could produce technological and organizational wonders, yet he worried that science was carrying us away from more basic questions about the meaning and purpose of human existence. Weber feared that rationalization, especially in bureaucracies, would erode the human spirit with endless rules and regulations.

CHECK YOUR LEARNING What did Weber mean by describing the modern world as "disenchanted"? In what ways are scientists, capitalists, and bureaucrats all "disenchanted"?

Some of Weber's critics think that the alienation Weber attributed to bureaucracy actually stemmed from social inequality. This issue leads us to the ideas of Karl Marx.

Karl Marx: Capitalism

For Karl Marx, modern society was synonymous with capitalism; he saw the Industrial Revolution primarily as a *capitalist* revolution. Marx traced the emergence of the bourgeoisie in medieval Europe

to the expansion of commerce. The bourgeoisie gradually displaced the feudal aristocracy as the Industrial Revolution gave it control of a powerful new productive system.

Marx agreed that modernity weakened small communities (as described by Tönnies), increased the division of labour (as noted by Durkheim), and encouraged a rational world view (as Weber claimed). But he saw these simply as conditions necessary for capitalism to flourish. According to Marx, capitalism draws population away from farms and small towns into an ever-expanding market system centred in the cities; specialization is needed for efficient factories; and rationality is illustrated by the capitalists' endless pursuit of profit.

Earlier chapters have painted Marx as a spirited critic of capitalist society, but his vision of modernity also includes a good bit of optimism. Unlike Weber, who viewed modern society as an "iron cage" of bureaucracy from which there was no escape, Marx believed that social conflict in capitalist societies would sow the seeds of revolutionary change, leading to an egalitarian socialism. Such a society, as he saw it, would harness the wonders of industrial technology to enrich people's lives and rid the world of social classes, the source of conflict and so much suffering. Although Marx's evaluation of modern capitalist society was highly negative, he imagined a future of human freedom, creativity, and community.

CRITICAL REVIEW Marx's theory of modernization is a complex theory of capitalism. But he underestimated the dominance of bureaucracy in shaping modern societies. In socialist societies, in particular, the stifling effects of bureaucracy have turned out to be as bad as, or even worse than, the dehumanizing aspects of capitalism. The upheavals in Eastern Europe and the

mass society a society in which prosperity and bureaucracy have weakened traditional social ties

class society (p. 454) a capitalist society with pronounced social stratification

former Soviet Union in the 1990s revealed the depth of popular opposition to oppressive state bureaucracies.

CHECK YOUR LEARNING Of the four theorists just discussed—Tönnies, Durkheim, Weber, and Marx—who comes across as the most optimistic about modern society? Who was the most pessimistic? Explain your choices.

Structural-Functional Analysis: Modernity as Mass Society

June 16, Shelbourne Street at McKenzie. From the car window, we see CIBC, Shell and Petro-Canada gas stations, Home Depot, Canadian Tire, Safeway, Boston Pizza, and Tim Hortons. This road stop happens to be in Victoria, British Columbia, but it could be just about any city in Canada.

The rise of modernity is a complex process involving many dimensions of change, described in earlier chapters and reviewed here in the Summing Up table on page 453. How can we make sense of so many changes going on at once? Sociologists have two broad explanations of modern society, one guided by the structural-functional approach and the other based on social-conflict theory.

The first explanation, guided by the structural-functional approach and drawing on the ideas of Tönnies, Durkheim, and Weber, understands modernity as the emergence of a *mass society* (Berger, Berger, & Kellner, 1974; Kornhauser, 1959; Nisbet, 1969; Pearson, 1993). A **mass society** is *a society in which prosperity and bureaucracy have weakened traditional social ties*. A mass society is productive; on average, people have more income than ever. At the same time, it is marked by weak kinship and impersonal neighbourhoods, leaving individuals to feel socially isolated. Although many people have material plenty, they are spiritually weak and often experience moral uncertainty about how to live.

The Mass Scale of Modern Life

Mass-society theory argues, first, that the scale of modern life has greatly increased. Before the Industrial Revolution, Europe and North America formed a mosaic of rural villages and small towns. In these local communities, which inspired Tönnies's concept of *Gemeinschaft*, people lived out their lives surrounded by kin and guided by a shared heritage. Gossip was an informal yet highly effective way of ensuring conformity to community standards. Such small communities tolerated little social diversity—the state of mechanical solidarity described by Durkheim.

For example, before 1690, English law demanded that everyone participate regularly in the Christian ritual of Holy Communion

(Laslett, 1984). On the North American continent, only Rhode Island among the New England colonies tolerated any religious dissent. Because social differences were repressed in favour of conformity to established norms, subcultures and countercultures were few, and change proceeded slowly.

Increasing population, the growth of cities, and specialized economic activity driven by the Industrial Revolution gradually altered this pattern. People came to know one another by their jobs (for example, as "the doctor" or "the bank clerk") rather than by their kinship group or hometown. People looked on most others simply as strangers. The face-to-face communication of the village was eventually replaced by the impersonal mass media: newspapers, radio, television, and computer networks. Large organizations steadily assumed more and more responsibility for the daily needs that had once been fulfilled by family, friends, and neighbours; public education drew more and more people to schools; police, lawyers, and courts supervised a formal criminal justice system. Even charity became the work of faceless bureaucrats working for various social welfare agencies.

Geographic mobility, mass communication, and exposure to diverse ways of life all weaken traditional values. People become more tolerant of social diversity, defending individual rights and freedom of choice. Treating people differently because of their race, sex, or religion comes to be defined as backward and unjust. In the process, minorities at the margins of society gain greater power and broader participation in public life. The appointment of Michaëlle Jean, a refugee from Haiti, as governor general of Canada and the election of Barack Obama, an African-American, to the highest office in the United States are surely indicators that ours is now a modern society (West, 2008).

The mass media give rise to a national culture that washes over the traditional differences that used to set off one region from another. As one analyst put it, "Even in Baton Rouge, La., the local kids don't say 'y'all' anymore; they say 'you guys' just like on TV" (Gibbs, 2000:42). Mass-society theorists fear that the transformation of people of various backgrounds into a generic mass may end up dehumanizing everyone.

The Ever-Expanding State

In the small-scale pre-industrial societies of Europe, government amounted to little more than a local noble. A royal family formally reigned over an entire nation, but in the absence of swift transportation and efficient communication, even absolute monarchs had far less power than today's political leaders.

As technological innovation allowed government to expand, the centralized state grew in size and importance. At the time of Confederation, the Canadian government was a tiny organization, its primary function being national defence. Since then, government has assumed responsibility for more and more areas of social life: schooling, regulating wages and working conditions, establishing standards for products of all sorts, and providing

SUMMING UP

Traditional and Modern Societies: The Big Picture

Elements of Society	Traditional Societies	Modern Societies
Cultural Patterns		
Values	Homogeneous; sacred character; few subcultures and countercultures	Heterogeneous; secular character; many subcultures and countercultures
Norms	Great moral significance; little tolerance of diversity	Variable moral significance; high tolerance of diversity
Time orientation	Present linked to past	Present linked to future
Technology	Pre-industrial; human and animal energy	Industrial; advanced energy sources
Social Structure		
Status and role	Few statuses, most ascribed; few specialized roles	Many statuses, some ascribed and some achieved; many specialized roles
Relationships	Typically primary; little anonymity or privacy	Typically secondary; much anonymity and privacy
Communication	Face to face	Face-to-face communication supplemented by mass media
Social control	Informal gossip	Formal police and legal system
Social stratification	Rigid patterns of social inequality; little mobility	Fluid patterns of social inequality; high mobility
Gender patterns	Pronounced patriarchy; women's lives centred on the home	Declining patriarchy; increasing share of women work in the paid labour force
Settlement patterns	Small-scale; population typically small and widely dispersed in rural villages and small towns	Large-scale; population typically large and concentrated in cities
Social Institutions		
Economy	Based on agriculture; much manufacturing in the home; little white-collar work	Based on industrial mass production; factories become centres of production; increasing white-collar work
State	Small-scale government; little state intervention in society	Large-scale government; much state intervention in society
Family	Extended family as the primary means of socialization and economic production	Nuclear family still has some socialization functions but is more a unit of consumption than of production
Religion	Religion guides world view; little religious pluralism	Religion weakens with the rise of science; extensive religious pluralism
Education	Formal schooling limited to elites	Basic schooling becomes universal, with growing share of people receiving advanced education
Health	High birth and death rates; short life expectancy because of low standard of living and simple medical technology	Low birth and death rates; longer life expectancy because of higher standard of living and sophisticated medical technology
Social Change	Slow; change evident over many generations	Rapid; change evident within a single generation

financial assistance to the elderly, the ill, and the unemployed. To pay for such programs, taxes have soared: Today's average worker in Canada labours more than six months each year just to pay for the broad array of services the government provides.

In a mass society, power resides in large bureaucracies, leaving people in local communities with little control over their lives. For example, government officials mandate that local schools must meet educational standards, local products must be government-certified, and every citizen must maintain extensive tax records. Although such regulations may protect people and enhance social equality, they also force us to deal more and more with nameless officials in distant and often unresponsive bureaucracies, and they undermine the autonomy of families and local communities.

CRITICAL REVIEW The growing scale of modern life certainly has positive aspects, but only at the cost of our cultural heritage. Modern societies increase individual rights, have greater tolerance of social differences, and raise living standards (Inglehart & Baker, 2000). But they are prone to what Weber feared most—excessive bureaucracy—as well as to Tönnies's self-centredness and Durkheim's anomie. The size, complexity, and tolerance of diversity of modern societies all

Canada has reached a very high standard of living but not all people have benefited. In December 2011, the United Nations special envoy for Aboriginal peoples criticized the Federal Government for its failure to respond to the terrible housing conditions in the Aboriginal community of Attawapiskat in northern Ontario.

but doom traditional values and families, leaving individuals isolated, powerless, and materialistic. As Chapter 12 ("Economics and Politics") noted, voter apathy is a serious problem in Canada. But should we be surprised that individuals in vast, impersonal societies such as ours end up thinking that no one person can make much of a difference?

Critics sometimes say that mass-society theory romanticizes the past. They remind us that many people in the small towns of our past were eager to set out for a better standard of living in cities. This approach also ignores problems of social inequality. Critics say that mass-society theory attracts social and economic conservatives who defend conventional morality and are indifferent to the historical inequality of women and other minorities.

○ **CHECK YOUR LEARNING** In your own words, state the mass-society analysis of modernity.

Social-Conflict Analysis: Modernity as Class Society

The second explanation of modernity derives mostly from the ideas of Karl Marx. From a social-conflict perspective, modernity takes the form of a **class society**, *a capitalist society with pronounced social*

stratification. While agreeing that modern societies have expanded to a mass scale, this approach views the heart of modernization as an expanding capitalist economy, marked by inequality (Buechler, 2000; Habermas, 1970; Harrington, 1984).

Capitalism

Class-society theory follows Marx in claiming that the increasing scale of social life in modern times has resulted from the growth and greed unleashed by capitalism. Because a capitalist economy pursues ever-greater profits, both production and consumption steadily increase.

According to Marx, capitalism rests on "naked self-interest" (Marx & Engels, 1972:337, orig. 1848). This self-centredness weakens the social ties that once united small communities. Capitalism also treats people as commodities: a source of labour and a market for capitalist products.

Capitalism supports science not just as the key to greater productivity but also as an ideology that justifies the status quo. Modern societies encourage people to view human well-being as a technical puzzle that can be solved by engineers and other scientific experts rather than through the pursuit of social justice. For example, a capitalist culture seeks to improve health through advances in scientific medicine rather than by eliminating poverty, despite the fact that poverty is a core cause of poor health.

Businesses also raise the banner of scientific logic, trying to increase profits through greater efficiency. As Chapter 12 ("Economics and Politics") explained, capitalist corporations have reached enormous size and control unimaginable wealth as a result of global expansion. From the class-society point of view, the expanding scale of life is less a function of *Gesellschaft* than the inevitable and destructive consequence of capitalism.

Persistent Inequality

Modernity has gradually worn away some of the rigid categories that divided pre-industrial societies. But class-society theory maintains that elites persist in the form of capitalist millionaires instead of nobles born to wealth and power. In Canada, we may have no hereditary monarchy, but the richest 20 percent of the population receives 40 percent of after-tax income after transfers and taxes (Grabb & Guppy, 2009; Statistics Canada, 2009).

What of the state? Mass-society theorists argue that the state works to increase equality and fight social problems. Marx disagreed; he doubted that the state could accomplish more than minor reforms because, as he saw it, real power lies in the hands of the capitalists who control the economy. Other class-society theorists add that to the extent that working people and minorities do enjoy greater political rights and a higher standard of living today, these changes were the result of political struggle, not government goodwill. Despite our

SUMMING UP

Two Interpretations of Modernity

	Mass Society	Class Society
Process of modernization	Industrialization; growth of bureaucracy	Rise of capitalism
Effects of modernization	Increasing scale of life; rise of the state and other formal organizations	Expansion of the capitalist economy; persistence of social inequality

pretensions of democracy, they conclude, most people are powerless in the face of wealthy elites.

CRITICAL REVIEW Class-society theory dismisses Durkheim's argument that people in modern societies suffer from anomie, claiming instead that most people deal with alienation and powerlessness. Not surprisingly, the class-society interpretation of modernity enjoys widespread support among liberals and radicals who favour greater equality and seek extensive regulation (or abolition) of the capitalist marketplace.

A basic criticism of class-society theory is that it overlooks the increasing prosperity of modern societies and the fact that discrimination based on race, ethnicity, religion, and gender is now illegal and is widely regarded as a social problem. In addition, many people in Canada do not want an egalitarian society; they prefer a system of unequal rewards that reflects personal differences in talent and effort.

Based on socialism's failure to generate a high overall standard of living, few observers think that a centralized economy would cure the ills of modernity. Many other problems in Canada—including unemployment, industrial pollution, and unresponsive government—are also found in socialist nations.

CHECK YOUR LEARNING In your own words, state the class-society analysis of modernity. What are several criticisms of it?

The Summing Up table compares views of modern society offered by mass-society theory and class-society theory. Mass-society theory focuses on the increasing impersonality of social life and the growth of government; class-society theory stresses the expansion of capitalism and the persistence of inequality.

Modernity and the Individual

Both mass- and class-society theories look at the broad patterns of change since the Industrial Revolution. From these macro-level approaches, we can also draw micro-level insights into how modernity shapes individual lives.

Mass Society: Problems of Identity

Modernity freed individuals from the small, tightly knit communities of the past. Most members of modern societies have the privacy and freedom to express their individuality. However, mass-society theory suggests that so much social diversity, widespread isolation, and rapid social change make it difficult for many people to establish any coherent identity at all (Berger, Berger, & Kellner, 1974; Wheelis, 1958).

Chapter 3 ("Socialization: From Infancy to Old Age") explained that people's personalities are mostly a product of their social experiences. The small, homogeneous, and slowly changing societies of the past provided a firm, if narrow, foundation for building a personal identity. Even today, Amish and Hutterite communities that flourish in Canada and the United States teach young men and women "correct" ways to think and behave. Not everyone born into such a community can tolerate such rigid demands for conformity, but most members establish a well-integrated and satisfying personal identity (Kraybill & Hurd, 2006; Kraybill & Olshan, 1994).

Mass societies are quite another story. Socially diverse and rapidly changing, they offer only shifting sands on which to build a personal identity. Left to make many life decisions on their own, people—especially those with greater wealth—face a confusing range of options. The freedom to choose has little value without standards to guide the selection process; in a tolerant mass society, people may find little reason to choose one path over another. As a result, many people shuttle from one identity to another, changing their lifestyles, relationships, and even religions in search of an elusive "true self." Given the widespread relativism of modern societies, people without a moral compass lack the security and certainty once provided by tradition.

To David Riesman (1970, orig. 1950), modernization brings changes in **social character**, *personality patterns common to members of a particular society*. Pre-industrial societies promote what Riesman calls **tradition-directedness**, *rigid conformity to time-honoured ways of living*. Members of such societies model their lives on those of their ancestors, so that "living the good life" amounts to "doing what people have always done."

social character (p. 455) personality patterns common to members of a particular society

tradition-directedness (p. 455) rigid conformity to time-honoured ways of living

other-directedness openness to the latest trends and fashions, often expressed by imitating others

Mass-society theory relates feelings of anxiety and lack of meaning in the modern world to rapid social change that washes away tradition. This notion of modern emptiness is captured in the photo on the left. Class-society theory, by contrast, ties such feelings to social inequality, by which some categories of people are made into second-class citizens (or not made citizens at all), an idea expressed in the photo on the right.

Tradition-directedness corresponds to Tönnies's *Gemeinschaft* and Durkheim's mechanical solidarity. Culturally conservative, tradition-directed people think and act alike. Unlike the conformity often found in modern societies, the uniformity of tradition-directedness is not an effort to imitate a popular celebrity or follow the latest trend. Instead, people are alike because they all draw on the same solid cultural foundation. Hutterite women and men exemplify tradition-directedness; in the Hutterite culture, tradition ties everyone to ancestors and descendants in an unbroken chain of righteous living.

Members of diverse and rapidly changing societies define a tradition-directed personality as deviant because it seems so rigid. Modern people prize personal flexibility, the capacity to adapt, and sensitivity to others. Riesman calls this type of social character **other-directedness**, *openness to the latest trends and fashions, often expressed by imitating others*. Because their socialization occurs in societies that are continuously in flux, other-directed people develop fluid identities marked by superficiality, inconsistency, and change. They try on different "selves" almost like new clothing, seek out role models, and engage in varied performances as they move from setting to setting (Goffman, 1959). In a traditional society, such "shiftiness" marks a person as untrustworthy, but in a changing, modern society, the chameleon-like ability to fit in almost virtually anywhere is very useful.

In societies that value the up-to-date rather than the traditional, people look to others for approval, using members of their own generation rather than elders as role models. Peer pressure can be irresistible to people without strong standards to guide them. Our society urges people to be true to themselves, but when social surroundings change so rapidly, how can people develop the self to which they should be true? This problem lies at the root of the identity crisis so widespread in industrial societies today. "Who am I?" is a nagging question that many of us struggle to answer. In truth, this problem is not so much us as the inherently unstable mass society in which we live.

Class Society: Problems of Powerlessness

Class-society theory paints a different picture of modernity's effects on individuals. This approach maintains that persistent inequality undermines modern society's promise of individual freedom. For some people, modernity serves up great privilege, but for many others, everyday life means coping with economic uncertainty and a gnawing sense of powerlessness (Ehrenreich, 2001; K.S. Newman, 1993).

For racial and ethnic minorities, the problem of relative disadvantage looms even larger. Similarly, although women participate more broadly in modern societies, they continue to run up against traditional barriers of sexism. This approach rejects mass-society theory's claim that people suffer from too much freedom; according to class-society theory, our society still denies a majority of people full participation in social life.

As Chapter 9 ("Global Stratification") explained, the expanding scope of world capitalism has placed more of Earth's

The firelight flickers in the gathering darkness. Chief Kanhonk sits, as he has done at the end of the day for many years, ready to begin an evening of animated talk and storytelling (Simons, 2007). This is the hour when the Kaiapo, a small society in Brazil's lush Amazon region, celebrate their heritage. Because the Kaiapo are a traditional people with no written language, the elders rely on evenings by the fire to pass along their culture to their children and grandchildren. In the past, evenings like this have been filled with tales of brave Kaiapo warriors fighting off Portuguese traders in pursuit of slaves and gold.

But as the minutes pass, just a few older villagers assemble for the evening ritual. "It is the Big Ghost," one man grumbles, explaining the poor turnout. The "Big Ghost" has indeed descended on them; its bluish glow spills from windows throughout the village. The Kaiapo children—and many adults as well—are watching sitcoms on television. Buying a television and a satellite dish several years ago has had consequences far greater than anyone imagined. In the end, what their enemies failed to do with guns, the Kaiapo may well do to themselves with prime-time programming.

The Kaiapo are among the 230 000 native peoples who inhabit Brazil. They stand out because of their striking body paint and ornate ceremonial dress. During the 1980s, they became rich from gold mining and harvesting mahogany trees. Now they must decide if their newfound fortune is a blessing or a curse.

To some, affluence means the opportunity to learn about the outside world through travel and television. Others, like Chief Kanhonk, are not so sure. Sitting by the fire, he thinks aloud, "I have been saying that people must buy useful things like knives and fishing hooks. Television does not fill the stomach. It only shows our children

and grandchildren white people's things." Bebtopup, the oldest priest, nods in agreement: "The night is the time the old people teach the young people. Television has stolen the night" (Simons, 2007:522).

The story of the Kaiapo shows us that change is not a simple path toward "progress." These people may be moving toward modernity, but this process will have both positive and negative consequences. In the end, they may enjoy a higher standard of living with better shelter, more clothing, and new technology. But their newfound affluence will come at the price of their traditions. The drama of these people is now being played out around the world as more and more traditional cultures are being lured away from their heritage by the affluence and materialism of rich societies.

WHAT DO YOU THINK?

1. Why is social change both a winning and a losing proposition for traditional people?

2. Do the changes described here improve the lives of the Kaiapo?

3. Do traditional people have any choice about becoming modern? Explain your view.

population under the influence of multinational corporations. As a result, 80 percent of the world's income is concentrated in high-income nations, where just 23 percent of its people live. Is it any wonder, class-society theorists ask, that people in poor nations seek greater power to shape their own lives?

The problem of widespread powerlessness led Herbert Marcuse (1964) to challenge Max Weber's claim that modern society is rational. Marcuse condemned modern society as irrational for failing to meet the needs of so many people. Although modern capitalist societies produce unparalleled wealth, poverty remains the daily plight of more than 1 billion people. Marcuse added that technological advances further reduce people's control over their own lives. The advent of high technology has generally conferred a great deal of power on a core of specialists—not the majority of people—who now dominate discussion of when to go to war, what our energy policy should be, and how people should pay for health care. Countering the popular view that technology *solves* the world's problems, Marcuse believed that science *causes* them. In sum, class-society theory asserts

that people suffer because modern societies have concentrated both wealth and power in the hands of a privileged few.

Modernity and Progress

In modern societies, most people expect and applaud social change. We link modernity to the idea of *progress* (from the Latin, meaning "moving forward"), a state of continual improvement. We equate stability with stagnation.

Given our bias in favour of change, members of our society tend to regard traditional cultures as backward. But change, particularly toward material affluence, is a mixed blessing. As the Thinking Globally box above shows, social change is too complex simply to equate with progress.

Even getting rich has both advantages and disadvantages, as the cases of the Kaiapo and Gullah show. Historically, among people in countries such as Canada and the United States, a rising standard of living has made lives longer and more comfortable. At the same time, many people wonder whether today's routines are too stressful, with families often having little time to relax or to spend time together. It is interesting in this respect that measures of happiness have declined in the United States but not Canada; Canadians are the second happiest group in the world, after Australians (Inglehart, Welzel, & Foa, 2010; Myers, 2000).

Science, too, has its pluses and minuses. People in North America are more confident than people living in most other industrial societies that science improves our everyday lives (Inglehart & Welzel, 2010). But surveys also show that many adults feel that science "makes our way of life change too fast" (NORC, 2009:1329).

New technology has always sparked controversy. Just over a century ago, the introduction of automobiles and telephones allowed more rapid transportation and more efficient communication, improving people's lives. At the same time, such technology also weakened traditional attachments to hometowns and even to families. Today, people may wonder whether computer technology will do the same thing: giving us access to people around the world but shielding us from the community right outside our doors; providing more information than ever before but in the process threatening personal privacy. In short, we all realize that social change comes faster all the time, but we may disagree about whether a particular change is good or bad for society.

Modernity: Global Variation

> October 1, Kobe, Japan. Riding the computer-controlled monorail high above the streets of Kobe or the 320-kilometre-per-hour bullet train to Tokyo, we see Japan as the society of the future, in love with high technology. Yet the Japanese remain strikingly traditional in other respects: Few corporate executives and almost no politicians are women, young people still show seniors great respect, and public orderliness contrasts with the relative chaos of many North American cities.

Japan is a nation both traditional and modern. This contradiction reminds us that although it is useful to contrast traditional and modern social patterns, the old and the new often coexist in unexpected ways. In the People's Republic of China, ancient Confucian principles are mixed with contemporary socialist thinking. In Saudi Arabia and Qatar, a love of the latest modern technology is mixed with respect for the ancient principles of Islam. Likewise, in Mexico and much of Latin America, people observe centuries-old Christian rituals even as they struggle to move ahead economically. In short, although we may think of tradition and modernity as opposites, combinations of traditional and modern are far from unusual, and they are found throughout the world.

Postmodernity

If modernity was the product of the Industrial Revolution, could the Information Revolution be creating a postmodern era? A number of scholars think so, and they use the term **postmodernity** to refer to *social patterns characteristic of post-industrial societies.*

Precisely what postmodernism is remains a matter of debate. The term has been used for decades in literary, philosophical, and even architectural circles. It has moved into sociology on a wave of social criticism that has been building since the spread of left-leaning politics in the 1960s. Although there are many variations of postmodern thinking, all share the following five themes (Hall & Neitz, 1993; Inglehart, 1997; Rudel & Gerson, 1999):

1. **In important respects, modernity has failed.** The promise of modernity was a life free from want. As postmodernist critics see it, however, the twentieth century was unsuccessful in solving social problems such as poverty because many people still lack financial security.

2. **The bright light of "progress" is fading.** Modern people look to the future expecting their lives to improve in significant ways. Members (and even leaders) of a postmodern society are less confident about what the future holds. The strong optimism that carried society into the modern era more than a century ago has given way to widespread pessimism, especially in recent years because of the weak economy.

3. **Science no longer holds the answers.** The defining trait of the modern era was a scientific outlook and a confident belief that technology would make life better. But postmodern critics argue that science has failed to solve many old problems (such as poor health) and has even created new problems (such as air and water pollution and declining natural resources).

   Postmodernist thinkers discredit science, claiming that it implies a singular truth. On the contrary, they maintain, there is no one truth. This means that objective reality does not exist; rather, many realities result from social construction.

4. **Cultural debates are intensifying.** Many people have all of the material things they really need. This creates a space for ideas to take on greater importance. In this sense, postmodernity is also a post-materialist era in which issues such as social justice, the environment, and animal rights command more and more public attention.

5. **Social institutions are changing.** Just as industrialization brought sweeping transformation to social institutions, the rise of post-industrial society is remaking society all over again. For example, the Industrial Revolution placed *material things* at the centre of productive life; the Information Revolution emphasizes *ideas.* Similarly, the postmodern family no longer conforms to any one pattern; on the contrary, individuals are choosing among many family forms.

Personal Freedom and Social Responsibility: Can We Have It Both Ways?

Shortly after midnight on a crisp March evening in 1964, Kitty Genovese drove into the parking lot of her New York apartment complex. She turned off the headlights, locked the car doors, and headed across the pavement toward the entrance to her building. Out of nowhere, a man holding a knife lunged at her and, as she shrieked in terror, he stabbed her repeatedly. Windows opened above as curious neighbours looked down to see what was going on. The attacker stopped for a moment, but when the windows closed, he went back to his deadly business. The attack continued for more than 30 minutes until Genovese lay dead in her doorway. A follow-up investigation failed to identify the assailant but did confirm a stunning fact: *dozens of neighbours had witnessed the attack on Kitty Genovese, but not one helped her or even called the police.*

Decades later, people still recall the Genovese tragedy in discussions of what we owe one another. As members of a modern, post-industrial society, we prize our individual rights and personal privacy, but we sometimes withdraw from public responsibility and turn a cold shoulder to people in need. When a cry for help is met with indifference, have we pushed our modern idea of personal freedom too far? How can "free" individuals keep a sense of human community?

These questions highlight the tension between traditional and modern social systems, which is evident in the writings of all of the sociologists discussed in this chapter. Tönnies, Durkheim, and others concluded that in some respects, traditional community and modern individualism don't go together. Society can unite its members as a moral community only by limiting their range of personal choices about how to live. In short, although we value both community and freedom, we can't have it both ways.

The sociologist Amitai Etzioni (1993, 1996, 2003) has tried to strike a middle ground. The communitarian movement rests on the simple idea that "strong rights presume strong responsibilities." Put another way, an individual's pursuit of self-interest must be balanced by a commitment to the larger community.

Etzioni claims that modern people have become too focused on individual rights. People expect the system to provide for them, but they are reluctant to support the system. Although most of us believe in the principle of trial by a jury of one's peers, fewer and fewer people today are willing to perform jury duty. Similarly, the public is quick to accept government services but increasingly reluctant to pay for these services through taxes.

Communitarians advance four proposals aimed at balancing individual rights with public responsibilities. First, our society should halt the expanding "culture of rights" by which people have placed their own interests ahead of social involvement (after all, nothing in the Canadian Charter of Rights and Freedoms allows us to do whatever we want to). Second, communitarians remind us, all rights involve responsibilities (we cannot simply take from society without giving something back). Third, some responsibilities, such as upholding the law or protecting the natural environment, are too important for anyone to ignore. Fourth, defending legitimate community interests may mean limiting individual rights (protecting public safety, for example, might mean subjecting workers to drug tests).

The communitarian movement appeals to many people who, along with Etzioni, seek to balance personal freedom with social responsibility. But critics from both ends of the political spectrum have attacked this initiative. To those on the left, problems ranging from voter apathy to street crime cannot be solved by some vague

idea of "social reintegration." Instead, we need expanded government programs to increase social equality. Specifically, these critics say, we must curb the political influence of the rich and actively fight racism and sexism.

Conservatives on the political right find fault with Etzioni's proposals for different reasons (Pearson, 1995). To them, the communitarian movement amounts to little more than a rerun of the 1960s leftist agenda. The communitarian vision of a good society favours liberal goals (such as protecting the environment) but says little about conservative goals such as allowing organized prayer in school or restoring the strength of traditional families. Conservatives ask whether a free society should permit the kind of social engineering that Etzioni advocates, such as instituting anti-prejudice programs in schools and requiring people to perform a year of national service.

Perhaps, as Etzioni himself has suggested, the fact that both the left and the right find fault with his views indicates that he has identified a moderate, sensible answer to a serious problem. But it may also be that people in a society as diverse as Canada will not easily agree about what they owe to themselves and to one another.

In today's world, people can find new ways to express age-old virtues such as concern for their neighbours and extending a hand to those in need. Habitat for Humanity, an organization with chapters in cities and towns across North America, is made up of people who want to help local families realize their dream of owning a home.

CONTINUE THE DEBATE . . .

1. Have you ever chosen not to come to the aid of someone in need or in danger? Why?

2. Some argue that young people today have a strong sense of "self-entitlement." Do you believe that you differ from your parents in this respect?

3. Do you agree or disagree that our society needs to balance rights with more responsibility? Explain your position.

CRITICAL REVIEW Analysts who claim that Canada and other high-income nations are entering a postmodern era criticize modernity for failing to meet human needs. In defence of modernity, there have been marked increases in longevity and living standards over the past century. Even if we were to accept postmodernist views that science is bankrupt and progress is a sham, what are the alternatives?

CHECK YOUR LEARNING In your own words, state the defining characteristics of a postmodern society.

Looking Ahead: Modernization and Our Global Future

Imagine the entire world's population reduced to a single village of 1000 people. About 230 residents of this "global village" are from high-income countries. Another 196 people are so poor that their lives are at risk.

The tragic plight of the world's poor shows that some desperately needed change has not yet occurred. Chapter 9 ("Global Stratification") presented two competing views of why 1 billion people around the world are so poor. *Modernization theory* claims that in the past, the entire world was poor and that technological change, especially the Industrial Revolution, enhanced human productivity and raised living standards in many nations. From this point of view, the solution to global poverty is to promote technological development and market economies around the world.

For reasons suggested earlier, however, global modernization may be difficult. Recall that David Riesman portrayed pre-industrial people as *tradition-directed* and likely to resist change. So modernization theorists claim that rich nations should help poor countries grow economically. Industrial nations can speed development by exporting technology to poor regions, welcoming students from these countries, and providing foreign aid to stimulate economic growth.

The review of modernization theory in Chapter 9 points to some success for these policies in Latin America and more dramatic results in the small Asian countries of Taiwan, South Korea, and Singapore and in Hong Kong (part of the People's Republic of China). But jump-starting development in the poorest countries of the world poses greater challenges. Even where dramatic change has occurred, modernization involves a trade-off. Traditional people, such as Brazil's Kaiapo, may gain wealth through economic development, but only at the cost of losing their traditional identity and values as they are drawn into a global "McCulture," which is based on Western materialism, pop music, trendy clothes, and fast food. One Brazilian anthropologist expressed optimism about the future of the Kaiapo: "At least they quickly understood the consequences of watching television. . . . Now [they] can make a choice" (Simons, 2007:523).

But not everyone thinks that modernization is really an option. According to a second approach to global stratification, *dependency theory*, today's poor societies have little ability to modernize, even if they want to. From this point of view, the major barrier to economic development is not traditionalism but global domination by rich capitalist societies.

Dependency theory asserts that rich nations achieved their modernization at the expense of poor ones, by taking their valuable natural resources and exploiting their human labour. Even today, the world's poorest countries remain locked in a disadvantageous economic relationship with rich nations, dependent on wealthy countries to buy their raw materials and in return provide them with whatever manufactured products they can afford. According to this view, continuing ties with rich societies will only perpetuate current patterns of global inequality.

Whichever approach you find more convincing, keep in mind that change in Canada is no longer separate from change in the rest of the world. At the beginning of the twentieth century, most people in today's high-income countries lived in relatively small settlements with limited awareness of the larger world. Today, the world has become one huge village because the lives of all people are increasingly interconnected.

The twentieth century witnessed unprecedented human achievement. Yet solutions to many problems of human existence—including finding meaning in life, resolving conflicts between societies, and eliminating poverty—have eluded us. The Seeing Sociology in Everyday Life box on page 459 examines one dilemma: balancing individual freedom and personal responsibility. To this list of pressing matters new concerns have been added, such as controlling population growth and establishing an environmentally sustainable society. In the coming years, we must be prepared to tackle such problems with imagination, compassion, and determination. Our growing understanding of human society gives us reason to be hopeful that we can get the job done.

CHAPTER 16 SOCIAL CHANGE: MODERN AND POSTMODERN SOCIETIES

IS TRADITION THE OPPOSITE OF MODERNITY? Conceptually, this may be true. But as this chapter explains, traditional and modern social patterns combine in all sorts of interesting ways in our everyday lives. Look at the photographs below, and identify elements of tradition and modernity. Do they seem to go together, or are they in conflict? Why?

These young girls live in the city of Istanbul in Turkey, a country that has long debated the merits of traditional and modern life. What sets off traditional and modern ways of dressing? Do you think such differences are likely to affect patterns of friendship? Would the same be true in Canada?

In Riyadh, Saudi Arabia, these young men are shopping for the latest in cellphones. Does such modern technology threaten a society's traditions?

HINT: Although sociologists analyze tradition and modernity as conceptual opposites, every society combines these elements in various ways. People may debate the virtues of traditional and modern life, but the two patterns are found almost everywhere. Technological change always has social consequences—for example, the use of cellphones changes people's social networks and economic opportunities; similarly, the spread of McDonald's changes not only what people eat but also where and with whom they share meals.

Applying Sociology in Everyday Life

1. How do tradition and modernity combine in your life? Point to several ways in which you are traditional and several ways in which you are thoroughly modern.

2. Ask people in your class or friendship group to make five predictions about Canadian society in 2050, when today's 20-year-olds will be senior citizens. Compare notes. On what issues is there agreement?

3. Do you think the rate of social change has been increasing? Do some research about modes of travel—including walking, riding animals, bicycles, trains, cars, airplanes, and rockets. At what point in history did each of these ways of moving come into being? What pattern do you see?

CHAPTER 16 Social Change: Modern and Postmodern Societies

What Is Social Change?

SOCIAL CHANGE is the transformation of culture and social institutions over time. Every society changes all the time, sometimes faster, sometimes more slowly. Social change often generates controversy.
pp. 440–41

social change (p. 441) the transformation of culture and social institutions over time

Causes of Social Change

CULTURE
- Invention produces new objects, ideas, and social patterns.
- Discovery occurs when people take notice of existing elements of the world.
- Diffusion creates change as products, people, and information spread from one society to another.
p. 441

SOCIAL CONFLICT
- Karl Marx claimed that class conflict between capitalists and workers pushes society toward a socialist system of production.
- Social conflict arising from class, race, and gender inequality has resulted in social changes that have improved the lives of working people.
p. 442

social movement (p. 442) an organized activity that encourages or discourages social change

claims making (p. 443) the process of trying to convince the public and public officials of the importance of joining a social movement to address a particular issue

relative deprivation (p. 445) a perceived disadvantage arising from some specific comparison

disaster (p. 446) an event, generally unexpected, that causes extensive harm to people and damage to property

IDEAS
Max Weber traced the roots of most social changes to ideas:
- The fact that industrial capitalism developed first in areas of Western Europe where the Protestant work ethic was strong demonstrates the power of ideas to bring about change.
p. 442

DEMOGRAPHIC FACTORS
Population patterns play a part in social change:
- The aging of Canadian society has resulted in changes to family life and the development of consumer products to meet the needs of the elderly.
- Migration within and between societies promotes change.
p. 442

DISASTERS

Disasters cause unexpected social change:
- natural disasters (examples: sinking of the *Ocean Ranger* and Hurricane Katrina)
- technological disasters (example: nuclear accident at the Chernobyl power plant)
- intentional disasters (example: Darfur genocide)
pp. 446–47

SOCIAL MOVEMENTS

TYPES OF SOCIAL MOVEMENTS
- Alterative social movements seek limited change in specific individuals (example: Promise Keepers).
- Redemptive social movements seek radical change in specific individuals (example: Alcoholics Anonymous).
- Reformative social movements seek limited change in the whole society (example: the environmental movement).
- Revolutionary social movements seek radical change in the whole society (example: the Communist party).
pp. 442–43

EXPLANATIONS OF SOCIAL MOVEMENTS
- Deprivation theory: Social movements arise among people who feel deprived of something, such as income, safe working conditions, or political rights.
- Mass-society theory: Social movements attract socially isolated people who join a movement to gain a sense of identity and purpose.
- Resource mobilization theory: Success of a social movement is linked to available resources, including money, labour, and the mass media.
- Culture theory: Social movements depend not only on money and resources but also on cultural symbols that motivate people.
- New social movements theory: Social movements in post-industrial societies are typically international in scope and focus on quality-of-life issues.
pp. 443–45

What Is Modernity?

MODERNITY refers to the social consequences of industrialization, which include the decline of traditional communities, the expansion of personal choice, increasing social diversity, and a focus on the future.
- **Ferdinand Tönnies** described modernization as the transition from *Gemeinschaft* to *Gesellschaft*, characterized by the loss of traditional community and the rise of individualism.
- **Emile Durkheim** saw modernization as a society's expanding division of labour. Mechanical solidarity, based on shared activities and beliefs, is gradually replaced by organic solidarity, in which specialization makes people interdependent.
- **Max Weber** saw modernity as the decline of a traditional world view and the rise of rationality. Weber feared the dehumanizing effects of rational organization.
- **Karl Marx** saw modernity as the triumph of capitalism over feudalism. Capitalism creates social conflict, which Marx claimed would bring about revolutionary change leading to an egalitarian socialist society.
pp. 448–50

modernity (p. 448) social patterns resulting from industrialization

modernization (p. 448) the process of social change begun by industrialization

division of labour (p. 449) specialized economic activity

anomie (p. 450) a condition in which society provides little moral guidance to individuals

Theoretical Analysis of Modernity

STRUCTURAL-FUNCTIONAL THEORY: MODERNITY AS MASS SOCIETY

- According to **mass-society theory**, modernity increases the scale of life, enlarging the role of government and other formal organizations in carrying out tasks previously performed by families in local communities.
- Cultural diversity and rapid social change make it difficult for people in modern societies to develop stable identities and to find meaning in their lives.

pp. 452–53

SOCIAL-CONFLICT THEORY: MODERNITY AS CLASS SOCIETY

- According to **class-society theory**, modernity involves the rise of capitalism into a global economic system resulting in persistent social inequality.
- By concentrating wealth in the hands of a few, modern capitalist societies generate widespread feelings of alienation and powerlessness.

pp. 454–55

mass society (p. 452) a society in which prosperity and bureaucracy have weakened traditional social ties

class society (p. 454) a capitalist society with pronounced social stratification

See the Summing Up tables on pages 453 and 455.

Modernity and the Individual

Both mass-society theory and class-society theory are macro-level approaches; from them, however, we can also draw micro-level insights into how modernity shapes individual lives.

p. 455

social character (p. 455) personality patterns common to members of a particular society

tradition-directedness (p. 455) rigid conformity to time-honoured ways of living

other-directedness (p. 456) openness to the latest trends and fashions, often expressed by imitating others

MASS SOCIETY: Problems of Identity

- Mass-society theory suggests that the great social diversity, widespread isolation, and rapid social change of modern societies make it difficult for individuals to establish a stable social identity.

David Riesman described the changes in social character that modernity causes:

- Pre-industrial societies exhibit **tradition-directedness**: Everyone in society draws on the same solid cultural foundation, and people model their lives on those of their ancestors.
- Modern societies exhibit **other-directedness**: Because their socialization occurs in societies that are continuously in flux, other-directed people develop fluid identities marked by superficiality, inconsistency, and change.

pp. 455–56

CLASS SOCIETY: Problems of Powerlessness

- Class-society theory claims that the problem facing most people today is economic uncertainty and powerlessness.
- Herbert Marcuse claimed that modern society is irrational because it fails to meet the needs of so many people.
- Marcuse also believed that technological advances further reduce people's control over their own lives.
- People suffer because modern societies have concentrated both wealth and power in the hands of a privileged few.

pp. 456–57

Modernity and Progress

Social change is too complex and controversial simply to be equated with progress:

- A rising standard of living has made lives longer and materially more comfortable; at the same time, many people are stressed and have little time to relax with their families; measures of happiness have declined in recent decades.
- Science and technology have brought many conveniences to our everyday lives, yet many people are concerned that life is changing too fast; the introduction of automobiles and advanced communication technology have weakened traditional attachments to hometowns and even to families.

pp. 457–58

Modernity: Global Variation

Although we often think of tradition and modernity as opposites, traditional and modern elements coexist in most societies.

pp. 458

Postmodernity

POSTMODERNITY refers to the cultural traits of post-industrial societies. Postmodern criticism of society centres on the failure of modernity, and specifically science, to fulfill its promise of prosperity and well-being.

pp. 458–59

postmodernity (p. 455) social patterns characteristic of post-industrial societies

MySocLab

Visit MySocLab at www.mysoclab.com to access a variety of online resources that will help you to prepare for tests and to apply your knowledge, including

- an eText
- videos
- self-grading quizzes
- glossary flashcards

Glossary

absolute poverty a lack of resources that is life-threatening.

achieved status a social position a person takes on voluntarily that reflects personal ability and effort.

age-sex pyramid a graphic representation of the age and sex of a population.

ageism prejudice and discrimination against older people.

agriculture large-scale cultivation using plows harnessed to animals or more powerful energy sources.

alienation the experience of isolation and misery resulting from powerlessness.

animism the belief that elements of the natural world are conscious life forms that affect humanity.

anomie a condition in which society provides little moral guidance to individuals.

anticipatory socialization learning that helps a person achieve a desired position.

ascribed status a social position a person receives at birth or takes on involuntarily later in life.

asexuality a lack of sexual attraction to people of either sex.

assimilation the process by which minorities gradually adopt patterns of the dominant culture.

authoritarianism a political system that denies the people participation in government.

authority power that people perceive as legitimate rather than coercive.

beliefs specific ideas that people hold to be true.

bisexuality sexual attraction to people of both sexes.

blue-collar occupations lower-prestige jobs that involve mostly manual labour.

bureaucracy an organizational model rationally designed to perform tasks efficiently.

bureaucratic inertia the tendency of bureaucratic organizations to perpetuate themselves.

bureaucratic ritualism a focus on rules and regulations to the point of undermining an organization's goals.

capitalism an economic system in which natural resources and the means of producing goods and services are privately owned.

capitalists people who own and operate factories and other businesses in pursuit of profits.

caste system social stratification based on ascription, or birth.

cause and effect a relationship in which change in one variable (the independent variable) causes change in another (the dependent variable).

charisma extraordinary personal qualities that can infuse people with emotion and turn them into followers.

church a religious organization that is well integrated into the larger society.

civil religion a quasi-religious loyalty linking individuals in a basically secular society.

claims making the process of trying to convince the public and public officials of the importance of joining a social movement to address a particular issue.

class society a capitalist society with pronounced social stratification.

class system social stratification based on both birth and individual achievement.

cohabitation the sharing of a household by an unmarried couple.

cohort a category of people with something in common, usually their age.

colonialism the process by which some nations enrich themselves through political and economic control of other nations.

community-based corrections correctional programs operating within society at large rather than behind prison walls.

concept a mental construct that represents some aspect of the world in a simplified form.

concrete operational stage Piaget's term for the level of human development at which individuals first see causal connections in their surroundings.

conspicuous consumption buying and using products because of the "statement" they make about social position.

corporate crime the illegal actions of a corporation or people acting on its behalf.

corporation an organization with a legal existence, including rights and liabilities, separate from that of its members.

correlation a relationship in which two (or more) variables change together.

counterculture cultural patterns that strongly oppose those widely accepted within a society.

crime the violation of a society's formally enacted criminal law.

crimes against property (property crimes) crimes that involve theft of money or property belonging to others.

crimes against the person (violent crimes) crimes that direct violence or the threat of violence against others.

criminal justice system the organizations—police, courts, and prison officials—that respond to alleged violations of the law.

criminal recidivism later offences by people previously convicted of crimes.

critical sociology the study of society that focuses on the need for social change.

crude birth rate the number of live births in a given year for every 1000 people in a population.

crude death rate the number of deaths in a given year for every 1000 people in a population.

cult a religious organization that is largely outside a society's cultural traditions.

cultural integration the close relationships among various elements of a cultural system.

cultural lag the fact that some cultural elements change more quickly than others, disrupting a cultural system.

cultural relativism the practice of judging a culture by its own standards.

cultural transmission the process by which one generation passes culture to the next.

cultural universals traits that are part of every known culture.

culture the ways of thinking, the ways of acting, and the material objects that together form a people's way of life.

culture shock personal disorientation when experiencing an unfamiliar way of life.

Davis-Moore thesis the functional analysis claiming that social stratification has beneficial consequences for the operation of society.

democracy a political system that gives power to the people as a whole.

demographic transition theory a thesis that links population patterns to a society's level of technological development.

demography the study of human population.

denomination a church, independent of the state, that recognizes religious pluralism.

dependency theory a model of economic and social development that explains global inequality in terms of the historical exploitation of poor, low-income nations by wealthier, high-income ones.

descent the system by which members of a society trace kinship over generations.

deterrence the attempt to discourage criminality through the use of punishment.

deviance the recognized violation of cultural norms.

direct-fee system a medical care system in which patients pay directly for the services of physicians and hospitals.

disaster an event, generally unexpected, that causes extensive harm to people and damage to property.

discrimination unequal treatment of various categories of people.

division of labour specialized economic activity.

dramaturgical analysis Erving Goffman's term for the study of social interaction in terms of theatrical performance.

dyad a social group with two members.

eating disorder an intense form of dieting or other unhealthy method of weight control driven by the desire to be very thin.

ecologically sustainable culture a way of life that meets the needs of the present generation without threatening the environmental legacy of future generations.

ecology the study of the interaction of living organisms and the natural environment.

economy the social institution that organizes a society's production, distribution, and consumption of goods and services.

ecosystem a system composed of the interaction of all living organisms and their natural environment.

education the social institution through which society provides its members with important knowledge, including basic facts, job skills, and cultural norms and values.

ego Freud's term for a person's conscious efforts to balance innate pleasure-seeking drives with the demands of society.

empirical evidence information we can verify with our senses.

endogamy marriage between people of the same social category.

environmental deficit profound long-term harm to the natural environment caused by humanity's focus on short-term material affluence.

environmental racism patterns of development that expose poor people, especially minorities, to environmental hazards.

ethnicity a shared cultural heritage.

ethnocentrism the practice of judging another culture by the standards of one's own culture.

ethnomethodology Harold Garfinkel's term for the study of the way people make sense of their everyday surroundings.

Eurocentrism the dominance of European (especially English) cultural patterns.

euthanasia assisting in the death of a person suffering from an incurable disease ; also known as *mercy killing.*

exogamy marriage between people of different social categories.

experiment a research method for investigating cause and effect under highly controlled conditions.

expressive leadership group leadership that focuses on the group's well-being.

extended family a family composed of parents and children as well as other kin; also known as a *consanguine family.*

faith belief based on conviction rather than on scientific evidence.

family a social institution found in all societies that unites people in co-operative groups to care for one another, including any children.

family violence emotional, physical, or sexual abuse of one family member by another.

feminism support of social equality for women and men.

feminism support of social equality for women and men, in opposition to patriarchy and sexism.

feminization of poverty the trend of women making up an increasing proportion of the poor.

fertility the incidence of child-bearing in a country's population.

folkways norms for routine or casual interaction.

formal operational stage Piaget's term for the level of human development at which individuals think abstractly and critically.

formal organizations a large secondary group organized to achieve its goals efficiently.

Freud's Model of Personality id Freud's term for the human being's basic drives.

functional illiteracy a lack of the reading and writing skills needed for everyday living.

fundamentalism a conservative religious doctrine that opposes intellectualism and worldly accommodation in favour of restoring traditional, otherworldly religion.

Gemeinschaft a type of social organization in which people are closely tied by kinship and tradition.

gender the personal traits and social positions that members of a society attach to being female or male.

gender the personal traits and social positions that members of a society attach to being female or male.

gender roles (also known as **sex roles**) attitudes and activities that a society links to each sex.

gender stratification the unequal distribution of wealth, power, and privilege between men and women.

gender-conflict approach a point of view that focuses on inequality and conflict between women and men.

generalized other Mead's term for widespread cultural norms and values we use as a reference in evaluating ourselves.

genocide the systematic killing of one category of people by another.

gerontocracy a form of social organization in which the elderly have the most wealth, power, and prestige.

gerontology the study of aging and the elderly.

Gesellschaft a type of social organization in which people come together only on the basis of individual self-interest.

global economy economic activity that crosses national borders.

global perspective the study of the larger world and our society's place in it.

global stratification patterns of social inequality in the world as a whole.

global warming a rise in Earth's average temperature due to an increasing concentration of carbon dioxide in the atmosphere.

government a formal organization that directs the political life of a society.

groupthink the tendency of group members to conform, resulting in a narrow view of some issue.

hate crime a criminal act against a person or a person's property by an offender motivated by racial or other bias.

health a state of complete physical, mental, and social well-being.

heterosexism a view that labels anyone who is not heterosexual as "queer."

heterosexuality sexual attraction to someone of the other sex.

high culture cultural patterns that distinguish a society's elite.

high-income countries nations with the highest overall standards of living.

holistic medicine an approach to health care that emphasizes the prevention of illness and takes into account a person's entire physical and social environment.

homogamy marriage between people with the same social characteristics.

homophobia discomfort over close personal interaction with people thought to be gay, lesbian, or bisexual.

homosexuality sexual attraction to someone of the same sex.

horticulture the use of hand tools to raise crops.

hunting and gathering the use of simple tools to hunt animals and gather vegetation for food.

ideology cultural beliefs that justify particular social arrangements, including patterns of inequality.

in-group a social group toward which a member feels respect and loyalty.

incest taboo a norm forbidding sexual relations or marriage between certain relatives.

income earnings from work or investments.

industry the production of goods using advanced sources of energy to drive large machinery.

infant mortality rate the number of deaths among infants under one year of age for each 1000 live births in a given year.

institutional prejudice and discrimination bias built into the operation of society's institutions.

instrumental leadership group leadership that focuses on the completion of tasks.

intergenerational social mobility upward or downward social mobility of children in relation to their parents.

interpretive sociology the study of society that focuses on discovering the meanings people attach to their social world.

intersection theory analysis of the interplay of race, class, and gender, often resulting in multiple dimensions of disadvantage.

intersexual people people whose bodies (including genitals) have both female and male characteristics.

intragenerational social mobility a change in social position occurring during a person's lifetime.

kinship a social bond based on common ancestry, marriage, or adoption.

labelling theory the idea that deviance and conformity result not so much from what people do as from how others respond to those actions.

language a system of symbols that allows people to communicate with one another.

latent functions the unrecognized and unintended consequences of any social pattern.

liberation theology the combining of Christian principles with political activism, often Marxist in character.

life expectancy the average lifespan of a country's population.

looking-glass self Cooley's term for a self-image based on how we think others see us.

low-income countries nations with a low standard of living in which most people are poor.

macro-level orientation a broad focus on social structures that shape society as a whole.

manifest functions the recognized and intended consequences of any social pattern.

marriage a legal relationship, usually involving economic co-operation, sexual activity, and child-bearing.

Marxist political-economy model an analysis that explains politics in terms of the operation of a society's economic system.

mass media the means for delivering impersonal communications to a vast audience.

mass society a society in which prosperity and bureaucracy have weakened traditional social ties.

master status a status that has special importance for social identity, often shaping a person's entire life.

matriarchy a form of social organization in which females dominate males.

measurement a procedure for determining the value of a variable in a specific case.

medicalization of deviance the transformation of moral and legal deviance into a medical condition.

medicine the social institution that focuses on fighting disease and improving health.

megalopolis a vast urban region containing a number of cities and their surrounding suburbs.

meritocracy social stratification based on personal merit.

metropolis a large city that socially and economically dominates an urban area.

micro-level orientation a close-up focus on social interaction in specific situations.

middle-income countries nations with a standard of living about average for the world as a whole.

migration the movement of people into and out of a specified territory.

military-industrial complex the close association of the federal government, the military, and defence industries.

minority any category of people distinguished by physical or cultural difference that a society sets apart and subordinates.

miscegenation biological reproduction by partners of different racial categories.

modernity social patterns resulting from industrialization.

modernization the process of social change begun by industrialization.

modernization theory a model of economic and social development that explains global inequality in terms of technological and cultural differences between nations.

monarchy a political system in which a single family rules from generation to generation.

monogamy marriage that unites two partners.

monopoly the domination of a market by a single producer.

mores norms that are widely observed and have great moral significance.

mortality the incidence of death in a country's population.

multiculturalism a perspective recognizing the cultural diversity of Canada and promoting equal standing for all cultural traditions.

multinational corporation a large business that operates in many countries.

natural environment Earth's surface and atmosphere, including living organisms, air, water, soil, and other resources necessary to sustain life.

neocolonialism a new form of global power relationships that involves not direct political control but economic exploitation by multinational corporations.

network a web of weak social ties.

non-verbal communication communication using body movements, gestures, and facial expressions rather than speech.

norms rules and expectations by which a society guides the behaviour of its members.

nuclear family a family composed of one or two parents and their children; also known as a *conjugal family*.

oligarchy the rule of the many by the few.

oligopoly the domination of a market by a few producers.

organizational environment factors outside an organization that affect its operation.

organized crime a business supplying illegal goods or services.

other-directedness openness to the latest trends and fashions, often expressed by imitating others.

out-group a social group toward which a person feels a sense of competition or opposition.

participant observation a research method in which investigators systematically observe people while joining them in their routine activities.

pastoralism the domestication of animals.

patriarchy a form of social organization in which males dominate females.

peer group a social group whose members have interests, social position, and age in common.

personal space the surrounding area over which a person makes some claim to privacy.

personality a person's fairly consistent patterns of acting, thinking, and feeling.

Piaget's Stages of Development sensorimotor stage Piaget's term for the level of human development at which individuals experience the world only through their senses.

plea bargaining a legal negotiation in which a prosecutor reduces a charge in exchange for a defendant's guilty plea.

pluralism a state in which people of all races and ethnicities are distinct but have equal social standing.

pluralist model an analysis of politics that sees power as spread among many competing interest groups.

political revolution the overthrow of one political system to establish another.

politics the social institution that distributes power, sets a society's goals, and makes decisions.

polygamy marriage that unites a person with two or more spouses.

popular culture cultural patterns that are widespread among a society's population.

pornography sexually explicit material intended to cause sexual arousal.

positivism a scientific approach to knowledge based on "positive" facts as opposed to mere speculation.

positivist sociology the study of society based on scientific observation of social behaviour.

post-industrial economy a productive system based on service work and high technology.

post-industrialism the production of information using computer technology.

postmodernity social patterns characteristic of post-industrial societies.

power the ability to achieve desired ends despite resistance from others.

power-elite model an analysis of politics that sees power as concentrated among the rich.

prejudice a rigid and unfair generalization about an entire category of people.

preoperational stage Piaget's term for the level of human development at which individuals first use language and other symbols.

presentation of self Erving Goffman's term for a person's efforts to create specific impressions in the minds of others.

primary group a small social group whose members share personal and lasting relationships.

primary sector the part of the economy that draws raw materials from the natural environment.

primary sex characteristics the genitals, organs used for reproduction.

profane included as an ordinary element of everyday life.

profession a prestigious white-collar occupation that requires extensive formal education.

proletarians people who sell their labour for wages.

prostitution the selling of sexual services.

queer theory a body of research findings that challenges the heterosexual bias in North American society.

race a socially constructed category of people who share biologically transmitted traits that members of a society consider important.

race-conflict approach a point of view that focuses on inequality and conflict between people of different racial and ethnic categories.

racism the belief that one racial category is innately superior or inferior to another.

rainforests regions of dense forestation, most of which circle the globe close to the equator.

rationality a way of thinking that emphasizes deliberate, matter-of-fact calculation of the most efficient way to accomplish a particular task.

rationalization of society the historical change from tradition to rationality as the main type of human thought.

reference group a social group that serves as a point of reference in making evaluations and decisions.

rehabilitation a program for reforming the offender to prevent later offences.

relative deprivation a perceived disadvantage arising from some specific comparison.

relative poverty the lack of resources of some people in relation to those who have more.

reliability consistency in measurement.

religion a social institution involving beliefs and practices based on recognizing the sacred.

religiosity the importance of religion in a person's life.

research method a systematic plan for doing research.

resocialization radically changing an inmate's personality by carefully controlling the environment.

retribution an act of moral vengeance by which society makes the offender suffer as much as the suffering caused by the crime.

role behaviour expected of someone who holds a particular status.

role conflict conflict among the roles connected to two or more statuses.

role set a number of roles attached to a single status.

role strain tension among the roles connected to a single status.

routinization of charisma the transformation of charismatic authority into some combination of traditional and bureaucratic authority.

sacred set apart as extraordinary, inspiring awe and reverence.

Sapir-Whorf thesis the idea that people see and understand the world through the cultural lens of language.

scapegoat a person or category of people, typically with little power, whom other people unfairly blame for their own troubles.

schooling formal instruction under the direction of specially trained teachers.

science a logical system that develops knowledge from direct, systematic observation.

scientific management the application of scientific principles to the operation of a business or other large organization.

secondary group a large and impersonal social group whose members pursue a specific goal or activity.

secondary sector the part of the economy that transforms raw materials into manufactured goods.

secondary sex characteristics bodily development, apart from the genitals, that distinguishes biologically mature females and males.

sect a religious organization that stands apart from the larger society.

secularization the historical decline in the importance of the supernatural and the sacred.

segregation the physical and social separation of categories of people.

self Mead's term for the part of an individual's personality composed of self-awareness and self-image.

sex the biological distinction between females and males.

sex ratio the number of males for every 100 females in a nation's population.

sexism the belief that one sex is innately superior to the other.

sexual harassment comments, gestures, or physical contacts of a sexual nature that are deliberate, repeated, and unwelcome.

sexual orientation a person's romantic and emotional attraction to another person.

sick role patterns of behaviour defined as appropriate for people who are ill.

significant others people, such as parents, who have special importance for socialization.

social change the transformation of culture and social institutions over time.

social character personality patterns common to members of a particular society.

social construction of reality the process by which people creatively shape reality through social interaction.

social control attempts by society to regulate people's thoughts and behaviour.

social dysfunction any social pattern that may disrupt the operation of society.

social epidemiology the study of how health and disease are distributed throughout a society's population.

social functions the consequences of a social pattern for the operation of society as a whole.

social group two or more people who identify with and interact with one another.

social institution a major sphere of social life or societal subsystem organized to meet human needs.

social interaction the process by which people act and react in relation to others.

social mobility a change in position within the social hierarchy.

social movement an organized activity that encourages or discourages social change.

social stratification a system by which a society ranks categories of people in a hierarchy.

social structure any relatively stable pattern of social behaviour.

social-conflict approach a framework for building theory that sees society as an arena of inequality that generates conflict and change.

socialization the lifelong social experience by which people develop their human potential and learn culture.

socialized medicine a medical care system in which the government owns and operates most medical facilities and employs most physicians.

societal protection rendering an offender incapable of further offences temporarily through imprisonment or permanently by execution.

society people who interact in a defined territory and share a culture.

socio-economic status (SES) a composite ranking based on various dimensions of social inequality.

sociobiology a theoretical approach that explores ways in which human biology affects how we create culture.

sociological perspective the special point of view of sociology that sees general patterns of society in the lives of particular people.

sociology the systematic study of human society.

state capitalism an economic and political system in which companies are privately owned but co-operate closely with the government.

state church a church formally linked to the state.

status a social position that a person holds.

status consistency the degree of uniformity in a person's social standing across various dimensions of social inequality.

status set all of the statuses a person holds at a given time.

stereotype a simplified description applied to every person in some category.

stigma a powerfully negative label that greatly changes a person's self-concept and social identity.

structural social mobility a shift in the social position of large numbers of people due more to changes in society itself than to individual efforts.

structural-functional approach a framework for building theory that sees society as a complex system whose parts work together to promote solidarity and stability.

subculture cultural patterns that set apart some segment of a society's population.

suburbs urban areas beyond the political boundaries of a city.

superego Freud's term for the cultural values and norms internalized by an individual.

survey a research method in which subjects respond to a series of statements or questions on a questionnaire or in an interview.

symbol anything that carries a particular meaning recognized by people who share a culture.

symbolic-interaction approach a framework for building theory that sees society as the product of the everyday interactions of individuals.

technology knowledge that people use to make a way of life in their surroundings.

terrorism acts of violence or the threat of violence used as a political strategy by an individual or a group.

tertiary sector the part of the economy that involves services rather than goods.

theoretical approach a basic image of society that guides thinking and research.

theory a statement of how and why specific facts are related.

Thomas theorem W. I. Thomas's claim that situations defined as real are real in their consequences.

total institution a setting in which people are isolated from the rest of society and controlled by an administrative staff.

totalitarianism a highly centralized political system that extensively regulates people's lives.

totem an object in the natural world collectively defined as sacred.

tradition values and beliefs passed from generation to generation.

tradition-directedness rigid conformity to time-honoured ways of living.

transsexuals people who feel they are one sex even though biologically they are the other.

triad a social group with three members.

urban ecology the study of the link between the physical and social dimensions of cities.

urbanization the concentration of population into cities.

validity actually measuring exactly what you intend to measure.

values culturally defined standards that people use to decide what is desirable, good, and beautiful and that serve as broad guidelines for social living.

variable a concept whose value changes from case to case.

victimless crimes violations of law in which there are no obvious victims.

war organized, armed conflict among the people of two or more nations, directed by their governments.

wealth the total value of money and other assets, minus outstanding debts.

welfare capitalism an economic and political system that combines a mostly market-based economy with extensive social welfare programs.

welfare state a system of government agencies and programs that provides benefits to the population.

white-collar crime crime committed by people of high social position in the course of their occupations.

white-collar occupations higher-prestige jobs that involve mostly mental activity.

zero population growth the rate of reproduction that maintains population at a steady level.

References

ABEL, G., L. FITZGERALD, and C. HEALY, eds. *Taking the Crime out of Sex Work: New Zealand Sex Workers' Fight for Decriminalisation*. Bristol, UK: Policy Press, 2010.

ABERLE, DAVID F. *The Peyote Religion among the Navaho*. Chicago: University of Chicago, 1982.

ADAMS, MICHAEL. *Sex in the Snow: Canadian Social Values at the End of the Millennium*. Toronto: Penguin Canada, 1997.

———. *Unlikely Utopia: The Surprising Triumph of Canadian Pluralism*. Toronto: Viking, 2007.

———. *Fire and Ice*. Toronto: Penguin Canada, 2009.

ADORNO, THEODORE W., ELSE FRENKEL-BRUNSWIK, DANIEL J. LEVINSON, and R. NEVITT SANFORD. *The Authoritarian Personality*. New York: Harper, 1950.

AKERS, RONALD L., MARVIN D. KROHN, LONN LANZA-KADUCE, and MARCIA RADOS-EVICH. "Social Learning and Deviant Behavior." *American Sociological Review*. Vol. 44, No. 4 (August 1979):636–55.

ALAN GUTTMACHER INSTITUTE. "U.S. Teenage Pregnancy Statistics: National and State Trends and Trends by Race and Ethnicity." Rev. September 2006. www.guttmacher.org/pubs/2006/09/12/USTPstats.pdf

ALLAN, EMILIE ANDERSEN, and DARRELL J. STEFFENSMEIER. "Youth, Underemployment, and Property Crime: Differential Effects of Job Availability and Job Quality on Juvenile and Young Adult Arrest Rates." *American Sociological Review*. Vol. 54, No. 1 (February 1989):107–23.

ALLARD, F.L., ET AL. "Maintien de l'engagement paternel après une rupture conjugale: point de vue des pères vivant en contexte de pauvreté. *Enfances, familles, générations*. Vol. 3 (2005):1–42.

ALLEN, MIKE. "Card Check Battle Starts Tomorrow." *Politico* (March 9, 2009). www.politico.com/news/stories/0309/19786.html

ALLEN, THOMAS B., and CHARLES O. HYMAN. *We Americans: Celebrating a Nation, Its People, and Its Past*. Washington, DC: National Geographic Society, 1999.

ALPHONSO, CAROLINE. "Girl's Death to Escape Bullying Shocks Town." *Globe and Mail* (November 17, 2000):A7.

AMATO, PAUL R. "What Children Learn from Divorce." *Population Today*. Vol. 29, No. 1 (January 2001):1, 4.

AMBERT, A. *Divorce: Facts, Causes & Consequences*. Ottawa: Vanier Institute of the Family, 2009. www.vifamily.ca/sites/default/files/divorce_facts_causes_consequences.pdf

AMERICAN PSYCHOLOGICAL ASSOCIATION. *Violence and Youth: Psychology's Response*. Washington, DC: American Psychological Association, 1993.

AMERICAN SOCIOLOGICAL ASSOCIATION. *The Importance of Collecting Data and Doing Social Scientific Research on Race*. Washington, DC: American Sociological Association, 2003.

AMNESTY INTERNATONAL. "The Death Penalty in 2008." 2010. www.amnesty.org/en/death-penalty/death-sentences-and-executions-in-2008

———. "The Death Penalty in 2010." 2011. http://www.amnesty.org/en/death-penalty

ANDERSON, ELIJAH. "The Code of the Streets." *Atlantic Monthly*. Vol. 273 (May 1994):81–94.

———. "The Ideologically Driven Critique." *American Journal of Sociology*. Vol. 197, No. 6 (May 2002):1533–50.

ANDERSON, JOHN WARD. "Early to Wed: The Child Brides of India." *Washington Post* (May 24, 1995):A27, A30.

ANGUS REID. *Canadians Reject Infidelity, Polygamy and Cloning*. 2009a. www.angus-reid.com/polls/37708/canadians_reject_infidelity_polygamy_and_cloning/

———. *Gender Shapes Views on Debate over Prostitution in Canada*. 2009b. www.visioncritical.com/public-opinion/3567/gender-shapes-views-on-debate-overprostitution-in-canada/

———. *Household Income Levels Define What Is Morally Acceptable for Canadians*. 2009c. www.visioncritical.com/wp-content/uploads/2009/11/2009.11.27_Morality.pdf

———. *Infidelity*. Public release (September 14, 1997b). [Online] www.angusreid.com/pressrel/FIDEL1.html

ANGUS REID GLOBAL MONITOR. *Canadians Reject Infidelity, Polygamy and Cloning*. 2009. www.angus-reid.com/polls/37708/canadians_reject_infidelity_polygamy_and_cloning/

———. *Most Canadians Generally Agree with Euthanasia*. 2010. www.angus-reid.com/polls/38352/most_canadians_generally_agree_with_euthanasia/

ANGUS REID GROUP INC. *The Federal Political Scene*. Public release (December 28, 1995). [Online] www.angusreid.com/pressrel/DecFedPolScene.html

———. *Canadian Views on the Public Education System*. Table accompanying public release (September 7, 1996a). [Online] www.angusreid.com/pressrel/pubedspt96.html

———. *Federal Political Trends and the Public Agenda*. Public release (December 9, 1996b). [Online] www.angusreid.com/pressrel/fedpoltrendsdec96.html

———. *Public Support for the Federal Gun Control Legislation*. Public release (December 23, 1996e). [Online] www.angusreid.com/pressrel/guncontrol.html

———. *The '97 Election: Late Campaign*. Public release (May 29, 1997c). [Online] www.angusreid.com/pressrel/97fedelect_latecampaign.htm

———. *Women in Politics*. Special report (May 13, 1997d). [Online] www.angusreid.com/wip/index.htm

———. *Canadians' Views on Including Sexual Orientation in Human Rights Legislation*. Public release (May 10, 1998b). [Online] www.angusreid.com/pressrel/pr100598.html

———. *Chrétien Continues to Ride High in Public Esteem, But Slight Majority (58%) Would Support Change in Party Leadership Before Next Election*. Tables accompanying press release (July 10, 1998c). [Online] www.angusreid.com/pressrel/pr100798.html

———. *Let's Talk About Sex, Tables*. Public release (March 3, 1998e). [Online] www.ipsos-reid.com/media/content/pdf/pr030398tb.pdf

———. *Canadian Teens Voice Their Opinions on Violence in Their Schools*. Public release (May 3, 1999a).

———. *Canadians' Assessment and Views of the Educational System*. Public release (June 22, 1999b).

———. *Federal Election Poll: November 24, 2000*. Tables accompanying press release (November 24, 2000b). [Online] www.ipsos-reid.com/media/content/pdf/mr001124_1t.pdf

ANGUS REID PUBLIC OPINION. *Canadians Review What Is Morally Acceptable*. 2007. www.angus-reid.com/polls/29842/canadians_review_what_is_morally_acceptable/

———. *Morality*. 2009. www.visioncritical.com/wp-content/uploads/2009/11/2009.11.27_Morality.pdf

ANNANDALE, ELLEN, and KATE HUNT, eds. *Gender Inequalities in Health*. Philadelphia, PA: Open University Press, 2000.

ANTI-SLAVERY INTERNATIONAL. 2008. "Slavery Remains Despite Years of Successes." www.antislavery.org/archive/press/latestpressrelease.htm

ANXO, DOMINIQUE, et al. *Parental Leave in European Companies*. Luxembourg, Belgium: European Foundation for the Improvement of Living and Working Conditions. Office for Official Publications of the European Communities, 2007.

APPLEBOME, PETER. "70 Years after Scopes Trial, Creation Debate Lives." *New York Times* (March 10, 1996):1, 10.

ARAT-KOC, SEDEF. "In the Privacy of Our Own Home: Foreign Domestic Workers as Solution to the Crisis in the Domestic Sphere in Canada." *Studies in Political Economy*. Vol. 28 (Spring 1989):33–58.

ARIÈS, PHILIPPE. *Centuries of Childhood: A Social History of Family Life*. New York: Vintage Books, 1965.

ARISTARKHOVA, I. "Ectogenesis and Mother as Machine." *Body and Society*. Vol. 11, No. 3 (2005):43–59.

ARMSTRONG, ELISABETH. *The Retreat from Organization: U.S. Feminism Reconceptualized*. Albany: State University of New York Press, 2002.

ARMSTRONG, PAT, and HUGH ARMSTRONG. *Wasting Away: The Undermining of Canadian Health Care*. Toronto: Oxford University Press, 1996.

———. *Wasting Away—The Undermining of Canadian Health Care*. 2nd ed. Toronto: Oxford University Press, 2002.

"Army Apologizes" (January 7, 2009). www.reuters.com/article/idUSTRE50674G 20090107

ARNETT, J. "The Developmental Context of Substance Abuse in Emerging Adulthood." *Journal of Drug Issues* (Spring 2005):235–54.

———. "Emerging Adulthood in Europe: A Response to Bynner." *Journal of Youth Studies*. Vol. 9, No. 1 (2006):111–23.

ARTZ, SIBYLLE. *Sex, Power, & the Violent School Girl*. Toronto: Trifolium Books, 1998.

ASANTE, MOLEFI KETE. *Afrocentricity*. Trenton, NJ: Africa World Press, 1988.

ASCH, SOLOMON. *Social Psychology*. Englewood Cliffs, NJ: Prentice Hall, 1952.

ASHFORD, LORI S. "Young Women in Sub-Saharan Africa Face a High Risk of HIV Infection." *Population Today*. Vol. 30, No. 2 (February/March 2002):3, 6.

ASPINALL, P. "The Conceptualisation and Categorisation of Mixed Race/Ethnicity in Britain and North America: Identity Options and the Role of the State." *International Journal of Intercultural Relations.* Vol. 27, No. 3 (2003):269–96.

ASTIN, ALEXANDER W., LETICIA OSEGUERA, LINDA J. SAX, and WILLIAM S. KORN. *The American Freshman: Thirty-Five-Year Trends.* Los Angeles: UCLA Higher Education Research Institute, 2002.

ASTONE, NAN MARIE, and SARA S. McLANAHAN. "Family Structure, Parental Practices and High School Completion." *American Sociological Review.* Vol. 56, No. 3 (June 1991):309–20.

ATKINSON, MICHAEL. *Tattooed: The Sociogenesis of a Body Art.* Toronto: The University of Toronto Press, 2003.

ATLAS, TERRY. "The Human Cost of China's Boom Times." *U.S. News and World Report* (March 12, 2007):21.

"Atomic Education Urged by Einstein." *New York Times* (May 25, 1946):13.

ATTORNEY GENERAL'S COMMISSION ON PORNOGRAPHY. *Final Report.* Washington, DC: U.S. Dept. of Justice, 1986.

AUCC (ASSOCIATION OF UNIVERSITIES AND COLLEGES OF CANADA). "Speaking Notes. Speech by Claire Morris, President Association of Universities and Colleges of Canada." 2008. www.aucc.ca/_pdf/english/speeches/2008/swaac_speech_claire_morris_05_02_bil.pdf

AUSTER, CAROL J., and MINDY MACRONE. "The Classroom as a Negotiated Social Setting: An Empirical Study of the Effects of Faculty Members' Behavior on Students' Participation." *Teaching Sociology.* Vol. 22, No. 4 (October 1994):289–300.

AXINN, WILLIAM G., and JENNIFER S. BARBER. "Mass Education and Fertility Transition." *American Sociological Review.* Vol. 66, No. 4 (August 2001):481–505.

BAGLEY, ROBIN. *Sexual Offences Against Children: Report of the Committee on Sexual Offences Against Children and Youth.* Ottawa: Canadian Government Publishing, 1984.

BAJAJ, VIKAS. "Bangladesh Garment Workers Awarded Higher Pay." *New York Times.* [Online] Available July 29, 2010, at http://www.nytimes.com/2010/07/29/business/global/29garment.html

BAKALAR, NICHOLAS. "Reactions: Go On, Laugh Your Heart Out." *New York Times* (March 8, 2005). www.nytimes.com/2005/03/08/health/08reac.html

BAKER, MAUREEN. *Canadian Family Policies: Cross-National Comparisons.* Toronto: University of Toronto Press, 1995.

BAKER, PATRICIA S., WILLIAM C. YOELS, JEFFREY M. CLAIR, and RICHARD M. ALLMAN. "Laughter in the Triadic Geriatric Encounters: A Transcript-Based Analysis." In Rebecca J. Erikson and Beverly Cuthbertson-Johnson, eds., *Social Perspectives on Emotion.* Vol. 4. Greenwich, CT: JAI Press, 1997:179–207.

BALAKRISHNAN, T.R., and FENG HOU. *The Changing Patterns of Spatial Concentration and Residential Segregation of Ethnic Groups in Canada's Major Metropolitan Areas 1981–1991.* Discussion Paper No. 95-2. London, ON: University of Western Ontario, Population Studies Centre, 1995.

BALAKRISHNAN, T.R., and GEORGE K. JARVIS. "Is the Burgess Concentric Zonal Theory of Spatial Differentiation Still Applicable to Urban Canada?" *Canadian Review of Sociology and Anthropology.* Vol. 28, No. 4 (November 1991):527–40.

BALAKRISHNAN, T.R., E. LAPIERRE-ADAMCYK, and K.J. KROTKI. *Family and Childbearing in Canada: A Demographic Analysis.* Toronto: University of Toronto Press, 1993.

BALDUS, BERND, and MEENAZ KASSAM. "'Making Me Truthful and Mild:' Values in Nineteenth-Century Ontario Schoolbooks." *Canadian Journal of Sociology.* Vol. 21, No. 3 (1996):327–57.

BALDUS, BERND, and VERNA TRIBE. "Children's Perceptions of Inequality." In Lorne Tepperman and James Curtis, eds., *Everyday Life: A Reader.* Toronto: McGraw-Hill Ryerson, 1992:88–97.

BALTZELL, E. DIGBY. *The Protestant Establishment: Aristocracy and Caste in America.* New York: Vintage Books, 1964.

———. "Introduction to the 1967 Edition." In W.E.B. Du Bois, ed., *The Philadelphia Negro: A Social Study.* New York: Schocken Books, 1967.

———. *Philadelphia Gentlemen: The Making of a National Upper Class.* Philadelphia: University of Pennsylvania Press, 1979; orig. 1958.

BANTING, K., T. COURCHENE, and L. SEIDLE, eds. *Belonging? Diversity, Recognition and Shared Citizenship in Canada.* Montreal: Institute for Research on Public Policy, 2007.

BARASH, DAVID P. *The Whisperings Within.* New York: Penguin Books, 1981.

BARNES, JULIAN E. "War Profiteering." *U.S. News & World Report* (May 13, 2002b):20–24.

BARON, JAMES N., MICHAEL T. HANNAN, and M. DIANE BURTON. "Building the Iron Cage: Determinants of Managerial Intensity in the Early Years of Organizations." *American Sociological Review.* Vol. 64, No. 4 (August 1999):527–47.

BARON, STEPHEN. "General Strain, Street Youth, and Crime: Testing Agnew's Revised Theory," *Criminology.* Vol. 42 (2004):57–483.

BAROVICK, HARRIET. "Tongues That Go Out of Style." *Time* (June 10, 2002):22.

BARTLETT, DONALD L., and JAMES B. STEELE. "Corporate Welfare." *Time.* Vol. 152, No. 19 (November 9, 1998):36–54.

———. "How the Little Guy Gets Crunched." *Time* (February 7, 2000):38–41.

BASSUK, ELLEN J. "The Homelessness Problem." *Scientific American.* Vol. 251, No. 1 (July 1984):40–45.

BAUER, P.T. *Equality, the Third World, and Economic Delusion.* Cambridge, MA: Harvard University Press, 1981.

BAYDAR, NAZLI, and JEANNE BROOKS-GUNN. "Effect of Maternal Employment and Child-Care Arrangements on Preschoolers' Cognitive and Behavioral Outcomes: Evidence from Children from the National Longitudinal Survey of Youth." *Developmental Psychology.* Vol. 27, No. 6 (November 1991):932–35.

BBC NEWS. "China Orders Bosses Down Mines." (November 7, 2005).

BEAMAN, L., and P. BEYER. *Religion and Diversity in Canada.* Boston: Brill, 2008.

BEARAK, BARRY. "Lives Held Cheap in Bangladesh Sweatshops." *New York Times* (April 15, 2001):A1, A12.

BEARMAN, PETER S., JAMES MOODY, and KATHERINE STOVEL. "Chains of Affection." *American Journal of Sociology.* Vol. 110, No. 1 (July 2004):44–91.

BEATTIE, KAREN. "Adult Correctional Services in Canada, 2003/04" *Juristat.* Vol. 25, No. 8 (December 2005):1–30.

BEAUJOT, R. *Earning and Caring in Canadian Families.* Toronto: Broadview, 2000.

BEAUJOT, RODERIC. "Gender Models of Family and Work." *Horizons Policy Research Initiative.* Vol. 8, No. 3 (April 2006):24–26.

BEAUPRÉ, PASCALE, and ELISABETH CLOUTIER. *Navigating Family Transitions: Evidence from the General Social Survey—2006.* Statistics Canada Catalogue no. 89-625-XIE, No. 002. 2007.

BECKER, ANNE E. "The Association of Television Exposure with Disordered Eating among Ethnic Fijian Adolescent Girls." Paper presented at the annual meeting of the American Psychiatric Association, Washington, DC, May 19, 1999.

BECKER, HOWARD S. *Outside: Studies in the Sociology of Deviance.* New York: Free Press, 1966.

BEEGHLEY, LEONARD. *The Structure of Social Stratification in the United States.* Needham Heights, MA: Allyn & Bacon, 1989.

BEGLEY, SHARON. "Gray Matters." *Newsweek* (March 7, 1995):48–54.

BELANGER, ALAIN, and ERIC CARON MALENFANT. *Population Projections of Visible Minority Groups, Canada, Provinces and Regions, 2001–2017.* Ottawa: Statistics Canada, Catalogue No. 91514-XIE. 2005a.

———. "Ethnocultural Diversity in Canada: Prospects for 2017." *Canadian Social Trends.* No. 79 (Winter 2005b):18–21.

BELL, ALAN P., MARTIN S. WEINBERG, and SUE KIEFER-HAMMERSMITH. *Sexual Preference: Its Development in Men and Women.* Bloomington: Indiana University Press, 1981.

BELL, DAVID, and LORNE TEPPERMAN. *The Roots of Disunity: A Look at Canadian Political Culture.* Toronto: McClelland & Stewart, 1979.

BELLAH, ROBERT N. *The Broken Covenant.* New York: Seabury Press, 1975.

BELLER, EMILY, and MICHAEL HOUT. "Intergenerational Social Mobility: The United States in Comparative Perspective." *The Future of Children.* Vol. 16, No. 2 (Fall 2006). www.futureofchildren.org/information2826/information_show.htm?doc_id=389282

BELTRAME, JULIAN, and BRENDA BRANSWELL. "The Enemy Within." *Maclean's.* Vol. 113, Issue 43 (October 23, 2000):36–38.

BEM, SANDRA LIPSITZ. *The Lenses of Gender: Transforming the Debate on Sexual Inequality.* New Haven, CT: Yale University Press, 1993.

BENEDICT, RUTH. "Continuities and Discontinuities in Cultural Conditioning." *Psychiatry.* Vol. 1, No. 2 (May 1938):161–67.

BENJAMIN, LOIS. *The Black Elite: Facing the Color Line in the Twilight of the Twentieth Century.* Chicago: Nelson-Hall, 1991.

BENNETT, STEPHEN EARL. "Left Behind: Exploring Declining Turnout Among Non-College Young Whites, 1964–1988." *Social Science Quarterly.* Vol. 72, No. 2 (June 1991):314–33.

BENOIT, CECILIA. "Rediscovering Appropriate Care: Maternity Traditions and Contemporary Issues in Canada." In David Coburn et al., eds., *Health and Canadian Society*. 3rd ed. Toronto: University of Toronto Press, 1998b.

———. *Women, Work and Social Rights: Canada in Historical and Comparative Perspective*. Scarborough, ON: Prentice Hall Canada, 2000a.

———. "Variation Within Post-Fordist and Liberal Welfare State Countries: Women's Work and Social Rights in Canada and the United States." In Thomas Boje and Arnlaug Leira, eds., *Gender, Welfare State and the Market: Towards a New Division of Labour*. London: Routledge, 2000b:71– 88.

BENOIT, CECILIA, and DENA CARROLL. "Aboriginal Midwifery in British Columbia: A Narrative Still Untold." *Western Geographic Series*. Vol. 30 (1995):221–46.

BENOIT, CECILIA, and H. HALLGRIMSDOTTIR, eds. *Valuing Care Work: Comparative Perspectives*. Toronto: University of Toronto Press, 2011.

BENOIT, CECILIA, M. JANSSON, and M. ANDERSON. "Understanding Health Disparities among Female Street Youth." In B. Leadbeater and N. Way, eds., *Urban Girls Revisited: Building Strengths*. New York: New York University Press, 2007:321–37.

BENOIT, CECILIA, M. JANSSON, H. HALLGRIMSDOTTIR, and E. ROTH. "Street Youth's Life Course Transitions." *Comparative Social Research*. Vol. 25 (2008): 329–57.

BENOIT, CECILIA, and ALISON MILLAR. *Dispelling Myths and Understanding Realities: Working Conditions, Health Status, and Exiting Experiences of Sex Workers*. Sponsored by Prostitutes Empowerment, Education and Resource Society (PEERS). Funded by BC Health Research Foundation, Capital Health District, and BC Centre of Excellence on Women's Health, 2001.

BENOIT, CECILIA, and F. SHAVER. "Critical Issues and New Directions in Sex Work Research." *The Canadian Review of Sociology and Anthropology*. Vol. 43 (2006):243–52.

BENOIT, CECILIA, L. SHUMKA, ET AL. "Explaining the Health Gap Between Girls and Women in Canada." *Sociological Research Online*. Vol. 14, No. 5 (2009). www.socresonline.org.uk/14/5/9.html

BENOKRAITIS, NIJOLE, and JOE R. FEAGIN. *Modern Sexism: Blatant, Subtle, and Overt Discrimination*. 2nd ed. Englewood Cliffs, NJ: Prentice Hall, 1995.

BERGAMO, MONICA, and GERSON CAMAROTTI. "Brazil's Landless Millions." *World Press Review*. Vol. 43, No. 7 (July 1996):46–47.

BERGER, PETER L. *Invitation to Sociology*. New York: Anchor Books, 1963.

———. *The Sacred Canopy: Elements of a Sociological Theory of Religion*. Garden City, NY: Doubleday, 1967.

———. *Facing Up to Modernity: Excursions in Society, Politics, and Religion*. New York: Basic Books, 1977.

———. *The Capitalist Revolution: Fifty Propositions about Prosperity, Equality, and Liberty*. New York: Basic Books, 1986.

BERGER, PETER L., BRIGITTE BERGER, and HANSFRIED KELLNER. *The Homeless Mind: Modernization and Consciousness*. New York: Vintage Books, 1974.

BERGESEN, ALBERT, ed. *Crises in the World-System*. Beverly Hills, CA: Sage, 1983.

BERNARD, JESSIE. *The Female World*. New York: Free Press, 1981.

———. *The Future of Marriage*. 2nd ed. New Haven, CT: Yale University Press, 1982.

BERRY, BRIAN L., and PHILIP H. REES. "The Factorial Ecology of Calcutta." *American Journal of Sociology*. Vol. 74, No. 5 (March 1969):445–91.

BERTEAU, CELESTE. "Disconnected Intimacy: AOL Instant Messenger Use among Kenyon College Students." Senior thesis. Kenyon College, 2005.

BERTRAND, JANE, MARGARET McCAIN, J. FRASER MUSTARD, and J. DOUGLAS WILLIAMS. "A First Tier for Canadian Children: Findings from the Early Years Study in Ontario." *Atlantic Centre for Policy Research*. Fredericton, NB: University of New Brunswick. No. 6 (July 1999):1–4.

BESECKE, KELLY. "Speaking of Meaning in Modernity: Reflexive Spirituality as a Cultural Resource." *Sociology of Religion*. Vol. 62, No. 3 (2003):365–81.

———. "Seeing Invisible Religion: Religion as a Societal Conversation about Transcendent Meaning." *Sociological Theory*. Vol. 23, No. 2 (June 2005):179–96.

BEST, RAPHAELA. *We've All Got Scars: What Boys and Girls Learn in Elementary School*. Bloomington: Indiana University Press, 1983.

BIAN, YANJIE. "Chinese Social Stratification and Social Mobility." *Annual Review of Sociology*. Vol. 28 (2002):91–116.

BIANCHI, SUZANNE M., and DAPHNE SPAIN. "Women, Work, and Family in America." *Population Bulletin*. Vol. 51, No. 3 (December 1996).

BIBBY, REGINALD W. *Fragmented Gods: The Poverty and Potential of Religion in Canada*. Toronto: Irwin, 1987.

———. *Unknown Gods: The Ongoing Study of Religion in Canada*. Toronto: Stoddart, 1993.

———. *Restless Gods: The Renaissance of Religion in Canada*. Toronto: Stoddart, 2002.

———. *A Survey of Canadian Hopes and Dreams*. Ottawa: The Vanier Institute of the Family, 2004. www.vifamily.ca/library/publications/futured.html

———. *The Emerging Millennials: How Canada's Newest Generation Is Responding to Change and Choice*. Lethbridge, AB: Project Canada Books, 2009.

BIBBY, REGINALD, and MERLIN BRINKERHOFF. "Circulation of the Saints 1966–1990: New Data, New Reflections." *Journal of the Scientific Study of Religion*. Vol. 33 (1994):273–80.

BIBLARZ, TIMOTHY J., and ADRIAN E. RAFTERY. "The Effects of Family Disruption on Social Mobility." *American Sociological Review*. Vol. 58, No. 1 (February 1993):97–109.

BIELSKI, ZOSIA. "Canada's Teen Birth and Abortion Rate Drops by 36.9 Per Cent." *Globe and Mail*. May 26, 2010.

BIGGS, LESLEY. "The Case of the Missing Midwives: A History of Midwifery in Ontario from 1795–1900." *Ontario History*. Vol. 75 (1983):21–35.

BLACK, CASSANDRA. "Survey Reports More Women Are Having Extramarital Affairs." *Associated Content* (May 4, 2007). [Online] Available April 19, 2009, at http://www.associatedcontent.com/article/231316/survey_reports_more_women_are_having.html

BLACKWOOD, EVELYN, and SASKIA WIERINGA, eds. *Female Desires: Same-Sex Relations and Transgender Practices across Cultures*. New York: Columbia University Press, 1999.

BLANTON, KIMBERLY. "Borrowers Sue Subprime Lender, Allege Race Bias." *Boston Globe*. July 13, 2007. www.boston.com/business/personalfinance/articles/2007/07/13/borrowers_sue_subprime_lender_allege_race_bias/

BLAU, JUDITH R., and PETER M. BLAU. "The Cost of Inequality: Metropolitan Structure and Violent Crime." *American Sociological Review*. Vol. 47, No. 1 (February 1982):114–29.

BLAU, PETER M. *Exchange and Power in Social Life*. New York: Wiley, 1964.

———. *Inequality and Heterogeneity: A Primitive Theory of Social Structure*. New York: Free Press, 1977.

BLAU, PETER M., TERRY C. BLUM, and JOSEPH E. SCHWARTZ. "Heterogeneity and Intermarriage." *American Sociological Review*. Vol. 47, No. 1 (February 1982):45–62.

BLISHEN, BERNARD. *Doctors in Canada*. Toronto: University of Toronto Press, 1991.

BLUMER, HERBERT G. "Collective Behavior." In Alfred McClung Lee, ed., *Principles of Sociology*. 3rd ed. New York: Barnes & Noble Books, 1969:65–121.

BOBO, LAWRENCE, and VINCENT L. HUTCHINGS. "Perceptions of Racial Group Competition: Extending Blumer's Theory of Group Position to a Multiracial Social Context." *American Sociological Review*. Vol. 61, No. 6 (December 1996):951–72.

BOETHUS, MARIA-PIA. "The End of Prostitution in Sweden?" Stockholm: Swedish Institute. No. 426 (October), 1999. [Online] www.si.se/eng/ esverige/cs426.html

BOGARDUS, EMORY S. "Social Distance and Its Origins." *Sociology and Social Research*. Vol. 9 (July/August 1925):216–25.

———. *A Forty-Year Racial Distance Study*. Los Angeles: University of Southern California Press, 1967.

BOHANNAN, CECIL. "The Economic Correlates of Homelessness in Sixty Cities." *Social Science Quarterly*. Vol. 72, No. 4 (December 1991):817–25.

BOHLEN, CELESTINE. "Facing Oblivion, Rust-Belt Giants Top Russian List of Vexing Crises." *New York Times* (November 8, 1998):1, 6.

BONANNO, ALESSANDRO, DOUGLAS H. CONSTANCE, and HEATHER LORENZ. "Powers and Limits of Transnational Corporations: The Case of ADM." *Rural Sociology*. Vol. 65, No. 3 (September 2000):440–60.

BONNER, JANE. Research presented in the Public Broadcast System telecast *The Brain #6: The Two Brains*. Videocassette VHS 339. Newark, NJ: Wnet-13 Films, 1984.

BOOTH, WILLIAM. The Myth of the Melting Pot, America's Racial and Ethnic Divides, Part 4, "Sweat of Their Brows Reshapes Economy," Fourth in a series of occasional articles, By William Booth, *Washington Post* Staff Writer (July 13, 1998): A01. http://www.washingtonpost.com/wp-srv/national/longterm/meltingpot/melt0713a.htm

BORIS, P. (2004). "Low Income among Immigrants and Visible Minorities." *Perspectives*. Statistics Canada Catalogue no. 75-001-XIE. www.statcan.gc.ca/pub/75-001-x/10404/6843-eng.pdf

BORITCH, HELEN. *Fallen Women: Female Crime and the Criminal Justice System in Canada*. Toronto: ITP Nelson, 1997.

BORMANN, F. HERBERT. "The Global Environmental Deficit." *BioScience*. Vol. 40, No. 2 (1990):74.

BOTT, ELIZABETH. *Family and Social Network*. New York: Free Press, 1971; orig. 1957.

BOUCHARD, BRIGITTE, and JOHN ZHAO. "University Education: Recent Trends in Participation." *Education Quarterly Review*. Vol. 6, No. 4 (August 2000):24–32.

BOURDIEU, P. *Language and Symbolic Power*. Cambridge, UK: Polity Press, 1993.

BOURGEAULT, IVY, CECILIA BENOIT, and ROBBIE DAVIS-FLOYD, eds. a *Reconceiving Midwifery*. Montreal-Kingston: McGill-Queen's University Press, 2004.

BOURGEAULT, I.L., and S. WREDE. *Caring Beyond Borders: Comparing the Relationship between Work and Migration Patterns in Canada and Finland.* Special Issue of *The Canadian Journal of Public Health* on "Finding Dignity in Health Care and Health Care Work." C. Benoit and H. Hallgrimsdottir, eds. Vol. 99 (Suppl. 2, 2008), S22–S26.

BOWLBY, G. "Provincial Dropout Rates—Trends and Consequences." *Education Matters.* Statistics Canada Catalogue no. 81-004-XIE, Vol. 2, No. 4 (2005).

BOWLBY, GEOFF. "The Labour Market Review." Perspectives on Labour and Income. Statistics Canada Catalogue no. 75-001-XIE. Vol. 2, No. 1 (January 2001):5–35.

BOWLES, SAMUEL, and HERBERT GINTIS. *Schooling in Capitalist America: Educational Reform and the Contradictions of Economic Life.* New York: Basic Books, 1976.

BOYCE, W. *Young People in Canada, Their Health and Well-Being.* Ottawa: Health Canada, 2004.

BOYCE, W., M. DOHERTY, C. FORTIN, and D. MACKINNON. *Canadian Youth, Sexual Health and HIV/AIDS Study: Factors Influencing Knowledge, Attitudes and Behaviours.* Toronto: Council of Ministers of Education, Canada, 2003.

BOYER, DEBRA. "Male Prostitution and Homosexual Identity." *Journal of Homosexuality.* Vol. 17, Nos. 1, 2 (1989):151–84.

BOYLE, ELIZABETH HEGER, FORTUNATA SONGORA, and GAIL FOSS. "International Discourse and Local Politics: Anti-Female-Genital-Cutting Laws in Egypt, Tanzania, and the United States." *Social Problems.* Vol. 48, No. 4 (November 2001): 524–44.

BOZICK, R., and S. DELUCA "Better Late Than Never? Delayed Enrollment in the High School to College Transition." *Social Forces.* Vol. 84 (2005):531–54.

BRADY CAMPAIGN. "Firearm Facts." April 2008. www.bradycampaign.org/issues/gvstats/firearmoverview/

BRAND, DIONNE. *No Burden to Carry: Narrative of Black Working Women in Ontario, 1920s to 1950s.* Toronto: Women's Press, 1992.

BRENNAN, S., and A. TAYLOR-BUTTS. *Sexual Assault in Canada: 2004 and 2007.* Ottawa: Statistics Canada, 2008.

BRETON, RAYMOND. *Ethnic Relations in Canada: Institutional Dynamics.* Montreal/Kingston: McGill-Queen's University Press, 2005.

BRETON, RAYMOND, NORBERT HARTMANN, JOS LENNARDS, and PAUL B. REED. *A Fragile Social Fabric? Fairness, Trust, and Commitment in Canada.* Montreal/Kingston: McGill-Queen's University Press, 2004.

BROCK, DEBORAH. *Making Work, Making Trouble: Prostitution as a Social Problem.* Toronto: University of Toronto Press, 1998.

BROCKERHOFF, MARTIN P. "An Urbanizing World." *Population Bulletin.* Vol. 55, No. 3 (September 2000):1–44.

BRODKIN, KAREN B. "How Did Jews Become White Folks?" In John J. Macionis and Nijole V. Benokraitis, eds., *Seeing Ourselves: Classic, Contemporary, and Cross-Cultural Readings in Sociology.* 7th ed. Upper Saddle River, NJ: Prentice Hall, 2007.

BRODY, L. *Gender, Emotion, and Family.* Cambridge, MA: Harvard University Press, 1999.

BROOKER, A., and I. HYMAN. "Time Use." *Canadian Index of Wellbeing.* 2010. www.ciw.ca/Libraries/Documents/Time_Use-Report_Highlights.sflb.ashx

BROOKS, B., J. JARMAN, and R.M. BLACKBURN. "Occupational Gender Segregation in Canada, 1981–1996: Overall, Vertical and Horizontal Segregation." *Canadian Review of Sociology and Anthropology.* Vol. 42, No. 2 (2003):197–213.

BROOKS, DAVID. *Bobos in Paradise: The New Upper Class and How They Got There.* New York: Simon & Schuster, 2000.

BROWN, LESTER R. "Reassessing the Earth's Population." *Society.* Vol. 32, No. 4 (May/June 1995):7–10.

BROWN, LESTER R., ET AL., eds. *State of the World 1993: A Worldwatch Institute Report on Progress toward a Sustainable Society.* New York: Norton, 1993.

BROWNING, CHRISTOPHER R., and EDWARD O. LAUMANN. "Sexual Contact between Children and Adults: A Life Course Perspective." *American Sociological Review.* Vol. 62, No. 5 (August 1997):540–60.

BRUXELLES, SIMON DE. "Crimespotting: The New Way to Make Money on the Internet." *London Times* (October 6, 2009). www.timesonline.co.uk/tol/news/uk/crime/article6862398.ece

BRYM, ROBERT J., and BONNIE J. FOX. *From Culture to Power: The Sociology of English Canada.* Toronto: Oxford University Press, 1989.

BUECHLER, STEVEN M. *Social Movements in Advanced Capitalism: The Political Economy and Cultural Construction of Social Activism.* New York: Oxford University Press, 2000.

BUNTING, T., P. FILION, and A. WALKS. "The Uneven Geography of Housing Affordability Stress in Canadian Metropolitan Areas." *Housing Studies.* Vol. 19 (2004):361–93.

BURKETT, ELINOR. "God Created Me to Be a Slave." *New York Times Magazine* (October 12, 1997):56–60.

BUSSOLLO, MAURIZIO, RAFAEL DE HOYOS, DENIS MEDVEDEV, and VICTOR SULLA. "Demographic Change, Economic Growth, and Income Distribution: An Empirical Analysis Using Ex-Ante Microsimulations." Paper prepared for Global Economic Prospects, 2007.

BUTLER, J. *Excitable Speech: A Politics of the Performative.* London: Routledge, 1997.

BUTLIN, GEORGE. " Determinants of University and Community College Leaving." *Education Quarterly Review.* Statistics Canada Catalogue no. 81-003-XIE. Vol. 6, No. 4 (August 2000):8–23.

CALIFORNIA NEWSREEL. "Race: The Power of an Illusion: Genetic Diversity Quiz." 2003. www.pbs.org/race/000_About/002_04_a-godeeper.htm

CAMERON, WILLIAM BRUCE. *Modern Social Movements: A Sociological Outline.* New York: Random House, 1966.

CAMPBELL, ROBERT A., and JAMES E. CURTIS. "Religious Involvement Across Societies." *Journal for the Scientific Study of Religion.* Vol. 33, No. 3 (September 1994):217–29.

CANADIAN CENTRE FOR DRUG-FREE SPORT. *Over 80 000 Young Canadians Using Anabolic Steroids.* Ottawa: News Release, 1993. [Online] www.hc-sc.gc.ca/main/hppb/nutrition/pube/vtlk/vitlk07.htm

CANADIAN CENTRE FOR JUSTICE STATISTICS. *Family Violence in Canada: A Statistical Profile 2007.* Catalogue no. 85-224-XIE. 2007. www.phac-aspc.gc.ca/ncfv-cnivf/pdfs/fv-85-224-XIE2007001.pdf

CANADIAN COUNCIL ON LEARNING. *The State of Post-secondary Education in Canada.* 2006. www.ccl-cca.ca/ccl/Reports/PostSecondaryEducation/Archives2006/index.html

———. *Gappers: Taking Time Off between High School and Post-Secondary Studies.* 2008. www.ccl-cca.ca/pdfs/LessonsInLearning/Jun-26-08-Gappers-Taking-time-off.pdf

CANADIAN INSTITUTE FOR HEALTH INFORMATION. *Health Care in Canada: A First Annual Report.* Ottawa: Statistics Canada, 2000.

CANADIAN NURSES ASSOCIATION. *Testing Solutions for Eliminating Canada's Registered Nursing Shortage.* 2009. www.cna-aiic.ca/CNA/documents/pdf/publications/RN_Highlights_e.pdf

CANADIAN PRESS NEWSWIRE. *Reporter Recovering from Murder Attempt Says Tougher Biker Laws Needed.* October 21, 2000.

CANADIAN SOCIOLOGY AND ANTHROPOLOGY ASSOCIATION. 1994. [Online] www.arts.ubc.ca/csaa/eng/englcode.htm

CANCER SOCIETY OF CANADA. *Cancer.* 2008. www.cancer.ca/Quebec/About%20us/Media%20centre/~/media/5967CE5F13054DEFBD0B96DB0B0E56A0.ashx

CAP INDEX. (2009). www.capindex.com

CAPLOW, THEODORE, et al. *Middletown Families.* Minneapolis: University of Minnesota Press, 1982.

CARLSON, NORMAN A. "Corrections in the United States Today: A Balance Has Been Struck." *American Criminal Law Review.* Vol. 13, No. 4 (Spring 1976):615–47.

CARMICHAEL, STOKELY, and CHARLES V. HAMILTON. *Black Power: The Politics of Liberation in America.* New York: Vintage Books, 1967.

CASTILLA, EMILIO J. "Gender, Race, and Meritocracy in Organizational Careers." *American Journal of Sociology.* Vol. 113, No. 6 (May 2008):1479–526.

CATALYST. "Research and Knowledge." 2010. www.catalyst.org/page/64/browsere search-knowledge

CBC NEWS. *Online Gambling.* 2003. www.cbc.ca/news/background/gambling/onlinegambling.html

———. *Canadians Split on Pot, Death Penalty: Poll.* 2010. www.cbc.ca/news/canada/story/2010/03/18/ekos-poll018.html

CENTER FOR RESPONSIVE POLITICS. "110th Congress Casualty List." 2009. www.opensecrets.org/index.php

———. "Overweight and Obesity: Economic Consequences." May 2007. www.cdc.gov/nccdphp/dnpa/obesity/economic_consequences.htm

———. "Trends in the Prevalence of Sexual Behaviors: National Youth Risk Behavior Survey, 1991–2007." 2008. www.cdc.gov/HealthyYouth/sexualbehaviors/index.htm

CENTERS FOR DISEASE CONTROL AND PREVENTION (CDC). "Trends in the Prevalence of Sexual Behaviors: National Youth Risk Behavior Survey, 1991–2007." 2008. http://www.cdc.gov/HealthyYouth/sexualbehaviors/index.htm

———. "Overweight and Obesity: Economic Consequences." May 2007. http://www.cdc.gov/nccdphp/dnpa/obesity/economic_consequences.htm

CENTRAL INTELLIGENCE AGENCY. *The World Factbook.* 2010 (updated biweekly). https://www.cia.gov/library/publications/the-world-factbook/index.html

———. *The World Factbook.* 2011 (updated biweekly). [Online] Available at http://www.cia.gov/library/publications/the-worldfactbook/index.html

CHAGNON, NAPOLEON A. *Yanomamö: The Fierce People.* 4th ed. Austin, TX: Holt, Rinehart and Winston, 1992.

CHANDLER, TERTIUS, and GERALD FOX. *3000 Years of Urban History.* New York: Academic Press, 1974.

CHANG, LESLIE T. *Factory Girls: From Village to City in a Changing China.* New York: Spiegel & Grau, 2008.

CHAPKIS, WENDY. *Live Sex Acts: Women Performing Erotic Labor.* New York: Routledge, 1997.

CHAPPELL, N.L. "Aging in Canada." In E. Palmore, ed., *International Handbook on Aging.* Westport, CT: Praeger Publishers, 2009.

CHAPPELL, NEENA, LYNN MACDONALD, and MICHAEL STONES. *Aging in Contemporary Canada.* 2nd ed. Toronto: Prentice Hall, 2005.

CHARLES, MARIA. "Cross-National Variation in Occupational Segregation." *American Sociological Review.* Vol. 57, No. 4 (August 1992): 483–502.

CHARLES, N., C.A. DAVIES, and C. HARRIS. *Families in Transition: Social Change, Family Formation and Kin Relationships.* Bristol, UK: Polity Press, 2008.

CHEN, SHAHUA, and MARTIN RAVALLION. "The Developing World Is Poorer than We Thought, but No Less Successful in the Fight against Poverty." 2008. http://go.worldbank.org/C9GR27WRJ0

CHEN, W., and BARRY WELLMAN. "Net and Jet: The Internet Use, Travel and Social Networks of Chinese Canadian Entrepreneurs." *Information, Communication and Society.* Vol. 12, No. 4 (2009):525–47.

CHILD AND FAMILY CANADA. How Families Are Doing in the '90s. (2003) [Online] www.cfc-efc.ca/docs/vocfc/00001083.htm

"China Faces Water Shortage." *Popline.* Vol. 23 (December 2001):1–4.

CHIRICOS, TED, RANEE MCENTIRE, and MARC GERTZ. "Perceived Racial and Ethnic Composition of Neighborhood and Perceived Risk of Crime." *Social Problems.* Vol. 48, No. 3 (August 2001):322–40.

CHODOROW, NANCY. *Femininities, Masculinities, Sexualities: Freud and Beyond.* Lexington: University of Kentucky Press, 1994.

CHOPRA, ANUJ. "Iranian Rap Music Bedevils the Authorities." *U.S. News & World Report* (March 24, 2008):33.

CHRISTIE, NANCY. *Engendering the State: Family, Work, and Welfare in Canada.* Toronto: University of Toronto Press, 2000.

CHURCH, S., and M. HENDERSON. "Violence by Clients towards Female Prostitutes in Different Work Settings." *British Medical Journal.* Vol. 322 (2001):524–25.

CIBC. "CIBC, Women Entrepreneurs: Leading the Charge." 2005. https://www.cibc.com/ca/pdf/women-entrepreneurs-en.pdf

CIHI (CANADIAN INSTITUTE FOR HEALTH INFORMATION). *National Health Expenditure Trends, 1975 to 2010.* 2010a. http://secure.cihi.ca/cihiweb/products/NHEX_Trends_Report_2010_final_ENG_web.pdf

———. *Regulated Nurses: Canadian Trends, 2005 to 2009.* 2010b. http://secure.cihi.ca/cihiweb/products/nursing_report_2005-2009_en.pdf

CIHR (CANADIAN INSTITUTES OF HEALTH RESEARCH). *CIHR Guidelines for Health Research Involving Aboriginal People.* 2007. [Online]. www.cihr-irsc.gc.ca/e/29134.html

CIHR (CANADIAN INSTITUTES OF HEALTH RESEARCH), NSERC (NATURAL SCIENCES AND ENGINEERING RESEARCH COUNCIL OF CANADA), AND SSHRC (SOCIAL SCIENCES AND HUMANITIES RESEARCH COUNCIL OF CANADA). *Tri-Council Policy Statement: Ethical Conduct for Research Involving Humans.* Ottawa: Her Majesty the Queen in Right of Canada, 2010. [Online] www.pre.ethics.gc.ca/pdf/eng/tcps2/TCPS_2_FINAL_Web.pdf

CIMINO, RICHARD, and DON LATTIN. "Choosing My Religion." *American Demographics.* Vol. 21, No. 4 (April 1999):60–65.

CITIZENS' FORUM ON CANADA'S FUTURE. *Report to the People and Government of Canada.* Ottawa: Minister of Supply and Services Canada, 1991.

CLARK, ANDREW. "Wal-Mart, the U.S. Retailer, Taking Over the World by Stealth." *Guardian* (January 12, 2010). www.guardian.co.uk/business/2010/jan/12/walmart-companiesto-shape-the-decade

CLARK, KIM. "Bankrupt Lives." *U.S. News & World Report* (September 16, 2002): 52–54.

CLARK, MARGARET S., ed. *Prosocial Behavior.* Newbury Park, CA: Sage, 1991.

CLARK, W. "Delayed Transitions of Young Adults." *Canadian Social Trends.* No. 84 (2007):14–22.

CLARK, W., and G. SCHELLENBERG. "Who's Religious?" *Canadian Social Trends* (Summer 2006). Statistics Canada Catalogue no. 11-008. www.statcan.gc.ca/pub/11-008-x/2006001/pdf/9181-eng.pdf

CLARKE, ROBIN. "Atmospheric Pollution." In Sir Edmund Hillary, ed., *Ecology 2000: The Changing Face of the Earth.* New York: Beaufort Books, 1984:130–48.

CLEMENT, WALLACE. *The Canadian Corporate Elite.* Toronto: McClelland and Stewart, 1975.

CLOSS, WILLIAM J., and PAUL F. MCKENNA. "Profiling a Problem in Canadian Police Leadership: The Kingston Police Data Collection Project." *Canadian Public Administration.* Vol. 49, No. 2 (2006):143–60.

CLOWARD, RICHARD A., and LLOYD E. OHLIN. *Delinquency and Opportunity: A Theory of Delinquent Gangs.* New York: Free Press, 1966.

CNN.COM, Women on Board: Breaking the "Bamboo Ceiling" (Video), by Kyung Lah, April 22, 2010. Available at: http://www.cnn.com/video/#/video/world/2010/04/15/lah.japan.women.on.board.cnn?iref=allsearch

COHEN, ALBERT K. *Delinquent Boys: The Culture of the Gang.* New York: Free Press, 1971; orig. 1955.

COHEN, MARK NATHAN. *Health and the Rise of Civilization.* New Haven, CT: Yale University Press, 1989.

COHEN, PHILIP N., and MATT L. HUFFMAN. "Individuals, Jobs, and Labor Markets: The Devaluation of Women's Work." *American Sociological Review.* Vol. 68, No. 3 (June 2003):443–63.

COLEMAN, JAMES S. "The Design of Organizations and the Right to Act." *Sociological Forum.* Vol. 8, No. 4 (December 1993):527–46.

COLEMAN, JAMES S., THOMAS HOFFER, and SALLY KILGORE. *Public and Private Schools: An Analysis of Public Schools and Beyond.* Washington, DC: National Center for Education Statistics, 1981.

COLEMAN, JAMES S., ET AL. *Equality of Educational Opportunity.* Washington, DC: U.S. Government Printing Office, 1966.

COLEMAN, RICHARD P., and LEE RAINWATER. *Social Standing in America.* New York: Basic Books, 1978.

COLLEGE BOARD. "Tables & Related Items, 2008." 2008. http://professionals.collegeboard.com/data-reports-research/sat/cb-seniors-2008/tables

———. "2009 College-Bound Seniors: Total Group Profile Report." 2009. http://professionals.collegeboard.com/profdownload/cbs-2009-national-TOTAL-GROUP.pdf

COLLEGE OF FAMILY PHYSICIANS OF CANADA." Patient-Centred Primary Care in Canada: Bring It on Home." Discussion paper. 2009. www.cfpc.ca/ProjectAssets/Templates/Resource.aspx?id=890

COLLEGE TOBACCO PREVENTION RESOURCE. "College Tobacco Resources, 1990–2005." 2006. www.ttac.org/college/pdfs/TTACFINALLitReview.pdf

COLLIN, C., and H. JENSEN. *A Statistical Profile of Poverty in Canada.* Ottawa: Parliamentary Information and Research Service Library of Parliament Publication, 2009. Catalogue no. PRB 09-17E. [Online] www.parl.gc.ca/Content/LOP/ResearchPublications/prb0917-e.htm#a8

COLLINS, RANDALL. *The Credential Society: A Historical Sociology of Education and Stratification.* New York: Academic Press, 1979.

———. *Sociological Insight: An Introduction to Nonobvious Sociology.* New York: Oxford University Press, 1982.

COLLYMORE, YVETTE. "Migrant Street Children on the Rise in Central America." *Population Today.* Vol. 30, No. 2 (February/March 2002):1, 4.

COLMAN, S. *The Ethics of Artificial Uteruses: Implications for Reproduction and Abortion.* Burlington, VT: Ashgate Publishing Company, 2004.

COLTON, HELEN. *The Gift of Touch: How Physical Contact Improves Communication, Pleasure, and Health.* New York: Seaview/Putnam, 1983.

COMTE, AUGUSTE. *Auguste Comte and Positivism: The Essential Writings.* Gertrud Lenzer, ed. New York: Harper Torchbooks, 1975; orig. 1851–54.

CONFERENCE BOARD OF CANADA. *Performance and Potential, 2000–2001.* Ottawa: The Conference Board of Canada, 2000. [Online] www.conferenceboard.ca/pdfs/pp_00kf.pdf

———. *Hot Topic: Advanced Skills & Innovation: How Much Do Advanced Skills Affect Innovation?* 2011. http://sso.conferenceboard.ca/hcp/hot-topics/innovation.aspx

CONNETT, PAUL H. "The Disposable Society." In F. Herbert Bormann and Stephen R. Kellert, eds., *Ecology, Economics, and Ethics: The Broken Circle.* New Haven, CT: Yale University Press, 1991:99–122.

COOLEY, CHARLES HORTON. *Human Nature and the Social Order.* New York: Schocken Books, 1964; orig. 1902.

CORAK, M. "Do Poor Children Become Poor Adults?" In John Creedy and Guyonne Kalb, eds., *Dynamics of Inequality and Poverty.* St. Louis, MO: Elsevier, 2006a:143–88.

CORAK, MILES. "Equality of Opportunity and Inequality across the Generations: Challenges Ahead." *Horizons: Policy Research Initiative.* Vol. 8, No. 3 (April 2006b): 43–50.

CORPORATE LIBRARY. "Executive Compensation." 2010. www.thecorporatelibrary .com/info.php?id=60ec

CORRELL, SHELLEY J. " Gender and the Career Choice Process: The Role of Biased Self-Assessment." *American Journal of Sociology.* Vol. 106, No. 6 (May 2001): 1691–730.

CORRIGAN, P.W. "How Stigma Interferes with Mental Health Care." *American Psychologist.* Vol. 59 (2004):614–25.

CORRIGAN, P.W., S.A. KUWABARA, and J. O'SHAUGHNESSY. "The Public Stigma of Mental Illness and Drug Addiction: Findings from a Stratified Random Sample." *Journal of Social Work.* Vol. 9, No. 2 (2009):139–47.

CORTESE, ANTHONY J. *Provocateur: Images of Women and Minorities in Advertising.* Lanham, MD: Rowman & Littlefield, 1999.

COULOMBE, S., J.F. TREMBLAY, and S. MARCHAND. *Literacy Scores, Human Capital and Growth Across 14 OECD.* Ottawa: Statistics Canada, 2004.

COWLEY, GEOFFREY. "The Prescription That Kills." *Newsweek* (July 17, 1995):54.

COX, HARVEY. *The Secular City.* Rev. ed. New York: Macmillan, 1971; orig. 1965.

CQ PRESS ELECTRONIC LIBRARY. *Political Handbook of the World Online Edition.* May 15, 2010. www.cqpress.com/product/PH-World-2008-OE.html

CROSSETTE, BARBARA. "Female Genital Mutilation by Immigrants Is Becoming Cause for Concern in the U.S." *New York Times International* (December 10, 1995):11.

CROUSE, JAMES, and DALE TRUSHEIM. *The Case against the SAT.* Chicago: University of Chicago Press, 1988.

CROWLEY, DAVID. "Where Are We Now? Contours of the Internet in Canada." *Canadian Journal of Communication,* Vol. 27, No. 4 (2002):469–507.

CTIA. "Quick Facts." June 2009. www.ctia.org/media/industry_info/index.cfm/AID/ 10323

CUMMINGS, SCOTT, and THOMAS LAMBERT. "Anti-Hispanic and Anti-Asian Sentiments among African Americans." *Social Science Quarterly.* Vol. 78, No. 2 (June 1997):338–53.

CURRIE, ELLIOTT. *Confronting Crime: An American Challenge.* New York: Pantheon Books, 1985.

CURTIS, BRUCE. *Building the Educational State: Canada West, 1831–1871.* London, ON: Althouse Press, 1988.

CURTIS, JAMES E., DOUGLAS E. BAER, and EDWARD G. GRABB. "Nations of Joiners: Explaining Voluntary Association Membership in Democratic Societies." *American Sociological Review.* Vol. 66, No. 6 (December 2001):783–805.

CURTIS, JAMES E., EDWARD G. GRABB, and NEIL GUPPY. *Social Inequality in Canada.* Scarborough, ON: Prentice Hall, 1999.

CURTISS, SUSAN. *Genie: A Psycholinguistic Study of a Modern-Day "Wild Child."* New York: Academic Press, 1977.

DAHL, ROBERT A. *Who Governs?* New Haven, CT: Yale University Press, 1961.

———. *Dilemmas of Pluralist Democracy: Autonomy vs. Control.* New Haven, CT: Yale University Press, 1982.

DAHRENDORF, RALF. *Class and Class Conflict in Industrial Society.* Stanford, CA: Stanford University Press, 1959.

DALMIA, SHIKRA. "Obama and Big Labor." *Forbes* (October 29, 2008). www.forbes .com/2008/10/28/obama-card-check-oped-cx_sd_1029dalmia.html

DARLING, ROSALYN, and BENJAMIN BRYANT. "Stigma of Disability." In D. Clifton, ed., *Encyclopedia of Criminology and Deviant Behavior.* Philadelphia, PA: Brunner-Routledge, 2001: 482–85.

DARROCH, JACQUELINE E., ET AL. "Teenage Sexual and Reproductive Behavior in Developed Countries: Can More Progress Be Made?" 2001. [Online] Available May 30, 2005, at www.guttmacher.org/pubs/eurosynth_rpt.pdf

DARWIN, CHARLES. *On the Origin of Species by Means of Natural Selection, or the Preservation of Favoured Races in the Struggle for Life.* London: Murray, 1859.

DAUVERGNE, M. "Crime Statistics in Canada, 2007." *Juristat.* Vol. 28, No. 7 (2008). Catalogue no. 85-002-X. [Online] www.statcan.gc.ca/pub/85-002-x/85-002-x2008007-eng.pdf

DAUVERGNE, M., K. SCRIM, and S. BRENNAN. 2008. *Hate Crime in Canada 2006.* Catalogue no. 85F0033M—No. 17. Ottawa: Canadian Centre for Justice Statistics, 2008.

DAUVERGNE, M., and S. TURNER. "Police-Reported Crime Statistics in Canada, 2009." *Juristat.* Vol. 20, No. 2 (2010). Catalogue no. 85-002-X. [Online] www.statcan.gc .ca/pub/85-002-x/2010002/article/11292-eng.pdf

DAVIDSON, JULIA O'CONNELL. *Prostitution, Power, and Freedom.* Ann Arbor: University of Michigan Press, 1998.

DAVIES, CHRISTIE. *Ethnic Humor around the World: A Comparative Analysis.* Bloomington: Indiana University Press, 1990.

DAVIES, JAMES B., SUSANNA SANDSTRÖM, ANTHONY SHORROCKS, and EDWARD N. WOLFF. *The World Distribution of Household Wealth.* Discussion Paper No. 2008/03. Helsinki: United Nations University–World Institute for Development Economics Research. February 2008. www.wider.unu.edu/publications/working-papers/ discussion-papers/2008/en_GB/dp2008-03/

DAVIES, JAMES B., ANTHONY SHORROCKS, EDWARD N. WOLFF, and SUSANNA SANDSTRÖM. "The Level and Distribution of Global Household Wealth." *The Economic Journal.* Vol. 121, No. 551 (February 2010):223–54.

DAVIES, JAMES C. "Toward a Theory of Revolution." *American Sociological Review.* Vol. 27, No. 1 (February 1962):5–19.

DAVIES, MARK, and DENISE B. KANDEL. "Parental and Peer Influences on Adolescents' Educational Plans: Some Further Evidence." *American Journal of Sociology.* Vol. 87, No. 2 (September 1981):363–87.

DAVIES, S., and F. HAMMACK. "The Channeling of Student Competition in Higher Education: Comparing Canada and the U.S." *The Journal of Higher Education.* Vol. 76, No. 1 (2005):89–106.

DAVIES, SCOTT, and NEIL GUPPY. "Race and Canadian Education" in Vic Satzewich, ed., *Racism & Social Inequality in Canada.* Toronto: Thompson, 1998:131–55.

DAVIS, DONALD M., cited in "TV Is a Blonde, Blonde World." *American Demographics,* special issue: *Women Change Places.* 1993.

DAVIS, KATHY. "A Dubious Equality: Men, Women and Cosmetic Surgery." *Body & Society.* Vol. 8, No. 1 (2002):49–65.

DAVIS, KINGSLEY. "Extreme Social Isolation of a Child." *American Journal of Sociology.* Vol. 45, No. 4 (January 1940):554–65.

———. "Final Note on a Case of Extreme Isolation." *American Journal of Sociology.* Vol. 52, No. 5 (March 1947):432–37.

———. "Sexual Behavior." In Robert K. Merton and Robert Nisbet, eds., *Contemporary Social Problems.* 3rd ed. New York: Harcourt Brace Jovanovich, 1971:313–60.

DAVIS, KINGSLEY, and WILBERT MOORE. "Some Principles of Stratification." *American Sociological Review.* Vol. 10, No. 2 (April 1945):242–49.

DAVIS, SCOTT, and NEIL GUPPY. "Fields of Study, College Selectivity, and Student Inequalities in Higher Education." *Social Forces.* Vol. 75, No. 4 (June 1997): 1417–38.

DAWSON, LORNE. *Comprehending Cults: The Sociology of New Religious Movements.* Toronto: University of Toronto Press, 1998.

DAWSON, LORNE L., ed. *Cults in Context: Readings in the Study of New Religious Movements.* Toronto: Canadian Scholar's Press, 1996.

DEATH PENALTY INFORMATION CENTER. "Innocence and the Death Penalty." 2010. www. deathpenaltyinfo.org/innocence-and-death-penalty

DEBROUKER, PATRICE, and LAVAL LAVALLEÉ. "Getting Ahead: Does Your Parents' Education Count?" *Education Quarterly Review.* Statistics Canada Catalogue no. 81-003XIE. Vol. 5, No. 1 (August 1998):22–28.

DECARLO, SCOTT, ed. "The Global 2000," Forbes.com. April 8, 2009. www.forbes.com/ lists/2009/18/global-09_The-Global-2000_Rank.html

DECKER, M., JAY SILVERMAN, and A. RAJ. "Dating Violence and Sexually Transmitted Disease/HIV Testing and Diagnosis among Adolescent Females." *Pediatrics.* Vol. 116, No. 2 (2005):e272–e276.

DEDRICK, DENNIS K., and RICHARD E. YINGER. "MAD, SDI, and the Nuclear Arms Race." Unpublished manuscript. Georgetown, KY: Georgetown College, 1990.

DEFINA, ROBERT H., and THOMAS M. ARVANITES. "The Weak Effect of Imprisonment on Crime, 1971–1998." *Social Science Quarterly.* Vol. 83, No. 3 (September 2002): 635–53.

DELACROIX, JACQUES, and CHARLES C. RAGIN. "Structural Blockage: A Cross-National Study of Economic Dependency, State Efficacy, and Underdevelopment." *American Journal of Sociology.* Vol. 86, No. 6 (May 1981):1311–47.

DE LINT, W. "Public Order Policing in Canada: An Analysis of Operations in Recent High Stakes Events." Unpublished paper. 2005.

DELUCA, TOM. "Joe the Bookie and the Class Voting Gap." *American Demographics.* Vol. 20, No. 11 (November 1998):26–29.

DEMERATH, N.J., III. "Who Now Debates Functionalism? From *System, Change,* and *Conflict* to 'Culture, Choice, and Praxis.'" *Sociological Forum.* Vol. 11, No. 2 (June 1996):333–45.

DEMUTH, STEPHEN, and DARRELL STEFFENSMEIER. "The Impact of Gender and Race-Ethnicity in the Pretrial Release Process." *Social Problems.* Vol. 51, No. 2 (May 2004):222–42.

DEPARTMENT OF JUSTICE CANADA. *Canadian Charter of Rights and Freedoms.* 1982. http://laws-lois.justice.gc.ca/eng/charter/

DERBER, CHARLES. *The Wilding of America: Money, Mayhem,* and *the New American Dream.* 3rd ed. New York: Worth, 2004.

DEUTSCHER, IRWIN. *Making a Difference: The Practice of Sociology.* New Brunswick, NJ: Transaction, 1999.

DEVINE, JOEL A. "State and State Expenditure: Determinants of Social Investment and Social Consumption Spending in the Postwar United States." *American Sociological Review.* Vol. 50, No. 2 (April 1985):150–65.

DEVRIES, R., C. BENOIT, E. VAN TEIJLINGEN, and SIRPA WREDE, eds. *Birth by Design: The Social Shaping of Maternity Care in Northern Europe and North America.* London: Routledge, 2001.

DICKASON, OLIVE PATRICIA. *Canada's First Nations: A History of Founding Peoples from Earliest Times.* Toronto: McClelland and Stewart, 1992.

DICKLER, JESSICA. "Best-Paid Executives: The Gender Gap Exaggerated." *Fortune: 50 Most Powerful Women in Business.* October 3, 2007. http://money.cnn.com/2007/ 10/02/ news/newsmakers/mpwpay/index.htm

DIDERICHSEN, F., M. WHITEHEAD, B. BURSTROM, and M. ABERG. "Sweden and Britain: The Impact of Policy Context on Inequities in Health." In T. Evans, M. Whitehead, F. Diderichsen, A. Bhuya, and M. Wirth, eds., *Challenging Inequities in Health: From Ethics to Action.* New York: Oxford University Press, 2001:241–55.

DISHION, T.J., and L.D. OWEN. "A Longitudinal Analysis of Friendships and Substance Use: Bidirectional Influence from Adolescence to Adulthood." *Developmental Psychology.* Vol. 38, No. 4 (2002):480–91.

DIXON, WILLIAM J., and TERRY BOSWELL. "Dependency, Disarticulation, and Denominator Effects: Another Look at Foreign Capital Penetration." *American Journal of Sociology.* Vol. 102, No. 2 (September 1996):543–62.

DOBYNS, HENRY F. "An Appraisal of Techniques with a New Hemispheric Estimate." *Current Anthropology.* Vol. 7, No. 4 (October 1966):395–446.

DOLLARD, JOHN, ET AL. *Frustration and Aggression.* New Haven, CT: Yale University Press, 1939.

DONAHUE, JOHN J., III, and STEVEN D. LEVITT. Research cited in "New Study Claims Abortion Is behind Decrease in Crime." *Population Today.* Vol. 28, No. 1 (January 2000):1, 4.

DONALD, LELAND. *Aboriginal Slavery on the Northwest Coast of North America.* Berkeley: University of California Press, 1997.

DONOVAN, VIRGINIA K., and RONNIE LITTENBERG. "Psychology of Women: Feminist Therapy." In Barbara Haber, ed., *The Women's Annual, 1981: The Year in Review.* Boston: Hall, 1982:211–35.

DOWNEY, DOUGLAS B., PAUL T. VON HIPPEL, and BECKETT A. BROH. "Are Schools the Great Equalizer? Cognitive Inequality during the Summer Months and School Year." *American Sociological Review.* Vol. 59, No. 5 (October 2004):613–35.

DOYLE, JAMES A. *The Male Experience.* Dubuque, IA: Brown, 1983.

DREW, S., M. MILLS, and B. GASSAWAY. *Dirty Work: The Social Construction of Taint.* Waco, TX: Baylor University Press, 2007.

DROLET, MARIE. "The Persistent Gap: New Evidence of the Canadian Gender Wage Gap." Ottawa: Statistics Canada, Business and Labour Market Analysis Division. Catalogue no. 11F0019MPE, No. 157. 2001. [Online] www.statcan.ca/english/ research/11F0019MIE/11F0019MIE2001157.pdf

DRUDY, S., and M. CHATHAIN. "Gender Effects in Classroom Interaction: Data Collection, Self-Analysis, and Reflection." *Evaluation and Research Education.* Vol. 16, No. 1 (2002):34–50.

DU BOIS, W.E.B. *The Philadelphia Negro: A Social Study.* New York: Schocken Books, 1967; orig. 1899.

DUBOS, RENÉ. *Man Adapting.* Enlarged ed. New Haven, CT: Yale University Press, 1980.

DU MONT, J., and M.J. MCGREGOR. "Sexual Assault in the Lives of Urban Sex Workers: A Descriptive and Comparative Analysis." *Women & Health.* Vol. 39 (2004):79–96.

DUNCAN, CYNTHIA M. *Worlds Apart: Why Poverty Persists in Rural America.* New Haven, CT: Yale University Press, 1999.

DUNCAN, GREG J., W. JEAN YEUNG, JEANNE BROOKS-GUNN, and JUDITH R. SMITH. "How Much Does Childhood Poverty Affect the Life Chances of Children?" *American Sociological Review.* Vol. 63, No. 3 (June 1998):406–23.

DUNN, S. "Police Officers Murdered in the Line of Duty, 1961 to 2009." *Juristat.* Vol. 30, No. 1 (2010). Catalogue no. 85-002-X. [Online] www.statcan.gc.ca/pub/ 85-002-x/2010003/article/11354-eng.pdf

DURKHEIM, EMILE. *The Division of Labor in Society.* New York: Free Press, 1964a; orig. 1893.

———. *The Rules of Sociological Method.* New York: Free Press, 1964b; orig. 1895.

———. *The Elementary Forms of Religious Life.* New York: Free Press, 1965; orig. 1915.

———. *Suicide.* New York: Free Press, 1966; orig. 1897.

DWORKIN, ANDREA. *Intercourse.* New York: Free Press, 1987.

EAGLY, A., and M. JOHANNESEN-SCHMIDT. "The Leadership Styles of Women and Men." *Journal of Social Issues.* Vol. 57, No. 4 (2001):781–97.

EAGLY, ALICE H., MARY C. JOHANNESEN-SCHMIDT, and MARLOES L. VAN ENGEN. "Transformational, Transactional, and Laissez-Faire Leadership Styles: A Meta-Analysis Comparing Women and Men." *Psychological Bulletin.* Vol. 129, No. 4 (July 2003):569–91.

EBAUGH, HELEN ROSE FUCHS. *Becoming an Ex: The Process of Role Exit.* Chicago: University of Chicago Press, 1988.

EBOH, CAMILLUS. "Nigerian Woman Loses Appeal against Stoning Death." *Yahoo! News* (August 19, 2002). http://news.yahoo.com

EDIN, KATHRYN, and LAURA LEIN. "Work, Welfare, and Single Mothers' Economic Survival Strategies." *American Sociological Review.* Vol. 62, No. 2 (April 1996): 253–66.

EDWARDS, TAMALA M. "Flying Solo." *Time* (August 28, 2000):47–55.

EHRENREICH, BARBARA. *The Hearts of Men: American Dreams and the Flight from Commitment.* Garden City, NY: Anchor Books, 1983.

———. "The Real Truth about the Female Body." *Time* (March 15, 1999):56–65.

———. *Nickel and Dimed: On (Not) Getting By in America.* New York: Henry Holt, 2001.

EICHLER, MARGRIT. *Nonsexist Research Methods: A Practical Guide.* Winchester, MA: Unwin Hyman, 1988.

———. *Family Shifts: Families, Policies, and Gender Equality.* Toronto: Oxford University Press, 1997.

EKMAN, PAUL. "Biological and Cultural Contributions to Body and Facial Movements in the Expression of Emotions." In A. Rorty, ed., *Explaining Emotions.* Berkeley: University of California Press, 1980a:73–101.

———. *Face of Man: Universal Expression in a New Guinea Village.* New York: Garland Press, 1980b.

ELECTIONS CANADA. Eventresults.txt [Electronic data file accessed June 19, 2011]. 2011. http://enr.elections.ca/DownloadResults.aspx

ELIAS, JAMES, VERN BULLOUGH, VERONICA ELIAS, and JOYCELYN ELDERS, eds. *Prostitution: On Whores, Hustlers, and Johns.* New York: Prometheus Books, 1998.

ELIAS, ROBERT. *The Politics of Victimization: Victims, Victimology, and Human Rights.* New York: Oxford University Press, 1986.

ELLIOTT, DELBERT S., and SUZANNE S. AGETON. "Reconciling Race and Class Differences in Self-Reported and Official Estimates of Delinquency." *American Sociological Review.* Vol. 45, No. 1 (February 1980):95–110.

ELLISON, CHRISTOPHER G., JOHN P. BARTKOWSKI, and MICHELLE L. SEGAL. "Do Conservative Protestant Parents Spank More Often? Further Evidence from the National Survey of Families and Households." *Social Science Quarterly.* Vol. 77, No. 3 (September 1996):663–73.

ELSON, JEAN. *Am I Still a Woman? Hysterectomy and Gender Identity.* Philadelphia, PA: Temple University Press, 2004.

EMERSON, JOAN P. "Behavior in Private Places: Sustaining Definitions of Reality in Gynecological Examinations." In H.P. Dreitzel, ed., *Recent Sociology.* Vol. 2. New York: Collier, 1970:74–97.

EMERSON, MICHAEL O., GEORGE YANCEY, and KAREN J. CHAI. "Does Race Matter in Residential Segregation? Exploring the Preferences of White Americans." *American Sociological Review.* Vol. 66, No. 6 (December 2001):922–35.

ENCYCLOPEDIA OF MUSIC IN CANADA." Rock 'n' roll and rock music, Anglo-Canadian." 2011. www.thecanadianencyclopedia.com/index.cfm?PgNm=tce&Params=U1ARTU0003007

ENEMARK, DANIEL. "Backstory: Tapping the World." *Christian Science Monitor.* March 22, 2006, edition. [Online] www.csmonitor.com/2006/0322/p20s01-sten.html

ENGELS, FRIEDRICH. *The Origin of the Family.* Chicago: Kerr, 1902; orig. 1884.

ENGLAND, PAULA. "Three Reviews on Marriage." *Contemporary Sociology.* Vol. 30, No. 6 (November 2001):564–65.

ENGLAND, PAULA, JOAN M. HERMSEN, and DAVID A. COTTER. "The Devaluation of Women's Work: A Comment on Tam." *American Journal of Sociology.* Vol. 105, No. 6 (May 2000):1741–60.

ENSIGN, JOSEPHINE, and MICHELLE BELL. "Illness Experiences of Homeless Youth." *Qualitative Health Research.* Vol. 14, No. 9 (2004):1239–54.

ENVIRONICS RESEARCH GROUP. "Canadians for Equal Marriage June 2006." (May 25–June 2, 2006) [Online] http://erg.environics.net/news/equal_marriage/

ERIKSON, KAI T. *Everything in Its Path: Destruction of Community in the Buffalo Creek Flood.* New York: Simon & Schuster, 1976.

———. *A New Species of Trouble: Explorations in Disaster, Trauma, and Community.* New York: Norton, 1994.

———. *Wayward Puritans: A Study in the Sociology of Deviance.* New York: Wiley, 2005b; orig. 1966.

———. "The Day the World Turned Red: A Report on the People of Utrik", *The Yale Review,* Volume 99, Number 1, 2011.

ERIKSON, ROBERT S., NORMAN R. LUTTBEG, and KENT L. TEDIN. *American Public Opinion: Its Origins, Content, and Impact.* 2nd ed. New York: Wiley, 1980.

ETOWA, J., J. WIENS, W.T. BERNARD, and B. CLOW. "Determinants of Black Women's Health in Rural and Remote Communities." *Canadian Journal of Nursing Research.* Vol. 39 (2007):56–76.

ETZIONI, AMITAI. *A Comparative Analysis of Complex Organization: On Power, Involvement, and Their Correlates.* Rev. and enlarged ed. New York: Free Press, 1975.

———. "How to Make Marriage Matter." *Time.* Vol. 142, No. 10 (September 6, 1993):76.

———. "The Responsive Community: A Communitarian Perspective." *American Sociological Review.* Vol. 61, No. 1 (February 1996):1–11.

———. *My Brother's Keeper: A Memoir and a Message.* Lanham, MD: Rowman & Littlefield, 2003.

EUROPEAN UNION. EUROPEAN COMMUNITIES STATISTICAL OFFICE. "Eurostat." 2010. http://epp.eurostat.ec.europa.eu/portal/

EXECUTIVE LEADERSHIP COUNCIL. "Women and Minorities on *Fortune* 100 Boards." January 28, 2008. www.elcinfo.com/reports.php

FALLON, A.E., and P. ROZIN. "Sex Differences in Perception of Desirable Body Shape." *Journal of Abnormal Psychology.* Vol. 94, No. 1 (1985):100–05.

FALLON, M., and L. JOME. "An Exploration of Gender-Role Expectations and Conflict among Women Rugby Players." *Psychology of Women Quarterly.* Vol. 31 (2007):311–21.

FEAGIN, JOE R., and VERA HERNÁN. *Liberation Sociology.* Boulder, CO: Westview Press, 2001.

FEDERAL BUREAU OF INVESTIGATION. CRIMINAL JUSTICE INFORMATION SERVICES DIVISION. *Crime in the United States, 2007.* 2008. www.fbi.gov/ucr/cius2007/index.html

———. *Crime in the United States, 2008.* 2009. www.fbi.gov/ucr/cius2008/index.html

FEINSTEIN, J. "The Relationship between Socioeconomic Status and Health: A Review of the Literature." *Milbank Quarterly.* Vol. 71 (1993):279–322.

FELLMAN, BRUCE. "Taking the Measure of Children's TV." *Yale Alumni Magazine* (April 1995):46–51.

"Female Opinion and Defense since September 11th." *Society.* Vol. 39, No. 3 (March/April 2002):2.

FENG HOU and JOHN MYLES. "The Changing Role of Education in the Marriage Market: Assortive Marriage in Canada and the United States since the 1970s." *Canadian Journal of Sociology.* Vol. 33, No. 2 (2008):335–64.

FERGUSSON, D., F. VITARO, B. WANNER, and M. BRENDGEN. "Protective and Compensatory Factors Mitigating the Influence of Deviant Friends on Delinquent Behaviours during Early Adolescence." *Journal of Adolescence.* Vol. 30 (2007): 33–50.

FERNANDEZ, ROBERTO M., and NANCY WEINBERG. "Sifting and Sorting: Personal Contacts and Hiring in a Retail Bank." *American Sociological Review.* Vol. 62, No. 6 (December 1997):883–902.

FERRARO, KENNETH F., and JESSICA A. KELLEY-MOORE. "Cumulative Disadvantage and Health: Long-Term Consequences of Obesity?" *American Sociological Review.* Vol. 68, No. 5 (October 2003):707–29.

FERREE, MYRA MARX, and BETH B. HESS. *Controversy and Coalition: The New Feminist Movement across Four Decades of Change.* 3rd ed. New York: Routledge, 1995.

FETTO, JOHN. "Down for the Count." *American Demographics.* Vol. 21, No. 11 (November 1999):46–47.

———. "Me Gusta TV." *American Demographics.* Vol. 24, No. 11 (January 2003):14–15.

FILION, P., K. MCSPURREN, and B. APPLEBY. "Wasted Density? The Impact of Toronto's Residential Density Distribution Policies on Transit Use and Walking." *Environment and Planning A.* Vol. 38 (2006):1367–92.

FINN, CHESTER E., JR., and REBECCA L. GAU. "New Ways of Education." *The Public Interest.* Vol. 130 (Winter 1998):79–92.

FIREBAUGH, GLENN. "Growth Effects of Foreign and Domestic Investment." *American Journal of Sociology.* Vol. 98, No. 1 (July 1992):105–30.

———. "Does Foreign Capital Harm Poor Nations? New Estimates Based on Dixon and Boswell's Measures of Capital Penetration." *American Journal of Sociology.* Vol. 102, No. 2 (September 1996):563–75.

FIREBAUGH, GLENN, and FRANK D. BECK. "Does Economic Growth Benefit the Masses? Growth, Dependence, and Welfare in the Third World." *American Sociological Review.* Vol. 59, No. 5 (October 1994):631–53.

FIREBAUGH, GLENN, and DUMITRU SANDU. "Who Supports Marketization and Democratization in Post-Communist Romania?" *Sociological Forum.* Vol. 13, No. 3 (September 1998):521–41.

FIRESTONE, S. *The Dialectic of Sex.* New York: William Morrow and Co., 1970.

FISHER, ELIZABETH. *Woman's Creation: Sexual Evolution and the Shaping of Society.* Garden City, NY: Anchor/Doubleday, 1979.

FISHER, ROGER, and WILLIAM URY. "Getting to Yes." In William M. Evan and Stephen Hilgartner, eds., *The Arms Race and Nuclear War.* Englewood Cliffs, NJ: Prentice Hall, 1988:261–68.

FLAHERTY, MICHAEL G. "A Formal Approach to the Study of Amusement in Social Interaction." *Studies in Symbolic Interaction.* Vol. 5. New York: JAI Press, 1984:71–82.

———. "Two Conceptions of the Social Situation: Some Implications of Humor." *Sociological Quarterly.* Vol. 31, No. 1 (Spring 1990):93–106.

FLOWERS, PAUL, MARK DAVIS, GRAHAM HART, MARSHA ROSENGARTEN, JAMIE FRANKIS, and JOHN IMRIE. "Diagnosis and Stigma and Identity amongst HIV Positive Black Africans Living in the UK." *Psychology & Health.* Vol. 21, No. 1 (2006):109–22.

FONDA, DAREN. "The Male Minority." *Time* (December 11, 2000):58–60.

FORBES. "Richest Canadians on Forbes." 2009. [Online] www.forbes.com/wealth/billionaires#p_1_s_arank_-1__-1

FORD, CLELLAN S., and FRANK A. BEACH. *Patterns of Sexual Behavior.* New York: Harper Bros., 1951.

FORTUNE. "Rankings: 2010 Fortune 500." 2010. http://money.cnn.com/magazines/fortune/rankings/

FOUCAULT, MICHEL. *The History of Sexuality: An Introduction.* Vol. 1. Robert Hurley, trans. New York: Vintage, 1990; orig. 1978.

FOWLER, BREE. "GM 3Q Global Sales Drop 11 Percent, Trail Toyota." *USA Today,* October 29, 2008. www.usatoday.com/money/economy/2008-10-29-1630144436_x.htm

FOX, B. *When Couples Become Parents: The Creation of Gender in the Transition to Parenthood.* Toronto: University of Toronto Press, 2009.

FOX, BONNIE, ed. *Family Patterns/Gender Relations.* Toronto: Oxford University Press, 2001.

FOX, BONNIE, and MEG LUXTON. "Conceptualizing Family." In Bonnie Fox, ed., *Family Patterns/Gender Relations.* Toronto: Oxford University Press, 2001:22–33.

FOX, JUSTIN. "Why Denmark Loves Globalization." *Time* (November 15, 2007). www.time.com/time/magazine/article/0,9171,1684528,00.html

FRAGER, RUTH A. *Sweatshop Strife: Class, Ethnicity, and Gender in the Jewish Labour Movement in Toronto, 1900–1939.* Toronto: University of Toronto Press, 1992.

FRANCIS, M. "The 'Civilizing' of Indigenous People in Nineteenth-Century Canada." *World History.* Vol. 9, No. 1 (1998):51–87.

FRANK, ANDRÉ GUNDER. *On Capitalist Underdevelopment.* Bombay: Oxford University Press, 1975.

———. Crisis in the World Economy. New York: Holmes & Meier, 1980.

———. Reflections on the World Economic Crisis. New York: Monthly Review Press, 1981.

FRAZIER, E. FRANKLIN. Black Bourgeoisie: The Rise of a New Middle Class. New York: Free Press, 1965.

FREEDMAN, ESTELLE B. No Turning Back: The History of Feminism and the Future of Women. New York: Ballantine Books, 2002.

FREEDOM HOUSE. "Freedom in the World Comparative and Historical Data." Freedom House, Inc., 2011. [Online] Available at http://www.freedomhouse.org/template.cfm?page=363&year=2011

FREEDOM HOUSE. "Freedom in the World Comparative and Historical Data." 2010. www.freedomhouse.org/template.cfm?page=439

FRENCH, MARILYN. Beyond Power: On Women, Men, and Morals. New York: Summit Books, 1985.

FRIEDMAN, MEYER, and RAY H. ROSENMAN. Type A Behavior and Your Heart. New York: Fawcett Crest, 1974.

FROHLICH, K., N. ROSS, and C. RICHMOND. "Health Disparities in Canada Today: Some Evidence and a Theoretical Framework." Health Policy. Vol. 79, Nos. 2–3 (2006):132–43.

FULLER, REX, and RICHARD SCHOENBERGER. "The Gender Salary Gap: Do Academic Achievement, Intern Experience, and College Major Make a Difference?" Social Science Quarterly. Vol. 72, No. 4 (December 1991):715–26.

FURSTENBERG, FRANK F., JR., and ANDREW CHERLIN. Divided Families: What Happens to Children When Parents Part. Cambridge, MA: Harvard University Press, 1991.

———. "Children's Adjustment to Divorce." In Bonnie J. Fox, ed., Family Patterns, Gender Relations. 2nd ed. New York: Oxford University Press, 2001.

GAGNÉ, PATRICIA, RICHARD TEWKSBURY, and DEANNA MCGAUGHEY. "Coming Out and Crossing Over: Identity Formation and Proclamation in a Transgender Community." Gender and Society. Vol. 11, No. 4 (August 1997):478–508.

GALANO, ANA MARIA. "Land Hungry in Brazil." Courier (July/August 1998). www.unesco.org/courier/1998_08/uk/somm/intro.htm

GALLUP ORGANIZATION, Special Reports: Global Study of Family Values. Princeton, NJ: The Gallup Organization, November 7, 1997.

GAMORAN, ADAM. "The Variable Effects of High-School Tracking." American Sociological Review. Vol. 57, No. 6 (December 1992):812–28.

GANS, HERBERT J. People and Plans: Essays on Urban Problems and Solutions. New York: Basic Books, 1968.

GARFINKEL, HAROLD. "Conditions of Successful Degradation Ceremonies." American Journal of Sociology. Vol. 61, No. 2 (March 1956):420–24.

———. Studies in Ethnomethodology. Cambridge, MA: Polity Press, 1967.

GAVE, ELENI N. "In the Indigenous Muxe Culture of Mexico's Oaxaca State, Alternative Notions of Sexuality Are Not Only Accepted, They're Celebrated." Travel and Leisure (November 2005. [Online] Available June 15, 2009, at http://travelandleisure.com/articles/stepping-out/page/2/print

GEDDES, J. "What Canadians Think of Sikhs, Jews, Christians, Muslims." Maclean's (April 28, 2009). www2.macleans.ca/2009/04/28/what-canadians-think-of-sikhs-jews-christians-muslims/

GEE, ELLEN. "Population." In Robert Hagedorn, ed., Sociology. 4th ed. Toronto: Holt, Rinehart & Winston, 1990:195–226.

GEERTZ, CLIFFORD. "Common Sense as a Cultural System." Antioch Review. Vol. 33, No. 1 (Spring 1975):5–26.

GERBER, THEODORE P., and MICHAEL HOUT. "More Shock than Therapy: Market Transition, Employment, and Income in Russia, 1991–1995." American Journal of Sociology. Vol. 104, No. 1 (July 1998):1–50.

GERLACH, MICHAEL L. The Social Organization of Japanese Business. Berkeley: University of California Press, 1992.

GESCHWENDER, JAMES A. Racial Stratification in America. Dubuque, IA: Brown, 1978.

GEWERTZ, DEBORAH. "A Historical Reconsideration of Female Dominance among the Chambri of Papua New Guinea." American Ethnologist. Vol. 8, No. 1 (1981):94–106.

GHOSH, RATNA. Redefining Multicultural Education. Toronto: Harcourt Brace Canada, 1996.

GIBBS, NANCY. "The Pulse of America along the River." Time (July 10, 2000):42–46.

———. "What Kids (Really) Need." Time (April 30, 2001):48–49.

GIDDENS, ANTHONY. The Transformation of Intimacy. Cambridge: Polity Press, 1992.

GILBERT, NEIL. "Family Life: Sold on Work." Society. Vol. 42, No. 3 (2005):12–17.

GILLESPIE, MARK. "Trends Show Bathing and Exercise Up, TV Watching Down." Gallup.com. January 2000. www.gallup.com/poll/3352/Trends-Show-BathingExercise-Up-Watching-Down.aspx

GILLIGAN, CAROL. In a Different Voice: Psychological Theory and Women's Development. Cambridge, MA: Harvard University Press, 1982.

GILLON, RAANAN. "Euthanasia in the Netherlands: Down the Slippery Slope?" Journal of Medical Ethics. Vol. 25, No. 1 (February 1999):3–4.

GIMENEZ, MARTHA E. "Silence in the Classroom: Some Thoughts about Teaching in the 1980s." Teaching Sociology. Vol. 17, No. 2 (April 1989):184–91.

GINSBURG, FAYE, and ANNA LOWENHAUPT TSING, eds. Uncertain Terms: Negotiating Gender in American Culture. Boston: Beacon Press, 1990.

GIOVANNINI, MAUREEN. "Female Anthropologist and Male Informant: Gender Conflict in a Sicilian Town." In John J. Macionis and Nijole V. Benokraitis, eds., Seeing Ourselves: Classic, Contemporary, and Cross-Cultural Readings in Sociology. 2nd ed. Englewood Cliffs, NJ: Prentice Hall, 1992:27–32.

GLEICK, ELIZABETH. "The Marker We've Been Waiting For." Time (April 7, 1997):28–42.

GLOBAL MARCH AGAINST CHILD LABOUR. Worst Forms of Child Labour Report, 2005. 2008. www.globalmarch.org/worstformsreport/world/index.html

GLOBE AND MAIL, THE. "Judge Decriminalizes Prostitution in Ontario, but Ottawa Mulls Appeal." September 28, 2010. www.theglobeandmail.com/news/national/ontario/judge-decriminalizesprostitution-in-ontario/article1730433/?cmpid=rss1

———. "Do School Hugging Bans Go Too Far?" January 20, 2011. www.theglobeandmail.com/life/parenting/teens/teen-discipline/do-school-hugging-bans-go-too-far/article1877794/page2/

GLUECK, SHELDON, and ELEANOR GLUECK. Unraveling Juvenile Delinquency. New York: Commonwealth Fund, 1950.

GOESLING, BRIAN. "Changing Income Inequalities within and between Nations: New Evidence." American Sociological Review. Vol. 66, No. 5 (October 2001):745–61.

GOFFMAN, ERVING. The Presentation of Self in Everyday Life. Garden City, NY: Anchor Books, 1959.

———. Asylums: Essays on the Social Situation of Mental Patients and Other Inmates. Garden City, NY: Anchor Books, 1961.

———. Stigma: Notes on the Management of Spoiled Identity. Englewood Cliffs, NJ: Prentice Hall, 1963.

———. Interactional Ritual: Essays on Face to Face Behavior. Garden City, NY: Anchor Books, 1967.

———. Gender Advertisements. New York: Harper Colophon, 1979.

GOLDBERG, BERNARD. Bias: A CBS Insider Exposes How the Media Distort the News. Washington, DC: Regnery, 2002.

GOLDBERG, STEVEN. The Inevitability of Patriarchy. New York: Morrow, 1974.

GOLDBERGER, PAUL. Lecture delivered at Kenyon College, September 22, 2002.

GOLDEN, FREDERIC, and MICHAEL D. LEMONICK. "The Race Is Over." Time (July 3, 2000):18–23.

GOLDSMITH, H.H. "Genetic Influences on Personality from Infancy." Child Development. Vol. 54, No. 2 (April 1983):331–35.

GOLDSTEIN, JOSHUA R., and CATHERINE T. KENNEY. "Marriage Delayed or Marriage Forgone? New Cohort Forecasts of First Marriage for U.S. Women." American Sociological Review. Vol. 66, No. 4 (August 2001):506–19.

GOODE, WILLIAM J. "The Theoretical Importance of Love." American Sociological Review. Vol. 24, No. 1 (February 1959):38–47.

———. "Encroachment, Charlatanism, and the Emerging Profession: Psychology, Sociology, and Medicine." American Sociological Review. Vol. 25, No. 6 (December 1960):902–14.

GORDON, JAMES S. "The Paradigm of Holistic Medicine." In Arthur C. Hastings et al., eds., Health for the Whole Person: The Complete Guide to Holistic Medicine. Boulder, CO: Westview Press, 1980:3–27.

GORDON, SOL, and CRAIG W. SNYDER. Personal Issues in Human Sexuality: A Guidebook for Better Sexual Health. 2nd ed. Boston: Allyn & Bacon, 1989.

GORE, AL. An Inconvenient Truth: The Crisis of Global Warming. Emmaus, PA: Rodale Books, 2006.

GORMAN, CHRISTINE. "Stressed-Out Kids." Time (December 25, 2000):168.

GOTHAM, KEVIN FOX. "Race, Mortgage Lending, and Loan Rejections in a U.S. City." Sociological Focus. Vol. 31, No. 4 (October 1998):391–405.

GOTTFREDSON, MICHAEL R., and TRAVIS HIRSCHI. "National Crime Control Policies." Society. Vol. 32, No. 2 (January/February 1995):30–36.

GOTTMANN, JEAN. Megalopolis. New York: Twentieth Century Fund, 1961.

GOULD, STEPHEN J. "Evolution as Fact and Theory." *Discover* (May 1981):35–37.

GOYDER, J. *The Prestige Squeeze*. Montreal: McGill-Queen's University Press, 2009, Table 4-1, pp. 106-10.

GRABB, E., and N. GUPPY. *Social Inequality in Canada: Patterns, Problems & Policies*. 5th ed. Don Mills, ON: Pearson Education Canada, 2009.

GRACE, A., and K. WELLS, "The Marc Hall Prom Predicament: Queer Individual Rights v. Institutional Church Rights in Canadian Public Education." *Canadian Journal of Education*. Vol. 28, No. 3 (2005):237–70.

GRANT, KAREN R. "The Inverse Care Law in the Context of Universal Free Health Insurance in Canada: Toward Meeting Health Needs through Public Policy." *Sociological Focus*. Vol. 17, No. 2 (April 1984):137–55.

GRAYBOW, MARTHA. "Women Directors Help Boost the Bottom Line." *Yahoo! News* (October 1, 2007). http://news.yahoo.com

GREELEY, ANDREW M. *Religious Change in America*. Cambridge, MA: Harvard University Press, 1989.

———. "Symposium: Neo-Darwinism and Its Discontents." *Society*. Vol. 45, No. 2 (2008):162–63.

GREEN, GARY PAUL, LEANN M. TIGGES, and DANIEL DIAZ. "Racial and Ethnic Differences in Job-Search Strategies in Atlanta, Boston, and Los Angeles." *Social Science Quarterly*. Vol. 80, No. 2 (June 1999):263–90.

GREENBERG, DAVID F. *The Construction of Homosexuality*. Chicago: University of Chicago Press, 1988.

GREENHOUSE, STEVEN. "Many Entry-Level Workers Find Pinch of Rough Market." *New York Times* (September 4, 2006). www.nytimes.com/2006/09/04/us/04labor.html

GREENSPAN, STANLEY I. *The Four-Thirds Solution: Solving the Child-Care Crisis in America*. Cambridge, MA: Perseus, 2001.

GREENSPOON, EDWARD. "Pay-Equity Costs Too High: Chrétien." *Globe and Mail* (August 18, 1998):A3.

GRIER, PETER. "How to Slow the Spread of the Bomb." *Christian Science Monitor* (June 5, 2006). http://news.yahoo.com/s/csm/20060605

GROSS, JANE. "New Challenge of Youth: Growing Up in a Gay Home." *New York Times* (February 11, 1991):A1, B7.

GU, BAOCHANG, ZHENZHEN ZHENG, FENG WANG, and YONG CAI. "Globalization, Policy Intervention, and Reproduction: Below Replacement Fertility in China." (2007). Annual Meeting of the Population Association of America.

GUINDON, HUBERT. "Quebec and the Canadian Question." In James Curtis and Lorne Tepperman, eds., *Images of Canada: The Sociological Tradition*. Scarborough, ON: Prentice-Hall, Inc., 1990:30–41.

GUTIERREZ, CARL. "Bear Stearns Announces More Job Cuts." *Forbes* (October 3, 2007). www.forbes.com/markets/2007/10/03/bear-stearns-layoffs-markets-equitycx_cg_1003markets23.html

GWARTNEY-GIBBS, PATRICIA A., JEAN STOCKARD, and SUSANNE BOHMER. "Learning Courtship Aggression: The Influence of Parents, Peers, and Personal Experiences." *Family Relations*. Vol. 36, No. 3 (July 1987):276–82.

GWYNNE, S.C., and JOHN F. DICKERSON. "Lost in the E-Mail." *Time* (April 21, 1997):88–90.

HABERMAS, JÜRGEN. *Toward a Rational Society: Student Protest, Science, and Politics*. Jeremy J. Shapiro, trans. Boston: Beacon Press, 1970.

HABTU, ROMAN, and ANDRIJA POPOVIC. "Informal Caregivers: Balancing Work and Life Responsibilities." *Horizons*. Vol. 8 (April 2006):27–34.

HACKEY, ROBERT B. "Competing Explanations of Voter Turnout among American Blacks." *Social Science Quarterly*. Vol. 73, No. 1 (March 1992):71–89.

HACKLER, JIM. "Criminalizing Sex." In Jim Hackler, ed., *Canadian Criminology: Strategies and Perspectives*. Scarborough, ON: Prentice Hall Canada, 1999:254–67.

HADAWAY, C. KIRK, PENNY LONG MARLER, and MARK CHAVES. " What the Polls Don't Show: A Closer Look at U.S. Church Attendance." *American Sociological Review*. Vol. 58, No. 6 (December 1993):741–52.

HADDEN, JEFFREY K., and CHARLES E. SWAIN. *Prime-Time Preachers: The Rising Power of Televangelism*. Reading, MA: Addison-Wesley, 1981.

HAGAN, JACQUELINE MARIA. "Social Networks, Gender, and Immigrant Incorporation: Resources and Restraints." *American Sociological Review*. Vol. 63, No. 1 (February 1998):55–67.

HAGAN, JOHN, and HOLLY FOSTER. "Profiles of Punishment and Privilege: Secret and Disputed Deviance during the Racialized Transition to American Adulthood." *Crime, Law, and Social Change*. Vol. 46 (2006):65–85.

HAGAN, JOHN, and BILL MCCARTHY. *Mean Streets: Youth Crime and Homelessness*. New York: Cambridge University Press, 1997.

HAGAN, JOHN, and FIONA KAY. *Gender in Practice: A Study of Lawyers' Lives*. New York Oxford University Press, 1995.

HALBERSTAM, DAVID. *The Reckoning*. New York: Avon Books, 1986.

HALL, JOHN R., and MARY JO NEITZ. *Culture: Sociological Perspectives*. Englewood Cliffs, NJ: Prentice Hall, 1993.

HALL, M., D. LASBY, S. AYER, and W. GIBBONS. *Caring Canadians, Involved Canadians: Highlights from the 2007 Canada Survey of Giving, Volunteering and Participating*. Ottawa: Statistics Canada, 2009.

HALL, STUART M. *Policing the Crisis: Mugging, the State, and Law and Order*. London: Macmillan. 1978.

HALLGRIMSDOTTIR, H., R. PHILLIPS, and C. BENOIT. "Fallen Women and Rescued Girls: Social Stigma and Media Narratives of the Sex Industry in Victoria, BC, from 1980 to 2005." *Canadian Review of Sociology and Anthropology*. Special Issue, Vol. 43, No. 3 (2006):265–80.

HAMER, DEAN, and PETER COPELAND. *The Science of Desire: The Search for the Gay Gene and the Biology of Behavior*. New York: Simon & Schuster, 1994.

HAMILTON, ANITA. "Speeders, Say Cheese." *Time* (September 17, 2001):32.

HAMILTON, BRADY E., JOYCE A. MARTIN, and STEPHANIE J. VENTURA. "Births: Preliminary Data for 2007." *National Vital Statistics Reports*. Vol. 57, No. 12 (March 18, 2009). www.cdc.gov/nchs/data/nvsr/nvsr57/nvsr57_12.pdf

HAMRICK, MICHAEL H., DAVID J. ANSPAUGH, and GENE EZELL. *Health*. Columbus, OH: Merrill, 1986.

HANEY, CRAIG, W. CURTIS BANKS, and PHILIP G. ZIMBARDO. "Interpersonal Dynamics in a Simulated Prison." *International Journal of Criminology and Penology*. Vol. 1 (1973):69–97.

HANEY, LYNNE. "After the Fall: East European Women since the Collapse of State Socialism." *Contexts*. Vol. 1, No. 3 (Fall 2002):27–36.

HANGO, D. *Taking Time Off between High School and Postsecondary Education: Determinants and Early Labour Market Outcomes*. Statistics Canada Catalogue no. 81-004-XIE 2008. Ottawa: Culture, Tourism and the Centre for Education Statistics, 2008.

HANKIVSKY, O., and R. CORMIER. *Intersectionality: Moving Women's Health Research and Policy Forward*. Vancouver: Women's Health Research Network, 2009.

HANKIVSKY O., et al. "Exploring the Promises of Intersectionality for Advancing Women's Health Research." *International Journal for Inequity in Health*. Vol. 9, No. 5 (2010).

HARLOW, HARRY F., and MARGARET KUENNE HARLOW. "Social Deprivation in Monkeys." *Scientific American* (November 1962):137–46.

HARRIES, KEITH D. *Serious Violence: Patterns of Homicide and Assault in America*. Springfield, IL: Thomas, 1990.

HARRIGAN, PATRICK J. "The Schooling of Boys and Girls in Canada." *Journal of Social History*. Vol. 23, No. 4 (Summer 1990):803–26.

HARRINGTON, MICHAEL. *The New American Poverty*. New York: Penguin Books, 1984.

HARRIS, CHAUNCY D., and EDWARD L. ULLMAN. "The Nature of Cities." *Annals of the American Academy of Political and Social Sciences*. Vol. 242, No. 1 (November 1945):7–17.

HARRIS, DAVID R., and JEREMIAH JOSEPH SIM. "Who Is Multiracial? Assessing the Complexity of Lived Race." *American Sociological Review*. Vol. 67, No. 4 (August 2002):614–27.

HARRIS, MARVIN. *Cultural Anthropology*. 2nd ed. New York: Harper & Row, 1987.

HARRISON, D. "The Role of Military Culture in Military Organizations Responses to Woman Abuse in Military Families." *The Sociological Review*. Vol. 54, No. 3 (2006):546–574.

HARRISON, DEBORAH, and LUCIE LALIBERTÉ. *No Life Like It: Military Wives in Canada*. Toronto: James Lorimer & Company, 1994.

HAYDEN, THOMAS. "Losing Our Voices." *U.S. News & World Report* (May 26, 2003):42.

HEALTH CANADA. *Federal Interdepartmental Working Group on Female Genital Mutilation: Female Genital Mutilation and Health Care—An Exploration of the Needs and Roles of Affected Communities and Health Care Providers in Canada*. Ottawa: Author, 1999.

———. *Infectious Syphilis in Canada*. Epi Update (February 2002). [Online] www.hc-sc.gc.ca/pphb-dgspsp/publicat/epiu-aepi/std-mts/infsyph_e.html

———. *Prevalent HIV Infections in Canada: Up to One-Third May Not Be Diagnosed*. Epi Update (April 2003c). [Online] www.hc-sc.gc.ca/pphb-dgspsp/publicat/epiu-aepi/hiv-vih/hivtest_e.html

———. *National HIV Prevalence and Incidence Estimates for 1999: No Evidence of a Decline in Overall Incidence*. Epi Update (April 2003d). [Online] www.hc-sc.gc.ca/pphb-dgspsp/publicat/epiu-aepi/hiv-vih/pdf/epiact_0403_e.pdf

———. *First Nations Comparable Health Indicators*. 2007. www.hc-sc.gc.ca/fniah-spnia/diseasesmaladies/2005-01_health-sante_indicat-eng.php#life_expect

———. *A Statistical Profile on the Health of First Nations in Canada: Self-Rated Health and Selected Conditions, 2002 to 2005*. Ottawa: Author, 2009. www.hc-sc.gc.ca/fniah-spnia/pubs/aborig-autoch/2009-stats-profil-vol3/index-eng.php#a2

HECKATHORN, DOUGLAS. "Respondent-Driven Sampling: A New Approach to the Study of Hidden Populations." *Social Problems*. Vol. 44, No. 2 (1997):174–99.

HELGESEN, SALLY. *The Female Advantage: Women's Ways of Leadership*. New York: Doubleday, 1990.

HELIN, DAVID W. "When Slogans Go Wrong." *American Demographics*. Vol. 14, No. 2 (February 1992):14.

HELLMICH, NANCI. "Environment, Economics Partly to Blame." *USA Today* (October 9, 2002):9D.

HENLEY, NANCY, MYKOL HAMILTON, and BARRIE THORNE. "Womanspeak and Manspeak: Sex Differences in Communication, Verbal and Nonverbal." In John J. Macionis and Nijole V. Benokraitis, eds., *Seeing Ourselves: Classic, Contemporary, and Cross-Cultural Readings in Sociology*. 2nd ed. Englewood Cliffs, NJ: Prentice Hall, 1992.

HENRY, WILLIAM A., III. "Gay Parents: Under Fire and On the Rise." *Time*. Vol. 142, No. 12 (September 20, 1993):66–71.

HERMAN, DIANNE. "The Rape Culture." In John J. Macionis and Nijole V. Benokraitis, eds., *Seeing Ourselves: Classic, Contemporary, and Cross-Cultural Readings in Sociology*. 5th ed. Upper Saddle River, NJ: Prentice Hall, 2001.

HERMAN, DIDI. *Rights of Passage: Struggles for Lesbian and Gay Legal Rights*. Toronto: University of Toronto Press, 1994.

HERON, MELONIE, ET AL. "Deaths: Final Data for 2006." *National Vital Statistics Reports*. Vol. 57, No. 14 (April 17, 2009). http://www.cdc.gov/nchs/data/nvsr/nvsr57/nvsr57_14.pdf

HERPERTZ, SABINE C., and HENNING SASS. "Emotional Deficiency and Psychopathy." *Behavioral Sciences and the Law*. Vol. 18, No. 5 (September/October 2000):567–80.

HERRNSTEIN, RICHARD J., and CHARLES MURRAY. *The Bell Curve: Intelligence and Class Structure in American Life*. New York: Free Press, 1994.

HERTZ, R. *More Equal Than Others: Women and Men in Dual-Career Marriages*. Berkeley: University of California Press, 1986.

HERTZMAN, C. "Framework for the Social Determinants of Early Child Development." In R.E. Tremblay, R.G. Barr, R.D. Peters, and M. Boivin, eds., *Encyclopedia on Early Childhood Development*. Montreal: Centre of Excellence for Early Childhood Development, 2010:1–9. [Online]. www.child-encyclopedia.com/documents/HertzmanANGxp.pdf

HERTZMAN, C., C. POWER, S. MATTHEWS, and O. MANOR. "Using an Interactive Framework of Society and Lifecourse to Explain Self-Rated Health in Early Adulthood." *Social Science & Medicine*. Vol. 53 (2001):1575–85.

HERTZMAN, CLYDE. "The Biological Embedding of Early Experience and Its Effects on Health in Adulthood." *Annals of the New York Academy of Sciences* 896, 1999:85–95.

HESKETH, T., and LU, L. "The Effect of China's One-Child Policy After 25 Years." *New England Journal of Medicine*. Vol. 353, No. 1 (September 2005):1171–76.

HESS, BETH B. "Breaking and Entering the Establishment: Committing Social Change and Confronting the Backlash." *Social Problems*. Vol. 46, No. 1 (February 1999):1–12.

HEWLETT, SYLVIA ANN, and CAROLYN BUCK LUCE. "Off-Ramps and On-Ramps: Keeping Talented Women on the Road to Success." *Harvard Business Review*. Vol. 83, No. 3 (March 2005):43–54.

HEYMANN, PHILIP B. "Civil Liberties and Human Rights in the Aftermath of September 11." *Harvard Journal of Law and Public Policy*. Vol. 25, No. 2 (Spring 2002):441–57.

HIER, S. *Panoptic Dreams: Streetscape Video Surveillance in Canada*. Vancouver: UBC Press, 2010.

HIGHTOWER, JIM. *Eat Your Heart Out: Food Profiteering in America*. New York: Crown, 1975.

HILL, MARK E. "Race of the Interviewer and Perception of Skin Color: Evidence from the Multi-City Study of Urban Inequality." *American Sociological Review*. Vol. 67, No. 1 (February 2002):99–108.

HIRSCHI, TRAVIS. *Causes of Delinquency*. Berkeley: University of California Press, 1969.

HIV/AIDS LEGAL NETWORK. *Sex, Work, Rights: Reforming Canadian Criminal Laws On Prostitution*. Toronto: Author, 2005.

HOCHSCHILD, ARLIE RUSSELL. "Emotion Work, Feeling Rules, and Social Structure." *American Journal of Sociology*. Vol. 85, No. 3 (November 1979):551–75.

———. *The Managed Heart*. Berkeley: University of California Press, 1983.

HOPE, TRINA L., HAROLD G. GRASMICK, and LAURA J. POINTON. "The Family in Gottfredson and Hirschi's General Theory of Crime: Structure, Parenting, and Self-Control." *Sociological Focus*. Vol. 36, No. 4 (November 2003):291–311.

HORTON, HAYWARD DERRICK. "Critical Demography: The Paradigm of the Future?" *Sociological Forum*. Vol. 14, No. 3 (September 1999):363–67.

HOUT, MICHAEL. "More Universalism, Less Structural Mobility: The American Occupational Structure in the 1980s." *American Journal of Sociology*. Vol. 95, No. 6 (May 1998):1358–400.

HOUT, MICHAEL, ANDREW M. GREELEY, and MELISSA J. WILDE. "The Demographic Imperative in Religious Change in the United States." *American Journal of Sociology*. Vol. 107, No. 2 (September 2001):468–500.

HOWDEN, DANIEL. "Latin America's New Socialist Revolution." *New Zealand Herald* (December 20, 2005). www.nzherald.co.nz

HOYT, HOMER. *The Structure and Growth of Residential Neighborhoods in American Cities*. Washington, DC: Federal Housing Administration, 1939.

HSU, FRANCIS L.K. *The Challenge of the American Dream: The Chinese in the United States*. Belmont, CA: Wadsworth, 1971.

HUCHINGSON, JAMES E. "Science and Religion." *Miami* (Florida) *Herald* (December 25, 1994):1M, 6M.

HUFFMAN, KAREN. *Psychology in Action*. New York: Wiley, 2000.

HUFFMAN, M. "Who's in Charge? Organizational Influences on Women's Representation in Managerial Positions." *Social Science Quarterly*. Vol. 80 (1999):738–56.

HUMAN RESOURCES AND SKILLS DEVELOPMENT CANADA. *2006 Designated Group Profiles*. 2006. www.hrsdc.gc.ca/eng/labour/equality/docs/designated_group_profiles.pdf

———. *Pan-Canadian Study of First Year College Students: Report 2: The Characteristics and Experience of Aboriginal, Disabled, Immigrant and Visible Minority Students*. 2008. www.hrsdc.gc.ca/eng/publications_resources/learning_policy/sp_890_12_08/sp_890_12_08.pdf

———. *Work—Unemployment Rate*. 2011. www4.hrsdc.gc.ca/.3ndic.1t.4r@-eng.jsp?iid=16

HUMPHRIES, HARRY LEROY. *The Structure and Politics of Intermediary Class Positions: An Empirical Examination of Recent Theories of Class*. Unpublished Ph.D. dissertation. Eugene: University of Oregon, 1984.

HUNTER, JAMES DAVISON. *American Evangelicalism: Conservative Religion and the Quandary of Modernity*. New Brunswick, NJ: Rutgers University Press, 1983.

———. "Conservative Protestantism." In Philip E. Hammond, ed., *The Sacred in a Secular Age*. Berkeley: University of California Press, 1985:50–66.

———. *Evangelicalism: The Coming Generation*. Chicago: University of Chicago Press, 1987.

HWANG, STEPHEN W. "Homelessness and Health." *Canadian Medical Association Journal*. Vol. 164, No. 2 (January 2001):229–33.

HYMEL, S., N. ROCKE HENDERSON, and R. BONANNO. "Moral Disengagement: A Framework for Understanding Bullying among Adolescents." *Journal of Social Sciences*. Vol. 8 (2005):1–11.

HYMOWITZ, KAY S. "Kids Today Are Growing Up Way Too Fast." *Wall Street Journal* (October 28, 1998):A22.

IACOVETTA, FRANCA. "Remaking Their Lives: Immigrants, Survivors, and Refugees." In Joy Parr, ed., *A Diversity of Women: Ontario, 1945–1980*. Toronto: University of Toronto Press, 1995:135–67.

IANNACCONE, LAURENCE R. "Why Strict Churches Are Strong." *American Journal of Sociology*. Vol. 99, No. 5 (March 1994):1180–211.

IBM. Web site by country/region and language. 2010. [Online] Available at http://www.ibm.com/planetwide/select/selector.html

IDE, THOMAS R., and ARTHUR J. CORDELL. "Automating Work." *Society*. Vol. 31, No. 6 (September/ October 1994):65–71.

IGNATIUS, ADI. "Why Putin Will Still Run Russia." *Time* (March 2, 2008). www.time.com/time/world/article/0,8599,1718775,00.html

INCIARDI, JAMES A. *Elements of Criminal Justice*. 2nd ed. New York: Oxford University Press, 2000.

INCIARDI, JAMES A., HILARY L. SURRATT, and PAULO R. TELLES. *Sex, Drugs, and HIV/AIDS in Brazil*. Boulder, CO: Westview Press, 2000.

INDIAN AND NORTHERN AFFAIRS CANADA. *Nisga'a Final Agreement—Issues and Responses*. 2008. www.ainc-inac.gc.ca/al/ldc/ccl/fagr/nsga/nfa/snr-eng.asp

Industry Canada. *Services Sector Overview—October 2006.* 2009. www.ic.gc.ca/eic/site/si-is.nsf/eng/ai02201.html

———. *Key Small Business Statistics—July 2010: How Many People Are Self-Employed?* 2011a. www.ic.gc.ca/eic/site/sbrp-rppe.nsf/eng/rd02501.html

———. *What Are the Characteristics of the Self-Employed?* 2011b. www.ic.gc.ca/eic/site/sbrp-rppe.nsf/eng/rd02354.html

INGLEHART, RONALD. *Modernization and Postmodernization: Cultural, Economic, and Political Change in 43 Societies.* Princeton, NJ: Princeton University Press, 1997.

INGLEHART, RONALD, and WAYNE E. BAKER. "Modernization, Cultural Change, and the Persistence of Traditional Values." *American Sociological Review.* Vol. 65, No. 1 (February 2000):19–51.

INGLEHART, RONALD and CHRISTIAN WELZEL . "Changing Mass Priorities: The Link Between Modernization and Democracy." *Perspectives on Politics.* June 2010 (Vol. 8, No. 2): 554.

———. "World Values Survey: Inglehart-Welzel Cultural Map of the World." 2010. www.worldvaluessurvey.com

INGLEHART, RONALD, CHRISTIAN WELZEL, and ROBERTO FOA. "Happiness Trends in 24 Countries, 1946–2006." 2010. www.worldvaluessurvey.org/wvs/articles/folder_published/article_base_106

INTERNAL REVENUE SERVICE. "SOI Tax Stats: Individual Statistical Tables by Tax Rate and Income Percentile." 2009. www.irs.gov/taxstats/indtaxstats/article/0,,id=133521,00.html

INTERNATIONAL CENTRE FOR PRISON STUDIES. "Entire World—Prison Population Rates per 100,000 of the National Population." 2011. [Online]. http://www.prisonstudies.org/info/worldbrief/wpb_stats.php?area=all&category=wb_poprate

INTERNATIONAL DEVELOPMENT RESEARCH CENTER. *Growing Better Cities: Urban Agriculture for Sustainable Development.* Ottawa, Canada. 2006.

INTERNATIONAL LABOUR ORGANIZATION. International Programme on the Elimination of Child Labour (ILO-IPEC). "Global Child Labour Trends, 2000–2004." June 2006. www.ilo.org/ipec/Informationresources/lang–en/index.htm

———. *Key Indicators of the Labour Market.* 6th ed. 2010. [Online] Available at http://www.ilo.org/public/english/employment/strat/kilm/index.htm

INTERNATIONAL PANEL ON CLIMATE CHANGE. *Climate Change, 2007.* New York: United Nations, 2007.

INTERNATIONAL TELECOMMUNICATION UNION. *World Telecommunication Development Report.* Data cited in World Bank, *2008 World Development Indicators.* Washington, DC: World Bank, 2008.

———. *World Telecommunication Development Report.* Data cited in World Bank, *2009 World Development Indicators.* Washington, DC: World Bank, 2009.

———. "ICT Database, 2009." 2010. http://www.itu.int

INTER-PARLIAMENTARY UNION. "Women in National Parliaments." October 31, 2009. www.ipu.org/english/home.htm

———. "Women in National Parliaments." 2011. www.ipu.org/wmn-e/world.htm

IPSOS-REID. "17-Country Poll on Taxes, Spending and Priorities." Media release (March 16, 2000a). [Online] www.ipsos-reid.com/media/dsp_displaypr_cdn.cfm?id_to_view=999

———. "Marital Infidelity." Public release (March 14, 2001a). [Online] www.ipsos-reid.com/media/dsp_displaypr_cdn.cfm?id_to_view=1186

———. "Federal Political Scene, March 2001." Tables accompanying press release March 12, 2001c. [Online] www.ipsos_reid.com/pdf/media/mr010312tb_5.pdf

———. "Federal Political Scene, Late April 2001." Tables accompanying press release April 27, 2001d. [Online] www.ipsos_reid.com/pdf/media/mr010427tb_8.pdf

———. "Federal Political Scene, July 2001." Tables accompanying press release July 9, 2001e. [Online] www.ipsos_reid.com/pdf/media/mr010709_3t.pdf

———. "Federal Liberals Lead in Every Province/Region in the Country." Tables accompanying press release August 29, 2001f. [Online] www.ipsos_reid.com/pdf/media/mr010829tb_3.pdf

———. "Two-thirds (63%) of Canadians Approve of Prime Minister's Performance." Tables accompanying press release September 28, 2001g. [Online] www.ipsos_reid.com/pdf/media/mr010928tb1.pdf

———. "Liberals Continue to Hold Support of Half (49%) of Decided Voters in the Country." Tables accompanying press release November 23, 2001h. [Online] www.ipsos_reid.com/pdf/media/mr011123_1tb.pdf

———. "Federal Liberals (47%) at Lowest Level Since 2000 Election—But Lead Still Comfortable with What Would Be a Sweeping Majority." Tables accompa-

nying press release, March 8, 2002a. [Online] www.ipsos_reid.com/pdf/media/mr020308tb.pdf

———. "Seven in Ten (68%) Canadians Say That Prime Minister Should Step Down—Including 58% of Liberal Supporters." Tables accompanying press release May 31, 2002b. [Online] www.ipsos_reid.com/pdf/media/mr020531_2tb.pdf

———. "Despite Continued Controversies, Liberal Vote (43%) Holds Static Since May." Tables accompanying press release June 21, 2002c. [Online] www. ipsos_reid.com/pdf/media/mr020621_1tb_2.pdf

——— "Despite Party In-Fighting, Support for Liberals (46%) Climbs." Tables accompanying press release July 19, 2002d. [Online] www.ipsos_reid.com/pdf/media/mr020719_2tb.pdf

———. "The Green Party (4%) Shows Up on Radar Screen... Especially in British Columbia." Tables accompanying press release October 11, 2002e. [Online] www.ipsos_reid.com/pdf/media/mr021011_1tb.pdf

———. "A Reader's Digest Poll: Marriage in Canada." Media release (March 24, 2003a). [Online] www.angusreid.com/media/dsp_displaypr_cdn.cfm?id_to_view=1777

———. "Slim Majority (54%) Support Same-Sex Marriages." Public release (June 13, 2003d). [Online] www.ipsos-reid.com/search/pdf/mediamr030613%2D1.pdf

———. "Same-Sex Marriage: The Debate Enjoined." Public release (August 8, 2003e). [Online] www.ipsos-reid.com/media/dsp_displaypr_cdn.cfm?id_to_view=1877

———. "Federal Liberals (50%) Continue to Hold Resounding Lead." Tables accompanying press release (April 27, 2003g). [Online] www.ipsos_reid.com/pdf/media/mr030427_1tb.pdf

———. "New PC Leader MacKay Convention Fallout." Tables accompanying press release (June 6, 2003h). [Online] www.ipsos_reid.com/pdf/media/mr030606_4tb.pdf

———. "Uniting the Right ...?" Tables accompanying press release (October 5, 2003i). [Online] www.ipsos_reid.com/pdf/media/mr031005_1tb.pdf

———. "Support for New Conservative Party Drops with Official Announcement of Merger." Tables accompanying press release (October 24, 2003j). [Online] www.ipsos_reid.com/pdf/media/mr031024_3tb.pdf

———. "Federal Politics: Bouncing Back." Vol. 19, No. 5 (September/October 2004a).

———. "Federal Liberals Reach 40% for First Time Since May 2004." News release dated October 13, 2004b.

———. "Federal Vote." News release dated November 2, 2004c.

———. "Following Loss of Confidence Vote." News release dated May 14, 2005a.

———. "The Federal Political Landscape." News release dated June 20, 2005b.

———. "At the One Year Anniversary of the Federal Election." News release dated June 28, 2005c.

———. "As Liberal Caucus Meets in Regina." News release dated August 22, 2005d.

———. "Federal Poll." News release dated October 3, 2005e.

———. "Majority of Canadians (57%) Feel Spring Is Best Time to Hold Elections." News release dated November 12, 2005f.

———. "Most Canadians (78%) Say Election Over Holidays Won't Affect Their Party Vote." News release dated November 17, 2005g.

———. "Liberals (34% v. 30% Tories) Hold Slim Lead on Eve of Election Call as Canadians Warm to Idea of Potential Harper Minority." News release dated November 17, 2005h.

———. "Decision Canada." News release dated November 29, 2005i.

———. "Decision Canada." News release dated December 3, 2005j.

———. "Grits (34%, +1 Point) Have Minor Edge." News release dated December 10, 2005k.

———. "Liberals (36%, +2 Points) Ahead of Conservatives." News release dated December 13, 2005l.

———. "Election Prelude Ends with Tight Race." News release dated December 24, 2005m.

———. "With Three Weeks to Election Day the Tight Race Tilts Tory." News release dated January 2, 2006a.

———. "As Final Week of 2006 Election Begins, Tories Within Close Striking Distance of Winning Majority Government." News release dated January 17, 2006b.

———. "Federal Landscape at One Month After Election." News release dated February 23, 2006c.

———. "Grits Get Post Convention Bounce as Ontario and Quebec Warms to Liberals." Public release dated December 9, 2006d.

————. "Federal Political Landscape: Calm amidst the Income Trust Storm." Public release dated November 4, 2006e.

————. "Canadians Assess the Performance of the Minority Conservative Government Under Prime Minister Stephen Harper." Public release dated September 2, 2006f.

————. "Conservative Vote Dips Slightly in Wake of Mid-East Turmoil." Public release dated July 31, 2006g.

————. "Conservatives Surge to 43% Support Nationally—Level Not Seen Since Mulroney Government in November of 1988." Public release dated May 23, 2006h.

————. "Federal Vote Support Remains Stable, but Approval Rating for Harper Government Climbs." Public release dated March 25, 2006i.

————. "Federal Landscape at One Month after Election." Public release dated February 23, 2006j.

————. "Only Coal for Harper's Tories (35%) as Liberal's (33%) Vote Stocking Up." Public release dated December 22, 2007a.

————. "Gap Narrows in Midst of Schreiber-Mulroney Affair." Public release dated November 26, 2007b.

————. "Prime Minister Stephen Harper (63%) Given Highest Ratings For Leadership Qualities and Skills of Any Federal Party Leader." Public release dated October 16, 2007c.

————. "Running Fast but Standing Still: After 18 Months of Governing, Conservatives Make No Progress on the Public Opinion Front." Public release dated August 2, 2007d.

————. "Little Momentum for Main Federal Parties." Public release dated June 18, 2007e.

————. "Voter Opinion Locked In." Public release dated May 26, 2007f.

————. "Majority Still Out of Reach for Harper." Public release dated April 23, 2007g.

————. "Will He or Won't He?" Public release dated March 22, 2007h.

————. "Grit Post-Convention Lead Evaporates—Tories and Grits Neck-in-Neck." Public release dated February 24, 2007i.

————. "Liberals Consolidate Lead." Public release dated January 23, 2007j.

————. "Harper Has Hammer, Even with New Grit Leader." Public release dated December 11, 2008a.

————. "Majority (68%) of Canadians from Every Part of Country Supports Governor General's Decision to Prorogue Parliament." Public release dated December 5, 2008b.

————. "Canadian Teenagers Are Leading the Online Revolution? Maybe Not . . . " Press release dated February 27, 2008c.

————. "Conservatives Crushed in Quebec (18%) as Bloc Soars (40%)." Public release dated October 4, 2008d.

————. "Election 2008: At the End of Week 1, Tories Lead but No Magic Breakthrough." Public release dated September 13, 2008e.

————. "If You Sabre Rattle in Summer, Does Anyone Hear It? Apparently Not." Public release dated August 2, 2008f.

————. "Grits (32%) and Tories (33%) in a Statistical Tie, but Grits Have Big Lead in Battleground Ontario." Public release dated July 12, 2008g.

————. "Despite Gaffs and a Sack, Harper's Tories Still Lead, but Having Country on the 'Right Track' Tumbles." Public release dated May 29, 2008h.

————. "Liberals (32%) Edge Closer to Conservatives (35%)." Public release dated May 10, 2008i.

————. "Antics in House of Commons Have Little Impact on Party Vote." Public release dated April 12, 2008j.

————. "Despite Gaffes and Woes, Tories (35%) Hold Narrow Lead over Grits (31%)." Public release dated March 10, 2008k.

————. "Tories (37%) Lead Grits (29%) by Eight Points." Public release dated January 27, 2008l.

————. "Liberals Drop to New Low (24%) under Ignatieff as NDP (19%) in the Hunt for Grit Votes." Public release dated November 19, 2009a.

————. "Tory Lead in Ontario Offset by Low Level Support in Quebec, Making Majority Elusive." Public release dated October 13, 2009b.

————. "NDP Falters to Mere 12% Support with All Eyes on Layton as He Determines Government's Fate." Public release dated September 15, 2009c.

————. "Arctic Tour and Economic Rebound Put Tories in Driver's Seat." Public release dated August 24, 2009d.

————. "Despite Election Rhetoric, Seven in Ten (68%) Canadians Say There's 'No Need for an Election', Majority (51%) Says Country Heading in 'Right Direction', Minority (41%) 'Wrong'." Public release dated June 4, 2009e.

————. "As Liberals Rally around Ignatieff in Vancouver, Grits (36%) Lead Tories (33%) Nationally, with 10-Point Lead in Seat-Rich Ontario." Public release dated May 2, 2009f.

————. "Ignatieff Liberals (33%) Continue to Edge Closer to Harper Conservatives (37%)." Public release dated March 5, 2009g.

————. "Vote Gap Narrows as Grits, Not Tories, Get Post-Budget Bounce." Public release dated February 7, 2009h.

————. "Amidst Deepening Economic Concern, Majority (55%) Still Believes Canada on Right Track." Public release dated January 8, 2009i.

————. "Tories Breaking Out of Stalemate." Public release dated December 10, 2010a.

————. "Yawn: Same Old, Same Old." Public release dated November 6, 2010b.

————. "Parliament Resumes to Same-Old Story." Public release dated September 23, 2010c.

————. "As Parliament Prepares to Return Next Week, Conservatives Hold Tenuous Lead." Public release dated September 14, 2010d.

————. "Barbecues and Bus Rides Bring Tories (34%), Grits (31%) Closer Together." Public release dated August 10, 2010e.

————. "National Vote Intentions Remain Relatively Flat Despite Excitement of G-20 Summit, Royal Visit and Canada Day." Public release dated July 10, 2010f.

————. "Merger Rejected by Party Faithful in all Parties." Public release dated June 12, 2010g.

————. "Canadians Split on Whether Opposition Parties Can Be Trusted (45%) or Not (49%) with Secret Afghan Detainee Issue Documents." Public release dated May 8, 2010h.

————. "Jaffer-Guergis Affair Leaves Little Impact on Voters." Public release dated April 22, 2010i.

————. "Harper's Tories (34%) Continue to Lead Ignatieff's Grits (28%) in Wake of Throne Speech, Budget." Public release dated March 20, 2010j.

————. "In Lead Up to Budget Day, Canadians Want a Long-Term Deficit-Reduction Strategy That Ensures Sustainability of Important Programs Like Health Care." Public release dated February 26, 2010k.

————. "Harper's Conservatives Hold Tenuous Lead amidst Haiti's Troubled Times." Public release dated January 25, 2010l.

————. "On Eve of Confidence Votes, Half (50%) of Canadians Say to Opposition Parties: Pass Budget, Avoid Election." Public release dated March 24, 2011a.

————. "Pre-Election Budget Sabre Rattling Masks Stagnant Party Vote Strength." Public release dated February 4, 2011b.

ISRAEL, GLENN D., LIONEL J. BEAULIEU, and GLEN HARTLESS. "The Influence of Family and Community Social Capital on Educational Achievement." *Rural Sociology*. Vol. 66, No. 1 (March 2001):43–68.

JACOBS, M. "Obsessed with Impression Management: A Critical Sociology of Body Image in Capitalist Society." *Human Architecture: Journal of the Sociology of Self-Knowledge*. Vol. II, No. 2 (2003):66–73.

JACOBSON, JENNIFER. "Professors Are Finding Better Pay and More Freedom at Community Colleges." *Chronicle of Higher Education* (March 7, 2003). http://chronicle.com/article/ Professors-Are-Finding-Better/18498/

JACQUET, CONSTANT H., and ALICE M. JONES. *Yearbook of American and Canadian Churches, 1991*. Nashville, TN: Abingdon Press, 1991.

JAFFE, A.J. *The First Immigrants from Asia: A Population History of the North American Indians*. New York and London: Plenum Press, 1992.

JAMES, CARL E. "Up to No Good: Black on the Streets and Encountering Police." In Vic Satzewich, ed., *Racism & Social Inequality in Canada*. Toronto: Thompson Educational Publishing Inc. 1998:157–76.

JAMIESON, KATHLEEN. "Sex Discrimination and the *Indian Act*." In J. Rick Ponting, ed., *Arduous Journey: Canadian Indians and Decolonialization*. Toronto: McClelland & Stewart, 1986:112–36.

JANIS, IRVING L. *Victims of Groupthink*. Boston: Houghton Mifflin, 1972.

————. *Crucial Decisions: Leadership in Policymaking and Crisis Management*. New York: Free Press, 1989.

JEFFRIES, T. "Sechelt Women and Self-Government." In G. Creese and V. Strong-Boag, eds., *British Columbia Reconsidered: Essays on Women*. Vancouver: Press Gang Publishers, 1992:90–95.

JENKINS, J. CRAIG. *Images of Terror: What We Can and Can't Know about Terrorism*. Hawthorne, NY: Aldine de Gruyter, 2003.

JENKINS, J. CRAIG, and MICHAEL WALLACE. "The Generalized Action Potential of Protest Movements: The New Class, Social Trends, and Political Exclusion Explanations." *Sociological Forum.* Vol. 11, No. 2 (June 1996):183–207.

JENSON, J. "Changing the Paradigm: Family Responsibility or Investing in Children." *Canadian Journal of Sociology.* Vol. 29, No. 2 (2004):169–92.

JHA, P., M. KESLER, R. KUMAR, F. RAM, U. RAM, L. ALEKSANDROWICZ, D. BASSANI, S. CHANDRA, and J. BANTHIA. "Trends in Selective Abortions of Girls in India: Analysis of Nationally Representative Birth Histories from 1990 to 2005 and Census Data from 1991 to 2011." *The Lancet* (2011). doi:10.1016/S0140-6736(11)60649-1

JHA, PRABHAT, RAJESH KUMARB, PRIYA VASAA, NEERAJ DHINGRAA, DEVA THIRUCHELVAMA, and RAHIM MOINEDDINA. "Low Male-to-Female Sex Ratio of Children Born in India: National Survey of 1.1 Million Households." *Lancet,* Vol. 367, No. 9506 (21 January 2006–27 January 2006):211–18.

JOHNSON, CATHRYN. "Gender, Legitimate Authority, and Leader-Subordinate Conversations." *American Sociological Review.* Vol. 59, No. 1 (February 1994):122–35.

JOHNSON, J., and L. GREAVES. *Better Science with Sex and Gender: A Primer for Health Research.* Vancouver: Women's Health Research Network, 2007.

JOHNSON, PAUL. "The Seven Deadly Sins of Terrorism." In Benjamin Netanyahu, ed., *International Terrorism.* New Brunswick, NJ: Transaction Books, 1981:12–22.

JOHNSTON, R.J. "Residential Area Characteristics." In D.T. Herbert and R.J. Johnston, eds., *Social Areas in Cities. Vol. 1: Spatial Processes and Form.* New York: Wiley, 1976:193–235.

JONES, CHARISSE. "Upon Release from Prison, Some Can Feel Lost." *USA Today* (December 14, 2007):5A.

JONES, D. GARETH. "Brain Death." *Journal of Medical Ethics.* Vol. 24, No. 4 (August 1998):237–43.

JORDAN, ELLEN, and ANGELA COWAN. "Warrior Narratives in the Kindergarten Classroom: Renegotiating the Social Contract?" *Gender and Society.* Vol. 9, No. 6 (December 1995):727–43.

JOSEPHY, ALVIN M., JR. *Now That the Buffalo's Gone: A Study of Today's American Indians.* New York: Knopf. 1982.

KAIN, EDWARD L. "A Note on the Integration of AIDS into the Sociology of Human Sexuality." *Teaching Sociology.* Vol. 15, No. 4 (July 1987):320–23.

KALBACH, WARREN E., and WAYNE W. MCVEY. *The Demographic Basis of Canadian Society.* 2nd ed. Toronto: McGraw-Hill, 1979.

KALLEBERG, ARNE L., BARBARA F. RESKIN, and KEN HUDSON. "Bad Jobs in America: Standard and Nonstandard Employment Relations and Job Quality in the United States." *American Sociological Review.* Vol. 65, No 2 (April 2000):256–78.

KAMINER, WENDY. "Volunteers: Who Knows What's in It for Them?" *Ms.* (December 1984):93–96, 126–28.

KANTER, ROSABETH MOSS. *Men and Women of the Corporation.* New York: Basic Books, 1977.

KANTER, ROSABETH MOSS, and BARRY A. STEIN. "The Gender Pioneers: Women in an Industrial Sales Force." In Rosabeth Moss Kanter And Barry A. Stein, eds., *Life in Organizations.* New York: Basic Books, 1979:134–60.

KAPLAN, DAVID E., and MICHAEL SCHAFFER. "Losing the Psywar." *U.S. News & World Report* (October 8, 2001):46.

KAPLAN-MYRTH, N. "Sorry Mates: Reconciliation and Self-Determination in Australian Aboriginal Health." *Human Rights Review.* Vol. 6, No. 4 (2005):69–83.

KAPTCHUK, TED. "The Holistic Logic of Chinese Medicine." In Berkeley Holistic Health Center, *The New Holistic Health Handbook: Living Well in a New Age.* Shepard Bliss et al., eds. Lexington, MA: Steven Greene Press, 1985:41.

KARATNYCKY, ADRIAN. "The 2001–2002 Freedom House Survey of Freedom: The Democracy Gap." In *Freedom in the World: The Annual Survey of Political Rights and Civil Liberties, 2001–2002.* New York: Freedom House, 2002:7–18.

KARP, DAVID A., and WILLIAM C. YOELS. "The College Classroom: Some Observations on the Meaning of Student Participation." *Sociology and Social Research.* Vol. 60, No. 4 (July 1976):421–39.

KAUFMAN, ROBERT L. "Assessing Alternative Perspectives on Race and Sex Employment Segregation." *American Sociological Review.* Vol. 67, No. 4 (August 2002):547–72.

KAUFMAN, WALTER. *Religions in Four Dimensions: Existential, Aesthetic, Historical, and Comparative.* Pleasantville, NY: Reader's Digest Press, 1976.

KAY, PAUL, and WILLETT KEMPTON. "What Is the Sapir-Whorf Hypothesis?" *American Anthropologist.* Vol. 86, No. 1 (March 1984):65–79.

KEISTER, LISA A. *Wealth in America: Trends in Wealth Inequality.* New York: Cambridge University Press, 2000.

KENT, MARY M., and MARK MATHER. "What Drives U.S. Population Growth?" *Population Bulletin.* Vol. 57, No. 4 (December 2002):3–40.

KENTOR, JEFFREY. "The Long-Term Effects of Foreign Investment Dependence on Economic Growth, 1940–1990." *American Journal of Sociology.* Vol. 103, No. 4 (January 1998):1024–46.

———. "The Long-Term Effects of Globalization on Income Inequality, Population Growth, and Economic Development." *Social Problems.* Vol. 48, No. 4 (November 2001):435–55.

KERR, RICHARD A. "Climate Models Heat Up." *Science Now* (January 26, 2005):1–3.

KERR, THOMAS, MARK TYNDALL, KATHY LI, JULIO S.G. MONTANER, and EVAN WOOD. "Safer Injection Facility Use and Syringe Sharing in Injection Drug Users." *Lancet.* Vol. 366 (2005):316–18.

KEYS, JENNIFER. "Running the Gauntlet: Women's Use of Emotional Management Techniques in the Abortion Experience," *Symbolic Interaction,* Vol. 33, No. 1, (Winter 2010): pp. 41–70. http://www.jstor.org/stable/10.1525/si.2010.33.1.41

KILBOURNE, BROCK K. "The Conway and Siegelman Claims against Religious Cults: An Assessment of Their Data." *Journal for the Scientific Study of Religion.* Vol. 22, No. 4 (December 1983):380–85.

KILGORE, SALLY B. "The Organizational Context of Tracking in Schools." *American Sociological Review.* Vol. 56, No. 2 (April 1991):189–203.

KING, KATHLEEN PIKER, and DENNIS E. CLAYSON. "The Differential Perceptions of Male and Female Deviants." *Sociological Focus.* Vol. 21, No. 2 (April 1988):153–64.

KINSEY, ALFRED, WARDELL BAXTER POMEROY, and CLYDE E. MARTIN. *Sexual Behavior in the Human Male.* Philadelphia, PA: Saunders, 1948.

KINSEY, ALFRED, WARDELL BAXTER POMEROY, CLYDE E. MARTIN, and PAUL H. GEBHARD. *Sexual Behavior in the Human Female.* Philadelphia, PA: Saunders, 1953.

KITTRIE, NICHOLAS N. *The Right to Be Different: Deviance and Enforced Therapy.* Baltimore MD: Johns Hopkins University Press, 1971.

KITZINGER, JENNY. "Media Templates: Patterns of Association and the (Re) Construction of Meaning Over Time." *Media, Culture, and Society.* Vol. 22 (2000): 61–84.

KIVANT, BARBARA. "Reassessing Risk." *Time* (November 17, 2008): Global 1–4.

KLUCKHOHN, CLYDE. "As an Anthropologist Views It." In Albert Deutsch, ed., *Sex Habits of American Men.* New York: Prentice Hall, 1948.

KOBASA, SUZANNE. "Stressful Life Events, Personality and Health: An Inquiry into Hardiness." *Journal of Personality and Social Psychology.* Vol. 37, No. 1 (1979): 1–11.

KOBAYASHI, K.M. "Midlife Crises: Understanding the Changing Nature of Relationships in Middle Age Canadian Families." In D. Cheal, ed., *Canadian Families Today.* 2nd ed. Don Mills, ON: Oxford University Press, 2010:84–97.

KOBAYASHI, K.M., D. CLOUTIER-FISHER, and M. ROTH. "The Link Between Social Isolation and Health Among Older Adults in Small City and Small Town, British Columbia." *Journal of Aging and Health.* Vol. 21 (2009):374–97.

KOGAWA, JOY. *Obasan.* Markham, ON: Penguin Books, 1981.

KOHEN, D.E., JEANNE BROOKS–GUNN, TAMA LEVENTHAL, and CLYDE HERTZMAN. "Neighborhood Income and Physical and Social Disorder in Canada: Associations with Young Children's Competencies." *Child Development.* Vol. 73, No. 6, (2002):1844–60.

KOHLBERG, LAWRENCE. *The Psychology of Moral Development: The Nature and Validity of Moral Stages.* New York: Harper & Row, 1981.

KOHLBERG, LAWRENCE, and CAROL GILLIGAN. "The Adolescent as Philosopher: The Discovery of Self in a Postconventional World." *Daedalus.* No. 100 (Fall 1971):1051–86.

KOHN, MELVIN L. *Class and Conformity: A Study in Values.* 2nd ed. Homewood, IL: Dorsey Press, 1977.

KONG, R., and K. AUCOIN. *Female Offenders in Canada.* Ottawa: Canadian Centre for Justice Statistics, 2008. Catalogue no. 85-002-XIE, Vol. 28, No. 1. [Online] www.statcan.gc.ca/pub/85-002-x/85-002-x2008001-eng.pdf

KONO, CLIFFORD, DONALD PALMER, ROGER FRIEDLAND, and MATTHEW ZAFONTE. "Lost in Space: The Geography of Corporate Interlocking Directorates." *American Journal of Sociology.* Vol. 103, No. 4 (January 1998):863–911.

KORNHAUSER, WILLIAM. *The Politics of Mass Society.* New York: Free Press, 1959.

KOZOL, JONATHAN. *Rachel and Her Children: Homeless Families in America.* New York: Crown, 1988.

———. *Savage Inequalities: Children in America's Schools.* New York: Crown Publishers, a division of Random House, Inc., 1991.

Krahn, Harvey J., and Graham S. Lowe. *Work, Industry, and Canadian Society.* 3rd ed. Toronto: ITP Nelson, 1998.

———. *Work, Industry, and Canadian Society.* 4th ed. Toronto: Nelson, 2002.

Kral, Brigitta. "The Eyes of Jane Elliott." *Horizon Magazine.* 2000. www.horizonmag.com/4/jane-elliott.asp

Kraybill, Donald B. *The Riddle of Amish Culture.* Baltimore: Johns Hopkins University Press, 1989.

———. "The Amish Encounter with Modernity." In Donald B. Kraybill and Marc A. Olshan, eds., *The Amish Struggle with Modernity.* Hanover, NH: University Press of New England, 1994:21–33.

Kraybill, Donald B., and James P. Hurd. *Horse-and-Buggy Mennonites: Hoofbeats of Humility in a Postmodern World.* University Park: Pennsylvania State University Press, 2006.

Kraybill, Donald B., and Marc A. Olshan, eds. *The Amish Struggle with Modernity.* Hanover, NH: University Press of New England, 1994.

Krieger, N. "Genders, Sexes, and Health: What Are the Connections—and Why Does It Matter?" *International Journal of Epidemiology.* Vol. 32 (2003):652–57.

Krieger, Nancy. "Embodiment: A Conceptual Glossary for Epidemiology." *Journal of Epidemiology and Community Health.* 59 (2005):350–57.

Kriesi, Hanspeter. "New Social Movements and the New Class in the Netherlands." *American Journal of Sociology.* Vol. 94, No. 5 (March 1989):1078–116.

Kroll, Luisa, Matthew Miller, and Tatiana Serafin. "Forbes Special Report: The World's Billionaires." Forbes.com. March 11, 2009. www.forbes.com/2009/03/11/worlds-richest-people-billionaires-2009-billionaires_land.html

Krugman, Paul. "For Richer: How the Permissive Capitalism of the Boom Destroyed American Equality." *New York Times Magazine* (September 20, 2002):62–67, 76–77, 141–42.

Kruks, Gabriel N. "Gay and Lesbian Homeless/Street Youth: Special Issues and Concerns." *Journal of Adolescent Health.* Special Issue, No. 12 (1991):515–18.

Krysan, Maria. "Community Undesirability in Black and White: Examining Racial Residential Preferences through Community Perceptions." *Social Problems.* Vol. 49, No. 4 (November 2002):521–43.

Kübler-Ross, Elisabeth. *On Death and Dying.* New York: Macmillan, 1969.

Kubrin, Charles E. "Gangstas, Thugs, and Hustlas: Identity and the Code of the Street in Rap Music." *Social Problems.* Vol. 52, No. 3 (2005):360–78.

Kunkel, Dale, et al. *Sex on TV, 2005.* Menlo Park, CA: Henry J. Kaiser Family Foundation, 2005. www.kff.org/entmedia/entmedia110905pkg.cfm

Kuumba, M. Bahati. "A Cross-Cultural Race/Class/Gender Critique of Contemporary Population Policy: The Impact of Globalization." *Sociological Forum.* Vol. 14, No. 3 (March 1999):447–63.

Kuznets, Simon. "Economic Growth and Income Inequality." *American Economic Review.* Vol. 14, No. 1 (March 1955):1–28.

———. *Modern Economic Growth: Rate, Structure, and Spread.* New Haven, CT: Yale University Press, 1966.

Kymlicka, W. "The Rise and Fall of Multiculturalism? New Debates on Inclusion and Accommodation in Diverse Societies." *International Social Science Journal.* Vol. 61 (2010):97–112.

Kwan, S. "Framing the Fat Body: Contested Meanings between Government, Activists, and Industry." *Sociological Inquiry.* Vol. 79, No. 1 (2008):25–50.

Lacey, Marc. "A Distinct Lifestyle: The Muxe of Mexico." *New York Times* (December 7, 2008.):4.

Ladd, John. "The Definition of Death and the Right to Die." In John Ladd, ed., *Ethical Issues Relating to Life and Death.* New York: Oxford University Press, 1979:118–45.

Lai, H.M. "Chinese." In *Harvard Encyclopedia of American Ethnic Groups.* Cambridge, MA: Harvard University Press, 1980:217–33.

Lambert, L. "Gendered Wage Gap Even More Pronounced for Aboriginal Women." *Pimatisiwin: A Journal of Aboriginal and Indigenous Community Health.* Vol. 8, No. 2 (2010). www.pimatisiwin.com/online/wp-content/uploads/2010/09/03Lambert.pdf

Land, Victoria and Celia Kitzinger. "Speaking as a Lesbian: Correcting the Heterosexist Presumption." *Research on Language and Social Interaction.* Vol. 38, No. 4 (2005):371–416.

Landsberg, Mitchell. "Health Disaster Brings Early Death in Russia." *Washington Times* (March 15, 1998):A8.

Langan, Patrick A., and David J. Levin. "Recidivism of Prisoners Released in 1994." Bureau of Justice Statistics Special Report. June 2002. bjs.ojp.usdoj.gov/index.cfm?ty=pbdetail&iid=1134

Langbein, Laura I., and Roseana Bess. "Sports in School: Source of Amity or Antipathy?" *Social Science Quarterly.* Vol. 83, No. 2 (June 2002):436–54.

Lapchick, Richard with Alejandra Diaz-Cameron and Derek Mcmechan. "The 2009 Racial and Gender Report Card: Major League Baseball." Orlando: Institute for Diversity and Ethics in Sports. University of Central Florida, 2009. web.bus.ucf.edu/sportbusiness/?page=1445

Lappé, Frances Moore, and Joseph Collins. *World Hunger: Twelve Myths.* New York: Grove Press/Food First Books, 1986.

Lareau, Annette. "Invisible Inequality: Social Class and Childrearing in Black Families and White Families." *American Sociological Review.* Vol. 67, No. 5 (October 2002):747–76.

Larossa, Ralph, and Donald C. Reitzes. "Two? Two and One-Half? Thirty Months? Chronometrical Childhood in Early Twentieth-Century America." *Sociological Forum.* Vol. 166, No. 3 (September 2001):385–407.

Laslett, Peter. *The World We Have Lost: England before the Industrial Age.* 3rd ed. New York: Scribner, 1984.

Laumann, Edward O., John H. Gagnon, Robert T. Michael, and Stuart Michaels. *The Social Organization of Sexuality: Sexual Practices in the United States.* Chicago: University of Chicago Press, 1994.

Leacock, Eleanor. "Women's Status in Egalitarian Societies: Implications for Social Evolution." *Current Anthropology.* Vol. 19, No. 2 (June 1978):247–75.

Leacy, F.H. *Historical Statistics of Canada.* 2nd ed., electronic ed. Statistics Canada Catalogue no. 11-516-XIE. Ottawa: Statistics Canada, 1999.

Leadbeater, B., and N. Way, eds. *Urban Girls: Building Strengths.* 2nd ed. New York: New York University Press, 2007.

Leavitt, Judith Walzer. "Women and Health in America: An Overview." In Judith Walzer Leavitt, ed., *Women and Health in America.* Madison: University of Wisconsin Press, 1984:3–7.

Lee, Z. "Korean Culture and Sense of Shame." *Transcultural Psychiatry.* Vol. 36 (1999):181–94.

Leira, Arnlaug. *Welfare States and Working Mothers: The Scandinavian Experience.* New York: Cambridge University Press, 1992.

———. "Combining Work and Family: Nordic Policy Reforms in the 1990s." In Thomas Boje and Arnlaug Leira, eds., *Gender, Welfare State and the Market: Towards a New Division of Labour.* London: Routledge, 2000:157–74.

Lelonde, Mark. *A New Perspective on the Health of Canadians: Working Paper.* Ontario: Health and Welfare Canada, 1974.

Lemert, Edwin M. *Social Pathology: A Systematic Approach to the Theory of Sociopathic Behavior.* New York: McGraw-Hill, 1951.

———. *Human Deviance, Social Problems, and Social Control.* 2nd ed. Englewood Cliffs, NJ: Prentice Hall, 1972.

Lemonick, Michael D. "The Search for a Murder Gene." *Time* (January 20, 2003):100.

Lengermann, Patricia Madoo, and Ruth A. Wallace. *Gender in America: Social Control and Social Change.* Englewood Cliffs, NJ: Prentice Hall, 1985.

Lenhart, Amanda. "Adults, Cell Phones, and Texting." Pew Research Center Publications. [Online] Available September 2, 2010, at http://pewresearch.org/pubs/1716/adults-cell-phones-text-messages

Lennon, Mary Clare. "Sex Differences in Distress; The Impact of Gender and Work Roles." *Journal of Health and Social Behavior.* Vol. 28, No. 3 (1987):290–305.

Lenski, Gerhard E. *Power and Privilege: A Theory of Social Stratification.* New York: McGraw-Hill, 1966.

Leonard, Eileen B. *Women, Crime, and Society: A Critique of Theoretical Criminology.* White Plains, NY: Longman, 1982.

Leopold, Evelyn. "Sudan's Young Endure 'Unspeakable' Abuse: Report." *Yahoo! News* (April 19, 2007). http://news.yahoo.com

Levay, Simon. *The Sexual Brain.* Cambridge, MA: MIT Press, 1993.

Lever, Janet. "Sex Differences in the Complexity of Children's Play and Games." *American Sociological Review.* Vol. 43, No. 4 (August 1978):471–83.

Levine, Michael. *Student Eating Disorders: Anorexia Nervosa and Bulimia.* Washington, DC: National Educational Association, 1987.

Levine, Michael P. "Reducing Hostility Can Prevent Heart Disease." *Mount Vernon* (Ohio) *News* (August 7, 1990):4A.

LEVINE, SAMANTHA. "Playing God in Illinois." *U.S. News & World Report* (January 13, 2003):13.

LEVINSON, F. JAMES, and LUCY BASSETT. "Malnutrition Is Still a Major Contributor to Child Deaths." Population Reference Bureau. 2007. www.prb.org/pdf07/Nutrition2007.pdf

LEWIN, TAMAR. "Girls' Gains Have Not Cost Boys, Report Says." *New York Times* (May 20, 2008). www.nytimes.com/2008/05/20/education/20girls.html?partner =permalink &exprod=permalink

LEWIS, J., and E. MATICKA-TYNDALE. *Escort Services in a Border Town: Methodological Challenges Conducting Research Related to Sex Work.* Health Canada, Ottawa: Division of STD Prevention and Control, 1999.

LEWIS, J., E. MATICKA-TYNDALE, F. SHAVER, and H. SCHRAMM. "Managing Risk and Safety on the Job." *Journal of Psychology and Human Sexuality.* Vol. 17 (2005): 147–67.

LEWIS, M. PAUL, ed. *Ethnologue: Languages of the World.* 16th ed. Dallas, TX: SIL International, 2009.

LEWIS, OSCAR. *The Children of Sachez.* New York: Random House, 1961.

LEWIS, PIERCE, CASEY MCCRACKEN, and ROGER HUNT. "Politics: Who Cares?" *American Demographics.* Vol. 16, No. 10 (October 1994):20–26.

LI, JIANG HONG, and ROGER A. WOJTKIEWICZ. "A New Look at the Effects of Family Structure on Status Attainment." *Social Science Quarterly.* Vol. 73, No. 3 (September 1992):581–95.

LIAZOS, ALEXANDER. "The Poverty of the Sociology of Deviance: Nuts, Sluts, and Perverts." *Social Problems.* Vol. 20, No. 1 (Summer 1972):103–20.

———. *People First: An Introduction to Social Problems.* Needham Heights, MA: Allyn & Bacon, 1982.

LICHTER, S. ROBERT, and DANIEL R. AMUNDSON. "Distorted Reality: Hispanic Characters in TV Entertainment." In Clara E. Rodriguez, ed., *Latin Looks: Images of Latinas and Latinos in the U.S. Media.* Boulder, CO: Westview Press, 1997: 57–79.

LIGHT, D., and R. KIRK. "High School Rugby, the Body and the Reproduction of Hegemonic Masculinity." *Sport, Education and Society.* Vol. 5, No. 2 (2000):163–76.

LIN, NAN, KAREN COOK, and RONALD S. BURT, eds. *Social Capital: Theory and Research.* Hawthorne, NY: Aldine de Gruyter, 2001.

LIN, NAN, and WEN XIE. "Occupational Prestige in Urban China." *American Journal of Sociology.* Vol. 93, No. 4 (January 1988):793–832.

LINDAUER, DAVID L., and AKILA WEERAPANA. "Relief for Poor Nations." *Society.* Vol. 39, No. 3 (March/April 2002):54–58.

LINDSTROM, BONNIE. "Chicago's Post-Industrial Suburbs." *Sociological Focus.* Vol. 28, No. 4 (October 1995):399–412.

LINK, BRUCE, and JO PHELAN. "Social Conditions as Fundamental Causes of Disease." *Journal of Health and Social Behavior.* Extra Issue, 1995:80–94.

———. "Conceptualizing Stigma." *Annual Review of Sociology.* Vol. 27 (2001):363–85.

LINO, MARK, and ANDREA CARLSON. "Expenditures on Children by Families, 2009." U.S. Department of Agriculture, Center for Nutrition Policy and Promotion. Washington, DC: U.S. Government Printing Office, 2010.

LINTON, RALPH. "One Hundred Percent American." *American Mercury.* Vol. 40, No. 160 (April 1937a):427–29.

———. *The Study of Man.* New York: Appleton-Century, 1937b.

LIPSET, SEYMOUR MARTIN. "Canada and the United States: The Cultural Dimension." In Charles F. Donan and John H. Sigler, eds., *Canada and the United States.* Englewood Cliffs, NJ: Prentice Hall, 1985.

LIPTAK, ADAM. "More than 1 in 100 Adults Are Now in Prison in U.S." *New York Times* (February 29, 2008):A14.

LISKA, ALLEN E., and BARBARA D. WARNER. "Functions of Crime: A Paradoxical Process." *American Journal of Sociology.* Vol. 96, No. 6 (May 1991):1441–63.

LITTLE, CRAIG, and ANDREA RANKIN. "Why Do They Start It? Explaining Reported Early-Teen Sexual Activity." *Sociological Forum.* Vol. 16, No. 4 (December 2001):703–29.

LIU, MELINDA, and DUNCAN HEWITT. "The Rise of the Sea Turtles." *Newsweek* (August 18, 2008):29–31.

LOCK, MARGARET. "Cultivating the Body: Anthropology and Epistemology of Bodily Practice and Knowledge." *Annual Review of Anthropology.* Vol. 22 (1993):133–55.

LOGAN, JOHN R., DEIDRE OAKLEY, and JACOB STOWELL. "School Segregation in Metropolitan Regions, 1970–2000: The Impacts of Policy Change on Public Education." *American Journal of Sociology.* Vol. 113, No. 6 (May 2008):1611–44.

LOOMIS, CAROL. "Getting Women to the Highest Levels." *Fortune: 50 Most Powerful Women in Business.* October 4, 2007. [Online] Available May 12, 2008, at http://money.cnn.com/2007/10/04/magazines/fortune/loomis_boards.fortune/index .htm

LORD, WALTER. *A Night to Remember.* Rev. ed. New York: Holt, Rinehart and Winston, 1976.

LOURY, G. *The Anatomy of Racial Inequality.* Cambridge, MA: Harvard University Press, 2002.

LOVEMAN, MARA. "Is 'Race' Essential?" *American Sociological Review.* Vol. 64, No. 6 (December 1999):890–98.

LOWE, GRAHAM S. *The Quality of Work: A People-Centred Agenda.* Toronto: Oxford University Press, 2000.

LOWE, GRAHAM, and HARVEY KRAHN. "Work Aspirations and Attitudes in an Era of Labour Market Restructuring: A Comparison of Two Canadian Youth Cohorts." *Work, Employment and Society.* Vol. 14, No. 1 (2000):1–22.

LOWMAN, J. "Prostitution Law Reform in Canada." In Institute of Comparative Law in Japan, ed., *Toward Comparative Law in the 21st Century.* Tokyo: Chuo University Press, 1998:919–46.

———. "Violence and the Outlaw Status of (Street) Prostitution in Canada." *Violence Against Women.* Vol. 6 (2000):987–1011.

LOWMAN, JOHN. "Taking Young Prostitutes Seriously." *Canadian Review of Sociology and Anthropology.* Vol. 24, No. 1 (1987):99–116.

———. "Notions of Equality Before the Law: The Experience of Street Prostitutes and Their Customers." *Journal of Human Justice.* Vol. 1, No. 2 (1990):55–76.

LOWMAN, JOHN, and CHRIS ATCHISON. "Men Who Buy Sex: A Survey in the Greater Vancouver Regional District." *Canadian Review of Sociology and Anthropology.* Vol. 43, No. 3 (2006):281–96.

LOWMAN, JOHN, and LAURA FRASER. *Violence Against Persons Who Prostitute: The Experience in British Columbia.* Technical Report No. TR1996-14e. Ottawa: Department of Justice Canada, 1995. [Online] http://mypage.uniserve.ca/~lowman/violence/title.htm

LUND, DALE A. "Caregiving." *Encyclopedia of Adult Development.* Phoenix, AZ: Oryx Press, 1993:57–63.

LUXTON, MEG. "Wives and Husbands." In Bonnie Fox, ed., *Family Patterns/Gender Relations.* Toronto: Oxford University Press, 2001:176–98.

LYND, ROBERT S., and HELEN MERRELL LYND. *Middletown in Transition.* New York: Harcourt, Brace & World, 1937.

LYNN, MARION, and MILANA TODOROFF. "Women's Work and Family Lives." In Nancy Mandell, ed., *Feminist Issues: Race, Class, and Sexuality.* 2nd ed. Scarborough, ON: Prentice Hall Allyn and Bacon Canada, 1998:208–32.

MABRY, MARCUS, AND TOM MASLAND. "The Man after Mandela." *Newsweek* (June 7, 1999):54–55.

MACE, DAVID, and VERA MACE. *Marriage East and West.* Garden City, NY: Doubleday/Dolphin, 1960.

MACIONIS, JOHN J. "Intimacy: Structure and Process in Interpersonal Relationships." *Alternative Lifestyles.* Vol. 1, No. 1 (February 1978):113–30.

———. *Social Problems.* 4th ed. Upper Saddle River, NJ: Prentice Hall, 2010.

MACIONIS, JOHN J., and VINCENT R. PARRILLO. *Cities and Urban Life.* 4th ed. Upper Saddle River, NJ: Prentice Hall, 2007.

MACIONIS, JOHN J., and KEN PLUMMER. *Sociology: A Global Introduction.* New York: Prentice Hall Europe, 1997.

MACKAY, JUDITH. *The Penguin Atlas of Human Sexual Behavior.* New York: Penguin, 2000.

MACKINNON, C.A. *Feminism Unmodified: Discourses on Life and Law.* Cambridge, MA: Harvard University Press, 1987.

MADDOX, SETMA. "Organizational Culture and Leadership Style: Factors Affecting Self-Managed Work Team Performance." Paper presented at the annual meeting of the Southwest Social Science Association, Dallas, February 1994.

MALAMUTH, N.M., and F. DONNERSTEIN. *Pornography and Sexual Aggression.* Orlando, FL: Academic Press, 1984.

MALTHUS, THOMAS ROBERT. *First Essay on Population 1798.* London: Macmillan, 1926; orig. 1798.

MANDELL, NANCY, and ANN DUFFY, eds. *Canadian Families: Diversity, Conflict, and Change.* 2nd ed. Scarborough, ON: ITP Nelson, 2000.

_____, eds. *Canadian Families: Race, Class, Gender and Sexuality.* 3rd ed. Toronto: Harcourt, Brace & Co., 2004.

MANZA, JEFF, and CLEM BROOKS. "The Religious Factor in U.S. Presidential Elections, 1960–1992." *American Journal of Sociology*. Vol. 103, No. 1 (July 1997):38–81.

MARATHONGUIDE.COM (2011). www.marathonguide.com/index.cfm?SRED=18

MARCUSE, HERBERT. *One-Dimensional Man*. Boston: Beacon Press, 1964.

MARKOFF, JOHN. "Remember Big Brother? Now He's a Company Man." *New York Times* (March 31, 1991):7.

MARQUAND, ROBERT. "Worship Shift: Americans Seek Feeling of 'Awe.'" *Christian Science Monitor* (May 28, 1997):1, 8.

MARQUAND, ROBERT, and DANIEL B. WOOD. "Rise in Cults as Millennium Approaches." *Christian Science Monitor* (March 28, 1997):1, 18.

MARQUARDT, ELIZABETH, and NORVAL GLENN. *Hooking Up, Hanging Out, and Hoping for Mr. Right*. New York: Institute for American Values, 2001.

MARSHALL, K. "Converging Gender Roles," by Katherine Marshall, *Perspectives on Labour and Income*, Vol. 7, No. 7, July 2006. See: http://www.statcan.gc.ca/pub/75-001-x/10706/9268-eng.htm

———. "Fathers' Use of Paid Parental Leave." *Perspectives on Labour and Income*. Catalogue no. 75-001-X. 2008. www.statcan.gc.ca/pub/75-001-x/75-001-x2008106-eng.pdf

MARSHALL, KATHERINE. "Part-time by Choice." *Perspectives on Labour and Income*. Statistics Canada Catalogue no. 75-001-XIE. Vol. 1, No. 2 (November 2000): 5–12.

MARSHALL, SUSAN E. "Ladies against Women: Mobilization Dilemmas of Antifeminist Movements." *Social Problems*. Vol. 32, No. 4 (April 1985):348–62.

MARTEL, L., and A. BÉLANGER. *An Analysis of the Change in Dependence-Free Life Expectancy in Canada between 1986 and 1996: Report on the Demographic Situation in Canada, 1998-1999*. Statistics Canada. Catalogue no. 91-209-XPE. 2000.

MARTIN, CAROL LYNN, and RICHARD A. FABES. "The Stability and Consequences of Young Children's Same-Sex Peer Interactions. *Developmental Psychology*. Vol. 37, No. 3 (May 2001):431–46.

MARTIN, JOYCE A., BRADY E.HAMILTON, PAUL D. SUTTON, STEPHANIE J.VENTURA, T. J. MATHEWS, and MICHELLE J. K. OSTERMAN. "Births: Final Data for 2008." *National Vital Statistics Reports*. Vol. 59, No. 1. Hyattsville,Md: National Center for Health Statistics, December 2010. [Online] Available at http://www.cdc.gov/nchs/data/nvsr/nvsr59/nvsr59_01.pdf

MARTINDALE, KATHLEEN. "What Makes Lesbianism Thinkable?: Theorizing Lesbianism from Adrienne Rich to Queer Theory." In Nancy Mandell, ed., *Feminist Issues: Race, Class, and Sexuality*. Scarborough, ON: Prentice Hall Allyn and Bacon Canada, 1998:55–76.

MARULLO, SAM. "The Functions and Dysfunctions of Preparations for Fighting Nuclear War." *Sociological Focus*. Vol. 20, No. 2 (April 1987):135–53.

MARX, KARL. *Karl Marx: Early Writings*. T.B. Bottomore, ed. New York: McGraw-Hill, 1964; orig. 1848.

———. *Capital*. Friedrich Engels, ed. New York: International Publishers, 1967; orig. 1867.

MARX, KARL, and FRIEDRICH ENGELS. "Manifesto of the Communist Party." In Robert C. Tucker, ed., *The Marx-Engels Reader*. New York: Norton, 1972:331–62; orig. 1848.

MASON, DAVID S. "Fairness Matters: Equity and the Transition to Democracy." *World Policy Journal*. Vol. 20, No. 4 (Winter 2003–04). 2004. www.worldpolicy.org/journal/articles/wpj03-4/mason.htm

MASON, MARY ANN, and MARC GOULDEN. "Do Babies Matter (Part II)? Closing the Baby Gap." *Academe* (November–December 2004) [Online] www.aaup.org/publications/Academe/2004/04nd/04ndmaso.htm

MASSEY, DOUGLAS S., and NANCY A. DENTON. "Hypersegregation in U.S. Metropolitan Areas: Black and Hispanic Segregation along Five Dimensions." *Demography*. Vol. 26, No. 3 (August 1989):373–91.

MATA, F. *Religion-Mix Growth in Canadian Cities: A Look at 2006–2031 Projections Data*. Report Prepared for Department of Canadian Heritage. 2010. [Online] www.ssc.uwo.ca/MER/MERcentre/conference%20presentations/Mata,Fernando.pdf

MATAS, ROBERT, and CRAIG MCINNES. "Critics of Nisga'a Treaty Demand Referendum." *Globe and Mail* (July 23, 1998):A1, A5.

MATICKA-TYNDALE, E. "Sexuality and Sexual Health of Canadian Adolescents: Yesterday, Today and Tomorrow." *Canadian Journal of Human Sexuality*. Vol. 17, No. 3 (2008):85–95.

MATTHIESSEN, PETER. *Indian Country*. New York: Viking Press, 1984.

MAXWELL, MARY PERCIVAL, and JAMES MAXWELL. "Going Co-Ed: Elite Private Schools in Canada." *Canadian Journal of Sociology*. Vol. 20, No. 3 (Summer 1995): 333–57.

MAYO, KATHERINE. *Mother India*. New York: Harcourt, Brace, 1927.

MCADAM, DOUG, JOHN D. MCCARTHY, and MAYER N. ZALD. "Introduction: Opportunities, Mobilizing Structures, and Framing Processes—Toward a Synthetic, Comparative Perspective on Social Movements." In Doug Mcadam, John D. Mccarthy, and Mayer N. Zald, eds., *Comparative Perspectives on Social Movements: Political Opportunities, Mobilizing Structures, and Cultural Framings*. New York: Cambridge University Press, 1996:1–19.

MCBROOM, WILLIAM H., and FRED W. REED. "Recent Trends in Conservatism: Evidence of Non-Unitary Patterns." *Sociological Focus*. Vol. 23, No. 4 (October 1990):355–65.

MCCARTHY, BILL, and TERESA CASEY. "Love, Sex and Crime: Adolescent Romantic Relationships and Offending." *American Sociological Review*. Vol. 73, No. 6 (2008):944–69.

MCCARTHY, BILL, and ERIC GRODSKY. "Sex and School: Adolescent Sexual Intercourse and Education." *Social Problems*. Vol. 58, No. 2 (2011):213–34.

MCCREARY CENTRE SOCIETY. *Healthy Youth Development: Highlights from the 2003 Adolescent Health Survey III*. Vancouver: Author, 2004.

MCCREATH, G. *The Politics of Blindness: From Charity to Parity*. Vancouver: Granville Island Publishing, 2011.

MCDANIEL, SUSAN A. "Women's Changing Relations to the State and Citizenship: Caring and Intergenerational Relations in Globalizing Western Democracies." *Canadian Review of Sociology and Anthropology*. Vol. 39, No. 2 (2002):1–26.

MCGEEHAN, PATRICK, and MATHEW R. WARREN. "Adding to Recession's Pain, Thousands to Lose Job Benefits." *New York Times* (January 11, 2009). www.nytimes.com/2009/01/12/nyregion/12benefits.html

MCKAY, ALEXANDER, and MICHAEL BARRETT. "Trends in Teen Pregnancy Rates from 1996–2006: A Comparison of Canada, Sweden, U.S.A., and England/Wales." *Canadian Journal of Human Sexuality*. Vol. 19, No. 1–2 (2010):43–52.

MCKEE, VICTORIA. "Blue Blood and the Color of Money." *New York Times* (June 9, 1996):49–50.

MCKIBBEN, BILL. *Deep Economy: The Wealth of Communities and the Durable Future*. New York: Times Books, 2007.

MCLANAHAN, SARA. "Life without Father: What Happens to the Children?" *Contexts*. Vol. 1, No. 1 (Spring 2002):35–44.

MCLAREN, ANGUS, and ARLENE TIGAR MCLAREN. *The Bedroom and the State: The Changing Practices and Politics of Contraception and Abortion in Canada 1880–1980*. Toronto: McClelland and Stewart, 1986.

MCLEOD, JANE D., and MICHAEL J. SHANAHAN. "Poverty, Parenting, and Children's Mental Health." *American Sociological Review*. Vol. 58, No. 3 (June 1993): 351–66.

MCLEAN, SCOTT. "Objectifying and Naturalizing Individuality: A Study of Adult Education in the Canadian Arctic." *Canadian Journal of Sociology*. Vol. 22, No.1 (Winter 1997):1–30.

MCLEOD, JAY. *Ain't No Makin' It: Aspirations and Attainment in a Low-Income Neighborhood*. Boulder, CO: Westview Press, 1995.

MCVEIGH, RORY, MICHAEL WELCH, and THORODDUR BJARNASON. "Hate Crime Reporting as a Successful Social Movement Outcome." *American Sociological Review*. Vol. 68, No. 6 (December 2003):843–67.

MCVEY, WAYNE W., JR., and WARREN E. KALBACH. *Canadian Population*. Toronto: Nelson Canada, 1995.

MEAD, GEORGE HERBERT. *Mind, Self, and Society*. Charles W. Morris, ed. Chicago: University of Chicago Press, 1962; orig. 1934.

MEAD, MARGARET. *Sex and Temperament in Three Primitive Societies*. New York: Morrow, 1963; orig. 1935.

MEADOWS, DONELLA H., DENNIS L. MEADOWS, JORGAN RANDERS, and WILLIAM W. BEHRENS III. *The Limits to Growth: A Report on the Club of Rome's Project on the Predicament of Mankind*. New York: Universe, 1972.

MELTZER, BERNARD N. "Mead's Social Psychology." In Jerome G. Manis and Bernard N. Meltzer, eds., *Symbolic Interaction: A Reader in Social Psychology*. 3rd ed. Needham Heights, MA: Allyn & Bacon, 1978.

MELUCCI, ALBERTO. *Nomads of the Present: Social Movements and Individual Needs in Contemporary Society*. Philadelphia, PA: Temple University Press, 1989.

MERTON, ROBERT K. "Social Structure and Anomie." *American Sociological Review.* Vol. 3, No. 6 (October 1938):672–82.

———. *Social Theory and Social Structure.* New York: Free Press, 1968.

METZ, MICHAEL E., and MICHAEL H. MINER. "Psychosexual and Psychosocial Aspects of Male Aging and Sexual Health." *Canadian Journal of Human Sexuality.* Vol. 7, No. 3 (Summer 1998):245–60.

MICHELS, ROBERT. *Political Parties.* Glencoe, IL: Free Press, 1949; orig. 1911.

MILAN, A., H. MAHEUX, and T. CHUI. "A Portrait of Couples in Mixed Unions." *Canadian Social Trends.* Catalogue 11-008-X No. 89. 2010. www.statcan.gc.ca/pub/11-008-x/2010001/article/11143-eng.htm#a1

MILANOVIC, BRANKO. "Global Inequality Recalculated: The Effect of New 2005 PPP Estimates on Global Inequality." World Bank. August 2009. http://siteresources.worldbank.org/INTDECINEQ/Resources/Global_Inequality_Recalculated.pdf

MILBRATH, LESTER W. *Envisioning a Sustainable Society: Learning Our Way Out.* Albany: State University of New York Press, 1989.

MILGRAM, STANLEY. "Behavioral Study of Obedience." *Journal of Abnormal and Social Psychology.* Vol. 67, No. 4 (November 1963):371–78.

———. "Group Pressure and Action against a Person." *Journal of Abnormal and Social Psychology.* Vol. 69, No. 2 (August 1964):137–43.

———. "Some Conditions of Obedience and Disobedience to Authority." *Human Relations.* Vol. 18, No. 1 (February 1965):57–76.

———. "The Small World Problem." *Psychology Today* (May 1967):60–67.

MILLER, ARTHUR G. *The Obedience Experiments: A Case of Controversy in Social Science.* New York: Praeger, 1986.

MILLER, FREDERICK D. "The End of SDS and the Emergence of Weatherman: Demise through Success." In Jo Freeman, ed., *Social Movements of the Sixties and Seventies.* White Plains, NY: Longman, 1983:279–97.

MILLER, TERRY, KIM HOLMES, and ANTHONY B. KIM. "2010 Index of Economic Freedom." January 20, 2010. www.heritage.org/index/Default.aspx

MILLER, WALTER B. "Lower-Class Culture as a Generating Milieu of Gang Delinquency." In Marvin E. Wolfgang, Leonard Savitz, and Norman Johnston, eds., *The Sociology of Crime and Delinquency.* 2nd ed. New York: Wiley, 1970:351–63; orig. 1958.

MILLER, WILLIAM J., and RICK A. MATTHEWS. "Youth Employment, Differential Association, and Juvenile Delinquency." *Sociological Focus.* Vol. 34, No. 3 (August 2001):251–68.

MILLIGAN, K. "The Evolution of Elderly Poverty in Canada." Social and Economic Dimensions of an Aging Population (SEDAP) Research Paper 170. Hamilton, ON: McMaster University, 2007.

MILLS, C. WRIGHT. *The Power Elite.* New York: Oxford University Press, 1956.

———. *The Sociological Imagination.* New York: Oxford University Press, 1959.

MINISTRY OF INDUSTRY. *A Guide to Research on the New Economy.* 2003. http://dsp-psd.pwgsc.gc.ca/Collection/Statcan/11-622-M/11-622-MIE2003001.pdf

———. *Women in Canada: Work Chapter Updates.* Catalogue no. 89F0133XIE. 2007. www.statcan.gc.ca/cgi-bin/af-fdr.cgi?l=eng&loc=89f0133x2006000-eng.pdf

MIRACLE, TINA S., ANDREW W. MIRACLE, and ROY F. BAUMEISTER. *Human Sexuality: Meeting Your Basic Needs.* Upper Saddle River, NJ: Prentice Hall, 2003.

MIROWSKY, JOHN. "The Psycho-Economics of Feeling Underpaid: Distributive Justice and the Earnings of Husbands and Wives." *American Journal of Sociology.* Vol. 92, No. 6 (May 1987):1404–34.

MITCHELL, CHRIS. "The Killing of Murder." *New York Magazine* (January 8, 2008). http://nymag.com/news/features/crime/2008/42603/

MODRCIN, NANCY K. "Slim Options for Battered Men." *Peak,* Simon Fraser University's Student Newspaper, Vol. 98, No. 5 (February 9, 1998). [Online] www.peak.sfu.ca/the-peak/98-1/issue5/battered.html

MOGHADAM, VALENTINE M. "The 'Feminization of Poverty' and Women's Human Rights." UNESCO Gender Equality and Development Section. July 2005. http://portal.unesco.org/shs/en/files/8282/11313736811Feminization_of_Poverty.pdf/Feminization%2Bof%2BPoverty.pdf

MONTAIGNE, FEN. "Russia Rising." *National Geographic.* Vol. 200, No. 5 (September 2001):2–31.

MOORE, GWEN, ET AL. "Elite Interlocks in Three U.S. Sectors: Nonprofit, Corporate, and Government." *Social Science Quarterly.* Vol. 83, No. 3 (September 2002):726–44.

MOORE, WILBERT E. "Modernization as Rationalization: Processes and Restraints." In Manning Nash, ed., *Essays on Economic Development and Cultural Change in Honor of Bert F. Hoselitz.* Chicago: University of Chicago Press, 1977:29–42.

———. *World Modernization: The Limits of Convergence.* New York: Elsevier, 1979.

MORELL, VIRGINIA. "Minds of Their Own: Animals Are Smarter than You Think." *National Geographic.* Vol. 213, No. 3 (March 2008):36–61.

MORETTI, M., M. JACKSON, and C. ODGERS, eds. *Girls and Aggression: Contributing Factors and Intervention Principles.* New York: Kluwer Academic Publishers, 2004.

MORRISETTE, RENE, GRANT SCHELLENBERG, and ANICK JOHNSON. "Diverging Trends in Unionization." *Perspectives on Labour and Income.* Vol. 6, No. 4 (April 2005):5–12.

MORISSETTE, RENE, XUELIN ZHANG, and MARIE DROLET. "Wealth Inequality." *Perspectives on Labour and Income.* Vol. 3, No. 2 (February 2002a): 5–12. (2002a) Statistics Canada Catalogue no. 75-001-XIE.

———. *The Evolution of Wealth Inequality in Canada, 1984–1999.* Analytical Studies Branch Research Paper Series No. 187. (2002b) Statistics Canada Catalogue no. 11F0019MIE2002187. [Online] www.statcan.ca/english/research/11F0019MIE/11F0019MIE2002187.pdf

MORRA, NORMAN, and MICHAEL D. SMITH. "Men in Feminism: Reinterpreting Masculinity and Femininity." In Nancy Mandell, ed., *Feminist Issues: Race, Class, and Sexuality.* 2nd ed. Scarborough, ON: Prentice Hall Allyn and Bacon Canada, 1998:160–78.

MOSHER, WILLIAM D., ANJANI CHANDRA, and JO JONES. *Sexual Behavior and Selected Health Measures: Men and Women 15–44 Years of Age, United States, 2002.* 2005. www.cdc.gov/nchs/products/pubs/pubd/ad/361-370/ad362.htm

MOSS, PETER, and MARGARET O'BRIEN, eds. *International Review of Leave Policies and Related Research 2006.* Employment Relations Research Series No. 57. London: Department of Trade and Industry, 2006.

MOUW, TED. "Job Relocation and the Racial Gap in Unemployment in Detroit and Chicago, 1980 to 1990." *American Sociological Review.* Vol. 65, No. 5 (October 2000):730–53.

MSNBC. "Cop-Killer Suspect Shot Dead by Officer." December 1, 2009. www.msnbc.msn.com/id/34194122/

"Much Ado about Evolution." *Time* (November 21, 2005):23.

MULLIGAN-FERRY, L., R. SOARES, J. COMBOPIANO, J. CULLEN, and L. RIKER. *2010 Catalyst Census: Financial Post 500 Women Senior Officers and Top Earners.* 2011. [Online] www.catalyst.org/publication/467/2010-catalyst-census-financial-post-500-women-senior-officers-and-top-earners

MUMFORD, LEWIS. *The City in History: Its Origins, Its Transformations, and Its Prospects.* New York: Harcourt, Brace & World, 1961.

MUNN, M. "Living in the Aftermath: The Impact of Lengthy Incarceration on Post-Carceral Success." *The Howard Journal of Criminal Justice.* Vol. 50 (2011). doi:10.1111/j.1468

MUNROE, SUSAN. "Abolition of Capital Punishment in Canada." About.com: Canada Online. July 2007. http://canadaonline.about.com/od/crime/a/abolitioncappun.htm

MURDOCK, GEORGE PETER. "Comparative Data on the Division of Labor by Sex." *Social Forces.* Vol. 15, No. 4 (May 1937):551–53.

———. "The Common Denominator of Cultures." In Ralph Linton, ed., *The Science of Man in World Crisis.* New York: Columbia University Press, 1945:123–42.

———. *Social Structure.* New York: Free Press, 1965; orig. 1949.

MYERS, DAVID G. *The American Paradox: Spiritual Hunger in an Age of Plenty.* New Haven, CT: Yale University Press, 2000.

MYERS, NORMAN. "Humanity's Growth." In Edmund Hillary, ed., *Ecology 2000: The Changing Face of the Earth.* New York: Beaufort Books, 1984a:16–35.

———. "Disappearing Cultures." In Sir Edmund Hillary, ed., *Ecology 2000: The Changing Face of the Earth.* New York: Beaufort Books, 1984c:162–69.

———. "Biological Diversity and Global Security." In F. Herbert Bormann and Stephen R. Kellert, eds., *Ecology, Economics, and Ethics: The Broken Circle.* New Haven, CT: Yale University Press, 1991:11–25.

MYERS, SHEILA, and HAROLD G. GRASMICK. "The Social Rights and Responsibilities of Pregnant Women: An Application of Parsons' Sick Role Model." Paper presented to the Southwestern Sociological Association, Little Rock, AR, March 1989.

MYLES, JOHN. "When Markets Fail: Social Welfare in Canada and the United States." In Gösta Esping-Andersen, ed., *Welfare States in Transition: National Adaptations in Global Economies.* London: Sage, 1996:116–40.

NACK, ADINA. "Bad Girls and Fallen Women: Chronic STD Diagnoses as Gateways to Tribal Stigma." *Symbolic Interaction.* Vol. 25 (2002):463–85.

NAGEL, JOANE. "Constructing Ethnicity: Creating and Recreating Ethnic Identity and Culture." *Social Problems.* Vol. 41, No. 1 (February 1994): 152–76.

NAJAND, N. "Ectogenesis: The Ethical Implications of a New Reproductive Technology." Unpublished Master thesis. Victoria, BC: University of Victoria, 2010.

NANCARROW CLARKE, JUANNE, and LAUREN NANCARROW CLARKE. *Finding Strength. A Mother and Daughter's Story of Childhood Cancer.* Toronto: Oxford University Press, 1999.

NATIONAL CONFERENCE OF STATE LEGISLATURES. "Marriages." 2009. www.ncsl.org/ programs/cyf/cousins.htm

NATIONAL HIGHWAY TRAFFIC SAFETY ADMINISTRATION. "2008 Traffic Safety Annual Assessment: Highlights." June 2009. http://www-nrd.nhtsa.dot.gov/Pubs/811172 .PDF

NATIONAL OCEANIC AND ATMOSPHERIC ADMINISTRATION. "State of the Climate Global Analysis: Annual 2009." February 12, 2010. www.ncdc.noaa.gov/sotc/ ?report=global&year= 2009&month=13gtemp

NATIONAL POST, THE DOMINION INSTITUTE, and INNOVATIVE RESEARCH GROUP. *The Canadian Values Study.* September 26, 2005. [Online] www.innovativeresearch.ca/ Canadian%20Values%20Study_Factum%20270905a.pdf

NATURAL RESOURCES CANADA. "Atlas of Canada: Foreign-Born Population, 2006." 2009a. http://atlas.nrcan.gc.ca/site/english/maps/peopleandsociety/immigration/ FB/1

NATURAL RESOURCES CANADA. "Atlas of Canada: Visible Minority Population, 2006." 2009b. http://atlas.nrcan.gc.ca/site/english/maps/peopleandsociety/population/ visible_minority/visible_minority_2006/1

NAVARRO, MIREYA. "For Younger Latinas, a Shift to Smaller Families." *New York Times* (December 5, 2004). www.nytimes.com/2004/12/05/national/05latina.html

NELSON, AMY L. "The Effect of Economic Restructuring on Family Poverty in the Industrial Heartland, 1970–1990." *Sociological Focus.* Vol. 31, No. 2 (May 1998):201–16.

NELSON, L., and C. BARRY. "Distinguishing Features of Emerging Adulthood: The Role of Self-Classification as an Adult." *Journal of Adolescent Research.* Vol. 20 (2005):242–62.

NETTLE, S. *The Sociology of Health and Illness.* 2nd ed. Cambridge, UK: Polity Press, 2006.

NEUHOUSER, KEVIN. "The Radicalization of the Brazilian Catholic Church in Comparative Perspective." *American Sociological Review.* Vol. 54, No. 2 (April 1989):233–44.

NEWMAN, KATHERINE S. *Declining Fortunes: The Withering of the American Dream.* New York: Basic Books, 1993.

NEWMAN, PETER. *The Canadian Establishment.* Vol. 1. Toronto: McClelland & Stewart, 1975.

NG, ROXANNE. "Racism, Sexism and Immigrant Women." In Sandra Burt, Lorraine Code, and Lindsay Dorney, eds., *Changing Patterns: Women in Canada.* 2nd ed. Toronto: McClelland and Stewart, 1993:279–307.

NG, ROXANNE, and TANIA DAS GUPTA. "Nation Builders? The Captive Labour Force of Non-English Speaking Immigrant Women." *Canadian Women's Studies.* Vol. 3, No. 1 (1993):83–85.

NIELSEN MEDIA RESEARCH. 2008. http://en-us.nielsen.com

Niesse, Mark. "Some Bars Pan Hawaii's Tough Smoking Ban." *Yahoo! News* (February 19, 2007). http://news.yahoo.com

NIPPERT-ENG, CHRISTENA E. *Home and Work: Negotiating Boundaries through Everyday Life.* Chicago: The University of Chicago Press, 1995.

NISBET, ROBERT A. *The Quest for Community.* New York: Oxford University Press, 1969.

NOLAN, PATRICK, and GERHARD E. LENSKI. *Human Societies: An Introduction to Macrosociology.* 10th ed. Boulder, CO: Paradigm, 2007.

NORC. *General Social Surveys, 1972–2006: Cumulative Codebook.* Chicago: National Opinion Research Center, 2007.

———. *General Social Surveys, 1972–2008: Cumulative Codebook.* Chicago: National Opinion Research Center, 2009. www.norc.org/GSS+Website/

NOSEK, MARGARET A., ROSEMARY B. HUGHES, NANCY SWEDLUND, HEATHER B. TAYLOR, and PAUL SWANK. "Self-Esteem and Women with Disabilities." *Social Science & Medicine.* Vol. 56 (2003): 1737–47.

NOVAK, VIVECA. "The Cost of Poor Advice." *Time* (July 5, 1999):38.

NULAND, SHERWIN B. "The Hazards of Hospitalization." *Wall Street Journal* (December 2, 1999):A22.

NUNN, CLYDE Z., HARRY J. CROCKETT, JR., and J. ALLEN WILLIAMS, JR. *Tolerance for Nonconformity.* San Francisco: Jossey-Bass, 1978.

OAKES, JEANNIE. "Classroom Social Relationships: Exploring the Bowles and Gintis Hypothesis." *Sociology of Education.* Vol. 55, No. 4 (October 1982):197–212.

———. *Keeping Track: How High Schools Structure Inequality.* New Haven, CT: Yale University Press, 1985.

OECD (ORGANISATION FOR ECONOMIC CO-OPERATION AND DEVELOPMENT). "Growing Unequal?: Income Distribution and Poverty in OECD Countries, Country Note: Canada." 2008. www.oecd.org/dataoecd/44/48/41525292.pdf

———. "Education at a Glance, 2009: OECD Indicators." 2009. www.oecd.org/edu/ eag2009

———. "A Family Affair: Intergenerational Social Mobility across OECD Countries. Economic Policy Reforms Going for Growth." 2010. www.oecd.org/dataoecd/3/ 62/44582910.pdf

———. "Women's Earnings as a Percentage of Men's Earnings, Ages 35 to 44, by Education, Selected Countries," 2010a. Table 14-2, from OECD Family database www .oecd.org/els/social/family/databaseOECD, http://www.oecd.org/dataoecd/29/63/ 38752746.pdf

———. "Education at a Glance 2010: OECD Indicators: Indicator A7: What Are the Economic Benefits of Education? Table A7.3a. Differences in earnings between females and males (2008 or latest available year)." 2010b. Electronic Data Base. http://dx.doi.org/10.1787/888932310206

———. "Economic Survey of China 2010: Improving the Health Care System." 2010c. www.oecd.org/document/13/0,3746,en_2649_34581_44482445_1_1_1,00.html

———. "Stat Extracts." 2010d. http://stats.oecd.org/WBOS/index.aspx

———. "OECD Statistics (GDP, Unemployment, Income, Population, Labour, Education, Trade, Finance, Prices...)." 2011a. http://stats.oecd.org/Index.aspx

———. "Harmonised Unemployment Rates." 2011b. www.oecd.org/dataoecd/60/12/ 46861245.pdf

———. "Incidence of Involuntary Part Time Workers." 2011c. http://stats.oecd.org/ Index.aspx?DataSetCode=INVPT_I

OGBURN, WILLIAM F. *On Culture and Social Change.* Chicago: University of Chicago Press, 1964.

OGMUNDSON, R., and J. MCLAUGHLIN. "Changes in An Intellectual Elite 1960–1990: The Royal Society Revisited." *Canadian Review of Sociology & Anthropology.* Vol. 31, No. 1 (February 1994):1–13.

O'HARROW, ROBERT, JR. "ID Theft Scam Hits D.C. Area Residents." *Yahoo! News* (February 21, 2005). http://news.yahoo.com

OLOTU, M., D. LUONG, A. BREWS, C. SCARFONE, A. NOLAN, L. PECARIC, B. MACDONALD, and M. HENIGHAN. *Evaluation Report: LifeLine Program.* Ottawa: Correctional Service of Canada, 2009.

OLSEN, DENIS. *The State Elite.* Toronto: McClelland and Stewart, 1980.

OLSEN, GREGG M. "Remodeling Sweden: The Rise and Demise of the Compromise in a Global Economy." *Social Problems.* Vol. 43, No. 1 (February 1996):1–20.

OLYSLAGER, FEMKE, and LYNN CONWAY. "On the Calculation of the Prevalence of Transsexualism." 2007. http://ai.eecs.umich.edu/people/conway/TS/Prevalence/ Reports/Prevalence%20of%20Transsexualism.pdf

OLZAK, SUSAN. "Labor Unrest, Immigration, and Ethnic Conflict in Urban America, 1880–1914." *American Journal of Sociology.* Vol. 94, No. 6 (May 1989):1303–33.

OMATSU, MARYKA. *Bittersweet Passage: Redress and the Japanese Canadian Experience.* Toronto: Between the Lines, 1992.

"Online Privacy: It's Time for Rules in Wonderland." *Business Week* (March 20, 2000):82–96.

OREOPOULOS, PHILIP. "The Compelling Effects of Compulsory Schooling: Evidence From Canada." *Canadian Journal of Economics.* Vol. 39, No. 1 (2006):22–52.

ORLANSKY, MICHAEL D., and WILLIAM L. HEWARD. *Voices: Interviews with Handicapped People.* Columbus, OH: Merrill, 1981.

ORHANT, MELANIE. "Human Trafficking Exposed." *Population Today.* Vol. 30, No. 1 (January 2002):1, 4.

ORNELAS, I., K. PERREIRA, and G. AYALA. "Parental Influences on Adolescent Physical Activity: A Longitudinal Study." *International Journal of Behavioral Nutrition and Physical Activity.* Vol. 4, No. 3 (2007). doi:10.1186/1479-5868-4-3 [Online] www .ijbnpa.org/content/4/1/3

OSTRANDER, SUSAN A. "Upper-Class Women: The Feminine Side of Privilege." *Qualitative Sociology.* Vol. 3, No. 1 (Spring 1980):23–44.

———. *Women of the Upper Class.* Philadelphia, PA: Temple University Press, 1984.

OUCHI, WILLIAM. *Theory Z: How American Business Can Meet the Japanese Challenge.* Reading, MA: Addison-Wesley, 1981.

"Our Cheating Hearts." Editorial. *U.S. News & World Report* (May 6, 2002):4.

OVADIA, SETH. "Race, Class, and Gender Differences in High School Seniors' Values: Applying Intersection Theory in Empirical Analysis." *Social Science Quarterly.* Vol. 82, No. 2 (June 2001):341–56.

OWEN, CAROLYN A., HOWARD C. ELSNER, and THOMAS R. MCFAUL. "A Half-Century of Social Distance Research: National Replication of the Bogardus Studies." *Sociology and Social Research.* Vol. 66, No. 1 (1977):80–98.

PACKARD, MARK. Personal communication (2002).

PACKER, GEORGE. "Smart-Mobbing the War." *New York Times Magazine* (March 9, 2003):46–49.

PAKULSKI, JAN. "Mass Social Movements and Social Class." *International Sociology.* Vol. 8, No. 2 (June 1993):131–58.

PAMMET, JON H., and LAWRENCE LEDUC. "Explaining the Turnout Decline in Canadian Federal Elections: A New Survey of Non-Voters." Ottawa: Elections Canada. (2003). [Online] www.elections.ca/loi/tur/tud/TurnoutDecline.pdf

PARK, ROBERT E. *Race and Culture.* Glencoe, IL: Free Press, 1950.

PARKER-POPE, TARA. "Love, Sex, and the Changing Landscape of Infidelity." *New York Times* (October 27, 2008). www.nytimes.com/2008/10/28/health/28.well.html?_r=1

PARRILLO, VINCENT, and CHRISTOPHER DONOGHUE. "Updating the Bogardus Social Distance Studies: A New National Survey." *Social Science Journal.* Vol. 42, No. 2 (April 2005):257–71.

PARSONS, TALCOTT. "Age and Sex in the Social Structure of the United States." *American Sociological Review.* Vol. 7, No. 4 (August 1942):604–16.

———. *The Social System.* New York: Free Press, 1951.

———. *Essays in Sociological Theory.* New York: Free Press, 1954.

———. *Societies: Evolutionary and Comparative Perspectives.* Englewood Cliffs, NJ: Prentice Hall, 1966.

PASSY, FLORENCE, and MARCO GIUGNI. "Social Networks and Individual Perceptions: Explaining Differential Participation in Social Movements." *Sociological Forum.* Vol. 16, No. 1 (March 2001):123–53.

PATEMAN, CAROLE. *The Sexual Contract.* Cambridge: Polity Press, 1988.

PATTERSON, ELISSA F. "The Philosophy and Physics of Holistic Health Care: Spiritual Healing as a Workable Interpretation." *Journal of Advanced Nursing.* Vol. 27, No. 2 (February 1998):287–93.

PAXTON, PAMELA, MELANIE M. HUGHES, and JENNIFER L. GREEN. "The International Women's Movement and Women's Political Participation, 1893–2003." *American Sociological Review.* Vol. 71, No. 6 (December 2006):898–920.

PEAR, ROBERT, and ERIK ECKHOLM. "When Healers Are Entrepreneurs: A Debate over Costs and Ethics." *New York Times* (June 2, 1991):1, 17.

PEARSON, DAVID E. "Post-Mass Culture." *Society.* Vol. 30, No. 5 (July/August 1993):17–22.

———. "Community and Sociology." *Society.* Vol. 32, No. 5 (July/August 1995): 44–50.

PEASE, JOHN, and LEE MARTIN. "Want Ads and Jobs for the Poor: A Glaring Mismatch." *Sociological Forum.* Vol. 12, No. 4 (December 1997):545–64.

PEAT MARWICK AND PARTNERS. "Canadians' Attitudes toward and Perceptions of Pornography and Prostitution." *Working Papers on Pornography and Prostitution #6.* Ottawa: Department of Justice, 1984.

PERLMUTTER, PHILIP. "Minority Group Prejudice." *Society.* Vol. 39, No. 3 (March/April 2002):59–65.

PERREAULT, S. *Violent Victimization of Aboriginal People in the Canadian Provinces, 2009.* Ottawa: Statistics Canada, 2011. Catalogue no. 85-002-X. [Online] www .statcan.gc.ca/pub/85-002-x/2011001/article/11415-eng.pdf

PERRUCCI, ROBERT. "Inventing Social Justice: SSSP and the Twenty-First Century." *Social Problems.* Vol. 48, No. 2 (May 2001):159–67.

PERRY, ALEX. "South Africa Looks for a Leader." *Time* (April 27, 2009):38–41.

PERRY, BARBARA. *In the Name of Hate: Accounting for Hate Crime.* New York: Routledge, 2001.

———. "Where Do We Go from Here? Future Directions in Hate Crime Scholarship." *Internet Journal of Criminology.* 2003. www.flashmousepublishing.com

PETERSEN, TROND, ISHAK SAPORTA, and MARC-DAVID L. SEIDEL. "Offering a Job: Meritocracy and Social Networks." *American Journal of Sociology.* Vol. 106, No. 3 (November 2000):763–816.

PEW CENTER ON THE STATES. "One in 100: Behind Bars in America 2008." 2008. www .pewcenteronthestates.org/uploadedFiles/One%20in%20100.pdf

PEW FORUM ON RELIGION & PUBLIC LIFE. "U.S. Religious Landscape Survey." February 2008b. http://religions.pewforum.org/reports

PEW RESEARCH CENTER. "As Marriage and Parenthood Drift Apart, Public Is Concerned about Social Impact." July 1, 2007a. http://pewsocialtrends.org/pubs/526/ marriage-parenthood

———. "Social and Demographic Trends: Reports." 2008. http://pewsocialtrends.org/pubs

PFIZER INC. *The Pfizer Global Study of Sexual Attitudes and Behaviors.* 2002.

PHILADELPHIA, DESA. "Tastier, Plusher—and Fast." *Time* (September 30, 2002):57.

PHILLIPS, RACHEL, and CECILIA BENOIT. "Social Determinants of Health Care Access among Sex Industry Workers in Canada." *Sociology of Health Care.* Vol. 23 (2005):79–104.

PINCHOT, GIFFORD, and ELIZABETH PINCHOT. *The End of Bureaucracy and the Rise of the Intelligent Organization.* San Francisco: Berrett-Koehler, 1993.

PINHEY, THOMAS K., DONALD H. RUBINSTEIN, and RICHARD S. COLFAX. "Overweight and Happiness: The Reflected Self-Appraisal Hypothesis Reconsidered." *Social Science Quarterly.* Vol. 78, No. 3 (September 1997):747–55.

PINKER, STEVEN. *The Language Instinct.* New York: Morrow, 1994.

———. "Are Your Genes to Blame?" *Time* (January 20, 2003):98–100.

PIVEN, FRANCES FOX, and RICHARD A. CLOWARD. *Poor People's Movements: Why They Succeed, How They Fail.* New York: Pantheon Books, 1977.

PODOLNY, JOEL M., and JAMES N. BARON. "Resources and Relationships: Social Networks and Mobility in the Workplace." *American Sociological Review.* Vol. 62, No. 5 (October 1997):673–93.

POLSBY, NELSON W. "Three Problems in the Analysis of Community Power." *American Sociological Review.* Vol. 24, No. 6 (December 1959):796–803.

PONTING, J. RICK. "Racial Conflict: Turning Up the Heat." In Dan Glenday and Ann Duffy, eds., *Canadian Society: Understanding and Surviving the 1990s.* Toronto: McClelland and Stewart, 1994:86–118.

PONTING, J. RICK, and JERILYNN KIELY. "Disempowerment: 'Justice,' Racism, and Public Opinion." In J. Rick Ponting, ed., *First Nations in Canada: Perspectives on Opportunity, Empowerment, and Self-Determination.* Whitby, ON: McGraw-Hill Ryerson, 1997.

POPENOE, DAVID. "American Family Decline, 1960–1990: A Review and Appraisal." *Journal of Marriage and the Family.* Vol. 55, No. 3 (August 1993a):527–55.

———. "Parental Androgyny." *Society.* Vol. 30, No. 6 (September/October 1993b): 5–11.

———. "Can the Nuclear Family Be Revived?" *Society.* Vol. 36, No. 5 (July/August 1999):28–30.

POPKIN, SUSAN J. "Welfare: Views from the Bottom." *Social Problems.* Vol. 17, No. 1 (February 1990):64–79.

POPULATION ACTION INTERNATIONAL. *People in the Balance: Population and Resources at the Turn of the Millennium.* Washington, DC: Population Action International, 2000.

POPULATION REFERENCE BUREAU. "2009 World Population Data Sheet." August 2009. www.prb.org/pdf09/09WPDS_Eng.pdf

———. "2010 World Population Data Sheet." July 2010. [Online] Available at http:// www.prb.org/Publications/Datasheets/2010/2010wpds.aspx

———. "Datafinder." 2010. www.prb.org/DataFinder.aspx

———. "Datafinder." 2010, 2011. [Online] Available at http://www.prb.org/ DataFinder.aspx

PORTER, JOHN. *The Vertical Mosaic.* Toronto: University of Toronto Press, 1965.

POSTEL, SANDRA. "Facing Water Scarcity." In Lester R. Brown et al., eds., *State of the World, 1993: A Worldwatch Institute Report on Progress toward a Sustainable Society.* New York: Norton, 1993:22–41.

POTTER, DENA. "Fear of Dem Crackdown Leads to Boom in Gun Sales." (November 8, 2008). www.dailyamerican.com/articles/2009/04/20/business/business091.txt

POWELL, BILL. "Postcard: Dongguan." *Time* (December 15, 2008):4.

PRENTICE, ALISON. *The School Promoters.* Toronto: McClelland and Stewart, 1977.

PRENTICE, ALISON, PAULA BOURNE, GAIL CUTHBERT BRANDT, BETH LIGHT, WENDY MITCHINSON, and NAOMI BLACK. *Canadian Women: A History.* 2nd ed. Toronto: Harcourt Brace & Company, 1996.

PRESSLEY, SUE ANNE, and NANCY ANDREWS. "For Gay Couples, the Nursery Becomes the New Frontier." *Washington Post* (December 20, 1992):A1, A22–23.

PRIMEGGIA, SALVATORE, and JOSEPH A. VARACALLI. "Southern Italian Comedy: Old to New World." In Joseph V. Scelsa, Salvatore J. La Gumina, and Lydio Tomasi, eds., *Italian Americans in Transition.* New York: American Italian Historical Association, 1990:241–52.

PRYOR, JOHN H., ET AL. *The American Freshman: National Norms for Fall 2007*. Los Angeles: UCLA Higher Education Research Institute, 2008.

———. *The American Freshman: National Norms for Fall 2009*. Los Angeles: UCLA Higher Education Research Institute, 2010.

PUBLIC HEALTH AGENCY OF CANADA. 2004 Canadian Sexually Transmitted Infections Surveillance Report: Pre-Release: STI Data Tables, Table 2.1 Reported Gonorrhea Cases and Rates in Canada by Age Group and Sex, 1980–2004. (2006) [Online] www.phac-aspc.gc.ca/std-mts/stddata_pre06_04/tab2-1_e.html

———. 2009. Analyses performed using Health Canada's DAIS edition of anonymized microdata from the *Canadian Community Health Survey 2009: Healthy Aging*, prepared by Statistics Canada.

———. *STI & Hepatitis C Statistics*. 2011a. www.phac-aspc.gc.ca/sti-its-surv-epi/surveillance-eng.php

———. *Reported Cases and Rates of Infectious Syphilis by Province/Territory and Sex, 1993 to 2009*. 2011b. www.phac-aspc.gc.ca/std-mts/sti-its_tab/syphilis_pts-eng.php

———. *HIV/AIDS Epi Updates—July 2010*. 2011c. www.phac-aspc.gc.ca/aids-sida/publication/epi/2010/1-eng.php

PUTKA, GARY. "SAT to Become a Better Gauge." *Wall Street Journal* (November 1, 1990):B1.

QUEENAN, JOE. "The Many Paths to Riches." *Forbes*. Vol. 144, No. 9 (October 23, 1989):149.

QUILLIAN, LINCOLN, and DEVAH PAGER. "Black Neighbors, Higher Crime? The Role of Racial Stereotypes in Evaluations of Neighborhood Crime." *American Journal of Sociology*. Vol. 107, No. 3 (November 2001):717–67.

QUINNEY, RICHARD. *Class, State and Crime: On the Theory and Practice of Criminal Justice*. New York: McKay, 1977.

RAND, MICHAEL R. "Criminal Victimization, 2008." National Crime Victimization Survey. (September 2009). http://bjs.ojp.usdoj.gov/content/pub/pdf/cv08.pdf

RECKLESS, WALTER C., and SIMON DINITZ. "Pioneering with Self-Concept as a Vulnerability Factor in Delinquency." *Journal of Criminal Law, Criminology, and Police Science*. Vol. 58, No. 4 (December 1967):515–23.

REID, ANGUS. *Shakedown: How the New Economy Is Changing Our Lives*. Toronto: Doubleday Canada, 1996.

REITZ, JEFFREY G. *The Survival of Ethnic Groups*. Toronto: McGraw-Hill Ryerson, 1980.

RESKIN, BARBARA, and IRENE PADAVIC. *Women and Men at Work*. Thousand Oaks, Calif.: Pine Forge Press, 1994.

RESKIN, BARBARA F., and DEBRA BRANCH MCBRIER. "Why Not Ascription? Organizations' Employment of Male and Female Managers." *American Sociological Review*. Vol. 65, No. 2 (April 2000):210–33.

RIDEOUT, VICTORIA. "Parents, Children, and Media: A Kaiser Family Foundation Survey." June 2007. www.kff.org/entmedia/upload/7638.pdf

RIDGEWAY, CECILIA L. *The Dynamics of Small Groups*. New York: St. Martin's Press, 1983.

RIDGEWAY, CECILIA L., and LYNN SMITH-LOVIN. "The Gender System and Interaction." *Annual Review of Sociology*. Vol. 25 (August 1999):191–216.

RIESMAN, DAVID. *The Lonely Crowd: A Study of the Changing American Character*. New Haven, CT: Yale University Press, 1970; orig. 1950.

RIIS, OLE. "Religion Re-Emerging: The Role of Religion in Legitimating Integration and Power in Modern Societies." *International Sociology*. Vol. 13, No. 2 (June 1998):249–72.

RILEY, S., C. GRIFFIN, and Y. MOREY. "The Case for 'Everyday Politics': Evaluating Neotribal Theory as a Way to Understand Alternative Forms of Political Participation, Using Electronic Dance Music Culture as an Example." *Sociology*. Vol. 44 (2010):345–63.

RISKA, ELIANNE. "The Rise and Fall of Type A Man." *Social Science & Medicine*, Vol. 51, No. 11 (2000):1665–74.

———. "From Type A Man to the Hardy Man: Masculinity and Health." *Sociology of Health & Illness*. Vol. 24, No. 3 (2002):347–58.

RISKA, ELIANNE, and KATARINA WEGAR, eds. *Gender, Work, and Medicine: Women and the Medical Division of Labour*. Newbury Park, CA: Sage, 1993.

RITZER, GEORGE. *The McDonaldization of Society: An Investigation into the Changing Character of Contemporary Social Life*. Thousand Oaks, CA: Pine Forge Press, 1993.

———. *The McDonaldization Thesis: Explorations and Extensions*. Thousand Oaks, CA: Sage, 1998.

———. "The Globalization of McDonaldization." *Spark* (February 2000):8–9.

RITZER, GEORGE, and DAVID WALCZAK. *Working: Conflict and Change*. 4th ed. Englewood Cliffs, NJ: Prentice Hall, 1990.

ROBERTS, J. DEOTIS. *Roots of a Black Future: Family and Church*. Philadelphia, PA: Westminster Press, 1980.

ROBERTSON, TODD. "Changing Patterns of University Finance." *Education Quarterly Review*. Vol. 9, No. 2. Catalogue no. 81-003-XIE (June 2003):9–17.

ROBINSON, THOMAS N., ET AL. "Effects of Reducing Children's Television and Video Game Use on Aggressive Behavior." *Archives of Pediatrics and Adolescent Medicine*. Vol. 155, No. 1 (January 2001):17–23.

ROCHER, GUY. "The Quiet Revolution in Quebec." In James Curtis and Lorne Tepperman, eds., *Images of Canada: The Sociological Tradition*. Scarborough, ON: Prentice Hall, 1990:22–29.

ROESCH, ROBERTA. "Violent Families." *Parents*. Vol. 59, No. 9 (September 1984): 74–76, 150–52.

ROGERS, RICHARD G., REBECCA ROSENBLATT, ROBERT A. HUMMER, and PATRICK M. KRUEGER. "Black-White Differentials in Adult Homicide Mortality in the United States." *Social Science Quarterly*. Vol. 82, No. 3 (September 2001):435–52.

ROOF, WADE CLARK, and WILLIAM MCKINNEY. *American Mainline Religion: Its Changing Shape and Future*. New Brunswick, NJ: Rutgers University Press, 1987.

ROSEN, JEFFREY. *The Unwanted Gaze*. New York: Random House, 2000.

ROSENBERG, MICA. "Mexican Transvestite Fiesta Rocks Indigenous Town." Reuters (November 23, 2008). www.reuters.com/article/lifestyleMolt/idUSTRE4AM1PB20081123

ROSENDAHL, MONA. *Inside the Revolution: Everyday Life in Socialist Cuba*. Ithaca, NY: Cornell University Press, 1997.

ROSENFELD, RICHARD. "Crime Decline in Context." *Contexts*. Vol. 1, No. 1 (Spring 2002):20–34.

ROSENTHAL, ELIZABETH. "Canada's National Health Plan Gives Care to All, with Limits." *New York Times* (April 30, 1991):A1, A16.

ROSSI, ALICE S. "Gender and Parenthood." In Alice S. Rossi, ed., *Gender and the Life Course*. New York: Aldine, 1985:161–91.

ROSTOW, WALT W. *The Stages of Economic Growth: A Non-Communist Manifesto*. Cambridge: Cambridge University Press, 1960.

———. *The World Economy: History and Prospect*. Austin: University of Texas Press, 1978.

ROTERMANN, M. "Trends in Teen Sexual Behaviour and Condom Use." *Health Reports*. Vol. 19, No. 3 (2008):1–5. Catalogue no. 82-003-XWE2008003; http://www.statcan.gc.ca/bsolc/olc-cel/olc-cel?lang=eng&catno=82-003-X

ROTHENBERG, PAULA. *White Privilege*. 3rd ed. New York: Worth, 2008.

ROTHMAN, STANLEY, and AMY E. BLACK. "Who Rules Now? American Elites in the 1990s." *Society*. Vol. 35, No. 6 (September/October 1998):17–20.

ROTHMAN, STANLEY, STEPHEN POWERS, and DAVID ROTHMAN. "Feminism in Films." *Society*. Vol. 30, No. 3 (March/April 1993):66–72.

ROUDI-FAHIMI, FARZANEH, and MARY MEDERIOS KENT. "Challenges and Opportunities: The Population of the Middle East and North Africa." *Population Bulletin*. Vol. 65, No. 2 (June 2007). Washington, DC: Population Reference Bureau, 2007.

ROUSSEAU, CARYN. "Unions Rally at Wal-Mart Stores." *Yahoo! News* (November 22, 2002). http://dailynews.yahoo.com

ROZELL, MARK J., CLYDE WILCOX, and JOHN C. GREEN. "Religious Constituencies and Support for the Christian Right in the 1990s." *Social Science Quarterly*. Vol. 79, No. 4 (December 1998):815–27.

RUBIN, JOEL. "E-Mail Too Formal? Try a Text Message." Columbia News Service, March 7, 2003. www.jrn.columbia.edu/studentwork/cns/2003-03-07/85.asp

RUBIN, LILLIAN BRESLOW. *Worlds of Pain: Life in the Working-Class Family*. New York: Basic Books, 1976.

RUDEL, THOMAS K., and JUDITH M. GERSON. "Postmodernism, Institutional Change, and Academic Workers: A Sociology of Knowledge." *Social Science Quarterly*. Vol. 80, No. 2 (June 1999):213–28.

RUDY, LAURA. "Under the Knife: Society's Quest for Perfection." *The McGill Tribune*. Issue date: 10/22/02 (April 4, 2006) [Online] www.mcgilltribune.com/media/storage/paper234/news/2002/10/22/Features/Under.The.Knife.Societys.Quest.For.Perfection-303273.shtml?norewrite 200605211931&sourcedomain=www.mcgilltribune.com

RULE, JAMES, and PETER BRANTLEY. "Computerized Surveillance in the Workplace: Forms and Delusions." *Sociological Forum*. Vol. 7, No. 3 (September 1992):405–23.

RUSSELL, D.E.H. *Dangerous Relationships: Pornography, Misogyny, and Rape*. Thousand Oaks, CA: Sage, 1998.

RYAN, WILLIAM. *Blaming the Victim*. Rev. ed. New York: Vintage Books, 1976.

RYMER, RUSS. *Genie*. New York: HarperPerennial, 1994.

SACHS-ERICSSON, NATALIE, and JAMES A. CIARLO. "Gender, Social Roles, and Mental Health: An Epidemiological Perspective." *Sex Roles.* Vol. 43, Nos. 9–10 (2000): 605–28.

SACHS, JEFFREY D. "The Case for Bigger Government." *Time* (January 19, 2009):34–36.

SACKS, VALERIE. "Women and AIDS: An Analysis of Media Misrepresentations." *Social Science and Medicine.* Vol. 42, No. 1 (1996):59–73.

SAINSBURY, DIANE. *Gender, Equality and Welfare States.* Cambridge, MA: Cambridge University Press, 1996.

SAINT JAMES, MARGO, and PRISCILLA ALEXANDER. "What Is Coyote?" 2004. www .coyotela.org/what-is.html

ST. JEAN, YANICK, and JOE R. FEAGIN. *Double Burden: Black Women and Everyday Racism.* Armonk, NY: M.E. Sharpe, 1998.

SALA-I-MARTIN, XAVIER. *The World Distribution of Income.* Working Paper No. 8933. Cambridge, MA: National Bureau of Economic Research, 2002.

SALE, KIRKPATRICK. *The Conquest of Paradise: Christopher Columbus and the Columbian Legacy.* New York: Knopf, 1990.

SALVATION ARMY. "Canada Speaks: The Dignity Project." 2011. http://intraspec.ca/ CanadaSpeaks_report_May2011.pdf

SANSOM, WILLIAM. *A Contest of Ladies.* London: Hogarth, 1956.

SAPIR, EDWARD. "The Status of Linguistics as a Science." *Language.* Vol. 5, No. 4 (1929):207–14.

———. *Selected Writings of Edward Sapir in Language, Culture, and Personality.* David G. Mandelbaum, ed. Berkeley: University of California Press, 1949.

SAPORITO, BILL. "Can Wal-Mart Get Any Bigger?" *Time* (January 13, 2003):38–43.

———. "Spotlight: Toyota's Recall." *Time* (February 15, 2010):17.

SAUL, S. *Feminism Issues and Arguments.* New York: Oxford University Press, 2003.

SAUNDERS, T. "Becoming an Ex-Sex Worker: Making Transitions Out of a Deviant Career." *Feminist Criminology.* Vol. 2, No. 1 (2007):74–95.

SAUVÉ, J. "Crime Statistics in Canada, 2004." *Juristat.* Canadian Centre for Justice Statistics, Statistics Canada. Catalogue no. 85-002-XPE, Vol. 25, No. 5 (2005).

SAX, LINDA J., ET AL. *The American Freshman: National Norms for Fall 2003.* Los Angeles: UCLA Higher Education Research Institute, 2003.

SAYER, A. *Method in Social Science: A Realist Approach.* 2nd ed. London: Routledge, 1992.

SCAMBLER, GRAHAM, and ANNETTE SCAMBLER. *Rethinking Prostitution: Purchasing in the 1990s.* London and New York: Routledge, 1997.

SCANLON, STEPHAN J. "Food Availability and Access in Less Industrialized Societies: A Test and Interpretation of Neo-Malthusian and Technoecological Theories." *Sociological Forum.* Vol. 16, No. 2 (June 2001):231–62.

SCHAFFER, MICHAEL. "American Dreamers." *U.S. News & World Report* (August 26, 2002):12–16.

SCHEFF, THOMAS J. *Being Mentally Ill: A Sociological Theory.* 2nd ed. New York: Aldine, 1984.

SCHEPER-HUGHES, NANCY. "Embodied Knowledge: Thinking with the Body in Critical Medical Anthropology." In Robert Borofsky, ed., *Assessing Cultural Anthropology.* New York. McGraw-Hill, 1993:229–39.

SCHILLER, BRADLEY. "Who Are the Working Poor?" *The Public Interest.* Vol. 155 (Spring 1994):61–71.

SCHISSEL, BERNARD. *Social Dimensions of Canadian Youth Justice.* Toronto: Oxford University Press, 1993.

SCHLOSSER, ERIC. *Fast-Food Nation: The Dark Side of the All-American Meal.* New York: Perennial, 2002.

SCHNEIDER, MARK, MELISSA MARSCHALL, PAUL TESKE, and CHRISTINE ROCH. "School Choice and Culture Wars in the Classroom: What Different Parents Seek from Education." *Social Science Quarterly.* Vol. 79, No. 3 (September 1998):489–501.

SCHOEN, ROBERT, and YEN-HSIN ALICE CHENG. "Partner Choice and the Differential Retreat from Marriage." *Journal of Marriage and the Family.* Vol. 68 (2006):1–10.

SCHOFER, EVAN, and MARION FOURCADE-GOURINCHAS. "The Structural Contexts of Civil Engagement: Voluntary Association Membership in Comparative Perspective." *American Sociological Review.* Vol. 66, No. 6 (December 2001):806–28.

SCHULENBERG, J.E., A.C. MERLINE, L. JOHNSTON, P. O'MALLEY, and J. BACHMAN. "Trajectories of Marijuana Use During the Transition to Adulthood: The Big Picture Based on National Panel Data." *Journal of Drug Issues.* Vol. 35, No. 2 (2005): 255–79.

SCHUTT, RUSSELL K. "Objectivity versus Outrage." *Society.* Vol. 26, No. 4 (May/June 1989):14–16.

SCHWARTZ, CHRISTINE R., and ROBERT D. MARE. "Trends in Educational Assortative Marriage from 1940 to 2003." July 2005. www.ccpr.ucla.edu/ccprwpseries/ ccpr_017_05.pdf

SCOTT, KATHERINE. *The Progress of Canada's Children 1996.* Ottawa: Canadian Council on Social Development, 1996.

SCUPIN, RAY. Personal communication (2000).

SEAGER, JONI. *The Penguin Atlas of Women in the World.* 3rd ed. New York: Penguin Putnam, 2003.

SEALE, CLIVE. "Health and Media: An Overview." *Sociology of Health and Illness* 25 (2003):513–31.

SEGALL, A., and C. FRIES. *Pursuing Health and Wellness Healthy Societies, Healthy People.* New York: Oxford University Press, 2011.

SEGALL, ALEXANDER, and NEENA CHAPPELL. *Health and Health Care in Canada.* Toronto: Prentice Hall, 2000.

SEN, AMARTYA. "Missing Women—Revisited: Reduction in Female Mortality Has Been Counterbalanced by Sex Selective Abortions." *British Medical Journal.* Vol. 327, No. 7427 (December 6, 2003):1297–98.

SENNETT, RICHARD. *The Corrosion of Character: The Personal Consequences of Work in the New Capitalism.* New York: Norton, 1998.

SENNETT, RICHARD, and JONATHAN COBB. *The Hidden Injuries of Class.* New York: Vintage Books, 1973.

SENTENCING PROJECT. "Felony Disenfranchisement Laws in the United States." September 2008a. www.sentencingproject.org/Admin%5CDocuments%5Cpublications%5 Cfd _bs_fdlawsinus.pdf

———. "Incarceration." 2008b. www.sentencingproject.org/IssueAreaHome.aspx? IssueID=2

SHAPIRO, JOSEPH P., and JOANNIE M. SCHROF. "Honor Thy Children." *U.S. News and World Report.* Vol. 118, No. 8 (February 27, 1995):39–49.

SHARPE, A., and J. HARDT. *Five Deaths a Day: Workplace Fatalities in Canada 1993–2005.* Ottawa: Centre for the Study of Living Standards, 2006.

SHARPE, R. "As Leaders, Women Rule." *Business Week* (November 20, 2000):74.

SHAVER, FRANCES. "Prostitution: A Female Crime?" In Ellen Adelberg and Claudia Currie, eds., *In Conflict with the Law: Women and the Canadian Justice System.* Vancouver: Press Gang Publishers, 1993.

SHEA, RACHEL HARTIGAN. "The New Insecurity." *U.S. News & World Report* (March 25, 2002):40.

SHELDON, WILLIAM H., EMIL M. HARTL, and EUGENE MCDERMOTT. *Varieties of Delinquent Youth.* New York: Harper Bros., 1949.

SHERMAN, LAWRENCE W., and DOUGLAS A. SMITH. "Crime, Punishment, and Stake in Conformity: Legal and Informal Control of Domestic Violence." *American Sociological Review.* Vol. 57, No. 5 (October 1992):680–90.

SHEVKY, ESHREF, and WENDELL BELL. *Social Area Analysis.* Palo Alto, CA: Stanford University Press, 1955.

SHIELDS, M., M.D. CARROLL, and C.L. OGDEN. *Adult Obesity Prevalence in Canada and the United States.* NCHS Data Brief no. 56, Hyattsville, MD: National Center for Health Statistics, 2011.

SHIELDS, M., and S. WHEATLEY PRICE. "Racial Harassment, Job Satisfaction and Intentions to Quit: Evidence from the British Nursing Profession." 2000. http://netec .mcc.ac.uk/WoPEc/data/Papers/izaizadpsdp164.html

SHILLINGS, C. *The Body in Culture, Technology & Society.* London: Sage, 2005.

SHIPLEY, JOSEPH T. *Dictionary of Word Origins.* Totowa, NJ: Rowman & Allanheld, 1985.

SHIVELY, JOELLEN. "Cowboys and Indians: Perceptions of Western Films among American Indians and Anglos." *American Sociological Review.* Vol. 57, No. 6 (December 1992):725–34.

SHOVELLER, J., J. JOHNSON, M. PRKACHIN, and D. PATRICK." "'Around Here, They Roll Up the Sidewalks at Night': A Qualitative Study of Youth Living in a Rural Canadian Community." *Health and Place.* Vol. 13 (2007):826–38.

SHOVER, NEAL, and ANDREW HOCHSTETLER. *Choosing White-Collar Crime.* New York: Cambridge University Press, 2006.

SHUPE, ANSON. *In the Name of All That's Holy: A Theory of Clergy Malfeasance.* Westport, CT: Praeger, 1995.

SIDEL, RUTH, and VICTOR W. SIDEL. *The Health Care of China.* Boston: Beacon Press, 1982b.

SIMMEL, GEORG. *The Sociology of Georg Simmel.* Kurt Wolff, ed. New York: Free Press, 1950; orig. 1902.

SIMON, JULIAN. *The Ultimate Resource.* Princeton, NJ: Princeton University Press, 1981.

————. "More People, Greater Wealth, More Resources, Healthier Environment." In Theodore D. Goldfarb, ed., *Taking Sides: Clashing Views on Controversial Environmental Issues.* 6th ed. Guilford, CT: Dushkin, 1995.

SIMON, R., and L. NATH. "Gender and Emotion in the United States: Do Men and Women Differ in Self-Reports of Feelings and Expressive Behavior?" *American Journal of Sociology.* Vol, 109, No. 5 (2004):1137–76.

SIMON, ROGER, and ANGIE CANNON. "An Amazing Journey." *U.S. News & World Report* (August 6, 2001):10–19.

SIMONS, MARLISE. "The Price of Modernization: The Case of Brazil's Kaiapo Indians." In Jerome L . Singer and Dorothy G. Singer. "Psychologists Look at Television: Cognitive, Developmental, Personality, and Social Policy Implications." *American Psychologist.* Vol. 38, No. 7 (July 1983):826–34.

SIMONS, MARLISE. "The Price of Modernization: The Case of Brazil's Kaiapo Indians." In John J. Macionis and Nijole V. Benokraitis, eds., *Seeing Ourselves: Classic, Contemporary, and Cross-Cultural Readings in Sociology.* 7th ed. Upper Saddle River, NJ: Prentice Hall, 2007.

SINGER, P., and D. WELLS. "Ectogenesis." In Scott Gelfand and John R. Shook, eds., *Ectogenesis: Artificial Womb Technology and the Future of Human Reproduction.* Amsterdam: Rodopi, 2006.

SIVARD, RUTH LEGER. *World Military and Social Expenditures, 1987–88.* 12th ed. Washington, DC: World Priorities, 1988.

SIZER, THEODORE R. *Horace's Compromise: The Dilemma of the American High School.* Boston: Houghton Mifflin, 1984.

SKOCPOL, THEDA. *States and Social Revolutions: A Comparative Analysis of France, Russia, and China.* Cambridge: Cambridge University Press, 1979.

SMAIL, J. KENNETH. "Let's *Reduce* Global Population!" In John J. Macionis and Nijole V. Benokraitis, eds., *Seeing Ourselves: Classic, Contemporary, and Cross-Cultural Readings in Sociology.* 8th ed. Upper Saddle River, NJ: Prentice Hall, 2010:413–17.

SMITH, ADAM. *An Inquiry into the Nature and Causes of the Wealth of Nations.* New York: Modern Library, 1937; orig. 1776.

SMITH, DOUGLAS A. "Police Response to Interpersonal Violence: Defining the Parameters of Legal Control." *Social Forces.* Vol. 65, No. 3 (March 1987):767–82.

SMITH, DOUGLAS A., and PATRICK R. GARTIN. "Specifying Specific Deterrence: The Influence of Arrest on Future Criminal Activity." *American Sociological Review.* Vol. 54, No. 1 (February 1989):94–105.

SMITH, DOUGLAS A., and CHRISTY A. VISHER. "Street-Level Justice: Situational Determinants of Police Arrest Decisions." *Social Problems.* Vol. 29, No. 2 (December 1981):167–77.

SMITH, TOM W. "Anti-Semitism Decreases but Persists." *Society.* Vol. 33, No. 3 (March/April 1996):2.

————. "Are We Grown Up Yet? U.S. Study Says Not 'til 26." *Yahoo! News* (May 23, 2003). http://news.yahoo.com

————. *American Sexual Behavior: Trends, Sociodemographic Differences, and Risk Behavior.* Chicago: National Opinion Research Center, March 2006. www.norc.org/NR/rdonlyres/2663F09F-2E74-436E-AC81-6FFBF288E183/0/AmericanSexualBehavior2006.pdf

SMITH-LOVIN, LYNN, and CHARLES BRODY. "Interruptions in Group Discussions: The Effects of Gender and Group Composition." *American Journal of Sociology.* Vol. 54, No. 3 (June 1989):424–35.

SNELL, MARILYN BERLIN. "The Purge of Nurture." *New Perspectives Quarterly.* Vol. 7, No. 1 (Winter 1990):1–2.

SNOWDON, G. "Women Still Face a Glass Ceiling." *The Guardian* (February 21, 2011). www.guardian.co.uk/society/2011/feb/21/women-glass-ceiling-still-exists-top-jobs

SNYDER, HOWARD N. "Sexual Assault of Young Children as Reported to Law Enforcement: Victim, Incident, and Offender Characteristics." U.S. Department of Justice. 2000. http://bjs.ojp.usdoj.gov/index.cfm?ty=pbdetail&iid=1147

SOBEL, RACHEL K. "Herpes Tests Give Answers You Might Need to Know." *U.S. News & World Report* (June 18, 2001):53.

SOUTH, SCOTT J., and STEVEN F. MESSNER. "Structural Determinants of Intergroup Association: Interracial Marriage and Crime." *American Journal of Sociology.* Vol. 91, No. 6 (May 1986):1409–30.

SOWELL, THOMAS. *Race and Culture.* New York: Basic Books, 1994.

————. "Ethnicity and IQ." In Steven Fraser, ed., *The Bell Curve Wars: Race, Intelligence, and the Future of America.* New York: Basic Books, 1995:70–79.

SPECTER, MICHAEL. "Plunging Life Expectancy Puzzles Russia." *New York Times* (August 2, 1995):A1, A2.

SPEIER, HANS. "Wit and Politics: An Essay on Laughter and Power." Robert Jackall, ed. and trans. *American Journal of Sociology.* Vol. 103, No. 5 (March 1998): 1352–401.

SPENCER, MARTIN E. "Multiculturalism, 'Political Correctness,' and the Politics of Identity." *Sociological Forum.* Vol. 9, No. 4 (December 1994):547–67.

SPENCER STUART. "Leading CEOs: A Statistical Snapshot of S&P 500 Leaders." December 2008. www.spencerstuart.com/research/articles/975

SPITZER, STEVEN. "Toward a Marxian Theory of Deviance." In Delos H. Kelly, ed., *Criminal Behavior: Readings in Criminology.* New York: St. Martin's Press, 1980:175–91.

SPREEN, MARIUS, and RONALD ZWAAGSTRA. "Personal Network Sampling, Outdegree Analysis and Multilevel Analysis: Introducing the Network Concept in Studies of Hidden Populations." *International Sociology.* Vol. 9 (1994): 475–91.

STACEY, JUDITH. *Patriarchy and Socialist Revolution in China.* Berkeley: University of California Press, 1983.

————. *Brave New Families: Stories of Domestic Upheaval in Late-Twentieth-Century America.* New York: Basic Books, 1990.

STACK, STEVEN, IRA WASSERMAN, and ROGER KERN. "Adult Social Bonds and the Use of Internet Pornography." *Social Science Quarterly.* Vol. 85, No. 1 (March 2004):75–88.

STAPINSKI, HELENE. "Let's Talk Dirty." *American Demographics.* Vol. 20, No. 11 (November 1998):50–56.

STARK, RODNEY. *Sociology.* Belmont, CA: Wadsworth, 1985.

STARK, RODNEY, and WILLIAM SIMS BAINBRIDGE. "Of Churches, Sects, and Cults: Preliminary Concepts for a Theory of Religious Movements." *Journal for the Scientific Study of Religion.* Vol. 18, No. 2 (June 1979):117–31.

STATISTICS CANADA. "The Violence against Women Survey: Highlights." *The Daily.* Ottawa: Minister of Industry, Science and Technology, 1993b.

————. *Women in Canada: A Statistical Report.* 3rd ed. Ottawa: Minister of Industry, 1995a.

————. *National Population Health Survey Overview, 1994–95.* Ottawa: Minister of Industry, 1995b.

————. "Street Prostitution in Canada." *Juristat.* Catalogue no. 85-002XPE. Vol. 17, No. 2 (February, 1997g):1–12.

————. *The Daily* (May 28, 1998j). [Online] www.statcan.ca/Daily/English/980528/d980528.htm

————. *The Daily* (June 2, 1998k). [Online] www.statcan.ca/Daily/English/980602/d980602.htm

————. *Statistical Report on the Health of Canadians.* Federal, Provincial and Territorial Committee on Population Health, 1999d.

————. "General Social Survey: Time Use." *The Daily* (Tuesday, November 9, 1999f) [Online] www.statcan.ca/Daily/English/991109/d991109a.htm

————. *The Daily* (Thursday, March 16, 2000d). [Online] www.statcan.ca/Daily/English/000316/d000316.pdf

————. *Education in Canada, 1999.* Statistics Canada Catalogue no. 81229-XIE, May 2000h.

————. *Women in Canada 2000: A Gender-based Statistical Report.* Ottawa: Housing, Family and Social Statistics Division. Catalogue no. 89-503XPE. Ottawa: Ministry of Industry, 2000m.

————. *Education in Canada, 2000.* Statistics Canada Catalogue no. 81229-XIB, May 2001c.

————. "2001 Census: Marital Status, Common-law Status, Families, Dwellings and Households." *The Daily* (October 22, 2002a) [Online] www.statcan.ca/Daily/English/021022/d021022a.htm

————. "Television Viewing." *The Daily* (December 2, 2002h) [Online] www.statcan.ca/Daily/English/021202/d021202a.htm

————. "Therapeutic Abortions." *The Daily.* (January 18, 2002i) [Online] www.statcan.ca/Daily/English/020118/d020118d.htm

————. *2001 Census: Analysis Series. Education in Canada: Raising the Standard.* Catalogue no. 96F0030XIE2001012, 2003c.

————. *Education Quarterly Review,* Vol. 9, No. 2. Catalogue no. 81-003XIE, June 2003d.

————. *The People: Student Indebtedness.* (2003f) [Online] http://142.206.72.67/02/02c/02c_007b_e.htm

————. *Overview: University Education, Experience Pay Off in Higher Earnings.* (2003g) [Online] www12.statcan.ca/english/census01/Products/Analytic/companion/earn/canada.cfm#9

————. Number and Average Employment Income (2) in Constant (2000) Dollars, Sex (3), Work Activity (3), Age Groups (7) and Historical Highest Level of Schooling (6) for Population 15 Years and Over With Employment Income, for Canada, Provinces, Territories, Census Metropolitan Areas and Census Agglomerations, 1995 and 2000—20% Sample Data. (2003h) [Electronic Data File.] Catalogue No. 97F0019XCB01002.

————. Profile of Canadian Families and Households: Diversification Continues. (2003l) Ottawa: Statistics Canada. Catalogue no. 96F0030XIE2001003. [Online] www12.statcan.ca/english/census01/products/analytic/companion/fam/pdf/96F0030XIE2001003.pdf

————. Family Violence in Canada: A Statistical Profile 2003. (2003m). Ottawa: Minister of Industry. Catalogue no. 85-224-XIE.

————. Canada's Ethnocultural Portrait: The Changing Mosaic. 2003t. Ottawa: Minister of Industry. Catalogue no. 96F0030XIE2001008.

————. Number and Average Wages and Salaries (2) in Constant (2000) Dollars, Sex (3), Work Activity (3), Historical Highest Level of Schooling (6), Age Groups (5) and Occupation—1991 Standard Occupational Classification (Historical) (706A) for Paid Workers 15 Years and Over with Wages and Salaries, for Canada, Provinces and Territories, 1995 and 2000—20% Sample Data. (2003ak) [Electronic Data File]. Catalogue no. 97F0019XCB01060.

————. Income Status (4) and Census Family Structure for Census Families, Sex, Age Groups and Household Living Arrangements for Non-family Persons 15 Years and Over and Sex and Age Groups for Persons in Private Households (87), for Canada, Provinces, Census Metropolitan Areas and Census Agglomerations, 1995 and 2000—20% Sample Data. (2003al) [Electronic Data File.] Catalogue no. 97F0020XCB01006.

————. "University Degrees, Diplomas and Certificates Awarded." The Daily, 2003be. [Online] www.statcan.ca/Daily/English/030708/d030708a.htm

————. Selected Income Characteristics (35), Aboriginal Identity (8), Age Groups (6) and Sex (3) for Population, for Canada, Provinces, Territories and Census Metropolitan Areas, 2001 Census—20% Sample Data (2003bu). [Electronic Data File.] Catalogue no. 97F0011XIE2001047.

————. "Pregnancies." The Daily (Wednesday, October 27, 2004b). [Online] www.statcan.ca/Daily/English/041027/d041027d.htm

————. The Daily. "Shelters for Abused Women: 2003/04." (Wednesday, June 15, 2005a). [Online] www.statcan.ca/Daily/English/050615/d050615a.htm

————. Education Indicators in Canada: Report of the Pan-Canadian Education Indicators Program 2005. Ottawa: Statistics Canada, 2005.

————. "Family Violence in Canada: A Statistical Profile." The Daily (July 14, 2005). [Online] www.statcan.ca/Daily/English/050714/d050714a.htm.

————. Learning a Living: First Results of the Adult Literacy and Life Skills Survey. Catalogue no. 89-603-XWE. Ottawa: Minister of Industry, Canada, and Organization for Economic Cooperation and Development (OECD), 2005.

————. Census Snapshot—Immigration in Canada: A Portrait of the Foreign-Born Population, 2006 Census. 2006a. [Online] www.statcan.gc.ca/pub/11-008-x/2008001/article/10556-eng.htm

————. "Television Viewing." The Daily (March 31, 2006b). [Online] www.statcan.gc.ca/daily-quotidien/060331/dq060331b-eng.htm

————. "Canadian Internet Use Survey." The Daily (August 15, 2006c). [Online] www.statcan.gc.ca/daily-quotidien/060815/dq060815b-eng.htm

————. Police Resources in Canada, 2006. Catalogue no. 85-225. 2006d. [Online] www.statcan.gc.ca/pub/85-225-x/85-225-x2006000-eng.pdf.

————. "The Teaching Profession: Trends from 1999 to 2005." Education Matters. Vol. 3, No. 4 (2006e). [Online] www.statcan.gc.ca/pub/81-004-x/81-004-x2006004-eng.htm

————. Measuring Violence against Women Statistical Trends. Catalogue no. 85-570-XIE. 2006f. [Online] www.statcan.ca/english/research/85-570-XIE/85-570-XIE2006001.pdf

————. "Study: Wives as Primary Breadwinners." The Daily (August 23, 2006g). [Online] www.statcan.gc.ca/daily-quotidien/060823/dq060823b-eng.htm

————. Canada's Ethnocultural Mosaic, 2006 Census: Highlights. 2006h. [Online] www12.statcan.ca/census-recensement/2006/as-sa/97-562/p1-eng.cfm

————. Low Income Cut-Offs for 2005 and Low Income Measures for 2004. Catalogue no. 75F0002MIE, Vol. 4. Ottawa: Statistics Canada, 2006an.

————. Women in Canada: A Gender-Based Statistical Analysis. 5th ed. Ottawa: Statistics Canada. Catalogue no. 89-503-XIE, 2006au.

————. Profile of Language, Immigration, Citizenship, Mobility and Migration for Canada, Provinces, Territories, Census Divisions and Census Subdivisions, 2006 Census. 2007a. [Online] www12.statcan.gc.ca/census-recensement/2006/dp-pd/prof/rel/Rp-eng.cfm?LANG=E&APATH=3&DETAIL=0&DIM=0&FL=A&FREE=0&GC=0&GID=0&GK=0&GRP=1&PID=89770&PRID=0&PTYPE=89103&S=0&SHOWALL=0&SUB=0&Temporal=2006&THEME=70&VID=0&VNAMEE=&VNAMEF=

————. "Ethnic Origins 2006 Counts for Canada Provinces and Territories—20% Sample Data (Table)." Ethnocultural Portrait of Canada Highlight Tables, 2006 Census. Catalogue no. 97-562-XWE2006002. 2007b.

————. Women in Canada: Work Chapter Updates 2006. Catalogue no. 89F0133XIE. 2007c. [Online] www.statcan.gc.ca/pub/89f0133x/89f0133x2006000-eng.pdf

————. Census Families by Number of Children at Home, by Province and Territory (2006 Census). 2007d. [Online] www40.statcan.ca/l01/cst01/famil50a-eng.htm

————. Family Portrait: Continuity and Change in Canadian Families and Households in 2006, 2006 Census. Catalogue no. 97-553-XIE. 2007e. [Online] http://dsp-psd.pwgsc.gc.ca/collection_2007/statcan/97-553-X/97-553-XIE2006001.pdf

————. A Portrait of Seniors in Canada, 89-519-XWE2006001, February 2007f, http://www.statcan.gc.ca/pub/89-519-x/2006001/c-g/4181481-eng.htm

————. Earnings and Incomes of Canadians over the Past Quarter Century, 2006 Census. 2008a. [Online] www.statcan.gc.ca/bsolc/olc-cel/olc-cel?catno=97-563-XIE2006001&lang=eng

————. Report on the Demographic Situation in Canada. 2008b. [Online] www.statcan.gc.ca/bsolc/olc-cel/olc-cel?catno=91-209-x&lang=eng

————. Educational Portrait of Canada, 2006 Census. Catalogue no. 97-560-X. Ottawa: Minister of Industry, 2008c.

————. Labour, 2006 Census. Catalogue no. 97-559-XCB2006027. 2008d. http://www.statcan.gc.ca/bsolc/olc-cel/olc-cel?lang=eng&catno=97-559-X2006027

————. "Median(1) 2005 Earnings for Full-Year, Full-Time Earners by Education, Both Sexes, Age 25 to 34, for Canada, Provinces and Territories—20% Sample Data (Table)." Income and Earnings Highlight Tables, 2006 Census. Catalogue no. 97-563-XWE2006002. 2008e. http://www.statcan.gc.ca/bsolc/olc-cel/olc-cel?lang=eng&catno=97-563-X2006002

————. 2006 Census: Earnings, Income and Shelter Costs. 2008f. [Online] www.statcan.gc.ca/daily-quotidien/080501/dq080501a-eng.htm

————. Study: Trends in Employment and Wages. 2008g. [Online] www.statcan.gc.ca/daily-quotidien/080926/dq080926c-eng.htm

————. "Survey of Earned Doctorates." The Daily (April 28, 2008h). [Online] www.statcan.gc.ca/daily-quotidien/080428/dq080428b-eng.htm

————. Gender Differences in Police-Reported Violent Crime in Canada, 2008. Catalogue no. 85F0033M, no. 24. 2008i. [Online] www.statcan.gc.ca/pub/85f0033m/2010024/part-partie1-eng.htm

————. Visible Minority Groups (15), Generation Status (4), Age Groups (9) and Sex (3) for the Population 15 Years and Over of Canada, Provinces, Territories, Census Metropolitan Areas and Census Agglomerations, 2006 Census—20% Sample Data. Statistics Canada Catalogue no. 97-562-XCB2006010. 2008j.

————. "2006 Census: Ethnic Origin, Visible Minorities, Place of Work and Mode of Transportation." The Daily (April 2, 2008k). [Online] www.statcan.gc.ca/daily-quotidien/080402/dq080402a-eng.htm

————. Ethnic Origin (247), Single and Multiple Ethnic Origin Responses (3) and Sex (3) for the Population of Canada, Provinces, Territories, Census Metropolitan Areas and Census Agglomerations, 2006 Census—20% Sample Data. Catalogue no. 97-562-XCB2006006. 2008l.

————. Employment Income Statistics (4) in Constant (2005) Dollars, Work Activity in the Reference Year (3), Age Groups (5A), Generation Status (4), Visible Minority Groups (15), Highest Certificate, Diploma or Degree (5) and Sex (3) for the Population 15 Years and Over with Employment Income of Canada, Provinces, Territories, Census Metropolitan Areas and Census Agglomerations, 2000 and 2005—20% Sample Data. Catalogue no. 97-563-XCB2006060. 2008m.

————. Employment Income Statistics (4) in Constant (2005) Dollars, Work Activity in the Reference Year (3), Aboriginal Identity, Registered Indian Status and Aboriginal Ancestry (21), Age Groups (5A), Highest Certificate, Diploma or Degree (5) and Sex (3) for the Population 15 Years and Over with Employment Income of Canada, Provinces, Territories, 2000 and 2005—20% Sample Data. Catalogue no. 97-563-XCB2006061. 2008n.

————. Work Activity in 2005 (14), Visible Minority Groups (15), Immigrant Status and Period of Immigration (9), Highest Certificate, Diploma or Degree (7), Age Groups (9)

and Sex (3) for the Population 15 Years and Over of Canada, Provinces, Territories, Census Metropolitan Areas and Census Agglomerations, 2006 Census—20% Sample Data [Electronic Data File]. Catalogue no. 97-562-XCB2006014. 2008o.

———. Public Sector Statistics, Financial Management System, 2007/2008. Catalogue no. 68-213-X. 2008p.

———. "Fathers' Use of Paid Paternal Leave." Perspectives on Labour and Income. Catalogue no. 75-001-X. 2008q. [Online] www.statcan.gc.ca/pub/75-001-x/75-001-x2008106-eng.pdf

———. Mobility Status 5 Years Ago (9), Mother Tongue (8), Age Groups (16) and Sex (3) for the Population Aged 5 Years and Over of Canada, Provinces, Territories, Census Metropolitan Areas and Census Agglomerations, 2006 Census—20% Sample Data. Catalogue no. 97-556-XCB2006006. 2008r.

———. Aboriginal Peoples in Canada in 2006: Inuit, Métis and First Nations, 2006 Census. Ottawa: Minister of Industry, 2008s. [Online] www12.statcan.ca/census-recensement/2006/as-sa/97-558/pdf/97-558-XIE2006001.pdf

———. Report on the Demographic Situation in Canada 2005 and 2006. Catalogue no. 91-209-X. 2008t. [Online] http://dsp-psd.pwgsc.gc.ca/collection_2008/statcan/91-209-X/91-209-XIE2004000.pdf

———. Educational Portrait of Canada, Census 2006. Catalogue no. 97-560-X2006001. 2008u.

———. "Ethnic Diversity and Immigration." January 13, 2009. www41.statcan.ca/2008/30000/ceb30000_000-eng.htm

———. 2006 Census: Family Portrait: Continuity and Change in Canadian Families and Households in 2006: National Portrait: Census Families. 2009a. [Online] www12.statcan.ca/census-recensement/2006/as-sa/97-553/p4-eng.cfm

———. Aboriginal Peoples of Canada, 2006 Census. Catalogue no. 92-593-XCB2006001. 2009b. [Online] www.statcan.gc.ca/bsolc/olc-cel/olc-cel?catno=92-593-XCB2006001&lang=eng&issnote=1

———. Earnings and Incomes of Canadians over the Past Quarter Century, 2006 Census: Earnings. 2009c. [Online] www12.statcan.ca/census-recensement/2006/as-sa/97-563/p5-eng.cfm

———. Postsecondary Enrolment and Graduation: Education Indicators in Canada: Fact Sheets. 2009d. [Online] www.statcan.gc.ca/pub/81-599-x/81-599-x2009003-eng.htm

———. Women in Canada: A Gender-Based Statistical Report, Paid Work. Catalogue no. 89-503-X. 2010a.

———. Police-Reported Hate Crimes. 2010b. [Online] www.statcan.gc.ca/daily-quotidien/100614/dq100614b-eng.htm

———. Police-Reported Crime Statistics 2009. 2010c. [Online] www.statcan.gc.ca/daily-quotidien/100720/dq100720a-eng.htm

———. 2006 Community Profiles. 2010d. [Online] www12.statcan.ca/census%E2%80%90recensement/2006/dp%E2%80%90pd/prof/92%E2%80%90591/search-recherche/lst/page.cfm?Lang=E&GeoCode=35

———. Projections of the Diversity of the Canadian Population. Catalogue no. 91-551-X. Ottawa: Minister of Industry, 2010e.

———. Father's Day... By the Numbers. 2010f. [Online] www42.statcan.gc.ca/smr08/2010/smr08_143_2010-eng.htm

———. University Enrolments by Registration Status and Sex, by Province. 2010g. [Online] www40.statcan.ca/l01/cst01/educ53a-eng.htm

———. Aboriginal Statistics at a Glance. Catalogue no. 89-645-XWE. 2010h.

———. "Trends in Dropout Rates and the Labour Market Outcomes of Young Dropouts." Education Matters: Insights on Education, Learning and Training in Canada. 2010i. [Online] www.statcan.gc.ca/pub/81-004-x/2010004/article/11339-eng.htm

———. Current Smoking. 2010j. [Online] www.statcan.gc.ca/pub/82-229-x/2009001/deter/cos-eng.htm

———. 2006 Census: Portrait of the Canadian Population in 2006: Findings. 2010k. [Online] www12.statcan.gc.ca/census-recensement/2006/as-sa/97-550/index-eng.cfm?CFID=3674780&CFTOKEN=64671080

———. Life Expectancy by Birth, by Sex, by Province. 2010l.

———. CANSIM Database Retrieval Output, Table 102-0551—Deaths and Mortality Rate, by Selected Grouped Causes, Age Group and Sex, Canada, Annual. 2011a.

———. Place of Birth for the Immigrant Population by Period of Immigration, 2006 Counts and Percentage Distribution, for Canada, Provinces and Territories—20% Sample Data. 2011b. [Online] www12.statcan.gc.ca/census-recensement/2006/dp-pd/hlt/97-557/T404-eng.cfm?Lang=E&T=404&GH=4&GF=1&SC=1&S=1&O=D

———. Persons in Low Income after Tax. 2011c. [Online] www40.statcan.gc.ca/l01/cst01/famil19a-eng.htm

———. Figure 15, More Young Adults in Their Twenties Live in the Parental Home in 2006. 2011d. [Online] www12.statcan.ca/census-recensement/2006/as-sa/97-553/figures/c15-eng.cfm.

———. Age Groups (14) and Sex (3) for the Population of Canada, Provinces, Territories, Census Divisions and Census Subdivisions, 2006 Census—100% Data [Electronic Data File]. Catalogue no. 97-551-XCB2006013.IVT. 2011e.

———. "Residential Telephone Service Survey." The Daily (April 11, 2011f).

———. CANSIM II Database Retrieval Output. Series v14225267. Ottawa: Statistics Canada, 2011g.

———. CANSIM II Database Retrieval Output. Series v14225271. Ottawa: Statistics Canada, 2011h.

———. CANSIM II Database Retrieval Output. Series v14225269. Ottawa: Statistics Canada, 2011i.

———. Legal Marital Status (6), Common-Law Status (3), Age Groups (17) and Sex (3) for the Population 15 Years and Over of Canada, Provinces, Territories, Census Divisions and Census Subdivisions, 2006 Census—100% Data. [Electronic Data File]. Catalogue no. 97-552-XCB2006009[1].IVT. 2011j.

———. Income in Canada. 2011k. [Online] www.statcan.gc.ca/bsolc/olc-cel/olc-cel?catno=75-202-x&lang=eng

———. Income in Canada 2009. Catalogue no. 75-202-XWE. Ottawa: Minister of Industry, 2011l.

———. Family Income Groups (22B) in Constant (2005) Dollars and Census Family Structure (11) for the Census Families in Private Households of Canada, Provinces, Territories, Census Metropolitan Areas and Census Agglomerations, 2000 and 2005—20% Sample Data. [Electronic Data File]. Catalogue no. 97-563-XCB2006071[1].IVT. 2011m.

———. CANSIM Table 202-0702: v32211870—Canada; Median Total Income; Economic Families, Two Persons Or More (Dollars). [Electronic Data File]. 2011n.

———. Modified Table 202-0703—Market, Total and After-Tax Income, by Economic Family Type and After-Tax Income Quintiles, 2007 Constant Dollars, Annual. [Electronic Data File]. Catalogue no: 703[1].ivt. 2011o.

———. Family Income (7) and Economic Family Structure (4) for the Economic Families in Private Households of Canada, Provinces, Territories, Census Divisions and Census Subdivisions, 2005—20% Sample Data. [Electronic Data File]. Catalogue no. 97-563-XCB2006031[1].IVT. 2011p.

———. Income Status after Tax (3A) and Economic Family Structure (4) for the Economic Families in Private Households of Canada, Provinces, Census Divisions and Census Subdivisions, 2005—20% Sample Data. [Electronic Data File]. Catalogue no. 97-563-XCB2006040[1].IVT. 2011q.

———. Table 102-0512—Life Expectancy, at Birth and at Age 65, by Sex, Canada, Provinces and Territories, Annual (Years). CANSIM Database. 2011r www5.statcan.gc.ca/cansim/a01?lang=eng

———. CANSIM II: Canadian Socio-Economic Information Management System [Computer File]. Series v2461476. Ottawa: Statistics Canada, 2011s.

———. CANSIM II: Canadian Socio-Economic Information Management System [Computer File]. Series v2461686. Ottawa: Statistics Canada, 2011t.

———. Profile of Labour Market Activity, Industry, Occupation, Education, Language of Work, Place of Work and Mode of Transportation for Canada, Provinces, Territories, Census Divisions and Census Subdivisions, 2006 Census [Electronic Database]. Catalogue no. 94-579-XCB2006001. 2011u.

———. Visible Minority Groups (15), Immigrant Status and Period of Immigration (9), Age Groups (10) and Sex (3) for the Population of Canada, Provinces, Territories, Census Divisions and Census Subdivisions, 2006 Census—20% Sample Data. [Electronic Data File]. Catalogue no. 97-562-XCB2006016[1].IVT. 2011v.

———. Aboriginal Identity (8), Area of Residence (6), Age Groups (12) and Sex (3) for the Population of Canada, Provinces and Territories, 2006 Census—20% Sample Data. [Electronic Data File]. Catalogue no. 97-558-XCB2006006[1].IVT. 2011w.

———. CANSIM II: Canadian Socio-Economic Information Management System [Computer File]. Series v2522952. Ottawa: Statistics Canada, 2011x.

———. CANSIM II: Canadian Socio-Economic Information Management System [Computer File]. Series v2522972. Ottawa: Statistics Canada, 2011y.

———. CANSIM II: Canadian Socio-Economic Information Management System [Computer File]. Series v2522982. Ottawa: Statistics Canada, 2011z.

———. CANSIM II: Canadian Socio-Economic Information Management System [Computer File]. Series v2522992. Ottawa: Statistics Canada, 2011aa.

———. CANSIM II: Canadian Socio-Economic Information Management System [Computer File]. Series v2523002. Ottawa: Statistics Canada, 2011ab.

———. CANSIM II: Canadian Socio-Economic Information Management System [Computer File]. Series v2523012. Ottawa: Statistics Canada, 2011ac.

———. CANSIM II: Canadian Socio-Economic Information Management System [Computer File]. Series v2523022. Ottawa: Statistics Canada, 2011ad.

———. Profile of Labour Market Activity, Industry, Occupation, Education, Language of Work, Place of Work and Mode of Transportation for Canada, Provinces, Territories, Census Divisions and Census Subdivisions, 2006 Census.[Electronic Data File]. Catalogue no. 94-579-XCB2006001[1].IVT. 2011ae.

———. Estimates of Census Families for Canada, Provinces and Territories. 2011af. [Online] www.statcan.gc.ca/cgi-bin/imdb/p2SV.pl?Function=getSurvey&SDDS=3606&lang=en&db=imdb&adm=8&dis=2#a2.

———. Population Groups (28), Age Groups (8), Sex (3) and Selected Demographic, Cultural, Labour Force, Educational and Income Characteristics (309), for the Total Population of Canada, Provinces, Territories, Census Metropolitan Areas and Census Agglomeration. [Electronic Data Base]. Catalogue no. 97-564-XCB2006009[1].IVT. 2011ag.

———. Divorces, by Age of Husband and Wife at Divorce. CANSIM Table 101-6507, v42136435 [Electronic Database]. 2011ah.

———. Vital Statistics, Divorces. CANSIM Table 053-0002, v107 [Electronic Database]. 2011ai.

———. Divorces and Crude Divorce Rates. CANSIM Table 101-6501, v42136127 [Electronic Database]. 2011aj.

———. Census Family Status (6), Age Groups (20) and Sex (3) for the Population in Private Households of Canada, Provinces, Territories, Census Divisions and Census Subdivisions, 2006 Census—20% Sample Data. [Electronic Data File]. Catalogue no. 97-553-XCB2006015[1].IVT. 2011ak.

———. Learning—Educational Attainment. 2011al. [Online] www4.hrsdc.gc.ca/.3ndic.1t.4r@-eng.jsp?iid=29#M_4

———. Highest Certificate, Diploma or Degree (14), Age Groups (10A) and Sex (3) for the Population 15 Years and Over of Canada, Provinces, Territories, Census Metropolitan Areas and Census Agglomerations, 2006 Census—20% Sample Data. [Electronic Data File]. Catalogue no. 97-560-XCB2006007. 2011am.

———. Employment Income Statistics (4) in Constant (2005) Dollars, Work Activity in the Reference Year (3), Occupation—National Occupational Classification for Statistics 2006 (720A) and Sex (3) for the Population 15 Years and Over with Employment Income of Canada, Provinces, Territories, Census Metropolitan Areas and Census Agglomerations, 2000 and 2005—20% Sample Data. [Electronic Data File]. Catalogue no. 97-563-XCB2006063. 2011an.

———. Aboriginal Identity (8), Highest Certificate, Diploma or Degree (14), Major Field of Study—Classification of Instructional Programs, 2000 (14), Area of Residence (6), Age Groups (10A) and Sex (3) for the Population 15 Years and Over of Canada, Provinces and Territories, 2006 Census—20% Sample Data. [Electronic Data File]. Catalogue no. 97-560-XCB2006028. 2011ao.

———. Canadian Health Measures Survey: Adult Obesity Prevalence in Canada and the United States. 2011ap. [Online] www.statcan.gc.ca/daily-quotidien/110302/dq110302c-eng.htm

———. Estimates of Births, Deaths and Marriages, Canada, Provinces and Territories, Quarterly (Number). CANSIM Table 530001, v62 [Electronic Data Base]. 2011aq.

———. Estimates of Population, by Age Group and Sex for July 1, Canada, Provinces and Territories, Annually (Persons Unless Specified). Cansim Table 510001, v466668 [Electronic Database]. 2011ar.

———. Estimates of Births, Deaths and Marriages, Canada, Provinces and Territories, Quarterly (Number). Cansim Table 530001, v77 [Electronic Database]. 2011as.

———. Infant Mortality, by Sex and Birth Weight. Cansim Table 102-0030, v5939542 [Electronic Database]. 2011at.

———. Canada, Place of Residence of Mother; Total, Month of Birth; Number of Live Births. CANSIM Table 102-4502, v21400536 [Electronic Database]. 2011au.

———. Life Expectancy, at Birth and at Age 65, by Sex. Cansim Table 102-0512, v52302198 [Electronic Database]. 2011av.

———. Life Expectancy, at Birth and at Age 65, by Sex. Cansim Table 102-0512, v52302200 [Electronic Database]. 2011aw.

———. Profile for Canada, Provinces, Territories, Census Divisions and Census Subdivisions, 2006 Census. [Electronic Data File.] Catalogue no. 94-581-XCB2006001. 2011ax.

———. Mode of Transportation (9), Age Groups (9) and Sex (3) for the Employed Labour Force 15 Years and Over Having a Usual Place of Work or No Fixed Workplace Address of Canada, Provinces, Territories, Census Metropolitan Areas and Census Agglomerations, 2006 Census—20% Sample Data. [Electronic Data File]. Catalogue no. 97-561-XCB2006012.IVT. 2011ay.

———. Income in Canada 2009. Catalogue no. 75-202-XWE (2011). Ottawa: Minister of Industry, 2011az.

———. Canadians in Context—Aging Population. 2011ba. [Online] www4.hrsdc.gc.ca/.3ndic.1t.4r@-eng.jsp?iid=33

———. Profile for Canada, Provinces, Territories, Census Divisions and Census Subdivisions, 2006 Census. [Electronic Data File]. Catalogue no. 94-581-XCB2006001. 2011bb.

STATISTICS CANADA and OECD. Learning a Living: First Results of the Adult Literacy and Life Skills Survey. 89-603-XWE2005001. May 2005. http://www.statcan.gc.ca/bsolc/olc-cel/olc-ccl?catno=89-603-X&lang=eng; Based on data from Table 2.2, from OECD/Statistics Canada (2005), Learning a Living: First Results of the Adult Literacy and Life Skills Survey, OECD Publishing, http://dx.doi.org/10.1787/9789264010390-en

STEBEN, MARC, and STEPHEN L. SACKS. "Genital Herpes: The Epidemiology and Control of a Common Sexually Transmitted Disease." Canadian Journal of Human Sexuality. Vol. 6, No. 2 (1997):127–34.

STEELE, SHELBY. The Content of Our Character: A New Vision of Race in America. New York: St. Martin's Press, 1990.

STEIN, ROB. "Fewer U.S. Deaths Linked to Obesity." Washington Post (April 20, 2005):A10.

STEPHENS T., C. DULBERG, and N. JOUBERT. "Mental Health of the Canadian Population: A Comprehensive Analysis." Chronic Diseases in Canada Vol. 20, No. 3 (1999):118–26.

STEVENSON, KATHRYN. "Family Characteristics of Problem Kids." Canadian Social Trends. Vol. 55 (Winter 1999):2–6.

STEYN, MARK. "Is Canada's Economy a Model for America?" Imprimis. Vol. 37, No. 1 (January 2008):1–7.

STIER, HAYA. "Continuity and Change in Women's Occupations following First Childbirth." Social Science Quarterly. Vol. 77, No. 1 (March 1996):60–75.

STOBBE, MIKE. "Cancer to Be World's Top Killer by 2010, WHO Says." Guardian (December 12, 2008). www.guardian.co.uk/uslatest/story/0,,-8147108,00.html

STOCKHOLM INTERNATIONAL PEACE RESEARCH INSTITUTE. SIPRI Yearbook, 2009: Armaments, Disarmament and International Security. Stockholm: SIPRI. June 2009. www.sipri.org/yearbook/2009

STORMS, MICHAEL D. "Theories of Sexual Orientation." Journal of Personality and Social Psychology. Vol. 38, No. 5 (May 1980):783–92.

STORY, LOUISE. "Top Hedge Fund Managers Do Well in a Down Year." New York Times (March 25, 2009). www.nytimes.com/2009/03/25/business/25hedge.html

STOUFFER, SAMUEL A., ET AL. The American Soldier: Adjustment during Army Life. Princeton, NJ: Princeton University Press, 1949.

STRAUS, MURRAY A. "Physical Assaults by Wives—A Major Social Problem." In Richard Gelles and Donileen Loseke, eds., Current Controversies on Family Violence. Newbury Park, CA: Sage, 1993.

STRAUS, MURRAY A., and Richard J. Gelles. "Societal Change and Change in Family Violence from 1975 to 1985 As Revealed By Two National Surveys." Journal of Marriage and the Family. Vol. 48, No. 4 (August 1986):465–79.

STROHSCHEIN, LISA A. "Parental Divorce and Child Mental Health Trajectories." Journal of Marriage and Family. Vol. 67 (2005):1286–300.

STUESSY, JOE, and SCOTT LIPSCOMB. Rock and Roll: Its History and Stylistic Development. 6th ed. Upper Saddle River, NJ: Prentice Hall, 2009.

SULLIVAN, ANDREW. Lecture delivered at Kenyon College, April 4, 2002.

SULLIVAN, BARBARA. "McDonald's Sees India as Golden Opportunity." Chicago Tribune (April 5, 1995):B1.

SUMNER, WILLIAM GRAHAM. Folkways. New York: Dover, 1959; orig. 1906.

SUMTER, S.R., C.L. BOKHORST, L. STEINBERG, and P.M. WESTENBERG. "The Developmental Pattern of Resistance to Peer Influence in Adolescence: Will the Teenager Ever Be Able to Resist?" Journal of Adolescence. Vol. 32 (2009):1009–21.

SUNG, BETTY LEE. Mountains of Gold: The Story of the Chinese in America. New York: Macmillan, 1967.

SURRATT, H.L., J.A. INCIARDI, S.P. KURTZ, and M.C. KILEY. "Sex Work and Drug Use in a Subculture of Violence." *Crime & Delinquency.* Vol. 50 (2004):43–59.

SUSSMAN, DEBORAH, and LAHOUARIA YSSAAD. "The Rising Profile of Women Academics." *Perspectives on Labour and Income.* Catalogue no. 75-001-XIE. Ottawa: Statistics Canada, 2005.

SUTHERLAND, EDWIN H. "White Collar Criminality." *American Sociological Review.* Vol. 5, No. 1 (February 1940):1–12.

SVEBAK, SVEN. CITED in MARILYN ELIAS, "Study Links Sense of Humor, Survival." [Online] Available March 14, 2007, at http://www.usatoday.com

SWANK, DUANE. *Global Capital, Political Institutions, and Policy Change in Developed Welfare States.* Cambridge, UK, and New York, USA: Cambridge University Press, 2002.

SYZMANSKI, ALBERT. *Class Structure: A Critical Perspective.* New York: Praeger, 1983.

SZASZ, THOMAS S. *The Myth of Mental Illness: Foundations of a Theory of Personal Conduct.* New York: Dell, 1961.

———. *The Manufacturer of Madness: A Comparative Study of the Inquisition and the Mental Health Movement.* New York: Harper & Row, 1970.

———. "Cleansing the Modern Heart." *Society.* Vol. 40, No. 4 (May/June 2003):52–59.

———. "Protecting Patients against Psychiatric Intervention." *Society.* Vol. 41, No. 3 (March/April 2004):7–10.

TAIT, H. *Aboriginal Peoples Survey, 2006: Inuit Health and Social Conditions.* Statistics Canada, Catalogue no. 89-637-X, No. 001. 2008. www.cwlc.ca/files/file/Aboriginal%20Peoples%20Survey%202006%20(Inuit%20health%20and%20social%20conditions).pdf

TAJFEL, HENRI. "Social Psychology of Intergroup Relations." *Annual Review of Psychology.* Palo Alto, CA: Annual Reviews, 1982:1–39.

TALLICHET, SUZANNE E. "Barriers to Women's Advancement in Underground Coal Mining." *Rural Sociology.* Vol. 65, No. 2 (June 2000):234–52.

TAMBLYN, ROBYN, cited in Sheldon Lewis, "Which Doctors Will Annoy Their Patients?" *Spirituality and Health.* Vol. 11, No. 2 (March/April 2008):28.

TANNEN, DEBORAH. *You Just Don't Understand: Women and Men in Conversation.* New York: Morrow, 1990.

———. *Talking from 9 to 5: How Women's and Men's Conversational Styles Affect Who Gets Heard, Who Gets Credit, and What Gets Done at Work.* New York: Morrow, 1994.

TANNER, JULIAN, HARVEY KRAHN, and TIMOTHY F. HARTNAGEL. *Fractured Transitions from School to Work: Revisiting the Dropout Problem.* Toronto: Oxford University Press, 1995.

TAUB, DIANE E., PENELOPE A. MCLORG, and PATRICIA L FANFLIK. "Stigma Management Strategies among Women with Physical Disabilities: Contrasting Approaches of Downplaying or Claiming a Disability Status." *Deviant Behavior.* Vol. 25, No. 2 (2004):169–90.

TAVRIS, CAROL, and CAROL WADE. *Psychology in Perspective.* 3rd ed. Upper Saddle River, NJ: Prentice Hall, 2001.

TAYLOR, ALISON, and HARVEY KRAHN. "Aiming High: Educational Aspirations of Visible Minority Immigrant Youth." *Canadian Social Trends.* No. 79 (Winter 2005):8–12.

TAYLOR, FREDERICK WINSLOW. *The Principles of Scientific Management.* New York: Harper & Brothers, 1911.

TAYLOR, S., and C. ASHWORTH. "Durkheim and Social Realism: An Approach to Social Health." In G. Scrambler, ed., *Sociological Theory and Medical Sociology.* London: Tavistock, 1987.

TAYLOR-BUTTS, ANDREA. "Private Security and Public Policing in Canada, 2001." *Juristat.* Vol. 24, No. 7 (August 2004):1–15.

TEENAGE RESEARCH UNLIMITED. Loveisrespect.org, National Teen Dating Abuse Helpline: Resource Center. 2008. www.loveisrespect.org/resource-center/

TERRY, DON. "In Crackdown on Bias, a New Tool." *New York Times* (June 12, 1993):8.

THOMAS, EVAN, and MARTHA BRANT. "Injection of Reflection." *Newsweek* (November 19, 2007):40–41.

THOMAS, JENNIFER. "Adult Correctional Services in Canada, 1998–99." *Juristat.* Statistics Canada Catalogue no. 85-002-XIE. Vol. 20, No 3 (June 2000):1–16.

THOMAS, PIRI. *Down These Mean Streets.* New York: Signet, 1967.

THOMAS, W.I. "The Relation of Research to the Social Process." In Morris Janowitz, ed., *W.I. Thomas on Social Organization and Social Personality.* Chicago: University of Chicago Press, 1966:289–305; orig. 1931.

THOMAS, W.I., and DOROTHY SWAINE THOMAS. *The Child in America: Behavior Problems and Programs.* New York: Knopf, 1928.

THOMMA, STEVEN. "Christian Coalition Demands Action from GOP." *Philadelphia Inquirer* (September 14, 1997):A2.

THOMPSON, DICK. "Gene Maverick." *Time* (January 11, 1999):54–55.

THOMPSON, MARK, and DOUGLAS WALLER. "Shield of Dreams." *Time* (May 8, 2001):45–47.

THORNBERRY, TERRANCE, and MARGARET FARNSWORTH. "Social Correlates of Criminal Involvement: Further Evidence on the Relationship between Social Status and Criminal Behavior." *American Sociological Review.* Vol. 47, No. 4 (August 1982):505–18.

THORNE, BARRIE, CHERIS KRAMARAE, and NANCY HENLEY, eds. *Language, Gender, and Society.* Rowley, MA: Newbury House, 1983.

THUROW, LESTER C. "A Surge in Inequality." *Scientific American.* Vol. 256, No. 5 (May 1987):30–37.

TILLY, CHARLES. "Does Modernization Breed Revolution?" In Jack A. Goldstone, ed., *Revolutions: Theoretical, Comparative, and Historical Studies.* New York: Harcourt Brace Jovanovich, 1986:47–57.

TITTLE, CHARLES R., WAYNE J. VILLEMEZ, and DOUGLAS A. SMITH. "The Myth of Social Class and Criminality: An Empirical Assessment of the Empirical Evidence." *American Sociological Review.* Vol. 43, No. 5 (October 1978):643–56.

TOCQUEVILLE, ALEXIS DE. *The Old Regime and the French Revolution.* Stuart Gilbert, trans. Garden City, NY: Anchor/Doubleday, 1955; orig. 1856.

TODD, D. "B.C. Residents Ready to Combat a Decade of High Poverty: Poll." *The Vancouver Sun.* 2011. [Online] http://communities.canada.com/vancouversun/blogs/thesearch/archive/2011/03/07/b-c-residents-ready-to-combat-a-decade-of-high-poverty.aspx

TOEWS, MIRIAM. *A Complicated Kindness.* New York: Counterpoint Press, 2005.

TOLSON, JAY. "The Trouble with Elites." *Wilson Quarterly.* Vol. 19, No. 1 (Winter 1995):6–8.

TOMKOWICZ, JOANNA, and TRACEY BUSHNIK. *Who Goes to Post-Secondary Education and When: Pathways Chosen by 20-Year-Olds.* Education Skills and Learning—Research Papers. Statistics Canada Catalogue No. 81-595-MIE. Ottawa: Statistics Canada, 2003 [Online] www.statcan.ca/english/research/81-595-MIE/81-595-MIE2003006.pdf

TÖNNIES, FERDINAND. *Community and Society (Gemeinschaft und Gesellschaft).* New York: Harper & Row, 1963; orig. 1887.

TOPPO, GREG, and ANTHONY DEBARROS. "Reality Weighs Down Dreams of College." *USA Today* (February 2, 2005):A1.

TORRES, LISA, and MATT L. HUFFMAN. "Social Networks and Job Search Outcomes among Male and Female Professional, Technical, and Managerial Workers." *Sociological Focus.* Vol. 35, No. 1 (February 2002):25–42.

TREAS, JUDITH. "Older Americans in the 1990s and Beyond." *Population Bulletin.* Vol. 50, No. 2 (May 1995).

TREVIÑO, JAVIER, ed. *Goffman's Legacy.* Lanham, MD: Rowman & Littlefield Publishers, Inc., 2003.

TRI TECHNOLOGY RESOURCES INC. "Solid Waste Composition Study: Executive Summary." Vancouver: Technology Resource Inc., 2005. Accessed June 12, 2006. [Online] www.gvrd.bc.ca/recycling-and-garbage/pdfs/2004CompositionExecSummary.pdf

TRIVENTI, M. "Something Changes, Something Not: Long-Term Trends in Gender Segregation of Fields of Study in Italy." *Italian Journal of Sociology of Education.* No. 2 (2010). www.ijse.eu/index.php/ijse/article/viewFile/71/76

TROELTSCH, ERNST. *The Social Teaching of the Christian Churches.* New York: Macmillan, 1931.

TUCKER, JAMES. "New Age Religion and the Cult of the Self." *Society.* Vol. 39, No. 2 (February 2002):46–51.

TUMIN, MELVIN M. "Some Principles of Stratification: A Critical Analysis." *American Sociological Review.* Vol. 18, No. 4 (August 1953):387–94.

TURCOTTE, PIERRE, and ALAIN BÉLANGER. *The Dynamics of Formation and Dissolution of First Common-Law Unions in Canada.* Research report. Ottawa: Statistics Canada, 1998.

TURNER, JONATHAN. *On the Origins of Human Emotions: A Sociological Inquiry into the Evolution of Human Emotions.* Stanford, CA: Stanford University Press, 2000.

TYLER, S. LYMAN. *A History of Indian Policy.* Washington, DC: U.S. Department of the Interior, Bureau of Indian Affairs, 1973.

UDRY, J. RICHARD. "Biological Limitations of Gender Construction." *American Sociological Review.* Vol. 65, No. 3 (June 2000):443–57.

UGGEN, CHRISTOPHER. "Ex-Offenders and the Conformist Alternative: A Job-Quality Model of Work and Crime." *Social Problems.* Vol. 46, No. 1 (February 1999): 127–51.

UGGEN, CHRISTOPHER, and JEFF MANZA. "Democratic Contraction? Political Consequences of Felon Disenfranchisement in the United States." *American Sociological Review.* Vol. 67, No. 6 (December 2002):777–803.

UNAIDS. "2008 Report on the Global AIDS Epidemic." August 2008b. www.unaids.org/en/KnowledgeCentre/HIVData/GlobalReport/2008/2008_Global_report.asp

——. "Fast Facts about HIV Prevention." 2011. [Online] Available at http://www.unaids.org/en/KnowledgeCentre/Resources/FastFacts

UNESCO. Data reported in "Tower of Babel Is Tumbling Down—Slowly." *U.S. News & World Report* (July 2, 2001):9.

UNESCO INSTITUTE OF STATISTICS. "Data Centre." 2009. http://stats.uis.unesco.org/unesco/TableViewer/document.aspx?ReportId=143

——. Data Centre. Custom Table, VAR: Adult literacy rate (%). 2010.

UNGERLEIDER, C.S. "Media, Minorities and Misconceptions: The Portrayal of Minorities in Canadian News Media." *Canadian Ethnic Studies.* Vol. 23, No. 3 (1991):158–64.

UNICEF. "Gender Equality: The Big Picture." August 25, 2004. www.unicef.org/gender/index_bigpicture.html

——. "ChildInfo Statistics by Area: Child Protection/Female Genital Mutilation/Cutting." November 2009.

——. "World Contraceptive Use, 2008." 2008d. www.un.org/esa/population/publications/contraceptive2008/WCU2008.htm

——. *The State of the World's Children 2011*, UNICEF, New York, 2011, pp. 120-23, Table 9: Child Protection (Child labour 2000 -2009). [Online] Available at: http://www.unicef.org/sowc2011/pdfs/Table%209%20CHILD%20PROTECTION_12082010.pdf

UNITED NATIONS. UN World Contraceptive Use 2007. 2008. [Online] Available at http://www.un.org/esa/population/publications/contraceptive2007/contraceptive2007.htm

UNITED NATIONS DEVELOPMENT PROGRAMME. *Human Development Report 1990.* New York: Oxford University Press, 1990.

——. *Human Development Report 2000.* New York: Oxford University Press, 2000.

——. "Human Development Indices: A Statistical Update." December 18, 2008. http://hdr.undp.org/en/statistics/data/

——. *Human Development Report 2009.* New York: Palgrave Macmillan, 2009. http://hdr.undp.org/en/reports/global/hdr2009/

——. *Human Development Report 2010.* Statistical Tables. [Online] Available at http://hdr.undp.org/en/statistics/data

UNITED NATIONS ENVIRONMENTAL PROGRAMME. "Vital Forest Graphics: Stopping the Downswing?" June 8, 2009. www.fao.org/forestry/home/en/

UNITED NATIONS FOOD AND AGRICULTURE ORGANIZATION. "Prevalence of Undernourishment in Total Population: Food Security Statistics." 2010. www.fao.org/faostat/foodsecurity/index_en.htm

UNITED NATIONS POPULATION DIVISION. "World Population Prospects: The 2006 Revision" and "World Urbanization Prospects: The 2007 Revision." 2008. http://esa.un.org/unup

——. "World Population Prospects: The 2008 Revision." March 2009. www.un.org/esa/population/unpop.htm

——. "World Population Prospects: The 2009 Revision." March 2010. www.un.org/esa/population/unpop.htm

UNITED NATIONS WORLD WATER ASSESSMENT PROGRAMME. "World Water Development Report 3: Water in a Changing World." March 2009. www.unesco.org/water/wwap/wwdr/

UNRUH, JOHN D., JR. *The Plains Across.* Urbana, IL: University of Illinois Press, 1979.

UPPAL, SHARANJI. "Unionization 2010." *Perspectives on Labour and Income.* Vol. 11, No. 10 (2010):18–27.

U.S. BUREAU OF INTERNATIONAL LABOR AFFAIRS. "Office of Child Labor, Forced Labor and Human Trafficking (OCFT)." 2008. www.dol.gov/ilab/programs/ocft/

U.S. BUREAU OF JUSTICE STATISTICS "Federal Justice Statistics Resource Center." 2010. http://fjsrc.urban.org/index.cfm

U.S. BUREAU OF LABOR STATISTICS. "International Comparisons of Manufacturing Productivity and Unit Labor Cost Trends, 2009." 2010. www.bls.gov/news.release/pdf/prod4.pdf

U.S. CENSUS BUREAU. "National Population Projections: Tables and Charts." August 14, 2008a. www.census.gov/population/www/projections/

——. "Who's Minding the Kids? Child Care Arrangements, Spring 2005." Rev. February 28, 2008b. www.census.gov/population/www/socdemo/child/ppl-2005.html

——. "American Community Survey, 2009." 2009. http://factfinder.census.gov/

——. "Foreign Trade Statistics." 2009. www.census.gov/foreign-trade/statistics/index.html

——. International Database. Summary Demographic Data—Yemen and Canada. Accessed May 4, 2006.

——. "International Data Base." December 2009. www.census.gov/ipc/www/idb/tables.html

——. "Current Population Survey." September 2010a. [Online] Available at http://www.census.gov/cps

——. *Statistical Abstract of the United States, 2010* (129th ed.). Washington, DC: U.S. Government Printing Office, 2009. www.census.gov/compendia/statab/

——. "Families and Living Arrangements." 2010. www.census.gov/population/www/socdemo/hh-fam.html

——. "Census 2010." 2011. [Online] Available at http://factfinder2.census.gov/faces/nav/jsf/pages/index.xhtml

U.S. DEPARTMENT OF HEALTH AND HUMAN SERVICES. SUBSTANCE ABUSE AND MENTAL HEALTH SERVICES ADMINISTRATION (SAMHSA). *Results from the 2008 National Survey on Drug Use and Health: National Findings.* DHHS Publication no. SMA 08-4343. Rockville, MD, 2010. http://oas.samhsa.gov/NSDUHlatest.htm

U.S. DEPARTMENT OF LABOR. "Employment Situation." December 9, 2009a. www.bls.gov/news.release/empsit.toc.htm

——. "Highlights of Women's Earnings in 2008." July 2009b. www.bls.gov/cps/cpswom2008.pdf

——. "List of Goods Produced by Child Labor or Forced Labor." September 2009c. www.dol.gov/ilab/programs/ocft/PDF/2009TVPRA.pdf

U.S. DEPARTMENT OF STATE. "Independent States in the World." August 19, 2008. www.state.gov/s/inr/rls/4250.htm

U.S. GEOLOGICAL SURVEY. "Estimated Use of Water in the United States in 2005." 2009. http://water.usgs.gov/watuse/

U.S. HOUSE OF REPRESENTATIVES. *1991 Green Book.* Washington, DC: U.S. Government Printing Office, 1991.

U.S. OFFICE OF MANAGEMENT AND BUDGET. "The Budget for Fiscal Year 2010." 2010. www.gpoaccess.gov/usbudget/fy10/pdf/summary.pdf

UPTHEGROVE, TAYNA R., VINCENT J. ROSCIGNO, and CAMILLE ZUBRINSKY CHARLES. "Big Money Collegiate Sports: Racial Concentration, Contradictory Pressures, and Academic Performance." *Social Science Quarterly.* Vol. 80, No. 4 (December 1999):718–37.

VAILLANCOURT, R. Gender Differences in Police-Reported Violent Crime in Canada, 2008. Catalogue no. 85F0033M, no. 24. Ottawa: Statistics Canada, 2010.

VALDEZ, A. "In the Hood: Street Gangs Discover White-Collar Crime." *Police.* Vol. 21, No. 5 (May 1997):49–50, 56.

VALLAS, STEPHEN P., and JOHN P. BECK. "The Transformation of Work Revisited: The Limits of Flexibility in American Manufacturing." *Social Problems.* Vol. 43, No. 3 (August 1996):339–61.

VALOCCHI, STEVE. "The Emergence of the Integrationist Ideology in the Civil Rights Movement." *Social Problems.* Vol. 43, No. 1 (February 1996):116–30.

VAN BIEMA, DAVID. "Parents Who Kill." *Time.* Vol. 144, No. 20 (November 14, 1994):50–51.

VANDIVERE, S., K. TOUT, J. CAPIZZANO, and M. ZASLOW. "Left Unsupervised: A Look at the Most Vulnerable Children." *Child Trends Research Brief* (2003):1–8.

VAN STERKENBURG, J., and A. KNOPPERS. "Dominant Discourses about Race/Ethnicity and Gender in Sport Practice ad Performance." *International Review for the Sociology of Sport.* Vol. 39, No. 3 (2004):301–21.

VAN WOLPUTTE, S. "Hang On To Your Self: Of Bodies, Embodiment, And Selves." *Annual Review of Anthropology* (2004), 33:251–69.

VAYDA, EUGENE, and RAISA B. DEBER. "The Canadian Health Care System: An Overview." *Social Science and Medicine.* Vol. 18, No. 3 (1984):191–97.

VEENSTRA, G. "Race, Gender, Class, and Sexual Orientation: Intersecting Axes of Inequality and Self-Rated Health in Canada." *International Journal for Equity in Health.* Vol. 10, No. 3 (2011). www.equityhealthj.com/content/10/1/3

VENTURA, STEPHANIE J., JOYCE C. ABMA, WILLIAM D. MOSHER, and STANLEY K. HENSHAW. "Estimated Pregnancy Rates for the United States, 1990–2005: An Update." *National Vital Statistics Reports.* Vol. 58, No. 4 (October 14, 2009). www.cdc.gov/nchs/data/nvsr/nvsr58/nvsr58_04.pdf

VISSER, JELLE. "Union Membership Statistics in 24 Countries." *Monthly Labor Review* (January 2006):38–49. www.bls.gov/opub/mlr/2006/01/art3full.pdf

VOGEL, EZRA F. *The Four Little Dragons: The Spread of Industrialization in East Asia.* Cambridge, MA: Harvard University Press, 1991.

VOGEL, LISE. *Marxism and the Oppression of Women: Toward a Unitary Theory.* New Brunswick, NJ: Rutgers University Press, 1983.

VOLD, GEORGE B., and THOMAS J. BERNARD. *Theoretical Criminology.* 3rd ed. New York: Oxford University Press, 1986.

WAIT, T. *Canadian Demographic and Social Values at a Glance: Impact on Strategic HR Planning.* Ottawa: Department of National Defence, 2002.

WALBY, KEVIN. "Open-Street Camera Surveillance and Governance in Canada." *Canadian Journal of Criminology and Criminal Justice.* Vol. 47, No. 4 (October 2005):655–83.

WALDFOGEL, JANE. "The Effect of Children on Women's Wages." *American Sociological Review.* Vol. 62, No. 2 (April 1997):209–17.

WALKER, KAREN. "'Always There for Me': Friendship Patterns and Expectations among Middle- and Working-Class Men and Women." *Sociological Forum.* Vol. 10, No. 2 (June 1995):273–96.

WALL, THOMAS F. *Medical Ethics: Basic Moral Issues.* Washington, DC: University Press of America, 1980.

WALLERSTEIN, IMMANUEL. *The Modern World-System: Capitalist Agriculture and the Origins of the European World-Economy in the Sixteenth Century.* New York: Academic Press, 1974.

———. *The Capitalist World-Economy.* New York: Cambridge University Press, 1979.

———. "Crises: The World Economy, the Movements, and the Ideologies." In Albert Bergesen, ed., *Crises in the World-System.* Beverly Hills, CA: Sage, 1983: 21–36.

———. *The Politics of the World Economy: The States, the Movements, and the Civilizations.* Cambridge: Cambridge University Press, 1984.

WALLERSTEIN, JUDITH S., and SANDRA BLAKESLEE. *Second Chances: Men, Women, and Children a Decade after Divorce.* New York: Ticknor & Fields, 1989.

WALMART. "Corporate Facts: Wal-Mart by the Numbers"; "Wal-Mart International Operational Data Sheet, April 2008"; and "2009 Annual Report to Shareholders." 2009. http://walmartstores.com/FactsNews/FactSheets/

WALSH, BRYAN. "How Business Saw the Light." *Time* (January 15, 2007):56–57.

WARNER, R. STEPHEN. "Work in Progress toward a New Paradigm for the Sociological Study of Religion in the United States." *American Journal of Sociology.* Vol. 98, No. 5 (March 1993):1044–93.

WARNER, W. LLOYD, and PAUL S. LUNT. *The Social Life of a Modern Community.* New Haven, CT: Yale University Press, 1941.

WARR, MARK, and CHRISTOPHER G. ELLISON. "Rethinking Social Reactions to Crime: Personal and Altruistic Fear in Family Households." *American Journal of Sociology.* Vol. 106, No. 3 (November 2000):551–78.

WATKINS, S. CRAIG, and RANA EMERSON. "Feminist Media Practices and Feminist Media Criticism." *Annals of the American Academy of Political and Social Science.* 571 (2000):151–66.

WATTS, C., and C. ZIMMERMAN. "Violence against Women." *Lancet.* Vol. 359 (2002):1232–37.

WATTS, DUNCAN J. "Networks, Dynamics, and the Small-World Phenomenon." *American Journal of Sociology.* Vol. 105, No. 2 (September 1999):493–527.

WEBER, ADNA FERRIN. *The Growth of Cities.* New York: Columbia University Press, 1963; orig. 1899.

WEBER, MAX. *The Protestant Ethic and the Spirit of Capitalism.* New York: Scribner, 1958; orig. 1904–05.

———. *Economy and Society: An Outline of Interpretive Sociology.* Guenther Roth and Claus Wittich, eds. Berkeley: University of California Press, 1978; orig. 1921.

WEBSTER, PAMELA S., TERRI ORBUCH, and JAMES S. HOUSE. "Effects of Childhood Family Background on Adult Marital Quality and Perceived Stability." *American Journal of Sociology.* Vol. 101, No. 2 (September 1995):404–32.

WEIDENBAUM, MURRAY. "The Evolving Corporate Board." *Society.* Vol. 32, No. 3 (March/April 1995):9–20.

WEINBERG, GEORGE. *Society and the Healthy Homosexual.* Garden City, NY: Anchor Books, 1973.

WEINBERG, MARTIN, FRANCES SHAVER, and COLIN WILLIAMS. "Gendered Sex Work in the San Francisco Tenderloin." *Archives of Sexual Behaviour,* 2000.

WEISBERG, D. KELLY. *Children of the Night: A Study of Adolescent Prostitution.* Lexington, MA: DC Heath, 1985.

WEISNER, THOMAS S., and BERNICE T. EIDUSON. "The Children of the '60s as Parents." *Psychology Today* (January 1986):60–66.

WEISS, M.G., and J. RAMAKRISHNA. "Stigma Interventions and Research for International Health." Stigma and Global Health: Developing a Research Agenda: An International Conference. September 2001.

WEITZMAN, LENORE J. *The Divorce Revolution: The Unexpected Social and Economic Consequences for Women and Children in America.* New York: Free Press, 1985.

———. "The Economic Consequences of Divorce Are Still Unequal: Comment on Peterson." *American Sociological Review.* Vol. 61, No. 3 (June 1996):537–38.

WELLMAN, BARRY, ed. *Networks in the Global Village.* Boulder, CO: Westview Press, 1999.

WELLS, HODAN FARAH, and JEAN C. BUZBY. *Dietary Assessment of Major Trends in U.S. Food Consumption, 1970–2005.* Economic Information Bulletin No. (EIB 33). Washington, DC: U.S. Department of Agriculture, March 2008.

WELLS, K. "Generation Queer: Sexuality Minority Youth and Canadian Schools." *Education Canada.* Vol. 48, No. 1 (2008):18–20, 22–23.

WENDLE, JOHN. "Russia's Millionaires Keep Their Heads Up." *Time* (January 12, 2009):4.

WESSELMAN, HANK. *Visionseeker: Shared Wisdom from the Place of Refuge.* Carlsbad, CA: Hay House, 2001.

WEST, C. *Doing Gender, Doing Difference: Inequality, Power, and Institutional Change.* New York: Routledge, 2002.

WEST, CORNEL. "The Obama Moment." *U.S. News & World Report* (November 17, 2008): 29.

WHEELIS, ALLEN. *The Quest for Identity.* New York: Norton, 1958.

WHITAKER, MARK. "Ten Ways to Fight Terrorism." *Newsweek* (July 1, 1985):26–29.

WHITE, JACK E. "I'm Just Who I Am." *Time* (May 5, 1997):32–36.

WHITE, RALPH, and RONALD LIPPITT. "Leader Behavior and Member Reaction in Three 'Social Climates.'" In Dorwin Cartwright and Alvin Zander, eds., *Group Dynamics.* Evanston, IL: Row & Peterson, 1953:586–611.

WHITEHEAD, M., G. DAHLGREN, and D. MCINTYRE. "Putting Equity Center Stage: Challenging Evidence-Free Reforms." *International Journal of Health Services.* Vol. 37 (2007):353–61.

WHITMAN, DAVID. "Shattering Myths about the Homeless." *U.S. News & World Report* (March 20, 1989):26, 28.

WHORF, BENJAMIN LEE . "The Relation of Habitual Thought and Behavior to Language." In *Language, Thought, and Reality.* Cambridge, MA: Technology Press of MIT; New York: Wiley, 1956:134–59; orig. 1941.

WHYTE, WILLIAM FOOTE. *Street Corner Society.* 3rd ed. Chicago: University of Chicago Press, 1981; orig. 1943.

WIDOM, CATHY SPATZ. "Childhood Sexual Abuse and Its Criminal Consequences." *Society.* Vol. 33, No. 4 (May–June 1996):47–53.

WILDAVSKY, BEN. "Small World, Isn't It?" *U.S. News & World Report* (April 1, 2002):68.

WILES, P.J.D. *Economic Institutions Compared.* New York: Halstead Press, 1977.

WILKES, RIMA, and JOHN ICELAND. "Hypersegregation in the Twenty-First Century." *Demography.* Vol. 41, No. 1 (February 9, 2004):23–36.

WILKINS, RUSSELL, JEAN-MARIE BERTHELOT, and EDWARD NG. *Trends in Mortality by Neighbourhood Income in Urban Canada from 1971 to 1996.* Supplements to Health Reports, Vol. 13. Statistics Canada Catalogue no. 82-003-SIE, 2002.

WILKINSON, R. *The Impact of Inequality: How to Make Sick Societies Healthier.* New York: The New Press, 2005.

WILKINSON, R., and M. MARMOT. *Social Determinants of Health: The Solid Facts.* 2nd ed. Geneva: World Health Organization, 2003.

WILLIAMS, CARA. "Family Disruptions and Childhood Happiness." *Canadian Social Trends.* No. 62 (Autumn 2002):2–4. Statistics Canada Catalogue no. 11-008-XPE.

WILLIAMS, D.R., H.W. NEIGHBORS, and J.S. JACKSON. "Racial/Ethnic Discrimination and Health: Findings from Community Studies." *American Journal of Public Health.* Vol. 93, No. 2 (2003):200–08.

WILLIAMS, JOHNNY E. "Linking Beliefs to Collective Action: Politicized Religious Beliefs and the Civil Rights Movement." *Sociological Forum.* Vol. 17, No. 2 (June 2002):203–22.

WILLIAMS, PETER W. *America's Religions: From Their Origins to the Twenty-First Century.* Urbana: University of Illinois Press, 2002.

WILLIAMS, RHYS H., and N.J. DEMERATH III. "Religion and Political Process in an American City." *American Sociological Review.* Vol. 56, No. 4 (August 1991): 417–31.

WILLIAMS, ROBIN M., JR. *American Society: A Sociological Interpretation.* 3rd ed. New York: Knopf, 1970.

WILLIAMSON, JEFFREY G., and PETER H. LINDERT. *American Inequality: A Macroeconomic History.* New York: Academic Press, 1980.

WILLIAMSON, SAMUEL H. "Seven Ways to Compute the Relative Value of a U.S. Dollar Amount, 1774 to Present." Measuring Worth. April 2010. www.measuringworth.com/uscompare

WILLIS, ANDREW, and GAYLE MACDONALD. "The Gap between the Rich and the Poor." *Globe and Mail* (July 5, 2003):F4.

WILSON, CLINT C., II, and FELIX GUTIERREZ. *Minorities and Media: Diversity and the End of Mass Communication.* Beverly Hills, CA: Sage, 1985.

WILSON, EDWARD O. "Biodiversity, Prosperity, and Value." In F. Herbert Bormann and Stephen R. Kellert, eds., *Ecology, Economics, and Ethics: The Broken Circle.* New Haven, CT: Yale University Press, 1991:3–10.

WILSON, S.J. *Women, Families and Work.* 4th ed. Toronto: McGraw-Hill Ryerson, 1996.

WILSON, THOMAS C. "Urbanism and Tolerance: A Test of Some Hypotheses Drawn from Wirth and Stouffer." *American Sociological Review.* Vol. 50, No. 1 (February 1985):117–23.

———. "Urbanism and Unconventionality: The Case of Sexual Behavior." *Social Science Quarterly.* Vol. 76, No. 2 (June 1995):346–63.

WILSON, WILLIAM JULIUS. *When Work Disappears: The World of the New Urban Poor.* New York: Knopf, 1996a.

———. "Work." *New York Times Magazine* (August 18, 1996b):26ff.

WINSHIP, CHRISTOPHER, and JENNY BERRIEN. "Boston Cops and Black Churches." *Public Interest* (Summer 1999):52–68.

WIRTH, LOUIS. "Urbanism as a Way of Life." *American Journal of Sociology.* Vol. 44, No. 1 (July 1938):1–24.

WOLF, NAOMI. *The Beauty Myth: How Images of Beauty Are Used against Women.* New York: Morrow, 1990.

WOLFF, EDWARD N. "Recent Trends in Household Wealth in the United States: Rising Debt and the Middle-Class Squeeze." Levy Economics Institute of Bard College. June 2007. www.levy.org/pubs/wp_502.pdf

WOLFE, JEANNE M. "Canada's Liveable Cities." *Social Policy.* Vol. 23, No. 1 (Summer 1992):56–65.

WOLFGANG, MARVIN E., ROBERT M. FIGLIO, and THORSTEN SELLIN. *Delinquency in a Birth Cohort.* Chicago: University of Chicago Press, 1972.

WOLFGANG, MARVIN E., TERRENCE P. THORNBERRY, and ROBERT M. FIGLIO. *From Boy to Man, from Delinquency to Crime.* Chicago: University of Chicago Press, 1987.

WONG, LLOYD, and RICARDO TRUMPER. "Canada's Guestworkers: Racialized, Gendered and Flexible" Race and Racism in 21st Century Canada: Continuity, Complexity, and Change. Peterborough: Broadview Press, 2007. 151–70.

WOOD, EVAN, THOMAS KERR, WILL SMALL, KATHY LI, DAVID C. MARSH, JULIO S.G. MONTANER, AND MARK W. TYNDALL. "Changes in Public Order After the Opening of a Medically Supervised Safer Injecting Facility for Illicit Injection Drug Users." *Canadian Medical Association Journal.* Vol. 170, No. 10 (May 2004):1551–56.

WOODWARD, KENNETH L. "Talking to God." *Newsweek.* Vol. 119, No. 1 (January 6, 1992):38–44.

———. "Feminism and the Churches." *Newsweek* (February 13, 1989):58–61.

WORKPLACE DIVERSITY UPDATE. "Ernst & Young: Recognized Diversity Pioneer." Vol. 12, No. 4 (April 2004):1–2.

WORLD BANK, THE. *World Development Report 1993.* New York: Oxford University Press, 1993.

———. *2008 World Development Indicators.* Washington, DC: World Bank, 2008.

———. "Education Statistics." 2009, 2010 (updated regularly). http://go.worldbank.org/ITABCOGIV1

———. *World Development Indicators, 2009.* Washington, DC: World Bank, 2009.

———. *World Development Indicators.* 2010. [Online] Available at http://data.worldbank.org/data-catalog/world-development-indicators

———. *Population.* 2011a. [Online] http://api.worldbank.org/datafiles/sp.pop.totl_Indicator_MetaData_en_Excel.zip

———. *GNI, PPP (current international $).* 2011b. [Online] http://api.worldbank.org/datafiles/NY.GNP.MKTP.PP.CD_Indicator_MetaData_en_EXCEL.zip

———. *Land Area (sq. km).* 2011c. [Online] http://api.worldbank.org/datafiles/AG.LND.TOTL.K2_Indicator_MetaData_en_EXCEL.zip

———. *GNI per Capita, PPP (current international $).* 2011d. [Online] http://api.worldbank.org/datafiles/NY.GNP.PCAP.PP.CD_Indicator_MetaData_en_EXCEL.zip

———. "EdStats." 2011e. [Online] Available at http://data.worldbank.org/data-catalog/ed-stats

WORLD HEALTH ORGANIZATION. *Constitution of the World Health Organization.* New York: World Health Organization Interim Commission, 1946.

———. *Mortality Country Fact Sheet 2006: Canada.* 2006a. www.who.int/whosis/mort/profiles/mort_amro_can_canada.pdf

———. *Mortality Country Fact Sheet 2006: Nigeria.* 2006b. www.who.int/whosis/mort/profiles/mort_afro_nga_nigeria.pdf

———. "Female Genital Mutilation: New Knowledge Spurs Optimism." *Progress in Sexual and Reproductive Health Research.* No. 72 (2006). [Online] Available May 13, 2008, at http://www.who.int/reproductivehealth/hrp/progress/72.pdf

———. "Eliminating Female Genital Mutilation: An Interagency Statement–OHCHR, UNAIDS, UNDP, UNECA, UNESCO, UNFPA, UNHCR, UNICEF, UNIFEM, WHO." 2008. http://www.who.int/reproductivehealth/publications/fgm/9789241596442/en/index.html

———. "Major Causes of Death: A Primer." Fact sheet No. 310. November 2008c. www.who.int/mediacentre/factsheets/fs310/en/index2.html

———. "WHO Report on the Global Tobacco Epidemic, 2009." 2009. www.who.int/tobacco/mpower/2009/en/index.html

———. "Suicide Rates per 100,000 by Country, Year and Sex." 2009a. [Online] www.who.int/mental_health/prevention/suicide_rates/en/index.html

WORLD VALUES SURVEY. "Inglehart-Welzel Cultural Map of the World." 2008. www.worldvaluessurvey.com

WORSLEY, PETER. "Models of the World System." In Mike Featherstone, ed., *Global Culture: Nationalism, Globalization, and Modernity.* Newbury Park, CA: Sage, 1990:83–95.

WORTLEY, SCOT, and LYSANDRA MARSHALL. *Race and Police Stops in Kingston, Ontario: Results of a Pilot Project.* Kingston, ON: Kingston Police Services Board, 2005.

WREDE, S., C. BENOIT, and T. EINARSDOTTIR. "Equity and Dignity in Maternity Care Provision in Canada, Finland and Iceland: Finding Dignity in Health Care and Health Care Work." *Canadian Journal of Public Health.* Vol. 99 (Suppl. 2, 2008):16–21.

WRIGHT, EARL, II. "The Atlanta Sociological Laboratory, 1896–1924: A Historical Account of the First American School of Sociology." *Western Journal of Black Studies.* Vol. 26, No. 3 (2002a):165–74.

———. "Why Black People Tend to Shout! An Earnest Attempt to Explain the Sociological Negation of the Atlanta Sociological Laboratory Despite Its Possible Unpleasantness." *Sociological Spectrum.* Vol. 22, No. 3 (2002b):325–61.

WRIGHT, JAMES D. "Ten Essential Observations on Guns in America." *Society.* Vol. 32, No. 3 (March/April 1995):63–68.

WRIGHT, QUINCY. "Causes of War in the Atomic Age." In William M. Evan and Stephen Hilgartner, eds., *The Arms Race and Nuclear War.* Englewood Cliffs, NJ: Prentice Hall, 1987:7–10.

WRIGHT, RICHARD A. *In Defense of Prisons.* Westport, CT: Greenwood Press, 1994.

WRIGHT, ROBERT. "Sin in the Global Village." *Time* (October 19, 1998):130.

WU, LAWRENCE L. "Effects of Family Instability, Income, and Income Instability on the Risk of a Premarital Birth." *American Sociological Review.* Vol. 61, No. 3 (June 1996):386–406.

WU, XIAOGANG, and DONALD G. TREIMAN. "Inequality and Equality under Chinese Socialism: The Hukou System and Intergenerational Occupational Mobility." *American Journal of Sociology.* Vol. 113, No. 2 (September 2007):415–45.

WU, ZHENG. "Premarital Cohabitation and the Timing of First Marriage." *Canadian Review of Sociology and Anthropology.* Vol. 36, No. 1 (February 1999):109–27.

———. *Cohabitation: An Alternative Form of Living.* Don Mills, ON: Oxford University Press, 2000.

XU, JIAQUAN, KENNETH D. KOCHANEK, and BETZAIDA TEJADA-VERA. "Deaths: Preliminary Data for 2007." *National Vital Statistics Reports.* Vol. 58, No. 1 (August 19, 2009). www.cdc.gov/nchs/data/nvsr/nvsr58/nvsr58_01.pdf

YABROFF, JENNIE. "The Myths of Teen Sex." *Newsweek* (June 9, 2008):55.

YAMADA, M. "Meanings of Tattoos in the Context of Identity-Construction: A Study of Japanese Students in Canada." *Japan Studies Review.* Vol. XII (2008):3–21.

YANG, FENGGANG, and HELEN ROSE FUCHS EBAUGH. "Transformations in New Immigrant Religions and Their Global Implications." *American Sociological Review.* Vol. 66, No. 2 (April 2001):269–88.

YARDLEY, JIM. "China Sticking with One-Child Policy." *New York Times* (March 11, 2008). www.nytimes.com/2008/03/11/world/asia/11china.html?_r=1

YEATTS, DALE E. "Creating the High Performance Self-Managed Work Team: A Review of Theoretical Perspectives." Paper presented at the annual meeting of the Southwest Social Science Association, Dallas, February 1994.

YEE, M. "Chinese Canadian Women: Our Common Struggle." In G. Creese and V. Strong-Boag, eds., *British Columbia Reconsidered: Essays on Women.* Vancouver: Press Gang Publishers, 1992.

YOELS, WILLIAM C., and JEFFREY MICHAEL CLAIR. "Laughter in the Clinic: Humor in Social Organization." *Symbolic Interaction.* Vol. 18, No. 1 (1995):39–58.

ZAGORSKY, JAY. "Divorce Drops a Person's Wealth by 77 Percent." Press release, January 18, 2006. www.eurekalert.org/pub_releases/2006-01/osu-dda011806.php

ZAMARIA, C., and F. FLETCHER. *Canada Online.* Toronto: Ryerson University and School of Radio and Television Arts, 2008. [Online] www.ciponline.ca/en/docs/2008/CIP07_CANADA_ONLINE-REPORT-FINAL%20.pdf

ZHANG, D., and E. BRUNING. "Personal Characteristics and Strategic Orientation: Entrepreneurs in Canadian Manufacturing Companies." *International Journal of Entrepreneurial Behaviour & Research.* Vol. 17, No. 1 (2011):82–103.

ZHAO, DINGXIN. "Ecologies of Social Movements: Student Mobilization during the 1989 Prodemocracy Movement in Beijing." *American Journal of Sociology.* Vol. 103, No. 6 (May 1998):1493–529.

ZIMBARDO, PHILIP G. "Pathology of Imprisonment." *Society.* Vol. 9, No. 1 (April 1972):4–8.

ZUCCHI, J. *A History of Ethnic Enclaves in Canada.* Ottawa: Canadian Historical Association, 2007. www.collectionscanada.gc.ca/obj/008004/f2/E-31_en.pdf

ZUCKERMAN, MORTIMER B. "The Russian Conundrum." *U.S. News & World Report* (March 13, 2006):64.

Credits

Photo Credits

Note: Page numbers followed by the alphabet b indicate a photo appearing inside a box banner.

CHAPTER 1: © Erik Isakson/CORBIS, 1; Caroline Penn/CORBIS, 7 (left); Paul Liebhardt, 7 (middle); © Alain Evrard/Maxx Images, 7 (right); Tanya Talaga/GetStock, 8; Azpworldwide/Dreamstime, 9; Art Resource/Schomburg Center for Research in Black Culture, 13b; Archives of Ontario/F2130, 14 (left); Helen C. Abell Collection, Archival & Special Collections, University of Guelph Library, 14 (right); Dreamstime, 16b; Thinkstock, 19b; © Bob Sacha/CORBIS, 22; iStockphoto/Thinkstock, 25; Michael Doolittle/The Image Works, 26; Victor Malfrone/Getty Images, 32 (left); Helga Esteb/Shutterstock.com, 32 (right).

CHAPTER 2: iStock, 37 (top left); © Marvin Dembinsky Photo Associates/Alamy, 37 (top middle); Jupiterimages/Thinkstock, 37 (top right); Jupiterimages/Thinkstock, 37 (center left); © Photononstop/SuperStock, 37 (center middle); © Suzy Bennett/Alamy, 37 (center right); HAZEL THOMPSON /The New York Times/Redux, 37 (bottom); © Herve Collart/CORBIS, 38; Stockbyte/Thinkstock, 39; Creatas Images/Thinkstock, 40b; Monty Brinton/CBS/Getty Images, 45; Michael Buckner/Discovery Channel/Getty Images, 47; Thomas Kelly / Aurora Photos, 52; Polka Dot Images/Thinkstock, 58; © Bettman/ CORBIS, 59 (left); Marvel/Sony Pictures/Picture Desk, Inc./Kobal Collection, 60 (left); Captain Canuck® © (Copyright) Richard Comely Art by Richard Comely, 60 (right).

CHAPTER 3: Copyright: the Estate of William Kurelek, courtesy of the Wynick/Tuck Gallery, Toronto, 65; Rima Gerlovina and Valeriy Gerlovin "Manyness", photography 1009 © gerlovin.com, 69; George Pimentel/WireImage/Getty Images, 78; © Remi Benali/CORBIS, 83 (left); Chung Sung-Jun/Getty Images, 83 (right).

CHAPTER 4: Jupiterimages/Comstock/Getty Images, 86; Jonathan Hayward/The Canadian Press, 88; Michael Hanson/Getty Images-Aurora, 89b; Thinkstock, 93; Stanton Winter/New York Times/Redux, 94 (left); Courtesy American Sociological Association www.asanet.org, 94 (right); Photograph by: Adrian Wyld, Reuters, 96; Paul Liebhardt, 97 (left); Paul Liebhardt, 97 (middle); Paul Liebhardt, 97 (right); iStockphoto/Thinkstock, 98 (left); Creatista / Dreamstime, 98 (second from left); Jupiterimages/Thinkstock, 98 (third from left); Shutterstock, 98 (third from right); Thinkstock, 98 (second from right); Thinkstock, 98 (right); stefanolunardi/Shutterstock, 99b; Digital Vision/Thinkstock, 100; Chris Young/The Canadian Press, 101; The Everett Collection/The Canadian Press, 103; saluha/iStock, 104; Craig Swatton/istock, 105.

CHAPTER 5: Michael Newman/PhotoEdit Inc, 110; Darren Calabrese/The Canadian Press, 113; Friends 1991, Acrylic on Masonite, 14" × 11" © Jonathan Green-Collection of Patric McCoy, 115; Chris Haston/NBCU/Photo Bank, 118; nuyl/Fotolia, LLC, 125; © Catherine Karnow/CORBIS, 127 (left); © David Levenson/Alamy, 127 (right); corepics/Shutterstock, 130 (left); © Ilene MacDonald/Alamy, 130 (right).

CHAPTER 6: Peter Wafzig/Getty Images, 133; ©John Cancalosi/Alamy, 135 (left); © Peter Adams/Alamy, 135 (middle); Pichugin Dmitry/Shutterstock, 135 (right); Gregg DeGuire/PictureGroup/The Canadian Press, 136; Brand X Pictures/Thinkstock, 138 (left); Vitaly M/Shutterstock, 138 (right); Shaul Schwarz/Getty Images, 144b; Kevin Fryer/The Canadian Press, 145; Darren Calabrese/The Canadian Press, 151b; AKG-Images, 153; Phakimata/Dreamstime, 156; Splash News/Newscom, 157 (left); NC1 WENN Photos/Newscom, 157 (right).

CHAPTER 7: iStockphoto/Thinkstock, 160; Melissa Moore/The Image Works, 162b; Jose Azel/Aurora Photos, 163; Robert Yager/Getty Images, 166; Shutterstock, 167b; Bob Gathany/The Huntsville Times/Landov, 170 (left); iStockphoto/Thinkstock, 170 (right); Jonathan Hayward/The Canadian Press, 171; Phil Snell/The Canadian Press, 175 (left); Frank Gunn/The Canadian Press, 175 (right); A. Ramey/Woodfin Camp and Assoc, 179; LAC, C-014078, 183; Don Healy/LEADER POST, 185b; Miguel Angel Morenatti/AP Images, 186 (left); Bill Greenblatt/UPI/Landov, 186 (right).

CHAPTER 8: Charlie Campbell/The Star-Democrat/AP Worldwide Photos, 189; William Albert Allard/NGS, 191; De Agostini Editore Picture Library/Getty Images, 193; Kevin Winter/Getty Images, 199; Ken Faught/Getstock, 200; Jupiterimages/Thinkstock, 208 (left); Thinkstock, 208 (right); © Russell Lee/CORBIS, 209; AP Images, 216; Ryan Remiorz/The Canadian Press, 222; David De Lossy/Thinkstock, 223 (left); Brand X Pictures/Thinkstock, 223 (right).

CHAPTER 9: Jay Directo/Getty Images, 226; Warwick Kent/Photolibrary.com, 229 (top left);Jan S./Shutterstock, 229 (top right); Paul Nevin/Photolibrary.com, 229 (bottom left); edro Cerda/UPI/Newscom, 230 (left); Claudia Dewald/iStock, 230 (right); © Alison Wright/CORBIS, 232b; © Sucheta Das/CORBIS, 235; © Joe McDonald/CORBIS, 240 (left); © Robert van der Hilst/CORBIS, 240 (middle); © Wolfgang Kaehler/CORBIS, 240 (right); © Maciej Dakowicz/Alamy, 241b; © Jenny Mathews/Alamy, 244; Fabio Liverani/Nature Picture Library, 245; RABIH MOGHRABI/AFP/Getty Images/Newscom, 248 (left); Typhoonski/Dreamstime.com, 248 (right).

CHAPTER 10 : © Suzanne Porter/Alamy, 254; Jean Louis Batt/Getty Images, 256; UNIMEDIA EUROPE\SND FILMS © De/Newscom, 257; Sonda Dawes/The Image Works, 267; ©Sven Hagolani/Zefa/CORBIS, 269; Hulton Archive/Getty Images, 272 (left); John Bazemore/AP Images, 272 (right); © Suzanne Porter/Alamy, 276 (left); © Janet Klinger Photography/Alamy, 276 (right).

CHAPTER 11: © Gedeon Mendal/Corbis, 279; AISPIX/Shutterstock, 281 (top left); Stockbyte/Thinkstock, 281 (top middle); Ryan McVay/Thinkstock, 281 (top right); © Charles O'Rear/CORBIS, 281 (bottom left); iStockphoto/Bartosz Hadyniak, 281 (bottom center); © Buddy Mays/Alamy, 281 (bottom right); The Slide Farm/Al Harvey, 291; David Rossiter/The Canadian Press, 292; ©Pierre Roussel/Images Distribution, 295, LAC, C-024452, 296; A.Ramey/Woodfin Camp and Assoc, 297; Photolibrary, 298 (left); iStockphoto/Thinkstock, 298 (right).

CHAPTER 12: © Antoine Serra/Sygma/Corbis, 301; Ingram Publishing/Thinkstock, 303; Goodshoot/Thinkstock, 307 (left); © Roberto Fumagalli/Alamy, 307 (right); National Geophysical Data Center, 308; Stockbyte/Thinkstock, 315; Vincent Thian/AP Images, 318; Kevin Van Paassen/The Globe and Mail/The Canadian Press, 322 (left); Joel Gordon Photography, 322 (right); David Hoffman/Photolibrary.com, 327; Time & Life Pictures/Getty Images, 329; Paul Warner/AP Images, 334 (left); Sean Kilpatrick/The Canadian Press, 334 (right).

CHAPTER 13: © Israel images/Alamy, 337; ABC via Getty Images, 339; BananaStock/Thinkstock, 341; AP Images, 344b; © The New Yorker Collection, 1983, Robert Weber, from cartoonbank.com. All rights reserved., 345; Mark J Barrett/Creative Eye/MIRA.com, 351; Ryan McVay/Thinkstock, 353; iStockphoto/Thinkstock, 354; © Life Issues Institute, Inc., 355b; © Micah Hanson/Alamy, 356; The Diocese of the Artic, 358; © David G Wells/CORBIS, 360; © Galen Rowell/CORBIS, 361; © Gary Braasch/CORBIS, 368b; Photos.com/Thinkstock, 369 (left); Ryan McVay/Thinkstock, 369 (right).

CHAPTER 14: Getty Images, 372; AnthonyNjuguna/REUTERS/Landov Media, 377 (left); PICTURE DESK KOBAL COLLECTION ART ARCHIVE ADV ARCHIVE TRAVELSITE/Baer Karin/Fox-TV, 377 (right); Cleve Bryant/Photo Edit Inc., 378 (left); © Jim Cummins/CORBIS, 378 (right); Spencer Grant/Photo Edit, 381b; LAC, PA-134110, 385; iStockphoto/Thinkstock, 388; © Gabe Palmer/CORBIS, 390; © imagebroker/Alamy, 395; Prado, Madrid, Spain/Giraudon/Bridgeman Art Library, 399; © Tom Nebbia/CORBIS, 400; Billy E. Barnes/PhotoEdit Inc., 402 (left); tefanolunardi/Dreamstime, 402 (right); Dan Rafla/Aurora Photos, 407 (left); Glenbow, NA-3965-66, 407 (right).

CHAPTER 15: © nick baylis/Alamy, 410; AP Images, 415; © David Turnley/CORBIS, 417; Aaron Harris/Toronto Star/GetStock, 422 (left); iStock / Reuben Schulz, 422 (right); © The Print Collector/Alamy, 424 (left); Art Resource/Smithsonian American Art Museum, Washington, DC, U.S.A., 424 (right); James King -Holmes/Science Photo Library/Photo Researchers, 427; John Macionis, 430b; Amit Dave/Reuters/Landov, 431; RICHARD B. LEVINE/Newscom, 436 (left); David Cooper/Getstock, 436 (right).

CHAPTER 16: AFP/Getty Images, 439; AFP/Getty Images, 441; AP Images/Hans Edinger, 445; EITAN ABRAMOVICH/AFP/Getty Images/Newscom, 446 (left); © Barry Lewis/Alamy, 446 (middle); AFP/Getty Images, 446 (right); © CORBIS, 447; © Lucas Payne/Alamy, 450 (left); Jupiterimages/Thinkstock, 450 (right); Oakland Ross/GetStock, 454; Hemera/Thinkstock, 456 (left); Zoran Karapancev/Shutterstock, 456 (right); Mauri Rautkari/Pictorium/plainpicture, 457; © Dennis MacDonald/Alamy, 459b; © paul prescott/Alamy, 461 (left); SHAWN BALDWIN/The New York Times/Redux, 461 (right).

Banner Photos: Rafael Ramirez Lee/Istockphoto, Seeing Sociology in Everyday Life box; Chris Schmidt/iStock, Thinking about Diversity: Race, Class, & Gender box; © Stylephotographs/Robert Kneschke/Dreamstime, Controversy & Debate box.

Table, Figure, & Box Credits

CHAPTER 1: Figure 1–1, Statistics Canada. Deaths and Mortality Rate, by Selected Grouped Causes, Age Group and Sex, Canada, 2011, CANSIM Data Base Retrieval Output, Table 102-0551, March 21, 2011; Figure 1–2, Statistics Canada. Deaths and Mortality Rate, by Selected Grouped Causes, Age Group and Sex, Canada, 2011, CANSIM Data Base Retrieval Output, Table 102-0551, March 21, 2011, and World Health Organization. "Suicide Rates per 100,000 by Country, Year and Sex." 2009 (Table) [Online] www.who.int/mental_health/prevention/suicide_rates/en/index.html © Copyright World Health Organization (WHO), 2011. All Rights Reserved; Sports: Playing the Theory Game, Courtesy of Richard Lapchick.

CHAPTER 2: Figure 2–2, Permission granted by Ronald Inglehart and Christian Welzel; National Map 2–1, Calculated based on Statistics Canada, Profile of Language, Immigration, Citizenship, Mobility and Migration for Canada, Provinces, Territories, Census Divisions and Census Subdivisions, 2006 Census, 2007. [Online] http://www12.statcan.gc.ca/census-recensement/2006/dp-pd/prof/rel/Rp-eng.cfm?LANG=E&APATH=3&DETAIL=0&DIM=0&FL=A&FREE=0&GC=0&GID=0&GK=0&GRP=1&PID=89770&PRID=0&PTYPE=89103&S=0&SHOWALL=0&SUB=0&Temporal=2006&THEME=70&VID=0&VNAMEE=&VNAMEF; Figure 2–3, Statistics Canada. Clark, Warren. "Delayed transitions of young adults," *Canadian Social Trends*, 11-008-XIE2007007, Winter 2007, no. 84, December 11, 2007. http://www.statcan.gc.ca/bsolc/olc-cel/olc-cel?lang=eng&catno=11-008-X; Early Rock-and-Roll: Based on Stuessy, Joe, Lipscomb, Scott D., Rock and Roll: Its History and Stylistic Development, 6th edition, © 2009. Pearson Education, Inc., Upper Saddle River, NJ, and Social Divisions and Cultural Change, *Encyclopedia of Music in Canada* (Historica-Dominion Institute, 2011).

CHAPTER 3: Table 3–1, Statistics Canada. "Ethnic Origins 2006 Counts for Canada Provinces and Territories—20% Sample Data (Table)." *Ethnocultural Portrait of Canada Highlight Tables*, 2006 Census. Catalogue no. 97-562-XWE2006002. 2007; Figure 3–2, Statistics Canada. *Family Portrait: Continuity and Change in Canadian Families and Households in 2006*, 2006 Census, 97-553-XWE2006001, September 12, 2007. http://www.statcan.gc.ca/bsolc/olc-cel/olc-cel?catno=97-553-XWE2006001&lang=eng; Figure 3–3, U.S. Census Bureau. "National Population Projections: Tables and Charts." August 14, 2008, http:// www.census.gov/population/www/projections/, and International Telecommunication Union. World Telecommunication Development Report. Data cited in WORLD BANK, World Development Indicators, 2008; Global Map 3–1, UNICEF. The State of the World's Children 2011, UNICEF, New York, 2011, pp. 120-123, Table 9: Child Protection (Child labour 2000–2009). [Online] Available at: http://www.unicef.org/sowc2011/pdfs/Table%209%20CHILD%20PROTECTION_12082010.pdf. Reproduced with permission of UNICEF, and International Bank for Reconstruction and Development/The World Bank: World Development Indicators, 2010. [Online] Available at http://data.worldbank.org/data-catalog/world-development-indicators; National Map 3–1, Calculated based on Statistics Canada, *Age Groups and Sex for the Population of Canada, Provinces, Territories, Census Divisions and Census Subdivisions, 2006 Census*—100% Data [Electronic Data File]. Catalogue no. 97-551-XCB2006013. IVT. 2011; Figure 3–4, Statistics Canada. *A Portrait of Seniors in Canada*, 89-519-XWE2006001, February 2007 http://www.statcan.gc.ca/pub/89-519-x/2006001/c-g/4181481-eng.htm.

CHAPTER 4: Managing Feelings: Women's Abortion Experiences, Courtesy of Jennifer Keys.

CHAPTER 5: Figure 5–1, Courtesy of Solomon Asch Center for Study of Ethnopolitical Conflict; Global Map 5–1, International Telecommunications Union. "ICT Database, 2009." 2010. http://www.itu.int; Figure 5–3, Statistics Canada. Morrisette, Rene, Grant Schellenberg and Anick Johnson. "Diverging Trends in Unionization." *Perspectives on Labour and Income*, Vol.6, No.4 (April 2005): 5-12, and Uppal, S. "Unionization 2010." *Perspectives on Labour and Income*, Vol.11, No.10 (2010):18-27; Figure 5–4, Statistics Canada. *Women in Canada: A Gender-Based Statistical Report, Paid Work*. Catalogue No. 89-503-X, December 2010.

CHAPTER 6: Chapter Overview Figure: *The American Journal of Sociology* by UNIVERSITY OF CHICAGO PRESS. Copyright 2004. Reproduced with permission of UNIVERSITY OF CHICAGO PRESS - JOURNALS in the formats Textbook and Other book via Copyright Clearance Center, Inc.; National Map 6–1, Statistics Canada, Legal Marital Status, Common-Law Status, Age Groups and Sex for the Population 15 Years and Over of Canada, Provinces, Territories, Census Divisions and Census Subdivisions, 2006 Census—100% Data. [Electronic Data File]. Catalogue no. 97-552-XCB2006009[1].IVT. 2011; Figure 6–1, Statistics Canada. Rotermann, M. "Trends in Teen Sexual Behaviour and Condom Use." *Health Reports*. Vol.19, No.3 (September 2008):1–5. Catalogue no. 82-003-XWE2008003, http://www.statcan.gc.ca/bsolc/olc-cel/olc-cel?lang=eng&catno=82-003-X; Global Map 6–1, Data from UN World Contraceptive Use 2007 © United Nations, 2008, http://www.un.org/esa/population/publications/contraceptive2007/contraceptive2007.htm. Reproduced with permission, and Population Reference Bureau. "Datafinder." 2010, 2011. [Online] Available at http://www.prb.org/DataFinder.aspx; Table 6–1, Vision Critical Communications Inc.; Figure 6–2, Adapted from Storms, Michael D. "Theories of Sexual Orientation." *Journal of Personality and Social Psychology.* Vol. 38, No. 5 (May 1980):783–92; Figure 6–3, Statistics Canada, 2006 Census: *Family Portrait: Continuity and Change in Canadian Families and Households in 2006: National Portrait: Census Families.* 2009, 97-553-XWE2006001; http://www12.statcan.ca/census-recensement/2006/as-sa/97-553/p4-eng.cfm; Figure 6–4, *The American Freshman: Thirty-Five-Year Trends.* © 2011 The Regents of the University of California. All Rights Reserved; Figure 6–5, Adapted from Statistics Canada, CANSIM database http://cansim2.statcan.ca, Table106-9002, and from Marital status, 2006 Census, Catalogue no. 97-552-XWE2006009. Retrieval date May 22, 2011, http://www.statcan.gc.ca/bsolc/olc-cel/olc-cel?lang=eng&catno=97-552-X2006009; Global Map 6–2, from THE PENGUIN ATLAS OF HUMAN SEXUAL BEHAVIOR by Judith MacKay, copyright © 2000 by Judith MacKay, text. © 2000 by Myriad Editions, Ltd., maps & graphics. Used by permission of Viking Penguin, a division of Penguin Group (USA) Inc; When Sex Is Only Sex: The Campus Culture of "Hooking Up", Institute for American Values.

CHAPTER 7: Deviant (Sub)Culture: Has It Become Okay to Do Wrong?, Based on "Our Cheating Hearts," Editorial. U.S. News & World Report (May 6, 2002):4. *U.S. News & World Report*, May 2002. Copyright 2002 by U.S. News & World Report. Reproduced by permission; Hate Crime Laws: Do They Punish Actions or Attitudes?, Terry (1993) and Sullivan (2002); National Map 7–1, Statistics Canada. Dauvergne, Mia and John Turner. "Police-Reported Crime Statistics in Canada, 2009." *Juristat*, Vol.20, No.2 (2010). Catalogue no. 85-002-X. [Online] http://www.statcan.gc.ca/pub/85-002-x/2010002/article/11292-eng.pdf; Figure 7–1, Dauvergne, M. "Crime Statistics in Canada, 2007." *Juristat*. Vol.28, No.7 (2008). Catalogue no. 85-002-XWE2008007. http://www.statcan.gc.ca/bsolc/olc-cel/olc-cel?lang=eng&catno=85-002-X; Global Map 7–1, "The Death Penalty in 2010." 2011. http://www.amnesty.org/en/death-penalty. © Amnesty International, 1 Easton Street, London WC1X 0DW, United Kingdom, http://www.amnesty.org; Figure 7–2, Roy Walmsley, Director of the World Prison Population List and World Prison Brief Online, International Centre for Prison Studies.

CHAPTER 8: Figure 8–1, U.S. Census Bureau. "Current Population Survey." September 2010. [Online] Available at http://www.census.gov/cps, and International Bank for Reconstruction and Development/The World Bank: World Development Indicators, 2010; Figure 8–2, Created by John Macionis, based on Kuznets (1955) and Lenski (1966); Global Map 8–1, Based on Gini coefficents obtained from International Bank for Reconstruction and Development/The World Bank: *World Development Indicators*, 2010. [Online] Available at http://data.worldbank. org/data-catalog/world-development-indicators, and Central Intelligence Agency. *The World Factbook*. 2010 (updated biweekly). https://www.cia.gov/library/publications/the-world-factbook/index.html; Figure 8–3, Adapted from Statistics Canada. *Income in Canada 2009*, Catalogue no. 75-202-XWE2009000, June 2011, http://www.statcan.gc.ca/bsolc/olc-cel/olc-cel?lang=eng&catno=75-202-X; Table 8–1, Adapted from Statistics Canada. *Income and Earnings, 2006 Census*, Catalogue no. 97-563-XWE2006071, September 2008, http://www.statcan.gc.ca/bsolc/olc-cel/olc-cel?lang=eng&catno=97-563-X2006071; Table 8–2, Goyder, John. *The Prestige Squeeze*. Montreal: McGill-Queen's University Press, 2009, Table 4-1, pp.106-110; Figure 8–4, Adapted from Statistics Canada CANSIM database http://cansim2.statcan.gc.ca, Table 202-0702: v32211870, June 16, 2011; Table 8-3, Adapted from Statistics Canada. *Labour, 2006 Census*, Catalogue no. 97-559-XCB2006027, October 2008 and *Income and Earnings, 2006 Census*, 97-563-XWE2006002, May 2008, http://www.statcan.gc.ca/bsolc/olc-cel/olc-cel?lang=eng&catno=97-559-X2006027, http://www.statcan.gc.ca/bsolc/olc-cel/olc-cel?lang=eng&catno=97-563-X2006002; National Map 8–1, Statistics Canada. *Family Income and Economic Family Structure for the Economic Families in Private Households of Canada, Provinces, Territories, Census Divisions and Census Subdivisions*, 2005—20% Sample Data. [Electronic Data File]. Catalogue no. 97-563-XCB2006031[1].IVT. 2011; Figure 8–5, Adapted from the Statistics Canada CANSIM database http://cansim2.statcan.gc.ca, Table 202-0703, June 16, 2011; National Map 8–2, Statistics Canada. *Income Status after Tax and Economic Family Structure for the Economic Families in Private Households of Canada, Provinces, Census Divisions and Census Subdivisions*, 2005—20% Sample Data. [Electronic Data File]. Catalogue no. 97-563-XCB2006040[1].IVT. 2011.

CHAPTER 9: Figure 9–1, International Bank for Reconstruction and Development/ The World Bank: Milanovic, Branko. "Global Inequality Recalculated: The Effect of New 2005 PPP Estimates on Global Inequality." World Bank. August 2009. http://siteresources.worldbank.org/INTDECINEQ/Resources/Global_Inequality_ Recalculated.pdf, and Davies, James B., Anthony Shorrocks, Edward N. Wolff, and Susanna Sandström. "The Level and Distribution of Global Household Wealth." *The Economic Journal*. Vol. 121, No. 551 (February 2010):223–254; Global Map 9–1, Data from *Human Development Report 2010*, United Nations Development Programme (UNDP). Reproduced with permission of Palgrave Macmillan; *Las Colonias*: Based on Schaffer, Michael. "American Dreamers." U.S. News & World Report (August 26, 2002):12–16. "America's Third World", *U.S. News & World Report*, August 2002. Copyright 2002 by U.S. News & World Report. Reproduced by permission; Figure 9–2, Estimated based on data from World Bank (2011a, 2011b). *Population*. 2011a. [*GNI, PPP (current international $)*. 2011b. [Online] http://api.worldbank. org/datafiles/NY.GNP.MKTP.PP.CD_Indicator_MetaData_en_EXCEL.zip; Table 9–1, World Bank. *World Development Indicators, 2009*: World Bank, 2009; World Bank. GNI, PPP (current international $). 2011. [Online] http://api.worldbank.org/datafiles/NY.GNP.MKTP.PP.CD_Indicator_MetaData_en_EXCEL.zip, World Bank. GNI per Capita, PPP (current international $). 2011d. [Online] http://api.worldbank.org/datafiles/NY.GNP.PCAP.PP.CD_Indicator_MetaData_en_EXCEL.zip, and *Human Development Report 2009*, United Nations Development Programme (UNDP). Reproduced with permission of Palgrave Macmillan; Figure 9–3, International Bank for Reconstruction and Development: World Bank. *World Development Indicators*, 2009; "God Made Me to Be a Slave", Reprinted by permission of International Creative Management, Inc. Copyright © [2012] by {Elinor Burkett}; Figure 9–5, *Human Development Report 2009*, United Nations Development Programme (UNDP). Reproduced with permission of Palgrave Macmillan.

CHAPTER 10: Figure 10–1, Marathonguide.com, 2011; Global Map 10—1, *Human Development Report 2010*, United Nations Development Programme (UNDP). Reproduced with permission of Palgrave Macmillan; Figure 10–2, Adapted from the Statistics Canada CANSIM database, http://cansim2.statcan.gc.ca, Table 282-0002: Series v2461476 and v2461686, June 7, 2011; Table 10–1, Statistics Canada. *Women in Canada: Work Chapter Updates 2006*. Catalogue No. 89F0133XIE. 2007. [Online] http://www.statcan.gc.ca/pub/89f0133x/89f0133x2006000-eng.pdf; Figure 10–3, Statistics Canada "Converging gender roles," by Katherine Marshall, *Perspectives on Labour and Income*, Vol. 7, No. 7, July 2006. See: http://www.statcan.gc.ca/pub/75-001-x/10706/9268-eng.htm; National Map 10–1, Calculated based on data in

Statistics Canada. *Profile of Labour Market Activity, Industry, Occupation, Education, Language of Work, Place of Work and Mode of Transportation for Canada, Provinces, Territories, Census Divisions and Census Subdivisions*, 2006 Census [Electronic Database]. Catalogue no. 94-579-XCB2006001. 2011; National Map 10–2, Calculated based on data in Statistics Canada. *Profile of Labour Market Activity, Industry, Occupation, Education, Language of Work, Place of Work and Mode of Transportation for Canada, Provinces, Territories, Census Divisions and Census Subdivisions*, 2006 Census [Electronic Database]. Catalogue no. 94-579-XCB2006001. 2011; Table 10–3, "Women in National Parliaments," http://www.ipu.org/wmn-e/classif.htm, 31 July 2011, and calculations by the authors; Female Genital Mutilation: Violence in the Name of Morality, Courtesy of Barbara Crossette and University of California Press; Figure 10–5, *The American Freshman: Thirty-Five-Year Trends*. © 2011. The Regents of the University of California. All Rights Reserved.

CHAPTER 11: Table 11–1, Adapted from Statistics Canada. *Ethnic Origin and Visible Minorities, 2006 Census*, Catalogue no. 97-562-XCB2006010, April 2008, http://www.statcan.gc.ca/bsolc/olc-cel/olc-cel?lang=eng&catno=97-562-X2006010; Table 11–2, Adapted from Statistics Canada. *Ethnic Origin and Visible Minorities, 2006 Census*, Catalogue no. 97-562-XCB2006006, April 2008, http://www.statcan.gc.ca/bsolc/olc-cel/olc-cel?lang=eng&catno=97-562-X2006006; National Map 11–1, Calculated based on data in Statistics Canada. *Visible Minority Groups, Immigrant Status and Period of Immigration, Age Groups and Sex for the Population of Canada, Provinces, Territories, Census Divisions and Census Subdivisions,2006 Census—20% Sample Data*. [Electronic Data File]. Catalogue no. 97-562-XCB2006016[1].IVT. 2011; Hard Work: The Immigrant Life in North America, Based in part on Booth (1998) and Wong et al. (2007); Figure 11–1, Parrillo, Vincent, and Christopher Donoghue. "Updating the Bogardus Social Distance Studies: A New National Survey." *Social Science Journal*. Vol. 42, No. 2 (April 2005):257–71. *Social Science Journal* by Western Social Science Association. Reproduced with permission of ELSEVIER SCIENCE in the format Journal via Copyright Clearance Center; Table 11–3, Adapted from Statistics Canada. *Aboriginal Peoples, 2006 Census*, Catalogue no. 97-558-XWE2006006, January 2008; http://www.statcan.gc.ca/bsolc/olc-cel/olc-cel?lang=eng&catno=97-558-X2006006; Should Certain Groups in Canada Enjoy Special Rights?, Reprinted with permission of *The Globe and Mail Inc.*, and Nisga'a Final Agreement: Issues and Responses, http://www.aadncaandc.gc.ca/DAM/DAM-INTER-HQ/STAGING/texte-text/snr_1100100031336_eng.pdf, Aborigial Affairs and Northern Development Canada, 2008. Adapted with the permission of the Minister of PublicWorks and Government Services Canada, 2011; Table 11–4, Adapted from Statistics Canada. *Income and Earnings, 2006 Census*, Catalogue no. 97-563-XCB2006060 and 97-563-XCB2006061, September/December 2008, http://www.statcan.gc.ca/bsolc/olc-cel/olc-cel?lang=eng&catno=97-563-X2006060, http://www.statcan.gc.ca/bsolc/olc-cel/olc-cel?lang=eng&catno=97-563-X2006061.

CHAPTER 12: Figure 12–1, International Bank for Reconstruction and Development: World Bank. *World Development Indicators*, 2009; Global Map 12–1, Data from International Labor Organization. *Key Indicators of the Labour Market. 6th ed. 2010.* [Online] Available at http://www.ilo.org/public/english/employment/strat/kilm/index.htm. Copyright © International Labour Organization (ILO Department of Statistics, http://laborsta.ilo.org/); Figure 12–3, *American Freshman: National Norms for Fall 2009*. © 2011 The Regents of the University of California. All Rights Reserved; National Map 12–1, Statistics Canada. *Profile of Labour Market Activity, Industry, Occupation, Education, Language of Work, Place of Work and Mode of Transportation for Canada, Provinces, Territories, Census Divisions and Census Subdivisions, 2006 Census*. [Electronic Data File]. Catalogue no. 94-579-XCB2006001[1].IVT. 2011; Figure 12–4, *Work - Unemployment Rate*, 2011, www4.hrsdc.gc.ca/.3ndic.1t.4r@-eng.jsp?iid=16. Human Resources and Skills Development Canada. Reproduced with the permission of the Minister of Public Works and Government Services Canada, 2012; Proportion of Visible Minority Canadians, Aged 15 through 64, 2006 and 2031, Statistics Canada. *Projections of the Diversity of the Canadian Population*. Catalogue No. 91-551-X2010001, March 2010. http://www.statcan.gc.ca/bsolc/olc-cel/olc-cel?lang=eng&catno=91-551-X; Global Map 12–2, "Freedom in the World Comparative and Historical Data." Freedom House, Inc., 2011. [Online] Available at http://www.freedomhouse.org/template.cfm?page=363&year=2011. www.freedomhouse.org; Figure 12–5, Based on data from "Stat Extracts." 2010, http://stats.oecd.org/WBOS/index.aspx; National Map 12–2, Adapted from Elections Canada.

CHAPTER 13: Figure 13–1, Habtu, Roman, and Andrija Popovic. "Informal Caregivers: Balancing Work and Life Responsibilities." *Horizons.* Vol. 8:3 (April 2006):27–34, Table 3, Consequences Related to Caregiving, p.30. http://www.horizons.gc.ca/doclib/HOR_v8N3_200604_e.pdf. Reproduced with the permission of the Minister of Public Works and Government Services Canada, 2011; Figure 13–2, Adapted from Statistics Canada. *Special Interest Profiles,* 2006 Census, Catalogue no. 97-564-XWE2006009, December 2008, http://www.statcan.gc.ca/bsolc/olc-cel/olc-cel?lang=eng&catno=97-564-X2006009; Figure 13–3, Adapted from the Statistics Canada CANSIM database http://cansim2.statcan.gc.ca, Table 101-6507 and 053-0002, June 17, 2011; National Map 13–1, Estimated based on data in Statistics Canada. *Census Family Status, Age Groups and Sex for the Population in Private Households of Canada, Provinces, Territories, Census Divisions and Census Subdivisions, 2006 Census—20% Sample Data.* [Electronic Data File]. Catalogue no.97-553-XCB2006015[1].IVT. 2011; Table 13–1, Mata, Fernando. *Religion-Mix Growth in Canadian Cities: A Look at 2006–2031 Projections Data.* Report Prepared for Department of Canadian Heritage. 2010. Table 1, "Population Counts of Religions Affiliations (in thousands), Canada and 33 Major Metropolitan Areas, 2006-2031" p.6. [Online] http://www.ssc.uwo.ca/MER/MERcentre/conference%20presentations/Mata,Fernando.pdf. Reproduced with the permission of the Minister of Public Works and Government Services Canada, 2011; Figure 13–5, Clark, W., and G. Schellenberg. "Who's Religious?" *Canadian Social Trends,* (Summer 2006). Statistics Canada, Catalogue No. 11-008. http://www.statcan.gc.ca/pub/11-008-x/2006001/pdf/9181-eng.pdf.

CHAPTER 14: Global Map 14–1, International Bank for Reconstruction and Development: World Bank. "EdStats." 2011. [Online] Available at http://data.worldbank.org/data-catalog/ed-stats; Table 14–1, Statistics Canada. *Education, 2006 Census.* Catalogue No. 97-560-XWE2006007. March 2008. http://www.statcan.gc.ca/bsolc/olc-cel/olc-cel?lang=eng&catno=97-560-X2006007; National Map 14–1, Statistics Canada. *Employment Income Statistics in Constant (2005) Dollars, Work Activity in the Reference Year, Occupation—National Occupational Classification for Statistics 2006, and Sex for the Population 15 Years and Over with Employment Income of Canada, Provinces, Territories, Census Metropolitan Areas and Census Agglomerations, 2000 and 2005—20% Sample Data.* [Electronic Data File]. Catalogue no. 97-563-XCB2006063. 2011; Schooling in the United States: Savage Inequality, From Savage Inequalities: Children In America's Schools by Jonathan Kozol, copyright © 1991 by Jonathan Kozol. Used by permission of Crown Publishers, a division of Random House, Inc.; National Map 14–2, Adapted from Statistics Canada. Hango, D., *Education Matters: Insights on Education, Learning and Training in Canada,* Catalogue no. 81-004-XIE2007005, Vol. 4, No. 5, January 2008. http://www.statcan.gc.ca/bsolc/olc-cel/olc-cel?lang=eng&catno=81-004-X; Figure 14–1, Adapted from the Statistics Canada CANSIM database http://cansim2.statcan.gc.ca, Table 101-6507 and 053-0002, June 20, 2011, and Adapted from Statistics Canada. *Education, 2006 Census,* Catalogue no. 97-560-XCB2006028, March 4, 2008. http://www.statcan.gc.ca/bsolc/olc-cel/olc-cel?catno=97-560-XCB2006028&lang=eng#formatdispb; Table 14–2, Based on data from OECD (2010) table 14-2 "Women's Earnings as a Percentage of Men's Earnings, Ages 35 to 44, by Education, Selected Countries" from OECD Family database www.oecd.org/els/social/family/databaseOECD, http://www.oecd.org/dataoecd/29/63/38752746.pdf; Figure 14–2, Adapted from Statistics Canada and OECD. *Learning a Living: First Results of the Adult Literacy and Life Skills Survey.* 89-603-XWE2005001. May 2005. http://www.statcan.gc.ca/bsolc/olc-cel/olc-cel?catno=89-603-X&lang=eng, and based on data from Table 2.2, from OECD/Statistics Canada (2005), *Learning a Living: First Results of the Adult Literacy and Life Skills Survey,* OECD Publishing, http://dx.doi.org/10.1787/9789264010390-en; Table 14–3, World Health Organization: Mortality Country Fact Sheet 2006: Canada. 2006 http://www.who.int/whosis/mort/profiles/mort_amro_can_canada.pdf, and Mortality Country Fact Sheet 2006: Nigeria. 2006. http://www.who.int/whosis/mort/profiles/mort_afro_nga_nigeria.pdf. © Copyright World Health Organization (WHO), 2011. All Rights Reserved; Figure 14–3, Adapted from Statistics Canada. *Aboriginal Statistics at a Glance,* Catalogue no. 89-645-XWE2010001, June 2010. http://www.statcan.gc.ca/bsolc/olc-cel/olc-cel?catno=89-645-XWE&lang=eng; Masculinity: A Threat to Health?, From Type A Behavior and Your Heart by Meyer Friedman and Ray H. Rosenman, copyright © 1974 by Meyer Friedman. Used by permission of Alfred A. Knopf, a division of Random House, Inc., and Courtesy of Michael Levine; Global Map 14–2, Population Reference Bureau. "2010 World Population Data Sheet." 2010. [Online] Available at http://www.prb.org/Publications/Datasheets/2010/2010wpds.aspx ; UNAIDS/ONUSIDA, and based on data from UNAIDS. "Fast Facts about HIV Prevention," 2011. [Online] Available at http://www.unaids.org/en/KnowledgeCentre/Resources/FastFacts.

CHAPTER 15: National Map 15–1, Statistics Canada. *Profile for Canada, Provinces, Territories, Census Divisions and Census Subdivisions, 2006 Census.* [Electronic Data File.] Catalogue no. 94-581-XCB2006001. 2011; Minorities Now a Majority in the Largest Canadian Cities, Based on Bélanger, Alain, and Eric Caron Malenfant. "Ethnocultural Diversity in Canada: Prospects for 2017." Canadian Social Trends. 11-008-XWE No. 79 (Winter 2005):18–21, and *Population Projections of Visible Minority Groups, Canada, Provinces and Regions, 2001–2017.* Ottawa: Statistics Canada, Catalogue No. 91-541-XIE. 2005; Figure 15–4, TRI Technology Resource Inc.; Figure 15–5, Adapted from Statistics Canada. *Place of work and commuting to work, 2006 Census,* Catalogue no. 97-561-XWE2006012, March 4, 2008; http://www.statcan.gc.ca/bsolc/olc-cel/olc-cel?lang=eng&catno=97-561-X2006012.

CHAPTER 16: National Map 16–1, Statistics Canada. *Profile for Canada, Provinces, Territories, Census Divisions and Census Subdivisions, 2006 Census.* [Electronic Data File]. Catalogue no. 94-581-XCB2006001. 2011; Figure 16–1, Permission of University of Chicago Press; A Never-Ending Atomic Disaster, Courtesy of Kai Erikson.

Name Index

Subject Index

Military Leadership Diversity Commission (2009, U.S.), 330
military-industrial complex, 330
Millennium Scholarship Fund (MSF), 383
Miller, Walter, 165
Milloy, John, 11
Mills, C. Wright, 5, 6, 7, 324
minority women, 266–267
　in Canada, 267
　intersection theory and, 267
　layers of disadvantage for, 267
minority-majority contact,
　assimilation, 290–291
　genocide, 291–292
　in Canada, 292
　pluralism, 290
　segregation, 291
miscegenation, 291
Mobuto, Sese Seko, 245
mode, 18
Modern Family (television show), 339
modernity, 450, 451
modernization theory, 239
　critical review of, 242, 246, 460
　cultural patterns and, 239
　demography and, 416
　historical perspective, 239
　Industrial Revolution and, 460
　mass consumption stage of, 240
　multinationals and, 316
　stages of, 240
　takeoff stage of, 240
　technological maturity stage of, 240
　technology partly cause of poverty, 239
　tradition as barrier and, 239
　traditional stage of, 240
modernization, 448
　capitalism and, 451–454
　centralized state and, 452
　characteristics of, 448–449
　class-society theory and, 454
　division of labour and, 449–450
　Durkheim's theory of, 449–450
　expansion of personal choice as characteristic of, 448
　future trends in, 457–458
　global variations, 458
　individual powerlessness in, 456–457
　individual problems of identify and, 455–456
　Marx's theory of, 451
　mass society theory of, 452
　orientation towards future as characteristic of, 449
　other-directedness from, 456
　persistent inequality and, 454–455
　progress and, 457–458

rationalization and, 450–451
　small community decline as characteristic of, 448
　social character changes from, 455
　social diversification as characteristic of, 448
　social-conflict analysis of, 454
　structural-functional analysis of, 452
　Tönnies; theory of, 449
　tradition-directedness in, 455–456
　Weber's theory of, 450–451
monarchy, 318
　absolute, 318
　constitutional, 318
　during Middle Ages, 318
　in agrarian societies, 318
　traditional, 318
monogamy, 340
　historical preferences for, 339
Moore, Demi, 330
Moore, Wilbert, 196, 197, 198
Morales, Evo, 309
Moranis, Rick, 103
mores, 44
Morgan, J. P., 198
mortality, 411–412, 413
Mother Teresa, 241, 442
Mott, Lucretia, 272
multi-centred model (of cities), 424
multiculturalism, 48
　advantages and disadvantages of, 48
　assimilation and, 291
　challenges of, 48
　crime rates and, 177
multinational corporations, 239, 243, 316
　dependency theory and, 316
　global economy and, 316
　low-income countries and, 316
　modernization theory and, 316
Mundugumor peoples, 253
Murdock, George, 54, 254
Murray, Charles, 288
Musuo peoples, 254
mutual assured destruction (MAD), 331
Muxes (transgender peoples) of Mexico, 143, 144
My Name is Khan (motion picture), 95
Myers, Norman, 433

N
Napoleon, 327
National Association for the Advancement of Colored People (NAACP), 13
National Basketball Association (NBA), 16
National Firearms Association, 324
National Football League (NFL), 16
National Forum on Health (1994), 401
National Health Service (U.K.), 400

natural environment, 426
　biodiversity loss, 433–434
　global perspective, 426–427
　pollution of, 431–432
　progress and, 434–435
　water supply, 431
Natural Sciences and Engineering Research Council of Canada (NSERC), 23
natural selection, 57
Nelson, Ricky, 55
Nenshi, Naheed, 5
neocolonialism, 239, 243
neolocality, 339
Netherlands,
　prostitution in, 149
networks (social), 117
　bases for, 115
　gender and, 117
　immigrants and, 116
　research into, 115–116
　sizes of, 117
New Age spiritual movement, 364, 366
　core values of, 366
New Deal (1930s), 316
New Democratic Party (NDP), 102, 295, 322
　social class and, 211
　social issues and, 322
New England Journal of Medicine, 397
New France, 293, 295
new social movements theory, 446
New Testament of *Bible*, 356, 357
New York Times, 218
New Zealand,
　prostitution in, 149
Newlywed, Nearly Dead (television show), 92
Newton, Isaac, 9
Nicaragua,
　revolution in agrarian, 202
Nisga'a peoples, 293
　treaty with BC and Canada, 294
Nocturne (painting), 424
non-governmental organizations (NGOs), 320
non-verbal communication,
　body language in, 95
　deceptive body language and, 96
　eye contact in, 96
　gestures in, 96
　presentation of self by, 95, 100
　smiling, staring and touching in, 97
Noriega, Manuel, 245
Norman Paterson School of International Affairs, Carleton University, 218
norms, 44, 186
　as just, 171
　as reflection of society, 163, 171
　deviance and cultural, 161, 162, 163, 164